Encyclopedia of World Cultures

Volume I

NORTH AMERICA

ENCYCLOPEDIA OF WORLD CULTURES

David Levinson
Editor in Chief

North America
Oceania
South Asia
Europe and the Middle East
East and Southeast Asia
Soviet Union and China
South America
Middle America and the Caribbean
Africa
Bibliography

The Encyclopedia of World Cultures was prepared under the auspices and with the support of the Human Relations Area Files at Yale University. HRAF, the foremost international research organization in the field of cultural anthropology, is a not-for-profit consortium of twenty-two sponsoring members and 300 participating member institutions in twenty-five countries. The HRAF archive, established in 1949, contains nearly one million pages of information on the cultures of the world.

Encyclopedia of World Cultures
Volume I
NORTH AMERICA

Timothy J. O'Leary
David Levinson
Volume Editors

G.K. Hall & Co.
Boston, Massachusetts

MEASUREMENT CONVERSIONS		
When You Know	Multiply By	To Find
LENGTH		
inches	2.54	centimeters
feet	30	centimeters
yards	0.9	meters
miles	1.6	kilometers
millimeters	0.04	inches
centimeters	0.4	inches
meters	3.3	feet
meters	1.1	yards
kilometers	0.6	miles
AREA		
square feet	0.09	square meters
square yards	0.8	square meters
square miles	2.6	square kilometers
acres	0.4	hectares
hectares	2.5	acres
square meters	1.2	square yards
square kilometers	0.4	square miles
TEMPERATURE		

$$°C = (°F - 32) \times .555$$
$$°F = (°C \times 1.8) + 32$$

© 1991 by the Human Relations Area Files, Inc.

First published 1991
by G.K. Hall & Co.
70 Lincoln Street
Boston, Massachusetts 02111

10 9 8 7 6 5 4 3 2 1

Library of Congress Cataloging-in-Publication Data

Encyclopedia of world cultures / David Levinson, editor in chief.
    p. cm.
    Includes bibliographical references and index.
    Filmography: p.
    Contents: v. 1. North America / Timothy J. O'Leary.
David Levinson, volume editors.
    ISBN 0-8161-1808-6
    1. Ethnology—North America—Encyclopedias.
  2. North America—Social life and customs—Encyclopedias.
I. Levinson, David. 1947-
GN550.E53 1991
305'.097—dc20   90-49123
                                               CIP

Contents

Contributors

Nabeel Abraham
Department of Anthropology
Henry Ford Community College
Dearborn, Michigan
United States

Arab Americans

William Y. Adams
Department of Anthropology
University of Kentucky
Lexington, Kentucky
United States

Navajo

Mary E. Andereck
Department of Psychology
Memphis State University
Memphis, Tennessee
United States

Irish Travelers

Elizabeth Andrews
Department of Fish and Game
State of Alaska
Fairbanks, Alaska
United States

Tanana

Molefi Kete Asante
Department of African-American Studies
Temple University
Philadelphia, Pennsylvania
United States

African Americans

Donald Bahr
Department of Anthropology
Arizona State University
Tempe, Arizona
United States

Pima-Papago

Garrick A. Bailey
Department of Anthropology
University of Tulsa
Tulsa, Oklahoma
United States

Osage

Marshall J. Becker   ***Delaware***
Department of Anthropology
West Chester University
West Chester, Pennsylvania
United States

Robert L. Bee   ***Quechan***
Department of Anthropology
University of Connecticut
Storrs, Connecticut
United States

Margaret B. Blackman   ***Haida***
Department of Anthropology
State University of New York College, Brockport
Brockport, New York
United States

John J. Bodine   ***Taos***
Department of Anthropology
American University
Washington, District of Columbia
United States

William Bright   ***Karok***
Department of Linguistics
University of Colorado
Boulder, Colorado
United States

Norman Buchignani   ***South and Southeast Asians of Canada***
Department of Anthropology
University of Lethbridge
Lethbridge, Alberta
Canada

Ernest S. Burch, Jr.   ***North Alaskan Eskimos***
Harrisburg, Pennsylvania
United States

Gregory R. Campbell   ***Cheyenne***
Department of Anthropology
University of Montana
Missoula, Montana
United States

Warren L. d'Azevedo   ***Washoe***
Department of Anthropology
University of Nevada–Reno
Reno, Nevada
United States

David Damas   ***Copper Eskimo***
Department of Anthropology
McMaster University
Hamilton, Ontario
Canada

William A. Douglass
Basque Studies Program
University of Nevada–Reno
Reno, Nevada
United States

Basques

Albert B. Elsasser
Lowie Museum of Anthropology
University of California, Berkeley
Berkeley, California
United States

Wiyot

Gerhard J. Ens
Department of History
University of Alberta
Edmonton, Alberta
Canada

Metis of Western Canada

Vincent O. Erickson
Department of Anthropology
University of New Brunswick
Fredericton, New Brunswick
Canada

Maliseet

Claire R. Farrer
Department of Anthropology
California State University, Chico
Chico, California
United States

Lipan Apache; Mescalero Apache

Ann Fienup-Riordan
Anchorage, Alaska
United States

Central Yup'ik Eskimos; Eskimo

Mark S. Fleisher
Department of Anthropology
Washington State University
Pullman, Washington
United States

Nootka

John E. Foster
Department of History
University of Alberta
Edmonton, Alberta
Canada

Metis of Western Canada

Catherine S. Fowler
Department of Anthropology
University of Nevada–Reno
Reno, Nevada
United States

Northern Paiute; Southern Paiute and Chemehuevi

Theodore R. Frisbie
Department of Anthropology
Southern Illinois University at Edwardsville
Edwardsville, Illinois
United States

Zuni

Merwyn S. Garbarino
Department of Anthropology
University of Illinois at Chicago
Chicago, Illinois
United States

Seminole

Rolf Gilberg
Department of Ethnography
National Museum of Denmark
Copenhagen
Denmark

Inughuit

Philip J. Greenfeld
Department of Anthropology
San Diego State University
San Diego, California
United States

Western Apache

Jeffery R. Hanson
Department of Sociology, Anthropology, and Social Work
University of Texas at Arlington
Arlington, Texas
United States

Hidatsa

June Helm
Department of Anthropology
University of Iowa
Iowa City, Iowa
United States

Dogrib

Frances Henry
Department of Anthropology
York University
North York, Ontario
Canada

Blacks in Canada

Thomas R. Hester
Department of Anthropology
University of Texas at Austin
Austin, Texas
United States

Yurok

Nancy P. Hickerson
Department of Anthropology
Texas Tech University
Lubbock, Texas
United States

Kiowa

Edward H. Hosley
Department of Anthropology
State University of New York College, Potsdam
Potsdam, New York
United States

Ingalik

John A. Hostetler
Center for Anabaptist and Pietist Studies
Elizabethtown College
Elizabethtown, Pennsylvania
United States

Amish; Hutterites

Charles C. Hughes   **Yuit**
Department of Anthropology
University of Utah
Salt Lake City, Utah
United States

Sue-Ellen Jacobs   **Tewa Pueblos**
Department of Women's Studies
University of Washington
Seattle, Washington
United States

Joel C. Janetski   **Ute**
Museum of Peoples and Cultures
Brigham Young University
Provo, Utah
United States

William B. Kemp   **Baffinland Inuit**
Orientations CGR
Montreal, Quebec
Canada

Inge Kleivan   **West Greenland Inuit**
Institute of Eskimology
University of Copenhagen
Copenhagen
Denmark

David L. Kozak   **Pima-Papago**
Department of Anthropology
Arizona State University
Tempe, Arizona
United States

Shepard Krech III   **Hare**
Department of Anthropology
Brown University
Providence, Rhode Island
United States

Ronald LaBelle   **Acadians**
Centre d'Études Acadiennes
Université de Moncton
Moncton, Nouveau-Brunswick
Canada

Charles H. Lange   **Keres Pueblo Indians**
Santa Fe, New Mexico
United States

David Levinson   **Jews**
Human Relations Area Files
New Haven, Connecticut
United States

Jeffrey Longhofer   **Mennonites**
Department of Sociology
University of Missouri–Kansas City
Kansas City, Missouri
United States

Nancy Oestreich Lurie
Milwaukee Public Museum
Milwaukee, Wisconsin
United States

Winnebago

M. Marlene Martin
Human Relations Area Files
New Haven, Connecticut
United States

Appalachians; Klamath

Thomas R. McGuire
Department of Anthropology
University of Arizona
Tucson, Arizona
United States

Walapai

F. Mark Mealing
Selkirk College
Castlegar, British Columbia
Canada

Doukhobors

James H. Merrell
Department of History
Vassar College
Poughkeepsie, New York
United States

Catawba

Donald Mitchell
Department of Anthropology
University of Victoria
Victoria, British Columbia
Canada

Kwakiutl

Mary H. Moran
Department of Sociology and Anthropology
Colgate University
Hamilton, New York
United States

Sea Islanders

Richard A. Morris
Woodburn, Oregon
United States

Old Believers

Andriy Nahachewsky
Department of Slavic and East European Studies
University of Alberta
Edmonton, Alberta
Canada

Ukrainians of Canada

Mary Christopher Nunley
Department of Anthropology
University of Wisconsin–Milwaukee
Milwaukee, Wisconsin
United States

Kickapoo

Robert L. Oswalt
Kensington, California
United States

Pomo

Peter Peregrine
Department of Sociology and Anthropology
Purdue University
West Lafayette, Indiana
United States

Miami

John H. Peterson
Department of Sociology and Anthropology
Mississippi State University
Mississippi State, Mississippi
United States

Choctaw

Lise Marielle Pilon
Département d'Anthropologie
Université Laval
Cité Universitaire, Québec
Canada

French Canadians

William K. Powers
Department of Anthropology
Rutgers University
New Brunswick, New Jersey
United States

Teton

Gerald F. Reid
Department of Sociology
Sacred Heart University
Fairfield, Connecticut
United States

Cherokee; Chipewyan; Fox; Iroquois; Jicarilla; Mohave; Montagnais-Naskapi; Ojibwa; Pawnee; Yokuts

Donald H. Rubinstein
Micronesian Area Research Center
University of Guam
Mangilao
Guam

Micronesians

Scott Rushforth
Department of Sociology and Anthropology
New Mexico State University
Las Cruces, New Mexico
United States

Slavey

Matt T. Salo
Center for Survey Methods Research
Bureau of the Census
Washington, District of Columbia
United States

Peripatetics; Rom

Alice Schlegel
Department of Anthropology
University of Arizona
Tucson, Arizona
United States

Hopi

Mary Jane Schneider
Department of Indian Studies
University of North Dakota
Grand Forks, North Dakota
United States

Mandan

William Shaffir
Department of Sociology
McMaster University
Hamilton, Ontario
Canada

Hasidim

Florence C. Shipek
San Diego, California
United States

Kumeyaay

James G. E. Smith
Museum of the American Indian
Heye Foundation
Bronx, New York
United States

Cree, Western Woods

Dean R. Snow
Department of Anthropology
State University of New York at Albany
Albany, New York
United States

Abenaki

Nicholas R. Spitzer
Office of Folklife Programs
Smithsonian Institution
Washington, District of Columbia
United States

Black Creoles of Louisiana

George D. Spindler
Department of Anthropology
Stanford University
Stanford, California
United States

Menominee

Louise S. Spindler
Department of Anthropology
Stanford University
Stanford, California
United States

Menominee

Daniel Strouthes
Department of Anthropology
Yale University
New Haven, Connecticut
United States

Micmac

Kenneth D. Tollefson
School of Social and Behavioral Sciences
Seattle Pacific University
Seattle, Washington
United States

Snoqualmie; Tlingit

Joan B. Townsend
Department of Anthropology
University of Manitoba
Winnipeg, Manitoba
Canada

Tanaina

Victor K. Ujimoto
Department of Sociology
University of Guelph
Guelph, Ontario
Canada

East Asians of Canada

Douglas W. Veltre
Social Sciences Division
University of Alaska, Anchorage
Anchorage, Alaska
United States

Aleut

Diego Vigil
Department of Anthropology
University of Southern California
Los Angeles, California
United States

Latinos

Preface

This project began in 1987 with the goal of assembling a basic reference source that provides accurate, clear, and concise descriptions of the cultures of the world. We wanted to be as comprehensive and authoritative as possible: comprehensive, by providing descriptions of all the cultures of each region of the world or by describing a representative sample of cultures for regions where full coverage is impossible, and authoritative by providing accurate descriptions of the cultures for both the past and the present.

The publication of the *Encyclopedia of World Cultures* in the last decade of the twentieth century is especially timely. The political, economic, and social changes of the past fifty years have produced a world more complex and fluid than at any time in human history. Three sweeping transformations of the worldwide cultural landscape are especially significant.

First is what some social scientists are calling the "New Diaspora"—the dispersal of cultural groups to new locations across the world. This dispersal affects all nations and takes a wide variety of forms: in East African nations, the formation of new towns inhabited by people from dozens of different ethnic groups; in Micronesia and Polynesia, the movement of islanders to cities in New Zealand and the United States; in North America, the replacement by Asians and Latin Americans of Europeans as the most numerous immigrants; in Europe, the increased reliance on workers from the Middle East and North Africa; and so on.

Second, and related to this dispersal, is the internal division of what were once single, unified cultural groups into two or more relatively distinct groups. This pattern of internal division is most dramatic among indigenous or third or fourth world cultures whose traditional ways of life have been altered by contact with the outside world. Underlying this division are both the population dispersion mentioned above and sustained contact with the economically developed world. The result is that groups who at one time saw themselves and were seen by others as single cultural groups have been transformed into two or more distinct groups. Thus, in many cultural groups, we find deep and probably permanent divisions between those who live in the country and those who live in cities, those who follow the traditional religion and those who have converted to Christianity, those who live inland and those who live on the seacoast, and those who live by means of a subsistence economy and those now enmeshed in a cash economy.

The third important transformation of the worldwide cultural landscape is the revival of ethnic nationalism, with many peoples claiming and fighting for political freedom and territorial integrity on the basis of ethnic solidarity and ethnic-based claims to their traditional homeland. Although most attention has focused recently on ethnic nationalism in Eastern Europe and the Soviet Union, the trend is nonetheless a worldwide phenomenon involving, for example, American Indian cultures in North and South America, the Basques in Spain and France, the Tamil and Sinhalese in Sri Lanka, and the Tutsi and Hutu in Burundi, among others.

To be informed citizens of our rapidly changing multicultural world we must understand the ways of life of people from cultures different from our own. "We" is used here in the broadest sense, to include not just scholars who study the cultures of the world and businesspeople and government officials who work in the world community but also the average citizen who reads or hears about multicultural events in the news every day and young people who are growing up in this complex cultural world. For all of these people—which means all of us—there is a pressing need for information on the cultures of the world. This encyclopedia provides this information in two ways. First, its descriptions of the traditional ways of life of the world's cultures can serve as a baseline against which cultural change can be measured and understood. Second, it acquaints the reader with the contemporary ways of life throughout the world.

We are able to provide this information largely through the efforts of the volume editors and the nearly one thousand contributors who wrote the cultural summaries that are the heart of the book. The contributors are social scientists (anthropologists, sociologists, historians, and geographers) as well as educators, government officials, and missionaries who usually have firsthand research-based knowledge of the cultures they write about. In many cases they are the major expert or one of the leading experts on the culture, and some are themselves members of the cultures. As experts, they are able to provide accurate, up-to-date information. This is crucial for many parts of the world where indigenous cultures may be overlooked by official information seekers such as government census takers. These experts have often lived among the people they write about, conducting participant-observations with them and speaking their language. Thus they are able to provide integrated, holistic descriptions of the cultures, not just a list of facts. Their portraits of the cultures leave the reader with a real sense of what it means to be a "Taos" or a "Rom" or a "Sicilian."

Those summaries not written by an expert on the culture have usually been written by a researcher at the Human Relations Area Files, Inc., working from primary source materials.

The Human Relations Area Files, an international educational and research institute, is recognized by professionals in the social and behavioral sciences, humanities, and medical sciences as a major source of information on the cultures of the world.

Uses of the Encyclopedia

This encyclopedia is meant to be used by a variety of people for a variety of purposes. It can be used both to gain a general understanding of a culture and to find a specific piece of information by looking it up under the relevant subheading in a summary. It can also be used to learn about a particular region or subregion of the world and the social, economic, and political forces that have shaped the cultures in that region. The encyclopedia is also a resource guide that leads readers who want a deeper understanding of particular cultures to additional sources of information. Resource guides in the encyclopedia include ethnonyms listed in each summary, which can be used as entry points into the social science literature where the culture may sometimes be identified by a different name; a bibliography at the end of each summary, which lists books and articles about the culture; and a filmography at the end of each volume, which lists films and videos on many of the cultures.

Beyond being a basic reference resource, the encyclopedia also serves readers with more focused needs. For researchers interested in comparing cultures, the encyclopedia serves as the most complete and up-to-date sampling frame from which to select cultures for further study. For those interested in international studies, the encyclopedia leads one quickly into the relevant social science literature as well as providing a state-of-the-art assessment of our knowledge of the cultures of a particular region. For curriculum developers and teachers seeking to internationalize their curriculum, the encyclopedia is itself a basic reference and educational resource as well as a directory to other materials. For government officials, it is a repository of information not likely to be available in any other single publication or, in some cases, not available at all. For students, from high school through graduate school, it provides background and bibliographic information for term papers and class projects. And for travelers, it provides an introduction into the ways of life of the indigenous peoples in the area of the world they will be visiting.

Format of the Encyclopedia

The encyclopedia comprises ten volumes, ordered by geographical regions of the world. The order of publication is not meant to represent any sort of priority. Volumes 1 through 9 contain a total of about fifteen hundred summaries along with maps, glossaries, and indexes of alternate names for the cultural groups. The tenth and final volume contains cumulative lists of the cultures of the world, their alternate names, and a bibliography of selected publications pertaining to those groups.

North America covers the cultures of Canada, Greenland, and the United States of America.
Oceania covers the cultures of Australia, New Zealand, Melanesia, Micronesia, and Polynesia.
South Asia covers the cultures of Afghanistan, Bangladesh, Burma, India, Pakistan, Sri Lanka, and the Himalayan states.

Europe and the Middle East covers the cultures of Europe, North Africa, the Middle East, and the Near East.
East and Southeast Asia covers the cultures of Japan, Korea, mainland and insular Southeast Asia, and Taiwan.
Soviet Union and China covers the cultures of Mongolia, the People's Republic of China, and the Union of Soviet Socialist Republics.
South America covers the cultures of South America.
Middle America and the Caribbean covers the cultures of Central America, Mexico, and the Caribbean islands.
Africa covers the cultures of Madagascar and sub-Saharan Africa.

Format of the Volumes

Each volume contains this preface, an introductory essay by the volume editor, the cultural summaries ranging from a few lines to several pages each, maps pinpointing the location of the cultures, a filmography, an ethnonym index of alternate names for the cultures, and a glossary of scientific and technical terms. All entries are listed in alphabetical order and are extensively cross-referenced.

Cultures Covered

A central issue in selecting cultures for coverage in the encyclopedia has been how to define what we mean by a cultural group. The questions of what a culture is and what criteria can be used to classify a particular social group (such as a religious group, ethnic group, nationality, or territorial group) as a cultural group have long perplexed social scientists and have yet to be answered to everyone's satisfaction. Two realities account for why the questions cannot be answered definitively. First, a wide variety of different types of cultures exist around the world. Among common types are national cultures, regional cultures, ethnic groups, indigenous societies, religious groups, and unassimilated immigrant groups. No single criterion or marker of cultural uniqueness can consistently distinguish among the hundreds of cultures that fit into these general types. Second, as noted above, single cultures or what were at one time identified as single cultures can and do vary internally over time and place. Thus a marker that may identify a specific group as a culture in one location or at one time may not work for that culture in another place or at another time. For example, use of the Yiddish language would have been a marker of Jewish cultural identity in Eastern Europe in the nineteenth century, but it would not serve as a marker for Jews in the twentieth-century United States, where most speak English. Similarly, residence on one of the Cook Islands in Polynesia would have been a marker of Cook Islander identity in the eighteenth century, but not in the twentieth century when two-thirds of Cook Islanders live in New Zealand and elsewhere.

Given these considerations, no attempt has been made to develop and use a single definition of a cultural unit or to develop and use a fixed list of criteria for identifying cultural units. Instead, the task of selecting cultures was left to the volume editors, and the criteria and procedures they used are discussed in their introductory essays. In general, however, six criteria were used, sometimes alone and sometimes in combination to classify social groups as cultural groups: (1) geographical localization, (2) identification in the social science literature as a distinct group, (3) distinct language, (4) shared traditions, religion, folklore, or values, (5) maintenance of group identity in the face of strong assimilative pressures, and (6) previous listing in an inventory of the world's cultures such as _Ethnographic Atlas_ (Murdock 1967) or the _Outline of World Cultures_ (Murdock 1983).

In general, we have been "lumpers" rather than "splitters" in writing the summaries. That is, if there is some question about whether a particular group is really one culture or two related cultures, we have more often than not treated it as a single culture, with internal differences noted in the summary. Similarly, we have sometimes chosen to describe a number of very similar cultures in a single summary rather than in a series of summaries that would be mostly redundant. There is, however, some variation from one region to another in this approach, and the rationale for each region is discussed in the volume editor's essay.

Two categories of cultures are usually not covered in the encyclopedia. First, extinct cultures, especially those that have not existed as distinct cultural units for some time, are usually not described. Cultural extinction is often, though certainly not always, indicated by the disappearance of the culture's language. So, for example, the Aztec are not covered, although living descendants of the Aztec, the Nahuat-speakers of central Mexico, are described.

Second, the ways of life of immigrant groups are usually not described in much detail, unless there is a long history of resistance to assimilation and the group has maintained its distinct identity, as have the Amish in North America. These cultures are, however, described in the location where they traditionally lived and, for the most part, continue to live, and migration patterns are noted. For example, the Hmong in Laos are described in the Southeast Asia volume, but the refugee communities in the United States and Canada are covered only in the general summaries on Southeast Asians in those two countries in the North America volume. Although it would be ideal to provide descriptions of all the immigrant cultures or communities of the world, that is an undertaking well beyond the scope of this encyclopedia, for there are probably more than five thousand such communities in the world.

Finally, it should be noted that not all nationalities are covered, only those that are also distinct cultures as well as political entities. For example, the Vietnamese and Burmese are included but Indians (citizens of the Republic of India) are not, because the latter is a political entity made up of a great mix of cultural groups. In the case of nations whose populations include a number of different, relatively unassimilated groups or cultural regions, each of the groups is described separately. For example, there is no summary for Italians as such in the Europe volume, but there are summaries for the regional cultures of Italy, such as the Tuscans, Sicilians, and Tyrolians, and other cultures such as the Sinti Piedmontese.

Cultural Summaries

The heart of this encyclopedia is the descriptive summaries of the cultures, which range from a few lines to five or six pages in length. They provide a mix of demographic, historical, social, economic, political, and religious information on the cultures. Their emphasis or flavor is cultural; that is, they focus on the ways of life of the people—both past and present—and the factors that have caused the culture to change over time and place.

A key issue has been how to decide which cultures should be described by longer summaries and which by shorter ones. This decision was made by the volume editors, who had to balance a number of intellectual and practical considerations. Again, the rationale for these decisions is discussed in their essays. But among the factors that were considered by all the editors were the total number of cultures in their region, the availability of experts to write summaries, the availability of information on the cultures, the degree of similarity between cultures, and the importance of a culture in a scientific or political sense.

The summary authors followed a standardized outline so that each summary provides information on a core list of topics. The authors, however, had some leeway in deciding how much attention was to be given each topic and whether additional information should be included. Summaries usually provide information on the following topics:

CULTURE NAME: The name used most often in the social science literature to refer to the culture or the name the group uses for itself.

ETHNONYMS: Alternate names for the culture including names used by outsiders, the self-name, and alternate spellings, within reasonable limits.

ORIENTATION

Identification. Location of the culture and the derivation of its name and ethnonyms.

Location. Where the culture is located and a description of the physical environment.

Demography. Population history and the most recent reliable population figures or estimates.

Linguistic Affiliation. The name of the language spoken and/or written by the culture, its place in an international language classification system, and internal variation in language use.

HISTORY AND CULTURAL RELATIONS: A tracing of the origins and history of the culture and the past and current nature of relationships with other groups.

SETTLEMENTS: The location of settlements, types of settlements, types of structures, housing design and materials.

ECONOMY

Subsistence and Commercial Activities. The primary methods of obtaining, consuming, and distributing money, food, and other necessities.

Industrial Arts. Implements and objects produced by the culture either for its own use or for sale or trade.

Trade. Products traded and patterns of trade with other groups.

Division of Labor. How basic economic tasks are assigned by age, sex, ability, occupational specialization, or status.

Land Tenure. Rules and practices concerning the allocation of land and land-use rights to members of the culture and to outsiders.

KINSHIP

Kin Groups and Descent. Rules and practices concerning kin-based features of social organization such as lineages and clans and alliances between these groups.

Kinship Terminology. Classification of the kinship terminological system on the basis of either cousin terms or generation, and information about any unique aspects of kinship terminology.

MARRIAGE AND FAMILY

Marriage. Rules and practices concerning reasons for marriage, types of marriage, economic aspects of marriage, postmarital residence, divorce, and remarriage.

Domestic Unit. Description of the basic household unit including type, size, and composition.

Inheritance. Rules and practices concerning the inheritance of property.

Socialization. Rules and practices concerning child rearing including caretakers, values inculcated, child-rearing methods, initiation rites, and education.

SOCIOPOLITICAL ORGANIZATION

Social Organization. Rules and practices concerning the internal organization of the culture, including social status, primary and secondary groups, and social stratification.

Political Organization. Rules and practices concerning leadership, politics, governmental organizations, and decision making.

Social Control. The sources of conflict within the culture and informal and formal social control mechanisms.

Conflict. The sources of conflict with other groups and informal and formal means of resolving conflicts.

RELIGION AND EXPRESSIVE CULTURE

Religious Beliefs. The nature of religious beliefs including beliefs in supernatural entities, traditional beliefs, and the effects of major religions.

Religious Practitioners. The types, sources of power, and activities of religious specialists such as shamans and priests.

Ceremonies. The nature, type, and frequency of religious and other ceremonies and rites.

Arts. The nature, types, and characteristics of artistic activities including literature, music, dance, carving, and so on.

Medicine. The nature of traditional medical beliefs and practices and the influence of scientific medicine.

Death and Afterlife. The nature of beliefs and practices concerning death, the deceased, funerals, and the afterlife.

BIBLIOGRAPHY: A selected list of publications about the culture. The list usually includes publications that describe both the traditional and the contemporary culture.

AUTHOR'S NAME: The name of the summary author.

Maps

Each regional volume contains maps pinpointing the current location of the cultures described in that volume. The first map in each volume is usually an overview, showing the countries in that region. The other maps provide more detail by marking the locations of the cultures in four or five subregions.

Filmography

Each volume contains a list of films and videos about cultures covered in that volume. This list is provided as a service and in no way indicates an endorsement by the editor, volume editor, or the summary authors. Addresses of distributors are provided so that information about availability and prices can be readily obtained.

Ethnonym Index

Each volume contains an ethnonym index for the cultures covered in that volume. As mentioned above, ethnonyms are alternative names for the culture—that is, names different from those used here as the summary headings. Ethnonyms may be alternative spellings of the culture name, a totally different name used by outsiders, a name used in the past but no longer used, or the name in another language. It is not unusual that some ethnonyms are considered degrading and insulting by the people to whom they refer. These names may nevertheless be included here because they do identify the group and may help some users locate the summary or additional information on the culture in other sources. Ethnonyms are cross-referenced to the culture name in the index.

Glossary

Each volume contains a glossary of technical and scientific terms found in the summaries. Both general social science terms and region-specific terms are included.

Special Considerations

In a project of this magnitude, decisions had to be made about the handling of some information that cannot easily be standardized for all areas of the world. The two most troublesome matters concerned population figures and units of measure.

Population Figures

We have tried to be as up-to-date and as accurate as possible in reporting population figures. This is no easy task, as some groups are not counted in official government censuses, some groups are very likely undercounted, and in some cases the definition of a cultural group used by the census takers differs from the definition we have used. In general, we have relied on population figures supplied by the summary authors. When other population data sources have been used in a volume, they are so noted by the volume editor. If the reported figure is from an earlier date—say, the 1970s—it is usually because it is the most accurate figure that could be found.

Units of Measure

In an international encyclopedia, editors encounter the problem of how to report distances, units of space, and temperature. In much of the world, the metric system is used, but scientists prefer the International System of Units (similar to the metric system), and in Great Britain and North America the English system is usually used. We decided to use English measures in the North America volume and metric measures in the other volumes. Each volume contains a conversion table.

Acknowledgments

In a project of this size, there are many people to acknowledge and thank for their contributions. In its planning stages, members of the research staff of the Human Relations Area Files provided many useful ideas. These included Timothy J. O'Leary, Marlene Martin, John Beierle, Gerald Reid, Delores Walters, Richard Wagner, and Christopher Latham. The advisory editors, of course, also played a major role in planning the project, and not just for their own volumes but also for the project as a whole. Timothy O'Leary, Terence Hays, and Paul Hockings deserve special thanks for their comments on this preface and the glossary, as does Melvin Ember, president of the Human Relations Area Files. Members of the office and technical staff also must be thanked for so quickly and carefully attending to the many tasks a project of this size inevitably generates. They are Erlinda Maramba, Abraham Maramba, Victoria Crocco, Nancy Gratton, and Douglas Black. At G. K. Hall, the encyclopedia has benefited from the wise and careful editorial management of Elizabeth Kubik and Elizabeth Holthaus, the editorial and production management of Michael Sims and Ara Salibian, and the marketing skills of Linda May and Lisa Pemstein. Finally, I would like to thank Melvin Ember and the board of directors of the Human Relations Area Files for their administrative and intellectual support for this project.

DAVID LEVINSON

References

Murdock, George Peter (1967). _Ethnographic Atlas_. Pittsburgh, Penn., University of Pittsburgh Press.

Murdock, George Peter (1983). _Outline of World Cultures._ 6th rev. ed. New Haven, Conn. Human Relations Area Files.

Introduction

This volume covers the cultures of Canada, Greenland (Kala-allit Nunaat), and the United States of America. Greenland, although administratively linked to Denmark, is included here because its native inhabitants, the Inuit, are related culturally to the Inuit of Canada. For the same reason, the cultures of Hawaii are covered in the Oceania volume, as native Hawaiians are related culturally to the Polynesian peoples of Oceania.

North America covers 8,254,654 square miles and had an estimated population of 276 million in 1989. The forty-eight contiguous U.S. states plus Alaska cover 3,562,864 square miles and in 1989 had an estimated population of 246,498,000. Canada covers 3,851,790 square miles with an estimated population of 25,334,000 in 1989. And Greenland covers 840,000 square miles, making it the largest island in the world, with an estimated population of 55,000 in 1989. Reaching nearly from the North Pole almost to the Tropic of Cancer, North America is a diverse physiographic and climatic region. It is also a complex cultural region. At the time of sustained European contact (ca. 1600) the native inhabitants of the New World spoke at least one thousand languages and were organized into as many distinct cultural groups. Since that time, people representing hundreds of different cultural traditions have immigrated to and settled in the United States and Canada, creating a mix of cultures perhaps without precedent in human history.

The cultures of North America now fall into three general categories: (1) Native Americans, the modern-day descendants of the original inhabitants of North America—the American Indian (Amerindian), Aleut, and Eskimo and Inuit cultures; Eskimo, as used here, refers to the native cultures of north and western Alaska, and Inuit to the native cultures of northern Canada and Greenland; (2) folk cultures, such as the Amish, who have maintained their unique cultural identity within the context of modern North American society; and (3) ethnic groups composed of people who share a common sense of identity on the basis of national origin, race, or religion. This volume covers cultures in all three of these categories.

When dealing with cultures, one central issue is the name that is used for the culture. Most have more than one name: usually they have a name for themselves, and outsiders use one or more different names. The name of each summary in this book, and thus the name used for each culture, is either the name preferred by the author of the summary or the name by which the culture is most commonly known. Ethnonyms or alternative names are provided in the summaries and in the ethnonym index. For immigrant-based groups such as Korean-Americans, we have hyphenated the names except in summaries where authors preferred the nonhyphenated form.

Native American Cultures

North America was settled by peoples migrating east from Siberia across the Bering Strait. Although it is clear that the first settlers arrived from Asia and were the ancestors of the contemporary native peoples of North, Middle, and South America, archaeologists are not certain of the date of first settlement of North America nor of the exact route taken by these migrants. As to the date, there are three views (Kehoe 1981). One, subscribed to by only a minority of experts, holds that Asian peoples migrated across the Bering Strait land bridge some 100,000 or more years ago. More widely accepted is the view that first settlement occurred between 40,000 and 15,000 years ago, through migration either across the land-covered Bering Strait or by boat, with peoples moving from island to island or along the coastline. A third and more cautious view places first settlement at about 12,000 years ago. The ancestors of the Eskimo/Inuit and Aleut arrived later, although again there is disagreement about the actual date, with 8,000 and 4,000 years ago both considered reasonable estimates by experts. The Aleut and Eskimo/Inuit are related peoples (they are also related to the native peoples of northeastern Siberia such as the Chukchi and Tungus) whose ancestors migrated in different directions after arriving in North America. The ancestors of the Aleut migrated south and west, settling the Aleutian Islands while the Eskimo/Inuit ancestors migrated east and north, settling the Arctic region from the west coast of Alaska to the southeast coast of Greenland.

The pre-European population of North America is unknown, with estimates suggesting a total of anywhere from 1 million to 12 million around the beginning of the sixteenth century (Waldman 1985). Compared to Central America, whose inhabitants numbered in the tens of millions, North America was sparsely inhabited. Under the pressure of deadly epidemics of European-introduced diseases, forced relocations, and private and government-sponsored genocide campaigns, the Native American population shrank to a low of about 250,000 around 1900.

Since that time the population has increased, partly owing to a lower death rate but also, in the last twenty years, to an increased desire by people to identify themselves as American Indians and an increased willingness of the U.S.

and Canadian governments to consider them as such. The 1980 U.S. census identified 1,364,033 American Indians, 42,162 Eskimos, and 14,205 Aleut. There are 279 federal Indian reservations in the United States with 339,836 American Indians living on them in 1980 plus another 30,265 living on tribal trust lands. Most American Indians in the United States live off of the reservations, and many live in cities, although a pattern of frequent returns to the reservations is not uncommon. In Canada in 1981 there were 367,810 status (legally defined) American Indians and 25,390 Inuit and perhaps as many as 750,000 non-status Indians and Métis (people of mixed Indian-European ancestry). About 70 percent of Canadian status Indians live on the 2,251 Canadian Indian reserves. In Greenland today about 46,000 of the entire population of 55,000 are Inuit and they live mainly in villages or small towns along the western, southern, and eastern coasts. It should be noted that any population figures for the native peoples of North America are only estimates. Because of varying definitions of who a Native American is and difficulties in counting those who are so classified, no accurate enumeration of Native Americans is possible.

In the United States and Canada today, some Native American groups are officially recognized as political entities. There were 307 American Indian groups so recognized by the U.S. government in 1988. These groups are often labeled tribes, nations, towns, communities, bands, reservations, rancherias, colonies, and pueblos (for example, the Tonto Apache Tribe of Arizona, Kialegee Tribal Town of the Creek Nation, Kalispel Indian Community of the Kalispel Reservation, Citizen Band of Potawatomi Indians of Oklahoma, Lookout Rancheria of Pit River Indians of California, Reno-Sparks Indian Colony of Nevada, and Pueblo of Taos, New Mexico). But some are identified only by their name and location (for example, Makah, Makah Reservation, Washington). Some 200 Eskimo and Aleut groups are also recognized by the federal government and since 1971 have been organized into twelve regional business corporations and thirteen nonprofit associations, which function alongside cultural, linguistic, and residential groupings. In Canada, the Inuit are organized into nine territorial/regional associations. Status American Indian groups in Canada are identified by band names. The bands generally live on or near their reserves.

Governmental recognition means that Native American groups and their members so recognized have a special relationship with both the federal and the state or provincial governments. These special relationships center around such issues as the holding of reservation or reserve land in trust, the return of land taken in the past, settlement of claims, provision of educational and health services, payment of taxes, and the applicability of federal or state law. At the same time, Native Americans are citizens of the respective nations. In the United States, definition as a Native American is usually left up to the individual, and membership in a group is left up to the particular Indian group he or she claims affiliation with. Access to various federal or state programs, however, may depend on official recognition of one's membership in a federally recognized group. In Canada, the government distinguishes between status and nonstatus Indians largely on the basis of such considerations as intermarriage with non-Indians, residence off reserve land, and assimilation into Canadian society. In 1985 the criteria for classification as a status Indian were relaxed, leading to a dramatic rise in the "official" Indian population of Canada. Métis are not recognized as Indian by the Canadian government. Although tied to Denmark, Greenland is self-governing, and many decisions about their own lives are in the hands of the native Inuit peoples.

Although these political/territorial divisions may help sort different groups into identifiable units for legal, political, or business purposes, they do not always correspond to the delineation of specific Native American groups as distinct cultural entities, in either the past or the present. In some cases two or more groups are lumped together and in other cases one group is subdivided into two or more groups. It is probably impossible to count precisely the number of Native American cultures that existed in the past or that exist today. The *Ethnographic Bibliography of North America* (Murdock and O'Leary 1975; Martin and O'Leary 1990) lists 251 native cultures for the United States, Canada, and Greenland at about the time of settlement of North America by Europeans. (This figure of 251 is a lumping, as groups that spoke dialects of the same language or were politically linked are usually treated as a single group.) Forty of these groups are now extinct, and a number of others are nearly so. Those that still exist exhibit a broad range of degree of cultural persistence, from those in which the language has disappeared and the traditional culture exists mostly in the memories of a few old people to those in which most people speak the native language and follow traditional beliefs and customs. Most cultures fall between these two extremes. Excluding the extinct ones and treating as distinct groups a few that were lumped with others by Murdock and O'Leary, we cover in this volume 223 Native American cultures. Many of these are now located in the western United States, especially in Arizona, California, and Oklahoma. Maps 2 and 3 show the large-scale relocations of eastern and midwestern American Indian groups that resulted from European settlement of the United States. In Canada, groups are spread across much of the continent as they were prior to European settlement (see map 4) mainly because early settlers were more interested in obtaining furs for the fur trade than in acquiring large tracts of land. Most bands are located in British Columbia. But many Canadian groups are now facing the same pressure on their land from settlers and developers that U.S. groups experienced from the early 1600s on.

At the time of European contact, Native American groups may have spoken as many as 2,000 languages, although some experts prefer a more conservative estimate of 1,000 (Beals and Hoijer 1965, 613; Driver 1969, 25). Of these, only 221 have survived for study by linguists and have been classified by Voegelin and Voegelin (1966) into seven language phyla and twenty-nine language families. Native Americans continue to speak about 100 of these languages, with many American Indians bilingual in their native language and in English or French in French-speaking parts of Canada. In the Southwest, English is replacing Spanish as the second language, though some American Indians are trilingual in all three languages.

Three levels of coverage are provided in this encyclopedia for these Native American groups: seventy groups are described in long summaries, ninety-nine in shorter summaries, and fifty-four in mentions. When we selected groups for long summaries, our major objective was to ensure that the full range of cultural variation among Native American cultures, past and present, is presented. Thus, the long summaries describe all fifteen major cultural patterns (see below) displayed by Native American cultures at the time of European contact as well as more recent variations such as those between acculturated and unacculturated groups. Short summaries and mentions are cross-referenced to longer entries when the groups described in each are culturally similar. In preparing these summaries as well as those on other North American cultures, we benefited from both the contributions of the summary authors and the resources and staff of the Human Relations Area Files (HRAF). The HRAF Archive is especially rich with materials on North American cultures and contains nearly two thousand documents describing seventy cultures. This material was used to prepare many short summaries and mentions. In addition, five members of HRAF's research staff have themselves conducted research on North American cultures, and they wrote a number of summaries and provided information for others.

Anthropologists conventionally divide the pre-European native cultures into regional groupings, on the basis of similarities among the cultures of each region and differences between regions. These regional groupings also reflect differences in terrain and climate, both of which were powerful determinants of cultural variation. One such classification delineates fifteen regions (Murdock and O'Leary 1975): (1) Arctic Coast, (2) Mackenzie-Yukon, (3) Northwest Coast, (4) Oregon Seaboard, (5) California, (6) Peninsula, (7) Basin, (8) Plateau, (9) Plains, (10) Midwest, (11) Eastern Canada, (12) Northeast, (13) Southeast, (14) Gulf, and (15) Southwest (see map 1).

Arctic Coast

This vast area, stretching from eastern Siberia to Greenland, includes a number of cultures whose members speak languages of the Eskimo-Aleut language family and have a general cultural adaptation to the rigors of life in Arctic coastal conditions. The primary subsistence pattern of these groups varies from dependency on sea mammal hunting to fishing to caribou hunting, depending upon local ecological conditions. The Western Eskimos, including the Aleut, the Alaskan Eskimos, and the Siberian Yuit, have been much influenced by the cultures of Siberia to the west and those of the Northwest Coast to the southeast, in contrast to the Central and Eastern Inuit, who have lived for a long period in relative isolation and are assumed to have preserved more of the traditional cultural patterns.

A major linguistic division occurs at Norton Sound in western Alaska, with the Siberian Eskimos and the Alaskan Eskimos living south of this area speaking a language (Yup'ik, Alaskan Eskimo) that is quite different from that of the Eskimo living to the north and east, who speak a language called Inupik, Inuit, or Central-Greenlandic. Linguistic differences occurring in the vast geographical spread of the latter language are comparatively insignificant. In addition to the above, there are two Aleut languages, Eastern Aleut (Unalaskan) and Western Aleut (Atkan, Attuan). It has been estimated that there are more than eighty thousand speakers of these four languages. Although subsistence is still based to some extent on sea mammal hunting and fishing, most of the

Arctic peoples have been slowly drawn into the American, Canadian, and Greenlandic economies. Most people now live in towns, purchase a fair amount of their food and other items, and through modern transportation and communication are linked to modern society.

Mackenzie-Yukon

This area includes the western part of the great boreal coniferous forest stretching across North America from Labrador to Alaska. It is a subarctic region, including patches of tundra as well as the forest. The peoples living in this region hunted (particularly moose and caribou) and fished for survival. The fur trade, beginning in the eighteenth century, brought about a cultural adaptation to trading post conditions and Western goods in much of the area and a partial breakdown of the aboriginal cultural pattern. This western section of the boreal forest has two major regions: (1) the Yukon Subarctic in Alaska and the Yukon Territory (the Pacific Drainage division), drained mainly by the Yukon River, and (2) the Mackenzie Subarctic in the Northwest Territories and the northern parts of British Columbia, Alberta, Saskatchewan, and Manitoba (the Arctic Drainage division), drained principally by the Mackenzie River. All the groups spoke Athapaskan languages. They were culturally quite similar, except that those living in the Pacific Drainage division had a relatively richer ceremonial culture than those of the Arctic Drainage division. The native population of this area is not large, although trustworthy figures are hard to find. Recent economic and cultural changes in this area are much the same as those in the Arctic.

Northwest Coast

This area stretches along the North Pacific coastline from the western Yakutat region in Alaska, along the southeastern Alaskan Panhandle and the coast of British Columbia, to the southern end of Puget Sound in northwestern Washington. It is an area with much rainfall and dense coniferous forest, which is warmed by the deflection southeastward of the Japan Current by the Aleutian Islands along the coast. The sea here is very rich in food, and the life of the inhabitants was oriented to the sea and to the coastal bays and estuaries. Salmon was the staple food, supplemented by cod and halibut, shellfish, seaweed, and sea mammals (whales and sea lions). The food from the sea provided such an economic surplus that life was relatively secure here, compared to the neighboring areas. The cultures shared features typical of societies with large food surpluses: social classes, including slaves, emphasis on the acquisition and display of material goods, and elaborate sculpture and other artistic expressions. The cultures also display a number of influences from Asia, such as rod and slat armor. Another characteristic of these cultures was the great use of wood in large plank houses, dugout canoes, boxes, and especially the totem poles of the northern groups (Tlingit, Haida, and Tsimshian). The cultures had diverse origins, as shown by the number of different languages spoken. Among them are representatives of the Wakashan, Chimakuan, and Salish language families and the Na-Dene and Penutian language phyla. There was a highly developed trading system and much raiding and warfare. Most of these groups still control some of their traditional lands, although many individuals have been attracted to cities such as Vancouver and Seattle.

The sea is still a basic source of income, although many people are involved in the market economy through the sale of fish and employment in canneries, some of which are tribally owned. Tourism, including the production of art objects, is also now important. In many ways, however, they are much integrated into modern society.

Oregon Seaboard

This area includes the coastal regions of southern Washington, western Oregon, and northern California. The environment is generally similar to that of the Northwest Coast, with a great deal of rainfall and a heavy coniferous forest. The groups who lived in this area were not ocean-going, but tended to keep to the bays and rivers. The general culture shared by these groups was an attenuated form of that found on the Northwest Coast: social classes, plank houses, the potlatch, woodworking, emphasis on material wealth, guardian spirits, and ceremonials. Moving from north to south, however, there was less and less emphasis on most of these traits, with many of them absent from the cultural repertory of groups in northern California. Fishing, particularly salmon fishing, was the basis of subsistence, with hunting of secondary importance. There was a good deal of trade up and down the coast, with dentalium shells in particular being used as a means of exchange. Many of these groups have lost much of their traditional culture and others have disappeared entirely as distinct cultural units, although a number of groups are making an effort to revitalize the traditional culture.

California

The California area includes about two-thirds of the state of California. It does not include the northwestern section, which forms part of the Oregon Seaboard area, nor most of the eastern border region, which is part of the Basin area. The southeastern part near the Colorado River is within the Southwest area, and southern California is part of the Peninsula area. This region is not large, but it contained a variety of cultures, languages, and physical types. The focus of the region is the interior valley, together with the flanking Sierra Nevada and Coast mountain ranges. All the groups living here were hunters and gatherers, the focal point of subsistence being the acorn, although there was a large variety of other food resources. On the coast, seafood was the staple when it was available. There was no great elaboration of sociopolitical organization or ceremonial life. The population was relatively dense, but the individual units were small in size. They usually lived in clusters of hamlets during the winter and in migratory bands during the summer, but a number of groups had permanent villages and a stronger territorial organization. Each group was quite independent and hostile to the encroachments of other groups. As a result, there was a good deal of intergroup warfare. Characteristic of California cultures were sophisticated basketry, cremation burial, subsistence based on acorns, and the general use of shell money in exchange. In the south and central coastal areas, many of these groups disappeared under the pressure of the Spanish missions. Those in the central valley and the Sierra Nevada were nearly exterminated by the gold miners and the settlers who followed after 1849. Surviving groups are now mostly scattered on small rancherias and reservations or have been assimilated.

Peninsula

This area includes southern California from approximately San Luis Obispo south to the Mexican border and eastward to near the Nevada-Arizona border as well as Baja California, whose cultures are covered in the Middle America volume. The climate of the area is generally dry, being part desert. The cultures of the northern part of the area are much like those of the California area, with some Basin and Southwestern elements added. In the northern part of the area, acorns were an important part of the diet along with agave and mesquite. Population density was low except in the North, where the food supply was more generous. The cultural inventory was much like that of the Basin area, including vegetal-fiber clothing, brush-covered dwellings, shell money in the North, and ceremonies based on events in the life cycle, especially puberty and death. All of these groups, except the Serrano and Cahuilla, were converted by Spanish missionaries in the eighteenth century with a subsequent destruction of the aboriginal culture. Apart from the Cahuilla and Kumeyaay, there are few groups left, although there are numerous small reservations scattered throughout southern California.

Basin

This area includes almost all of Nevada and Utah, western Colorado, western Wyoming, southwestern Montana, southern Idaho, southeastern Oregon, and eastern California. This is one of the driest regions of the United States, and during the glacial period it formed the bed of a series of lakes. The surrounding mountains keep out rain, and the rivers within the basin have no means of egress to the sea and drain instead into sinks and swamps. The whole area is a sagebrush-juniper steppe, with generally sparse vegetation that could not support a large population. The peoples of this region were food gatherers rather than hunters because of the scarcity of animal food aside from rabbits and other rodents, reptiles, birds, and some deer and antelope. The basis of the diet in the southern Basin area was piñon nuts, with other seeds, nuts, bulbs, and wild vegetable foods replacing the piñon when it was not available. Virtually all activities of the groups living in this region were carried out by individual families. They lived in small family groups or bands and had regular territories but no permanent villages. There was no large-scale sociopolitical organization, no permanent leaders, and little war. There was also little ceremonial life, except for that associated with rabbit or antelope drives. Their houses were domed wickiups or brush shelters. They used a minimal amount of clothing and household equipment, although basketry was highly developed in many areas. In historic times, a number of cultural influences came in from the Plains area, including the use of the horse (where there was enough pasturage), and clothing and customs, including hide tipis. All the groups in this area were speakers of Shoshonean languages, except for the Washoe in the West, who spoke a Hokan language. The only large population group was the Ute, most of whom are now living on a number of reservations, with the traditional culture surviving in various degrees.

Plateau

This area, named for the plateaus drained by the Fraser, Columbia, and Snake rivers, stretches from north-central British

Columbia in the north to northern Oregon in the southwest and northwestern Montana in the southeast. According to Kroeber (1939), it can be divided into three provinces. The first is the Middle Columbia, which forms the southern part of the Plateau and is the great area of groups speaking Sahaptin languages (such as Nez Percé, Yakima, Umatilla), as well as some groups speaking Salish and other languages. It is the region that received the greatest amount of cultural influence from the Plains area in historic times, resulting in the acquisition of skin tipis, parflêches, floral beadwork, and a version of the Sun Dance among some groups. The second province is the Upper Columbia, which was the region of the Interior Salish-speaking groups, but also includes the Kutenai in the east. The third province is the drainage of the Fraser River inland from the coast and is also a region of Interior Salish-speaking groups, with the exception of the Athapaskan-speaking Nicola.

Over the entire area, the diet staple was fish, particularly salmon. Aside from this staple, the subsistence pattern varied with the local resources. In the North, the pattern was similar to that in the subarctic, with moose and other large game forming a major part of the diet. In the South, where subsistence patterns were similar to those in the neighboring Basin, there was a greater dependence on plant foods. In the East, groups depended on big game in addition to fish. Generally the peoples settled in tribelets or groups of villages. There was no great emphasis on rank. Village chieftainship could be hereditary or based on personal exploits, and most of the groups had village councils to assist the leaders. The area might be characterized (with exceptions) by a few traits such as peacefulness, democracy, fear of the dead, dependency on salmon fishing, and girls' puberty rites. These groups today live mostly on reservations and reserves, with some still engaged in lumbering and salmon fishing.

Plains

This large area stretches from central Alberta to southern Texas and from the eastern foothills of the Rocky Mountains to the western Mississippi River region. From east to west the Plains area can be divided into three major environmental provinces: the tall-grass prairies, the short-grass plains, and the Rocky Mountain foothills. The inhabitants of the prairies were basically sedentary farmers, whereas the dwellers in the short-grass plains and the foothills were nomadic hunters. Bison meat was the basis of subsistence throughout most of the area, with maize, beans, and squash supplanting it in the east. After A.D. 1600 the horse was available for hunting and warfare, which in the western part of the area provoked a cultural florescence culminating in the nineteenth century in a way of life familiar as a stereotype to most readers. Some of the highlights of this culture were bison hunting on horseback, nomadism with definite territories, the skin tipi, the Sun Dance, war bonnets, coup counting, and constant warfare with other groups and with the U.S. government. This contrasted greatly with the life of the sedentary farmers in the eastern sections, who had permanent villages and horticulture, and were relatively more peaceful.

Most of these groups had a complex sociopolitical organization, but a few, such as the Comanche, Kiowa Apache, and Teton Dakota, were organized as bands. They occupied fairly well-defined territories that were defended against enemies.

The nomads often assembled for communal bison hunts and religious rituals, and representatives from many different groups would gather for the Sun Dance ceremonial. Most groups were led by chiefs and councils, with military and other societies maintaining order.

As in the Northeast and the Southeast areas there was extensive migration of individual Plains groups during the historic period. The Plains was also an area of great dislocation of population with the advent of European settlement. The wars fought by most of the Plains groups with the federal government are famous in U.S. history, the last major conflicts occurring in the 1880s. As a result of these wars, the Plains groups were resettled on reservations scattered throughout the area.

Midwest

This area covers the general region of the north-central United States east of the Mississippi River from the Upper Peninsula of Michigan on the north to western Tennessee on the south, eastward to eastern Kentucky, and north along the general Ohio-Indiana boundary into the Lower Peninsula of Michigan. In other words, it is the southern upper Great Lakes region, together with the drainages of the Illinois River and part of the Ohio River. This is generally an area of groups speaking languages of the Central branch of Algonkian, in addition to the Siouan-speaking Winnebago. These groups usually lived in permanent villages and farmed much of the year. They also hunted bison and other large game, with many groups conducting large-scale bison hunts in the autumn. Maize, beans, and squash were the principal crops, with wild rice forming a staple food in the northwestern part of the area. Around the Great Lakes, fishing was as important as hunting. Government usually featured a weak village system, with separate civil and war leaders and village councils. Throughout the historic period there was a great deal of migration in the area, with much of the eastern part being almost unoccupied a good deal of the time. Most of the people have been resettled on reservations outside this area. Because of these movements, the aboriginal cultures are not well known and many cultural features have disappeared through assimilation.

Eastern Canada

This area includes the eastern part of the great boreal coniferous forest stretching across northern North America, as well as portions of other ecological areas. There is a general dependency on game (especially moose and caribou), fish, and wild fruit throughout the region. In the southern sections, in the area of the northern Great Lakes and in the North Atlantic Slope region of the Maritime Provinces, some groups practiced agriculture and absorbed cultural influences from the South. The area can be divided into three subareas. The largest is the eastern Canadian subarctic, which includes the Hudson Bay and Atlantic drainages and the area north of the Height of Land, which separates Hudson Bay from the Great Lakes drainages. This area is ecologically similar to that of the Mackenzie-Yukon area and includes the Cree, Beothuk, Montagnais-Naskapi, and Northern Ojibwa groups. The second subarea is that of the northern Great Lakes, which had limited agriculture and was exposed to direct contacts with agricultural areas to the south. It includes the Southern

Ojibwa, Ottawa, and Algonkin proper. The third subarea is that of the North Atlantic Slope, which lies south of the St. Lawrence River in Maine, Nova Scotia, New Brunswick, and the Gaspé, and is the territory of the Abenaki, Maliseet, and Micmac. It had some agriculture, but subsistence was based upon hunting, fishing, and gathering.

In contrast to the Mackenzie-Yukon area, which is populated by Athapaskan speakers, all the native peoples of this area were speakers of Algonkian languages of the Eastern and Central types. The Abenaki, Maliseet, and Micmac spoke languages of the Eastern type, and the remainder spoke Central Algonkian languages. One branch of the latter is Cree-Montagnais-Naskapi. The area covered by speakers of this branch is immense, stretching from British Columbia to Labrador. Because of dialect similarities, it is difficult at times to assign individual groups to larger units. Most of these groups now live on or near reserves in their traditional territories, although their participation in Canadian society is often limited to being the recipients of government aid programs.

Northeast

This area includes the northeastern United States with adjacent areas of Canada. It consists basically of two provinces, the lower Great Lakes region, which contained groups speaking Iroquoian languages, and the North Atlantic Coast region, including New England and the Middle Atlantic states, which were inhabited by Algonkian-speaking groups. The whole region is heavily forested, with deciduous species predominating, and with no grasslands and little open space. It has a fairly uniform rainfall, not a very bold physiographic relief, and a generally long growing season for crops. It was an area of sedentary farmers, large political units, and large fortified towns. Subsistence was based on maize, beans, and squash horticulture, with hunting also important. Gathering of wild plant foods was secondary to hunting and farming. The groups living near the coasts spent the summers fishing and collecting shellfish and the winters inland, hunting large game (deer, elk, and so on). Political organization was complex, with most groups organized in confederacies, the climax being reached with the League of the Iroquois in central New York State. Matrilineal descent prevailed in the area, with leadership often inherited in this manner. Clans and sibs were strongly developed, and religious and political leadership often went along with membership in these units. There was a great deal of warfare, with torture of captives, cannibalism, and scalping often part of the pattern. Warfare reached its strongest development with the Iroquois, who used it as an instrument of political policy. Because this was an area of early and heavy European settlement, there are few survivors of the original inhabitants still remaining, except for the Iroquois in New York State, Quebec, and Ontario. Most of the other groups are fragmented, removed to reservations in the West, or extinct.

Southeast

This is a very large area, consisting of all the southeastern United States, running south and west from Chesapeake Bay around the coast to the Mississippi River Delta, north to the confluence of the Ohio River with the Mississippi, and north-

east from that point, excepting the territory of the Western Shawnee of the lower Ohio River region, which is considered to be a part of the Midwest. The whole area is a region of warm, temperate climate and heavy forest, partly deciduous and partly coniferous. Subsistence was based on maize, beans, and squash horticulture, with hunting secondary, although important. Fish and shellfish formed a large part of the diet in the coastal areas. Towns were usually permanent, and often large and fortified. The cultures featured complex sociopolitical organizations. There were great confederacies of linguistically related groups. Descent was usually matrilineal, with clans, sibs, moieties, and phratries forming the basis of the political organization. Large groups of native peoples engaged in a good deal of movement during historic times, such as the Tuscarora who moved from North Carolina to New York State in the eighteenth century. As in the Northeast, this was an area of early and intense European settlement, with the result that most of the aboriginal groups were destroyed or removed to distant reservations. Most notable of these was the forced removal of the Five Civilized Tribes to reservations in the present state of Oklahoma during the 1840s. There are still large groups of Indians remaining, however, including Cherokee and Creek populations, as well as groups formed during historic times, such as the Seminole in Florida. This area and the Northeast also contain numerous bi- or triracial groups, referred to as American Isolates.

Gulf

This area includes the territory between approximately the Río Grande in extreme southern Texas and the Vermilion River in southern Louisiana, including part of southwestern Louisiana and southeastern Texas as far west as the Edwards Plateau. The groups inhabiting this large area were mostly hunters and gatherers who coped with a very limiting, semiarid environment. Small bands united by kinship bonds were the basic social units, with little social differentiation by status or rank. Groups so characterized inhabited what has been termed the Western Gulf area, which is generally the region from the Trinity River in northeast Texas southward to the Río Grande. As a whole, Gulf culture groups are very poorly known, most having become extinct as functioning cultures by the nineteenth century.

Southwest

This area includes most of Arizona and New Mexico, and parts of Texas, Colorado, Utah, and California. Most of the area is desert or mountainous and is semiarid to arid in climate. Settlements tend to cluster close to water supply as a result. Most of the Indians were farmers, although there were hunters and collectors in the eastern parts as well. Maize agriculture was the basis of subsistence throughout most of the area, with reliance on maize being greatest among the Puebloan peoples of Arizona and New Mexico. Squashes, beans, and sunflower seeds also characterized the diet. Meat was not plentiful in most of the area. In the arid regions, plant collecting formed a large part of the subsistence base.

There was a wide range of sociopolitical organization, from a weak band organization among the Desert Yumans and the Athapaskans (Apache and Navajo), through the village and town organizations of the Puebloan peoples, to the tribal organization of the River Yumans. Raiding and warfare were endemic until the Spanish government managed to put an end to most of these activities. Dislocation and reduction of the population has not been as great as in other parts of the country. The Navajo, for instance, are now among the largest Indian groups in the United States, and most of the other groups have a relatively stable population. Involvement in the American cash economy has replaced traditional subsistence practices, but many Pueblo groups have managed to retain much of their traditional culture.

Folk Cultures

North America is the home of a number of cultural groups who have remained culturally distinct, a considerable accomplishment given the strong assimilationist policies at work in the United States. In the face of these assimilative pressures, such as compulsory education and English as the primary language, such groups as the Amish have maintained their unique cultures through a number of strategies including endogamous marriage, strict adherence to their unique religious beliefs and practices, residence in isolated communities, socialization practices that encourage a strong sense of cultural solidarity, and an economic system that allows the culture to be largely self-sufficient. Folk cultures covered here fall into two groups: (1) those that developed elsewhere and have maintained their distinct culture and identity in North America (Basques, Rom Gypsies, Irish Travelers, Amish, Hutterites, Hasidim, Old Believers, Acadians, Molokans, Doukhobors, Mennonites, and Sea Islanders), and (2) those that developed in North America (Appalachians, Cajuns, Mormons, Ozarkers, and Shakers). The current locations of some of these folk cultures are shown on map 5.

Ethnic Groups

North America is mostly populated by people whose ancestors arrived in the New World from Europe. But though most earlier immigrants came from Europe, during the past two decades the majority have arrived from Asia and Latin America. The _Harvard Encyclopedia of American Ethnic Groups_ (Thernstrom 1980) covers 106 ethnic groups in the United States, though this number could easily be tripled if groups were defined in terms of regional origin (such as Sicily, Tuscany, Piedmont) rather than national origin (Italy). Ethnic groups in the United States and Canada fall into four general categories, although some groups can be placed in more than one. Our purpose here is not to sort these groups into rigid categories, but simply to give an idea of the diversity of ethnicity in North America.

(1) A _national-origin group_ is an ethnic group formed and maintained through group members sharing a common affiliation based on their tracing their ancestry to the same nation. Because the nations of origin were often European, these groups are sometimes referred to as "White ethnics" or "hyphenated Whites" (Italian-Americans, Greek-Americans). It is important to keep in mind that there is considerable variation both among the different ethnic groups and within groups in the degree to which the traditional beliefs and customs have disappeared and the people have assimilated into North American society. Across groups, degree of assimilation is reflected by such factors as extent of use of the native language, residential localization, and the rate of intermarriage. Within all groups, internal cultural variation ranges from one extreme—ethnic neighborhoods or towns exist in which the traditional culture is maintained—to the other extreme—large numbers of group members are almost completely assimilated into mainstream society. Within nearly all ethnic groups there are some ethnic communities—sometimes urban neighborhoods, other times rural settlements—where the traditional culture survives. But, at the same time, in nearly all groups, most of the individual members are assimilated into either U.S. or Canadian society.

(2) An _ethnic minority group_, like a national-origin group, is based on members affiliating on the basis of national or regional origin. But ethnic minorities are also identified as distinct groups because their members have been the object of economic, cultural, or political discrimination on the ground of their race or religion. Included here are African-Americans, Chinese-Canadians, and Latinos, among others. Again, as with national-origin groups, many of these groups display considerable internal cultural variation, although many individuals often live outside or on the periphery of the mainstream economic, political, and social system because of discrimination based on religion or race.

(3) An _immigrant group_ is an ethnic group whose members have recently arrived in North America and are largely unassimilated into mainstream society, as reflected in continued use of the native language, residential isolation, and endogamous marriage. Included here are groups such as Central Asian Jews in New York, West Indians in Toronto, and Tongans in Los Angeles. Over time in the United States, European immigrant groups have tended to become ethnic groups, non-European groups have become minority groups, and a few, such as the Amish or Sea Islanders, have become folk cultures. In Canada the history of assimilation is not as clear and needs to be analyzed in the context of Canada as an officially bilingual and multicultural nation (Anderson and Frideres 1981).

(4) A _syncretic ethnic group_ is formed through the blending of the people and the cultural features of two or more distinct groups. Included here are the Lumbee in the United States, Métis in Canada, Creoles in Louisiana, and American Isolate groups in the eastern United States. Groups, such as the Seminole, that formed through the blending of two or more Native American groups are classified as Native Americans.

These four types of ethnic groups numbering over one hundred in the United States and Canada are covered in three ways in the encyclopedia. First, this volume provides thirteen general summaries (African Americans, Arab Americans, Blacks in Canada, East Asians of Canada, East Asians of the United States, European-Americans, European-Canadians, Jews, Latinos, Micronesians, Polynesians, South and Southeast Asians of Canada, and South and Southeast Asians of the United States). Second, the cultures covered in these general summaries are described in summaries in the appropriate regional volumes. So, for example, the Irish are covered in the Europe volume, and separate summaries describe the Northern Irish, Irish, Gaels, and Irish Travellers. Third, separate summaries are provided for French

Canadians, Haitians, Black West Indians in the United States, and Ukrainians of Canada.

Reference Resources

The literature on Native Americans, North American folk cultures, and ethnic groups is voluminous. Here we discuss and list the basic reference resources that lead the reader to the relevant literature.

Native Americans

The three basic directories to scholarly research on Native Americans are *The Ethnographic Bibliography of North America*, 4th ed. (Murdock and O'Leary 1975), *The Ethnographic Bibliography of North America, Supplement to the 4th Edition* (Martin and O'Leary 1990), and the *Handbook of North American Indians* (Sturtevant 1978–) The two bibliographies provide citations to over sixty thousand books, articles, doctoral dissertations, and government documents pertaining to Native Americans. They also include bibliographic essays telling the reader where to find more about Native Americans. The *Handbook* is a projected twenty-volume collection of thematic essays and cultural summaries covering Native American groups, past and present. Eight volumes are in print, with all expected to appear by the year 2000. Also of note is Hodge's *Handbook of American Indians North of Mexico* (1959). Although Hodge's cultural summaries are being superseded by those in the *Handbook of North American Indians*, he provides much valuable information on American Indian history, beliefs, and customs. The *Indian Reservations: A State and Federal Handbook* (Confederation of American Indians 1986) is a useful guide to Indian reservations in the United States. The *Native American Directory* (1982) is invaluable as a guide to groups, organizations, media, museums, and so on. Other general or regionally focused sources are Driver's (1969) *Indians of North America*, Leitch's (1979) *A Concise Dictionary of Indian Tribes of North America*, Jorgensen's (1980) *Western Indians*, Krech's (1986) *Native Canadian Anthropology and History: A Selected Bibliography*, Kroeber's (1925) *Handbook of the Indians of California*, Ruby and Brown's (1986) *A Guide to the Indian Tribes of the Pacific Northwest*, and Swanton's (1952) *The Indian Tribes of North America*. A comprehensive guide to films on Native Americans is *Native Americans on Film and Video* (Weatherford and Seubert 1988).

Folk Cultures and Ethnic Groups

As with Native Americans, it is easy to be quickly overwhelmed by the amount of information available on ethnic groups and folk cultures in the United States and Canada. Basic bibliographies are *European Immigration and Ethnicity in the United States and Canada: A Historical Bibliography* (Brye 1983), *Immigrants and Their Children in the United States: A Bibliography of Doctoral Dissertations* (Hogland 1986), *American and Canadian Immigrant and Ethnic Folklore: An Annotated Bibliography* (Georges and Stern 1982), *A Comprehensive Bibliography for the Study of American Minorities* (Miller, 1976), and *Minorities in America: The Annual Bibliography* (Miller 1976–1978). In addition, the journal *Canadian Ethnic Studies/Études Ethniques au Canada* publishes a continuing bibliography emphasizing Native Americans and ethnic groups in Canada. The *Harvard Encyclopedia of American Ethnic Groups* (Thernstrom 1980) provides demographic/social history profiles of 106 U.S. ethnic groups and thematic essays on topics such as assimilation, immigration, and ethnicity. *We the People* (Allen and Turner 1988) provides demographic profiles of U.S. ethnic groups and maps marking the locations and concentrations of these groups in 1980. Burnet and Palmer's (1988) *Coming Canadians: An Introduction to Canada's Peoples* provides a general history of Canadian ethnicity. *The Ethnic Almanac* (Bernardo 1981) provides population and other information of more general interest, and the *Ethnic Directory of Canada* (Markotic and Hromadiuk 1983) provides much information on Canadian groups. Scholarly journals that regularly publish articles and book reviews on Canadian and American ethnic groups include *Canadian Ethnic Studies/Études Ethniques au Canada, Ethnic Groups, Ethnic and Racial Studies, International Migration Review, Journal of American Ethnic History,* and the *Journal of Ethnic Studies*. Dozens of regional, state, and local historical society journals as well as journals published by ethnic associations also publish articles on ethnic groups. *Encyclopedia Canadiana* (Robbins 1965) and *The Canadian Encyclopedia* (Marsh 1988) provide descriptions of ethnic and folk cultures in Canada. Three continuing book series are the *Immigrant Communities and Ethnic Minorities in the United States and Canada* (Theodoratus 1989), which now includes sixty-seven monographs, with many describing specific ethnic communities; the *Immigrant Heritage of America Series* (Archdeacon 1984–), which provides social histories of more than a dozen ethnic groups; and the *Generation Series* (Burnet and Palmer 1976–), which does the same for Canadian ethnic groups.

The interests of many ethnic groups, which often include the preservation and celebration of ethnic customs, are represented by ethnic associations. Names and addresses of these associations and other information sources can be found in the *Encyclopedia of Associations* (Burek, Koek, and Novallo 1990), *Minority Organizations: A National Directory* (Garrett Park Press 1987), *Ethnic Information Sources of the United States* (Wasserman and Kennington 1983), and the *Corpus Almanac and Canadian Sourcebook* (Sova 1987).

Acknowledgments

First, we would like to thank the contributors, whose knowledge and willingness to share that knowledge have made this volume possible. We also want to thank Gerald Reid, Marlene Martin, and Nancy Gratton of the HRAF Research Staff for their various contributions to this volume. A number of individuals also merit thanks for other contributions—Professor James Frideres for his recommendations on experts to write about Canadian ethnic groups, Professor James P. Allen for his advice on how to cover U.S. ethnic groups, and Professor Jack Glazier for his comments on the Jews in North America summary.

References

Allen, James P., and Eugene J. Turner (1988). *We the People: An Atlas of America's Ethnic Diversity*. New York: Macmillan.

Anderson, Alan B., and James S. Frideres (1981). _Ethnicity in Canada: Theoretical Perspectives._ Toronto: Butterworths.

Archdeacon, Thomas J., ser. ed. (1984–). _Immigrant Heritage of America Series._ Boston: Twayne Publishers.

Beals, Ralph L., and Harry Hoijer (1965). _An Introduction to Anthropology._ 3rd ed. New York: Macmillan.

Bernardo, Stephanie, ed. (1981). _The Ethnic Almanac._ Garden City, N.Y.: Doubleday & Co.

Brye, David L., ed. (1983). _European Immigration and Ethnicity in the United States and Canada: A Historical Bibliography._ Santa Barbara, Calif.: ABC-Clio Information Services.

Burek, Deborah M., Karen E. Koek, and Annette Novallo, eds. (1990). _Encyclopedia of Associations._ 24th ed. Detroit: Gale Research.

Burnet, Jean R., and Howard Palmer, ser. ed. (1976–) _Generation Series._ Toronto: McClelland and Stewart.

Burnet, Jean R., with Howard Palmer (1988). _Coming Canadians: An Introduction to Canada's Peoples._ Toronto: McClelland & Stewart.

Confederation of American Indians (1986). _Indian Reservations: A State and Federal Handbook._ Jefferson, N.C.: McFarland & Co.

Driver, Harold E. (1969). _Indians of North America._ 2nd ed., rev. Chicago: University of Chicago Press.

Garrett Park Press (1987). _Minority Organizations: A National Directory._ 3rd ed. Garrett Park, Md.: Garrett Park Press.

Georges, Robert A., and Stephen Stern, comps. (1982). _American and Canadian Immigrant and Ethnic Folklore: An Annotated Bibliography._ New York: Garland Publishing.

Hodge, Frederick W., ed. (1959). _Handbook of American Indians North of Mexico._ New York: Pageant Books. Originally published, 1907–1910.

Hogland, A. W. (1986) _Immigrants and Their Children in the United States: A Bibliography of Doctoral Dissertations._ New York: Garland Publishing.

Jorgensen, Joseph G. (1980). _Western Indians._ San Francisco: W. H. Freeman and Co.

Kehoe, Alice B. (1981). _North American Indians: A Comprehensive Account._ Englewood Cliffs, N.J.: Prentice-Hall.

Krech, Shepard, III (1986). _Native Canadian Anthropology and History: A Selected Bibliography._ Winnipeg: Rupert's Land Research Centre, University of Winnipeg.

Kroeber, Alfred L. (1925). _Handbook of the Indians of California._ Smithsonian Institution, U.S. Bureau of American Ethnology, Bulletin no. 78. Washington, D.C. Reprint, Berkeley, Calif.: California Book Co., 1953; New York: Dover Books, 1976.

Kroeber, Alfred L. (1939). _Cultural and Natural Areas of Native North America._ University of California Publications in Archaeology and Ethnology, no. 38. Berkeley: University of California Press.

Leitch, Barbara A. (1979). _A Concise Dictionary of Indian Tribes of North America._ Algonac, Mich.: Reference Publications.

Markotic, Vladimir, and Bob Hromadiuk (1983). _Ethnic Directory of Canada._ Calgary: Western Publishers.

Marsh, James H., ed. (1988). _The Canadian Encyclopedia._ 2nd ed. Edmonton: Hurtig Publishers.

Martin, M. Marlene, and Timothy J. O'Leary, comps. (1990). _Ethnographic Bibliography of North America. Supplement to the Fourth Edition._ New Haven: HRAF Press.

Miller, Charles W., ed. (1976). _A Comprehensive Bibliography for the Study of American Minorities._ New York: New York University Press.

Miller, Charles W., ed. (1976–1978). _Minorities in America: The Annual Bibliography._ University Park, Pa.: Pennsylvania State University Press.

Murdock, George P., and Timothy J. O'Leary, comps. (1975). _Ethnographic Bibliography of North America._ 4th ed. New Haven: HRAF Press.

Native American Directory (1982) San Carlos, Ariz.: National Native American Co-operative.

Robbins, John E., ed. (1965). _Encyclopedia Canadiana._ Toronto: Grolier of Canada.

Ruby, Robert H., and John A. Brown (1986). _A Guide to the Indian Tribes of the Pacific Northwest._ Norman: University of Oklahoma Press.

Sova, Gordon, ed. (1987). _Corpus Almanac and Canadian Sourcebook._ Don Mills, Ontario: Southam Communications.

Sturtevant, William C., gen. ed. (1978–). _Handbook of North American Indians._ Washington, D.C.: Smithsonian Institution.

Swanton, John R. (1952). _The Indian Tribes of North America._ U.S. Bureau of American Ethnology, Bulletin no. 145. Washington, D.C.

Theodoratus, Robert, ser. ed. (1989). _Immigrant Communities and Ethnic Minorities in the United States and Canada._ New York: AMS Press.

Thernstrom, Stephan, ed. (1980). *Harvard Encyclopedia of American Ethnic Groups*. Cambridge: Harvard University Press, Belknap Press.

Voegelin, Charles F., and Florence M. Voegelin (1966). *Map of North American Indian Languages, Revised*. American Ethnological Society, Publication no. 20. Bloomington, Ind.

Waldman, Carl (1985). *Atlas of the North American Indian*. New York: Facts on File.

Wasserman, Paul, and Alice E. Kennington (1983). *Ethnic Information Sources of the United States*. 2nd ed. Detroit: Gale Research Co.

Weatherford, Elizabeth, and Emelia Seubert, eds. (1988). *Native Americans on Film and Video*. New York: Museum of the American Indian/Heye Foundation.

TIMOTHY J. O'LEARY
DAVID LEVINSON

MAP 1: AMERICAN INDIAN REGIONS (CIRCA 1600)

ARCTIC OCEAN

GREENLAND

ICELAND

BERING SEA

MACKENZIE–YUKON

ARCTIC COAST

HUDSON BAY

NORTHWEST COAST

PACIFIC

OCEAN

EASTERN CANADA

PLATEAU

OREGON SEABOARD

PLAINS

NORTHEAST

CALIFORNIA

BASIN

MIDWEST

ATLANTIC

PENINSULA

SOUTHWEST

SOUTHEAST

OCEAN

GULF

GULF OF MEXICO

CARIBBEAN SEA

MILES

0   500   1000

MAP 2: NATIVE AMERICAN CULTURES (CIRCA 1600)[1]

ARCTIC OCEAN

U.S.S.R.

BERING SEA

GREENLAND

ICELAND

INUGHUIT

EAST GREENLAND INUIT

YUIT

NORTH ALASKA ESKIMOS

CENTRAL YUP'IK ESKIMO

KOYUKON

INGALIK

TANANA

IGLULIK INUIT

WEST GREENLAND INUIT

ALEUT

TANAINA

AHTNA

3

HAN

KUTCHIN

MACKENZIE INUIT

HARE

NETSILIK INUIT

BAFFINLAND INUIT

PACIFIC ESKIMO

TUTCHONE

2

BEAR LAKE

COPPER ESKIMO

CARIBOU INUIT

SOUTHAMPTON INUIT

DOGRIB

YELLOWKNIFE

KASKA

SLAVE

LABRADOR INUIT

HUDSON BAY

4

5

SEKANI

BEAVER

CHIPEWYAN

MONTAGNAIS

BEOTHUK

CARRIER

SARSI

CREE

PACIFIC

1

OCEAN

MICMAC

MALISEET

See INSET A.

BLACKFOOT

ASSINIBOIN

OJIBWA

ALGONKIN

ABENAKI

See INSET E.

9

OTTAWA

IROQUOIS

28

MASSACHUSET

10 12

20

25

MAHICAN

26

8

22

CROW

YANKTON

SANTEE

23

21

NEUTRAL

24

27

See INSET B.

NO. SHOSHONE

NO. PAIUTE

BANNOCK

39

TETON

19

18

ERIE

METOAC

DELAWARE

15

14

IOWA

MIAMI

NANTICOKE

See INSET C.

7

6

UTE

ARAPAHO

CHEYENNE

PAWNEE

OTO

13

ILLINOIS

MOSOPELEA

34

POWHATAN

MONO

SO. PAIUTE

KANSA

OSAGE

SHAWNEE

CHEROKEE

37

PAMLICO

KIOWA

11

WICHITA

QUAPAW

31

CATAWBA

38

ATLANTIC

See INSET D.

CUSABO

See INSET F.

17

16

CADDO

30

36

CREEK

YAMASEE

OCEAN

COMANCHE

35

33

CHOCTAW

29

32

TIMUCUA

CALUSA

COAHUILTECO

ATAKAPA

CHITIMACHA

ACOLAPISSA

HUMA

BILOXI

MOBILE

APALACHEE

LEGEND

1.	CHILCOTIN	14.	OMAHA	27.	MOHEGAN
2.	MOUNTAIN	15.	PONCA	28.	PENNACOOK
3.	NABESNA	16.	KARANKAWA	29.	ALABAMA
4.	TAHLTAN	17.	TONKAWA	30.	CHAKCHIUMA
5.	TSETSAUT	18.	FOX	31.	CHICKASAW
6.	WESTERN	19.	KICKAPOO	32.	HITCHITI
	SHOSHONE	20.	MENOMINI	33.	HUMA
7.	WASHOE	21.	POTAWATOMI	34.	MONACAN
8.	ARIKARA	22.	SAUK	35.	NATCHEZ
9.	GROS VENTRE	23.	WINNEBAGO	36.	TUNICA
10.	HIDATSA	24.	CONESTOGA	37.	TUSCARORA
11.	KIOWA APACHE	25.	HURON	38.	YUCHI
12.	MANDAN	26.	MAHICAN	39.	EASTERN
13.	MISSOURI				SHOSHONE

GULF OF MEXICO

CARIBBEAN SEA

75

MILES

0   500   1000

[1]See also MAP 2 INSETS.

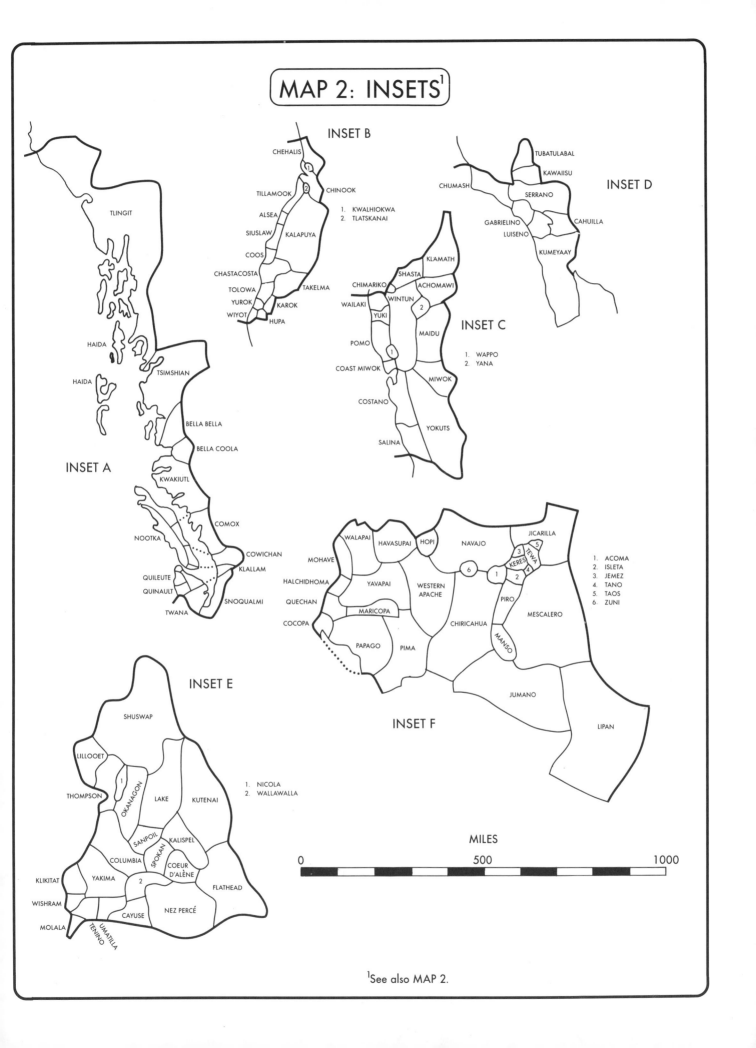

MAP 2: INSETS[1]

INSET B

CHEHALIS
TILLAMOOK — CHINOOK
ALSEA
SIUSLAW — KALAPUYA
COOS
CHASTACOSTA
TOLOWA — TAKELMA
YUROK — KAROK
WIYOT — HUPA

1. KWALHIOKWA
2. TLATSKANAI

INSET D

TUBATULABAL
KAWAIISU
CHUMASH — SERRANO
GABRIELINO — CAHUILLA
LUISENO
KUMEYAAY

INSET A

TLINGIT
HAIDA
HAIDA
TSIMSHIAN
BELLA BELLA
BELLA COOLA
KWAKIUTL
COMOX
NOOTKA
COWICHAN
KLALLAM
QUILEUTE
QUINAULT
SNOQUALMI
TWANA

INSET C

KLAMATH
SHASTA
CHIMARIKO — ACHOMAWI
WAILAKI — WINTUN
YUKI
POMO — MAIDU
COAST MIWOK
MIWOK
COSTANO
SALINA — YOKUTS

1. WAPPO
2. YANA

INSET F

WALAPAI — HAVASUPAI — HOPI — NAVAJO — JICARILLA
MOHAVE
HALCHIDHOMA — YAVAPAI — WESTERN APACHE — KERES — TEWA
QUECHAN
COCOPA — MARICOPA — PIRO
PAPAGO — PIMA — CHIRICAHUA — MANSO — MESCALERO
JUMANO
LIPAN

1. ACOMA
2. ISLETA
3. JEMEZ
4. TANO
5. TAOS
6. ZUNI

INSET E

SHUSWAP
LILLOOET
THOMPSON
OKANAGON
LAKE
KUTENAI
SANPOIL — KALISPEL
COLUMBIA — SPOKAN
COEUR D'ALÈNE
KLIKITAT
YAKIMA
FLATHEAD
WISHRAM
CAYUSE
NEZ PERCÉ
MOLALA
UMATILLA
TENINO

1. NICOLA
2. WALLAWALLA

MILES

0   500   1000

LEGEND FOR MAPS 3 AND 4

1. ABENAKI
2. ACHUMAWI
3. AHTNA
4. ALEUT
5. ALGONKIN
6. ARAPAHO
7. ARIKARA
7A. BAFFINLAND INUIT
8. BANNOCK
9. BEARLAKE
10. BEAVER
11. BELLABELLA
12. BELLA COOLA
13. BLACKFOOT
14. CADDO
15. CAHUILLA
16. CARIBOU INUIT
17. CARRIER
18. CATAWBA
19. CAYUGA
20. CENTRAL YUP'IK ESKIMO
21. CHEROKEE
22. CHEYENNE
23. CHICKASAW
24. CHINOOK
25. CHIPEWYAN
26. CHIRICAHUA
27. CHOCTAW
28. CHUMASH
29. COCOPA
29A. COEUR D'ALENE
30. COMANCHE
31. COMOX
32. COPPER INUIT
33. COWICHAN
34. CREE (WESTERN)
35. CREEK
36. CROW
37. DELAWARE

38. DOGRIB
39. EAST GREENLAND INUIT
40. EASTERN SHOSHONE
41. FLATHEAD
42. FOX AND SAUK
43. GROS VENTRE
44. HAIDA
45. HARE
46. HAVASUPAI
47. HIDATSA
48. HOPI
49. HOPI-TEWA
50. HUPA
51. HURON
52. IGLULIK INUIT
53. INGALIK
54. INUGHUIT
54A. IOWA
54B. IROQUOIS
55. JICARILLA
56. KALAPUYA
56A. KANSA
57. KAROK
58. KASKA
59. KERES
60. KICKAPOO
61. KIOWA
62. KIOWA APACHE
63. KLALLAM
64. KLAMATH
65. KUMEYAAY
66. KUTCHIN
67. KUTENAI
68. KWAKIUTL
69. LABRADOR INUIT
70. LIPAN
71. LILLOOET
72. LUISENO
73. LUMBEE

74. MALISEET
75. MANDAN
76. MARICOPA
77. MENOMINI
78. MESCALERO
79. MIAMI
80. MICMAC
81. MIWOK
82. MOHAVE
83. MOHAWK
84. MONTAGNAIS
85. NAVAJO
86. NETSILIK INUIT
87. NEZ PERCE
88. NOOTKA
89. NORTH ALASKA ESKIMOS
90. NORTHERN PAIUTE
91. NORTHERN SHOSHONE
92. OJIBWA
93. OKANAGON
94. OMAHA
95. ONEIDA
96. ONONDAGA
97. OSAGE
97A. OTO AND MISSOURI
98. OTTAWA
99. PACIFIC ESKIMO
100. PASSAMAQUODDY
101. PAWNEE
102. PENOBSCOT
103. PIMA/PAPAGO
104. POMO
105. PONCA
106. POTAWATOMI
107. POWHATAN
107A. QUAPAW
108. QUECHAN
109. SANTEE
110. SARSI

111. SEKANI
112. SEMINOLE
112A. SEMINOLE-OKLAHOMA
113. SENECA
114. SHAWNEE
115. SHUSWAP
116. SLAVEY
117. SNOQUALMIE
118. SOUTHERN PAIUTE
119. SPOKANE
120. TANAINA
121. TANANA
122. TAOS
123. TETON
124. TEWA
125. THOMPSON
126. TLINGIT
127. TOLOWA
128. TONKAWA
129. TSIMSHIAN
130. TUBATULABAL
131. TUSCARORA
132. UTE
133. WALAPAI
134. WASHOE
135. WEST GREENLAND INUIT
136. WESTERN APACHE
137. WESTERN SHOSHONE
138. WICHITA
139. WINNEBAGO
140. WINTUN
141. WIYOT
142. YANKTON
143. YAVAPAI
144. YOKUTS
145. YUIT
146. YUROK
147. ZUNI

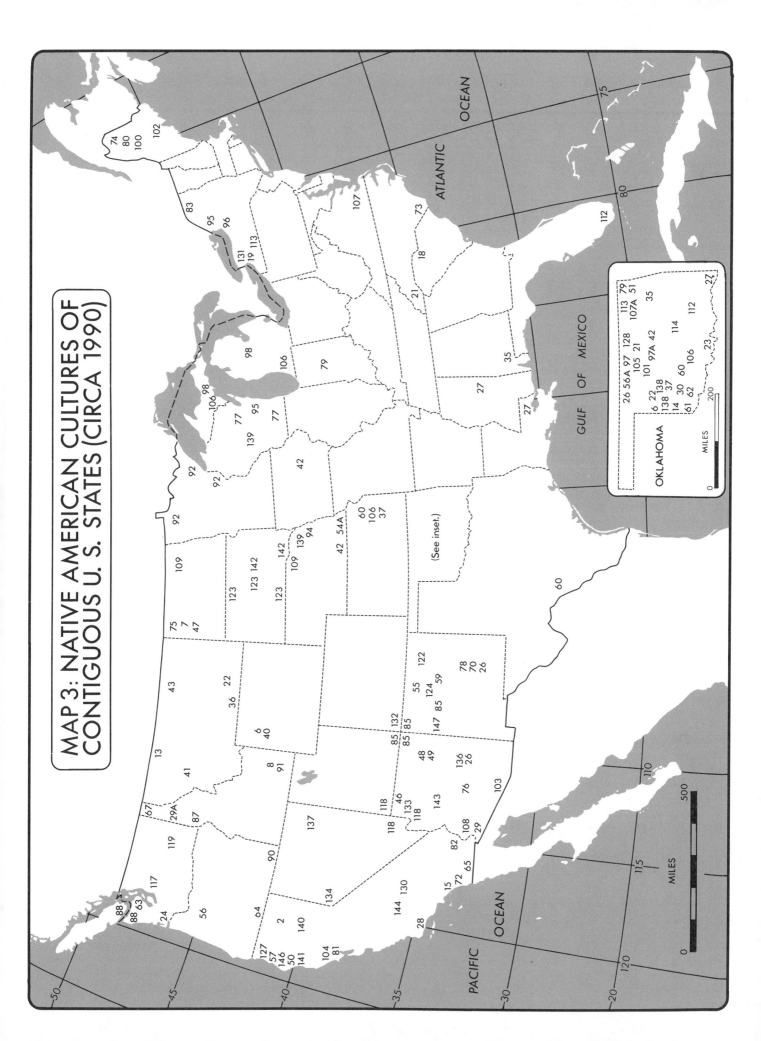

MAP 3: NATIVE AMERICAN CULTURES OF
CONTIGUOUS U. S. STATES (CIRCA 1990)

LEGEND FOR MAPS 3 AND 4

1. ABENAKI	38. DOGRIB	74. MALISEET
2. ACHUMAWI	39. EAST GREENLAND INUIT	75. MANDAN
3. AHTNA	40. EASTERN SHOSHONE	76. MARICOPA
4. ALEUT	41. FLATHEAD	77. MENOMINI
5. ALGONKIN	42. FOX AND SAUK	78. MESCALERO
6. ARAPAHO	43. GROS VENTRE	79. MIAMI
7. ARIKARA	44. HAIDA	80. MICMAC
7A. BAFFINLAND INUIT	45. HARE	81. MIWOK
8. BANNOCK	46. HAVASUPAI	82. MOHAVE
9. BEARLAKE	47. HIDATSA	83. MOHAWK
10. BEAVER	48. HOPI	84. MONTAGNAIS
11. BELLABELLA	49. HOPI-TEWA	85. NAVAJO
12. BELLA COOLA	50. HUPA	86. NETSILIK INUIT
13. BLACKFOOT	51. HURON	87. NEZ PERCE
14. CADDO	52. IGLULIK INUIT	88. NOOTKA
15. CAHUILLA	53. INGALIK	89. NORTH ALASKA ESKIMOS
16. CARIBOU INUIT	54. INUGHUIT	90. NORTHERN PAIUTE
17. CARRIER	54A. IOWA	91. NORTHERN SHOSHONE
18. CATAWBA	54B. IROQUOIS	92. OJIBWA
19. CAYUGA	55. JICARILLA	93. OKANAGON
20. CENTRAL YUP'IK ESKIMO	56. KALAPUYA	94. OMAHA
21. CHEROKEE	56A. KANSA	95. ONEIDA
22. CHEYENNE	57. KAROK	96. ONONDAGA
23. CHICKASAW	58. KASKA	97. OSAGE
24. CHINOOK	59. KERES	97A. OTO AND MISSOURI
25. CHIPEWYAN	60. KICKAPOO	98. OTTAWA
26. CHIRICAHUA	61. KIOWA	99. PACIFIC ESKIMO
27. CHOCTAW	62. KIOWA APACHE	100. PASSAMAQUODDY
28. CHUMASH	63. KLALLAM	101. PAWNEE
29. COCOPA	64. KLAMATH	102. PENOBSCOT
29A. COEUR D'ALENE	65. KUMEYAAY	103. PIMA/PAPAGO
30. COMANCHE	66. KUTCHIN	104. POMO
31. COMOX	67. KUTENAI	105. PONCA
32. COPPER INUIT	68. KWAKIUTL	106. POTAWATOMI
33. COWICHAN	69. LABRADOR INUIT	107. POWHATAN
34. CREE (WESTERN)	70. LIPAN	107A. QUAPAW
35. CREEK	71. LILLOOET	108. QUECHAN
36. CROW	72. LUISENO	109. SANTEE
37. DELAWARE	73. LUMBEE	110. SARSI

111. SEKANI
112. SEMINOLE
112A. SEMINOLE-OKLAHOMA
113. SENECA
114. SHAWNEE
115. SHUSWAP
116. SLAVEY
117. SNOQUALMIE
118. SOUTHERN PAIUTE
119. SPOKANE
120. TANAINA
121. TANANA
122. TAOS
123. TETON
124. TEWA
125. THOMPSON
126. TLINGIT
127. TOLOWA
128. TONKAWA
129. TSIMSHIAN
130. TUBATULABAL
131. TUSCARORA
132. UTE
133. WALAPAI
134. WASHOE
135. WEST GREENLAND INUIT
136. WESTERN APACHE
137. WESTERN SHOSHONE
138. WICHITA
139. WINNEBAGO
140. WINTUN
141. WIYOT
142. YANKTON
143. YAVAPAI
144. YOKUTS
145. YUIT
146. YUROK
147. ZUNI

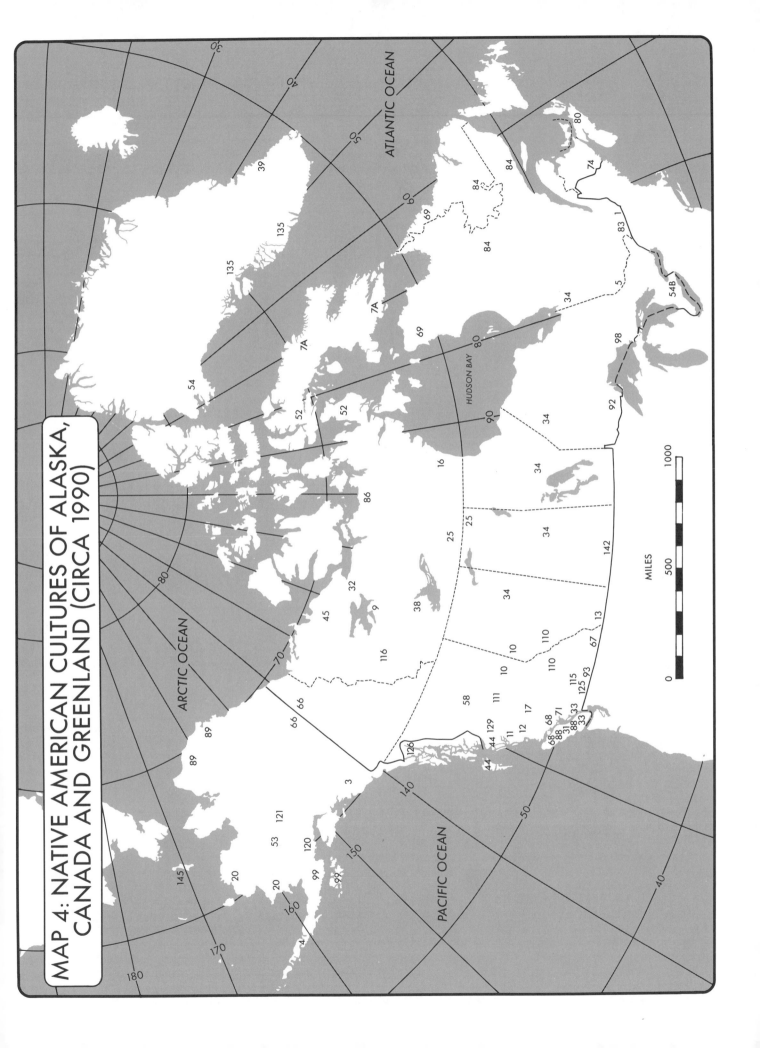

MAP 4: NATIVE AMERICAN CULTURES OF ALASKA, CANADA AND GREENLAND (CIRCA 1990)

Encyclopedia of World Cultures

Volume I

NORTH AMERICA

Abenaki

ETHNONYMS: Abenaque, Abenaquioicts, Abenaquois, Abnaki, Eastern Indians, Mawooshen, Moasham, Obenaki, Openango, Oubenaki, Wabnaki

Orientation

Identification. The Abenaki appear first as "Abenacquiouoict" on Champlain's map of 1632; they were located in the interior of Maine between the Kennebec and Penobscot rivers. In 1604, Champlain had called the Indians of modern New Brunswick and Maine "Etechemins" (lumping the Indians of southeastern New England under the term "Armouchiquois"). Because "Etchemin" was later applied more specifically to the modern Maliseet and Passamaquoddy of New Brunswick and easternmost Maine, some scholars have concluded that the communities Champlain found in Maine in 1604 subsequently withdrew eastward and were replaced by Abenaki expanding from the interior. Others, including this writer, have favored the view that the apparent shift was more likely due to confusion resulting from the changing mix of place-names, personal names, and ethnic identifications that alternated and overlapped in time and space in New England.

Location. In the *Handbook of North American Indians* (1978) a distinction is drawn between the Western Abenaki of interior New Hampshire and Vermont and the Eastern Abenaki of western and central Maine. The Western Abenaki included people of the upper Connecticut River called the "Sokoki." The Eastern Abenaki can be further subdivided from west to east into the Pequawket, Arosaguntacook, Kennebec, and Penobscot, reflecting community clusters along the Presumpscot, Androscoggin, Kennebec, and Penobscot rivers. All through the devastating epidemics and wars of the seventeenth and eighteenth centuries, many survivors from the first three divisions, as well as many Western Abenaki, relocated to the Penobscot. Most Western Abenaki, along with some Eastern Abenaki, eventually settled at Odanak (Saint Francis), near the St. Lawrence River in Quebec. Most Eastern Abenaki survived at Old Town and in other communities of central Maine, where they are known today as the Penobscot Indians. Both communities have absorbed people from southern New England and to a lesser extent from the Maritime Provinces over the last three centuries.

Demography. There were probably around 14,000 Eastern Abenaki and 12,000 Western Abenaki in 1600. These populations collapsed quickly to around 3,000 and 250, respectively, owing largely to epidemics and migration early in the seventeenth century. Further demographic changes took place as refugees arrived from the south, the number of violent deaths increased in the course of colonial warfare, and communities became consolidated at a few locations. In 1973 there were probably no more than 1,000 Western Abenaki, 220 of whom lived at Odanak. Others remain scattered in Vermont and in other portions of their original homeland. The population at Old Town was 815 in 1970, with many people of Penobscot descent living elsewhere.

Linguistic Affiliation. Abenaki dialects belong to the Eastern Algonkian subdivision of the Algonkian-Ritwan language family. Depopulation and family relocations have so confused Abenaki history that it may be impossible to ever reconstruct the contents and distributions of seventeenth-century dialects.

History and Cultural Relations

The Abenaki were contacted sporadically by Basque and perhaps French fishermen during the sixteenth century. Their hostility to Giovanni da Verrazano in 1524 suggests that there had been earlier unfriendly contacts. By the time of more intense French and English exploration just after 1600, the Abenaki were accustomed to dealing with Europeans, and there was brisk trading of furs for European manufactured goods. Kidnapped Abenaki were introduced to fascinated English audiences by their captors. The French took a different approach, sending Jesuit missionaries to convert the Abenaki to Roman Catholicism. An epidemic of hepatitis or some similar disease wiped out the communities of eastern Massachusetts after 1616, opening the way for English settlement in that area in 1620. Meanwhile, the French established themselves at Port Royal (in modern Nova Scotia) and on the St. Lawrence in Quebec, with Abenaki territory then becoming a zone of contention between the European powers. The Abenaki were drawn into six colonial wars between 1675 and 1763. English settlement of the Maine coast was largely abandoned during King Philip's War (1675–1676). Thereafter the Abenaki increasingly became economically tied to the English, but religiously tied to the French. Although they were dependent in different ways upon each, the Abenaki managed to remain independent from both through King William's War (1688–1697), Queen Anne's War (1702–1713), King George's War (1744–1748), and the Seven Years' War (1756–1763), each of which was an American counterpart to wars in Europe. Dummer's War (1721–1725) was a conflict between the Indians and the English that despite French support for the Indian cause had no counterpart conflict in Europe. The Jesuit missionary Sébastien Râle was killed during this war, and afterward many Abenaki from western Maine began moving to safer communities in Quebec and on the Penobscot River. From this time on, the Penobscot were principal spokesmen for the Abenaki in dealings with the English. After the defeat of the French in 1763, the Penobscot joined with six other former French allies in a confederation that had its headquarters at Caughnawaga, Quebec. By this time the western and coastal region of Maine had been lost to English settlement. The Abenaki sided with American rebels in the American Revolution, and those remaining in the United States retained most of interior Maine. New treaties with Massachusetts (which then held the Province of Maine) began to be negotiated in 1786. By 1833 the Penobscot were reduced to a few islands in the Penobscot River. These were unconstitutional agreements, however, and recent land claims by the Penobscot and other Maine Indians have led to very large settlements in compensation for the lost land.

Settlements

Abenaki villages based on hunting, fishing, and collecting were probably always more permanent than those of horticultural communities to the south and west. The Abenaki were unwilling to risk serious horticulture as long as they were at the mercy of frequent crop failures so far north. Thus, the Abenaki settlement pattern does not feature a large number of village sites, each the result of a short occupation. On the other hand, both the coast and the interior lakes are dotted with the traces of temporary camps that were used for seasonal hunting and gathering by family groups. At the time of first contact with Europeans, village houses appear to have been wigwams. These were large enough to accommodate an average of ten people each, although the range of three to twenty-seven people per house suggests considerable variation in house size. Houses at hunting camps were either small versions of the domed wigwam or pyramidal structures having square floor plans. In all cases these early houses were shingled with sheets of bark. Later Penobscot houses combined European log walls with bark roofs, and later villages were palisaded. Still later, in the nineteenth century, frame houses of European design replaced the earlier forms entirely.

Economy

Subsistence and Commercial Activities. The late prehistoric subsistence system probably featured family excursions from the main village to coastal camps during the warm months to hunt and gather maritime resources. Spring and fall runs of migratory fish were harvested from the main villages, which were located mainly at strategic points on major estuaries. Families dispersed upstream to traditional areas along the tributaries of the main streams in the colder months. There were probably midwinter reunions at the main villages when families returned to exchange canoes and other fall hunting equipment for snowshoes, toboggans, and other equipment appropriate for hunting over snow and ice. After 1600, the development of a regular fur trade led to the conversion of traditional family hunting areas into more carefully defined family hunting and trapping territories. As the human and beaver populations shrank, the demand for furs and the importance of their trade for the acquisition of manufactured goods increased. By the nineteenth century, family territories had grown to about a hundred square miles each. The fur trade collapsed and the Penobscot gave up most of their interior lands by 1818. Thereafter they worked in lumbering and the production of splint baskets and canoes for cash income.

Industrial Arts. Birchbark was perhaps the single most important aboriginal material and was used to make shelters, canoes, moose calls, trays, and containers, among other things. Baskets made from ash splints and sweetgrass, for which the Abenaki are still known, provided an alternative source of income. The technique was apparently introduced by European settlers on the Delaware River in the seventeenth century and spread outward from there as it came to be adopted by Indian craftspeople in one community after another. Penobscot men were known as skilled canoe makers, and it is no accident that the Old Town canoe manufacturing company got its start across the Penobscot River from Indian Island. Other crafts were typical of the Eastern Algonkians of New England.

Trade. Although some limited trade with other nations probably occurred prehistorically, the clan system that facilitated trade elsewhere in the Eastern Woodlands was not developed among the Abenaki. After 1600, however, trade flourished with Europeans as the Abenaki were drawn into the world economic system as an important source of beaver pelts. Copper pots replaced native bark containers and earthenware, guns replaced bows, and glass beads replaced porcupine quills very quickly in these decades. Both French and English trading posts were established in and around Abenaki territory, and these led to the construction of forts designed to protect these trading interests through and between the colonial wars.

Division of Labor. Primary distinctions were made on the basis of age and sex. Men were hunters, fishermen, leaders, and shamans. Women were gatherers, hide workers, followers, and curers. Boys and girls aspired to and practiced at these roles.

Land Tenure. Land ownership was not an issue before the development of the fur trade and the historic establishment of farming. By the early nineteenth century, the Abenaki were aware of the advantage of the exclusive ownership of trapping territories and knew from experience the consequences of conveying title to Europeans. Yet by 1818 the disappearance of the fur trade made the ownership of the Maine forests appear useless to them, and they gave up everything but the right to hunt, fish, and collect ash splints over most of their former territory. Meanwhile, the ownership of individual plots became more important for managing gardens and house lots on remaining reservation land.

Kinship

Kin Groups and Descent. The nuclear family was the primary kin group in traditional Abenaki culture. At the end of the nineteenth century, local lineages were often identified with specific animal totems. Those with aquatic totems usually had trapping territories toward the coast and were known as saltwater families. Those with terrestrial totems were found in the more remote interior. Unlike true clans, the common ancestries of these family units were often known, or at least discoverable. Moreover, the ancient trading functions of true clans appear not to have given rise to the totemic groups of the Penobscot. The kinship system was bilateral, with some preference for the patrilineal side. Family (lineage) identities were usually inherited patrilineally, but a young couple who chose to reside with the wife's family would assume that family identity over time.

Kinship Terminology. One's mother and father were distinguished from their siblings, but there was a tendency to lump cousins and siblings together.

Marriage and Family

Marriage. Lineage exogamy was customary, which was expressed as a prohibition against marrying first or second cousins. There was, however, no system of exogamy based on family totems. Dominant men often had more than one wife. The levirate and sororate were common. Polygyny but not polyandry was allowed, partly in recognition of male dominance, partly as social security for widowed people. Households were led by dominant men. A young married couple might reside matrilocally if the husband's father was dead or weak or already had many sons or if the wife's father was strong or lacked sons. Older dominant men might have large households under their control, but the maturation of strong sons could lead to the breakup of such a household.

Domestic Unit. The domestic unit was made up of one to four adult male warriors, a nearly equal number of wives, and a mix of children and elderly. This was the unit that moved to the interior woods in winter and to coast camps in the summer. It was probably also the basic production unit for fishing and gathering activities even when in residence in the main village.

Inheritance. Aboriginally, families made their own houses, tools, and clothing. Sharing and gift giving were important mechanisms for redistributing items produced by specialists within and perhaps between families. Hunting and trapping territories, houses, and perhaps some portable goods were considered the property of the family as a whole, a concept that obviated the issue of inheritance.

Socialization. Sisters were treated with formality and respect by brothers. Boys often took practical instruction from their father's brothers. Women were isolated during menstruation. Young men were also isolated for long periods and given special food if they were identified as gifted runners. Dominant fathers, caring mothers, kind uncles, and fun-loving aunts were familiar figures in the socialization of Abenaki children.

Sociopolitical Organization

Social Organization. The basic social unit was traditionally the residential family. Individuals maintained close relations with others sharing the same family totem. Families fell into a natural division between saltwater and terrestrial totems, but there is little evidence that this division was ever formalized. Men often established lifelong partnerships that went beyond the ties of kinship or close residence. Exchange couched as giftgiving served to maintain such relationships while at the same time facilitating the redistribution of prized items.

Political Organization. Prior to the nineteenth century, village leadership normally resided with a dominant local family. A strong man, or sagamore, usually emerged from such a family to hold a leadership position for life. There was often a second sagamore who also held his position for life. John Attean and John Neptune held these positions at the Penobscot village of Old Town until 1866. Up to that time resistance had been building among members of saltwater families, who referred to themselves as the "New Party." State intervention led to an annual (later biennial) cycle of alternating leadership by the New Party and the Old Party until 1931. Since then leadership has been by election.

Social Control. Leadership and social order were traditionally maintained through the force of strong personalities. Sagamores depended upon broad consensus and lacked the formal power to act without it. But political power, personal charisma, virility, and shamanistic power were nearly interchangeable concepts. Consequently, a strong man had much real power even though it was not defined formally.

Conflict. Abenaki concepts of shamanistic power allowed for the diversion of conflict into the realm of the supernatural. This eliminated much open physical conflict within the community as did warfare with non-Abenaki communities.

Religion and Expressive Culture

Religious Beliefs. Supernatural beings included Pamola, a powerful monster who was believed to live atop Mount Katahdin, the highest mountain in Maine. Gluskabe was a trickster and culture hero whose exploits were more humorous than frightening. Many living men and some women had their own shamanistic powers that allowed them to leave their bodies and enter the realm of the supernatural, usually in animal forms. Strange occurrences involving animals were customarily interpreted as being the acts of shamans in their animal forms.

Religious Practitioners. All shamans possessed at least one animal form into which they could transform themselves. Seven forms were attributed to John Neptune, the most powerful of the last shamans. Such men were virile and had strong personalities. Their powers were often expressed through polygyny and political leadership. The rare female shamans were especially feared and respected in this male-dominated society.

Ceremonies. Dancing was an important part of impromptu ceremonies, including the installation of sagamores, marriages, and occasions when visiting brought people together temporarily. Ceremonies appear to have been irregular compared to the periodic seasonal societies to the southwest. Death and mourning brought any current festivities to an abrupt end, and close relatives mourned for a year.

Arts. Elaborate stitching and curvilinear incised designs decorated prized bark artifacts. In recent centuries, ash splint basketry has been taken up, along with the use of metal-toothed gauges for splitting the splints. The use of tubular wampum was as important here as elsewhere in the Northeast in the seventeenth and eighteenth centuries, and several Penobscot collars and belts survive. Later artisans favored glass seed beads sewn on trade cloth. Bead designs included floral and geometric motifs, as well as the well-known double-curve motif. Other crafts were the more standard ones shared by various Northeast Indian societies.

Medicine. Curers, a class of individuals separate from shamans, understood the medicinal characteristics of various plants, but did not necessarily possess shamanistic powers.

Death and Afterlife. The dead were buried in their best clothes in individual interments. Ideas about an afterlife were probably consistent with shamanistic beliefs, but centuries of Catholic missionizing have greatly modified traditional beliefs.

Bibliography

Day, Gordon M. (1978). "Western Abenaki." In *Handbook of North American Indians*. Vol. 15, *Northeast*, edited by Bruce G. Trigger, 148–159. Washington, D.C.: Smithsonian Institution.

Eckstorm, Fanny H. (1945). *Old John Neptune and Other Maine Indian Shamans*. Portland, Maine: Southworth-Anthoensen Press.

Snow, Dean R. (1968). "Wabanaki 'Family Hunting Territories.'" *American Anthropologist* 70:1143–1151.

Snow, Dean R. (1978). "Eastern Abenaki." In *Handbook of North American Indians*. Vol. 15, *Northeast*, edited by Bruce Trigger, 137–147. Washington, D.C.: Smithsonian Institution.

Speck, Frank G. (1940). *Penobscot Man: The Life History of a Forest Tribe in Maine*. Philadelphia: University of Pennsylvania Press.

DEAN R. SNOW

Acadians

ETHNONYM: Acadiens

Orientation

Identification. "Acadia" ("Acadie") was the name given to the first permanent French colony in North America. Historians disagree as to the origins of the name. One possibility is that it derives from "Arcadia," a name given to a land that was considered a sort of earthly paradise in ancient Greece. The Italian explorer Giovanni da Verrazzano gave the name "Arcadie" to an area he explored along the eastern seaboard of North America in 1524. The other, more likely, possibility is that "Acadie" was borrowed from the Micmac people of the present-day Maritime Provinces of Canada: it is found in many Micmac place names such as "Tracadie," "Shunenacadie," and "Tanacadie." Today, "Acadie" is used to refer to areas in the Maritime Provinces that are populated by French-speaking descendants of the original inhabitants of the colony of Acadia.

Location. The Maritime Provinces include New Brunswick, Prince Edward Island, and Nova Scotia. Being Canada's three smallest provinces, together they cover just over 1 percent of Canada's land surface. The territory predominantly inhabited by Acadians includes almost half of the province of New Brunswick, where French is the majority language both in the three northern counties and on the east coast. Elsewhere, Acadians form a scattered population living in isolated pockets in western Prince Edward Island, southwestern Nova Scotia, and eastern Nova Scotia. The sea forms a natural boundary around the Maritime Provinces, except New Brunswick, which touches upon the province of Quebec to the north and the state of Maine to the west.

Given their position on Canada's Atlantic coast, the Maritimes have a cool, temperate climate: cold continental air masses from the northwest alternate with warmer, humid maritime air from the southwest. Winters are long and cold, and snowfalls abundant. The city of Moncton, in the geographical center of the region, has an average annual snowfall of ninety-two inches. Typically, spring and summer are short seasons, and the autumn is long and pleasant, with cool nights. Summers are very warm in inland areas and along the Gulf of St. Lawrence, but cooler on the Atlantic coast. The average temperature in Moncton is 18° F in January and 64° F in July, although high temperatures occasionally reach 86° F in July. Average annual precipitation is thirty-nine inches. The growing season lasts on the average 133 days, beginning in early May and ending in September. Within the Acadian areas of the Maritime Provinces are two regions with distinctly different weather patterns. Northern New Brunswick has a colder, more continental climate, with a shorter growing season. In Campbellton, for example, the average growing season lasts only 110 days. Southwestern Nova Scotia, in contrast, has a humid, temperate climate with rainy winters and few extremes in temperature.

Demography. In 1986, the total population of the Maritime Provinces was 1,709,000. In census returns, the main indicator used to identify the Acadian population is the mother tongue. In 1986 the total population with French as the mother tongue was 295,000, or 17 percent of the population of the Maritimes. The vast majority of Acadians now live in New Brunswick. Those whose mother tongue in 1986 was French numbered 248,925 in New Brunswick, 39,630 in Nova Scotia, and 6,525 in Prince Edward Island.

There is no city where the Acadians form a majority of the population. The largest concentration of urban Acadians is in Moncton, where they form a third of the population of 80,000.

Linguistic Affiliation. Recent figures have shown that the French language is in sharp decline in Nova Scotia and Prince Edward Island, where Acadians form only 5 percent of the population. Though almost all New Brunswick Acadians used French as their first language in 1986, one-third of Nova Scotia Acadians and almost one-half of those living in Prince Edward Island indicated that English was the main language spoken at home. The rate of acculturation is highest in urban areas where Acadians form a small minority, such as Halifax, St. John, and Charlottetown, although the recent opening of

French-language schools in these cities may influence the trend.

The French language, as spoken by Acadians, includes many archaic elements that originated in the seventeenth-century dialects spoken in western France. The strongest linguistic affiliations are found between Acadia and the Loudun area in the northern part of Poitou. There are several regional linguistic differences in Acadia itself. In northern New Brunswick, for example, the proximity of the province of Quebec has influenced the spoken language, whereas isolated areas such as Chéticamp, on Cape Breton Island, Nova Scotia, have maintained a more archaic form of speech. In the Moncton area, constant intermingling between Acadians and English speakers has spawned a hybrid form of speech, known as Chiac. In French-language schools, modern standard French is taught, and students are strongly encouraged to avoid mixing French and English. Educational institutions also tend to condemn the use of archaic expressions no longer accepted in modern French usage, although in recent years many voices have been raised in the Acadian community calling for the maintenance of the distinctive elements of the Acadian dialect.

History and Cultural Relations

The first French colonists arrived in Acadia in 1604. After ill-fated attempts to establish colonies on Île Sainte-Croix (Dotchet Island, Maine) and at Port-Royal (Nova Scotia), Acadia was abandoned and Britain seized control of the area, naming it Nova Scotia in 1621. In 1632, the Treaty of Saint-Germain-en-Laye returned Acadia to French jurisdiction and permanent colonization began. Between 1632 and 1654, when Acadia once again fell to the British, about fifty families of colonists arrived from France, and those few families formed the nucleus of the present-day Acadian population.

Politically, the next hundred years continued to be marked by instability. Because of the weak position it occupied on the margins of both the French and the British North American empires, Acadia changed hands several times. In 1713, the Treaty of Utrecht gave Britain permanent control of peninsular Nova Scotia, and with the Treaty of Paris in 1763, France lost the rest of what had been the colony of Acadia. During the tense period between these two treaties, the Acadians were referred to by the British as the "French neutrals" because of their desire to avoid all involvement in military conflicts. But despite the Acadians' avowed neutrality, the British began to deport them in 1755, with the goal of destroying their culture and placing settlers from New England on their lands. Among a total population of about thirteen thousand, at least ten thousand were deported between 1755 and 1763. The rest either fled to Quebec or were captured and detained in military camps.

Once a permanent peace had been established, a new Acadia was born, as prisoners being released from detention searched for lands on which to settle. They were joined by a number of Acadians returning from exile, although most of these were drawn toward Quebec, which remained a French-speaking territory, or Louisiana, where they settled in large numbers and became known as "Cajuns." For two centuries, the Acadian population in the Maritime Provinces increased both in numbers and in proportion of the total population, until the 1960s, when the Acadian percentage of the population leveled off in New Brunswick and began to decline in Nova Scotia and Prince Edward Island. Today's Acadians have a whole range of social, educational, and cultural institutions and are active participants in the political process, both provincially and federally, although their political influence is significant only in New Brunswick.

Settlements

In Acadian rural communities long lines of houses stretch along both sides of a main road. Land is divided into parallel strips beginning at the road and continuing beyond the cleared area into the woods. Livestock used to be branded and left to roam free in the woods during grazing season, but now all pastureland is fenced in. The main outbuilding is a barn constructed of vertical wooden boards. The parish church is usually found at the center of the village, with local institutions such as the post office, credit union, and cooperative store nearby. Except in communities with a population of over a thousand, there is rarely a cluster of houses in the center of the village. Rather, the population is evenly spread out along the main road. This is true in both farming and fishing communities, as Acadians in coastal areas traditionally practiced both activities. Rather than living in a clustered community around a harbor, fishing families lived on farms and often traveled several miles to reach the local harbor during fishing season.

The average rural house is quite small and made of wood. The kitchen, the largest room, is the center of activity for the household. Nineteenth-century houses usually included a small room beside the kitchen and two upstairs bedrooms. Acadians have always had a tendency to modify their houses as needed. Often, small houses were enlarged with the addition of a new wing as the family grew. For exterior wall covering, modern clapboard has now replaced cedar or spruce shingles, and asphalt shingles have replaced the original wooden ones on the roof.

Urban houses show various influences in style. Again, wood is the most important element used in construction. In urban areas occupied by Acadians, the main signs of their presence are the Catholic church, the French school, and the credit union.

Economy

Subsistence and Commercial Activities. Until the late nineteenth century, rural Acadian communities had a subsistence economy based on a combination of mixed farming, fishing, and forestry. The development of the commercial fishery, and particularly the lobster industry, brought a modest revenue to rural Acadians beginning in the 1880s. Similarly, the development of the forest industry permitted Acadians to earn money cutting wood during the winter, when farming and fishing activities had ceased. In inland areas, where subsistence agriculture was the main activity, cutting wood in remote lumber camps during the winter provided the only source of cash income. After World War II, subsistence agriculture ceased and the more marginal inland communities became depopulated. In some areas, successful commercial farming has been developed, the main crop being potatoes. An important dairy industry also now exists. The relative success of commercial fishing and farming has prevented massive depopulation in rural areas, although a tendency to move to industrial centers outside the region has existed since the late nineteenth century and still continues.

The traditional diet of Acadians consisted of salt pork, salt fish, wild game (deer, moose, and rabbit), and a limited amount of vegetables such as potatoes, turnips, carrots, and string beans, as well as tea, bread, and molasses. Products such as tea, flour, sugar, and molasses were obtained from local stores and were often bartered for such farm products as butter and eggs.

Industrial Arts. Weaving and knitting are important craft activities for women. Colorful hooked rugs have been produced in large quantities since the early twentieth century, when traveling merchants began yearly trips to Acadian communities in order to exchange manufactured goods for rugs. Today, rugs and hand-woven goods are sold primarily through craft outlets.

Trade. Since the Great Depression, when many Acadians found themselves indebted to local merchants, the cooperative movement has had a strong following. Consumer coops are found throughout Acadia, and many people also belong to producer coops, marketing such diverse products as children's clothing, potato chips, and frozen fish.

Division of Labor. Traditionally, men tended to leave their homes in order to engage in seasonal activities such as lumbering and fishing while the women carried out not only work activities in the home but also much of the farm work. Most women now seek salaried employment outside the home to contribute to the domestic economy, but in farm households women still tend to participate actively in agricultural work.

Land Tenure. Land is privately held, although large tracts of land in the wooded interior are government-owned Crown Lands that may be leased for forest exploitation. Most Acadians tend to be small landowners, and even in cities private ownership of dwellings, rather than renting, is the norm.

Kinship

Kin Groups and Descent. The nuclear family is at the center of the social structure of Acadians. Apart from identifying strongly with their immediate family, people also identify with their extended family, or *parenté*, including grandparents, cousins, aunts, and uncles, and even to a certain extent with distant relations with whom they share a common lineage. Because of the limited number of families that gave rise to the Acadian people in the seventeenth century, the community today can be considered a type of large, extended family, where multiple alliances have been formed among individual kin groups over the years. The fact that they are a minority group with no distinct territory has contributed to making Acadians aware of the importance of maintaining the bonds existing among families. In the past, knowledge of one's lineage was maintained orally by a family elder. Today, Acadians use archival sources to trace their family trees, often seeking to trace both their male and their female lineages.

Kinship Terminology. It is common practice to refer to an individual by his or her father's first name rather than by family name. For instance, in a village where there are several families sharing the name Bourgeois, the son of Georges Bourgeois may be known as Léandre à Georges, rather than Léandre Bourgeois.

Marriage and Family

Marriage. Acadian society long maintained, both through church and parental influences, a taboo regarding marriage outside the Acadian Catholic community. Pressure to marry within one's own cultural group has now diminished, but Acadians still tend to follow the established practice. Couples now usually marry in their midtwenties, whereas the norm used to be the early twenties, and even younger in the case of females. Although the Catholic church disapproves of divorce, Acadians have followed the national trend toward an increase in the divorce rate. The birthrate, which in the past was very high by Canadian standards, has decreased significantly since the 1960s.

Domestic Unit. The single-family household is the basic domestic unit. Aged parents often live with a son or daughter, although it is becoming a common practice to send elderly parents to nursing homes when their health deteriorates. In the past, young married couples often lived with the groom's parents until they had the means to build their own home.

Inheritance. Early Acadians divided their landholdings among their sons. When the land parcels became too small to sustain a family, the sons moved away to settle on new lands. In the twentieth century, the tendency is for one of the children to inherit the land, while the rest of the estate is shared among all the children.

Socialization. In rural communities, an unwritten code of behavior exists, and those who transgress it meet with disapproval that may be expressed in different ways. Physical punishment has always been rare, and rejection, either temporary or permanent, from local society is the most common form of punishment.

Sociopolitical Organization

Social Organization. In the past, immediate authority in each community was held by the parish priest. Since the early 1960s, the church has relinquished its authority in temporal matters, and a new educated elite has filled the void. Acadian nationalist organizations such as La Société Nationale des Acadiens attempt to represent and influence public opinion, with varying success.

Political Organization. Each Canadian province has a democratically elected legislature, with each member representing a riding (district) in his or her province. The provincial legislatures share power with the federal government. Voters elect members to both their provincial legislature and the federal parliament in separate elections.

Social Control. With the modernization of Acadian society, it is difficult to maintain social control through community-imposed sanctions, and there is a greater dependence on the Canadian legal system.

Conflict. Since the end of the conflict between the British and the French in 1763, Acadia has been a peaceful land. By establishing themselves in separate areas, Acadians and English-speaking citizens in the Maritimes largely avoided conflict. A strong element of anti-French prejudice persists, however, and this is most evident in towns, such as Moncton, where the two groups now interact on a regular basis.

Religion and Expressive Culture

Religious Beliefs. Acadians have always been Roman Catholics. Their attachment to the church endured even during the difficult years of resettlement in the late eighteenth century, when church services were held only during rare visits by missionaries from Quebec. In the absence of a priest, it was customary for villagers to gather for Sunday prayers led by an elder of the community. Though adhering strictly to Roman Catholic practices, Acadians traditionally had a strong belief in sorcery, associating sorcerers with the power of the devil. There was also a strong belief that the souls of the deceased in purgatory could manifest themselves to the living. To protect themselves from evil influences, Acadians used the power of prayer, as well as holy objects and holy water, and occasionally requested a priest to perform an exorcism. With the changes in dogma the church has undergone since the 1960s, religious beliefs have tended to become more rationalized.

Religious Practitioners. Parish priests, though still highly respected figures in the community, no longer have the absolute authority they once held in Acadian society. Until the middle of the twentieth century, it was not uncommon for people to believe a priest could heal a sick person or stop a forest fire by reciting certain prayers.

Ceremonies. Christmas and Easter are the most important religious holidays, but traditional feast days have tended to coincide with less important dates on the religious calendar. For example, a festive celebration marking the middle of the winter was held on Candlemas Day, February 2, and the third Thursday in Lent was known as _Mi-Careme_ (Mid-Lent), with people excused from their Lenten obligations for the day. The patron saint of Acadia is Our Lady of Assumption, and August 15, Assumption Day, is the Acadian national holiday.

Arts. Acadians possess a rich oral literature consisting of songs, folktales, and legends. Ballads and tales brought from France by the original settlers have been preserved to a remarkable extent. The Acadians' propensity for music is a distinctive cultural trait, and in almost every family there are singers and musicians who play folk or country music.

Medicine. Before the middle of the twentieth century, Acadians rarely consulted professional medical practitioners. The midwife had an important role in the community, and traditional herbal medicinal cures were widely used. Regional medical clinics have now replaced the village midwife, but herbal medicine is still used in rural areas, and people considered to have the gift of stopping bleeding or curing specific ailments are commonly consulted.

Death and Afterlife. It was once customary for Acadians to hold all-night wakes in their homes, but the establishment of funeral parlors, with their set hours, has now changed the form of the wake. Acadians like to keep mementos of the dead—for example, photographs of the deceased at the funeral parlor. The month of November used to be referred to as _le mois des morts_, and religious ceremonies would then take place in cemeteries. There has been a recent decline in religious observances regarding the dead, but it is still common to celebrate a mass in memory of a deceased person on the anniversary of the death.

See also Cajuns, French Canadians

Bibliography

"Acadians." (1988). In _The Canadian Encyclopedia._ 2nd ed. Edmonton: Hurtig Publishers.

Daigle, Jean, ed. (1982). _The Acadians of the Maritimes._ Moncton: Centre d'etudes acadiennes.

Lapierre, Jean-William, and Muriel Roy (1983). _Les Acadiens._ Paris: Presses Universitaires de France.

Tremblay, Marc-Adelard, and Marc Laplante (1971). _Famille et parente en Acadie._ Ottawa: National Museum of Man.

Vernex, Jean Claude (1978). _Les Francophones du Nouveau-Brunswick._ Paris: Librairie Honore Champion.

RONALD LABELLE

Achumawi

ETHNONYMS: Achomawi, Pit River Indians, Pitt River Indians

The Achumawi are an American Indian group located in northeast California. "Achumawi" means "river people" and referred, aboriginally, to only one subgroup. Today, both the Achumawi and Whites commonly use "Pit River Indians" in reference to the entire society. "Pit River" is derived from the Achumawi practice of trapping deer in deep pits. An aboriginal population of about three thousand has been reduced to about one thousand, although the exact population is unknown owing to the group's dispersed settlement pattern and its mixing with the neighboring Atsugewi. Along with Atsugewi, Achumawi forms the Palaihnihan branch of the Hokan language family.

Little is known about the Achumawi prior to the twentieth century. First contact was probably with trappers in the early 1800s, followed later in the century by an influx of gold miners and settlers which disrupted the traditional culture. Because the group lacked centralized leadership and was marred by factionalism and regional self-interest, much of its aboriginal land was lost to Whites. Since the 1950s members have conducted a series of legal battles to regain some of this land. The Achumawi were in close and regular contact with the Atsugewi, who were bilingual in the two languages. Contacts with other groups were infrequent.

The Achumawi were divided into eleven named subtribes or tribelets, with each occupying a distinct territory. Villages were located on or near water such as rivers or marshlands. The typical winter dwelling was the semisubterranean longhouse, with tule mat–covered conical dwellings used in the summer. Today, about five hundred Achumawi live on the Round Valley and XL Ranch Reservations, with the remainder dispersed among the White population.

The Achumawi occupied a rich and varied ecological region that included pine and oak forests, sagebrush lands, swamps, streams, lakes, meadows, and grasslands. All provided resources for food and manufactures obtained through hunting, fishing, and gathering. Fish, birds, bird eggs, and deer, badgers, and other animals were taken for food and for raw materials for tools, utensils, and clothing. Tubers, roots, and bulbs were dug, and sunflowers, tobacco, and other plant foods and materials collected. In regions with large oak forests, acorns were the dietary staple. Twined basketry was a highly developed craft that survived into the twentieth century.

The aboriginal kinship system has not been well described. Evidently, descent was bilateral and marriage partners were expected to be nonrelatives, which in practice meant people living outside of one's own or nearby villages. Marriage was marked by gift exchange, and both widows and widowers were seen as "property" of the deceased spouse's family. Marriage between members of different tribelets was apparently encouraged as a means of building cross-tribelet solidarity. Puberty rites for boys were minimal, and a girl's first menstruation was marked by a ten-day rite.

Achumawi society was divided into eleven named tribelets, each controlling a distinct territory. Ties between tribelets were based on the common use of the Achumawi language and tribelet exogamy.

Religious beliefs and practices focused on the identification and treatment of illness and misfortunes. Male and female shamans, the central figures in this process, sought to effect cures through contact with the powerful *tamakomi* forces. Each male sought contact with and protection from a personal *tinihowi*, "guardian spirit." Death was unmarked and the soul was thought to travel to the western mountains, where the Achumawi hoped it would remain.

Bibliography

Garner, Van Hastings (1982). *The Broken Ring: The Destruction of the California Indians.* Tucson, Ariz.: Westernlore Press.

Olmsted, David L., and Omer C. Stewart (1978). "Achumawi." In *Handbook of North American Indians.* Vol. 8, *California,* edited by Robert F. Heizer, 225–235. Washington, D.C.: Smithsonian Institution.

African Americans

ETHNONYMS: (contemporary): Black Americans, Afro-Americans; (archaic): Colored, Negro

Orientation

Identification.   African Americans constitute the largest non-European racial group in the United States of America. Africans came to the area that became the United States in the sixteenth century with the Spaniards, but their first appearance as a group in the English colonies occurred in 1619, when twenty Africans were brought as indentured servants to Jamestown, Virginia. Subsequent importations of Africans from western Africa stretching from Morocco on the north to Angola on the south over a period of two hundred years greatly increased the African population in the United States. By the time of the Emancipation Proclamation in 1863, they numbered 4.5 million people. A composite people, comprised of numerous African ethnic groups including Yoruba, Wolof, Mandingo, Hausa, Asante, Fante, Edo, Fulani, Serer, Luba, Angola, Congo, Ibo, Ibibio, Ijaw, and Sherbro, African Americans have a common origin in Africa and a common struggle against racial oppression. Many African Americans show evidence of racial mixture with Native Americans, particularly Creek, Choctaw, Cherokee, and Pawnee, as well as with Europeans from various ethnic backgrounds.

Location.   African Americans were predominantly a rural and southern people until the Great Migration of the World War II era. Thousands of Africans moved to the major urban centers of the North to find better jobs and more equitable living conditions. Cities such as Chicago, New York, Philadelphia, and Detroit became magnets for entire southern communities of African Americans. The lure of economic prosperity, political enfranchisement, and social mobility attracted many young men. Often women and the elderly were left on the farms in the South, and husbands would send for their families, and children for their parents, once they were established in their new homes. Residential segregation became a pattern in the North as it had been in the South. Some of these segregated communities in the North gained prominence and became centers for culture and commerce. Harlem in New York, North Philadelphia in Philadelphia, Woodlawn in Detroit, South Side in Chicago, and Hough in Cleveland were written into the African Americans' imagination as places of high style, fashion, culture, and business. The evolution of the African American communities from southern and rural to northern and urban has been going on since 1945. According to the 1980 census, the largest populations are found in New York, Chicago, Detroit, Philadelphia, Los Angeles, Washington, D.C., Houston, Baltimore, New Orleans, and Memphis. In terms of percentage of population, the five leading cities among those with populations of over 300,000 are Washington, D.C., 70 percent; Atlanta, 67 percent; Detroit, 65 percent; New Orleans, 55 percent; and Memphis, 49 percent. (East St. Louis, Illinois, is 96 percent African American, but its population is less than 100,000.)

Demography.   The 1990 population of African Americans is estimated to be 35 million. In addition to those in the United States, there are approximately 1 million African Americans abroad, mainly in Africa, Europe, and South America. African Americans constitute about 12 percent of the American population. This is roughly equal to the percentages of Africans in the populations of Venezuela and Colombia. The largest population of African people outside the continent of Africa resides in Brazil; the second largest is in the United States of America. The following countries have the largest populations of Africans in the world: Nigeria, Brazil, Egypt, Ethiopia, Zaire, and the United States. The cities with the largest populations of African Americans are New York, 2.1 million; Chicago, 1.4 million; Detroit, over

800,000; Philadelphia, close to 700,000; and Los Angeles, more than 600,000. Seven states have African American populations of more than 20 percent. These are southern and predominantly rural: Mississippi, 35 percent; South Carolina, 30 percent; Louisiana, 29 percent; Georgia, 27 percent; Alabama, 26 percent; Maryland, 23 percent; and North Carolina, 22 percent.

Linguistic Affiliation.   African Americans are now native speakers of English. During the seventeenth century, most Africans in the Americas spoke West African languages as their first languages. In the United States, the African population developed a highly sophisticated pidgin, usually referred to by linguists in its creolized form as Ebonics. This language was the prototype for the speech of the vast majority of African Americans. It was composed of African syntactical elements and English lexical items. Use of this language made it possible for Africans from various ethnic and linguistic groups (such as Yoruba, Ibo, Hausa, Akan, Wolof, and Mande) to communicate with one another as well as with the Europeans with whom they came in contact.

The impact of the African American language on American society has been thorough and all-embracing. From the ubiquitous "O.K.," a Wolof expression from Senegal, to the transformations of words like "bad" and "awesome" into different and more adequate expressions of something entirely original, one sees the imprint of African American styles that are derived from the African heritage. There are more than three thousand words, place names, and concepts with African origins found in the language of the United States. Indeed, the most dynamic aspects of the English language as spoken in the United States have been added by the popular speakers of the African American idiom, whether contemporary rap musicians, past jazz musicians, or speakers of the street slang that has added so much color to American English. Proverbs, poems, songs, and hollers, which come with the historical saga of a people whose only epics are the spirituals, the great songs, provide a rich texture to the ever-evolving language of the African American people.

History and Cultural Relations

African Americans did not come freely to America. Theirs is not a history of a people seeking to escape political oppression, economic exploitation, religious intolerance, or social injustice. Rather, the ancestors of the present African Americans were stolen from the continent of Africa, placed on ships against their wills, and transported across the Atlantic. Most of the enslaved Africans went to Brazil and Cuba, but a great portion landed in the southern colonies or states of the United States. At the height of the European slave trade, almost every nation in Europe was involved in some aspect of the enterprise. As the trade grew more profitable and European captains became more ambitious, larger ships with specially built "slave galleries" were commissioned. These galleries between the decks were no more than eighteen inches in height. Each African was allotted no more than a sixteen-inch wide and five-and-a-half-foot-long space for the many weeks or months of the Atlantic crossing. Here the Africans were forced to lie down shackled together in chains fastened to staples in the deck. Where the space was two feet high, Africans often sat with legs on legs, like riders on a crowded sled. They were transported seated in this position with a once-a-day break for exercise. Needless to say, many died or went insane.

The North made the shipping of Africans its business; the South made the working of Africans its business. From 757,208 in 1790 to 4,441,830 in 1860, the African American population grew both through increased birthrates and through importation of new Africans. By 1860, slavery had been virtually eliminated in the North and West, and by the end of the Civil War in 1865, it was abolished altogether. After the war, 14 percent of the population was composed of Africans, the ancestors of the overwhelming majority living in the United States today.

During the Reconstruction period after the Civil War, African American politicians introduced legislation that provided for public education, one of the great legacies of the African American involvement in the legislative process of the nineteenth century. Education has always been seen as a major instrument in changing society and bettering the lives of African American people. Lincoln University and Cheyney University in Pennsylvania, Hampton in Virginia, and Howard University are some of the oldest institutions of learning for the African American community. Others, such as Tuskegee, Fisk, Morehouse, Spelman, and Atlanta University, are now a part of the American educational story of success and excellence.

The Great Civil Rights Movement of the 1950s and 1960s ushered in a new generation of African Americans who were committed to advancing the cause of justice and equality. Rosa Parks refused to give her seat to a White man on a Montgomery city bus and created a stir that would not end until the most visible signs of racism were overthrown. Martin Luther King, Jr., emerged as the leading spokesperson and chief symbol of a people tired of racism and segregation and prepared to fight and die if necessary in order to obtain legal and human rights. Malcolm X took the battle a step further, insisting that the African American was psychologically lost as well and therefore had to find historical and cultural validity in the reclamation of the African connection. Thus, out of the crucible of the 1960s came a more vigorous movement toward full recognition of the African past and legacy. Relationships with other groups depended more and more on mutual respect rather than the African Americans acting like clients of these other groups. African Americans expressed their concern that the Jewish community had not supported affirmative action, although there was a long history of Jewish support for African American causes. Accepting the role of vanguard in the struggle to extend the protection of the American Constitution to oppressed people, African Americans made serious demands on municipal and federal officials during the civil rights movement. Voting rights were guaranteed and protected, educational segregation was made illegal, and petty discriminations against African Americans in hotels and public facilities were eradicated by the sustained protests and demonstrations of the era.

Economy

African Americans have been key components in the economic system of the United States since its inception. The initial relationship of the African American population to the economy was based upon enslaved labor. Africans were instrumental in establishing the industrial and agrarian power of the United States. Railroads, factories, residences, and places of business were often built by enslaved Africans. Now African Americans are engaged in every sector of the American economy, though the level of integration in some sectors is less than in others. A considerable portion of the African American population works in the industrial or service sectors. Others are found in the professions as opposed to small businesses. Thus, teachers, lawyers, doctors, and managers account for the principal professional workers. These patterns are based upon previous conditions of discrimination in businesses throughout the South. Most African Americans could find employment in communities where their professional services were needed; therefore, the above-mentioned professions and others that cater to the African American population provide numerous opportunities for employment. During the past twenty years, the number of businesses opened by African Americans has begun to increase again. During the period of segregation, many businesses existing solely for the convenience of the African American population flourished. When the civil rights movement ended most of the petty discriminations and it became possible for African Americans to trade and shop at other stores and businesses, the businesses located in the African American community suffered. There is now a greater awareness of the need to see businesses as interconnected and interdependent with the greater American society. A larger and more equitable role is being played by women in the African American community. Indeed, many of the chief leaders in the economic development of the African American community are and have been women. Both men and women have always worked in the majority of African American homes.

Kinship, Marriage and Family

Marriage and Family.   African American marriage and kinship patterns are varied, although most now conform to those of the majority of Americans. Monogamy is the overwhelming choice of most married people. Because of the rise of Islam, there is also a growing community of persons who practice polygyny. Lack of marriageable males is creating intense pressure to find new ways of maintaining traditions and parenting children. Within the African American population, one can find various arrangements that constitute family. Thus, people may speak of family, aunts, uncles, fathers, mothers, and children without necessarily meaning that there is a genetic kinship. African Americans often say "brother" or "sister" as a way to indicate the possibility of that being the actual fact. In the period of the enslavement, individuals from the same family were often sold to different plantation masters and given the names of those owners, creating the possibility that brothers or sisters would have different surnames. Most of the names borne by African Americans are derived from the enslavement period. These are not African names but English, German, French, and Irish names, for the most part. Few African Americans can trace their ancestry back before the enslavement. Those that can do so normally have found records in the homes of the plantation owners or in the local archives of the South. African Americans love children and believe that those who have many children are fortunate. It is not uncommon to find families with more than four children.

Socialization.   African American children are socialized in the home, but the church often plays an important role. Parents depend upon other family members to chastise, instruct, and discipline their children, particularly if the family members live in proximity and the children know them well. Socialization takes place through rites and celebrations that grow out of religious or cultural observances. There is a growing interest in African child socialization patterns with the emergence of the Afrocentric movement. Parents introduce the *mfundalai* rites of passage at an early age in order to provide the child with historical referents. Increasingly, this rite has replaced religious rites within the African American tradition for children. Although it is called mfundalai in the Northeast, it may be referred to as the Changing Season rite in other sections of the United States. This was done in the past in the churches and schools, where children had to recite certain details about heroines and heroes or about various aspects of African American history and culture in order to be considered mature in the culture. Many independent schools have been formed to gain control over the cultural and psychological education of African American children. A distrust of the public schools has emerged during the past twenty-five years because African Americans believe that it is difficult for their children to gain the self-confidence they need from teachers who do not understand or are insensitive to the culture. Youth clubs established along the lines of the African age-set groups are popular, as are drill teams and formal youth groups, often called "street gangs" if they engage in delinquent behavior. These groups are, more often than not, healthy expressions of male and sometimes female socialization clubs. Church groups and community center organizations seek to channel the energies of these groups into positive socialization experiences. They are joined by the numerous Afrocentric workshops and seminars that train young people in traditional behaviors and customs.

Sociopolitical Organization

Social Organization.   African Americans can be found in every stratum of the American population. However, it remains a fact that the vast majority of African Americans are outside of the social culture of the dominant society in the United States. In a little less than 130 years, African Americans who were emancipated with neither wealth nor good prospects for wealth have been able to advance in the American society against all odds. Considered determined and doggedly competitive in situations that threaten survival, African Americans have had to outrun economic disaster in every era. Discrimination against African Americans remains in private clubs, country clubs, social functions, and in some organizations. Nevertheless, African Americans have challenged hundreds of rules and regulations designed to limit choice. Among the major players in the battle for equal rights have been the National Association for the Advancement of Colored People (NAACP) and the Urban League. These two organizations have advanced the social integration of the African American population on the legal and social welfare fronts. The NAACP is the major civil rights organization as well as the oldest. Its history in the struggle for equality and justice is legendary. Thurgood Marshall, the first African American to sit on the Supreme Court, was one of the organization's most famous lawyers. He argued twenty-four cases before the Supreme Court as a lawyer and is credited with winning twenty-three. Although there is no official organization of the entire African American population, and no truly mass movement that speaks to the interests of the majority of the people, the NAACP comes closest to being a conscience for the nation and an organized response to oppression, discrimination, and racism. At the local level, many communities have organized Committees of Elders who are responsible for various activities within the communities. These committees are usually informal and are set up to assist the communities in determining the best strategies to follow in political and legal situations. Growing out of an Afrocentric emphasis on community and cohesiveness, the committees are usually composed of older men and women who have made special contributions to the community through achievement or philanthropy.

Political Organization.   African Americans participate freely in the two dominant political parties in the nation, Democratic and Republican. Most African Americans are Democrats, a legacy from the era of Franklin Delano Roosevelt and the New Deal Democrats who brought about a measure of social justice and respect for the common people. There are more than six thousand African Americans who are elected officials in the United States, including the governor of Virginia and the mayors of New York, Los Angeles, Philadelphia, and Detroit. A previous mayor of Chicago was also an African American. Concentrated in the central cities, the African American population has a strong impact on the political processes of the older cities. The national Democratic party chairperson is of African American heritage, and some of the most prominent persons in the party are also African Americans. The Republican party has its share, though not as large, of African American politicians. There is no independent political party in the African American community, although it has remained one of the dreams of leading strategists.

Social Control and Conflict.   Conflict is normally resolved in the African American community through the legal system, although there is a strong impetus to use consensus first. The idea of discussing an issue with other members of the community who might share similar values is a prevalent one within the African American society. A first recourse when problems arise is another person. This is true whether it is a personal problem or a problem with family members. Rather than calling a lawyer first, the African American is most likely to call a friend and seek advice. To some extent, the traditional African notion of retaining and maintaining harmony is at the heart of the matter. Conflicts should be resolved by people, not by law, is one of the adages.

Religion and Expressive Culture

Religious Beliefs.   African Americans practice the three main monotheistic religions, as well as Eastern and African religions. The predominant faith is Christian, the second largest group of believers accept the ancestral religions of Africa—Vodun, Santeria, Myal—and a third group of followers practice Islam. Judaism and Buddhism are also practiced by some people within the community. Without understanding the complexity of religion in the African American community, one should not venture too deeply into the nature of the culture. While the religions of Christianity and Islam seem to attract attention, the African religions are present everywhere, even in the minds of the Christians and Muslims. Thus, traditional practitioners have introduced certain rites that have become a part of the practices of the Christians and Muslims, such as African greetings and libations to ancestors. The African American is spiritually oriented; having given to the American society the spirituals, the master songs, the African American people have learned how to weave religion into everything so that there is no separation between religion and life. Many of the practitioners of the African religions use the founding of Egypt as the starting date for the calendar; thus 6290 A.F.K. (After the Founding of Kemet) is equivalent to 1990. There is no single set of beliefs to which all African Americans subscribe.

Ceremonies.   Martin Luther King, Jr.'s, birthday, January 15, and Malcolm X's birthday, May 19, are the two most important days in the African American calendar. Kwanzaa, a celebration of first fruits, initiated by the philosopher Maulana Karenga, is the most joyous occasion in the African American year. Kwanzaa is observed from December 26 to January 1, and each day is named after an important virtue.

Death and Afterlife.   There is no wide acceptance of cremation in the African American culture; the majority of African Americans choose burial. Funerals are often occasions of sadness followed by festivities and joyousness. "When the Saints Go Marching In" was made famous as the song to convey African Americans to the other world by African American musicians in New Orleans. Sung and played with gusto and great vigor, the song summed up the victorious attitude of a people long used to suffering on earth.

See also Black Creoles of Louisiana, Sea Islanders

Bibliography

Asante, Molefi, and Mark Mattson (1990). _The Historical and Cultural Atlas of African Americans_. New York: Macmillan.

Baughman, E. Earl (1971). _Black Americans_. New York: Academic Press.

Frazier, Thomas R. (1988). _Afro American History: Primary Sources_. 2nd ed. Chicago: Dorsey Press.

Harding, Vincent (1981). _There Is a River_. New York: Vintage.

Henry, Charles (1990). _Culture and African American Politics_. Bloomington: Indiana University Press.

McPherson, James, et al. (1971). _Blacks in America: Bibliographic Essays_. Garden City, N.Y.: Anchor Books.

MOLEFI KETE ASANTE

Ahtna

ETHNONYMS: Ahtena, Ahtnakotana

The Ahtna, an Athapaskan-speaking American Indian group, were located in the eighteenth century in the Copper River basin of Alaska and numbered about five hundred. First European contact was with Russians in the eighteenth century, but it was the discovery of gold in their territory in 1899 that opened the group to intensive and sustained outside contact. In 1980 the Ahtna numbered three hundred and continued to live in the Copper River basin where they persisted in the practice of some of their traditional subsistence and religious activities. The Ahtna were and are culturally related to the neighboring Tanaina.

In the eighteenth century the Ahtna fished, hunted, and gathered for their subsistence and were heavily involved in the fur trade. Salmon, caught with traps, nets, weirs, and spears, was their most important food source. The Ahtna were divided into three geographical groups, each speaking a separate dialect and composed of several villages. Each village was made up of several families and was led by its own chief, or *tyone*. Each family occupied a semisubterranean wood and pole frame house covered with spruce bark. Within Ahtna society there was a complex social structure consisting of village leaders, shamans, commoners, and a servant class. Religious life centered around the potlatch.

Bibliography

Goniwiecha, Mark C., and David A. Hales (1988). "Native Language Dictionaries and Grammars of Alaska, Northern Canada and Greenland." *Reference Services Review* 16:121–134.

Hanable, William S., and Karen W. Workman (1974). *Lower Copper and Chitina River: An Historic Resources Study.* Juneau: Alaskan Division of Parks, Department of Natural Resources.

Laguna, Frederica de, and Catharine McClellan (1981). "Ahtna." In *Handbook of North American Indians.* Vol. 6, *Subarctic,* edited by June Helm, 641–663. Washington, D.C.: Smithsonian Institution.

Alabama

The Alabama (Alibamu), with the Kaskinampo, Koasati (Alabama-Coushatta), Muklasa, Pawokti, and Tawasa, lived in south central Alabama and the northwestern tip of Florida. Their descendants now live principally on the Polk County Reservation in Texas (the Alabama-Coushatta Tribe of Texas), in the Alabama-Quassarte tribal town in Oklahoma, and in the Coushatta Community in Louisiana. They spoke Muskogean languages. The population of the Alabama-Coushatta tribe of Texas was 494 in 1980, and that of the Coushatta Community was 196 in 1966. A tourism-based economy has given economic stability to the community.

Bibliography

Bounds, John H. (1971). "The Alabama-Coushatta Indians of Texas." *Journal of Geography* 70:175–182.

Roth, Aline T. (1963). *Kalita's People: A History of the Alabama-Coushatta Indians of Texas.* Waco, Tex.

Aleut

ETHNONYMS: Aleutian, Alyoot

Orientation

Identification.   The origin of the name "Aleut" is uncertain. It is possibly derived from the Olutorski tribe, on the Olutorsk River, in northeast Kamchatka, and was applied by early Russian fur hunters to residents of the Aleutian Islands. But it may instead be derived from the Chukchee word for "island," *aliat.* Finally, it is possible that "Aleut" comes from the name the westernmost Aleuts, on Attu Island, used to refer to themselves, "Aliut," which was then extended eastward by the Russians. Today, Aleuts infrequently refer to themselves with the Aleut word "Unangin" (or "Anĝaĝin"), meaning approximately "we, the people."

Location.   At the time of initial Russian contact in 1741, Aleuts occupied all the Aleutian Islands west to Attu Island, the western tip of the Alaska Peninsula, and the Shumagin Islands south of the Alaska Peninsula. In the late 1700s and early 1800s, Aleuts were settled on the Pribilof Islands in the Bering Sea. Today, some thirteen Aleut villages remain, mostly in the Pribilofs and eastern Aleutians.

Demography.   At contact, there were an estimated twelve thousand to fifteen thousand Aleuts, but this number quickly and dramatically declined in the first decades of Russian occupation. Today fewer than two thousand live in several small communities in the Aleutian and Pribilof Islands, while approximately another fifteen hundred reside elsewhere in Alaska or other states.

Linguistic Affiliation.   The Aleut language belongs to the Eskimo-Aleut (or Eskaleut) language family. Eastern, central, and western dialects existed until quite recently; now only the first two are spoken to any degree, and those mostly by adults.

History and Cultural Relations

Archaeological evidence is clear that Aleuts have lived in the Aleutian archipelago for at least the last four thousand years.

Although the oldest archaeological site in the Aleutians dates to eight thousand years ago, it is not certain that the cultural, biological, and linguistic affiliations of its occupants were Aleut. Very few sites are known from between eight thousand and four thousand years ago. Because of their residence in a geographic cul-de-sac, Aleuts had only infrequent and largely inconsequential contact with other peoples except their Eskimo neighbors to the east on the Alaska Peninsula and Kodiak Island, with whom Aleuts both traded and fought.

Settlements

Prior to Russian contact, Aleuts maintained coastal villages and seasonal subsistence camps. Prime village locations had safe access to the sea, a number of important food resources close at hand, and often lookout locales from which offshore resources or attacking enemies could be spotted. Villages varied a great deal in size, from just a few families in one or two houses to many families in several houses. The homes were semisubterranean, roofed over with rafters of driftwood and whalebone, and covered with a layer of sod. With the coming of the Russians in the mid-1700s and the Americans a century later, the Aleut population dwindled and settlements were consolidated. By the early twentieth century, houses were nearly all above-ground frame structures in which nuclear families lived.

Economy

Subsistence and Commercial Activities. The sea was the direct and indirect provider of virtually all of the Aleuts' subsistence needs. These gatherer-hunters depended on a broad spectrum of plentiful resources, including marine mammals (like sea lions, harbor seals, and sea otters), marine invertebrates (like sea urchins, clams, and mussels), birds and eggs (like murres, puffins, ducks, and geese), and fish (like cod, halibut, and several species of salmon). Plant foods, primarily berries, provided only a small part of their diet. With Russian contact came a few imported foodstuffs, but the major economic changes resulted from the subsequent loss of population and most of the men being forced to work for the Russian fur hunters as procurers of sea otter and other animal pelts. Beginning in the late 1700s, some Aleuts were relocated seasonally, eventually resettling permanently on the Pribilof Islands north of the Aleutian archipelago. The Pribilofs are the breeding grounds of the northern fur seal, and Aleut labor was crucial to Russian efforts to harvest these pelts. In the late nineteenth century and the first half of the twentieth, Aleuts from the Aleutian Islands found seasonal employment in the Pribilof fur seal harvest, and others pursued fox trapping, commercial fishing, and traditional subsistence activities. Today, many Aleuts continue hunting, gathering, and fishing for the traditional food items, but all are involved to some degree in the Western cash economy. Many work away from their villages at seasonal construction and fishing, since employment in the villages is generally limited.

Industrial Arts. Prior to Russian contact, Aleut material culture consisted primarily of tools manufactured from local stone and sea mammal and bird bone. Other important raw materials included grass for baskets and matting and drift-wood for boats, houses, masks, and other carved objects. Today, traditional crafts are limited mostly to the very finely woven grass baskets made by just a few women for sale.

Trade. Aboriginally, trade within the Aleutian region was apparently confined largely to items of localized availability: amber, obsidian, and walrus ivory. During the Russian period, Aleuts became increasingly dependent on metal tools and, to a certain extent, imported foodstuffs.

Division of Labor. Although traditionally there was general division of labor by both age and sex, a feature of the Aleut food economy was that most members of a community could make an important contribution to their families' food supplies. Thus, though younger, able-bodied Aleut men traditionally did all the hunting at sea, few other subsistence pursuits were restricted to only one group. This basic pattern continues to the present: men are still the only ones who go out in their skiffs to hunt, while all members of the community fish, collect marine invertebrates, gather eggs, and so on.

Land Tenure. Prior to Russian contact, land, strictly speaking, had much less value than coastline, and Aleuts likely maintained rights to hunt, fish, and gather along specific portions of the coast. With the 1971 passage of the federal Alaska Native Claims Settlement Act, each Aleut village selected a certain amount of land within the Aleutian Islands region to own, and the regional Aleut Corporation likewise was given title to certain lands.

Kinship

Kin Groups and Descent. Prior to contact, Aleut kinship was likely matrilineal, though the ethnohistoric information on this is not altogether clear. It is doubtful that kin groups beyond the matrilineage, such as moieties or phratries, existed. Within a few decades of Russian contact, this system ceased to function.

Kinship Terminology. The pattern of precontact Aleut kinship terminology has not been adequately determined.

Marriage and Family

Marriage. Precontact Aleut matrilineages were likely exogamous, with a boy's preferred marriage partner being the daughter of his mother's brother. Polygamy occurred, with polygyny more common than polyandry. Postmarital residence was flexible; a couple might live matrilocally at first and then patrilocally, perhaps after the birth of their first child.

Domestic Unit. Aleut houses (_barabaras_) were multifamily units. Although some houses were occupied by perhaps a pair of related nuclear families, others were larger and served as home to dozens of individuals from many related families. By the later Russian period and today, nuclear family households are the norm.

Inheritance. The aboriginal pattern of inheritance is unclear. Some material possessions might be buried with the deceased individual; others could be passed on to family members or friends. It is possible that the house was passed down to the eldest daughter. Contemporary inheritance patterns have not been described.

Socialization. Traditionally, as today, children depended on close relatives for their care and training. Although generally permissive, parents provide discipline in various ways, including telling stories of the dangerous "outside men." Schools in most communities extend through high school, though relatively few students attend college.

Sociopolitical Organization

Social Organization.   Aboriginal Aleut society was ranked, with the highest status going to those individuals having the greatest wealth (including Aleut and Eskimo slaves), the largest families, the most local kin support, and the closest proximity to important subsistence resources. This system changed rapidly and radically with the coming of the Russians. Many Russian men married Aleut women, they and their families remaining in Alaska after it was sold to the United States. The children of these marriages, often termed "Creoles" in the literature of the times, frequently received special education and assumed skilled technical positions with the Russian-American Company. Today, no Creoles per se exist; however, those Aleuts who have gained experience outside the villages through formal education, military service, or other means serve in positions of leadership on the regional or village level.

Political Organization.   Aboriginally, villages were probably the basic political unit, though larger, regional, political affiliations did exist. With the tremendous population decline and resettlement during the Russian period, these political entities were essentially abolished. In the 1960s and 1970s, regional Aleut organizations were formed. Today, the Islands Association represents Aleuts on a regional basis, and similar village-based for-profit and nonprofit corporations operate in each community.

Social Control.   Prior to contact, Aleuts maintained social control through the informal pressure of ridicule and gossip, with village leaders deciding upon more formal punishments.

Conflict.   Aleuts traditionally warred among themselves as well as against neighboring Eskimo peoples to the east on the Alaska Peninsula and Kodiak Island. Personal revenge and the capture of slaves were likely the primary motivations for warfare. In the first decades of the Russian period, Aleuts often attempted to defend themselves against foreign violence and hostility, but were subdued by the late 1700s.

Religion and Expressive Culture

Religious Beliefs.   Because Russian contact quickly devastated much of Aleut culture, we know relatively little about the group's traditional religion. It was animistic, with spirits of humans, animals, and natural entities requiring placation. Russian Orthodoxy was introduced by the early Russian fur hunters, and the first missionaries arrived at the end of the eighteenth century. By the mid-1800s, Russian Orthodoxy had likely replaced virtually all the precontact Aleut religion.

Religious Practitioners.   Shamans were the aboriginal specialists in dealing with the supernatural. They cured the sick, foretold the future, brought success in hunting and warfare, and performed other similar tasks. With Russian Orthodoxy came priests, though from the beginning the church emphasized native involvement and leadership, and to this day there has been a large proportion of Aleuts educated and trained as priests. Today, most Aleuts are members of the Russian Orthodox church.

Ceremonies.   Prior to contact, Aleut ceremonies were likely held in the winter. Through singing, dancing, drumming, and wearing masks, the people entertained themselves and honored deceased relatives. Social rank was likely bolstered through bestowal of gifts. Today, Aleut ceremonies are those of the Russian Orthodox church.

Arts.   Artistic expression took many forms, among them singing, dancing, storytelling, and carving in wood, ivory, and bone. Except for grass baskets made for sale by some Aleut women, few traditional arts survive today.

Medicine.   Traditional Aleut medical knowledge was extensive. Aleuts were aware of the similarities of human anatomy to that of sea mammals, and they sometimes autopsied their dead to determine the cause of death. Sickness was treated in various spiritual and practical ways, including forms of acupuncture and bloodletting. By the mid-1800s, aboriginal spiritual aspects of healing were lost. Today, Aleuts can obtain limited medical care in their home communities or obtain full care by traveling to larger cities.

Death and Afterlife.   Aleuts believed that death stemmed from both natural and supernatural causes. The dead were treated in a range of ways, including mummification and cave burial of high-ranking men, women, and children, burial in special stone and wooden burial structures, and interment in small holes in the ground adjacent to habitations. Spirits of deceased individuals continued to "live," although details of any notion of an afterlife or of reincarnation are scanty.

Bibliography

Lantis, Margaret (1970). "The Aleut Social System, 1750 to 1810, from Early Historical Sources." In *Ethnohistory in Southwestern Alaska and the Southern Yukon: Method and Content*, edited by Margaret Lantis, 139–301. Lexington: University of Kentucky Press.

Lantis, Margaret (1984). "Aleut." In *Handbook of North American Indians*. Vol. 5, *Arctic*, edited by David Damas, 161–184. Washington, D.C.: Smithsonian Institution.

Laughlin, William S. (1980). *Aleuts: Survivors of the Bering Land Bridge*. New York: Holt, Rinehart & Winston.

Veniaminov, Ivan (1984). *Notes on the Islands of the Unalashka District*. Kingston, Ontario: Limestone Press.

DOUGLAS W. VELTRE

Algonkin

ETHNONYM: Algonquin

"Algonkin" is the name used here for a number of related groups who lived in southwestern Quebec and southeastern Ontario, from the Ottawa River to Lake Nipissing to the north of Georgian Bay. These groups included those known today as Abitibi, Kitcisagi (Grand Lake Victoria), Maniwaki, Nipissing, Temiscaming, and Weskarini, as well as other probably extinct bands. The cover name is derived from a Maliseet term meaning "they are our relatives (or allies)." Each band or group spoke closely related dialects of Algonkian, the language still used today, in addition to English and French. At present there may be as many as six thousand Algonkin of whom twenty-five hundred to three thousand live on about a dozen reserves in Canada.

First contact with French traders apparently predated 1570. Relations with the French were generally peaceful from that time onward. There was, however, almost continual strife with the Iroquois until the peace of 1701 between the Iroquois and the French and their Indian allies. Missionization by Roman Catholic missionaries, particularly the Jesuits and Sulpicians, began in the early seventeenth century, with mission stations being established at that time. A government reserve was established at Golden Lake, Ontario, in 1807 with a number of others added throughout the nineteenth century.

Not a great deal is known about traditional Algonkin culture. Subsistence was based upon hunting and fishing, although a simple form of swidden horticulture featuring maize, beans, and squash and, later, European peas was practiced wherever possible. They constructed longhouses and other smaller structures. Twentieth-century Algonkin bands share many characteristics of Boreal Forest Peoples, including a belief in a supreme being; the Windigo; a trickster culture hero; the vision quest; scapulimancy; and the construction of canoes and other items in birchbark, toboggans, showshoes, and moose- and deerhide clothing. Specific family hunting territories have continued to exist in the twentieth century.

Bibliography

Day, Gordon M. (1978). "Nipissing." In _Handbook of North American Indians._ Vol. 15, _Northeast,_ edited by Bruce G. Trigger, 787–791. Washington, D.C.: Smithsonian Institution.

Day, Gordon M., and Bruce G. Trigger (1978). "Algonquin." In _Handbook of North American Indians._ Vol. 15, _Northeast,_ edited by Bruce G. Trigger, 792–797. Washington, D.C.: Smithsonian Institution.

Speck, Frank (1929). "Boundaries and Hunting Groups of the River Desert Algonquin." _Indian Notes_ (Museum of the American Indian, Heye Foundation) 6:97–120. New York.

American Isolates

ETHNONYMS: Aframerindians, Creoles, Half-Breeds, Marginal Peoples, Mestizos, Metis, Micro-Races, Middle Peoples, Quasi-Indians, Racial Islands, Racial Isolates, Southern Mestizos, Submerged Races, Tri-Racials, Tri-Racial Isolates

This generic label covers some two hundred different groups of relatively isolated, rural peoples who live in at least eighteen states mainly in the eastern and southern United States. In general, the label and the various alternatives refer to distinct peoples thought to have a multiracial background (White-Indian-African-American, African-American-White or Indian-White, Indian-Spanish) who historically have been unaffiliated with the general White and African-American population or with specific American Indian groups. Estimates place the number of people in these groups at about seventy-five thousand, although some groups have disappeared in recent years through a combination of migration to cities and intermarriage with Whites and African-Americans. The best known of these groups is the Lumbee Indians, numbering over thirty thousand mainly in North and South Carolina.

Classification of a group as an American Isolate rests on (1) real or ascribed mixed racial ancestry of group members; (2) a social status different from that of neighboring White, African-American, or American Indian populations; and (3) identification as a distinct local group with the assignment of a distinct group name.

American Isolates existed prior to the American Revolution, perhaps as long ago as the early eighteenth century, and they increased in number throughout the nineteenth century as they came to public attention in the areas where they lived. Among factors leading to group formation were the presence of offspring of African-American male slaves and White women and the offspring of Indians and free or enslaved African-Americans. Once a small community of multiracial members began, it grew primarily through a high fertility rate and became more and more isolated both socially and physically as its members were rejected by Whites and chose, themselves, to shun African-Americans. The movement of Indian groups west also contributed to their isolation. More recently, isolation was maintained in part through government action, most significantly through the banning of Isolate children from public schools. Most Isolate groups were and continue to be described by outsiders in such stereotypical terms as lazy, shiftless, criminals, violent, illiterate, poor, or incestuous.

Groups known to have still existed in the 1950s and 1960s include the following, listed by state:

Alabama: Cajans, Creoles, Melungeons (Ramps)

Delaware: Moors, Nanticoke

Florida: Dominickers

Georgia: Lumbee Indians (Croatans)

Kentucky: Melungeons, Pea Ridge Group (Coe Clan, Black Coes)

Louisiana: Natchitoches Mulattoes, Rapides Indians, Red Bones, Sabines, St. Landry Mulattoes, Zwolle-Ebard People

Maryland: Guineas, Lumbee Indians, Melungeons, Wesorts (Brandywine)

Mississippi: Creoles

New Jersey: Gouldtowners, Ramapo Mountain People (Jackson Whites), Sand Hill Indians

New York: Bushwhackers, Jackson Whites

North Carolina: Haliwa Indians, Lumbee Indians, Person County Indians, Portuguese, Rockingham Surry Group

Ohio: Carmel Indians, Cutler Indians, Darke County Group, Guineas, Vinton County Group

Pennsylvania: Karthus Half-Breeds, Keating Mountain Group, Nigger-Hill People, Pooles

South Carolina: Brass Ankles, Lumbee Indians, Turks

Tennessee: Melungeons

Virginia: Adamstown Indians, Brown People, Chickahominy Indians, Issues, Melungeons, Potomac Indians, Rappahannock Indians, Rockingham Surry Group

West Virginia: Guineas

While it is difficult to generalize across all Isolate groups or individuals, most live in rural areas and derive their income from farming and unskilled or semiskilled labor. Social status within a group is based on wealth, access to the White community, primarily through intermarriage, and residence in a settled, named Isolate community.

Bibliography

Berry, Brewton (1963). *Almost White.* New York: Macmillan.

Blu, Karen (1977). "Varieties of Ethnic Identity: Anglo-Saxons, Blacks, Indians, and Jews in a Southern County." *Ethnicity* 4:263–286.

Greissman, B. Eugene, subed. (1972). "The American Isolates." *American Anthropologist* 74:693–734.

Amish

ETHNONYMS: Mennonites, Pennsylvania Dutch, Pennsylvania Germans

Orientation

Identification.   Old Order Amish Mennonites in North America are a Germanic people with origins in the radical Swiss Anabaptist movement that developed between 1525 and 1536 during the Reformation. Among the Anabaptist groups who have persisted in their beliefs for over three centuries are the Amish, the Mennonites, and the Hutterites. These groups believe in adult baptism and pacifism, maintain a strict religious community and reject participation in the world to varying degrees. Their adherence to simple, or "plain," living is widely known.

Location.   The Amish migrated to America from Switzerland, Alsace-Lorraine, the Palatinate (in what is now western Germany), France, and Holland. During the first period of their migration, between 1727 and 1790, approximately five hundred Amish, along with other Germanic groups, settled in Pennsylvania. Between 1815 and 1865, a second influx of three thousand Amish immigrated to Ohio, New York, Indiana, and Illinois.

Demography.   In 1990 there were approximately 130,000 Amish living in twenty states and one province of Canada (Ontario). Seventy percent of all Amish live in Pennsylvania, Ohio, and Indiana. At a 3 percent rate of population increase annually, the Amish are doubling their numbers every twenty-three years. This growth rate results from large families in which seven or eight children are typical.

Linguistic Affiliation.   The Amish speak a dialect of German among themselves, use biblical High German in religious services, and speak standard English with outsiders.

History and Cultural Relations

The Amish were established as a separate sect between 1693 and 1697 on the basis of religious principles that continue to guide their communities. These rules, laid down by Jacob Ammann, a leader of a dissenting faction of the Swiss Anabaptists, include shunning (the social avoidance of excommunicated members), ceremonial foot washing as part of the communion service, and simplicity in dress and grooming. Today the rules are interpreted locally by the members of each congregation. The Amish, like other Anabaptist groups in Europe, suffered severe persecution and imprisonment. If they remained in their own countries, they were not allowed to own land and were denied citizenship. These restrictions prevented them from forming permanent settlements. As a result, those who stayed in their European homelands have largely been assimilated into the dominant religious groups there.

The bases for Amish existence as a distinct American subculture are their nonconformity in dress, homes, speech, attitudes toward education, and resistance to modernization and change. The Amish adhere to traditions that include living in rural areas, using horses for farming, marrying within the group, and dressing in a manner reminiscent of seventeenth-century Europeans. The Amish lead lives that are socially distinct as well. Since the Amish are secure in their tradition of separation from the outside world, their relations with their non-Amish neighbors appear to be free of the judgmental attitudes of other separatist sects. Rules for Amish living prohibit more than an elementary school education, the ownership (but not always the use) of automobiles and telephones, and the use of electricity and modern conveniences. The Amish are aware of their position with respect to the larger cultural environment. Farmers especially consider that using technological farm implements would have a devastating impact on their ability to maintain a separate society.

Conformity to the consensual rules (*Ordnung*) for behavior serves to unify Amish communities. Their religious perspective emphasizes commitment to a self-sufficient community of believers who reject worldly values. As part of a religious ethic based on their interpretations of Biblical scripture, the Amish ideal is to provide totally for members of their congregations throughout the life cycle. The Amish therefore remain committed to the home as the locus of their church services and for the care of the sick, the orphaned, the indigent, the elderly, and the mentally retarded. Important values that are the result of socialization in the home rather than in school are the ability to cooperate with others and to work as a contributing member to the society.

Outside industries have moved to Amish districts in Indiana and Pennsylvania in order to take advantage of their reputation for hard and reliable work. The Amish, though, tend to maximize their interactions with members of their group through the spatial arrangements in their communities, for example, while reducing interactions with outsiders. Like other rural communities, the encroachment of industrialization has diminished the possibility of isolation desired by the Amish.

Settlements

The Amish are located in regions that are compatible with their ideal of continuing a farming life-style. Within a settlement, the church district encloses a certain area. The size of the district is determined by the number of persons who can be accommodated in a single farm dwelling for church services. About twenty-five to thirty-five married couples plus their children compose a district. The steady growth rate of the Amish population and the need for more farmland accessible to the younger generation for purchase have required movement to new settlements. Amish homes tend to be large, functional dwellings dedicated to simplicity. Interiors are neatly kept and, in compliance with church rules, there is minimal decoration or ornamentation other than quilts and decorative china. The emphasis is on functional space that will allow homes to become churches for the bimonthly Sunday worship.

Economy

Subsistence and Commercial Activities. Farming is the occupation desired by most Amish. All family members are integrated into an agricultural way of life. Beginning at an early age, the young assist in farm and household chores. The Amish keep their farms small enough to be handled by the family unit. Family-size farms have consistently been productive, serving to meet the needs of the community rather than to earn large profits. Farms average between fifty and ninety-six acres; the larger acreage occurs in midwestern areas rather than in eastern regions such as Lancaster, Pennsylvania. The lack of concern with high-income productivity is evident in Amish farmers' choosing to concentrate on raising livestock in small numbers and on growing a variety of crops. Farm size is limited not only by the amount of land that can be managed by one family but also by the prohibition on the use of electricity.

On New York farms, if tractors are used at all, they provide the power source for other types of farm machinery. Often these vehicles are outdated and have steel wheels instead of rubber tires. In some parts of Ohio, for example, the prohibition on technological dairy farming has meant the abandonment of farming, resulting in a change in the nature of the Amish community. Some nonfarming Amish work within their communities, serving traditional needs such as the repair of farm and household equipment and operating horse-and-buggy trades. Work outside of farming in some regions has become increasingly necessary because of the declining availability of affordable land. Ironically, however, nonagricultural employment has also created the financial security that allows many young families to remain within the Amish fellowship. Newer occupational opportunities include service industries and shops where Amish work for non-Amish ("English") employers, often saving their earnings to buy a farm. More women are now being trained as teachers for Amish schools.

The Amish depend on outsiders for medical and legal services. When making loans to Amish clients, bank managers rely on the system of mutual aid for church members to back up buyers who become financially overburdened.

Division of Labor. Mainly, women are employed in the home. Besides attending to children, house, garden, and chickens, the Amish woman also sews clothes for her family, cooks and cans food, and engages in quilt and rug making and embroidery. Both sexes handle household finances; children have both parents as role models for learning behavior appropriate to Amish society. Members of the congregation, both male and female, work cooperatively to build and rebuild houses and barns.

Land Tenure. The Amish are often forced to migrate to areas where cheaper farmland is available. They save to buy additional farms for their children, giving young married couples financial and other forms of assistance in establishing their own farms. It is not uncommon for members of the community to provide low-interest loans to young people starting out.

Kinship

Kin Groups and Descent. The Amish tend to maintain social relations mainly but not exclusively with members of their group. In-group marriages and kinship solidarity reinforce the family-based social structure. Amish marriages occur in what is essentially a large kin group. The extent of intermarriage that has resulted in the intermingling of genealogies for more than two centuries is evident in various Amish localities by the relatively few surnames. In naming their children, Amish parents may recognize both maternal and paternal sides of the family. Children have their fathers' surnames and middle names that are often their mothers' maiden names.

Several hereditary diseases have been studied among Amish populations. Although they are not a single, genetically closed population, the Amish have separate inbreeding communities within the larger group. The inbred character is indicated by the history of their migration patterns, by the unique family names in each community, and by the distribution of blood types. Of at least twelve "new" recessive diseases ascertained, several are especially pronounced: dwarfism, a rare blood cell disease, hemophilia, muscular dystrophy, and diseases associated with metabolism. The low rate of some hereditary diseases that are common in the general population has also been noted.

Marriage and Family

Marriage. Amish couples are expected to remain married to the mates they select as young adults. The Amish church depends on the biological reproduction of its members rather than on acquiring new members through proselytization. There is thus a strong commitment to marrying within the church, although females tend to move outside the district since males usually inherit the family farm. Despite the fact that mate choice is limited to other church members, the young people do not necessarily choose to marry close relatives. The high inbreeding of the Amish population results not from marriages between first cousins but from the inter-marriages that have occurred over generations within a genetically isolated group.

Baptism into the church is preliminary to marriage. Courtship tends to be a private matter prior to the wedding announcement by the minister. A wedding, on the other hand, is a public affair celebrated in anticipation of certain benefits that will accrue to the entire community. Members of the congregation see the marriage as an end to a sometimes spirited adolescence and expect to have the couple's home as a new place for the Sunday service; they also look forward to more children who will be raised in the Amish way. Guests give household gifts; parents may provide livestock, furniture, and equipment to help the young people get started.

Where a newlywed couple resides depends on the opportunity to continue farming in the traditional manner. This may mean working in a factory until enough savings have been accumulated to invest in a farm of their own. If the couple remains on the family farm, their parents may, at retirement, move to a separate house on the property and eventually leave the management of the farm to the younger couple. No provision is made for divorce, nor is separation a part of Amish expectations for conformity to church-based rules of behavior.

Domestic Unit.   As previously mentioned, each family member contributes to the working of the family farm. Although married couples share in the responsibilities of child rearing and of running the household and farm, the prevailing authority rests with the husband.

Inheritance.   Land tends to be kept within families and is usually passed on to sons rather than to daughters and to younger rather than to older sons.

Socialization.   Individuals are prepared for all stages of life, including aging, under Amish patterns of socialization. The primary goals of child rearing are the acquisition of practical skills, the instilling of responsibility to the Amish community, and an emphasis on respect for hard work. Young people may be hired out to relatives or other church members after they are trained on the family farm and in the household. Parents often allow adolescents to explore the outside world and test the boundaries of Amish identity. Family and community may therefore overlook the ownership of radios, cameras, even automobiles, by young people as well as their going to the movies and wearing non-Amish clothes. Such deviations are ignored in order that the young may freely decide on marriage and membership within the church community. About one-quarter leave the church, but most join more progressive Amish or Mennonite churches.

Sociopolitical Organization

Social Organization.   Amish communities are not entirely self-sufficient. Support for state and local government may be given through voting and paying taxes, but church rules prohibit them from participating in politics as officeholders. They also comply with church rules forbidding military service and government assistance in the form of insurance or subsidies.

Resistance to compulsory school attendance beyond the eighth grade is perhaps the most controversial issue that has brought the Amish into direct confrontation with state and local authorities recently. Amish in certain communities were subjected to fines and imprisonment because they rejected secondary school education for their children. Finally, the dilemma was resolved in the 1972 Supreme Court decision *Wisconsin v. Yoder et al.*, which found that laws that required Amish children to attend school beyond the elementary level were a violation of their religious convictions. Conflicts between Amish and mainstream American goals in education were not an issue when one-room schoolhouses were the norm in a primarily rural United States. Today, the change to consolidated schools and to a deemphasis on basic skills has prompted the Amish to establish their own schools. According to Hostetler there are more than seven hundred one- and two-room schools that uphold Amish traditions and lifestyles.

Political Organization.   Old Order Amish churches are not organized around a central authority. Rather, the church districts serve as the governing units for each congregation. Men who hold the offices of deacon (*Armen Diener*), preacher (*Diener zum Buch*), and bishop (*Volle Diener*) are chosen by lot from among the members of the congregation themselves. The three ministers have charge of various aspects of church activities. The bishop performs baptisms and marriages; the preacher assists in the communion service and delivers the bimonthly sermon when asked; the deacon is responsible for distributing funds to the needy. Bishops meet informally to discuss matters pertaining to their congregations, and visiting by congregants also helps maintain bonds between church districts.

Social Control.   When a member breaks a moral or church code, the minister presents the question of discipline to the congregation. It is the church community that has the final decision. Shunning (*Meidung*), an extreme censure placed on violators, requires that no church member engage in social dealings with the individual until the ban is lifted.

Religion and Expressive Culture

Religious Beliefs.   The Amish conceive of their church-community (*Gemeinde*) as being composed of those who are truly repentant and duly baptized. Members are joined communally in an effort to become righteous Christians and reject worldly values. Amish moral imperatives also account for their desire to be close to the soil and to nature.

Ceremonies.   The communion service to celebrate the Lord's Supper is held twice a year in the fall and spring. Preparations for communion include prayer, meditation, and fasting. As part of the service, the ceremonial foot washing, introduced by Ammann in the seventeenth century, takes place as a sign of fellowship.

Arts.   Women combine quilt making and visiting as an acceptable means of artistic expression. Other forms of artistic endeavor, like photography, are forbidden. Whitewashed houses with decorative paint trim and brightly colored flowers are also evidence of artistry among the Amish.

Medicine.   The Amish have access to a variety of practitioners, including folk healers as well as modern physicians and surgeons. They also consider the reputation of practitioners and, taking for granted the competency of providers, they select ones whom they feel they can trust.

Death and Afterlife. Death is a solemn occasion, but is accepted as a matter of course. The dead are usually buried on the third day after death. Respect for someone who has died is often shown in a large funeral attendance. Funeral establishments may be asked to prepare the body, but afterward, church members dress the body at home in special garments. Preparation of the grave, notification of the ministers, and selection of pallbearers are duties that are divided between more or less distant relatives, friends, and neighbors of the deceased. Amish bereaved are comforted by their belief in heaven and life after death. Although the Amish want to be ready for Judgment Day, they are not especially preoccupied with the nature of an afterlife.

Bibliography

Gallagher, Thomas E., Jr. (1982). *Clinging to the Past or Preparing for the Future? The Structure of Selective Modernization among Old Order Amish in Lancaster County, Pennsylvania.* Ann Arbor: University Microfilms International.

Hostetler, John A. (1980). *Amish Society.* 3rd ed. Baltimore: Johns Hopkins University Press.

Hostetler, John A. (1980) "Amish." In *Harvard Encyclopedia of American Ethnic Groups*, edited by Stephen Thernstrom, 122–125. Boston: Harvard University Press, Belknap Press.

Keim, Albert N., ed. (1975). *Compulsory Education and the Amish: The Right Not to Be Modern.* Boston: Beacon Press.

Kraybill, Donald B. (1989). *The Riddle of Amish Culture.* Baltimore: Johns Hopkins University Press.

McKusick, Victor A. (1978). *Medical Genetic Studies of the Amish.* Baltimore: Johns Hopkins University Press.

JOHN A. HOSTETLER

Appalachians

ETHNONYMS: Briars, Highlanders, Hillbillies, Mountaineers, Mountain Whites, Plain Folks, Southern Appalachians

Orientation

Identification. "Appalachians" refers to a largely rural people who reside in the southern Appalachian region covering about 110,000 square miles in the states of Maryland, Virginia, West Virginia, Kentucky, Tennessee, North Carolina, South Carolina, Georgia, and Alabama. Although these rural people are only a minority of the regional population, the region has long been defined in terms of their traditional culture. Geographically isolated throughout much of their history, they are thought to have retained cultural traditions of early nineteenth-century pioneers. Their language and music are thought by some to be "pure" survivals of Elizabethan forms, although many scholars believe that this is something of an exaggeration. It is no exaggeration, however, that White inhabitants of southern Appalachia were cut off from the mainstream of American culture and that their culture is conservative. Their ethos and values center on those traditionally associated with small, rural communities in the United States including individualism, familism, loyalty in personal relationships, and egalitarianism. Appalachians are known to the general American population through television and comic-strip stereotypes as "hillbillies."

Location. As noted above, Appalachians are spread through the Appalachian Mountains in nine states. This area consists of three physiographic regions. The Blue Ridge Mountains, with the highest peaks in the area, constitute the eastern region; the central, southern, East Tennessee, and Southwest Virginia valleys and their ridges constitute the central region; and the Appalachian plateau forms the western region. Settled areas and cultivable land are scattered along streams and their basins, coves, and hollows.

Demography. At the time of the first U.S. census in 1790, the population of southern Appalachia was 175,000 with most of these people settled in what is now Virginia. Settlement throughout the rest of southern Appalachia was completed after the removal of the Cherokee in 1836 and the discovery of gold in northern Georgia. The area remained largely isolated until the Civil War. By 1960 there were 5.7 million people living in the southern Appalachians, with the population expanding steadily up to that time because of a high birthrate that offset periodic population declines stemming from outmigration. Outmigration has produced large Appalachian enclaves in industrial towns in Ohio and Kentucky as well as in cities such as Atlanta, Cleveland, Chicago, Pittsburgh, and Columbus. The southern Appalachian population is now thought to be either stable or increasing. There are relatively few African-Americans in the region, compared to the rest of the South, although a number of biracial American Isolate groups are found in Appalachia.

Linguistic Affiliation. Appalachians speak a regional dialect of English that is described by some as being difficult for outsiders to understand.

History and Cultural Relations

The early settlers of the region were primarily of English, Scots-Irish, and Highland Scots ancestry with some Germans and Dutch. The life-style of the early settlers was much like that of other rural southerners and centered on farming, livestock herding, and hunting, both for subsistence and for a surplus to sell in nearby villages. When much of the South shifted to large-scale cotton growing after the Civil War, the soil and terrain in southern Appalachia could not support intensive agriculture and the prewar economy and life-style survived. Eventually, isolation from the regional economy, early pioneers' methods of clearing land for farming, and coal-mining and lumbering activities left the southern Appalachians an area of severe economic depression and the inhabitants labeled as "hillbillies." Since then, Appalachia has often been identified as an area characterized by widespread poverty, with less attention given to the growing middle class. Although education, health care, transportation, and economic conditions have all improved since the 1960s, the region still lags behind the nation. In the 1980s little of the traditional culture survives, save that which is exhibited for tourists.

Settlements

Those identified as still adhering in some ways to the traditional culture live mostly in rural settlements in the valleys and in the larger basins, coves, and hollows. These settlements vary from scattered houses constituting a neighborhood, to small villages with a general store, to incorporated towns serving as county seats and commercial centers. Isolated homes, however, constitute the way of life for many. They are found in remote areas and contact with any but close family members is unusual. The residential groups that inhabit the coves and hollows are usually described as neighborhoods rather than communities. Throughout the history of the area, neighborhoods have been impermanent owing to large families and agricultural practices that rapidly deplete the soil.

Economy

Traditional Appalachians relied on subsistence farming, with the mountain terrain allowing only scattered farming on relatively small amounts of tillable land. Commercialization, which revolutionized farming elsewhere in the nation, had little impact in Appalachia. Early in the twentieth century, lumbering and coal mining lured Appalachians off the land with the promise of steady employment. With the decline of these industries, people have been forced to migrate, commute to jobs, or find work in other industries. Almost everyone maintains family gardens, with corn and tobacco common crops. Cattle, chickens, and hogs are widely raised.

Large-scale commercial exploitation of the forests began after the Civil War when the national demand for timber increased and the spread of rail lines made the transportation of lumber possible. Lumbering was managed by outside syndicates who hired local labor. Production peaked in 1909, but by 1920, with the forests nearly depleted, the large companies were moving out. Small companies, relying on small mills and circular saws, took over what was left of the industry. By the 1960s only temporary work at low wages was available, and workers, who might have two or more lumbering jobs each year, had to supplement their wages through other forms of employment.

Coal mining is the largest mineral industry in southern Appalachia, although manganese, zinc, lead, copper, pyrite, marble, feldspar, kaolin, and mica are also mined or quarried. Large-scale coal mining began in the late 1800s, boomed during World War I, declined during the Great Depression, and then boomed again during World War II. Since then, owing to competition from other fuels and the mechanization of the industry, coal mining has declined as a primary source of employment. The declines in agriculture, mining, and lumbering have forced Appalachians to look elsewhere for income, migrating to cities, commuting to towns, receiving government assistance, selling land, or cultivating and marketing shrubbery.

Kinship, Marriage and Family

Kin Groups and Descent.   The rural neighborhoods of southern Appalachia are kin-based. The "clans" that inhabit the hollows are actually large extended families with a patriarchal authority structure and patrilineal inheritance of surnames. There are no corporate kin groups, and kinship is reckoned bilaterally.

Marriage.   Marriages are often contracted when the individuals are quite young, and they are usually locally endogamous, if not within the "clan." Postmarital residence is said to be up to the couple. Some children in every generation move away, but there is a clear preference for residence near kin. Usually the husband's family will offer the couple land; if this is not possible, the wife's family will make the offer, leading to the development of the large, extended family neighborhoods.

Domestic Unit.   The nuclear family is the ideal, though there is much variation in actual household composition. There are six or seven children in the average family, although families with ten or more children are not uncommon. Inbreeding is reported to be very common.

Sociopolitical Organization

Neighborhood residence is sometimes based on a common occupation, and residents of a neighborhood usually share a church, school, and grist mill. They also tend to interact more often with each other than with outsiders, and there is some limited sense of neighborhood unity. Neighborhoods are often named after family names, geographic features, or man-made features. The combination of the strong family ethic, the familial basis of the neighborhoods, and lack of trust in the judicial system provided a social environment conducive to the development of "clan" feuds. The feuds grew largely from divided loyalties during the Civil War. Although the southern Appalachians have been described as an island of Union sympathy within the otherwise united South, there was considerable difference of opinion within neighborhoods and even within families. The feuds began shortly after the Civil War and continued until about 1915, with the most famous being the one between the Hatfields and the McCoys. Today, with social relations still much the same, disputes often force individuals to side with their family and grudges can run deep.

Religion and Expressive Culture

Religion.   Most Appalachians are fundamentalists, with the Southern Baptist church and the Methodist church the major denominations. The current tone of Appalachian religion was set by a series of revivals that took place through the 1800s. Basic characteristics include a puritanical sense of morality, biblical fundamentalism, revivalism, fatalism, and a clergy that differs from the laity only in the extent of its zeal for universal salvation. Church organization is very informal, with neighborhoods sharing a minister who makes a monthly series of rounds. The primary goal of religious behavior is salvation or conversion through a personal experience of God. These experiences most often occur at the summer revivals, which include spirited preaching, hymn singing that builds in intensity to the point of trance, hand waving toward heaven, speaking in tongues, and faith healing.

Arts. Appalachian art, handicrafts, amusements, dance, music, and folkways in general have been brought to the attention of the general population thorough a variety of publications, including the *Foxfire* series of books.

Bibliography

Bryant, Frances C. (1981). *We're All Kin: A Cultural Study of a Mountain Neighborhood.* Knoxville: University of Tennessee Press.

Ford, Thomas R., ed. (1962). *The Southern Appalachian Region: A Survey.* Lexington: University of Kentucky Press.

Hicks, George L. (1976). *Appalachian Valley.* New York: Holt, Rinehart & Winston.

Keefe, Susan Emley, ed. (1988). *Appalachian Mental Health.* Lexington: University of Kentucky Press.

Speer, Jean Haskell (1989). *The Appalachian Photographs of Earl Palmer.* Lexington: University of Kentucky Press.

M. MARLENE MARTIN

Arab Americans

ETHNONYMS: Arab Muslims, Chaldeans, Copts, Druze, Lebanese, Palestinians, Shia, Syrians, Yemenis

Orientation

Identification. Americans of Arab ancestry are a heterogeneous amalgam of national and religious subgroups. Their link is a common Arab cultural and linguistic heritage, which has profoundly influenced the Middle East for over fourteen centuries. Historically, "Arab" referred exclusively to the Arabic-speaking tribes of the Arabian Peninsula and parts of the Fertile Crescent. Today, the term is understood to be a cultural/linguistic and political designation. It embraces various national, religious, and regional groups that share overlapping histories and national political aspirations, although significant differences and regional loyalties remain strong. No single set of racial or physical traits defines all Arabs. Nor can they be identified with a single religion (Islam), as is often mistakenly done, for not all Arabs are Muslims (about 6 to 10 percent are non-Muslims, mostly Christians and some Jews). In fact, although Islam originated in the Arabian Peninsula, and the Qur'an (its holy book) was written in Arabic, the vast majority of Muslims are not Arabs, but Indonesians, Pakistanis, Asian Indians, and Persians.

Arab Americans hail from only a handful of the twenty-one countries that compose the modern Arab world: Leba-non, Syria, Palestine, Iraq, Egypt, Yemen, and Jordan. In terms of recency of arrival, Arab Americans fall into three diverse groups: recent arrivals, long-term immigrants, and native-born descendants of earlier generations of immigrants.

Location. Arab Americans live primarily in cities or adjacent suburbs. Many recent arrivals tend to gravitate to Arab neighborhoods, where ethnic grocery stores, restaurants, bakeries, clubs, and religious centers are concentrated. These neighborhoods tend to be working class and lower middle class in character. The largest is found in the Detroit suburb of Dearborn, Michigan; others are located in New York and Chicago. These "Arab Towns" have largely replaced the "Little Syrias" of earlier immigrant generations. The more assimilated long-term immigrants and native-born Arab Americans tend to eschew the ethnic neighborhoods for the middle-class suburbs. The major concentrations of Arab Americans are found in Detroit, New York, Los Angeles, Boston, Chicago, and Houston. Smaller communities are also found throughout the Northeast and Middle West.

Demography. Exact population figures are difficult to ascertain owing to imprecise immigration and census data. Scholars tend to agree on 2 million as the number of persons of Arab ancestry in the United States, with another 80,000 in Canada. In comparison, the population of the Arab world is over 150 million. The largest single concentration of Arabs in North America is in Detroit, which is reputed to have about 250,000 Arabs. Native-born Arab Americans and long-established immigrants make up the largest share of the population, which was fairly stable through the mid-1960s. Beginning in the late 1960s, the population in North America witnessed rapid growth owing largely to the influx of tens of thousands of new immigrants.

Linguistic Affiliation. Most assimilated Arab Americans use English as their primary language or only domestic language. Many recent arrivals use Arabic as their primary language, employing English as needed in contacts outside the home and the ethnic community. Arabic speakers converse in the regional dialect of their home village or town. Some Iraqi Chaldeans speak Chaldean (a Semitic language) as their only domestic language; others know only Iraqi Arabic or combine the two languages. Second-generation Arab Americans usually reach adulthood retaining very little of their parents' native tongue.

History and Cultural Relations

The first Arabic-speaking immigrants in the United States were a handful of nineteenth-century adventurers and sojourners. It was not until the end of the century that significant numbers of Arab immigrants began making their way to the United States. Their numbers were minuscule by the standards of the day, averaging several thousand per year, with the highest recorded number reaching nine thousand in 1913–14. World War I brought immigration to a virtual standstill. In the years immediately following the war, Arab immigration returned to its prewar level only to be restricted again by the legislation of the 1920s.

Many of the early immigrants left homes in Greater Syria, an Arab province of the Ottoman Empire until the end of World War I. In the postwar period, the province was partitioned into separate political entities (Syria, Lebanon, Palestine, Transjordan) under British and French rule. Although the area remains predominantly Arab and Muslim culturally, Christian, Islamic, and Jewish ethnoreligious minorities constitute its cultural mosaic. Many of the early immigrants were drawn from these minorities, especially certain Christian denominations (Maronites, Melkites, and Eastern Orthodox). Others included a small number of Muslims and Druze, as well as smaller numbers of Iraqi Chaldeans and Yemeni Muslims.

In general, the early immigrants were mostly illiterate or semiliterate, unskilled, single males, who emigrated without their families. Of the approximately 60,000 who entered the United States between 1899 and 1910, some 53 percent were illiterate, and 68 percent were single males. A notable exception was a small group of literati (writers, poets, artists, journalists) who settled in places like New York and Boston. Politically rather than economically motivated, this group spawned an important school of modern Arabic literature. They formed the Pen League (al-Rabita al-Qalamiyya) under the leadership of Kahlil Gibran (1883–1931), the celebrated author of The Prophet.

The early immigrants tended to settle in the cities and towns of the Northeast and Midwest, in states like New York, Massachusetts, Pennsylvania, Michigan, and Ohio. By 1940 about a fifth of the estimated 350,000 Arabs lived in just three cities—New York, Boston, and Detroit—mostly in ethnic neighborhoods ("Little Syrias"). Many worked their way across America as peddlers of dry goods and other sundry items, reaching virtually every state of the Union. Some homesteaded on the Great Plains, and others settled in southern rural areas.

A second wave of Arab immigration to the United States occurred after World War II. The influx included many more Muslims than the previous one. It also included refugees who had been displaced by the 1948 Palestine war, as well as professionals and university students who elected to remain permanently in the United States. These trends accelerated after the June 1967 Arab-Israeli War, a watershed for both the Middle East and Arab immigration to the United States. The 1970s and 1980s witnessed a massive influx of Arab immigrants from Lebanon, Iraq, the Israeli-occupied West Bank, Yemen, Egypt, and other Arab countries. Many had been displaced by war and political upheaval.

The early Arab immigrants followed a fairly smooth assimilation into mainstream society. Several generations later their descendants have achieved high social mobility. Some are household names: Danny Thomas, Ralph Nader, Christa McAuliffe, Paul Anka, Casey Kasem, Bobby Rahall, F. Murray Abraham. In comparison, the second-wave immigrants have had a mixed time of it. Many have prospered economically, especially those in the professions and business. But others, particularly in the period following the June 1967 war, have had to contend with demeaning stereotypes, prejudice, and discrimination stemming from the oil crisis, Middle East terrorism, and U.S. involvement in the region. These problems are more pronounced in areas where large numbers of recent arrivals reside.

Economy

Arab Americans are highly integrated into the U.S. and Canadian economies. Both immigrant and assimilated Arabs are heavily involved in the retail business trade. In many urban areas, they own and manage grocery stores, supermarkets, candy stores, gasoline stations, and restaurants. Some native-born Arabs own small and medium-sized manufacturing and commercial enterprises; most, however, choose careers in the professions (medicine, law, accounting, engineering, teaching). Many unskilled immigrants, particularly recent arrivals, can be found working in factories or restaurants, but they usually remain in such jobs only until they accumulate sufficient means to enter the retail business world. Although Arabs as a group have not faced economic discrimination, individuals have encountered discrimination in hiring and on the job, mostly in the professions.

Kinship, Marriage and Family

Marriage and Family.   Arab marriage and kinship practices vary somewhat by religion and recency of arrival, but usually stress lifelong marriages, a preference for religious and ethnic group endogamy, marriage of cousins, extended families, patrilineal descent, and bifurcate-collateral (descriptive) kinship terminology. Surnames are patrilineal. Data on intermarriage with non-Arabs are virtually nonexistent. Generally, recency of immigration, degree of ethnic group cohesiveness, and religiousness mitigate against interreligious marriages, though marriages across Arab regional and national lines are allowed as long as religious group endogamy is maintained. Arab affiliation is usually traced patrilineally, though women are delegated the responsibility of transmitting ethnic and religious awareness to the children. In many mixed marriages, particularly of Arab men to non-Arab women, the wives often play important roles in promoting Arab cultural heritage within the family and the ethnic community.

Socialization.   As with North Americans generally, early socialization takes place in the immediate family. Arab parents are extremely indulgent, though they may resort to physical punishment. Socialization as an Arab takes place in the home, through attendance at "Arabic school" on weekends, and in youth groups at the mosque or church. Weddings, funerals, and other community gatherings offer occasion for further socialization into the ethnic group.

Sociopolitical Organization

Social Organization.   Traditionally, the primary loyalties and affiliations of Middle Eastern peoples have been to local areas, the village or urban quarter, which were usually homogeneous religious and ethnic units. Not surprisingly, Arabs in America tended to establish ethnically homogeneous church- and mosque-centered communities. In addition, they formed hometown and village clubs and associations. Because immigrants from the same village or town were often scattered in many parts of the United States and elsewhere, these associations often acquired a national or even international scope. Hometown and village affiliations remain strong among recent arrivals and the immigrant population generally, and less so among assimilated Arab Americans.

Political Organization.   There is no overarching political structure that groups all Arab Americans. The Christian denominations are separately organized in hierarchical groups that are essentially extensions of churches based in the Middle East. Lacking the hierarchical structure of the Christian churches, local congregations of Muslims are loosely federated with one another according to sect (Sunni, Shia) and to competing Islamic federations in the Middle East.

In the late 1960s Arab Americans began establishing national organizations that transcend religious and hometown/ village affiliations. The Association of Arab-American University Graduates (AAUG), founded by a group of academics and professionals, was the first such organization. Eventually larger organizations appeared in the 1970s and 1980s (American-Arab Anti-Discrimination Committee; National Association of Arab-Americans; American Arab Institute). The impetus behind the emergence of these organizations was the perceived need to present an Arab-American voice on U.S. foreign policy, combat demeaning stereotypes and discrimination, and encourage Arab Americans to become actively involved in the electoral process. Although these groups are highly visible, they represent only a small fraction of the Arab American population.

Social Control and Conflict.   Arab Americans generally resolve disputes through the legal system. The population is law-abiding, and contrary to popular images, Arab Americans have not been involved in terrorist activities. Rather, they have been the targets of sporadic intentional violence, including several bombings and arson fires that killed two people and injured nearly a dozen others in the 1980s.

Religion

Religious Beliefs and Practices.   Islam is the youngest of the monotheistic religions. Established in the seventh century, Islam's central tenet is the oneness of God. Humankind is called on to obey God's law and prepare for the Day of Judgment. Muslims view the Prophet Muhammad as the last in a long succession of prophets going back to Abraham. Muslims accept Jesus as a prophet who possessed miracle-working powers. The Qur'an places emphasis on his virgin birth. Muslims do not, however, recognize the divinity of Christ or accept that he was crucified, claiming instead that God intervened at the last moment. Shia Muslims differ from Sunni (orthodox) Islam over the rightful succession of the Caliphate (leader) of the early Muslim community and over the role and powers of the _ulama_ (religious scholars or clergy). The majority of Arab American Muslims are Sunni; Arab American Shia Muslims are mostly from Lebanon and to a lesser extent from North Yemen and Iraq.

Arab Christians are divided between Eastern rite churches (Syrian Antiochian Orthodox, Greek Orthodox, and Coptic) and Latin rite Uniate churches (Maronite, Melkite, and Chaldean). Originally, all Middle Eastern denominations belonged to churches that followed Eastern rites. The Uniate churches eventually split from the Eastern churches and affiliated with the Latin church in Rome. Although they formally recognize the authority of the Roman pope and conform to Latin rites, the Uniate churches maintain their own patriarchs and internal autonomy. The Middle Eastern churches, Eastern as well as Uniate, allow priests to marry, though not bishops, and maintain their separate liturgies, often in an ancient language (Coptic, Aramaic, Syriac, and so on).

Religious Practitioners.   Islam lacks a hierarchical church structure. The ulama are essentially teachers or scholars, lacking real authority, though Shia Islam as practiced in non-Arab Iran invests the ulama with special occult powers and authority in social matters. The Middle Eastern churches are structured in rigid hierarchies, and priests often command substantial respect and authority in local affairs.

Ceremonies.   Strictly speaking, Islam recognizes only three religious holidays: Ramadan, Eid al-Fitr, and Eid al-Adha. Other holidays, like the Prophet's birthday, are celebrated by some communities and not others. Ramadan, the ninth month of the Islamic lunar calendar, is the time of fasting that precedes Eid al-Fitr. The fast requires complete abstinence from food, drink, tobacco, and sex from sunrise to sunset during the entire month. Eid al-Fitr ("End of the Fast") marks the end of Ramadan. Eid al-Adha ("Feast of the Sacrifice") commemorates Abraham's willingness to sacrifice his son Ishmael in obedience to God. The holiday at the end of the Hajj, or pilgrimage to Mecca, falls on a different day each year owing to the differences between the Islamic lunar calendar and the Western solar calendar. The Eastern rite churches differ from the Latin churches on the timing of Easter and Christmas celebrations. Easter is celebrated the Sunday after Passover, and Christmas is celebrated on the Epiphany, which falls on January 6.

Bibliography

Abraham, Sameer Y., and Nabeel Abraham, eds. (1983). _Arabs in the New World_. Detroit: Center for Urban Studies, Wayne State University.

Abu-Laban, Baha (1980). _An Olive Branch on the Family Tree: The Arabs in Canada_. Toronto: McClelland & Stewart.

Abu-Laban, Baha, and Michael W. Suleiman, eds. (1989). _Arab Americans: Continuity and Change_. Belmont, Mass.: Association of Arab-American University Graduates.

Hooglund, Eric J. (1987). _Crossing the Waters: Arabic-Speaking Immigrants to the United States before 1940_. Washington, D.C.: Smithsonian Institution Press.

Naff, Alixa (1985). _Becoming American: The Early Arab Immigrant Experience_. Carbondale: Southern Illinois University Press.

Orfalea, Gregory (1988). _Before the Flames_. Austin: University of Texas Press.

NABEEL ABRAHAM

Arapaho

ETHNONYMS: Arapahoe, Dog Eaters, Hitänwoiv, Inuñaina, Suretika

The Arapaho are an Algonkian-speaking tribe who at the time of first contact with the Americans lived around the headwaters of the Arkansas and Platte rivers in southwestern Wyoming and eastern Colorado. In the mid-nineteenth century, the tribe split into two groups. The Northern Arapaho now live with the Eastern Shoshone on the Wind River Reservation in Wyoming, and the Southern Arapaho, with the Southern Cheyenne as the Cheyenne-Arapahoe Tribes of Oklahoma on a federal trust area in southwestern Oklahoma. The U.S. Bureau of the Census estimated that there were at least forty-four hundred Arapaho living in the United States in 1980. Their language is distantly related to Blackfoot, Cheyenne, and the other Algonkian languages. The Gros Ventre (Atsina) were formerly an Arapaho band and speak a dialect of Arapaho.

The earliest evidence indicates the Arapaho were agriculturalists living near the headwaters of the Mississippi River in Minnesota around 1600. From there they moved westward, acquiring the horse and becoming typical bison-hunting horse nomads on the Great Plains. They were noted as warriors and fought with many other tribes as well as with the U.S. Army. After the split into two groups around 1835, the Southern Arapaho agreed to settle with the Cheyenne on an Oklahoma reservation in 1869, and the Northern Arapaho were placed on the Wind River Reservation in Wyoming with their old enemies the Eastern Shoshone. The Southern Arapaho are now governed by the Cheyenne-Arapahoe Tribal Business Committee, which has elected officials from each of the tribes; on the Wind River Reservation, affairs are carried on by a joint business council. The major Arapaho business on this reservation is the Arapaho Ranch Enterprise, a beef-breeding operation that brings in over $3 million annually. Income is also derived from coal mining, forestry, and payments for grazing rights.

After the Arapaho moved to the plains, their economy was based almost entirely on bison hunting and the use of the horse, with men doing the hunting and carrying on warfare and the women concerned with domestic chores, gathering vegetable foods, raising children, and building the conical bison-hide-covered tipis characteristic of the society. They originally had five major divisions, although the Gros Ventre broke away from the others around the beginning of the eighteenth century. Each division had a chief, not formally elected but chosen from among the Dog Company, one of the age-grade societies which were characteristic of Arapaho social organization. These societies no longer survive, but their general structure continues today in modified form and their values still determine social and political behavior to some extent.

While living on the plains, the tribe was nearly fully nomadic, with communities having populations of two hundred to four hundred people. They had bilateral descent but no descent groups. The communities were exogamous, and postmarital residence was generally uxorilocal. There were strict mother-in-law/son-in-law and father-in-law/daughter-in-law taboos, as well as great respect between brothers and sisters.

Polygyny was frequent, very often sororal. There were no strict rules of inheritance. Religion was largely bound up with the ceremonials of the age-grade societies, with the Sun Dance and the peyote worship also being important.

Bibliography

Elkin, Henry (1940). "The Northern Arapaho of Wyoming." In *Acculturation in Seven American Tribes*, edited by Ralph Linton, 207–258. New York: D. Appleton-Century Co.

Fowler, Loretta D. (1982). *Arapahoe Politics, 1851–1978: Symbols in Crises of Authority*. Lincoln: University of Nebraska Press.

Kroeber, Alfred L. (1983). *The Arapaho*. Lincoln: University of Nebraska Press. Originally published, 1902–1907.

Trenholm, Virginia Cole (1970). *The Arapahoes, Our People*. Norman: University of Oklahoma Press.

Arikara

ETHNONYMS: Pandani, Panimaha, Ree, Ricari, Ricaree, Sanish, Starrahhe

The Arikara are a group of Caddoan-speaking American Indians who in historic times lived along the Missouri River in northern South Dakota and west-central North Dakota. The Arikara are culturally related to the Pawnee. They are believed to have originated in the Southeast and migrated north along the Missouri River before reaching the Dakotas sometime around 1770. At that time they numbered between three thousand and four thousand people. In 1837 the Arikara were severely affected by a smallpox epidemic, and in 1862, their numbers much reduced, they joined the Mandan and Hidatsa tribes. In about 1870 all three groups were settled on the Fort Berthold Reservation in North Dakota. In the 1980s they numbered about one thousand.

The Arikara were primarily an agricultural people living in permanent villages of semisubterranean earth lodges located on bluffs overlooking the Missouri River. They cultivated maize, beans, squash, pumpkins, and sunflowers and also hunted bison, deer, and antelope and gathered wild foods. Politically, the Arikara were organized into a loose confederacy of villages led by a head chief assisted by a tribal council of village chiefs. Religious life and ceremonies centered around the planting, cultivation, and harvesting of maize, the principal food resource.

See also Hidatsa; Mandan

Bibliography

Abel, Annie Heloise, ed. (1939). *Tabeau's Narrative of Loisel's Expedition to the Upper Missouri*. Norman: University of Oklahoma Press.

Macgowan, E. S. (1942). "The Arikara Indians." *Minnesota Archaeologist* 8:83–122.

Meyer, Roy W. (1977). *The Village Indians of the Upper Missouri: The Mandans, Hidatsas, and Arikaras.* Lincoln: University of Nebraska Press.

Assiniboin

ETHNONYMS: Assiniboine, Assinipwat, Fish-Eaters, Hohe, Stoneys, Stonies

The Assiniboin are a Siouan-speaking group who separated from the Nakota (Yanktonnai) in northern Minnesota sometime before 1640 and moved northward to ally themselves with the Cree near Lake Winnipeg. Later in the century they began to move westward, eventually settling in the basins of the Saskatchewan and Assiniboine rivers in Canada, and in Montana and North Dakota north of the Milk and Missouri rivers. With the disappearance of the bison (the mainstay of their subsistence) in the middle of the nineteenth century, they were forced to relocate to several reservations and reserves in Montana, Alberta, and Saskatchewan. Population estimates for the tribe ranged from eighteen thousand to thirty thousand in the eighteenth century. Today there are perhaps fifty-five hundred living on the Fort Belknap and Fort Peck reservations in Montana and in Canadian reserves, the largest being at Morley on the upper Bow River in Alberta.

The Assiniboin were a typical plains bison-hunting tribe; they were nomadic and lived in hide tipis. They usually employed the dog travois for transporting goods, although the horse was sometimes used. Famed as the greatest horse raiders on the Northern Plains, the Assiniboin were also fierce warriors. They were generally on friendly terms with Whites but regularly engaged in warfare against the Blackfoot and Gros Ventre. Many were converted to Methodism by Wesleyan missionaries during the nineteenth century, but the Grass Dance, Thirst Dance, and Sun Dance remained important ceremonials. After the Second World War, the Alberta Stoneys became much involved in political activism and cultural betterment through the Indian Association of Alberta. An Assiniboin-language school and university-level courses are offered at the reserve at Morley.

Bibliography

Dempsey, Hugh A. (1978). "Stoney Indians." In *Indian Tribes of Alberta*, 43–50. Calgary: Glenbow-Alberta Institute.

Kennedy, Dan (1972). *Recollections of an Assiniboine Chief*, edited and with an introduction by James R. Stevens. Toronto: McClelland & Stewart.

Lowie, Robert H. (1910). *The Assiniboine.* American Museum of Natural History, Anthropological Papers 4, 1–270. New York.

Notzke, Claudia (1985). *Indian Reserves in Canada: Development Problems of the Stoney and Peigan Reserves in Alberta.* Marburger Geographische Schriften, no. 97. Marburg/Lahn.

Whyte, Jon (1985). *Indians in the Rockies.* Banff, Alberta: Altitude Publishing.

Writers' Program, Montana (1961). *The Assiniboines: From the Accounts of the Old Ones Told to First Boy (James Larpenteur Long).* Norman: University of Oklahoma Press.

Baffinland Inuit

Orientation

Identification.   The Baffinland Inuit constitute the easternmost group of what is commonly referred to as the Central Eskimo, a designation that also includes the Copper, Iglulik, Netsilik, and Caribou Inuit. The Baffinland Inuit are a hunting people who have occupied their land for over four thousand years. They refer to their territory as *Nunaseak,* which means "beautiful land." Today, the Baffinland Inuit are under the jurisdiction of the Northwest Territories government. There is, however, an active movement toward a reinterpretation of their political status within Canada, which is based on the settlement of land claims, the creation of a system of self-government, and the recognition of aboriginal rights within the constitution of Canada. The rather massive changes that have occurred over the last twenty-five years have resulted in many disruptions to traditional social patterns that must be dealt with by all segments of the population as the Baffinland Inuit struggle to reconcile tradition with change and to create a new form of adaptation.

Location.   The Baffinland Inuit occupy the southern two-thirds of Baffin Island. Their territory extends from approximately 62° to 72° N. The northeastern sector of their territory is mountainous with small glaciers, the southern sector has rolling terrain, and to the west the surface becomes flat. The climate is marked by intense cold in the winter with daytime temperatures averaging about -30° F. Summer temperatures average 50° F and except for the areas of glaciers most of the snow melts each season. The sea freezes in October and begins break-up in July. In some years, however, pack ice never clears from the area.

Demography.   In 1988 the population of the Baffinland Inuit was approximately 7,200. The largest community, Iqaluit (Frobisher Bay), is the transportation, supply, and government center for the territory and has a population of 3,625. The Davis Strait communities of Kangitugaapiq (Clyde) and Qikitarjuaq (Broughton Island) have populations of approximately 550 and 450, respectively; Pangnirtung, about 1,100; Kingmiruit (Lake Harbor), about 350 and, farther west, Kingait (Cape Dorset), about 1,100. The population is growing at a rate of 2.8 percent per year, which is a significant decrease from earlier estimates of over 4 percent. In all communities there is a predominance of young people, with almost 45 percent of the total population under eighteen years of age. The existence of settlements of even 400 people, coupled with this shift in age composition, is a new development with major social and economic consequences.

Linguistic Affiliation.   The Baffinland Inuit speak Inuktituk, which is the language spoken from northern Alaska to Greenland. Although there are dialects and changes from region to region, the Baffinland Inuit can communicate with all the Central Eskimo groups as well as with the Inuit of Quebec and Labrador. Inuktituk is now written by using syllabic symbols that were developed by missionaries. English is the second language of most young Baffinland Inuit, but there is a deep concern about maintaining the language and ensuring its use in the workplace as well as in the home.

History and Cultural Relations

The Baffinland Inuit have prehistoric origins that date back to approximately 2200 B.C. Many material culture traits as well as the seasonal use of territory have remained amazingly consistent over this long period of time. The earliest Inuit to occupy the territory are referred to as the pre-Dorset and Dorset cultures. The Inuit usually refer to this cultural phase as Tunit. Dorset adaptation was based on small, well-crafted stone, ivory, and bone implements used to harvest and process marine and land mammals, freshwater fish, and migratory birds. Sometime during the first thousand years the kayak, snowhouse, and dogsled came into use through a process of diffusion combined with local development. Around A.D. 1200, a different cultural adaptation called the Thule culture became evident throughout the territory and centered on the hunting of whales. Archaeological findings indicate that the Thule culture, like the population that preceded it, originated in Alaska and spread rapidly eastward. The Thule Inuit are the direct ancestors of the Baffinland Inuit of today.

Sustained contact with Europeans began around 1750, when whalers first entered the area. They introduced trade goods and disease and altered to some extent the general pattern of seasonal adaptation, especially after 1850, when they began to overwinter near the present-day communities of Pangnirtung and Kingmiruit. Whalers were the primary European presence until the early 1900s, when the decline of whales ended this activity. Whalers were replaced by fur traders, who first entered some parts of the territory around 1910 and remained a powerful economic and social force until about 1965. Although whalers introduced bartering and the seasonal employment of Inuit as crew members, it was the fur traders who instituted formal exchange and a system of economic control based on debit and credit. The trading era brought about occasional periods of prosperity, especially in the 1920s, but for the most part resulted in difficult economic times and a deterioration of the Baffinland Inuit's independent pattern of subsistence. Nevertheless, when the elders of today refer to traditional times, or even to "the good old days," they mean life during the fur trade era.

Around 1912, the first missionaries entered the region and the evidence points to a rapid replacement of a shamanistic-based system of belief by that of Anglican Christianity. The missionaries were soon followed by the Royal Canadian Mounted Police who represented the government of Canada and looked after Canadian sovereignty of the territory. A more active government representation started to develop in the late 1950s when it became apparent that the living conditions and health of Inuit had deteriorated. Tuberculosis was the major health problem, although influenza and even common colds could cause hardship and death. By the mid-1950s, a medical ship would visit all Baffinland Inuit communities each year and seriously ill individuals of any age were evacuated to spend one to several years recuperating in a southern hospital or sanatorium. By the 1970s, small nursing stations were built in the communities, with a regional hospital in Iqualuit. The rate of tuberculosis has been significantly slowed, but evacuation, now carried out by airplane, is still relied upon.

The development of the six present-day communities began in 1960 when the government started to implement a wider range of programs. The first communities comprised shacks without water, sewage treatment, or other services. By 1965, government housing programs were initiated and as services accumulated the community became more permanent. Schools were created for primary grades, but some teenage youth would be sent to boarding schools outside the region for vocational training or academic upgrading.

Settlements

The settlement pattern of the Baffinland Inuit was based on small reasonably permanent winter encampments that were the primary residence for family groups ranging in size from twenty-five to fifty individuals. Family groups identified themselves geographically and socially by the suffix -_miut_ which means "the people of a particular place." The territory utilized by Inuit was defined geographically through the designation of many place names, and there was a network of trails and travel routes, indicating the potential for the movement of people over long distances. The winter residence was the central point from which smaller, seasonal camps would be established in order to harvest specific resources. The pattern of occupation was formed by groups of related families living within a region. Certain activities such as the late winter breathing-hole hunting of the seal could support larger groups and tended to bring people together. At other times, especially during inland trips for caribou, smaller social units, usually composed only of male hunters from closely related families, were more productive. During much of this century, the presence of fur traders throughout the region had an influence on settlement since they encouraged or coerced Inuit to maintain smaller social groups over a larger territory and to locate their settlement with respect to potential benefits from trapping rather than hunting.

The settlement pattern and territoriality of particular Baffinland Inuit groups did not necessarily exclude other individuals or family groups from using territory, but since kinship linkages within one particular area were better defined than between areas, there was a tendency to maintain loose boundary distinctions. Certain of these boundary distinctions are still maintained today through the arrangement of family housing units within the new settlements. Older patterns can also be recognized in the political structure and influence of particular individuals or families on the economic and social life in these new communities.

Today, the Baffinland Inuit live in six centralized communities and practice a mixed economy of hunting and wage labor. Children attend primary and secondary schools, the families are housed in centrally heated government-built dwellings that are serviced for water and sewage, and there is access to social programs and basic health services. All the communities are linked together and to southern Canada by a system of air transport, but there has been no substantial migration to southern Canada.

Economy

The traditional economy of the Baffinland Inuit was based on seasonal harvesting that took place within the framework of settlement and territoriality described above. Marine mammals were the primary species harvested by the Baffinland Inuit, including, in general order of importance, ringed and bearded seals, beluga whale, walrus, and polar bear. A very generalized description of the seasonal economic cycle can be applied to the Baffinland Inuit as a whole, though each area had a particular pattern. In the winter, the primary activity was hunting for seals at their breathing holes or along the floe edge where permanent ice gives way to open water. Winter was the time of lowest productivity, and traditionally the ease of survival was often a function of the amount of food that could be stored from fall hunting and fishing. As winter gave way to spring, seals began to sun themselves on top of the ice, making them easier to find and harvest. In May, beluga whale and migratory birds would begin to move into the region and anadromous fish move to the ocean. Spring was an important hunting time, since surpluses of food could be obtained. When dogsleds were in wide use, these surpluses would be stored for dog food. During the summer families relied on fishing near coastal or inland lakes or rivers and on the gathering of seaweed and clams, as well as berries and roots. By September, the weather often made coastal travel difficult, so people moved to fishing sites for Arctic char, but on calm days seal hunting was often productive. Early fall was marked by long inland hunts for caribou, with caribou fur at its best for the preparation of winter clothing. The transition from fall to winter was marked by the movement of beluga whale and, in certain areas, walrus along the coast. These species could often be harvested in large quantities and stored for winter use.

Dogsleds were the primary means of land transportation until about 1965, when the snowmobile was introduced. Introduction of the snowmobile, along with the motor-powered freighter canoes and, most recently, the four-wheel drive overland vehicles, meant that new economic strategies needed to be created since this technology had to be purchased and supported through large sums of money. At present, it costs an Inuit hunter approximately thirty thousand dollars (Canadian) to obtain and operate the minimal equipment needed. Since the Arctic environment is hard on equipment, full replacement, at least of snowmobiles, is necessary every two to three years. The types of economic activity used to generate income have changed over time. The reliance on the debit and credit system of the fur trade began to disappear around 1965. At that time, universal programs of social assistance such as family allowances and old-age benefits were applied to the Inuit, and there was also the creation of more permanent wage employment in the new settlements.

The transition between the reliance on trapping and the employment patterns of today was bridged for many Inuit by the creation of an industry based on Inuit soapstone carving. This industry still flourishes in some of the Baffinland communities, especially Kingait and Kingmiruit. The economy of Iqaluit is based on the provision of services to the inhabitants of this community and the region. The economy of Pangnirtung has recently been supported through the development of a tourist industry based on the creation of a unique national park supplemented by commercial fishing in winter. The national park has also affected Broughton Island on Davis Strait. Throughout the territory, there continues to be an emphasis on hunting in part because of its importance to the food economy but also because of its values for maintaining and enjoying a more traditional life-style. The sale of furs and sealskin has been badly damaged by pressures from the animal rights movement. Even though many Inuit now participate in wage employment that may range from driving trucks or heavy equipment to serving as community mayor or administrator, many jobs are still held by nonnatives. The development of schools and the creation of academic vocational programs should bring about a shift in this situation. It is now possible for Inuit to look forward to employment as pilots, managers, and politicians, and a number of small business ventures have been attempted. Nevertheless, the economic outlook is still not secure, and there is the persistent question of how the youth of today will be able to support themselves.

Kinship

Kin Groups and Descent.   The pattern of social cohesion, or division, within Baffinland Inuit society is determined to a large measure by the density and type of kin-based relationships that exist within any one segment of the population. The nuclear family is a primary social unit, but it is the extended family that is the most important social entity when considering the integration that occurs between the social and economic roles of individuals. Extended families are also linked through kinship to form the larger territorial group that is often referred to as a band. The Baffinland system of kinship is bilateral and recognizes positions for two ascending and two descending generations. The kinship system encourages interpersonal behavior based on respect, affection, and obedience. Although these categories of behavior apply only to pairs of individuals, they also play a part within the larger system since they help to regulate or channel the sharing of food and materials including money, the flow of information, the age or sexual division of roles, and the expression of leadership within a social group. The structure of kinship groups indicates a bias toward relationships between males, yet not to the extent that could be called a patrilineal form of social organization.

Kinship Terminology.   Within Baffinland Inuit society, two types of terminological processes operate to create a kinship network. The first is that which establishes the formal or ideal set of terms that identify fixed kinship positions in relationship to a speaker. These positions are based on the consanguineal ties of biological family and on the affinal ties acquired through marriage. The second, and in relation to everyday usage, the more important process, is the alternative way in which the terms of the formal or ideal system are incorporated into an alternative, or "fictive," system of relationships. Because of this second process, there is often a major distinction between the true consanguineal or affinal relationship and the term that is actually used. The name is the primary factor that creates this apparent contradiction. Throughout Baffinland, newborn children are named after a deceased person or persons—a child can have as many as seven names. A speaker will therefore refer to this child on the basis of the kinship relationship that existed between the speaker and the deceased person. Because of this process, most individuals are recognized by many different fictive kinship terms. The fictive kinship established through the name also means that the behavior follows the fictive rather than the actual kinship designation, and this can cross sexual lines. Although such reckoning is often used in a symbolic sense, especially as the child grows older, it is nevertheless important and persistent.

Marriage and Family

Marriage.   Traditionally, marriage took place through an arrangement made for children by adults when the two children were young. Since the rigors of life could not guarantee the eventual joining of these individuals, it was not uncommon for parents to create such an arrangement just prior to the marriage. Men usually moved to the village of the wife's parents. The duration of this depended on the social position and economic circumstances of the two families and on the overall availability of either eligible males or females. Polygamous unions existed, and there could be unions that represented significant age differences between the partners.

Domestic Unit.   New domestic units were created when a couple had their first child. This nuclear unit usually remained within the parental dwelling, but as the number of children increased, a new residence would be created usually close to the parental home. Since adoption of grandchildren by grandparents was common, the actual development of new nuclear families could be delayed. In the new communities there has been a breakdown of arranged marriages, and young adults often express their independence through exercising their own choice of partner. There is also a tendency especially for young women to remain unmarried, but pregnancies often occur and the child is usually adopted by parents or other members of the extended family.

Socialization.   The socialization of children has undergone significant change since the creation of modern communities. In the past, the immediate family, including especially the grandparents, was responsible for much of the socialization. Children were involved in a continuous process of education that tended to shift its emphasis as the child matured. The early stages of development were defined by tolerance and affection. As a child grew older, affection was replaced by a stress on independence. Learning took place by example and was often integrated with play. Male roles and female roles were part of this play. As a child grew older, play gave way to more useful work, and there was an emphasis on tasks that would be incorporated into their older and more productive stages of life. The productive stage could begin before marriage and lasted until age set limits on the type of activities a male or female could carry out. At this point they moved into a stage in which they became more valuable as possessors of information, including family history and myth. In today's world the complexity of community life means that this process has broken down. The primary exception is during the spring and summer when children, parents, and elders are often together in smaller hunting camps. For the most part, however, the school, television, and other imported institutions have either replaced or, more often, come into conflict with traditional ways of socializing the young.

Sociopolitical Organization

In traditional Inuit society there was no active political level of organization. The kinship system operated to maintain social control and resolve conflict. The leadership noted above was neither persistent nor acquired through any formal process. Most leadership was exercised most effectively only within the extended family. Territory did not carry political connotation or boundaries. Again, it was social organization that tended to limit or facilitate access to territory. There was no ownership of either land or resources. A tendency toward possessing "rights" to a particular territory was simply a function of the size of a social unit and the time in which it had persisted in the use of a particular territory. Rights to resources were part of everyone's heritage, and these rights were best expressed through the almost universal process of sharing. The lack of traditional political and leadership roles within the culture of the Baffinland Inuit has meant that the development of new political realities within the areas of land claims, self-government, or community organization has been difficult to create. Although young people have attempted to develop politically, it is still hard for them to express leadership across a large segment of the population.

Religion and Expressive Culture

In the traditional world of the Baffinland Inuit, spirits permeated every aspect of life. Some of these spirits were benevolent and helpful; others were not. The powers of certain spirits were integrated with the powers of certain individuals in order to create a shamanistic power. Ceremonies, feasts, and celebrations were held, most of which were linked to different phases of the ecological or natural cycle. Amulets were widely used and a wide range of taboos observed. Direct intervention between the spirit world and living Inuit was carried out through the shaman. The change to Christianity within the framework of the Anglican church began in the early 1900s and rapidly spread through all of the population. The role of the Christian religion has continued to develop, and the Bible remains the only piece of literature that is available to the Inuit in their own language.

Bibliography

Anders, G., ed. (1967). _Baffinland-East Coast: An Economic Survey_. Ottawa: Department of Indian Affairs and Northern Development, Industrial Division.

Boas, Franz (1888). _The Central Eskimo_. Sixth Annual Report of the Bureau of American Ethnology for the Years 1884–1885, 399–669. Washington, D.C.

Freeman, Milton M. R. (1976). _Inuit Land Use and Occupancy Project: Report_. 3 vols. Ottawa: Department of Indian and Northern Affairs.

Graburn, Nelson H. H. (1963). _Lake Harbour, Baffin Island: An Introduction to the Social and Economic Problems of a Small Eskimo Community_. Ottawa: Department of Northern Affairs and National Resources, Northern Co-Ordination and Research Centre.

Higgins, G. M. (1967). _South Coast–Baffinland: An Area Economic Survey_. Ottawa: Department of Indian Affairs and Northern Development, Industrial Division.

Kemp, William B. (1984). "Baffinland Eskimo." In _Handbook of North American Indians_. Vol. 5, _Arctic_, edited by David Damas, 463–475. Washington, D.C.: Smithsonian Institution.

McElroy, Ann (1977). _Alternatives to Modernization: Styles and Strategies of Acculturative Behavior of Baffin Island Inuit_. 3 vols. New Haven, Conn.: Human Relations Area Files.

WILLIAM B. KEMP

Bannock

ETHNONYMS: Banac, Nimi, Punnush

The Bannock are a Northern Paiute-speaking minority population among the Northern Shoshone, both of whom in the past lived in southern Idaho south of the Salmon River and extending eastward into northwestern Wyoming and southwestern Montana. Most now live with the Northern Shoshone on the Fort Hall Indian Reservation near Pocatello, Idaho. They apparently lived originally in northeastern Oregon, but migrated into the general region of the Snake River where they lived among the Shoshone speakers in peaceful cooperation. In the nineteenth century they were loosely organized in seminomadic bands. They had band chiefs who inherited office through the male line subject to community approval. They shared most of their culture traits with the Northern Shoshone. Their culture was basically Basin Shoshonean with an admixture of Plateau Indian and Plains Indian traits, such as the use of the horse and of bison-hunting parties. There were about 2,500 Bannock and Shoshone Indians living on the Fort Hall Reservation in 1980. It is not known what the population breakdown is.
See also Northern Shoshone

Bibliography

Madsen, Brigham D. (1958). _The Bannock of Idaho_. Caldwell, Idaho: Caxton Printers.

Murphy, Robert F., and Yolanda Murphy (1986). "Northern Shoshone and Bannock." In _Handbook of North American Indians_. Vol. 11, _Great Basin_, edited by Warren L. d'Azevedo, 284–307. Washington, D.C.: Smithsonian Institution.

Basques

ETHNONYMS: Bascos, Eskualdunak, Euskaldunak, Vascos

Orientation

Identification. The European Basque homeland is in the western Pyrenees and straddles the French-Spanish border. Although frequently designated as either French or Spanish

Basques, the Basque people constitute one of Europe's most distinctive ethnic groups in their own right. The seven traditional regions within the Basque country, further distinguished by dialectical differences in spoken Basque, provide subethnic distinctions within the Basque population. Basques entered North America as either Spanish or French nationals, but Basque-Americans invoke Basqueness as their primary ethnic identity.

Location.   There are small numbers of Basques in British Columbia, Quebec, and the eastern seaboard in Canada. Basques are present in every state of the United States but are concentrated in California, Idaho, and Nevada. Basques are particularly noted for an identification with sheepherding and are therefore present to some degree in the open-range livestock districts of all thirteen states of the American West. Florida, New York, and Connecticut have significant Basque populations as well.

Demography.   The Basque-Canadian population as such has not been enumerated, but probably numbers no more than 2,000 to 3,000 individuals. The 1980 U.S. census estimated the Basque-American population at slightly more than 40,000. The three largest concentrations by state include California (15,530), Idaho (4,332), and Nevada (3,378). The Basques of North America are primarily rural and small-town dwellers, although there are urban concentrations in New York City (port of entry), Miami, Greater San Francisco, Greater Los Angeles, Stockton, Fresno, Bakersfield, Boise, and Reno.

Linguistic Affiliation.   First-generation Basque immigrants are usually fluent in Basque (*Euskera*), an agglutinative language employing the Roman alphabet but with no known affinity with any other tongue. Basque immigrants are also fluent in Spanish and/or French. Basque-Canadians and Basque-Americans are more likely to be bilingual in Basque and English (French in the case of Quebec) than to retain their parents' fluency in Spanish or French. It is rare for the second generation of New World–born individuals to retain fluency in a second language. Rather, they are fully assimilated linguistically into the American mainstream.

History and Cultural Relations

Basques, as Europe's earliest and most efficient whalers, may have entered North America prior to the voyages of Columbus. There is documentation of Basque whaling and cod-fishing activity along the Labrador coast by the early sixteenth century and evidence of Basque loan words in some of the Atlantic coastal Canadian Native American languages. Canadian archivists and archaeologists have discovered a sixteenth-century Basque whaling station (used seasonally) and sunken whaling ship at Red Bay, Labrador. Place names such as Port-aux-Basques, Placentia, and Biscay Bay also testify to a Basque presence in Canadian coastal waters. This activity remained intense through the eighteenth century and lasted well into the nineteenth. With the exception of this maritime involvement, the Basque presence in Canada remains virtually unstudied. Some French Basques became established in Quebec as part of that area's overall French immigration. In recent years there has been a Basque festival in the town of Trois Pistoles. In the twentieth century, a small colony of Basques (associated with the timber industry) has

emerged in western British Columbia, and several of its families have relocated to the Vancouver area.

Basques entered the western United States as part of the Spanish colonial endeavor. Several administrators, soldiers, explorers, and missionaries in the American Southwest and Spanish California were Basques. After Mexican independence and subsequent American annexation of the area, there was a renewal of Basque immigration as part of the California gold rush. Many of the prospectors came from southern South America, where Basques were the established sheepmen on the pampas. Some saw an opportunity to repeat in California a sheep-raising pattern under frontier conditions. By 1860, there were established Basque sheep outfits roaming the public lands in southern California. In the 1870s they spread throughout California's central valleys and had expanded into parts of Arizona, New Mexico, and western Nevada. By the first decade of the twentieth century, Basques were present in the open-range districts of all thirteen western states. The Basque sheepherder was the preferred employee in Basque- and non-Basque-owned sheep outfits alike.

Restrictive immigration legislation in the 1920s, with its anti-southern-European bias, severely limited Basque immigration into the United States, and by the 1940s, the Basque-American community was evolving away from its Old World cultural roots. But a labor shortage during World War II and the unwillingness of Americans to endure the privations of the sheepherding way of life prompted the U.S. government to exempt prospective Basque sheepherders from immigration quotas. Between 1950 and 1975, several thousand Basques entered the United States on three-year contracts. The general decline of the sheep industry over the past fifteen years, coupled with full recovery of the Spanish and French economies, has all but interdicted the immigration of Basques into the American West. Today there are fewer than one hundred Basques herding sheep in the United States.

A secondary source of twentieth-century Basque immigration derived from the Basque game of jai alai. Nuclei of professional players who have married U.S. citizens or otherwise gained permanent residency have formed around the legalized jai alai frontons in Florida, Connecticut, and Rhode Island. Political refugees form a third modern, if modest, stream of Basque immigration in North America, as some individuals rejected Franco's Spain and others fled Castro's Cuba.

Settlements

Basque involvement in sheepherding is limited to the arid and semiarid open-range districts of the American West, where sheep husbandry entails transhumance—that is, the herds are wintered on the valley floors and then trailed into adjacent or distant mountain ranges for summer pasturage. The annual trek might involve covering as much as five hundred miles on foot, although today the animals are more likely to be trucked if the distance between the summer and winter ranges is considerable. For the herder, while on the winter range, home is a sheep wagon containing little more than a bunk, table, and stove. The wagon is moved about the desert winter range with either horses or a four-wheel drive vehicle. In the summer months the herder lives in a tipi camped along streambeds in high mountain canyons. He is visited every several days by a camptender who brings him supplies on mule-back or by pickup truck. The herder's life is characterized by extreme isolation, the loneliness being relieved only by the camptender's brief visit, the portable radio, a few magazines and books, and the occasional letter from a fiancée or family. Some former sheepherders acquired their own ranch properties. These were established holdings and therefore have no architectural features that might be regarded as uniquely Basque. Most small towns of the open-range districts have one or more Basque hotels, which are likely located within sight of the railroad station (to facilitate the travel of newly arrived herders from Europe). Again, they tend to be purchased rather than constructed by their proprietors and are therefore largely consonant with western American small-town architecture, although some of the hotels have added a fronton or handball court. The typical hotel contains a bar; a dining room where meals are served family-style at long tables to boarders and casual guests alike; and a second floor of sleeping rooms usually reserved for permanent boarders, sheepherders in town for a brief visit, vacation, or employment layoff, and herders in transit to an employer.

Economy

Subsistence and Commercial Activities. The Basque fishermen in Canada were seasonal sojourners, who crossed the Atlantic to hunt whales and fish for cod. The former were rendered into oil and the latter were salted for transport back to Europe. In the United States, Basques, as much as any and more than most immigrant groups, have been identified with a single industry—sheep husbandry. By the beginning of the present century, they were present in all phases of it, dominating the ranks of the sheepherders and nomadic outfits that moved about the public lands throughout the year. Some Basques also acquired their own ranch properties; others worked as camptenders and ranch foremen. Still others became involved as wool and lamb buyers and in livestock transportation. In recent years, open-range sheep husbandry in the United States has declined owing to increased labor costs and herder shortages, the abolition of certain predator control measures, the success of environmentalists in limiting livestock numbers on public lands, declining demand for wool versus synthetic fabrics, and foreign competition for meat products. Consequently, the Basque involvement in sheep husbandry is now more historic than actual. Many former herders and owners returned to Europe; others converted sheep ranches to cattle; and still others moved to nearby small towns to engage in construction work or establish small businesses (bars, bakeries, motels, gasoline stations, and so on). In San Francisco, Basques work as gardeners, specializing in caring for dozens of urban, postage-stamp-sized yards. They wrested this occupational niche from Japanese-Americans when the latter were interned during World War II. In the Greater Los Angeles area, several Basques work as milkers in large commercial dairies. Wherever jai alai (words that mean "happy festival" in Basque) is legalized, Basque players are recruited from Europe. They tend to be true sojourners, playing part of the year in the Basque country and the remainder in the United States. Basque-Americans are assimilated into the wider culture and therefore display the full range of American occupations and professions. There are Basque attorneys, medical doctors, and university professors, as well as a few owners and chief executive officers of major businesses and financial institutions. It is also true, however, that Basque-Americans have tended to cluster in small businesses, trades, and unskilled occupations. In part, this is a reflection of the Old World rural origins of their forebears and their own upbringing in rural and/or small-town America.

Trade. In the American West there is a Basque ethnic network that, if far from absolute, provides a certain Basque clientele to Basque-owned businesses and tradespeople. The Basque hotels are particularly patronized by Basque-Americans, although all depend upon their wider American clientele as well. In this regard, they trade on the excellent reputation of Basque cuisine and their fame for providing a unique ethnic atmosphere.

Division of Labor. In both Old World and Basque-American society there is considerable egalitarianism between the sexes. Although domestic tasks remain largely the purview of women, they are not regarded as demeaning for men. Conversely, whether running a ranching operation, a Basque hotel, or a town business, women work alongside their menfolk performing virtually any task.

Land Tenure. In Old World Basque society, farm or business ownership is a point of personal pride and social prestige, an attitude discernible among Basque-Americans. Practically none entered the United States with the intention of remaining salaried sheepherders. Rather, the occupation was seen as a stepping-stone providing savings either to return to Europe and purchase land or to acquire a ranch or town business in the United States. Those Basques who remain salaried employees manifest an extremely high level of home ownership.

Kinship

Kin Groups and Descent. The Basque-American community is stitched together by extended consanguineal (reckoned bilaterally) and affinal ties. Recruitment of herders from Europe typically involved sending for or receiving a request from a brother or cousin willing to come to the United States. Therefore, each Basque-American colony is more likely to be made up of family clusters rather than unrelated families and individuals. The degree of interrelatedness is enhanced by local endogamy involving an Old World–born ex-herder and a Basque-American spouse or two first-generation Basque-Americans. Extended Basque-American families tend to maintain close ties, gathering for baptisms, graduations, weddings, and funerals, and is further integrated by godparental ties.

Kinship Terminology. Basque kinship terms are of the Eskimo variety. Sibling terms differ according to whether the speaker is male or female. Basque kinship reckoning is quite consonant with that in the wider North American mainstream.

Marriage and Family

Marriage. Few Basques entered the United States with the intention of staying. Also, the immigrants were mainly young males. The sheepherding occupation was inimical to family life, and the only married herders were sojourners who had left their spouses and children in Europe. Gradually, some Basques became oriented to an American future and either sent back or went back to Europe for brides (few married non-Basques). Many of the brides were of the "mail-order" variety, the sister or cousin of an acquaintance made in the United States. As Basque hotels proliferated they became a source of spouses. The hotel keepers sent back to Europe for women willing to come to America as domestics, and few remained single for long. In this fashion, the basis of Basque-American family life and community was established.

Domestic Unit. Most Basque-American households are of the nuclear family variety and are largely indistinguishable from their American counterparts. For those Basques engaged in ranching, the notion of family, or at least of family privacy, is stretched to include ranch employees. The latter sleep in a bunkhouse, but they are likely to take their meals in the kitchen of the main house. If the outfit includes Old World–born herders with limited or no English skills, they are likely to be afforded special attention by the family. For families engaged in the hotel business, home is the entire establishment, which is truly a family enterprise. Special attention is likely to be accorded to the permanent boarders—retired herders with no interest in returning to Europe.

Inheritance. In Europe, farm property is transmitted to a single heir in each generation. This is less noticeable among Basque-Americans. Few Basque-American businesses or ranches remain in the same family for two or more generations.

Socialization. Child rearing among Basque-Americans is similar to that in mainstream American society. The exception is that first-generation American-born children are imbued with an urgency to excel in academics and athletics through the secondary school level. This has been interpreted as the need to prove oneself in American terms as a countermeasure to anti-immigrant and, at times, specifically anti-Basque prejudice.

Sociopolitical Organization

Social Organization. After the family, the most important social institution is the hotel or boarding house. For the Old World–born herder it is a town address, a bank, an employment agency, an ethnic haven, a source of advice and translation assistance when dealing with the wider society, a place to leave one's city clothes while on the range and one's saddle, rifle, and bedroll when on a return visit to Europe, a possible source of a bride, and a potential retirement home. For the Basque-American, it is a place to recharge one's ethnic batteries, practice one's rusty Basque, learn something about Old World Basque culture, dance to Basque music, eat Basque cuisine, hire help, possibly board one's children during the school year, and hold baptism and wedding receptions as well as wakes. Over the past four decades, Basque social clubs have emerged in many small towns and cities of the American West. There is now a Basque festival cycle in the region, lasting from late May through early September, with many of the social clubs sponsoring a local event. Several of the clubs have their own folk-dance group. In Bakersfield, Boise, and San Francisco, the Basque club has its own physical plant for meetings, dances, and banquets.

Political Organization. Basque-Americans tend to reflect the conservative politics of rural western America, usually registering as Republicans. The most notable Basque politi-

cians include Nevada's former governor and U. S. senator Paul Laxalt and Idaho's Secretary of State Peter Cenarrusa. Basque-Americans have minimal interest in and knowledge of political developments in the European Basque homeland. In the 1980s, representatives of the government of Euskadi (*Eusko Jaurlaritza*), including its president, several parliamentarians, and ministers have visited the Basque settlements of the United States. The Basque government has provided some financial aid to Basque-American organizations and cultural endeavors and currently publishes an English-language newsletter regarding events in the Basque homeland. In 1974, the Basque clubs of the United States formed NABO, or North American Basque Organizations, Inc. Each of the nineteen member clubs elects a NABO delegate. The organization meets periodically to coordinate the Basque festival cycle and to promote special events. These include sponsorship of national handball and *mus* (a Basque card game) championships, the U. S. tours of Old World Basque performing artists, and an annual summer music camp for Basque-American children at which they learn Basque folk music and are instructed in the *txistu* (a flutelike instrument played simultaneously with the drum).

Social Control. Peer pressure among Basque-Americans is pronounced. Basques have a group reputation for honesty (one's word is deemed to be as good as a written contract) and hard work. Anyone jeopardizing this perception through scandalous or frivolous behavior is likely to be both criticized and ostracized.

Conflict. Basques have experienced a degree of discrimination in the United States. They are sometimes perceived to be Latins or Hispanics by persons ignorant of the subtleties of southern European ethnic differentiation. The close identification of Basques with sheepherding, a denigrated occupation in the American West, and the activities of the nomadic ("tramp" to their detractors) sheep bands in competing with settled livestock interests for access to the range were additional sources of anti-Basque sentiment and even legislation. More recently, the sensationalized newspaper coverage of conflict in the Basque country, and particularly the activities of the ETA organization, have made Basque-Americans sensitive to the possible charge of being terrorist sympathizers.

Religion and Expressive Culture

Religious Beliefs. Basques are Roman Catholics, with strong Jansenist overtones. On occasion, the church has assigned a Basque chaplain to minister to the Basques of the American West. In Old World Basque society there was a belief in witchcraft and supernatural dwellers in mountain caverns and forest fastnesses. There is little carryover of this tradition to the Basque-American context.

Religious Practitioners. With some exceptions, Basque-Americans are not particularly devout. The isolation of sheep camp and ranch life precluded regular church attendance. Basque-American demographics in which a small population is scattered over an enormous geographic expanse militated against the development of a Basque ethnic church. Conversely, few Basques have converted to other religions and a number of Basque-Americans attend parochial schools and Catholic universities.

Arts. There are several Basque folk-dance groups and txistu players in the American West. There are also a few *bertsolariak*, or versifiers, who spontaneously comment on any subject in sung verse. The literary spokesman of the Basque-American experience is Robert P. Laxalt, whose book, *Sweet Promised Land*, described his father's life as a sheepman in the American West and his return visit to his natal village. The Basque festival incorporates several Old and New World features including a mass, folk dancing, social dancing, barbecue, athletic events (woodchopping, stone lifting, weight carrying, tugs-of-war) and possibly sheep hooking and sheepdog trials. In 1989, the National Monument to the Basque Sheepherder was dedicated in a public park in Reno, Nevada. It contains a seven-meter-high contemporary sculpture by the noted European Basque sculptor Nestor Bastarretxea.

Medicine. There is nothing distinctively Basque about their New World medical beliefs or practices.

Death and Afterlife. Standard Christian beliefs in heaven, purgatory, and hell obtain. Funerals are taken seriously and mobilize the widest range of kinship and friendship ties. Basque-Americans will travel hundreds of miles to attend the funeral of a family member, fellow villager, or former companion.

Bibliography

Douglass, William A., and Jon Bilbao (1975). *Amerikanuak: Basques in the New World.* Reno: University of Nevada Press.

Douglass, William A., and Beltran Paris (1979). *Beltran: Basque Sheepman of the American West.* Reno: University of Nevada Press.

Laxalt, Robert P. (1986). *Sweet Promised Land.* Reno: University of Nevada Press.

WILLIAM A. DOUGLASS

Bearlake Indians

ETHNONYMS: Sahtú gotine, Satudene, Gens du Lac d'Ours

The Bearlake Indians are an Athapaskan-speaking population made up of the descendants of Dogrib, Hare, Slavey, and other groups who were in contact with Europeans after the establishment of trading posts at or near Great Bear Lake in the northern Canadian Northwest Territories. Their culture is similar to that of the Dogrib, Hare, and Slavey.

There has apparently been no change in land use and settlement patterns since they were first studied in 1928. Fort Norman on the Mackenzie River was the focal point of trade for the Bearlake Indians from the 1820s until 1950 when a Hudson's Bay Company post was established at Fort Franklin on the Keith Arm of the Lake. The Bearlake settlement at Fort Franklin has expanded since then: the town is a government center, with a school, a nursing station, a government-sponsored housing program, and a Roman Catholic church. There are about seven hundred Bearlake Indians in the area today.

See also Dogrib, Hare, Slavey

Bibliography

Gillespie, Beryl C. (1981). "Bearlake Indians." In *Handbook of North American Indians.* Vol. 6, *Subarctic,* edited by June Helm, 310–313. Washington, D.C.: Smithsonian Institution.

Osgood, Cornelius (1931). *The Ethnography of the Great Bear Lake Indians.* National Museum of Canada Bulletin no. 70, 31–97. Ottawa.

Beaver

ETHNONYMS: Tsattine, Castors

The Beaver are an American Indian group numbering about nine hundred located in northeast British Columbia and northwest Alberta in Canada. They are closely related to the Sekani, their neighbors to the west. Today, the Beaver reside in the same area, on or near the Prophet River, Beaton River, Doig River, Blueberry River, and West Moberly Lake reserves in British Columbia and the Child Lake, Boyer, Clear Hills, and Horse Lakes Reserves in Alberta. Beaver is an Athapaskan language.

The Beaver were nomadic hunter-gatherers. Beaver was the most important game, first as the basic food and later for both food and the fur trade. In accordance with the nomadic way of life, band composition was flexible, with the bilaterally extended family the basic social and economic unit. Early contacts with Whites included involvement in the fur trade and Roman Catholic missionaries, producing a syncretic religion composed of Catholic and traditional beliefs and practices. Extensive contacts with Whites began in the twentieth century and have included the farming of traditional Beaver lands, compulsory education (which led to English replacing Beaver as the primary language), and the establishment of the reserves. Wage labor now competes with hunting and trapping as the major source of income.

Bibliography

Ridington, Robin (1968). "The Environmental Context of Beaver Indian Behavior." Ph.D. diss., Harvard University.

Ridington, Robin (1981). "Beaver." In *Handbook of North American Indians.* Vol. 6, *Subarctic,* edited by June Helm, 350-360. Washington D.C.: Smithsonian Institution.

Bellabella

ETHNONYMS: Elkbasumh, Heiltsuk, Milbank Sound Indians, Northern Kwakiutl

The Bellabella are a Kwakiutl-speaking group related to the Southern Kwakiutl and the Nootka, neighboring groups to the south. The Bellabella live on the coast of British Columbia in the area from Rivers Inlet to Douglas Channel. The name "Bellabella" is an Indian rendering of the English word *Milbank*, taken back into English. The Bellabella numbered about three hundred in 1901 and number about twelve hundred today. Bellabella, along with Nootka and Kwakwala, form the Wakashan linguistic family. The Bellabella were divided into two distinct dialect groups—the Haisla, including the Kitamat and Kitlope; and the Heiltsuk, including the Bellabella proper (with the Kohaitk, Oealitk, and Oetlitk), the Nohuntsitk, Somehulitk, and Wikeno. The Xaihais may have constituted a third linguistic division.

The Bellabella were visited by explorers and traders beginning in the late 1700s, with a Hudson's Bay Company post established in 1833. The traders were soon followed by Protestant missionaries and settlers, leading to rapid assimilation and the disappearance of much of the traditional culture. Because of the rapid assimilation and resistance to intrusions by researchers, little is known about the traditional culture. From what is known, however, they were evidently quite similar to the Southern Kwakiutl.

See also Kwakiutl

Bibliography

Lopatin, Ivan A. (1945). *Social Life and Religion of the Indians in Kitimat, British Columbia*. University of Southern California Social Science Series, no. 26. Los Angeles.

Olson, Ronald (1954). *Social Life of the Owikeno Kwakiutl*. University of California Anthropological Records 14, 169–200. Berkeley.

Bella Coola

ETHNONYMS: Bellacoola, Belhoola, Bilqula

The Bella Coola are a North American Indian group numbering about six hundred who live on and near a reserve at Bella Coola, British Columbia. The Bella Coola language is classified in the Salishan-language family. In the late nineteenth century the Bella Coola numbered about fourteen hundred and occupied the shores of the Bella Coola River and its tributaries in British Columbia. Contact with White traders was limited until the discovery of gold in the Bella Coola territory in 1851. During the late nineteenth century, the tribe was decimated by smallpox, liquor, and starvation.

Subsistence was based on fishing, hunting, and gathering and included some trade. The social structure was complex, consisting of chiefs, shamans, an aristocracy, commoners, and slaves. The Bella Coola were divided into five geographical groups, with the main political units being autonomous village communities headed by chiefs.

The traditional Bella Coola cosmology consisted of two heavens above the earth and two hells below and was ruled over by a supreme female deity named QAma'its.

Bibliography

Boas, Franz (1900). *The Mythology of the Bella Coola Indians*. American Museum of Natural History, Memoir no. 2, 25–127. New York.

Kopas, Cliff (1970). *Bella Coola*. Vancouver: Mitchell Press.

McIlwraith, T.F. (1948). *The Bella Coola Indians*. Toronto, University of Toronto Press, 1948.

Black Creoles of Louisiana

ETHNONYMS: Afro-French, Black Creoles, Black French, Creoles, Créoles, Créoles Noirs, Creoles of Color

Orientation

Identification. Black Creole culture in southern Louisiana derives from contact and synthesis in the region over nearly three centuries between African slaves, French and Spanish colonists, *gens libres de couleur* (free people of color), Cajuns, and Indians, among others. Today, people in this dominantly African-French population have a range of ethnic styles and associations depending upon residence, family history, economic status, and perceived ancestry. Creole culture shows syncretism in areas such as folk Catholicism (home altars, voodoo, and *traiteurs*, or "traditional healers"), language use (French Creole), music/dance (New Orleans jazz and zydeco), the festival observed (Mardi Gras), and foodways (congris, jambalaya, gumbo). As a result of the internal cultural diversity and overlapping boundaries of group affiliation that characterize southern Louisiana society as a whole, Creole ethnic identity is particularly fluid and situation-derived. As Black Creoles gauge their relations to African-Americans, Cajuns, and other Whites (Italian, German, Irish, Isleno, French) among the major ethnic groups in the region, they make multiple group associations and show singular group pride in their diverse heritage. The name "Creole" has a polysemic history, and its meaning remains heavily context-bound to the present. The word derives from the Latin *creare* (to create) and entered French via Portuguese *crioulo* in the slave/plantation sphere of West Africa and the tropical New World. In the French colony of Louisiana, it originally referred to European descendants born in the colony. Over time its meaning extended to all people and things of domestic rather than foreign origin. Today, the old association of "Creole" with strictly European populations of the ancien régime is vestigial—though clung to by some Whites. Although the ethnic meaning of Creole varies in Louisiana, its primary public association is now with people of African-French/Spanish ancestry.

Location. The Creole "homeland" is semitropical French Louisiana in the southern part of the state along the Gulf of Mexico. Creole communities are found in downtown New Orleans neighborhoods; the plantation regions along the Mississippi River to the north and inland bayous, particularly Bayou Teche in Iberia, St. Martin, and St. Landry parishes; and the prairie region of southwest Louisiana, especially including Lafayette, St. Landry, Evangeline, and Calcasieu parishes. The rural southwest portion of this region is also called "Cajun Country" or "Acadiana," names derived from the dominant presence of Cajuns, who were descended ancestrally from French-speaking Acadians of what is now Nova Scotia and were displaced to southern Louisiana in the mid-eighteenth century. Although many Creoles reject Cajun sociocultural dominance reflected in the naming of the region, there is no doubt that Cajuns and rural Black Creoles (outside New Orleans) have interacted culturally to a great degree as evidenced in Cajun/Creole music, food, and language. Historic rural outlier settlements are also found on the north shore of Lake Pontchartrain and in northern Louisiana in the Cane River area south of Natchitoches. Major twentieth-century migrations have occurred into southeast Texas, particularly Beaumont, Port Arthur, and Houston, where the Fifth Ward is called "Frenchtown." Post–World War II migrants fleeing racial discrimination and seeking economic opportunity also established major Creole populations in the Los Angeles and San Francisco areas.

Demography. Early Louisiana census reports used racial terms like _mulâtre_ and FMC (free man of color) to indicate Black Creoles, but modern population studies do not specifically identify Black Creoles. The 1980 census does note over 250,000 people who speak some form of French or Creole, mostly in southern Louisiana parishes. Judging from the identification of Black population in these parishes, probably one-third of the French speakers are Black Creoles. A much larger number of English-dominant speakers affiliate ethnically as Black Creole in Louisiana, Texas, and California.

Linguistic Affiliation. Historically, three varieties of French in Louisiana have been identified: Colonial/Continental French, Cajun French, and French Creole. Although English is increasingly the dominant language among Creoles under forty, all these language varieties have been and are spoken in different Creole communities today. French Creole historically is a language discrete from French. Also called _Gombo_ and _couri-veni_ (for "to go"/"to come" in contrast to _aller_ and _venir_ of standard and dialectical French), various forms of French Creole originated from contact pidgin language in the slave/plantation spheres of West Africa and the New World. Louisiana Creole bears parallel and possibly historical relations to similar Creoles spoken in the French Caribbean, French West African, and Indian Ocean areas. As the Creole language expanded from the more limited pidgin form to become a mother tongue, it retained a mostly French lexicon, with African-influenced phonology and a restructured grammar not unlike that of other African-European Creole languages. The stronghold of Creole speaking in southern Louisiana is the plantation region along Bayou Teche, where it is sometimes the first language

of Whites as well as Blacks. There are also elder Creole speakers in New Orleans. Cajun French is the most widely spoken French language variety throughout rural southern Louisiana. It is used by Creoles in prairie settlements of southwest Louisiana, though they may speak it with influence from French Creole. Creole and Cajun language use do not correlate to ethnicity on an exact basis. Further, the long-term interaction with and dominance of Cajun French, as well as the larger assimilative tendency of English, have made Creole closer to Cajun French. Colonial/Continental French derives from the speakers of French among colonial settlers, planters, mercantilists, and non-Acadian farmer-laborers of the seventeenth and eighteenth centuries. Of the linguistic varieties, this "old Louisiana French" is the least used, although some upper-caste plantation area and urban Creoles speak the language, and its elements are maintained through Catholic schools and French-speaking social clubs in New Orleans.

History and Cultural Relations

Perhaps as many as twenty-eight thousand slaves arrived in eighteenth-century French- and then Spanish-held Louisiana from West Africa and the Caribbean. The early population dominance of Africans from the Senegal River basin included Senegalese, Bambara, Fon, Mandinka, and Gambian peoples. Later came Guinean, Yoruba, Igbo, and Angolan peoples. Owing to the high ratio of slaves to Whites and the nature of slavery in the French/Spanish regimes, New Orleans today is culturally the most African of American cities. The African–West Indian character of this port city and nearby plantation region was reinforced at the turn of the nineteenth century by the arrival of nearly ten thousand slaves, free Blacks, and planters from St. Domingue (Haiti).

Among those eighteenth- and nineteenth-century Louisiana Creoles with African ancestry, a higher percentage than in the rest of the American South was freed from slavery in Louisiana, owing in part to French and Spanish attitudes toward acknowledgment of social and biological mingling. These cultural differences from the Anglo South were expressed in laws (such as _Le Doce Noir_ and _Las Siete Partidas_ in Louisiana and the Caribbean) that governed relations to slaves and their rights and restrictions and provided for manumission in a variety of circumstances. Of those freed from slavery, a special class in the French West Indies and Louisiana resulted from relationships characteristically between European planter/mercantile men and African slave or free women. This formative group for Black Creoles was called _gens libres de couleur_ in antebellum times. In New Orleans, these "free people of color" were part of the larger Creole (that is, not American) social order in a range of class settings from French slaves, laborers, and craftsmen to mercantilists and planters. Some of these "Creoles of color," as they were also sometimes called, owned slaves themselves and had their children educated in Europe.

Various color terms, such as _griffe_, _quadroon_, and _octoroon_, were used in color/caste-conscious New Orleans to describe nineteenth-century Creoles of color in terms of social categories for race based on perceived ancestry. Given the favored treatment of lighter people with more European appearance, some Creoles would _passe blanc_ (pass for White) to seek privileges of status, economic power, and education denied to non-Whites. In times of racial strife from the Civil War to the civil rights movement, Black Creoles were often pressured to be in one or another of the major American racial categories. Such categorization has often been a source of conflict in Creole communities with their less dichotomized, more fluid Caribbean notion of race and culture.

Settlements

In New Orleans, Creoles have tended to remain strongly affiliated with neighborhoods such as the Treme area near the French Quarter as well as in the Gentilly area. Creole neighborhoods are centered around involvement in social clubs and benevolent societies as well as Catholic churches and schools. Black Creole sections of varied class/caste affiliations are found in most southern Louisiana towns of any size. In rural plantation areas, Creoles may reside in rows of worker housing or in some cases in inherited owners' homes. In southwestern Louisiana prairie farming regions, small settlements on ridges of high ground or pine forest "islands" may be entirely composed of descendants of Black Creoles who were freed or escaped from plantations to the east. Although Houston has a Creole-influenced Black neighborhood, in West Coast cities people are affiliated through networks maintained in Catholic churches, schools, and dance halls.

In rural plantation areas and some New Orleans neighborhoods, Creole houses are a regionally distinctive form. These cottage dwellings combine Norman influences in roofline and sometimes historic construction with half-timbering and *bousillage* (mud and moss plastering), with Caribbean influences seen in porches, upturned lower rooflines (false galleries), louvered doors and windows, and elevated construction. Most Creole cottages are two rooms wide, constructed of cypress with continuous pitch roofs and central chimneys. They were expanded and decorated according to the wealth and needs of the family. The basic Creole house, especially more elite plantation versions, has become a model for Louisiana suburban subdivisions. Other major house types include the California bungalow, shotgun houses, and mobile homes. Of these, the shotgun shows particular Louisiana characteristics that relate it to the dwellings in the Caribbean and West Africa. It is one room wide and two or more rooms long. Although shotgun houses are often associated with plantation quarters, they have frequently been gentrified in construction for middle-class Creoles and others by being widened, elevated, trimmed with Victorian gingerbread, and otherwise made fancier than the unpainted board-and-batten shacks of slaves and sharecroppers. All these house forms and their many variations, often painted in deep primary colors and rich pastels, create a Louisiana Creole-built environment look that has come to symbolize the region as a whole.

Economy

Subsistence and Commercial Activities.   In rural French Louisiana, Creoles have historically been farmers and itinerant agricultural laborers raising sugar cane, rice, sweet potatoes, and, more recently, soybeans. Chickens, ducks, pigs, cattle, and goats are found in plantation regions and prairie farmsteads. Hunting and, to a lesser extent, fishing may also add to the household economy. In towns and New Orleans, many Creoles have worked as artisans and craftspeople. Today, oil-related jobs and construction and service industries are added to the mix. Creoles also hold an array of mainstream jobs, such as teaching, law enforcement, medicine, and so on. While some Creoles run grocery and sundries stores, most people outside New Orleans neighborhoods or rural Creole settlements are not merchants.

Industrial Arts.   Urban Creoles and town dwellers have a long association in the skilled crafts. In New Orleans there is a tradition of Creole plaster work, wrought iron, and carpentry. In rural areas also, carpentry is often a Creole occupation.

Division of Labor.   In rural areas, women oversee the domestic sphere, raising children, cooking, washing clothes, and tending to yard-related animals and gardens. Men are more oriented toward work in cash jobs or as farmers, with additional subsistence derived from hunting, fishing, and gathering firewood. Girls and small children tend to assist their mother, and older boys and young men may work with their father. Increasing urbanization in employment venue and penetration of mainstream society with less gender-specific work roles is transforming the rural division of labor. In an established urban setting like New Orleans, men have similarly tended to be those who labored outside the home in the crafts previously noted, while women have been primary in the domestic sphere. When women do work outside the home, roles as teachers, nurses, and professional support services dominate. Particularly in New Orleans, middle-class Creoles have entered all layers of professional society, though discrimination remains a problem there and throughout the region.

Land Tenure.   A wide variety of situations obtains. Some Creoles inherited extensive family holdings that date to antebellum days. Other holdings, particularly on the prairies, derive from nineteenth-century settlement claims. Some families obtained land after the Civil War through "forty acres and a mule" redistribution.

Kinship

Kin Groups and Descent.   Extensive work on Creole kinship has not been done except for historical genealogical studies. In a society where much is made of perceived race and free ancestors, Creole concern often focuses on powerful forebears who were free in the antebellum era. In some cases, well-known female ancestors receive special attention. Women in *placage* relationships to White planters and mercantilists were often granted freedom and, as such, became symbols of family settlement and economic power for succeeding generations. Connection to European ancestry is also often stressed, though since the civil rights era and in a time of heightened ethnic awareness, pride in African ancestry has increased.

Kinship Terminology.   Most Creole kinship terms are from the French, as in *mere, pere, frere, belle soeur, beau-pere,* and so on. Special focus is placed upon *marraine* and *parrain* (godmother/godfather) relationships characteristic of Mediterranean societies. Avuncular figures called *nonc*, often fictive uncles, are common in rural communities as sources of respected male wisdom and support. Nicknaming is common, with attributes from childhood or physical appearance as a focus, such as *'Tite Boy, Noir, 'Tite Poop.* Some families appear to have African-rooted nicknames such as *Nene, Soso,* or *Guinee.*

Marriage and Family

Marriage within the Catholic church usually takes place during the partners' teens and early twenties. Among upper-caste Creole families, a marriage into a similar status family or with a White may be regarded as successful. As social boundaries with African-Americans are increasingly blurred, marriage outside the Creole community in this direction can serve as an affirmation of connection to the Black American mainstream. Because Louisiana civil law derives in part from the Napoleonic Code, common-law marriage based on a period of cohabitation is generally accorded legal status. There is a tendency to stay within or near Creole settlements and neighborhoods. In rural areas, families may divide land to assist a new couple. Childbearing is encouraged and families with an agrarian base are large by American standards. Extended families in close proximity allow for mutual child rearing with assistance from older girls. Widowed elders often reside with children and grandchildren. Within the domestic sphere, much respect is accorded women and elders who emphasize values of self-improvement through church attendance, education, and hard work. Young men may challenge these values of respectability by associating outside family settings with people in bars and dance halls, and in work situations with other men. Creole men in groups may assert their reputation as great lovers, sportsmen, cooks, dancers, talkers, and workers, but over time they are expected to settle into a respectable home life. Much is made of the distinction between individuals who choose the street and club life over home and church life.

Sociopolitical Organization

Louisiana is distinguished from the rest of the Anglo-Protestant South and the United States by its French/Spanish Catholic heritage. Thus, parishes rather than counties exist, with police juries as consular boards. Parish sheriffs and large landowners wield much political power. Creoles generally are not at the top of regional power structures, though they do serve on police juries and school boards and as mayors and in the Louisiana state house. In New Orleans, two Creole mayors have served in the last decade. Creole landowners, independent grocers, dance hall operators, priests, and educators are power figures in rural Creole communities. Such respected men are usually public articulators of social control, upward mobility, Creole cultural equity, and relations to government entities. In addition, social advancement and community support and expressive recreation is organized through associations such as Mardi Gras crews, Knights of Peter Klaver (Black Catholic men's society), burial societies, and, particularly in New Orleans, social aide and pleasure clubs. Recently, official ethnic organizations and events have emerged, such as Creole Inc. and the Louisiana Zydeco Festival.

Religion and Expressive Culture

It is especially in the realms of ritual, festival, food, and music as expressive cultural forms that Creole identity within the region is asserted and through which the culture as a whole is recognized, though often misrepresented, nationally and internationally.

Religious Beliefs. Creoles are, like most southern Louisianians, predominantly Catholic. Southern Louisiana has the largest per capita Black Catholic population in the country. Historically, the Creole churches and parishes, especially those in rural areas and some poorer urban neighborhoods, have been viewed by the church as missionary districts. In addition to various Irish and French-Canadian clergy who have worked in Louisiana, the Baltimore-based Josephite Fathers have long operated in the Black Creole communities. Beyond the official dogma and structures of the Catholic church, a wide range of folk religious practices has flourished, drawing upon African influences, medieval Catholicism, African-American belief and ritual systems, and Native American medicinal and belief systems. Home altars with saints, statues, and holy water are widely used. Houses are trimmed with blessed palms or magnolias in the form of crosses over the doors. Creole Louisiana is probably best known for its association with voodoo (_voudun_ in Haiti) as an Afro-Catholic set of religious practices. Unlike Haiti, Louisiana Black Catholics have remained more connected to official church practices; thus African retentions are less marked. Still, within the context of the United States, southern Louisiana Catholicism is unique. The practices of healers, spiritualists, and voodoo specialists who utilize an eclectic mix of prayers, candles, special saints, and charms for good or ill is carried on in settings that range from grossly commercial to private within neighborhoods and communities. Probably the strongest carrier of African-based religious tradition in both Creole and non-Creole Black communities in New Orleans are the spiritual churches. These locally based institutions emphasize spirit possession and ecstatic behavior as part of their service, and unlike such churches elsewhere, they utilize a wide range of Catholic saints and syncretic altars for power figures like Martin Luther King, Jr., St. Michael the Archangel, and Chief Blackhawk. In rural areas, the new charismatic Catholicism has also been influential.

Religious Practitioners. Traditional healers in rural Black Creole and Cajun communities are called _traiteurs_.

Ceremonies. Although linked to Catholicism, Mardi Gras has pre-Christian roots which in turn combined with African and a variety of New World traditions to become the major celebratory occasion of the year. In New Orleans, the festival draws large numbers of tourists and has a public focus on elite parades. Blacks and Black Creoles participate in two significant forms of public carnival celebration. One is the Zulu parade, which involves middle- and upper-middle-class participants parodying the White carnival and stereotypes of Blacks by painting their own faces black, wearing wooly wigs and grass skirts, and carrying spears while throwing coconuts to the crowds. The other major group includes dozens of bands of working-class men dressed in fanciful versions of Plains Indians costumes of beads, feathers, and ribbons. The Mardi Gras Indians associate under names like Creole Wild West, White Eagles, or Yellow Pocahontas. These hierarchical groups use esoteric language, call/response singing, and complex drumming to express personal worth through performance and pride among associations of men who are often otherwise excluded from mainstream social acceptance. Rural Creole Mardi Gras influenced by Cajun culture involves more of a French mumming tradition of going from house to house with men dressed as women, devils, Whites, and strangers to the community. Taking the role of beggar-clowns, the men ask for *charité* in the form of a live chicken, which they must catch and kill. Those householders giving charité then are invited to a communal supper. Mardi Gras is not exclusive to Black Creoles, but in both urban and rural instances they are occasions utilized to express Creole style and social boundaries through traditional public performances.

Arts.   Creole music is often associated with carnival occasions. In New Orleans, jazz has long been created and played by Creoles from Sidney Bechet to Jelly Roll Morton and the Marsalis family. Jazz conjoins European melodies and performance occasions (cotillion, ball, military parade) with African sensibilities of rhythm, ritual/festival performance (originally slave gatherings in public squares), and style. In its mingling of styles to create a new music, jazz is analogous to Black Creole history and culture and is truly a Creole music that has transformed America and the world. Zydeco is the music of Black Creoles in southwestern Louisiana. It is a synthesis of Cajun tunes, African-American blues, and Caribbean rhythms. The word *zydeco* (*les haricots*) literally translates from Creole as "snapbeans." The word may have African root forms, but in Louisiana folk etymology it is attributed to the proverbial phrase *les haricots sont pas salés* ("no salt in the beans") referring to hard times when no salt meat was available. Performed on accordion and violin with Creole vocals and a rhythm section augmented by a hand-scraped *frottoir* (rubbing board), zydeco music brings together the full range of the Creole community for weekly dances at bars and church halls, the only exception being the Lenten season. All these Creole expressive cultural forms of festival and music (to which could be added Creole cuisine) have come to mark this African-Mediterranean cultural group as unique within America but related to other Creole societies in the Caribbean, South America, and West Africa. Creoles and creolization of cultural elements set much of the regional tone for southern Louisiana. Their expressive culture has been national and worldwide in impact.

Death and Afterlife.   Death and burial practices that stand out are the jazz funerals of New Orleans—generally linked to West African traditions of celebrating the passage of an acclaimed elder. Such funeral processions involve jazz bands playing dirges as they follow the body to the cemetery and then breaking into upbeat parade tunes after burial as they return home. In rural and urban Creole Louisiana cemeteries, the dead are remembered particularly on *Toussaint*, or All-Saints' Day (November 1 on the liturgical calendar). Families clean, paint, and decorate the vaulted white, above-ground tombs that characterize the region. In some areas candlelit ceremonies are held.

Bibliography

Domínguez, Virginia R. (1986). *White by Definition: Social Classification in Creole Louisiana*. New Brunswick: Rutgers University Press.

Fiehrer, Thomas Marc (1979). "The African Presence in Colonial Louisiana." In *Louisiana's Black Heritage*, edited by

Robert R. McDonald, John R. Kemp, and Edward E. Haas, 3–31. New Orleans: Louisiana State Museum.

Jacobs, Claude F. (198). "Spirit Guides and Possession in the New Orleans Black Spiritual Churches." *Journal of American Folklore*, 102(403):45–67.

Neumann, Ingrid (1985). *Le Creole de Breaux Bridge, Louisiane*. Hamburg: Helmut Buske Verlag.

Spitzer, Nicholas R. (1984). *Zydeco: Creole Music and Culture in Rural Louisiana*. Color film; 56 minutes. Distributed by Flower Films, El Cerrito, Calif.

Spitzer, Nicholas R. (1986). "Zydeco and Mardi Gras: Creole Performance Genres and Identity in Rural French Louisiana." Ph.D. diss., University of Texas at Austin.

Sterkx, Herbert E. (1972). *The Free Negro in Ante-Bellum Louisiana*. Rutherford, N.J.: Fairleigh Dickinson University Press.

NICHOLAS R. SPITZER

Blackfoot

ETHNONYMS: Blood, Kainah, Northern Blackfoot, Peigan, Piegan, Pikuni, Siksika

Orientation

Identification.   The Blackfoot of the United States and Canada consisted aboriginally of three geographical-linguistic groups: the Siksika (Northern Blackfoot), the Kainah (Blood), and the Pikuni or Piegan. The three groups as a whole are also referred to as the "Siksika" (Blackfoot), a term that probably derived from their practice of coloring their moccasins with ashes. The term *Kainah* means "many chiefs" and *Piegan* refers to "people who had torn robes." Although the three groups are sometimes called a confederacy, there was no overarching political structure and the relations among the groups do not warrant such a label. Actually, the three groups had an ambiguous sense of unity, and they gathered together primarily for ceremonial purposes.

Location.   Before the Blackfoot were placed on reservations and reserves in the latter half of the nineteenth century, they occupied a large territory that stretched from the North Saskatchewan River in Canada to the Missouri River in Montana, and from longitude 105° W to the base of the Rocky Mountains. The Plains Cree were located to the north, the Assiniboin to the east, and the Crow to the south of the Blackfoot. The Piegan were located toward the western part of this territory, in the mountainous country. The Blood were located to the northeast of the Piegan, and the Northern Blackfoot were northeast of the Blood. The Blackfoot now live mainly on or near three reserves: the Blackfoot Agency (Northern Blackfoot), the Blood Agency, and the Peigan Agency (Northern Peigan) in Alberta, Canada, and the Blackfeet Indian Reservation in Montana, inhabited by the Southern Piegan.

Demography. In 1790 there were approximately 9,000 Blackfoot. In 1832 Catlin estimated that the Blackfoot numbered 16,500, and in 1833 Prince Maximilian estimated that there were 18,000 to 20,000. During the nineteenth century, starvation and repeated epidemics of smallpox and measles so decimated the population that by 1909 the Blackfoot numbered only 4,635. Evidence indicates that the Piegan were always the largest of the three groups. In 1980 in Montana, the Blackfoot population was about 15,000 with 5,525 on the Blackfeet Reservation and the remainder living off the reservation. In Canada they numbered about 10,000.

Linguistic Affiliation. Blackfoot is an Algonkian language and is on a coordinate level with Arapaho and Cheyenne. Dialects of Blackfoot are Siksika, Blood, and Piegan.

History and Cultural Relations

Horses, guns, and metal as well as smallpox were probably present among the Blackfoot early in the eighteenth century, although they did not see a White person until the latter part of that century. The introduction of horses and guns produced a period of cultural efflorescence. They were one of the most aggressive groups on the North American plains by the mid-nineteenth century. Allied with the Sarsi and the Gros Ventre, the Blackfoot counted the Cree, Crow, and Assinboin as enemies. Warfare between the groups often centered on raiding for horses and revenge. The U. S. government defined Blackfoot territory and promised provisions and instructions in the Judith Treaty of 1855. The westward movement of White settlers in the following decade led to conflicts with the Blackfoot. By 1870 the Blackfoot had been conquered and their population weakened by smallpox. The bison had become virtually extinct by the winter of 1883–1884, and by 1885 the Southern Piegan had settled on the Blackfeet Reservation. The Canadian government signed a treaty with the Blackfoot in 1877. The three reserves were established some time later, and they are under jurisdiction of the Canadian Indian Department.

Settlements

The conical bison-hide tipi supported by poles was the traditional dwelling. During the summer, the Blackfoot lived in large tribal camps. It was during this season that they hunted bison and engaged in ceremonial activities such as the Sun Dance. During the winter they separated into bands of some ten to twenty households. Band membership was quite fluid. There might be several headmen in each band, one of whom was considered the chief. Headmanship was very informal, with the qualifications for office being wealth, success in war, and ceremonial experience. Authority within the band was similar to the relationship between a landlord and a tenant. As long as the headman continued to provide benefits, people remained with him. But if his generosity slackened, people would simply pack up and leave. When bands congregated during the summer, they formed distinct camps, which were separated from other band camps by a stream or some other natural boundary when available. When the Piegan, Blood, and Northern Blackfoot joined together for ceremonial purposes, each one of the three groups camped in a circle.

Economy

Subsistence and Commercial Activities. The Blackfoot were the typical, perhaps even the classic example of the Plains Indians in many respects. They were nomadic hunter-gatherers who lived in tipis. The bison was the mainstay of their economy, if not the focus of their entire culture. They hunted other large mammals and gathered vegetable foods. Traditions indicate that the bison were hunted in drives, although hunting practices changed when horses and guns were introduced. Deer and smaller game were caught with snares. Fish, although abundant, were eaten only in times of dire necessity and after the disappearance of the bison. Today, the economy at Blackfeet Reservation, Montana, is based on ranching, farming, wage labor, welfare, and leased land income. There is potential for oil and natural gas production and for lumbering. Poverty is a major problem, with the more acculturated doing better economically than the less acculturated as a general rule. Describing the Blackfeet during the 1960s, Robbins refers to them as an "underclass" and their economic position as "neo-colonial." On the Canadian reserves the current economic situation is similar to that in the United States, with the Blackfoot now marginally integrated into the White economy.

Industrial Arts. In traditional times, the bison was the primary food source as well as the source of raw material for many material goods including clothing, tipi covers, cups, bowls, tools, and ornaments. After trade was established with Whites, metal tools and cloth rapidly replaced the traditional manufactures.

Trade. Trade within the group or among the three Blackfoot groups was more common than trade with other groups. Horses, slaves, food, tipis, mules, and ornaments were common trade items. Trade with Whites involved the Blackfoot trading bison hides and furs for whiskey, guns, clothes, food, and metal tools.

Division of Labor. There was a rigid division of labor on the basis of sex. Men hunted, made war, butchered animals, made weapons, made some of their own clothing, and painted designs on the tipis and shields. Women did most of the rest, including moving camp, bringing wood and water, preparing and storing food, cooking meals, making clothing, and producing most implements and containers.

Land Tenure. Traditionally, there were no formal rules relevant to access or use of lands. Under the reservation system, about 15 percent of the reservation land is owned by the tribe, with the remainder allotted to individuals. In some cases, the inheritance by numerous heirs of what were once large parcels of land has resulted in ownership of small pieces of land of no economic value.

Kinship

Kin Groups and Descent. The aboriginal kinship and social systems have been characterized as reflecting "anarchistic individualism." The kinship system was multilineal and multilocal, with a very slight tendency toward patrilineality. The basic social unit was the "orientation group," which consisted of the household of one's parents and one's own household.

Kinship Terminology.   Kin terms were of the Hawaiian type.

Marriage and Family

Marriage and Domestic Unit.   Marriage brought increased status to both the husband and the wife. Although most marriages were monogamous, polygyny was practiced and was preferred, especially among wealthier men. Marital and kinship relationships in general were governed by rigid rules of etiquette and behavior including mother-in-law avoidance, age-grading, and the use of formal speech with older kin. Husbands were exceedingly sexually jealous, and a wife suspected of adultery might be beaten, mutilated, or even killed. Today, family relationships and structures remain amorphous, unstable, and fluid. At Blackfeet Reservation, the formation of large households made up of related families and the tendency for the families to live near each other is associated with the scarcity of economic resources. These groups of relatives form cooperative economic units. A similar situation obtains at the Northern Blackfoot Reserve, with independent households occurring only under conditions of financial security.

Inheritance.   Traditionally, men would leave their property to kin through a verbal will. Horses were the most valuable property and were most often left to the man's oldest brother. In the past, women inherited little, although today they more often receive an equitable share.

Socialization.   Children were and are viewed as individuals worthy of respect. They are expected to be quiet and deferential with adults but assertive with peers. Admonishing, teasing, ridiculing, and scaring are preferred to corporal punishment which is considered abusive. Girls are taught by women and boys by men, generally learning the appropriate sex-typed behavior and skills first by imitation, then by helping, and finally by instruction. The extended family plays a central role in child rearing and care; it is not uncommon for children to live with their grandmother or grandparents. Adoption or the "bringing up" of children raised by relatives is also fairly common.

Sociopolitical Organization

Social Organization.   Like other Plains Indian cultures, the Blackfoot aboriginally had age-graded men's societies. Prince Maximilian counted seven of these societies in 1833. The first one in the series was the Mosquito society, and the last, the Bull society. Membership was purchased. Each society had its own distinctive songs, dances, and regalia, and their responsibilities included keeping order in the camp. There was one women's society.

Political Organization.   For each of the three geographical-linguistic groups, the Blood, the Piegan, and the Northern Blackfoot, there was a head chief. His office was slightly more formalized than that of the band headman. The primary function of the chief was to call councils to discuss affairs of interest to the group as a whole. The Blackfeet Reservation is a business corporation and a political entity. The constitution and corporate charter were approved in 1935. All members of the tribe are shareholders in the corporation. The tribe and the corporation are directed by a nine-member tribal council.

Social Control and Conflict.   Intragroup conflict was a matter for individuals, families, or bands. The only formal mechanism of social control was the police activities of the men's societies in the summer camp. Informal mechanisms included gossip, ridicule, and shaming. In addition, generosity was routinely encouraged and praised.

Religion and Expressive Culture

Religious Beliefs.   Aboriginally, the religious life of the Blackfoot centered upon medicine bundles, and there were more than fifty of them among the three main Blackfoot groups. The most important bundles to the group as a whole were the beaver bundles, the medicine pipe bundles, and the Sun Dance bundle. Christianity is practiced now by most Southern Piegan with Roman Catholicism predominating. The Blackfoot apparently never adopted the Ghost Dance, nor is the Peyote Cult present. The Sun Dance and other native religious ceremonies are still practiced among most of the Blackfoot groups.

Ceremonies.   By the middle of the nineteenth century, the Sun Dance had become an important ceremony. It was performed once each year during the summer. The Sun Dance among the Blackfoot was similar to the ceremony that was performed in other Plains cultures, though there were some differences: a woman played the leading role among the Blackfoot, and the symbolism and paraphernalia used were derived from beaver bundle ceremonialism. The Blackfoot Sun Dance included the following: (1) moving the camp on four successive days; (2) on the fifth day, building the medicine lodge, transferring bundles to the medicine woman, and offering of gifts by children and adults in ill health; (3) on the sixth day, dancing toward the sun, blowing eagle-bone whistles, and self-torture; and (4) on the remaining four days, performing various ceremonies of the men's societies.

Arts.   Singing groups were an important form of social intercourse. Porcupine quillwork was considered a sacred craft and some men were highly skilled painters of buffalo-skin shields and tipi covers. Today, achievement in traditional arts and crafts is valued as a sign of Indian identity. Consequently, there are skilled Blackfoot dancers, artists, carvers, leather- and beadworkers, orators, and singers whose work is known both within and beyond Blackfoot society.

Medicine.   Illness was attributed to an evil spirit entering the body. Treatment by the shaman was directed at removing the spirit through singing, drumming, and the like. Some practitioners specialized in treating certain illnesses, setting broken bones, and so on.

Death and Afterlife.   The dead were placed on a platform in a tree or the tipi, or on the floor of the tipi. Some property was left with the body for use in the next life. The Blackfoot feared the ghosts of the dead, and if a person died in a tipi, that tipi was never used again.

Bibliography

Hanks, Lucien M., and Jane R. Hanks (1950). *Tribe under Trust: A Study of the Blackfoot Reserve of Alberta.* Toronto: University of Toronto Press.

Hungry Wolf, Adolf (1977). *The Blood People, a Division of the Blackfoot Confederacy: An Illustrated Interpretation of the Old Ways.* New York: Harper & Row.

Hungry Wolf, Beverly (1980). *The Ways of My Grandmothers.* New York: William Morrow.

McFee, Malcolm (1972). *Modern Blackfoot: Montanans on a Reservation.* New York: Holt, Rinehart & Winston.

Robbins, Lynn A. (1972). *Blackfoot Families and Households.* Ann Arbor, Mich.: University Microfilms. Ph.D. diss., University of Oregon, 1971.

Wissler, Clark (1910). *Material Culture of the Blackfoot Indians.* New York: American Museum of Natural History.

Blacks in Canada

ETHNONYMS: African-Canadians, Blacks, People of Color

Orientation

Identification. The Black population in Canada today is derived from several migratory streams. The largest group, numbering approximately 195,000, are relatively recent migrants from the Caribbean. Blacks have, however, been in Canada since the early eighteenth century. The major division in the population is that between the descendants of earlier Black settlers and those of more recent Caribbean origin. The major home countries have been Jamaica, Guyana, Haiti, and Trinidad and Tobago. Divisions based on country of origin affect the first-generation migrant community, but these become increasingly less important to the new generation of Canadian-born.

Location. Black migrants from the Caribbean live primarily in Toronto, Montreal, and Vancouver. Smaller numbers now live in other urban centers. Descendants of the earlier settlers live mostly in the province of Nova Scotia in its capital city of Halifax (and Bedford) and in smaller rural communities spread throughout the province. In the mid-eighteenth century, a small group of Blacks from the United States settled in Amber Valley, Alberta, where a few of their descendants still live, and a similar group found its way to Vancouver Island.

Demography. The Black population of Canada is, according to the 1986 census, 239,000, of whom 193,440 are of Caribbean origin. These census figures, however, are not regarded as accurate because they do not differentiate between racial status and place of origin. In addition, persons of mixed race status may be counted in several categories and Black persons migrating from Great Britain (or other countries) are designated as British. The best estimates suggest that approximately 300,000 Blacks live in Canada today, and the vast majority are of recent Caribbean origin. There are approximately 123,000 Black (and Caribbean) people in Toronto, nearly 50,000 in Montreal, and about 15,000 in Halifax.

Linguistic Affiliation. The Black population in Canada is English-speaking, with the exception of migrants from Haiti who have settled in Quebec, primarily in the city of Montreal. They speak French and Creole as spoken in Haiti.

History and Cultural Relations

Slavery was legal in New France between 1689 and 1709, and it was also permitted in Upper Canada. In 1793, an attempt was made in Upper Canada to abolish slavery; though this failed, Blacks were nevertheless protected by the same laws as Whites. Slavery was abolished throughout the British Empire in 1833. It did not become an important institution in early Canadian history because conditions of climate and geography prevented the development of a plantation system of agriculture. Although small numbers of Blacks have lived in Canada since 1628, the first major group was composed of slaves brought to Nova Scotia by residents of New England after the expulsion of the Acadians. Moreover, as a result of the American Revolution in 1776, White loyalists escaping from the colonies also brought their slaves with them to Nova Scotia. The next group of migrants was that of refugee Blacks fleeing from the War of 1812, who settled in Nova Scotia and Ontario. The passage of the Fugitive Slave Act in the United States in 1850 brought another group of refugee slaves, who used the Underground Railroad to reach southern Ontario. By 1860, there were approximately seventy-five thousand Blacks in the province of Ontario, but most of them returned to the United States after the Civil War.

The last and most substantial group of Blacks to come to Canada were from the Caribbean. This migration began in the early 1960s and reached its peak during the 1970s. At this time, approximately ten thousand migrants from the Caribbean come to Canada each year. The largest numbers come from the Commonwealth Caribbean and are English-speaking, but smaller numbers have migrated from French-speaking Haiti.

Economy

Blacks are essentially integrated into the larger economy. In earlier periods of history, employment ghettoization marginalized the majority of Blacks into the service sector and on the railways. In more recent times, middle-class Blacks occupy professional and managerial positions in medicine, nursing, accountancy, and the like. Those with less education, and more recently arrived Caribbean migrants, are still clustered into the service and unskilled-labor sectors.

Kinship, Marriage and Family

Traditional patterns of family organization have, to a certain extent, been retained by the first generation of Caribbean migrants. Single-mother-headed households are still fairly common, especially among the working class. In the middle-class migrant population, legal marriage and nuclear families predominate. In all Caribbean migrant groups, regardless of class status, a significant incidence of marriage or relationship failure is apparent; this is probably related to the stress of migrating to a predominantly White host society. The marriage and family organization of descendants of the earlier Black settlers is, in most respects, similar to that of the mainstream society.

Sociopolitical Organization

Although racial discrimination in Canada was not as institutionalized as in the United States, racism has played a major role in constraining the lives and experiences of Black Canadians. Even in earlier times, Blacks were victims of racial discrimination. Free Black settlers in Nova Scotia were given the most rocky and infertile land and, as a result, were barely able to maintain themselves. Blacks in Nova Scotia soon became wards of the government and have lived in a condition of dependency through most of their history. Today, the result of generations of neglect and poverty can be seen in the lack of development in the Black communities of that province. In Nova Scotia and Ontario, school segregation was practiced and Black children were denied equal access to educational facilities. The last segregated, all-Black school in Ontario finally closed its doors in 1965. Although most provinces have enacted human rights and antidiscrimination legislation, and the federal government of Canada has legislated a Charter of Rights and Freedoms as well as Multicultural and Employment Equity legislation, patterns of racism can still be detected in Canadian society. Overt racism in the form of incidents such as personal assaults, police harassment, name-calling, and racial slurs are evident in the large cities of the country where Blacks have tended to settle. There is also considerable evidence for systemic employment and housing discrimination. The Black population is part of the larger sociopolitical structure of Canadian society. In former times, the small Black communities were not particularly active in political arenas. More recently, however, a greater sense of political awareness is developing, as Blacks form substantial residential communities in the larger cities. More Black candidates are standing for political office, although with relatively little success so far. At the moment, the province of Ontario has a Black lieutenant governor who acts as the representative of the queen.

Religion and Expressive Culture

The descendants of earlier Black settlers for the most part belong to Protestant denominational churches as well as fundamentalist, independent churches derived from Protestantism. Many of the more recently arrived migrants from the Caribbean practice Roman Catholicism. Membership in fundamentalist Protestant churches is, however, on the increase among this group. In addition, some Haitian migrants in Montreal have retained aspects of the traditional Haitian vodun religion. Jamaican-derived Rastafarianism is practiced, especially in the larger cities such as Toronto and Montreal. The majority of Rastafarians are relatively young. Because Rastafarianism is associated with reggae music, it is especially appealing to the youth. Symbols associated with Rastafarianism, such as traditional colors, dreadlocks hairstyles, and other emblems, are particularly attractive to Black youth searching for the African roots of their ethnic identities.

Bibliography

Christiansen, J. M., et al. (1980). *West Indians in Toronto*. Toronto: Family Service Association of Metropolitan Toronto.

Clairmont, D. H., and D. W. Magill (1974). *Africville: Life and Death of a Canadian Black Community*. Toronto: McClelland & Stewart.

Henry, Frances (1973). *The Forgotten Canadians: The Blacks of Nova Scotia*. Don Mills, Ontario: Longman Canada.

Walker, James W. St. G. (1976). *The Black Loyalists: The Search for a Promised Land in Nova Scotia and Sierra Leone, 1783–1870*. New York: Africana.

Winks, Robin W. (1971). The Blacks in Canada: A History. New Haven, Conn., Yale University Press; McGill-Queen's University Press.

FRANCES HENRY

Black West Indians in the United States

ETHNONYMS: Jamaicans, Trinidadians, Bahamians, Guyanese, West Indians

Orientation

Identification.   Blacks in the United States of West Indian ancestry come mainly either from the British West Indies (Bahamas, Barbados, Bermuda, British Virgin Islands, Jamaica, the Leeward Islands, Trinidad and Tobago, and the Windward Islands) or from Haiti, in the French West Indies. Blacks from Guyana, on the northeast coast of South America, are also classified as British West Indians. The majority of those from the British West Indies are from Jamaica. The history of Black West Indians and Haitians and their experiences in the United States differ from each other and also from that of African-Americans descended from slaves brought directly to North America from Africa. Blacks in the West Indies are descendants of African slaves brought to the Caribbean to work on sugar plantations in the eighteenth and early nineteenth centuries. Blacks make up 80 percent of the population of the British West Indies and 90 percent of the population of Haiti. Other major ethnic groups on the British islands are the English, Chinese, Asian Indians, and Syrians. Contact between the Black slaves and English rulers has produced unique cultural and linguistic forms in the

Black Caribbean cultures as well as people of mixed White and Black ancestry, leading to the use of the term _mulatto_ to identity segments of the population.

Location.　British West Indian Blacks in the United States live primarily in cities on the east coast, from New York south to the southern Florida coast, with concentrations in New York City, southeastern Florida, and Hartford, Connecticut. There is also a growing Jamaican community in Los Angeles. About 50 percent of Jamaicans live in New York City.

Demography.　According to the 1980 census, there were 223,652 Americans of Jamaican ancestry, 66,062 of Trinidadian, Tobagonian and Guyanese ancestry, and 39,513 of other British West Indian ancestry. In addition, there were 48,592 Americans of Black British West Indian and other ethnic ancestry. All these figures are undercounts, as a large though undetermined number of Black West Indians are undocumented immigrants.

Linguistic Affiliation.　The West Indies are officially English-speaking, but actually display a post-Creole linguistic continuum. On the islands, indigenous Creole languages developed through contact between the English plantation owners and Black slaves, with elements from Asian languages added later in some places. Speech varies according to social class and social context from Creole to Standard English. Black West Indians generally speak English with a British accent.

History and Cultural Relations

Although some came earlier, most Black West Indians immigrated to the United States after 1900 and especially after World War I. They looked to emigrate because of limited economic opportunities at home and chose the United States because of its proximity, the promise of economic opportunity, and U.S. immigration quotas that favored British subjects. The majority of the nearly 100,000 who came in the first thirty years of the twentieth century were literate in English, young, single, and able to find work in skilled occupations, though racial discrimination often forced them to take jobs beneath their qualifications. Some dealt with this problem by pooling financial resources to start small businesses and stores, many of which prospered in northern cities. Immigration decreased during the Great Depression and World War II, but increased from 1948 to 1954, decreased again under restrictive legislation, and then increased again after 1965 when quotas were abolished.

Immigrants since 1965 have again been mostly young and single, but in general are less skilled and educated than those who came before them. There has also been a trend toward less concentrated settlement, though West Indians remain mainly in the Northeast and Florida. Relations between African-Americans and Black West Indians before the increased migration beginning in the 1960s were generally hostile. At the same time, however, West Indians were active in politics and many African-American leaders such as Malcolm X, Roy Innis, James Farmer, Shirley Chisholm, and Stokely Carmichael were of West Indian ancestry. In recent years, though tensions still exist, there has been a merging of African-American and Black West Indian interests, and cooperation as well as conflict is now evident.

Settlements

In the post–World War II years, Black West Indians in U.S. cities often lived near one another in African-American neighborhoods. There was, for example, a large Black West Indian community in Harlem. In southern farming regions, Blacks were segregated from the White population. On sugar cane plantations where Black West Indian men work as contract laborers, they live in dormitories on the farm. In recent years, as the demographic composition of the Black West Indian immigrant population has changed, they have become more widely dispersed among the African-American population, though distinct West Indian communities still exist and new immigrants often settle in those communities. In Washington, D.C., for example, a West Indian community has formed around Georgia Avenue in the northwest quarter of the city. These communities often contain, in addition to the West Indian population, West Indian restaurants, food stores, clothing stores, record stores, and bakeries.

Economy

Included in the Black West Indian population who settled in the United States before World War II were a large number of highly educated or skilled individuals. Because of racial discrimination, however, many were unable to secure professional or skilled employment and took lower-level work as cooks, domestics, and so on until opportunities became available. Some eventually found employment as doctors, dentists, lawyers, accountants, and teachers, with most of their clientele coming from the African-American and Black West Indian communities. Others began small businesses, usually retail stores or rental real estate properties, financed through partnerships or often through rotating credit associations that provided members with access to capital. Black West Indian business ownership continues today, with estimates in the 1970s indicating that 50 percent of Black-owned businesses in New York were owned by Black West Indians.

In the 1960s, the trend of well-educated Black West Indians immigrating to the United States continued. Many now found it easier to use their professional skills immediately, although the African-American and Black West Indian communities continued to provide most clients. A sizable percentage of the 1960s immigrants were female nurses. By that decade, the composition of the immigrant population had begun to change, and it now contains a larger percentage of younger, less-skilled people. Many are women, a large number of whom immigrate to work as domestics or providers of child care. This growing population of young, unskilled Black West Indians has led to tensions with the African-American and Latino communities as they are seen as competing for service jobs with men and women in the latter two groups.

The Black West Indian population in the United States also includes a group of about eight thousand to ten thousand men who are imported each year from Jamaica, Barbados, St. Lucia, St. Vincent, and Dominica to cut sugar cane in southern Florida. They enter the country under five- or six-month temporary work visas and are paid on the basis of a minimum wage and piece-work system. At least 25 percent of their income is remitted to the local communities from which they were recruited.

Kinship, Marriage and Family

The organization of Black West Indian kinship and marriage in the United States is a function of length of residence in the country (pre– versus post–World War II) and the social status of the family (working class versus middle or upper class). Because most Black West Indians come from islands that were once colonies of England, middle- and upper-class people usually follow mainstream European practices including bilateral descent, monogamous marriage, small nuclear families, and Eskimo kin terms. For the pre–World War II population, the family was the most important social institution, and cooperation and loyalty among family members were expected with the husband/father the head of the family. The family remains a vital institution in the West Indian community, although the husband/father leadership role has weakened and mother-child households are now more common, with the arrival of many younger female immigrants since the late 1960s. Since that time, perhaps the most common form of immigration entailed a young woman arriving first and then later bringing her children and sometimes her husband.

American marriages among Black West Indians are highly endogamous with a marked preference for a marriage partner from the same island as oneself. Marriage to African-Americans usually involves a West Indian man and an African-American woman.

Sociopolitical Organization

Social Organization.   The West Indians' place in American society and their status vis-à-vis African-Americans is a complex topic. West Indians came from societies in which they were the racial majority, in which a British-imposed social class system was a feature of everyday life, and in which they had greater educational, economic, and political opportunities than did African-Americans in the United States. In the United States they found and continue to find a much different situation. They are classified by Whites as Black and are subject to the same racial discrimination, though both Black West Indians and African-Americans believe that Whites treat the former somewhat differently than they do the latter. But though they are treated as if the same as African-Americans, Black West Indians distinguish themselves from African-Americans, and though they often live in the same areas, there are noticeable differences in speech, dress, cuisine, religious beliefs, and life-style.

West Indian ethnic identity is tied to the island from which one emigrated rather than to a general pan–West Indian identity and is reflected in marriage mainly to people from the same island and the various island ethnic associations formed in the 1920s and 1930s.

Political Organization.   Black West Indians who came to the United States in the early 1900s brought with them a tradition of political activism and some experience as officials in the British colonial governments. In the United States political activism for racial equality flourished in the Black West Indian community. Marcus Garvey, an immigrant from Jamaica who was eventually sent back there, and his Universal Negro Improvement Association is the best-known but not the only Black West Indian political movement in the United States. As noted above, many leaders of the civil rights movement were or are of West Indian ethnic ancestry. Today, because they are lumped by Whites with African-Americans and because they also often live in the same communities, West Indian political interests are often merged with those of African-Americans.

Religion and Expressive Culture

Many of those who settled in the United States in the early twentieth century were Anglicans who became Episcopalians in America and established their own churches. With the large migration since the 1960s has come a broader range of religious affiliation, and Black West Indians in the United States now include Roman Catholics, Seventh-Day Adventists, Pentecostals, and Rastafarians. In general, West Indians continue to form their own churches rather than affilate with existing ones in either the African-American or the White communities.

The Rastafarian movement, based in Jamaica, has had much influence in the United States, as evidenced by the popularity of reggae music, the dreadlock hairstyle, and clothing featuring African designs and coloring.

See also Black Creoles in Louisiana, Blacks in Canada, Haitians

Bibliography

Bonnett, Aubrey W. (1981). *Institutional Adaptation of West Indian Immigrants to America: An Analysis of Rotating Credit Associations.* Washington, D.C.: University Press of America.

Bryce-Laporte, Roy S., and Delores M. Mortimer (1976). *Caribbean Immigration to the United States.* Washington, D.C.: Research Institute on Immigration and Ethnic Studies, Smithsonian Institution.

Foner, Nancy (1985). "Race and Color: Jamaican Migrants in London and New York City." *International Migration Review* 19:708–727.

Ueda, Reed (1980). "West Indians." In *Harvard Encyclopedia of American Ethnic Groups*, edited by Stephan Thernstrom, 1020–1027. Cambridge: Harvard University Press, Belknap Press.

Wood, Charles H., and Terry L. McCoy (1985). "Migration, Remittances and Development: A Study of Caribbean Cane Cutters in Florida." *International Migration Review* 19:251–277.

Caddo

ETHNONYMS: Ceni, Caddoquis, Teja

"Caddo" is the name used for a number of related and perhaps affiliated groups who lived in the lower Red River Valley and surrounding sections of what are now Louisiana, eastern Texas, and southern Arkansas. The number of Caddo subgroups is unknown and may have ranged from six to more than a dozen, including the Adai, Natchitoches, Kadohadacho, Hasinai, Hainai, and Eyeish. The name "Caddo" is an Anglicization of the French corruption of "Kadohadacho," the name of one of the subgroups. Each subgroup spoke a dialect of the Caddo language; only Kadohadacho and Hasinai are spoken today. The Caddo now live mainly on allotted land in Caddo County, Oklahoma, where they are affiliated with the Wichita and Delaware and are largely assimilated into European-American society. In 1984 there were about three thousand Caddo.

First contact was evidently with Hernando de Soto's expedition of 1540. Subsequent contacts with the Spanish and French were generally peaceful, though the Caddo were drawn into the wars between the French and Spanish and depopulated by disease. Following the Louisiana Purchase, the Caddo ceded their land to the federal government and moved first to Texas and then, in 1859, to their present locale in what is now Oklahoma.

The Caddo lived in settled villages of large earthlodges and grass-covered lodges similar to those of the Wichita. They subsisted through a combination of horticulture, hunting, and gathering. Maize and beans were the major crops and deer and bison the primary game animals. The Caddo were well known for their highly developed manufactures including baskets, mats, cloth, and pottery. Their religion centered on a supreme deity and lesser deities. The ceremonial cycle closely followed the annual subsistence cycle. Leadership rested with hereditary chiefs and subchiefs. The tribe is governed today by elected tribal officers and a council, which operates independently of the similar bodies that govern the Delaware and Wichita.

Bibliography

Gregory, H. F. (1986). _The Southern Caddo: An Anthology._ New York: Garland Publishing.

Pertulla, Timothy K. (1980). "The Caddo Indians of Louisiana: A Review." _Louisiana Archaeology_ 7:116–121.

Cahuilla

ETHNONYMS: Cahahaguillas, Coahuillas, Cowela, Dancers, Jecuches, Kahuilla, Kawia

The Cahuilla are an American Indian group who lived aboriginally and continue to live in south-central California in a region bordered roughly by the San Bernardino Mountains on the north and Borrego Springs and the Chocolate Mountains on the south. Neighboring groups were the Mohave, Tipai-Ipai, Serrano, Gabrielino, Juaneño, and Luiseño. Estimates of the precontact population range from thirty-six hundred to ten thousand. Today, the Cahuilla number about fifteen hundred and live on or, more often, near ten reservations in southern California. The Cahuilla language is classified in the Cupan subgroup of the Takic family of Uto-Aztecan languages. Although it had nearly become extinct, efforts are now underway through language programs for Cahuilla children to maintain its use. Because of their inland location, the Cahuilla were directly influenced by Europeans later than other more western groups. First contact with the Spanish was indirect through other Indian groups where missions were established and probably mostly involved the spread of European diseases to the Cahuilla. Regular contact began in about 1819 and led to the Cahuilla's adopting farming and cattle raising, working for the Spanish, and converting to Roman Catholicism. In 1863 the Cahuilla were seriously depopulated by a smallpox epidemic. The reservation period began in 1877, and since that time and until the last twenty years the Cahuilla have been generally dependent on and under the influence of the federal government. Despite major changes in their economy, religion, and social and political organization, the Cahuilla continue to stress their cultural identity while also identifying with the pan-Indian movement.

Aboriginally, the Cahuilla lived in permanent villages in sheltered valleys near water sources, with seasonal excursions to gather acorns. Because they occupied an ecologically diverse region, major food sources varied from one area to another. The Cahuilla, were, however, basically hunter-gatherers with rabbits, deer, mountain sheep, and small rodents hunted and acorns, cacti roots, mesquite, berries, and numerous other plant foods gathered. Basketry was highly developed, with four types of coiled baskets made and decorated. Today, the Cahuilla are integrated, though somewhat marginally, into the White economy and derive income from wage labor, salaried positions, business ownership, farming, and cattle raising.

Aboriginal social and political organization rested on patrilineages, clans, and moieties. Both the lineages and clans were landowning units. Reciprocity was a central value and permeated all relationships, both between humans and between humans and the supernatural world. The key leadership positions were the lineage leader, his administrative assistant, and the shamans. Tribal affairs are today managed by reservation business councils and administrative committees and through participation in interreservation associations.

The traditional religion emphasized the performance of individual rituals as a means of maintaining balanced relationships between all things and events in the universe. Traditional practices are still used in funeral ceremonies, though most Cahuilla are now Roman Catholics and some are Protestants.

Bibliography

Bean, Lowell J. (1978). "Cahuilla." In *Handbook of North American Indians*. Vol. 8, *California*, edited by Robert F. Heizer, 575–587. Washington, D.C.: Smithsonian Institution.

Bean, Lowell J., and Harry W. Lawton (1965). *The Cahuilla Indians of Southern California*. Banning, Calif.: Malki Museum Press.

Cajuns

ETHNONYMS: Acadians of Louisiana

Orientation

Identification.   The Cajuns are a distinct cultural group of people who have lived mainly in south-central and southwestern Louisiana since the late eighteenth century. In the past, because of their Acadian heritage, residential localization, unique language, and Roman Catholicism, it was relatively easy to distinguish Cajuns from other groups in Lousiana. Today, their identity is less clear. It usually applies to those who are descended from Acadians who migrated in the late 1770s and early 1800s from Canada to what is now Louisiana, and/or live or associate with a Cajun life-style characterized by rural living, family-centered communities, the Cajun French language, and Roman Catholicism. Cajuns in Louisiana today are a distinct cultural group, separate from the Acadians of Nova Scotia. Like the Appalachians and Ozarkers, they are considered by outsiders to be a traditional folk culture with attention given to their arts and crafts, food, music, and dance. The name "Cajuns" is evidently an English mispronunciation of "Acadians." Cajun and Black Creole culture share a number of common elements, some of which are discussed in the entry on Black Creoles of Louisiana.

Location.   In 1971 the Louisiana legislature designated twenty-two parishes as Acadiana: Acadia, Ascension, Assumption, Avoyelles, Calcasieu, Cameron, Evangeline, Iberia, Iberville, Jefferson Davis, Lafayette, Lafourche, Pointe Coupee, St. Charles, St. James, St. John, St. Landry, St. Martin, St. Mary, Terrebonne, Vermilion, and West Baton Rouge. This region includes coastal marshes, swamps, prairies, and levee land. In recent decades, as the region has experienced economic development and population shifts, the boundaries of Acadiana have blurred. And the Cajuns are not the only residents of these parishes, which include non-Cajun Whites of various ethnic backgrounds, African-Americans, Black Creoles, and others.

Demography.   In the 1970s there were about 800,000 Cajuns in Louisiana. After Acadians began arriving in Louisiana, perhaps as early as 1756, the population increased rapidly, from about 6,000 in 1810 to 35,000 in 1815 to 270,000 in 1880.

Linguistic Affiliation.   Language use by Cajuns is a complex topic, with the relationship between the speakers and the social context often determining what language is spoken. Cajun French is the language commonly associated with the Cajun culture, though many Cajuns no longer speak it fluently and its use has declined markedly in the younger generation. Older Cajuns speak Cajun French in the home and with other Cajuns. Cajun French differs from standard French in the use of some archaic forms of pronunciation, the inclusion of various loan words from English, American Indian, Spanish, and African languages, and a simplified grammar. Cajuns usually use English as the contact language and as the domestic language in an increasing number of homes. In some homes and communities, Creole French is spoken as well.

History and Cultural Relations

Cajun culture began with the arrival of French Acadians (the French-speaking people of the territory that is now mainly Nova Scotia in Canada) who migrated to and settled in what is now Louisiana mainly between 1765 and 1785. Some migrated directly from Acadia, whereas others came after stays in France and the West Indies. All came as part of the Acadian Diaspora, which resulted from their forced exile by the British from Acadia in 1755. Because of additional migrants who arrived in the early 1800s and a high birth rate, the Acadians increased in numbers rapidly and were soon the most numerous group in many locales where they settled. Once settled in Lousiana, in environments very different from Acadia and in contact with other cultures including Black Creoles, American Indians, Germans, Spaniards, and Italians, the Acadian culture began to change, eventually becoming what has come to be called Cajun culture. With the exception of those in the levee-land region who lost their land to Anglos, most Cajuns lived in relative isolation in rural communities where they farmed, fished, or raised cattle.

It was not until after World War I that mainstream society entered Acadiana and began to influence Cajun life. Mechanization of farming, fishing, and cattle raising, the building of roads linking southern Louisiana to the rest of the state, mass communication, and compulsory education changed local economic conditions and exposed Cajuns to mainstream Louisiana society. Contact also meant that the use of Cajun French decreased, and in 1921 it was banned from use in public schools.

The end of World War II and the return of Cajun veterans to their homes was the beginning of a new era in Cajun culture, one characterized by continuing involvement in mainstream life and by the birth of Cajun ethnicity, reflected in pride in one's heritage and efforts to preserve some traditional beliefs and practices. In 1968 Lousiana created the Council for the Development of French in Louisiana (CODOFIL) as a mechanism to encourage the teaching of French in public schools. Because of conflicts over which French to teach—standard French or Cajun French—the program has not been a total success, though many Cajun children do participate in French-language programs.

Acadians are one of a number of groups of French ancestry in Louisiana, which also include the French-Canadians, Creoles, and those who emigrated directly from France. Relations between the Cajuns and other groups in Louisiana including Anglos, Creoles, Black Creoles, and others were generally peaceful because the Cajuns were largely self-sufficient, lived in distinctly Cajun regions, were numerically dominant in those regions, and chose to avoid conflict. That they were Roman Catholic while others were mainly Protestant further contributed to group segregation. Within the regional class structure, Cajuns were considered better than Blacks but the lowest group of Whites. In general, they were seen as poor, uneducated, fun-loving backwoods folk. Cajuns generally viewed themselves as superior to the poor rural Whites referred to as Rednecks.

Settlements

Acadian settlements in the past varied in size, style, and structure among the four major environmental zones. Settlements included isolated houses, small farms, towns, ranches, and families living on houseboats. Population relocations, the arrival of non-Cajuns, and changes in economic activities have all produced changes in settlement patterns. In recent years, there has been a marked trend to settlement in towns and cities through migration from the rural areas. The Acadian cottage, a small, nearly square dwelling with a covered front porch and high-pitched roof, was a distinctively Cajun house type in the 1800s. It was raised a few feet above the ground and constructed from cypress wood and infilled with clay and moss. Some later styles of dwellings were elaborations on the basic style, though all have now been replaced by modern-style homes made from mass-produced materials.

Economy

Subsistence and Commercial Activities.   In Canada, the Acadians lived by farming (wheat, oats, rye, vegetables), raising cattle, and fishing, and by selling surplus crops and cattle and buying manufactured products. Louisiana had a markedly different environment, with four environmental regions, none exactly the same as Acadia. These new environments led to the development of new subsistence and commercial pursuits in Louisiana as well as variation in activities from one region to another. In the levee-land region, the early Cajun settlers grew maize and rice for consumption and cotton for sale. They also grew vegetables and raised cattle. Non-Cajuns began settling in the region around 1800, however, and took much of the land for large plantations. Most Cajuns moved elsewhere; those that stayed lived by subsistence farming in the backwaters until well into the twentieth century. In the swampland region, fishing and the hunting and gathering of crawfish, ducks, crabs, turtles, frogs, and moss were the major economic activities. By the late 1800s, most Cajuns in this region were involved in the commercial fishing industry, and many still are today, though they have modernized their equipment and methods and often live outside the swamps. The Cajuns who settled on the Louisiana prairies developed two economic adaptations. Those in the east grew maize and cotton, supplemented by sweet potatoes. Those in the west grew rice and raised cattle, with local variation in terms of which was the more important. In the marshland region, on the Chernier Plain, Cajuns raised cattle, trapped, and gardened; on the Deltaic Plain they farmed, fished, hunted, and trapped.

Regular contact with the outside economy, which influenced all regions by about 1920, has changed the traditional economy. Cattle ranching has declined, and sugar cane, rice, cotton, and maize are now the major crops. As towns have developed and compulsory education laws have been enforced, Cajuns have been employed in service-sector jobs, and many now work in the oil and gas industries that have entered the southern part of the region. With public interest in the Cajuns as a folk culture developing in the 1960s, tourism has also become a source of income.

Industrial Arts.   Aspects of the traditional subsistence technology of the 1800s that draw attention today are mainly adaptations to life in the swamp and marshlands. The traditional technology has been modernized, although traditional knowledge and skills are still valued. Aspects of the traditional technology that are of interest today are the Cajun cottage, the various tools and techniques used in collecting crawfish, crabs, and moss, and the *pirogue* (a narrow canoe made from a dugout log or planks).

Trade.   The intinerant traders (*marchand-charette*) who once supplied most household supplies are a thing of the past. Most Cajun families are now integrated into the mainstream economy and purchase goods and services.

Division of Labor.   The traditional economy centered on cooperation among members of the extended family and kindred. Men generally had responsibility for subsistence activities, and women managed the household. As the Cajuns have been drawn into American society, traditional sex roles have weakened, with women now working outside the home and often taking the lead in "Americanizing" the family.

Land Tenure.   Despite their early settlement in Louisiana, Cajuns own relatively little land. This is the result of a number of factors, including dishonest land agents, Cajun ignorance or misunderstanding of real estate laws, and patrilineal inheritance of property coupled with patrilocal residence which meant that once sizable farms were divided into smaller and smaller units over the generations. Today, lumbering, fossil fuel, and agricultural corporations own much land in the Cajun region, and in some locales, many Cajuns lease the land they farm.

Kinship

The basic social and economic unit in traditional times was the patrilineally extended family, whose members often lived near one another. Nearby residence was encouraged by patrilocal postmarital residence which involved fathers giving newly married sons a piece of the family land. Wider ties were also maintained with the local community, which often involved homesteads located some miles from one another. Preferential community endogamy meant that others in the community often included the wife's kin. People were involved with this kinship network throughout their lives.

Marriage and Family

Marriage and Domestic Unit.   Although community and in-group endogamy was preferred, some women did marry non-Cajun men who were rapidly and easily assimilated into the group. Marriage usually occurred at a young age. Divorce was rare and difficult to justify. Although the nuclear family unit lived in the same dwelling as part of the extended family, the extended family was the basic social and economic unit. Kin worked together, helped build each other's houses, went to the same church, had to approve the marriage of female kin, cared for each other's children, and socialized and celebrated together. Both the country butchery (*la boucherie de campagne*), where kin met every few days to butcher hogs for meat, and the weekly public dance (*fais do-do*) provided opportunities for regular socializing by family members. Men were the major decision makers in their homes, but if a man died, his wife, not his sons, assumed control. Children lived at home until they married.

This traditional pattern of marriage and family began to change after World War I and then changed even more rapidly after World War II. Today, nuclear families have replaced extended ones, with economic ties now far less important than social ones in kinship groups. Husbands no longer dominate families, as women work outside the home and establish lives for themselves independent of their families. The prohibition of the teaching of French in Louisiana schools has created a generation gap in some families with grandparents speaking Cajun French, parents speaking some Cajun French, and the grandchildren speaking only English. Marriage to outsiders has also become more frequent, and is often the reverse of the former pattern, with Cajun men now marrying non-Cajun women who acculturate their husbands into mainstream society.

Socialization.   Traditionally, children were raised by the extended family. Cajuns rejected formal education outside the home except for instruction provided by the church. Parents emphasized the teaching of economic and domestic skills and participation in the activities of the kinship network. In 1916 school attendance up to age fifteen became compulsory, although the law was not rigorously enforced until 1944. Public school education played a major role in weakening the traditional culture, as it resulted in many children never learning or even forgetting Cajun French and provided skills and knowledge useful in mainstream society, thus giving younger Cajuns the opportunity for upward socioeconomic mobility. Today, Cajun children attend both public and parochial schools and tens of thousands participate in French-language programs in elementary schools. The rapid growth of the University of Southwestern Louisiana, McNeese State University, and Nicholls State University is evidence that many Cajuns now attend college as well.

Sociopolitical Organization

Social Organization.   Social cohesiveness in Cajun communities as well as a general sense of being Cajun was maintained through various informal mechanisms that brought Cajuns together both physically and symbolically. The Roman Catholic church was a major unifying force, as it provided the belief system that supported many Cajun practices as well as differentiated Cajuns from their mostly Protestant neighbors. As noted above, the extended family and the somewhat larger kinship network were the basic social groupings in Cajun society. These social units were maintained through daily participation of members and through regularly scheduled get-togethers such as the boucherie and the fais do-do and the cockfights that brought the men together. There was no formal class structure, though a Cajun elite, the "Genteel Acadians" emerged in the early 1800s. They were

mainly a few families who had become wealthy as farmers, merchants, or professionals. They tended to marry non-Cajuns, lived among Anglos and Creoles, and looked down upon the poor, rural Cajuns. Within the Cajun group in general, there was a continuum of wealth, though most were poor. Today, as the Cajuns have shifted from being a distinct cultural group to an ethnic group, group cohesiveness has weakened, with a sense of "being Cajun" derived from membership in a group that shares a common tradition.

Political Organization.   There was no overarching political structure governing Cajun life, nor was there any purely Cajun political organization at the local level. Rather, Cajuns generally participated in Louisiana and national politics as voters. Two governors and other state officials came from the Genteel Acadian ranks in the 1880s. In the 1900s, Edwin Edwards, "the Cajun Governor" was first elected in 1972.

Social Control and Conflict.   Conflicts were preferably handled by the local group, through mediators, or through fighting between men when matters of honor were involved.

Religion and Expressive Culture

Religious Beliefs.   The Cajuns were and are mainly Roman Catholic. Experts suggest that the traditional culture cannot be understood unless the central role of the Catholic church is considered. On the one hand, their Roman Catholic beliefs set the Cajuns apart from the surrounding population, which was mainly Baptist and Methodist. On the other hand, the church was a visible and active participant in family and social life in every community. The priest was often a major figure in the community, setting the moral tone and serving as a confidant and adviser as necessary. All life events such as birth, marriage, and death required church rituals as did many daily events, with the blessing of fields, tools, boats, and so on an integral part of the work cycle. There were also numerous festivals and feast days of religious significance. Perhaps more important, the church teachings formed the belief system underlying Cajun social organization. Male dominance in the home, stable marriages, large families, and so on were all in accord with the requirements of the church. In addition, Roman Catholicism as practiced in Acadiana created an atmosphere that allowed the celebration of life, or "la joie de vivre," so characteristic of Cajun culture.

Ceremonies.   All the major Roman Catholic holidays were celebrated by the Cajuns. Mardi Gras was the most important festival, with local communities celebrating in ways often much different than that in New Orleans. Public dances (*bals*), festivals, and feasts were regularly held in Cajun communities. All usually involved community dinners, dancing, playing, drinking beer, and music making, and all were family affairs with the entire family participating. Although they occur now less often, public dances, especially the fais do-do, are still important social events for the extended family. Dances, parties, and other opportunities to have a good time are an integral element of the Cajun life-style. Numerous other festivals are held in Acadiana each year, many of which are harvest festivals focusing on local crops such as sugar cane, rice, crawfish, and shrimp.

Arts.   With their current status as a folk culture, considerable interest has developed in the expressive elements of traditional Cajun culture, especially the music and food. Both are unique cultural forms, with a French base combined with elements drawn from American Indian, Spanish, African, British, and German cultures. Both have also changed over the years as new features have been added. Today, Cajun music comes in a variety of styles, the two most prominent being the country-western style and zydeco, which reflects the influence of Black rhythm and blues. Cajun music involves a band, singing, and sometimes foot-stomping. The particular instruments vary with the style, though the fiddle and accordion have been basic instruments for some time. As with their music, Cajun food reflects the combining of elements from a number of cultural traditions on a rural French base. Traditional Cajun cuisine was also influenced, of course, by the foods grown or available locally. From this combination of influences, we find, for example, the heavy use of cayenne pepper for a piquant taste, an oil and flour roux, gumbo, dirty rice, jambalaya, _boudin_ (stuffed hog intestine casings), and crawfish as distinctive elements of Cajun food.

See also Acadians, Black Creoles of Louisiana

Bibliography

Conrad, Glenn R., ed. (1983). _The Cajuns: Essays on Their History and Culture_. Lafayette: Center for Louisiana Studies, University of Southwestern Louisiana.

Del Sesto, Steven L., and Jon L. Gibson, eds. (1975). _The Culture of Acadiana: Tradition and Change in South Louisiana_. Lafayette: University of Southwestern Louisiana.

Dorman, James H. (1983). _The People Called Cajuns_. Lafayette: Center for Louisiana Studies, University of Southwestern Louisiana.

Rushton, William Faulkner (1979). _The Cajuns: From Acadia to Louisiana_. New York: Farrar, Straus & Giroux.

Caribou Inuit

ETHNONYM: Kinnepatoo

Caribou Inuit refers to five independent groups (Qairnirmiut, Harvaqtuurmiut, Hauniqtuurmiut, Paallirmiut, and Ahiarmiut) of central Canadian Inuit located on and inland from the west shore of Hudson Bay between 61° and 65° N and 90° and 102° W. The name "Caribou" was applied by Europeans on the Fifth Danish Thule Expedition (1921–1924) and reflects the groups' reliance on the caribou for food and raw materials. The five groups did not view themselves as part of any larger overarching group. The Caribou Inuit today number about three thousand located in the villages of Chesterfield Inlet, Rankin Inlet, Whale Cove, Eskimo Point, and Baker Lake. They speak dialects of the Inuit-Inupiaq language.

The prehistory of the Caribou Inuit is unclear. First contact with Whites was in 1612–1613, although regular contact began only after the founding of what was to become Churchill, Manitoba, in 1717. From then on, the Caribou Inuit have undergone a slow but steady acculturation into Canadian society, involving the use of guns in hunting and the introduction of trapping, regular trade, and whaling. Acculturative pressure intensified following resettlement in the permanent villages after 1950 and the introduction of Canadian schools, television, and wage labor. In response to these forces and White claims on traditional Inuit land, the Caribou Inuit have been actively involved in Inuit political organizations.

The traditional winter dwelling was the snow house, replaced by the skin-covered snow house and then the conical skin tent in the warmer months. Camps numbered from a few people to as many as fifty, and split or coalesced as food supplies allowed. Beginning in 1950, the Caribou Inuit along with some Netsilik and Iglulik Inuit were settled by the Canadian government in prefabricated housing in the five villages listed above.

The traditional economy centered on the caribou, which was the primary source for food and raw material for clothings, tents, tools, and containers. Caribou hunting remains an important activity, though the traditional methods of herding and lancing from kayaks have been replaced by rifles and snowmobiles. Fishing was and is also important, again with traditional methods and equipment giving way to modern ones. Although each group was associated with a particular region, land was generally open to all who wanted to exploit it. Today, wage labor, craft production for the tourist trade, and welfare have become important sources of income.

The patrilocally extended family residing in one large or several adjacent dwellings was the basic social unit. The oldest capable male was the group leader (_ihumataq_). Polygynous marriage (especially sororal polygyny) was common, and polyandry has been reported. Intermarriage between different groups was evidently common. Patrilocal residence was the norm, though other arrangements were permitted.

No centralized authority existed for any of the five groups nor for the Caribou Inuit in general. Cooperation in hunting and trade was based on kinship and residential patterns. Partnerships of various types common in other Inuit groups were relatively unimportant.

Caribou Inuit myths are similar in focus to those other central Inuit groups, though somewhat less elaborated. The caribou figured centrally in the supernatural world; it was protected by Pingna (a female supernatural figure who also protected other living things) and was the object of various taboos. Hela (air) was the source of misfortune. Shamans treated illness and predicted the future. Singing and song feasts were important and frequent expressive activities.

Bibliography

Arima, Eugene Y. (1984). "Caribou Eskimo." In _Handbook of North American Indians_. Vol. 5, _Arctic_, edited by David Damas, 447–462. Washington, D.C.: Smithsonian Institution.

Birket-Smith, Kaj (1929). _The Caribou Eskimos: Material and Social Life and Their Cultural Position_. Report of the Fifth Thule Expedition, 1921–24. Vol. 5, Pt. 2. Copenhagen, Denmark.

Carrier

ETHNONYM: Takulli

The Carrier are an American Indian group located in north-central British Columbia along the numerous lakes and rivers in the region. The estimated precontact population of roughly eighty-five hundred decreased to a low of about fifteen hundred by 1890 and has since increased to about six thousand. The Carrier were composed of fourteen named subtribes, which on the basis of cultural, territorial, and linguistic evidence have been classified into two or three divisions such as the northern, central, and southern Carrier. Seventeen bands are recognized by the Canadian government today. The Carrier use the subtribe names in reference to themselves. They speak an Athapaskan language.

Carrier prehistory is unclear. The Carrier were involved in intensive trade relations with groups to the west, which eventually involved indirect trade with White traders making port on the northwest coast to seek beaver, fox, and other furs supplied by the interior groups. Contact with Northwest Coast groups such as the Gitksan and Bellacoola resulted in the Carrier adopting the social stratification/potlatch complex of these groups. First contact with Whites was in 1793. Within fifteen years, North West Company fur trade posts were established in Carrier territory and the traditional Carrier hunting and fishing economy began to change. Fur trade activity was joined by gold mining in 1858, then farming and ranching, and finally lumbering of Carrier lands.

Prior to White settlement, families followed an annual cycle of congregating in settlements to visit, potlatch, prepare food for storage, and live off of stored food or separating in order to hunt and trap. Beginning in the late 1800s, the government began setting aside land for the Carrier, which now includes some sixty-three thousand acres in over two hundred reserves. Traditional dwellings included A-frame houses and plank houses modeled after those of the Northwest Coast.

The Carrier were hunters, fishers, and fur trappers. Salmon was the primary fish taken in basket traps, and beaver, bear, caribou, and other animals were hunted. The fur trade, at first indirect through the Northwest Coast groups and later direct with the North West Company and then Hudson's Bay Company, quickly replaced hunting and fishing as the primary economic activity. As the fur trade became more and more lucrative, purchase of food and equipment replaced hunting for food and traditional manufactures to a large extent. Today wage labor (mostly seasonal work in canneries, on ranches, or in lumbering) and government assistance are the major sources of income supplemented by trapping and crafts by some families.

Prior to extensive contact with Northwest Coast groups, the patrilineally extended family (sadeku) was probably the basic social unit. Northwest Coast influences produced somewhat different forms of social organization among the northern and southern Carrier subtribes. Though subtribe variation existed, in the North social organizational units went from subtribe to phratries to clans to matrilineages. Social ranking was based on wealth (largely obtained through the fur trade) and was signified by personal and clan crests and potlatching. Control of subtribe land was allocated to the phratries. In the South, the system was less elaborate with crest groups (who conducted potlatches), bilateral descent groups, and sadeku. Potlatching, banned by the government and discouraged by Catholic missionaries, has largely disappeared. Marriage was usually preceded and followed by a period of bride-service. Polygyny, the sororate, and levirate were practiced in the past.

The Carrier are now mostly Roman Catholic in belief, if not entirely in practice. Traditional beliefs and practices (taboos, dreaming, quests, and so on) focused on spirits.

Bibliography

Jenness, Diamond (1943). *The Carrier Indians of the Bulkley River: Their Social and Religious Life.* U.S. Bureau of American Ethnology Bulletin no. 133. Anthropological Papers, no. 25, Washington, D.C.

Morice, Adrien G. (1905). *The History of the Northern Interior of British Columbia (Formerly New Caledonia), 1660–1880.* 3rd ed. Toronto: William Briggs.

Tobey, Margaret L. (1981). "Carrier." In *Handbook of North American Indians.* Vol. 6, *Subarctic,* edited by June Helm, 413–432. Washington, D.C.: Smithsonian Institution.

Catawba

ETHNONYMS: Anitakwa, Esaw, Issa, Kadapau, Kuttawa, Oyadagahroene, Toderichroone, Ushery

Orientation

Identification. The Catawba are an American Indian group who live in North and South Carolina. The meaning of the name "Catawba" is unclear. It may be derived from the Choctaw *katapa,* meaning "separated" or "divided." Other scholars have traced it to a Catawba word meaning "people on the edge (or bank) of a river," or "people of the fork." The Catawba called themselves "Nieye" (people), or "Ye iswa'here" (people of the river).

Location. Aboriginally the Catawba lived in the southern Piedmont between 34° and 36° N and 79° and 82° W, an area now occupied by North and South Carolina. Most Catawba today live in these two states.

Demography. Today the Catawba population is approximately fourteen hundred. At the beginning of frequent contact with Europeans in the late seventeenth century, after 150 years of sporadic contact (and, presumably, losses to European diseases), Catawba numbers may have approached ten thousand.

Linguistic Affiliation. The Catawba aboriginal language was a branch of Siouan, often termed Eastern Siouan. The last known speaker of the language died in 1959.

History and Cultural Relations

Ancestors of the historic Catawba probably migrated to the southern Piedmont from across the Appalachian Mountains several centuries before Columbus. When Europeans arrived, the Catawba bordered on the Cherokee to the west, the Cheraw, Occaneechi, Saponi, Tutelo, and other Siouan-speaking Piedmont groups to the north, the Tuscarora to the east, and the Mississippian chiefdom of Cofitachique to the south. Contact with their fellow Piedmont peoples appears to have been peaceful; relations with other neighbors were marked by conflict. Initial contact with Europeans came with Hernando de Soto's exploratory army in 1540, but continuous contact with Europeans did not begin until the middle of the following century, when traders from Virginia (and, after 1670, South Carolina) pushed into the Piedmont.

Mutually beneficial trade relations induced the Catawba to ally with the English colonists against the Tuscarora in 1711, but in 1715 abuses by colonial traders led the Catawba to join Yamasee, Creeks, and others in a war against South Carolina. Following their defeat, Catawba relations with the English intruders were peaceful. Catawba warriors fought on the side of the British in the Seven Years' War and allied with the Patriot cause in the American Revolution.

In a 1763 treaty with representatives of the British Crown, the Catawba Nation agreed to give up its claims to much of the Carolina Piedmont in exchange for a reservation of 225 square miles (144,000 acres) along the Catawba River. In 1840, however, the Indians, under intense pressure from settlers (to whom they had leased much of the reservation), signed the Treaty of Nation Ford with South Carolina, relinquishing these lands in exchange for promises of money and the purchase of land somewhere else. Efforts to settle them elsewhere—including an abortive attempt to remove them across the Mississippi River with other Southeastern Indians—were unsuccessful. After a short stay among the neighboring Cherokee, the Catawba returned to the Catawba River, where in 1842 South Carolina purchased a 630-acre reservation for them. In 1943 the Catawba established a relationship with the federal government that included the addition of 3,500 acres to the reservation. This relationship with the federal government was terminated in 1962, and the "new" (federal) reservation was broken up. Today many Catawba remain on or near the "old" reservation established by South Carolina in 1842.

Settlements

During the aboriginal and early contact periods the Catawba built settlements along the Piedmont's rivers and streams. At one time these villages probably were widely dispersed, but by the early eighteenth century European diseases and raids by enemy Indians had helped create a tight cluster of six or seven towns, with perhaps four hundred persons in each, near the junction of the Catawba River and Sugar Creek. Palisades were a common feature, as were open areas in the center for communal activities. Most towns had a large "state house," which was used for ceremonies and for greeting and housing guests. By the late eighteenth century, disease had reduced the number of settlements to one or two, and a decline in enemy raids made palisades superfluous. A century later the towns themselves were gone, and the Catawba were scattered across the landscape—some on farms, others in nearby towns—as they are today.

The aboriginal Catawba house was a circular or oval structure framed of bent saplings and covered with bark or skins. Around the time of the American Revolution they began to imitate their White neighbors and build log cabins. Today their houses are indistinguishable from those of the surrounding population.

Economy

Subsistence and Commercial Activities. The Catawba pursued a subsistence routine that balanced agriculture with hunting, fishing, and gathering. The staples of their diet were maize and venison. The peltry procured by the hunters was in great demand by European traders, who arrived in the late seventeenth century. By the middle of the eighteenth century, however, the deerskin trade had declined, and the Catawba had to find other ways to acquire the European goods—firearms, clothing, kettles—that had become necessities. While continuing to hunt, farm, and fish, they also leased reservation land to Whites after 1763 and peddled household goods, especially pottery, throughout the region. With the loss of the reservation in 1840, many became sharecroppers on nearby farms or earned a living selling firewood. Today most Catawba are employed in local industry; many are professionals or tradespeople.

Industrial Arts. Aboriginal craftspeople produced pottery, baskets, and other items. Today some thirty Catawba potters continue to practice their ancient craft regularly, and another sixty do so occasionally.

Trade. In aboriginal times Catawba carried on an extensive trade with neighboring groups in deerskins, natural dyes, and other products. Trade with European colonists included slaves, peltry, and baskets in exchange for firearms, alcohol, cloth, beads, and other items. The pottery trade, which began in the late eighteenth century, continues today.

Division of Labor. Until the end of the eighteenth century, women were responsible for farming, dressing animal skins, cooking, making pottery and baskets, and raising the children. The men hunted, fished, traded, and cleared new fields. The decline of the deerskin trade reduced the men's economic importance without substantially altering the division of labor; not until the end of the nineteenth century did men begin to replace women in performing agricultural tasks. Making and peddling pottery, which was primarily the responsibility of the women, was central to the Catawba economy until World War II. Today the division of labor mirrors that of the surrounding society.

Land Tenure. Little is known of Catawba land tenure in aboriginal times, but usufruct probably prevailed, with ultimate ownership residing in the community, but individual or familial rights to a tract respected as long as that tract was used. The reservation established in 1763 placed all lands under tribal authority, though particular families may have held the right to collect rent from certain tracts leased to Whites. On the state and federal reservations individuals "owned" a tract of land, with the right to rent it out and leave it to their heirs. When the "new" federal reservation was sold in 1962, Catawbas could choose a cash settlement or a tract of land; 286 of the 631 people on the tribal roll chose cash.

Today on the "old" (state) reservation, a Catawba must apply to the tribal council for an allotment.

Kinship

Kin Groups and Descent. Catawba society was matrilineal at least until the early twentieth century. Extended kinship groups were clearly important in determining an individual's place in society—serving to protect one from harm, determining whom one could marry, and so on—but there is no clear evidence of clans.

Kinship Terminology. Efforts to fit Catawba kinship terms into an accepted kinship classification category have been unsuccessful. Fragmentary evidence, however, suggests that the Tutelo, a Siouan-speaking Piedmont tribe living near the Catawba in colonial times, followed the Dakota system.

Marriage and Family

Marriage. Catawba marriage rules in aboriginal and early-contact times probably forbade first-cousin marriages. Polygamy was neither unknown nor condemned, but most marriages were monogamous. In courtship, a man or his relations approached the woman's parents to ask permission, though the woman's consent was also required. Marriages were matrilocal, and divorce was easily effected by either party.

Domestic Unit. Extended families have been and continue to be the norm.

Inheritance. Matrilineal inheritance was the rule in earlier times; bilateral inheritance obtains today.

Socialization. Catawba child-rearing practices were permissive, with ostracism, ridicule, and example the rule. Folktales were (and to some degree still are) an important educational tool, setting out proper modes of behavior and warning of punishment by native enemies or supernatural beings for those who disobey. Today, formal education is highly valued: there was a primary school on the reservation from 1898 to 1966, and beginning in the 1930s Catawba were attending the local high school. Today many go on to college.

Sociopolitical Organization

Social Organization. Until the early nineteenth century, men achieved status through their skills as hunters, warriors, and speakers. Age conferred status on both men and women. Women, who enjoyed equal status with men, may also have acquired status through their skills as potters—a status that may have increased in the nineteenth century as pottery's economic role became more important. Although surrounded after 1750 by a slave-owning culture, the Catawba owned few slaves themselves. Indeed, they tended to shun African-Americans.

Political Organization. Towns were largely independent before the arrival of Europeans, with each town possessing a council of elders, a headman, and a war captain. At some point in the early colonial period the six or seven villages that came to compose the core of the Catawba Nation developed a tribal government along the same lines as the town political organization: a chief (*eractasswa*), apparently always drawn from a specific kin group, was selected by a council made up of leaders from each town. During the eighteenth century, refugee groups—Cheraw, Wateree, and others—from other parts of the Piedmont arrived in the Catawba Nation, built their own towns, and participated in this national council until eventually they were thoroughly incorporated into Catawba culture.

In 1944, as part of their agreement with the federal government, the Catawba drew up a formal constitution along the lines laid down in the Indian Reorganization Act (1934). Federal termination ended this constitutional government, but the basic political structure of chief and council continues today, with every adult member of the tribe eligible to vote for these officers.

Social Control. Until the late nineteenth century the maintenance of order among Catawbas was left to the tribe. Ostracism and ridicule were vital elements in ensuring good behavior, but more serious crimes such as homicide often led to revenge by the kin of the victim. Since the late nineteenth century the Catawba have been subject to the laws of the surrounding society. In addition, Mormon codes of conduct have been important in setting the standards of behavior.

Conflict. Alcohol was a common cause of violence in the eighteenth century; early in the next century, rights to land leases on the reservation were a point of contention between families. Apparently the decision to sell the reservation in 1840 was also a source of conflict, as was the debate about whether to remove to the west. The decision to terminate the nation's relationship with the federal government divided the Catawba in 1959, and today there are disagreements over the best strategy for seeking compensation for the Treaty of Nation Ford, which was never ratified by Congress as federal law requires.

Religion and Expressive Culture

Religious Beliefs. In aboriginal times the Catawba were polytheistic, with the emphasis on the maintenance of harmony and balance among the various forces governing the universe. The Indians as a rule rebuffed Christian missionaries until the nineteenth century, when some of the Catawba became Baptists or Methodists. In the 1880s, Mormon missionaries visited the nation, and by the 1920s virtually all the Catawba had converted to Mormonism. They remain largely Mormon today. Fragmentary evidence hints that Catawba religion had a supreme being that was associated with the sun. In addition, there were numerous spirits—personal, animal, and elemental—whose powers could be used for good or ill. Today vestiges of these spirits remain in the stories of *yehasuri*, or "wild Indians," who are said to live in the woods on the reservation.

Religious Practitioners. Priests, or "conjurers," enjoyed great prestige in the aboriginal and early-contact era for their powers as healers and diviners. How long the position lasted is unclear, though certainly not past the middle of the nineteenth century. From the 1840s to 1962, the Catawba had a state-appointed physician; today many of the Indians still visit the last man to hold this office.

Ceremonies. In addition to the numerous rituals to be performed by individuals (such as hunters) during the course of daily life, the Catawba had communal ceremonies to celebrate the harvest and pray for future success in planting. The fate of their ceremonial round is unknown; during the early nineteenth century the harvest ceremony may have evolved into an annual meeting in late summer to discuss the leases of reservation lands. "Powwows" were said to have been held into the late nineteenth century, though their form and function are unknown.

Arts. Singing, accompanied by tortoise-shell rattles and pot-drums, was common at ceremonies.

Medicine. Sickness could be caused by ghosts, evil spirits, or the violation of certain taboos. Cures combined medicinal plants applied through proper rituals. Today the Catawba rely exclusively on Western medical practices.

Death and Afterlife. Death was ascribed to the same causes as sickness. The afterworld was said to be divided into good and bad spheres, though the influence of Christianity on this belief cannot be discounted. Heaven was said to have four levels. Elaborate funeral ceremonies, including speeches, feasts, and periods of mourning, were the norm in aboriginal and early-contact times. As late as the end of the nineteenth century, funerals included a fast, a three-day wait for the departure of the soul, and a taboo on speaking the name of the deceased. Today, Catawba practice mirrors that of the nation's neighbors, except that potters may be buried with a piece of their pottery.

Bibliography

Blumer, Thomas J. (1987). _Bibliography of the Catawba._ Native American Bibliography Series, no. 10. Metuchen, N.J.: Scarecrow Press.

Brown, Douglas Summers (1966). _The Catawba Indians: The People of the River._ Columbia: University of South Carolina Press.

Hudson, Charles M. (1970). _The Catawba Nation._ University of Georgia Monographs, no. 18. Athens: University of Georgia Press.

Merrell, James H. (1989). _The Indians' New World: Catawbas and Their Neighbors from European Contact through the Era of Removal._ Chapel Hill: University of North Carolina Press.

JAMES H. MERRELL

Cayuga

The Cayuga were one of the original member tribes of the League of the Iroquois or Five Nations Confederacy. The Cayuga, living mostly in Ontario, New York, Wisconsin, and Oklahoma in the 1980s, numbered more than three thousand. In late aboriginal and early historic times the Cayuga occupied a narrow strip of territory centering on Cayuga and Owasco lakes in New York and stretching south from Lake Ontario toward the Susquehanna River. In 1660 they numbered approximately fifteen hundred.

The Cayuga were drawn into the American Revolution on the side of the British, and in 1779 their villages were destroyed by American forces. Subsequently, many of the Cayuga migrated to Canada and established two villages on the Six Nations Reserve, while others scattered among other of the Iroquois tribes in New York. In the early nineteenth century some of the Cayuga remaining in New York migrated to Ohio, and from there to Indian Territory (Oklahoma) in 1831. Others joined the Oneida in migrating to Wisconsin in 1832.

Traditionally, the Cayuga were a hunting and farming people, but gathering and fishing were also important subsistence activities. The Cayuga held ten of the fifty hereditary sachem positions in the council of the League of the Iroquois and, along with the Oneida, were known as "Younger Brothers" of the confederacy.

See also Iroquois

Bibliography

Wait, Mary Van Sickle, and William Heidt, Jr. (1966). _The Story of the Cayugas, 1609-1809._ Ithaca, N.Y.: De Witt Historical Society of Tompkins County.

Cayuse

The Cayuse (Wailatpa, Wailatpu) lived around the heads of the Wallawalla, Unatilla, and Grand Ronde rivers and extended from the Blue Mountains to Deschutes River in the general area of Pendleton and La Grande in northeastern Oregon. They spoke a language isolate in the Penutian phylum and probably number about three hundred today on the Umatilla Indian Reservation in Oregon, where they live among the Wallawalla and Umatilla.

Bibliography

Ruby, Robert H., and John A. Brown (1972). _The Cayuse Indians: Imperial Tribesmen of Old Oregon._ Norman: University of Oklahoma Press.

Central Yup'ik Eskimos

ETHNONYMS: Aglurmiut, Akulmiut, Askinarmiut, Bering Sea Eskimos, Canineqmiut, Kiatagmiut, Kuigpagmiut, Kusquqvagmiut, Marayarmiut, Nunivaarmiut, Pastulirmiut, Qaluyaarmiut, Southwest Alaska Eskimos, Tuyuryarmiut, Unaliqmiut, West Alaska Eskimos

Orientation

Identification. The name "Eskimo" probably originated from Montagnais, although the belief that it was a pejorative term meaning "eater of raw flesh" is erroneous. The people refer to themselves as "Yup'ik" or "Cup'ik" (the real people). This self-designation derives from the word for "person" (*yuk*) plus the postbase *piak*, meaning "real" or "genuine."

Location. The physical environment of the Central Yup'ik Eskimos is a rich and varied one, and not at all the frozen wasteland of popular imagination. The Yup'ik occupy the lowland delta of western Alaska, including the drainages of the Yukon, Kuskokwim, Togiak, and Nushagak rivers, as well as the Bering Sea coast lying between them. Innumerable sloughs and streams crisscross the coastal tundra, covering close to half the surface of the land with water and creating the traditional highways of its native population. Along the coastline between the Yukon and Kuskokwim rivers, the sea is shallow and the land is flat. Volcanic domes provide relief on Nelson and Nunivak islands, and mountains meet the coast in the vicinity of Bristol Bay and the Togiak River.

Demography. In early postcontact times, the Central Yup'ik Eskimos may have numbered as many as fifteen thousand persons. This number was reduced by over one-half by the smallpox epidemic of 1838–1839 as well as subsequent epidemics. Close to eighteen thousand Yup'ik Eskimos live in western Alaska today, as well as several thousand living outside the region.

Linguistic Affiliation. The Central Yup'ik speak the Central Alaskan Yup'ik language, which aboriginally was one of five Yup'ik languages. Together with the Inupiaq language, spoken by the Eskimos living to the north and east across Canada and Greenland, they constitute the Eskimo branch of the Eskimo-Aleut family of languages. At present, Central Alaskan Yup'ik is internally divided into four major dialects, all of which are spoken in western Alaska today.

History and Cultural Relations

The ancestors of the contemporary Yup'ik Eskimos were originally shore dwellers, settling primarily on the coastal headlands of western Alaska three thousand years ago. Population pressure combined with the need for a more reliable food supply produced migrations of these shore dwellers up the drainages of the coastal rivers around A.D. 1400. At the beginning of the 1900s, Yup'ik Eskimos were still moving slowly but surely upriver, intermarrying with and gradually displacing the Ingalik Athapaskan population that bordered them on the west and with whom they shared largely friendly relations.

The first nonnatives to make a direct impact on the region were Russian traders and explorers who sought to expand the fur trade into western Alaska prior to 1850. The traders were accompanied by Russian Orthodox priests. After the purchase of Alaska by the United States in 1867, the hegemony of the Orthodox mission was challenged by the establishment of a Roman Catholic mission along the Bering Sea coast in 1888 and a Moravian mission on the Kuskokwim River in 1885. Together the missions constituted the major nonnative influence in the region until 1900, when the discovery of gold on the Yukon River inspired a dramatic increase of traffic on both the Yukon and Kuskokwim rivers.

Although rich deposits of gold were never discovered in western Alaska, the decades between 1900 and 1920 saw a steady increase in the nonnative population at the same time the influenza epidemics of 1900 and 1919 continued to undercut the region's native population. Government and mission schools, regular steamship and air transportation, and, in the 1960s, increased federal and state subsidy of housing, health care, and social services also worked to increase nonnative influence. But the region's geographical isolation, as well as the lack of large amounts of commercially valuable resources, limited nonnative activity. The region is at present dominated by Yup'ik-speaking natives, and the only significant populations of nonnatives live in the regional centers of Bethel and Aniak on the Kuskokwim River and Dillingham on Bristol Bay.

Settlements

Prior to the arrival of the Russians in the early 1800s, the substantial population of western Alaska was socially divided into a number of overlapping extended family networks, which in turn were united into territorially centered village groups, ranging in size from 50 to 250 people. At various seasons family groups, married couples, or groups of hunters moved to outlying camps for resource extraction. During the more settled winter season, extended families gathered together into large permanent winter villages, residentially divided between a communal men's house (*qasgiq*) and smaller individual women's houses. The population moved annually, but within a fixed range; it was thus relatively settled compared to other Eskimo peoples. Exchanges of food, women, names, feasts, and visits also served to unify village groups into at least thirteen larger, more comprehensive regional confederations, which alternately traded and warred with each other.

The population decline owing to diseases introduced from the early 1800s on put an end to interregional warfare and undercut interregional social distinctions. Beginning in the early 1900s along the rivers and somewhat later along the more isolated Bering Sea coast, people began to gather into permanent year-round villages focused on a school, cannery, store, church, and post office. At present the population is divided into some seventy year-round villages ranging in size from one hundred to six hundred, along with two major regional centers, Bethel and Dillingham.

The aboriginal Yup'ik winter dwelling was a semi-subterranean sod-insulated log structure with a central smokehole and underground tunnel entryway. These well-insulated but damp sod houses began to be replaced by airier log cabins along the rivers where timber was more accessible beginning in the early 1900s and somewhat later along the coast. Beginning in the 1950s, cabins were replaced by frame houses, often government-subsidized. Although log cabins are still used in timbered areas, standardized frame dwellings are the dominant form of housing in the region today.

Economy

Subsistence and Commercial Activities. Traditionally, the Central Yup'ik Eskimos were hunters and gatherers, relying on the region's varied ecology to support a social and ceremonial complexity unmatched in any other part of the Eskimo world. The shallow coastline is rich in seals, walrus, beluga whales, and saltwater fish including herring, halibut, and cod. The rivers were the spawning grounds for no less than five species of salmon. The coastal wetlands hosted millions of migratory waterfowl during the summer season. Small furbearers including fox, muskrat, mink, and otter were trapped, and caribou were hunted along the river drainages. From the establishment of Russian trading posts in the early 1800s, trapping provided supplemental income to native residents. Reindeer herding was also introduced around 1900 but had disappeared everywhere by the 1940s except on predator-free Nunivak Island. Commercial fishing began to play a major role in the economy of the region in the 1890s in Bristol Bay and by the 1930s along the Yukon and Kuskokwim rivers. The rich salmon fishery and the relatively new herring and bottom fisheries are the most important private-sector commercial activities in the region today. Along with the commercial fishery, income is largely derived from employment in state and federally funded jobs and public assistance programs on which the regional population is markedly dependent. This cash income is in turn used to support the substantial harvest of fish and game for local use.

Except for dogs, there were no important domesticated animals in aboriginal times. Reindeer herding was introduced by missionaries at the end of the nineteenth century but continues only on Nunivak Island. Musk-oxen were also introduced onto Nunivak Island in the 1940s and a small herd subsequently begun on nearby Nelson Island. Both of these herds have prospered and are now the subject of regulated hunting by both nonnative and local hunters.

Industrial Arts.   Aboriginally, all men carved both wood and ivory, and all women were adept at sewing skins and weaving grass into articles for household use. Today some men continue to carve ivory jewelry and wooden fish traps and women to knit and sew skins both for home use and for sale. Men also carve decorative wooden masks, and women weave grass baskets for sale to tourists and collectors.

Trade.   Precontact trade in native articles, including furs and sea mammal products, was maintained between riverine and coastal groups within the region as well as between the Central Yup'ik Eskimos and the Athapaskan peoples to the east. Russian trade goods first entered the region by Siberian trade routes across the Bering Strait, and in the mid-1800s Russian trading stations were established along the rivers. During the nineteenth century, trade largely consisted of luxury goods, including tea, tobacco, and beads. By the early 1900s, the increased river traffic resulting from the Klondike gold rush along with rising fur prices dramatically increased both native buying power and the inventory of goods that were available for trade.

Division of Labor.   Just as men and women lived and worked in different social spaces in the traditional winter village, they were responsible for different productive activities. Men hunted and fished during the day. In the men's house they carved and repaired tools, kayak frames, and objects of everyday use, as well as training young men and boys in these tasks. Women's work included processing their husbands' catch, preparing food, gathering plant materials, making clothes, fashioning pottery, weaving grass, and rearing children. Ritual and medicinal activities were assigned to both men and women. This basic division of labor remained in effect until the modern era. Today women are increasingly employed outside the home, although they retain primary responsibility for food preparation and child care. Men also continue to actively harvest fish and game.

Land Tenure.   Aboriginally, land tenure and land use were based on prior use. An individual had the right to use a particular site because of his relationship to previous generations of users who had harvested at that site in the past. Early nonnative interest in the region focused on small mining claims and trading and cannery sites, and these claims rarely conflicted with traditional patterns of land use. In 1971, the Alaska Native Claims Settlement Act created regional and village native corporations, which were given corporate title to a portion of their traditional holdings, while substantial acreage was retained for state and federal use. At the same time, federal and state laws increasingly regulated the harvesting of fish and game in the region. These regulatory constraints and new legal boundaries are increasingly in conflict with historic patterns of land use and are the focus of considerable controversy in the region today.

Kinship

Kin Groups and Descent.   Aboriginally, the bilateral extended family was the basic social unit. This unit consisted of from two to four generations, including parents, offspring, and parents' parents. Married siblings of either the parents or their offspring might also be included as family members. These extended family networks lived in a number of territorially centered village groups, members of which were joined by overlapping ties of blood and marriage. For the larger village groups, most marriages were within the village. Although the extended family continues to be an important social and productive unit in western Alaska today, increased emphasis on the nuclear family household, intermarriage with nonnatives, and a decline in the importance of intrafamily sharing and exchange networks have undercut its importance.

Kinship Terminology.   The Yup'ik Eskimos follow the Iroquois system of kinship terminology. Although many nuances of the traditional system have been abandoned, Yup'ik kinship terms continue to be used in both reference and address. The traditional practice of addressing persons named for a deceased relative by the kinship term (in either English or Yup'ik) appropriate to that relative is also still widely employed.

Marriage and Family

Marriage.   Traditionally, marriage was encouraged between descendants of cross cousins. Most marriages were monogamous, with occasional polygamy, and serial marriages were common. Before the advent of Christianity, the marriage ceremony consisted of the bride serving food to her new husband in the men's house while wearing newly made clothing presented to her by the family of the groom. Duolocal residence was the norm. A woman raised her daughters in the house where she was born, while at age five her sons went to live in the men's house with their father. When a young man was married, he moved into the men's house of the father of his bride while the woman remained in her mother's house where she in turn would raise her children. Traditionally marriages were dissolved easily by either spouse failing to provide for and/or moving away from their partner. Missionaries report that a number of "trial marriages" ending in divorce were usually preliminary to a stable union.

Domestic Unit. Aboriginally, men lived in a communal men's house while the women and children resided in separate dwellings. The nuclear family lived together in the same house only at the fish or hunting camp. Beginning in the late nineteenth century, missionaries worked to replace this residential separation. Today, the nuclear family household predominates, but owing to increasing costs of maintaining a household as well as increasing rates of illegitimacy, three-generation households are also common.

Inheritance. Traditionally the goods of the deceased were either left at the grave site or distributed among members of the community outside the immediate family of the deceased. The turn-of-the-century missionaries did their best to discourage this practice, and at present property is retained by the deceased's immediate family.

Socialization. Contrary to the general perception of Eskimo child rearing as permissive, Yup'ik children from their earliest years were carefully trained in a multitude of prescriptions and proscriptions circumscribing culturally appropriate thought and deed. These they learned through the observation of adult behavior as well as through countless lessons introduced by their adult care givers. Failure on the child's part to follow the rules was and still is met with teasing, ridicule, and finally the threat of abandonment. At present, as in the past, child rearing discourages overt and direct expressions of hostility and aggression to avoid injuring the mind of the offender. With the recent emphasis on public education, socialization is increasingly in the hands of nonnative teachers in the public schools.

Sociopolitical Organization

Social Organization. In aboriginal times, class distinctions were absent. An individual, male or female, achieved standing within the community from a combination of factors including age, family connections, generosity, and demonstrated skill and knowledge. These same factors control status within the community today. Women occupied a position of equality with men. Slavery did not exist, although during the historic period, orphans were often required to perform innumerable menial jobs within the community. Intermarriage with nonnatives has not resulted in marked class distinctions and at present accounts for fewer than one out of ten marriages.

Political Organization. Traditionally, Yup'ik Eskimos had no formal organization to make political decisions. Leadership was vested in the elder heads of large and well-respected families. When major decisions were required or serious problems arose in a village, residents responded in unison but only when numerous extended families were affected. In the case of interregional hostilities, two or more villages might form an alliance for the purpose of a retaliatory raid against the opposing group. Although interregional alliances changed over time, their relative stability prior to the arrival of the Russians indicates their strength and importance in organizing interregional relations. The arrival of the Russians did little to alter the principles of village and regional political organization, al-

though the subsequent population decline decreased the size and influence of leading families.

Federal oversight of the region expanded in proportion to the growth of the nonnative population after 1900. Under the Indian Reorganization Act (IRA) of 1934, traditional councils, as well as IRA councils, were formed in some villages and began to act as governing bodies within the community. Permanent villages began to acquire municipal governments in the 1950s, and city councils were established. Recently a number of villages have disbanded their municipal governments in favor of the traditional and IRA councils. By this action, they hope to divest themselves of state control and reassert their sovereign rights in a nation-to-nation relationship with the federal government.

Social Control. The moral guidelines for life, which were taught to children from their earliest years, produced a high degree of social control within traditional Yup'ik society. If these rules were broken or ignored, gossip, ostracism, teasing, ridicule, and social withdrawal were traditionally important mechanisms of social control, and they still are today. Fear of retribution by a member of either the human or the spirit world was also a powerful control mechanism. In the case of homicide, blood vengeance by a close relative of the deceased prevailed. At the turn of the century, Yup'ik Eskimos were for the first time subject to American civil and criminal law, and formal sanctions began to be levied against offenders. Civil offenders were brought before the city council. Later regional magistrates were employed to decide local civil offenses, while more serious crimes were referred to the state and federal judicial systems. At present, local village public safety officers and state troopers take offenders into custody. Individual villages and regional organizations are working to regain local jurisdiction over civil issues and increased community control.

Conflict. Interregional hostilities, including bow-and-arrow warfare, were a regular aspect of traditional life in western Alaska. Ironically, warfare was brought to an abrupt halt by death itself when the epidemics of the early 1900s dramatically reduced the native population. Neither Russian nor early American activity in the region produced an organized aggressive response by the Yup'ik people, and the history of native-nonnative interaction in the region has been largely peaceful. In 1984, however, villages along the middle Kuskokwim and lower Bering Sea coast organized into the Yupiit Nation, a political entity representing a nonviolent but nonetheless aggressive response to increasing nonnative control over their lives.

Religion and Expressive Culture

Religious Beliefs. The traditional worldview of the Yup'ik Eskimos has encompassed a system of cosmological reproductive cycling: nothing in the universe ever finally dies away, but is instead reborn in succeeding generations. This view was reflected in elaborate rules circumscribing naming practices, ceremonial exchanges, and daily living. These rules required careful attitudes and actions to maintain the proper relationship with the human and animal spirit worlds and so ensure their return in successive generations. Over the past one hundred years, the Yup'ik Eskimos have become active practitioners of Russian Orthodoxy, Catholicism, and Moravianism. Although they have abandoned many traditional practices, many have been retained and the traditional generative worldview remains apparent in many aspects of contemporary village life.

Religious Practitioners.   Traditionally, shamans exercised considerable influence as a result of their divinatory and healing roles. When the missionaries arrived in the nineteenth century, they viewed the shamans as their adversaries, and many of the shamans actively resisted the new Christian influence. Others, however, converted and went on to become native Christian practitioners. Today the major Christian denominations in western Alaska are run by native pastors and deacons.

Ceremonies.   The traditional winter ceremonial cycle consisted of six major ceremonies and a number of minor ones. Individually, the ceremonies served to emphasize different aspects of the relationships among humans, animals, and the spirit world. Among other things, the ceremonies ensured the rebirth and return of the animals in the coming harvest season. Through dramatic ritual reversals of the normal productive relationships, the human community was opened to the spirits of the game as well as the spirits of the human dead, who were invited to enter and receive recompense for what they had given and would presumably continue to give in their turn. Masked dances also dramatically re-created past spiritual encounters to elicit their participation in the future. Together the ceremonies constituted a cyclical view of the universe whereby right action in the past and the present reproduces abundance in the future. Over the years, Christian missionaries would dramatically challenge the expression of this point of view, although they have never fully replaced it.

Arts.   Singing, dancing, and the construction of elaborate ceremonial masks and finely crafted tools were an important part of traditional Yup'ik life. Although the ceremonies are no longer practiced, traditional recreational dancing and intervillage exchange dances continue in many coastal communities. A rich oral literature was also present traditionally. Although many of the stories have been lost, the region still possesses a number of knowledgeable and expert orators.

Medicine.   The Yup'ik people traditionally understood disease to be the product of spiritual malevolence brought on by a person's improper thought or deed in relation to the spirit world. Curing techniques consisted of herbal medicines, ritual purification, and the enlistment of spirit helpers to drive out the malevolent forces. At present, Western clinical medicine is the primary means of handling sickness and disease, although traditional herbal remedies are still often employed.

Death and Afterlife.   Death was not viewed as the end of life, as some spiritual aspects of each man and animal were believed to be reborn in the following generation. The traditional Yup'ik Eskimos also believed in a Skyland as well as an underworld Land of the Dead, both of which housed the souls of dead humans and animals. It was from these worlds that the spirits were invited to participate in the ceremonies held in their honor in the human world.

Bibliography

Fienup-Riordan, Ann (1983). *The Nelson Island Eskimo.* Anchorage: Alaska Pacific University Press.

Lantis, Margaret (1984). "Nunivak Eskimo." In *Handbook of North American Indians.* Vol. 5, *Arctic,* edited by David Damas, 209–223. Washington, D.C.: Smithsonian Institution.

Nelson, Edward W. (1899). *The Eskimo About Bering Strait.* U.S. Bureau of American Ethnology, 18th Annual Report (1896–1897). Washington, D.C. Reprint. Washington, D.C.: Smithsonian Institution Press, 1983.

Oswalt, Wendell (1966). "The Kuskowagamiut: Riverine Eskimos." In *This Land Was Theirs,* edited by Wendell Oswalt, 106–147. Mountain View, Calif.: Mayfield Publishing Co.

VanStone, James W. (1984). "Mainland Southwest Alaska Eskimo." In *Handbook of North American Indians.* Vol. 5, *Arctic,* edited by David Damas, 224–242. Washington, D.C.: Smithsonian Institution.

ANN FIENUP-RIORDAN

Chastacosta

The Chastacosta, including the Coquille, Galice (Taltushtuntude), Tututni (Lower Rogue River Indians), and the Umpqua, lived in southwestern Oregon along the Lower Rogue, Coquille, and Illinois rivers. They spoke Athapaskan languages and numbered less than fifty in 1970. They are now nearly extinct.

Bibliography

Bakken, Lavola J. (1973). *Land of the North Umpquas: Peaceful Indians of the West.* Grants Pass, Oreg.: Te-Cum-Tom Publications.

Hall, Roberta L. (1984). *The Coquille Indians: Yesterday, Today, and Tomorrow.* Lake Oswego, Oreg.: Smith, Smith, & Smith Publishing Co.

Chehalis

The Chehalis, including the Upper Chehalis (Kwaiailk), Lower Chehalis, Copalis, Cowlitz, Humptulip, Oyhut, Satsop, and Shoalwater Salish, lived in southeastern Washington along the Chehalis, Satsop, and Cowlitz rivers. They spoke Halkomelem languages of the Coast Salish division and numbered 382 in 1984. They were living among the Chinook on the Chehalis and Shoalwater Indian Reservations.

Bibliography

Haeberlin, Hermann, and Erna Gunther (1930). *The Indians of Puget Sound*. University of Washington Publications in Anthropology, 4(1). Seattle.

Marr, Carolyn J., Donna Hicks, and Kay Francis (1980). *The Chehalis People*. Oakville, Wash.: Confederated Tribes of the Chehalis Reservation.

Cherokee

ETHNONYMS: Chalaque, Cheraqui, Manteran, Oyata'ge Ronon, Rickahochan, Tallige', Tsa'lagi', Tsa'ragi

Orientation

Identification. The Cherokee are an American Indian group who now live in North Carolina and Oklahoma. The name, "Cherokee" is apparently of foreign origin, perhaps from the Choctaw *chiluk,* meaning "cave," an allusion to the Cherokees' mountainous homeland. Historically the Cherokee sometimes referred to themselves as "Ani'-Yun'-wiya'" (real people) or "Ani'-kitu' hwagi" (people of Kituwha) in reference to one of their important ancient settlements.

Location. Aboriginally the Cherokee occupied the region of the southern Appalachian Highlands from 34° to 37° N and 80° to 85°W, mainly in the present-day states of Tennessee and North Carolina in the southeastern United States. Most Cherokee now live in Oklahoma and North Carolina.

Demography. In 1970 the Cherokee population was estimated at 66,150, with 27,197 in Oklahoma, 6,085 in North Carolina, and 32,878 in other states, mainly California, New Mexico, and Texas. In early postcontact times the Cherokee numbered approximately 20,000. In a 1989 Bureau of the Census publication, it was noted that in 1980 there were over 230,000 Cherokee enumerated, which would make them the largest Native American group in the United States.

Linguistic Affiliation. The Cherokee language is classified in the Iroquoian family. In aboriginal and early postcontact times there were three dialects: the Eastern or Lower dialect is now extinct; the Middle or Kituwha dialect is spoken in North Carolina; and the Western or Upper dialect in Oklahoma.

History and Cultural Relations

Linguistic, archaeological, and mythological evidence suggest that the Cherokee migrated to the southern Appalachian Highlands from the north prior to European contact in 1540. Native groups bordering the Cherokee territory at that time included the Powhatan and Monacan to the northeast, the Tuscarora and Catawba to the east and southeast, the Creek to the south, the Chickasaw and Shawnee to the west, and the now-extinct Mosopelea to the north. Generally speaking, Cherokee relations with all these groups during the early historic period were contentious.

Continuous contact with Europeans dates from the mid-seventeenth century when English traders from Virginia began to move among native groups in the southern Appalachians. Following contact, the Cherokee intermarried extensively with Whites. Peaceful Cherokee-White relations ended when war broke out with South Carolina in 1759. During the American Revolution the Cherokee allied with the British and continued hostilities with Americans until 1794. White encroachments on their territory led a large number of Cherokee to migrate west between 1817 and 1819. In 1821, after many years of effort, Sequoyah, a mixed-blood Cherokee, developed a Cherokee syllabary, which had the important result of extending literacy throughout the population. In 1835 gold was discovered in the Cherokee territory and White encroachments increased.

In that same year the Treaty of New Echota arranged for the sale of Cherokee lands to the U.S. government and the removal of the Cherokee to Indian Territory (Oklahoma) and Kansas. As the treaty was opposed by most Cherokee, the removal had to be carried out by force involving seven thousand federal troops. Over four thousand Cherokee, intermarried Whites, and African-American slaves died en route or as a result of the removal. A band of several hundred Cherokee escaped the roundup and in 1842 were granted permission to remain on land set aside for them in North Carolina. The descendants of these two groups make up the present-day Western (Oklahoma) and Eastern (North Carolina) Cherokee.

Settlements

In aboriginal and early-contact times settlements were clustered near streams and rivers. Because of the rugged topography, they were often separated by considerable distances but were linked by intricate trade networks. Up to sixty towns existed, with populations of 55 to 600, but averaging 250–300 persons. Larger towns were built around a council house and a field for stickball and served as economic, social, and religious centers for smaller surrounding towns. Warfare, disease, and trade attending European contact undermined the nucleated settlement pattern and resulted in more linear, dispersed settlements.

Since the removal, mixed-blood Cherokee in Oklahoma have tended to settle on rich bottomlands near railroad centers while full-bloods have tended to settle in small isolated villages in the Ozark foothills. At the Qualla Boundary Reservation in North Carolina, the Cherokee population is concentrated in four bottomland areas comprising five townships. Each township has a small center, but most families live on isolated farmsteads on the edges of the bottomlands and along creeks and streams. The community of Cherokee in the Yellow Hill township is the site of numerous tourist attractions, shops, and restaurants. The aboriginal Cherokee house was of wattle-and-daub construction, oval or oblong, with a single door, no windows, and a pitched roof of thatch, reeds, or poles. Today, much Cherokee wood-frame housing is substandard, although improvements have been made recently.

Economy

Subsistence and Commercial Activities. The Cherokee were horticulturalists, raising cereal and vegetable crops on a swidden basis and supplementing their subsistence through hunting, fishing, and collecting. The primary cultigen was maize and the most important game animal the white-tailed deer. Contact with Europeans resulted in the addition of new grains, vegetables, and domesticated animals. During the seventeenth century the European fur trade became a central factor in the Cherokee economy. But the trade declined in the mid-eighteenth century, and the Cherokee adopted more intensive forms of agriculture and animal husbandry.

Prior to contact each Cherokee town maintained a mutual aid society known as the gadu:gi (later known as the Free Labor Company), which coordinated agricultural activities. After contact the cooperative functions of the gadu:gi expanded to include relief to those in need of emergency assistance. In North Carolina the gadu:gi remained a permanent organization until very recent times, while in Oklahoma it became a temporary group constituted to perform specific tasks.

Today the majority of the Eastern Cherokee continue general subsistence farming, with tobacco, garden crops, and beef occasionally raised for cash. At Qualla Boundary, tourism provides income through retail shops, restaurants, motels, museums, and exhibitions; however, these are not sufficient to provide all families with adequate incomes. Other income is derived from logging, seasonal wage labor, and government assistance. Among the Western Cherokee there is little industry, tourist or otherwise, and they often rent their land to White ranchers rather than farm it themselves. Cash income is from ranching and other wage labor, government work projects, and government assistance.

Industrial Arts. Aboriginal crafts included metalworking, potting, soapstone carving, and basket weaving. Copper, then brass, then silver were used by Cherokee metalsmiths. Today basket weaving persists among Cherokee women at Qualla Boundary, where the products are sold to tourists.

Trade. A considerable precontact trade was maintained with neighboring Indian groups. Trade with Europeans in the seventeenth century was indirect and inconsequential, but by the early eighteenth century it had become an integral part of the economy. Salt obtained by the Cherokee from saline streams and licks was an important trade item in both pre- and postcontact times.

Division of Labor. Prior to the mid-eighteenth century women did most of the farming, while men were responsible for hunting, fishing, and clearing fields for planting. Women also prepared food, made clothes, made pottery and baskets, and raised the children. Ritual and medicinal activities were carried out mainly by males. After contact, both men and women conducted trade with Europeans. The decline of hunting and the adoption of more intensive agriculture in the eighteenth century altered the traditional division of labor, and men replaced women in the fields and women's work was increasingly confined to the household. Today, at least among the Eastern Cherokee, most women continue to work in the home. Some, however, are employed in tourist services, crafts, factory work, and farm and domestic labor.

Land Tenure. Aboriginally, individuals had the right to occupy, hunt, and cultivate the land with ownership vested in local clan sections. After contact the Cherokee were under constant pressure to sell their lands to Whites, and as a result in the early nineteenth century the Cherokee Nation adopted a system of property law, placing all Cherokee lands under tribal authority. In 1906, tribal land in Indian Territory was allotted to individuals by the U.S. government. In North Carolina after the removal the Cherokee were prohibited from owning land, and for a time all their lands were recorded under the name of their White benefactor, Will Thomas. Today, the federal government is the trustee of the Eastern Cherokee lands, with actual ownership vested in the Eastern Band itself.

Kinship

Kin Groups and Descent. Cherokee society was divided into seven matrilineal, exogamous clans, or sibs. Within each town, clan sections formed corporate groups that held and allocated land, regulated marriage, and controlled conflict among local clan members. Age stratification within the clan section constituted the first level of local decision making. Clans rarely, if ever, acted as corporate groups on a tribewide basis. Since the time of contact, intermarriage with Whites and acculturation has gradually undermined the clan system. Among the Eastern Cherokee, clans are no longer meaningful social units except among the very elderly.

Kinship Terminology. Traditional kinship terminology followed the Crow system.

Marriage and Family

Marriage. In the traditional marriage system, members of the mother's and father's matrilineage were forbidden as marriage partners, while marriage to members of the father's father's and mother's father's matrilineage was permitted and even favored. Few modern Eastern Cherokee marriages conform to these rules. Marriages were usually monogamous, but polygyny was permitted and occasionally practiced. In the eighteenth century the marriage ceremony was an informal affair in which a man obtained the consent of the prospective bride and her mother before accompanying her to a previously prepared dwelling place. Matrilocal residence was the traditional norm. Divorce was common and could be affected easily by either party.

Domestic Unit. Until recently, small extended families were common. Among contemporary Cherokee the nuclear family tends to predominate. Owing to poverty and high rates of illegitimacy, however, three-generation households also are common.

Inheritance. Since the nineteenth century, property has usually passed to the person who took care of the owner in his or her last years. Since that person has often been the youngest son, ultimogeniture has prevailed by custom.

Socialization. Generally speaking, children were and are raised permissively. Ostracism, ridicule, and the threat of external sanctioning agents—"boogers"—were and still are used to discipline and control children. Overt and direct expressions of hostility and aggression are discouraged. Parents, many of whom are themselves well educated, encourage their children to remain in high school and often to continue with postsecondary training.

Sociopolitical Organization

Social Organization.   In aboriginal and early-contact times age conferred status and the oldest, "beloved" men enjoyed the greatest prestige. Women occupied a position of equality with men, but as the traditional division of labor shifted during the eighteenth century their economic independence lessened and their influence and status diminished. Institutionalized slavery appeared in the form of African slaves before 1700 and became widespread in the nineteenth century. Intermarriage with Whites resulted in a class of mixed-blood Cherokee who, after the American Revolution, increasingly controlled power and wealth within the society. In the nineteenth century they formed a class of wealthy, educated, and acculturated planters set apart from full-blood Cherokee by language, religion, life-style, and values. This class division persists in contemporary Cherokee society.

Political Organization.   Prior to contact with Europeans each town was politically independent from the others and had two distinct governmental structures—a White, or peace, government and a Red, or war, government. During the course of the eighteenth century an overarching tribal government based on the traditional town model was created in response to European expansion. In 1827 a constitution was adopted creating a republican form of government modeled after that of the United States, which remained active until 1906 when it was abolished by the U.S. Congress. In 1948 the Cherokee Nation in Oklahoma was reestablished. The Eastern Cherokee incorporated as the Eastern Band of Cherokee Indians in 1889.

Social Control.   Eschewing face-to-face conflict, the Cherokee have employed gossip, ostracism, and social withdrawal as important forms of social control. Fear of divine retribution was a powerful form of social control in the past and remains so among some conservative Cherokee today. Conjuring or witchcraft declined in importance during the eighteenth century. In aboriginal and early-contact times serious crimes were adjudicated by the White government. Homicide often led to blood revenge by clan members. In 1898 the Cherokee judicial system was dissolved by the federal government and the group was placed under the jurisdiction of the U.S. federal courts.

Conflict.   In the eighteenth century the Cherokee were divided mainly along lines of age over what the relationship to the European colonies should be. In addition, the introduction and gradual acceptance of the money economy and European values introduced an element of aggression and competition between individuals and towns that previously was unknown in the society. Even more significant was the split over the removal to Indian Territory, first in 1817–1819 and then more seriously in 1838–1839. In general, mixed-bloods favored removal while full-bloods did not. This split broke out into civil war after arrival in Indian Territory and resurfaced during the American Civil War. Beginning in 1896 many full-bloods took part in the nativistic Nighthawk Keetoowah movement to resist the reallotment of tribal lands

and mixed-blood support for reallotment. For several decades the Nighthawk movement exercised a powerful force among conservative full-blood Cherokee, but beginning about 1935 its influence waned, owing to internal divisions and the opposition of militant Christian Cherokee. Today the mixed-blood/full-blood division persists, and on occasion the hostility has erupted in violence.

Religion and Expressive Culture

Religious Beliefs.   The aboriginal religion was zootheistic and guided by a deep faith in supernatural forces that linked human beings to all other living things. Evil was understood to be the result of a disharmony with nature. Beginning in the early nineteenth century Christian missionaries succeeded in driving native religious beliefs underground, and today the Baptist denomination predominates among Christian Cherokee in Oklahoma and North Carolina. The existence of a supreme being in the native religion is not clear; however, there were numerous animal, elemental, personal, and inanimate spirits. These spirits were believed to have created the world and to reside in seven successive tiers of heaven, on earth, and in the water, where they remain until the exercise of their powers is properly petitioned.

Religious Practitioners.   In aboriginal times priests received no special material considerations, although they did exercise considerable influence as a result of their divining and healing roles. In the nineteenth century Christian Cherokee pastors were an important factor in the conversion process.

Ceremonies.   The native ceremonial cycle consisted of a series of six festivals, the last three of which were held in quick succession in the autumn, simultaneously with important meetings of town councils. The Propitiation Festival, held ten days after the first new moon of autumn and the Great New Moon Feast, was the most important and was devoted to ritually eliminating ill will among villagers and promoting local unity. The six festivals have been collapsed into a single Green Corn Festival.

Arts.   Singing was an important part of aboriginal and postcontact ceremonial life. For religious and other purposes texts are sung in Cherokee, but tunes and the manner of harmonizing are derived from nonnative sources.

Medicine.   In the aboriginal culture disease was understood to be the product of spiritual malevolence brought on by violating taboos. Curing techniques consisted of herbal medicines, ritual purifications, and the enlistment of spirit helpers to drive out the malevolent forces. Western clinical medicine is now the treatment approach, although native conjurors still persist.

Death and Afterlife.   Native beliefs ascribed death, like disease, to evil spirits and witches. Death was feared and so, too, were the evil spirits connected with death. There was also a belief in an afterworld, or "nightworld," to which the ghosts or souls of the deceased desired to go. A successful journey to the nightworld, however, depended on one's actions in life on earth. Funeral ceremonies had great religious significance, and among Eastern Cherokee the funeral is the most important life cycle ritual.

Bibliography

Gearing, Frederick O. (1962). *Priests and Warriors: Social Structures for Cherokee Politics in the Eighteenth Century.* American Anthropological Association, Memoir 93. Menasha, Wis.

Gulick, John (1973). *Cherokees at the Crossroads.* Chapel Hill: University of North Carolina Institute for Research in the Social Sciences.

King, Duane H., ed. (1979). *The Cherokee Indian Nation: A Troubled History.* Knoxville: University of Tennessee Press.

GERALD REID

Cheyenne

ETHNONYMS: Sha-hi'ye-la, Itasi'na, Chien, Schian, Chayenne, Shyenne

Orientation

Identification. The name "Cheyenne" derives from the Dakota word sha-hi'ye-la, meaning "red talkers" or "people of an alien speech." The Cheyenne refer to themselves as "Tsetsehese-staestse" (People), although today the Northern Cheyenne also are known as the "Notame-ohmeseheetse" (Northern-eaters) and the Southern Cheyenne are called "Heevaha-tane" (Rope-people).

Location. Throughout the late-eighteenth and midnineteenth centuries, the Cheyenne occupied a region that extended from the Yellowstone River, Montana, to the upper Arkansas River in present-day Colorado and Kansas. In all, their territory extended over 500,000 square miles, covering nearly eight states. The high plains is characterized by shortgrass vegetation, occasionally interrupted by riparian forests and shrubs along the more perennial waterways. Evergreen stands predominate at higher elevations. The climate is one of hot summers and harsh, cold winters, with an average annual precipitation of ten to fourteen inches. Although the region was not conducive to horticulture, it did support a large bison population.

Demography. At contact (c. 1780) population estimates indicate that there were about 3,500 Cheyenne. Despite four known major epidemics and a number of massacres inflicted by the U.S. military forces, the 1888 Cheyenne reservation population was 3,497. Of that number, 2,096 were Southern Cheyenne living in Indian Territory (now Oklahoma) and 1,401 were Northern Cheyenne residing on the Tongue River Reservation, Montana, and the Pine Ridge Reservation, South Dakota. In 1989, the Northern Cheyenne numbered 5,716. An exact Southern Cheyenne population figure is more difficult to obtain. Currently 9,525 Southern Cheyenne

and Arapaho are enrolled at Concho Agency; at least 50 percent identify themselves as Southern Cheyenne.

Linguistic Affiliation. The Cheyenne language is one of five main Algonkian languages spoken on the Great Plains. In the postcontact period, there were at least two major Cheyenne dialects, Tse-tsehese-staestse and So'taa'e, the latter spoken by a tribe incorporated into the Cheyenne. Today only Tse-tsehese-staeste is spoken, but So'taa'e words have been adopted into the language.

History and Cultural Relations

Cheyenne history and cultural relations are linked to their shifting adaptations from a woodland people to equestrian nomads on the Great Plains. Although the Cheyenne have never been associated with a specific archaeological focus, oral tradition and ethnohistorical evidence confirm that the protohistoric Cheyenne occupied the woodland-prairie country of the upper Mississippi Valley, where they inhabited semisedentary villages located along lakes and rivers. As early as 1680, the Cheyenne initiated contact with the French in an attempt to establish trade relations. Their desire for trade provoked attacks from the Sioux and Chippewa, who were competing for domination. Outnumbered and possessing no firearms, the Cheyenne were forced westward into the Minnesota Valley and eventually onto the northeastern plains. On the plains, the Cheyenne established at least twelve fortified earthlodge villages along the Sheyenne and Missouri rivers. Allied with the Mandan and Arikara, they continued to war with the Chippewa, Assiniboin, and expanding Sioux. During this period, the Cheyenne incorporated the So'taa'e, intermarried Arikara, and the Moiseyu, a Siouan group from Minnesota. Although forced out of the Great Lakes fur market, the Cheyenne continued to trade, serving as middlemen between more westwardly nomadic Plains groups and the Missouri River village people. Between 1742 and 1770, the Cheyenne acquired horses and became equestrian nomads. By 1820, the Cheyenne had stabilized their geographical and political position in the Black Hills region, allying themselves with the Arapaho and Oglala. From here, the tribe expanded in a southwesterly direction. Their separation into northern and southern divisions began as early as 1790 and was accelerated in the 1830s by the establishment of Bent's Fort on the Arkansas River and Fort William on the North Platte River.

Formal relations with the U.S. government was marked by the signing of the 1825 Friendship Treaty and White-Cheyenne relations were generally amicable until the 1840s. During this decade, the Cheyenne witnessed a flood of Whites migrating along the Oregon Trail and the destruction of their environment and bison herds; they also contracted infectious diseases at this time. The Cheyenne and their allies responded by conducting a series of minor raids. To end Indian-Indian and Indian-White hostilities, the U.S. government negotiated the Treaty of 1851, making the division between the Northern and Southern Cheyenne permanent. The reduction of their land base, the continuing invasion of Whites, and the construction of forts prompted the Cheyenne to fight. For the next twenty-five years, they waged war against the U.S. military and White settlers; the Southern Cheyenne surrendered in 1875 and Northern Cheyenne resistance ended in 1879. With the Southern Cheyenne settled on their reservation, the U.S. government attempted to reconsolidate the tribe by forcibly removing the Northern Cheyenne to Indian Territory. Culturally alienated, starving, and infected with dysentery, measles, and malaria, 257 Northern Cheyenne broke out and avoided capture until crossing the North Platte River. There they divided into two bands, both of which were eventually captured, with the remnants allowed to relocate in 1881 from Indian Territory to Pine Ridge Agency. In 1884, the Tongue River Reservation was established by executive order in southeastern Montana and all the Northern Cheyenne were reunited. In 1892 the Southern Cheyenne–Arapaho Reservation was dissolved through allotment. The Northern Cheyenne Reservation was allotted in 1932, although the land was never opened to White homesteading, thus preserving the integrity of the reservation. Presently, both tribes continue to struggle to establish the legal and cultural rights they have lost over the centuries.

Settlements

For most of the year, the ten Cheyenne bands traveled independently throughout their territory. Camping locations were usually near the confluence of two waterways, near adequate game, wood, and grazing land for the horses. During the early summer, the bands congregated to conduct tribal ceremonies. Afterwards, the bands dispersed to their territories, settling in wooded areas along waterways for winter. After being placed on their reservations the Cheyenne continued to settle along waterways, although eventually communities were formed near government buildings or White towns. Aboriginal Cheyenne housing on the plains was a three-pole tipi replaced during the reservation period by cabins. Today, most Cheyenne live in governmental housing, mobile homes, or converted older reservation structures. Some of the homes are substandard, although improvements have been made since the 1960s.

Economy

Subsistence and Commercial Activities. Although casual gardening continued among some bands as late as 1850, the primary focus was the bison. Besides meat, the bison provided materials for shelter, clothing, and manufactured goods and was a trade item. Of over forty food plants gathered, the most important were the Indian turnip, chokecherries, and plums. European contact resulted in the adoption of trade foods into the Cheyenne diet. Coffee, sugar, bacon, and bleached flour became important commodities, especially during the dramatic decline of the bison. Cheyenne involvement in the nineteenth-century bison robe trade resulted in a further dependency on European goods. On reservations, rations, gardening, and marginal wage labor became the mainstay of the Cheyenne economy. Today the majority of the Southern and Northern Cheyenne income is derived through the federal government. Among the Northern Cheyenne, tribal enterprises such as logging, ranching, growing alfalfa, seasonal wage labor, and governmental assistance provide most of their income. The Southern Cheyenne are involved in wheat raising, oil exploitation, some ranching, and governmental work projects. Both tribes continue to be underemployed and dependent on governmental support. The most important domesticated animal was the horse, which was used for transportation, warfare, and hunting, and became a source of wealth in Cheyenne society.

Industrial Arts. Cheyenne skills included leatherworking, woodworking, quillworking, featherworking, and stone carving. After direct trade with Europeans, metal objects, glass beads, cloth, and other items to decorate replaced articles of native manufacture. Today the Cheyenne continue to make objects for personal use, powwows, ceremonial purposes, and sale to non-Indians.

Trade. The extent of precontact trade is not fully known, but by the historical period the Cheyenne were involved in a complex trading network. As middlemen, the Cheyenne traded horses, dried bison meat, pemmican, dehydrated *pomme blanche,* and decorated robes, shirts, and leather pouches with the Missouri River tribes. In exchange, the Cheyenne obtained European items such as guns, powder, and foodstuffs as well as native maize and tobacco. By 1830, they had become involved in the bison robe trade with Europeans, which ended in the 1880s, leading to complete economic dependency on the U.S. government.

Division of Labor. The division of labor was based on age and sex. Men's work included hunting, raiding, ceremonial activities, and manufacturing all items associated with these pursuits. Young boys and elder men in the household were often in charge of caring for the horse herd. Women's tasks were associated with domestic activities: gathering food and fuel, caring for children, butchering meat, making pemmican, erecting and dismantling the lodge, manufacturing all household objects, and preparing bison hides for use or trade. Young girls assisted their mothers with these tasks, and elder women relieved the mother of child-care duties. During the bison hide trade period, men's and women's labor focused on acquisition and production of hides. During the reservation period, the division of labor was altered radically with women's work increasingly devalued and confined to the household. Since World War II, Cheyenne men and women have been employed in a variety of occupations ranging from trapping to law.

Land Tenure. Aboriginally, any Cheyenne had the right to resources within their territory. Although portions of their territory were contested by other Plains Indians, the Cheyenne claimed and actively defended the region from the Yellowstone River to the Arkansas River. Within this territory, each band occupied and utilized a favored location, usually near major rivers.

Kinship

Kin Groups and Descent. Descent was bilateral. Although clans probably existed when the Cheyenne resided in sedentary earthlodge villages during the 1700s, clans no longer existed after they became equestrian nomads.

Kinship Terminology. Prior to the alteration of the kinship system during the reservation period, terminology followed the Hawaiian system, emphasizing horizontal classification along generational levels.

Marriage and Family

Marriage. Marriage was a formal matter. Premarital sex was strictly prohibited and a girl's virginity was carefully guarded by her family. Because a young man postponed marriage until he had horses and a respectable war record, courtship often lasted for several years. The most respectable marriages were arranged between families, although elopement took place. Until the pattern was interrupted by epidemic disease and warfare, marriage was forbidden to a relative of any degree. Most marriages were monogamous, but polygyny was permitted, often of the sororal type, with the levirate also practiced. Today there is still concern about the degree of relatedness between a couple wanting to marry. Traditionally, postmarital residence was uxorilocal. With the incorporation of the Dog Soldiers into the tribal circle, residence shifted in that portion of Cheyenne society to patrilocality, resulting in two residence patterns after 1860. Divorce could be initiated by either the husband or wife for mistreatment, adultery, or other marital transgressions. A man could publicly disgrace his wife by "throwing her away" at a public gathering.

Domestic Unit.   The primary unit of cooperation and subsistence was the *vestoz*, a residential extended family of related women and their conjugal families. Although the nuclear family is the predominant pattern today, extended families still exist, often as an adaptation to the high unemployment rates, poverty, illegitimacy, and other socioeconomic factors associated with social disadvantage.

Inheritance.   Some of a man's personal possessions were buried with him, but all the remaining property was given to nonrelatives. The widow and her children retained nothing. At funerals today, give-aways are still held before the body is buried and one full year after the death. Contemporary inheritance patterns are defined by legal stipulation and kinship.

Socialization.   Children were generally raised permissively. Social ideals were taught through advice, counsel, and demonstration. Although physical punishment was rarely used, gossip, teasing, and sometimes ostracism acted as negative sanctions if the child misbehaved. Many of these mechanisms are used today, but physical punishment is also now used to correct undesirable behavior.

Sociopolitical Organization

Social Organization.   Although kinship was the foundation of Cheyenne society, there coexisted four types of social organization: the *vestoz* (a camp), the *manhastoz* (a bunch), the *notxestoz* (military society), and the *manhao* (a sacred band). The manhastoz was structurally similar to the vestoz, but was larger and usually organized around a chief's household; it was organized for trade rather than strictly subsistence pursuits. The manhao, the largest traditional Cheyenne social unit, was composed of numerous vestoz and manhastoz led by council chiefs. Most important, these ten "sacred bands" were recognized as having a camping position in the Cheyenne tribal circle when they came together to conduct ceremonies. The 1849 cholera and 1850–1851 smallpox epidemics and White expansion resulted in three "sacred bands" becoming extinct and others being depopulated. In response, a notxestoz, the Dog Soldier Military Society, merged with the remnant Mas'kota band and was added to the Cheyenne tribal circle. Aside from kin-based groups, there were various sodalities for men and women. The most famous male sodality was the Contraries; other male sodalities included the Buffalo Men and Horse Men. Women's sodalities focused on

skill and achievement in manufactured articles, the most important being the Quillwork Society. In modern times, the War Mothers Association was organized to honor Cheyenne veterans.

Political Organization.   Cheyenne political organization was unique among Plains equestrian peoples. They maintained a Council of Forty-four, leaders who made decisions for the entire tribe consisting forty headsmen (four from each of the ten bands) and four councilmen known as the old man chiefs. They were considered the wisest men and were often the tribal religious authorities. Each council member had equal authority and served for ten years. The Council of Forty-four met during the summer when the tribe congregated for ceremonies and decided on future tribal movements, relations with other tribes, the schedule of tribal ceremonies, and important internal tribal matters. To carry out their decisions, the Council of Forty-four relied upon the six Cheyenne military societies. Membership in any of the military societies was open to all young men, although most boys joined their father's society. In addition, each society selected several young women, known for their chastity and virtue, who served as assistants in society ceremonial functions.

Social Control.   The mechanisms of social control ranged from public ridicule, social withdrawal, songs, and ostracism to physical punishment carried out by the military societies. Such mechanisms were replaced during the reservation period. After allotment and Oklahoma statehood in 1906, the Southern Cheyenne came under the legal jurisdiction of state law enforcement agencies. Since that time, the Southern Cheyenne, like the Northern Cheyenne, have instituted a tribal police force and tribal court system.

Conflict.   Forced onto the plains through conflict, the Cheyenne, between 1790 and 1850, warred against the Crow, Shoshone, Pawnee, and numerous other tribes to establish hunting territories, to acquire new land, and to maintain an advantageous position in their trade relations with other tribes and Europeans. Other reasons for going to war were more individualistic, usually to acquire horses, take captives, or gain revenge. After 1850, the nature of warfare changed and the growing conflict with Whites became a fight for survival.

Religion and Expressive Culture

Religious Beliefs.   The Cheyenne world was a dynamic, operative system with interrelated components. Within the Cheyenne universe (*Hestanov*), the world was divided into seven major levels. Spirit-beings (*maiyun*) reside in this universe and their sacredness is relative to their relationship to Ma'heo'o, the creator of all physical and spiritual life in Hestanov. These levels are intersected by the Maiheyuno, a personal spirit residing at each of the cardinal directions. Various animals, birds, and plants are manifestations of these spirit-beings. In Cheyenne religious expression, aspects of these spirit-beings or the spirit-beings themselves are entwined symbolically with plant and animal forms portrayed in Cheyenne ceremonies. Many Cheyenne today view the world's ecological crisis as an end to Hestanov. Christian missionary activity has been continuous among the Cheyenne for a century, especially the Mennonites and Catholics. Today there is a variety of religious beliefs and expressions including Christianity and the American Indian church, although Sacred Arrows (*Mahuts*) and the Medicine Hat (*Isiwun*) remain the most venerated sacred objects.

Religious Practitioners.   Aside from the Keepers of Mahuts and Isiwun and the arrow priests, there were numerous Cheyenne shamans and doctors, each possessing a particular religious or healing power.

Ceremonies.   There were four major religious ceremonies: the renewal of Mahuts, the *Hoxehe-vohomo'ehestotse* (New Life Lodge or Sun Dance), the *Massaum* (Animal Dance), and Isiwun. Mahuts was given to the Cheyenne by their cultural hero, Mutsoyef (Sweet Medicine). The four Sacred Arrows included two "Man Arrows" for warfare and two "Bison Arrows" for hunting. The Arrows were renewed every few years, unless a murder took place or a pledger needed their blessing. Presently, the renewal of the Mahuts, the New Life Lodge, and ceremonies surrounding Isiwun are still performed.

Arts.   Aboriginal arts featured a particular musical style, songs, and an artistic tradition, all important parts of Cheyenne social and ceremonial life. The Cheyenne artistic tradition reflected not only the sacred but the socioeconomic pursuits of men and women. Presently, there are a number of prominent Cheyenne artists, and Cheyenne songs are still performed at various functions.

Medicine.   Disease arose from both natural and supernatural causes. Curing techniques involved the use of herbal and root remedies, ritual purification, the sweat lodge, smoking, prayer, and sometimes surgery. Both men and women were healers. Treatment of sickness was designed to restore the patient not only biologically but spiritually as well. Presently, most Cheyenne use Western clinical medicine to cure afflictions, but native healers are still used by many people.

Death and Afterlife.   Cheyenne believed that death, like disease, could have a natural or spiritual causation. As a cultural phenomenon, death was a spiritual process. At birth, Ma'heo'o provided the child with the "gift of breath/power" (*omotome*) and "spiritual potential" (*mahta'sooma*). These two gifts are developed through life. As a person ages, the process is reversed. Mahta'sooma leaves the body, resulting in behavior and cognitive changes. Next omotome departs, bringing on death. The spirit of the deceased then travels up the long fork of the Milky Way to *Seana*, the camp of the dead. If the dead individual was an outcast, died in a violent accident or by suicide, or was an unredeemed sinner, he or she would travel the "suicide road," the short fork of the Milky Way. Others would return to earth as malevolent spirits. The concern for following the "good life," and so to have a "good death," is still prevalent among the Cheyenne.

Bibliography

Grinnell, George Bird (1923). *The Cheyenne Indians: Their History and Ways of Life.* 2 vols. New Haven: Yale University Press.

Moore, John H. (1987). *The Cheyenne Nation: A Social and Demographic History.* Norman: University of Oklahoma Press.

Schlesier, Karl H. (1987). *The Wolves of Heaven: Cheyenne Shamanism, Ceremonies, and Prehistoric Origins.* Norman: University of Oklahoma Press.

Weist, Tom (1977). *A History of the Cheyenne People.* Billings: Montana Council for Indian Education.

GREGORY R. CAMPBELL

Chickasaw

The Chickasaw are a Muskogean-speaking American Indian group whose aboriginal homeland was located in present-day northeastern Mississippi. The Chickasaw, one of the so-called Five Civilized Tribes, numbered about five thousand in 1600 and about seven thousand in 1980.

By the nineteenth century the expansion of White settlement and resulting pressure on land and animal resources had forced the Chickasaw to abandon hunting and take up farming on a full-time basis. Continued White expansion and desire for the Chickasaws' land slowly pushed the group to give up their lands and migrate to Indian Territory (Oklahoma), a process that was completed by 1832. In 1906 the tribal governments of the Chickasaw and the other Civilized Tribes were dissolved by the federal government. In the 1980s the descendents of the Chickasaw located in Oklahoma numbered approximately seven thousand, and their tribal affairs were overseen by a tribal governor and ten-member advisory council.

The Chickasaw subsisted through a combination of hunting, fishing, gathering, and agriculture. Bison, deer, and bear were the most prized game animals, and hunting expeditions often took the Chickasaw men on long excursions throughout the Mississippi valley region.

Chickasaw society was characterized by a moiety organization, each half of which was divided into a number of exogamous matrilineal clans. Each moiety was headed by a priest whose primary responsibility was to oversee religious ceremonies. Political leadership was vested in a head chief whose position was inherited within the leading clan and who was advised by a council of clan leaders and elders. At the bottom of Chickasaw society was a class of slaves taken in battles with neighboring tribes.

The supreme deity of the Chickasaw was Ababinili, beneath whom there were numerous lesser deities, witches, and evil spirits. The Chickasaw believed that after death those who had led a good life found reward in the heavens, and those who were evil wandered endlessly in a land of witches.

Bibliography

Gibson, Arrell M. (1971). *The Chickasaws.* Norman: University of Oklahoma Press.

Kniffen, Fred B., Hiram F. Gregory, and George A. Stokes

(1987). *The Historic Indian Tribes of Louisiana: From 1542 to the Present*. Baton Rouge: Louisiana State University Press.

Chilcotin

The Chilcotin (Tsilkotin) are an Athapaskan-speaking group who live in the valley region of the Chilcotin River in south-central British Columbia. Their culture is basically of the Subarctic Athabaskan type, but they have been strongly influenced by the culture of the neighboring groups of the Plateau area of northwestern North America. There were seventeen hundred Chilcotin in 1978.

Bibliography

Lane, Robert R. (1981). "Chilcotin." In *Handbook of North American Indians*. Vol. 6, *Subarctic*, edited by June Helm, 402–412. Washington, D.C.: Smithsonian Institution.

Chinook

ETHNONYMS: Cheenook, Tchinouks, Tsniuk

The Chinook are an American Indian group who joined the Chehalis Indians and other tribes of Oregon and Washington in the mid-nineteenth century following the decimation of their tribe by smallpox epidemics in 1782–1783, 1830–1833, and 1853. In the 1970s the descendants of the Chinook resided on or near the Chehalis Indian Reservation in Washington. The Chinook language is classified in the Penutian language phylum. In the late 1700s the Chinook numbered about two thousand and occupied the region of the lower Columbia River and the adjoining coastal area in Oregon and Washington. The Chinook included the Lower Chinook groups (Chinook, Clatsop, and Shoalwater) and the Middle groups (Clackamas, Cathlamet, and Wahkiakum).

Salmon fishing was their principal economic activity, but gathering berries and nuts and hunting deer, elk, and small game were also important. Autonomous villages were led by chiefs, and local society was divided into an upper class of chiefs, shamans, warriors, and traders, a class of commoners, and a slave class. Traditional religious life centered around guardian spirits sought through fasting and prayer in adolescence.

Bibliography

Boas, Franz (1911). *Chinook*. U.S. Bureau of American Ethnology Bulletin no. 40, 559–678. Washington, D.C.

Ruby, Robert H., and John A. Brown (1976). *The Chinook Indians*. Norman: University of Oklahoma Press.

Chipewyan

ETHNONYMS: Orchipoins, Otchipiweons

Orientation

Identification. The Chipewyan are a Subarctic group whose name is derived from a Cree word meaning "pointed skins," a reference to the cut of the caribou-skin hunting shirt traditionally worn by the men. The Chipewyan referred to themselves as "Dene," meaning "human" or "the people."

Location. In aboriginal times Chipewyan territory extended west from Hudson Bay along the Seal River to Lake Athabasca and north above the Arctic Circle to near the mouth of the Coppermine River at Coronation Gulf. During the nineteenth century the Chipewyan abandoned the northernmost parts of this territory while pushing westward to Great Slave Lake and the Slave River and southward to the Athabasca River. In the north this region consists of rolling, boulder-strewn, and lichen-covered hills and valleys interlaced with numerous lakes, rivers, and streams. To the south this barren-ground environment gives way to a spruce-dominated boreal forest transition zone that includes bogs, patches of tundra, and stands of juniper, aspen, and birch.

Demography. In the late eighteenth and early nineteenth centuries the Chipewyan numbered between thirty-five hundred and four thousand, an estimate that probably reflects the effects of smallpox epidemics in 1781–1782 and 1819. In the twentieth century tuberculosis has been a major health problem for the Chipewyan, and they were severely affected by influenza outbreaks in the 1920s and a measles epidemic in 1948. In 1982 the Chipewyan numbered approximately five thousand.

Linguistic Affiliation. Chipewyan is classified in the Northern Athapaskan subfamily of the Athapaskan language family.

History and Cultural Relations

At the beginning of the historic period the native groups neighboring the Chipewyan included Western Woods Cree to the south, Inuit to the north, and Dogrib, Slavey, and Beaver to the west. To the northwest was a regional group of Chipewyan usually identified as the Yellowknife. Aboriginally and in historic times the Inuit and Western Woods Cree were considered enemies. Even today, in settled Cree-Chipewyan communities, ethnic relations are usually strained.

Direct contact with Europeans was initiated in the late seventeenth century when French and English traders encountered Chipewyan women and children who had been taken captive by the Cree. Direct trade with the English was established in 1715, and in 1717 the English established a post at Churchill (Prince of Wales Fort) on Hudson Bay for the purposes of carrying on this trade. In response to the pressures of the fur trade and the desire for European trade goods, during the late eighteenth and early nineteenth centuries some groups of Chipewyan moved permanently into the boreal forest zone, where fur-bearing game was more plentiful. Those groups became known as the Boreal Forest Chipewyan, and those who continued to occupy the forest edge and the barren grounds and hunt caribou became known as the Caribou Eater Chipewyan. In 1846 Roman Catholic missionaries established a mission at Lake Isle à la Cross, and in 1912 an Anglican mission was founded at Churchill.

In 1899 and 1907 treaties with the Dominion of Canada extinguished Chipewyan land titles in exchange for annuity payments and other considerations. Many of the lifeways of the early-contact period persisted among the Caribou Eater Chipewyan well into the twentieth century. During the 1950s and 1960s, however, repeated government efforts to relocate, settle, and acculturate these traditional Chipewyan resulted in rapid and disruptive culture change. Nevertheless, even in the 1970s some Chipewyan still were committed to the caribou-hunting way of life.

Settlements

The Chipewyan were highly mobile, with the movement and dispersal of camps and hunting groups determined by the nature and availability of resources, especially caribou. In the winter and early spring camps were located at elevated points on the forest edge in areas frequented by the caribou. In the summer, when caribou were sometimes scarce, camps were located near lakes and streams containing fish. Trade with Europeans and the establishment of European trading posts undermined the traditional pattern of mobility and gradually led to permanent clustered settlements. In the twentieth century this trend has been reinforced by government relocation programs, the establishment of schools and other services, increased commerce, and limited wage labor opportunities. The traditional dwelling was a conical structure built of a framework of wooden poles covered with sewn caribou skins. As the settlement pattern became more permanent, the traditional dwellings were replaced by canvas tents and log homes, which were still common in the 1970s.

Economy

Subsistence and Commercial Activities. The seasonal round of economic activities in aboriginal and early-contact times centered on the movement of the caribou herds. In the spring when the herds moved out of the boreal forest to their breeding grounds on the tundra and in the late autumn when they returned, local and regional bands coalesced and situated themselves along the migration routes and killed large numbers of caribou in communal hunts. Traditionally, hunting parties employed the chute and pound method and killed the caribou with spears and arrows. In the summer on the tundra and in the winter in the boreal forest the herds dispersed and were pursued in small, scattered hunting groups;

at these times of the year fishing with nets, weirs, spears, bows and arrows, and hook and line was also an important subsistence activity. Other animals hunted included ducks, geese, bears, beaver, squirrels, and wolverines. Fur trapping from late autumn through early winter was added to the aboriginal subsistence pattern after the Chipewyan became involved in the European trade. The Boreal Forest Chipewyan, as a consequence of involvement in fur trade, abandoned seasonal migrations to the barren grounds in search of caribou and hunted moose and woodland caribou instead. In the 1960s limited wage labor and commercial hunting and fishing became important factors in the Chipewyan economy.

Industrial Arts. Besides being the main source of food, the caribou also provided the raw material for hunting and fishing equipment, lodge coverings, clothing, bedding, and snowshoe webbing. This material culture complex was considerably modified quickly by the introduction of European firearms and metal tools. Dogs are used as beasts of burden.

Trade. The Chipewyan were not at first heavily involved in the fur trade owing to the scarcity of fur-bearing game in their territory. Nevertheless, they did play an active middleman role in connecting European traders with native groups farther west, a role that continued to earn them considerable profits into the early nineteenth century.

Division of Labor. Men's work was concerned primarily with hunting and fishing. Women erected lodges, set and broke camp, hauled supplies, prepared fires and food, prepared skins, made clothing, dried meat, cared for children, snared small game, and gathered plant foods. The hard lot of women reflected their low status in Chipewyan society.

Land Tenure. In aboriginal and early-contact times regional bands were associated with the vaguely defined wintering territories and migration routes of different caribou herds. Involvement in the fur trade led to the development of a concept of land use rights in trapping areas, but not to actual land ownership. Land ownership was made more concrete in 1958 when the Manitoba government required the registration of trap lines.

Kinship

Kin Groups and Descent. Traditionally, bilateral personal kindreds were the basis for networks of cooperation and sharing.

Kinship Terminology. Kinship terminology has changed from Iroquois to the Eskimo type as a consequence of European contact and acculturation.

Marriage and Family

Marriage. First marriages were arranged by parents, and girls were often betrothed in childhood. Patrilateral cross-cousin marriage may have been preferred. Polygyny, usually of a sororal type, was permitted and occurred most often among group leaders and skilled hunters. In aboriginal and early-contact times marriage was unaccompanied by ceremony, but today is attended by a Roman Catholic service. In the past the newly married couple resided with the bride's family until the birth of their first child, at which time they might take up residence with the husband's family. In more recent times bilocal and neolocal residence patterns have become prevalent.

The option of divorce was available to both husband and wife, but was rarely exercised. Divorce is rare among present-day Chipewyan as well.

Domestic Unit. In the historic period and probably in aboriginal times as well, the basic unit of social organization was the hunting group, consisting of a male head and his wife, their unmarried children, and, depending on the male head's hunting skill and influence, their married children and their families. Throughout the seasonal round of subsistence activities, this basic unit remained intact. Involvement in the fur trade, sedentization, and acculturation undermined this traditional pattern and in the twentieth century has resulted in greater emphasis on the nuclear family. Even among those Chipewyan who continue to hunt and trap, the traditional pattern has been broken as men leave their families behind in the villages and hunt alone or in small groups.

Inheritance. In aboriginal and early contact times an individual's property was destroyed at death. Today property is divided evenly between the deceased's survivors.

Socialization. As in adult life, the work responsibilities of adolescents and children fell most heavily on females. There was no rite of initiation recognizing puberty or adulthood for males; for females first menses was marked by a period of isolation. Among contemporary Chipewyan, boys and girls are allowed to play together until about age ten and then are kept apart in separate play groups.

Sociopolitical Organization

Social Organization. Aboriginally, hunting groups linked by ties of marriage and descent constituted local bands averaging between fifty and sixty persons. Several local bands, in turn, made up regional bands of two hundred to four hundred persons who identified with particular caribou wintering areas and migration routes. In the mid-nineteenth century five such regional bands existed. The organization of local and regional bands remained fairly well intact until the mid-twentieth century when increasing sedentization resulted in the deterioration of larger group identity and solidarity.

Political Organization. Positions of leadership embodying power and authority were not present among the aboriginal and early-contact Chipewyan; however, individuals with unique proven ability were accorded respect and influence. Such men were often hunting group and band leaders. After contact, participation in the fur trade and the desire of Europeans to deal with groups rather than individuals led to the development of the trading chief whose responsibility it was to command small expeditions to European trading posts. In 1900 the Canadian government created the position of chief in order to facilitate its official dealings with the Chipewyan. Until the 1930s this elected position was occupied by respected leaders, but since that time the position has lost much of its influence as Chipewyan have tended to interact with the government on a more individual basis.

Conflict and Social Control. In the past the fluidity of local and regional band structure served to diffuse group tensions. This outlet, however, has become increasingly less available as the Chipewyan have settled in permanent villages. In the mid-twentieth century the tensions resulting from settled life and the concentration of large groups of people from different local bands have been exacerbated by the breakdown of traditional patterns of sharing and cooperation under the influence of a cash economy. In response to these tensions, some families have returned to the more nomadic hunting and trapping way of life in the bush.

Religion and Expressive Culture

Religious Beliefs. Chipewyan religious beliefs were based on the idea of power being given to human beings in dreams by animal spirits. This power could be used to cure sickness or control game and other natural phenomena and was a factor in leadership. Today most Chipewyan are practicing Roman Catholics.

Religious Practitioners. Shamans, in particular, were believed to possess supernatural powers.

Arts. Drums are the only musical instruments known to have existed in aboriginal times.

Medicine. Illness was believed to be the result of hostile, usually non-Chipewyan sorcerers. In curing ceremonies the shaman sang and danced to summon his spirit helpers. It was believed, however, that he would be successful only if his powers exceeded those of the sorcerer causing the sickness.

Death and Afterlife. Except in the case of the very old, death, like illness, was thought to be the work of a hostile sorcerer. The Chipewyan believed that the dead are reincarnated and return to earth as men or wolves and often with supernatural powers. In aboriginal and early-contact times hunting groups abandoned their camp after a member's death and left the deceased unburied.

Bibliography

Birket-Smith, Kaj (1930). _Contributions to Chipewyan Ethnology_. Translated by W. E. Calvert. Report of the Fifth Thule Expedition, 1921–24. Vol. 6, Pt. 3. Copenhagen, Denmark.

Bone, Robert M., Earl N. Shannon, and Stewart Ruby (1973). _The Chipewyan of the Stony Rapids Region: A Study of the Changing World with Special Attention Focused upon Caribou_. University of Saskatchewan, Institute of Northern Studies, Maudsley Memoir no. 1. Saskatoon, Canada.

Oswalt, Wendell H. (1966). "Chipewyan: Hunters and Fishermen of the Subarctic." In _This Land Was Theirs: A Study of the North American Indian_, 17–63. New York: John Wiley.

Smith, James G. E. (1981). "Chipewyan." In _Handbook of North American Indians_. Vol. 6, edited by June Helm, 271–284. Washington, D.C.: Smithsonian Institution.

VanStone, James W. (1965). _The Changing Culture of the Snowdrift Chipewyan_. National Museum of Canada Bulletin no. 209. Anthropological Series, no. 74. Ottawa.

GERALD F. REID

Chiricahua

ETHNONYM: Aiaho

The Chiricahua are an Athapaskan-speaking American Indian group whose traditional homeland was located in present-day southeastern Arizona, southern New Mexico, southwestern Texas, and the adjacent areas of northern Mexico. At the beginning of the nineteenth century they numbered about one thousand.

During the latter half of that century the Chiricahua engaged in an extended period of warfare with the United States that finally ended in 1886 when they surrendered and began serving a twenty-seven-year term as prisoners of war in Indian Territory (Oklahoma). In 1913 they were freed and given the choice of remaining in Oklahoma or relocating to the Mescalero Reservation in southern New Mexico. In the 1980s about five hundred Chiricahua were living in Oklahoma and an indeterminate, but small number were living with Mescalero and Lipan Apache on the Mescalero Reservation. The tribal government on this reservation consists of an elected president, vice president, and an eight-member advisory council.

Originally, the Chiricahua earned their subsistence primarily through hunting and gathering, but in later historic times they also practiced some agriculture. Deer, taken with bows and arrows, were the most important game animals.

Chiricahua society was organized into three bands, each of which was composed of several extended families. Formal political authority extended no further than the level of band leaders who wielded influence on the basis of their recognized wisdom and skill in warfare. The Chiricahua believed in numerous supernatural beings; religious leadership was provided by male and female shamans who specialized in certain types of ceremonies and cures.

See also Mescalero Apache

Bibliography

Betzinez, John, with Wilbur Sturtevant (1987). *I Fought with Geronimo*. Lincoln: University of Nebraska Press.

Opler, Morris E. (1965). *An Apache Life-Way*. New York: Cooper Square Publishers.

Chitimacha

The Chitimacha (Shetinasha) live in southern and southwestern Louisiana, principally on the Chitimacha Indian Reservation on Grand Lake near Charenton, Louisiana. In the 1980s they spoke a language isolate in the Macro-Algonkian phylum and numbered about six hundred.

Bibliography

Hoover, Herbert T. (1975). *The Chitimacha People*. Phoenix, Ariz.: Indian Tribal Series.

Stouff, Faye, and W. Bradley Twitty (1971). *Sacred Chitimacha Indian Beliefs*. Pompano Beach, Fla.: Twitty & Twitty.

Choctaw

ETHNONYMS: Chacktaws, Chaquita, Chat-Kas, Tchatakes, Tchiactas

Orientation

Identification. The Choctaw are an American Indian group who lived aboriginally in Mississippi. "Chahta," the Choctaw's name for themselves, is probably a term of native origin derived from *Hacha Hatak*, "River People."

Location. In the eighteenth century, the Choctaw population was centered in central and southern Mississippi. Most Choctaw now live in Oklahoma and Mississippi.

Demography. Historically, the Choctaw were one of the largest tribes in the Southeast. In spite of major population losses through warfare and disease in the early historical period, the population in 1831 was 19,554. In 1980, there were 6,000 Choctaw in Mississippi and 10,000 in Oklahoma. Over 100,000 people in Oklahoma claim some Choctaw ancestry, however. Small numbers of Choctaw have migrated to urban areas in Texas, California, and Illinois.

Linguistic Affiliation. The Choctaw language belongs to the Muskogean family, which also includes Creek and Chickasaw.

History and Cultural Relations

Choctaw origin legends describe a migration of the Choctaw and Chickasaw from farther west, but there is no known archaeological evidence for this. Native groups bordering the Choctaw territory at the time of European contact included the Creek east of the Tombigbee River, the Chickasaw in northern Mississippi, and the Natchez to the west on the Mississippi River. Along the Gulf Coast were closely related Choctaw-speaking tribes: the Pascagoula, the Acolapissa, and the Bayogoula. Choctaw relations with other major tribes were characterized by customary warfare associated with the receiving of young males into adulthood.

The first written account of the Choctaw is in the chronicles of the Hernando de Soto expedition in 1540. Permanent European contact began with French settlements on the Gulf Coast in 1699. The Choctaw were rapidly plunged into a complicated colonial rivalry as European powers sought to utilize Indian allies to carry out their territorial designs and to profit from the trade in guns, deerskins, and slaves. The Choctaw allied with the French operating from New Orleans in efforts to get European goods as well as guns to protect themselves from the English and their allies. With the ending of colonial rivalry and the establishment of the American nation, warfare was curtailed.

The Choctaw joined with the United States in the War of 1812 against their traditional enemies, the Creeks, and the British. But the Treaty of Fort Adams in 1801 had begun a pattern of progressive loss of Choctaw land, which resulted in removal thirty years later. In each treaty, the Choctaw were forced to cede more land and more prerogatives to the United States. Choctaw leaders such as Pushmataha were aware of the threat imposed by the growing number of White settlers in the Southeast and consciously decided to adopt White ways as a means of survival. Missionaries established schools in response to a Choctaw request. With the spread of literacy, the Choctaw adopted formal written rules passed in district councils in the place of customary law. But these changes did not affect the demand for Indian removal that resulted in the Treaty of Dancing Rabbit Creek in 1831 requiring the removal of the Choctaw to Oklahoma.

Under this treaty, Choctaws could elect to remain in Mississippi with individually owned lands, but when large numbers attempted to use this provision, the treaty agent deliberately failed to record their claims. In the coming years, the remaining Choctaw were robbed of their possessions, and most eventually were forced to go to Oklahoma. Some Choctaw remained as subsistence farmers on unoccupied marginal lands in east central Mississippi. The descendants of these two groups compose the current Oklahoma and Mississippi Choctaw populations.

Settlements

The basic Choctaw social unit was the town, usually located along tributaries of major rivers. Approximately ninety towns were divided into three major districts clustered in the upper reaches of the Pearl River, the western tributaries of the Tombigbee River, and the Chickasawhay River in southern Mississippi. Settlements ranged from fifty to five hundred people. Larger towns were fortified and had a physical center including a council house and field for stickball. These larger towns served as social, economic, and religious centers for surrounding settlements. With the end of colonial warfare, the population dispersed from the towns and from the centers of the districts. Following removal to Oklahoma, the more acculturated mixed-blood Choctaw settled in the rich bottomlands, while the more traditional Choctaw settled in isolated communities in hill country. The Mississippi Choctaw remained on marginal land protected by hills and swamps. The purchase of lands for the current Mississippi Choctaw Reservation centered on lands where Choctaw were located, resulting in a dispersed pattern of six major reservation communities. In Oklahoma, the Choctaw are concentrated in what was the old Choctaw Nation in southeastern Oklahoma. Here traditional Choctaw rural communities still exist on more marginal lands.

The aboriginal Choctaw house was of wattle-and-daub construction, oval or square, with a single door, no windows, and a steeply sloping roof of thatch. This was usually accompanied by one or more open roofed structures, referred to as summer houses, and by granaries. In this century, most rural Choctaw have lived in poorly constructed frame houses, but public housing programs have made great improvements.

Economy

Subsistence and Commercial Activities. In the latter half of the eighteenth century the Choctaw were among the most accomplished farmers in the Southeast, but this was only an intensification of the basic Southeastern pattern of maize, beans, and squash cultivation supplemented by hunting, fishing, and collecting. The arrival of Europeans brought additional vegetables, cattle, horses, and cotton. During the eighteenth century the trade in deer skins resulted in first an expansion of hunting and then an increase in agriculture and cattle as the deer population declined. In the nineteenth and early twentieth centuries, rural Choctaw remained subsistence farmers, often in debt to the cotton sharecropping system. Agriculture was supplemented by work in forestry and agricultural day labor. In the 1970s and 1980s, the Mississippi Choctaw successfully established tribal industries including construction and electronic component and greeting card assembly. Lacking a reservation land base, the Oklahoma Choctaw have been less successful in establishing economic enterprises and are largely dependent on employment in forestry, seasonal wage work, and governmental assistance.

Industrial Arts. Aboriginal crafts included pottery, carving of wood, stone, and shell, and basket and textile weaving. Today basket weaving continues among the Choctaw, but the number of skilled craftspeople is declining because of limited markets. Making traditional nineteenth-century Choctaw clothing to wear at special events remains important.

Trade. The Choctaw participated in the complex of aboriginal trade linking the shell of the coastal areas with stone and related products of the interior. Competition over the trade for deerskins and guns was a major factor in eighteenth-century Choctaw affairs. By the nineteenth century, the replacement of Indians by African slaves and the decline in deer led to an expansion of peaceful trade in agricultural products and cattle.

Division of Labor. Aboriginally, women and children cared for the crops, while the men cleared fields and helped with planting and harvesting. Women prepared food, made clothes, pottery, and baskets, and cared for the children. Men hunted, built houses, and performed ritual activities. Both women and men practiced medicine. Men became more involved in agriculture with the use of domesticated animals for cultivating crops, but subsistence farming involved both men and women in major shared activities. With the rise of an industrial economy, men and women were able to gain employment outside the home.

Land Tenure. Aboriginally, individual ownership was limited to use rights for homesites and lands under cultivation or improvement. Although men cleared land and built houses, these were the property of the wife and her female descendants as long as the land and house were being utilized. Those Choctaw remaining after removal had to register land in the name of the male head of household, but most of these land titles were quickly lost, leaving the Mississippi Choctaw largely without land until the establishment of the Choctaw Agency in 1918. The reservation is held by the federal government as trustee for the Mississippi Choctaw. Individual homesites are allocated by the Tribal Council. In the Choctaw Nation in Oklahoma, the traditional land use patterns were lost with the abolishment of the Choctaw Nation and allocation of Choctaw lands to individuals by the U.S. government. Most of this land soon passed to White ownership leaving the Oklahoma Choctaw without a reservation land base.

Kinship

Kin Groups and Descent.   Choctaw society was divided into two matrilineal exogamous moieties and six matrilineal clans. The remaining kinship unit was the locality group similar to the "house names" of the Chickasaw. Members of different clans lived together in the same town. But since inheritance rules followed the female line, it is probable that residency was matrilocal. With the disruption of removal and increasing White contact, the clan system was undermined, and matrilineality was largely replaced by patrilineality.

Kinship Terminology.   Traditional terminology followed the Crow system.

Marriage and Family

Marriage.   In the traditional marriage system, exogamy applied to the matrilineally based moieties. Marriages were usually monogamous, but polygyny was permitted. Marriage required the consent of the bride and her mother, and involved a ceremony involving members of both kinship groups. Divorce was common and could be obtained easily by either party.

Domestic Unit.   Until this century extended families were common. While the nuclear family predominates, three-generation families often occur because of poverty and illegitimacy.

Inheritance.   Traditionally, all property except individual personal property passed through the female line. After the abolishment of Choctaw governments in Mississippi in 1830 and Oklahoma in 1906, patrilineal patterns of inheritance came to dominate.

Socialization.   Children are raised permissively with little direct punishment or direct orders. Ridicule, ignoring, and threat of external forces are used to discipline children. Direct aggression and hostility are discouraged. Parents encourage their children to continue their education, but such encouragement rarely is expressed directly or forcefully.

Sociopolitical Organization

Social Organization.   Choctaw social organization was based on two geographic units: the three districts and ninety towns, and three social units: moieties, clans, and locality groups. The relationships among these units are not completely clear. Early descriptions of the Choctaw show a confusion of names of geographic division, moieties, clans, and locality groups. At all levels, leadership was by older proven warriors called "beloved" men.

Political Organization.   The two matrilineal exogamous moieties of the Choctaw resemble the White, or peace, moiety and the Red, or war, moiety of other Southeastern tribes. The moiety and clan divisions were basic to kinship, ceremony, and political affairs. The heads of respective clans were

responsible for adjudicating disputes. If the principal men in two divisions could not agree on the outcome of a case, it was referred to the leading men of the next larger divisions. Major officials within a town were selected from the leaders of the local groups within the town. Each town had a chief who, with his spokesman, supervised civil affairs and ceremonies. A war chief and his assistants led the men in time of war. The leadership pattern at the town level was duplicated at the district level. Early in the eighteenth century there may have been a central district and head chief for the tribe as a whole, but if so this had been abandoned by midcentury as a result of civil strife. The primary means of achieving consensus on major courses of action was the council. District councils were called by the district chief, and national councils were called by the three district chiefs acting jointly. In 1834, the Choctaw adopted a constitution for the Choctaw Nation in Oklahoma that was in force until the Choctaw Nation was abolished as a territorial government by the U.S. Congress in 1906. Nevertheless, the Choctaw Nation of Oklahoma continues to exist as a nonterritorial organization conducting activities and enterprises for the Choctaw there. The remaining Mississippi Choctaw did not adopt a constitution until 1945, but since then they have operated a tribal government with jurisdiction over the reservation lands in Mississippi.

Social Control.   Avoiding direct conflict, gossip, and avoidance have been important forms of social control. Witchcraft declined in importance in the eighteenth century. Tribal judicial authority was ended in Mississippi with removal, and in Oklahoma with the abolishment of the Choctaw Nation in 1906. But local judicial control under tribal courts was reestablished on the Mississippi Choctaw reservations in 1978 through a ruling of the U.S. Supreme Court.

Conflict.   In the eighteenth century the Choctaw were divided over the proper relationship with European powers. In the nineteenth and twentieth centuries the expansion of the money economy resulted in conflicts over participation in the White-dominated market economy. While this social class discord involved conflict between mixed-bloods and full-bloods in Mississippi prior to removal and later in Oklahoma, the same dissension exists among the predominantly full-blood Mississippi Choctaw. For the latter a major external conflict arose from the acute racism of surrounding White society, which did not noticeably improve until the 1970s.

Religion and Expressive Culture

Religious Beliefs.   Choctaw traditional religion was largely unrecorded before early nineteenth-century Christian missionaries influenced traditional practices. The Choctaw maintain a deep faith in supernatural forces linking humans and other living creatures. The importance of maintaining harmony with nature, fellowmen, and the supernatural world is central to Choctaw beliefs. The status of a supreme being in traditional Choctaw religion prior to the spread of Christianity is not clear. Their belief in numerous animal and anthropomorphic spirits who influenced human affairs continued, however, after the coming of Christianity. Today the Baptist denomination predominates among Choctaw in Oklahoma and Mississippi.

Religious Practitioners. In aboriginal times, the influence of Choctaw prophets and doctors was considerable, and the belief in witchcraft was strong. By the nineteenth century, the influence of Christian Choctaw pastors was important in most Choctaw communities in Oklahoma and Mississippi.

Ceremonies. Choctaw ceremonies were similar to other Southeastern tribes, with the Green Corn ceremonies being most important. Observers noted that the Choctaw held fewer religious ceremonies and more social dances than their neighbors. Both dances and ceremonies were closely associated with the very popular stickball game similar to lacrosse.

Arts. In addition to their industrial arts, the Choctaw were well known for singing and storytelling. In addition to traditional music, the Choctaw enjoy country music.

Medicine. The Choctaw believe serious persistent illnesses to be a product of spiritual evil often associated with witchcraft. Curing consisted of herbal medicines, ritual purifications, and the enlistment of spirit helpers to drive out evil forces. Western clinical medicine is generally used today, but native Choctaw doctors are still consulted.

Death and Afterlife. Death, like disease, could be the result of either natural or supernatural forces. Choctaw believed in an afterworld to which spirits of the dead go and in which individuals experience reward or punishment depending on their life on earth. Funeral ceremonies are the most important life cycle ritual.

Bibliography

Debo, Angie (1934). _The Rise and Fall of the Choctaw Republic._ Norman: University of Oklahoma Press.

DeRosier, Arthur H., Jr. (1970). _The Removal of the Choctaw Indians._ Knoxville: University of Tennessee Press.

Kidwell, Clara S., and Charles Roberts (1981). _The Choctaws: A Critical Bibliography._ Bloomington: Indiana University Press.

Peterson, John H. (1979). "Three Efforts at Development among the Choctaws of Mississippi." In _The Southeastern Indians since Removal,_ edited by Walter L. Williams, 142–153. Athens: University of Georgia Press.

Swanton, John R. (1931). _Source Material for the Social and Ceremonial Life of the Choctaw Indians._ U.S. Bureau of American Ethnology Bulletin no. 103. Washington, D.C.

JOHN H. PETERSON

Chumash

ETHNONYM: Santa Barbara Indians

The Chumash are a Hokan-speaking American Indian group who in the late eighteenth century was located in present-day southern coastal California near Santa Barbara and numbered between ten thousand and eighteen thousand. The Chumash were primarily gatherers whose food staple was the acorn. In addition, inland groups hunted deer and rabbits, while coastal groups fished, hunted waterfowl, and harvested shellfish.

The Chumash were missionized by the Spanish during the late 1700s and thereafter were divided into six local groups, each associated with a specific mission station and led by a chief who inherited his position. Shamans cured the sick with a combination of herbal medicines and powers obtained from guardian spirits. Missionization was complete by the beginning of the nineteenth century and was accompanied by a dramatic decline in the population as a result of disease. In 1980 an unknown number of Chumash were assimilated into the general population of southern California, while about 120 of their number lived on the small Santa Ynez Indian Reservation near Santa Barbara. The tribal government on the reservation consists of a general council of all members twenty-one years of age or older and an elected five-member business council.

Bibliography

Landberg, Leif C. W. (1965). _The Chumash Indians of Southern California._ Los Angeles: Southwest Museum.

McCall, Lynn, and Rosalind Perry (1986). _California's Chumash Indians._ Santa Barbara, Calif.: John Daniel, Publisher.

Coast Miwok

The Coast Miwok (Olamentke), including the Lake Miwok, lived on the California coast north of San Francisco and inland to Clear Lake. They spoke languages of the Miwok family of the Penutian phylum. There are a few descendants of the Coast Miwok still living in California, but the culture has disappeared.
See also Miwok

Bibliography

Callaghan, Catherine A. (1978). "Lake Miwok." In _Handbook of North American Indians._ Vol. 8, _California,_ edited by Robert F. Heizer, 264–273. Washington, D.C.: Smithsonian Institution.

Kelly, Isabel (1978). "Coast Miwok." In *Handbook of North American Indians*. Vol. 8, *California*, edited by Robert F. Heizer, 414–425. Washington, D.C.: Smithsonian Institution.

Cocopa

ETHNONYMS: Cocapa, Cocopah, Cucapá, Kokwapá

The Cocapa are a Yuman language–speaking group in the lower Colorado River region and its delta in southwestern Arizona and southeastern California, and northwestern Sonora and northeastern Baja California Norte in Mexico. The Cocopa continue to maintain their identity as an ethnic group, although many elements of their material culture have disappeared in the delta because of upstream diversions and dam construction. The U.S. Cocopa have a tribal council consisting of five members and a chairman with jurisdiction over the Cocopah Indian Reservation. One group of Mexican Cocopa still lives in the area of the Hardy River in Baja California Norte. Others live in Sonora—most of these very conservative Indians being in Pozos de Arvizu. There were about eight hundred Cocopa living in the United States and Mexico in 1980.

Contact with Europeans began early with Hernando de Alarcón and Melchior Diaz noting a heavy Indian population at the river mouth in 1540. There was intermittent contact with Spanish missionaries, with the Cocopa resisting at least one attempt at missionization. After the Gadsden Purchase in 1853, which put the international boundary in the middle of the Cocopa territory, the Cocopa became heavily involved in the river trade until the end of the nineteenth century. In 1917, a reservation was established near Somerton, Arizona, but little happened with the government until 1961 when development programs began. Similar programs exist in Mexico. Most Cocopa are now trilingual in Cocopa, English, and Spanish.

The Colorado River provided ample moisture, particularly with the summer floods. During the winter months food was scarce. After the floodwaters receded the Cocopa planted maize, squash, and beans, some of which was irrigated. Prior to 1900, mesquite was probably the most important wild food, supplemented by screw beans, cattail pollen, tule roots, and grass seeds. Animals hunted included deer, wild boar, rabbits, dove, quail, and duck. American Cocopa can no longer count on fish as a food owing to a lack of river access, but Mexican Cocopa still rely on them heavily.

The Cocopa have patrilineal, exogamous, nonlocalized, nonautonomous clans or lineages. Each is associated with a particular totem (plant, animal, natural phenomenon). Leaders are selected for their ability to speak well and to be counselors to the people. Elaborate rites and ceremonies were associated with death and the dead, with cremation of the body and personal possessions usually being involved. Cremation of the corpse is now illegal in Mexico, but still followed in the United States.

Bibliography

Gifford, Edward Winslow (1933). *The Cocopa*. University of California Publications in American Archaeology and Ethnology, 31(5), 257–334. Berkeley.

Kelly, William H. (1977). *Cocopa Ethnography*. Anthropological Papers of the University of Arizona, no. 29. Tucson, Ariz.: University of Arizona Press.

Williams, Anita Alvarez de (1983). "Cocopa." In *Handbook of North American Indians*. Vol. 10, *Southwest*, edited by Alfonso Ortiz, 99-112. Washington, D.C.: Smithsonian Institution.

Coeur D'Alène

The Coeur d'Alène (Skitswish, Schitzui) lived around the headwaters of the Spokane River and Coeur d'Alène Lake in northern Idaho in the 1700s, and numbered about three thousand. They speak an Interior Salish language and number about eight hundred on or near the Coeur d'Alène Indian Reservation in northern Idaho, where they have been largely assimilated into American society.

Bibliography

Teit, James A. (1930). *The Salishan Tribes of the Western Plateaus*. U.S. Bureau of American Ethnology, 45th Annual Report (1927-1928), 37-197. Washington, D.C.

Columbia

The Columbia (Middle Columbia Salish, Sinkiuse), including the Chelan, Methow, Sinkakaius (Sinkaquaiius), and Wenatchi (Pisquow, Moses' Columbia), lived in northwestern Washington from the Columbia River region to the Cascades Range and from Wenatchee north to the Canadian border. They speak an Interior Salish language, probably number about two hundred, and live with other groups on Colville Indian Reservation in Washington.

Bibliography

Teit, James A. (1928). *The Middle Columbia Salish*. University of Washington Publications in Anthropology 2:83–128. Seattle.

Comanche

ETHNONYMS: Nimenim, Numinu, Numu, Padouca, Snake Indians, Tête Pelée

In historical times, the Comanche were a nomadic bison-hunting tribe dominating the southern and southwestern Great Plains and famous for their war exploits against the Mexican and U.S. armies, the state of Texas, and other tribes. They spoke a Central Numic language closely related to those spoken by the Eastern Shoshone, Northern Shoshone, and Western Shoshone. They apparently separated from other Shoshonean groups in Wyoming in the seventeenth century, moving to the plains area of southeastern Wyoming and eastern Colorado, and later spreading into western Oklahoma, Texas, eastern New Mexico, and northern Mexico, as far south as Zacatecas and Durango. In the late eighteenth century they were allied with the Kiowa and have remained close to them to the present day. During the first half of the nineteenth century there was continual strife with Mexicans, Texans, and the U.S. Army. In 1867 the Medicine Lodge Treaty with the United States was signed and the Comanche, along with the Kiowa and Kiowa-Apache moved to a reservation (now a federal trust area) in southwest Oklahoma, where they remain today. The tribe's present constitution and bylaws were approved by the Bureau of Indian Affairs in 1966, being represented as a tribe on the Kiowa-Comanche-Apache Intertribal Business Committee. Of a total of about nine thousand Comanche noted in the 1980 census, about thirty-six hundred lived in the trust area.

Before being placed on the reservation, the Comanche in historical times were nomadic bison hunters organized into numerous bands, of which five were always prominent—the Quahadi (Kwahadi), the Penateka (Penande), the Nokoni (Detsanayuka), the Yamparika, and the Kotsoteka. The bands were nearly autonomous and interconnections were very loose. Bison were the subsistence mainstay from the time the Comanche moved onto the plains. After the horse was acquired, they usually staged communal hunts under the direction of a hunt leader. Bison were shot with bows and arrows (later with rifles), stabbed with lances, or sometimes driven over a cliff. Men did the hunting and women the butchering. Other game hunted included elk, deer, black bear, antelope, and, at times, wild horses. In times of necessity, their own horses would supply the food. Numerous wild plants were collected by the women, and agricultural products could be traded for with other tribes. Today they are mainly agriculturalists. The bison-hide-covered tipi was the basic dwelling, with wooden frame bungalows and houses replacing them in modern times.

Descent was bilateral with no descent groups being present. Kinship terminology for cousins was Hawaiian in type. Marriage was usually endogamous within the band community with uxorilocal postmarital residence. The husband was obliged to provide food for his wife's parents. Polygyny, often sororal, was practiced to a high degree, with the levirate also being present. Children were cherished, although abnormal babies were abandoned, as very often were one or both of a set of twins. Grandparents, especially grandmothers, played a central role in the rearing of children.

As noted above, the political structure was loosely organized, but each band had an elected nonhereditary chief. The most famous of these was Quanah Parker (1845–1911) who led the Comanche on the reservation from the 1870s until his death. Comanche religious practice was very individualistic, with emphasis being laid on the male vision quest. The quest gave power to individuals but entailed restrictive practices and taboos. There were no priests and few group ceremonies. The Comanche believed in a creator spirit and its counterpart, an evil spirit, and accepted the Sun, the Earth, and the Moon as deities. The religion was animistic with natural objects and animal spirits (except for dogs and horses) having various powers. Medicine men served as intermediaries and helpers with the spirits and also served practically as curers. The Comanche had few ceremonies, but had developed or practiced the Beaver Ceremony and the Eagle Dance. Unlike most of the other Plains tribes, they never accepted the Sun Dance.

Bibliography

Cash, Joseph H., and Gerald W. Wolff (1976). *The Comanche People*. Phoenix, Ariz.: Indian Tribal Series.

Hoebel, E. Adamson (1940). *The Political Organization and Law-ways of the Comanche Indians*. American Anthropological Association, Memoir 54. Menasha, Wis.

Wallace, Ernest, and E. Adamson Hoebel (1952). *The Comanches: Lords of the South Plains*. Norman: University of Oklahoma Press.

Comox

ETHNONYM: Coast Salish

Comox is the language spoken by the Comox, Homalco, Klahoose, and Sliammon American Indians of British Columbia. The Comox were located on the east coast of Vancouver Island; the one hundred or so remaining Comox currently reside on or near the Comox Indian Reserve in Comox Harbor. The Homalco, Klahoose, and Sliammon were located on both coasts of the northern Strait of Georgia in British Columbia. Today, these three groups, numbering about eight hundred, reside primarily on the Sliammon Indian Reserve. Comox is a Coast Salish language. The Comox spoke the island dialect; the other three groups speak the mainland dialect. These three groups refer to themselves by their respective group names rather than "Comox." The Comox on Vancouver Island were largely absorbed by the Lekwiltok, a Kwakiutl tribe, and are now essentially extinct as a culture. Culturally, the Comox were a transitional group between the other Coast Salish groups to the south and the Kwakiutl to the north.

First European contact was with Spanish explorers in the mid-seventeenth century, though sustained contact did not begin until 1843, leading to depopulation and relocations. The traditional and, to a large extent, the modern economy is based on the sea. Salmon fishing was the most important activity, supplemented by shellfish gathering, deer hunting, birding, plant gathering, and other activities. The Comox culture displayed many features typical of Northwest Coast groups—permanent coastal villages, plank houses, large wooden canoes, totem poles, potlatching, trade with interior groups, and social classes. The extended patrilineal family was the primary kinship group. Traditional religious beliefs centered on the acquisition and help of individual guardian spirits and curing powers of the shaman. Today most Comox are Roman Catholics.

Bibliography

Barnett, Homer G. (1944). *The Coast Salish Indians of British Columbia.* Eugene: University of Oregon Press.

Kennedy, Dorothy, and Randy Bouchard (1983). *Sliammon Life, Sliammon Lands.* Vancouver: Talonbooks.

Copper Eskimo

ETHNONYMS: Kidlineks, Killinirmiut, Nagyuktogmiut, Qidliniks

Orientation

Identification. The people of the Canadian Arctic most often referred to as "Copper Eskimos" had no name for themselves as a whole group, but rather referred only to local groups. All names for the entire population are those used by outsiders. Their nearest neighbors to the west, the Mackenzie Eskimo, called them "Nagyuktogmiut" (the people of the caribou antler). Their eastern neighbors, the Netsilik Inuit, called them "Killinirmiut" (also rendered "Kidlineks" or "Qidliniks," people of the boundary). The American explorer Schwatka appears to have first used "Copper Eskimo," an association clearly based on the deposits of copper in their region and their use of copper implements. Recently some anthropologists and popular writers have used "Copper Inuit."

Location. The Copper Eskimo occupied the coastal and adjoining inland regions of much of Victoria Island and the opposite shores of the Canadian Arctic mainland. Some also

hunted off the southeastern shores of Banks Island. Extremes of their normal hunting range were 66° to 72° N and 101° to 122° W. Temperatures for the coldest month, February, average from −25° to −30° F and almost all Copper Eskimo country lies north of the July 50° F isotherm. Gulfs and straits are ice-free for only about three months of the year and snow covers the ground usually from some time in September until June. Although not a region of extremely high winds, the frequent storms pack the snow firmly throughout winter. The sun remains below the horizon for varying periods around the winter solstice and there are also substantial periods of continuous daylight. Much of the treeless land is flat with numerous lakes. Several large rivers reach the coasts. Here and there hills or small mountains interrupt the monotony of the landscape.

Demography. Estimates and censuses from the early twentieth century suggest about 800 people, a figure that may well represent an average for the precontact period. Later, during the fur trade era beginning in 1916, there was a slow growth in numbers until improved health facilities and the abandonment of infanticide brought a rapid expansion after about 1950. By 1980 there were about 1,750 Copper Eskimo.

Linguistic Affiliation. The Copper Eskimo speak a dialect of Inuit, one of the three major languages of the Eskaleut language family.

History and Cultural Relations

Archaeological evidence indicates a derivation from the Thule culture with a regional focus based on seal and caribou hunting as opposed to the classical Thule association with whaling. First European contact came when Samuel H. Hearne reached the mouth of the Coppermine River in 1771. Contacts with explorers during the nineteenth century were so limited that when the ethnologist Vilhjalmur S. Stefansson entered the area in 1910 he encountered natives who had not previously seen White men. This may have been the last such encounter in North America. During the first quarter of the twentieth century trading schooners and some Western Eskimos entered the area from the west. Relations with other Eskimo peoples were of a fleeting nature. Earlier contacts with the Mackenzie Eskimo were broken off before the middle of the nineteenth century, and those with their Netsilik neighbors to the east were often tense with woman stealing and other hostilities intermingled with trade. Caribou Eskimo were also contacted for trade. The massacre of Copper Eskimo by Hearne's Indian companions was only one of several such bloody encounters. In the summer of 1910 Stefansson brought some of the Copper Eskimo together with some Slavey Indians, producing more harmonious relations.

Settlements

Aboriginally, the Copper Eskimo were nomadic. During winter months the snowhouse villages built on the sea ice were shifted about once a month as locales were hunted out. These aggregations averaged about one hundred people and split into smaller groups in spring. During the summer months, units as small as the nuclear family often shifted their camps on an almost daily basis. Longer stays of perhaps two weeks were spent by somewhat larger aggregates at fishing places. In the autumn, groups of fifty or more people gathered at points of land for periods of two to four weeks.

The Copper Eskimo had no permanent dwellings, using the snowhouse in winter, skin tents in summer, and a combination of snow walls with tents in spring. Men built snowhouses by cutting blocks vertically from a drift and arranging them in a circle around the builder and then cutting a slanting section from the first tier to commence a spiral of blocks which culminated in a keystone block, thus forming an unsupported dome. Tents were made from either caribou skin or sealskin and could be of tipi or ridged form. Canvas quickly replaced skin as summer tent material after the advent of the fur trade, but some inland dwelling people then used wall tents of caribou skin in the winter. With the concentration of most Copper Eskimo into large communities of both Whites and natives in the 1950s and 1960s, government-sponsored building programs provided oil-heated, insulated, wooden houses.

Economy

Subsistence and Commercial Activities. Vegetable products played practically no role in Copper Eskimo life. Though heather and brush were used as fuel in summer, the seal oil lamp was the most important source of heat and light for most of the year. Seals were hunted by a group of men stationed over breathing holes in the ice located by their dogs. They also hunted polar bears and musk-oxen, but these animals were available in only a few locales. As spring approached, the people moved inland to fish through lake ice and hunt small game and migrating wild fowl. About the end of July, caribou hunting began as the animals fattened and their hides reached a condition suitable for clothing. These hunts, which extended through the period of the southward migrations of caribou in the fall, were interrupted by a short period of intensive weir fishing about the end of August as arctic char returned upstream. After a period of living on stored food, the winter sealing season began again in December.

This seasonal cycle was changed in most places by the introduction of rifles, nets, steel traps, and small wooden boats. In some mainland locales caribou hunting was especially successful with firearms, and camps were located at sites of big caribou kills, with nets placed under river or lake ice and traps set for the arctic fox. These people often remained inland for most of the year. Elsewhere, as on Victoria Island, sea mammal hunting became important year-round with seals hunted from small boats that replaced the kayak, a craft that has not been used in the sea in this area. Trading arctic fox furs provided access to these important fishing and hunting tools as well as to tea, tobacco, and flour, commodities that became necessities in the 1920s. With centralization, some hunting and trapping continued outward from the large settlements, and a few outpost camps still survived.

Attempts were made to develop local craft industries, and together with export of frozen fish, they provided modest sources of income. More significant amounts of money came from wage labor and social legislation funds. For a brief period in the 1960s a sharp rise in the price of sealskin and sealskin products brought a time of modest prosperity for the Copper Eskimo, but this relative affluence was short-lived as the price of skins fell once more.

The Eskimo dog was of great importance, but given the marginal subsistence of the aboriginal period, few men owned more than two. They served both for hunting and for transport. In winter travel, because of the scarcity of dogs, women and men pulled ahead or beside sleds together with their animals. In summer, both dogs and humans carried packs. After the establishment of the fur trade and the corresponding general economic improvement, men were able to support teams of five or more dogs, which greatly increased mobility.

Industrial Arts. Women sewed clothing, and each man made his own hunting gear including harpoons, lances, bows and arrows, and sleds. Men also manufactured lamps and pots from steatite (soapstone), which was found in quantity in various places as was the copper that was used for most of the tools with cutting edges.

Trade. Within Copper Eskimo country, trade of local materials such as copper and steatite was lively as was trade in wood and wooden products, which were accessible at the southern limits of the normal range of Copper Eskimo hunting grounds. Trade with the Netsilik Eskimos to the east brought iron objects into the country after the abandonment of Sir John Ross's ship _Victory_, which was locked in ice, stimulated intertribal trade in that item. The Netsilik were eager for wood items, as their territory was without trees. Before posts were established in their own country, some Copper Eskimo also traded fox furs to the Caribou Eskimo for guns, ammunition, and other European goods.

Division of Labor. The major subsistence animals—seal and caribou—were killed by men only, with women participating in fishing at the weirs as well as with hooks through the ice and the snaring of fowl and small game. Women and children served as beaters in caribou hunts. Men did the actual work of snowhouse building, cutting and placing the blocks, but women filled the chinks between blocks with soft snow and arranged furnishings inside. Tents were struck and set up by women and men together, and women made them as well as all the clothing. Cooking and other domestic chores were the province of women. There was no specialization of labor beyond that related to sex and age. Today, fox trapping is men's work as is most wage labor and craft production in the centralized communities.

Land Tenure. Although groups of Copper Eskimo were identified by name with their summer hunting ranges or other locals by the affix -_miut_, there was no actual sense of ownership or defense of territory. The membership of groups who inhabited specific regions changed frequently, and locales could be abandoned for periods of a year or longer.

Kinship

Kin Groups and Descent. The basic kin group was the nuclear family with little development of any group that could be labeled an extended family. On the other hand, in the large winter encampments on the sea ice, there was a network of continuous bilateral kinship links created in part by extensive marriage ties. The smaller summer hunting groups contained various combinations of kin or nonkin. The kinship system is bilateral with a recognized kindred (*ilagiit*) composed of both consanguines and affines, but with no definable limits. The concept of descent is lacking.

Kinship Terminology. All cousins are distinguished from siblings, but the children of the father's brother have a separate term. Each sex distinguishes between older and younger siblings of their own sex and have separate sets of terms for the children of brothers or sisters, which are also extended to male or female cousins. There are four aunt/uncle terms, all separate from parental designations, and some terms in the parental generation are also applied to spouses of some of these relatives. There is a complex set of affinal terms that show complementary variations between males and females.

Marriage and Family

Marriage. Although they do not state so explicitly, the Copper Eskimo appear to prefer marrying people classed as cousins of varying degrees of closeness. Getting married was informal, with the couple merely setting up a separate domicile. Most marriages were arranged while the potential spouses were still children. Because of the shortage of women, owing to female infanticide, there was often a considerable gap in age between bride and groom. In such cases a young man might live in the household of a prospective father-in-law for a period of several years while waiting for a girl to reach puberty, working in a form of premarital brideservice. At other times, gifts of important objects like sleds could be used as bride-purchase. Before the birth of children, young couples often separated in a casual fashion with the woman simply transferring her household articles. On the other hand, given the shortage of women, marriage was sometimes broken through wife stealing, a practice that often led to homicide and the likelihood of a blood feud. Tensions created by this demographic imbalance resulted in short-lived polygynous marriages, with polyandry even more rarely practiced.

Domestic Unit. Since it was considered normal for the newly married to break away from parents, residence was usually neolocal. Sometimes single or dependent relatives might attach themselves to such units, forming stem nuclear family households. At times such nuclear or stem nuclear units joined their snowhouses or tents with those of others, but there was no regular pattern of relationships that persisted in such arrangements, and indeed the arrangements were often contracted between units lacking kinship ties.

Inheritance. There was little inheritable property, and valuable objects were often buried with the deceased. Those goods that were passed on were transferred (usually to close relatives) according to no special pattern.

Socialization. Children were treated with considerable indulgence. Disciplining took the form of ridicule or threats of supernatural punishment similar to the "bogey man" phenomenon. Parents taught adult pursuits patiently over long periods. Imitation of male and female occupations like dog driving, care of infants, archery, or cooking were encouraged. When a boy killed his first seal, the body of the animal was dragged over him by his father or another close male relative at the scene of the hunt, marking his graduation to the status of a hunter. For females, puberty usually coincided with marriage.

Sociopolitical Organization

Social Organization. Although the ties of kinship beyond the nuclear family were less pronounced than in other Eskimo societies, there were several ways of extending such linkages. One was spouse exchange, as the children of couples engaged in this practice were regarded as quasi siblings. Adoption also served to create ties between the parental donor and recipient couples. There were, in addition, a number of dyadic relationships that taken together created a multiplicity of ties exclusive of or incidental to kinship. Partnerships in dancing, together with the creation of spouse exchange partnerships, provided mechanisms whereby travelers could gain peaceful entry into aggregations of Copper Eskimo other than their usual groups of association. Joking partnerships and song partnerships were other means of formalizing friendships. Given the absence of compulsory sharing of meat beyond the nuclear family, the system of seal-sharing partnerships was the most important insurance against shortages. Each hunter had a roster of men with whom he exchanged specific parts of the seal, a practice that helped compensate for the vagaries of the hunt. Meat was also shared through communal eating, which, though not compulsory, was widely practiced within local groupings during any season.

Political Organization. The Copper Eskimo cannot be said to have had anything that could be properly labeled political organization or government. There were no chiefs. Shamans were believed to have supernatural powers, but their secular influence was limited. Certain men were respected for their judgment or helped organize hunts, but such status did not extend automatically beyond the immediate situation.

Social Control and Conflict. Certain men were feared for their aggressiveness or violent tendencies, but they almost invariably met with violent ends themselves. The high rate of homicide among the Copper Eskimo attests to the ineffectiveness of social control mechanisms. The vengeance acts of the blood feud were one area of kinship that extended beyond the nuclear family. During the earlier years of the Royal Canadian Mounted Police (RCMP) presence, a number of homicides were investigated and several individuals punished under Canadian law. But in traditional times, about the only means of social control were executions of especially troublesome individuals, derision singing, and, simply, withdrawal from local groups where one might feel antagonisms. In the recent period of centralized living the Copper Eskimo have been involved in only a few conflict situations, most related to alcohol-induced violence. While early contacts between Whites and Copper Eskimo were usually of a peaceful nature, there were several early homicides that did involve priests, traders, and the RCMP.

Religion and Expressive Culture

Religious Beliefs. One central theme of Copper Eskimo beliefs relates to the separation of sea and land animals. The sea goddess, Arnapkapfaluk, was believed to be in control of sea creatures and certain precautions had to be observed to keep them from contamination by land animals. Most important was the custom of sewing the caribou skin garments only in the period before the seal-hunting season began. There were other deities, but most Copper Eskimo beliefs revolved around threats of witchcraft and fear of ghosts.

Religious Practitioners.   The shaman acted as an intermediary between the human and the spirit world. Powers were believed to come from the deity of the air, Hilap Inui. Some sort of visionary experience was needed to qualify as a shaman, with training from established practitioners also important. In addition to the main functions of controlling weather, bringing game, and healing, the shaman had to perform certain feats from time to time such as those involving ventriloquism, in order to prove his powers.

Ceremonies.   Aside from shamanistic performances, most social events centered around recreational activities involving singing, dancing, or athletic events and were accompanied by communal eating in times of plenty.

Arts.   The Copper Eskimos wore ceremonial garments more elaborate in design than those of most Eskimo groups. Women also practiced tattooing for cosmetic purposes and to mark marriage or marriageability. Far more developed was the oral literature of the Copper Eskimo. The Danish ethnologist Knud Rasmussen, who visited nearly every Eskimo group from Greenland to Siberia, proclaimed the Copper Eskimo the most poetically gifted of any of these far-flung people. From his recordings and the work of Diamond Jenness we have available a large body of material on the songs, legends, and mythology, which gives important insights into their psychology and worldview.

Medicine.   In addition to attempts to combat sickness through supernatural means, shamans also used some practical medical skills, such as setting and splinting broken or dislocated bones, lancing swellings, and amputating frozen limbs. Headaches were treated by bleeding.

Death and Afterlife.   Copper Eskimo beliefs concerning the afterworld were vague, but there was a definite belief in and fear of ghosts of the recently deceased, and places of death were quickly abandoned. In winter, a corpse might be left in a snowhouse or snowblock enclosure and in summer within a tent, which was also abandoned. In either case some implements that might be useful in a possible afterlife were usually left in the grave, though in many cases these objects were in miniature, given the value of actual implements.

Bibliography

Damas, David (1984). "Copper Eskimo." In _Handbook of North American Indians_. Vol. 5, _Arctic_, edited by David Damas, 397–414. Washington, D.C.: Smithsonian Institution.

Jenness, Diamond (1922). _The Life of the Copper Eskimos._ Report of the Canadian Arctic Expedition, 1913–1918. Vol. 12. Ottawa: F. A. Acland (King's Printer).

Rasmussen, Knud (1932). _Intellectual Culture of the Copper Eskimos._ Report of the Fifth Thule Expedition, 1921–24. Vol. 9. Copenhagen: Gyldendalske Boghandel.

Stefansson, Vilhjalmur (1913). _My Life with the Eskimo._ New York: Macmillan.

DAVID DAMAS

Cowichan

ETHNONYMS: Halkomelem, Humaluh, Kawichan

The Cowichan lived aboriginally and continue to live on the southeastern coast of Vancouver Island between Nanoos Bay and Saanich Inlet (the Cowichan proper) and on the mainland on the lower Fraser River. There were numerous subdivisions (more than forty in all), including the Muskwium (Musqueam), Nanaimo (Snanaimux), and Sanetch (Saanich). Today, there are about six thousand Cowichan living mainly on small reserves in their traditional territory. Cowichan is one of the principal language groups of the Coast Salish language family.

They may have been contacted as early as 1592 by Juan de Fuca and were in contact with later Spanish and English explorers. Hudson's Bay Company traders entered the region in the early 1800s, and Victoria was founded in 1843, a major event in the history of the Northwest Coast peoples.

The Cowichan were culturally similar to other southern Northwest Coast groups such as the Comox, Kwakiutl, Nootka, and Snoqualmie. They lived in permanent villages with rectangular cedar-plank houses; subsisted mainly on salmon and herring, supplemented by gathered plant foods and deer and elk; had social classes with nobles, commoners, and slaves; warred with other groups; had hereditary village chiefs; and were organized into patrilineal extended families.

Bibliography

Barnett, Homer G. (1955). _The Coast Salish of British Columbia._ University of Oregon Monographs, Studies in Anthropology, vol. 4. Eugene: University of Oregon Press.

Duff, Wilson (1952). _The Upper Stalo Indians of the Fraser Valley, British Columbia._ Anthropology in British Columbia, Memoir no. 1. Victoria, B.C.: British Columbia Provincial Museum of Natural History and Anthropology.

Jilek, Wolfgang G. (1974). _Salish Indian Mental Health and Culture Change: Psychohygienic and Therapeutic Aspects of the Guardian Spirit Ceremonial._ Toronto: Holt, Rinehart & Winston of Canada.

Cree, Western Woods

ETHNONYMS: Ne·hiyawak, Ne·hiδawak (we speak the same language), Maskegan [from omaske·ko·wak (swamp or muskeg)], Rocky Cree or Asini·ska·wiδiniwak (people of the place where there is an abundance of rock), Bush Cree or Saka·wiyiniwak (bush people)

Orientation

Identification. The Cree are a Subarctic group whose name is derived from the name of specific bands in the region between Lake Superior and Hudson Bay, known to the French, from Ojibwa, as "Kiristino," later shortened to "Cree." The meaning is unknown. The regional designations are those by which they know themselves.

Location. Aboriginally the Western Woods Cree occupied the subarctic or boreal forest from Hudson and James bays westward to the Peace River in what is now Canada. This is the Precambrian or Canadian Shield, except for westernmost northern Alberta, with a mixed-wood boreal forest. The subarctic has long cold winters, during which temperatures may fall to −60° F or lower, and short moderately warm summers. "Freeze-up," the period during which the lakes, rivers, and streams freeze over, is a time of limited travel, and "break-up," or spring thaw, is the harbinger of summer. The severity of the subarctic climate makes its mark on the cultures, which are closely tied to the environment. In only a few favored areas is horticulture even marginally possible.

Demography. Reliable population estimates are for recent times only, and these figures include only those having legal status under the provisions of the Indian Act. Cree were seriously affected by great smallpox epidemics in 1781 and later and other European-introduced diseases to which they had no immunity. After World War I, influenza epidemics struck at various times and places across the subarctic. In 1970, there were approximately forty thousand Western Woods Cree with legal status and an unknown number of people of mixed Cree and European ancestry who were not legally classified as Indian.

Linguistic Affiliation. The Cree language or dialect group is the northern variant of Central Algonkian, extending from the Montagnais-Naskapi of the Labrador Peninsula to the Rocky Mountains. Swampy Cree is the /n/dialect, Rocky Cree the /δ/ dialect, and Bush and Plains Cree speak /y/ dialects. An /r/ dialect was spoken south of Lake Athabasca until the late eighteenth century.

History and Cultural Relations

Historical traditions, linguistic evidence, and a growing amount of archaeological data confirm oral traditions that the Cree occupied the boreal forest from Hudson Bay to approximately the Peace River, with some protohistoric, probably seasonal expansion north of Lake Athabasca to the south shore of Great Slave Lake. In addition, there may have been some expansion into Beaver areas near Peace River. The Cree were bounded on the north by Athapaskan-speaking peoples including the Chipewyan, on the northwest by the Slavey, and on the west by the Beaver. To the south were Algonkian speakers, including Blackfeet, Piegan, Blood, Ojibwa, and Gros Ventre. Later, Siouan-speaking Assiniboin occupied part of the adjacent prairies. Until the early nineteenth century, relationships with Athapaskan-speaking groups and those Inuit near Hudson Bay were hostile. Warfare on the Plains periphery continued until the late nineteenth century.

Earliest contacts with Europeans were with the French near Lake Superior, beginning after 1640, and with the English at Hudson's Bay Company forts on Hudson and James bays after 1670. French exploration reached the Rocky Mountains by 1751, but ended after the cession of New France to the British in 1763. Thereafter, fur trade competition involved the Scots partnerships that became the Northwest Company out of Montreal. European exploration increased in the western hinterland of Hudson Bay, and trading posts were established by the competing fur companies. The sanguinary contest was resolved in 1821 by the merger of the two companies under the royal charter of the Hudson's Bay Company. The stabilization of the fur trade economy coincided with the end of intertribal warfare and endured until the impact of Canada's national policies in the mid and late twentieth century was felt. The gradual diminishing of the big-game and fur-bearing animal populations in the late eighteenth century led many Cree, Ojibwa, and Iroquois to move west. Intermarriage between fur traders and Cree led to a new population element, and from the Algonkian-French combination emerged the first and culturally distinctive Metis of the Red River.

In 1870 the Hudson's Bay Company ceded Rupert's Land to the new Dominion of Canada and the era of treaty making began. Through treaties, Canada attempted to end aboriginal title to Indian lands in return for reserves and small annuities, but a number of remote and isolated Bush Cree bands were overlooked. They neither entered into treaty relations nor surrendered their lands or sovereignty; the discovery and exploitation of oil on their lands was the source of much tension later (1988). In recent times, many Cree have received varying degrees of education and have taken positions of leadership with their own people and in the larger Canadian society in the economic, political, and artistic arenas.

Settlements

Cree settlement patterns varied seasonally. As nomadic hunters, local bands were widely distributed among camps in their small autumn-winter-spring hunting ranges. The camps were located near water, usually on the windward side of a lake where they were protected from the cold winds. In summer they gathered in large regional bands, widely spread out along the leeward side of a favorable lake, where winds blew the voracious flies and mosquitoes into the bush. The basic shelter was a conical lodge, made of moose or caribou hides. It usually held an extended family, including several hunters. Animal hides were later replaced by canvas coverings, often made into ridge pole tents. About the end of the nineteenth century log cabin settlements developed, reflecting a higher degree of sedentism. In very recent times, federal and provincial governments have provided relatively modern houses, band offices, schools, and health facilities.

Economy

Subsistence and Commercial Activities. The Cree were basically hunters of big game, especially moose. In some areas, moose were supplemented by woodland caribou or barren-ground caribou (reindeer), and in others by white-tailed or Virginia deer. Bear were hunted and were also ritually important. Waterfowl, geese, and ducks, were seasonally available in favored localities and flyways. Fish were apparently taken by women in the vicinity of the camps, but fishing by men did not become important until the decline of big-game populations, especially among the inhabitants of the Shield. Except for beaver, small fur-bearing animals became valuable only after the beginning of the European fur trade. The early trade introduced an increasing variety of goods. Metal items were of great value and included awls, axes, kettles, knives, muskets, fishhooks, and other items, such as alcohol, beads, and mirrors. Blankets and cloth were introduced and became common. Cree bands became oriented to specific trading post–mission complexes. Low-cost trade goods had ended with the establishment of the Hudson's Bay Company monopoly, but toward the end of the century independent or "free traders" entered the region. In the midtwentieth century commercial fishing was added to trapping as a basis of the cash economy.

By the mid-twentieth century, government programs induced subarctic peoples to concentrate in nucleated villages, for "administrative convenience," where the social institutions of Canadian industrial society were located. This increasingly brought an end to or weakened traditional socioeconomic adjustments and social control mechanisms, as well as many cultural institutions; it also increased unemployment, alcohol abuse, and other social problems, leading to greater dependence upon social welfare programs.

The only aboriginally domesticated animal was the dog, used in hunting or as a pack animal. By the end of the nineteenth century, dog teams were increasingly used for hauling toboggans. In some areas on the southern margins of the forest, horses came into use as pack animals, saddle horses, and draft animals, until they were replaced by motorized toboggans and pickup trucks.

Industrial Arts.   The women were expert in preparing hides and making clothing, storage bags, lodge coverings, and other items. They also made baskets of birchbark and were potters until ceramics were replaced by metal. Men made weapons, snowshoes, and birchbark canoes.

Trade.   There was probably trade between friendly Algonkian-speaking bands in prehistoric times, although the archaeological record is incomplete. With the establishment of trading centers on the Great Lakes and Hudson and James bays, some Cree were employed seasonally as "home-guard" Indians, hunting, fishing, and carrying messages between forts. Others became middlemen, bringing furs to the traders and trade goods to the Indians of the interior. This phase lasted until the trading companies expanded throughout the forest. Trade was so important that many bands were oriented toward specific posts, and some new bands came into existence around such places.

Division of Labor.   Men were responsible for hunting, trapping, fishing with nets, and traveling to the trading posts. Women were responsible for processing the game, preparing food and hides, making clothing and other items such as baskets, and caring for girls and small boys. Shamans were usually men, and they were concerned with ritual, while female shamans were often skilled in the use of herbal medicine. As a result of concentration in villages and the decline of traditional activities, this division of labor is disappearing and new patterns may be emerging.

Kinship

Kin Groups and Descent.   The Cree were typical subarctic band societies. The basic unit was a small hunting group or local band made up of one or more extended families and numbering about twenty-five persons. Unity was based on father-son relationships, or cooperation among brothers. The life expectancy of such a band was limited, as sons became adults and developed highly valued personal autonomy. The leader was usually the eldest active male hunter. These winter bands dispersed to hunt the widely distributed nomadic game and to trap relatively sedentary fur-bearing animals. They were usually known by the name of the best-known lake. Regional bands were the largest and most permanent groups, named after some feature of the area, usually a lake at which the people assembled during the summer or some common animal. The regional band was a bilateral grouping, made up of individuals, families, and hunting groups related by primary ties of consanguinity and affinity. They probably numbered from one hundred to two hundred or more. Descent was bilateral, with paternal and maternal relatives equally recognized.

Kinship Terminology.   The kinship system was bilateral, with bifurcate merging terminology in the first ascending generation, and Iroquois cousin terminology in one's own generation. Males and females were both differentiated on the basis of relative age and sex.

Marriage and Family

Marriage.   Marriages were arranged by parents between opposite-sex cross cousins. Marriage with parallel cousins, first or classificatory, was prohibited, as they were considered siblings. Arranged marriages ensured that the son-in-law would be a good hunter and provider. The levirate and sororate were practiced. Sororal polygyny was permitted and was an indication of the bride's parental approval. Bilateral crosscousin marriage tended to establish or maintain cooperative relations between hunting groups, and the marriage of sibling pairs (two brothers to two sisters, or a brother and sister to a sister and brother) was considered exceptionally good. Some marriages were arranged with more distant groups, and with the advent of the fur trade, marriage of a daughter to an important fur trader was highly desirable. Following marriage, there was temporary matrilocal residence involving brideservice, until a child was born. The groom hunted for his parents-in-law and performed other services. After the birth of a child, residence was patrilocal. Divorce in the past was highly informal, but marriages are now performed in Roman Catholic or Anglican churches or by civil authorities and are subject to religious restraints and civil law.

Domestic Unit.   The typical residential unit was an extended family, adjacent to another related unit.

Inheritance.   Property was minimal and on the death of an individual was abandoned. Later, as material goods accumulated, survivors inherited appropriate items, but Canadian law is now applicable in the new village and urban context.

Socialization.   Children were raised permissively, and control and discipline were instilled gradually. Mothers trained their daughters, and boys were gradually taught hunting and trapping skills by their fathers. A boy usually killed his first big game at about the age of fourteen, marking him a true hunter. Girls were secluded at first menses and regularly thereafter. These traditional practices are rapidly disappearing. In recent generations, many Cree children were sent to boarding schools, but now elementary and secondary schools are commonly found on the reserves, and some children go on to university or other postsecondary institutions.

Sociopolitical Organization

Social Organization.   Traditional Cree hunting society was egalitarian, with status distinctions based on relative age or abilities, as in hunting success, and on one's sex. In summer, regional bands were normally the largest social aggregation and gathered at lake shores. At the end of the summer, regional bands dispersed into constituent hunting groups to exploit the seasonally dispersed game. The pattern was only slightly altered when the Cree began to hunt and trap fur-bearing animals, although the orientation was to a trading post center which later included a Christian mission. Intermarriage with Whites created no problems until treaties were made, after which the patrilineal provisions of the Indian Act of 1869 separated status Indians from nonstatus or Metis.

Political Organization.   Leadership was based on age, with the eldest active male the head of the extended family, and informal councils of elders reaching consensus on behalf of the members of regional bands. During the treaty-making period, chiefs and councilors had to be elected. At first these were respected elders, but with the increase in importance of government authorities, younger and more articulate men skilled in English became the formal chiefs, principally acting as foreign ministers or ambassadors. The elders remained extremely important in decision making, however.

Social Control and Conflict.   The socialization of children and informal pressures were usually enough to prevent serious problems. Face-to-face conflict was always avoided, and interpersonal tensions were resolved by families leaving one local band and realigning with another. Belief in conjuring and witchcraft was also important, but there is little information available about specific practices. In the contemporary period, order is maintained by special constables or the Royal Canadian Mounted Police.

Religion and Expressive Culture

Religious Beliefs.   Throughout history, Cree have always been reticent about sharing their beliefs with scoffing outsiders. Beliefs in a Great Spirit (*misi-manito*) or Evil Spirit (*maci-manito· w*) may be of postcontact origin. The cannibal giant (*wi-htiko· w*) was greatly feared. The religion was animistic, and all living beings and some inanimate objects had spirits, or *manitowak*. Humans, through dreams and visions, were able to secure the help of powerful animal spirits in such activities as hunting, warfare, and love. Since all beings, including humans, had spirits, there was no concept of the supernatural.

Religious Practitioners.   All individuals had some power, but some men or women had more. There was no priesthood.

Ceremonies.   No ceremonies are recorded for the earliest periods, but in recent history tea dances of thanksgiving were held in spring and autumn. Feasts and dancing were held following successful hunts. Christian rituals are now common.

Arts.   There was a rich oral tradition that included both sacred and secular tales. *Wi· sake· ca· hk* was the hero of the popular trickster or transformer tales. In the past, the face and body were tattooed and painted with elaborate designs. Women worked with quills and, later, beads.

Medicine.   Sickness and injury were considered the result of personal malevolent forces, for which treatment by a shaman was necessary. Treatment included herbal medicines and setting broken limbs, but the spiritual help invoked in the ritual of the shaking tent or the sweatbath was equally important.

Death and Afterlife.   Fatal illness was greeted with equanimity, but the dying person required that his survivors avenge his death, for death was believed to be the result of witchcraft. Burial was in a grave or on a scaffold. A gun was fired in the tent to drive away the spirit.

Bibliography

Helm, June, ed. (1981). *Handbook of North American Indians.* Vol. 6, *Subarctic.* Washington, D.C.: Smithsonian Institution.

Isham, James (1949). *Observations on Hudson's Bay, 1743–1749,* edited by E. Rich. Toronto: Champlain Society.

Mandelbaum, David G. (1940). *The Plains Cree.* American Museum of Natural History, Anthropological Papers 37, 155–316. New York.

Mason, Leonard (1967). *The Swampy Cree: A Study in Acculturation.* National Museum of Canada, Anthropological Paper no. 13. Ottawa.

Smith, James G. E. (1987). "Western Woods Cree: Anthropological Myth and Historical Reality." *American Ethnologist* 14:434–448.

Smith, James G. E. (1981). "Western Woods Cree." In *Handbook of North American Indians.* Vol. 6, *Subarctic,* edited by June Helm, 256–270. Washington, D.C.: Smithsonian Institution.

JAMES G. E. SMITH

Creek

ETHNONYMS: Muscogee, Muskogee

Prior to European settlement, the Creek were a confederacy of tribes who lived in about fifty villages mainly in central Georgia and in other locations from the Atlantic coast to central Alabama. Included in the confederacy were the Kawita (Coweta), Kasihta, Abihka, Hilibi, Kusa (Coosa), Wakokai, and Huhliwahli. The groups spoke six languages—Muskogee, Hitchiti, Koasati, Yuchi, Natchez, and Shawnee. The Creeks were so named by the English because of the large number of streams and creeks in the region. When met by Hernando De Soto in 1540, the confederacy had already been formed as a means of defense against attacks from powerful northern groups.

Between 1836 and 1840 nearly twenty thousand Creeks were removed from their homeland and settled in the Indian Territory (present-day Oklahoma). Today, there are four main groups of Creeks in Oklahoma—the Creek Nation, the Alabama-Quassarte (Coushatta), the Kialegee, and the Thopthlocco Creek, each governed by a tribal council. Together, they form the modern Creek Confederacy, with about fifty thousand members. There is also a small community near Atmore, Alabama.

Traditional villages in the Southeast contained irregular clusters of four to eight houses each, with as many as twenty-five different matriclans represented in a village. Subsistence was based on the cultivation of maize, beans, and squash supplemented by hunting and gathering. Each tribe or village was governed by an elected chief (_miko_), subchief, and a council. The military was under civilian control, with war chiefs leading war parties while governing was left to the chiefs who were chosen for their wisdom and skills. The major religious ceremony was the Busk or Green Corn Dance (_puskita_) held in midsummer to celebrate the ripening of the new maize crop. The lighting of the new fire and drinking of the ritual black drink as well as the forgiving of all grudges and most offenses were important accompaniments.

Bibliography

Green, Donald E. (1973). _The Creek People_. Phoenix: Indian Tribal Series.

Swanton, John R. (1928). _Social Organization and Social Usages of the Indians of the Creek Confederacy_. U.S. Bureau of American Ethnology, 42nd Annual Report (1924–1925), 23—472. Washington, D.C.

Crow

ETHNONYMS: Absarokee, Apsaalooke, Apsaroke

The Crow are an American Indian group who today live primarily on the Crow Reservation in Big Horn and Yellowstone counties, Montana. The 1980 U.S. census counted 7,074 Crow of whom 4,846 were in Montana, with about 4,000 living on the reservation. The Crow and Hidatsa are closely related linguistically and evidently formed one group in the past before the Crow split off and moved west where they eventually adopted a nomadic bison-hunting life-style typical of the Plains culture of the 1800s. The Crow and Hidatsa languages are classified as a subfamily in the Siouan language family. The Crow language is still spoken regularly on the reservation. The Crow were often at war with the Blackfoot and Teton but maintained generally peaceful trade relations with the Shoshone and Hidatsa. Regular contact with Whites, which began in the early 1800s, was usually peaceful, with the Crow often serving as scouts for the U.S.

Army. In 1851 the Crow were given a 38-million-acre reservation, which was much reduced in size in 1868. The Crow Reservation today contains 335,951 acres of tribal land, with an additional 1,229,628 acres allotted to individuals.

As with other Plains groups, Crow life centered on hunting bison from horseback to obtain food and most other material objects. The tipi was the major type of dwelling. The Crow were divided into thirteen exogamous matrilineal clans and six phratries. There were also named military and social societies, with membership through election. The camps were governed by a council of esteemed warriors and a head chief, who achieved this status through succesful military exploits. Governance today rests with the tribal council composed of all adults on the reservation and an executive committee comprising seventeen district representatives. Special commissions oversee specific activities or projects such as water and utilities and industrial development. Following the decline of the bison after 1880, the Crow turned to horse and cattle raising and farming on the reservation. Today, compared to many other American Indian groups, the Crow are well-off financially, although the poverty and unemployment rates are several times higher than the national averages. Individual and tribal income is derived from ranching, farming, manufacturing, commercial establishments, wage and salaried labor, and tourism, with many tourists visiting the Custer Battlefield National Monument on the reservation and the fairs and rodeos run by the Crow. The tribe also operates Little Big Horn College at Crow Agency, Montana.

The traditional religion centered on beliefs in various spirits, the Trickster (Coyote), visions, and vision quests. Shamanism, although not highly developed, existed. Shamans were those who had acquired stronger supernatural powers in certain endeavors through especially important visions. The Sun Dance and Tobacco Society ceremonies were the most important, and both are still performed today. Most Crow have now been converted to either Roman Catholicism or Protestantism, though traditional beliefs and practices continue.

Bibliography

Frey, Rodney (1987). _The World of the Crow Indians: As Driftwood Lodges_. Norman: University of Oklahoma Press.

Lowie, Robert H. (1935). _The Crow Indians_. New York: Farrar & Rinehart.

Delaware

ETHNONYMS: Lenape, Munsee, River Indians, Turkey Tribe, Unami

Orientation

Identification. By the end of the eighteenth century the name "Delaware" had become associated with three groups of native people who originally occupied the valley of the Delaware River. The first Europeans called the various people living along the Delaware River by the collective term "River Indians." Years later, when the river was named the Delaware after Sir Thomas West, Lord de la Warr, the first governor of the Virginia colony, the "River Indians" became known by the same name. The few remaining speakers of the Delaware language and the descendants of these people who still strongly identify themselves as Delaware live in two "communities" in Oklahoma. Like their ancestors, they continue to maintain a dispersed residential pattern, but now the areas between individual households are occupied by other Americans. The concentrations of modern "Delaware" can be found in the northeast of Oklahoma in the Bartlesville area, and in the western part of the state around Anadarko. Although these contemporary Delaware appear quite similar to the other Americans around them, many old cultural traits are embedded in their life-styles.

Location. In aboriginal times the three cultures (Lenape, Munsee, "Jerseys") now popularly known as Delaware occupied separate parts of the river valley. The Lenape, the best known of these groups, are the focus of this description. The Lenape inhabited the area along the west side of the lower Delaware River, from old Duck Creek in northern Delaware up to Tohiccon Creek, which flows south of and parallel to the Lehigh River. Lenape territory ran inland as far as the sources of these feeder streams and all of those in between. Today the remnants of the Lenape traditionalists, including eight people who still speak the language, live in Oklahoma. The people who lived on the east side of the lower Delaware River, occupying all of southern New Jersey south of the Raritan River, are identified only as the "Jerseys" in early documents. When these "Jerseys" left their territory they migrated north and northwest, and most of their descendants now live in Canada. The Munsee, or Minsi, occupied the upper Delaware River drainage. By the end of the seventeenth century they had separated into several groups, some of which moved in concert with the Lenape while other Munsee chose different cultures to live among. A small group of approximately 250 was still living in Kansas in the 1970s. The true Lenape, often referred to as "Unami" after 1750, became known as the "Turtles." The "Jerseys," who after 1780 were sometimes called the "Unalachtigo," later became known as the "Turkeys," and the Munsee (or Minsi) became identified as the "Wolf."

Demography. In 1600 the total aboriginal population of the foraging Lenape was between 250 and 500. The population of the "Jerseys" was somewhat larger, possibly numbering 800 to 1,000 individuals. The Munsee also may have had as many as 1,000 members, but their early history is less clear. Today, thousands of Delaware maintain an ethnic identity through various organizations. These groups, primarily located in the south-central part of the country, include over 25,000 members. The two largest are the Delaware Tribe of Western Oklahoma and the Delaware Tribe of Indians, living in northeastern Oklahoma.

Linguistic Affiliation. The languages of the three cultures called Delaware are included within the Eastern Algonkian family. The Lenape and the "Jerseys" spoke dialects of the same language, while the Munsee language was sufficiently distinct that interpreters were required.

History and Cultural Relations

The Lenape appear to have been in their territory for centuries, if not millennia, prior to 1500. The Lenape and "Jerseys" must have been more closely aligned, but by 1600 marriages and other activities were sufficiently distinct to prevent cooperation in land sales or migration. The Lenape were bounded on the south by the Cinconicin, a low-level chiefdom which had their main village where Lewes, Delaware, now stands. To the west, in central Pennsylvania, were the powerful Susquehannock, who controlled the fur trade throughout the area and beyond the Monongahela and Ohio rivers to the Mississippi. The heartland of the Iroquois territory lay to the north of the Munsee, and to the north of the "Jerseys" were various independent groups foraging along the Hudson and other rivers and waterways surrounding Manhattan Island. The Susquehannock and Iroquois had grown powerful through fur trading and overshadowed these foraging peoples living along the major rivers. All the people of the Delaware valley formed an economic backwater with minimal participation in the fur trade during the entire sixteenth century.

In 1622 the uprising of the Potomac confederacy stimulated the Susquehannock to seek other outlets for their furs. The most convenient route ran from the head of the Chesapeake up the Elk River and, by a portage, down Minquas Creek through Lenape territory. This brought the Susquehannock to the lower end of the Delaware River where Dutch traders from New Amsterdam (New York) established a trading post. From the earliest records left by these traders, beginning in 1623, we have clear evidence that the Susquehannock abused and controlled the Lenape during this period, and the Lenape remained in their shadow for nearly forty years.

During this period, Dutch traders and Swedish colonists purchased small plots of land from the Lenape on which to establish several outposts. The Swedes erected a small village where Wilmington, Delaware, now stands. Swedish farmers spread throughout the lower half of the Lenape range, and many intermarried with Lenape. Owing to the low level of funding provided to the Swedish colonists, they could not compete in the fur trade, and they soon focused their attention on tobacco production. Swedish needs for food had stimulated the foraging Lenape, who usually gardened a bit of maize at their summer stations, to increase production for sale to the colonists. Between 1640 and 1660, maize became an important cash crop for the Lenape, providing access to European goods which other nations procured with furs. By 1660, imports of grain from other colonies had captured the local market.

By that time the wars of the Susquehannock, primarily with the Seneca, had created stresses that caused them to become allied with the Lenape and allowed the Lenape to participate more extensively in the fur trade. When English immigrants began settling the area around 1660 they also made small purchases of land from the Lenape on which to establish farms. These immigrants stimulated the formation of new alliances in the region. In 1674 the Maryland colonists joined with the Seneca and turned on the Susquehannock, who had formerly been their allies. The Susquehannock nation was defeated and scattered, and their power lost forever.

Their lands in central Pennsylvania and to the west became available for Lenape use, although the Maryland colony and some of the Five Nations now held claim to them by right of conquest. Lenape became increasingly active in the fur trade, and a growing number relocated into this vast open area which in 1680 was uncluttered by European immigrants. The political events that led the English Crown to grant a charter for this region to William Penn (1681) at first had little significance for the Lenape. Penn's policy for just treatment of the native peoples led him to contact every Lenape band and to purchase all their holdings in the Delaware valley. This program began in 1681 and continued until 1701. Although Penn assiduously protected Lenape rights to lands on which they were seated, the foraging life-style depended on access to forest resources and to the abundant fish runs in the streams feeding the Delaware River. Gradually the various Lenape bands relocated their foraging areas and summer stations farther inland, and by 1750 all the Lenape bands had relocated to the west of their homeland, joining their kin who, in some cases, had moved west more than fifty years previously. Many of those who had left in the 1600s had moved even farther to the west by 1740, where they bought lands from other Native American groups. This established a pattern of movement in which the Lenape made purchases directly from aboriginal landholders and later sold these lands to colonists or, after 1780, to the U.S. government.

Over the years various Lenape bands established settlements and villages in Ohio, Indiana, Illinois, Kansas, and even Texas. Innumerable Lenape splinter groups moved into still other areas, and many individuals simply settled down among and married with the immigrants who were advancing close behind them. In the second half of the nineteenth century most of the Lenape then in Kansas made a purchase of land (sometimes seen as land rights) from the Cherokee in Indian Territory, which later became Oklahoma. Lenape settlements among those of the western Cherokee provided a stable environment, but one increasingly susceptible to outside influences. By the 1920s most of the Lenape had come to speak English, and fewer households were to be found where the Lenape language was maintained.

Settlements

The foraging Lenape had no permanent settlements and no villages, and the "Jerseys" in the historic period may have had a similar settlement pattern. The Munsee built small villages similar to those of the Iroquois. Each Lenape band dispersed into nuclear family units for winter hunting. In the spring these families regathered at a summer station near the mouth of the stream that served as the focus of their band's territory. About a dozen such bands can be recognized, each averaging nearly twenty-five members. All the various Lenape bands gathered in late fall for annual renewal rites, just before dispersing for winter hunting. Families or individuals often oper-

ated alone even in aboriginal times, and after 1675 this pattern of independence and entrepreneurial activity became pronounced.

From several historic descriptions we know that each aboriginal Lenape family lived in a wigwam, less than nine feet in diameter and under five feet high. The walls were formed from thin bent poles tied at the top. These were covered with bark and grass, as well as with mats woven from reeds. A hearth area occupied the center of the floor area. Such shelters must have served the Lenape traditionalists well into the nineteenth century, although those Lenape who were becoming more sedentary were building cabins as early as the late eighteenth century.

Economy

Subsistence and Commercial Activities. The Lenape were foragers with a seasonal pattern of band aggregation and dispersion geared to effective recovery of naturally available resources within their range. In the early spring they set up their summer stations to take advantage of six species of anadromous fish which spawned in the fresh waters of the Delaware valley watershed. In March the shad were the first of these to arrive from the sea, with a run often lasting as long as four weeks. The other five species came in sequence throughout the summer and into early fall, with the last species spawning in September and October. These fish, plus the catadromous eel and migratory waterfowl resources, provided an abundant and extremely rich protein source for nearly eight months of the year. The winter months, during which deer hunting was the principal activity, were less rich, but sufficient to supply the population with food needs when supplemented by extensive gathering. Aside from the period from 1640 to 1660 when Lenape bands cash-cropped maize, complex technology was available only through the sale of a few furs and the barter of venison and other native-made products. After 1680 the Lenape became important in the fur trade, but the demand for this resource had declined. Lenape became known as expert and reliable guides and were important in opening the frontier straight out to the Pacific Coast. Lenape adoption of the horse in the eighteenth century facilitated their movement west, and they also became horse traders of note.

The independence and individuality that characterized the foraging ancestors of these people are reflected today in a number of economic factors. Private ownership of their own homes, a reluctance to be part of big businesses, and avoidance of financial encumbrances make the Delaware appear to be secure members of the American mainstream. Although many collectively receive government payments for old treaty obligations, there are none of the difficulties that are noted among other Native American groups where such support has become the mainstay of the economy.

Industrial Arts. The aboriginal Lenape were extraordinarily skilled at leather and quillwork and at carving wooden objects that were often traded to the colonists. Outstanding early examples of these crafts exist in European museum collections. Basketry was one of the skills used by Lenape settled among the seventeenth-century colonists, but aspects of this skill may have been European imports. Much later, ribbonwork applique became a major technique for decorating clothing among the Lenape as it did among many other Native American peoples.

Trade.   The Lenape always maintained a relatively low level of trade, both with their aboriginal neighbors and with the later European colonists. Although industrially produced metals, cloth, guns, and glass were immediately of interest to the Lenape, their low level of demand never generated a large-scale trading dependence as was often the case with other native cultures.

Division of Labor.   The women of the matrilineal Lenape performed traditional female roles and did whatever gardening was done at their summer stations, including preparing the small plots. Their gathering also included nestlings and eggs, and they shared in harvesting fish during the big runs. Men focused on fishing and were of greater economic importance during the winter hunting when they provided most of the winter food supply. These male roles expanded over the years as men became full-time trappers, guides, scouts, and horse traders.

Land Tenure.   Land usage was held in common among all the members of the band, which could be equated with the core members of the lineage and their in-marrying spouses. The aboriginal lands were sold by each of these bands, with all the adult males (over thirteen or fourteen years of age) signing the land transfer documents. After 1740 most of these groups held land in common among much larger social units, equated with towns. Land sales were made by these larger groups, and sometimes by a series of these groups acting as a single political body.

Kinship

Kin Groups and Descent.   The Lenape bands were matrilineally related clusters of nuclear families, but with high interband mobility. The "clans" of the Delaware described after 1750, sometimes referred to as "phratries," reflected the three cultures living in the Delaware valley prior to 1700. By the early nineteenth century, these cultures had become identified as being of three "totemic clans," still reflecting their traditional cultural borders.

Kinship Terminology.   Both the Lenape and Jerseys seem to have used Hawaiian cousin terminology by the early nineteenth century and semibifurcate terminology for the first ascending generation. This had evolved from the earlier aboriginal system, which remains to be clarified.

Marriage and Family

Marriage.   The traditional groups were lineage exogamous, and residence was matrilocal. Polygamy was permitted, but after contact women seem to have preferred to marry or live among the colonists rather than to become secondary wives. Divorce was common and could be initiated by either party.

Domestic Unit.   Nuclear families have always been the rule among the Lenape.

Inheritance.   In the 1600s most of a person's belongings were placed in the grave. By 1700 the relatives contributed food to a feast and secured goods to bury with the deceased as well as to distribute to participants in the burial rituals, not all of whom were close kin.

Socialization.   Children were seldom punished. Low-level social controls plus the rigors of foraging life provided sufficient behavioral controls in the past.

Sociopolitical Organization

Social Organization.   In aboriginal times the egalitarian Lenape generally, but not always, equated status with age.

Political Organization.   The independent and highly fluid aboriginal bands became more politically united after 1750, with towns being named for individuals who were in effect chiefs.

Social Control.   The Lenape have always avoided conflict: any situation that could produce stress is called *kwulacan*. Even in the face of changing economics and modern sedentary life-styles, Lenape withdraw from controversy and difficulties on any level.

Conflict.   Withdrawal from problematical situations has characterized the Lenape since they were first described by Europeans. This encouraged the fissioning of social groups and a tendency to avoid acting as a single political entity. The history of the Lenape, as with some of their neighbors, has been a series of splits among groups, with each group or even family then operating as an independent unit. Such groups often fused with others in complex patterns that render the collective history of these people difficult to follow.

Religion and Expressive Culture

Religious Beliefs.   The aboriginal Lenape were animistic, but individuals held strong beliefs about the unity of all living as well as inanimate things. By 1800 the Lenape had adopted many Munsee and Christian beliefs. Today, most practice various Protestant religions, but many still retain a fundamentally animist worldview largely indistinct from that which their distant ancestors would have found appropriate. Many Europeans interpreted the Manitou of the Lenape to be a supreme deity. Various other beings, particularly those associated with the creation myth, suggest that "Manitou" may have been a generic term applied to spirits of all kinds.

Religious Practitioners.   No individuals held strong ritual power, but some people were blessed with the ability to heal.

Ceremonies.   The complex rituals held before going on their winter hunting rounds were associated with annual renewal gatherings. These became still more complex as the Lenape adopted increasing numbers of introduced behaviors, particularly as they became more sedentary.

Medicine.   Illness could be dispersed by driving out spirits that caused disease. Specially designated curers assisted in this process, aided by herbal remedies and the powers of collective chants and prayers.

Death and Afterlife.   Death was caused by evil spirits, and the polluted dead were buried in graves lined with rushes, bark, and mats several hundred meters from their summer encampments. Complex funeral ceremonies involved transportation of the corpse to a prepared burial site, ritual lamentation, and participation in a ritual feast for the dead. Mourning periods varied depending on degrees of kinship, with the surviving spouse continuing for a full year. Some of these aspects of Lenape society continue to this day, ensuring that the souls of the departed will find their way to the west where hunting is good and they will have an easy afterlife.

Bibliography

Becker, Marshall J. (1983). "Boundary between the Lenape and the Munsee: The Forks of Delaware as a Buffer Zone." _Man in the Northeast_ 26:1–20.

Becker, Marshall J. (1989). "Lenape Population at the Time of Contact." _Proceedings of the American Philosophical Society_ 133:112–122.

Goddard, Ives (1978). "Delaware." In _Handbook of North American Indians_. Vol. 15, _Northeast_, edited by Bruce G. Trigger, 213–239. Washington, D.C.: Smithsonian Institution.

Newcomb, William W., Jr. (1956). _The Culture and Acculturation of the Delaware Indians_. University of Michigan Museum of Anthropology, Anthropological Papers, no. 10. Ann Arbor.

Weslager, Clinton A. (1978). _The Delaware Indian Westward Migration_. Wallingford, Pa.: Middle Atlantic Press.

MARSHALL JOSEPH BECKER

Dogrib

ETHNONYMS: Atimopiskay (in the Cree language), Done, Thlingchadinne (an English misconstruction for "dog rib people"), Tlicho

Orientation

Identification. The English term "Dogrib" is a translation of a Cree term. "Tlicho" (dog rib) was probably not a term of tribal self-reference aboriginally but came into use by Dogribs in the contact era, especially to distinguish themselves from neighboring Athapaskan peoples. The term "Done" (people) is the self-designation that emphasizes the Indianness of the Dogrib.

Location. The Dogrib have continued to occupy their aboriginal lands. Their hunting-trapping range is between 62° and 65° N and 110° and 124° W in the Northwest Territories, Canada. South to north, Great Slave Lake and Great Bear Lake border the Dogrib traditional range. The greater portion is in the rocky outcrop of the Canadian Shield, where the boreal forest cover becomes progressively more sparse and stunted toward the east. The westernmost range of the Dogrib includes the eastern edge of the Mackenzie River lowlands. The continental subarctic climate is one of brief warm summers with long hours of daylight and long cold winters when temperatures may drop to −40° F or below. "Freeze-up" of lakes and streams begins in early October and "break-up" comes in May.

Demography. In 1970 the Dogrib numbered about seventeen hundred persons, contrasted to only about one thousand in 1949. European-derived epidemics throughout the nineteenth century helped hold the Dogrib population to between approximately eight hundred and one thousand from 1858, when the first actual count was made, to 1949. The Canadian government's introduction of effective treatment for tuberculosis and expanded medical services in the late 1950s spurred population growth, which continues to the present. In the 1960s, by providing subsidized housing and through other means, the government succeeded in getting many Dogribs to settle in Rae, to which in former times, as the trading post and mission site, Dogribs had resorted only seasonally. Rae-Edzo (Edzo is an ancillary government-created complex) is now the major Dogrib settlement, although some live at Detah near the town of Yellowknife and in the small bush settlements of Lac la Martre, Rae Lakes, and Snare Lake, which the government began to provide with infrastructural support in the 1970s.

Linguistic Affiliation. The Dogrib speak a language of the northeastern Athapaskan language group, with some dialectic variation across the Dogrib regional groups.

History and Cultural Relations

The Dogrib are one division of the widespread population of the Dene or Athapaskan-speaking peoples who, by archaeological and linguistic evidence, first entered western Alaska from Siberia by way of the Bering land bridge that existed during late Pleistocene times. They subsequently spread throughout interior Alaska and the western Canadian subarctic. As a distinctive linguistic-tribal entity, the Dogrib emerged after their ancestors' entry, at an indeterminate period in prehistoric times, into the area they occupy today. The neighboring Athapaskan-speaking peoples to the east, the Chipewyan, and to the north, the Copper Indians, were distinguishing the Dogrib from themselves in the eighteenth century, but whether some groups ancestral to the present-day Slavey were, in that period, included in this appellation is not clear. By the mid-eighteenth century a few European goods were being traded to the Dogrib for furs by Chipewyan middlemen.

With the Slavey to the west and the Hare Indians north of Great Bear Lake, also Athapaskan speakers, the Dogrib seem always to have been on peaceful terms. Those groups as well as the Dogrib suffered intermittent predations by the Algonkian-speaking Cree from the southeast in the late eighteenth century and by the Copper (Yellowknife) Indians up to 1823. In 1823 a successful attack by the Dogrib on a band of the small Copper Indian tribe brought first an uneasy and then an enduring peace. By then a few fur trade posts were established in the South Great Slave Lake and Mackenzie River region. There was no trading post in Dogrib territory, however, until Old Fort Rae (down the North Arm of Great Slave Lake from the site of the present Rae) was established by the Hudson's Bay Company in 1852. The first Roman Catholic missionary, of the Oblats de Marie Immaculée, reached Old Fort Rae in 1859. Within ten years most of the Dogrib had accepted Roman Catholicism and it remains their religion today.

With the other Dene peoples north of Great Slave Lake the Dogribs trading into Rae "signed" Treaty No. 11 in 1921.

(The southernmost Dogribs, most of whose descendants live at Detah, had long traded into Fort Resolution on the south side of Great Slave Lake and had there "signed" Treaty No. 8 in 1899.) The treaty marked the advent of official Canadian government relations with the Dogrib.

Settlements

As mobile hunters of the northern forest, the Dogrib used temporary lodges or tipis covered with bark, spruce boughs, or caribou hide to shelter two or more families through the nineteenth century. Then some families began to build log cabins, often clustered at a good fishing locale, which became the base from which men or family groups went on fur-trapping and hunting tours. Canvas replaced caribou hide for the tipi and about 1920 the commercial canvas tent was introduced. In the 1960s houses of lumber and plywood were erected as permanent habitations by the government.

Economy

Subsistence and Commercial Activities.   Into the late twentieth century, the Dogrib relied on the game and fish of the land, increasingly supplemented by flour and lard from the trading post. Caribou were a major resource from September through March when the caribou retreated to the farther reaches of the barren grounds. Moose were taken year round. A large game kill was shared among all families in the local group. Contingent on its ten-year population cycle, the snowshoe hare was the major small game. With the introduction in the nineteenth century of commercial twine for gill nets, fish became an important resource. The Dogrib were drawn into the fur trade after the end of the eighteenth century and by the middle of the nineteenth century were committed to a dual economy of subsistence hunting, fishing, and snaring combined with the taking of fur animals (such as beaver, marten, fox) whose skins they traded for metal implements, guns, cloth, clothing, and so on. As Rae expanded in population and services after 1950, a few Dogrib, especially those who were bilingual, found employment as trading store clerks and janitors in government installations. Bush clearing and fire fighting are seasonal summer employments for men. In the 1980s, an Indian-operated fishing lodge for tourists was opened at the Dogrib bush hamlet of Lac la Martre. The dog was the only domestic animal aboriginally. Dogs did not become significant in transport until the nineteenth century, once firearms and twine for fish nets allowed families to provision a multidog team.

Industrial Arts.   The making of snowshoes, toboggans, and birchbark canoes by men and the processing of caribou and moose hides for clothing and footgear by women were aboriginal crafts vital to survival. Decorative art rested in the hands of the women, as adornment on apparel. Aboriginal porcupine quill decoration largely gave way to silk floss embroidery and beadwork in historic times. Containers of birchbark, of furred and unfurred hides, and of rawhide netting, often handsomely executed, were women's work as well.

Trade.   There was no consequential precontact trade between the Dogrib and neighboring Indian peoples. The fur trade was regularized in the early nineteenth century and remains the single dominant trade relation in Dogrib history.

Division of Labor.   Into recent times men were the hunters of the large game without which the people could not survive. Husband and wife might share the task of gill-net fishing which became increasingly important after net twine was introduced. Women made dry meat and dry fish, processed hides for clothing and, sometimes aided by their husbands, the fur pelts for the fur trade. Rabbit snaring, firewood gathering, cooking, and other activities that could take place close to the hearth were ordinarily the responsibility of women. Especially in bush communities, all these tasks remain important economic activities.

Land Tenure.   There was no ownership of land by either individuals or groups aboriginally, and so it has remained to the present day. The resources of the land were open to all. Government-registered trap lines were never established among the Dogrib.

Kinship

Kin Groups and Descent.   A Dogrib's relatives are embraced by the term *sehot'in,* "my people." As it conveys the Dogribs' sense of kinship, those with whom one lives in relationship, sehot'in includes relatives by marriage as well as consanguines and can also refer to one's band or hamlet group. Kinship is reckoned bilaterally. Clans or any other form of descent group are absent.

Kinship Terminology.   Dogrib distinguish older brother from younger brother and older sister from younger sister. The brother/sister terms are extended to cousins, cross and parallel. Parents are distinguished from aunts and uncles. Men's nieces and nephews are addressed or referred to by a single term and grandchildren of either sex by another. The same pattern holds for women's nieces/nephews and grandchildren, but women's terms are different from men's.

Marriage and Family

Marriage.   Prior to the introduction of Roman Catholic wedding rites, marriage was unmarked by ceremony. Courtship became de facto marriage, which stabilized after the birth of a child. At least until then, temporary matrilocality was the norm and has continued to be observed by tradition-minded families. After that, the young family might join the band or hunting-trapping group of one of the husband's primary relatives or remain with that of the wife. Before conversion to Catholicism, some superior providers took more than one wife. Once the Dogrib became Roman Catholics divorce was unacceptable. An individual may, however, leave a church-sanctioned spouse to establish an enduring common law marriage with another person.

Domestic Unit.   Aboriginally, probably two or more related conjugal pairs and their children occupied the temporary shelter. Permanent housing has always been in short supply; the log cabins and the more recent government house were and are apt to be occupied by two or three related generations.

Inheritance.   Into the nineteenth century, the death of a significant adult was accompanied by the destruction of not only the deceased's property but that of the bereaved relatives. In more recent times, inheritance of economically important goods—houses, guns, toboggans, canoes—is according to the needs of the immediate family members.

Socialization. Children have always absorbed moral values and standards of behavior by listening to the comments and gossip of their elders. In the bush camp or isolated hamlet where people still rely heavily on the products of the land, little girls by the age of six or seven begin to help their mother in fetching firewood and water. They also "pack" and tend their infant siblings. Boys observe the activities of their fathers but are not pressed into chores as early as girls, although they may be tending the rabbit snares by age ten or twelve. At about fourteen, boys join with their father or older brother on hunting-trapping tours. In contemporary times, with primary-grade schooling available even in the bush communities, Dogrib parents hold the ideal of having their children learn English and gain other advantages of White schooling. There is, however, a high rate of truancy that is not effectively restrained by parents. Since the 1950s, a minority of young Dogribs have gone on to high school and postsecondary education "outside."

Sociopolitical Organization

Social Organization. From aboriginal times to the present, the Dogrib have been without class distinctions. Among men, the good hunter-trapper commands approbation, as does the hardworking woman. Some persons of mixed Indian-White ancestry are regarded as fully Indian by their fellows; others, whose families have operated as cultural brokers between Indians and Whites, are viewed as a distinctive sector of the society, but are not accorded higher status by the Indians.

Political Organization. Aboriginally, the several socioterritorial groups or regional bands of Dogribs were autonomous. Leaders, whose roles were tied to economic pursuits and in historic times to White-Dogrib contact relations, were consensually accepted on the basis of demonstrated energy, intelligence, and ability. Regional bands had recognized leaders. During the period of the Hudson's Bay Company fur trade monopoly, a "trading chief," Ekawi Dzimi, emerged as spokesman and negotiator with the company at Fort Rae. With the "signing" of Treaty No. 11 at Rae in 1921, the government required an official installation of "chief" and "councilors." (The Detah Dogrib already had an official chief under Treaty No. 8.) Monphwi, who had succeeded the trading chief as prime leader of the Rae Dogrib, became "chief" and the regional band leaders, "councilors". Chief and councilors continued to be chosen consensually by their male peers until 1971 when, upon the retirement of the aged Rae chief, Jimmy Bruneau, the first formal elections were held for those offices. In 1969, the Indian Brotherhood of the Northwest Territories was formed. Several young educated and bilingual Dogrib played prominent roles in the Brotherhood as they have in the Dene Nation, which in 1978 succeeded the Brotherhood as the representative body for all the Dene peoples of the Northwest Territories in dealing with the Canadian government in respect to land claims, control of resources, and native rights.

Social Control and Conflict. Dogribs avoid confrontational behavior, a norm that may be abrogated under conditions of drunkenness. Internalized standards, gossip, and public opinion usually serve to keep individuals in line. Differences of opinion or goals between individuals, factions, or regional groups are characteristically muted. The Dogrib ideal has always been that people should "listen to one another" and come to consensus on issues. The recent exposure of young people to White-style schooling and pop culture has promoted a generational and cultural gap in values and outlook. Government police power is vested in the Royal Canadian Mounted Police; the post at Rae was established in 1924. Crimes by Canadian legal definition are tried in territorial courts, administered from the territorial capital at Yellowknife.

Religion and Expressive Culture

Religious Beliefs. Aboriginal religious beliefs, which have endured in attenuated form into present times, centered on the individual attaining a relationship with an animal or animal-like spirit, such as Raven, Spider, Thunderbird, through which he gained *ink'on*, "power." Summoning the enabling spirit with drum and song, the adept might control the weather or the hunt, cure illness, or divine the whereabouts of travelers. Until the acceptance of Christian divinities, the Dogrib had no concept of a supreme being or the idea of worship of a supernatural entity. With the advent of the Roman Catholic missionaries in the 1860s, the Dogribs quickly accepted the teachings of the church. In the opinion of the early missionaries, they became the most devoted Catholics among the Dene peoples of the Northwest Territories.

Religious Practitioners. Although many Dogribs had a relationship with a spirit, from aboriginal times into the twentieth century a few became recognized as having exceptional powers for curing, hunting, and so on. No Dogribs have entered the Roman Catholic priesthood.

Ceremonies. There is no evidence that aboriginally the Dogrib had any form of group religious ceremony. Roman Catholic observances came to include not only those directed by the priest but also Sunday prayer services initiated by Dogribs when in the bush apart from church and priest.

Arts. Dogribs take great pleasure, as they must have aboriginally, in group dance on occasions when regional groups come together at such times as the annual treaty payments each summer. The tea dance goes on through the night as a great inward-facing circle of dancers moves clockwise to the accompaniment of melodic song by the dancers. In the drum dance, less popular among old-timers, the drummers sing and the people dance front to back rather than side by side. The Dogrib hand game, a fast-paced hidden-object guessing game between two teams of players accompanied by drumming-chanting, is another major event when different regional groups of Dogribs assemble at Rae or another locale. The Dogrib hand game players and drummers have become a feature of territories-wide assemblies of the Dene peoples.

Medicine. In aboriginal understanding, sickness resulted from the transgression of moral norms, including violation of an interdiction imposed by one's enabling animal spirit, or from the ink'on of another malevolently directed against the sufferer. An adept in curing was called in to diagnose, with the aid of his spirit helper, the cause of the illness. In case of the violation of a taboo or a moral norm, the confession of the ailing person was required in order to restore health. For some minor physical ailments, certain botanical products were believed to have curative properties. Dogribs have generally been receptive to modern medical services.

Death and Afterlife. There is no real information about aboriginal beliefs regarding afterlife. Death as well as sickness might be caused by an individual's transgression or the malevolent power of an enemy. In contemporary times, all belief and ritual relating to death and the afterlife fall within the purview of Roman Catholic dogma and practice.

Bibliography

Helm, June (1972). "The Dogrib Indians." In *Hunters and Gatherers Today*, edited by Mario C. Bicchieri, 51–89. New York: Holt, Rinehart & Winston. Reprint, Waveland Press, 1988.

Helm, June (1981). "Dogrib." In *Handbook of North American Indians*. Vol. 6. *Subartic*, edited by June Helm, 291–309. Washington, D.C.: Smithsonian Institution.

Helm, June, and Nancy O. Lurie (1966). *The Dogrib Hand Game*. National Museum of Canada Bulletin no. 205. Anthropological Series, no. 71. Ottawa.

JUNE HELM

Doukhobors

ETHNONYMS: Bozhi Ludi (People of God), Svobodniki (Freedomites), Sini Svobodi (Sons of Freedom)

Orientation

Identification. Canadian Doukhobors, an ethnic-confessional group, originated in seventeenth-century Russia. Their distinctive belief is in the moral primacy of the Voice of God within the self; hence they are pacifists, refusing to take human life and thus extinguish the divine Voice. They first named themselves "Bozhi Ludi" (People of God), but Orthodox clergy labeled them "Dukhoborfsy" (Spirit Wrestlers) about 1785. They are presently divided into four related subsects: Community Doukhobors, Independents, Reformed, and Freedomites. They identify themselves by specific styles of worship and musical performance; by the ritual and social use of a Russian dialect; by vegetarian diet including "traditional" foods; by pacifist ideals; by at least the endorsement of communal ideals; and by the motto *Trud i Mirnaia zhizn'* "Toil and Peaceful Life."

Location. Doukhobors first settled near Yorkton in east-central Saskatchewan, shortly moved to the West Kootenay region of southeastern British Columbia, and later set up villages in the Pincher Creek region of southwestern Alberta. They have since expanded into the lower Fraser valley region and the Vancouver area; some live elsewhere. In the West Kootenay region, many Doukhobors dwell near their original communal villages, but elsewhere they choose their homes where they want. The only community institution still found everywhere is the *Molenie Dom*, "prayer home" or "community hall."

Demography. The 6,747 Doukhobors who arrived in Canada, mostly in 1899, increased to about 25,000. About 9,000 live primarily in the Yorkton area. At least 10,000 live in the West Kootenay region, and another 4,000 or so in the lower Fraser valley and the Vancouver area. Perhaps 1,000 more live in other parts of Canada, particularly in the Pincher Creek region of southwestern Alberta, the prairie capitals, and Toronto. A few families also live in rural parts of Washington and Oregon in the United States, and a few have settled in San Francisco and Los Angeles since the 1910s, but maintain some contact with their British Columbia congeners. A few individuals and families have emigrated from Russia between the turn of the century and the 1950s. While the topic of a return to Russia has been discussed by Community Doukhobors since World War I, none has returned permanently.

Linguistic Affiliation. Most Canadian Doukhobors are bilingual, speaking a moderately accented English as the business language and a fairly strong Russian dialect (including a number of Ukrainian and other loan words) in the community. Doukhobor Psalms are in a more archaic dialect nearer in structure to Old Church Slavonic. Most people in their forties or younger are fluent in English and some young people speak little Russian. Although loan words occur occasionally, their lexicon is too fluid to suggest permanency. Macaronic speech is not unusual in community contexts. The community expresses concern over the loss of Russian among their youth and supports local Russian-language programs in the school system. There is an ongoing debate regarding the religious importance of Russian, as most elders hold that the religion cannot be expressed in any other language.

History and Cultural Relations

Doukhobors originated in the Russian *Raskol*, or Schism of the 1650s, but did not become a distinct sect until the early 1700s. During the eighteenth century they were persecuted by both church and state as schismatics and pacifists. They developed a principle of spiritual leadership, which by the 1800s tended to be hereditary. Under the reign of Czar Alexander I, persecutions ended and they were granted land in the Crimea, where they developed a structured social system. Persecutions resumed within a generation and the Doukhobors were moved east of the Black Sea, where they again prospered until the Russo-Japanese War, when persecution intensified during a religious revitalization marked by the Burning of Arms (c. June 24, 1895). Leo Tolstoy worked for their relief, and the Society of Friends in London, Philadelphia, and Toronto supported emigration to Canada through 1899 for the most committed third of the Doukhobor population.

The Doukhobor homesteaded in hamlets on reserved lands in what is now east-central Saskatchewan. They established the Christian Community of Universal Brotherhood (CCUB), developed both out of great need for cooperative enterprise and upon doctrine charted by their spiritual leader,

Peter Gospodnie (Lordly) Verigin, still in exile in Russia until 1904. With a land rush and changes in federal government attitudes, the Doukhobors' refusal to complete their homesteading by swearing the oath of allegiance resulted in the loss of their lands and of their improvements as well.

Most migrated to the West Kootenay region in British Columbia between 1907 and 1912, once pioneers had begun the construction of novel community villages. The inhabitants farmed root, field, and orchard crops and produced their own food, clothing, and furnishings. During this period two major subsects appeared. About a third of the Doukhobors drifted out of the community organization and homesteaded independently; they were given the name of "Farmali" (Farmers), or Independents, and they are the largest subsect today. In 1902 a small group took literally a letter of Peter Gospodnie that speculated on the natural life of ideal Christians: seeing the CCUB as a secularizing of Doukhobor society, they withdrew from the community, preaching extreme views. They were named "Svobodniki" (Freedomites).

Between 1912 and 1929 the economic functions of the CCUB were successful, if not markedly so, but the whole community was shocked when, in late 1924, Peter Gospodnie and other passengers died when a still-unexplained explosion destroyed the railroad car in which he was riding from Brilliant, B.C., to Grand Forks, B.C. The event deeply scarred Doukhobor views of their new country and compounded their historic fear of secular governments. Not until three years later did Gospodnie's son Peter Chistiakov (Purger) travel from Russia to Canada to take control of the CCUB. Intending Doukhobor reunification, he organized a blanket structure, the Society of Named Doukhobors, which in 1934 produced the Declaration, an important manifesto. With the depression of 1929 the CCUB's mortgages were called, and between 1938 and 1940 the Doukhobors lost their land and improvements through foreclosures involving a balance of no more than $310,000 owed on an estimated $6 million in property. Peter Chistiakov died at this time. The provincial government paid off the greater part of the debt and seized the Doukhobors' lands and improvements.

Shortly after Peter's arrival, the Freedomite group had grown from about seventy to about twelve hundred individuals, and took the name "Sini Svobodi" (Sons of Freedom). From the 1910s through the 1930s they demonstrated, sometimes violently, against their brethren, the CCUB, the government, and the Canadian Pacific Railway. These acts increased in the 1940s in the wake of the collapse of the CCUB, the death of Peter Chistiakov, the loss of his son Peter Iastrabov (Hawk) Verigin in Russia, and the onset of World War II. Peter Chistiakov's grandson, John J. Verigin, who despite adulation never took up the title of spiritual leader, became secretary and eventually honorary chairman of the Society of Named Doukhobors, which changed its name to Union of Spiritual Communities of Christ in the early 1940s. In 1949, Stephan Sorokin, a Russian Baptist, arrived in Canada and displaced John Lebedoff as the Pastor of the Sons of Freedom. Over the next twenty years, Sorokin's policies and teaching, and repeated incarcerations, gradually ended the protests and most of them took up the new organizational title of members of the Christian Community and Brotherhood of Reformed Doukhobors, or Reformed. By 1964 the provincial government had sold back all the seized land,

though imprisoned Sons of Freedom were excluded from the deal. This small group returned to political protest, which finally ended in the early 1980s through the mediation efforts of members of the regional community.

Over the past twenty years, Doukhobors in Saskatchewan and the West Kootenays have revitalized their culture through the construction of local museums, new diverse-function community halls, and publication of songs and hymns and a bimonthly bilingual journal, _Iskra_ (the Spark); choirs from all groups have frequently taken part in regional and provincial events. Cultural exchanges with the USSR have been arranged, and a number of publications, journals, and recordings produced. Doukhobors continue to integrate themselves effectively into Canadian society, even though they eschew the notion of assimilation.

Economy

Doukhobors in Russia were primarily peasant farmers, though some exercised professional skills. In the Saskatchewan and British Columbia communes they usually farmed, though some men were carpenters and joiners, shoemakers, blacksmiths, harnessmakers, and so on; and women not only cooked and farmed but wove, embroidered, and made clothing. To pay the mortgages in British Columbia, many men went out of the communal villages to work on railroad section gangs, highway construction and maintenance, and in the forest industry. When the CCUB collapsed, many remained in the forest industry or drifted into related trades, taking work as builders or suppliers of building materials. By the 1950s, Doukhobors were retail merchants, teachers, and nurses; by the 1960s, some had entered legal, medical, journalistic, and academic professions. Independent Doukhobors had already entered the mainstream economy, some reaching the professional level by the 1930s. Sons of Freedom either took mostly working-class positions or depended on their vegetable gardens and some welfare for subsistence. Most Doukhobors not living within cities buffer themselves economically by maintaining large vegetable gardens; these represent some of the most intensive noncommercial horticulture on the continent. Much is eaten, almost as much may be contributed to community events, and a further amount is given to neighbors, friends, and guests. During the community period, all labor was divided reasonably between men and women, though the latter did fairly heavy work. Since World War II, patterns have come to resemble those in the majority culture. Elders tend to remain active and productive as long as possible, conditioned by the community motto: "Toil and Peaceful Life."

Kinship, Marriage and Family

Kinship. Canadian Doukhobor kinship patterns are typical of North American society, except that family status, connections, and history are a significant component of individual status in community settlement and political patterns. This is probably a heritage of Russian village life.

Marriage. Doukhobor marriage traditions are unclear before the late eighteenth century, when there was a period of significant informal rites and free choice among young people. Through the nineteenth century and into the early years of Canadian settlement, arranged marriages became the norm, with individual choice now the norm. Doukhobor marriage rites are oral with a variety of verbal rituals and community recognition of a union. Such marriages were not recognized in British Columbia until the late 1950s, and many injustices resulted. Marriages with non-Doukhobors have occurred since earliest times in Canada, increasing significantly since the 1940s. By the 1960s, ritual practices were North American to a marked degree. Today, traditional practices are used for marriage within the community and for joint rituals for intermarriages.

Socialization. During the communal period, there was broad resistance to public schooling, which was seen as assimilative at best and a tool of the Antichrist at worst. In the 1920s some public schools were burned, but after provincial government reprisals the community gradually accepted and then embraced public education. Freedomites resisted until the 1950s, when such draconian measures as the forcible placement of their children in an isolated fenced school broke resistance. Today only a couple of families conduct home education, while most Freedomites and Reformed find the public schools tolerable if not beneficial. Socialization always began within the family, where children have their highest value. In the 1930s a Sunday school movement was begun which continues to the present. In the 1950s, the USCC sponsored Russian-language classes in the community, usually after hours in local schools. In the last decade, local school districts have introduced Russian language and immersion classes into the general curriculum.

Sociopolitical Organization

Social Organization and Conflict. Doukhobors began as active sectarians, and persecution inured them to the maintenance of unity though the same forces from time to time cast up dissidents who sought (and seek) the establishment of their own regimes, not always unsuccessfully. Shortly after Doukhobors arrived in Canada, the Christian Community of Universal Brotherhood came into being, the offspring of vision and necessity. Within six months individual families began to drift away, to become the Independents, many of whom now adhere to the Canadian Society of Doukhobors. The Freedomites first appeared in 1902, became the Sons of Freedom about 1928, and evolved into their leading faction, the Christian Community and Brotherhood of Reformed Doukhobors in the 1960s, splitting off the new Freedomites in 1974. Peter Chistiakov's umbrella organization, the Society of Named Doukhobors, survived the collapse of the CCUB and changed its name in the early 1940s to the Union of Spiritual Communities of Christ. The debates and disputes between these organizations have been many, various, and sometimes bitter. External response has included vigilantism, police action, repressive legislation, royal commissions, and, more recently and less ineffectively, a standing consultative and mediative forum, the Kootenay Committee on Intergroup Relations. This structure, begun in 1979 and meeting irregularly since then, assembles representatives of the Doukhobor groups, provincial and federal agency officials, and local community resource people under the chairmanship of a very senior administrator of the attorney-general's ministry.

Political Organization. Doukhobors held the Russian state to be the Antichrist—that is, both religious and secular arms opposed to the Doukhobor spiritual vision. Toleration under Czar Alexander I only threw the usual practices of the Russian government into darker shadow. When governments in Canada were perceived to have betrayed Doukhobor hopes, the traditional view was reinforced by the British Columbia government's action to deprive Doukhobors (and others) of the voting franchise in the 1930s. At this point, Community Doukhobors formally repudiated involvement in anything above local government (which they perceived as a legitimate community-housekeeping function). Although the restoration of the franchise after World War II helped matters, the policy remains in place. Community Doukhobors do give strong verbal and some material support to the United Nations in its global and local forms, and have recently strongly reinforced their involvement in various arms of the North American pacifist movement. They also make pacifism a primary theme in their communications with Soviet institutions.

Social Control. During the communal period, contact with outside agencies was avoided as far as possible, and the spiritual leader and his lieutenants arbitrated a wide range of issues, occasionally beating offenders. Today, conflicts are usually handled conventionally, the ancient practices of comment, gossip, public debate, advice of elders, and spirited shouting matches followed by honest tolerance if not reconciliation being preferred to police and the courts.

Religion and Expressive Culture

Religious Beliefs. The Doukhobors' central belief is in the presence of God in each conscious person, obviating the need for scriptures, priests, prelates, liturgy, churches, and church paraphernalia, which Doukhobors perceive as unnecessary if not traps of Satan. Nevertheless, they worship corporately in a formal manner, refer to biblical scripture though not always accurately, and possess a magnificent repertoire of sacred music. The religious revitalization of the 1980s introduced some puritan values: alcohol and tobacco, formerly tolerated, were proscribed, and because animals cannot be held to be devoid of consciousness, vegetarianism also became obligatory. These strictures are today more preached than performed, though the vegetarian practice survives most strongly, partly as an ethnic marker. Today, the Doukhobor community is marked by a remarkably broad range of belief, ranging from near-fundamentalism to abstract and universalist deism and agnosticism.

Religious Practitioners. Despite the egalitarian implications of Doukhobor spirituality, various social forces of the 1700s confirmed for most the role of the spiritual leader, the individual in whom the presence of God, most honored, is most manifest. Though it is now a commonplace that "the time of spiritual leaders is past," both John Verigin and in his day Stephan Sorokin certainly have attracted expectations and obligations from those followers who doubt that the time is over. In the conduct of worship, though, even the most respected figures may do no more than occupy a conspicuous position; spoken and sung prayers are begun by respected elders and immediately carried by the congregation. In the home, women are most likely to take spiritual roles, though any individual may choose profound meditation, usually through silently reviewed Doukhobor psalms.

Ceremonies. All Doukhobor ritual is related to *Molenie* (prayer), the usual title of Sunday morning worship, which, briefly, consists of formal greetings, the recitation and singing of Doukhobor psalms, the kiss of peace, the singing of hymns, and final greetings. This is usually followed by the Sobrania (community meeting), a less formal discussion period. Funeral rites conflate the recitation and singing of psalms and hymns; festival occasions greatly expand the singing of hymns and include traditional secular songs on days other than Sunday and doctrinal addresses. All Doukhobors observe the remembrance of the Burning of Arms, usually on or about June 28, the Day of Saints Peter and Paul; Christmas; and Easter. Community Doukhobors add a number of festivals, including the Peminki (commemoration) for Peter Gospodnie and Peter Chistiakov Verigin, Declaration Day in August, and the youth and Sunday school festivals in May and June. Reformed Doukhobors have also celebrated Sorokin's birthday, November 27, but now observe his commemoration, November 15. These events are all sacred in character, although there is occasion for secular performance. Community choirs appear in large and diverse numbers and perform traditional music; visitors come from the region and farther, and regional and foreign dignitaries may be present. These are times of profound cultural expression and unification.

Arts. The primary mode of Doukhobor expression is music, and here they are remarkable, preserving the most complex folk tradition of oral polyphony known, that of their psalms. A high percentage—about 17 percent—of the population are competent choral performers. A hymn tradition is extremely lively, incorporating both Doukhobor and adapted tune and song texts. Musical instruments are used, but are barred from sacred performance. Many women still embroider distinctive Slavic designs; and older men may follow custom by carving wooden spoons, not only as trade curios but as a mark of continuing productivity. Weaving and joinery were significant and admirable during the community period but have since declined.

Medicine. Most Doukhobors use the conventional medical system, though there is a preference for access to masseurs, chiropractors, naturopaths, and similar schools emphasizing prophylaxis, as well as an old connection with the health-food tradition. Some elders also still preserve a folk-healing tradition using "healing psalms" and related practices, with reliable evidence given of their effectiveness.

Death and Afterlife. Here views tend to be conventional and correspond to the balance of religious views, ranging from understandings typical of the European Protestant tradition to broadly (and vaguely) universalist agnosticism. Traditional texts integrate conventional ideas of heaven and hell with the affirmation that these states are present rather than future. In practice, burial is followed by a six-week (when the soul is presumed to have left the vicinity of the corpse) and subsequently annual Peminki at the gravesite.

Bibliography

Bonch-Breuvich, Vladimir (1954). *Zhivotnaiia kniga Dukhobortsev.* [From the Book of Life of the Doukhobors]. Winnipeg, Manitoba: Regehr's Printing. Reprint of 1909 Petrograd edition.

Hawthorne, Harry B., ed. (1955). *The Doukhobors of British Columbia*. Vancouver: University of British Columbia.

Legebokoff, P., and Anna Markova, eds. (1978). *Psalmy, stikhn' pesni.* [Psalms, hymns, songs]. Grand Forks, B.C.: U.S.C.C.

Mealing, F. Mark (1972). "Our People's Way: A Study of Doukhobor Hymnody and Folklife." Ph.D. diss., University of Pennsylvania.

Tarasoff, Koozma (1977). *Traditional Doukhobor Folkways*. National Museum of Man, CCFCS Mercury Series, no. 20. Ottawa, Ontario.

Tarasoff, Koozma (1982). *Plakun Trava: The Doukhobors*. Grand Forks, B.C.: Mir Publishing Society.

Woodcock, George, and I. Avakumovic (1968). *The Doukhobors*. Toronto, Ontario: Oxford University Press.

F. MARK MEALING

East Asians of Canada

ETHNONYMS: Chinese, Japanese, Koreans, Filipinos, Nikkei (Japanese), Orientals

Orientation

Identification.   As used here, "East Asians in Canada" refers to Canadians of Chinese, Japanese, Korean, or Filipino ethnic ancestry. The Chinese in Canada can be divided into two major subgroups—those who came before 1947 and those who have come since then. The earlier group was composed almost totally of men who lived in western Canada. They came primarily from Guangdong Province in southern China. Those who have arrived since 1947 have more often been families, with a substantial percentage emigrating from Hong Kong. Within each subgroup further distinctions can be made on the basis of time of migration to Canada, social status, and place of birth. The Japanese in Canada are a heterogeneous group, consisting of the *issei, nisei, sansei, yonsei,* and the *shin eijusha.* The issei, or first generation, in Canada is made up of the early immigrants who came to Canada roughly between 1877 and 1907. The nisei are the children of the issei who as a group were born between about 1908 and 1940. In Japanese, *nisei* means "second generation," *sansei,* "third generation," and *yonsei,* "fourth generation." The Japanese immigrants who came to Canada after World War II are called the "shin eijusha." Theoretically, these new immigrants can be called "issei," but they prefer to be known as the new immigrants because they are mostly technicians and professionals, unlike the issei before the war who were mostly laborers, farmers, and fishermen. The Koreans and Filipinos are more homogeneous groups, as many are skilled technicians or professionals who have settled in Canada only in the last few decades and have assimilated easily into the Canadian economy.

Location.   Prior to the post–World War II influx, East Asians in general lived mainly in British Columbia and other western provinces. The Chinese were concentrated in British Columbia as well, though Chinese communities did form in large cities elsewhere (for example, Toronto) prior to World War II. In 1986, Ontario contained the largest number of people in each of the four groups with 156,170 Chinese, 44,195 Filipinos, 17,200 Koreans, and 16,150 Japanese. British Columbia is home for 112,605 Chinese, 15,905 Japanese, 15,810 Filipinos, and 5,065 Koreans. Alberta also has many East Asians, and Manitoba has a sizable (15,815) Filipino population. There are relatively few East Asians in the Maritime Provinces or in Quebec, with the exception of the Chinese who number 23,205 in the latter.

Demography.   According to estimates from the 1986 census, there are 360,320 Chinese, 93,285 Filipinos, 40,995 Japanese, and 27,285 Koreans in Canada. East Asians constitute about 2 percent of the population of Canada. Their number has increased rapidly in the last thirty years, both through natural population growth and through increased immigration under the Immigration Act of 1952 and subsequent amendments. For the Japanese, intermarriage of the sansei and younger nisei with non-Japanese has contributed to the natural population growth. The younger group in the Japanese-Canadian demographic profile provides a contrasting pattern to the general Canadian population profile in that the population pyramid base is wider indicating the population as a whole is younger. Filipinos in Canada today are mostly young with a high percentage of females, many of whom have arrived since the 1960s.

Linguistic Affiliation.   Prior to the end of World War II, when they were isolated from the general population, the Chinese and Japanese maintained their native languages. Full participation in their community often required knowledge of the local or regional dialect of Japanese or Cantonese or Mandarin. But those who have settled in Canada in the last thirty years and their children are more often bilingual in the native language and English, with many Chinese from Hong Kong speaking Hong Kong Chinese. Many recent Filipino and Korean immigrants have arrived already speaking English along with their native language.

History and Cultural Relations

The history of the Chinese and Japanese in Canada is essentially one of racial discrimination from the time of arrival to after the Second World War. Koreans and Filipinos, because they have arrived recently during the period when Canada has embraced an official policy of multiculturalism, have suffered much less from racial discrimination. There has been little organized cooperation among any of the four East Asian groups, either in the past or today.

Chinese.   Chinese first immigrated to Canada in the 1850s to participate in the Fraser River gold rush. When the mines gave out, some moved on to California and others returned to China, but the majority stayed on in British Columbia where they worked in low-level service jobs. In the 1880s a second wave of Chinese men arrived in Canada. In all, about seventeen thousand came, with most recruited to work on the extension of the Canadian Pacific Railroad through British Columbia. Whites in British Columbia expected that once the railroad was completed, the laborers would return to China. But many could not afford the trip back and instead settled in British Columbia where they worked as wage laborers in coal mining, fish canning, and agriculture. Always viewed as less than equal by Whites in British Columbia, their willingness to work hard for low wages and thus take jobs many thought belonged to Whites led to further resentment, harassment, and the formation of anti-Chinese organizations such as the Workingman's Protective Association and the Knights of Labour.

   White resentment also led the British Columbia government to seek changes in national immigration laws that would effectively end Chinese immigration to Canada. In 1885 a head tax of fifty dollars was placed on immigrating Chinese; in 1901 it was raised to one hundred dollars and in 1905 to five hundred dollars. Because the tax failed to prevent immigration, the Chinese Immigration [Exclusion] Act was amended in 1923 and immigration ceased until the act was repealed in 1947. Between 1923 and 1947 only forty-four Chinese had immigrated to Canada. The repeal of the act and subsequent measures over the next twenty years gave Chinese the opportunity for full participation in Canadian society, including the right to vote which had previously been denied them. It also opened up immigration, with many of those arriving since 1947 coming as families from Hong Kong, Taiwan, and elsewhere, such as Southeast Asia, the Caribbean, and South America.

Japanese.   The first Japanese in Canada was Manzo Nagano, a sailor, who arrived in 1877 and after sojourns back to Japan and to the United States eventually settled in Victoria in 1892. The early period of emigration from Japan (1877–1907) was one in which conflict resulting from racial and cultural differences culminated in the race riots of 1907 in Vancouver. During this period there was considerable hostility toward both the Chinese and Japanese in British Columbia. As noted above, various measures were enacted by the British Columbia government to restrict Chinese immigration and participation in Canadian society. Although aimed at the Chinese, these restrictions applied to the Japanese as well and led to disfranchisement and efforts to restrict naturalization. These various attempts to enact discriminatory and racist legislation were not occurring in a vacuum. Public agitation in the province had been increasing gradually.

The perception of Whites in British Columbia that the Japanese were an economic threat rested on several basic cultural differences. The Japanese emphasis on frugality and hard work was reflected in their day-to-day activities and in their customs and habits all of which were based on the traditional Japanese value system. Japanese social organization centered on shared needs as well as on a sense of group consciousness. Group solidarity within the Japanese community was further strengthened by its physical and social segregation from White society. Within this bounded territorial space, it was not difficult to retain the highly systematic and interdependent social relations that were based on the principle of social and moral obligation and traditional Japanese practices of mutual assistance such as *oyabun-kobun* (parent-child) and *sempai-kohai* (senior-junior) relationships. Another aspect of traditional Japanese social relations that characterized both the oyabun-kobun and sempai-kohai systems was the emphasis placed on one's sense of duty, loyalty, and obligations to one's employers. Out of a sense of unquestioning loyalty, the kobun or kohai blindly followed the orders given by the oyabun or sempai. Ironically, these traditional values and customs, which led to the relatively successful adaptation by the Japanese in western Canada, became the main reason that the White community prevented the Japanese from becoming equal members of Canadian society.

Japanese laborers who came to Canada around 1907 were recruited to work for the Canadian Pacific Railway and the Wellington Colliery. The period from 1908 to 1940 was one of controlled immigration, the major feature of which was the "Gentlemen's Agreement" of 1908, which restricted immigration to returning immigrants, wives and children, and immigrants specifically hired by Canadians. Because of the Anglo-Japanese alliance and labor shortages, anti-Japanese sentiment decreased before and during World War I. It increased again during the depression after the war and led to restrictions on Japanese involvement and ownership rights in the fishing and other industries, professional employment, and access to higher education. As Adachi has noted, to Japanese-Canadians citizenship was meaningless or, at best, symbolized the "status of second-class citizenship."

From 1941 to 1948 the situation worsened, and Japanese-Canadians were deprived of their civil rights. The threat of war with Japan and then the war itself increased anti-Japanese feelings and led the government beginning in late 1941 to impound the property of Japanese-Canadians, close their language schools, and halt publication of Japanese-language newspapers. In 1942, 20,881 Japanese-Canadians were rounded up and removed to detention camps in interior British Columbia, Alberta, Manitoba, and Ontario. Restrictions were relaxed beginning in 1943, motivated in part by the need for Japanese workers in other parts of Canada. In July 1947 a commission was established to compensate Japanese-Canadians for the property that had been confiscated. It was not until September 1988, however, that all property and civil rights claims were settled, with the final settlement reached by the National Association of Japanese Canadians and the government of Canada. The wartime experience effectively destroyed the Japanese community in Canada, but revitalization has started through the efforts of those who have arrived in the last few decades.

Settlements

East Asians have always been and continue to be mostly urban. Early Chinese and Japanese immigrants tended to form distinct ethnic communities—"Chinatowns" and "Little Tokyos"—in large cities. Because of their larger numbers, the Chinatowns have been more visible and have drawn more attention. In the nineteenth and early twentieth centuries, these communities were typical urban immigrant ghettos. Since the 1950s, as the Chinese and Japanese populations in Canada have increased and become more mobile spatially and socially, the urban communities have become social, political, and symbolic centers as well as residential ones. At the same time, as discrimination has lessened, more Chinese and Japanese have chosen to live outside the traditional communities. For the Japanese, Toronto has in some ways replaced Vancouver as the center of Japanese culture in Canada. Koreans and Filipinos have also settled mainly in urban areas (two-thirds of Filipinos live in the Toronto area), but they have not formed distinctive residential enclaves. Filipinos, perhaps more so than the other groups, have settled in the suburbs.

Economy

Chinese and Japanese laborers who came to British Columbia around 1907 were brought in mainly through contractual arrangements between emigration companies and Canadian importers of labor such as the Canadian Pacific Railway and the Wellington Colliery. Many of these men worked for the railroad, on farms, in the fishing industry, and in wood pulp mills. For the Chinese, White Canadians expected that they would return to China once their work on the railroad was completed. When most stayed in Canada and took low-level work at low wages, White resentment resulted and was directed both at the Chinese and Japanese. A labor shortage during World War I dampened anti-Asian feelings, but they increased again after the war as a result of a depression and unemployment that became marked upon the return of soldiers.

The strong control of the fishing industry on the west coast by the Japanese at this time became a matter of concern for British Columbia politicians, and in 1919 they attempted to limit the number of fishing licenses issued to Japanese fishermen. As part of the attempt to restrict immigration, the provincial legislature asked the dominion government to amend the British North America Act so that provincial governments would have the "power to make laws prohibiting Asiatics from acquiring proprietary interest in agricultural, timber and mining lands or in fishing or other industries, and from employment in these industries." Between 1923 and 1925, the Department of Marine and Fisheries took away close to one thousand fishing licenses from the Japanese, and they were prohibited even from using gasoline-powered fishing boats in order to give White fishermen a competitive advantage. Such economic harassment continued to plague the Japanese fishermen, and consequently, many went into farming.

Laws that denied Chinese and Japanese the right to a provincial vote prevented them from participating fully in several areas of professional employment because of a requirement that one must be on the voters' list. For example, to secure a logging license, one had to be twenty-one years of age and on the voters' list. These employment restrictions also applied to education, and it was not until the fall of 1945 that McGill University in Montreal accepted a nisei. This delayed access to education has had serious consequences for the nisei in terms of their occupational mobility. Chinese professionals, because of these restrictions, confined their business to the Chinese community. After release from the detention camps, some Japanese chose to remain in Alberta, Manitoba, and Saskatchewan where they became farmers. The Japanese who have arrived since World War II are more highly educated than both the prewar Japanese and Canadians in general and are found in relatively large numbers working in the professions, academia, and the arts. The Chinese today are still heavily involved in service industries (restaurants, laundries, garment-making), although recent immigrants are less likely to enter these traditional occupations. The economic nature of the Chinatowns has been transformed in the last two decades from what were essentially residential enclaves that provided products and services to the Chinese community to major economic centers that provide products and services to Canadian society.

Many Koreans came to Canada to find economic independence, and many have succeeded. Unemployment is rare among Korean-Canadians and about 50 percent own their own home, a far greater percentage than in Korea. Many are university-educated and work as physicians, lawyers, and professors, while perhaps some 50 percent own small businesses such as food stores, gasoline stations, restaurants, and real estate agencies. In Toronto, for example, Koreans run about twelve hundred convenience stores. The success of these enterprises rests in part on the willingness of family members to staff the establishments so that they can remain open for long hours.

Kinship, Marriage and Family

Chinese.   Chinese kinship, marriage, and family in Canada have gone through three distinct stages. From the 1880s to 1947, the Chinese in Canada formed a "bachelor community" composed almost entirely of unmarried men or men whose wives and families were in China. These men usually lived in collective households called *fang-k'ou-* in the Chinatowns. A few fang-k'ou- still exist, though they are disappear-

ing as the few remaining old Chinese bachelors die off. They were organized into numerous associations or fictive kin groups with affiliation based on a common place of birth, surname, or dialect. The second stage took place roughly from 1947 to 1967 and involved the arrival of the wives and children of some of the bachelors and the formation of nuclear families.

The third stage began in 1967 and continues today with nuclear families that are similar in size and composition to Canadian families in general. Perhaps the major differences between the contemporary Chinese-Canadian family and other Canadian families are the extent to which adult Chinese children provide financial support for their parents and the frequency with which grandparents live with their children and their important contribution to child rearing.

Japanese.   Many of the Japanese laborers who came to Canada in the early 1900s were unmarried men. Unable to return to Japan, they relied upon arranged marriages or on "picture bride" arrangements, a system whereby pictures of the prospective bride and groom were exchanged and the decision to marry made after consultation with relatives and possibly the *nakodo,* or go-between. As these brides immigrated to Canada, the demographic composition of the Japanese community gradually changed.

Kobayashi has observed that the most significant characteristic of Japanese-Canadian marriages today is that Japanese-Canadians are marrying Canadians of other ethnic backgrounds at a rate that suggests that this is the norm rather than the exception. Her analysis of immigrant marriages also reveals that immigrants, too, are intermarrying frequently with non-Japanese Canadians. About 42 percent of Japanese women under the age of forty-four are married to non-Japanese men.

In these mixed marriages, however, there are indications that not all aspects of traditional Japanese culture have disappeared. Certain traditional festivals such as *hina-matsuri* (dolls festival) on May 3, *tango-no-sekku* (boys festival) on May 5, and *keiro-no-hi* (a day set aside to respect the aged) are still celebrated. The celebration of these festivals reinforces Japanese family values. For example, the elderly issei and nisei place considerable emphasis on *gaman* (forebearance) and *enryo* (modesty). Gaman means the suppression of emotions, the ability to grin and bear all pain, to remain calm and carry out one's task regardless of the circumstances. Enryo means much more than modesty as it encompasses codes of behavior concerning moderation and nonaggression. Self-effacement, self-control, reticence, humility, and denigration of oneself are all included in enryo. With the aging of the issei and nisei, the Japanese-Canadian family is attempting to come to terms with some traditional family values such as *oyakoko* and *kansha*. Oyakoko (filial piety) rests on the feeling of kansha (gratitude to one's parents) and children are obliged to fulfill their filial duties to take care of their aging parents. This responsibility often falls on the eldest son or daughter. But in many families, because of the vast geographic distances that often separate the generations in Canada, it can be extremely difficult to fulfill one's filial obligations.

Koreans and Filipinos.   Because of their recent arrival, middle-class socioeconomic status, and residential dispersal, Korean and Filipino families are generally similar to the average Canadian family. Many Koreans, however, own small businesses, which are often staffed by family members from three generations, making economic cooperation between extended kin important. And despite economic assimilation, many traditional Korean family values such as the importance of ties to clan members, patriarchal authority, and respect for the elderly remain important. Filipino families in Canada are often formed through a chain migration, with the first immigrant being a young woman with job skills marketable in Canada. She subsequently arranges for her parents, children, siblings, and other relatives to emigrate.

Sociopolitical Organization

Because of their isolation within Canadian society, both the Chinese and Japanese developed distinct ethnic communities with their own social, economic, and religious institutions, which reflected both the values and customs of the homeland and adaptational needs in Canada.

Chinese.   The basic social unit in Chinese communities in pre–World War II Canada, the fictive clan (clan association or brotherhood), reflected the reality that 90 percent of the population was male. These associations were formed in Chinese communities on the basis of shared surnames or combinations of names or, less often, common district of origin or dialect. They served a wide range of functions: they helped maintain ties to China and to the men's wives and families there; they provided a forum for the settlement of disputes; they served as centers for organizing festivals; and they offered companionship. The activities of clan associations were supplemented by more formal, broader-based organizations such as the Freemasons, the Chinese Benevolent Association, and the Chinese Nationalist League. With the growth and demographic change in the Chinese community after World War II, the type and number of organizations in Chinese communities have proliferated. Most are now served by many of the following: community associations, political groups, fraternal organizations, clan associations, schools, recreational/athletic clubs, alumni associations, music/dance societies, churches, commercial associations, youth groups, charities, and religious groups. In many cases, membership in these groups is interlocking; thus special interests are served while community cohesion is reinforced. In addition, there are broader groups that draw a more general membership, including the Chinese Benevolent Association, the Kuomintang, and the Freemasons.

Japanese.   Group solidarity within the post–World War II Japanese community was strengthened by their social and physical segregation in their work and residential environments. Within this bounded territorial space, it was not difficult to retain the highly systematized and interdependent social relations that were based on the principle of social and moral obligations and the traditional practices of mutual assistance such as the oyabun-kobun and sempai-kohai relationships. The oyabun-kobun relationship promoted non-kin social ties on the basis of a wide-ranging set of obligations. The oyabun-kobun relationship is one in which persons unrelated by kin ties enter into an agreement to assume certain obligations. The kobun, or junior person, receives the benefits of the oyabun's wisdom and experience in dealing with day-to-day situations. The kobun, in turn, must be ready to

offer his services whenever the oyabun requires them. Similarly, the sempai-kohai relationship is based on a sense of responsibility whereby the sempai, or senior member, assumes responsibility for overseeing the social, economic, and religious affairs of the kohai, or junior member. Such a system of social relations provided for a cohesive and unified collectivity, which enjoyed a high degree of competitive power in the economic sphere. With the removal of the Japanese during World War II, subsequent relocations, and the arrival of the shin eijusha after World War II, there has been a weakening of these traditional social relations and obligations.

The sizable Japanese population, which shared a common language, religion, and similar occupations, led to the formation of various social organizations. Friendship groups and prefectural associations numbered about eighty-four in Vancouver in 1934. These organizations provided the cohesive force necessary to maintain the formal and informal social networks operative in the Japanese community. Prefectural association members were able to secure social and financial assistance, and this resource plus the strong cohesive nature of the Japanese family enabled early immigrants to remain competitive in numerous service-oriented businesses. Japanese-language schools were an important means of socialization for the nisei, until the schools were closed by the government in 1942. In 1949 the Japanese finally won the right to vote. Today, both the sansei and shin eijusha are active participants in Canadian society, although their involvement in the academic and business sectors is more noticeable than in the political sector. The National Association of Japanese Canadians has played a major role in settling the claims of the Japanese removed during World War II and in representing Japanese-Canadian interests in general.

Koreans and Filipinos.   Koreans and Filipinos in Canada have formed a variety of local and regional associations, with the church (United church for Koreans and Roman Catholic church for Filipinos) and affiliated organizations often the most important institution serving the community.

Religion and Expressive Culture

The majority of Chinese, Japanese, Koreans, and Filipinos in Canada are Christians.

Chinese.   Traditional Chinese religious beliefs centered on ancestor worship, which is reported as declining in Canada. But because ancestor worship is practiced in private, just how important it still is is unclear. The majority of Chinese are now Christians, with various denominations (Presbyterian, Roman Catholic, Anglican, Lutheran, Baptist, Pentecostal) represented in the larger Chinese communities. The United church is the most important and is the center of social and recreational activities in many communities. Major holidays other than Christian ones are the Lunar New Year, Bright-Clear, and Mid-Autumn. Chinese cultural traditions remain strong in Canada and are reflected in Chinese opera, martial arts, food, and traditional crafts such as paper folding. These traditions are maintained in part through regular cultural exchanges between Chinese-Canadian communities and the People's Republic of China, Taiwan, and Hong Kong.

Japanese.   The early issei or Japanese immigrants preferred Buddhism, but by the early 1900s, Christian missionaries were beginning to have some success in winning converts.

Both the United church of Canada and the Methodists were making considerable inroads especially with the Canadian-born nisei. Although churches in Canada did not take a stand when Japanese property was confiscated and the Japanese were interned during World War II, the Roman Catholic, Anglican, and United churches provided elementary school education for children in British Columbia camps. The 1986 census indicates that this education experience helped win converts to the churches, with 10,680 Japanese members of the United church, 3,425 Anglicans, and 1,625 Roman Catholics in comparison to 10,330 Buddhists. There are also Japanese who are Seventh-day Adventists, Pentecostals, Baptists, Methodists, Mormons, Lutherans, and other Protestant denominations. More than 25 percent claim no religious affiliation. Recent immigrants reflect the changing religious affiliations of modern Japan in that several *shinko shukyo*, or "new religions" such as Soka Gakkai, Tenrikyo, P. L. Kyodan, Rissho Kosei Kai, and Konkokyo, are beginning to flourish in such cities as Vancouver, Toronto, and Montreal. These new religions, however, have their roots in Shintoism and Buddhism.

Koreans.   For Koreans, earliest contacts with Canada date to 1890 and the arrival of Canadian missionaries in Korea. These missionaries later arranged for the immigration of Koreans to Canada. Koreans belong mainly to the Korean United church, the Korean Presbyterian church, and the Korean Roman Catholic church, with the United church being the most influential. At the same time, Korean traditions are maintained and Korean food, dance, music, and martial arts are highy visible in Canadian society. In addition to the major Christian holidays, Korea's National Independence Day is celebrated on March 1.

Filipino.   The overwhelming majority of Filipinos in Canada are Roman Catholics, and their churches are the centers for organized activity outside the family. The Christian holidays are major religious and social events and are celebrated with the incorporation of traditional foods, dance, music, and other customs.

See also East Asians of the United States

Bibliography

Adachi, Ken (1976). *The Enemy that Never Was*. Toronto: McClelland & Stewart.

Chan, Anthony B. (1983). *Gold Mountain: The Chinese in the New World*. Vancouver: New Star Books.

Johnson, Graham E. (1979). "Chinese Family and Community in Canada: Tradition and Change." In *Two Nations, Many Cultures: Ethnic Groups in Canada*, edited by Jean L. Elliot, 358–371. Scarborough: Prentice-Hall of Canada.

Kim, Uichol (1989). "Acculturation of Korean Immigrants: What Are the Hidden Costs?" *Korea Observer* 20:431–454.

Kobayashi, Audrey (1989). *A Demographic Profile of Japanese Canadians*. Winnipeg: National Association of Japanese Canadians.

LaViolette, Forrest E. (1948). *The Canadian Japanese and World War II*. Toronto: University of Toronto Press.

Li, Peter S., and B. Singh Bolaria, eds. (1983). *Racial Minorities in Multicultural Canada*. Toronto: Garamond Press.

Saito, Shiro (1977). *Filipinos Overseas: A Bibliography*. New York: Center for Migration Studies.

Sugimoto, Howard H. (1972). "The Vancouver Riots of 1907: A Canadian Episode." In *East across the Pacific*, edited by Hilary Conroy and T. Scott Miyakawa, 92–126. Honolulu: University of Hawaii Press.

Sunahara, Ann (1981). *The Politics of Racism*. Toronto: James Lorimer & Co.

Ujimoto, K. Victor (1979). "Postwar Japanese Immigrants in British Columbia: Japanese Culture and Job Transferability." In *Two Nations, Many Cultures: Ethnic Groups in Canada*, edited by Jean L. Elliot, 338–357. Scarborough: Prentice-Hall of Canada.

Wickberg, Edgar, ed. (1982). *From China to Canada: A History of the Chinese Communities in Canada*. Toronto: McClelland & Stewart.

K. VICTOR UJIMOTO

East Asians of the United States

ETHNONYMS: Chinese, Japanese, Koreans, Filipinos, Orientals

Orientation

Identification.   The general category of East Asians in the United States includes Americans of Chinese, Filipino, Japanese, and Korean ancestry. Neither East Asians in general nor any of the four East Asian–American groups is a homogeneous cultural group in the United States. Within each are a number of identifiable subgroups, with perhaps the most sigificant being those who arrived before World War II and their descendants and those who have arrived since, the latter, except for Japanese-Americans, making up the overwhelming majority of East Asian–Americans. Other important divisions are based on the region of origin in the sending nation, language, religion, generation, and occupation.

Location.   Prior to the post–World War II population increase East Asian–Americans were concentrated in Hawaii and California, with small numbers in Washington and Oregon. Since World War II, the percentage of East Asians has increased dramatically, partly through immigration to the United States and partly through migration from Hawaii to the mainland. Japanese-Americans remain heavily concentrated in the West (80.3 percent in 1980), mainly in the Los Angeles, San Francisco, and San Jose areas, though sizable numbers now live in Chicago, Washington, D.C., and New York City. In 1980, 42.9 percent of Korean-Americans lived in the West, with the other 60 percent distributed almost evenly in the northeastern, north-central, and southern regions. In 1980, 52.7 percent of Chinese-Americans lived in the West with 26.8 percent in the East, with major communities in New York City and Boston. Filipino-Americans remain a largely West Coast group with 68.8 percent settled there in 1980. Large Filipino communities also exist in Detroit, Chicago, New York City, and Boston as well as in San Diego, Norfolk, New London, Connecticut, and other cities with large naval bases, reflecting a tradition of Filipino service in the U.S. Navy dating to 1901.

Demography.   Estimates for 1985 indicate that there were 1,079,400 Chinese, 1,051,600 Filipino, 766,300 Japanese, and 542,400 Korean-Americans in the United States. If immigration figures for 1986 through 1989 are considered, it is likely that Filipinos are now the largest East Asian group in the United States as the number of Filipino immigrants was more than double the number of Chinese ones during this period. The number of East Asians has increased dramatically since the 1950s. In 1940, there were 285,115 Japanese, 106,334 Chinese, 98,535 Filipino, and 8,568 Korean-Americans. Reflecting this heavy recent immigration, the East Asian population contains a majority of immigrants (in 1980, 63.3 percent of the Chinese, 64.7 of the Filipinos, 81.9 percent of the Koreans), and they are a young population (about 60 percent are under forty-four years of age in these three groups). Japanese-Americans were a larger population than the other groups before 1950 and have had a lower rate of immigration since then; thus they have a lower percentage of immigrants (28.4 percent) and are a somewhat older population group.

Linguistic Affiliation.   The first generation of East Asian immigrants generally spoke the language of their homeland. Thus, Japanese spoke Japanese; Koreans spoke Korean; Chinese spoke Cantonese, various Mandarin dialects, or Hakka; and Filipinos spoke Ilocano, Visayan, or Tagalog, with most recent immigrants speaking Tagalog, now the offical language of the Philippines. In the second generation of recent immigrants, relatively few speak the native language regularly or remain fluent in it as adults. Instead, they prefer to speak English. Native language maintenance is a major concern of the first generation of recent immigrants, though language school programs have met with only limited success.

History and Cultural Relations

The nature of East Asian immigration to and settlement in the United States is a function of a variety of factors including politics and economic conditions in the sending nation, the relationship between the sending nation and the United States, the need for cheap labor in the United States, and the racial prejudice encountered by East Asians in the United States. The Chinese were the first East Asian group to settle in America in significant numbers, with 322,000 arriving between 1850 and 1882. Most were men who worked as laborers in mines, in factories, and on farms to earn money that would enhance their economic status when they returned home.

While initial settlement was in the western states, some later were sent east under a contract labor system designed to exploit the Chinese as a source of low-paid labor, and others settled in the south. In response to demands for control of Chinese immigration and settlement that began in California in the 1860s, Congress passed the Chinese Exclusion Act which in 1882 effectively ended their immigration until 1943. During this period, the Chinese population in the United States decreased from 107,448 to 61,639. It was also during this period, however, that Chinatowns developed in cities near where the men worked.

Unlike Chinese immigrants, the first influx of Filipino, Japanese, and Korean immigrants went to Hawaii where they were recruited to work on the sugar and pineapple plantations. Later, some moved on to California and the Northwest Coast while others immigrated directly from their homelands, again to work as laborers on farms and in factories and canneries. The Japanese came first, and by 1890 there were 12,000 in Hawaii and 3,000 in California. By 1920 300,000 had come to these two areas. The gentlemen's agreement between the United States and Japan in 1907 placed quotas on and slowed Japanese immigration. Between 1903 and 1905, 7,226 Koreans immigrated to Hawaii; however, Korean immigration virtually disappeared for forty years when the Japanese government (which then ruled Korea) ended emigration from the country in 1905. Filipinos were recruited and began immigrating to Hawaii in 1906 in place of the Koreans and Chinese. Between 1909 and 1931 113,000 Filipinos immigrated to Hawaii, with 55,000 settling there, 39,000 returning home, and 18,600 moving on to the mainland. Some Filipinos also immigrated directly to California and the Northwest Coast, where they were used as farmworkers in place of the declining numbers of Japanese and Chinese. The Immigration Act of 1924 through quotas virtually eliminated immigration from East Asia. Most immigrants between 1924 and the 1940s were wives of men already in the United States. Many of these were "picture-brides" selected through an exchange of photographs handled by a matchmaker. Nearly all East Asian men and women lived in distinctively Chinese, Japanese, or Filipino communities in which the native languages and many traditional beliefs and practices were maintained. The marriages also produced a second generation in the United States who were citizens and who spoke English and were much less interested in maintaining the traditional cultures.

During World War II, the four East Asian communities had different experiences. Filipinos were classified as nationals and therefore could not serve in the U.S. armed forces, though the rules were changed during the war to allow Filipinos to serve. The Chinese-American community benefited in some ways from the war, as job opportunities opened up. In 1943 the Exclusion Act was repealed, migration increased, and anti-Chinese sentiments lessened. Because Korea was ruled by Japan, Korean-Americans were classified as Japanese, although they were strong supporters of the war and vehemently anti-Japanese. Despite their being seen as Japanese, they were not classified as enemy aliens or removed to internment camps.

The bombing of Pearl Harbor served as a catalyst to turn years of anti-Japanese feeling on the West Coast into action designed to destroy the Japanese-American community on the mainland. Japanese-Americans (including those who were citizens) were classified as enemy aliens and rounded up; by the end of 1942 110,000 from California, Oregon, and Washington had been interned in camps in the California desert, Idaho, Arizona, Utah, and Arkansas. All except those who chose and were allowed to serve in the military and those who chose to resettle in the Midwest and East were kept in the camps until 1945. This mass violation of Japanese-Americans' civil rights nearly destroyed the Japanese community in the United States. After release from the camps most returned to California, with many reestablishing farms in the central part of the state. It was not until the late 1980s that the U.S. Congress voted to pay survivors of the camps $20,000 each as compensation for their losses.

As noted above, since the end of World War II, there has been a multifold increase in the number of East Asians immigrating to the United States. The repeal of restrictive immigration laws, closer ties between the United States and South Korea, the Philippines, Taiwan, and Japan, and the Hart-Cellar Immigration Act of 1965 which essentially ended the national-origin quota system all encouraged immigration to and settlement in the United States. East Asians who have come to America since World War II are a much different population than those who came earlier. They are younger, include a larger number of women and families, are often highly educated professionals and technicians, and expect to stay in the U.S.

The one constant in the settlement histories of the four groups was the economic exploitation and discrimination they experienced. In addition to major discriminatory actions—the Chinese Exclusion Act, the Immigration Act of 1924, and Japanese-American internment during World War II—East Asians were subject to numerous other discriminatory practices. For example, in California they were barred from certain businesses and professions, antimiscegenation laws prevented marriage to Whites, residential restrictions confined East Asians to their own communities, various laws limited their right to own land, Chinese miners (and Mexican miners) had their profits taxed, and so on. Today, although overtly racist policies and laws have essentially disappeared, racism continues. East Asian–American men, for example, make less than White counterparts with equal experience and education, and few have made it to the top level of American businesses. There is also growing resentment among other Americans about East Asian and especially Japanese investment in the U.S. economy and ownership of properties in the United States. The depiction of East Asian–American groups as "model minorities" troubles some East Asian–Americans, as it suggests that equality has been achieved while contrasting East Asian economic success with other minorities' alleged failures and thus creating conflict between the groups.

Settlements

East Asian–Americans are mainly an urban-suburban group, with the place of residence now largely determined by socioeconomic status. The two major nonurban groups are Japanese-Americans in the farming and nursery and related businesses in central California and Filipino-American farm workers in California. Today, Koreatown in Los Angeles is the center of Korean life for the 150,000 Korean-Americans in southern California and the home for many elderly Korean-Americans and recent immigrants. The large Chinatowns that developed early in the century in cities such as San Francisco, Portland, Boston, Los Angeles, and New York City have been transformed into major economic zones providing products and services both to the regional Chinese-American population and to the general economy. The tourist trade has also become a major source of income in Chinatowns. Their economic growth has been accompanied by or perhaps was stimulated by their decline as residential districts. As with Koreatown in Los Angeles, most residents are either elderly or are recent immigrants and many are poor. "Little Tokyo" in Los Angeles, which serves Japanese-American communities in southern California, has also undergone the same transformation. Filipino-Americans, except for the mostly male communities in Hawaii and California early in the century, have not formed distinct ethnic enclaves comparable to Chinatowns.

Economy

In general, the economic circumstances of Koreans, Japanese, Chinese, and Filipinos in Hawaii and on the mainland in the late nineteenth and early twentieth centuries were much the same. The majority were low-paid, unskilled, male workers on sugar plantations in Hawaii and in the railroad, agriculture, fishing, logging, and mining industries on the mainland. When demand for their work diminished and East Asian immigration decreased, those who remained in the United States and their children tended to settle in cities and became involved in service industries. Filipinos worked as domestics in hotels and as kitchen workers in restaurants and many men joined the Merchant Marine or the U.S. Navy where they worked as mess stewards or in other low-level service jobs. At the same time, many Filipinos were employed seasonally as farm workers and eventually became active in the unionization movement. The Chinese were also employed in service industries as well as founding their own businesses, with restaurants, laundries, and garment factories being most common. In Hawaii, many Chinese sugar workers went on to work in the rice industry, and a sizable percentage became business owners or professionals. The Japanese also found work as domestics, gardeners, and farmers, with some finding ways to circumvent laws that prohibited them from owning land. Many of those who owned farms returned to rebuild them after they were released from the World War II internment camps. Both the Japanese and Chinese businesses have been described as "middleman minority" adaptations characterized by self-ownership of family-staffed businesses that provide a unique product or service to the community.

The arrival of the post–World War II immigrants has changed the position of East Asian–Americans in the U.S. economy. Many of those who have arrived since 1965 have been highly educated professionals or skilled technicians, and the children of the earlier settlers have had greater access to advanced education and professional employment. These two developments have improved the economic position of East Asian–Americans. Both men and women are now employed at about the same rates as Americans in general. The percentages of East Asian–American women who work (55 percent of Koreans, 58 percent of Chinese, 59 percent of Japanese, and 68 percent of Filipinos in 1980) are especially noteworthy. As of 1980, the men were employed in significant numbers in managerial and professional positions (22.5 percent for Filipinos to 38 percent for Chinese), with the largest percentages of women being employed in administrative support and service jobs. Unique occupation patterns include 22 percent of Chinese-American men in service jobs, 30.4 percent of Filipino-American men in service and administrative support positions, and 14.4 percent of Korean-American men in sales. For women, 18.2 percent of Chinese-American and 24 percent of Korean-American women work in low-level laborer positions. Gross figures indicate that full-time Chinese-American and Japanese-American men have higher incomes and Filipino-American and Korean-American men have lower incomes than Whites. The Chinese and Japanese figures are somewhat misleading, however, in that they do not reflect the fact that men in these groups often have more education and work longer hours than do Whites. Korean-Americans have drawn considerable attention as owners of small businesses, often grocery stores or vegetable stands, in minority neighborhoods, suggesting a middleman minority role similar to the Chinese and Japanese earlier.

Kinship, Marriage and Family

Kinship. In the early Korean, Chinese, and Filipino communities, which were composed almost entirely of men, ties to families and wider kin networks were maintained through return visits, correspondence, and the remittance of a percentage of the man's earnings. In the communities that formed in this country, the absence of East Asian women and antimiscegenation laws made marriage and the formation of families and kin groups difficult. Some community cohesion was created through fictive kin groups modeled on clan and extended family structures in the homeland. Chinese men formed fictive clans with recruitment and membership based on immigration from the same village or province or possession of the same surname. When Chinese families began to form later in the early twentieth century with the arrival of Chinese women, these clan associations became less important. Filipinos organized _compang_, fictive extended families composed of men who immigrated from the same village, with the oldest man usually heading the family. As more Filipino women immigrated to the United States, Filipino-American families became more common (though before World War II Filipino-American men still outnumbered women by nearly three to one), and the _compadrazgo_ (godparent) system was transferred to the United States with each individual then enmeshed in a network of actual and fictive kin.

The situation for Japanese-Americans was different, as beginning in 1910 stable families began to form and Japanese urban and rural communities also become relatively stable. Although the second-generation Japanese-Americans, the nisei, were being acculturated into American society, the first-generation-based family (issei) was still strong enough to maintain traditional beliefs regarding appropriate behavior between superiors and inferiors as well as filial duties.

Marriage and Family. The most noteworthy trend in East Asian–American marriages is the shift from ethnic endogamous to ethnic exogamous marriage. In all groups since the 1950s there has been a large increase in the number of marriages to non–ethnic group members, and especially to Whites. Contemporary East Asian–American families are generally small nuclear families. Korean-American and Filipino-American households are somewhat larger because of the larger number of children in the former and the presence of non–nuclear family members in the latter. East Asian–American families are notably stable, with over 84 percent of children in all four groups living with both of their parents. Nonetheless, there are concerns in the Chinese-American community about juvenile delinquency and in the Korean-American about what is considered a high divorce rate. There is a major difference in household composition between those already settled in the United States and recent immigrants. Households among the latter frequently contain additional relatives beyond the nuclear family or friends, as these households are often part of the chain migration process through which relatives immigrate to the United States.

Within households in all four East Asian–American groups, decision making has become more egalitarian as patriarchal authority has diminished. Women, however, still bear the major responsibility for household tasks, even though a majority of both men and women are employed. Educational opportunities are afforded both boys and girls, and both sexes are encouraged to excel in school.

Socialization. As with Americans in general, socialization takes place through the family, the local community, and the formal education system. Many East Asians in the past came to America with a high school education and many of the recent immigrants have college and/or professional education or technical training. The children of recent immigrants make full use of educational opportunities in the United States; in fact education for their children is a major reason many East Asians resettle. Programs designed to maintain the traditional culture, such as language classes, youth groups, and cultural programs are offered in all major East Asian communities by ethnic associations and churches. One major problem facing many recent immigrant families is a generational gap between parents who prefer to speak the native language and eat native foods, stress family obligations, and associate mainly with other ethnic group members and their children who see themselves as Americans, speak English, and make friends among non-Asian-Americans.

Sociopolitical Organization

Social Organization. Each of the four East Asian–American groups is a diverse ethnic group composed of a number of distinct subgroups. Across all four groups, two internal divisions are most obvious. First is the distinction between those who settled before World War II and their descendants and those who arrived after the war. Second is the distinction in the post–World War II group between the parental and second generation, with the latter composed of those who were born in the United States or came when they were young. Beyond these two categories, each East Asian group displays additional diversity as well as various social institutions developed in the United States.

Chinese. Major divisions within the Chinese-American community include those based on place of origin (Hong Kong, Taiwan, Southeast Asia), Cantonese or non-Cantonese ethnicity, rural or urban residence, and support for Taiwan or recognition of the People's Republic of China. Localized in Chinatowns and excluded from full participation in American society for over one hundred years,

Chinese-Americans developed a complex set of interlocking organizations that enabled them to maintain elements of their traditional culture while adapting to their new life. In the early years, when the population was mostly male, clan and regional associations with affiliation based on surname and region of origin served to affiliate men in the United States and maintain ties with the homeland. Other organizations including secret societies (tongs), guilds, and credit associations were also developed, all of which served economic, political, and social functions. With the arrival of more women and the formation of families in the twentieth century, the second generation of Chinese-Americans appeared. Although they were socially and economically isolated from mainstream society, they learned English in school and formed organizations based on mainstream models and interests. At the same, they were less interested in the traditional culture, and membership in the clan and regional associations declined. In the post–World War II immigrant group, the clan and regional associations and tongs have declined in importance as the focus has shifted to forming organizations that will help Chinese-Americans secure full rights as American citizens.

Filipinos. For Filipino-Americans, the major internal distinction is based on the region from which one emigrated: the Ilocanos from northern Luzon, the Tagalogs from central Luzon, and the Visayans from the central Philippines. Although the three groups are no longer as separate as they once were, regional endogamy is still stressed by the post–World War II parental generation, and a preference for affiliation with people from the same region has contributed to the absence of a pan-Filipino organization in the United States. In the mostly male pre–World War II Filipino community, few social organizations developed. Instead, social cohesion was achieved through the maintenance of family and kin groups based on traditional practices. Today, the Roman Catholic church is the social center of many Filipino communities, and kinship and friendship networks are also important agents of social cohesion.

Japanese. Within the Japanese-American community a major distinction is made on the basis of generation in the United States with the issei being the first generation, the nisei the second, the sansei the third, and the yonsei the fourth. These categories are applied to those who arrived before World War II. Those who arrived after the war are technically issei, but are not referred to as such. Japanese in the United States also include Japanese businessmen and wives or ex-wives of Americans who worked in Japan after World War II. Both these groups exist outside the Japanese-American community. In the prewar years in California, Japanese-Americans formed a network of interlocking businesses, such as rooming houses, laundries, groceries, and so on, which served the Japanese-American and other East Asian–American communities. At the same time, the issei maintained a cohesive community through educational and cultural organizations, a credit association, and regional associations. The nisei moved away from the more traditional groups and chose instead to form their own organizations often based on existing mainstream models and activities such as recreation leagues. Today, the Japanese-American community is socially complex with distinctions made on the basis of generation, age, political affiliation, life-style, and oc-

cupation. At the same time, Japanese values emphasizing group interests over individual interests, deference, loyalty, and reciprocity govern everyday behavior for many Japanese-Americans and are a major source of social cohesion.

Koreans. The Korean-American community today is composed mainly of people who immigrated to the United States after World War II and their children. One basic distinction in the community is made among those born in Korea (Ilse), those born in the United States (*Ese* or *samse*), and those who came to the United States when they were young. The Ilse tend to speak Korean rather than English, have strong ties to Korea, and emphasize the role and authority of the family and the husband/father. Those in the younger generation are more assimilated into American society. Unlike the other East Asian groups, organizations based on kinship or regional affiliations rarely formed among Korean-Americans. Rather, most organizations have formed on the basis of common interests and include clubs, churches, associations, and political groups. One of the more important are the alumni associations (high school and college) which enmesh Korean-Americans in lifelong social and economic networks. Living outside the Korean-American community are perhaps as many as 100,000 wives or ex-wives of American servicemen who served in Korea, their children, and thousands of Korean children adopted into White families.

Political Organization.   Because they were denied citizenship and the right to vote, East Asian–Americans before World War II were essentially powerless to directly influence local, state, or federal policies and actions that affected them. Within the mostly male, relatively isolated East Asian-American communities, social control and decision making was based on traditional beliefs and customs that usually accorded much authority to the older men in the community. At the same time, the regional and clan associations, guilds, secret societies, and other organizations served as special interest groups to advance the interests of their members. East Asian–American interests within American society were often handled by umbrella organizations, which included the Chinese Consolidated Benevolent Association and later the Chinese-American Citizens Alliance, the Japanese-American Citizen's League, and the Korean Association. A pan-Filipino political organization did not develop, though Filipinos were active in labor movements in Hawaii and California.

Politics in the homeland have and continue to be a major concern and a source of conflict especially in the Chinese-American and Korean-American communities. Some Korean-Americans affiliate on the basis of ties to factions in Korea, and a major division in the Chinese-American community involves those who emphasize ties to Taiwan versus those who recognize and want ties strengthened with the People's Republic of China.

Japanese-Americans have been active in Hawaiian politics and hold many elective offices, a development that has sometimes led to conflict with other ethnic groups. On the mainland, especially since the 1960s and to some extent as a result of the civil rights movement, Chinese and Japanese-Americans especially have been more active in voicing their concerns, participating in the major political party politics, running for office, and seeking government employment.

Religion and Expressive Culture

Religious Beliefs. Religious beliefs and institutions have been a major force in all East Asian–American communities, both past and present, though the particular beliefs and institutions vary among the four groups. Most Koreans who settled in the United States had already been converted to Christianity (usually Protestantism) in Korea before arriving. In the contemporary Korean-American community the the Korean Christian churches are often the center of community activity and provide many programs of special appeal to women, the elderly, and children. They have also been the locus of language and cultural maintenance programs. In many churches the services are conducted in Korean.

Nearly all Filipinos in the United States are Roman Catholics, their ancestors having been converted some generations ago in the Philippines. Because of their dispersed residence pattern, Filipino-Americans do not form their own churches but instead affiliate with the local church.

The first generation of Japanese-Americans believed in Buddhism and/or Shintoism. Many were converted in the United States by missionaries to various Protestant denominations, and today the Japanese-American community has perhaps the widest range of religious affiliations of the four East Asian–American groups. Recent immigrants have brought with them some of the new Japanese religions, although all have roots in Buddhism and Shintoism.

The religious beliefs and practices of the early Chinese immigrants centered on ancestor worship, Buddhism, and Taoism. Ancestor worship was especially important as a source of community cohesion and as a mechanism to maintain ties with the homeland. Efforts by Protestant missionaries with these immigrants largely failed, and today only about 20 percent of Chinese-Americans are Christians. Recent immigrants have brought with them some of the revived Chinese folk religions and have formed Buddhist and Taoist associations.

Expressive Culture. The post–World War II immigration has revitalized the expressive elements of East Asian culture in the United States. In all four groups, traditional dance, music, theater, and art are flourishing and are a major focus of ethnic solidarity and pride, as are the public celebration of traditional holidays. Some aspects of expressive culture have also become part of the mainstream culture, most notably Chinese and Japanese cuisines, martial arts, architecture, and artistic styles and designs.

See also East Asians of Canada

Bibliography

Almirol, Edwin B. (1983). _Ethnic Identity and Social Negotiation: A Study of a Filipino Community in California._ New York: AMS Press.

Bonacich, Edna, and John Modell (1980). _The Economic Basis of Ethnic Solidarity: Small Business in the Japanese American Community._ Berkeley: University of California Press.

Daniels, Roger (1988). _Asian America: Chinese and Japanese in the United States since 1850._ Seattle: University of Washington Press.

Hurh, Won Moo, and Kwang Chung Kim (1984). _Korean Immigrants in America: A Structural Analysis of Ethnic Confinement and Adhesive Adaptation._ Rutherford, N.J.: Fairleigh Dickinson University Press.

Kendis, Kaoru O. (1988). _A Matter of Comfort: Ethnic Maintenance and Ethnic Style among Third-Generation Japanese-Americans._ New York: AMS Press.

Kim, Ilsoo. (1981). _New Urban Immigrants: The Korean Community in New York._ Princeton, N.J.: Princeton University Press.

Kitano, H. L. (1977). _Japanese Americans: The Evolution of a Subculture._ Englewood Cliffs, N.J.: Prentice-Hall.

Loewen, James W. (1971). _The Mississippi Chinese: Between Black and White._ Cambridge: Harvard University Press.

Pido, A. J. A. (1985). _The Pilipinos in America: Macro-Micro Dimensions of Immigration and Integration._ Staten Island, N.Y.: Center for Migration Studies.

Sung, Betty Lee (1967). _Mountain of Gold._ New York: Macmillan.

Takaki, Ronald (1989). _Strangers from a Different Shore: A History of Asian Americans._ Boston: Little, Brown & Co.

Thernstrom, Stephan (1980). _Harvard Encyclopedia of American Ethnic Groups._ Cambridge: Harvard University Press, Belknap Press.

Tsai, F. W. (1980). "Diversity and Conflict between Old and New Chinese Immigrants in the United States." In _Sourcebook on the New Immigration: Implication for the United States and the International Community,_ edited by Roy S. Bryce-Laporte, 329–337. Washington, D.C.: Research Institute on Immigration and Ethnic Studies, Smithsonian Institution.

Wong, Bernard (1983). _Patronage, Brokerage, Entrepreneurship, and the Chinese Community of New York._ New York: AMS Press.

Xenos, Peter S., Robert W. Gardner, Herbert R. Barringer, and Michael J. Levin (1987). "Asian Americans: Growth and Change in the 1970s." In _Pacific Bridges: The New Immigration from Asia and the Pacific Islands,_ edited by James T. Fawcett and Benjamin V. Cariño, 249–284. Staten Island, N.Y.: Center for Migration Studies.

Yanagisako, S. (1985). _Transforming the Past: Tradition and Kinship among Japanese Americans._ Stanford: Stanford University Press.

Yu, Eui-Young (1989). "Korean American Community in 1989: Issues and Prospects." _Korea Observer_ 20:275–302.

Eastern Shoshone

ETHNONYMS: Green River Snakes, Plains Shoshone, Washakie's Band, Wind River Shoshone

Orientation

Identification. The Eastern Shoshone have lived in western Wyoming, particularly in the valleys of the Wind, Green, and Big Horn rivers, since about the fifteenth century, combining the general culture type of the Great Basin with those of the pre-horse and post-horse Great Plains. In addition, they have been influenced by Spanish, American, and other sources. In the early 1980s, there were perhaps three thousand of their descendants living on the Wind River Reservation in Wyoming and its environs.

Location. The Eastern Shoshone can be divided into two groups, the Buffalo Eaters (Sage Brush People) and the Mountain Sheep Eaters (Mountaineers). The former occupied the Green River and Wind River valleys and had a pattern of annual movement with concurrent tribal concentration and dispersal. In earlier times they were under continual attack from the Plains tribes, including the Arapaho, Blackfoot, and Sioux. The Mountain Sheep Eaters used the central Rocky Mountain region, including the Yellowstone Lake area. The Wind River Reservation, which they now share with the Northern Arapaho, was established in 1863. It is a generally dry mountainous area with rainfall averaging about thirteen inches a year, and with average temperatures ranging from 10° to 80° F.

Linguistic Affiliation. The Shoshone spoke dialects of the Central Numic language, a branch of the Uto-Aztecan language family, and had affinities to the languages of the Northern and Western Shoshone groups.

History and Cultural Relations

Their history since about 1500 can be described in a number of phases, beginning with their pre-horse penetration of the High Plains and their adoption of large-scale bison hunting; then with the acquisition of horses around 1700 came a second phase of widespread raiding through the plains. A third phase, around the beginning of the nineteenth century, was marked by a losing war with the Blackfoot, smallpox epidemics, and the introduction of the Sun Dance. This was followed by a period of alliances with the Whites and renewed tribal viability under Chief Washakie. Reservation life in the later nineteenth century was characterized by intense hardship and population losses. The first half of the twentieth century showed cultural and demographic stabilization, and innovation in religious institutions. Since 1945, there has been population growth and a general adaptation to mainstream White culture as well as to a growing Arapaho political dominance on the reservation.

Settlements

In the nineteenth century, the Eastern Shoshone had a complex pattern of land use. The Buffalo Eaters did not have a single set of specified boundaries, but a number of different ones of varying significance. The valleys of the Green and Wind rivers were their core area, with the plains and mountains used at times. They had a pattern of annual movements with concurrent tribal concentrations and dispersals. The Mountain Sheep Eaters held the central Rocky Mountain region but also had reciprocal relations with the Buffalo Eaters. In the early days, the dwellings were bison-skin tipis. The tipis' pole framework was covered by a complex arrangement of bison hides, and the covering was decorated with paintings celebrating the husband's accomplishments. Small menstrual huts were also used. Dwellings on the reservation today are generally wooden bungalows.

Economy

Subsistence and Commercial Activities. There was a large variety of fauna available to the Eastern Shoshone, supplemented by berries and roots, with seeds being of minor importance. Access to these resources was limited somewhat by natural conditions, and by the actions of hostile tribes. Hunters had a right to their kill, with a special sequence of sharing followed for bison. Sites for fish weirs or game traps involved only temporary property rights, and plant gathering involved none. Food was ritualized to only a minor extent, the most important being a taboo on meat eating by women in menstrual or birthing seclusion. Staples were the bison, fish (especially trout), elk, beaver, and mule deer. Major but only occasionally available game included the antelope, jackrabbit, mountain sheep, marmot, and sage hen. These were supplemented by many minor food sources. Lynx, mink, otter, and weasel were not eaten but were valued for their furs. Women, especially in the late summer and fall, picked currants, rose hips, haws, and gooseberries. They dug up roots, camas bulbs, and wild onions. Greens and the sugar content of various honey plants enlivened the diet. Thistles and some kinds of sunflowers served as the only source of seeds. The seasonality of foodstuffs ruled the annual congregating, movement, and dispersal of the various Shoshone groups. The bison was by far the greatest resource but was available only briefly in the spring and for a longer period in the fall. The women were skilled and rapid butchers and were efficient at drying the meat. But the Shoshone could only rarely gain as much as half their annual food supply from bison. The principal food fish were cutthroat trout, Montana grayling, and Rocky Mountain whitefish, taken primarily in the spring and either eaten fresh or preserved by sun-drying or smoking. The basic method of catching fish was by driving them into a weir. After bison and fish in importance were elk, which were run down like bison, or single elk being tracked like mule deer. Berries were eaten fresh, in soups, or pounded with meat and fat to be preserved as pemmican. Roots were cooked in an earth oven. Prickly pear in drier areas was eaten on rare occasions.

The horse, mule, and dog were the domestic animals, with cattle being added in the later nineteenth century. They prized horses and dogs as aids in transportation, hunting, and war; neither animal was eaten except in great need, nor were the hides and bones put to other uses. Both animals were well cared for, with the bison-hunting horse often being sacrificed on a man's grave. Men cared for war horses, women for pack horses and baggage. They used rawhide-lashed wood-handled whips but not spurs, transported the infirm with a horse travois, and raided other tribes for horses. They had a relatively low incorporation of the horse into religion and the formal social structure. The Buffalo Eaters kept dogs for hunting and as guards, and the Mountain Sheep Eaters used dog transport on a large scale.

Industrial Arts.   The Eastern Shoshone made a wide variety of leather goods. Tipis, clothing, and containers, as well as hides or furs primarily for trade, were the major manufactures. The latter were of three types: sumptuary, ritual, and craft products; utilitarian objects (coiled basketry, drinking horns, bear-paw snowshoes); and improvised expedient productions (temporary housing, bullboats, scrapers). In later years they were heavily involved in the fur trade and in intermarriage with traders and White settlers.

Division of Labor.   Bison-skin tipis were made by the women and decorated by their husbands. Leatherworking, except for shields, bowstrings, drums, and rattles, was women's work. Women possessed special skills in plant gathering, household crafts, curing, household transportation, and gambling. They were socially subordinate to the men who were engaged in hunting, fishing, warfare, working with horses, and trade.

Kinship

The Eastern Shoshone used Hawaiian kinship terminology, all cousins being equated with siblings or called by terms derivative from those used for siblings. In the terminology, which is still being used, there are distinctions between primary and descriptive terms. Collective and quasi-kin terms indicate focal and indefinitely extended relationships. Most primary terms refer to consanguineal kin. They distinguish the kinsman's line of descent and generation, and, in part, the sex of the speaker. Both parallel and cross cousins are considered to be more distant siblings.

Marriage and Family

Marriage.   In the past, bride-service was common, especially through a young groom's living initially with his wife's parents. There used to be a high degree of polygyny, and sibling exchange marriages were also probably common. According to Shimkin, however, in the period 1850–1930, only 3 cases of polygyny, 2 of sibling exchanges, and 3 of marriage with consanguineal kin were reported out of 239 marriages. These changes were likely due to Christian influence. Marriage was forbidden with any first or second cousin. Premarital sex relations were freely permitted and subject to no sanctions.

Inheritance.   There was an absence of individual property rights in land or movable property, or of any rule of inheritance governing the transmission of such rights.

Socialization.   Infants and very young boys and girls were dependents undifferentiated by sex. They were rarely punished, but kept quiet through fears of monsters and enemies. Larger boys joined peer groups, with aggression being much encouraged. Adolescence for boys was not formally marked, and the search for supernatural power began at this time. Marriage and joining a military society connoted a man's status. A girl would stay with her mother, helping in household chores, caring for younger siblings, and playing girls' games. Menarche required isolation in the family menstrual hut, avoidance of meat and of daytime sleeping, and the obliga-

tion to gather firewood. Shortly after menarche, a girl's parents or, if they were dead, her older brother or maternal uncle, would arrange her marriage—usually to a good hunter, stable and reliable.

Sociopolitical Organization

Social Organization.   Age and sex largely determined roles and status within the traditional society, with inheritance playing a small role. Social positions, however, were earned in warfare or attributed to the acquisition of supernatural power. Women were socially subordinated to men and menstruation stigmatized women as sources of dangerous ritual pollution. Polygyny (never sororal) involved conflicts and the economic exploitation of younger wives. In middle and older ages, midwifery, curing, or gambling earned prestige for women. In modern times, large bilateral kindreds have become key sociopolitical elements. Berdaches, of low status, were also present.

Political Organization.   The whole tribe was gathered at times for winter shelter. In winter and early spring, the tribe could break up into three to five bands, each having a loose association with a particular region in western Wyoming, but not named or bounded. Membership in each band was flexible, with extended family groups joining one or another of the bands or sometimes another tribe entirely. Effective leadership was necessary in the bison hunt, warfare, trade, and winter shelter. In the tribe, and to a varying extent in each band, the conduct of chieftainship was aided by two military societies and by a variety of temporary aides, such as heralds. The chief was a middle-aged or older man of military and shamanic distinction who gave orders affecting the tribal march or a collective hunt. He also gave counsel on issues of joint decision, but had little to do with internal disputes. There was evidence of an active tribal council in earlier times, but on the reservation now, they maintain a business council of six members. The business of the reservation as a whole is carried out by a joint business council with the Northern Arapaho tribe, also residents of the reservation. The two military societies, the Yellow Brows and the Logs, were complementary rather than competitive.

Social Control and Conflict.   War was a continuing state among them, and war gains and losses directly affected tribal viability. In the early nineteenth century, the Shoshone were badly battered by smallpox and were threatened by Sioux, Cheyenne, and Gros Ventre raiders. They countered these threats by alliances with fur traders and the U.S. government, but they continued to lose small parties to raiders until well into the late nineteenth century. The demographic effects of warfare were severe. Eventually, there was a low adult male/female sex ratio, as a result of which they were forced to recruit trappers, Metis, and Indians from other tribes into marriages. Features evident in Shoshone warfare were war honors, which were the greatest source of prestige, suicide in combat, and horse-stealing raids on foot. Chiefs were in charge of large actions and peacemaking.

Religion and Expressive Culture

Religious Beliefs.   Prior to extensive Christian missionary efforts and the introduction of the Peyote religion in the late nineteenth century, the Eastern Shoshone practiced two forms of religious beliefs and behavior. The first was directed toward personal success and survival through the acquisition of supernatural power from the world of spirits. The second was designed for the welfare of the community and of nature and to ward off impending prophesized disasters. The mythological beings and animations of nature and their powers were of central importance, with the relation between shaman and power being of supplication and dependency. A successful quest for power was expressed by a vision in which the power appears bestowing skills or protections, fetishes to call forth the power, a song, and individual taboos. Water Ghost Beings and Rock Ghost Beings were feared. The domain of ghosts included not only Ghost Beings, but old women, great-grandparents, apparitions, and whirlwinds.

Ceremonies.   The Father Dance, the Shuffling Dance (Ghost Dance), and the Sun Dance were supplications addressed to beneficent beings, particularly Our Father. The Father Dance and the Shuffling Dance were especially a tradition among the Mountain Sheep Eaters and were usually nighttime events in the fall, winter, or spring in which both men and women participated in the singing of sacred songs. The Sun Dance, probably acquired from the Plains tribes, was a day-and-night event of the summer, restricted to men, with dancing and thirsting to exhaustion.

Medicine.   It was believed that illness came from breach of taboos, malevolent dwarf people, and sorcery. On the other hand, they were pragmatic about childbirth, snake bites, minor ailments, and wounds and fractures. Houses where death had occurred were often abandoned.

Bibliography

Johnson, Thomas Hoevet (1975). *The Enos Family and Wind River Shoshone Society: A Historical Analysis.* Ann Arbor: University Microfilms.

Lowie, Robert Harry (1915). *Dances and Societies of the Plains Shoshone.* American Museum of Natural History, Anthropological Papers, 11, 803–835. New York.

Shimkin, Demitri B. (1947). *Wind River Shoshone Ethnogeography.* University of California Anthropological Records, 5(4). Berkeley.

Shimkin, Demitri B. (1947). *Childhood and Development among the Wind River Shoshone.* University of California Anthropological Records, 5(5). Berkeley.

Shimkin, Demitri B. (1986). "Eastern Shoshone." In *Handbook of North American Indians.* Vol. 11, *Great Basin,* edited by Warren L. d'Azevedo, 308–335. Washington, D.C.: Smithsonian Institution.

Trenholm, Virginia C., and Maurine Carley (1964). *The Shoshonis: Sentinels of the Rockies.* Norman: University of Oklahoma Press.

East Greenland Inuit

ETHNONYM: Tunumiut

The East Greenland Inuit are found in the Ammassalik (65°40′ N) and Scoresbysund (70° N) regions on the east coast of Greenland. Two other east Greenland groups, the Northeast and the Southeast Greenland Inuit, are now extinct. In 1980 the East Greenlanders numbered some three thousand with about twenty-four hundred in the Ammassalik region and four hundred in Scoresbysund. The East Greenlandic language is a dialect of Central Greenlandic and is mutually intelligible with the West Greenlandic dialect.

East Greenland was settled by peoples migrating east from West Greenland, beginning as early as the fourteenth century and continuing to modern times. As Europeans preferred to settle in the west, the East Greenlanders come under sustained European influence only after 1900. Early contacts were in the form of schools and churchs, followed by stores and colonial rule by Denmark. Scoresbyund was settled in 1925 by migrants from Ammassalik. Since about 1950, the East Greenlanders have experienced considerable cultural change—most significantly, a shift from a subsistence hunting economy to a money economy based on the sale of sealskins and cod fishing.

Prior to Danish rule, there were no permanent settlements, with new winter settlements established every year or so and more frequent movements in the warmer months. The extended family longhouse with nuclear families occupying "apartments" was the typical dwelling in the winter village. Tents were used in the summer. Traditional housing has now been replaced by expensive wood houses that have led to a more settled life, but that have also put new financial burdens on East Greenlanders.

The traditional subsistence economy was based heavily on seal meat and skin as well as whale, sea birds, and fish. Productive equipment included dog sleds, umiaks, kayaks, wooden boats, harpoons, knives, sealskin floats, and seal nets. The motor boat has replaced traditional modes of transportation, though the kayak remains important for sealing. Sale of sealskins and cod along with craft sales, wage labor, and welfare are sources of income today.

The basic social unit is the patrilocally extended family usually consisting of three generations residing in one dwelling. The oldest male heads the family, though leadership in most activities vests in those who are most skilled or knowledgeable. A few households formed a settlement, although ties between the family units were loose and families could join or leave a settlement as they chose. The Ammassalik and Scoresbysund regions are governed by municipal councils and represented on the Greenland Municipal Council.

Missionary activity in East Greenland was very successful, and most East Greenlanders are now Christians. The traditional religion included beliefs in a tripart universe, a soul (*tarneq*), and various gods and spirits. Shamanism was not highly developed, as individuals could use magic to approach the supernatural world directly.

Bibliography

Petersen, Robert (1984). "East Greenland before 1950." _In Handbook of North American Indians._ Vol. 5, _Arctic,_ edited by David Damas, 622–639. Washington, D.C.: Smithsonian Institution.

Petersen, Robert (1984). "East Greenland after 1950." In _Handbook of North American Indians._ Vol. 5, _Arctic,_ edited by David Damas, 718–723. Washington, D.C.: Smithsonian Institution.

Trap, Jens P. (1970) _Grønland._ 5th ed. Edited by Niels Nielsen, Peter Skautrup, and Christian Vibe. Danmark, Vol. 14. Copenhagen, Denmark: G.E.C. Gads Forlag.

Eskimo

ETHNONYMS: Esquimox, Esquimaux

The name "Eskimo" has been applied to the native peoples of the Arctic since the sixteenth century; ironically, it is not an Eskimo word. For close to a century both anthropological and popular sources, including the _Oxford English_ and _Webster's New World_ dictionaries, maintained that the name "Eskimo" derived from a proto-Algonkian root translating as "eaters of the raw flesh." In fact, the name originated in the Montagnais language and had no such meaning. Eskimos refer to themselves with terms that translate as "real people" or "authentic human beings." These self-names vary from one Eskimo language to another and include the names "Inuit," "Inummaariit," "Inuvialat," "Inupiat," "Yup'ik," "Suxpiat," and "Unangan." The strength of the belief by Eskimos themselves in the pejorative connotations of their name was a major factor in its replacement, in Canada and Greenland since the 1970s, by the designation "Inuit," an ethnonym used by eastern Arctic Eskimos and Canadian Arctic Eskimos. In Alaska and Siberia, however, the term has never taken root. Although the Eskimos of the western Arctic are indeed members of the larger family of Eskimo cultures, they refer to themselves in their own language as "Yup'ik," "Inupiat," or "Unangan." To call them "Inuit" is inaccurate, and there is no all-encompassing native name for the entire native population of the Arctic.

ANN FIENUP-RIORDAN

European-Americans

About 80 percent of Americans are descended from people of European ethnicity. The short summaries that follow present information on the population, distribution, migration history, and cultural persistence of thirty-seven European ethnic groups in the United States. Appended to some summaries are short lists of publications, most of which are recent studies of a particular ethnic community or a general historical or cultural survey of the ethnic group. Some of the information in these summaries is derived from _The Harvard Encyclopedia of American Ethnic Groups_ and _We the People._ These are the basic reference resources for information about American ethnic groups and should be consulted for additional information and references.

See also Acadians, Amish, Appalachians, Basques, Doukhobors, French Canadians, Hasidim, Hutterites, Irish Travelers, Jews, Mennonites, Molokans, Mormons, Old Believers, Ozarks, Peripatetics, Rom, Shakers

ALBANIANS. In 1980, 21,687 Americans claimed Albanian ethnic ancestry and another 16,971 claimed Albanian and other ethnic ancestry. Because of underreporting in the past, this is likely an undercount, with Americans of Albanian ancestry probably numbering no less than 70,000. Pre-World War II Albania was inhabited by two major cultural groups—the Ghegs (Gegs) in the mountainous North and the Tosks (Toscs) in the South. Both groups spoke mutually intelligible dialects of Albanian, although there were clear economic, religious, and social differences between the two groups. In the United States, in-group variation is reflected more in religious differences (Greek Orthodox, Muslim, Roman Catholic) than in the Gheg/Tosk dichotomy. Most Albanians settled in the United States in the early 1900s, with Boston the major community. Other communities formed in Detroit, Chicago, Worcester (Massachusetts), and Connecticut. After World War II, a community of Catholic Albanians formed in the Bronx, New York, and continues to exist as a distinct ethnic enclave. The traditional culture centered on the patriarchal family, a strong sense of family honor, clans, and blood feuds has mostly given way to an American middle-class life-style. But a strong sense of Albanian identity survives through ethnic associations, the church, traditional celebrations and foods, and kin ties. Albanian political identity is perhaps centered more on concern over the status of Albanians in the Kosovo region of Serbian Yugoslavia than on anticommunism.

Bibliography

Nagi, Dennis L. (1987). _The Albanian-American Odyssey: A Pilot Study of the Albanian Community of Boston, Massachusetts._ New York: AMS Press.

ARMENIANS. In 1980, 155,693 Americans claimed Armenian ancestry and another 56,928 claimed Armenian and other ethnic ancestry. In Europe and the Near and Middle East, Armenians have lived under the control of the Turks, Russians, and Iranians and have formed distinct ethnic minorities in countries such as Lebanon. Economic and cultural variations among Armenian groups in these locales was transferred by Armenian immigrants to the United States. Industrial cities in the East and Midwest, the California central valley, and Los Angeles are major Armenian population centers, with 42 percent of Armenian-Americans in 1980 living in California. Settlers in industrial cities first worked in the steel, automobile, and textile industries, but quickly moved up the economic ladder, using business and technical skills brought with them from Armenia to the New World. The first Armenians in central California were farm workers, and they, too, quickly moved up the economic ladder, as shop and landowners. In both locations, the rapid economic mobility was accompanied by rapid assimilation, reflected in the loss of the Armenian language and a high rate of intermarriage. The most recent arrivals are those who have emigrated from the Soviet Union (and indirectly from Turkey and the Middle East) since 1976 to the Los Angeles area. Since the 1960s, there has been a strong ethnic revival reflected in Armenian schools, language programs, contacts with Armenians in the Soviet Union, and concern over the continuing Armenian-Azerbaijani conflict there.

Bibliography

Henry, Sheila A. (1978). *Cultural Persistence and Socioeconomic Mobility: A Comparative Study of Assimilation among Armenians and Japanese in Los Angeles*. San Francisco: R and E Research Associates.

Mirak, Robert (1983). *Torn between Two Lands: Armenians in America, 1890 to World War I*. Cambridge: Harvard University Press.

Phillips, Jenny K. (1987). *Symbol, Myth, and Rhetoric: The Politics of Culture in an Armenian-American Population*. New York: AMS Press.

Rollins, Joan H., ed. (1981). *Hidden Minorities: The Persistence of Ethnicity in American Life*. Washington, D.C.: University Press of America.

AUSTRIANS. In 1980, 339,789 Americans claimed Austrian ancestry and another 608,769 claimed Austrian and other ancestry. Unlike many other Euopean nations, Austria was not formed on a distinct ethnic population base, and thus Austrians are more accurately described as a nationality than as an ethnic group. Austrians who have settled in the United States, including a sizable minority of Jews, have assimilated rapidly into American society and tend to see their Austrian identity as a variant of German identity.
See also Germans

BELGIANS. In 1980 there were 122,814 Americans who claimed Belgian ancestry and another 237,463 who claimed Belgian and other ethnic ancestry. The nation of Belgium was and is inhabited by two distinct groups—the Flemish in the coastal northwest (in the region commonly called Flanders), who speak a language closely related to Dutch, and the Walloons in the east and southeast, who speak French. This distinction has been maintained in the United States and is reflected in the separate settlements established by immigrants from each group in the nineteenth and twentieth centuries. Most of the pre-1920 immigrants were Flemish and they tended to settle in areas already settled by the Dutch (especially in Michigan and Wisconsin), although they were often excluded from Dutch communities because of Dutch anti-Catholicism. Walloons tended to settle near French or French-Canadian communities, and the large Walloon community near Green Bay, Wisconsin, began in this way. Although some features of Walloon or Flemish culture survived into the mid-twentieth century such as cycling clubs, choral societies, and community newspapers, both groups are now largely assimilated into American society and are seen by others as of Belgian rather than of distinctively Flemish or Walloon ancestry.

BYELORUSSIANS. (Belorussians, Kryvians, White Russians, White Ruthenians). There are about 200,000 people of Byelorussian ethnic ancestry in the United States today. This is very likely an underestimate, as those who arrived prior to World War I (and whose descendants are the majority of Byelorussians in the United States today) were identified as either Russians or Poles. Byelorussia is the region that today is located in the Soviet Union south and east of Lithuania and Latvia. As with many peoples from Eastern Europe, the Byelorussians arrived in two major waves: 1880 to World War I and after World War II. Both groups tended to settle in large industrial cities in the Northeast and Midwest. The descendants of the first wave are now much assimilated into American society. Those who arrived after World War II and their children have emphasized their Byelorussian identity through formation of their own church communities, parochial schools, associations, anti-Soviet sentiment, a language preservation program, and the celebration of ethnic holidays and life-cycle events following traditional customs.

Bibliography

Kipel, Vitaut (1982). *Byelorussian Americans and Their Communities of Cleveland*. Cleveland: Cleveland State University.

CARPATHO-RUSYNS. (Carpatho-Russians, Carpatho-Ukrainians, Rusnaks, Ruthenians, Uhro-Rusyns). Carpatho-Rusyns in the United States today are mainly third- or fourth-generation descendants of Carpatho-Rusyns who immigrated to North America between 1880 and 1914. Carpatho-Rusyns spoke East Slavic dialects closely related to Ukrainian. In 1980 about 600,000 Americans were of Carpatho-Rusyn ancestry, although only 8,485 claimed such ancestry in the 1980 census. This is in part because many identify themselves as Ukrainians or Russians and because the U.S. census no longer considers the Carpatho-Rusyns as a distinct group. The homeland of the Carpatho-Rusyns is the Carpathian mountains in what are the modern nations of Poland and Czechoslovakia and the Ukrainian Soviet Socialist Republic. Initial settlement was in the mining and industrial regions of Pennsylvania, New York, New Jersey, Ohio, Illinois, and Connecticut. Ethnic identity was closely tied to their identity as Eastern Christians, expressed through membership in the Byzantine Rite Catholic church or Orthodox churches. Carpatho-Rusyn services contained a number of unique practices, most notably a liturgical chant using folk melodies still sung by groups today. Partly because of the absence of a distinct country of national origin, a sense of Carpatho-Rusyn ethnic identity has largely disappeared in the United States. In the Ukrainian Soviet Socialist Republic, people of Carpatho-Rusyn ancestry now see themselves as Ukrainians. In 1931, a subgroup called the Lemkians, composed of people from the Lemkian region of southeastern Poland formed a separate ethnic association. They have made a strong effort to maintain their ethnic identity through an active press, concern about their national identity, and the maintenance of some traditional practices.

See also Ukrainians

Bibliography

Magocsi, Paul R. (1984). _Our People: Carpatho-Rusyns and Their Descendants in North America_. Toronto: Multicultural History Society of Ontario.

CROATS (Croatians). In 1980, 107,855 Americans claimed Croatian ancestry and another 145,115 claimed Croatian and other ethnic ancestry. This is probably a gross undercount, as many Croats are identified as Yugoslavians or Serbs. A figure of at least 500,000 is probably a more accurate estimate of the number of people of Croatian ancestry in the United States. Croatia is one of the six constituent republics of the modern nation of Yugoslavia. The U.S. census has usually classified Dalmatians, who live on the Adriatic coast of Yugoslavia, as Croats. In the late 1700s and early 1800s Dalmatian fishermen settled in Louisiana, where they were able to continue their maritime traditions. The major migration of Croats occurred between 1880 and World War I when they formed Croatian communities in industrial and mining towns and cities in Pennsylvania, Ohio, Illinois, and Indiana. Most Croats are Roman Catholic, although church membership did not play a major role in the establishment of Croatian communities as it did with other groups. Croats have assimilated more slowly into American society than many other groups, and it was not until the mid-1950s that inner-city Croatian neighborhoods began to break up through outmigration to the suburbs. Factors involved in the maintenance of Croat communities were strong extended family ties and a pattern of sons settling in the same community and working in the same factories as their fathers. Since World War II at least 60,000 Croats have settled in the United States and have led a renewal of Croat ethnic identity, through ties maintained with the homeland and a revitalized Croatian press.

Bibliography

Bennett, Linda (1978). _Personal Choice in Ethnic Identity Maintenance: Serbs, Croats and Slovenes in Washington_. Palo Alto, Calif.: R and E Research Associates.

Kraljec, Francis (1978). _Croation Migration to and from the United States_. Palo Alto, Calif.: Ragusan.

Prpic, G. J. (1978). _South Slavic Immigration in America_. Boston: Twayne.

CZECHS. In 1980, 788,724 Americans claimed Czech ancestry and another 1,103,732 claimed Czech and other ethnic ancestry. This figure may be somewhat inflated as it includes both ethnic Czechs and Czechoslovaks, some of whom may be ethnically Slovak rather than Czech. Czechs in the United States today are mainly descendants of people who emigrated from Bohemia and Moravia between 1850 and 1914, the two major regions of the Czech area of the nation of Czechoslovakia. Czechs settled both in farming communities (in Wisconsin, Minnesota, Nebraska, Iowa, South Dakota, and Texas) and in cities (New York, Cleveland, Chicago, and Omaha). Czech settlers differed from other European ethnic groups in a number of ways. First, they had an unusually low return-migration rate. Second, many left the Roman Catholic church and either converted to Protestantism or eschewed formal religious affilation altogether. Third, although they never were a unified group, they assimilated relatively slowly, in part because of values that stressed individual and family self-reliance and because of ties to the homeland. After the 1920s, Czech identity began to weaken as few new immigrants arrived, children attended public schools, and intermarriage became common.

After the communist takeover of Czechoslovakia in 1948, 35,000 Czechoslovakians fled to the United States and an additional 10,000 or so arrived after the failed 1968 revolution. These groups contained many professionals who often stayed apart from the established Czech communities in the United States. The Czech presence still reflects considerable internal diversity (rural/urban, early/later immigrants).

Bibliography

Bicha, Karel D. (1980). "Community of Cooperation? The Case of the Czech-Americans." In _Studies in Ethnicity: The East European Experience in America_, edited by C. A. Ward, P. Shashko, and D. E. Pienkos, 93–102. Boulder: East European Monographs.

Jerabek, Esther (1976). _Czechs and Slovaks in North America: A Bibliography_. New York: Czechoslovak Society of Arts and Sciences in America.

Skrabanek, R. L. (1985). _We're Czechs_. College Station: Texas A&M University Press.

DANES. In 1980, 428,619 Americans claimed Danish ancestry and another 1,089,654 claimed Danish and other ancestry. Most Danes immigrated to the United States in the last half of the nineteenth century. Mormon missionaries were active in Denmark after 1850, and a sizable contingent of Danes settled in farm communities in Utah and southern Idaho. The descendants of these Danish Mormons account today for about 9 percent of Danes in the United States. Most immigrants settled in the Midwest, primarily in Wisconsin, Iowa, and Minnesota. There is also a sizable Danish ancestry population in California, mostly the product of migration west following initial settlement elsewhere. Danes assimilated more quickly than other Scandinavian peoples, in part because of their relatively few numbers and wide dispersal, which encouraged marriage to non-Danes and a more rapid loss of the Danish language and adoption of English. Today, a sense of Danish ethnicity survives through the Dansk Samvirke (the Association of Danes Abroad), tours to Denmark, and Danish customs as part of the Christmas celebration.

Bibliography

Hale, Frederick, ed. (1984). _Danes in North America_. Seattle: University of Washington Press.

Mackintosh, Jette (1988). "'Little Denmark' on the Prairie: A

Study of the Towns of Elk Horn and Kimballton in Iowa." *Journal of American Ethnic History* 7:46–68.

Nielsen, George R. (1981). *The Danish Americans*. Boston: Twayne.

DUTCH. In 1980, 1,404,794 Americans claimed Dutch ancestry and another 4,899,705 claimed Dutch and other ethnic ancestry. In the United States, Frisians, who form a distinct ethnic group in the Netherlands and West Germany are classified as Dutch. After Henry Hudson "discovered" the Hudson River during his exploration of 1610–1611, the Dutch established the colony of New Netherland in the Hudson and Delaware river valleys and the city of New Amsterdam on lower Manhattan Island. Following the loss of the colony to the English in 1664, some Dutch settlers removed to adjacent areas in what are now New York State and New Jersey. Many people of Dutch ancestry still live in these areas, although their numbers have been swelled by later Dutch immigrants who worked in the factories in northern New Jersey. Most Dutch immigrants (80 percent) were Protestants, with the densest concentration being Dutch Calvinists who continue to be a major political-economic-social force in a four-hundred-square-mile region of southwestern Michigan. The major concentration of Dutch Roman Catholics is found across Lake Michigan in eastern Wisconsin. Other Dutch settlements were started and continue to flourish in Bozeman, Montana, and northwestern Washington State. The most recent Dutch immigrants are mostly native Indonesians who fled to the Netherlands from their country in the 1960s, with some subsequently immigrating to the United States. The large number of negative phrases with the word *Dutch* such as *Dutch treat* or *Dutch courage* can be attributed to the anti-Dutch sentiments of the early English colonists.

Bibliography

Bratt, James D. (1984). *Dutch Calvinism in Modern America: A History of a Conservative Subculture*. Grand Rapids, Mich.: William B. Eerdmans.

Swierenga, Robert P., ed. (1985). *The Dutch in America: Immigration, Settlement, and Cultural Change*. New Brunswick, N.J.: Rutgers University Press.

Van Hinte, Jacob (1985). *Netherlanders in America: A Study of Emigration and Settlement in the 19th and 20th Centuries in the United States of America*. Robert P. Swierenga, general editor. Adriaan de Wit, chief translator. Grand Rapids, Mich.: Baker Book House.

ENGLISH. In 1980, 23,748,772 Americans claimed English ancestry and another 25,849,263 claimed English along with other ethnic ancestry. These figures include those claiming Cornish ancestry but not those of Manx ancestry, who numbered 50,000 in 1970. Americans of English ancestry are sometimes referred to as White Anglo-Saxon Protestants (WASPs) and those in New England, as Yankees. The English were the primary colonizers of what became the United States and were the major shapers of the American economy, political system, society, and culture. Although American society is now a blending of beliefs and practices from dozens of cultures, the most fundamental features of American life, such as the use of the English language and the legal system, reflect English traditions. People of English ancestry are settled across the entire United States with major concentrations in Maine, the Appalachian and Ozark regions, and the Mormon region of Utah and southern Idaho. The few areas with relatively low percentages of English-Americans are New York City, areas of Southwest Texas with large Mexican-American populations, and those sections of Nevada and the Dakotas with large American Indian reservations.

See also Appalachians, Mormons, Ozarks, Shakers

Bibliography

Ewart, Shirley (1987). *Cornish Mining Families of Grass Valley, California*. New York: AMS Press.

ESTONIANS. Because emigrants from Estonia arriving before 1922 were usually listed as Russians, the number of Estonians who came to the United States and the number of current Estonian-Americans are unknown. Estimates place their number at about 200,000, with over half in the Mid-Atlantic and New England regions, 19 percent on the West Coast, and 15 percent in the Great Lakes area. The homeland is currently the Estonian Soviet Socialist Republic. The Estonian language is related to Finnish, and Estonian culture has been strongly influenced by Scandinavian traditions. Most Estonian-Americans are descendants of people who arrived between 1890 and World War I. An influx of about 15,000 Estonians after World War II has both increased the population and stimulated a rebirth of Estonian ethnic identity. The Estonians today are unified by strong nationalistic and anticommunist sentiments and active local, regional, national, and international ethnic associations. At the same time, a high intermarriage rate and a middle-class life-style are drawing many people in the younger generations into mainstream society.

Bibliography

Parming, Tönu, and Imre Lipping (1979). *Aspects of Cultural Life*. Estonian Heritage in America Series. New York: Estonian Learned Society in America.

Walko, Ann M. (1988). *Rejecting the Second-Generation Hypothesis: Maintaining Estonian Ethnicity in Lakewood, New Jersey*. New York: AMS Press.

FINNS. In 1980, 267,902 Americans claimed Finnish ancestry and another 347,970 claimed Finnish and other ethnic ancestry. Finnish immigration took place mainly from the 1860s on, with most settling and continuing to live in northern Michigan, Wisconsin, and Minnesota. In 1980, 38 percent of Finnish-Americans lived in this area. The original lure for many Finnish men was work in mining and the sawmills and on the railroads, although many eventually established small farms. Up to about 1920, Finnish identity remained strong and was maintained by the interlocking ties of churches, temperance groups, labor unions, and political parties. The membership and influence of these groups, however, waned after 1920, leading to rapid assimilation.

Bibliography

Finnish Americana: A Journal of Finnish American History and Culture. New York Mills, Minnesota.

Kivitso, Peter (1984). _Immigrant Socialists in the United States: The Case of Finns and the Left_. London, Ontario, and Toronto: Associated Universities Press.

FRENCH. In 1980, 3,504,542 Americans claimed French ancestry and another 10,168,192 claimed French and other ethnic ancestry. The general category of Americans of French ancestry includes people of French, French-Canadian, Acadian (Cajun), and Creole ancestry. It can also be stretched to include Bretons, Alsatians, and French Basques, although these groups are not French-speaking nor do they identify themselves as French; they are simply from areas that are today located in France. The two largest groups are the French-Canadians and those of direct French ancestry; the former outnumber the latter by a ratio of five to two. People who emigrated directly from France often came alone or in small groups and were rapidly assimilated into the general population through both intermarriage and wide dispersal, with a significant number settling in California. Those from the other French cultural traditions have tended to maintain their traditional culture for longer periods of time.

La Salle claimed what is now Louisiana for France in 1682, and Louisiana has since been known as the "French" region of the United States. The French influence in Louisiana is seen in the continued use of French in some areas, adherence to Roman Catholicism, French-style architecture and cuisine, and so on. This region was first settled by French-Canadians, who traveled down the Mississippi River and settled New Orleans, and then by Acadians, who fled from eastern Canada and numbered over 1,000 in Louisiana by 1800. Some of the Acadians eventually returned to Canada, but most remained in Louisiana and are today called Cajuns. They reside mostly in a region centered around Lafayette. These groups were added to by French arriving directly from France and French Creoles, Whites, and Blacks from French Caribbean colonies, most important, Saint Dominique (Haiti). In their travels south, the French Canadians also founded other French settlements including a number in Missouri.

The Northeast is the second major area of French settlement in the United States, with people of French-Canadian ancestry found in large numbers in the northern sections of Maine, New Hampshire, Vermont, and New York. The first French-Canadian settlers were mostly farmers, loggers, and traders. After 1860 they began moving farther south and found factory work in the leather goods, jewelry, cutlery, and brick industries that flourished in New England. They fought hard to maintain their French-Canadian heritage through intermarriage, residential isolation in distinctively French neighborhoods, use of the French language, and Roman Catholic parochial schools. But with the demise by the mid-twentieth century of the industries in which they worked, isolation from mainstream society became more difficult and assimilation increased.

See also Acadians, Cajuns, Black Creoles of Louisiana, French Canadians, Haitians

Bibliography

Brault, Gerard J. (1986). _The French-Canadian Heritage in New England_. Hanover, N.H.: University Press of New England.

Breton, Raymond, and Pierre Savard, eds. (1982). _The Quebec and Acadian Diaspora in North America_. Toronto: Multicultural History Society of Ontario.

Carroll, R. (1987). _Cultural Misunderstanding: The French-American Experience_. Chicago: University of Chicago Press.

Dominguez, Virginia R. (1986). _White by Definition: Social Classification in Creole Louisiana_. New Brunswick, N.J.: Rutgers University Press.

GERMANS. In 1980, 17,943,485 Americans claimed German ancestry and another 31,280,661 claimed German and other ethnic ancestry. Next to the English, the Germans are the largest ethnic population group in the United States. German immigration began in the 1600s, was especially heavy during the early and mid-nineteenth century, peaking in the 1890s. Because relatively few Germans have arrived since then, most of them in the United States today are third- or fourth-generation Germans. Germans settled in rural areas, small cities, and urban centers. Today, areas with heavy German populations include Pennsylvania, southeastern Wisconsin, south-central Texas, and the Midwest. During the twentieth century, there has been a movement from rural areas to cities, with most recent arrivals also settling in cities.

Despite their large numbers and long settlement history, Germans are among the most assimilated of all European ethnic groups, and German neighborhoods, publications, associations, architecture, meeting halls, and so on have mostly disappeared. A number of factors account for this assimilation. First, German immigrants never formed a homogeneous linguistic, religious, or cultural group. Second, the early peaking of immigration in the 1890s means that few first- or second-generation Germans live in the United States. And, third, for some Germans, German ethnicity was a means to economic and political ends and, thus, became less important when German identity was not helpful such as during and after World Wars I and II.

A distinct group who have maintained their ethnic identity are the German-Russians (Russian-Germans, Germans from Russia). German-Russians are German-speaking peoples whose ancestors settled in the Volga and Black Sea regions of Russia in the 1700s. In the late 1800s, many of the Germans in Russia left in order to find political and religious freedom elsewhere. By the 1920s, at least 300,000 had settled in the United States. Those from the Volga region settled in Colorado, Kansas, and Nebraska where many were involved in sugar beet agriculture and processing. Many of those from north of the Black Sea became wheat farmers in the Dakotas. Today, there are over a million German-Russians in the United States. Their long tradition of independence, residential localizations, and desire to stay separate from other Germans has enabled them to maintain their distinct ethnic identity.

See also Amish, Austrians, Hutterites, Mennonites, Pennsylvania Dutch, Sorbs, Swiss

Bibliography

America and the Germans: An Assessment of a Three-Hundred-Year History. (1986). Philadelphia: University of Pennsylvania Press.

Arends, S. F. (1989). *The Central Dakota Germans: Their History, Language, and Culture.* Washington, D.C.: Georgetown University Press.

Miller, Randall M., ed. (1984). *Germans in America: Retrospect and Prospect.* Philadelphia: German Society of Pennsylvania.

Prewitt, Terry J. (1988). *German-American Settlement in an Oklahoma Town: Ecological, Ethnic and Cultural Change.* New York: AMS Press.

Rippley, LaVern J. (1976). *The German-Americans.* Boston: Twayne.

Sallet, Richard (1974). *Russian-German Settlements in the United States.* Translated by LaVern J. Rippley and Armand Bauer. Fargo: North Dakota Institute of Regional Studies.

GREEKS.   In 1980, 615,882 Americans claimed Greek ancestry and another 343,974 claimed Greek and other ethnic ancestry. The nearly two-to-one ratio of full to partial Greek ancestry indicates that Greek-Americans continue to stress their Greek cultural identity. The first Greek immigrants arrived in Florida in 1768, although the current Greek-American population is composed mostly of the descendants of emigrants from Greece who arrived in the United States between 1880 and 1920. Greek-Americans were and remain a largely urban group and at 93 percent, have the highest urban-suburban settlement rate of any European-American group. Major concentrations of Greek-Americans live today in and around New York City, Boston, Washington, D.C., Chicago, and Tarpon Springs, Florida, with sizable populations in Los Angeles, San Francisco, Detroit, Pittsburgh, and Houston. In some locations the Greek population is associated with a particular economic specialization such as sponge fishing in Tarpon Springs and restaurant ownership in New England. Although Greektowns were never as prevalent as other ethnic enclaves, Greek identity was and is maintained through male socialization at coffeehouses, the Greek Orthodox religion and church, a strict division of labor with men working outside and women in the home, the continued use of the Greek language, marriage within the group, and economic cooperation among Greek-American businesspeople.

Bibliography

Georgakais, D. (1987). "The Greeks in America." *Journal of the Hellenic Diaspora* 14:131–143.

Kiriazis, James W. (1989). *Children of the Colossus: The Rhodian Greek Immigrants in the United States.* New York: AMS Press.

Patterson, George J., Jr. (1988). *The Unassimilated Greeks of Denver.* New York: AMS Press.

Psomiades, Harry J., and Alice Scourby (1982). *The Greek American Community in Transition.* New York: Pella Publishing.

Scourby, Alice (1984). *The Greek Americans.* Boston: Twayne.

HUNGARIANS.   In 1980, 727,223 Americans claimed Hungarian and another 1,049,679 claimed Hungarian and other ethnic ancestry. Hungarians, also called Magyars, are ethnic Hungarians. The label "Hungarian" also sometimes includes people of Romanian, Slovak, Polish, Ukrainian, German, or Jewish ancestry who lived in what was the large territory that was Hungary prior to World War I. Ethnic Hungarians who came to the United States mostly between 1880 and World War I also displayed religious variation, with about 60 percent being Roman Catholic and the others Protestant, Greek Christian, and Eastern Orthodox. The immigrants, many of whom were single men, settled in regions offering the opportunity of heavy industrial work such as mining and steel production. Thus, the majority settled in four states—New Jersey, New York, Pennsylvania, and Ohio. Since 1950 there has been a gradual dispersal of Hungarians, especially to California and the South. The revolution against communist rule in Hungary in 1956 led the U.S. government to allow 35,000 Hungarians to immigrate since then. Better educated than Hungarians already settled in the United States, they tended to assimilate quickly into the American economy. Hungarians never established distinct neighborhoods comparable to those of other European immigrants. Rather, a strong sense of Hungarian identity resulted from the putting aside of religious and regional differences for economic solidarity and the formation of insurance associations, churches, and Magyar-language newspapers. Hungarian identity was further strengthened by Hungarian government programs designed to prevent assimilation in the United States and to encourage a return to Hungary. World War I was the effective end of this strong sense of Hungarian ethnicity in the United States, as Austro-Hungary was the enemy. After the war, ties to Hungary (now substantially reduced in size) weakened, and by the Second World War, English had essentially replaced or existed alongside Magyar in Hungarian associations, churches, newspapers, and schools. Although the post-1956 arrivals have remained concerned about Hungary and have been strongly anticommunist, their presence has not produced a rebirth of Hungarian ethnicity.

Bibliography

Vardy, Steven B. (1985). *The Hungarian-Americans.* Boston: Twayne.

Weinberg, Daniel E. (1977). "Ethnic Identity in Industrial Cleveland: The Hungarians, 1900–1920." *Ohio History* 86:171–186.

IRISH.   In 1980, 10,337,353 Americans claimed Irish ancestry and another 29,828,349 claimed Irish and other ethnic ancestry. Included in these figures are 17,000 people who claimed Scots-Irish identity (Northern Irish, Ulster Scots) who are mostly descended from Irish Protestants who settled in North America in the 1700s. This is probably a gross undercount as over half of the Irish in the United States are Protestants, and most of these are likely descended from the 1700s immigrants. Most people of Scots-Irish ancestry live in the rural South, Appalachia, and the Ozarks. Any unique Scots-Irish identity has now been lost, and they are generally lumped and lump themselves with other Americans of either Irish or English ancestry.

People thought of as ethnic Irish in the United States

today are the descendants of the Roman Catholic Irish who arrived mainly between 1830 and World War I. Many of these immigrants were poor and fled to the United States to escape famine in Ireland. They formed distinctively Irish neighborhoods in eastern and midwestern cities, often centered around the parish church and large, stable families dominated by the wife/mother. It was in reference to these urban Catholic Irish that the negative stereotype of the drunken, violent Irishman developed. Involvement in the Roman Catholic church through social assistance programs, parochial schools, colleges and universities, and local and national religious leaders and involvement in local politics brought the Irish into the mainstream of American society. These involvements also benefited the Irish community and have given them much influence in American life.

The Irish are now dispersed across the United States in a pattern typical of the general American population. They were and remain a strongly urban-suburban group, however, with major concentrations in the Mid-Atlantic states, New England, Chicago, and Los Angeles. Despite their settlement across the nation, Irish cultural identity and influence on American society remains strong.

Bibliography

Akenson, Donald H. (1985). _Being Bad: Historians, Evidence, and the Irish in North America._ Port Credit, Ontario: P. D. Meany.

Cahill, Kevin M., ed. (1984). _The Irish American Revival._ Port Washington, N.Y.: Associated Faculty Press.

Clark, Dennis (1986). _Hibernia America: The Irish and Regional Cultures._ Westport, Conn.: Westview Press.

Greeley, Andrew M. (1982). _The Irish Americans._ New York: Harper and Row.

McCaffrey, Lawrence J., Ellen Skerrett, Michael F. Funchion, and Charles Fanning (1987). _The Irish in Chicago._ Urbana: University of Illinois Press.

Miller, Kerby A. (1985). _Emigrants and Exiles: Ireland and the Irish Exodus to North America._ New York: Oxford University Press.

ITALIANS. In 1980, 6,883,320 Americans claimed Italian ethnic ancestry and another 5,300,372 claimed Italian and other ethnic ancestry. Italian immigration to the United States can be divided into two periods. Prior to 1880, most immigrants were from northern Italy (Tuscany, Lombardy, Piedmont) and represented only a minority of those coming to the New World, with most settling in Brazil and Argentina. Most of the men were skilled craftsmen (masons and stonecutters), and the families lived in small communities often composed of people from the same town in Italy. The second period, beginning in 1880 and continuing to World War I, was a time of major Italian immigration to and settlement in the United States. After 1880 most Italian immigrants were poor men or families from the southern provinces and Sicily. In competition for low-level factory jobs with Eastern European immigrants, the Italians tended to settle in cities where the Eastern Europeans were less numerous. Thus, Italian

communities formed in Portland, Maine; Rochester, New York; Philadelphia, Pennsylvania; Newark, New Jersey; New Castle, Pennsylvania; Staten Island, New York; Chicago, Illinois; and New York City. Other Italian communities formed in midwestern cities, and a few farming communities formed in central California, Louisiana, Illinois, and Arkansas. But the Italian immigrants were mostly an urban group, with at least 85 percent settling in cities.

Italy became a unified nation only in 1870; thus Italian immigrants generally felt only a weak identity with Italy and lacked an overarching cultural tradition typical of other immigrant groups. This led to two unique developments in the United States. First, strong ties were maintained with the town from which emigration took place, and a weaker sense of Italian identity prevailed. Second, within the first two generations of settlement, a syncretic Italian-American culture developed in the United States. Key features of the new cultural identity were an Americanized dialect of Italian that replaced the regional languages and dialects, a distinctly Italian tradition within the Irish-dominated American Roman Catholic church featuring a more "emotional-celebratory" set of practices, involvement in local politics, and the formation of associations, banks, and labor unions that served the Italian community. At the same time, the large patriarchal families were giving way to small families, with intermarriage to non-Italian Roman Catholics increasing in frequency.

Assimilation has progressed rapidly since World War II, and the Italians are now a middle-class, urban-suburban group. Although much of the population has shifted to suburbs, distinct Italian neighborhoods remain in many cities, including Philadelphia, New York, Chicago, St. Louis, Newark, and Providence. At the same time, the Italian-American cultural identity is maintained through extended family ties, the church, unique food preferences and practices, and a general sense of respect for the family and its oldest members.

Bibliography

Alba, Richard D. (1985). _Italian Americans._ Englewood Cliffs, N.J.: Prentice-Hall.

Belfiglio, C. V. (1983). _Italian Experience in Texas._ Austin: Eakin Press.

Cinel, Dino (1982). _From Italy to San Francisco: The Immigrant Experience._ Stanford: Stanford University Press.

di Leonardo, Micaela (1984). _The Varieties of Ethnic Experience: Kinship, Class, and Gender among California Italian-Americans._ Ithaca: Cornell University Press.

Martinelli, Phyllis C. (1987). _Ethnicity in the Sunbelt: Italian-American Migrants in Scottsdale, Arizona._ New York: AMS Press.

Mormino, Gary R. (1986). _Immigrants on the Hill: Italian-Americans in St. Louis, 1882–1982._ Urbana: University of Illinois Press.

Nelli, Humbert S. (1983). _From Immigrants to Ethnics: The Italian Americans._ New York: Oxford University Press.

Schoener, Allon (1987). *The Italian Americans.* New York: Macmillan.

Tomasi, Lydio F., ed. (1985). *Italian Americans: New Perspectives in Italian Immigration and Ethnicity.* New York: Center for Migration Studies.

Tricarico, Donald (1984). *The Italians of Greenwich Village.* New York: Center for Migration Studies.

LATVIANS. In 1980, 55,563 Americans claimed Latvian ancestry and another 36,578 claimed Latvian and other ethnic ancestry. Latvians are people who trace their ethnic identity to the territory that is now the Latvian Soviet Socialist Republic. Latvian is an Indo-European language closely related only to Lithuanian. Latvians came to the United States in two major migrations. The first group, composed mainly of peasants and artisans looking for better opportunities, emigrated from Russia between 1905 and World War I. They were mostly Lutherans or Baptists and initially took unskilled work in the Northeast and in communities in Wisconsin and Minnesota. Some returned to Latvia after the Russian Revolution, and the descendants of those who remained in the United States are now largely assimilated into American society. The second group contained about 40,000 emigrants who arrived after World War II, with many classified as displaced persons seeking refuge from war-ravaged Europe and Soviet rule. Because of their more recent arrival and strong Latvian nationalistic feelings, they have resisted assimilation and make up the majority of Latvian-Americans today. About 50 percent still speak Latvian and 85 percent are members of Latvian ethnic organizations. Latvian culture is a mix of native, Slavic, Scandinavian, and German elements that have been combined over the centuries into a unique Latvian cultural tradition. To outsiders, Latvian culture is most notable for its rich collection of folk songs (*dainas*), unique art and design motifs, and native peasant dress.

Bibliography

Karklis, Maruta, Liga Streips, and Laimonis Streips, comps. (1974). *The Latvians in America, 1640–1973: A Chronology and Fact Book.* Dobbs Ferry, N.Y.: Oceania Publications.

LITHUANIANS. In 1980, 339,438 Americans claimed Lithuanian ethnic ancestry and another 403,338 claimed Lithuanian and other ancestry. The majority of Americans of Lithuanian ancestry are descendants of immigrants who settled in the United States between 1880 and World War I. They came mainly from the eastern sections of the territory that is now the Lithuanian Soviet Socialist Republic. Most were Roman Catholics, and they often settled near Polish communities in industrial cities and towns in the Northeast and Midwest where the men worked in the mines and factories. Beginning about 1890, Lithuanians began to distance themselves from the Poles and distinct Lithuanian communities formed around their own parishes, kin and friendship networks, local and national associations, and the Lithuanian-language press. From about 1900 on, their economic role began changing, as Lithuanians were often involved in labor unions, strikes, and other efforts to improve working conditions. Since then, the Lithuanians have assimilated into American society, though distinct Lithuanian eth-

nic enclaves, such as the Marquette Park area of Chicago, still exist. New arrivals after World War I and World War II brought strong nationalistic and anticommunist sentiments with them. Even in this group, however, a distinct Lithuanian cultural identity is disappearing.

Bibliography

Baskauskas, Liucija (1983). *An Urban Enclave: Lithuanian Refugees in Los Angeles.* New York: AMS Press.

Gedmintas, Aleksandras (1988). *An Interesting Bit of Identity: The Dynamics of Ethnic Identity in a Lithuanian-American Community.* New York: AMS Press.

Jonitis, Peter P. (1983). *The Acculturation of the Lithuanians of Chester, Pennsylvania.* New York: AMS Press.

NORWEGIANS. In 1980, 1,260,997 Americans claimed Norwegian ancestry and another 2,192,842 claimed Norwegian and other ethnic ancestry. Starting in 1840, Norwegians began forming church-based farming communities in western Wisconsin, Minnesota, and North Dakota, regions that provided the settlers with affordable farmland. A migration of younger people from the Midwest farther west led to the formation of a Norwegian community in Washington. Today, over 20 percent of Norwegian-Americans live in Minnesota, mostly in and around Minneapolis. Beginning in 1853, the Norwegian Evangelical Lutheran Church (the Norwegian Synod) became the focal point for the continuation of Norwegian culture in the New World. In 1962, the church merged with the German and Dutch churches to form the American Lutheran church, though Norwegian identity continues in rural Norwegian communities in the Midwest. Although most Americans of Norwegian ancestry are assimilated into American society, Norwegian ethnic identity is notably strong, because of a combination of factors including the rural church-based communities, Norwegian colleges, ethnic organizations, and Norwegian social and business networks in some Midwest cities.

Bibliography

Gjerde, Jon (1985). *From Peasants to Farmers: The Migration from Balestrand, Norway, to the Upper Middle West.* Cambridge: Cambridge University Press.

Lovoll, Odd S. (1984). *The Promise of America: A History of the Norwegian-American People.* Minneapolis: University of Minnesota Press in cooperation with the Norwegian-American Historical Association.

Strickon, Arnold, and R. A. Ibarra (1983). "The Changing Dynamics of Ethnicity: Norwegians and Tobacco in Wisconsin." *Ethnic and Racial Studies* 6:174–197.

PENNSYLVANIA DUTCH. This general label refers to the Amish, Mennonites, Moravians, Dunkers, Schwenkfelders, and others who settled mostly in Pennsylvania. These peoples, fleeing religious persecution, were either German or Swiss (all were German speakers), not Dutch. The reference to "Dutch" is a modern-day confusion resulting from the word *Deutsch* meaning "German." Thus, the Pennsylvania

Dutch are actually Pennsylvania Germans and are sometimes correctly labeled as such. Most Pennsylvania Dutch are today found in Pennsylvania and North Carolina.
See also Amish, Mennonites

Bibliography

Reimensnyder, Barbara L. (1988). _Powwowing in Union County: A Study of Pennsylvania German Folk Medicine in Context_. New York: AMS Press.

Swank, Scott (1983). _Art of the Pennsylvania Germans_. New York: W. W. Norton.

POLES. In 1980, 3,805,740 Americans claimed Polish ancestry and another 4,422,297 claimed Polish and other ethnic ancestry. The Poles are one of the largest and, in some ways, the least assimilated of the European-American groups. Poles in the United States are mostly ethnic Poles whose ancestors spoke Polish, German, and Russian. Distinct ethnic minorities in Poland, including the Carpatho-Rusyns, Kashubians, Górali, Mazurians, Silesians, and Galicians are also represented in the United States, and they have tended to remain somewhat separate from the ethnic Polish majority. The majority of Poles have arrived since 1850. The first large group of settlers was composed of German-speaking Poles who settled in cities already inhabited by Germans. Later arrivals, though from non-German sections of Poland, settled near those already in the United States. This migration pattern led to the formation of major Polish communities in cities with large German communities such as Buffalo, Milwaukee, Chicago, New York, and Cleveland. Other major Polish communities formed in Pittsburgh, Detroit, Philadelphia, and the Connecticut River valley in New England. Poles have remained an urban group, with 80 percent still living in urban areas. Small rural communities based on farming formed in south-central Texas, the northern Midwest, Missouri, and Nebraska.

Polish men generally found relatively low-level physical work such as mining, steel-working, meat-packing, automobile manufacturing, and factory labor. From 1865 through World War II the Poles remained a relatively homogeneous group, with their lives centered around the Roman Catholic parish and parochial schools, extended family ties, associations, multiple-family housing, Polish neighborhoods and stores, the Polish press, and Polish beliefs and customs at holidays and life-cycle celebrations. A religious schism developed around the turn of the century, leading to the formation of the independent Polish National Catholic Church of America, which now has about 300,000 members. Since the end of World War II, Poles have been assimilating more rapidly into American society, fueled primarily by upward social mobility from a working-class to a middle-class life-style. Today, the majority of Poles work in white-collar and skilled occupations. Still, Polish assimilation has been slower than among other groups, with intermarriage mostly with other Eastern European Catholics, a slower loss of the Polish language, the continued existence of Polish neighborhoods in large cities, and ties often maintained with relatives in Poland. A reaction to the negative stereotype of Poles and the Solidarity movement in Poland have also contributed to a strong sense of Polish identity in recent years.

Bibliography

Bodnar, John, Roger Simon, and Michael P. Weber (1982). _Lives of Their Own: Blacks, Italians, and Poles in Pittsburgh, 1900–1960_. Urbana: University of Illinois Press.

Obidinski, Eugene, and Helen Stankiewicz Zand (1987). _Polish Folkways in America: Community and Family_. Polish Studies Series 5. Lanham, Md.: University Press of America.

Mocha, Franck, ed. (1978). _Poles in America_. Stevens Point, Wis.: Worzalla Publishing.

Polish-American Studies: A Journal of Polish-American History and Culture. Binghamton, N.Y.: Polish American Historical Association.

PORTUGUESE. In 1980, 616,362 Americans claimed Portuguese ancestry and another 407,989 claimed Portuguese and other ethnic ancestry. Americans of Portuguese descent came either from Portugal or from the Portuguese Azores and Madeira islands. Portuguese immigration patterns are different from most other European-American groups in that a large percentage arrived in recent years (about 39 percent since 1959) and a large number (29 percent) settled in California. The Portuguese are essentially bicoastal with major concentrations in Hawaii (descendants of Azorean whalers and Madeiran sugar plantation workers), farming communities in central California, and fishing and industrial communities in southern New England and the northern Mid-Atlantic states. The early arrivals were mostly Azoreans and Madeirans who settled and formed communities populated by immigrants from the same islands. With life centered around the patriarchal family and family financial obligations, the traditional culture has survived to some extent even among the third and fourth generations. The more recent arrivals have resisted integration into these communities and have instead directed their efforts at maintaining political and economic ties with Portugal, activities of less interest to the descendants of the earlier settlers.

Bibliography

Cabral, Stephen L. (1988). _Tradition and Transformation: Portuguese Feasting in New Bedford_. New York: AMS Press.

Gilbert, Dorothy A. (1987). _Recent Portuguese Immigrants to Fall River, Massachusetts_. New York: AMS Press.

Pap, Leo (1981). _The Portuguese-Americans_. Boston: Twayne.

ROMANIANS. (Roumanians, Rumanians). In 1980, 141,675 Americans claimed Romanian ancestry and another 173,583 claimed Romanian and other ethnic ancestry. Most Romanians who arrived in the United States before 1895 were Jewish. Romanian immigrants since 1895 include Jews and non-Jews, with both groups included in the above figures. Romanians settled mainly in industrial cities such as Cleveland, East Chicago, Gary, and Detroit where men worked in the steel and auto industries. Although the Romanian church, clubs, and press were active for some years, the descendants of these immigrants are now largely assimilated into American society. More recent arrivals have lived apart from these communities and have focused their attention on anticommunist activities and Romanian-U.S. relations. The community has recently coalesced around the overthrow of the communist leadership of Romania in 1989–1990.

Bibliography

Bobango, Gerald J. (1978). "The Union and League of Romanian Societies: An 'Assimilating Force.'" *East European Quarterly* 12:85–92.

Roceris, Alexandra (1982). *Language Maintenance within an American Community: The Case of Romanian.* Grass Lake and Jackson, Mich: Romanian-American Heritage Center.

RUSSIANS.   In 1980, 1,379,585 Americans claimed Russian ancestry and another 1,401,847 claimed Russian and other ancestry. The category "Russian" generally includes people who emigrated from what was the Russian Empire and is now the Soviet Union. This includes a number of culturally distinct groups including ethnic Russians, Ukrainians, Georgians, Latvians, Lithuanians, Estonians, Belorussians (Byelorussians, White Russians), Galicians, Russian Jews, Doukhobors, Old Believers, Molokans, Carpatho-Rusyns, and Cossacks. Stretched to its limits, Russians can also include peoples from non-European regions of the Soviet Union such as the Azerbaijani, Kalmyk, and Turkestani who do not consider themselves Russian. In short, "Russians" is more correctly viewed as a territorial-political label than an ethnic one, except when applied specifically to ethnic Russians.

Russians immigrated to the United States in five stages. The first group was composed of traders who settled in Alaska to trade for furs with the local American Indian groups. When Russia sold Alaska to the United States in 1867, they either returned home or migrated to California. From the 1880s to World War I, Russians settled in industrial cities in the East and Midwest. After the Russian Revolution of 1917, a large influx of mostly middle-class, anticommunist Russians also settled in large cities. After World War II, Russian displaced persons and refugees made their way to the United States, often with stays in other countries first. Finally, a small number of Russians have immigrated to the United States since the 1950s. In the past, participation in the Eastern Orthodox church was a major factor in maintaining Russian ethnic identity. Red scares in the twentieth century (1919–1920, 1950s) led to sometimes hostile relations between Russian-Americans and mainstream society. But the cold war and the resultant interest in Russian life have somewhat lessened hostility toward Russian-Americans. Today, the Russians do not form a viable, cohesive ethnic entity in the United States, partly because of internal variations and partly because of the relatively few Russians who have arrived in the past forty years.

See also Byelorussians, Carpatho-Rusyns, Doukhobors, Estonians, Jews, Latvians, Lithuanians, Molokans, Old Believers, Ukrainians

Bibliography

Gerber, Stanford N. (1983). *Russkoya Celo: The Ethnography of a Russian-American Community.* New York: AMS Press.

Townsend, Joan B. (1975). "Mercantilism and Societal Change: An Ethnohistoric Examination of Some Essential Variables." *Ethnohistory* 22:21–32.

SCOTS.   In 1980, 1,172,904 Americans claimed Scottish ancestry and another 8,875,912 claimed Scottish and other ethnic ancestry. The distinction between Lowland and Highland Scots, though still important in Scotland, has not been of concern for some years in the United States. Because of their early settlement beginning in the late 1600s, high intermarriage rate, and dispersal across the entire United States, Scots are largely assimilated into American society and no longer display the degree of ethnic identity found in non-English-speaking ethnic groups of later arrival.

Bibliography

Chalker, Fussell M. (1976). "Highland Scots in the Georgia Lowlands." *Georgia Historical Quarterly* 60:35–42.

MacDonell, M. (1982). *The Emigrant Experience: Songs of Highland Emigrants in North America.* Toronto: University of Toronto Press.

SERBS.   In 1980, 49,621 Americans reported Serbian ethnic ancestry and another 51,320 reported Serbian and other ancestry. These figures are probably a gross undercount, as many people of Serbian background often identified themselves as Yugoslavians. A more realistic estimate of Americans of Serbian ancestry is 200,000. Serbia is one of the regions of the modern nation of Yugoslavia. The other major regions are Slovenia, Montenegro, Bosnia, Macedonia, and Croatia. Most immigrants of Serbian background came from the Bosnia, Montenegro, Croatia, and Vojvodina regions, primarily between 1903 and 1909. While Serbs and Croats came from different villages in Europe, they tended to settle near one another in the United States, mainly in the iron and steel-producing cities of Detroit, Chicago, Milwaukee, and Cleveland and the western Pennsylvania and eastern Ohio regions, which provided men with employment opportunities. Since World War II, about 50,000 Serbs, many of them displaced persons, have settled in the United States. Better educated and more urban than the earlier generation of immigrants, they have tended to remain separate from the already established Serbian communities. Although many Serbs have assimilated into mainstream life, the opportunity for maintaining a strong Serbian identity is readily available for those who so choose. A strong, politically conservative Serbianism ethos still exists in the United States, ties are maintained with the homeland, Serbian social organizations at all levels are highly organized, and Serbian music, epic poetry, and traditions provide a unifying bond.

Bibliography

Brkich, Lazar (1980). "Serbian Fraternal, Social, and Cultural Organizations in America." In *Studies in Ethnicity: The East European Experience in America*, edited by C. A. Ward, P. Shashko, and D. E. Pienkos, 103–114. Boulder: East European Monographs.

Padgett, Deborah (1988). *Settlers and Sojourners: A Study of Serbian Adaptation in Milwaukee, Wisconsin.* New York: AMS Press.

SLOVAKS. In 1980, 361,384 Americans reported Slovak ethnic ancestry and another 415,422 reported Slovak and other ancestry. These figures are almost certainly undercounts, as Slovaks who reported Czechoslovakian ancestry were classified as Czechs. Slovaks are people from the Slovakia region, which is today part of the modern nation of Czechoslovakia. The major Slovak immigration to the United States began in the 1870s, with the Slovaks settling in the anthracite mining region of eastern Pennsylvania and the coal mining and steel areas of western Pennsylvania and eastern Ohio. By the 1920s, the Slovaks had settled in the towns and cities where they continue to live today, with the only major population shift being a movement by the post–World War II generation to the suburbs. The Slovaks display a high degree of geographical persistence, with only 3 percent living in California, the lowest percentage of any European ethnic group. The pre–World War II ethnic culture was centered on family-based communities, wage labor in what was often the only factory or mine in the town, the Roman Catholic church, local clubs, and home ownership. Cohesion was reinforced by a general disinterest in education and the settlement of people from the same Slovak villages near one another in the United States. Today, a strong sense of Slovak identity remains, focused on the church, Slovak cuisine, and holiday rituals, although intermarriage has increased, family visits have replaced the two-generation domestic unit, and Slovak is spoken by only a few.

Bibliography

Stolarik, Mark M. (1985). _Growing up on the South Side: Three Generations of Slovaks in Bethlehem, Pennsylvania, 1880–1976._ Lewisburg, Pa.: Bucknell University.

Stolarik, Mark M. (1988). _Immigration and Urbanization: The Slovak Experience._ New York: AMS Press.

SLOVENES (Slovenians). In 1980, 63,587 Americans claimed Slovenian ancestry and another 62,876 claimed Slovenian and other ethnic ancestry. Slovenes are people from Slovenia, the northwestern section of the modern nation of Yugoslavia. The major arrival of Slovenes took place before World War I with major population centers forming in the mining areas of Colorado, northern Minnesota, and western Pennsylvania and in the industrial cities of Cleveland and Chicago. Slovene cultural identity was maintained through the Roman Catholic church, fraternal insurance societies, singing societies, and the Slovene press. Assimilation has been slowed by the arrival of a second large wave of immigrants in the 1950s, who are much concerned about and involved in political developments in Yugoslavia.

Bibliography

Prisland, Marie (1968). _From Slovenia to America._ Chicago: Slovenian Women's Union of America.

Susel, Rudolph M. (1983). "The Perpetuation and Transformation of Ethnic Identity among Slovene Immigrants in America and the American-Born Generations: Continuity and Change." In _The Dynamics of East European Ethnicity outside of Eastern Europe,_ edited by Irene P. Winner and Rudolph M. Susel, 109–132. Cambridge, Mass.: Schenkman.

Voynick, S. M. (1984). _Leadville: A Miner's Epic._ Missoula, Mont.: Mountain Press.

SORBS. (Wends). The Sorbs are a distinct cultural group in Germany. The Sorbian territory is located in the Lusatia region in the southeastern corner of what was the German Democratic Republic (East Germany). Sorbian is a West Slavic language, with Lower and Upper dialects spoken in northern and southern Sorbia, respectively. The number of Sorbs in North America is unknown, as they have usually been counted as German. Most are descendants of Sorbs who emigrated in the last half of the nineteenth century and settled in Texas near already existing German communities in present-day Lee County. Smaller communities also formed in Nebraska and Canada, although the Texas ones were the largest and most distinctly Sorbian. In recent years, some Sorbs have moved to cities in Texas, including Houston, San Antonio, and Austin. Initially close to the Germans through intermarriage, nearby residence, and language (most Sorbs also spoke German), self-identification as Americans began with World War I, in part as an effort to distance themselves from Germany. The traditional culture centered on distinct religious customs and holiday and life-cycle celebrations, although assimilation has increased rapidly in recent years.

SPANIARDS. Spaniards should be differentiated from Latinos who are people of Latin American ancestry. Because Spanish immigrants either were not counted at all or were at times lumped with Latinos, it is impossible to say how many Spaniards have immigrated to and settled in the United States—one estimate suggests about 250,000. Major population centers are in New York City, southern California, Louisiana, and Florida. The American Southwest has had an especially strong Spanish influence, dating to Coronado's expedition of 1540, though Mexican (which is also partly Spanish) and American Indian influences are also important in the region. For the most part, Spanish immigrants and their descendants have rapidly assimilated into American society and no strong sense of Spanish identity or culture has ever emerged. This is in part because they were few in number compared to other immigrant groups also arriving in the early twentieth century and in part because regional cultural identities (such as Galician, Catalonian) were more important in Spain than any sense of a national culture. In the United States these regional identities have been manifested in regional associations.

Bibliography

Brophy, Don, and Edythe Westenhauer, eds. (1978). _The Story of Catholics in America._ New York: Paulist Press.

Williams, James C. (1978). "Cultural Tension: The Origins of American Santa Barbara." _Southern California Quarterly_ 60:349–377.

SWEDES. In 1980, 1,288,341 Americans claimed Swedish ancestry and another 3,057,051 claimed Swedish and other ethnic ancestry. Swedes began immigrating to the United States in sizable numbers after 1840, settling mostly in the Midwest, where they often formed communities based on kin ties, or in areas where work similar to that in Sweden (such as metalworking, iron mining) was available. Illinois, Minnesota, Wisconsin, Iowa, Nebraska, and Kansas were areas of heavy settlement, with smaller communities forming in New England and New York where specialized work was available. Chicago and Minneapolis were the major centers for urban Swedes, with ties maintained with the Norwegian and German communities. Although Swedes resisted intermarriage (except with Norwegians), they nonetheless rapidly assimilated into American society. They learned English quickly (most Swedes were literate), desired U.S. citizenship, valued public education, and were upwardly mobile, moving from the cities to the suburbs. The 1970s saw a revival of interest in Swedish identity, reflected in public celebrations of Swedish holidays, Scandinavian study programs at colleges, and the economic success of Swedish retail outlets.

Bibliography

Kastrup, Allan (1975). *The Swedish Heritage in America*. St. Paul, Minn.: The Swedish Council of America.

Moe, M. L., ed. (1983). *Saga from the Hills: A History of the Swedes of Jamestown, New York*. Jamestown, N.Y.: Fenton Historical Society.

Wheeler, Wayne (1983). *An Analysis of Social Change in a Swedish-Immigrant Community*. New York: AMS Press.

SWISS. In 1980, 235,355 Americans claimed Swiss ancestry and another 746,188 claimed Swiss and other ancestry. Switzerland is a pluralistic country populated by four linguistic-cultural groups: French speakers in the West, German speakers in the center and North, Romansch speakers in the East, and Italian speakers in the South. Nearly 90 percent of Swiss settlers in the United States prior to 1900 were German speakers (German-speaking Swiss are also the most numerous group in Switzerland), although some had lived in other European countries prior to their migration to the New World, which may have blurred their sense of Swiss identity. The concentrations of Swiss in the United States today represent four distinct cultural traditions. The largest concentration of Swiss is the Old Order Amish and Mennonites in Pennsylvania, Ohio, Indiana, and Kansas. A second large concentration is the Swiss Mormons in northern Utah whose ancestors converted to Mormonism in the 1880s. A third group is the Italian Swiss in northern and central California whose ancestors settled in the San Francisco area. Last is the best-known Swiss concentration centered in and around Madison, Wisconsin, known as "the Swiss capital of the United States" and a major tourist attraction. The first Swiss settlement was formed in 1845 by immigrants who at first made their living from dairy farming and cheese making, two occupations associated also with other Swiss settlements.
See also Amish, Mennonites, Mormons

Bibliography

Kuhn, W. Ernst (1976). "Recent Swiss Immigration into Nebraska: An Empirical Study." *Swiss American Historical Society Newsletter* 12:12–20.

Lewis, Brian A. (1973). "Swiss-German in Wisconsin: The Impact of English." *American Speech* 48:211–228.

UKRAINIANS. In 1980, 381,084 Americans claimed Ukrainian ethnic ancestry and another 348,972 claimed Ukrainian and other ancestry. The relatively low percentage of Ukrainians claiming mixed ethnic ancestry indicates that the Ukrainians continue to exist as a distinct cultural group in the United States. Among the Ukrainian immigrants who arrived between 1880 and World War I, 85 to 95 percent were classified as Carpatho-Rusyns (Ruthenians), and few saw themselves as ethnically Ukrainian. After the end of World War I and the establishment of the Ukrainian Soviet Socialist Republic, descendants of this first wave of immigrants who were from Galicia have often preferred to define themselves as Ukrainian. The more than 100,000 Ukrainians who came to the United States after World War I were mainly from the center of the Ukraine, and their presence has strengthened Ukrainian identity. Fifty percent of Ukrainians lived in either New York State or Pennsylvania in 1980, with the New York City area being the major population and cultural center, especially with many immigrants since World War II settling there. The Ukrainians continue to exist as a distinct cultural group within American society, although many are, at the same time, active participants in the national economic system. Ukrainian schools, social clubs, associations, churches (Catholic, Protestant, and Orthodox), resorts, and publications all provide the opportunity for a full life within the Ukrainian community. A shared sense of identity is further maintained through continued use of the Ukrainian language, a high rate of endogamous marriage, and strong and active membership in fraternal organizations. External forces also play a role in maintaining group identity, especially involvement in political movements to establish a free Ukrainian nation and continued estrangement from the Polish- and Russian-American communities.
See also Ukrainians (Canada)

Bibliography

Stachin, Matthew (1976). "Ukrainian Religious, Social and Political Organization in the U.S. Prior to World War II." *Ukrainian Quarterly* 32:385–392.

WELSH. In 1980, 308,363 Americans claimed Welsh ancestry and another 1,356,235 claimed Welsh and other ethnic ancestry. Although the Welsh began arriving in North America in the late 1600s, the major migrations were in the mid- and late-1800s. Those who came first were largely farmers who sought to escape assimilation into English society by forming Welsh-speaking communities in North America. Those who came after 1880 were largely miners who settled in the coal-mining areas of northeast Pennsylvania, eventually moving from coal mining into work in the steel and related industries. Sizable populations of Welsh-Americans still live in this region, although most people of Welsh ancestry are assimilated into American society, as indicated by the high intermarriage rate and migration of many Welsh to the West Coast.

Bibliography

Ashton, Elwyn T. (1984). *The Welsh in the United States*. Shoreham, England: Elwyn T. Ashton.

Ellis, David M. (1973). "The Assimilation of the Welsh in Central New York State." *Welsh Historical Review* 6:424–447.

Thomas, R. D. (1983). *Hanes Cymry America: A History of the Welsh in America.* Translated by Phillips G. Davies. Washington, D.C.: University Press of America. (Originally published, 1872.)

European-Canadians

In 1986, about 78 percent of Canadians were descended from people of European ethnicity. The short summaries that follow present information on the population, distribution, migration history, and cultural persistence of thirty-three European ethnic groups in Canada. Appended to many of these summaries are short lists of publications, most of which are recent studies of a particular ethnic community or a general historical or cultural survey of the ethnic group. The population information in these summaries for 1981 is taken from the 1981 census of Canada, and that for 1986, from the estimates (based on a 20 percent sample) from the 1986 census of Canada as reported in the *Canada Year Book 1990.*

See also Acadians, Amish, Basques, Doukhobors, French Canadians, Hasidim Jews, Hutterites, Mennonites, Old Believers, Ukrainians in Canada

ALBANIANS.   In 1981, 1,265 Canadians claimed Albanian ethnic ancestry. This is probably an undercount, as many Albanians do not identify themselves as such and others identify themselves as Yugoslavians. The distinction between Gheg and Tosk Albanians, which was significant in pre–World War II Albania, has disappeared in Canada. Most present-day Albanian-Canadians are descendants of Albanians who settled in Canada between 1900 and World War I. Given their small numbers and third- and fourth-generation status, they are now much assimilated into Canadian society. Ethnic identity is expressed mainly within the the context of small family groups.

ARMENIANS.   In 1986, an estimated 22,525 Canadians claimed Armenian ancestry, 60 percent of whom lived in the Montreal area and 35 percent in the Toronto-Hamilton area. Armenia is today a unit of the Soviet Union, as the Armenian Soviet Socialist Republic, and in the past Armenians have been under the control of various other peoples, including the Turks, Russians, and Iranians. Armenians began immigrating to Canada in the late 1880s, and by 1915 1,000 Armenians were living in the country. The major period of Armenian immigration came in the 1950s and 1960s when thousands arrived from the Middle East and Mediterranean countries. Many of these were professionals or business people who settled in urban areas. As in other nations where they have settled, Armenian ethnicity remains strong in Canada, centered around the memory of the genocide of 1915–1922 by the Turks and ongoing concern over the possible loss of their traditional homeland. Armenian institutions include the Armenian National Apostolic church, the Armenian National Committee, the Armenian-language press, and language-maintenance programs.

Bibliography

Kaprielian, Isabel (1987). "Migratory Caravans: Armenian Sojourners in Canada." *Journal of American Ethnic History* 6:20–38.

AUSTRIANS.   In 1986, an estimated 24,900 Canadians claimed Austrian ancestry with over 40 percent living in Ontario. Unlike many other European nations, Austria was not formed on a distinct ethnic population base, and thus Austrians are more accurately described as a nationality rather than an ethnic group. Austrians who have settled in Canada, including a sizable minority of Jews, have assimilated rapidly into Canadian society and tend to affiliate with the much larger German community.

Bibliography

Keyserlingk, Robert H. (1983). "Policy or Practice: Canada and Austria 1938–1948." In *Roots and Realities among Eastern and Central Europeans,* edited by Martin L. Kovacs, 25–39. Edmonton, Alberta: Central and East European Studies Association of Canada.

BELGIANS.   In 1986, an estimated 28,395 Canadians claimed Belgian ethnic ancestry. The nation of Belgium is inhabited by two distinct groups—the Flemish in the Northwest (in the region commonly called Flanders), who speak a language closely related to Dutch, and the Walloons in the South and Southeast, who speak French. This distinction was maintained in Canada, with the Walloons settling primarily in Quebec and the Flemish settling in Ontario and forming Belgian communities in the western provinces of Alberta, Manitoba, Saskatchewan and British Columbia. Because of their small numbers, wide dispersal, and cultural similarity to British and French Canadians, the Belgians are highly assimilated into Canadian society.

Bibliography

Magee, Joan (1987). *The Belgians in Ontario: A History.* Toronto and Reading: Dundurn Press.

BYELORUSSIANS.   (Belorussians, Kryvians, White Russians, White Ruthenians). Estimates place the number of people of Byelorussian ethnic ancestry in Canada today at from 30,000 to more than 100,000. No accurate count of Canadians of Byelorussian ancestry is possible, as those who arrived prior to World War I were often identified as either Russians or Poles and they were not enumerated separately in the census until 1971. Byelorussia is the region that today is located in the Soviet Union, south and east of Lithuania and Latvia. The Byelorussians arrived in three major waves. Those coming in the first decade of the twentieth century mainly settled in cities in northern Ontario where they worked as industrial laborers. Often identified by themselves and others as Poles, they were rapidly absorbed by the Canadian Polish community. The group that arrived after World War I settled in the prairies where they often established farming communities. The group arriving after World War II were more educated and skilled than the earlier groups and settled in cities. This latter group is also much involved in maintaining their Byelorussian identity through associations, festivals, Byelorussian publications, and a strong desire for an independent Byelorussian homeland.

Bibliography

Sadouski, John (1981). *A History of the Byelorussians in Canada.* Belleville, Ontario: Mika Publishing Co.

CROATS. (Croatians). In 1986, an estimated 35,115 Canadians claimed Croat ethnic ancestry. Since it is estimated that at least 75,000 Croats have immigrated to Canada in the twentieth century, this figure is a gross undercount. Most Canadians of Croat ancestry are now identified by themselves or others as simply Canadians or Yugoslavians. (Croatia is one of six republics that form the modern nation of Yugoslavia.) Croats in Canada today are mostly people who immigrated there in the 1900s or are their descendants. The first wave of immigration preceded World War I and consisted mainly of men who took mining, railroad, and logging work in the western provinces. Those who came between the world wars settled in both rural and urban areas where they established distinctively Croat neighborhoods, displaying many of the communal and cooperative features of the *zadruga*, the extended family homestead common in rural Croatia. By the 1950s, the Croatian identity of these groups and their children had eroded, and many had adopted a middle-class lifestyle. After World War II, and especially after 1955, there was a third major immigration of Croats to Canada, which has led to a fragmentation of the Canadian Croat population into the assimilated earlier arrivals and the post–World War II group, which strives to maintain its Croat ethnic identity. The latter group is largely urban; its members have founded new Croatian Catholic churches, economic and political associations, social clubs, and music and art groups, and are served by a revitalized Croatian press, language maintenance programs, and family-based businesses and partnerships that rely on cooperative features of the zadrugas. There is also considerable interest and involvement in efforts to establish an independent Croatian homeland.

Bibliography

Rasporich, A. W. (1982). *For a Better Life: A History of the Croatians in Canada.* Toronto: McClelland & Stewart.

CZECHS. In 1981, 67,695 Canadians claimed Czechoslovakian ethnic ancestry, but this figure requires a number of qualifications. First, Czechoslovakian is not an ethnic category, but a national one, referring to the citizens of the modern nation of Czechoslovakia (Czecho-Slovakia), whose two major ethnic groups are the Czechs and the Slovaks. Second, it is likely an underestimate of the number of ethnic Czechs and Slovaks in Canada, as prior to 1918 they were often identified as Austrians or Hungarians. And, third, the number of people of Slovak ancestry is probably two to three times greater than those of Czech ancestry. Substantial Czech immigration to Canada began in the 1880s, with the first settlers relocating from the United States to form farming communities in the prairies and to mine in the Rockies. A large number came in the late 1800s and early 1900s, again from the United States, but also now directly from the Czech region of Austro-Hungary. They settled mainly in Alberta and Manitoba. The greatest influx occurred after World War I, with many of these immigrants working in factories in cities such as Toronto, Montreal, Windsor, Hamilton, and Vancouver, though distinctively Czech neighborhoods rarely formed. Following World War II and the establishment of communist rule in Czechoslovakia, more Czechs arrived in Canada. In the absence of ethnic communities, Czech identity was maintained through the church (Roman Catholic and Baptist), economic and political associations, social clubs, and the Czech and Czechoslovakian press. At the same time, Czechs have become well integrated into Canadian society.

Bibliography

Gellner, John, and John Smerek (1968). *The Czechs and Slovaks in Canada.* Toronto: University of Toronto Press.

Horna, Jarmila L. A. (1979). "The Entrance Status of Czech and Slovak Immigrant Women." In *Two Nations, Many Cultures: Ethnic Groups in Canada,* edited by Jean L. Elliott, 270–279. Scarborough, Ontario: Prentice-Hall of Canada.

DANES. In 1986, an estimated 39,950 Canadians claimed Danish ethnic ancestry. Most Danes immigrated to Canada either between 1870 and World War I or in the 1950s. Those who came before World War I moved directly from Denmark or indirectly from Danish settlements in the United States. The former often settled in the Maritime Provinces and Ontario; many of the latter settled in the Prairie provinces. Those who came in the 1950s settled mainly in cities, especially in Alberta, British Columbia, and Ontario. Because many of these immigrants eventually returned to Denmark, the Danish population in Canada has been relatively unstable, doubling in the years between 1951 and 1961 and then decreasing by at least 50 percent between 1961 and 1986. Because of the previous residence of many in the United States, their wide dispersal across Canada, and the return of many to Denmark, Danes did not develop a distinct ethnic identity in Canada, and most are assimilated into Canadian society.

Bibliography

Paulsen, Frank M. (1974). *Danish Settlements on the Canadian Prairies: Folk Traditions, Immigrant Experiences, and Local History.* National Museum of Man, Centre for Folk Culture Studies, Paper no. 11. Ottawa: National Museums of Canada.

DUTCH. In 1986, an estimated 351,765 Canadians claimed Dutch ethnic ancestry. Of these, 171,151 lived in Ontario, 62,945 in British Columbia, 55,920 in Alberta, and 27,875 in Manitoba. Dutch settlement in Canada can be divided into three periods. From 1890 to 1914 Dutch emigrated from the United States and the Netherlands mostly to the western provinces where they worked on or established farms. In the 1920s, the Dutch continued to settle in the West, but now sought industrial work in cities in the East as well, especially in southern Ontario. After World War II about 150,000 Dutch settled in cities with a heavy concentration in Ontario. Despite being the sixth largest ethnic group in Canada and the large number of recent arrivals, the Dutch are among the most assimilated of all ethnic groups in Canada. Dutch is rarely spoken anymore, the Dutch Catholic and Protestant churches, with the exception of the Dutch Calvinists, have become Canadian churchs, and associations attract only a minority of Dutch-Canadians. Integration into Canadian society has come through a strong work ethic, a willingness to intermarry, and little attachment to Dutch traditions that are sometimes seen as an impediment to full participation in Canadian life.

Bibliography

Ganzevoort, Herman, and Mark Boekelman, eds. (1983). _Dutch Immigration to North America._ Toronto: Multicultural History Society of Ontario.

Ishwaran, K. (1977). _Family, Kinship, and Community: A Study of Dutch Canadians, a Developmental Approach._ Toronto: McGraw-Hill Ryerson.

ENGLISH. The number of Canadians of English ethnic ancestry is unknown, as the English are classified as British, along with the Scots, Irish, and Welsh. Estimates from the 1986 census indicate that 6,332,725 Canadians claimed British ethnic ancestry. An additional 2,073,830 claimed mixed British ancestry and 3,401,870 claimed British and other ethnic ancestry. Prior to 1850, most English immigration to Canada involved soldiers stationed there to combat the French influence, Loyalists who fled north both before and following the American Revolution, and those encouraged to emigrate by the English government. English settlement in Canada accelerated after 1850, with immigrants arriving in three major groups. Between 1867 and 1920 many indigent English children were sent to live in the care of various societies in Canada. Between 1890 and 1914 many English also settled in the prairies, as did numerous other immigrants. After World War II, English immigration increased again. The English have settled heavily all across Canada, except in Quebec, with major concentrations in the Maritime Provinces, British Columbia, and Ontario. Modern Canadian society has been shaped in important ways by English institutions; these include the language, the legal system, the parliamentary form of government, the Anglican church, the Royal Canadian Mounted Police, social clubs, labor unions, and various cultural activities. Because English customs and beliefs are so common, if not dominant, English immigrants have easily and quickly assimilated into Canadian society.

Bibliography

Arnopoulos, Sheila, and D. Clift (1980). _The English Fact in Quebec._ Montreal: McGill-Queen's University Press.

Cowan, Helen (1967). _British Immigration to British North America._ Toronto: University of Toronto Press.

Dunae, Patrick A. (1981). _Gentlemen Emigrants: From the British Public Schools to the Canadian Frontier._ Vancouver, British Columbia: Douglas & McIntyre.

Weaver, Jack W. (1986). _Immigrants from Great Britain and Ireland: A Guide to Archival and Manuscript Sources in North America._ Westport, Conn.: Greenwood Press.

ESTONIANS. In 1986, an estimated 13,200 Canadians claimed Estonian ethnic ancestry. Estonians are mostly recent arrivals in Canada, with 14,310 arriving between 1947 and 1960 and 11,370 of those between 1948 and 1952. Most were displaced persons who fled Estonia in 1944 and afterward for Sweden and Germany and then immigrated to Can-

ada and other nations. The first permanent Estonian settlements were farm communities formed in Alberta in the first decade of the twentieth century. The subsequent arrival of other Canadians led to rapid assimilation into Canadian society. Today, Estonians are an urban group, with 85 percent living in cities such as Toronto, Montreal, Hamilton, and Vancouver. Many are professionals or entrepreneurs who own small or medium-sized businesses. While participating in Canadian society, the Estonians are attempting to maintain their ethnic identity through clubs, schools, summer camps, credit unions, the Estonian-language press, and associations who maintain contact with similar associations in other nations where Estonians have settled.

Bibliography

Aun, K. (1985). _The Political Refugees: A History of the Estonians in Canada._ Toronto: McClelland & Stewart.

FINNS. In 1986 an estimated 40,565 Canadians claimed Finnish ethnic ancestry. This is probably a large undercount, with Canadians of Finnish ancestry more likely numbering more than 100,000. Over 50 percent of self-identified Finnish-Canadians live in Ontario, and about 20 percent live in British Columbia. There have been three major eras of Finnish migration to Canada. The small number who came before World War I, either directly from Finland or after initial settlement in the United States, included some socialists who stressed community cooperation. A major influx occurred after World War I, but these Finns were mainly antisocialist and often formed rural communities centered around the Finnish Lutheran church. Between 1950 and 1960, a third group arrived. More urban and skilled than the earlier settlers, they more often settled in cities. The Finns have been active participants in the Canadian economy and political system. At the same time, a strong Finnish identity has been maintained, especially in smaller towns that were initially settled by Finns emigrating from the same areas in Finland. In the early years, temperance societies, the churches, sports and social clubs, a Finnish-language press, and participation in national organizations were sources of Finnish identity. More recently, as the use of Finnish has declined and the Finns have become economically assimilated, Finnish identity revolves more around such core values as personal freedom, pride, determination, and strongly held political and religious views that both Finns and others see as uniquely Finnish in the Canadian context.

Bibliography

Karni, Michael G., ed. (1981). _Finnish Diaspora. Vol. 1, Canada, South America, Africa, Australia and Sweden._ Toronto: Multicultural History Society of Ontario.

Nilsen, Kirsti (1985). _The Baker's Daughter: Memoirs of a Finnish Immigrant Family in Timmins._ Toronto: Multicultural History Society of Ontario.

Roninila, Mike (1987). "Language Retention in the Finnish Identification of Winnipeg's Finnish Population." _Siirtolaisuus-Migration_ 2:6–11.

GERMANS. In 1986, an estimated 896,720 Canadians claimed German ethnic ancestry. Germans are the third largest ethnic population group in Canada, behind the British and French. German-Canadians are heavily concentrated in the western provinces, with 182,870 in Alberta, 148,280 in British Columbia, 128,850 in Saskatchewan, and 96,160 in Manitoba. There are also 285,155 in Ontario. The majority of German-speaking people who came to Canada emigrated not from territory that is now part of the two German nations but from territory now in other nations such as Austria (and the Austro-Hungarian Enmpire), Switzerland, the Netherlands, Russia, and the United States. German immigration to Canada goes back to the seventeenth century when German soldiers who fought with the French and then the British settled in Canada. In the eighteenth century, German settlement in Canada continued, but then by families from Europe and others resettling from the United States. In the first half of the 1800s most settlement was in Ontario. From about 1880 to World War I immigration was mainly to the western provinces, and it was during this period that many German communities were founded in the West.

Germans have never formed a cohesive ethnic group in Canada. Rather, there have been a number of major divisions within the German population group, including those based on religion (Roman Catholic or Protestant), nation or region of origin, rural or urban settlement in Canada, and social class. In addition, intermarriage with non-Germans has been common, Germans are highly integrated into the Canadian economy, and German identity became less desirable during and after World War I when Germans were often treated as the enemy. Only in the last twenty years as part of the revival of ethnic pluralism in Canada has a strong sense of German ethnic identity reemerged. German ethnicity has perhaps been stronger in rural communities where land is often seen as family property, the traditional division of labor by sex prevails, and children are raised less permissively. Despite their almost full participation in Canadian society, Germans are generally not seen by experts as fully assimilated, perhaps because of their large numbers and also because of their large concentrations and visibility in the western provinces.

As much as 25 percent of the German-Canadian population is of German-Russian (Russian-German, Germans from Russia) ancestry. They are German-speaking peoples whose ancestors settled in the Volga and Black Sea regions of Russia in the 1700s. In the late 1800s, many of them left Russia in order to find political and religious freedom elsewhere, some of them in western Canada. Others arrived later, after World I and again after World War II. Because of their rural background in Russia and settlement of farm communities in western Canada, they are perhaps somewhat less assimilated than other German-Canadians.

See also Amish, Austrians, European-Americans (Pennsylvania Dutch, Sorbs), Hutterites, Mennonites, Swiss

Bibliography

Bassler, Gerhard (1986). *The German Canadians, 1750–1937: Immigration, Settlement and Culture*. Translated by Heinz Lehmann. St John's, Newfoundland: Jesperson Press.

Eberhardt, Elvire (1985). "The Growth of the German Population in Medicine Hat, Alberta, from 1885 to the Present." *Deutsch Kanadisches Jahrbuch/German-Canadian Yearbook* 6:62–65.

Helling, Rudolf A. (1984). *A Socio-Economic History of German-Canadians: They, Too, Founded Canada*. Edited by Bernd Hamm. Wiesbaden: Franz Steiner Verlag.

Kloberdanz, Timothy J. (1988). "Symbols of German-Russian Ethnic Identity on the Northern Plains." *Great Plains Quarterly* 8:3–15.

Lee-Whiting, Brenda (1985). *Harvest of Stones: The German Settlement in Renfrew County*. Toronto: University of Toronto Press.

GREEKS. In 1986 an estimated 143,780 Canadians claimed Greek ethnic ancestry. Of these, 80,320 lived in Ontario, 47,450 in Quebec, and 7,295 in British Columbia. Most Greeks came to Canada after 1900, with perhaps no more than 1,000 arriving before then. From 1900 to 1945 Greek immigration to Canada was relatively steady, with Greeks generally settling in cities. After 1945, in reaction to the political and economic instability in Greece, the immigration increased, leading to the formation of distinct neighborhoods with a strong sense of Greek identity in cities such as Montreal, Toronto, and Vancouver. With the Greek population today composed of many of these post–World War II immigrants and their children, Greeks remain relatively unassimilated into Anglo-Canadian society. Greek is still spoken by many of them, they have a relatively low level of identification with Canadian society, they tend to socialize mostly with other Greeks, and they are not highly integrated into the work force. Factors leading to the persistence of Greek culture include Greek schools, the Greek Orthodox church, the family and its strong resistance to exogamy, the Greek-language press, and the survival of Greek neighborhoods. In addition, traditional Greek values focusing on hard work, economic cooperation, and family authority have been maintained while more mainstream Canadian values have been rejected. Although the Greeks in Canada form a relatively homogeneous cultural group, it should be noted that the Macedonians are culturally distinct and see themselves as a separate ethnic group. In 1986 there were an estimated 11,355 Canadians of Macedonian ancestry, with nearly all residing in Ontario.

Bibliography

Chimbos, Peter D. (1980). *The Canadian Odyssey: The Greek Experience in Canada*. Toronto: McClelland & Stewart.

Chimbos, Peter D. (1987). "Occupational Distribution and Social Mobility of Greek-Canadian Immigrants." *Journal of the Hellenic Diaspora* 14:131–143.

Constantinides, Stephanos (1983). *Les Grecs du Québec*. Montreal: Les Éditions Le Métèque.

Ioannov, Tina (1983). *La Communauté Grecque du Québec*. Quebec: Quebecoise Recherche sur la Culture.

Vasiliadis, Peter (1988). *Whose Are You? Identity and Ethnicity among the Toronto Macedonians*. New York: AMS Press.

HUNGARIANS. In 1986, an estimated 97,850 Canadians claimed Hungarian ethnic ancestry. Of these, 51,255

lived in Ontario, 12,780 in Alberta, and 13,000 in British Columbia. Hungarian immigration to Canada has taken place in three stages. From 1885 to World War I, Hungarian peasants, many of whom moved north from the United States, established rural farming communities in the plains. Settlement was so concentrated in Saskatchewan that before 1914 it was labeled Little Hungary. Between World Wars I and II, Hungarian immigrants settled in cities across Canada, leading to a more dispersed and more urban Hungarian population. Following World War II, Hungarian immigration increased again and included Jews, Nazi sympathizers, anticommunists, and those who fled after the 1956 revolution. These new arrivals have produced a far more heterogeneous Hungarian population and have stimulated a revitalization of Hungarian ethnicity manifested in schools, clubs, theater and dance groups, and a Hungarian-language press. At the same time, the internal diversity has hindered a broad sense of shared Hungarian identity.

Bibliography

Blumstock, Robert (1985). "Est Vita Hungariam: Hungarians in Canada." *Hungarian Studies Review* 12(1):33–41.

Dreisziger, N. F. (1985). "The Hungarian Experience in Toronto." *Hungarian Studies Review* 12:1–88.

Dreisziger, N. F., with M. L. Kovacs, Paul Bödy, and Bennett Kovrig (1982). *Struggle and Hope: The Hungarian-Canadian Experience.* Toronto: McClelland & Stewart.

Miska, John, comp. (1987). *Canadian Studies on Hungarians, 1886–1986: An Annotated Bibliography of Primary and Secondary Sources.* Regina: Canadian Plains Research Centre, University of Regina.

ICELANDERS. Contemporary Icelanders are descendants of Norwegians who migrated to Iceland and established an independent republic there in A.D. 874. After failed attempts in 1873 and 1874 to establish settlements in Quebec and Ontario, a group of Icelanders settled in the interlake region of what is today Manitoba in 1875 where they founded the republic of "New Iceland." Later arrivals settled in and around Winnipeg where they were joined by people moving south from New Iceland. When the boundaries of Manitoba were extended northward, New Iceland became part of the province.

The major unifying feature among Icelanders in Canada has been their rich oral and written literary tradition, with many sagas recounting the settling of Iceland in the ninth century. Icelanders are partially assimilated into Canadian society in that most speak English as their primary language, are highly educated, intermarry readily, and often hold professional positions. At the same time, a long history of factionalism involving kin group and regional distinctions, Lutherans versus Unitarians, and political differences has kept much of the group focus inward and helped maintain Icelander identity.

Bibliography

Lindal, Walter J. (1967). *The Icelanders in Canada.* Ottawa and Winnipeg: National Publishers and Viking Printers.

Matthiasson, John S. (1979). "The Icelandic Canadians: The Paradox of an Assimilated Ethnic Group." In *Two Nations, Many Cultures: Ethnic Groups in Canada,* edited by Jean L. Elliott, 195–205. Scarborough, Ontario: Prentice-Hall of Canada.

IRISH. There are at least 2 million people of Irish ethnic ancestry in Canada today. The exact number of Irish-Canadians is unknown, as the many descendants of Irish immigrants who arrived in the early 1880s are now assimilated into Canadian society and no longer see themselves as members of a distinct ethnic group. The Irish have been a sizable population and major contributor to Canadian society since Canada was under French control in the seventeenth century. But the major period of Irish immigration was the first half of the nineteenth century. Those who came before 1840 tended to settle in the Maritime Provinces where they often worked as laborers. Those who came after 1847, the "Famine Irish," more often settled in towns and cities across Canada, but especially in Ontario and the Maritime Provinces and less so in the West.

The Irish who came to Canada included both Protestants and Roman Catholics who represented different cultural traditions and experienced different assimilation processes. The Protestants associated with the British tradition and quickly and easily assimilated into British Canadian society. There probably never was and certainly is not now a distinct Protestant Irish ethnic group in Canada. Many of the Catholics arrived later than the Protestants, were less educated and less well-off economically, and were at odds with both the Protestants and the Catholic French-Canadians, making assimilation more difficult. Nevertheless, assimilation did occur for several reasons: they spoke English, the Catholic church was a major force in Canadian society, and, from the 1860s on, many Irish Catholics moved south to the United States. Thus, Irish urban neighborhoods rarely formed in Canada. Today, both the Protestants and the Catholics are integrated socially, economically, and politically into Canadian society.

Bibliography

Akenson, Donald H. (1984). *The Irish in Ontario: A Study in Rural History.* Kingston and Montreal: McGill-Queen's University Press.

Elliott, Bruce S. (1988). *Irish Migrants in the Canadas: A New Approach.* Montreal: McGill-Queen's University Press.

Nicolson, Murray W. (1985). "The Irish Experience in Ontario: Rural or Urban?" *Urban History Review/Revue d'Histoire Urbaine* 14:37–45.

O'Driscoll, Robert, and Lorna Reynolds, eds. (1988). *The Untold Story: The Irish in Canada.* 2 vols. Toronto: Celtic Arts of Canada.

ITALIANS. In 1986, an estimated 709,590 Canadians claimed Italian ethnic ancestry. Italians are the fourth largest ethnic group in Canada. They are a largely urban group with the largest concentrations in 1981 in Toronto (297,205) and Montreal (156,535) and sizable communities in Hamilton, Vancouver, St. Catherines, Windsor, Ottawa, Calgary, and

Edmonton. Although Italian contact with Canada goes back to the late fifteenth century, most immigration occurred between either 1900 and 1914 or 1950 and 1970, with the majority of Italian-Canadians having entered or descended from people who entered in the latter period. Over 90 percent of Italian-Canadians are Roman Catholics. About three-quarters of all immigrants came from southern Italy, mainly from Abruzzi-Molise and Calabria, and the majority were peasants.

Italians have participated in and contributed to Canadian society, but they have also resisted assimilation and in important ways remain a distinct cultural group. Ethnic associations, clubs, the Roman Catholic church, the Italian press, and language programs have all played a role since the early 1900s in maintaining Italian ethnicity. Perhaps more important were the Italian neighborhoods ("Little Italies") that formed in cities with large Italian populations. These communities were often based on extended family and nuclear family ties as well as ties to regions and villages in Italy that provided a social context in which basic core values such as loyalty, reciprocity, respect for the elderly, and family honor could be expressed. Although there has been considerable population relocation to the suburbs and second- and third-generation Italian-Canadians have moved rapidly up the socioeconomic ladder, kin and family ties and obligations remain strong as does a shared sense of Italian identity.

Bibliography

Campenella, M., ed. (1977). *Proceedings of Symposium '77: On the Economic, Social and Cultural Conditions of the Italian Canadian in the Hamilton-Wentworth Region.* Hamilton: Italian Canadian Federation of Hamilton.

Harney, Robert F. (1978). *Italians in North America.* Toronto: Multicultural History Society of Ontario.

Multicultural Society of Ontario (1985). "Italians in Ontario." *Polyphony* 7(2):1–147.

Razzolini, Maria (1983). "All Our Fathers: The North Italian Colony in Industrial Cape Breton." *Ethnic Heritage Series* 8:1–55.

Sturino, Franc, comp. (1988). *Italian-Canadian Studies: A Select Bibliography.* Toronto: Multicultural History Society of Ontario.

Zucchi, John E. (1988). *Italians in Toronto: Development of a National Identity.* Montreal: McGill-Queen's University Press.

LATVIANS.   In 1986, an estimated 12,615 Canadians were Latvians—people who trace their ethnic identity to the territory that is now the Latvian Soviet Socialist Republic. Latvian is an Indo-European language closely related only to Lithuanian. Most Latvians in Canada are immigrants who arrived after World War II, many of them classified as displaced persons seeking refuge from war-ravaged Europe and Soviet rule. Most settled in Ontario and especially in Toronto where many who were professionals integrated easily into the Canadian work force. Because of their recent arrival and strong Latvian nationalistic feelings, they have resisted cultural as-

similation and have formed associations, clubs, language schools, and churches (mostly Lutheran). Latvian culture is a mix of native, Slavic, Scandinavian, and German elements that have been combined over the centuries into a unique Latvian cultural tradition. To outsiders, Latvian culture is most notable for its rich collection of folk songs (*dainas*), unique art and design motifs, and native peasant dress.

LITHUANIANS.   In 1986 an estimated 14,625 Canadians claimed Lithuanian ethnic ancestry. Lithuanians are people from the territory that is now the Lithuanian Soviet Socialist Republic in the Soviet Union. Lithuanian-Canadians can be divided roughly into those or the descendants of those who arrived before World War II and those who came after. Many of those who arrived before World War II (mainly early in the century and in the 1920s and 1930s) settled initially in rural areas, but many eventually relocated to cities (usually Toronto and Montreal) where the men often worked in factories. Those who came after World War II numbered about 20,000 and were primarily displaced persons and refugees. They tended to settle in cities, with most Lithuanians now in Ontario but some also in Quebec, Alberta, and British Columbia. Lithuanian ethnic identity remains strong in Canada, with perhaps a majority still speaking Lithuanian, a strong sense of national community, and numerous well-organized clubs, associations, and societies that promote Lithuanian identity, culture, and language.

Bibliography

Danys, Milda (1986). *Lithuanian Immigration to Canada after the Second World War.* Toronto: Multicultural History Society of Ontario.

NORWEGIANS.   In 1986, an estimated 61,575 Canadians claimed Norwegian ethnic ancestry. During the nineteenth century hundreds of thousands of Norwegians immigrated to Canada, although very few stayed as most continued on to the United States. The Norwegians who settled in Canada did so mostly before 1930. From 1886 to 1929, Norwegians arriving from both Norway and the United States settled mostly in rural communities in the western provinces where they farmed, logged, mined, and worked for railroads. The rate of Norwegian immigration increased again after World War II but decreased and has remained low since about 1960. Up to about fifty years ago, Norwegians maintained a strong sense of ethnic identity centered around the rural communities, membership in the Lutheran church, associations and clubs, and ties to the Norwegian community in the United States. Over time, however, the effects of relocations to cities, intermarriage, public education, and the use of English in place of Norwegian have led to assimilation into Canadian society. In recent years there has been a marked revival of Norwegian ethnic identity, tied less to the past and the traditional culture than to an association with the modern nation of Norway.

Bibliography

Loken, Gulbrand (1980). *From Fjord to Frontier: A History of the Norwegians in Canada.* Toronto: McClelland & Stewart.

POLES.   In 1986, an estimated 222,260 Canadians claimed Polish ethnic ancestry. Of these, 117,570 lived in Ontario, 28,500 in Alberta, 19,305 in British Columbia,

18,835 in Quebec, and 13,325 in Saskatchewan. Nearly 90 percent of Poles live in urban centers, with Toronto, Winnipeg, Montreal, Edmonton, Hamilton, and Vancouver having the largest numbers. Today, there are no uniquely Polish urban ghettos nor any Polish rural communities. In the early years of immigration, Poles were often distinguished as Kashubians, Galicians, German Poles, and so on. These distinctions have now largely disappeared. The first wave of Polish immigration took place from 1858 to 1913, with most arriving after 1895 and settling on farms in the prairie provinces. Those who arrived in the interwar years also settled on the prairies. The end of World War II brought a third wave of Polish immigrants, including many men who had served in the Polish military, displaced persons, and refugees. From 1957 on, Poles have continued to settle in Canada, many immigrating in search of better economic conditions and political freedom. Most of the post–World War II immigrants have settled in cities, about half in Ontario. The Roman Catholic church (about 70 percent of Canadian Poles are Roman Catholic; others are mainly United church or Polish Catholic) and various Polish associations and clubs have played a major role in maintaining Polish ethnic identity. There is considerable variation within the group regarding the strength of Polish identity, with the strongest identity expressed by those who have arrived since World War II and share an interest in and concern about the Polish homeland.

Bibliography

Boski, Pawel (1987). "On Turning Canadian or Remaining Polish: Stability and the Change of Ethnic Identity among Polish Immigrants to Canada." *Przeglad Polonijny* 13:25–54, 128.

Heydenkorn, Benedykt (1985). *A Community in Transition: The Polish Group in Canada.* Toronto: Canadian Polish Research Institute.

Kusharska, Jadwiga (1986). "Kaszubi W Kanadzie: Mechanizmy Identyfikacji Ethniczncj" (Kashubs in Canada: The mechanism of ethnic identification). *Etnografia Polska* 30:163–179.

Radecki, Henry, and Benedykt Heydenkorn (1976). *A Member of a Distinguished Family: The Polish Group in Canada.* Toronto: McClelland & Stewart.

Renkiewicz, Frank, ed. (1984). *Polish Presence in Canada and America.* Toronto: Multicultural History Society of Ontario.

PORTUGUESE. In 1986, an estimated 199,595 Canadians claimed Portuguese ethnic ancestry, with about 139,220 living in Ontario, 29,700 in Quebec, and 15,535 in British Columbia. About 38 percent live in Toronto. The Portuguese have been coming to maritime Canada since the late 1400s, first as explorers and later as fishermen. Few actually settled there, however, and in 1951 there were only about 1,000 Portuguese in Canada. After 1950, Canada became a preferred place for Portuguese settlement, and large numbers of immigrants arrived from mainland Portugal and the Azores. Much of the migration was in the form of chains of extended family members who formed communities and neighborhoods populated mostly by people from the same communities or regions in Portugal. Portuguese communities are mainly working class (the first generation often found only unskilled work), although there has been a steady movement into small-business ownership, and jobs in the service, technical, and professional sectors. With nearly all Portuguese being either first- or second-generation Canadians, ethnic identity remains strong and is a major concern of the first generation. This identity is reflected mainly in Portuguesismo, "being Portuguese." Among central elements of this identity are a strong sense of family, distinct sex roles, respect for the elderly, and food and music preferences. At the same time, however, a strong pan-Canadian Portuguese cohesiveness has not developed, perhaps because Portuguese regional distinctions are still important and because of the social class cleavages appearing in the Portuguese community.

Bibliography

Anderson, Grace M., and Davis Higgs (1976). *A Future to Inherit: The Portuguese Communities of Canada.* Toronto: McClelland & Stewart.

Joy, Annamma (1988). *Ethnicity in Canada: Social Accommodation and Cultural Persistence among the Sikhs and the Portuguese.* New York: AMS Press.

ROMANIANS (Roumanians, Rumanians). In 1986, 18,745 Canadians claimed Romanian ethnic ancestry. This is probably an undercount, as some who arrived around the turn of the twentieth century came from Austria, Hungary, and Russia and were not listed as Romanian. The largest number of Romanians live in Ontario (7,385), with concentrations also in Saskatchewan (2,695), Alberta (2,790), and British Columbia (1,840). The major periods of Romanian immigration to Canada were the late 1880s to World War I, the 1920s, and post–World War II. Early immigrants settled in rural communities mainly in the western provinces, whereas the post–World War II group more often settled in cities in Ontario. The Romanian Orthodox church, the Romanian press, and local units of national organizations have long provided a focus for Romanian identity, but such identity has weakened in recent years, especially in urban areas, where many post–World War II immigrants settled.

Bibliography

Patterson, G. James (1977). *The Romanians of Saskatchewan: Four Generations of Adaptation.* National Museum of Man, Canadian Centre for Folk Culture Studies, Paper no. 23. Ottawa: National Museums of Canada.

RUSSIANS. In 1986, an estimated 32,080 Canadians claimed Russian ethnic ancestry. Russians in Canada live mainly in the western provinces, with 14,170 in British Columbia (many of whom are Doukhobors), 4,185 in Alberta, 4,130 in Saskatchewan, and 1,755 in Manitoba. There are also 5,780 in Ontario. Russians in Canada represent a number of distinct groups: (1) White Russians who fled after the Russian Revolution in 1917, (2) Old Believers, (3) Doukhobors, (4) Russians from Poland, (5) Russian peasants, (6) displaced persons and refugees after World War II, and (7) Russian Jews. Russian immigration to Canada began in the late eighteenth century with fur trappers and traders in Alaska, then a Russian territory, and on the Pacific coast; they, however, moved elsewhere after the sale of Alaska to the United States. After the Russian Revolution a large number immigrated to Canada, as did many displaced persons and refugees after World War II. Most of these latter two groups settled in cities. Russians have never formed a cohesive ethnic entity in Canada, partly because of internal variations and partly because of the relatively few Russians who have arrived in the past forty years. In those areas where a sense of Russian identity does exist, it tends to center on participation in the Russian Orthodox church or in anticommunist organizations.

See also Byelorussians, Doukhobors, Estonians, Jews, Latvians, Lithuanians, Old Believers, Ukrainians in Canada

Bibliography

Jeletzky, T. F., ed. (1983). *Russian Canadians, Their Past and Present*. Ottawa: Borealis Press.

Jones, David C. (1987). "So Pretty, So Middle Europe, So Foreign—Ruthenians and Canadianization." *History of Education Review* 16:13–30.

Tarasoff, Koozma J. (1988). *Spells, Splits, and Survival in a Russian Canadian Community: A Study of Russian Organizations in the Greater Vancouver Area*. New York: AMS Press.

SCOTS.   The number of Canadians of Scottish ethnic ancestry is unknown, as the Scots are classified as British, along with the English, Irish, and Welsh. Estimates from the 1986 census indicate that 6,332,725 Canadians claimed British ethnic ancestry. An additional 2,073,830 claimed mixed British ancestry and 3,401,870 claimed British and other ethnic ancestry. In 1961, 1,894,000 Canadians claimed Scottish ancestry. The earliest sizable groups of Scottish settlers were the men from the Orkney Islands who worked for the Hudson's Bay Company in western Canada and soldiers who served in the British army. From 1770 to 1815 a substantial number of Roman Catholic, Gaelic-speaking Highland Scots settled in eastern Canada where their distinctive communities continued to exist for a number of generations, though most have now disappeared into mainstream society. Since about 1815, Scottish migration to Canada has been dominated by the Protestant, English-speaking Lowland Scots who have settled all across Canada except for Newfoundland and Quebec. Since that time Scots have constituted about 10 percent of the Canadian population. Scots have been successful at both playing a major role in the development of Canadian society and maintaining a distinct sense of ethnic identity. Scots have participated in all areas of Canadian life but have been most visible in the religious, educational, business, and political sectors where they have brought such values as respect for education, intellectual inquiry, hard work, and thrift into the Canadian national culture. Today, Scottish identity is manifested through proud self-identification as a Scot as well as Scottish literary traditions, music, dance, sports such as curling, and educational and other institutions.

Bibliography

Emmerson, Frank (1987). *Peoples of the Maritimes: The Scots*. Four East Publications.

Hill, Douglas (1972). *The Scots in Canada*. London: Gentry Books.

McRae, Ellen (1986). "The Glens of Glengarry: 'Aye, 'Tis Not Scotland, but, Achh Now It'll Do!'" *Canadian Geographical Journal* 106:66-71.

Reid, W. Stanford, ed. (1976). *The Scottish Tradition in Canada*. Toronto: McClelland & Stewart.

SERBS.   In 1986, an estimated 9,510 Canadians claimed Serbian ethnic ancestry. They are people from the territory that is now Serbia, one of the six republics of the modern nation of Yugoslavia. Serbs in Canada, since they first arrived, have been sometimes misidentified, first as Hungarians, Austrians, or Turks, and later as Yugoslavians (a political, not a cultural category). Thus, the figure above underestimates the number of people of Serbian ancestry in Canada. Serbs began immigrating to Canada (both from Serbia and other regions of Yugoslavia and later from the United States) in 1850, and those who arrived before the early 1900s settled mainly in the western provinces. Those who arrived afterward—before World War I, between the wars, and since World War II— have more often settled in cities in Ontario. Serbian identity remains strong in Canada and is supported by associations, clubs, societies, Serbian-language radio, numerous publications, and the Serbian Orthodox church. The majority of Serbs in Canada still speak Serbian.

Bibliography

Skoric, Sofija, and George Vid Tomashevich, eds. (1987–1988). *Serbs in Ontario: A Socio-Cultural Description*. Toronto: Serbian Heritage Academy.

SLOVAKS.   In 1981, 67,695 Canadians claimed Czechoslovakian ethnic ancestry. This figure requires a number of qualifications. First, Czechoslovakian is not an ethnic category, but a national one, referring to the citizens of the modern nation of Czechoslovakia (Czecho-Slovakia), whose two major ethnic groups are the Czechs and the Slovaks. Second, it is likely an underestimate of the number of ethnic Czechs and Slovaks in Canada, as prior to 1918 they were often identified as Austrians or Hungarians. And, third, the number of people of Slovak ancestry is probably two to three times greater than those of Czech ancestry, with 43,070 Canadians being identified as of Czech ancestry in 1981. Slovaks came to and settled in Canada during four periods. Those who came first, from 1885 to World War I, settled in the West, where they farmed, mined, and worked for railroads. The second group came after World War I, and they too farmed and mined, settling in the West and also in Ontario and Quebec. The third and fourth waves of immigration took place after World War II and after the revolt against communist rule in 1968 and brought displaced persons and refugees to Canada. Although more than a third of the Slovaks in Canada have married non-Slovaks and Slovaks value Canadian citizenship, the Slovaks remain a distinct ethnic group. Their ethnic identity has been maintained in a variety of ways, including participation in ethnic organizations and church parishes and a shared concern about their homeland.

Bibliography

Kirschbaum, Joseph M. (1967). *Slovaks in Canada*. Toronto: Canadian Ethnic Press Association.

Stolarik, M. Mark (1988). "From Field to Factory: The Historiography of Slovak Immigration to the U.S. and Canada (1976–1987)." *Ethnic Forum* 8:23–39.

Sutherland, Anthony X. (1984). *The Canadian Slovak League: A History, 1932–1982*. Toronto: Canadian Slovak League.

SLOVENES. (Slovenians). In 1986, an estimated 5,890 Canadians claimed Slovenian ethnic ancestry. Slovenes are people from the territory that is now Slovenia, one of the six republics of the modern nation of Yugoslavia. Slovenes in Canada, since they first arrived, have been sometimes misidentified, first as Hungarians, Italians, or Turks, and later as Yugoslavians (a political, not a cultural category). Thus, the figure above underestimates the number of people of Slovenian ancestry in Canada. Slovenian immigration to Canada can be divided into two periods: before and after World War II. Those who came before the war, especially in the late 1800s and early 1900s, settled mainly in rural communities, often in the western provinces. Many of those who came after World War II were political refugees who settled mainly in cities, especially Toronto. They have stimulated a revival of Slovenian ethnic identity, centered around their Roman Catholic parishes and anticommunist sentiments.

SPANIARDS. In 1986, an estimated 57,125 Canadians claimed Spanish ethnic ancestry. This figure includes both Spaniards and Latinos. Spaniards are people who migrated directly from Spain (perhaps with a short stop elsewhere) or whose ancestors did so. They should be differentiated from Latinos who are people of Latin American ancestry. But because Spanish immigrants either have not been counted at all or were at times lumped with Latinos, it is impossible to say how many Spaniards have settled in Canada. The major population centers are Ontario and Quebec, with 78 percent of the Spanish population in those two provinces. For the most part, Spanish immigrants and their descendants have rapidly assimilated into Canadian society, and no strong sense of Spanish identity or culture has ever emerged. Assimilation has been especially rapid in French Canada. This is in part because Spaniards were few in number compared to other immigrant groups also arriving in the twentieth century and also because regional cultural identities (Galician, Catalonian, and so on) were more important in Spain than a sense of a national culture.

See also Latinos

Bibliography

Anderson, Grace M. (1979). "Spanish and Portuguese-Speaking Immigrants in Canada." In *Two Nations, Many Cultures: Ethnic Groups in Canada*, edited by Jean L. Elliott, 206–219. Scarborough, Ontario: Prentice-Hall of Canada.

SWEDES. In 1981, 78,360 Canadians claimed Swedish ethnic ancestry. The major period of Swedish settlement in Canada was from 1868 to 1914. Most of these people came after having first settled in Minnesota and North Dakota. In Canada, they settled mainly in the western provinces, with Winnipeg becoming the hub of Swedish activities and British Columbia today having the largest Swedish population. The majority of these early settlers were farmers, although many of their descendants have moved to cities where they work in industry and business. Other, smaller influxes of Swedes followed World Wars I and II, with these people settling mainly in Ontario. The rural Swedish communities were joined together through various organizations including the Swedish Lutheran church, labor unions, temperance groups, societies, and clubs. Today, Swedes are much assimilated into Canadian society, a result of their movement to cities, active participation in the public education system, and the relatively few new arrivals in the last few decades.

SWISS. In 1986, an estimated 19,130 Canadians claimed Swiss ethnic ancestry. Ontario is home to the largest number, followed by British Columbia, Alberta, and Quebec. The Swiss came to Canada from both Switzerland and the United States, and a substantial number arrived before the twentieth century. The majority were from the German-speaking region of Switzerland, and they tended to affiliate with Germans in Canada; those from the French-speaking region affiliated with French-Canadians. Today, a strong sense of Swiss identity has disappeared, and the Swiss are generally assimilated into Canadian society.

See also Mennonites

WELSH. In 1981, 46,620 Canadians claimed Welsh ethnic ancestry. This is almost certainly a large undercount (only twenty years earlier nearly three times as many claimed Welsh ethnicity) and is mostly the result of many Welsh being classified as British or as English (they had departed from Liverpool). Welsh immigration to Canada began with Welsh soldiers who served with the British in the American Revolution. The influx peaked after 1862 when gold miners settled in British Columbia, in 1902 when the Patagonian Welsh relocated from Argentina, after World War I, after World War II, and in the mid-1950s. The Welsh in Canada have never formed a national organization, although local societies and associations have existed since the early days of settlement in Canada. Perhaps the most visible signs of Welsh identity today are the Gymanfa Ganu (hymn-singing festival) and *eisteddfod* (arts festival) regularly held by various Welsh societies. In general, the Welsh lump themselves and are lumped by others under the general category of British, and, as such, are much assimilated into Canadian society.

Bibliography

Bennett, Carol (1985). *In Search of the Red Dragon: The Welsh in Canada*. Renfrew, Ontario: Juniper Books.

Thomas, Peter (1986). *Strangers from a Secret Land: The Voyages of the Brig "Albion" and the Founding of the First Welsh Settlements in Canada*. Toronto: University of Toronto Press.

Flathead

ETHNONYMS: Salish, Selish

The Flathead are an American Indian group numbering about four thousand who live with members of the Kalispel and Kutenai American Indian groups on the Flathead Indian Reservation in northwestern Montana.

The Flathead are a Salishan-speaking group who in the seventeenth and eighteenth centuries numbered between three thousand and six thousand and inhabited the region of western Montana and Wyoming north of the Gallatin River between the Rocky Mountains and the Little Belt range.

Aboriginally, the Flathead hunted bison on the plains and other large game in the mountains; fishing and gathering supplemented their diet. Bison hunting increased in importance after horses were acquired in 1700, and fur trading became an important part of the economy beginning in the early nineteenth century. The Flathead were loosely organized into bands composed of several related families and led by a chief.

Tribal government on the reservation today consists of a ten-member elected tribal council, which is responsible for selecting a tribal chairman and vice chairman. Forest industries are the main source of income on the reservation.

Religious life centered around guardian spirits obtained in dreams or visions induced by fasting and prayer. The Flathead believed that after death good souls journey to an upper world inhabited by the deity, Amo'tken, while bad souls go to live in an underworld inhabited by the evil deity, Amte'p.

Bibliography

Bigart, Robert J. (1971). "Patterns of Cultural Change in a Salish Flathead Community." *Human Organization* 30:229–237.

Old Person, Earl (1984). "Problems, Prospects, and Aspirations of the 'Real People' in America." In *Pathways to Self-Determination*, edited by Leroy Little Bear et al., 148–151. Toronto: University of Toronto Press.

Turney-High, Harry H. (1937). *The Flathead Indians of Montana*. American Anthropological Association, Memoir 48. Menasha, Wis.

Fox

ETHNONYMS: Mesquakie, Outagami

Orientation

Identification. The Fox were a hunting and agricultural society whose name for themselves was "Meskwahki-haki," meaning "Red earths" or "People of the red earth." Their identity is often confused with the Sauk. But even after the development of a close alliance between the two groups in the eighteenth century, the Fox have remained a single, clearly defined group.

Location. In aboriginal times the Fox were located in present-day southern Michigan or northwestern Ohio. Prior to European contact they were driven by the Iroquois into Wisconsin, where they were located at the time of first direct contact with Europeans in the mid-seventeenth century. Their territory at that time centered on the Wolf River and spread from Lake Superior south to the Chicago River and from Lake Michigan west to the Mississippi River.

Demography. In 1650 the Fox numbered approximately 2,500, and in the early nineteenth century, between 1,600 and 2,000. By 1867 the Fox population had declined to but 264 persons. In 1932 they numbered 403, and in 1955, 653. In the 1980s the Fox numbered about 1,000, with some 500 on the Sac and Fox Reservation in Tama County, Iowa.

Linguistic Affiliation. The Fox spoke an Algonkian language, which those in Iowa still speak.

History and Cultural Relations

In the mid to late seventeenth century the establishment of a French trading post at Green Bay drew the Fox to the Wolf River area. Almost from the start, tension and conflict characterized Fox-French relations. This stemmed in part from Fox opposition to the French extending the fur trade to their traditional enemies, the Dakota. In 1712, twenty-five years of continuous warfare were initiated when the Fox who had moved to Detroit and were presumed by the French post there to be planning an assault were attacked by a coalition of tribes organized and incited by the French commander. During this period the Fox were nearly wiped out by warfare and disease. In 1733 they took refuge with the Sauk at Green Bay and soon thereafter both tribes fled to Iowa. Shortly after the cessation of hostilities in 1737 the Fox returned to Wisconsin, but by the late eighteenth century they were living on the Iowa side of the Mississippi River.

Between 1832 and 1842, Fox and Sauk ceded their lands to the United States and moved to a reservation in Kansas. On the Kansas reservation, relations between the two groups were marked by tension, and between 1856 and 1859 the Fox returned to Iowa and settled near Tama. The federal government opposed this move, but was unsuccessful in returning them to Kansas.

The descendants of the Fox have maintained many elements of the traditional culture, including their language and clan-organized ritual activities. An important factor in this process has been tribal ownership of land and resistance to land allotment.

Settlements

In the early nineteenth century, the Fox settlement pattern alternated between large semipermanent villages occupied during the summer planting and fall harvesting seasons and small dispersed camps used during the winter and early spring hunting seasons. The semipermanent villages were located in river bottoms near agricultural fields and moved periodically as firewood resources were depleted. Generally, fewer than twenty dwellings or lodges made up a village, with the lodges aligned in parallel rows along an east-west axis. A typical summer lodge consisted of an elm-bark-covered pole scaffolding measuring forty to sixty feet long and twenty feet wide. Winter camps varied in size from one to a few extended families, with dwellings consisting of dome-shaped, pole-framed structures covered with cattail mats. On the 3,476-acre reservation, the Fox now live in scattered modern housing.

Economy

Subsistence and Commercial Activities. The Fox were hunter-farmers whose subsistence focused on deer, bison, maize, squash, beans, and pumpkins. Trapping and hunting for the fur trade became an important part of the economic pattern very soon after European contact. At the beginning of the nineteenth century the seasonal pattern of economic activities included planting crops in May and June and harvesting in the early autumn, after which the summer villages dispersed and the people journeyed to their hunting grounds. Hunts were also carried out during the summer growing season. Midwinter was spent in temporary camps in sheltered river bottoms where the people remained until hunting activities were renewed in the early spring. In April the dispersed families returned to their summer village and initiated a new cycle of agricultural activities.

Since the 1950s, commuting to work in nearby cities has been an important part of the economic pattern of Fox living near Tama, Iowa. Tribal income is derived from renting tribal lands to local farmers.

Industrial Arts. The Fox displayed a typical Woodland pattern, relying on the bow and arrow for hunting and warfare. Clothes were made from deerskin. Aboriginal manufactures were quickly replaced with items obtained from Europeans.

Trade. Apart from furs taken to obtain European trade goods, hides and tallow, a by-product of deer hunting, and lead ore obtained through surface mining were important trade items for the Fox during the historic period.

Division of Labor. Traditionally men hunted, and women were responsible for growing crops and gathering roots, nuts, berries, and animal by-products such as honey and beeswax.

Land Tenure. When they settled near Tama, Iowa, in 1857, the Fox purchased 80 acres of land; since that time additional land purchases have brought tribal holdings to 3,476 acres.

Kinship

Kin Groups and Descent. Fox kin groupings consisted of numerous exogamous patrilineal clans, the corporate features of which focused on ritual activities and rights to clan names. In theory, each clan was descended from a vision seeker who had been blessed by a spirit. Lineages composing the clans were the primary means for the inheritance of rights to ritual positions and political offices and also served to regulate secondary marriages. Descent was patrilineal.

Kinship Terminology. Kinship terminology followed the Omaha system.

Marriage and Family

Marriage. Marriage within one's clan was forbidden. Whether arranged by the couple, a go-between, or through negotiations between families, marriage was validated by an exchange of gifts between families. Polygyny was permitted; however, its frequency is unclear. After marriage, the couple resided with the wife's parents for one year or until the birth of their first child; thereafter they might live in their own lodge or with the husband's parents. Widows and widowers were expected to replace their deceased spouse with a member of the spouse's lineage; failure to do so brought retribution from the women of the offended lineage in the form of the destruction of the offender's property.

Domestic Unit. Each household consisted of an extended family of between five and thirty persons. Each extended family constituted an economic unit whose members cooperated in hunting and agricultural activities.

Inheritance. Ritual positions and political offices were controlled by lineages and inherited patrilineally.

Socialization. Corporal punishment of children was rare, the preferred method being forced fasting to instill correct behavior. During her first menstruation, a girl was isolated in a separate lodge for ten days as a precaution against endangering others and herself; during subsequent menstrual periods she was similarly isolated but for shorter periods of time. For boys, puberty was marked by a vision quest, undertaken in isolation, with the object of gaining spiritual power. Girls also sought visions, but not in isolation nor as part of menstrual seclusion.

Sociopolitical Organization

Social Organization. Fox society was split into two divisions whose lines crosscut clan and lineage divisions. The two divisions were represented by the colors white and black and organized the people for games, ceremonies, dances, and warfare. The firstborn child of a couple was assigned to the division to which the father did not belong, and subsequent children were assigned to alternate divisions according to their order of birth. Numerous permanent and temporary voluntary associations existed for raiding, ritual, and other purposes.

Political Organization. Politically, Fox society was divided into peace and war organizations, each with its own chief and subordinate officeholders. The peace chief had little authority and functioned primarily as a moderator; he was selected for the position from a specific lineage which controlled rights to the office by a tribal council. During times of war and other threatening periods, the war chief and the war organization held considerable power. For the war chief, this stemmed from his control over the camp police, an organization of warriors that enforced decisions made by the tribal council. In the early nineteenth century, the war chief acquired office through successful leadership in warfare. At an earlier time, however, clan affiliation may have been an important factor in access to the office. Membership in the tribal council was controlled by a specific lineage and its responsibilities included issues such as peace and war, relations with other tribes, and the selection of winter hunting grounds.

Today, an elected tribal council of seven members meets monthly to manage tribal affairs.

Social Control and Conflict. In addition to enforcing the decisions of the tribal council, the camp police regulated tribal movements and patrolled the campgrounds during bison hunts. Their unquestioned right to destroy the property of anyone who disobeyed them enabled the camp police to function effectively as a mechanism of social control. Currently, tension exists between the traditional and progressive factions who disagree about the extent to which the tribe should follow White economic and political practices.

Religion and Expressive Culture

Religious Beliefs. Fox cosmology included a belief in an upper world in the sky, associated with good, and a lower world beneath the earth, associated with evil. The Fox believed themselves to be the grandchildren of the earth and all that grew on it. Fox supernatural beings included Great or Gentle Manitou, who ruled the upper world. Other important supernatural beings included spirits associated with the four cardinal directions and the earth.

Religious Practitioners. Certain prescribed actions could be undertaken to gain the attention and favor of the spirits and place them under obligation. These actions included blackening one's face, fasting, wailing, and smoking or offering tobacco, which was believed to be greatly desired by the spirits, but accessible to them only through human beings. Successful vision questers were believed to be able to draw on supernatural powers contained in sacred packs they assembled following their vision experience. In some instances, individuals experienced multiple intense visions; the sacred packs associated with these visions were believed to be extremely powerful, with benefits extending to the clan and lineage of the vision quester.

Ceremonies. Two ceremonies were held annually in order to maintain the powers of the sacred packs of clans and lineages. One of these, a winter ceremony, was small and lacked elaborate ritual and social activities. The second, held in the summer, was rich in such activities, including prayers, songs, the telling of the histories of the sacred packs, dancing, and feasting.

Arts. Body ornamentation was important to the Fox. They were highly skilled in ribbon applique and silverwork and the production of beaded ornaments.

Medicine. The Fox developed a rich pharmacopoeia, and curers used over two hundred plant materials in curing, most of which were used for intestinal disorders. Most were taken internally, some applied externally, and a few burned for the therapeutic value of the smoke.

Death and Afterlife. Death was announced by a village crier and followed by an all-night mourning ceremony at the deceased's lodge by the deceased's clan members. The corpse was dressed in the finest clothing and wrapped in bark or reed mats prior to burial. Interment was usually in the ground, with the corpse extended and oriented along an east-west axis, the feet to the west. Noted warriors were commonly buried in a seated position. The burial ceremony included an address by a funeral director and tobacco offerings by the director and mourners; the earth-filled grave was covered over by a small wooden shed and marked with a post at the head that indicated the deceased's clan affiliation. Grave goods were few, and the deceased's property was divided by burial attendants and the deceased's surviving relatives.

Within four years of an individual's death, an adoption ceremony was held that served to release mourners from their obligations and bring into the deceased's lineage a friend or other person chosen by the surviving relatives. Usually the adoptee was a person of the same sex and age of the deceased, and the ceremony of adoption included feasts, games, dancing, and the exchange of gifts.

Bibliography

Callender, Charles (1978). "Fox." In *Handbook of North American Indians*. Vol. 15, *Northeast*, edited by Bruce G. Trigger, 636–647. Washington, D.C.: Smithsonian Institution.

Hagan, William T. (1950). *The Sac and Fox Indians*. Norman: University of Oklahoma Press.

Jones, William (1939). *Ethnography of the Fox Indians*. U.S. Bureau of American Ethnology Bulletin no. 125. Washington, D.C.

GERALD F. REID

French Canadians

ETHNONYMS: Francophones (outside of Quebec), Québecois

Orientation

Identification. French Canadian is a generic term applied to all descendants of French settlers in Canada. They form two groups: Québecois in the province of Quebec, and Francophones outside of Quebec. The former identify themselves as a distinct society and culture. The latter form a diaspora having a minority status, namely, Acadians in the Maritime Provinces and French Canadian communities in Ontario and the western provinces.

Location. Quebec Province is bounded by Hudson Bay and Ontario on the west, New Brunswick on the east, Labrador and the Arctic Ocean on the north, and New York on the south. Its area is 1,540,680 square kilometers. Geographically, the St. Lawrence lowlands separate the Canadian Plateau from the Appalachians. An Arctic climate, vegetation, and fauna are found in the north; subarctic climate in the center; and continental humid with mixed forest and a growing season of 60 to 160 days in the south.

Demography. The total population is about 6.4 million persons in Quebec and 500,000 outside Quebec. Francophones form 90 percent and Anglophones 10 percent of the population of Quebec. The Francophone population is now mainly urban, living in Montreal and Quebec City metropolitan areas. The remainder of the population of Quebec is sparsely distributed in regional cities of less than 10,000 persons and in rural areas. Francophones outside Quebec live in small localities and rural areas, but some have migrated recently to cities.

Linguistic Affiliation. French has been the official language of Quebec Province since 1974. In the 1970s the status of the French language became an important political issue: Quebec governments adopted linguistic laws. In other provinces, French Canadian communities must struggle to have their own institutions in order to preserve their language and culture and avoid assimilation. In New Brunswick and Ontario they now have access to French-language governmental services, education, and radio and television. The language spoken in Quebec differs from that in France in its vocabulary and pronunciation. The Quebec government decided in 1979 to translate English technical terms and promote Frenchification of all enterprises in Quebec so that French would be predominant. A special effort was also made to introduce immigrants to the language in order to protect the French character of the province.

History and Cultural Relations

In 1534, a French navigator took possession of the eastern part of Quebec in the name of France. Because of France's involvement in wars, it was not until 1608 that Samuel de Champlain, following the St. Lawrence River, founded Quebec City, the first settlement of the colony named New France. From 1608 to 1760, only ten thousand persons migrated from France to the colony, and present-day French Canadians are almost all descended from these first settlers. New France differed from New England in significant ways. France was a feudal society, which transplanted the seigneurial system, French law, and the Roman Catholic church to New France. The territory was divided between seigneuries headed by a seignor collecting seigneurial dues for granting land to *censitaires*, or peasant settlers. The New France economy rested on subsistence agriculture and the fur trade, all furs being exported to France. The territory was then much larger than now, covering the Maritime Provinces, the Great Lakes region, the central part of the United States along the Mississippi River, and Louisiana.

In 1760, New France became an English colony. Since French Canadians formed a distinct society and culture, they resisted assimilation, and in 1774 the English compromised, with the Act of Quebec recognizing French Canadian distinctiveness and affording them the right to live by their laws, religion, and language. From 1774 to 1854, the seigneurial system and the Catholic church dominated the social and economic life of French Canadians. The church allied itself with the seignors and English rulers. This situation was resented by the professional and merchant class, leading to the 1837–1838 revolt, which was put down by the English army. The leaders were killed or jailed and the peasant population demoralized and subordinated to the Catholic church. From 1840 to 1867 the colony had two governments: Upper Canada with Anglophone settlers, and Lower Canada, the French Canadian territory. Each had its own somewhat autonomous parliament to manage its internal affairs. In 1867, a federation of five provinces was founded. Lower Canada

then became the province of Quebec. From 1867 to 1949, five other provinces joined Canada. In the federation, Quebec Province maintained its cultural distinctiveness.

A strong nationalist movement seeking more political autonomy for Quebec has developed since 1945. The Duplessis government (1945–1959) obtained its own provincial taxation system. In 1960, a Liberal party government decided to modernize the economic, educational, and health systems, marking the end of the social and political power of the Catholic church and the beginning of a secular society in which the state plays the dominant role. Nationalist aspirations reached their high point in the 1970s. The *Parti Québecois* was elected in 1976 on a nationalist platform. It lost a referendum to negotiate the independence of Quebec in 1980 but remained in power until 1984. In 1982, the province was excluded from the new constitution of Canada. The Liberal party government was elected in 1984 with the mission to reintegrate Quebec into the Constitutional Act.

Isolated for one hundred years from France, *franco-québecois* cultural, economic, and political relations have existed since the 1960s and have been extended to all Francophone countries in Europe and elsewhere through the regular participation by the Quebec government in the Francophone Summit for the past twenty years. Québecois have been influenced almost equally by France and the United States, and their intellectual and organizational life is a synthesis of the two. Relations with English Canada have been more limited because of cultural and linguistic differences but also because of strained relations.

Settlements

Two settlement patterns have shaped the Quebec landscape. Since the St. Lawrence River and its tributaries were once the only means of transportation, all farms fronted the river in a pattern called *rangs*. Social life took place in these rangs and small villages. Settlements spread from the river to interior lands. From 1608 to 1850, the French Canadians lived in the rangs of seigneuries on each shore of the St. Lawrence River between Quebec and Montreal. In the 1840s, Scottish and Irish settlers colonized the eastern townships outside the seigneuries according to the English pattern. In the 1860s, peripheral regions of Quebec were colonized from the seigneuries. During this same period, thousands of French Canadians migrated to work in New England factories where they formed the Franco-American diaspora.

Economy

Subsistence and Commercial Activities. Quebec has been industrialized since the 1920s. Before 1939, more than 20 percent of the population worked in agriculture, industry being mostly textile- and local-market-oriented. World War II accelerated industrialization. Today, Quebec is an industrially advanced society. Since 1960, Quebec governments have encouraged a diversified industrial base of Québecois-owned enterprises through a social-democratic policy (social assistance, free health services, Health and Security Commission) and an interventionist economic policy (statist financial institutions; direct subventions to industries; nationalization of electricity, automobile insurance, and asbestos companies; construction of dams). Agriculture has been modernized and only 2 percent of the population is now engaged in farm work.

The main products are milk, pork, beef, fruits, and vegetables, grains, and greenhouse crops. Forests have attracted pulp and paper companies.

Industrial Arts. French Canadians make traditional and modern crafts. The traditional crafts focus on re-creations of folk objects. The modern is creative and functional. Craftwork is taught in technical schools and organized in associations holding annual expositions.

Trade. Cities and suburbs have shopping centers and American-style stores. There are also open-air markets during the summer for fruits and vegetables, but most people buy their food in supermarket chains. A recent trend, however, is to buy fruits, vegetables, and meat directly from the farm.

Division of Labor. Traditionally, women working on the farm performed a great variety of tasks. Many handled all the farm responsibilities while their husbands lumbered in the forests for months. They also received more education than men and managed the family money. Outside of agriculture, they could work only as teachers, nurses, or industrial workers. This rigid division of labor was challenged by a strong feminist movement during the 1970s. Since 1975, steps have been taken to give women equal access to university education, professions, and traditionally male jobs. The Quebec government has followed affirmative action guidelines for women since 1981, and the feminist movement has been institutionalized through the formation of a Consultative Council on the status of women in 1977, and a Feminine Condition Ministry in 1979. Important changes have resulted in the division of labor between the sexes in the workplace and in the family, with the younger generation now taking sexual equality for granted.

Land Tenure. Quebec is a capitalist society. Private ownership is the rule for agricultural, industrial, and commercial property. Family farms are predominant with a single farm owner or a partnership between spouses or among relatives.

Kinship, Marriage and Family

Kinship. French Canadians reckon descent bilaterally. Kinship terminology distinguishes the paternal from the maternal line by adding the term *paternel* and *maternel* to terms like uncle, aunt, or cousin. First, second, and third cousins are recognized. Genealogical knowledge is an important social asset in which women excel. In rural areas, women can easily state every kinship tie they have with hundreds of persons for five or six generations. Residence was traditionally patrilocal for the son inheriting the paternal farm but neolocal for other sons and daughters. Now it is neolocal for all.

Marriage. Traditionally, men and women had to either marry or remain celibate, taking care of their elderly parents or entering religious communities. Marriage was religious and divorce prohibited by the church. Sexuality was severely repressed and only allowed as a means to produce children. Married couples felt obligated to have a great number of children to ensure the survival of the French Canadian nation. A radical change has taken place since 1960, with fewer men and women entering religious communities and civil marriage, birth control, and divorce now the norm. The typical family now has only two children, and 50 percent of new marriages end in divorce. Sexuality has been liberalized, and a woman's economic status in marriage has been recognized by civil law in marriage contracts and in divorce settlements.

Domestic Unit. *Famille-souche,* consisting of a married couple, their numerous children, grandparents, and unmarried brothers or sisters on the paternal farm, was the traditional pattern. For sons and daughters leaving the famille-souche, the nuclear family was the rule. The nuclear family with five persons or less is now prevalent, with a growing proportion of single-parent families as a consequence of the large number of divorces. Agricultural families have followed the urban pattern.

Inheritance. Patrilineal land transmission was the rule, with only one son (usually one of the younger ones) inheriting the paternal farm, the other sons having been given land earlier by their father. Women were not allowed to inherit land, though they now can. For inheritance of other goods, English practices have been followed since the nineteenth century.

Socialization. Traditionally, children in rural areas received only a minimal formal education for three to six years. They worked on the farm from the age of twelve to the time of their marriage. Emphasis was placed on capacity to work hard and on respect for adults and church authority. Only a minority had an opportunity to attend the colleges and universities controlled by the clergy. Since 1960, religious educational institutions have been nationalized, and universal access to formal education has been promoted. Familial education is more liberal and permissive since families are now smaller. With the changing roles of men and women, a greater emphasis has been put on the socialization of boys and girls free of sexual stereotypes in families and at school.

Sociopolitical Organization

Social Organization. The class structure of modern Quebec is complex and consists of several strata: (1) an Anglophone bourgeoisie; (2) a French Canadian middle bourgeoisie having interests in financial institutions, middle-sized industries, and controlling statist economic institutions, which supports the federalist political position with minimal nationalist claims; and (3) a petty bourgeoisie including public-sector managers and employees, professionals, and small entrepreneurs in industry and commerce, which supports the nationalist party. The working class is numerically important and is divided into two groups: workers organized in strong assertive unions that have won acceptable salaries and working conditions, and poorly paid nonunionized workers. In agriculture, family farms are the majority. Farmers are organized and control the sale of agricultural products through quotas. Quebec has more unemployed persons than other provinces; almost 15 percent of the population collects unemployment insurance or social security payments.

Political Organization. Quebec is a province with its own parliament within a federation. According to the Canadian Constitution, the provincial parliament has jurisdiction over educational, health, agricultural, economic, and social policy in the province. Quebec governments have sought additional autonomy from the federal government since the 1940s. The political system is bipartisan with two major political parties and a third and fourth of marginal influence. The dominant political party has been the Liberal party (1960–1976; 1984–

1990). A conservative party in power in the 1950s disappeared in the 1970s, replaced by the _Parti Québecois_, which governed from 1976 to 1984.

The Quebec government makes decisions concerning education, health, and economic matters. Municipalities have power over local matters. All decisions regarding zoning, the environment, transportation, and economic development are centralized at the government level. Municipalities receive a part of their budget from the central government and are grouped into regional units to coordinate decision making. Deputies are important intermediaries between the people and the government. Ministries have delegated some of their power to semi-autonomous commissions like the Health and Security Commission, the Right of Persons Commission, the Agricultural Markets and Agricultural Credit Commission, the French Language Commission, and the Zoning Commission.

Social Control.   Quebec operates under two legal systems: French civil law and English criminal law. The provincial court system has three levels: the Ordinary Court, the Provincial Court, and the Superior Court. Since 1981, a provincial Charter of Person's Right predominates over all laws. Quebec citizens can obtain a Supreme Federal Court judgment when they have passed through the three levels of provincial courts. A national police corps has jurisdiction over all of Quebec.

Conflict.   Armed conflict has been rare in Quebec history with the exception of the 1837 revolt. In 1970, when a terrorist group kidnapped two politicians, war powers were enacted by the federal government, leading to the arrest of hundreds of persons and the military occupation of Quebec. The main conflicts in Quebec are not ethnic, but protracted conflicts involving unions are a consequence of the unions' aggressiveness in defending their interests. Racism and any kind of discrimination are overtly condemned and they occur only rarely. Québecois are on the whole tolerant and pacific people who will fight for respect but who generally live in peace with other groups.

Religion and Expressive Culture

Religious Beliefs.   The Catholic religion occupied a central place in French Canadian life from the beginnings of New France until 1960. The authority of the Catholic church was not only religious but also social through the religious community's monopolization of educational and health institutions; economic through the wealth of the clergy; political through the partisan position and alliance of the clergy with English rulers and seignors in the nineteenth century and with the conservative federal and provincial governments in the 1940s and 1950s; and ideological because of the church's strong opposition to liberal and democratic ideas, helping those with conservative and elitist ideas to remain in control. With the Quiet Revolution in the 1960s, the Catholic church lost its social and political influence. Québecois abandoned religious practices and beliefs en masse and rapidly accepted a pluralistic value system. But schools remained confessional, and the governments have lost the battle for the complete secularization of the school system.

Arts.   Québecois culture has been flourishing during the last thirty years in literature, poetry, popular songs, theater, cinema, painting, sculpture, and music. The Quebec govern-ment encourages arts with subsidies and aid for travel abroad. Cultural relations with France have helped artists to become known in Europe and to build an international reputation. Quebec culture is now celebrated internationally for its diversity and creativity. Canadian Francophones outside Quebec followed the same path. Acadians have developed their own literature, theater, and popular song, as is the case with Franco-Ontarians and Franco-Manitobans.

Medicine.   The Quebec health system was nationalized in 1960, and in 1969 the Health Insurance Commission was created by law to provide free health services for the people. Physicians are paid for their services by the commission. With the aging of the population, a debate has now begun because the costs are constantly increasing. Alternative medical practices are developing, but most are still illegal.

Death and Afterlife.   Traditionally, the deceased was displayed at home or later in funeral homes for two days for viewing by kin and friends. A religious funeral ceremony was performed on the third day and a banquet organized after the ceremony. Catholic funerals have been the norm for many years. Recently, cremation was introduced as an alternative with the religious ceremony retained. Beliefs regarding life after death followed the teachings of the Catholic church, which insisted in the 1960s that those who did not conform were condemned to eternal fire. This view was rejected as a manipulative attempt by the church to maintain its waning power.

See also Acadians

Bibliography

Anthropologie et sociétés. Quebec: Presses de l'Université Laval.

Hamilton, Roberta (1988). _Feudal Society and Colonization: The Historiography of New France_. Gananoque, Ontario: Langdale Press.

Moniere, Denis (1981). _Ideologies in Quebec: The Historical Development_. Translated by Richard Howard. Toronto: University of Toronto Press.

Recherches sociographiques. Quebec: Presses de l'Université Laval.

Revue d'histoire de l'Amérique française. Montreal: Institut de l'Amérique français.

Ryan, William F. (1966). _The Clergy and the Economic Growth of Quebec, 1896–1914_. Quebec: Presses de l'Université Laval.

Sociologie et sociétés. Montreal: Presses de l'Université de Montréal.

Wade, Mason (1968). _The French Canadians, 1760–1967_. 2 vols. Toronto: Macmillan.

LISE PILON

Gosiute

The Gosiute (Goshute) live in the area around the Great Salt Lake and to the west in Utah and Nevada. They speak a Shoshonean language. About 450 of them now survive in Utah and Nevada on the Goshute and Skull Valley Indian Reservations and in nearby communities. *See* Western Shoshone

Bibliography

Thomas, David Hurst, Lorann S. A. Pendleton, and Stephen C. Cappanari (1986). "Western Shoshone." In *Handbook of North American Indians*. Vol. 11, *Great Basin,* edited by Warren L. d'Azevedo, 262–283. Washington, D.C.: Smithsonian Institution.

Gros Ventre

ETHNONYMS: Atsina, Fall Indians, Gros Ventre of the Prairie, Hitunena, Minnetarees of Fort de Prairie, Rapid Indians, White Clay People

The Gros Ventre (Aaninena, Haaninin) are an Algonkian-speaking American Indian group closely related to the Arapaho. In the eighteenth century they lived on the Canadian plains in the forks of the Saskatchewan River region. Late in the century, weakened by the smallpox epidemic of 1780, they moved south to the Milk River region in north-central Montana and have remained there ever since. From 1818 to 1823 some moved further south and lived with the Arapaho, but later rejoined the group. Their long alliance with the Blackfoot effectively ended when they aligned themselves with the Crow, and both groups were defeated by the Blackfoot in 1867.

The U.S. government established the Fort Belknap Reservation for them and the Assiniboin in Montana Territory in 1888, and they have mostly remained on the reservation since then. Estimates place the 1950 Gros Ventre reservation population at 1,100 and the combined Gros Ventre–Assiniboin population at 1,870 in 1980. On the reservation, the Fort Belknap Community Council is the governing body. It has twelve members from four districts with the Gros Ventre and Assiniboin having equal representation. Tribal income derives mainly from land leases. There are some small Indian-owned stores and a tribally owned utility commission. There are large deposits of gravel, bentonite, gas, and oil on the reservation, with only gravel extracted and sold. The Labor Day Celebration and the Mid-Winter Fair are the two major reservationwide festivals.

Aboriginally, the Gros Ventre were divided into twelve autonomous bands. Each band was led by a chief who usually made decisions in consultation with other male members of the band. Each band also had other chiefs, afforded that status because of their prowess in war. In winter, the bands camped separately, usually in wooded areas along waterways as protection from the harsh weather. In the warmer months they coalesced for the spring and fall bison hunts, and for various ceremonies, including the Sun Dance. At these times, they camped in a circle, with an opening facing to the east, and with each band having its own place in the circle. Subsistence was based on the bison, every part of the animal being used in some way—the meat was roasted, boiled, or dried, the hides used for clothing, tipi covers, and trade with Whites. The tipi covers could also be converted into round boats for crossing large rivers. Deer, elk, and antelope were also hunted, and berries, fruits, and roots were collected by women. There was once a tradition of pottery making, but almost none has been made in the last two centuries. Men engaged in hunting and warfare, while women did most of the work around the camp.

All girls were given in marriage before puberty to older men, but men usually delayed marriage until they were twenty years old. Polygyny was common, as was divorce, which was usually initiated by the husband. Most women married three or four times during their lifetime. The sororate and levirate were customary. Each child belonged to the band of his or her father. There was strict mother-in-law avoidance, with mother-in-law and son-in-law forbidden to speak, look, or be in the same tipi with each other. Father-in-law avoidance was less restrictive. At adolescence, boys entered one of the age-graded societies and also became a member of either the Star Society or the Wolf Society, each of which had peacekeeping and social functions. At death, the individual had a scaffold burial, in a tree or in a cave, with some personal possessions. The Flat Pipe and Feathered Pipe Rites were important ceremonies, with personal supernatural powers and visions also significant. Today, the Gros Ventre are predominatly Roman Catholic.

Bibliography

Cooper, John M. (1956). *The Gros Ventre of Montana.* Pt. 2, *Religion and Ritual.* Catholic University of America, Anthropological Series, no. 16. Washington, D.C.

Flannery, Regina (1953). *The Gros Ventre of Montana.* Pt. 1, *Social Life.* Catholic University of America, Anthropological Series, no. 15. Washington, D.C.

Fowler, Loretta (1987). *Shared Symbols, Contested Meanings: Gros Ventre Culture and History.* Ithaca, N.Y.: Cornell University Press.

Kroeber, Alfred L. (1907). *Ethnology of the Gros Ventre.* American Museum of Natural History, Anthropological Papers 1, 145–281. New York.

Haida

ETHNONYMS: Haidah, Hydah, Hyder

Orientation

Identification. The Haida are an American Indian group whose traditional territory covered the Queen Charlotte Islands off the coast of British Columbia and a section of the Alexander Archipelago in southeastern Alaska. The name "Haida" is an Anglicized version of the Northern Haida's name for themselves, meaning "to be human, to be a Haida."

Location. The Queen Charlotte Islands, which includes 2 large and about 150 small islands, lie from thirty to eighty miles off the north coast of British Columbia, between 52° and 54° 15' N. Haida territory in southeastern Alaska extended to about 55° 30' N. This is an ecologically diverse territory, with considerable variation from one locale to another in rainfall, flora, fauna, topography, and soil. At the time of first contact with Europeans in the late 1700s, the Haida were settled in a number of towns that formed six regional-linguistic subdivisions: the Kaigani people, the people of the north coast of Graham Island, the Skidegate Inlet people, the people of the west coast of Moresby Island, the people of the east coast of Moresby Island, and the southern (Kunghit) people. In the 1970s, four divisions were still recognized.

Demography. A census conducted from 1836 to 1841 suggested a total Haida population of about 8,000. By 1901 the population had declined to about 900 and then to 588 in 1915. Since that time, it has gradually increased, and today there are about 2,000 Haida in Canada and 1,500 in southeastern Alaska.

Linguistic Affiliation. The Haida language is apparently unrelated to any other known language, although at one time it was classified in the Na Dene language family. Before European settlement, there were Northern and Southern dialects and a number of subdialects spoken in specific towns or regions. Today, there are few Haida speakers left.

History and Cultural Relations

The first known European contact was with the Spanish explorer Juan Pérez in 1774. For the next fifty years, the Haida traded sea otter pelts with European trading ships for iron, manufactured goods, and potatoes, which the Haida then began to cultivate themselves. In 1834 the Hudson's Bay Company established the Fort Simpson trading post in Tsimshian territory which became the center of Indian-White trade as well as trade among the various Indian groups for the next forty years. The trading trips disrupted the traditional economy, led to warfare with the Kwakiutl, and brought a smallpox epidemic to the Queen Charlotte Islands that led to a rapid population decline in the late nineteenth century. By 1879 the Haida were so reduced in number that they had all resettled in the communities of Skidegate and Masset. The first missionary to visit the Haida came in 1829, but the first to establish residence on the Queen Charlottes did not arrive until 1876 (in Marret); the first missionary to the Kaigani Haida arrived in 1880 (Howkan). The Skidegate mission was founded in 1883. From 1875 to 1910 the Haida underwent considerable culture change, largely in the direction of acculturation into the adjacent White society. The potlatch was outlawed, many features of the traditional religion disappeared, White-style housing replaced the cedar plank houses, and totem-pole raising was discontinued; wage labor increasingly replaced traditional economic pursuits. The Queen Charlotte Haida were granted a number of reserves that reflect their many subsistence places. The two largest reserves are the Skidegate and Haida (Masset) reserves, which were laid out initially in the 1880s and added to in 1913. The Kaigani Haida are not reservation Indians.

Settlements

At the time of European contact, the Haida lived in a number of "towns," although it is not clear how large or permanent these towns really were. Winter villages, consisting of one or two rows of cedar plank dwellings facing the sea, were more permanent and substantial settlements. In a row in front of the dwelling houses were the totem housepoles. Today, Haida house styles are like those of their White neighbors.

Economy

Subsistence and Commercial Activities. The traditional economy rested on a combination of fishing, shellfish gathering, hunting, and the gathering of plant foods. Because of seasonal variations in food availability, much effort was expended on extracting as much food as possible and preserving foodstuffs by drying, smoking, wrapping in grease, and so on for use in lean seasons. Halibut and salmon were the most important preserved foods (by drying, smoking), and sea mammals (which were also preserved) were more important than land mammals for food. Dozens of species of berries, plant stalks, tree fibers, seaweed, and roots were harvested and preserved. Current jobs and sources of income include the commercial fishing industry (fishing and fish and shellfish processing), logging, and arts and crafts (wood carving, argillite carving, graphics, jewelry, weaving, and so on).

Trade. The Haida traded heavily with the Coast Tsimshian and Tlingit. With the former they traded canoes, slaves, and shells for copper, Chilkat blankets, and hides; with the latter they traded canoes, seaweed, and dried halibut for eulachons and soapberries. There was also some internal trade between Haida communities.

Industrial Arts. Wood was used for a wide variety of objects including canoes of several sizes for different purposes, totem poles, houses, boxes, dishes, and weapons. Spruce roots and the inner bark of the red cedar were used by women to twine baskets for various uses and to make spruce root hats.

Division of Labor. Labor was divided on the basis of sex and, to a lesser extent, on the basis of social class distinctions. Women gathered plant foods and plant materials for manufactures, preserved food, prepared skins, made clothing, and twined baskets. Men hunted, fished, made canoes, built the houses, and carved and painted. Both sexes collected shellfish and hunted birds. Fishing, canoe making, and carving were viewed as prestigious occupations. Slaves did much of the heavy work, although people who did not work were looked down upon.

Land Tenure.   The lineage was the basic property-owning unit. Lineages controlled rights to streams, lakes, plant patches, trees, sections of coastline, and winter house sites. Lineages also owned names (personal and object such as canoe names), dances, songs, stories, and crest figures.

Kinship

Kin Groups and Descent.   The Haida had a moiety structure, with a Raven and an Eagle moiety, each composed of a number of lineages. There were no clans. The lineages traced their origins to supernatural women associated with the two moieties. The lineages were usually named after the site of the lineage origin, and a few were further divided into sublineages. Villages usually were inhabited by members of different lineages, and sometimes both moieties were represented as well. Each lineage was marked by its several crests, usually animals but sometimes other environmental features such as a rainbow or clouds. Crests were widely displayed—on totem poles, the body, boxes, utensils, drums, and canoes.

Kinship Terminology.   Kin terms followed the Crow system. Affinal kin were distinguished from consanguines.

Marriage and Family

Marriage.   Marriages were arranged, often by the parents when the betrothed were still children. Polygyny was permitted for chiefs but was rare. The preferred partner was someone in one's father's lineage, and there is some evidence of bilateral cross-cousin marriage.

Inheritance.   A man's property went to his younger brothers and nephews. The widow was usually left with little more than her own property. A woman's property went to her daughter.

Socialization.   Girls were evidently preferred as they guaranteed the perpetuation of the lineage. Much of child rearing involved formal instruction, with boys being taught male tasks and behaviors by their fathers and mother's brothers, and girls taught female tasks and behavior by their mothers. The puberty rites for girls involved seclusion, food restrictions, and various taboos. There was no comparable rite for boys.

Sociopolitical Organization

Social Organization.   Although there was no ranking of lineages, there is some evidence that some lineages were considered to be wealthier or more powerful than others. At the individual level, there were three social categories—nobles, commoners, and slaves. Nobles owned the houses, were generally wealthier, inherited chieftanships, used high-rank names, and hosted potlatches. Commoners did not have access to these signs of status. Slaves were war captives and their children.

Political Organization.   There was no overarching political structure above the lineage level of organization. Each lineage was led by a chief who inherited the position through the matriline. That is, the title was passed on to next oldest brother, other younger brothers, or the oldest sister's oldest son. Chiefs made decisions regarding property use, internal lineage business, and war. The owner of the dwelling was the house chief who managed the affairs of the domestic unit. In multilineage settlements, the "town master" or "town mother" was the highest ranking, wealthiest house chief.

Conflict.   The Haida were feared warriors and fought with the Coast Tsimshian, Bellabella, and Southern Tlingit, among others, for plunder, revenge, or slaves. Internal warfare also existed.

Social Control.   Social control was maintained at the lineage, town, and household levels by the appropriate chiefs. The fairly rigid class system served to reinforce expectations about appropriate behavior.

Religion and Expressive Culture

Religious Beliefs.   Animals were classified as special types of people, more intelligent than humans and with the ability to transform themselves into human form. Animals were thought to live on land, in the sea, and in the sky in a social order that mirrored that of the Haida. Traditional beliefs have been largely displaced by Christianity, although many Haida still believe in reincarnation.

Ceremonies.   The Haida prayed and gave offerings to the masters of the game animals and to the beings who gave wealth. Major ceremonial events were feasts, potlatches, and dance performances. High-ranking men were expected to host these events. Property was distributed through the potlatch on a number of occasions including the building of a cedar house, naming and tattooing of children, and death. Potlatches also included feasts and dance performances, although a feast might be given apart from the potlatch.

Arts.   As with other Northwest Coast groups, carving and painting were highly developed art forms. The Haida are renowned for their totem poles in the form of house-front poles, memorial poles, and mortuary columns. Painting usually involved the use of black, red, and blue-green to produce highly stylized representations of the zoomorphic matrilineal crest figures. The body of a high-ranking individual was often tattooed and faces were painted for ceremonial purposes.

Death and Afterlife.   Treatment of the deceased reflected status differentials. For those of high rank, after lying in state for a few days in the house, the body was buried in the lineage gravehouse where it remained either permanently or until it was placed in a mortuary pole. When the pole was erected, a potlatch was held both to honor the deceased and to recognize his successor. Commoners were usually buried apart from the nobles, and carved poles were not erected. Slaves were tossed into the sea. The Haida believed strongly in reincarnation, and sometimes before death an individual might choose the parents to whom he or she was to be reborn. At death, the soul was transported by canoe to the Land of the Souls to await reincarnation.

Bibliography

Blackman, Margaret B. (1981). *Window on the Past: The Photographic Ethnohistory of the Northern and Kaigani Haida.* National Museum of Man, Canadian Ethnology Service, paper no. 74. Ottawa.

Blackman, Margaret B. (1982). *During My Time: Florence*

Edenshaw Davidson, a Haida Woman. Seattle: University of Washington Press.

Boelscher, Marianne (1988). _The Curtain Within: Haida Social and Mythical Discourse._ Vancouver: University of British Columbia Press.

MacDonald, George F. (1983). _Haida Monumental Art: Villages of the Queen Charlotte Islands._ Vancouver: University of British Columbia Press.

Stearns, Mary Lee (1981). _Haida Culture in Custody._ Seattle: University of Washington Press.

Swanton, John R. (1905). _Contributions to the Ethnology of the Haida._ American Museum of Natural History, Memoir no. 5, 1–300.

MARGARET B. BLACKMAN

Haitians

Orientation

Identification.   Haitians are Blacks from the island of Haiti, which occupies one-third of the island of Hispaniola in the Caribbean Sea. The other two-thirds of Hispaniola is occupied by the Dominican Republic. Contemporary Haitians are descendants of African slaves imported by the French colonists to work on the sugar plantations in the eighteenth century. Haiti has been an independent nation since 1804 when a slave revolt overthrew the French government. Haitians in Haiti are a homogeneous group, with the major distinctions based on social class and urban-rural residence. Ninety percent of the population is rural, and the other 10 percent is mostly mulatto and forms the elite. In the United States, the Haitian population is composed of naturalized U.S. citizens, legal immigrants, legal nonimmigrants (students, government workers), children born in the United States, and undocumented aliens and refugees. The large number of Haitians who have come to North America since the mid-1970s has made the group highly visible and has resulted in their being the victims of economic, political, and residential racial discrimination. Haitians see themselves as distinctively Haitian, with the identities of West Indian or Black being of secondary importance.

Location.   In the United States, Haitians live primarily in New York City, Chicago, Washington, D.C., Philadelphia, Boston, and Miami. Perhaps as many as one-half live in New York City. In Canada, Haitians live mainly in Montreal.

Demography.   Estimates place the Haitian population in the United States at about 800,000 with perhaps as many as one-half that number classified as undocumented aliens or refugees. About a quarter are children born in the United States. In Canada, Haitians number about 25,000. In both countries, most Haitians have arrived in the last thirty years.

Linguistic Affiliation.   Haitians speak Haitian Creole, which is a distinct language, not a dialect of French. About 8 percent, most of whom are the elite, also speak French. Because of regular contact with the United States, the use of English, especially in cities, is increasing. In North America, most recent immigrants speak Haitian Creole, while those who came earlier and their American-born children speak English.

History and Cultural Relations

Haiti is unique in a number of ways: it is the second oldest independent nation in the New World; it is the only nation in history to achieve independence through a slave revolt; it is the poorest nation in the hemisphere; and its culture is the most strongly African culture in the New World. Migration to North America went through four stages. During the period of French colonization in the 1700s some French and their slaves migrated to the southern colonies and settlements. The period of the Haitian Revolution (1791–1803) brought some 50,000 Whites and Blacks to North America, with most settling in cities in the East and the South. From 1915 to 1934 Haiti was occupied by the United States and thousands of middle-class Haitians immigrated to the United States. Most settled in cities, establishing businesses or obtaining professional employment, and eventually assimilated into mainstream society. From 1957 to 1986 Haiti was ruled by the Duvaliers, first François "Papa Doc" and then his son, Jean-Claude. The Duvaliers' repressive rule drove thousands of middle-class Haitians north from 1957 to 1971.

Beginning in the early 1970s, Haitian "boat people" began arriving in Florida. Unlike most of the earlier immigrants, they were mainly rural, poor, uneducated, and male. After 1977 the number of these immigrants increased dramatically, making them highly visible and leading to often repressive government action including deportation or internment in detention camps. Although the courts put an end to most of these abuses, the public stereotyped Haitians as poor, illiterate, illegal aliens. Haitians were then identified as an at-risk group for contracting the AIDS virus, a classification that was later rescinded by the government. Not surprisingly, Haitians who have arrived since the 1970s and constitute the majority of those in North America, are subject to various forms of racial and cultural discrimination. Because of linguistic and cultural differences, they usually do not affiliate with the African-American community or with Black West Indians. The children born in the United States, however, adopt English as their primary language and associate with African-Americans.

Settlements

In the cities where they have settled, Haitians tend to live in the same neighborhoods and often on the same blocks and in the same buildings. In New York, the major Haitian communities are in Queens and Brooklyn, with Queens seen as the home for those who are more affluent and own their own homes. "Little Haiti" in Miami is probably the most distinctively Haitian community in North America, with numerous businesses operated by Haitians and with an almost exclusively Haitian clientele.

Economy

As mentioned above, Haitians who settled in North America before the 1970s often started small businesses or found skilled or professional employment. They either became part of mainstream economy or continued to serve the Haitian community. Those who have arrived since the 1970s include some with business experience in Haiti who have opened businesses in Haitian communities. But most of the recent immigrants have been poor and uneducated and work at low-level, low-paying jobs. Unskilled factory work and maintenance work are common for men, and many women work as domestics. Many Haitians live in poverty in slum neighborhoods, often sharing dwelling units and pooling resources to help pay the various legal and travel costs involved in bringing relatives to North America. In some cities, economic self-help organizations and church or government-backed programs have developed to provide economic and other assistance. For undocumented immigrants, who seek to avoid government contact, finding and holding regular employment is even more difficult. Among Haitians immigrating to Florida, some have become migrant farm workers, following the crops as they ripen up and down the eastern United States.

Kinship, Marriage and Family

The networks of kin ties and various family forms in rural Haiti have largely disappeared in urban North America. In fact, many Haitian families in North America are fragmented, with some having members still in Haiti, and others with members in two or more places in North America or elsewhere. Ties are regularly maintained among such kin, however, with the ultimate goal of family members settling near one another. Household composition in North America is often determined by the economic status of the household and its role in the chain migration process. In the North American context, male dominance in the family has disappeared and Haitian families are more egalitarian. In two-generation families, in which the children have been born in North America, conflict has emerged between parents who speak Haitian Creole and emphasize Haitian culture and children who speak English and identify with the African-American community. Education has been markedly difficult for Haitian children because of the language difference and because Haitian parents, while valuing education, traditionally vest considerable authority in the schools and play a less active role than do White American parents.

Sociopolitical Organization

Social Organization.   Haitians identify themselves as such and generally do not identify with the African-American, Black West Indian, or other Caribbean communities in North America. They have also chosen not to seek political or economic representation through established African-American or Latino political channels. Whatever their self-identity, once Haitians enter public schools or the work force, they are identified by Whites as Blacks and treated as such. In

Canada, Haitians were encouraged to settle in Quebec and Montreal because they were thought to be French-speaking. But rather than learn French, some have chosen to affiliate with English-speaking Canadians through their choice of churches and schools for their children.

There are clear distinctions in the Haitian-American community between those who arrived in the past and those who arrived recently and between the poor and the wealthy (*bon moun*). These distinctions are manifested in behavior, speech, place of residence, and degree of identification with the Haitian community. The wealthier, and more recently, the economically stable tend to live in suburbs, whereas the poor remain in the inner cities. In some communities there is a division between those who prefer to speak French and those who prefer Creole.

Political Organization.   Haitian neighborhoods, including Little Haiti in Miami, are notable for the relatively few Haitian associations and organizations that have developed. In Miami, for example, the Haitian Chamber of Commerce is the only Haitian business association of any importance. Haitian neighborhoods are also notable for their peacefulness and the absence of conflict. Haitian politics center on political developments in Haiti. From Duvalier's taking of power in 1957 until the present, the Haitian community in the United States has been active in opposing his regime and attempting to replace him. Haitians have also tried to become active politically in the United States, with only limited success.

Religion and Expressive Culture

The major religion in Haiti is Voodoo, an ancient religion that combines elements of ancestor worship with the worship of the recently deceased. Voodoo rituals often take place at the time of illness or death and involve healing the sick and appeasing angry ancestors. In Haiti, some Haitians are Roman Catholics or Protestants. In North America, Haitians belong to or form their own Roman Catholic, Baptist, and other churches. Some are Jehovah's Witnesses. The existence of Voodoo in North America is poorly documented; when it is practiced it is evidently in private so as not to draw attention from the outside community, which sees it as a pagan cult rather than a legitimate religion.

As in other areas of life, Haitians in North America provide the Haitian community with its own music, dance, entertainment, social clubs, theater, and radio programs.
See also Black Creoles in Louisiana, Blacks in Canada

Bibliography

Laguerre, Michel S. (1984). *American Odyssey: Haitians in New York City*. Ithaca: Cornell University Press.

Lawless, Robert (1986). "Haitian Migrants and Haitian-Americans: From Invisibility into the Spotlight." *Journal of Ethnic Studies* 14:29–70.

Richman, Karen E. (1984). "From Peasant to Migratory Farmworker: Haitian Migrants in U.S. Agriculture." In *Haitian Migration and the Haitian Economy*, edited by Terry L. McCoy, 52–65. Gainesville: Center for Latin American Studies, University of Florida.

Stepick, Alex (1982). "Haitian Boat People: A Study in the Conflicting Forces Shaping U.S. Refugee Policy." *Law and Contemporary Problems* 45:163–196.

Woldemikael, Tekle M. (1988). *Becoming Black American: Haitians and American Institutions in Evanston, Illinois.* New York: AMS Press.

Halchidhoma

The Halchidhoma lived along the Colorado River in Arizona near the mouth of the Gila River and spoke a Yuman language. They now live with the Maricopa in Arizona on the Gila River Indian Reservation.
See Maricopa

Bibliography

Harwell, Henry O., and Marsha C. S. Kelly (1983). "Maricopa." In *Handbook of North American Indians.* Vol. 10, *Southwest,* edited by Alfonso Ortiz, 71–85. Washington, D.C.: Smithsonian Institution.

Han

The Han (Hankutchin) are an Athapaskan-speaking group who live in the western part of the Yukon Territory in Canada and the east-central part of Alaska in the upper Yukon River drainage area. It has been estimated that there are about thirty-five speakers of the Han language who, along with a few hundred others, are assimilated into White society.

Bibliography

Crow, John R., and Philip R. Obley (1978). "Han." In *Handbook of North American Indians.* Vol. 6, *Subarctic,* edited by June Helm, 506–513. Washington, D.C.: Smithsonian Institution.

Hare

ETHNONYMS: Kancho, Kawchodinne, Kah-cho-tinneh, K'a-tchô-gottinè, Kk ayttchare Ottine, Peaux de Lievre, Rabbit Skins, Tä-nä'-tinne; Bâtards Loucheux (one band), Dene, Tinne, Slave (with other northeastern Northern Athapaskans)

Orientation

Identification. The Hare refer to themselves as "Ka šo goͬinè," (which may mean big willow people), or as "gahwié goͬinè" (rabbitskin people, which is a recent translation from English). The suffix *-goͬinè* means "the people of"; *hare, willow,* and *arrow* have similar roots, and the Hare have been called "the people of" all three. The names "Hare" and "Peaux de Lievre," which Whites have used for over two hundred years, refer to the extreme dependence some Hare Indians placed on the varying hare *Lepus americanus* for food and clothing.

Location. The Hare live today where they lived when first contacted by Whites: in what is now the Canadian Northwest Territories, north of Great Bear Lake and on both sides of the Mackenzie River. Since 1806, Fort Good Hope, located today at 66°16' N and 128°38' W, has evolved from a trading post visited by most Hare Indians several times a year for economic and, after 1860, religious reasons into the settlement where most of the Hare live today.

Demography. In 1978, 430 Hare Indians were registered on the Canadian Indian band roll at Fort Good Hope and Colville Lake. The first census, in 1827, estimated the population of the Hare as approximately 300, but by that time they had been strongly affected by epidemic disease from which, apparently, mortality was significant.

Linguistic Affiliation. The Hare speak an Athapaskan language that shares high mutual intelligibility with and differs in only minor dialectical ways from Mountain, Bearlake, and Slavey. Divergence from neighboring Kutchin is sharp with the exception, perhaps, of one enigmatic nineteenth-century band that apparently was a cultural and biological amalgam of Hare and Kutchin—the "ne la goͬinè" (end of the earth people or Bâtards Loucheux).

History and Cultural Relations

There is no evidence that the Hare have lived anywhere other than where they are today. Their neighbors are the Kutchin and Inuvialuit or Mackenzie Delta Inuit to the north, the Yellowknife to the east, the Slavey and Bearlake to the south, and the Mountain to the west. Relations with these various groups have varied widely: the Hare greatly feared and avoided the Inuit, and they were bullied by the Yellowknife in the fur trade; some Hare Indians were formerly Mountain Indians, and others in the nineteenth century became part of the group then emerging as the so-called Bearlake Indians. Before the early nineteenth century, the Hare were only indirectly affected by the European fur trade. By 1806, fifteen years after Alexander Mackenzie's voyage of exploration down the river that bears his name, a trading post had been established in the territory of the Hare. From that year on, the

Hare participated directly in the trade, and many annually visited Fort Good Hope to exchange pelts and provisions for European goods. In 1859, the Roman Catholic Oblates arrived and several years later built a mission and church for the Hare, who in time became nominal Catholics, many gathering for three religious celebrations each year. Throughout the nineteenth century, the Hare were periodically affected by epidemic diseases.

In 1921, the Hare signed Treaty 11 with Canada. After World War II, the government became involved in almost every aspect of Hare life through health, education, game, and social welfare programs and regulations. The numbers of Whites living among the Hare increased—by 1972, to 50 Whites in a population of about 370 Hare Indians at Fort Good Hope.

Settlements

In aboriginal days, the Hare most probably lived in bands composed flexibly and on the basis of kinship and affinity. Their sites were located at advantageous fishing and hunting spots, and the bands ranged in size from small to large—the latter if a task demanded cooperation as did the annual hunt for caribou for clothing and food. After European traders came, the activities of the Hare and their camp locations were adjusted to accommodate. In the nineteenth century, one major settlement grew at Fort Good Hope, itself originally positioned and moved several times for the convenience of transportation and the trade; but few Hare Indians lived there for any length of time before 1900.

At Fort Good Hope today are the permanent residences of over 3,509 native people, two missions, the Hudson's Bay Company, and various governmental services—school, police, nursing station, and administration. In the twentieth century, a major aggregation of Hare at Colville Lake (67°2' N, 126°5' W) initially declined because of deaths and because the store and mission were located at Fort Good Hope. But since 1960 the establishment of a mission and trading post have again made Colville Lake a small permanent independent settlement. The construction of a winter road has eased travel to and from Fort Good Hope.

Economy

Subsistence and Commercial Activities.   Traditionally, the Hare were hunters and fishers. Both large and small game and birds were shot with bows and arrows, speared, snared, surrounded, or netted. Formerly, a cooperative August-September hunt for caribou was very important, as was a second hunt in April. The rest of the year, the Hare fished for lake trout, whitefish, and other species and hunted small game like birds and hares. For some Hare Indians who lived near the Mackenzie River, the dependence on hares was so great that when the population of these ruminants crashed, which occurred cyclically, starvation and on occasion cannibalism were the results. After European fur traders arrived, the Hare adjusted their annual cycle to accommodate trapping: marten, lynx, and mink in winter, beaver and muskrats in late winter and spring. Dogs increased in importance and numbers as fur trapping did. Before 1900, musk-oxen were important to the diet; in recent years, moose have repopu-

lated Hare territory and many are shot. For the last one hundred years, the Hare have supplemented their diet with tea, flour, sugar, and other store-purchased foods.

Today, few Hare Indians depend on the bush alone for fulfilling all their needs, and most spend summer months in town, hoping for fire-fighting jobs. The ideal is to combine wage labor with subsistence activities, including trapping, during the course of the year. Indeed, though the replacement value of fish and game consumed is substantial, the bulk of any person's or family's income is from wage labor or welfare and transfer payments.

Industrial Arts.   From wood, roots, caribou and hare skins, sinew, bone, antler, and stone, the aboriginal Hare made and used spruce-framed birchbark canoes, snowshoes, nets and snares, bows and arrows, clothing, baskets in which liquid, with the aid of hot stones, was boiled, scrapers, and other products. Today, store-purchased goods have replaced most of the aboriginal technology. Formerly, some clothing was decorated with porcupine quill weaving; today, silk embroidery and beadwork in floral and geometric designs adorn jackets, vests, moccasins, gauntlets, and mukluks.

Trade.   Unlike their neighbors, the Kutchin and the Yellowknife, the Hare were not known to be interested traders or middlemen. Nevertheless, they participated in the trade with European fur traders from the late eighteenth century on and annually brought the skins and meat of caribou and musk-oxen and furs of beavers, martens, and muskrats to exchange for European goods and, after 1890, tea, flour, and other foods. In the nineteenth century, middlemen Hare Indians traded European goods occasionally with Mackenzie Delta Inuit.

Division of Labor.   Although few tasks were the exclusive province of either men or women throughout the historic period, women have tended to be principally responsible for taking care of young children, making clothing, collecting berries, preparing food, drying fish, and pulling toboggans; and men for hunting, fishing, trapping, and making drums. Even today, some women do not handle or use boats on their own because to do so would bring bad luck.

Land Tenure.   There is no permanent ownership of land or resources. The Hare have always been able to hunt, fish, and trap where they wish, as long as they feel secure and as long as no one else has habitually used, and plans to continue to use, a specific area. In 1950, the Hare were assigned a game area northwest of Great Bear Lake as their exclusive hunting and trapping area, which represented a fraction of their former range.

Kinship

Kin Groups and Descent.   There is no concrete indication that descent has been other than bilateral, despite certain terminological and marriage patterns linked elsewhere to unilineality. The Hare have used both consanguineal and affinal ties to join a specific residential group, which usually has as a core several people closely related by blood. No descent groups form.

Kinship Terminology.   For the traditional Hare, terminology in the first ascending generation was a mixture of bifurcate collateral (females) and bifurcate merging (males). In one's own generation, Iroquois cousin terms were used; and teknonymy was common.

Marriage and Family

Marriage. Monogamy, perhaps serial, was probably the most common traditional marriage pattern; polyandry, which was sometimes fraternal, occurred, and polygyny, especially sororal, may have been preferred but was uncommon. The Hare observed a nuclear family incest taboo, and marriage proscription extended to parallel cousins. Marriage to cross cousins was preferred. Bride-service was performed, and initial uxorilocality might be continued or followed by virilocality; bilocality seemed the ultimate pattern. The levirate and, perhaps, the sororate were both observed. Because of missionary influence, polygyny, polyandry, actual cross-cousin marriage, and child betrothal have disappeared. Marriage in adulthood, church ceremony, monogamy, absence of divorce, living out of wedlock with a partner who may be doing the same, and initial uxorilocality and ultimate neolocality are the rule.

Domestic Unit. The nuclear family has always been the basic unit of economic cooperation. The household has always consisted of a nuclear family, of a family extended by bride-service or initial uxorilocality or a widow or widower and adopted child, of a bilateral extended family (usually with a sibling core), or of individuals who have joined each other for some task like hunting, trapping, or trade.

Inheritance. There is no set of rules for inheritance, perhaps because land and rights are not individually owned. Traditionally, individuals destroyed much of their own property at the death of a relative. Today, property like a cabin is inherited by a spouse, child, close relative who is in need, or a friend.

Socialization. Young children, males more than females, are indulged and treated with affection. Sanction is largely through ridicule; spanking is very rare and occurs only when a child puts himself in danger. Young children begin their attempts to use adult technology at an early age and learn mainly by trial and error and imitation. Today, when children and adolescents are not in school, they are expected to help with a range of increasingly gender-specific household chores. Children enculturate emotional restraint, independence, resourcefulness, flexibility, and reciprocity. Formerly, girls underwent exclusion and observed a number of taboos at menarche. There exists considerable ambivalence today about formal education. To participate fully has meant, for parents, residence in town and, for adolescents who continue with high school, both life in a hostel away from town and gaps in their knowledge about the bush. To drop out, however, means risking nonparticipation in the new economy.

Sociopolitical Organization

Social Organization. Distinctions of status and wealth seem always to have been minimal among the Hare. The nuclear family was the basic unit of social life, joining with (or departing from) others on the basis of kinship and affinity in a highly flexible fashion. In the class society that emerged in the post-European-contact era, patron-client relations developed between, on the one hand, traders, missionaries, and governmental agents who controlled the distribution of valued imported resources and, on the other, the Hare. In some instances, the control was so great that castelike relations developed.

Political Organization. Hare leaders lack power but possess authority, which, however, may be highly ephemeral. Their leadership derives from special hunting, fighting, trading, or shamanic skills, from their ability to influence others suggestively, or from their kinship connections. This has always been the case. Political action at the level of "the Hare" is unknown. Whereas a particular band might take action, the same principals are not consistently involved because band membership fluctuates. The Hudson's Bay Company introduced the position of trading chief and, later, the Canadian government the band chief; in each case, the title has been a misnomer because the person in whom it resided has been a spokesman at best. In 1921, the Hare signed Treaty 11 with the Canadian government, and the Hare Band at Fort Good Hope was created. Today, the Hare count themselves, with other Northwest Territories Athapaskans, as members of the Dene Nation, which for years has been pressing for the settlement of outstanding and conflicting treaty rights and for self-determination. In 1988, the Dene Nation and the Metis Association of the Northwest Territories signed an agreement-in-principle with the government of Canada in which the former would receive cash, surface rights to (and a share of mineral royalties from) over seventy thousand square miles of land, and other guarantees.

Social Control. The Hare depended heavily on gossip, ridicule, and other diffuse negative sanctions to effect control. Shamans, who had the power to kill, could also exercise social control. In the twentieth century, the Royal Canadian Mounted Police and Northwest Territories courts have provided formal sanctions for the Hare, although the informal diffuse negative sanctions have remained important in daily life.

Conflict. In their relations with others, especially the Inuit, the Hare traditionally have possessed a reputation for timidity. They have withdrawn rather than fought. Perhaps because of the emphasis placed on emotional restraint and the dependence on diffuse negative sanctions, drinking today—culturally constructed as a sociable, generous activity up to a point—frequently becomes violent as suppressed conflicts find expression. Since 1970, the Hare and other native people in the Northwest Territories have become increasingly vocal concerning the exploitation of natural resources and treaty and political rights.

Religion and Expressive Culture

Religious Beliefs. Insofar as can be ascertained, the aboriginal religion was animistic, and the Hare believed also in the existence of a host of supernaturals and in the powers of medicine men or shamans. The Hare lived in an animistic universe in which certain animals had to be respected by observance of a series of taboos. In addition, a poorly understood host of supernaturals peopled the universe: a river monster, bushmen, a thunderbird, a spirit of the moon, a master of animals, ghosts, and perhaps a creator. Today, the Hare are baptized and confirmed into Roman Catholicism, variably observe the Sabbath and say rosaries, and believe in the Christian God and in heaven and hell. Some traditional beliefs persist—in reincarnation, ghosts, the power of shamans to cure some ailments, the efficacy of dreams and amulets, bad luck if certain taboos are broken.

Religious Practitioners.   Hare medicine men, or shamans, were visionaries who could predict the future, locate lost objects, counteract the malevolence of non-Hare shamans, relieve hunger, and cure and kill. A shaman gained his power in dreams and could sing to an animal like a wolf, wolverine, or caribou (with whom he maintained a transformative and tutelary relationship), which would help him achieve success. Some Hare shamans had reputations that reached their neighbors. Since the 1860s, Oblate priests have spread Roman Catholicism and lived among the Hare. While the decline in shamanism is linked to the arrival of Christianity, the belief in the special power of shamanism endured over a hundred years later.

Ceremonies.   Aboriginal ceremonies were probably few and ranged from highly individualistic rites (when, for example, a Hare left an offering on a deceased relative's grave to appease the spirit) to ones of concern to a family or the entire band (such as foretelling future events or combating starvation or sickness that affected all). Today, some Hare Indians say their rosaries every night, in town or in camps in the bush, and some—in particular older people—go regularly to church, whereas others neither say rosaries nor attend services. Sunday Mass at Fort Good Hope regularly attracts one-fifth of the population; a much higher proportion attends services at Christmas and Easter, which are the focal points of weeks-long gatherings that, for the last hundred years, have brought many to Fort Good Hope.

Arts.   By the twentieth century, traditional ring and pin and hand games had given way to card games and cribbage, although gambling has been a feature of both traditional and modern games. The Hare have adopted the square dance, but it has not supplanted the traditional drum dance that accompanies important community events.

Medicine.   The traditional Hare combated ailments by using certain herbs and by turning to their medicine men, who sang and either extruded the disease through sucking or demanded confession of breaches of taboo. In the mid-twentieth century, some Hare Indians have continued to rely on traditional medicine men to sing over, touch, and cure some sick people, but for illnesses like tuberculosis they have depended upon the White man's medicine. Today, the Hare make use of the nursing station or, in the bush, of traditional techniques unless the problem is clearly one that demands treatment in a hospital or by modern medicine.

Death and Afterlife.   Formerly, the dead were placed on scaffolds, but interment by burial has occurred since the Oblates arrived. The body is prepared by the most distant kin or nonkin who observe taboos and henceforth to some degree are avoided by the kin of the deceased. The belief in the need to appease and feed the ghost of the deceased continues today, but self-mortification and destruction of property, both formerly common, no longer occur.

Bibliography

Broch, Harald Beyer (1986). *Woodland Trappers: Hare Indians of Northwestern Canada.* Bergen Studies in Social Anthropology, no. 35. Bergen, Norway: University of Bergen, Department of Social Anthropology.

Hara, Hiroko Sue (1980). *The Hare Indians and Their World.* National Museum of Man, Mercury Series, Canadian Ethnology Service Paper 63. Ottawa: National Museums of Canada.

Hultkrantz, Åke (1973). "The Hare Indians: Notes on Their Traditional Culture and Religion." *Ethnos* 38(1–4):113–152.

Osgood, Cornelius (1932). "The Ethnography of the Great Bear Lake Indians." *Annual Report for 1931, National Museum of Canada Bulletin* 70:31–97.

Savishinsky, Joel S. (1974). *The Trail of the Hare: Life and Stress in an Arctic Community.* New York: Gordon & Breach.

Savishinsky, Joel S., and Hiroko Sue Hara (1984). "Hare." In *Handbook of North American Indians.* Vol. 6, *Subarctic,* edited by June Helm, 314–325. Washington, D.C.: Smithsonian Institution.

SHEPARD KRECH III

Hasidim

ETHNONYM: Chassidim

Orientation

Identification.   Hasidim are ultrareligious Jews who live within the framework of their centuries-old beliefs and traditions and who observe Orthodox law so meticulously that they are set apart from most other Orthodox Jews. Even their appearance is distinctive: the men bearded in black suits or long black coats, and women in high-necked, loose-fitting dresses, with kerchiefs or traditional wigs covering their hair. They are dedicated to living uncontaminated by contact with modern society except in accord with the demands of the workplace and the state. They do not, for the most part, own radio or television sets, nor do they frequent cinemas or theaters. They dress and pray as their forefathers did in the eighteenth century, and they reject Western secular society, which they regard as degenerate. They do not, however, constitute a uniform group but are divided into a number of distinctive sects and communities, each organized around the teachings of a particular rebbe, or charismatic religious leader. Although the various Hasidic sects share a desire to maintain the integrity of Orthodox Judaism, they are sometimes sharply divided on practice, points of philosophy, and the personality of their religious leaders. In spite of their differences, all attach great importance to preventing assimilation by insulating their members from the secular influences of the host culture, which they perceive to be disruptive of the lifestyle they wish to observe. To outsiders, the Hasidim are a homogeneous entity whose life-style and religious practices mirror those of previous generations. Such a view exaggerates the reality. Despite the perception of Hasidic society as relatively static, and as unresponsive to social, political, economic, and technological changes over the past decades, a more precise appraisal is that it is an ongoing sociocultural entity constantly adapting to events in the larger society and is, in the process, becoming transformed. Owing to their persistent and organized efforts, the Hasidim have both maintained their distinctive way of life and adapted to societal influences that in the case of other ethnic and religious minorities have resulted in their assimilation.

Location and Demography. Although the estimation of numbers is difficult, the Lubavitcher and Satmar constitute the two largest groups, with approximately 25,000 followers in their respective areas of Brooklyn, New York. A current estimate of the number of Hasidic Jews in North America is between 90,000 to 100,000. The Hasidic population of Montreal is but a fraction of its New York counterpart—it numbers some 4,000 persons. Outside of New York and Montreal, the Hasidic population is relatively small. The exception is the Lubavitch sect, which has created nuclei of communities throughout North America. Several Hasidic sects have established enclaves to remain shielded from the urban environment. Three such settlements include New Square, near Spring Valley, New York; Kiryas Yoel, in Monroe County, New York, named after the previous Satmar rebbe; and Tash in Boisbriand, Quebec, established by the Tasher rebbe.

History and Cultural Relations

The Hasidic movement began in the middle of the eighteenth century in Galicia on the Polish-Romanian border and in the Volhynia region of the Ukraine. It was founded by Rabbi Israel Ben Eliezer (1700–1760) who became known as the Baal Shem Tov (Master of the Good Name). The movement emerged as a populist reaction against what its followers considered the elite, remote, and formal character of rabbinic leaders. In contrast to the mechanical and rigid forms of worship, the Baal Shem Tov preached piety of heart and service of God through the emotions. To serve God, the duty of every Jew, was not confined exclusively to the study of Talmud but embraced every aspect of daily life. The Baal Shem Tov's ministry stressed the joyful affirmation of life and counseled against asceticism and self-affliction. It was only after his death, however, that the systematic dissemination of Hasidism began. The movement evolved into a number of dynastic courts, comprising a rebbe and his followers. As the rebbe's power was inherited by his sons, in succeeding generations the number of rebbeim (plural of *rebbe*) multiplied and dynastic courts were established in villages and towns throughout Eastern and Central Europe.

In essence, Hasidic institutions are only comparatively autonomous and are connected with, and affected by, those in the larger Jewish community and surrounding society. The very presence of the non-Hasidic Jewish population contributes to the development of the Hasidic community by offering financial support for its various institutions. It also provides the Hasidim with a market for their products, including kosher baked goods, kosher meat, and religious articles. The precise nature of the relationship is influenced by the particular sect's views of the threats posed by such contacts. The differing cases of the Lubavitcher and Satmarer illustrate this point. Although the differences between them are few—their appearance and religious practice are nearly identical and both strictly observe Jewish laws—their styles and outlooks in crucial ways are vastly different. The Satmar group is an insular community that seeks no publicity and shuns outsiders. It also staunchly opposes the State of Israel on the ground that the Jewish state cannot rightly come into existence until the arrival of the Messiah. In contrast, under Rabbi Schneerson, the Lubavitcher rebbe, this sect has altered the Hasidic pattern by looking outward. They have sent vans ("*mitzveh tanks*") into Manhattan and the suburbs, offering, to Jews only, religious books and items and a place to pray. They have also recruited many young Jews at colleges in New York and California, offering intellectual programs, drug clinics, and outreach houses. Aimed at intensifying less observant Jews' identification with Orthodox Judaism, the Lubavitch sect is unique in its involvement with the wider Jewish community. Their outreach activities, however, have offended the more extremist Hasidic sects whose relations with outsiders, both Jewish and Gentile, are governed pragmatically. They are viewed by the larger Jewish community as ultra-Orthodox and fanatical as a result of their zealous observance of the Code of Jewish Law. While acknowledging that contact with the outside world cannot be avoided completely, they believe it can be controlled.

Settlements

For the most part, Jerusalem and B'Nai Brak in Israel and Brooklyn, New York, were the choices of residence of the Hasidic Jews who survived World War II. A sizable community was also established in Montreal, Quebec. The arrival of the Hasidim in the 1940s and 1950s differed from the previous settlements of Hasidic Jews in North America, since, for the first time, a number of Hasidic rebbeim settled in the New York area: for instance, the Satmarer rebbe and the Klausenburger rebbe established themselves in Williamsburg, and the Lubavitcher rebbe and the Bobover rebbe moved to the Crown Heights area. In 1990, Williamsburg, Crown Heights, and Boro Park, all in Brooklyn, serve as the center of Hasidic Jewry and include a diverse set of institutions catering to the Hasidim's needs.

Economy

Commercial Activities. As with other activities in the Hasidic world, employment is balanced on the scale of religious values. Hasidic Jews do not pursue occupational careers as is the norm in Western culture, but organize their livelihood so that it does not interfere with their religious obligations, such as refraining from work on the Sabbath and major Jewish holidays. As a rule, following their yeshiva studies but sometimes concurrent with them, young men usually learn a trade or business, or are taken into a family business if conditions permit. Most Hasidim are skilled workers and are employed in various facets of the diamond industry, particularly in the New York area, but also hold such jobs as electricians, carpenters, wholesalers, operators of small businesses, and manufacturers. Many as well are employed in religious-oriented occupations and serve as religious teachers, ritual slaughterers, overseers of food products requiring rabbinical supervision, scribes for religious letters and documents, and the manufacturers of religious articles such as phylacteries, prayer shawls, and *mezzuzoths*. To better control their hours of employment so as to meet their religious obligations, Hasidim prefer either to be self-employed or to work for an Orthodox Jew who will be sympathetic to their religious requirements. While the number of business enterprises in the Hasidic community is increasing, the professional class remains very small since Hasidim restrict secular educational opportunities for their members. Since in only the rarest of cases do Hasidim attend college or university, professionals among the Hasidim received their secular training prior to affiliating with the Hasidic community.

Division of Labor. Attitudes toward women working outside the home have undergone modification. As the value of conspicuous consumption has taken root among young married couples, it is generally expected that in the absence of small children at home a woman ought to be employed. Aside from serving as teachers in their own schools, women are usually employed in some secretarial capacity in small businesses.

Kinship, Marriage and Family

Marriage. Boys and girls are segregated at a very early age and never participate in activities where the sexes are mixed. Ideally neither male nor female has any sexual experience before marriage, the average age of which is young—usually between the ages of eighteen and twenty—but varies with the particular Hasidic sect. Dating and falling in love are as foreign to the Hasidim as they are the norm in the larger secular culture. The selection of a mate is arranged through the aid of friends and members of the community who act in the capacity of *shadchan*, or marriage broker. There is a tendency to prefer marriages within the same sect or at least within sects sharing a similar ideology. Although intermediaries bring the couple together, the latter do meet and are given the opportunity to talk and judge the other's suitability as a marriage mate. Such encounters often consist simply of conversations in the living room of the girl's family, although some might take a stroll unescorted. In some instances, notably among the Lubavitcher, the couple might go for a drive or meet in a public setting. After a few meetings between a prospective bride and groom, a decision regarding marriage is reached. It will require approval by the respective families, and the rebbe's blessing will be sought. Procreation, God's commandment, is one of the most important functions of the Hasidic family, and couples strive to have children as soon as possible. Most forms of birth control are religiously forbidden and the tendency is toward large families. Although rates of separation and divorce remain low, they may increase as the Hasidim respond to social and economic changes in the world around them.

Domestic Unit. The family is a central institution in the Hasidim's efforts to ensure conformity to a prescribed lifestyle, as it is the first and most enduring locus of the socialization process. It is the mediator or communicator of social values and links the individual to the larger social structure. In this capacity, it becomes one of the cornerstones of community cohesion, continuity, and survival. Structurally speaking, the Hasidic family appears to be much like its traditional North American counterpart. Its organization shows a division of labor whereby the husband and father serves as the overall supervisor in religious matters, and the wife and mother is charged with keeping the house and ensuring that the children adhere to the prescribed religious precepts.

Socialization. The religious education of the young is a central consideration in the Hasidic community. From childhood on, parents are instrumental in communicating to their children the appropriate attitudes and behavior. The ultimate objective of the religious training is to produce a God-fearing person who is well socialized into the sect's normative structure. Since Hasidic norms demand a strict separation of the sexes, separate schools are available for boys and girls and their formal education differs. For males, the central activity of the school day, until they are sixteen or seventeen, consists of learning Torah. The primary subject matter is the Pentateuch, and this, together with the Babylonian Talmud and some biblical commentaries, constitutes the core curriculum. Following graduation from the elementary division, the young man moves to the yeshiva—upper division—where the same basic subject matter is emphasized, except that more commentaries are added, and the coverage increases. The girls' religious curriculum does not parallel the boys'. Although it has undergone some changes in recent years, the general rule against teaching Torah to girls has resulted in a diluted curriculum, which emphasizes a knowledge of Hebrew reading for prayer, Bible stories, moral teachings, and simplified law and custom codes. For both, the language of instruction is Yiddish.

A feature common to all Hasidic sects is the view that secular education threatens their traditional values; in order to shield their children from its potentially harmful influences, they run their own schools where secular classes are closely supervised to ensure that the pupils will not encounter any conflict with the contents of their religious studies. Secular programs exist alongside the religious curriculum in the schools, but they are hardly accorded equal importance. Textbooks are censored in advance and purged of all suspect stories and pictures. Nonacademic subjects such as music and physical education are totally absent. Those hired for secular studies—virtually all are outsiders since Hasidim do not pursue higher education to qualify for teacher accreditation—are specifically informed about the constraints within which they must operate. The secular studies program for girls is generally more liberal than the boys', since the former are permitted to have a greater amount of diversion from their religious studies. In the case of boys, only minimal time is devoted to secular education—usually not more than a couple of hours late in the afternoon—and by age sixteen such studies are terminated for both sexes. The coordination of secular education helps the Hasidim uphold community boundaries, screening out potentially harmful secular influences and contributing to the maintenance of their particular life-style. Secular studies programs are not seen as bearing any relationship to occupational choice in adulthood.

Sociopolitical Organization

The rebbe occupies a unique position in the Hasidic community. He is in every way the leader of his flock and that fact is central in the organization of the group and the dynamics of change within it. His followers turn to him for advice not merely on spiritual and ethical problems but also on a wide range of practical matters such as taking a new job, moving to another city, or even consulting a physician. Because he is believed to be a *tzaddik*—a righteous person—possessing special qualities of insight, he is viewed as a mediator between his followers and God. In addition to seeking a personal audience with him, the Hassid may also send a *kvitl*, or prayer note, to the rebbe requesting his advice and blessing. It is common for Hasidim who are geographically distanced from their rebbe to visit him particularly during religious holidays. A rebbe's authority is inherited from his father or some other close relative but is believed ultimately to come from God. Perceived by his followers as unable to do wrong, it is impossible to have a disconfirmation of the rebbe's advice.

See also Jews

Bibliography

Mintz, Jerome (1968). *Legends of the Hasidim: An Introduction to Hasidic Culture and Oral Tradition in the New World.* Chicago: University of Chicago Press.

Poll, Solomon (1962). *The Hasidic Community of Williamsburg.* New York: Free Press of Glencoe.

Rubin, Israel (1972). *Satmar: An Island in the City.* Chicago: Quadrangle Books.

Shaffir, William (1974). *Life in a Religious Community: The Luvaitcher Chassidim in Montreal.* Montreal: Holt, Rinehart, & Winston of Canada.

WILLIAM SHAFFIR

Havasupai

ETHNONYMS: Coconino, Kanina, Kokonino, Nation of the Willows, Supai

A Yuman-speaking American Indian group, the Havasupai, both past and present, have been located in Cataract Canyon in northwestern Arizona. Except in modern times, the Havasupai have never numbered more than about three hundred people.

In 1880 the U.S. government established a reservation for the Havasupai, but subsequently much of the land set aside was transferred to the Navajo, Hopi, and Whites. In 1974 some of this land was restored to the Havasupai. In 1980 those living on the 3,058-acre Havasupai Reservation in Cataract Canyon numbered 267.

The Havasupai were agriculturalists who cultivated maize, beans, squash and melons in irrigated fields. In addition, women gathered pine nuts, mesquite pods, honey, berries, and other wild foods and men hunted rabbits, antelope,

deer, and mountain sheep. During the growing season from April to October the Havasupai settled alongside their fields at the canyon bottom and then after harvest ascended to the top of the canyon and followed a more nomadic hunting and gathering pattern of life. Trade with the Hopi, Walapai, Navajo, and Mohave were also an important part of their economy.

The Havasupai lived in bands composed of related but autonomous families and were led by a head chief, whose position tended to be inherited patrilineally and was filled by an individual of demonstrated bravery and wisdom. Religious leadership was provided by several types of shamans who were believed to have received special powers in their dreams. The Havasupai were strongly influenced by the Hopi, and this was especially evident in their religious ceremonies, which focused on planting and rain and involved prayer sticks and masked dancers.

Bibliography

Euler, Robert C. (1980). *Grand Canyon Indians.* Dillon: Western Montana College Foundation.

Hirst, Stephen (1976). *Life in a Narrow Place.* New York: David McKay.

Hidatsa

ETHNONYMS: Agutchaninnewug, Ameshe, Gros Ventres of the Missouri, Hewaktokto, Minitari, Wanukeyena, Wetitsaan

Orientation

Identification. The Hidatsa are an American Indian group currently located in North Dakota. The name "Hidatsa" is a term of their own derivation that means "willow people," and was used by them to refer to one of their three village subgroups. Two other subgroups were called "Awatixa" and "Awaxawi." The merging of these latter village groups with the more numerous Hidatsa group led to the use of the latter term as the collective referent for the tribe.

Location. Aboriginally the Hidatsa occupied three villages in the Missouri River valley near the confluence of the Knife River in present-day west-central North Dakota, roughly between 47° and 48° N and 100° and 102° W.

Demography. As of 1976, the Three Affiliated Tribes (Hidatsa, Mandan, and Arikara) of North Dakota numbered 2,750. From a precontact high of perhaps 5,000, the Hidatsa decreased to about 3,000 during the early 1800s and approximately 400 by 1876, after which the population began a slow increase to its modern level of about 1,200 in North Dakota. Hidatsa population decline was the result of infectious epidemic diseases of European origin to which the Hidatsa and other tribes had little or no immunity.

Linguistic Affiliation. The Hidatsa language belongs to the Siouan language family. It is most closely related to the Crow language, which was a divergent dialect of Hidatsa. It is more distantly related to Mandan, a separate language spoken by a tribe culturally and geographically close to the Hidatsa. The Hidatsa language is spoken today.

History and Cultural Relations

Mythological evidence suggests that the Hidatsa migrated into the Missouri River valley from the northeast, near present-day Devils Lake, North Dakota. Acquiring maize agriculture from the Mandan, the Hidatsa established several villages nearby. Archaeological evidence suggests that some Hidatsa were present in their historically known location by the early 1600s. Nearby groups included the Mandan and Crow, with whom the Hidatsa were allied, and the Dakota, Cheyenne, Assiniboin, and Arikara, all of whom the Hidatsa counted as enemies.

Sustained contact with Europeans began during the late eighteenth century, when the Hidatsa were brought into the fur trade. In 1804, the Hidatsa established peaceful relations with the United States as a result of the Lewis and Clark expedition. While initially prospering from the fur trade, frequent intertribal warfare with the Dakota, coupled with extensive loss of life from the 1837 smallpox epidemic, caused the Hidatsa to relocate into a single village near the relative safety of Fort Berthold in 1845. The Hidatsa were subsequently joined by the Mandan and Arikara, resulting in the formation of the Three Affiliated Tribes and the Fort Berthold Reservation during the 1860s within traditional Hidatsa territory. Throughout the historic period, the Hidatsa have maintained peaceful relations with the United States.

Settlements

Aboriginally, Hidatsa villages were built on flood-free terraces of the Missouri River. These permanent villages were located adjacent to bottomland gardening areas and valuable timber stands. Villages were compact and fortified by ditches and palisades. Houses were large, circular, earth-covered structures built upon a substantial foundation of timber beams and posts. The Hidatsa also constructed more temporary versions of earthlodge encampments in the wooded bottomlands that served as winter quarters.

During the early 1800s, the three Hidatsa subgroups, the Hidatsa proper, Awatixa, and Awaxawi, lived in villages that numbered approximately eighty, fifty, and twenty earthlodges respectively, with populations of about one thousand, seven hundred, and three hundred. By the late 1860s, when the Hidatsa had relocated into a single village and were experiencing the acculturative influences of reservation policies, the square log cabin began to replace the traditional earthlodge. By this time, family size had declined significantly and the Hidatsa were being encouraged to alter their family structure to the nuclear family model of rural American agrarian life. The cohesive, nucleated earthlodge settlement plan disappeared in the 1880s, when the village was dismantled and the Hidatsa were placed on family allotments and scattered along the Missouri Valley. The creation of Garrison Dam in the 1950s inundated the small farming and ranching communities that the Hidatsa developed in the rich bottomlands of the reservation, and they have been relocated to towns or isolated homes in the upland prairie.

Economy

Subsistence and Commercial Activities. The Hidatsa were horticulturists, raising maize, beans, squash, and sunflowers using swidden techniques in fertile alluvial bottomlands. Hunting was of equal importance, with major game animals consisting of bison, elk, pronghorn, mule deer, and white-tailed deer. The Hidatsa were able to produce and store surpluses of vegetable crops, which were valuable trade commodities in a widespread Plains intertribal trade system. By the mid-1800s, the Hidatsa began to experience economic hardship as a result of several factors: the military ascendancy of nomadic pastoralist tribes such as the Lakota and Yanktonai Sioux, depopulation from epidemic diseases, and changing fortunes of the fur trade. Beginning with the reservation era in the 1860s, the Hidatsa incorporated ranching and commercial farming of wheat and other grains into their economy while maintaining subsistence horticulture. The disappearance of bison from North Dakota relegated the hunting of deer and other game to secondary importance. Today, the Hidatsa continue to work as ranchers and commercial farmers, while commercial/industrial enterprises, government employment, and public assistance augment their economy. As of 1975, however, their unemployment rate stood at approximately 50 percent.

Industrial Arts. Aboriginal crafts included pottery, basket making and mat weaving, porcupine quillwork, and painted representational art applied to tanned hides, robes, clothing, and containers. After European contact, the Hidatsa incorporated bead manufacture and beadwork as crafts, which, along with quillwork and quiltmaking, are currently practiced.

Trade. In precontact times the Hidatsa carried on an important trade with nomadic tribes, exchanging maize and other garden produce for dried meat and leather products. Historic trade in horses and European technology such as firearms, iron hoes, metal arrowpoints, and beads was superimposed onto this precontact intertribal trade system. Hidatsa villages served as trading centers where numerous tribes would come to exchange goods. The trade in horses was especially lucrative as the Hidatsa amassed short-term surpluses in horses, which served as capital for barter.

Division of Labor. Prior to the reservation period, Hidatsa women were primarily responsible for farming, including clearing fields, harvesting, and processing vegetables. Women also constructed the earthlodges, with men assisting in heavy labor. Women made pottery and baskets, butchered game animals and processed hides into clothes, tipi covers, robes, and other accoutrements. They also engaged in beadwork and quillwork. Men hunted, fished, conducted warfare, trapped eagles, and conducted religious rituals. The alteration of the Hidatsa economy during the reservation period resulted in men becoming storekeepers, farmers, ranchers, and ministers.

Land Tenure. In aboriginal times, hunting and timber-bearing lands were theoretically open to all within the Hidatsa tribe, although each village does appear to have had favored areas that were open to other villages by request. Ownership of garden lands was vested in local clan segments, with individual extended family households exercising rights of usufruct on lands they cultivated. With the advent of the reservation system, Hidatsa lands reverted to tribal ownership under the control and supervision of the Bureau of Indian Affairs (BIA). During the 1880s, tribal lands were allotted by the BIA to individuals. Today, Hidatsa land on the Fort Berthold Reservation is owned by individuals as well as the tribe.

Kinship

Kin Groups and Descent. Hidatsa society was divided into eight exogamous matrilineal clans. Within each village these clans functioned as corporate groups that controlled land, arranged marriages, sponsored ceremonies and ritual feasts, and generally served to integrate the population. Clans were aggregated into two moieties. Depopulation, intermarriage with other tribes and with Whites, and forced acculturation has resulted in a breakdown of the clan system.

Kinship Terminology. Hidatsa aboriginal kinship terminology followed the Crow system.

Marriage and Family

Marriage. Traditionally, marriages between members of the same clan or moiety were frowned upon. Historic Hidatsa villages were agamous, as intervillage marriages were common. Marriages functioned as a bond between both individuals and kin groups, and occurred by arrangement, purchase, or elopement. Monogamy was rare as polygyny was the prevailing form of marriage. The sororate and levirate also were practiced. Postmarital residence was theoretically matrilocal, but depopulation during the historic period resulted in multilocal residence as households attempted to widen their strategies for incorporating male and female residents.

Domestic Unit. Traditionally, the domestic unit was the matrilocal extended family, an earthlodge household consisting of a core of matrilineally related women. Since reservation times the domestic unit has been influenced by the nuclear family model, but bilateral extended families are common.

Inheritance. Traditionally, patrilineal and matrilineal inheritance occurred with the former applying mainly to medicine bundles.

Socialization. Aboriginally, much of Hidatsa socialization was informal and provided by the matrilineal extended family. Children were reared permissively into male and female roles. Generosity, self-reliance, and patience were values inculcated by parents. Males during adolescence and young adulthood were taught to be assertive and competitive as preparation for warfare and entrance into age-grade societies. Fasting, ritual self-torture, and mock combat underscored these values. Young girls were taught modesty, diligence, and patience in preparation for adulthood and marriage. Today cooperation, noninterference, kin support, and tribalism are important socialization values.

Sociopolitical Organization

Social Organization. Aboriginally, the status and prestige of individual Hidatsas depended on personal accomplishments, acquisition of wealth, and membership in male and female age-grade societies. Male status was determined primarily by hunting skills, war honors, and ownership of medicine bundles. Highest status went to older men who belonged to the upper age grades and had fulfilled the social and ceremonial expectations of Hidatsa society. These men owned the important medicine bundles and had great political and social influence. As a matrilineal society, women held relatively high status, particularly those who belonged to the higher age grades and were skilled potters, healers, architects, or basket makers. Acquisition of wealth and influence became easier as a result of equestrianism and the fur trade. Depopulation and acculturation resulted in a breakdown of the age-grade system and a shift in status and role determinants to employment opportunities, cash income, education, and church affiliation.

Political Organization. Prior to about 1797, the Hidatsa villages were politically independent, with each village containing a village council of chiefs made up of influential high-ranking men. These were achieved status positions. Each village also contained an age grade called the Black Mouths, who served as camp police, administered council decisions, and policed bison hunts. After 1797, the Hidatsa villages formed an overarching tribal council composed of the most distinguished warriors of the three subgroups. This council acted as a common cause structure in areas of diplomacy and warfare. Today the Three Affiliated Tribes are governed by an elected tribal council headed by a tribal chairperson.

Social Control. Traditionally, social control was a blend of informal mechanisms, such as gossip, ostracism, and peer pressure, and the formal police functions of the Black Mouth society, which had the authority to administer severe punishments, such as whipping or destruction of property, for violating community rules. Today, social control is maintained by the tribal courts and tribal police, except in the commission of major crimes, such as murder, armed robbery, or arson, which fall under federal jurisdiction.

Conflict. The Hidatsa were by and large an internally peaceful and cohesive tribe, although mythology holds that the Hidatsa proper and Awaxawi subgroups once fought over disputed village settlement areas. In the 1870s, conflict between Hidatsa chiefs led to a rift, resulting in the separation of a large contingent of Hidatsas, known as the Crow-Flies-High band, from the Fort Berthold group. This separation lasted for several years before ending in the late 1880s.

Religion and Expressive Culture

Religious Beliefs. Traditionally, the Hidatsa believed in a pervasive supernatural force that existed in all animate and inanimate objects. Through vision experiences, fasting, and self-torture, this power could be harnessed by individuals. Personal and tribal medicine bundles were the repositories and symbolic expressions of the Hidatsa spiritual world. This power could be used for good or evil, and successful hunting, war exploits, and healing were defined in terms of strong medicine or power. The Hidatsa supernatural world consisted of a vast array of human personifications, spirits, game keepers, and inanimate forces. Three important culture heroes in Hidatsa origin traditions are Charred Body (founder of the Awatixa Hidatsa), First Creator, and Only Man (both of whom created the earth in Awaxawi tradition). The Awatixa are believed to have descended from the sky, led by Charred Body, whereas the Awaxawi are believed to have emerged from the underground after the earth was created.

Religious Practitioners. Religious and medical practitioners were those men and women who held special medicine bundles and associated songs and rites. Many of these bundles dealt with specialties such as buffalo calling, healing of wounds, or child birth. "Priests" were those influential older men who held the important clan and tribal bundles, which gave them control of major mythological and ceremonial knowledge. They were charged with maintaining harmony between the tribe and the array of supernatural forces and spirits. Since the reservation era, many Hidatsas have converted to various denominations of Christianity, and some have retained portions of the aboriginal religion.

Ceremonies. Major ceremonies included the Naxpike or the Hidatsa variant of the Sun Dance, the Big Bird rainmaking ceremony, and the Red Stick buffalo-calling ceremony.

Medicine. Traditional Hidatsa medicine was a blend of practical knowledge in treating ailments and injuries like frostbite, wounds, snow blindness, and broken bones and supernatural intervention through shamanistic healing. Hidatsa doctors were paid for their skills, and the healing process was accompanied by sacred songs, symbolic healing, and sweatbaths. Modern medical etiology and practice now dominate among the Three Affiliated Tribes, although traditional practices such as the use of the sweatlodge and its associated ritual are still followed.

Death and Afterlife. Traditionally, at the death of an individual, the father's clan was responsible for making funeral arrangements. Forms of disposition included scaffolds, interment, and placing the deceased in trees or under rock overhangs. Concepts of the afterlife varied, although generally it mirrored earthly existence. Murderers were excluded from the villages of the dead and were believed to become aimless wanderers, an eternal banishment. Some Hidatsa (the Awatixa) believed that at death one returned to the sky, the origin place of the culture hero Charred Body. Others, like the Awaxawi, believed that they would return to their traditional homeland on Knife River or to their mythical homeland near Devils Lake. In general, death was attributed to supernatural causes and related violations of ritual prescriptions.

Bibliography

Bowers, Alfred (1965). *Hidatsa Social and Ceremonial Organization.* U.S. Bureau of American Ethnology Bulletin no. 194. Washington, D.C.

Gilman, Carolyn, and Mary Jane Schneider (1987). *The Way to Independence; Memories of a Hidatsa Indian Family, 1840–1920.* St. Paul: Minnesota Historical Society.

Hanson, Jeffery R. (1987). *Hidatsa Culture Change, 1780–1845: A Cultural Ecological Approach.* Lincoln, Nebr.: J&L Reprint Co.

Meyer, Roy W. (1977). *The Village Indians of the Upper Missouri.* Lincoln: University of Nebraska Press.

Wilson, Gilbert L. (1917). *Agriculture of the Hidatsa Indians.* Studies in the Social Sciences, no. 9. Minneapolis: University of Minnesota Press.

JEFFERY R. HANSON

Hopi

ETHNONYMS: Moqui, Tusayan

Orientation

Identification. The Hopi are an American Indian group in Arizona. The term "Hopi" means "one who behaves" or "one who follows the proper way."

Location. The Hopi lived aboriginally in the same location they now inhabit, the northeastern quadrant of Arizona. Their reservation is completely surrounded by the Navajo reservation.

Demography. The Hopi tribal enrollment was 6,624 in 1988. At first contact in 1540, there may have been a similar number. The population estimate in 1887 was about 2,200. Until recently, intermarriage with outsiders was rare, with only an occasional Navajo or person from another tribe marrying in.

Linguistic Affiliation. The Hopi language belongs to the Shoshonean branch of Uto-Aztecan. There are minor dialectical differences among the three Mesas (First, Second, and Third) on which Hopi villages are situated.

History and Cultural Relations

Hopi culture as known from the time of first contact came out of long tradition of Pueblo and pre-Pueblo culture, known archaeologically as Anasazi. Francisco Vasquez de Coronado's expedition in 1540 brought them their first contact with the Spanish. After a few other brief contacts, three missions were established, the first in 1629. These were destroyed in the Pueblo Revolt of 1680; after that date, there was little effort toward resuming contact and the Hopi were left alone. Contact with Americans began in the early nineteenth century and became intensive after 1850. An agency under the Department of the Army was established at Keams Canyon, near First Mesa, in 1873, and a reservation was set up in 1882. The first school was opened in 1887, and schooling became a central issue in the early factions of "Hostiles" and "Friendlies," or those opposed to or favorable toward accommodation with the Americans. Oraibi, the largest Hopi village, split in 1906 with much acrimony over this and other issues. A tribal constitution was adopted in 1936, providing for a tribal council with elected representatives from each village.

Settlements

The Hopi lived in compact villages, ranging in population from less than a hundred to perhaps two thousand persons. In 1850 there were seven villages; now there are eleven. Today as formerly, houses cluster about a central plaza where public ceremonies take place. Interspersed among the houses are kivas, or ceremonial chambers, which function as centers for esoteric ceremonies and as clubhouses for men. Traditional houses were built of stone and plastered with mud. Today, many people live in housing constructed of modern materials.

Economy

Subsistence and Commercial Activities. Aboriginal Hopis were horticulturalists, hunters, and gatherers. The major crop was maize. Hopis traded widely with neighboring peoples and were well known for the textiles that men wove of the cotton they grew. European articles were accepted and traded; and after coming under American rule, Hopi participated enthusiastically in wage labor and established numerous small businesses. Today, wage labor, commercial cattle ranching (begun in the 1920s), pensions, and welfare are major economic resources for those who live on the reservation. Commercial craft production has been a supplementary source of income for both men and women since the 1860s, and tourism is a major source of income for a small percentage of the population. Dogs were used for hunting aboriginally. Sheep and cattle supplemented hunting until the early twentieth century.

Industrial Arts. Cotton garments were woven for home consumption and external trade. Basketry was important for home use and for ceremonial exchange. Painted pottery, a traditional craft that had fallen into decline, was revived as a commercial craft in the late nineteenth century. Modern clothing, tools, and household goods began to be used in the late nineteenth century. Today, the traditional crafts are made for ceremonial use, sale, and to some degree household decoration.

Division of Labor. Men did most of the subsistence labor, in addition to weaving textiles and working wood and leather. Women performed mainly processing tasks and made pottery and baskets. After contact, both sexes took advantage of wage labor opportunities on and off the reservation. Today, women and men hold a variety of jobs in teaching, administration, clerical tasks, and commerce as well as skilled and unskilled labor. Both sexes did and do perform ritual activities.

Land Tenure. Land close to the village was owned by clans and was divided up among matrilocal clan households. Men cultivated land they received through their wives, and the harvested crops belonged to their wives. In addition, plots of land accompanied certain ceremonial positions. Since the horse and wagon and later the pickup truck were introduced, men have cleared fields in unclaimed territory farther from the village. These become their private property, which is often passed on to their sons.

Kinship

Kin Groups and Descent. Hopi society is divided into exogamous matrilineal ranked clans, the number varying over time. Clans are associated into exogamous phratries. Clans own farmland close to the villages and claim eagle-nesting grounds away from the village where eagles are captured for ceremonial use. High-ranking clans control ceremonial and traditional political offices and are in charge of ceremonies. Clan affairs are directed by a male and female pair, the clan elder and the clan mother. The elder is responsible for directing any male activities and ceremonies controlled by the clan and for representing the clan to the village, particularly in land boundary disputes. The clan mother directs female activities and ceremonies, makes the final decision in clan land distribution, and is responsible through prayer and ritual for the well-being of clan members. Although most clans are represented in most of the villages, each clan is a corporate group only within its village. Today, the importance of clans has diminished as land ownership and political office are achieved through other means, although clans are still active in ceremonial matters and exogamy is still the norm.

Kinship Terminology. Hopi kin terms follow the Crow system.

Marriage and Family

Marriage. Marriage was monogamous and was believed to last into the afterlife. In theory, people chose their own spouses, but high-ranking families to some extent controlled the marriage choices of their children. The marriage ceremony involved a short period of groom-service by the bride and an elaborate exchange of goods from both sides. The leading families of high-ranking clans tended to intermarry. Today, social class rather than clanship is a factor in selecting mates as it is in mainstream society, and some persons marry Whites or Indians of other tribes whom they meet at college or at work. Matrilocal residence was the rule. By the mid-1920s, a number of people lived in neolocal households, which predominate today. Marriages dissolved with some frequency. Sexual fidelity was expected, but infidelity was known and often a subject of gossip and conjecture. It was not punished, though separation frequently resulted.

Domestic Unit. During the early nineteenth century, the small extended family was probably most common. By the late nineteenth century and into the twentieth, the matrilocal stem family was the accepted form, with usually the youngest daughter remaining as older daughters and their husbands built houses contiguous or near to the maternal home.

Inheritance. Clan land and ceremonial and political positions pass within the clan. Livestock usually goes from parents to children of both sexes, most commonly sons. Daughters inherit houses.

Socialization. Early socialization was permissive. After about age four, children were expected to begin to do small tasks and were shamed or threatened if they did not obey. Boys were treated more harshly than girls, the preferred sex. From the 1880s to about the 1920s, there was much conflict over sending children to school, and even children eager to go were sometimes taken out to work on the family farm or to prevent them from being acculturated. In recent years, education has been recognized as valuable.

Sociopolitical Organization

Social Organization. The Hopi community could be seen as a federation of ranked clans. Upward mobility by a clan occurred when a lower-ranking clan took over the position of a higher-ranking one within the phratry. Women were equal to men, each gender having its own area of control: women controlled most aspects of the economy through their control over land and produce, and men controlled most aspects of village decision making. The ideology of gender gave women a higher value than men. Sexual equality still exists, although gender roles have changed considerably.

Political Organization. Prior to the late nineteenth century, each village was autonomous and was governed by a chief and a council of elders from the leading clans. The major areas of political discussion were clan land disputes, over which the chief had final adjudication, and warfare. Every man belonged to a kiva, which he used as a social club; and through kiva discussions the village leaders could read village opinions. Women played an active, although indirect, role in decision making, as men represented the wishes of sisters and wives as well as their own. The traditional system was undercut by the reservation system and suffered a death blow with the establishment of an elected tribal council.

Social Control.   Before contact, control was probably informal: gossip, teasing, fear of being labeled a witch, and mocking by ceremonial clowns at village ceremonies. Today, local crimes and misdemeanors are handled through the tribal court system. Serious crimes like murder are adjudicated in federal court.

Conflict.   Before American domination, war sometimes erupted between villages over land boundaries or vengeance. Navajos raided Hopi villages from the 1700s until they were pacified in the late nineteenth century. Warfare involved all village males under the leadership of the hereditary war chief. Since American pacification, much conflict within and between villages is expressed in terms of acceptance or rejection of accommodation to White ways, although its causes may lie elsewhere. In recent years, conflict with Navajos has intensified as the two tribes dispute their share of jointly held land, but this time the conflict is being resolved through the U.S. federal court system rather than by warfare. The Hopi have a reputation for nonviolence, but domestic and other forms of interpersonal violence seem to have increased in recent years.

Religion and Expressive Culture

Religious Beliefs.   The Hopi universe consists of earth, metaphorically spoken of as "our mother," the upper world, and the under world from which the Hopi came and to which their spirits go after death. Although the concept of original creation is unclear, there are various accounts of the Emergence into this present world from three preceding ones, the place of emergence, or the *sipapu,* being located in the Grand Canyon. Each of the preceding worlds came to an end because of some evil done by witches, and the present world will someday come to an end also. In order to forestall this and to keep the world in harmony, ceremonies are performed by ceremonial societies and by kiva members. The universe is balanced between a feminine principle, the earth, and a masculine one, manifested in the fructifying but dangerous powers of sun, rain, and lightning. Evil is caused by the deliberate actions of witches, called "two-hearts" because they have bargained away their hearts for personal gain and must steal another's heart to prolong their own lives. When a ceremonial leader is believed to "steal" the heart of a relative to ensure that the ceremony will be successful, there is an element of magical human sacrifice in this belief.

There are three major classes of supernatural. The most individualized are the gods and goddesses, each having his or her special area of concern. Figures or impersonations of these deities are used in ceremonial activity. The next category is the kachinas. A few of the kachinas are individuals, but most of them are classes of beings each with its different character and appearance. In kachina dances the dancers wear the costume appropriate to the kachina type they por-

tray. Some types are more popular than others; new ones are invented and old ones drop out of use. Finally, there are the generalized spirits of natural objects and life-forms, who will be offended if one of their earthly representatives is treated improperly. Thus, when a game animal is killed, its spirit, and the generalized spirits of that animal type, must be placated.

Religious Practitioners.   The leaders of the clans that control ceremonies are the chief priests or priestesses of these ceremonies and clan members take leading roles in them. Every Hopi is initiated into one of the two kachina societies, which are responsible for putting on the kachina dances. In former times, every man joined one of the four fraternities that put on the Emergence ceremony, and most women joined one of the three sororities. There are also special-purpose societies, controlled by clans but open to membership to anyone in the village, which conduct ceremonies. Villages vary in the number of societies still in existence, but all put on kachina dances, which are organized through kiva membership.

Ceremonies.   The Hopi follow a ceremonial calendar determined by solar and stellar positions. The ceremonial year begins with Wuwtsim, the Emergence ceremony, in November. Soyal, occurring at the time of winter solstice, is conducted by the village chief, and its officers are the men holding the leading ceremonial positions in the village. It is at this time that ceremonial arrangements for the coming year are planned. Powamuya, in February, is a planting festival in which beans are sprouted in the kivas in anticipation of the agricultural season. This is a great kachina festival, with many types being represented. Kachina dances begin after Soyal and continue until July, when Niman or Home Dance is held. This celebrates the return of the kachinas to their unearthly homes in the mountain peaks and the under world. Snake-Antelope and Flute Dances alternate biennially in August, the first emphasizing war and the destructive element and the second emphasizing the continuity of life after death. In September, Mamrawt, or the principal women's ceremony, is held. This contains many elements found in Wuwtsim. The other women's societies hold their ceremonies in October. Along with these ceremonies, there are some that are held only from time to time and others that have been defunct for many years. In addition, there are many small rituals. Accounts of the late nineteenth century indicate that hardly a day passed without some ritual activity taking place somewhere in each village. While ceremonies have specific purposes, all are in some way thought to bring rain, which is valued both for itself and as a symbol of abundance and prosperity. The kachinas, especially, are rain-givers. Kachina dances are joyous public events, consisting of carefully choreographed dance sets interspersed with comical performances of clowns. The clowns, like ignorant children, mock everything and understand nothing. Social deviants are shamed by the clowns' mockery.

Arts.   Traditional objects are produced as art objects as well as for use. Kachina dolls, nonsacred representations of kachinas given to girls and women as symbols of fertility and for toys, became tourist items in the late nineteenth century and have undergone several stylistic revisions since then. Modern techniques of silverwork were introduced by American artists associated with the Museum of Northern Arizona in Flagstaff in the 1920s. Using Hopi designs, this is a flourishing craft. There are several contemporary Hopi painters in oil and other media, as well as poets and art photographers. Aesthetic standards for dance, song, and costume are high and clearly articulated.

Medicine. Sickness can be brought on by witchcraft, by contact with dangerous forces like lightning, or, more commonly, by sad or negative thoughts, such as anger or jealousy, which disturb the harmony of the body. Curing is done by shamans who diagnose and heal the ailment or by members of ceremonial societies that control the cures for certain diseases. Today, most Hopis make use of government hospitals along with native home remedies and shamanistic treatment.

Death and Afterlife. A peaceful death in old age is a natural death. Other deaths may be attributed to witchcraft or the other factors causing disease. Burial by a son or other close relative is completed as soon as possible outside of the village. During its journey to the under world, the spirit of the dead may try to induce others to come with it, and various rites protect against this. Once safely in the under world, the dead are friendly to the living and will return to earth along with the kachinas to bring rain.

Bibliography

Laird, W. David (1977). *Hopi Bibliography.* Tucson: University of Arizona Press.

Nagata, Shuichi (1960). *Modern Transformations of Moenkopi Pueblo.* Urbana: University of Illinois Press.

Schlegel, Alice (1977). "Male and Female in Hopi Thought and Action." In *Sexual Stratification,* edited by Alice Schlegel, 245–269. New York: Columbia University Press.

Titiev, Mischa (1944). *Old Oraibi: A Study of the Hopi Indians of Third Mesa.* Papers of the Peabody Museum, Harvard University, 22(1) Cambridge.

ALICE SCHLEGEL

Hopi-Tewa

ETHNONYM: Tano

The Hopi-Tewa are a Tewa-speaking American Indian group who live in the pueblo of Hano on First Mesa on the Hopi Indian Reservation in northeastern Arizona. From the fourteenth to the seventeenth centuries the ancestors of the Hopi-Tewa occupied several pueblo communities in the Galisteo Basin, south of present-day Santa Fe, New Mexico. In the fourteenth century their ancestors are estimated to have numbered between fourteen hundred and four thousand people.

About 1692, following the return of the Spanish after the Pueblo Revolt of 1680, many Tano took refuge among their northern neighbors, the Tewa. About 1696 some Tano migrated to Hopi territory and settled there, establishing the

pueblo of Hano (Tewa Village) on First Mesa; thereafter they are known as the Hopi-Tewa. The Hopi-Tewa maintained much of the Tano cultural pattern, but added herding to their economic activities and some Hopi elements to their own religious beliefs and practices. In 1975 the Hopi-Tewa numbered about 625 and were located in several villages in northeastern Arizona.

The Hopi-Tewa were primarily horticulturalists who raised maize, beans, and squash; however, hunting and gathering were also important in their subsistence pattern. Herding, horticulture, and other traditional activities remained the subsistence base for the majority of the Hopi-Tewa up until the 1950s. Since that time wage work has increasingly become the most important source of income and subsistence. Hopi-Tewa society was organized into matrilineal, matrilocal, exogamous clans. Clan affiliation determined membership in one of two kiva groups, and the winter solstice ceremony was the most important religious rite.
See also Tewa

Bibliography

Dozier, Edward P. (1954). *The Hopi-Tewa of Arizona.* University of California Publications in American Archaeology and Ethnology, 44. Berkeley.

Stanislawski, Michael B. (1979). "Hopi-Tewa." In *Handbook of North American Indians.* Vol. 9, *Southwest,* edited by Alfonso Ortiz, 587–602. Washington, D.C.: Smithsonian Institution.

Huma

The Huma (Houma, Sabine) lived on the east side of the Mississippi River near the present Louisiana-Mississippi border. They are now settled in several communities around Houma, Louisiana, in Terrebonne and Lafourche parishes. They speak a Muskogean language and numbered 2,221 in 1966, 2,600 in 1980.

Bibliography

Curry, Jan (1979). "A History of the Houma Indians and Their Story of Federal Nonrecognition." *American Indian Journal* 5(1):8–28.

Stanton, Max E. (1971). "A Remnant Indian Community: the Houma of Southern Louisiana." In *The Not So Solid South,* edited by J. Kenneth Morland, 82–92. Athens, Ga.: Southern Anthropological Society.

Hupa

ETHNONYMS: Hoopa, Nabiltse, Natano, Trinity Indians

The Hupa are an American Indian group who lived at the time of contact and continue to live on the lower course of the Trinity River in northwestern California. Culturally, they were closely related to the neighboring Yurok and Karok and the Chilula, Whilkut, and South Fork Hupa, the latter three no longer existing as distinct cultural entities. At the time of contact in 1850 there were about 1,000 Hupa. In 1980 there were 1,502 Hupa living on the 84,703-acre Hoopa Valley Reservation in Humboldt County, California. Hupa is an Athapaskan language and is still spoken by many people, though English is the primary language for most Hupa today. The Hupa have successfully retained their cultural identity while benefiting financially from participation in the mainstream economy. The annual tribal income is about $1.5 million, with some 80 percent derived from forestry, and the Hupa enjoy the highest standard of living of all California Indian groups. First contact with Whites was in 1850 when White gold miners moved into northern California. In 1864 the Hoopa Valley Reservation was authorized by Congress, and the Hupa began a steady transition from a life based on fishing and acorn gathering to one based first on farming and livestock raising and finally to one based on logging, millwork and other types of wage labor.

The traditional economy was based on fishing for salmon and the gathering of acorns for processing into flour. The twelve Hupa villages were located about a mile apart from one another along the Trinity River. Each village contained a number of cedar-plank dwellings, each housing a nuclear family of about seven people, and several sweat lodges. The residential family was the basic social group, though several such patrilineally related units often lived in the same village and cooperated in various activities. There was no political organization at either the village or the tribal level and no tribal leadership. Today, tribal affairs are managed by an elected seven-member tribal council and a tribal chairman elected by the council. Though lacking true social classes, the Hupa were much concerned about individual wealth and the prestige that such wealth carried with it. With missionary activity commencing soon after contact, many Hupa converted to Christianity, though traditional dances are still performed, including the White Deerskin and Jumping renewal dances, which are performed every other year.

See also Karok, Yurok

Bibliography

Goddard, Pliny E. (1903-04). *Life and Culture of the Hupa.* University of California Publications in American Archaeology and Ethnology, 1, 1-88. Berkeley.

Wallace, William J. (1978). "Hupa, Chilula, and Whilkut." In *Handbook of North American Indians.* Vol. 8, *California,* edited by Robert F. Heizer, 164-179. Washington, D.C.: Smithsonian Institution.

Huron

ETHNONYMS: Huron of Lorette, Wendat, Wyandot

The Huron were a confederacy of Northern Iroquoian-speaking American Indians who in the early seventeenth century were located southeast of Georgian Bay in present-day Ontario, Canada. At that time they numbered about thirty thousand, but following smallpox epidemics in the 1630s were reduced to about ten thousand by 1639.

In 1648 and 1649 the Huron confederacy was destroyed by the Iroquois in a war for control of the fur trade. After their defeat the Huron dispersed, with some joining other tribes or being adopted by the Iroquois. One group of the defeated Huron took refuge with Jesuit missionaries and were eventually established on a reserve near Quebec, Canada, in 1697. They became known as the Huron of Lorette. In the eighteenth century a small group of Huron known as the Wyandot who had fled west after the defeat of the confederacy settled in Ohio and southeastern Michigan. Later, in the early 1840s, the Wyandot were forced to remove to Kansas. In 1857 and 1858 the Wyandot removed once again to Oklahoma and settled on land given to them by the Seneca. In the 1980s the Wyandot in Oklahoma and the Huron of Lorette numbered about two thousand.

The annual cycle of Huron subsistence activities included deer hunting, fishing, gathering, and the cultivation of maize, beans, squash, tobacco, and other crops. The Huron were strategically situated in the indigenous trade networks connecting farming peoples to their south and hunting peoples to their north, and thus trade was also an important part of their economy. Agriculture and gathering were the responsibility of the women; the men were responsible for trading, hunting, fishing, and warfare.

Huron society was organized into eight exogamous matrilineal clans, which cut across tribal and village boundaries. Each localized clan segment had a civil and a war chief. Village affairs were governed by independent war and civil councils made up of the senior warriors and elderly men of the clan segments. In the village councils the civil and war chiefs of the clan segments acted as spokesmen, and decisions were made by consensus. Above the level of the village the Huron were organized into four or five tribes united by a council of clan segment chiefs from each of the villages. The tribal council met at least once every year and could be brought together on the initiative of the clan segment chiefs on any matters involving the interests of more than one village.

The Huron believed that all animate and inanimate things had a spirit, the most powerful of which was the spirit of the sky controlling the wind, seasons, and other natural phenomena. In addition, they were greatly concerned with the interpretation of dreams, which were viewed as omens or the desires of one's soul that would result in illness if left unfulfilled. Shamans served to interpret and fulfill dreams and cure illness.

Bibliography

Delage, Denys (1982). "Conversion et identité: Le cas des Hurons et des Iroquois (1634-1664)." Culture 2:75-82.

Tooker, Elisabeth (1964). *An Ethnography of the Huron Indians, 1615–1649*. U.S. Bureau of American Ethnology Bulletin no. 190. Washington, D.C.

Hutterites

ETHNONYM: Hutterite Brethren

Orientation

Identification. The Hutterites in Canada and the United States are a Germanic people with origins in the Swiss Anabaptist movement that developed between 1525 and 1536 during the Reformation. Along with the Old Order Amish and Mennonites, the two other Anabaptist groups in North America, the Hutterites reject childhood baptism, are pacifists, maintain a closed religious community, and reject full participation in the Canadian and American societies. Unlike the two other Anabaptist groups, however, the Hutterites strictly adhere to community ownership of property and communal living patterns in farm communities (colonies) of from 60 to about 150 people each. Since settling in North America, the Hutterites have divided into three Leut (groups of colonies): the Dariusleut (mostly in Alberta, Saskatchewan, and Montana), the Schmiedeleut (mostly in Manitoba and South Dakota), and the Lehrerleut (in Alberta, Montana, and Saskatchewan).

Location. Hutterites (colonies) are found mainly in the provinces of Alberta, Manitoba, and Saskatchewan in Canada (253 colonies in 1989) and the states of South Dakota, Montana, North Dakota, Washington, and Minnesota in the United States (103 in 1989). Because of a high birth rate and a desire to keep colonies small, new colonies are regularly being formed.

Demography. About 1,265 Hutterites fled to what is now South Dakota from Russia in 1874. Only 443 chose to live communally. The population has increased to 31,521 in 1990. The rapid population growth at a rate of 4 percent per year is attributable to a high birth rate (completed family size of nine children) and a low attrition rate (less than 2 percent). Few outsiders are recruited through conversion and the Hutterites do not missionize.

Linguistic Affiliation. The Hutterites speak the Huttrish dialect of German, use biblical High German in religious services, and speak English with outsiders.

History and Cultural Relations

The first Hutterites were religious refugees who fled from the South Tyrol to Moravia (in what is now Czechoslovakia) and, as followers of Jacob Hutter, chose to hold their material goods in common. Hutter organized them into colonies (*Brüderhöfe*) of married adults and their children to live communally, a pattern of social organization that has remained a basic feature of the Hutterite culture since that time. As Ana-

baptist refugees flocked to Moravia, the early Hutterites managed to survive persecution and flourish, growing to over twenty thousand adherents by the early 1600s. Since 1590, however, the Hutterites have been a regular target of religious persecution, which precipitated a series of relocations first to Slovakia, then Hungary, then Romania, and finally to Russia in 1770. In the 1870s the group left Russia and settled in Dakota Territory, or what is now South Dakota. Their final mass relocation occurred during World War I when the men were persecuted for refusing military induction and all but one colony fled to Canada (during World War II Hutterite men performed alternative service). After the war, some colonies moved back, but the bulk of the population has remained in the plains provinces of Canada.

As suggested by their frequent forced relocations, Hutterite relations with mainstream society have often been less than friendly and the Hutterites have often been the target of violence. Their residential isolation, communal social and economic organization, Anabaptist beliefs, and economic success combined with the economic necessity of routinely interacting with outsiders have produced tense, distant Hutterite/non-Hutterite relations, which continue today. The desire of outsiders to develop Hutterite land and the issue of compulsory education are two recent sources of conflict.

Settlements

For the Hutterites, the colony is the center of their world, and each must be laid out in accord with the basic principles of order and proper relationships. The colonies are named and are essentially large, self-sufficient prairie farms usually located not too close to one another so as to reduce friction but not too far so as to inhibit the exchange of services. Colonies are also located away from towns, although near enough that Hutterites can conveniently shop for equipment and supplies. Each colony has about fifty buildings including longhouses with three-room family apartments, a central kitchen, a kindergarten, school buildings, shops, sheds, and barns. Most colonies do not have a separate church building and services are usually held in a school building or community dining hall in the kitchen building. Colony landholdings range from a few thousand to sixteen thousand acres of land. When colonies reach their optimal size (about 130 to 150 people) a "daughter" colony is formed through a carefully planned and managed process, with half the costs borne by the parent colony.

Economy

Subsistence and Commercial Activities. Owing to their use of highly mechanized farming techniques, a large work force, and fertile land, Hutterite colonies are very efficient and productive. Barley, wheat, oats, and hay are major crops, used primarily to feed the colony livestock with the excess sold for cash. Beef and dairy cattle, pigs, chickens and eggs, geese, turkeys, and sheep are raised and their products used in the colony and sold. The colonies are carefully planned and managed business enterprises with most decisions made in consideration of the supply and demand of the external economy.

Industrial Arts. Production of crafts for sale is no longer important, although bookbinding, clock repairing, tinsmithing, shoemaking, furniture making, and other industrial arts are sources of income for some colonies.

Trade.   Although the colonies are largely self-sufficient, they are integrated into the U.S. and Canadian economies through the sale of farm products and services and the purchase of equipment and raw materials. Cooperation in the loaning of services and materials is common between colonies located nearby, and especially between parent and daughter colonies.

Division of Labor.   All people able to work are expected to do so. Work is allocated on the bases of age, sex, and authority patterns. In general, men do the income-producing work, while women handle the domestic chores.

Land Tenure.   All land, buildings, and productive equipment is purchased and owned by the colony. A fairly detailed though flexible set of rules govern the distribution and ownership of material goods by individuals. Personal property is defined by the Hutterites as something given to the individual by the colony for the person to use, not to own.

Kinship, Marriage and Family

Kin Groups and Descent.   The recognized kin groups are the nuclear family, the patrinomial family (kin with the same surname), and clans (intermarrying family lines). Leuts are considered not kin groups but, rather, historical branches of the same large group. Brothers and their father often cooperate in many activities. Descent is bilateral with a patrilineal emphasis.

Marriage.   Marriage is colony exogamous and Leut endogamous. Within these bounds, freedom of choice of spouses is the norm, although sibling exchange marriages are preferred. Postmarital residence is patrilocal, and a woman's ties to her family are usually overridden by patriarchal authority patterns. Divorce is not allowed.

Domestic Unit.   The nuclear family is the primary residential unit, occupying an apartment in one of the longhouses. It is not, however, the primary economic unit nor the primary arena for socialization. Patriarchal authority is the norm and the in-marrying wives are greatly influenced both by their husbands and their mothers-in-law. Large families are strongly encouraged.

Inheritance.   As there is no ownership of personal property, there is no inheritance.

Socialization.   Children are seen as gifts of God who belong to the colony and ultimately to the church. Thus, much of child rearing and socialization occurs in the colony context. Hutterite values and ways are taught and reinforced informally through participation in colony activities and formally through school attendance. Kindergarten children (ages three to five) attend *Klein-Schul* and schoolchildren (ages six to fifteen) attend German school (*Gross-Schul*), English school, and Sunday school. Except for English school, the emphasis in school is on inculcating Hutterite values and ways of life. English school is taught by a non-Hutterite, though various restrictions are placed on the curriculum and teaching methods so as not to contradict Hutterite teachings.

Sociopolitical Organization

Social Organization.   The basic social unit is the colony. Colonies are communal organizations where equality and the meeting of group rather than individual needs are core values. Sex and age are important determinants of authority patterns, with these patterns evident in the social organization of virtually all colony activities. Community integration is achieved through communal song, prayer, and worship as well as through the cooperative nature of economic activities.

Political Organization.   There is no overarching political structure governing all Hutterites, though each of the three Leut has an elected head elder. Within each colony, there is a clear authority structure: (1) the colony; (2) the *Gemein* (church) composed of all baptized adults; (3) the council of five to seven men which serves as the colony's executive board; (4) the informal council of some council members which makes day-to-day decisions; (5) the head preacher ("elder") who serves as the contact with the outside world; and the *Diener der Notdurft* (steward or boss) who is the economic manager of the colony.

Social Control and Conflict.   Hutterite socialization is designed to produce responsible, submissive, hardworking adults who can live cooperatively in the communal colonies. Social control is maintained through the daily reinforcement of these behaviors and adherence to the well-defined rules governing authority and decision making. Misconduct is handled through a progression of sanctions, from individual reproach to a hearing before the council to excommunication followed by reinstatement. Shedding the blood of another and deserting the colony are the worst crimes, neither of which can be forgiven. No murder has ever occurred among the Hutterites. Alcohol abuse has been a minor social problem since the 1600s.

Religion and Expressive Culture

Religious Beliefs.   Hutterite religious beliefs are the major force shaping their values and behavior. Hutterite religion follows Christianity, with some significant differences in belief and practice. The major difference is the Hutterite belief that humans can be "saved" or "returned to God" only through communal living in a Christian community. The universe is seen as composed of a heaven (*Himmel*) and a lower part composed of earth (*Erde*) and hell (*Ort des Gefangniss*). God is seen as omnipotent.

Religious Practitioners.   The head preacher of each colony is responsible for all aspects of colony life. He is supervised by his colony church and other colony head preachers in his Leut. Head preachers are always men and only baptized men may vote on colony issues and select leaders. The head preacher is assisted by an assistant preacher.

Ceremonies.   The evening church service is an integral part of Hutterite life. Services are led by the head preacher and involve the singing of hymns, a sermon, and prayer. Sunday services are somewhat more involved and elaborate, and in many colonies Sunday is a day of rest and no or little work is performed. The major annual spiritual event is Holy Communion, taken by all baptized men and women on the day after Easter. Church attendance generally requires the wearing of special church clothes. Baptism at about age nineteen for women and from ages twenty to twenty-six for men is the most important rite of passage for Hutterites. It signifies adult status, is a prerequisite for marriage, and often creates closer bonds between the now-adult children and their parents.

Arts. Traditional crafts such as pottery making and decorative sewing have now largely disappeared, though clothing style is an important indicator of Leut identity. Sports and dancing are virtually absent, and individual hobbies tend toward productive activities such as electrical wiring. Singing is the central expressive activity. Hutterites sing in church, at school, at home, and during group activities. There is a rich and varied repertoire of songs and hymns.

Medicine. Medical care is largely free of religious content and physicians are routinely used. Hutterite chiropractors are used by both colony members and outsiders. The Hutterites have been the object of intense study by mental health researchers and display an unusually high incidence of affective psychoses and low incidence of schizophrenia when compared to other groups and the U.S. population in general. The Hutterites also display a culture-specific disorder called *Anfechtung*, characterized by a feeling of having sinned. Treatment is through talk with the preacher, prayer, and confession, usually producing a cure.

Death and Afterlife. Death is seen as the step leading to paradise for those who have lived a faithful life. Burial usually follows three days after the death and is preceded by a wake and an in-gathering of colony members and baptized members of other colonies. The communal life provides emotional support for the family of the deceased.

Bibliography

Bennett, John A. (1967). *Hutterian Brethren: The Agricultural Economy and Social Organization of a Communal People.* Stanford: Stanford University Press.

Hostetler, John A. (1974). *Hutterite Society.* Baltimore: Johns Hopkins University Press.

Hostetler, John A., and Gertrude Huntington (1970). *The Hutterites in North America.* New York: Holt, Rinehart & Winston.

Martens, Helen (1968). "Hutterite Songs: The Origins and Aural Transmission of Their Melodies from the Sixteenth Century." Ph.D. diss., Columbia University.

JOHN A. HOSTETLER

Iglulik Inuit

ETHNONYMS: Aivilingmiut, Iglulingmiut, Tununirmiut

The term "Iglulik" refers to the Iglulingmiut, Aivilingmiut, and Tununirmiut, Inuit-Inupiaq-speaking peoples located north of Hudson Bay in the Canadian Northwest Territories. Formerly, the Iglulik ranged over a wide territory that included parts of northern Baffin Island, Melville Peninsula, and northern Southampton Island. In the 1820s they numbered between four hundred and six hundred, approximately the same as in the 1980s.

The Iglulik were in contact with Whites in the 1820s, but it was not until regular visits by whaling crews during the second half of the nineteenth century that contact had a significant impact on their way of life. After 1920 acculturation was accelerated with the establishment of Hudson's Bay Company trading posts and Anglican and Catholic mission stations, and the presence of the Royal Canadian Mounted Police. Since the 1960s the number of Iglulik who depend on hunting and gathering for their livelihood has been diminishing rapidly as adults find employment in the mining and oil industries.

Traditionally, the Iglulik engaged in a seasonal pattern of subsistence activities and movement involving whale, seal, and walrus hunting in the summer, caribou hunting and salmon and trout fishing in the autumn, seal hunting on the sea ice in the winter, and seal and walrus hunting in the spring. Kayaks and umiaks were employed in the summer hunting of marine animals, and caribou were stalked and killed with bows and arrows or driven into the water and speared from kayaks. Birds, foxes, wolves, and polar bears were also hunted.

The nuclear family in which the husband was food provider and toolmaker and the wife was cook and clothesmaker was the basic unit of Iglulik society. Formerly, when the Iglulik moved inland in the autumn to hunt caribou and fish, they assembled in small camps of several families each. The camp's leader or leaders were respected and mature men who advised the camp with regard to group movements and subsistence activities.

Shamans cured the sick and practiced divination by calling upon the aid of spirits in trances. In some instances a single man filled the roles of both camp leader and shaman. The notion of the soul was fundamental to the beliefs of the Iglulik, and they held that the world around them was populated by a host of supernatural beings, ghosts, and spirits.

Bibliography

Kleivan, Inge (1985). *Eskimos: Greenland and Canada.* Leiden: E. J. Brill.

Mathiassen, Therkel (1928). *Material Culture of the Iglulik Eskimos.* Report of the Fifth Thule Expedition, 1921–24. Vol. 6, Pt. 1. Copenhagen, Denmark.

Rasmussen, Knud (1929). *Intellectual Culture of the Iglulik Eskimos.* Report of the Fifth Thule Expedition, 1921–24. Vol. 7, Pt. 1. Copenhagen, Denmark.

Illinois

The Illinois, including the Cahokia, Kaskaskia, Michigamea, Peoria, and Tamaroa, with the related Mascouten, lived principally along the Illinois and Mississippi rivers in the states of Illinois, Iowa, and Missouri. The remnants of the Illinois, together with the Wea and Piankashaw, now live on or near the former Peoria Indian Reservation in northeastern Oklahoma, and are largely assimilated with the European-American population.
See Miami

Bibliography

Callender, Charles (1978). "Illinois." In *Handbook of North American Indians.* Vol. 15, *Northeast,* edited by Bruce G. Trigger, 673–680. Washington, D.C.: Smithsonian Institution.

Goddard, Ives (1978). "Mascouten." In *Handbook of North American Indians.* Vol. 15, *Northeast,* edited by Bruce G. Trigger, 668–672. Washington, D.C.: Smithsonian Institution.

Ingalik

ETHNONYMS: Deg Hit'an, Inkality, Inkiliki, Ingelete, Inkiliki-iugel'nut, Kaiyuhkhotana, Ten'a

Orientation

Identification.   The Ingalik are an American Indian group in Alaska. The term "Inkiliki" in several variations first appears in the Russian literature of the 1830s and 1840s. The name appears borrowed from Yup'ik Eskimo "Ingqiliq," a general term for Indians of the interior and meaning "having louses' eggs." Ingalik call themselves "Deg Hit'an" (the people from here).

Location.   At the time of Russian contact in the 1830s the Ingalik lived in several villages on the lower Yukon and Innoko rivers, and on the middle Kuskokwim River, in southwestern Alaska. Their territory was bounded by Eskimo groups downriver and in the coastal regions, and other Athapaskans upstream—Koyukon on the Yukon, Kolchan on the Kuskokwim. Major settlements in historic times included the villages of Shageluk on the Innoko, Anvik, Bonasila, and Holy Cross on the lower Yukon, Kvygympaynagmyut and Georgetown on the middle Kuskokwim. The environment was subarctic boreal forest, characterized by short warm summers and long cold winters.

Demography.   In the 1830s, the Ingalik had a population estimated at between fifteen hundred and two thousand. Following the introduction of European diseases, numbers fell to six hundred by 1900. Particularly devastating was the small-pox epidemic of 1838–1839. The present population is over five hundred, although this figure does not take into account significant intermarriage with Eskimo and other groups.

Linguistic Affiliation.   The Ingalik language is one of the Northern Athapaskan languages, a subgroup of the Athapaskan family. There are two dialects, one spoken on the Yukon, the second restricted to the Kuskokwim. The Kuskokwim dialect has largely been replaced by other Athapaskan languages, Eskimo, and English. The Yukon dialect is presently spoken only by the older generation.

History and Cultural Relations

The Athapaskan cultures are likely related to microblade tool horizons, which appeared in Alaska from Asia around 8000 B.C. By 4800 B.C., this culture had expanded over much of Alaska and northwestern Canada, areas subsequently occupied by the Northern Athapaskans. Linguistic and cultural evidence suggests that the Proto-Athapaskan language was that of an interior hunting people, probably centered in the eastern Alaskan, upper Yukon River, and northwestern Canadian cordilleran region. Between 500 B.C. and A.D. 500, Athapaskans expanded into western Alaska and languages began to differentiate. Athapaskan core cultural elements included an emphasis on upland, big-game hunting, a matrilineal descent system, commemorative feasts for the dead, semisubterranean dwellings, and use of snowshoes and toboggans. Fishing was of secondary importance. As the ancestors of the Ingalik moved into riverine areas of southwestern Alaska, they came into contact with Eskimos. Exposure to the cultures of these efficient coastal sea-mammal hunting and fishing specialists led to considerable Eskimoization of the Athapaskan core culture, with the Ingalik adopting a fishing economy and a bilateral kinship system. By 1900, through intermarriage with Eskimo, the Kuskokwim Ingalik had ceased to exist as a cultural entity, and by 1980, Holy Cross village on the Yukon was at least 50 percent Eskimo.

Situated between Athapaskans and Eskimos, the Ingalik traded with both. Following Russian contact, the Ingalik occasionally visited posts such as Nulato on the middle Yukon to trade. Not as warlike as other groups, the Ingalik's traditional enemies were the Koyukon, although there was occasional friction with Eskimo and the Kolchan.

Settlements

The Ingalik established winter villages on major streams, often at the mouth of a tributary. A typical village contained a single large kashim or semisubterranean ceremonial men's house, five to ten smaller semisubterranean winter dwellings, raised pole food caches, and racks for canoes and sleds. Winter dwellings were occupied by more than one family, and a winter village would contain fifty to a hundred or more people. Spring and summer fishing camps, several miles from the winter village, consisted of less substantial A-frame or gabled dwellings built of logs covered by planks or bark.

Economy

Subsistence and Commercial Activities.   The Yukon Ingalik were primarily subsistence fishermen, supplementing this by hunting and trapping caribou, moose, bear, and a variety of other fur-bearing animals. The predictable salmon runs permitted a more sedentary life and larger populations than among Athapaskan groups who relied on big game. The Kuskokwim Ingalik in aboriginal times stressed hunting more than did the Yukon Ingalik. Occupying winter villages from September through April, the Ingalik used nets and traps set in the ice to take a variety of fish. Caribou were hunted using the surround and fences, and fur bearers were trapped and snared for food, clothing, and trade. In April and May, families moved inland to lakes for fishing and, following break-up of the ice, moved to summer fishing camps on the main streams. Here they used a variety of traps, nets, and weirs to take quantities of salmon and whitefish, which they dried for winter use. By the late 1800s, possibly because of hunting pressure and use of the repeating rifle, caribou numbers declined sharply. This forced an increased emphasis upon fishing, particularly on the Kuskokwim. By 1914, the European fish wheel had been introduced into the region and by the 1930s had largely replaced the use of fish traps. In recent years paid employment, including fire-fighting and work at fish canneries, has provided a source of income.

Industrial Arts. Traditional Ingalik crafts included extensive woodworking in the manufacture of containers, sleds, birchbark canoes, snowshoes, dwellings, and weapons. Simple pottery, some twined basketry, stone and bone tools, birchbark containers, tailored skin clothing, snares, nets, and fish traps were common products for use and trade.

Trade. Although the Ingalik traded with other groups, most exchange was with Eskimo. The Yukon Ingalik traded with the Eskimo of Norton Sound, exchanging wooden utensils and furs for beluga and seal oil, sealskins, and Siberian reindeer skins. Tobacco, tea, and metal tools reached the Ingalik via Siberian trade routes. The Kuskokwim Ingalik traded primarily with the Kuskowagamiut Eskimo downstream, exchanging furs and birchbark canoes for seal oil, sealskins, fish, and dentalium shells. During the Russian and early American period, metal tools, firearms, and cloth became increasingly significant as trade items. The availability of European trade goods led to a dependence upon the fur trade to acquire them, with significant changes in subsistence patterns and traditional social relations. The importance of trade tempered traditional hostilities between the Ingalik and their neighbors.

Division of Labor. Ingalik men were the primary providers, responsible for trading, most hunting, fishing, and the construction of dwellings, tools, sleds, and snowshoes. Both sexes cooperated in making birchbark canoes. Women snared small game and tended fish nets near the village, made clothing, prepared food, and manufactured pottery and baskets.

Land Tenure. Individuals and families had the right to occupy and use land within the territory of their village group. Rights to use certain fish-trapping and caribou-hunting sites belonged to families.

Kinship

Kin Groups and Descent. While most Alaskan Athapaskans had matrilineal descent and a tripartite matriclan structure, the Ingalik were bilateral. Formerly matrilineal, they changed through contact and intermarriage with the bilateral Eskimo. Clans were unknown, although the Ingalik "partner" system—a special relationship between two people in separate villages—was a widespread Athapaskan trait and may have been a vestige of the clan system.

Kinship Terminology. Ingalik kinship terms follow the Eskimo system with identical parallel and cross-cousin terms, which are differentiated from those for siblings. Kin terms imply generational differences, and lineal kin are distinguished from collateral. Also present is the Athapaskan distinction between older and younger siblings.

Marriage and Family

Marriage. The aboriginal Ingalik practiced local endogamy and avoided marriage to first cousins. Marriage was monogamous, with occasional polygyny by wealthy men. The levirate and sororate were practiced, the latter rarely. Residence after marriage was initially with the wife's family. The couple then lived with the husband's family until the man could build his own house. Divorce was uncommon, particularly when there were children. A divorced woman returned to her mother's house.

Domestic Unit. The typical winter village house was occupied by two or more nuclear families, usually fifteen to twenty persons. Units in the spring and summer fishing camps were smaller. In the winter villages, groups of men cooperated in caribou hunting and some fishing activities. Contemporary Ingalik live predominantly in single and extended family units.

Inheritance. Songs, dances, and the right to wear certain masks at ceremonies passed from father to son. At death, most property was inherited by the spouse and children, although that of a wealthy person would later be distributed at a potlatch. Some items were burned or placed in the coffin for use by the deceased in the afterlife. The house of a deceased adult was temporarily abandoned and sometimes burned. Rights to family hunting and fishing sites were inherited.

Socialization. Children were weaned after they began to walk. The Ingalik were gentle and tolerant with their offspring, with mild punishments and threats for misbehavior. Children learned various taboos, and older adults taught them moral tales. In aboriginal times, most learning came from imitating adult activities. Today, children attend public schools, and increasing numbers continue their education beyond high school.

Sociopolitical Organization

Social Organization. Status came from the ownership of material objects, especially fish. Furs, a large house, canoes, red ocher, and dentalium shells were also prized. In aboriginal times leadership was situational, with some men excelling in subsistence activities, others in ritual, trade, or warfare. Rich men and shamans were often leaders.

Political Organization. Villages were independent, recognized nearby communities as linguistically and culturally similar, and sometimes intermarried and shared potlatches with them. Russian and American agents introduced the idea of chiefs during the early-contact period. Today, elected leaders and participaion in collective political and economic oranizations have replaced traditional patterns.

Social Control.   Common methods of social control included taboos, ostracism, and fear of revenge or supernatural retaliation. Habitual unacceptable behavior would lead to a meeting of the older men, who decided on an appropriate punishment. A murder or accidental killing usually led to revenge by a male relative and sometimes a blood feud. Shamans were considered powerful and often served as opinion leaders. Joking relationships, kinship, and the partner system also served as social control mechanisms.

Conflict.   Interpersonal aggression arose from disputes, often over the opposite sex. Wrestling, beatings, and verbal insults were the result. When a murder occurred between the Ingalik and other groups, it could lead to warfare. Although travel in another group's territory for trading purposes was permitted, relationships were sometimes tense. Raids were group decisions, often in retaliation for an earlier raid, a dispute over caribou hunting grounds, or some other long-standing animosity. Raids were surprise attacks carried out at night during the fall or early spring. Attackers would blockade house and kashim entrances, and shoot arrows through smoke holes. All men were killed if possible, the village looted, and women and children abducted. Warfare was probably infrequent, mitigated by the importance of trade between groups. During the early-contact period, attacks also took place on Russian trading posts. Beginning in the American period, conflict was conrolled through a system of marshals and courts.

Religion and Expressive Culture

Religious Beliefs.   The Ingalik shared the Northern Athapaskan worldview of a universe in which all objects had a spirit or soul, *yeg*. In the beginning, men, animals, and inanimate objects lived together and shared many traits. They later separated and lost the ability to communicate. People were dependent on animals for food and thus had to remain on good terms with them. This they did by observing taboos and treating animals with respect so they would continue to be available for food. Increase ceremonies were performed to attract game and ensure a steady supply. The Ingalik also used a variety of "songs" or magical chants to maintain the balance between the human and spiritual worlds. These songs could be purchased, and both sexes had them. Songs were used to gain good hunting and fishing luck, enhance skills, cure illness and communicate with the spirits. Through possession of songs, nearly everyone had a little shamanistic power. Amulets, often bits of animal skin, bone, or feathers, were worn by all and were often associated with animal songs. Amulets brought specific kinds of luck or conferred special abilities. There were numerous taboos and prohibitions, many of which related to animals. The Ingalik had a rich mythology in which animals and the ritual number 4 were prominent.

Russian Orthodox priests arrived among the Ingalik in 1845 and baptized 437 Indians in two years, though understanding of Christianity remained superficial. By 1887–1888, Episcopal and Roman Catholic missionaries had appeared on the lower Yukon, mission schools had been established, and the Orthodox faith largely replaced. Today, the Ingalik are nominal Christians, with the last mission school closing in 1957. The Ingalik world was created by Denato, an otiose father figure. Many spirits and beings inhabited the Ingalik world, the most dangerous being Giyeg, the spirit of death.

Helpers of the Giyeg included the Nakani, a malevolent forest spirit common among Northern Athapaskans. Particularly important were the various animal and salmon people.

Religious Practitioners.   All Ingalik, through ceremonies and ownership of songs and amulets, participated to some degree in the supernatural world. Shamans were the primary practitioners, and they sometimes became powerful and wealthy individuals with many followers. Shamans derived their power from dreams, often of animals, and had animal spirit helpers. Shamans were of either sex and owned particularly powerful songs. Shamanistic power could be used for either good or evil, to kill people or to cure illness, to attract fish and game, and ensure success in warfare. Russian and American priests viewed shamanism as pagan and worked to eradicate it. By the 1930s, it was no longer a significant feature in Ingalik culture.

Ceremonies.   The Ingalik ceremonial cycle consisted of seven major observances, the majority concerned with ensuring a plentiful food supply. In the fall, a shaman conducted a brief Doll ceremony, using dolls to predict the game supply. A Bladder ceremony was performed at any time during the winter, offering animal bladders food to increase game. The peak of the ceremonial calendar came at midwinter, with the Potlatch for the Dead. This festival honored a deceased relative of the giver through a four-night ceremony of gifts of food and clothing to guests. Often preceding or following the Potlatch for the Dead was the Animal's ceremony. Given by one village and attended by others, this was a series of symbolic and imitative dances and singing intended to enhance the game supply. The Hot Dance was an evening of dancing and sexual license often occurring on the fourth night of the Potlatch for the Dead. In spring, the Mask Dance was given for guests from another village, with feasting and giving of gifts. The Partner's Potlatch could be given at any time of year to bring prestige to a village. These were reciprocal with nearby villages and involved the exchange of food and gifts between "partners" from the two communities. Several lesser rituals were given to please important spirits, and there were a variety of "putting down" ceremonies involving presentation of food or gifts to mark rites of passage. Neither the Doll ceremony nor the Bladder ceremony has been performed since the late 1800s. Others survive only in simplified form or have merged with Christian observances.

Arts.   Working primarily in spruce wood, the Ingalik produced a variety of masks, bowls, and ceremonial objects. Clothing was decorated with strips of fur and caribou skin. Porcupine quills, feathers, and dentalium shells were also used for ornamentation. Wooden objects often had painted designs in red or black, and skins were sometimes dyed. Pottery was incised with lines and dots. Ingalik women were traditionally tattooed with short, straight lines on their chins or hands, and the men wore carved labrets or lip plugs. Dancing and singing to the accompaniment of tambourine drums and wooden clapper sticks was characteristic of most ceremonies.

Medicine.   The Ingalik believed people became ill and died because the Giyeg and his helpers trapped them. Minor afflictions were treated with a variety of herbal and animal remedies, but the more serious soul-loss caused by the Giyeg required shamanistic therapy. A shaman would use his spirit helpers, songs, sucking, and blowing to recover the soul and effect a cure.

Death and Afterlife. The Ingalik believed all deaths ultimately resulted from the loss of the spirit, or *yeg*. In aboriginal times warfare, periodic famine, accidents and suicide were more proximate causes. Following death, the body was placed in a sitting position in the kashim. After four days of symbolic feeding, singing, and dancing, the deceased was traditionally given a coffin burial. Cremation and exposure were also practiced. At death, a person's spirit traveled to the underworld, a journey of four days. There, the deceased joined other spirits who lived in villages. A person's property was disposed of by burning, inhumation, giving it away, or inheritance. Close relatives observed a period of mourning and observance of taboos. Together with the increase ceremonies, death and its commemoration was a principal feature of the Ingalik ceremonial round.

Bibliography

Hosley, Edward H. (1981). "Environment and Culture in the Alaska Plateau." In *Handbook of North American Indians.* Vol. 6, *Subarctic,* edited by June Helm, 533–545. Washington, D.C.: Smithsonian Institution.

Hosley, Edward H. (1981). "Intercultural Relations and Cultural Change in the Alaska Plateau." In *Handbook of North American Indians.* Vol. 6, *Subarctic,* edited by June Helm, 546–555. Washington, D.C.: Smithsonian Institution.

Osgood, Cornelius (1940). *Ingalik Material Culture.* Yale University Publications in Anthropology, no. 22. New Haven, Conn.: Department of Anthropology, Yale University.

Osgood, Cornelius (1958). *Ingalik Social Culture.* Yale University Publications in Anthropology, no. 53. New Haven, Conn.: Department of Anthropology, Yale University.

Osgood, Cornelius (1959). *Ingalik Mental Culture.* Yale University Publications in Anthropology, no. 56. New Haven, Conn.: Department of Anthropology, Yale University.

Snow, Jeanne H. (1981). "Ingalik." In *Handbook of North American Indians.* Vol. 6, *Subarctic,* edited by June Helm, 602–617. Washington, D.C.: Smithsonian Institution.

EDWARD H. HOSLEY

Inughuit

ETHNONYMS: Arctic Highlanders, Avanersuarmiut, Cape York Inuit, Itanere, Kap Yorkere, Polar Eskimo, Polareskimoer, Polargroenlaendere, Smith Sound Inuit, Thuleeskimoer, Thulegroenlaendere, Whale Sound Inuit

Orientation

Identification. The Inughuit are a Greenland minority constituting about 1 percent of the general population. They speak a unique Inuit dialect and exist as a distinct subculture. Very much aware of their unique identity, they are proud people and strongly believe that survival in their harsh environment depends on the use of Inughuit ways and experience. The Inughuit feel uncomfortable outside their native communities and territory and choose not to live elsewhere in Greenland or Denmark. Over the decades, the Inughuit have been renamed a number of times by White visitors. "Polar Eskimo," the most common name, was given by Knud Rasmussen in 1903. The Inughuit call themselves "the great and real human beings," and until White contact in 1818, they believed that they were the only humans in the world. "Thule Inuit" is a misnomer, as it refers to the prehistoric culture antecedent to all current Inuit groups.

Location. The Inughuit live in the high Arctic on the west coast of North Greenland between 75° to 80° N and 58° to 74° W. Once called the "Thule District," the region is officially labeled Avanersuup Kommunia. There are four sunlight seasons: dark (twenty-four hours of darkness) from mid-October to mid-February; daylight (twenty-four hours of sunlight) from mid-April to mid-August; and two day/night seasons in between. There are also four climate seasons: summer (no sea ice) from mid-July to mid-September; fall (unsafe sea ice) from mid-September to mid-October; winter (total sea ice) from mid-October to mid-May (with dark and light periods); and spring from mid-May to mid-July. The average temperature is −31° F in winter and +41° F in summer.

Demography. Estimates place the pre-1880 population at 100–200 people, the 1880–1930 population at about 250, and the 1980 population at 700. The sex ratio, once favoring males 60 percent to 40 percent, has been balanced for the past sixty years.

Linguistic Affiliation. The Inughuit speak their own dialect of the Inuit language, with "s" replaced by "h."

History and Cultural Relations

The Inughuit are descendants of the Thule culture people who migrated from Canada to Greenland about A.D. 900. In the mid-1880s several polar expeditions visited Inughuit territory in search of Sir John Franklin, who was missing in his attempt to find the Northwest Passage. In the 1860s a small band of Canadian Eskimo settled in Inughuit territory and taught the Inughuit to build kayaks, to hunt from kayaks, to fish with leisters, and to hunt caribou with bows and arrows. Prior to that time caribou were believed to be poison and were not eaten. With the kayak, food shortages became less of a threat to survival with only one crisis period in late winter before the sun returned. From 1891 to 1909 Robert Peary spent much time among the Inughuit during his quests to reach the North Pole, which he claimed to reach in 1909 accompanied by Matthew Henson and four Inughuit, Odaq, Iggianguaq, Sigdluk, and Ukujaq. Frederick Cook also may have reached the North Pole in April 1908 with two Inughuit, Apilaq and Itukusuk. Among changes brought by Peary were rifles and ammunition for hunting, iron sewing needles and other Western tools, coffee, tea, sugar, and other processed foods.

Following his 1903–1904 visit, Knud Rasmussen became

the protector of the Inughuit, introducing Christianity and establishing a Lutheran mission in 1909. Baptisms for adults were actively conducted from 1912 to 1934. To ensure the regular flow of European goods, Rasmussen had a store built at Uummannaq in 1910 with Peter Freuchen serving as the first storekeeper until 1920. In 1927 Rasmussen established the Hunter's Council with the non-Inughuit storekeeper, minister, and physician and three of the best Inughuit hunters as members. The council established the Thule Law in 1929 which regulated hunting, settled conflicts, and provided assistance to the poor. The Thule Law lasted until 1963 when the West Greenland municipal system became the central authority.

In 1930 Uummannaq housed a government center, a new store, a church, a hospital, a school, and homes for the minister and physician. In 1937 Inughuit territory was incorporated into the Danish Greenland colony, with the Inughuit, like other Greenlanders, becoming Danish citizens in 1953. Between 1951 and 1955 the United States built Thule Air Base near Uummannaq. Pollution from the base made hunting poor and the village population had to move to Qaanaaq in 1953. In 1968 a B-52 bomber with four atomic bombs crashed, leaving ground radiation that restricted hunting in the area. In May 1979 the Inughuit along with other Greenlanders were given home rule, with only defense and foreign relations matters resting with Denmark. In the 1980s the Inughuit joined other members of the Inuit Circumpolar Conference to fight against the Canadian Arctic Pilot Project (APP), fearing that their hunting grounds would be destroyed by year-round oil-tanker traffic. The APP was eventually discontinued.

Settlements

Villages are on the coast facing the sea. Up until the early 1900s, many families moved from one settlement to another each winter. Settlements included as many as five families of relatives and friends, with anyone free to settle where they wanted and to use whatever dwellings already existed. Summer settlements were smaller and occupied only for hunting purposes. Today, with the presence of stores and access to wood for house construction, the Inughuit are relatively permanently settled in six communities—Qaanaaq (the capital), Siorapaluk, Qeqertarsuaq, Qeqertaq, Moriusaq, and Sivissivik. Another one hundred or so formerly used settlements lie abandoned. The traditional dwelling was a bulb-shaped stone house built into a slope with an entranceway measuring approximately ten feet by sixteen-and-a-half feet facing the sea. A small roof hole allowed ventilation, while the long low entranceway kept warm air trapped inside. The temperature ranged from 32° F at floor level to near 80° F near the ceiling of the single room, heated by a soapstone lamp. The dwelling housed a single family of from five to ten individuals. Sealskin tents were used in the summer because of drips into the stone house and because the tents were easy to move from one settlement to another. On hunts in winter, the men built snow houses. Beginning in the 1950s the stone houses were first replaced by wooden houses covered with sod and turf and then by all-wood houses raised on poles to avoid permafrost problems. The stone houses had belonged to the user; the wood houses now belong to the person who buys the wood.

Economy

Subsistence and Commercial Activities. The Inughuit are still hunters, although some work for the government or in stores, the hospital, the school, and so on. Unlike West Greenlanders who rely on fishing, the Inughuit hunt seal and walrus, which are available all year. Contrary to popular belief, they do not kill baby seals. Migrating beluga and narwhals are also hunted in the winter sun season and the skin eaten raw as a source of vitamin C. Migrating birds, and especially the plentiful small auks, are also hunted. An Inughuit delicacy, *kivioq*, is made by stuffing small auks in a sealskin with blubber and left to sit for six months. When the skin is cut open, the feathers are removed and the tender auk meat is eaten; it tastes much like mature cheese. Other game include arctic fox, polar bear (now under a government quota), hare, ptarmigans, reindeer, and musk-ox. The dog is of vital importance as the power for the sleds used in hunting. A dog team consists of eight to ten male and female dogs hitched to the sled in a fan shape with each dog on its own harness line. The Inughuit hunters are among the best dog sledders in the world. Kayaks and motor boats are both used for hunting today.

Division of Labor. Men hunt and women treat skins, sew clothing, and care for the household. As both men's and women's work is necessary for survival, the sexes are accorded equal status.

Land Tenure. No individual or group owns land or hunting grounds. All are free to hunt or build a dwelling where they want.

Kinship

The Inughuit have the traditional bilateral Inuit kinship system and terminology. There are no clans or exogamous groups. Traditionally, cousin marriage was not allowed, although cousin marriages have occurred since the 1940s with the doubling of the population.

Marriage and Family

Marriage. There was no formal wedding ceremony. Couples simply informed their neighbors that they were married, although it was usual to ask for the parents' consent. Couples who acted as if they were married were treated as such. A skilled person was preferred as a marriage partner, although romantic love was a consideration as well. Monogamy was the rule, with the few polygynous marriages lasting only a few years. Numerous deaths owing to accidents and illness meant that many men and women married more than once. A girl who had already shown her ability to have children was a desirable partner. Newlyweds would first settle with the parental family that had room and then establish their own home. Divorce was not common, and trial marriages were used to encourage marital stability. Childlessness was reason for divorce.

Domestic Unit. Small extended families were common. A young couple would follow their parents, and the parents, when old, would follow their children; thus, it was important to have children. Boys, seen as future providers, were preferred, although female infanticide for that reason alone was not practiced. Infanticide, once used in times of starvation, has now been abandoned with the availability of food in stores.

Inheritance. In traditional times, the few personal possessions of the deceased were placed on the grave. Danish law is now followed.

Socialization. Children learned the requisite skills by imitating their parents or other relatives of the same sex. Children were treated as adults with parents either suggesting a better way to do something or allowing the children to learn from their mistakes. Because Inughuit are now Danish citizens, school is mandatory and is taught in either West Greenlandic or Danish.

Sociopolitical Organization

Social Organization. The family was the basic social unit, with no tribal structure or leadership. Especially skilled hunters might have a say in matters, but no one was obligated to follow their suggestions. Although they lived over a broad area, frequent traveling made for frequent contact and all Inughuit were well informed about happenings in the society.

Political Organization. The Inughuit are Danish citizens and governed by Danish law.

Social Control and Conflict. Public opinion and ridicule were used both to prevent and to end conflicts. Problems were often settled by outside parties in order to avoid escalation into an open conflict. Only rarely would hunters join together to kill a troublesome person who tyrannized people. Neighbors would intervene in family fights only if it seemed a matter of life or death.

Religion and Expressive Culture

Religious Beliefs. The Inughuit, like other Inuit groups, believed in the Mother of the Sea (_Nerrivik_) and the Moon Man. She controlled the sea mammals and he made sure that taboos were followed. If someone violated a taboo, the Moon Man would appear in a dream or in the guise of a polar bear to remind the wrongdoer. The central belief in pre-Christian Inughuit religion was that everything in nature was alive and had a soul (_inua_). Incorrect human behavior could offend the souls and lead to calamities such as a poor hunt or starvation. Protection from such disasters was provided by wearing amulets or reciting spells in the proper tone, although spells could lose their power if used too often. Amulets and spells were also used to bring good luck. The Inughuit believed that humans had three parts—the immortal soul, the name, and the body. In 1903, Majaq, the hunter, told Rasmussen (1908): "The human soul is what makes you beautiful, what makes you into a human being. The soul alone makes you will, act, be enterprising. It is the soul that gives you drive in your life. Therefore, the body must collapse when the soul leaves it." An individual's personal name had its own force and was tabooed after the person died in order to save its power until it could be given to a newborn of the same sex. The qualities of the deceased name's owner were believed to follow the name to the next bearer. Thus, infants were often named for deceased friends and relatives of their parents. Those who shared the name of someone who died had to change the name until it was put into use again.

Religious Practitioners. Any member of the society could be a shaman (_angakkoq_), although the spirits would not work through just anyone. Special qualities were needed, and the best hunters were often shamans, with their power measured by the number and power of the helping spirits they controlled.

Medicine. Traditionally, some illnesses were attributed to a loss of the human soul, with recovery contingent on the shaman traveling to the spirit world and bringing back the lost soul. Other maladies such as broken bones and cuts were treated by experienced adults. Persons with serious handicaps had much difficulty surviving. Since 1928, however, a physician has served Inughuit communities.

Death and Afterlife. After a death, the settlement was tabooed for five days, with no activities save food preparation permitted. The Inughuit did not fear death, for it was seen as a stage between life in this world and life in the next. The next world was much like this one, except that it was free of illnesses, unsuccessful hunts, and other problems. There were two pleasant afterworlds, one in the sea and one in the sky. The notion of hell was introduced by the Christian missionaries. As all evil was thought to stay in the corpse, anyone who touched it was restricted from some activities for a year. The task of removing the body usually fell to a relative who carried it through a hole or side window so that the soul would not be able to find its way back. The corpse was then covered by stones and personal objects set on the grave. Grave robbing was forbidden, although objects could be substituted for valuable hunting tools so they could be used. The soul of the deceased remained near the grave to make sure all rules were followed and to frighten any violators.

Bibliography

Gilberg, Rolf (1976). _The Polar Eskimo Population, Thule District, North Greenland. Appendix: Polar Eskimo Bibliography._ Meddelelser om Grønland, 203(3):1–87. Copenhagen, Denmark.

Gilberg, Rolf (1984). "Polar Eskimo." In _Handbook of North American Indians._ Vol. 5, _Arctic,_ edited by David Damas, 577–594. Washington, D.C.: Smithsonian Institution.

Herbert, Wally (1981). _Hunters of the Polar North: The Eskimos._ Time-Life Books: Peoples of the Wild. Amsterdam: Elsevier.

Holtved, Erik (1967). _Contributions to Polar Eskimo Ethnography._ Meddelelser om Grønland, 182(2):1–180. Copenhagen, Denmark.

Rasmussen, Knud (1908). _People of the Polar North: A Record,_ edited by G. Herring. London: K. Paul, Trench, Trübner.

ROLF GILBERG

Inuit

See Eskimo

Iowa

The Iowa (Pahodja) lived throughout much of the present state of Iowa and in adjoining parts of Minnesota and Missouri and were culturally related to the neighboring Oto and Missouri. They now live principally on the Iowa Indian Reservation (which straddles the Kansas-Nebraska state boundary along the Missouri River) and in a federal trust area in central Oklahoma. They speak a Chiwere Siouan language and numbered about one thousand in the mid-1980s.

Bibliography

Gussow, Zachary (1974). *Sac, Fox, and Iowa Indians. Vol. I.* New York: Garland Publishing.

Skinner, Alanson (1926). "Ethnology of the Ioway Indians." *Bulletin of the Public Museum of the City of Milwaukee* 5:181–354.

Irish Travelers

ETHNONYMS: Irish Gypsies, Travelers

Orientation

Identification.   Irish Travelers are a small, itinerant ethnic group in the United States. Distinct from present-day Irish Travellers in the Republic of Ireland, Irish Travelers in the United States earn their living as itinerant workers, spray painting, asphalting, or laying linoleum. Irish Travelers are identified by non-Travelers as Gypsies because of their itinerant life-styles, but Travelers consider the term a derogatory one. Nevertheless, Irish Travelers will often introduce themselves to non-Travelers as Irish Gypsies because of the continuing use of the label by non-Travelers.

Location.   Irish Travelers divide themselves into three groups based on historical residence: Georgia Travelers, Mississippi Travelers, and Texas Travelers. There is also a group called Ohio Travelers that migrated to the Midwest in the late 1800s while other Irish Travelers moved south. Contact between the Ohio Travelers and the Travelers in the southern United States is minimal.

Demography.   Population figures on Irish Travelers in the United States are unavailable. The U.S. Census does not recognize Irish Travelers as a unique ethnic group. The amount of itinerancy and the level of secrecy of the group make enumeration very difficult. According to my research and Irish Travelers' estimates, the Georgia Travelers' camp is made up of about eight hundred families, the Mississippi Travelers, about three hundred families, and the Texas Travelers, under fifty families. The birthrate among Irish Travelers is surprisingly low for a very strict Roman Catholic group, with an average of two to three children per family.

Linguistic Affiliation.   Irish Travelers in the United States speak English and an argot they call Cant. Cant is a combination of Shelta, derived from Irish Gaelic, Romanes (the language of Romany Gypsies), and English. Travelers use their Cant among themselves in the presence of non-Travelers. Irish Travellers residing in Ireland also speak a similar Cant, but in the United States the Cant, over generations, has developed into more of a pidgin English. Younger Travelers are not as fluent as previous generations and often know only a few phrases or words.

History and Cultural Relations

According to oral history, Irish Travelers believe that eight families emigrated separately from Ireland or England to the United States in the mid-1800s. Traveler families spread throughout the urban areas of the Northeast, practicing itinerant occupations such as tinsmithing and peddling various goods, but gradually entered the mule trading business. Many Irish itinerants in Ireland were horse and mule traders, so the occupation was not new to those in the United States. Irish Travelers increased their numbers by marrying other Irish itinerants in the mule business, and more rarely, Romany Gypsies they encountered in their travels. Before the Civil War, Irish Travelers began trading in the southern states because of heavy use of horse and mule power on southern farms. Irish Travelers would spend winters in the South, trading horses and mules, and return to the North for the warmer months. As the need for horse and mule power decreased in the North but continued in the South, Irish Travelers began to set up their home bases in Nashville, Tennessee, and later Atlanta, Georgia, where the Irish Travelers began using the label "Georgia Travelers." Once in Georgia, Irish Travelers began to migrate to other areas of the South. A group of families moved to Mississippi for economic reasons and were then called "Mississippi Travelers." The two groups, Georgia Travelers and Mississippi Travelers, consisted of families who worked different stock centers. Communication and interaction between the two groups was and is still constant. A third group, Texas Travelers, has since emerged and is composed of both Georgia Traveler and Mississippi Traveler families who became interested in asphalting. Moving to Texas allowed them to conduct business in the growing urban areas affected by the oil boom of the 1970s.

Settlements

Prior to the 1930s, Irish Travelers moved throughout the Northeast and South in horse-drawn barrel-shaped wagons like those used by Irish Tinkers in Ireland. With the increased use of automobiles by the general population, Irish Travelers began using trucks after 1927 and camping in large tents with wooden floors. Gradually tents were replaced with small trailers, and since the 1960s, Irish Travelers have purchased large mobile homes. The size of the mobile homes has made it difficult to pull the homes on a regular basis, leading Irish Travelers to set up what they call camps or villages. Some of the more affluent Georgia Travelers have been building large homes worth over $200,000 in their villages, but this is unique to the Georgia Travelers and cause of much suspicion by non-Travelers concerning the source of the money. Mississippi, Georgia, and Texas Travelers have their own villages in the South, although they remain itinerant in terms of occupation. Families will travel throughout the year for work and return periodically to their villages.

Economy

Subsistence and Commercial Activities. Irish Travelers began their itinerant occupations in the mid-1800s, tinsmithing or trading horses and mules. By the mid-1920s, some Irish Travelers began peddling linoleum and spray painting, while others continued to work with livestock. During World War II, a number of Irish Traveler families who owned stables provided the U.S. government with mules for the war. Most Irish Travelers were spray painting and peddling linoleum by the 1960s and continue the occupations today. Many elderly Travelers receive Social Security benefits and also financial support from family members. Travelers are very proud of the fact that they do not take part in the welfare system in the United States.

Division of Labor. Irish Traveler women are not expected to work outside the home. Throughout their history in the United States, the women have peddled various items such as Irish lace and handbags. Only recently have younger, unmarried women entered the labor force with non-Travelers. Owing to their low educational level, lack of skills, and the suspicions held by non-Travelers, Irish Traveler women must often take factory jobs, but are expected by the Traveler community to quit their jobs once they are married. Traveler women are responsible for all aspects of the home and the children, including managing the money earned by their husbands. Most transactions are in cash, from paying for dinner to purchasing a new truck. Trading and bartering are still used by Travelers in business dealings. Irish Traveler men are expected to work until their health becomes a problem. Elderly women are not expected to peddle goods, but are responsible for helping raise the grandchildren. Many elderly women remain in the villages throughout the year and do not travel with their married children as was the practice in the past.

Kinship

Irish Traveler descent and inheritance is bilateral, although the children, as is the general custom in the United States, take the father's last name. Travelers recognize each other as close relatives compared to outsiders. Kinship responsibilities within the group, however, are usually limited to immediate family members and first and second cousins. Working partnerships for Irish Traveler men are varied and may include fathers and sons, brothers, or fathers-in-law and sons-in-law. Cousins become partners only when a more immediate family relation is absent. Beause of the residential pattern of each group of Irish Travelers, whenever a party or ceremony involving a Traveler occurs, the entire village is invited.

Marriage and Family

Marriage. Irish Travelers are endogamous. There are more females than males within the Traveler communities, so competition for marriage partners is strong. Marriages are still arranged by the mothers, sometimes at birth, although these early agreements are often broken. The young couple may have a say in finalizing the match, and rarely do the mothers arrange a marriage without prior approval from the couple. Traveler men are usually over twenty-one years of age when they marry, but their brides may be as young as twelve with the average being between fifteen and eighteen. An exchange of money, up to $200,000 in cash for the young man, is not uncommon among the more affluent Traveler families. Among the less affluent Georgia Travelers, the number of women marrying outside the group has been steadily increasing. Without a large dowry to offer a boy's family, these girls must choose between the possibility of remaining unmarried for life or marrying outside the group. Mississippi, Georgia, and Texas Travelers do marry across groups, but the growing population of each group contributes to a reduction in the exchange. Marriage between second cousins is allowed by Irish Travelers and is within the law of most southern states. Local officials have adapted to the cultural practices of the Irish Travelers by waiving the requirement for a court order from juvenile court for a marriage involving someone under fifteen. Weddings are usually held after Christmas because of the likelihood of a large number of Travelers being in the villages for the holidays. The holidays provide the Travelers with a chance to arrange marriages and then to organize the ceremony before the families return to the road.

Domestic Unit. Residential units are usually composed of nuclear family members. Grandparents, even when widowed, may maintain their own residence unless disabled. The grandparent whose health is poor will live with a daughter and her family. The unmarried children continue to live with their parents until marrying.

Socialization. Traveler children from age five are socialized to their future roles in the community. The young girls learn to take care of younger siblings or cousins, clean the home, and manage money. The young boys begin helping their fathers in their occupations at an early age, often traveling with the older men for long periods of time.

Sociopolitical Organization

Social and Political Organization. Irish Travelers in the United States are not politically active on their own behalf. Although they have been victims of discrimination and prejudice since their early itinerant days, Irish Travelers react to outsiders by withdrawing into the group and reinforcing the boundary rules. For example, Irish Travelers now enroll their children in school for a longer period of time than earlier generations did, but because of their increased contact with non-Travelers, Travelers are marrying each other at younger ages.

Social Control.   Irish Travelers have very strict boundary rules against outsiders. Close social contacts with non-Travelers are prohibited unless the non-Traveler is a religious person such as a priest or nun. If a Traveler is even suspected of befriending a non-Traveler for any reason other than business, the Traveler and the family may be ostracized by the entire village for a short or even permanent period. The chance of being ostracized has proven to be a very successful method of social control. The prejudice and discrimination Travelers feel from non-Travelers only reinforce the need for acceptance by fellow Travelers.

Religion and Expressive Culture

Religious Beliefs and Practices.   Irish Travelers are Roman Catholic and continue to raise their children in the Catholic church. But because of the lack of formal instruction, most Travelers have integrated into their observances a number of their own religious practices. Some, such as novenas or praying for several days for a special intention, are older Catholic practices that are not widely encouraged by the church, because of the tendency of the practitioners to show signs of superstition rather than affirm their faith. Traveler women's religiousness is strong, whereas the men participate in the sequence of sacraments but do not regularly attend church. All Travelers are baptized as infants, receive first communion around eight years of age, and are confirmed between thirteen and eighteen. The women continue to attend mass, receive communion, and often go to confession throughout their lives. Most men attend mass only on holidays and for special events. The older Traveler women attend mass daily for "extra graces" or special intentions. There are four major concerns for which Travelers, especially women, pray, in order of importance: that their daughters marry; that their daughters, once married, become pregnant; that their husbands or sons quit drinking; and that any health problems in the family are overcome. Because of the amount of time Traveler men are on the road and the fatalities that have occurred from automobile accidents, Traveler women worry about the level of social drinking practiced by the men. Pressure from the women has resulted in Irish Traveler men "taking the pledge." They ask a local priest to witness in front of the church altar their taking the pledge or promising to quit drinking for a specific amount of time. This is done inside the church with no other witnesses.

Death and Afterlife.   Irish Travelers believe, as the Roman Catholic church teaches, that there is an afterlife. Travelers do not believe anything that diverges from the mainstream Catholic way of thinking. In the past, Traveler funerals were held once a year to enable as many Travelers as possible to attend. The distance Travelers must travel from their villages to obtain work has made it difficult for some families to attend all the activities held by other Travelers. Because of the difficulty in including all Travelers in the funeral plans and the increase in funeral costs, funerals are now being held within six months of the person's death. Irish Travelers continue to bury their dead in cemeteries used by their ancestors, although recently, Travelers have begun to bury their relatives in local cemeteries.

Bibliography

Andereck, Mary E. (1988). "Irish Travelers in a Catholic Elementary School." Ph.D. diss., Texas A&M University, College Station.

Harper, Jared V. (1969). "Irish Traveler Cant: An Historical, Structural, and Sociolinguistic Study of an Argot." M.A. thesis, University of Georgia, Athens.

Harper, Jared V. (1971). "'Gypsy' Research in the South." In *The Not So Solid South*, edited by J. Kenneth Morland, 16–24. Athens, Ga.: Southern Anthropological Society.

Harper, Jared V. (1977). "The Irish Travelers of Georgia." Ph.D. diss., University of Georgia, Athens.

MARY E. ANDERECK

Iroquois

ETHNONYMS: Five Nations, League of the Iroquois, Six Nations

Orientation

Identification.   The League of the Iroquois was originally a confederacy of five North American Indian tribes: the Mohawk, Oneida, Onondaga, Cayuga, and Seneca. A sixth tribe, the Tuscarora, joined the League in 1722 after migrating north from the region of the Roanoke River in response to hostilities with White colonists. In the 1980s members of the six Iroquoian tribes lived in Quebec and Ontario, Canada, and New York, Pennsylvania, Wisconsin, and Oklahoma in the United States.

Location.   On the eve of European contact the Iroquois territory extended from Lake Champlain and Lake George west to the Genesee River and Lake Ontario and from the St. Lawrence River south to the Susquehanna River. Within these boundaries each of the original five tribes occupied a north-south oblong strip of territory; from east to west, they were the Mohawk, Oneida, Onondaga, Cayuga, and Seneca. The region was primarily lake and hill country dissected by numerous rivers. Deciduous forests of birch, beech, maple, and elm dominated the region, giving way to fir and spruce forests in the north and in the higher elevations of the Adirondack Mountains. In aboriginal times fish and animal species were diverse and abundant.

Demography.   In 1600 the population of the Five Nations is estimated to have been about fifty-five hundred and that of the Tuscarora about five thousand. By 1904 the six Iroquois tribes numbered at least sixteen thousand, not including several thousand persons of mixed blood. In the 1980s the total population of the six tribes was estimated to be over twenty thousand.

Linguistic Affiliation.   The languages of the six tribes are classified in the Northern Iroquoian branch of the Iroquoian language family. The languages of all six tribes are still spoken.

History and Cultural Relations

The Iroquoian confederacy was organized sometime between 1400 and 1600 for the purpose of maintaining peaceful relations between the five constituent tribes. Subsequent to European contact relations within the confederacy were sometimes strained as each of the five tribes sought to expand and maintain its own interests in the developing fur trade. For the most part, however, the fur trade served to strengthen the confederacy because tribal interests often complemented one another and all gained from acting in concert. The League was skillful at playing French and English interests off against one another and thereby was able to play a major role in the economic and political events of northeastern North America during the seventeenth and eighteenth centuries. The Iroquois aggressively maintained and expanded their role in the fur trade and as a result periodically found themselves at war with their neighbors, such as the Huron, Petun, and the Neutral to the west and the Susquehannock to the south. Much of the fighting was done by the Seneca, the most powerful of the Iroquoian tribes.

From 1667 to the 1680s the Iroquois maintained friendly relations with the French, and during this time Jesuit missions were established among each of the five tribes. Iroquois aggression and expansion, however, eventually brought them into conflict with the French and, at the same time, into closer alliance with the English. In 1687, 1693, and 1696 French military expeditions raided and burned Iroquois villages and fields. During Queen Anne's War (1702–1713) the Iroquois allied with the English and at the war's end were acknowledged to be British subjects, though they continued to aggressively maintain and extend their middleman role between English traders at Fort Orange (Albany) and native groups farther west. The victory of the English over the French in North America in 1763 weakened the power of the Confederacy by undermining the strategic economic and political position of the tribes and by promoting the rapid expansion of White settlement.

When the American Revolution broke out in 1775 neither the League as a whole nor even the tribes individually were able to agree on a common course of action. Most of the Iroquois allied with the British and as a result during and after the Revolution were forced from their homelands. In the period following the American Revolution the members of the Iroquois tribes settled on reservations in western New York state, southern Quebec, and southern Ontario, where many of their descendants remain today.

Settlements

Villages were built on elevated terraces in close proximity to streams or lakes and were secured by log palisades. Village populations ranged between three hundred and six hundred persons. Typically, an enclosed village included numerous longhouses and several acres of fields for growing crops; surrounding the village were several hundred more acres of cropland. Longhouses were constructed of log posts and poles and covered with a sheathing of elm bark; they averaged twenty-five feet in width and eighty feet in length, though some exceeded two hundred feet in length. Villages were semipermanent and in use year round. When soil fertility in the fields declined and firewood in the vicinity became scarce, the village was moved to a new site. This was a gradual process, with the new village being built as the old one was gradually abandoned. The settlements of the five tribes lay along an east-west axis and were connected by a system of trails.

Economy

Subsistence and Commercial Activities.   Traditionally, the Iroquois were farmers and hunters who practiced a slash-and-burn form of horticulture. In addition, they fished and gathered berries, plants, and roots. Before the arrival of Europeans the primary weapons were bows and arrows, stone axes, knives, and blowguns; however, by the late seventeenth century European trade goods had almost completely replaced the traditional weapons and tools. The principal crops were maize, beans, and squash which, in addition, were prominent in ceremonial activities. In good years surplus crops were dried and stored for future use. After the harvest of crops in the late summer, the seasonal round included fall hunting that lasted until the winter solstice, early spring fishing and hunting of passenger pigeons, and then spring and summer clearing and planting of fields. Farming has now been largely abandoned by the Iroquois, although the annual cycle of festivals and ceremonies associated with planting, harvesting, and other traditional economic activities persist. In the 1980s most Iroquois who are employed work off the reservations because economic opportunities are so limited on them. Some men, for example, work in high steel construction, which has been an important source of employment for the Iroquois since the late nineteenth century.

Industrial Arts.   The Iroquois knew how to bend and shape wood when green or after steaming. House frames, pack frames, snowshoes, toboggans, basket rims, lacrosse sticks, and other wood products were made using these techniques. Rope was made from the inner bark of hickory, basswood, and slippery elm, and burden straps and prisoner ties were made from the braided fibers of nettle, milkweed, and hemp. Pipes of fired clay were among the many types of items manufactured by the Iroquois. They are known for making ash and maple splint baskets, although this craft may be of European origin.

Trade.   Long before European contact the Iroquois, as mentioned above, were involved in an intricate trade network with other native groups. Clay pipes were an important trade item that reached other native groups all along the east coast of North America. The aggressive behavior the Iroquois exhibited toward their neighbors during the fur trade period has been interpreted by some as the result of their aim to protect and expand their middleman role. Others have suggested that the behavior was related to the scarcity of furs in their own territory and the resulting difficulty in obtaining European trade goods. According to this theory, the Iroquois warred primarily to obtain the trade goods of their neighbors who were in closer contact with Europeans. After the center of fur trading activities had moved farther west, the Iroquois continued to play an important role as voyageurs and trappers.

Division of Labor. Traditionally, men hunted and fished, built houses, cleared fields for planting, and were responsible for trade and warfare. In addition, men had the more visible roles in tribal and confederacy politics. Farming was the responsibility of women, whose work also included gathering wild foods, rearing children, preparing food, and making clothing and baskets and other utensils.

Land Tenure. Matrilineages were the property-holding unit in traditional Iroquoian society.

Kinship

Kin Groups and Descent. Matrilineages were organized into fifteen matrisibs. Among the Cayuga, Onondaga, Seneca, and Tuscarora, the matrisibs were further organized into moieties. Among the Mohawk and the Oneida, no moiety division was recognized. Descent was matrilineal. In modern times, the stress placed on patrilineal inheritance by Canadian authorities has undermined the traditional system.

Kinship Terminology. Traditional kinship terminology followed the Iroquoian pattern. In one's own and the first ascending and descending generations parallel relatives were classed with one's lineal relatives and cross relatives were referred to separately.

Marriage and Family

Marriage. At one time marriages were a matter of individual choice, but in the historic period the matrilineage, particularly the mother, played an increasingly important role in the arrangement of marriages. Postmarital residence was matrilocal. Polygyny was practiced, but by the late eighteenth century had entirely disappeared. Divorce was possible, and when it occurred the mother retained full control over her children.

Domestic Unit. The basic economic unit consisted of matrilineally extended family groups of women, their spouses, and their children. Each extended family group occupied a longhouse within which individual nuclear families occupied designated sections and shared common hearths. Each longhouse was under the control and direction of the elder women in the extended family group.

Inheritance. Traditionally, property was inherited matrilineally. In the 1980s matrilineal inheritance continued to be practiced among Iroquois on reservations in the United States, but not so for those in Canada, where the government has enforced a patrilineal system of inheritance.

Socialization. The life cycle pattern of the Iroquois is not well understood. There was a clear dividing line between the activities of men and women and the ideals of male and female behavior, and roles were communicated to children by elders through oral traditions. Except for those who achieved political office, no formalized rites of passage marked the transition to adulthood for boys or girls.

Sociopolitical Organization

Social Organization. The members of matrisibs cooperated in economic activities and were obligated to avenge the death or injury of any other member. Moieties had reciprocal and complementary ceremonial functions and competed against one another in games. Matrisibs cut across tribal boundaries so that members were found in each tribe and village and often within each longhouse.

Political Organization. The Iroquois confederacy operated under a council of fifty sachems representing the five original tribes. When the Tuscarora joined the League in 1722, no new sachem positions were created for it. The council was a legislative, executive, and judicial body that deliberated only on the external affairs of the confederacy, such as peace and war, and on matters common to the five constituent tribes. The council had no voice in the internal affairs of the separate tribes. Tribal representation on the council was unequally distributed among the five tribes, although abuse of power was limited by the requirement of unanimity in all council decisions. Below the level of the League council were separate tribal councils concerned with the internal affairs of each tribe and each tribe's relations with external groups. The tribal council was composed of the sachems who represented the tribe on the League council. Sachem positions were hereditary within each tribe and belonged to particular matrisibs. The women of the matrisib nominated each new sachem, who was always a male, and had the power to recall or "dehorn" a chief who failed to represent the interests of his people. Theoretically, each sachem was equal to the others in power, but in practice those with better oratorical skills wielded greater influence. After the confederacy had been functioning for a period of time a new, nonhereditary office of pine tree chief was created to provide local leadership and to act as adviser to the council sachems, although later they actually sat on the League council and equaled the sachems in power. Pine tree chiefs held their position for life and were chosen by the women of a matrisib on the basis of skill in warfare. Iroquois involvement in the fur trade and war with the French increased the importance and solidarity of the League council and thereby strengthened the confederacy. Its strength continued to grow until the time of the American Revolution when Iroquois alliances were divided between the British and the American colonists.

Social Control. Part-time religious specialists known as keepers of the faith served in part to censure antisocial behavior. Unconfessed witches detected through council proceedings were punished with death, while those who confessed might be allowed to reform.

Conflict. Witchcraft was the most serious type of antisocial behavior. The Iroquois believed that witches, in concert with the Evil Spirit, could cause disease, accident, death, or other misfortune. Because witches were thought to be able to transform themselves into other objects, they were difficult to catch and punish.

Religion and Expressive Culture

Religious Beliefs. The supernatural world of the Iroquois included numerous deities, the most important of which was Great Spirit, who was responsible for the creation of human beings, the plants and animals, and the forces of good in nature. The Iroquois believed that Great Spirit indirectly guided the lives of ordinary people. Other important deities were Thunderer and the Three Sisters, the spirits of Maize, Beans, and Squash. Opposing the Great Spirit and the other forces of good were Evil Spirit and other lesser spirits responsible for disease and other misfortune. In the Iroquois view ordinary humans could not communicate directly with Great Spirit, but could do so indirectly by burning tobacco, which carried their prayers to the lesser spirits of good. The Iroquois regarded dreams as important supernatural signs, and serious attention was given to interpreting dreams. It was believed that dreams expressed the desire of the soul, and as a result the fulfillment of a dream was of paramount importance to the individual.

Around 1800 a Seneca sachem named Handsome Lake received a series of visions which he believed showed the way for the Iroquois to regain their lost cultural integrity and promised supernatural aid to all those who followed him. The Handsome Lake religion emphasized many traditional elements of Iroquoian culture, but also incorporated Quaker beliefs and aspects of White culture. In the 1960s, at least half of the Iroquoian people accepted the Handsome Lake religion.

Religious Practitioners. Full-time religious specialists were absent; however, there were part-time male and female specialists known as keepers of the faith whose primary responsibilities were to arrange and conduct the main religious ceremonies. Keepers of the faith were appointed by matrisib elders and were accorded considerable prestige.

Ceremonies. Religious ceremonies were tribal affairs concerned primarily with farming, curing illness, and thanksgiving. In the sequence of occurrence, the six major ceremonies were the Maple, Planting, Strawberry, Green Maize, Harvest, and Mid-Winter or New Year's festivals. The first five in this sequence involved public confessions followed by group ceremonies which included speeches by the keepers of the faith, tobacco offerings, and prayer. The New Year's festival was usually held in early February and was marked by dream interpretations and the sacrifice of a white dog offered to purge the people of evil.

Arts. One of the most interesting Iroquoian art forms is the False Face Mask. Used in the curing ceremonies of the False Face Societies, the masks are made of maple, white pine, basswood, and poplar. False Face Masks are first carved in a living tree, then cut free and painted and decorated. The masks represent spirits who reveal themselves to the mask maker in a prayer and tobacco-burning ritual performed before the mask is carved.

Medicine. Illness and disease were attributed to supernatural causes. Curing ceremonies consisted of group shamanistic practices directed toward propitiating the responsible supernatural agents. One of the curing groups was the False Face Society. These societies were found in each village and, except for a female keeper of the false faces who protected the ritual paraphernalia, consisted only of male members who had dreamed of participation in False Face ceremonies.

Death and Afterlife. When a sachem died and his successor was nominated and confirmed, the other tribes of the League were informed and the League council met to perform a condolence ceremony in which the deceased sachem was mourned and the new sachem was installed. The sachem's condolence ceremony was still held on Iroquois reservations in the 1970s. Condolence ceremonies were also practiced for common people. In early historic times the dead were buried in a sitting position facing east. After the burial, a captured bird was released in the belief that it carried away the spirit of the deceased. In earlier times the dead were left exposed on a wooden scaffolding, and after a time their bones were deposited in a special house of the deceased. The Iroquois believed, as some continue to believe today, that after death the soul embarked on a journey and series of ordeals that ended in the land of the dead in the sky world. Mourning for the dead lasted a year, at the end of which time the soul's journey was believed to be complete and a feast was held to signify the soul's arrival in the land of the dead.

Bibliography

Fenton, William N. (1971). "The Iroquois in History." In *North American Indians in Historical Perspective*, edited by Eleanor B. Leacock and Nancy O. Lurie, 129–168. New York: Random House.

Fenton, William N. (1978). "Northern Iroquoian Culture Patterns." In *Handbook of North American Indians*. Vol. 15, *Northeast*, edited by Bruce G. Trigger, 296–321. Washington, D.C.: Smithsonian Institution.

Morgan, Lewis H. (1901). *League of the Ho-de-no-sau-nee or Iroquois*. Edited by Herbert M. Lloyd. 2 vols. New York: Dodd, Mead. Originally published, 1851.

Oswalt, Wendell H. (1966). "The Iroquois." In *This Land Was Theirs: A Study of North American Indians*, edited by Wendell H. Oswalt, 397–461. New York: John Wiley.

Tooker, Elisabeth (1978). *The League of the Iroquois: Its History, Politics, and Ritual*. In *Handbook of North American Indians*. Vol. 15, *Northeast*, edited by Bruce G. Trigger, 418–441. Washington, D.C.: Smithsonian Institution.

GERALD F. REID

Jews

ETHNONYMS: Ashkenazim, Hebrews, Sephardim

Orientation

Identification.   The Jews of North America are a relatively assimilated ethnic group in the United States and Canada. The name "Jew" is an Anglicized version of the Hebrew word *yehudi*, meaning "Hebrew, the language of the kingdom of Judah," and originally referred to the members of the tribe of Judah, one of twelve tribes of Israel in the Middle East about four thousand years ago. Jewish self-identity rests on a number of factors including a unique set of religious beliefs and practices, ancestry from Jewish peoples, a shared understanding of the Holocaust, and a belief in Israel as the Jewish homeland.

Location.   Jews in North America live primarily in cities or adjacent suburbs. Although urban Jewish ghettos no longer exist, a pattern of residential isolation persists, with many city neighborhoods or suburban communities defined as "Jewish" because of the large number of Jews who reside there and the Jewish institutions such as synagogues, community centers, and kosher food stores located there. Sixty percent of Jews live on the East Coast of the United States and about 20 percent on the West Coast, with relatively few, save those in major cities, in the South and Midwest. In Canada, the same pattern holds, with two-thirds of the Jewish population living in or near Toronto or Montreal.

Demography.   In 1986 the Jewish population in North America was about 6.3 million, with 5.9 million in the United States and 305,000 in Canada. Thus, North American Jews constitute about 43 percent of the 14.5 million Jews in the world. By way of comparison, in Europe there are 4.1 million Jews, in Asia 3.3 million, in South America 600,000, in Africa 159,000, and in Oceania 72,000. The United States has the largest Jewish population in the world and Canada the seventh largest. In North America, the majority of Jews live in twelve large cities, with 1.9 million in the metropolitan New York City region (over 30 percent of U.S. Jews), 500,000 in Los Angeles, 300,000 in Philadelphia, 250,000 each in Miami and Chicago, over 100,000 each in Boston, Washington, D.C., Montreal, and Toronto, and over 50,000 each in Baltimore and San Francisco. In Canada, the other Jewish population centers are Winnipeg, 15,000, and Vancouver, 14,000. The Jewish population has been relatively stable for the past decade, despite a relatively low birth rate, offset somewhat by recent emigrations of Jews from the Soviet Union and Israel to the United States and Canada.

Linguistic Affiliation.   The overwhelming majority of North American Jews use English as their primary or only domestic language, or French in the French-speaking provinces of Canada, with about 20 percent of Canadian Jews bilingual in the two languages. Recent immigrants from Europe and the Middle East often speak the language of their homeland, those from the Soviet Union speaking Russian, those from Syria speaking Arabic, and those from Israel speaking Hebrew. Hasidic Jews use Yiddish, written with Hebrew characters, and some Jews of central and eastern European ancestry speak Yiddish at home. Yiddish, the traditional language of Jews of Eastern Europe, shares common medieval roots with High German and contains Slavic loan-words, although it is usually written with Hebrew characters and from right to left as is Hebrew. A number of Yiddish words have become part of the U.S. English lexicon, including *blintze, chutzpah, goy, kibitz, landsman, mensh, nebbish, shlemiel, shlock, shnook,* and *shmooz.*

Hebrew is the religious language for Orthodox and some Conservative Jews, with prayerbooks written in and prayers chanted in Hebrew. Hebrew is a branch of the Canaanite group of Semitic languages. Reform Jews use English in their religious services.

History and Cultural Relations

The immigration history of Jews to the U.S. and Canada differs as does the nature of cultural relations between Jews and other groups in those nations.

United States.   The first Jews in North America—23 Sephardic Jews from South America—arrived in New Amsterdam (now New York City) in 1654. Since then Jews have continued to immigrate to North America, with the bulk arriving in three periods: 1830–1880, 1881–1924, and 1935–1941. Prior to 1830 most Jews in North America were Sephardic (see "Social Organization" below) and numbered about six thousand in 1830. From 1830 to 1880 the Jewish population increased to 250,000, most of whom were Ashkenazi Jews who emigrated from Germany, as part of a larger movement of Germans to North America. Not only did these immigrants, largely young, rural or small-town peoples escaping religious persecution, swell the Jewish population, but they also spread across the continent establishing communities in dozens of cities. The second period of migration from 1880–1924 closed with a Jewish population of over 4 million in the United States, mostly urban and mostly on the East Coast. This time the immigrants were mostly Ashkenazi Jews from eastern and central European countries such as Poland, Romania, Hungary, and especially western Russia. These immigrants were the forebears of about 80 percent of Jews in North America today. Restrictive immigration laws in the United States and the depression slowed immigration, but beginning in the mid-1930s until the late 1940s, some 200,000 Jews fleeing Nazi-controlled Europe and extermination in concentration camps arrived in the United States. The 1900–1950 period was also a time of upward (socially and economically) and outward (from the cities to the suburbs) mobility for the eastern European Jews. Since the establishment of the state of Israel in 1948, Jews have arrived in the United States mainly from the Middle East, the Soviet Union, and most recently from Israel. One key feature of Jewish immigration is that most of the immigrants stayed, with only one in fourteen returning to their homelands as compared to about one in three returns for most other ethnic groups.

Despite overt discrimination in education and employment in the past and organized anti-Semitism in some sectors of American society, laws have generally guaranteed Jews religious freedom and relations with other ethnic and religious groups have been generally peaceful if not friendly. Political ties to the African-American community are no longer as strong as they once were. Current tensions with the African-

Americans reflect, in part, Jewish concerns over African-American support for the Palestinians in the Middle East and African-American concerns over Jewish ties to South Africa and lack of Jewish support for affirmative action programs. Jews generally distinguish themselves from all non-Jews who are classified and referred to as *goyim*, commonly understood to mean "non-Jew." Some scholars suggest that Jews in the United States today are more apt to stress the secular aspects of Jewishness, such as the use of Yiddish words, as opposed to the religious aspects such as following Jewish law regarding dietary restrictions.

Canada. In contrast to the immigration history in the United States, the majority of Jewish immigrants to Canada arrived after 1945, with about 40 percent of the current Canadian Jewish population composed of recent arrivals as compared to about 20 percent for the United States. In 1900 there were 15,000 Jews in Canada, but by 1915 the population had grown to 100,000 through mass emigrations from eastern Europe. Few Jews immigrated to Canada in the years before World War II, and about 200,000 have arrived since then. These include Jews fleeing war-torn Europe, Hungarian Jews escaping from Hungary in 1956, French-speaking Jews coming from North Africa, and, most recently, about 22,000 arriving from Israel and 8,000 from the Soviet Union.

Largely because Canada is a bicultural nation with distinct French- and English-speaking populations and because of greater acceptance of cultural diversity, Jews in Canada, like other ethnic groups, are relatively less assimilated than their counterparts in the United States. While this has led to a more visible emphasis on religious elements of Jewishness and the survival of European customs, it has also placed Jews outside the two mainstream Canadian religious traditions of Catholicism and Protestantism. This position as a third religion and other factors have sometimes subjected Jews to laws interfering with traditional religious practices. Laws introduced after World War II removed most of these restrictions. Today, Canadian Jews are slowly becoming more like U.S. Jews, with the use of European customs and languages disappearing.

Economy

Jews are now largely integrated into the U.S. and Canadian economic systems. Although they work in most trades and professions, they are overrepresented (as a percentage of the population) in several, including ownership of small and middle-sized businesses, the communication and entertainment industries, public service, and professions such as medicine, dentistry, law, accounting, teaching, and scientific research. Past and present discrimination has been cited by some as the cause of the relatively few Jews found in the upper echelons of the banking industry and large corporations in general. Civil rights legislation of the 1960s and 1970s has outlawed old laws and private covenants that restricted Jewish ownership of land or membership in private associations. The traditional Jewish division of labor with men working outside the home and women working in the home has given way to many women having professional employment.

Kinship, Marriage and Family

Marriage and Family. Jewish marriage and kinship practices conform to those of mainstream North American culture: monogamous marriage, nuclear families, bilateral descent, and Eskimo-type kinship terms. Surnames are patrilineal, although there is a trend toward women keeping their own surnames at marriage or hyphenating their husbands' surnames and their own. The importance of family continuity is emphasized by the custom of naming children after deceased relatives. Although marriage with non-Jews (goyim) was proscribed and sanctioned by ostracism in the past, the intermarriage rate today is increasing as among North Americans in general. Though Jewish families have fewer children, they are often described as child-oriented, with family resources freely expended on education for both boys and girls. Jewish identity is traced matrilineally. That is, if one's mother is a Jew, then that person is Jewish according to Jewish law and entitled to all the rights and privileges that status brings, including the right to emigrate to and settle in Israel as citizens.

Socialization. As with most Americans and Canadians, early socialization takes place in the home. Jewish parents are indulgent and permissive and rarely use physical punishment. Socialization as a Jew takes place in the home through storytelling and participation in Jewish rituals, and through attendance at Hebrew school in the afternoon or evening and participation in Jewish youth groups at the synagogue or community center. Orthodox Jews often run their own grammar and high schools, whereas most non-Orthodox Jews attend public or private secular schools. Acquisition of knowledge and the open discussion of ideas are important values and activities for Jews, and many attend college and professional schools.

The Bar Mitzvah ceremony for a boy at age thirteen is an important rite of passage as it marks him as an adult member of the community for religious purposes, and the Bat Mitzvah ceremony for a Reform or Conservative girl at age twelve or thirteen serves the same purpose. In the past the Bar Mitzvah ceremony was much more elaborate and spiritual in focus; today both ceremonies have become important social as well as religious events for many Jews.

Sociopolitical Organization

Social Organization. Today, Jews are highly integrated into the North American class system, with Jews found in the upper, middle, and working classes. Upward social mobility is an important value, and has been achieved for about three generations largely through education. Although Jews are often thought to be concentrated in the upper-middle and lower-upper classes, there is still a sizable number in the working class and some elderly Jews live below the poverty line. Vestiges of discrimination remain and Jews are still excluded from some social organizations open to non-Jews. In communities with large Jewish populations, exclusively or largely Jewish social organizations such as community centers, the Young Men's and Young Women's Hebrew Associations (YMHA, YWHA), B'nai B'rith, and Hadassah are important. And in some communities the synagogue (*shul*) plays an important social and recreational role. Many Jews are also involved in or contribute to national or international organizations that support Jewish causes such as the Anti-Defamation League of the B'nai B'rith, the United Jewish Appeal, and the United Jewish Welfare Fund.

Internally, Jews have no formal social or political organization, although they can be and are often divided into subgroups on the basis of three overlapping criteria: degree of religiousness, place of one's own or one's ancestor's birth, and Ashkenazic or Sephardic ancestry. Degree of religiousness is reflected in the labels Orthodox, Conservative, or Reform Judaism. Orthodox Jews generally follow and resist changes in traditional religious beliefs and practices, which they base on the *halakhah*, the Jewish literature that covers ethical, religious, civil, and criminal matters. Conservative Judaism comprises a combination of thought reflecting different philosophical, ethical, and spiritual schools. In general, Conservatives stress change from within, Zionism, and an ingathering of all Jews. Because of the diversity of opinion, Conservative religious practices run a wide gamut, although most are less traditional than those of Orthodoxy. Reform Judaism, as the name suggests, reflects a modification of Orthodoxy in light of contemporary life and thought. Thus, Reform Jews do not believe that Jewish law is divinely revealed and eschew many practices central to Orthodoxy such as eating only kosher foods, wearing a skull-cap (*yarmulke*) when praying, and using Hebrew in prayer. The differences among Orthodox, Conservative, and Reform Jews go well beyond religion and are manifested in many day-to-day activities and events and the degree to which members of each are assimilated into North American society. Other categories of Jews based on degree of religiousness include Hasidic (ultra-Orthodox) Jews, Reconstructionists, and "Civil" Jews.

As mentioned above, Jews arrived in North America in waves, largely from European nations and these places of ancestry are used to delineate one Jew or group of Jews from another. Thus, for example, one speaks of German Jews, Russian Jews, Polish Jews, Syrian Jews, and so on, or in a more general sense, eastern, central, or southern European Jews. These distinctions are no longer especially important, although German Jews are still looked upon as wealthier and of higher status than other Jews.

The final major distinction is between Jews of Ashkenazic (Ashkenazim) or Sephardic (Sephardim, Sfardim) ancestry. Ashkenazim Jews are those descended from the Ashkenazic Jews of eastern and central Europe and currently make up about 90 percent of North American Jews. Sephardim are descended from the Sephardic Jews who lived in southern Europe from about the seventh to the fifteenth century when they were expelled from Spain by Queen Isabella and King Ferdinand. Most of the exiles settled in the Middle East and North Africa. Beyond a difference in place of ancestry, Ashkenazic and Sephardic Jews differed and in some ways continue to differ in language (Yiddish or European languages versus Judeo-Spanish or Middle Eastern languages), the pronunciation and spelling of Hebrew, liturgy, and surnames. But members of both groups freely acknowledge that members of the other group are Jews, although some Ashkenazim were less accepting of Sephardim in the past. Although North American Judaism is dominated by Ashkenazim because of their large numbers, there are important Sephardic communities in New York, Los Angeles, Seattle, Atlanta, Chicago, Montreal, Rochester, and Indianapolis.

These communities derive from a migration occurring from 1900 to 1925 when Sephardic Jews left areas that are now Turkey, Greece, Yugoslavia, Rhodes, and other territories of the Ottoman Empire.

Finally, mention should be made of other Jewish groups such as Karaites (Qaraites), Israeli, and Russian Jews who have recently immigrated to North America from their respective countries, and Black Jews who have formed their own sects (though by Jewish-defined criteria most of these sects are not considered Jews). These groups, who sometimes follow an ultra-Orthodox life-style or a life-style different from that of assimilated Jews, also sometimes choose to live in relatively isolated urban communities and form their own synagogues. The recent emigrants from Israel are looked upon by some with puzzlement, as they seem to be rejecting the *aliyyah*, or ascent to the land of Israel, a marker of Jewish identity if not a goal for many Jews.

Political Organization.   Although North American Judaism has no overarching political structure similar to that of Roman Catholicism or the Church of the Latter-Day Saints (Mormons), the Orthodox, Conservative, and Reform synagogues are aligned with central organizations—the Union of Orthodox Congregations of America, the United Synagogue of America (Conservative), and the Union of American Hebrew Congregations (Reform). Although in the past the synagogue played an important organizational and leadership role, it no longer does so for most Jews. Similarly, the rabbi, the spiritual and moral leader of the synagogue congregation, now rarely plays a leadership role in the community, based solely on his status as the rabbi.

Jews have been seen (often by anti-Semitic commentators) as aligned with liberal or radical political philosophies including socialism, communism, unionization, and the New Deal and tended to vote heavily in favor of candidates of the Democratic party in the United States; in the past decade or two, a marked trend toward conservatism and identification with the Republican party has been noted among a minority of Jews. Jews, despite being only about 2 percent of the population, are an important voting bloc because large numbers vote and because they make up a sizable percentage of the population in some large states such as New York and Florida and the Canadian provinces of Ontario and Quebec. Jews run for and have been elected to numerous local and state offices.

Social Control and Conflict.   Integrated as they are into U.S. and Canadian society, Jews generally resolve legal conflicts with Jews or non-Jews through the legal system. Legal remedies available through Jewish agencies are rarely used. Among the Orthodox there is recourse to some religiously sanctioned social control such as Orthodox divorce. Although overt discrimination against Jews is waning in North America, there is a long tradition of anti-Semitism, reflected in limited access to certain professions and residential isolation. Within the Jewish communities in both nations, there are long traditions of supporting Jewish causes and institutions through charitable donations to and work for synagogues, schools, community centers, social welfare agencies, and the state of Israel.

Religion and Expressive Culture

Religious Beliefs. Judaism is the oldest monotheistic religion to survive to modern times. To Jews, God is the Supreme Being, the Creator of the Universe, and ultimate Judge of Human Affairs. Some importance is also given to particular prophets and angels. The Hebrew calendar is a lunar calendar (based on the movement of the moon around the earth) and has 354 days, 12 months of 29 or 30 days each with extra days added so that the lunar calendar conforms to the solar (Gregorian) calendar, and seven days in a week. The Hebrew calendar is based on the date 3761 B.C.E., the year traditional Jewish scholars believed the world began. Thus, the years 5748–5749 are the equivalent of 1989 in the Gregorian calendar. Jewish weekly synagogue attendance is relatively low at about 20 percent compared to other religions. Because of the wide divergence of religious belief and practice (Orthodox/Conservative/Reform, Ashkenazic/Sephardic, and so on), no single all-encompassing system of Jewish belief and practice can be described.

Religious Practitioners. There is no hierarchy of religious leaders. The rabbi (master, teacher) is the spiritual leader of the synagogue congregation. Today, the role and status of the rabbi is roughly the same as that of a Protestant minister or Catholic priest and involves pastoral, social, educational, and interfaith responsibilities. Reform Jews and Reconstructionalists permit women to be ordained as rabbis. Cantors are also important, leading the congregation in the chanting of prayers (prayers are chanted, not recited) and in training boys for the Bar Mitzvah.

Ceremonies. Rosh Hashanah (New Year) and Yom Kippur (the Day of Atonement), the High Holy Days, usually fall in September. Pesach (Passover), Shavout (Festival of Weeks), and Succot (Feast of the Ingathering) were originally harvest festivals involving pilgrimages to the Temple. Passover today marks the escape of the Hebrews from ancient Egypt about 3,500 years ago and is widely celebrated. Minor holy days or festivals include Hanukkah (dedication Feast of Lights), Purim (Festival of Lots), and Tisha B'Av (Ninth Day of Av). Although of less importance today, Rosh Hodesh (Beginning of a New Moon) is still noted and marked by special prayers. Shabbat (the Sabbath) is the only Holy Day mentioned in the Ten Commandments and is celebrated from sundown Friday to sundown Saturday each week of the year. The Sabbath is a day of rest and reflection. In addition to these Holy Days and festivals, all major life-cycle events—birth, age of religious majority, marriage, and death—are marked by prayer and ritual observances.

Death and Afterlife. Jewish law requires that the deceased be buried within twenty-four hours of death. Some Reform Jews allow cremation. For close relatives there is a seven-day mourning period (shivah) involving prayer and restrictions on the activities of the mourner. Regular prayer in memory of the deceased follows at set intervals following the mourning period. Jewish beliefs concerning the soul and afterlife are vague and vary from one group to another.
See also Hasidim, and entries on Jews in the Europe and Middle East, Soviet Union and China, and South Asia volumes

Bibliography

Cohen, Steven (1983). _American Modernity and Jewish Identity_. New York: Tavistock.

Goren, Arthur A. (1980). "Jews." In _Harvard Encyclopedia of American Ethnic Groups_, edited by Stephan Thernstrom, 571–598. Cambridge: Harvard University Press, Belknap Press.

Gross, David C. (1981). _The Jewish People's Almanac_. Garden City, N.Y.: Doubleday.

Rosenberg, Stuart E. (1970–1971). _The Jewish Community in Canada_. Toronto: McClelland & Stewart.

Rosenberg, Stuart E. (1985). _The New Jewish Identity in America_. New York: Hippocrene Books.

Tillem, Ivan L., comp. and ed. (1987). _The 1987–88 Jewish Almanac_. New York: Pacific Press.

Weinfeld, M., W. Shaffir, and I. Cotler, eds. (1981). _The Canadian Jewish Mosaic_. Toronto: John Wiley.

DAVID LEVINSON

Jicarilla

ETHNONYM: Tinde

Orientation

Identification. The Jicarilla are an American Indian group whose names for themselves, "Haisndayin" and "Dinde," have been translated as "people who came from below" and "people." The name "Jicarilla" was used first by the Spanish in 1700 in reference to a hill or peak associated with the location of the tribe at that time.

Location. The homelands of the Jicarilla were located in the high country of present-day southern Colorado and north-central New Mexico. The Sangre de Cristo Mountains, ranging in height from two thousand to fourteen thousand feet, roughly bisect the former Jicarilla territory from north to south and are flanked on the east and west by high plains. The considerable variation in the topography of this region results in a varied climate, but one that is generally moderate with low annual precipitation. Summers are hot and dry and winters cold and snowy. The principal rivers in the region are the Rio Grande, the Arkansas, the Canadian, and the Chama. Spruce, fir, aspen, juniper, and piñon trees are found at the higher elevations, while short grasslands predominate on the high plains and in the intermontane basins.

Demography. In 1860 the Jicarilla numbered 860. By 1900 their numbers had declined to 815 and continued to decline to 588 in 1920. This decline in population was due most directly to tuberculosis, but the spread of the disease itself was the result of poverty and poor nutrition associated with limited employment and insufficient rations on their New Mexico reservation. In the 1920s government programs to improve health and economic conditions on the reservation helped reverse the population decline. By 1955 the number of Jicarilla exceeded 1,000 and in 1981 stood at 2,308 on the Jicarilla Reservation in north-central New Mexico.

Linguistic Affiliation.   The Jicarilla language is a dialect of the Apachean group of Southern Athapaskan languages.

History and Cultural Relations

The Jicarilla are descendants of Southern Athapaskan hunters who migrated from the subarctic region west of Hudson Bay to the Southwest between 1300 and 1500. The probable route of migration was through the plains along the eastern edge of the Rocky Mountains. The Apacheans in general came into contact with the Spanish in the mid-sixteenth century, and until the beginning of the eighteenth century contacts with the Spanish were limited and generally friendly. During the 1700s Hispanic settlement of Jicarilla lands gradually increased through land grants by the Mexican government to its citizens. The Jicarilla never agreed to these land grants. After the Jicarilla territory passed to the jurisdiction of the United States in 1848, American settlement of Jicarilla lands also increased.

The expansion of Hispanic and American settlement rendered the Jicarilla's traditional way of life impossible, and in response they began to raid White wagon trains and settlements. In 1854 the government of New Mexico declared war on the Jicarilla and the following year forced them to sign a peace treaty providing for their removal to a reservation. The plan for the Jicarilla reservation did not materialize until 1887. When it did, the system of individual land allotments intended to transform the people into farmers failed owing to the unfavorable climate and terrain of the reservation site, which led to social dislocation and dependence on government welfare. After the turn of the century the federal government added new lands to the reservation in an unsuccessful attempt to promote livestock raising. At this time living conditions on the reservation reached their low point, with widespread unemployment, poverty, malnutrition, and disease. Finally, in the 1920s the federal government succeeded in introducing sheep raising, and conditions on the reservation improved.

Culturally, the Jicarilla were heavily influenced by the Plains Indians to their east and the Pueblo Indians to their west, with the result that their own culture exhibited a combination of nomadic hunting and settled farming characteristics. One of the Plains Indian traits prominent in Jicarilla culture was an emphasis on raiding and warfare. After Spanish contact raiding increased in frequency and intensity with the use of and need for horses. At the beginning of the eighteenth century the Jicarilla commonly raided the Plains tribes to their east and used the fruits of their successes to trade with the Pueblo Indians and the Spanish. During the second decade of the eighteenth century Comanches who had obtained guns from the French drove the Jicarilla out of Colorado and into the foothills and mountains of northern New Mexico. Subsequently, the Jicarilla sought help from the Spanish by offering allegiance to the king of Spain, but with little result. In 1779 a combined force of Jicarilla, Ute, Pueblo, and Spanish soldiers defeated the Comanche, who, after another seven years and several more military campaigns, finally sued for peace. Thereafter the Jicarilla were able to reestablish themselves in southern Colorado.

Settlements

The Jicarilla lived in local groups of 150 to 400 people who occupied semipermanent, dispersed settlements or camps usually situated along the banks of rivers and streams and from which they conducted their hunting and raiding activities. Dwellings were low, dome-shaped structures, called wickiups, which consisted of a pole frame covered over with leaves and bark. Animal skins were laid over the structure for additional protection from the cold.

Economy

Subsistence and Commercial Activities.   The Jicarilla economy was based on hunting and gathering, but agriculture was also practiced and increased in importance over time. Animals hunted included large game such as bison, mountain sheep, antelope, deer, elk, and small game such as beaver, rabbit, squirrel, porcupine, and prairie dog. Antelope were killed in communal drives, and bison (after Spanish contact) were hunted on horseback and dispatched with bows and arrows and lances. Turkey, grouse, and quail were also hunted, and fish were taken in shallow pools, with the use of baited nooses and bows and arrows. Gathered foods included juniper berries, mesquite beans, yucca fruit, chokecherries, prickly pears, acorns, and piñon nuts. Cultivation was practiced by the Jicarilla after the late 1600s and resulted from contact with the Pueblo Indians. Crops included maize, beans, squash, pumpkins, peas, and melons, which were planted in plots along river and stream banks. Over time agriculture increased in importance and became more sophisticated. By the time of the American occupation of the Jicarilla territory in the mid-1800s, irrigation dams and ditches were constructed and used to supplement the region's scanty rainfall. Agricultural tools included crude wooden plows and implements for clearing irrigation ditches. Sheep raising became popular in the 1920s, but was eclipsed in importance in the 1950s by revenues from tribal-owned oil, gas, and timber resources. Since that time nonagricultural wage labor has increased with the development of small businesses and industries subsidized by the tribe's natural resource revenues.

Industrial Arts.   A chief Jicarilla industry was basket making, the products of which were an important item of barter in trade with other native groups. Some baskets were sealed with pitch and used as water vessels. The Jicarilla also made pottery and ceremonial clay pipes.

Trade.   Baskets, meat, salt, and tanned bison hides were traded to Pueblo Indians for maize and other agricultural products. The Indians of San Juan Pueblo, from whom the Jicarilla also obtained songbird feathers, were special trading partners.

Division of Labor.   Men hunted and women gathered. In farming, men prepared the fields, worked the irrigation ditches, and helped with the harvest, and women were responsible for planting, hoeing, weeding, and harvesting.

Land Tenure. Local groups of homesteads maintained somewhat ill-defined territories or camping grounds associated with some familiar geographical landmark. In 1891 lands on the Jicarilla reservations were allotted on an individual basis. In 1939 the allotted lands were returned to tribal ownership.

Kinship

Kin Groups and Descent. Local groups of extended families had a base in marriage and blood ties. However, kin groups with economic or political functions above the level of the local group did not exist. Kinship ties were reckoned bilaterally.

Kinship Terminology. Jicarilla kinship terminology followed the Iroquoian system. The father and the father's brother were classed under a single term, as were the mother and the mother's sister. Parallel cousins were grouped with siblings and cross cousins were classed separately. No terminological distinction was made between maternal and paternal grandparents nor between male and female grandchildren.

Marriage and Family

Marriage. Young women were eligible for marriage after reaching puberty and young men when they proved themselves capable of supporting a family. In arranging a marriage, the man was required to obtain the permission of the parents of his prospective bride, and it was completed when a dowry was offered and gifts were exchanged. Marriages were usually monogamous, though polygyny was practiced on a limited basis with the sister or cousin of the first wife as a preferred second mate. Postmarital residence was matrilocal. Divorce was common and second marriages were allowed. When a spouse died the survivor could marry again only after a period of mourning and after proper purification rituals were performed. In such cases, levirate and sororate marriages were preferred. A widower was considered unlucky and could remarry only after a temporary union with a woman whom he was not permitted to wed. The temporary union lasted less than a year and was believed to bring the widower back from his state of ill fortune.

Domestic Unit. The basic unit of Jicarilla society was the extended family consisting of parents, their unmarried children, and their married daughters and their husbands and children. Within the extended family each nuclear family unit occupied a separate household. Among modern Jicarilla the nuclear family has replaced the extended family as the basic social unit.

Inheritance. Property was inherited, but not according to any specific rules.

Socialization. Grandparents, especially on the maternal side, played an important role in the training of the young. Boys' training for hunting began in childhood when they were taught the use of the bow and arrow and the techniques of trapping, calling animals, and reading animal signs. At about age twelve they were taken on their first hunt and, if successful, were initiated into the fraternity of hunters and taught the rules and rituals of successful hunting. For girls, upon reaching puberty an adolescent rite was held in which the origins of the Jicarilla and the traits each woman should personify were revealed to them in prayers and songs related by elderly men. The purpose of the rite was to ensure initiates a long and fruitful life.

Sociopolitical Organization

Social Organization. The Jicarilla were divided into two bands, the Olleros, or "potters," in the west, and the Llaneros or "plains people," who ranged east of the Rio Grande. These two bands have been referred to by some authors as moieties. There were no important cultural differences between the bands, and their members intermarried freely. Each band was composed of several local groups, of which there were fourteen in the mid-nineteenth century, six belonging to the Olleros and eight to the Llaneros. Each local group, consisting of a geographical cluster of extended families associated by ties of blood, marriage, and strong friendship, formed a cooperative unit for economic and ceremonial activities for which the individual extended family was too small.

Political Organization. Political authority was weakly developed. Within each local group an influential elderly head of an extended family usually acted as a leader, but his authority was quite limited. Such leaders had no coercive power and their position was not inherited. Above the level of the local group there was no formal political hierarchy, although a few respected individuals such as religious leaders and warriors sometimes took responsibility for dealing with other native groups, the Spanish, and the Americans. This system changed somewhat during the period of American occupation when several inherited chieftainships existed within each of the two bands. During the period from 1888 to 1896 the Jicarilla were under the direct control of the Bureau of Indian Affairs, which shared some authority with the native leaders. In 1937, under the provisions of the Indian Reorganization Act, the Jicarillas adopted a tribal government consisting of an elected tribal council.

Social Control. Disputes over matters such as land and revenge within and between local groups were usually negotiated by local group leaders.

Conflict. In the late 1800s the Olleros and the Llaneros opposed each other over the location of the Jicarilla Reservation. Once settled, they occupied separate areas of the reservation. The animosities stemming from this period have persisted into the twentieth century, with the Olleros usually identified as progressives and the Llaneros as conservatives.

Religion and Expressive Culture

Religious Beliefs. The Jicarilla held that a strong tie existed between themselves and the land because all natural objects and all living things were representations of the power of their chief deity, Hascin. Hascin was believed to have been born of the union of Black Sky and Earth Mother, two supernaturals who lived in the inner womb of the earth and who had existed since the beginning of time. In Jicarilla mythology Hascin was responsible for the creation of Ancestral Man and Ancestral Woman and also for the creation of the animals and the sun and moon. Sun and Moon were considered important supernaturals. According to their mythology the Jicarilla were the sole descendants of the first people to emerge from the underworld, the abode of Ancestral Man and Ancestral Woman who produced the first people. Animals were revered and entreated by the Jicarilla with special ceremonies prior to hunting because it was believed they were descended from the first animals who had used their powers to facilitate the emergence of the first people from the underworld. In the 1970s approximately 70 percent of Jicarillas continued to hold to their traditional religious beliefs.

Religious Practitioners. The Jicarilla believed that at birth a child might receive a special power from an animal, a celestial body, or some natural phenomenon. In later years this power would appear to the select individual who then had to decide whether to accept the power and become a shaman. If the person accepted it, he or she underwent a test of courage and then a period of training under the guidance of an experienced shaman during which prayers, songs, and rituals were learned. The shaman's power could be either good or evil and was believed to be a finite resource, the effectiveness of which diminished with too frequent use.

Ceremonies. Jicarilla religious ceremonies were of two types, personal or shamanistic ceremonies and long-life ceremonies. Shamanistic ceremonies included curing and divining rituals that required the shaman's special power. Long-life ceremonies did not require such special personal power. One of the most important long-life ceremonies was the annual autumn Relay Race that pitted the young men of the Ollero and Llanero bands against one another. The purpose of the race was to ensure an abundant food supply during the coming year. Participants were painted and decorated with feathers and yucca leaves according to their band affiliation and raced on an east-west-oriented course. If the Olleros won the race, it was believed that plant foods would be abundant; if the Llaneros, animal foods. In the 1930s long-life ceremonies enjoyed much popularity among the Jicarilla, and in the 1970s the Relay Race was still active and supported by the tribal council.

Arts. Ground drawings were an integral part of the Relay Race ceremony. On the evening preceding the race each band selected a leader who, with his assistants, "painted" colorful drawings in the ground with pollen and colored materials. The drawings usually included the images of the sun and moon and two fast birds. The evening also included a good deal of singing, with the bands competing with one another and singing songs to the race participants.

Medicine. The Jicarilla attributed a variety of sicknesses and ailments afflicting children to contact with birds and other animals. For example, the shadow of a turkey vulture flying overhead could make a child sick and die. Contact with eagles or the tracks of snakes and bears could give a child rheumatism. Contact with menstrual blood could also cause rheumatism. Some sicknesses were believed to be caused by ghosts. Ghost sickness was marked by nervousness, hysteria, and derangement. Curing ceremonies were of both the shamanistic and the long-life type. One of the most important long-life ceremonies, the Holiness Rite, was a curing ceremony. Held three days prior to the appearance of a full moon, this ceremony was conducted inside a tipi within a brush enclosure. Patients were confined to the tipi and were the object of extended periods of singing by shamans for three successive nights. On the fourth night sacred clowns entered the tipi and participated in the cure with special prayers. On

the morning of the fifth day the patients and participants received a blessing within the tipi and then exited the tipi and the brush enclosure to the east where they "deposited" their ailments on a tree especially prepared by a medicine man. At the conclusion of the ceremony all returned to the brush enclosure without looking back and had their faces painted by a shaman.

Death and Afterlife. The Jicarilla believed that in the process of dying an individual's ghost or spirit was conducted northward to the edge of the earth where it was offered fruit. If the ghost refused the offer, it returned to its physical body and life, but if it accepted, it slid down into the afterworld and death occurred. Upon death close relatives of the deceased went into mourning and one or two relatives prepared the corpse. Burial took place during the daytime as soon after death as possible. Some personal possessions were buried with the deceased, and the person's horse was killed at grave side. The burial party returned from the grave site by a route different from that by which it had come, being careful not to look back and refraining from discussing the location of the grave with others when they returned. The burial party then discarded their clothes and washed themselves thoroughly. These elaborate precautions by the burial party were followed in order to avoid the vengeful, evil nature of the ghost of the deceased. The Jicarilla believed that the evil of ghosts was the result of the accumulation of its frustrations, conflicts, and disappointments while living and that ghosts could return to the living to avenge some past injury. Ghosts were believed to visit the living in the form of coyotes, which were considered an omen of one's own death or the death of a close relative.

Bibliography

Gunnerson, Dolores A. (1974). *The Jicarilla Apaches: A Study in Survival.* De Kalb: Northern Illinois University Press.

Opler, Morris (1936). "A Summary of Jicarilla Apache Culture." *American Anthropologist,* n.s. 38:202–223.

Opler, Morris (1971). "Jicarilla Apache Territory, Economy, and Society in 1850." *Southwestern Journal of Anthropology* 27(4):309–329.

Tiller, Veronica E. (1982) *The Jicarilla Apache Tribe: A History, 1846–1970.* Lincoln: University of Nebraska Press.

Tiller, Veronica E. (1983) "Jicarilla Apache." In *Handbook of North American Indians.* Vol. 10, *Southwest,* edited by Alfonso Ortiz, 440–461. Washington, D.C.: Smithsonian Institution.

GERALD F. REID

Kalapuya

ETHNONYM: Calapooya

The Kalapuya are an American Indian group who in the late eighteenth century numbered about three thousand and occupied the Willamette Valley of western Oregon. The Kalapuya language belonged to the Penutian language phylum. A smallpox epidemic in 1782–1783 wiped out an estimated two thousand Kalapuya, and between 1850 and 1853 large numbers were again taken by the disease. After being removed to reservation lands in 1854 and 1855, the Kalapuya dwindled to near extinction by the early twentieth century and today number no more than about a hundred.

The Kalapuya subsisted mainly as hunters of deer, elk, bear, and beaver and gatherers of nuts and berries, although they also fished with spears and traps. The group consisted of nine tribes or subdivisions, each of which was further subdivided into small villages led by chiefs.

Religious life centered around personal quests for guardian spirits. According to traditional customs, the dead were buried with their personal possessions, mourners cut their hair, and widows painted their faces red for a month.

Bibliography

Mackey, Harold (1974). _The Kalapuyans: A Sourcebook on the Indians of the Willamette Valley._ Salem, Oreg.: Mission Hill Museum Association.

Kalispel

The Kalispel (Kulleespelm, Pend d'Oreilles), including the Semteuse (Sematuse), lived around Pend d'Oreille River and Lake and around Priest Lake in northern Idaho. They now live on the Flathead Indian Reservation in Montana and the Colville Indian Reservation in Washington. They are largely assimilated into European-American society. They speak an Interior Salish language and probably number about 250.

Bibliography

Teit, James A. (1930). _The Salishan Tribes of the Western Plateaus._ U.S. Bureau of American Ethnology, 45th Annual Report, (1927–1928), 295–396. Washington, D.C.

Carriker, Robert C. (1973). _The Kalispel People._ Phoenix, Ariz.: Indian Tribal Series.

Kansa

The Kansa (Kaw, Hutanga) lived in the general area of the Kansas River in northeastern Kansas and in the adjoining part of Missouri. They now live in a federal trust area in north-central Oklahoma, where they are largely assimilated into the White community. They spoke a Dhegiha Siouan language and numbered about nine hundred in the 1980s.

Bibliography

Unrau, William E. (1971). _The Kansa Indians: A History of the Wind People, 1673–1873._ Norman: University of Oklahoma Press.

Karok

ETHNONYMS: Arra-Arra, Ehnek, Karuk, Pehtsik, Quoratem

Orientation

Identification. The Karok are an American Indian group located in northern California. The name "Karok" is from _karuk,_ "upriver," by contrast with the name "Yurok" for a neighboring tribe, from _yuruk,_ "downriver." The Karok's name for themselves is simply "'Araar," (human being). "Karuk" is now the official name for the tribe.

Location. Aboriginally, the Karok lived along the Klamath River in Humboldt and Siskiyou counties, northwestern California, and on the tributary Salmon River. Since the nineteenth century, Karok have also lived in Scott Valley, farther east in Siskiyou County. The region is characterized by steep forested slopes and a moderate climate, with abundant fish, game, and plant foods.

Demography. The aboriginal Karok population was estimated at 2,700 in 1848. In 1930, the U.S. Census reported 755 people of Karok descent. In 1972, the state of California identified 3,781 individuals of at least partly Karok ancestry.

Linguistic Affiliation. The Karok language is not closely related to any other language, but may be distantly related to other languages of California that have been classified as Hokan.

History and Cultural Relations

The Karok have lived on the middle course of the Klamath River for as long as we know, in close contact with the Yurok downstream, and with the Hupa on the tributary Trinity River. These groups shared most elements of a culture typical of northwestern California, with relationships to the Pacific Northwest cultural area of coastal Oregon and Washington. The Karok had little contact with Whites until gold miners arrived in 1850 and 1851, resulting in widespread disease, violence, social dislocation, and cultural breakdown. By 1972, however, ceremonials were being revived, and there were renewed prospects for the preservation of Karok identity.

Settlements

Since aboriginal times, the Karok have lived on small areas of flat land, locally called "river bars," which border the Klamath River. Families were grouped into villages, some of which have become modern communities such as Orleans and Happy Camp. Transportation was formerly via river canoe or overland trails. Certain larger villages, such as Orleans, served as ceremonial centers for villages upriver and downriver from them. At present the Karok live either in the towns or on individual homesteads. The "living house," one per family, and the sweat house, which served as a men's clubhouse and dormitory for a whole community, were the major structures. Traditional houses were semisubterranean; modern Karok usually live in wood frame houses.

Economy

Subsistence and Commercial Activities.   The aboriginal Karok subsisted by fishing, hunting, and gathering wild plant foods; the only cultivated crop was tobacco. Salmon, whose yearly upriver runs were the basis of ceremonial activity, were generally caught in nets from platforms on the riverbank. The prize game was deer, the hunting of which was also encompassed by ritual activities. The major plant food was the acorn of the tanbark oak prepared by cracking, drying, and grinding to flour, and then leaching to remove the bitter flavor of tannic acid. The resulting dough was diluted and boiled by placing it with heated rocks in a large basket to make "acorn mush" or "acorn soup." Hazel twigs and pine roots were used in basketry. Present-day Karok still fish and hunt, and occasionally make acorn soup. Subsistence is difficult for many modern Karok, as agriculture, industry, and tourism are very limited in the area where they live. In aboriginal times, the dog was the only domestic animal. After White contact, horses, cattle, pigs, and cats became familiar parts of Karok life.

Industrial Arts.   The principal art of the aboriginal Karok was basketry, practiced by the women; baskets were woven so tightly they held water. Much care was lavished on intricate decorative designs, woven as overlays. Men carved wood with stone tools, producing storage boxes and household objects, and they carved various utensils from soapstone, horn, and shell. Obsidian was chipped to make knives and arrowheads; large blades of chipped obsidian were prized wealth objects. In modern days, basketry survived for a time, but is in danger of extinction. There are no current sales of Karok art to tourists.

Trade.   Aboriginal trade was of minor importance, since most commodities were available locally. But the Karok traded with the downstream Yurok for redwood dugout canoes, for ornamental shells, and for edible seaweed. The principal Indian money was dentalium shells, which originated in British Columbia, but circulated among many tribes as a medium of exchange, with larger shells important in displays of wealth.

Division of Labor.   Men hunted, fished, and carved, while women gathered plant resources and wove baskets. Strict taboos forbade female contact with men engaged in hunting and fishing.

Land Tenure.   In aboriginal times, individual families owned the land closest to the river where they lived and had rights to particular fishing sites on the river. Hunting and gathering lands were used communally. The Karok are one of the few tribes in California for whom reservation land was never set aside. Most of Karok territory today is national forest land, with some plots owned privately either by Indians or by Whites.

Kinship

Kin Groups and Descent.   The aboriginal Karok recognized no social groups other than the family, within which descent was patrilineal.

Kinship Terminology.   The basic terms *father*, *mother*, *son*, and *daughter* are used without extensions of meaning. Grandparents and grandchildren are designated by three reciprocal terms: *male grandrelative through a woman* (mother's father or daughter's son), *female grandrelative through a woman*, and *grandrelative through a man*. Siblings are distinguished as male and female, older and younger. There is a complex set of terms referring to deceased relatives, and another for relatives through a deceased person—corresponding to a taboo on reference to the dead.

Marriage and Family

Marriage.   In aboriginal times, marriage was largely a financial transaction: the bridegroom struck a bargain with the bride's father, and the prestige of a family depended on how much money had been paid for the wife. If a man could not pay a full bride-price, he could become "half married"—that is, go to live with and work for his father-in-law. Monogamy was the norm; however, a widow was expected to marry either her husband's brother or her sister's husband, and this could result in polygyny. The newly married couple lived in the husband's parents' home. Later a husband might acquire his own house, usually adjacent to that of his parents. Either partner could seek a divorce on grounds of unfaithfulness or incompatibility; the central process was a repayment of money, with negotiation of the amount depending on the number of children.

Domestic Unit.   Small extended families commonly shared a house or a group of adjacent houses.

Inheritance.   The bulk of an estate was divided among a man's sons, with smaller shares to daughters and other relatives.

Socialization.   From around three years old, male children left the family living house to sleep with adult males in the sweat house, where they were indoctrinated in the virtues of thrift and industry, and taught fishing, hunting, and ritual. Girls remained in the living house, learning female skills from their mothers. The recitation of myths, typically by grandparents in the family house on winter nights, was another important means of socialization.

Sociopolitical Organization

Social Organization.   No formal distinctions of social class were recognized by the Karok, although prestige was associated with wealth.

Political Organization.   There was no formal political organization, either for villages or the Karok as a whole; the group can be delineated only by its shared language and habitat. In keeping with the general prestige associated with wealth, however, individuals and families who were considered rich tended to be regarded as community leaders. Tribal names were used to identify neighboring peoples such as the Yurok and Hupa, but the Karok had no name for themselves other than "'Araar" (people). After White contact, the U.S. government failed for over a century to recognize the Karok as a tribe. It was not until the 1970s that federal recognition was obtained; a tribal headquarters now exists at Happy Camp.

Social Control.   Behavior was regulated by the set of values that tribal members shared, and no crimes against the tribe or community were recognized. Instead, undesirable behavior was interpreted as either (1) transgression against the supernatural, by the breaking of taboos, which would bring retribution to the wrongdoer in the form of bad luck, or (2) transgression against private persons or property, which would have to be paid for through indemnities to the offended individuals or families. If one refused to pay, he would likely be killed by the offended party; and this killing could in turn result either in immediate compensation or in further feuding between the families concerned until a final settlement was negotiated.

Conflict.   What is sometimes called "war" among the Karok refers to the feuding described above, expanded to involve fellow villagers of the aggrieved parties. Such feuds could be settled with the help of a paid go-between. When a financial settlement was reached, opposing parties would face each other and do an armed "war dance" while singing songs to insult the other side. If this did not provoke a renewal of violence, then the settlement would conclude with a breaking of weapons. Following White contact, the Karok suffered greatly in clashes with miners, settlers, and soldiers, but there was no organized warfare. At the present time, White policy toward the Karok is mainly one of "benign neglect." Differences of opinion among the modern Karok themselves are associated with the degree of adherence to traditional values, but there are no sharp dividing lines.

Religion and Expressive Culture

Religious Beliefs.   No creation myth has been recorded for the Karok; however, many myths relate the deeds of the _'ikxareeyavs_, a prehuman race which ordained the characteristics of the present world. At a certain moment, the human species came spontaneously into existence, and at the same time the 'ikxareeyavs were transformed into prototypes of the animals and plants that now exist (and, in some cases, into geographical features or disembodied spirits). In an especially large and popular class of myths, Coyote ordains the principal features of human culture, but is at the same time trickster and buffoon. The recitation of certain myths and the singing of associated songs were believed to confer magical success in hunting, gambling, and love. Following White contact, many Karok became Christians, at least nominally; but native beliefs survived underground and have surfaced in the present-day revival of interest in ritual and shamanism.

Religious Practitioners.   Annual ceremonies were presided over by priests, with their male and female assistants; these positions were not permanent, but were assigned each year by community consensus. Shamans were of two types: (1) the "sucking doctor," usually female, who used a spirit helper to extract disease objects from the bodies of patients, and (2) the "herb doctor," of either sex, who administered herbal medicine along with recitation of magical formulas. Finally, some individuals (of either sex) were believed to have secret powers of witchcraft, which they could use maliciously to make their neighbors sicken and die; these witches were greatly feared.

Ceremonies.   The principal Karok rites concerned "renewing the world" and ensuring its stability between annual observances. These were correlated with the seasonal availability of major food resources such as salmon and acorns and involved ritual activity by priests and priestesses, along with feasting, display of wealth, and dancing to the accompaniment of songs. Best known is the autumn Deerskin Dance, when the skins of albino deer were displayed as wealth objects. Less important were the Brush Dance, held to cure a sick child; the Kick Dance, to initiate a sucking doctor; and the Flower Dance, celebrating a girl's first menstruation. In modern times, the Brush Dance has survived partly as a social and recreational function; and since the 1970s, the autumn ceremony of world renewal, with its Deerskin Dance, has been performed in several traditional sites.

Arts.   Singing was considered to have magical power—as an accompaniment to ceremonial dances, as an interpolation in the recitation of myths and magical formulas, and as an accompaniment to gambling. The recitation of myths itself was of considerable ritual importance. Visual arts were limited to body ornamentation (important in ceremonies) and basketry design. In modern times, knowledge and interest continue particularly in Brush Dance songs and performance.

Medicine.   The two major types of aboriginal shamanism have been described above. It was believed that serious illness was usually caused by a supernatural "pain" or disease object, lodged in the patient's body. In children, illness could also be caused by wrongdoing on the part of a family member; when the shaman elicited a public confession, the child would recover. Shamans' fees were paid before treatment, but had to be refunded if the patient died. Since White contact, native medical practice has declined in importance, but nowadays some interest exists in reviving it.

Death and Afterlife.   The bodies of the dead were buried with the observance of many taboos—for example, mourners were forbidden to engage in hunting, gathering, basket making, travel, sex, or gambling. After five days, the spirit of the deceased was believed to go to the sky, where an especially happy place was reserved for rich people and ceremonial leaders. If anyone in a community wished to sponsor a dance within a year after someone's death, the mourners had to be paid an indemnity. Uttering the name of a dead person was a serious insult; whether done deliberately or by accident, it had to be compensated by payments to the survivors.

Bibliography

Bright, William (1957). *The Karok Language*. University of California Publications in Linguistics, no. 13. Berkeley.

Bright, William (1978). "Karok." In *Handbook of North American Indians*. Vol. 8, *California*, edited by Robert F. Heizer, 180–189. Washington, D.C.: Smithsonian Institution.

Kroeber, Alfred L. (1925). "The Karok." In *Handbook of the Indians of California*. U.S. Bureau of American Ethnology Bulletin no. 78, 98–108. Washington, D.C.

Kroeber, Alfred L., and Edward W. Gifford (1980). *Karok Myths*. Berkeley: University of California Press.

WILLIAM BRIGHT

Kaska

ETHNONYMS: Casca, Kasa, Nahane, Nahani

The Kaska, a group of Athapaskan-speaking Indians closely related to the Tahltan, live in northern British Columbia and southeastern Yukon Territory in Canada. Formerly spread out thinly over a wide area, most now live on several reserves in the region. There are four bands or subgroups: Frances Lake, Upper Liard, Dease River, and Nelson Indians (Tselona). Most Kaska today are relatively fluent in English. There may be as many as twelve hundred Kaska now living on the reserves in the general area.

Continuous contact with Whites began early in the nineteenth century when the Hudson's Bay Company established trading posts at Fort Halkett and other locations. Roman Catholic and Protestant missionization has been in progress since the first part of the twentieth century. A Roman Catholic mission was established at McDame Creek in the Dease River area in 1926. Today most Kaska are nominally Roman Catholics, although they are not particularly devout. Few vestiges of the aboriginal religion seem to remain, most of them changed by exposure to Christianity.

Traditionally, the Kaska built sod- or moss-covered conical lodges made from closely packed poles, and A-frame buildings made from two lean-tos placed together. In recent times they have lived in log cabins, tents, or modern frame houses, depending on the season and location. Traditional subsistence was based on the collecting of wild vegetable foods by the women while the men secured game by hunting (including caribou drives) and trapping; fishing provided the primary source of protein. With the advent of the trading posts and fur trapping, the technological and subsistence systems changed radically. Traditional technology, based on the working of stone, bone, horn, antler, wood, and bark gave way to the White man's hardware, clothing (except for that made of tanned skins), and other material items, obtained in exchange for furs. Traditional travel by snowshoes, toboggans, skin and bark boats, dugouts, and rafts has generally given way to motorized scows and trucks, although dogsleds and snowshoes are still used in running the winter traplines.

The local band—generally an extended family group plus other individuals—was part of the amorphous regional band. Only the local band had headmen. The Kaska "tribe" as a whole, however, has a government-appointed chief who exercises little political control. Most Kaska belong to one or the other exogamous matrimoieties named Crow and Wolf, whose main function seems to have been preparing for burial the bodies of persons belonging to the opposite moiety.

Bibliography

Honigmann, John J. (1949). *Culture and Ethos of Kaska Society*. Yale University Publications in Anthropology, no. 40. New Haven, Conn.: Department of Anthropology, Yale University. (Reprint, Human Relations Area Files, 1964.)

Honigmann, John J. (1954). *The Kaska Indians: An Ethnographic Reconstruction*. Yale University Publications in Anthropology, no. 51. New Haven, Conn.: Department of Anthropology, Yale University.

Honigmann, John J. (1981). "Kaska." In *Handbook of North American Indians*. Vol. 6, *Subarctic*, edited by June Helm, 442–450. Washington, DC: Smithsonian Institution.

Kawaiisu

The Kawaiisu live in the Tehachapi and Piute mountains to the northeast of Los Angeles, California. They speak a Shoshonean language and probably number less than fifty.

Bibliography

Zigmond, Maurice L. (1986). "Kawaiisu." In *Handbook of North American Indians*. Vol. 11, *Great Basin*, edited by Warren L. d'Azevedo, 398–411. Washington, D.C.: Smithsonian Institution.

Keres Pueblo Indians

ETHNONYMS: Keresans, Qqueres, Queres, Queresans

Orientation

Identification. The name "Keres" refers to seven present-day Keresan-speaking Pueblo Indian tribes of New Mexico. Acoma and Laguna are commonly designated as Western Keresans as contrasted with the Eastern Keresan villages, or pueblos, of Santa Ana, Zia (Sia), San Felipe, Santo Domingo, and Cochiti. Each pueblo, together with its satellites, constitutes an independent tribe with its own political, ceremonial, and social structures.

Location. The Western Keresan villages, Acoma and Laguna, lie, respectively, some sixty and forty miles west of Albuquerque, in west-central New Mexico. Santa Ana and Zia are located on the Jemez River some miles above its confluence with the Rio Grande and twenty-seven and thirty miles north of Albuquerque. Cochiti, Santo Domingo, and San Felipe are on the Rio Grande and lie, respectively, twenty-five, thirty, and thirty-five miles southwest of Santa Fe.

Demography. The Keresan Pueblos, individually, have varied in size and also in comparison with one another at any particular time through the historic centuries. Dutton gave the following population figures for the Keresan tribes as of the census of 1980: Acoma, 3,592; Laguna, 6,233; Santa Ana, 517; Zia, 645; San Felipe, 2,145; Santo Domingo, 2,857; and Cochiti, 918.

Linguistic Affiliation. The Keresan language is regarded as standing alone by most linguists; connections with other linguistic stocks are not generally accepted. Within the group of seven Keresan Pueblos, there are significant differences between the Western and Eastern subgroups. Communication between the subgroups is commonly regarded as difficult at best. Within each of the two subgroups, minor dialectic distinctions are generally recognized. Members of the several tribes chide other Keresan speakers for speaking strangely. Under the impact of television, increasing numbers of marriages with non-Keresan spouses, and the overall influence of outside relationships, the smaller Keresan tribes are currently greatly concerned over the imminent loss of their native language: without this language, the ceremonial or religious life of the tribe suffers, and without a viable religious life, the way of life of the entire native culture is threatened with extinction.

History and Cultural Relations

Laguna Pueblo was founded by refugees from various Rio Grande Keresan villages and from Acoma in the late seventeenth and early eighteenth centuries. The other six Keresan Pueblos of today, along with at least some of their satellite villages, are in approximately the same locations where the Spaniards first contacted them in the sixteenth century. The Keresans have occupied a central position along the Rio Grande and the Jemez River between other Puebloan tribes to the north and also the south; they have served as something of a cultural filter between these Rio Grande, or Eastern, tribes and the Western Pueblos of Zuni in New Mexico and Hopi in Arizona.

Settlements. As noted, the Keresans have remained, for the most part, where the Spaniards first found them. Some tribes have shown a tendency to divide and establish new villages as a result of abandoning an old site that had become unhealthful (bewitched) or depleted of resources (deforested, or increasingly desiccated and unable to support the needs of their rudimentary agriculture). Archaeological findings reveal a slow but continual reoccupation of sites where conditions had improved with the passage of years or decades. For the late nineteenth and early twentieth centuries, there are documented instances in which economic and/or political considerations have caused segments of tribes to migrate en masse to villages where other languages are spoken—for example, the Laguna migration to Isleta (Tiwa speakers) and a group of San Ildefonso Pueblo Indians (Tewa speakers) moving to Cochiti. Apparently, the overriding factor was the availability of arable land at the new home or a greater compatibility in the political or some other phase of life in the new community. Size of the migrant group, in itself, does not seem to have been important in arriving at the decision either to move or to receive newcomers into the community.

Economy

Subsistence and Commercial Activities. For centuries prior to the arrival of the Spaniards in the area, the Keresans depended for the most part on an agricultural economy. Among the Western Keresans, herding was a significant addition to the economy; this was less true of the Eastern Keresans. All Pueblo tribes, however, benefited from the introduction of sheep and cattle by the Spanish. Oxen, mules, and horses were also involved, but in lesser numbers in the beginning. Of essentially equal importance were the metal-tipped agricultural implements—shovels, hoes, rakes, plows, and other tools—that enabled the Pueblo Indians to improve their relatively primitive ditch systems and expand the acreage of fields served by these ditches. New crops—a variety of grains and alfalfa—were also important additions to the agricultural scene.

In the years following World War II, there has been a steady growth in nonagricultural pursuits. Some of these involvements have taken the Keres to such Anglo-Spanish centers as Albuquerque, Santa Fe, Los Alamos, Grants, and other communities, some at considerable distances, where wage-earning has assumed increasing significance. Another important economic development has occurred in the area of arts and crafts, or, as some observers have noted, fine arts. This has involved painting and the making of pottery, jewelry, drums, leather goods, and other creations. Potters have expanded their products to include figurines such as the famous "Story Tellers" introduced by Helen Cordero of Cochiti Pueblo and now widely made, both among other Cochiti potters and potters elsewhere. With the unexpected and disastrous seepage from the recently completed Cochiti Dam on the Rio Grande a mile north of Cochiti Pueblo, agriculture at that pueblo has virtually ceased—being replaced by wage-earning and a variety of arts and crafts.

Trade. Through the centuries, the trading of agricultural produce and other material goods—pottery, baskets, woven belts and blankets, jewelry, and other items—has served to establish relations between pueblos and also to reinforce these ties over time by repeated visits, generally reciprocal in nature.

Division of Labor.   From aboriginal times until at least the post–World War II period, the division of labor between the sexes was rigidly observed. In recent decades, however, the line between male and female activities has been all but obliterated. Pottery making and decorating are no longer exclusively the bailiwick of women; jewelry making and other crafts have become essentially bisexual endeavors. Artists of both sexes have achieved wide recognition for their paintings, sculptures, and other creations.

Land Tenure.   Traditions in land tenure—land and crops in the field belonging to the man, and harvested produce and the house belonging to the woman—have remained little changed. There has been, nonetheless, a gradual shift away from the old customs. In such cases, there has been a tendency to switch to Spanish-Anglo practices when the situation seems better served by such changes. Rules of inheritance, as an integral facet of land tenure, have shown a similar tendency to switch when circumstances indicate the advisability of making changes.

Kinship

Kin Groups and Descent.   The kinship systems of the Western Keresans differ from one another and also from the systems of the Eastern Keresans. Matrilineal exogamous clans prevail in both the Western and Eastern tribes. Both Acoma and Laguna lack the patrilineal moieties, or kiva organizations, that are found among the Eastern Keresans. Laguna shows a tendency to link clans in what can be considered rudimentary phratries. Among the Eastern Keresans, clans and kiva groups operate independently; it has been suggested that the kiva groups were once endogamous, making the clans in each moiety distinct. Today, where moieties, or kiva groups, are concerned, each moiety normally contains a number of clans that are also present in the other group. A major distinction between the Keresan clan and the moiety is the ease with which a kiva affiliation may be changed; adoption from one clan into another still involves considerable ceremony. The literature on Santa Ana Pueblo suggests a unique relationship between clan and kiva that is found in no other Keresan tribe. Kiva membership, because it may be easily switched, is sometimes discussed under the heading of non-kin associations. Marriages can occur within the kiva group; if not, the wife shifts to the kiva of her husband. Later, under certain circumstances, the couple may change their memberships to the other kiva.

Kinship Terminology.   The Western Keresans show greater variability between themselves and also when compared to the Eastern Keresans. Terms of kinship tend to be similar among the several Eastern Keresan tribes. Distinctions are commonly made between terms of address used by the two sexes, and recognition of age-generational differences has also been noted.

Marriage and Family

Marriage.   Keresan marriages have always been monogamous, and they have traditionally occurred in accordance with the rule of clan exogamy. Upon marriage, each spouse retains his or her affiliation, and children belong to her clan. As noted above, the wife changes to the kiva of her husband if she is not already a member of the same kiva group. Children take their kiva affiliation from their father. Occasionally, when a clan is numerically strong, a marriage between clan members may occur; here, the rules of Catholicism concerning incest are followed. Most marriages are performed by a Catholic priest, with native rites usually following. With Catholicism present in all villages and observed to varying degrees of faithfulness by families and individuals, divorce tends to be unusual. When it does occur, it is commonly a matter of the couple no longer living together rather than any formal procedure. The man often leaves the village and takes up residence elsewhere.

Domestic Unit.   The nuclear family continues to be the basic domestic unit. In addition, within the household, there are often unmarried siblings of the couple, usually the wife, present. Single grandparents are often included. Extended family units may occupy adjacent or nearby houses, although this practice is being followed less and less.

Inheritance.   The passing of real and/or personal property from one generation or individual to another continues to be somewhat traditional. There is, however, an increasing tendency to pass possessions on by sex and by more personal considerations than strictly adhering to traditional ways.

Socialization.   In contrast to the pre–World War II period, when most children were born at home in the pueblo with the aid of midwives or, in difficult cases, the assistance of medicine men, such births are almost unknown today, the mother being able to reach the hospital in most instances. Upon arrival in the pueblo, infants today experience varying blends of traditional and modern practices. Cradle boards are still used, but cribs are sometimes favored by mothers or families with a tendency to emulate modern ways. Young children are commonly raised by the extended family, the members of which still enjoy participating in feeding, watching, and generally caring for and interacting with these newest members of the household.

Sociopolitical Organization

Social Organization.   The typical family continues to consist, in most cases, of the father, mother, and children. Variations would include single-parent units, families with stepchildren and stepparents where remarriages have occurred, and households with relatives who share in much of the activities. As explained above the family's kin affiliations are shaped by the wife's (mother's) clan membership and by the couple's kiva membership. In families where a non-Cochiti is a parent, there are obvious deviations, particularly when the spouse is not only non-Cochiti but non-Indian. If the alien spouse is from another Pueblo, especially a Keresan tribe, the adjustments are easily made. If the spouse is a non-Pueblo person, or even a non-Indian, accommodation is not as readily made.

Political Organization.   For the Eastern Keresans, the political structure reflects the general Puebloan pattern of dualism. The political organization is balanced against the ceremonial organization. In the political organization, presumably largely implanted by the Spaniards, there are the war captain, lieutenant war captain, governor, lieutenant governor, fiscale, and lieutenant fiscale. The captains are assisted throughout the year by eight young men, the *alguacilitos*; similarly, the governors and fiscales are aided by eight fiscalitos. These assistants are chosen for their potential and are essentially on trial vis-à-vis their possible future service as major officers. A common feature of these offices is that the senior officers are all from the same kiva, and the junior officers are from the other kiva. Senior and junior officers are traditionally appointed by medicine men, who are prominent in the ceremonial organization of each tribe. The selections for these offices are made anew at the end of each calendar year and announced to the tribe. The senior and junior positions alternate every year, again a feature of the characteristic balance maintained between the two kivas. Traditionally these officers serve without monetary compensation, their rewards coming from the fact that each has served to the best of his ability and the community acknowledges this fact. But in recent years, several of the tribes have begun to pay some of these officers for their efforts in behalf of all the people.

For many years, the tribal council was composed of the major officers. Once a man became a council member, he served for the remainder of his life. In recent years, younger men who have some particular experience and knowledge have been invited to serve on the council even though they have not yet served in a major office. Governing has long been conducted by the council. Unanimous decisions once were required, but majority votes have begun to be recognized—a result of the need to reach decisions more rapidly, time-consuming debate no longer being affordable. Decisions by the major officers often are made in accordance with council decisions made in past times. When precedents are not feasible, the matter in question is taken up by the entire council. Common law has been satisfactory over the years, but some tribes have become increasingly interested in the possible advantages of a written constitution. Beyond the boundaries of the respective tribes, there are such bodies as the All-Indian Pueblo Council, in which the various Puebloan tribes participate without exception.

Social Control. Traditionally, social controls have been those employed in many small societies—gossip, ridicule, and ostracism. From time to time, more drastic measures such as public whippings or confiscation of property have been employed. Trials held before the council convened to hear allegations of misdeeds have led to such penalties as whippings, or sentences of so many hours or days of community labor. Here, the larger pueblos have been able to be more rigid or stringent. In the smaller villages, however, matters must be carefully weighed. If an imposed penalty is deemed too harsh, the guilty person may take offense to the extent that he leaves the village, either alone or taking his family with him. This is something the tribal officers try to avoid. It is a delicate balancing act—making the punishment sufficient to serve as a deterrent and yet not running the risk of driving one or more people from the tribe. As acculturation progresses with the changing times, maintaining the tribe's numerical strength is a genuine concern. The old ways of dealing with deviations have proved less and less effective in recent years; often the officer attempting to enforce a judgment is, in effect, penalized as severely as the wrongdoer.

Conflict. As the forces of acculturation gather momentum and most of the Keresan Pueblos become involved with residents whose origins are from outside the particular tribal culture, there are increasing numbers and varieties of conflicts. Such clashes also arise when different generations are involved. More exposures to the mainstream educational system and its different values have led to dissonance that sometimes results in alienation and at least a temporary departure from the tribal culture.

Religion and Expressive Culture

Religious Beliefs. The Keresan Pueblos, both Western and Eastern, practice a blend of their native religious practices and beliefs and those of Roman Catholicism. Some Protestant sects are present, but they have remained relatively insignificant in the overall religious picture. Because of stringent requirements in terms of time, energy, and dedication, the numbers of members in the various secret societies are slowly declining rather than growing. As these societies lose members, there comes a time when one or another disappears from the ceremonial scene. Subsequently, some of its practices may be taken over by another society. If not, the tribe simply carries on without the services of the defunct society. In time, however, if there is sufficient interest, members of that tribe may go to another tribe where there is such a society and learn what is necessary to reinstate the society in their own tribe. There are still widespread beliefs, especially among the older people, in the supernaturals traditionally respected in the tribe. These are commonly revered along with the Christian beliefs acquired through contacts with the Franciscan priests who have served the Keresan Pueblos since the Spanish reconquest in the 1690s. The feast days of the various patron saints associated with the missions, the Christmas season, and the Easter season are all celebrated. Variations in the intensity of these observances are found when pueblos are compared; similarly, the degree of intensity varies among the residents of any one village—the same as one would find in mainstream communities or among families within a community. Among the Keresans, Christian practices are often combined with dances and other activities from the native religious life. No conflict is seen in this blending of the two religious traditions.

Religious Practitioners. As explained above, religious duties are carried on at present much as they have been performed traditionally. There are, however, continual losses among personnel with the result that portions of the old ways have been lost to the tribe. Newcomers in the religious structure may have sufficient training to continue; in other instances, these apprentices may not have had time to learn their roles completely. Accordingly, content is lost unless it can be made up with the aid of society members in another tribe.

Ceremonies. The ceremonial observances referred to in the previous section may occur as separate and distinct activities, or they may be combined, as noted. Outsiders are usually welcome to attend and observe such ceremonies; exceptions are in the cases of secret dances or rites, at which time the performers may be either masked or unmasked. Although the Hopi and Zuni Pueblos allow outsiders to witness aspects of such masked dances, the Keresans rarely, if ever, do. Unlike the Tewa Pueblos to the north of Santa Fe, the Keresans permit no photography, sketching, recording, or note-taking at their ceremonies even when they do allow the ceremonies to be watched. Ceremonial information is jealously guarded from the non-Indian, or nonbeliever; one can detect some erosion and loss of knowledge over the years. It is claimed that if there is knowledge of a ce"remonial, or any part of it, it cannot be termed extinct. But there are increasing instances in which the qualified personnel or necessary paraphernalia can no longer be called into play, despite the fact that the ceremony, at least in its broad outlines, can be recalled.

Arts. As is the case in essentially all cultures having a nontechnological base, the Keresans have made their material items from wood, bone, leather, clay, stone, feathers, and various fibers. For items not easily handcrafted, trading networks were established among the Keresans themselves or with other Puebloan and non-Puebloan groups. At times, trade involved travel to the Gulf of California, the Pacific coast, or the Gulf of Mexico; if not actually covering such distances, tribes living in the intervening areas often served as middlemen, facilitating the exchanges between the Keresan villages and the more distant sources of desired goods. In the years since World War II, Keresan Indians have been among the leaders from the pueblos in general in the conversion of these former utilitarian products to objects aimed at the tourist and collector trade. Many of these have been termed "objects of fine art rather than 'arts and crafts.'"

Medicine. Traditionally, illnesses and injuries were treated by medicine men or medicine societies, usually those present in the particular village. If circumstances permitted, such practitioners would be sought in neighboring pueblos. In cases of childbirth, midwives usually took care of matters; however, if the birth were difficult, the assistance of a medicine man was sought. In recent times, since about 1950, more and more use has been made of hospitals, trained nurses, and doctors. At present, the health and health care enjoyed by the people are greatly improved over what existed prior to mid-century. Today, very few babies are born away from the hospital and modern medical care. Older people still have a tendency to consult the native medicine men for more psychological problems or what might be termed psychosomatic ailments.

Death and Afterlife. When death occurs with little or no warning, the body is prepared by the family or medicine men, and burial (in a blanket rather than a casket) takes place in a matter of hours. Time usually does not permit the summoning of the Catholic priest, and the sacristan will officiate. The priest blesses the grave when he is next in the village. The Keresan Indians, if one may generalize, vary in their beliefs between the teachings of the Catholic church or other Christian faiths and the traditional ideas of the soul going to live with the ancestors and/or becoming a kachina, in some cases returning to the pueblo in the generic form of rain-bringing clouds. Much of this has to do with the degree of acculturation attained by individual Indians and by the pueblos in which they live.

Bibliography

Dozier, Edward P. (1983). *The Pueblo Indians of North America*. Prospect Heights, Ill.: Waveland Press. Originally published, 1970.

Dutton, Bertha P. (1983). *American Indians of the Southwest*. Albuquerque: University of New Mexico Press.

Ortiz, Alfonso, ed. (1979). *Handbook of North American Indians*. Vol. 9, *Southwest*. Washington, D.C.: Smithsonian Institution.

Parsons, Elsie Clews (1939). *Pueblo Indian Religion*. Chicago: University of Chicago Press.

CHARLES H. LANGE

Kickapoo

ETHNONYMS: Igabu, Kikapu, Kiikaapoa, Kiwegapaw, Kiwikapawa, Ontarahronon, Shakekahquah, Shikapo

Orientation

Identification. The name "Kickapoo" no longer has any evident meaning to the Kickapoo people other than that is how they refer to themselves. The variety of the other names by which they are known, however, demonstrates the extent of their contacts with other groups, ranging from the Great Lakes region to Mexico. These far-reaching migrations were probably responsible for an earlier translation that indicated that the term *Kiwikapawa* meant "he moves about, standing here, now there," today known to be linguistically impossible.

Location. Because of their nomadic nature, the Kickapoo cannot be assigned to a specific geographic area. Aboriginally, they ranged throughout the southern Great Lakes region, eventually being pushed west and south in the wake of European contact. Today they comprise three groups living respectively near Horton, Kansas; McCloud, Oklahoma; and Melchor Muzquiz, Coahuila, Mexico. Many members of the last group have dual residency near Eagle Pass, Texas, and continue a migratory life-style that takes them throughout Colorado, Utah, Wyoming, Montana, and North Dakota as agricultural workers.

Demography. Owing to the Kickapoo's migratory adaptation and their tendency to disperse and recombine in different groups, accurate population figures have always been difficult to obtain. It has been estimated that they numbered 2,000 in 1650. This population was probably split into at least three bands. At present, all three groups are roughly equal in population with between 650 and 750 members each.

Linguistic Affiliation. The Kickapoo language is of the Algonkian family. It is most closely related to Sauk and Fox and is also similar to other central Algonkian languages such as Shawnee, Potawatomi, Menominee, and Ojibwa. Virtually all Kickapoo in Mexico and Oklahoma, and a significant number in Kansas, retain the aboriginal language, although there are slight dialectical variations to be found among the three groups.

History and Cultural Relations

The Kickapoo may have been seen as early as 1612 by Samuel de Champlain, but continuous contact can be traced only from the mid-seventeenth century. The present existence of three decidedly different bands is representative of the cultural pattern of the tribe since precontact times. For over three centuries the Kickapoo have undergone a series of migrations, fragmentations, and reassociations. During the seventeenth century, constant attacks by the Iroquois, who were expanding their territory farther west to maintain their fur trade with the French, sent the Kickapoo and other tribes fleeing to the west and south. In their attempts to secure their own territory and interest in the fur trade, the Kickapoo shifted loyalties and alliances with other tribal groups as well as the French, British, and Spanish.

After the American Revolution, increased pressures to settle created divisions among the Kickapoo. Those who favored a more acculturated life-style became known as the "Progressives," whereas those who wished to maintain the traditional life-ways were called the "Kicking Kickapoo." The Progressives became associated with an Indian prophet, Kenekuk, and settled on reservation land in Kansas in about 1834. That reservation remains the home of the Kansas Kickapoo with whom the Potawatomi merged in 1851. The more traditional Kickapoo moved south into Texas, at that time a part of Mexico, where they settled among a combined group of Cherokee, Delaware, and Shawnee.

The anti-Indian policy that was established after Texas won independence, and ultimately became a state, drove the Kickapoo, along with a contingent of Seminoles and escaped African-American slaves, into Mexico. In 1852 they were given land by the Mexican government in return for protection against the Apache and Comanche. During the next two decades, the Kickapoo were repeatedly charged with raiding Texas ranches from their settlements across the Rio Grande. In 1873 the Fourth U.S. Cavalry crossed the Mexican border to decimate an undefended Kickapoo village. Captives were taken to Indian Territory (now Oklahoma). Eventually, approximately half the tribe agreed to remain in their village of El Nacimiento, Coahuila, Mexico. This last group became a tribe recognized by the U.S. government in 1983 and, in addition to their holdings in Mexico, now have a reservation near Eagle Pass, Texas. In the United States they are officially known as the Kickapoo Traditional Tribe of Texas, and in Mexico, where they spend most of their time, as the Mexican Kickapoo (*Tribu Kikapu*), the term by which they still refer to themselves.

Settlements

In aboriginal and early historic times the Kickapoo were seminomadic and this remains true for the conservative Mexican group today. Aboriginally, the Kickapoo summer villages were semipermanent, being associated with nearby agricultural fields. After crops were planted, a few residents, usually

elderly, remained to care for them while most of the population set out on communal hunts. In winter, the village residents broke into smaller band units and established temporary hunting camps. The semipermanent villages were associated with an area for dancing and games and a burial place. The houses (*wiikiaapi*) were constructed of elm bark or rush mats placed over a vertical framework of saplings. They were usually rectangular in shape with a covered, but open-sided extension on the front. The domed winter houses were oval in shape and covered with the same mats. The mats were readily transportable so that new camps could be constructed with ease.

Bark is no longer available, but the same construction techniques for both summer and winter houses are utilized in the Mexican village of Nacimiento today. A few of the traditional houses are still constructed by members of the Oklahoma Kickapoo, although this is rare and even rarer in Kansas. In Mexico, compounds are small and arranged in a close communal pattern. A typical compound consists of at least one wiikiaapi, a cook house, a menstrual hut (*nianotegaani*), and perhaps some facility for storage. Women build and own the houses, and several related women and their nuclear families often share a compound. There may also be a Mexican-style house in the compound. In Oklahoma, settlement is more dispersed as the reservation land was allotted in 1894 and many of the Kickapoo people have since lost any right to land ownership. In Kansas, the pattern is generally that common to a rurally fixed reservation that is agriculturally oriented.

Economy

Subsistence and Commercial Activities. The Kickapoo practiced a pattern of subsistence that combined a preferred hunting and gathering adaptation with less favored horticultural activity. Deer and bison were the major sources of meat, but other game animals, such as bear, elk, and small animals, were also utilized. Wild plants and nuts were supplemented by the maize, beans, and pumpkins they planted in the spring. In the wake of European contact, the Kickapoo became involved in the fur trade and later dealt in other goods as well, ultimately becoming known as shrewd traders.

All these activities remain evident to some degree in the economy of the Kickapoo who live in Mexico today. A significant portion of their food still comes from hunting, gathering, and home-grown products, although some commodities are purchased. Cash income is provided primarily through their employment as agricultural laborers in the United States, an activity that allows them to maintain their pattern of seasonal migration. Many of those who maintain a residence in the United States also receive Department of Agriculture food stamps and Aid to Families with Dependent Children. Still others are eligible for Social Security benefits as a result of their seasonal employment. These government benefits are also available to members of the Oklahoma and Kansas Kickapoo. Among these more acculturated groups, subsistence activities are more varied and there is a greater dependence on wage labor. Unemployment and underemployment remain a problem, especially in Oklahoma where many Kickapoo lack formal education and some do not speak English. Those who own land generally lease it to White farmers rather than working it themselves. On the Kansas reservation, development projects have provided some jobs, but many of the same problems found among the Oklahoma Kickapoo exist there as well.

Industrial Arts.   In addition to weapons, aboriginal crafts included many skillfully made wooden objects such as deer calls, cradle boards, and ladles. Baskets and mats were made from rushes. With the introduction of European beads, the Kickapoo began to produce ornately beaded moccasins. These crafts are still commonly practiced among the Mexican Kickapoo.

Trade.   Trade among the Kickapoo and neighboring tribes was well established prior to and after European contact. The Kickapoo traded with Europeans as well, but avoided the strong dependency observed among other Indian groups. As the importance of fur trading decreased and the Kickapoo moved south, emphasis shifted to the trading of horses and livestock during the nineteenth century. Their ability to supply these and other trade items was a valuable asset after they settled in Mexico. Some Mexican Kickapoo still carry on a brisk trade in used clothing and other items picked up at flea markets along their migrant route.

Division of Labor.   Aboriginally, all Kickapoo followed the traditional division of labor, which placed hunting activities as well as the protection of the village or camp in the charge of men. Men also cleared new fields for planting. Women were primarily responsible for gathering wild plant foods, planting and tending crops, building houses, cooking, and child care. On large hunting campaigns, everyone cooperated, the women processing the meat and later the hides of the animals that the men killed.

The division of labor changed for the Kansas and Oklahoma Kickapoo when they settled. Sedentary agriculture and eventually wage labor took precedence over hunting, and it was men who began to fulfill these tasks. For the Kickapoo in Mexico, the traditional divisions have undergone less change. Hunting remains important, although it has been replaced to some degree by agricultural wage labor. Nonetheless, it has allowed the continuation of the seasonal migratory pattern in which the male contribution to subsistence has been emphasized. Women take primary responsibility for the subsistence crops planted in the village at Nacimiento. During the migrations they work in the fields whenever child care and cooking allow. But it is the role of men, who cooperate in patrilineal crews just as they traditionally did for hunting, that is paramount. Religious rituals remain primarily the responsibility of men in both Oklahoma and Mexico, although healing practices are conducted by both men and women.

Land Tenure.   Prior to European encroachment, the nomadic movements of the Kickapoo precluded emphasis on land tenure. Tribal groups had traditional hunting territories over which they ranged and their fields were planted near their semipermanent villages. The Kansas Kickapoo now live on communally held federal reservation lands. The reservation lands of the Oklahoma Kickapoo were allotted individually in 1894 and excess lands sold, so that there is no actual Kickapoo settlement. The Mexican Kickapoo village of Nacimiento is classified as an *ejido* and administered according to the Mexican *Codigo Agrario*. The original families who settled there still maintain rights to the land, but in general, usufruc-

tory rights are respected. The reservation provided for this group in Texas is federally administered.

Kinship

Kin Groups and Descent.   Kickapoo social organization features thirteen groups that direct the inheritance of personal names. These nonunilineal, nonexogamous groups may have constituted patrilineal clans in the past. Association is now based on a personal name, or eponym, which is conferred by a namer who is of the same naming group. These eponymous units are groups in a system that determines reciprocal obligations among them. There are also dual divisions, which were probably true moieties in the past. The various name groups are divided into one or the other of these: *kiiskooha* is symbolized by the color white and the direction north, and *oskasa* is associated with black and south. The dual divisions provide rival teams for ball games and contests, and thereby redirect competitions and rivalries away from family, lineage, and name group. The Kickapoo are also divided into four bundle societies, which are essentially different "denominations" of the Kickapoo religion.

Kinship Terminology.   Traditional kin terms follow the Omaha system.

Marriage and Family

Marriage.   In earlier times, clans were exogamous and marriage among relatives was prohibited. An exchange of gifts established the marital ties. There was some polygyny. Usually a year's bride-service was required during which the groom simply lived with the bride's family and contributed to the economy of the household. Divorce was a very simple matter as matrimonial bonds were severed without ceremony. Today, marriages and divorces are likely to be legally sanctioned for the Kansas Kickapoo and, to a lesser extent, among those in Oklahoma. The Mexican Kickapoo, however, retain many of the traditional customs, which are not based on a formal state legal system. There is little ceremony attached to marriage. Use of a whistle language for courtship is still practiced in Mexico. After a courtship period, the groom passes a night with the bride in her house. His discovery by the bride's family on the following morning establishes the marital union. There is still a de facto period of bride-service. The newly married couple resides with the bride's family, usually until the first child is born, at which time the wife builds a house for them in or near the compound of her maternal female relatives. During the period of migratory agricultural labor, however, matrilocal residence gives way to temporary residency established around patrilineally organized bands, which also form field and orchard work crews.

Domestic Unit.   The household was traditionally the basic unit of production, with women tending to gathering and agricultural activities and men hunting. This pattern, which alternated matrilocal compounds with patrilocal camps, effectively created extended cooperative groups, although the nuclear household was the norm. This same pattern can be observed among the Kickapoo in Mexico today. Nuclear family households are more customary in Kansas and Oklahoma, but extended families are also common.

Inheritance.   Most property is passed on according to the wishes of the deceased. This includes real property, vehicles, livestock, and so on. The traditional Kickapoo house is built and owned by women, and on a woman's death, ownership usually passes to her oldest daughter. Personal belongings are divided among those who dig the grave and prepare the body for burial.

Socialization. Children are raised in a permissive fashion and are allowed to make decisions for themselves even at an early age. Fear of witches and supernatural phenomena are used by adults to control and sanction behavior, particularly among the Kickapoo in Oklahoma and Mexico. Children in Kansas and Oklahoma attend school, some going on to vocational training or college. Until recently, members of the very conservative Mexican Kickapoo have sought to avoid the acculturative effects of formal education and have purposely prevented their children from attending school. This attitude is changing owing to a closer association with the United States, which resulted from the newly established reservation in Eagle Pass, Texas, made available to them in 1986.

Sociopolitical Organization

Social Organization. Traditionally, the Kickapoo were a nonstratified society in which both material wealth and cogent authority were largely nonexistent. A religiously conservative people, individual Kickapoo acquire influence and prestige primarily from skills, accomplishments, and religious devotion and knowledge. Although ritual activities are primarily organized by and around men, women also have responsibilities through which their devotion and competence can be observed. As religion is an integral part of all aspects of Kickapoo life, carrying out any task in an appropriate and responsible manner constitutes performance of religious duties. This condition is still characterized by the Mexican Kickapoo. Increased stratification, which is due to socioeconomic factors and acculturation, is more obvious among individual members of the Oklahoma and Kansas Kickapoo.

Political Organization. Historically, the Kickapoo had a hereditary chief, who operated through influence rather than power, and a loosely structured council. This civil chief was primarily responsible for establishing hunting territories and deciding alliances. In time of war, control of the village passed to another chief who directed a council of warriors known for their military success. This group also acted as camp police, maintaining order and carrying out punishments. Today, political leadership for both the Kansas and Oklahoma Kickapoo comes from an elected tribal council. There is also a council, much more loosely structured, among the Mexican group. Business decisions notwithstanding, major influence comes from the religious leader.

Social Control. Fear of retribution from supernatural beings has always been a strong deterrent of disapproved behaviors among the Kickapoo. This remains so, particularly in Mexico and Oklahoma, where fear of witchcraft is strong. Fear of gossip and ostracism also plays an indirect role in social control, but in the case of serious crimes, direct control is now left to local non-Indian authorities, whether in Kansas, Oklahoma, Texas, or Mexico.

Conflict. The Kickapoo are a remarkably cohesive group despite an almost inherent factionalism that has persisted since contact. The Kickapoo have traditionally been very fluid, with bands breaking away and recombining. This pro-

tean pattern has served as a pressure valve to preserve intragroup solidarity. Since contact, there have been two permanent splits, however, and a third is developing. These divisions are formed between progressives and conservatives. The progressives are characterized by a tendency to settle permanently and a tolerance for cultural change and intervention by the Bureau of Indian Affairs. The conservatives are associated with a tendency to migrate as well as a stringently selective acceptance of outside cultural elements and a rejection of outside interference by non-Kickapoo. On a continuum, the Kansas Kickapoo are at the progressive end, the Mexican Kickapoo at the conservative end, and the Oklahoma Kickapoo in between. It is important to note that the Kickapoo identity is so strong that, except for disputes between individuals, there is no record of violent discord between factions. Groups of individuals who become sufficiently discordant in their cultural goals simply break away and form a new community without severing ties with the old.

Religion and Expressive Culture

Religious Beliefs. Traditionally, the Kickapoo religion has been an intrinsic part of every facet of life. The religion is animistic and includes a belief in manitous or spirit messengers. The supreme deity is Kisiihiat, who created the world and lives in the sky. Kisiihiat is assisted by a pantheon of manitous, or _manitooaki_ (plural), who are embodied in the earth, objects of nature, and natural forces, and who serve as spirit messengers. There is also a culture hero, Wisaaka, the son of Kisiihiat, who created the Indian world and taught the Kickapoo to build their houses, which are a vital element of the Kickapoo religion. Religious practice is organized around sacred bundles, _misaami_, for clans and herbal societies. The religion is protected and practiced almost fanatically among the Mexican Kickapoo, whereas the Kansas Kickapoo have been strongly affected by Christianity. Most Oklahoma Kickapoo practice the traditional religion, but some other religions, such as the Native American church and Protestant denominations, have made some impact.

Religious Practitioners. Each bundle society and clan has a leader to perform the various rituals associated with its respective sacred pack. Religious leaders have long years of training in order for them to attain the knowledge necessary to the performance of rituals, and they exercise considerable influence socially and politically.

Ceremonies. A highly ritualized cycle of ceremonies plays a part in maintaining the cultural integration of Kickapoo society in Mexico and Oklahoma, but less so in Kansas. A display of lightning and thunder, usually in early February, signifies the beginning of the New Year and hence the cycle of ceremonies. Festivals include clan and bundle rituals as well as ceremonies and dances that encompass all village members. Special ceremonial foods play a role in these feasts and are eaten with ceremonial ladles.

Arts. Dancing and singing are important to Kickapoo ceremonial life as are the instruments of accompaniment such as drums, flutes, and rattles. Some dances and songs are owned by individuals and may be performed only at their invitation.

Medicine. Religious ritual and herbal treatments are combined in traditional medical practices. A wide variety of plants are used in curing rituals and may be conducted by clan leaders, members of bundle societies, and individuals. The Buffalo Dance and Woman's Dance are often associated with treatment of illness and infertility. Modern medicine is accepted by all three Kickapoo groups, sometimes in combination with traditional healing.

Death and Afterlife.   Death is accepted with some equanimity and is surrounded with little display of emotion or prolonged mourning. The spirit will journey to a place in the West and reside there happily. There is some fear of the spirits of the dead, however, and children and surviving spouses are considered at risk. Burial takes place after an all-night wake during which chants and prayers are performed. Several times a year, clan members gather to "feed the ghosts" of deceased relatives in the belief that they, too, get hungry. Between four days and four years of death, a special friend of the same sex and approximate age will be adopted into the role of the deceased among his or her consanguineal kin.

Bibliography

Callender, Charles, Richard K. Pope, and Susan M. Pope (1978). "Kickapoo." In *Handbook of North American Indians*. Vol. 15, *Northeast*, edited by Bruce G. Trigger, 656–667. Washington, D.C.: Smithsonian Institution.

Latorre, Felipe, and Dolores Latorre (1976). *The Mexican Kickapoo Indians*. Austin: University of Texas Press.

Nunley, Mary Christopher (1986). *The Mexican Kickapoo Indians: Avoidance of Acculturation through a Migratory Adaptation*. Ann Arbor: University Microfilms International.

MARY CHRISTOPHER NUNLEY

Kiowa

ETHNONYMS: Caigua, Kioway, Manrhoat, Watapahato

Orientation

Identification.   "Kae-gua" (Kiowa plural) is an inflected form of an unanalyzable base; most historic appellations are variants of this form. Other traditional terms of self-reference include "Kwu' da" and "Tepda," both translated as "coming out, emerging"; and "Kompabianta," "big tipi-flaps" (explained as a reference to large smoke-hole flaps on Kiowa tipis).

Location.   Throughout their recorded history, the Kiowa heartland has been between 35° and 37° N and 98° and 100° W in present-day Oklahoma, the Texas Panhandle, and southern Kansas. This territory, intersected by tributaries of the Arkansas, Canadian, and Red rivers, was the region within which tribal summer encampments were located; at other times, bands could be more widely dispersed, and hunting, trading, and war parties traveled far from the heartland. Most Kiowa still live in this region of Oklahoma, centered around the towns of Anadarko and Carlisle.

Demography.   Population may have been from 2,000 to 2,500 before contact. The first census, in 1875, reported 1,070 members, and numbers remained low in succeeding decades, reaching 1,699 in 1920. A 1970 tribal count of 6,250 included persons of part-Kiowa ancestry and the descendants of non-Kiowa individuals who were affiliated with the tribe in the treaty period; it is likely that no more than half of this number are of predominantly Kiowa descent. The 1980 census lists 7,386 individuals claiming Kiowa descent.

History and Cultural Relations

The Kiowa are identifiable by name beginning around 1800; earlier evidence is complicated by the uncertainty of some identifications (for example, the "Manrhoat" of 1682). Kiowa cultural identity was forged in the Great Plains after the adoption of the horse into the regional culture and possibly after the entry of European traders. The time, place, and circumstances of ethnogenesis present problems to scholars. Tradition points to a northern homeland, located in the Yellowstone region of the Rocky Mountains; legendary accounts of emergence from an underworld and a long southward migration continue to have strong emotional appeal to the Kiowa people. But serious efforts to trace Kiowa origins must also take into account their linguistic kinship to the Tanoan peoples of New Mexico, a connection that is echoed in cultural traits, including folklore motifs and details of ceremonial life. On the other hand, sociopolitical organization shows convergence to a Plains type, with strongest points of similarity to north Plains and Plateau tribes such as the Teton Dakota, Kutenai, and Sarsi. A preliminary model of Kiowa ethnogenesis must locate the ancestral population in the south plains, adjacent to related Tanoans of the Rio Grande valley, at a time prior to the entry of Apacheans into the region, about A.D. 1100 to 1300.

Subsequent expansion of the Apache in the plains had the effect of separating the ancestral Kiowa from their cogeners, forcing their retreat eastward and northward. A part of this population remained as far south as the Arkansas-Canadian drainage, within or marginal to their aboriginal hunting range, while others, either as refugees or in pursuit of trade, traveled as far as the Yellowstone valley. Historical records, including the journal of Lewis and Clark, confirm Kiowa claims of contacts with the Crow, Sarsi, and Cheyenne, and an association with the Black Hills region early in the nineteenth century. During the same years, Kiowa further south formed an alliance with the Comanche, who had displaced the Apache in the New Mexican borderlands region and were able to reestablish contacts with New Mexico. Throughout historic times, the Kiowa had a close relationship with the Kwahadi band of Comanche; they also maintained friendly ties with Taos and other New Mexican Pueblos in the west, and with the Wichita and other Caddoans in the east. They traded with most Plains tribes, claiming a special tie with the Crow. Although closely associated with the Kiowa Apache, relations were usually hostile with western Apachean groups, including the Navajo. In the east, the Osage were long-time enemies with whom the Kiowa finally made peace in 1837 under U.S. government pressure. Their geographical position enabled the Kiowa to deal with White traders in New Mexico and in the Mississippi valley; however, both hunting and trade declined before the treaty period.

In 1867, the Treaty of Medicine Lodge was made between the United States and the Comanche, Kiowa, and Kiowa Apache, who received combined reservation lands in Oklahoma. Despite outbreaks of violence during the following decade, and the arrest and imprisonment of their leaders, the Kiowa remained settled on lands within their traditional heartland. In 1892, under the Jerome Agreement, they accepted individual allotments of 160 acres plus a tribal bloc of grazing land; the agreement is unique in making provisions for non-Kiowa attached to the tribe to receive a share in tribal lands.

Settlements

The nineteenth-century Kiowa followed a pattern of seasonal nomadism which was, at least in part, determined by the need for pasturage for their horse herds. From fall to early summer, the tribe dispersed; extended family groups formed the nuclei of bands, led by influential men or at times by brothers. The bands were flexible; small families and isolated individuals, whether related or not, might join the camp of a successful chief. During the summer months, the bands camped together for a period of several weeks; during this time, the Sun Dance ceremony was held. The site was always on a sizable stream and was chosen for its access to grass, firewood, and game—especially bison. At an appointed time, the subtribes arrived in a prescribed order and took designated places in the camp circle. In the 1880s there were five Kiowa subtribes, with the Kiowa Apache occupying a sixth place in the circle. Until bison became scarce, the Sun Dance was the prelude to a communal hunt. Plans for the coming year were made during the summer encampment; band movements must have been coordinated, since messengers were able to travel quickly and directly between the scattered winter camps; a circuit to announce the time and place of the Sun Dance could be completed in about three days.

Economy

Subsistence and Commercial Activities. The early Kiowa were hunters on a large scale and processed products of the hunt (robes, leather, horn, sinew, meat) both for subsistence use and for trade. They also raised and bred horses, supplementing their herds by raids into alien territories. The diet included bison, deer, and other game; wild plant foods such as berries and wild potatoes; and a substantial amount of maize, dried pumpkin, and other foods obtained in trade from both Indian and Hispanic populations of New Mexico.

Industrial Arts. The most notable traditional craft was the processing of leather, mainly performed by women. Clothing, moccasins and boots, and parfleches and other containers were made of bison and deerskins, and decorated with paint and beads.

Trade. The Kiowa were active traders and could be considered a semispecialized trading group. Trade parties traveled to New Mexico and all parts of the Great Plains, and are known to have gone frequently into Canada and Mexico. The natural pastures of the Kiowa provided a source of horses for northern tribes such as the Blackfoot, Sarsi, and Crow. From the time of La Salle, horses were delivered to White purchasers; in the nineteenth century, the Kiowa often dealt with U.S. military parties. Raiders returned from Mexico with horses and mules to supplement the herds and with other goods. Mexican textiles, weapons, and musical instruments were valued and became important as ceremonial attire; further, the Kiowa were known as purveyors as well as users of peyote, which they transported from Mexico. In 1835, the Kiowa in Oklahoma had a relationship with the Chouteau trading company of St. Louis, which built trading posts in Kiowa territory in the next decade. It is possible that an earlier tie to U.S. or British trading companies in the Missouri drainage led the Kiowa to the north, explaining their traditional claim to the Yellowstone country.

Division of Labor. Traditionally, men were hunters, horsemen, warriors, and traders; women collected plants, processed foodstuffs and hides, made clothing, and erected and maintained the skin lodges. In reality, male and female roles probably overlapped, and many men were frequently away for war or trade. Numerous captives did not form a servile class, but were adopted by Kiowa families; they did have a special ceremonial status, given the task of handling sacred artifacts that were taboo to full tribal members.

Land Tenure. Like other nomadic peoples, the Kiowa had a strong identification with their land but did not acknowledge individual tenure. The subtribes were essentially regional divisions; there is no indication that their territories were exclusive or strictly delimited. Private ownership of land began when treaty lands were apportioned in 1892.

Kinship

Kin Groups and Descent. There are indications of an early shift from patrilineal to the bilateral descent that has prevailed since the nineteenth century. The kindred, as defined by prohibition of marriage, extended to third cousins or beyond. There is no indication of the existence of corporate descent groups.

Kinship Terminology. Early Kiowa kinship terminology is not well documented. A list published in 1923 reveals a bilateral system with Hawaiian cousin terminology. In the first ascending generation, bifurcate merging terminology suggests an original Iroquois system. Certain sibling and in-law terms were differentiated for male and female speaker; grandparent and grandchild terms were identical; and sibling terms were used between great-grandparent and great-grandchild. Kin terms were extended to all band members.

Marriage and Family

Marriage. Bands were, in effect, exogamous, since marriage was prohibited to all classed as kin. Polygyny (usually sororal) was practiced; important chiefs often had several wives. The levirate was common, but not obligatory. Horses were the usual marriage gift, the number signifying the wealth and status of the groom. Divorce was common: a wife's kin might, with cause, remove her from the husband's household, or a marriage could end with absconding or elopement, followed by payment of compensation.

Domestic Unit. Residence was normally patrilocal; as one exception, a chief would give away a daughter to a promising young man, who then joined the camp of his father-in-law.

Inheritance. At death, personal possessions were destroyed. Horses (the only important form of private property) would normally pass from a man to his brother or son. Inheritance of a position—for example, as band chief or *Taime* (priest)—was preferably patrilineal but, in practice, was selective within the kindred. Custodanship of a medicine bundle might ideally go to a son, but in known cases this position passed to a variety of relations, male and female; a willingness to comply with the rigid demands of the position could influence the decision.

Socialization. Small children were, by all accounts, treated with affection and indulgence. The tie between siblings was emphasized; the brother-sister relationship took precedence over that of husband and wife. A favored child, male or female, was raised in status by a give-away of horses and property, and received special care and privileges. At around six years, all boys became members of the Rabbit Society and were instructed as a group in horsemanship and other skills; in adolescence they joined the adult military societies. Bravery, restraint, wisdom, and generosity were qualities admired in men and, to a degree, in women as well.

Sociopolitical Organization

Social Organization. Status distinctions reflected wealth, warfare honors, and political power. Highest prestige went to chiefs of the largest bands and to religious leaders. The fact that many historic Kiowa chiefs bore names that were eponymous of the bear (such as White Bear, Many Bears, Sitting Bear) and were passed from generation to generation suggests a continuity in leadership that may, at an earlier time, have been vested in a lineage or other descent group. Women had fewer opportunities to achieve individual prestige; however, folklore and personal histories indicate that a high value was placed on strong, resourceful Kiowa women, whose importance in community life should not be underestimated. Ex-captives had a marginal position but were able to achieve distinction in warfare and other pursuits.

Political Organization. Through most of the year, bands were largely independent; successful chiefs, who attracted and retained the largest following, had the greatest renown and influence. During the summer season, the Taime priest was in charge of the Sun Dance camp; order was maintained in the camp and during the hunt by military societies, which cut across the band membership but included all adult men of the tribe. For at least four generations, the Kiowa were politically unified under a head chief; the last to hold this rank was Dohasan (Little Bluff), who died in 1866. After his death, at the beginning of the reservation period, leadership became factionalized between chiefs such as Satanta (White Bear) and Lone Wolf, who resisted surrender, and others, including Kickingbird, who favored compromise. After a brief period of reservation life, the Kiowa were given individual allotments of land in 1892, and the area was opened to White settlement. A Kiowa Tribal Council, formed in 1969, represents Kiowa concerns in health, education, and economic development.

Social Control. The secular power of chiefs and military societies was complemented by the spiritual authority of the Taime and medicine bundle priests. Within the tribe, a serious affront might provoke revenge, but intervention by a priest prevented the escalation of quarrels. Offering the pipe and appealing to the fetishes served to invoke supernatural sanctions; violation of vows or a sanction imposed under these circumstances was potentially fatal, resulting in *taido*, an irreversible spiritual decline.

Conflict. In historic times, the importance attached to horses promoted intertribal raiding; hostilities often escalated through the avenging of death or injury. The Kiowa usually sought an intermediary to make peace with an enemy group. Chronic enmity toward the Apache and more recent hatred of Texans may have resulted from their expansion into Kiowa territory. Like other Plains tribes, the Kiowa suffered from the inroads of eastern Indians, such as the Cherokee and Shawnee, as these were moved westward in the nineteenth century.

Religion and Expressive Culture

Religious Beliefs. A pervasive underlying supernatural power was seen primarily in natural phenomena, which were personified and at times deified. The Kiowa revered the Sun, constellations such as the Pleiades, and natural forces such as the Cyclone, and gave special respect to the bison, bear, and eagle. Sendeh (or Sainday) is the main protagonist in Kiowa tales, as both culture hero and trickster; he has human rather than animal attributes. Spider Woman, Twin Heroes (Split Boys), and Coyote, suggestive of Southwestern affinities, appear in origin and explanatory tales. Personified natural forces and animal spirits were encountered in visionary experiences. Individuals sought power through the Sun Dance and personal visionary experiences. The Taime, an anthropomorphic effigy; medicine bundles; and several other fetishes were prominent in hunting, curing, and purification rites. In 1873, Quaker mission efforts began among the Kiowa, followed by Methodist, Baptist, and other denominations. The Native American Church also increased in importance as the Sun Dance and other hunting and war ceremonies declined. Protestant affiliation is now the norm; however, traditional practices continue and have experienced revival. As in earlier days, tribal ceremonies are concentrated in the summer, now centered on July 4.

Religious Practitioners. The Taime and medicine bundle priests were subject to numerous taboos and requirements of circumspect behavior. The Taime was housed in a special tipi and carried in public display by its priest; a select group of men, who had received visions, assisted him. Owners of the ten medicine bundles were called upon to intervene in disputes and could give sanctuary. Buffalo doctors were especially qualified to treat illness attributed to violation of taboos on the bear.

Ceremonies. The Sun Dance was held annually until 1887 when it was prohibited by the government and halted by military force. Other traditional dances, such as those of the warrior societies, also performed in the summer season, are now part of the July 4 celebration. A scalp dance followed the return of men from war; curing ceremonies were held at any time. The Feather Dance, the Kiowa response to the Ghost Dance movement, became institutionalized as the Invisible 00Church and held semiannual dances until prohibited in 1916; beliefs and iconography were a blend of Kiowa tradition and Christian influences. Some vestiges of this movement carried over into sectarian Christian churches. Peyotism now follows the pan-Indian ceremonialism of the Native American Church.

Arts. Tipi covers were often decorated with designs that symbolized the accomplishments of the owner; these designs, handed down through generations of the same family, constituted a type of heraldic emblem. The painted designs of Sun Dance shields also had symbolic significance, related to membership in warrior or medicine societies. Calendar histories, painted on buffalo hide, depicted important events of successive summer and winter periods; these are a valuable source of information about the nineteenth-century Kiowa. More recently, individual Kiowa have shown remarkable talent in graphic arts; a group known as the "Kiowa Five" (Spencer Asah, Stephen Mopope, Jack Hokeah, James Auchiah, and Monroe Tsatoke) became internationally recognized early in the present century, setting a pattern for Kiowa successes in the arts; literary artists include the poet N. Scott Momaday. Kiowa craftsmen have been active in the production of jewelry and silverwork based on traditional designs and marketed through the Oklahoma Indian Arts and Crafts Cooperative.

Medicine. The sweatbath was used for curing and for ritual purification. Ill health as well as misfortune was often seen as the result of supernatural harm or the violation of taboo. Certain older women served as herbalists and midwives, assisting with difficult births. Buffalo doctors and other curers received power through visionary experiences; shamanistic methods were used in healing.

Death and Afterlife. The elderly and disabled were abandoned if they could no longer travel. Mourning involved slashing of clothing, gashing the skin, cropping the hair; women might amputate finger joints. The dead were buried, preferably in a remote, isolated spot. Personal property of the deceased was destroyed and the name tabooed, unless bestowed on an heir before death.

Bibliography

Boyd, Maurice, ed. (1981–1983). _Kiowa Voices._ 2 vols. Fort Worth: Texas Christian University Press.

Mooney, James (1898). _Calendar History of the Kiowa Indians._ U.S. Bureau of American Ethnology, 17th Annual Report (1895–1896), 129–445. Washington, D.C.

Parsons, Elsie C. (1929). _Kiowa Tales._ American Folklore Society, Memoir no. 22. New York.

Richardson, Jane (1940). _Law and Status among the Kiowa Indians._ American Ethnological Society, Monograph no. 1. New York.

NANCY P. HICKERSON

Kiowa Apache

ETHNONYMS: Prairie Apache, Semat

The Kiowa Apache are a small Athapaskan group who at the time of sustained contact with Europeans in the early nineteenth century lived in the northwestern plains. Later they relocated to the general area of the Oklahoma Panhandle and adjoining sections of Kansas, Colorado, Texas, and New Mexico. They now number about nine hundred and are associated with the Kiowa and Comanche in southwestern Oklahoma. The Kiowa Apache speak an Athapaskan language closely related to Jicarilla Apache and Lipan Apache. All other Apache groups were forced to migrate to the southwest under pressure from the Comanche, but the Kiowa Apache remained on the plains and since that time have not had any political connection with other Apache tribes. They were able to resist the Comanche through their close relationship with the Kiowa. The Kiowa Apache became one of the seven bands of the Kiowa, camping with them in the summer to hunt bison and celebrate common rituals. There was also some intermarriage with the Kiowa. Along with the Kiowa they obtained horses early, and as a result the bison became the mainstay of their subsistence economy. Agricultural products were obtained through trade with the Pueblos and other sedentary peoples.

Throughout the nineteenth century, the Kiowa Apache maintained generally friendly relations with Whites. In the twentieth century, they at first shared a joint tribal constitution with the Kiowa and Comanche and then in 1972 ratified their own constitution, placing tribal governance in the hands of a tribal business council. Most Kiowa Apache children now attend public schools, and many continue their education at vocational schools or college.

See also Kiowa

Bibliography

Bittle, William E. (1971). "A Brief History of the Kiowa Apache." _University of Oklahoma, Papers in Anthropology_ 12:1–34.

McAllister, J. Gilbert (1970). _Dä vé ko: Kiowa-Apache Medicine Man._ Texas Memorial Museum Bulletin no. 17. Austin.

Whitewolf, Jim (1969). _Jim Whitewolf: The Life of a Kiowa Apache Indian._ New York: Dover Publications.

Klallam

ETHNONYMS: Clallam, Tlalem

As described here, "Klallam" refers to an American Indian group that includes the Klallam proper, the Lummi, Nootsack (Nooksack), Samish, Samiamoo (Semiahmoo),

Songish (Lkungen), and the Sooke. They live in the general area of the shores of northern Puget Sound, more specifically on the northeastern part of the Olympic Peninsula in Washington, on the southeastern tip of Vancouver Island, and on the adjacent coast and islands of northwestern Washington. Today, they reside on a number of reservations in the United States, among them the Lower Elwha Reservation, the Lummi Reservation, and the Port Gamble Reservation, with others living on reserves in British Columbia. Numerous individuals and families have relocated to cities such as Vancouver, Victoria, Port Angeles, and Seattle. There are about twenty-five hundred Klallam living in the region today.

First contact with Europeans was probably with Juan de Fuca in 1592, although it was another two hundred years before contacts with the Spanish explorer Manuel Quimper and the British captain George Vancouver led to sustained contact. Much change to the traditional culture resulted from the establishment of the city of Victoria on Vancouver Island in 1843, as it became a meeting place for Whites and numerous Indian tribes.

The traditional Klallam culture was similar to that of other Northwest Coast groups. Subsistence was based on fishing, mainly for various species of salmon, but also for herring, smelt, cod, flounder, halibut, and trout. Whales and seals were hunted when available, and several types of shellfish were gathered. Women collected berries and nuts, camas bulbs, and fern roots. Wood, especially the red cedar, was a key resource and was the basic material in house and canoe building. Steamed and bent cedar strips and cedar bark were made into boxes, utensils, dishes, clothing, rope, and furnishings.

Like most other Northwest Coast groups, Klallam society was stratified into classes of nobles, commoners, and slaves. There were numerous villages along the coastline, each ruled by a chief who ruled on the basis of heredity and wealth. Chiefs gave potlatches to enhance their prestige, often organizing them at the time of marriages and girls' puberty rites and to honor the dead. The Klallam waged war with the Makah, Squamish, and other neighboring groups as well as northern groups such as the Haida and Tsimshian who raided them for slaves. They were regularly involved in trade, both with neighboring groups and with groups on the eastern side of the Cascade Mountains. Items traded include horses, dried clams, blankets, skins, oils, dried fish, and venison.

Most of the Klallam groups have been converted to Christianity, the Lummi being mainly Roman Catholic and the others Protestant. They are largely assimilated into White society. The Lummi are noted for their aquacultural project, growing amd harvesting food from the nearby waters, and for their fish hatchery program.

Bibliography

Gunther, Erna (1927). *Klallam Ethnography*. University of Washington Publications in Anthropology 1(5). Seattle.

Nugent, Ann, ed. (1979). *The History of Lummi Fishing Rights*. Bellingham, Wash.: Lummi Communications.

Nugent, Ann, and Evan Kinley, eds. (1982). *Lummi Elders Speak*. Lynden, Wash., and Ferndale, Wash.: Lynden Tribune

and the Lummi Education Center, Lummi Historical Publications.

Stern, Bernard J. (1969). *The Lummi Indians of Western Washington*. New York: AMS Press. Originally published, 1934.

Klamath

ETHNONYMS: Clamath, Lutuami, Maklaks

Orientation

Identification. The Klamath were an American Indian group who lived in southern Oregon and northern California. Although the Klamath no longer exist as a distinct cultural entity, descendants of the Klamath who are identified as ethnically Klamath still live in their aboriginal territory. During the reservation period from 1864 to 1954 the Klamath were closely tied to the Modoc and the Yahuskin Paiute, with the latter two groups being largely assimilated into the Klamath during this period. The Klamath name for themselves is "Maklaks," meaning "people" or "community."

Location. As far can be determined, the Klamath had lived for some time before contact in what is today southern Oregon and northern California. The Modoc were situated mostly in northern California. Prior to the reservation period, the Klamath and Modoc claimed over 20 million acres of land in this region. The Klamath Reservation was located in Klamath County, Oregon, at about 121° to 122° W and 42° to 43° N. This region, with elevations over four thousand feet, is characterized by streams and marshes, and long, snowy winters. Fish, mussels, and water fowl were abundant. Culturally, this area is on the boundaries of the Great Basin, Plateau, and California regions. The Klamath displayed a number of cultural features typical of the aboriginal Plateau groups and, in later times, of the Northwest Coast region. The Modoc displayed some cultural features of northern California groups.

Demography. Estimates in the late 1700s placed the number of Klamath at from 400 to 1,000. In 1848 there were about 1,000. In 1930, 2,034 Klamath and Modocs were counted, and in 1958, shortly after the Klamath Reservation was terminated, the Klamath numbered 2,133. Since they were mixed with other Indian groups and Whites after being placed on the reservation, accurate population counts are not possible.

Linguistic Affiliation. The Klamath and the Modoc spoke dialects of the Lutuami language, which is classified in the Klamath-Sahaptin family of Penutian languages. There are probably no more than a few speakers of Klamath alive today.

History and Cultural Relations

The Klamath and Modoc believe that they entered the southern Oregon region as one people, later separating as the Modoc settled farther to the south. That they spoke dialects of the same language provides some support for this belief. The earliest influences of European society were indirect, primarily through trade relations with Northern Great Basin groups who had obtained horses and other goods from Plains tribes. Sustained contact began in 1826, and the Klamath were quickly drawn into a trading network with Whites and other Indian groups at The Dalles and other trading centers. Unlike many other groups, the Klamath did not suffer from European-introduced epidemic diseases nor from hostilities with White settlers.

In 1864 the Klamath entered into a treaty with the federal government, ceding their aboriginal land in return for the over one-million-acre Klamath Reservation, where they were joined by the Modoc and Yahuskin Paiute. In 1866 the Klamath Agency was established, leading to federal government control of Klamath life that was to continue until termination in 1954. Beginning in 1895, reservation land began to be allotted to individual Klamath and later to Modocs who returned from Oklahoma where they had been sent following their defeat by the federal government in the war of 1872–1873.

In the first half of the twentieth century, Klamath society underwent profound economic and political changes through contacts with neighboring Whites and the policies of the various federal agents who administered the reservation. During this same period, they were involved in a series of land claims and natural resource suits with the federal and state governments and local land companies. In August 1954 a majority of the Klamath agreed to a federal proposal to end federal oversight and administration of the reservation. This led to serious problems as federal and Bureau of Indian Affairs programs were ended, individual Klamath were awarded large cash payments, and many individuals lost a sense of Klamath identity. Beginning in 1964, the Klamath were involved in a series of legal battles about old land claims and the sale of the reservation land and were eventually awarded over $20 million in settlements. Efforts to reverse termination and regain federal recognition as an Indian tribe have so far been unsuccessful.

Settlements

Prior to the reservation period, the Klamath lived in settled villages during the cold, snowy winter months. These villages were often located along streams or in sheltered spots and contained anywhere from a few to dozens of semisubterranean earthlodges. Major villages were located at Klamath Lake, Klamath Marsh, and on the Williamson and Sprague rivers. In the spring and summer they generally moved to fishing spots and lived in mat-covered lodges. Once on the reservation, the population shifted to a number of towns: Chiloquin, Modoc Point, and Klamath Agency at the southern end and Sprague River and Beatty at the northern end. Over time, many Klamath also settled off the reservation, though near it, in search of jobs, schools, and stores. Since many Whites also settled in the reservation towns, the Klamath were usually a minority in the communities where they lived.

Economy

Subsistence and Commercial Activities. Aboriginally, the Klamath were fishers, gatherers, and hunters. Fish and pond lily seeds (*wokas*), which were ground into flour, were the dietary staples. Fruit, berries, and roots were gathered and deer, antelope, and waterfowl hunted. A surplus was obtained and stored in communal pits or in the earthlodges for consumption in the winter months. Once on the reservation and under agency control, the economy changed markedly. Although fishing, gathering, and hunting continued, the Klamath entered the regional cash economy as their economic base diversified. Stock raising became an important activity, with cattle raised for beef and for sale, and horses, mules, and pigs also raised. Attempts to introduce farming were less than successful and eventually focused on growing hay to feed the livestock. Rich in timberlands, the Klamath early on entered the logging industry and cut and hauled timber for their own use and for sale to Whites. Since federal rules forbade the cutting of live trees on the reservation, the Klamath and their customers developed schemes to circumvent this restriction. Hauling of freight, day labor, and work in the service sector also provided income during the reservation period. As more and more Klamath moved off the reservation, day labor, particularly as farm workers, became more important.

Industrial Arts. The Klamath made use of the variety of raw materials in their relatively rich environment. Woodworking was relatively unimportant, with the dugout canoes fashioned largely through burning. Mats from tule and swamp grass were used for inner and outer earthlodge covers and as bedding. Basketry was highly developed and was the source of most household utensils. Clothing, especially for the wealthy, was sewn from hides. The bow and arrow was used for hunting, supplemented by clubs, spears, and body armor for warfare.

Trade. After contact in 1826 the Klamath were active participants in the trade network with other Indian groups and Whites. They traded slaves taken from California groups and *wokas* for horses, blankets, buffalo skins, and dried salmon mainly with groups from the Northwest Coast and Plateau. After settlement on the reservation, trade gave way to involvement in the regional cash economy.

Division of Labor. Aboriginally, men hunted, women gathered, and both participated in fishing. Under the agency system, much of the new work went to men, leaving mostly domestic chores and traditional activities to the women.

Kinship, Marriage and Family

Kinship Terminology. Kin terms followed the Hawaiian system.

Marriage. Marriage was by gift exchange, with the bride's family generally giving more than the groom's. Since marriage to kin was forbidden, village exogamy predominated, with a slight tendency toward marriage within the tribelet. Wealthy men might take more than one wife, with sororal polygyny and the levirate present. Postmarital residence was generally patrilocal, though matrilocal residence did occur, particularly when the groom was poor. Divorce was easy and common.

Domestic Unit. Earthlodges housed a number of nuclear families, with the residents all related to one another. In addition, most residents of a village were kin.

Socialization. Daughters of chiefs and other wealthy families were afforded a puberty dance at first menstruation. Other girls followed the same food taboos and other restrictions, but did not dance in public. Boys at puberty were sent on a five-day dream quest.

Sociopolitical Organization

Social Organization. The winter village was the basic social unit, with the same families returning to their earthlodges each year. Although true social classes were absent, a distinction was made between the wealthy and the remainder of the population and slaves were kept. Wealth was symbolized by the possession of horses, slaves, beads, archers' equipment, canoes, furs, hides, large lodges, and other material items. In 1864 the slaves were freed, and many returned to their native groups.

Political Organization. There were five or six geographical subdivisions or tribelets of the Klamath. The major tribelets were those living on Klamath Marsh and the middle Williamson River. Other tribelets were located near Agency Lake, Pelican Bay, Klamath Falls, and the Sprague River valley. These divisions disappeared after settlement on the reservation. Chieftainship was weakly developed, with some villages having chiefs and others having none. Chiefs were men who had acquired prestige through warfare or wealth, were able public speakers and had some spirit experiences. The intensification of trade before placement on the reservation led a few men to acquire much wealth and increase their authority. During the reservation period, the Klamath had a general council, though they were largely under the control of the succession of agents at Klamath Agency.

Social Control and Conflict. The Klamath warred with other groups. All Klamath tribelets fought together, perhaps under the direction of a principal chief. War was motivated by plunder, a desire for slaves, and for revenge. Traditional enemies included the Shasta, Northern Paiute, Takelma, Kalapuya, and Pit River groups. Relations were close with the Modoc and peaceful with the Molala and Wishram-Wasco. Blood feuds between tribelets were not uncommon and were often precipitated by the murder of a man living with a wife of another tribelet. The feuds were usually ended by a negotiated payment of compensation.

Religion and Expressive Culture

Religious Beliefs. Every Klamath sought spiritual power in vision quests, which took place at life crises such as puberty and mourning. The spirits were poorly defined, but primarily took the form of nature spirits or anthropomorphic beings. Klamath mythology was dominated by the culture hero Kemukemps, a trickster figure who had created men and women.

Religious Practitioners. Shamans enjoyed considerable prestige and authority, often more than did chiefs. Shamans were people who had acquired more spiritual power than had others. Shamanistic performances, during which the shamans became possessed, were the main forms of Klamath ceremonialism. These performances were held in the winter and lasted five days and nights. The shamans' services could be invoked at any time during the year for such purposes as prophecy, divination, or weather control, in addition to curative funtions.

Arts. The Klamath made a flute, three types of rattles, and a hand drum. Basketry was decorated with geometric designs.

Death and Afterlife. The deceased were cremated, and their possessions and valuables given by others in their honor burned with the body. Mourning was a personal matter with a mourning period and behavioral restrictions without public ceremony.

Bibliography

Ray, Verne F. (1963). *Primitive Pragmatists: The Modoc Indians of Northern California*. American Ethnological Society Monograph no. 38. Seattle: University of Washington Press.

Spier, Leslie (1930). *Klamath Ethnography*. University of California Publications in American Archaeology and Ethnology, 30. Berkeley.

Stern, Theodore (1965). *The Klamath Tribe: A People and Their Reservation*. American Ethnological Society Monograph no. 41. Seattle: University of Washington Press.

M. MARLENE MARTIN

Klikitat

The Klikitat (Klickitat, Qwulhhwaipum), including the Mical and the Taidnapam (Taitnapam, Upper Cowlitz), lived in southwestern Washington on the north side of the Columbia River between The Dalles and Kelso, Washington. Most of them now live on the Yakima Indian Reservation, and are largely absorbed into the Yakima. They speak a Sahaptin language and numbered twenty-one in 1970.

Bibliography

Beach, Margery Ann (1985). "The Waptashi Prophet and the Feather Religion: Derivative of the Washani." *American Indian Quarterly* 9:325–333.

Koyukon

The Koyukon (Coyukon), including the Kolchan-Teneyna, both Athapaskan-speaking groups, live in the Yukon River basin south of the mouth of the Tanana River in central Alaska. There are about five hundred Koyukon speakers living in communities in their traditional area.

Bibliography

Clark, Annette McFadyen (1981). "Koyukon." In _Handbook of North American Indians._ Vol. 6, _Subarctic,_ edited by June Helm, 582–601. Washington, D.C.: Smithsonian Institution.

Kumeyaay

ETHNONYMS: Diegueño, Ipai, Kamia, Nytipai, Quemaya, Tipai, Yaguin

Orientation

Identification. The Kumeyaay are an American Indian group located in southern California and often called the "Diegueño" or "Tipai-Ipai." The Spanish recorded dialect variants of "Kumayaay," the people's name for themselves. "Kamia" is a Mohave variant. The San Diego Mission named the nearby Indians "Diegueño." Dialect variants of "Ipai" mean "people." Some sib names: "Kwash," "Kwamaay," "Kuñeil," "Akwa'ala" (southerners) used by Kumeyaay for southern villages.

Location. At contact, Kumeyaays held the area from below Todos Santos Bay, Baja California, to above Agua Hedionda Lagoon, California, approximately 31° to 33°15′ N. The northern boundary extended along the southern divide above San Luis Rey River to Palomar Mountain, across Valle de San Jose, to the desert along the northern divide above San Felipe Creek, then to the sand hills west of the Colorado River, and south to the river below Yuma. From south of Todos Santos Bay, the southern boundary angled northeast to the Colorado River above the Cocopa. Today, the Kumeyaay have thirteen small reservations in San Diego County and four in Baja California.

Demography. In 1980, approximately 1,700 lived on or near Kumeyaay reservations in San Diego County and 350 in Baja California. These figures exclude those on mixed-tribe reservations and those living away, possibly another 1,700. In 1769, approximately 20,000 existed, based on mission birth and death records and the 1860 federal census.

Linguistic Affiliation. Kumeyaay belongs to the Yuman language family, Hokan stock. Each village had its dialect with differences increased by distance.

History and Cultural Relations

Linguistically, about two thousand years seem to separate the Kumeyaay from the Quechan on the Colorado River. Some archaeologists recognize a gradual material culture change from 5000 B.C. to that recognized as "Diegueño" by 100 B.C. Mythology and southern band territories suggest that the ancestors of some Kumeyaays were there by 5000 to 8000 B.C. At contact, tribal neighbors in Baja California were speakers of Yuman languages: Cochimi, Kiliwa, Paipai, and Cocopa; to the east were Quechan and Mohave. On the north, Takic-speaking Shoshonean peoples entered about two thousand years ago, Luiseño on the coast, Cupeño at Warner Springs, and Cahuilla in the mountains and desert. Relations with neighbors alternated between war, trade, intermarriage, and ceremonial exchange.

In 1769, continuous contact with Europeans began when Franciscans founded San Diego Mission with a military post, San Diego Presidio. Soon after, Dominicans established missions in northern Baja California. Except for the 1818 foundation of Santa Ysabel Assistancia, Spanish and Mexicans controlled only coastal and near-coastal areas. Raids, revolts, and fugitivism characterized Kumeyaay-mission relations. Unlike other missions, San Diego and San Luis Rey kept only unmarried women, the sick, and the elderly at the missions owing to lack of agricultural land nearby. They brought in a group, taught them Catholicism, European agriculture, and crafts, and then returned them to the village except for labor drafts and special ceremonies. After mission secularization, most Kumeyaay fled and revolted, holding Mexicans to the coast.

America's entrance in 1846 did not cause much land loss until the Civil War ended. The few 1875 executive order reservations were insecure until trust-patented in 1891, when additional lands were reserved for some villages. By then, most were pushed to dry slopes above their original well-watered agricultural valleys. Many received no reservation: some took refuge in a cemetery, Jamul, receiving federal recognition in 1976, and others fled to Baja California, where non-Indian settlers did not crowd them until after 1940.

Settlements

Until evicted by settlers, villages were near permanent water sources, rivers, or springs. Depending upon a valley's richness, band territory extended ten to thirty miles on both sides of a stream to divides above the valley. Band population ranged from three hundred to more than five hundred persons. The _Kwaaypaay_ (band chief), priests, and environmental specialists lived in a central village; each family had a separate homestead near subsidiary water sources. Central villages held ceremonial grounds and meeting areas, and were surrounded by a cactus fence or nearby palisade refuge. Mountain villages were near fortified rocky peaks. Large villages had an area for trade or ceremonial visitors. European disease and starvation owing to land loss drastically reduced the number of villages and populations. On reservations, families follow the pattern of scattered homesteads with a central ceremonial and meeting area. If possible, economic developments are away from homes.

House structures varied with the environment: earth-covered in the desert, A-frame covered with cedar bark in mountains, and brush- or reed-covered willow branch domes near the coast. Building size varied from those holding four or five people to those holding forty. Settlers evicted them from the rectangular adobe homes introduced by the Spanish. Most modern reservation houses were built by Indians. The Bureau of Indian Affairs built some with the cost charged against Indian claims awards. Some Department of Housing and Urban Development housing also exists.

Economy

Subsistence and Commercial Activities. Southern California Indians had a mixed economy: plant husbandry, agriculture, and collecting, combined with hunting and fishing. They tried all food, medicinal, and technological plants in every ecological niche from the Colorado River to the coast, increasing plant diversity to protect against famine during droughts. Techniques included planting seeds, vegetative cuttings, transplanting, various water guidance systems, and controlled burning in sequences of from one to fifteen years according to foods planted in an area. Staples were acorns, an extinct grain, and a small white bean, with maize and squash added in mountain and desert areas having summer rain or irrigation water. Game included deer, antelope, mountain sheep, rabbit, and fowl. European crops, fruits, and domestic animals expanded beyond the missions. When American armies and settlers entered, southern California Indians began commercial agriculture along immigration routes and near settlements. By 1870, settlers had taken their best land. In 1891, commercial farming and ranching started again on trust reservations, combined with wage labor. Crops included fruits, nuts, vegetables, chickens, sheep, and cattle. Then non-Indians diverted water from reservations and the Indians lost their orchards, crops, and animals. Labor for non-Indians increased to include skilled and professional positions. Now income comes from off-reservation employment, reservation economic development, Social Security, retirement pensions, and some government jobs and grants.

Industrial Arts. Finely coiled baskets designed in tans, red, and black ranged from a few inches to over two feet in diameter. Women from leadership families made ceremonial basket hats with small colored feathers woven in the design. Abalone pendants and elaborate shell necklaces were made. Other crafts included pottery, manufacture of stone beads, pendants, and arrowshaft straighteners.

Trade. Using shell money or barter, extensive intra- and intertribal trade existed between coastal and inland villages and the Southwest. The Spanish complained of the Indians' trading acumen.

Division of Labor. Women planted and harvested most crops, gathered shellfish, and caught small game. They prepared and cooked food, made clothes, basketry, pottery, nets, and the tools they used. Men made their own tools, nets, weapons, and sacred equipment, and hunted, fished at sea, participated in the harvest of grain, acorn, and pine nut crops, cleared fields, and managed controlled burning. Men

were political, military, and religious leaders, healers, and economic (ecological) specialists; many women were also healing specialists. The missions and Mexicans demanded heavy labor from both men and women, such as pulling plows and making adobes. Now both men and women are in skilled and professional positions, and participate in tribal government.

Land Tenure. National, band, family, and individual territory existed. National territory, open to all Kumeyaay, included trails between villages, sacred mountains, and certain mountain, desert, and coastal areas considered wild, except for tribal controlled burning. Each band had a primary village territory and specific mountain, desert, and coastal areas. Within the band territory, the band-owned land included trails, religious and band meeting areas, and harvest areas used and tended by the group under the chief's direction. Bands had sacred solstice and equinox mountains, sacred healing areas, and an eagle's nest. Each sib lineage owned land divided between families as strips extending from valley bottom to ridge top. Each family tended and harvested its own land. Specialists individually used and owned specific sacred or healing plants or other resources. Water sources and springs were owned at each level from individual to tribal. Some reservations were allotted when trust-patented, and each allottee received inheritable trust ownership of the allotment. Some had trust homesteads outside reservation boundaries. The federal government is trustee of reservation land, allotted and unallotted, and homesteads. Few allotments have been taken out of trust or sold (a sole-survivor claimant took one reservation out of trust). Some have used wages to purchase and pay taxes on nontrust land.

Kinship

Kin Groups and Descent. In A.D. 1769 an estimated fifty to seventy-five patrilineal sibs existed as named groups, each descended from a mythical ancestor. Each village, or band, had ten to fifteen sibs represented by a lineage within which descent was traced and kinship terms used. A sib managed inheritance only if family or lineage lacked direct heirs. The sib system facilitated visiting and movement between bands and ecological areas.

Kinship Terminology. While data are unclear, a variant of the Omaha system seems to have existed.

Marriage and Family

Marriage. The traditional system forbade marriage to a sib mate. Today, Kumayaays claim marriage was forbidden to all traceable relatives of both parents. But in the traditional system, cross cousins were not related and mission records reveal cross-cousin marriage was possibly favored. The levirate and sororate provided a replacement for a deceased or disabled spouse. Leaders often had several wives. Leaders' families intermarried with those of distant bands and tribes. Formerly, families arranged marriages and the groom presented gifts to the bride's parents. Residence is generally patrilocal, though a couple may reside on either spouse's reservation or elsewhere. Children are likewise registered on either reservation.

Domestic Unit. Traditional extended families consisted of grandparents, one or two sons, their spouses, and children.

Nuclear families now predominate with relatives' homes nearby.

Inheritance.   Individual and family lands, water, and resources were inherited. Originally land went to whichever child remained to care for elderly parents, often the youngest son or daughter. Leadership, religious, and specialist positions were inherited by the most capable son or daughter trained in the specialty. At death all personal property was destroyed, including the house, clothing, tools, songs, stories, and dances. Today, personal property is burned and household furnishings given away. If a will is absent, the federal government follows state probate law.

Socialization.   Grandparents trained children to participate in hunting, fishing, and harvesting, and to be able to survive alone by age five. Village members shamed unruly children who were strictly taught to be polite to elders, obey religious leaders, and not interfere with adults. Keeping children in Indian boarding or day schools and forbidding all religious practices destroyed the strict socialization customs. A permissive system similar to that of non-Indians now exists.

Sociopolitical Organization

Social Organization.   Organization was hierarchical, with status conferred by inherited position and special knowledge. Those developing new environmental knowledge, craft skill, or running speed acquired status. Hard work, precision, neatness, and industriousness contributed to status and wealth. Individuals could shift from band to band if land were available and the new group willing. Subservient landless persons existed and had no voice in band affairs.

Political Organization.   Each band was independent, but was part of a Kumeyaay federation under a tribal leader, _Kuchut Kwataay_, who managed relations and ceremonies with other tribes, participated in solving interband disputes, organized defense, and managed tribal communications with a system of lookouts and relay runners carrying messages or warning of enemies. Each band also had a _Kwaaypaay_ (capitan or leader), who managed band social, economic, political, and religious affairs aided by a council of shamans (priests, singers, sun, and ecological specialists). Unlike the case in some neighboring tribes, a leader did not command, but was followed when found competent and knowledgeable. A primary duty was to adjudicate disputes within the band. At his death, all Kwaaypaay met to choose a successor from among their trained sons, one without sib mates or close kin in the band. By 1885, tribal and band leadership was underground, suppressed by Indian agents' requirements for annual elections of men obedient to the agent and by the attack on religion. Traditional leaders began organizations opposing government actions and bringing lawsuits against the government. Public Law 280 ended the need for opposition; gradually, elected councils and chairmen began managing reservation affairs. Often they are descendants of traditional leaders.

Social Control.   Social control devices included shaming and teasing for minor offenses, fear of witchcraft, whipping, and exile for major offenses, and death for murder and witchcraft. Under the Indian agents, untrained police were often abusive as were the opposition tribal police. Now civil and criminal offenses are under state law ineffectually enforced by county sheriffs and local courts. Because traditional sanctions are not allowed, in effect none exist.

Conflict.   Conflict occurred over trespass by stealing plants from family, band, or tribal land, or hunting on another band's land. After 1846, conflict developed over how to deal with Indian agents—whether to obey them or fight them in courts and Congress. While most agree on desired results, disagreements continue over economic development and preservation of land, and for some, over major issues resulting from Bureau of Indian Affairs actions.

Religion and Expressive Culture

Religious Beliefs.   The Kumeyaay worshiped a high god and his prophet, Kuuchamaa, who taught moral rules and proper behavior. Eagles, red-tailed hawks, and ravens were messengers between chiefs and God. Lesser spirits in all living things were placated by rituals. The spirits of the mythology resided in sacred places and were potentially available for aid. Secondary spirits dealing with humans and all other things were also recognized. Witchcraft caused evil and disease. Many myths taught children expectations of the behavior of others in an unstable, erratic, untrustworthy world. They saw Spanish missionaries and soldiers as evil, thieving witches. Most Kumeyaay are now Catholics, viewing their God as identical with the Catholic God and their prophets as valid as biblical prophets.

Religious Practitioners.   Priests and singers were paid for services with valuables or food, as were ecological and curing specialists who managed their specialty through rituals validated by the religion.

Ceremonies.   Ceremonies managed all life crises: naming, puberty (boys and girls), marriage, death, year after death, and a _keruk_ for all who died over a several years' period. Ceremonials celebrated solstices, equinoxes, and new moons, called for and stopped rain, dew, and fog. Others prepared for war or celebrated victory and peace. Ritual began and ended all ecological activity: controlled burning, planting, harvesting, and group hunts. Now Catholic baptisms, marriages, funerals, and memorials have varying combinations of Kumeyaay and Catholic ritual. Major events and yearly fiestas begin with a combination of Catholic and Kumeyaay prayer and ritual.

Arts.   Rock art was probably ceremonial and included geometric designs, large mazes, and human and animal figures; some related to solstice ceremonies. Singers performed many elaborate four- and five-day rituals with songs timed by the movement of sun and stars. Men performed elaborate ritual dances, and women, complex social dances.

Medicine.   Although all Kumeyaay used herbs for common ailments, men and women healers specialized in specific diseases, experimenting with the medicinal qualities of herbs. Improper behavior or witchcraft caused serious diseases. Some rituals were for psychological illness; others were combined with herbal medicine. Many still use efficacious herbs or modern medicine, depending on the problem.

Death and Afterlife.   Formerly, at death a cremation ceremony aided the spirit's journey to an afterworld in the south. Memorial services returned the spirits for a last time to enjoy life's activities: singing, dancing, peon (a gambling game of skill). Today, funerals and memorials are important to honor an individual and free the spirit from the earth.

Bibliography

Couro, Ted, and Margaret Langdon (1975). *Let's Talk 'liPaay Aa.* Banning, Calif.: Malki Museum Press.

Gifford, Edward W. (1931). *The Kamia of Imperial Valley.* U.S. Bureau of American Ethnology Bulletin no. 97. Washington, D.C.

Luomala, Katharine (1978). "Tipai and Ipai." In *Handbook of North American Indians.* Vol. 8, *California,* edited by Robert F. Heizer, 592–609. Washington, D.C.: Smithsonian Institution.

FLORENCE C. SHIPEK

Kutchin

ETHNONYMS: Dindjié, Gwich'in, Kootchin, Loucheux

The Kutchin are a group of Athapaskan-speaking Indians living in northeastern Alaska and extending eastward across the Mackenzie River in Canada in the northern Yukon Territory and northwestern Northwest Territories. Contact with Europeans began with Alexander Mackenzie's exploring party in 1789. Trading posts were established by the North West Company in the early nineteenth century and by the Hudson's Bay Company in mid-century and later. Roman Catholic and Anglican missionaries began their work in the area in the 1860s. Other European influences included epidemics in the 1860s and 1870s, whaling along the north coast, the Klondike gold rush at the turn of the century, the arrival of government police in 1903, and the establishment of schools in the early twentieth century.

In Canada, the Department of Indian Affairs and Northern Development was established in 1953, leading to much house and other construction under its auspices. In Alaska, cooperative movements began in the late 1950s, and the results of the Alaska Native Claims Settlement Act resulted in some economic development. Earlier probable native cultural influences from the Northwest Coast had been noted in some bands, specifically potlatching and slavery. Most Kutchin are now fluent in a Kutchin-influenced variety of English, although there are some who still speak only Kutchin.

It has been estimated that there were over five thousand Kutchin in the mid-eighteenth century. The population probably dropped to below one thousand in the nineteenth century, but has now rebounded to around twenty-two hundred. Most now live in fairly acculturated fixed communities, although many still feel they belong to one of the remaining bands.

At the time of contact, Kutchin speakers were grouped into nine or ten regional bands, each centered in the drainage of a major river. Over the years certain areas have been depopulated with bands being forced to move because of pressure from other ethnic groups or possibly because of inaccessibility to trading posts. In the late 1970s there were six bands remaining as well as subcommunities in the Mackenzie Delta in Canada and Birch Creek in Alaska. Each of the regional bands had a chief with limited authority—either hereditary or chosen for wealth or wisdom. The Kutchin were divided into three clans, which extended across tribal (ethnic group) lines to some extent.

Marriage was usually outside the clan and often outside the band, with children belonging to the mother's band. The nuclear family was fundamental. Some local groups of six to eight households existed, living within a few miles of each other. There was a general dichotomous wealth-ranking of families, with some marriage restrictions ensuing. Most marriages were monogamous, but some wealthy headmen were polygynous, with polyandry also being reported.

Early basic house types seem to have been semisubterranean rectangular log houses roofed with moss, and a portable dome-shaped skin house. The basic house type for most of the historical period has been the surface rectangular log house, frame houses becoming more frequent since the second quarter of the twentieth century. Canvas tents are used in warm weather and while traveling.

Subsistence was based upon a wide variety of flora and fauna, with the hunting of large mammals being very important in terms of prestige, although daily subsistence depended largely on the taking of fish, small mammals, and birds.

Religious and cosmological ideas were not systematically developed. There were no full-time religious practitioners. Shamans existed but were not particularly important. There was a close relationship to the natural world, especially with the caribou. Many supernatural beings and monsters were thought to exist.

Bibliography

McKennan, Robert A. (1965). *The Chandalar Kutchin.* Arctic Institute of North America Technical Paper no. 17. Montreal.

Nelson, Richard K. (1973). *Hunters of the Northern Forest: Design for Survival among the Alaska Kutchin.* Chicago: University of Chicago Press.

Osgood, Cornelius (1936). *Contributions to the Ethnography of the Kutchin.* Yale University Publications in Anthropology, no. 14. New Haven, Conn.: Department of Anthropology, Yale University. (Reprint, Human Relations Area Files, 1970.)

Slobodin, Richard (1981). "Kutchin." In *Handbook of North American Indians.* Vol. 6, *Subarctic,* edited by June Helm, 514–532. Washington, D.C.: Smithsonian Institution.

Kutenai

ETHNONYMS: Kitonaqa, Kootenay, Sanka, Tunaha

The Kutenai are an American Indian group living on the Kootenai Indian Reservation in Idaho, the Flathead Indian Reservation in Montana, and various reserves in British Columbia. In the nineteenth century the North West Company and Hudson's Bay Company established trading posts in the Kutenai territory. The Kutenai lived on peaceful terms with Whites during this time; their population, however, was gradually but greatly reduced by disease and alcohol-related problems. In 1895 the remainder of the tribe was removed to the reservations in Idaho and Montana. The Kutenai language is classified as a language isolate in the Algonkian-Wakashan language phylum.

On the Flathead Indian Reservation in Montana the Kutenai reside with the Flathead tribe and operate under a tribal council of ten elected officials. Income is derived mainly from forestry. In Idaho the Kutenai operate under a five-member tribal council headed by a chief with life tenure. In the late eighteenth century the Kutenai numbered about two thousand and inhabited the region of the Kootenay and Columbia rivers and Arrow Lake in Washington, Idaho, and British Columbia. At that time they were divided into an upper division subsisting mainly as bison hunters and a lower division living mainly as fishers. The upper and lower divisions were further subdivided into eight bands each headed by a nonhereditary chief.
See also Flathead

Bibliography

Turney-High, Harry H. (1941). _Ethnography of the Kutenai._ American Anthropological Association, Memoir 56. Menasha, Wis.

Kwakiutl

ETHNONYMS: Kwagulth, Kwakiool, Kwawkewlth, Kwawkwak-awakw, Southern Kwakiutl

Orientation

Identification. "Kwakiutl" was initially and properly applied only to one local group, the Walas Kwakiutl of Queen Charlotte Strait, British Columbia, but was subsequently used by fur traders and others to designate the four groups (including the Walas Kwakiutl) that assembled at the Hudson's Bay Company's Fort Rupert in the 1850s. By extension, missionaries, government officials, and ethnologists identified all speaking obviously related dialects and languages as "Kwakiutl." The word _Kwakiutl_ is native and variously interpreted as "smoke of the world," "smoke from their fires," and "beach at north side."

Location. Groups covered in this summary are those collectively referred to as the Southern Kwakiutl: occupants of Vancouver Island, the neighboring mainland, and the numerous intervening islands. Their territory lies between approximately 50° to 51°30′ N and 125° to 127° W. Most Kwakiutl remain in this area today: a few in their traditional winter villages, more in larger settlements to which small groups have been attracted.

Demography. Hudson's Bay Company estimates for around 1835 put the population at about 8,575, but by then the numbers had already been reduced by disease. The population declined steadily during the nineteenth and early twentieth centuries. When Franz Boas's studies began, there were about 2,000 Kwakiutl, and at lowest ebb in 1929, half that number. Approximately 4,000 now live in the area.

Linguistic Affiliation. Kwakwala, the language of the Southern Kwakiutl, belongs to the North Wakashan division of the Wakashan stock. It contained at least three dialects: Koskimo, on the west coast of Vancouver Island centering on Quatsino Inlet; Newetee (or Nawitti), on the northern tip of Vancouver Island; and Kwakiutl for the balance of the area—predominantly the shores of Queen Charlotte and Johnstone straits and adjoining fjords and channels. Newetee is likely extinct.

History and Cultural Relations

Southern Kwakiutl border the Chickliset Nootka and Comox Salish on Vancouver Island and Homathco and Klahuse Salish and Owikeno Kwakiutl on the mainland. Relations with all these neighbors were similar to those that obtained among the Southern Kwakiutl groups themselves: a mixture of bellicose raiding and amicable feasting, marriage, and trade. The taking of slaves and other plunder had undoubtedly long characterized relations with neighbors. At least in historic times, territorial acquisition also rose to prominence as the Lekwiltok Kwakiutl drove Comox Salish from the southern reaches of Johnstone Strait. Early contact with Europeans began for some groups in the 1780s with maritime fur traders, for others, with American, British and Spanish voyages of exploration in 1792. Through those groups on the north end of Vancouver Island there was direct participation in the early fur trade, but significant economic impact did not begin until the establishment of Fort Rupert (1849)—for many decades the economic and ceremonial focus of the Southern Kwakiutl. In the 1870s, an Anglican missionary assembled his Fort Rupert converts at Alert Bay, where he later established a sawmill to employ natives in the developing timber industry. Native participation, as fishermen and cannery workers, in the even more rapidly expanding fishing industry grew through the later years of the nineteenth century. Early contact was marked by few incidents of conflict between Whites and native partners in the fur trade. Later, church and government, recognizing the pivotal role played by potlatching in Kwakiutl culture, curbed this activity through arrests and confiscation of regalia.

Settlements

Each of the twenty-nine Southern Kwakiutl local groups occupied a village in the winter months and moved, seasonally, to settlements situated at specific resource locales. At the winter village and such repeatedly used locations as the eulachon and salmon fisheries stood the permanently erected, heavy timber house frames on which the villagers placed split plank cladding carried with them on their seasonal moves. Short-term camps, such as those used as bases for shellfish or seaweed gathering, typically were occupied by village segments. Shelters here were smaller and commonly formed of planks over a light pole framework. Winter village populations ranged from 100 to 750; aggregations at the eulachon fisheries could reach several thousands. Lesser resource locales might attract but one or two households. Dwellings were customarily ranged along the shores of a bay, protected channel, or lower reaches of a river. Within the houses, which could be up to 29.5 feet square, mats, screens, and piled belongings formed compartments for the occupant households.

In the mid- to late-nineteenth century, the Hudson's Bay Company post, sawmills, and canneries drew people into three principal settlements. Since formal establishment as reserve communities, these three have expanded, attractive for the amenities and social services offered. Only four of the original groups remain at their traditional winter locations. Reserve housing stock has improved greatly in recent years and can now generally be described as of good rural standard. Large communities have one or more modified old-style big houses as a focus for traditional ceremonies and often a recreation center for more recently adopted activities. Separate band office structures and churches are found in all but the smallest reserve settlements. Two communities have attractive, well-equipped, and professionally staffed museums.

Economy

Subsistence and Commercial Activities.   Fishing for salmon, herring, eulachon, and halibut, hunting such sea mammals as seal and porpoise, gathering shellfish and other marine invertebrates, and foraging for wild plant foods characterized subsistence activities. For taking these predominantly seasonal resources, the Kwakiutl possessed a wide variety of devices, many specifically designed for particular species and circumstances. The most productive and efficient fishing techniques involved weirs and traps, of which there were several kinds. Movement from one resource locale to another matched subsistence activities with the highly localized resources, and preservation techniques (mainly based on drying) permitted accumulation of surpluses for off-season consumption. They participated in the early maritime fur trade through direct contact at the north end of Vancouver Island and indirectly through exchanges across the island with the Nootka. Subsequently, with establishment of Fort Rupert, barter for food staples and goods increased in importance. Late in the nineteenth century, Kwakiutl became full participants in a cash economy as commercial fishermen, cannery workers, and loggers. Although no canneries now operate in the Southern Kwakiutl area, commercial fishing remains the principal vocation. Others find employment in logging, the region's small-scale service industries, and with various levels of government. A periodic government-regulated "food fishery" remains an important contributor to subsistence.

Industrial Arts.   Woodworking was of prime importance for the production of a very broad range of products, from dishes and spoons to houses and watercraft. The textile arts produced baskets, mats, and blankets. Many objects were richly decorated, a tradition that has continued in this century through production of small carved tourist items. A few artists now specialize in two-dimensional paper art: paintings and prints in traditional or modified traditional style.

Trade.   Precontact trading patterns reflected only some local groups having direct access to eulachon fisheries. Eulachon oil was widely traded both among Kwakiutl and with Nootka. The region's nineteenth-century fur trade centered on Fort Rupert. Many outlying groups dealt through native middlemen, at least some of whom, in later years, became Hudson's Bay Company rivals, traveling south to Victoria for their stock.

Division of Labor.   A gender-based division of labor prevailed. Women gathered plants and shellfish, processed all kinds of foods for storage, prepared meals, and manufactured nets, mats, fabrics, clothing, and baskets. Men built traps, made and used other hunting and fishing equipment, and did all woodworking, including manufacture of canoes and construction of houses. Men might be part-time specialists in the making of such items as masks, boxes, canoes, or crest poles. Women's specializations included blanket weaving and fine basketwork. Slaves were employed at menial tasks, including carrying water, gathering firewood, drying fish, and paddling canoes. In the early decades of the commercial fishery, men worked in the troller, gillnet, or purse-seine fleets and women in the canneries. With the removal of fish-processing plants to urban British Columbia, females have found local employment principally in the service industry and government. Males are still mainly employed as commercial fishermen.

Land Tenure.   Descent groups controlled all significant resource locations and owned such constructions as traps and weirs. They were also identified with specific segments of the local group's winter and other seasonal villages. When reserves were allocated in the late nineteenth century, plots of land at many traditional resource locations, winter village sites, and burial areas were attributed to "bands"—remnants or amalgamations of the old local groups. Title to reserve land is held for each band by the Canadian government. As Kwakiutl signed no treaties ceding their land, they continue to press for compensation or restitution.

Kinship

Kin Groups and Descent.   Each local group comprised several loosely structured, exogamous, nonunilineal descent groups (numayms). Affiliation with these was nominally ambilineal with pronounced patrilineal bias. Numayms disappeared several generations ago.

Kinship Terminology.   Cousin terminology was of Hawaiian type; aunt terms, lineal.

Marriage and Family

Marriage.   Preferred spouses were from other similarly ranked numayms. High-ranking, wealthy individuals might engage in polygynous unions. Divorce was effected by return of property equivalent to those gifts exchanged by families at the time of marriage. For several generations, marriage practices have conformed to those prescribed by the Anglican church and Canadian law.

Domestic Unit. Independent households, centering on a nuclear or polygynous composite family but including otherwise unattached relatives and slaves, were fundamental units of production and consumption. They shared a single large dwelling with three to five or more other such units, forming an extended household usually linked by a core of patrilineally related male heads. For much of the year, there was little activity in which these larger domestic units collectively engaged, but seasonally they cooperated in some hunting and fishing activities and shared food surplus to any independent household's needs. The typical domestic unit is now the nuclear family-centered household.

Inheritance. Most personal effects closely identified with an individual were burned at death. More valuable kinds of property (houses, coppers, ceremonial regalia, crests, dances, privileges, and titles) were transferred to heirs during one's lifetime. The usual path of inheritance and succession was defined by a rule of primogeniture with no distinction made between a male or female heir. If there was no child, property seems rightfully to have gone to the eldest offspring of the next oldest sibling, although that next oldest sibling might assert a claim. Many items could be passed on only within the numaym; others (especially titles, dances, coppers) that had been received from in-laws could be conveyed to other in-laws. Positions as functionaries or performers in the winter ceremonies were patrilineally transmitted.

Socialization. Children were raised with comparatively few restrictions until puberty, after which a girl was expected to become skilled at basket making and other women's work. Girls were instructed by older female members of the household. Boys learned appropriate skills from their fathers. Children continue to be raised in a setting of affection and permissiveness with the major responsibility for guidance falling on the parents, especially the mother. In later childhood, peer group influences predominate. Gender stereotyping begins early but becomes particularly evident during adolescence. Missionary schools on many reserves and a government residential school at Alert Bay were the main sources of instruction until the 1950s, after which time these were gradually replaced by secular instruction in provincial schools serving the region's Indian and non-Indian communities. Some in small remote villages rely on the province's correspondence program. Postsecondary enrollment has increased with recent establishment of nearby branch college campuses.

Sociopolitical Organization

Social Organization. Major divisions of society separated free and slave castes and, within the free population, distinguished title-holders and their families from other people. Title-holders were ranked within and among numayms and were under continual obligation to maintain and, if possible, advance the status of their names. Relative rank was readily apparent at potlatches where seating arrangement, order of distribution of food and property, and size or worth of gift all reflected relative positions of the assembled guests. The host's display of affluence was an assertion of worth, but only the position assigned him when he was a guest at a subsequent potlatch could tell him if fellow title-holders agreed. There may also have been broad distinctions between the group holding the most important titles, those who had held these titles formerly but had given them up to their successors, and the group holding lesser titles. Numayms were ranked with respect to one another within and among local groups, and there was a ranked order for local groups, themselves. During the winter months, these social divisions were partly eclipsed by ones related to organization of the winter ceremonies. The uninitiated formed a segment of society distinct from the group managing the ceremonies ("sparrows") and the performers ("seals"). Sparrows were subdivided into several groups on the basis of gender and age and seals into ranked dancing societies, each of which contained several ranked categories of performers.

Political Organization. The largest politically autonomous units were the local groups, loosely governed by informal consultation and consensus among the highest ranking title-holders of each numaym. Numayms were more significant political units and were each led by the highest ranking title-holder. Present-day bands have elected councillors and a chief councillor, and all but the smallest, an appointed band manager.

Social Control. There were several sources of constraint on individual action. A shaman's magic was available to control difficult members of society, and one shaman, a sorcerer, assisted the highest ranking title-holder of each numaym when his wishes were opposed. Mistakes or inappropriate behavior at potlatches, during winter ceremonies, or at any time for high-ranking people constituted shame that could be erased only by a formal distribution of property to those witnessing the embarrassing action. A killing called for revenge, which might be visited on any available member of the killer's numaym or local group, although properly it involved someone of similar rank.

Conflict. From early contact until the 1920s, numaym and local group rivalry was stimulated by and took the form of competitive potlatching, where the objective was to outdo opponents in the number and quality of possessions given away or destroyed. In earlier times, such competition may more commonly have been expressed by raids and fighting. Perceived excesses in potlatching and drinking led to a split among those gathered at Fort Rupert and withdrawal of many to Alert Bay.

Religion and Expressive Culture

Religious Beliefs. There was general recognition that most natural phenomena and all spirit beings possessed supernatural power, and the existence of such power made many activities and contacts potentially dangerous. Prayers might be offered or rituals followed to enlist supernatural assistance and affect the outcome of various pursuits. At the same time, the Kwakiutl attitude toward much of the world in which they lived was pragmatic and secular. There were numerous unearthly beings, including some identified with specific numayms and others with dancing societies. None was seen as particularly active in affecting the outcome of human affairs. Normally invisible, they might assume forms humans could see. Since missionization, most Kwakiutl have been Anglican. Some are members of evangelical Protestant churches.

Religious Practitioners. Shamans, of which there were several categories, were called on to impel or express spirit-induced sickness and to foretell or affect the outcome of events, cure bodily ills, or work sorcery.

Ceremonies. Winter was a period of intensive religious activity when the various dancing societies initiated new members and reenacted the first contact with their supernatural guardians. Performances—dramatizations of myth-time events—were often staged with cleverly constructed props. Potlatching accompanied the initiations and was in other seasons offered as a ceremony in its own right. It involved host and guest groups, lavish feasting, formal speeches, and distribution of gifts to guests. Life-cycle events (including bestowal of names, marriage, assumption of titles, and commemoration of the dead), launching of a large canoe, or construction of a new house were all occasions for potlatches.

Arts. The most intensely developed arts were those of sculpture, painting, dance, theater, and oratory. Prevalent themes and contexts were religious, including a distinctive and largely religious-based heraldry. Sculpture and painting conformed to conventionalized representations of animals and supernatural beings. Art was an applied form, richly decorating house fronts, mortuary and other commemorative monuments, boxes, seat backs, canoes, paddles, feast dishes, household utensils, tools, and personal possessions. Elaborate masks, robes, and other costume parts and complicated mechanical devices were important accompaniments of dance and theatrical performances. After a long period of languor, the arts have been revived in modified form, with sculpture holding most closely to tradition. Limited edition prints are the basis of a lively art especially popular with collectors. At least one Kwakiutl dance troupe offers costumed performances incorporating traditional themes and movements.

Medicine. Illness caused by soul loss or magic was treated by a shaman. Many ailments were attended to by specialized curers who might use plant, animal, or mineral compounds or decoctions or might prescribe bathing, sweating, or cauterization.

Death and Afterlife. The body, in a decorated bentwood box, was placed in the branches of a tree, in a rectangular plank gravehouse, or a sheltered rock cleft or cave. The soul of the departed, at first a threat to the well-being of survivors, was after about a year content in its new home and no longer dangerous. The afterworld resembled the earthly one, with people living in villages and harvesting the abundant animals, fish, and berries.

Bibliography

Boas, Franz (1897). *The Social Organization and Secret Societies of the Kwakiutl Indians.* United States National Museum Annual Report, 1895, 311–738. Washington, D.C.

Boas, Franz (1909). *The Kwakiutl of Vancouver Island.* American Museum of Natural History, Memoir no. 8, 307–515. New York.

Boas, Franz (1966). *Kwakiutl Ethnography.* Edited by Helen Codere. Chicago: University of Chicago Press.

Curtis, Edward S. (1915). *The North American Indian.* Vol. 10. Norwood, Mass. Reprint. Johnson Reprint Corp., 1970.

Rohner, Ronald P. (1967). *The People of Gilford: A Contemporary Kwakiutl Village.* National Museum of Canada Bulletin no. 225. Ottawa.

DONALD MITCHELL

Labrador Inuit

ETHNONYM: Labrador Eskimo

Orientation

"Labrador Inuit" refers to the native Inuit people of Labrador, a section of Canada that is now within the provinces of Quebec and Newfoundland. Scholars have recently suggested that the Inuit of Labrador are more accurately classified as two groups: the Labrador Inuit, on the coast of the Labrador Sea in Newfoundland, and the Inuit of Quebec, on the coasts of Hudson Bay and Hudson Strait and in the interior of Labrador. Aboriginally, the Labrador Inuit lived along the coast of the Labrador Sea from the Button Islands south to Cape Charles. In 1772–1773 there were about 1,460 Labrador Inuit in this region. Today, they live primarily north of Cape Harrison, in the villages of Postville, Makkovik, Hopedale, and Nain and number about 2,000. Also found in this region are people labeled "Settlers" who are descendants of Inuit-White marriages that occurred with considerable frequency after 1763. Settlers are generally not considered Inuit and have had greater access to European-Canadian society and a more stable socioeconomic position than the Inuit. Aboriginally, the Inuit of Quebec were composed of three regional bands: the Siqinirmiut on the coastline of Ungava Bay; the Tarramiut in the northernmost section of Quebec Labrador; and the Itivimiut on the coast of Hudson Bay and inland, south of the Tarramiut. In the early nineteenth century, they numbered about 2,000 and in 1969, numbered 3,561.

History and Cultural Relations

Contacts with the Labrador Inuit before 1700 generally involved hostilities with European whalers and fishermen. Initial relations with French traders who began arriving in 1700 were also characterized by hostility, but eventually gave way to peaceful trade, with the Inuit supplying cod and seal to the trading posts in southern Labrador. From 1763 to 1949, the Inuit were in contact with the British, and over that period the culture was transformed from an isolated hunter-gatherer one to one reliant on European-Canadian society. The Moravian missionaries who established a mission in 1771 were a key influence, and effectively replaced the traditional religion with Christianity and involved the Inuit in a trading post–based settlement and economic system. After 1926 the Hudson's Bay Company replaced the mission store as the central trading post.

As regards the Inuit of Quebec, the first trading post was established near their territory in 1750. From then on, the Inuit were slowly drawn into the European-Canadian economy, a process that was essentially completed by the twentieth century. Central players in this were the Anglican missionaries, the Hudson's Bay Company, and whaling and fishing stations. After 1900, the Inuit were caught in the middle of fur trade competition involving the Hudson's Bay Company and the French fur company, Révillon Frères, which further involved the Inuit in the fur trade.

Since the 1950s in Labrador and the 1960s in Quebec, the Inuit have been drawn further into European-Canadian society and enmeshed in an administrative and economic framework involving both the two provincial and the national governments. Among major changes are the formation of permanent communities, involvement in commercial fishing and wage labor, compulsory education, and English or French replacing Inuit as the primary language.

Settlements

The Labrador Inuit were seminomadic, usually spending the winter months in small villages of multifamily semisubterranean dwellings and the warmer months in tents. The Inuit of Quebec made more extensive use of snowhouses than did those in Labrador who used them only occasionally. Today, the Labrador Inuit are mostly settled in a number of villages and towns.

Economy

The traditional economy rested on the hunting of sea mammals (whales, seals, walruses) on the coast and caribou inland. These activities were supplemented by fishing, collecting of shellfish, and hunting of birds and small animals. Men hunted, women gathered, and both men and women fished. Although there was no ownership of land, specific bands or regional groupings might have priority to certain territories and such groups might coalesce at various times to hunt caribou. After the entrance of fur traders, trapping became an important activity, and the Labrador Inuit became progressively more dependent on European trade goods. Travel was by umiak, kayak (for hunting sea mammals), and dogsled; these have now been largely replaced by motorboats and snowmobiles, and the rifle has replaced the harpoon, darts, and bow and arrow.

Marriage and Family

Marriage was preferentially polygynous, and many such marriages were reported by early explorers, traders, and missionaries in the area. Postmarital residence was patrilocal, though kin ties were maintained with the wife's family as well. The typical domestic unit was either a polygynous family or a nuclear family with various other relatives added on. Winter dwellings housed about twenty people. Under the pressure of the fur trade, European settlers, and missionaries, there has been a shift to smaller, nuclear family domestic units.

Sociopolitical Organization

Neither the Labrador Inuit nor the Inuit of Quebec were organized as distinct cohesive units. Rather, the families, multifamily settlements, bands, and sometimes regional groupings of bands were the basic sociopolitical units. Leadership by older men was recognized at the household and family levels, and sometimes a broader leadership role might be given a man recognized as a great hunter or as a powerful shaman. Disputes at the local level were usually settled in informal village councils composed of the older men in the village. After establishment of the Moravian church, the elected church councils served as the governing bodies of the Labrador communities. After 1970, community councils and various committees replaced the church councils. Since 1973 the Labrador Inuit Association has been involved in fighting for aboriginal rights as well as serving as a forum for the joining of Inuit and Settler concerns. As regards the Inuit in Quebec, the James Bay and Northern Quebec Agreement of 1975 led to a division in the group between the majority who favored acceptance of compensation for giving up aboriginal rights and those who opposed the settlement. The agreement resulted in the formation of various Inuit corporations, some of which have failed, and others that have been successful.

Religion and Expressive Culture

The Labrador Inuit and, perhaps more so, the Inuit of Quebec had a rich mythology and spirit world, with giants, guardian spirits, animal spirits, dwarfs, and other mythological forms. Important spirits included Torngarsoak, the spirit of seals and whales, Superguksoak, the spirit of land animals, and Nerchevik, the sea goddess. Shamans were central figures in Labrador Inuit life. Men or women could be shamans, though they were more often men. Shamans invoked their guardian spirits to cure the sick, increase hunting success, and predict and control the weather. The Labrador Inuit came under the influence of the Moravian missionaries in the late 1700s, and by the mid-1800s, virtually all had been converted to Christianity. Traditional beliefs and practices continued for some years, often in secret, but have now been largely replaced by Christianity.

Bibliography

Brantenberg, Anne B., and Terje Brantenberg (1984). "Coastal Northern Labrador after 1950." In *Handbook of North American Indians*. Vol. 5, *Arctic*, edited by David Damas, 689–699. Washington, D.C.: Smithsonian Institution.

Saladin d'Anglure, Bernard (1984). "Contemporary Inuit of Quebec." In *Handbook of North American Indians*. Vol. 5, *Arctic*, edited by David Damas, 683–688. Washington, D.C.: Smithsonian Institution.

Saladin d'Anglure, Bernard (1984). "Inuit of Quebec." In *Handbook of North American Indians*. Vol. 5, *Arctic*, edited by David Damas, 476–507. Washington, D.C.: Smithsonian Institution.

Taylor, J. Garth (1984). "Historical Ethnography of the Labrador Coast." In *Handbook of North American Indians*. Vol. 5, *Arctic*, edited by David Damas, 508–521. Washington, D.C.: Smithsonian Institution.

Lake

The Lake (Senijextee, Gens des Lacs) lived on both sides of the Columbia River from Kettle Falls in northeastern Washington into British Columbia to the Arrow Lakes, on the Kettle River, and on the lower Kootenay River. Their culture was of the general Plateau type and they spoke an Interior Salish language. Most of them now live on or near the Colville Indian Reservation in northeastern Washington as part of the Confederated Tribes of the Colville Reservation and are generally assimilated into European-American society. Their current population is unknown, but they probably number about three hundred.

Bibliography

Curtis, Edward (1911). *The North American Indian*. Vol. 11. Norwood, Mass. Reprint. Johnson Reprint Corp., 1970.

Teit, James A. (1930). *The Salishan Tribes of the Western Plateau*. U.S. Bureau of American Ethnology, 45th Annual Report (1927–1928), 37–396. Washington, D.C.

Latinos

ETHNONYMS: Central Americans, Chicanos (alternative for Mexican Americans), Cuban Americans, Dominicans, El Salvadorians, Guatemalans, Hispanics, Marielitos, Mexican Americans, Nicaraguans, Puerto Ricans

Orientation

Identification. Latinos in the United States are a diverse group and, collectively, the second largest ethnic minority population in the country. Latino groups include, principally, Mexican Americans, who are the largest and (in historic terms) the oldest group; Puerto Ricans, Cuban Americans, Dominicans (from the Dominican Republic) and in recent years Central Americans, mainly from El Salvador, Nicaragua, and Guatemala. Most Latino Americans came to the United States as a result of one of the many wars of the last 150 years. Puerto Ricans and many Mexican Americans are descendants of residents whose homelands were annexed by the United States; many more Mexican, Cuban, and Central American refugees fled from civil wars and revolutionary upheavals. Others, however, came with or without government visas to seek economic opportunities. The U.S. Bureau of the Census has used the term "Hispanic" to designate all such persons, and use of the label has become widespread. An Hispanic is anyone in the United States who has a Spanish surname and comes from a Spanish-speaking background. Most people, however, prefer other labels that reflect where they came from, where they live, when they came, and how they have adapted to the dominant culture of the United States. In short, there are many Hispanics, and even within the broader subgroupings, there are very wide spectrums of historical experience and tradition. An understanding of the way these spectrums have come into being requires an appreciation of the importance of time, place, and history. Thus, "Latino" (a generic term created by the people themselves) identity is a varied and complex process that has created a fascinating mosaic.

Location.   Place has been crucial to the formation of the many Latino identities. For one thing, geography determines proximity to cultural roots in Latin America. Just as important, the U.S. government's acquisition and integration of Latinos was episodic, and the political and social conflicts that resulted from that process varied by region and by time period. Mexican Americans live principally in the southwestern states of California, Texas, Arizona, Colorado, and New Mexico, all of which were, before 1848, part of northern Mexico. Puerto Ricans outside of the island territory have settled mostly in New York City and large midwestern cities. Dominicans are located principally in New York, Cuban Americans, in Florida, and Central Americans, in California and Houston. Beyond these concentrations, members of each group also live in most major American cities.

Demography.   Estimates of the 1989 population based on 1985 figures indicate that there were 21 million Latinos constituting just under 10 percent of the U.S. population. The estimated 1989 populations of the largest Latino groups were 13 million Mexican Americans, 3 million Puerto Ricans, 1 million Cuban Americans, and 4 million other Latin American immigrants and their descendants. In recent decades, the influx of immigrants has sharply increased the total Latino population, so that 12 percent of Mexicans, for example, are first-generation immigrants. The immigration and settlement experiences of Latinos have varied from one group to another and also over time within groups. At the beginning of this century, Mexican immigrants were largely a rural, migrant worker population who joined a settled population that predated the 1846–1848 Mexican-American War by 250 years. Since the 1950s, however, Mexican Americans have become about 90 percent urban, concentrated in California and Texas. Among Puerto Ricans and Cubans, in contrast, initial migration was primarily to the urban areas, with the major Puerto Rican immigration beginning between the two world wars and Cubans mostly arriving after the 1959 Cuban Revolution. Central Americans, primarily settling in California and Houston, have arrived after the social upheavals of the 1970s and 1980s in their countries.

Linguistic Affiliation.   Spanish is the national language of each of the nations from which Latinos emigrated and in which their cultures developed. The Spanish spoken by American Latinos, however, has been transformed by the cultural changes, mixtures and attitudes, and other local and historical accidents and syncretisms that marked conditions in the New World. Mexican, Puerto Rican, Cuban, and other national language habits and customs differ; features of American Indian and African languages, for just one example, have variously influenced each of them. Many regional and urban/rural linguistic contrasts exist within each of the groups. With exposure and integration into American society, however, many Latinos' Spanish-speaking abilities and styles have been "Anglicized" (been affected by the English language), and many even forswore the use of Spanish to speak English, especially Latinos raised primarily in the United States.

Language usage is an important component of Latino ethnic identity. Certain Latino populations, especially recent immigrants and those of high social status, derive much pride from their ability to speak fluent Spanish. Where Spanish usage is expected, some enjoy the opportunity to demonstrate their bilingual flair. For both social and political (as well as aesthetic and practical) reasons, proficiency in Spanish has become a key component in an emerging ethnic "management" style, particularly in the border areas or where Latinos are heavily concentrated such as in Los Angeles (Mexicans and Central Americans), New York (Puerto Ricans and Dominicans), and Miami (Cubans). Speaking Spanish has also resulted at times in negative personal and group experiences, for it has been used by outsiders to stigmatize many people because they are different.

History and Cultural Relations

Mexicans can trace their roots to settlements in what is now the southwestern United States as early as 1598; this area was once the northern reaches of Mexico proper and was colonized before the settlement of New England by people from Europe. The region was prospering when Anglo-Americans began arriving in the early nineteenth century, setting in motion events that led to the Mexican-American War of 1846–1848. In the aftermath of the war, relations between Anglo-Americans and Mexicans were often characterized by culture conflict and intercultural hostility. With increased immigration in the wake of the 1910 Mexican Revolution, the Mexican population burgeoned in all previously established settlements, a process that has continued to this day.

Puerto Ricans and Cubans became associated with the United States as a result of the 1898 Spanish-American War. Puerto Rico became a territory of the United States and now has limited sovereignty within its commonwealth status. A migrant stream, increasing considerably after World War II, connected Puerto Ricans with the city of New York and brought the eastern seaboard its first large Latino population. Like Mexicans, Puerto Ricans have had a problematic relationship with Anglo-Americans, in their case further aggravated by the issue of national independence versus commonwealth status, which has strained both intergroup and intragroup relations. Cubans immigrated to the United States in large numbers after the socialist revolution of 1959. The first waves were primarily from the upper-middle and upper classes and most immigrants were people of European racial backgrounds; the second wave began in 1980 and involved mostly poorer, darker-hued "Marielitos," including many expelled from Cuban prisons. American foreign policy and actions have been affected by events in Cuba, especially the rise of anticommunism.

Large-scale immigration from the Dominican Republic occurred in the early 1960s. Central Americans, mostly from Guatemala, Nicaragua, and El Salvador, made their entrance in the late 1970s and early 1980s. Coupled with the changes brought by Cuban events, the radical upheavals in Central America have tended to generate even more anticommunist fears. Political and economic refugees from these nations have accounted for a substantial proportion of recent immigration to the United States.

American military conquests in the nineteenth century made Mexican residents of the southwest and Puerto Ricans on their island subjugated peoples. For subsequent migrants from Mexico and Puerto Rico, this intensified the scorn and discrimination that has been the traditional lot of poor immigrant populations in the United States. Cuban immigrants were initially comparatively well-off economically, especially because of federal government subsidies for refugee resettlement, which ameliorated economic problems for them. In all instances, however, the dynamic processes of immigration and adaptation have affected all groups in the direction of assimilation and acculturation. Latinos' relations with other racial minorities have been less antagonistic than with Anglo-Americans, although not tension-free, largely because Latinos and other minorities internalize Anglo-American stereotypes of each other. Civil rights measures and changing public attitudes over the last twenty-five years have substantially reduced these interethnic problems, but tensions remain, especially with regard to language and immigration issues.

Settlements

Initially, Mexicans established missions and small rancherias (hamlets) in what is now the Southwest; in California, a mission-pueblo-presidio structure ordered religious, civil, and military life for both American Indians as well as the Spanish/ Mexican newcomers. In the twentieth century, immigration enlarged some of these locales, but more often new settlements were established near work sites such as ranches, mines, railroad tracks, cash crop fields, and light industries. The railroad network helped create a migrant stream to the Midwest to Chicago and other industrial cities. The word *barrio* (neighborhood) came to be associated with these settlements in both rural and urban regions. Since the end of World War II, the Latino population has become increasingly urban, a trend that continues today, though pockets of traditional culture still exist, especially in areas such as New Mexico and south Texas. Puerto Ricans have established their own barrios in the eastern and midwestern cities. World War II was a watershed period as it created a demand for more workers and soldiers, and Puerto Rican communities expanded as a result. A unique arrangement facilitating travel between the mainland and island has tended to strengthen Puerto Rican culture and community. Arriving much later than the other Latino groups, Cubans and Central Americans have settled mainly in cities. Cubans, in fact, have achieved major economic and political influence in Miami, Florida. The U.S. government attempted to widely disperse the recent Marielitos wave, but in time even these immigrants gravitated to established Cuban enclaves.

Economy

Subsistence and Commercial Activities. Small pockets of Mexican Americans who trace their heritage to the early centuries have maintained their self-sufficient ranches and farmlands, but the majority earn wages as mine, farm, railroad, construction, and light industry laborers. Puerto Ricans have filled the garment district and light industry jobs of the cities. Cubans arrived with some money but, more important, with skills and training and have had much success in various business enterprises and professions. In recent decades there has been a slight increase in employment in white-collar service and professional occupations, but Latinos generally lag behind the Anglo population in employment in these sectors. A large agricultural migrant-worker population exists in states such as California, Texas, and Florida. Mexican Americans were a major force in the unionization effort by farm workers in California.

Latino foods vary and reflect the syncretic Spanish/ Indian/African mixture noted above, but beans, rice, and various stews prepared with pork, beef, and seafood are found in all groups. Chilies are also widely used in Latino cuisines. Corn products are of particular importance in Mexican and Mexican American culture (although bread and wheat flour tortillas have replaced corn tortillas on many Mexican American tables). Cubans and Puerto Ricans, as islanders, generally favor various seafood dishes characterized by Latino methods of preparation and spices.

Industrial Arts. The original settlements in New Mexico produced excellent wood carving, weaving, jewelry, and other artistic traditions. Today, this Latino bent is found among auto paint-and-body, upholstery, and seamstress craftspeople.

Trade. Barrios have shopping centers and stores that cater to the tastes of the local population, and some of these districts have become ethnic centers for social, cultural, and political activities. Latinos also use many of the malls that dot urban and suburban regions. Small family-operated stores are common among Latino entrepreneurs, and some have grown into multimillion-dollar enterprises. The Cuban American community has become a major economic force in the Miami area.

Division of Labor. A shift from low-skilled to skilled blue-collar jobs has emerged as an important trend, as has the increase of two-wage-earner households with many women now having the dual roles of breadwinner and breadmaker. Although the middle class has grown, with many professionals and educated people, especially among Cuban Americans, there are still relatively few Latinos of middle- or upper-class status. Because of traditional beliefs and the Spanish colonial influence, there has been particular strain involving changing gender relations and traditionally defined status in Latino communities. Many women have moved out of traditional female roles, and some men have found it very difficult to adjust to this change. Similarly, status distinctions based on the traditional "patron-peon" arrangements are slowly disappearing in an open, class-structured society.

Land Tenure. Since the late nineteenth century, most of the extensive land holdings owned by Mexican Americans has been lost to Anglo-Americans. The few pockets that remain are in rural areas such as New Mexico. As recently as 1966, attempts to raise public attention to the corrupt way in which these lands were acquired have failed. Nevertheless, Chicano (an ethnic name for Mexicans in the United States) activists still offer reminders of the abrogation of the Treaty of Guadalupe Hidalgo of 1848, which ended the Mexican-American War with assurances that land rights would be respected. Puerto Ricans have largely retained ownership of both large and small farms in Puerto Rico, but are predominantly renters in their urban U.S. communities. Cuban Americans, in contrast, are rapidly purchasing large blocs of real estate in Miami.

Kinship

Kin Groups and Descent. Family life is important to Latinos, especially extended kin networks, even though Anglo-American influences have altered traditional patterns. Family interests are valued over individual well-being. A syncretic mixture of indigenous and Catholic religious beliefs and practices undergirds this sense of familism. Although somewhat revamped in the United States, the *compadrazgo* (co-parenthood) institution of Latin America is widely practiced in baptisms, where godmothers and godfathers become *comadres* and *compadres* of the baptized child's parents. Descent is bilateral with a strong emphasis on patriarchy in how the family sets standards for status, respect, and authority. Generally, a sex and age hierarchy prevails, and often elder kin, especially grandparents, are vested with complete authority in family affairs; they sometimes take over primary care of grandchildren when parents falter. There are some intragroup Latino differences in family structure that stem from time, place, and history. For example, female-headed households are more common among Puerto Ricans; Mexican Americans have larger families on average, and Cuban Americans tend to have the smallest families. Mexican Americans in rural enclaves in south Texas and New Mexico generally embrace traditional family practices and beliefs, such as are found in Mexico proper.

Marriage and Family

Marriage.   Each person is allowed to seek his or her own mate, but traditionally the elder family members keep close watch to make sure that the choice is an appropriate one. The average age of marriage has increased lately, but typically it is lower than the overall average in the United States. Separate Latino groups have their own marriage customs, but even with American innovations, the wedding and celebrations are large, well-attended, often catered affairs hosted by the bride's family. Postmarital residence is almost always neolocal, although financial necessity allows for temporary living arrangements with either the bride's or the groom's parents. American-born Latinos who are upwardly socially mobile tend to intermarry more with Anglos, and exogamous marriage is slightly more common among Latinas of a higher status.

Domestic Unit.   Modernization and Americanization, of course, have changed Latino households. Nevertheless, the sense of obligation and responsibility that one owes to family elders and parents remains. This takes many forms, but emphasizes affording them respect and caring for them until death. Machismo, or manliness, is among the traits associated with the patriarchy complex, and male-female relations are often conditioned by the public assertion of male control, especially the positive qualities of providing care and protection for one's home and family. These practices are tempered somewhat by Marian Catholic ideology which places females, especially mothers and wives, in an exalted position.

Inheritance.   Land and property is usually transferred to the eldest son, although senior females also have rights. Most traditional practices in the area, however, have given way to American practices.

Socialization.   Social class differences account for considerable variation among the Latino groups in their approaches to child rearing. But beliefs in personal honor, respect for the aged, and proper courtship behavior are still stressed by many people in all groups. The bulk of the population follows working-class practices, and new immigrants attempt to continue native ways. Social and economic pressures on family life, however, have weakened parental control in many communities, with juvenile and adolescent street peers taking on many tasks of socialization.

Sociopolitical Organization

Social Organization.   There are a small number of well-to-do Latinos, with Cuban Americans disproportionately represented among them. The number of Latino entrepreneurs and professionals in the middle class is also relatively small, but increasing. The majority of the population is divided almost equally between American-born, working-class families and immigrant families headed by low-skilled and unskilled workers.

"Mestizaje," the mixing and amalgamation of Spanish, Indian, and African racial groups, was widespread in various places in Latin America. Terms like *mestizo, mulatto, cholo, moreno,* and *castizo* were originally created to categorize the subtle differences in the "hybrid" population mixes. Thus, there is a wide spectrum of racial appearance reflected within the Latino communities. Historically, such diversity has created considerable strain and conflict. As racial appearance and racial attitudes became increasingly important in interpersonal relations, people were made to feel different on the basis of their racial appearance. A kind of "pigmentocracy" was established throughout much of Latin America to shape people's attitudes—about others and, even more important, about themselves. Feelings of inferiority and superiority were implanted in people's heads and these feelings helped determine the extent to which they would have a common heritage and shared experiences.

Political Organization.   Latinos vary widely in their access to and inclination toward participation in the political process in the United States. Undocumented and documented aliens—who are unable to vote—are limited to publicizing their concerns. Many avoid even these activities out of fear of deportation. Recent immigrants often follow political developments in their homelands more closely than those of the United States. Latinos are sharply underrepresented in federal, state, and local governments despite the efforts of organizations such as NALEO (National Association of Latino Elected and Appointed Officials), which have attempted, with some success, to unite all Latinos and especially to find common ground for political lobbying. Latinos are also profoundly divided in political orientations. Cuban Americans are largely drawn to conservative causes, especially on foreign affairs issues. A majority of Mexican Americans and Puerto Ricans align themselves with the Democratic party, but the issues that concern them in part reflect their regional differences. Two political positions that Latinos largely support are improved, less punitive immigration legislation and increased support for bilingual education programs.

Social Control and Conflict.   Traditional familial constraints and respect for authority and, of course, the local, state, and federal legal systems operate to maintain social order. But there is still a residue of instability and uncertainty remaining from the past and especially from the negative side effects of immigration. Racial diversity has contributed to continuing social conflict, and frictions with major social control institutions, such as schools and police, have also persisted.

Local, regional, and sometimes national efforts to resist and change discriminatory practices are common occurrences. The Latino social movements of the 1960s, however, have resulted in continued improvements in such areas as bilingual education, increased hiring in public jobs, and a rise of public interest in Latino issues. The wars of the past continue to affect Latino-Anglo relations in the United States: Mexican Americans deplore violations of the Treaty of Guadalupe Hidalgo; many Puerto Ricans aspire to statehood or independence; Cubans, because of its recency, talk of recapturing the "revolution"; and Central Americans lament the contemporary wars from which many are refugees.

Religion and Expressive Culture

Religious Beliefs. As with the Spanish language, Roman Catholicism dominates throughout Latin America, but varies in form and practice from country to country and region to region, owing largely to syncretic mixing with other religious traditions. Latinos in the United States also display this variation, with patron saints, special days of observance, and rituals of baptism, marriage, and death varying among different Catholic Latino groups. For example, the Virgin of Guadalupe, a brown-appearing icon associated with the Indian-Mestizo segment of the population in Mexico, is of little interest among Cuban Americans and Puerto Ricans, and *santeria* (worship of African gods clothed in Catholic dogma) beliefs and practices in those groups are far less common among Mexican Americans. Although most Latinos adhere to the Catholic church, evangelical Protestantism has gained many followers in recent decades.

Arts. Folk art traditions in murals, woodwork, music, oral lore, and pottery, as well as modern stylized forms reinterpreting these traditions, characterize a rich artistic cultural element. Afro-Cuban and Puerto Rican percussion instruments and rhythms have effected a new American salsa style of music. Recently an increase in Latino American plays, theater, and cinema has brought a new awareness to the population; particularly important are the sociopolitical content of these works, such as demonstrated by the early Teatro Campesino (Peasant Theater) "actos" (politically charged skits) during the United Farm Worker movement in California.

Medicine. Traditional folk practices continue to vie with Western medicine in many Latino communities, although most Latinos seek medical help for serious injuries or acute illness. Still, one can readily find *curanderos* (folk healers) who offer old indigenous and syncretized herbal and physical remedies for virtually any ailment.

Death and Afterlife. Latinos generally subscribe to Christian beliefs of an afterlife in which one is rewarded or punished for having led a good or evil life. The significance of death and afterlife is symbolized most clearly in Mexican American celebrations of *El Dia de Los Muertos* (literally "Day of the Dead," but known as All Saints' Day in English), which feature masks, dolls, and cakes adorned with figures of skulls and skeletons. Funeral rites vary as other syncretized religious ceremonies do among Latinos, but typically include large gatherings of real and fictive kin.

Bibliography

Borjas, G., and M. Tienda, eds. (1985). *Hispanics in the U.S. Economy*. New York: Academic Press.

Boswell, Thomas D., and James R. Curtis (1984). *The Cuban-American Experience*. Totowa, N.J.: Rowan & Allanheld.

Hendricks, Glenn L. (1974). *The Dominican Diaspora: From the Dominican Republic to New York—Villagers in Transition*. New York: Teachers College Press.

Moore, Joan W., and Harry Pachon (1985). *Hispanics in the United States*. Englewood Cliffs, N.J.: Prentice-Hall.

Padilla, Felix (1987). *Puerto Rican Chicago*. South Bend, Ind.: University of Notre Dame Press.

Rodriquez, Clara (1989). *Puerto Ricans: Born in the U.S.A.* Boston: Unwin Hyman.

Vigil, James Diego (1984). *From Indians to Chicanos: The Dynamics of Mexican American Culture*. Prospect Heights, Ill.: Waveland Press.

JAMES DIEGO VIGIL

Lillooet

ETHNONYMS: Chin Nation, Lilowat, Lil'wat

The Lillooet were one of the four principal tribes in the interior plateau of British Columbia. They are sometimes referred to as the Lower Lillooet, including the Douglas and Pembroke Meadows bands, and the Upper Lillooet, including all other bands. They occupied the southwestern part of the province in the basin of the Lillooet River, the upper part of Harrison Lake, and environs.

In the early 1900s there were thirteen bands, with the number reduced to ten today. There were many villages, each governed by a hereditary band chief. Today there are about twenty-five hundred Lillooet living on reserves in their traditional territory and in nearby cities. The Lillooet speak an Interior Salishan language related to the languages of the Okanagon, Shuswap, and Thompson Indians.

Lillooet culture displayed many features typical of Northwest Coast groups: the potlatch, clan names, mythology, prestige afforded the wealthy and generous, and totem poles in some areas. They had several types of dwellings—long plank houses, winter earthlodges, and summer bark- or mat-covered lodges. Salmon and other fish were the basis of the economy, and numerous animals (bear, sheep, caribou, deer, and small mammals) were hunted and trapped, and berries and fruit were gathered. Warfare with other groups was unusual, with intensive intertribal trade the more typical state of affairs. The guardian spirit vision quest was important, as was a long training period for adolescents in preparation for adulthood.

Bibliography

Stryd, Arnoud H., ed. (1978). *Reports of the Lillooet Archaeological Project. Number 1. Introduction and Setting.* National Museum of Man, Mercury Series, Archaeological Survey of Canada, Paper 73. Ottawa.

Teit, James A. (1906). *The Lillooet Indians.* American Museum of Natural History, Memoir no. 4, 193–300.

Teit, James A. (1912). "Traditions of the Lillooet." *Journal of American Folklore* 25:287–371.

Lipan Apache

ETHNONYMS: Chipayne, Flechas de Palo Apaches, Hipandis, Ipande, Lipane, Lipianis, Lipyane, Lypanes, Ypande

Orientation

Identification.   The Lipan Apache had ceased to exist as a separate tribe by 1905, when the last of them moved to the Mescalero Apache Indian Reservation in south-central New Mexico. Anthropological fieldwork with Eastern Apache did not begin until Morris Opler's work in the 1930s, by which time the Lipan were virtually extinct. See the entry on the Mescalero Apache for all contemporary information. The following is a brief historical sketch reconstructed from archival documents and secondary sources. Usually, the name "Lipan" is said to have come from the name of a grand chieftain with a version of the suffix *-ndé*, "The People," appended. Archival documents, however, lead to an equally plausible explanation, since early mention (eighteenth century) of Lipans is often spelled with one of the variations of "Lipiyane." *Lii* is the Apachean word for "horse," and *' iyane* is the word for "bison"; thus, their name could well have referred to their primary subsistence pattern: that of following bison herds on horseback.

Location.   In the early eighteenth century, Lipan Apache were in central and western Texas, from approximately the Trinity River (east of present-day Waco, Texas) westward to the Pecos River, where they joined their Mescalero Apache "cousins." They were reported as far north as the Canadian River in the Texas Panhandle and as far south as the Santander area of Mexico. Most reports of Lipan place them either in the vicinity of bison herds or occupying river bottom lands. Like most Apachean groups, they roamed over vast areas, but always they were reported in desert or coastal plains sites rather than in mountains, as were some other Apache groups. In general they lived in very warm to hot climates; night in desert areas, however, is usually cool and can be cold in the winter.

Linguistic Affiliation.   Lipan Apache, still spoken by perhaps two dozen or so people on the Mescalero Apache Indian Reservation, is a Southern Athapaskan language. As such it can be understood by speakers of other Apachean languages, although most of them maintain that Lipan speakers speak more slowly and with broader vowels than do speakers of other Apachean languages. The Southern Athapaskan languages are related to other Athapaskan languages spoken on the north coast of California and in the Pacific Northwest, and through parts of northern Canada and Alaska. Despite attempts to record Lipan Apache, it remains largely unknown in a scholarly sense. The contemporary speakers are adamant that it not be recorded or written, believing that if the language is meant to survive them, then it will do so, but that it is inappropriate for people to interfere with a process directed by the Creator.

Demography.   Currently numbered with the Mescalero and Chiricahua, it is difficult to obtain precise numbers of Lipan. A reasonable estimate is that there are fewer than fifty people alive today claiming Lipan ancestry as their primary ethnicity. At their height, they probably numbered no more than five thousand, divided into about a dozen bands.

History and Cultural Relations

As with the other Apache groups, the Lipan were engaged in a protracted struggle over land use and settlement patterns with the Spanish, Mexican, and U.S. governments from the first mention of them in the early 1700s to their virtual extinction in 1905. Prior to the 1700s there was a plethora of names used for the Apachean people of eastern New Mexico, western Texas, and the Panhandle; it is likely, although not definitively demonstrated, that some of these (Trementina, Limita) were later called "Lipan." Unlike most Apache, the Lipan were missionized in the 1700s in the northeastern reaches of the Spanish empire, in the areas of Eagle Pass and San Antonio, Texas. The missionization effort cannot be termed a success, for the missions were poorly supplied and their inhabitants often left to pursue subsistence activities only to return when supplies were again available in the missions. For the most part, the Lipan were at war with the invaders until there were no longer enough of them left to fight.

Settlements and Economy

The Lipan were the most sedentary of the Apachean groups, for they planted crops, especially maize. The Spanish described them as living in rancherias, but also as living off bison. It appears that there were semipermanent dwellings of wickiups near fields during sowing and harvesting, and portable tipi dwellings used when following bison herds. They were probably transhumant, although this is an inference from documentary evidence rather than a generally accepted fact. In addition to reliance upon bison and maize, the Lipan Apache also gathered wild foods, especially varieties of cacti and agave. By the late eighteenth century, after generations of war with the Spanish and after acquiring the horse, the Lipan seem to have forsaken agriculture in favor of raiding; they maintained their bison protein resource, however.

Social Organization

Lipan were matrilineal and maintained close associations with their matrilaterally extended relatives. A household unit was usually composed of a woman and her husband or consort and her children; often unmarried sisters and brothers of the woman or her matrilineal relatives in the ascending generation were also present. Unmarried grandchildren might be a part of the household, too. Band membership seems to have followed matrilineal and matrilateral principles as well. But though women ruled in the family, men were in charge of the band.

Religion and Expressive Culture

The Lipan are usually credited with introducing peyotism into Native North America. Despite the paucity of Lipan information, Opler managed to collect their mythology.

Bibliography

Opler, Morris E. (1940). *Myths and Legends of the Lipan Apache Indians.* Memoirs of the American Folklore Society, vol. 36. New York.

Tunnell, Curtis D., and W. W. Newcomb, Jr. (1969). *A Lipan Apache Mission: San Lorenzo de la Santa Cruz, 1762–1771.* Texas Memorial Museum, Bulletin no. 14. Austin.

CLAIRE FARRER

Luiseño

ETHNONYM: Juaneño

The Luiseño and Juaneño, who culturally and linguistically are one group, are an American Indian group located in southern California. The Luiseño were associated with Mission San Luis Rey and the Juaneño with Mission San Juan Capistrano, from which the two groups take their respective names. Neither group evidently had a distinct name for themselves in precontact times. The precontact population, estimated as high as ten thousand, decreased to about seven hundred in 1940 and had increased to about two thousand in the 1980s. The Luiseño language is classified in the Takic subfamily of the Uto-Aztecan language family. An active effort is being made to maintain the language.

A distinct Luiseño culture has been traced back archaeologically to about A.D. 1400. Neighboring groups were the Gabrielino and Serrano to the north, Cahuilla to the east, and Ipai and Cupeño to the south. Following the establishment of Mission San Juan Capistrano in 1776 and Mission San Luis Rey in 1798, much of the traditional culture was replaced by Spanish, then Mexican and, beginning in the 1850s, European-American culture. Following years of inconsistent federal policy, most Luiseño today live on or near La Jolla, Rincon, Pauma, Pechanga, Pala, and Soboba Indian reservations. Despite the depopulation, external influences, and resettlement on reservations, much of the traditional culture regarding religion and expressive culture has survived.

Luiseño society was composed of localized village groups, each of which exploited food resources in their territory, though they also traveled to find food elsewhere. A semisubterranean earthlodge was the typical village dwelling.

The subsistence economy was based on gathering of acorns and other seeds, collecting greens, hunting small game and marine mammals, fishing, and digging roots and bulbs. The subsistence territory was owned and protected by the village group. Today, many Luiseño work in semiskilled and skilled occupations, with their wages supplemented by occasional participation in traditional subsistence activities.

Traditional kinship rules and practices disappeared rapidly under Spanish influence before they could be described. Evidently, each village group was a patrilineal clan group, with arranged village-exogamous marriage preferred as a means of affording villages access to other subsistence territories. Both boys and girls underwent elaborate initiation ceremonies, suggesting the central economic contributions made by both sexes.

Each village group was governed by a hereditary chief who exercised religious, political, and warfare authority, an assistant chief, and a village council. The political structure may have been more elaborate in the larger villages located on or near the Pacific coast. Warfare was often the result of boundary disputes between villages. Today, reservation decisions are made by the entire adult population on the reservation, although many Luiseño serve on the boards of various local, reservation, regional, and state organizations.

Elaborate ceremonies led by paid ritual specialists from other villages and involving dramatic recitations, feasting, and distribution of goods were a central feature of Luiseño life. Sixteen ceremonies have been reported, including those for initiation, hunting, fertility, death, marriage, conception, and peace. Some of these rites are still celebrated in addition to Catholic holidays.

Bibliography

Bean, Lowell John, and Florence C. Shipek (1978). "Luiseño." In *Handbook of North American Indians.* Vol. 8, *California,* edited by Robert F. Heizer, 550–563. Washington, D.C.: Smithsonian Institution.

Shipek, Florence C. (1985). "California Indian Reactions to the Franciscans." *Americas* 41:480–492.

Lumbee

ETHNONYMS: Cherokees, Croatans, Indians of Robeson County, Scuffletonians

The Lumbee are English-speaking descendants of the remnants of various Native American groups who now live principally along the Lumbee River in Robeson County, North Carolina, and in adjacent counties in North and South Carolina. The Lumbee number about forty thousand, making them the fifth largest American Indian group in the United States and the largest in the East. Today Lumbee are found in small concentrations in Greensboro, North Carolina, Baltimore, Philadelphia, and Detroit, although most migrants do return to Robeson County. Lumbee ancestry includes tribal groups that largely disappeared from the Carolinas in the eighteenth century and perhaps some African and European intermixture as well, leading to their classification as American Isolates. Lumbee oral tradition traces their ancestry to Sir Walter Raleigh's lost colony at Roanoke. Today, Lumbee self-identity is based on having a socially defined Lumbee parent and no socially defined African-American parent.

In the nineteenth century the Lumbee shared a common culture and life-style with their White neighbors that included landownership, farming, and Baptist and Methodist religious affiliation. Until 1835 they also shared the same civil rights, but in that year the Lumbee, along with other "free persons of color" in North Carolina, were stripped of most of those rights and began to suffer discrimination and impoverishment at the hands of Whites that persisted until well after the Civil War. In the 1880s the prejudice they faced lessened to a degree and some of their civil rights were restored. During the 1960s Lumbee began to develop a pan-Indian consciousness and increasingly became politically active.

From the late 1800s well into the twentieth century the Lumbee were employed mostly as farm laborers and share-croppers and occupied a depressed social stratum in a society dominated by White farmers and landowners. Beginning early in the twentieth century the modernization of farming in the region reduced labor demands, resulting in unemployment and underemployment for the Lumbee. In the 1960s industrial development in Robeson County offered some hope. Most Lumbee, however, were not able to take advantage of the new job opportunities as they lacked the necessary skills and education, a product of more than a century of "separate, but equal" schools. In the 1960s Lumbee began to move into white-collar and skilled blue-collar occupations, but those doing so have been forced to migrate to urban areas to find employment.

Bibliography

Blu, Karen I. (1980). *The Lumbee Problem: The Making of an Indian People.* Cambridge: Cambridge University Press.

Evans, W. McKee (1979). "The North Carolina Lumbees: From Assimilation to Revitalization." In *Southeastern Indians,* edited by Walter L. Williams, 49–71. Athens: University of Georgia Press.

Makofsky, Abraham (1980). "Tradition and Change in the Lumbee Indian Community in Baltimore." *Maryland Historical Magazine* 75:55-71.

Mahican

The Mahican (River Indians, Canoe Indians), together with the Wappinger, lived along the Hudson River in eastern New York from Lake Champlain to Manhattan Island and eastward to the Housatonic Valley in Massachusetts and the Connecticut River in Connecticut. Descendants of these groups now live on the Stockbridge-Munsee Indian Reservation in Wisconsin and in the Brotherton Indian Community in Winnebago and Calumet counties, Wisconsin. They spoke Algonkian languages. The Stockbridge-Munsee number about one thousand, and the Brotherton Community numbers about three hundred, with the traditional culture and language essentially extinct.

Bibliography

Brasser, T. J. (1978). "Mahican" In *Handbook of North American Indians.* Vol. 15, *Northeast,* edited by Bruce G. Trigger, 198–212. Washington, D.C.: Smithsonian Institution.

Maidu

The Maidu (Pujunan), including the Nisenan (Southern Maidu, Nishinam) and Konkau (Concow, Konkow), live in the drainage area of the Feather and American rivers in north-central California among other Indians and Whites. They spoke languages of the Maidu (Pujunan) family of the Penutian phylum. The number of Maidu today is not known, but may be over one thousand.

Bibliography

Riddell, Francis A. (1978). "Maidu and Konkow." In *Handbook of North American Indians.* Vol. 8, *California,* edited by Robert F. Heizer, 387–397. Washington, D.C.: Smithsonian Institution.

Maliseet

ETHNONYMS: Amelecite, Etechemin, Malecite, Marisiz, Saint John River Indians, Wδlastδkwiyδk

Orientation

Identification. The Maliseet are an American Indian group located in New Brunswick and southern Quebec in Canada and northern Maine in the United States. The name "Maliseet" appears to have been given by the neighboring Micmac to whom the Maliseet language sounded like faulty Micmac; the word "Maliseet" may be glossed "lazy, poor or bad speakers." The term the Maliseet use for themselves, Wδlastδkwiyδk," is derived from the name they gave to the St. John River, in the drainage area of which they dwell; it means "people of the St. John River" or, more exactly, "people of the beautiful, good, pleasant river."

Location. The ancestors of the Maliseet (the sixteenth- and seventeenth-century Etechemin) occupied not only the St. John River drainage region but also the west shore of the Bay of Fundy and the Gulf of Maine, as well as the rivers flowing into it south to about the sixty-eighth meridian. During the 1600s and 1700s the Etechemin or Maliseet shared use of the south shore of the St. Lawrence River with the Micmac, the Montagnais, and the Abnaki upstream to near Quebec City. Today the Maliseet live primarily in New Brunswick, northern Maine, and southeastern Quebec and form one language group with the Passamaquoddy who live to the south in Maine near the New Brunswick border. The region is one of mixed deciduous and evergreen forests, interspersed with rivers, streams, and interconnected lakes. Intervales along the St. John River provided the opportunity for some horticulture from the late 1600s on. Precipitation is generally abundant throughout the year. In the interior, it is hot and humid in summer, cold and snowy in winter, with less extreme weather along the Bay of Fundy and to a lesser degree along the St. Lawrence.

Demography. In 1612 the Etechemin numbered less than 1,000, and their numbers declined greatly in the 1600s and 1700s, owing to epidemics and the loss of traditional lifeways. Early in the 1970s, 1,812 Maliseets were enumerated on official band lists, representing a steady increase since around 1870. Better employment opportunities attracted Maliseets to southern New England during World War II, although many families have since returned to New Brunswick.

Linguistic Affiliation. The Maliseet speak a language of the eastern subdivision of Algonkian. The Abnaki (Penobscot) of Maine and Quebec (St. Francis Abnaki) speak languages closest to that of the Maliseet and Passamaquoddy.

History and Cultural Relations

There has been much intermarriage between the Maliseet and the neighboring Micmac, Passamaquoddy, and Penobscot and, since the early historical period, the French in Maliseet communities in northern New Brunswick and Quebec as well. Elsewhere Maliseet intermarriage with neighboring English-speaking persons has continued since the 1830s. Since White contact, relations among the Maliseet and their Algonkian-speaking neighbors have generally been peaceful. The Mohawk were their traditional enemies. Contact with Europeans dates to at least the mid-sixteenth century, with more or less continuous contact with the French since the seventeenth century. The Maliseet allied with the French against the British, although in the revolutionary war they sided with the British. Because of this support, the Maliseet were granted the first reserve established in Atlantic Canada. With the arrival in New Brunswick of Loyalists from New England and the Mid-Atlantic states in 1783, the Maliseet were displaced from several areas of traditional settlement along the St. John River. Encroachment on other lands by later White settlers led to further problems of access to traditional hunting territories.

When reserves were established, most were too small to accommodate the full range of traditional economic pursuits and the Maliseet were forced into the White economic world, becoming more and more dependent upon income from wage labor and the tourist trade and White products. Today the Maliseet live on six reserves along the St. John River in New Brunswick and off reserve at numerous places in Maine, Quebec, and New Brunswick.

Settlements

In the early historical period settlement patterns varied seasonally. Winters were spent in family hunting bands, composed of a few adult males plus their wives, children, and occasionally other dependent kin; band composition varied from year to year. Each spring, family bands returned to one or more intervales along the St. John River and formed larger fishing, gathering, and horticultural communities. The location of these communities varied in the historical period, but Medoctec is viewed by the Maliseet as their ancient village and Ekwpahak as a second important summer settlement. With the arrival of Roman Catholic priests the Maliseet settled near newly established mission stations, giving rise to St. Basile and Kingsclear as areas of Maliseet concentration.

With the establishment of reserves in the nineteenth century, and with the arrival of large numbers of Irish Catholic immigrants and a greater number of priests and Catholic churches, the Maliseet reserve communities acquired a more permanent character. Opportunities both for the sale of crafts and for wage labor in the larger European settlements made the lower St. John River areas as well as the south shore of the St. Lawrence River at Cacouna most attractive. By the early twentieth century most Maliseet families had moved to a reserve. A countertendency, however, had occurred at Woodstock and Tobique where families associated with these reserves moved to northern Maine to be closer to a more predictable employment as day laborers in the potato industry. The aboriginal Maliseet residence was the circular birchbark wigwam, but rectangular dwellings with a pitched roof tended to replace wigwams in the 1800s. More permanent cabins and frame houses became common by the end of the nineteenth century. A lean-to served as a temporary overnight shelter for men on hunting or trapping trips. Today, Maliseet housing represents a wide range of styles and is often indistinguishable from that of their White neighbors.

Economy

Subsistence and Commercial Activities. Traditionally the Maliseet were hunters, fishers, and gatherers. In the seventeenth century they adopted some horticulture, particularly maize cultivation, which remained of secondary importance into the twentieth century. Some had gardens where potatoes and other root vegetables were grown for family consumption and a very few had small acreage in oats and wheat. The caribou and moose were the major large game animals taken, with the white-tailed deer replacing the caribou in the early twentieth century. Beavers had always been taken by the Maliseet, but the demands of the fur trade led to scarcity by the end of the eighteenth century. Muskrat, considered a delicacy by the Maliseet, has been a more important food source than the beaver since the nineteenth century. Salmon, bass, and sturgeon were taken with spears when the species made their runs up the St. John River. Eels, smelt, and other smaller fish were taken as well. The Maliseet, unlike the Passamaquoddy, think of themselves as inland hunters and freshwater fishers rather than salt-water and coastal hunters and fishers. The manufacture of crafts, especially splint ash work baskets, birchbark canoes, and snowshoes made by the men and fancy baskets of splint ash and sweet hay made by the women, supplemented income from trapping, guiding, employment on river drives, stevedoring and other day or seasonal labor for nineteenth- and early-twentieth-century Maliseet men. Until the 1950s many families worked in the potato harvest for White farmers in northern Maine and New Brunswick each autumn. Increasingly, Maliseet are finding employment both on and off the reserve. A few families, particularly those who make baskets, maintain craft shops at or near their homes. But despite increasing participation in the White economy and government work projects, unemployment remains high even by the standards of the Maritime Provinces.

Industrial Arts. Pottery making was known prehistorically. Carved stone pipes were made by some men until about 1940. Though birchbark containers were formerly made, splint ash basketry supplanted it at the beginning of the nineteenth century and remains an important source of income for some families. Victorian tastes of neighboring White settlers and tourists contributed to the patterns selected by female basket makers. Male basket makers produced more utilitarian objects—potato baskets, clothes hampers, cradles, and, more recently, backpacks and wood baskets. The manufacture of barrels, casks, and firkins was also carried out. Embroidery with moose hair, glass beads, and porcupine quills has long been a tradition of the female craftsperson. Preparation of deerskin for clothing and its decoration with beads has been reintroduced recently.

Trade. Little is known of prehistoric trade with other groups. Shells from the mouth of the St. John River were used in the preparation of wampum. The barter (later sale) of furs with the Europeans for European products began at least as early as the sixteenth century and continued with dwindling significance into the twentieth century.

Division of Labor. Women gathered and prepared food, sewed and repaired clothing, moved camp, constructed the wigwam, fetched the larger game after a kill, cared for the children, and prepared homeopathic medicines. Men were the hunters, fishers, and warriors and almost always the shamans, political leaders, canoe and snowshoe makers, and religious leaders. Men apparently were the farmers in the early nineteenth century. Today both men and women may be employed, but if one person has the responsibility for care of the home and children, it is the woman.

Land Tenure. Recent research suggests that the traditional view that all land was controlled by the tribe is an oversimplification, especially in peripheral areas where families from other tribes or mixed families were free to use the land so long as it was not contested by Maliseet families. Each autumn families announced whether or not they would be returning to the spots they had formerly used, with free spots then open to any family.

Kinship

Kin Groups and Descent. The extended family was the basis of Maliseet social organization. In addition to their European names, many families had nicknames derived from animal names. For example, the Pauls were the "Pikswicik" (people of the pig), and the Sappiers were the "Kahkakuswicik" (people of the crow). Only a few families have a legend and/or a myth that accounts for the origin of the nickname. In most cases membership in these groupings is through the male line. Traditional family nicknames are no longer very important, but at the beginning of the twentieth century they connoted ethnicity. Families carrying the nickname of a nondomesticated animal were regarded as ethnically more Maliseet. Today, membership in a large family unit is important for gaining band office, since relatives are expected to vote for relatives.

Kinship Terminology. The terms for mother, mother's sister, and father's sister are distinct. Cousin terms, however, follow the Iroquois system, although kin term usage bristles with exceptions. At the present time Maliseet kin terms have largely disappeared unless their references closely parallel English usage.

Marriage and Family

Marriage. At time of contact most marriages were monogamous, although a chief might have had more than one wife. A young man was required to perform bride-service for his future father-in-law for a period of one year. With the acceptance of Catholicism, polygyny disappeared and bride-service fell into decline, although at the beginning of the twentieth century, the Maliseet still felt that a man should live with his wife's parents until at least the birth of the first child. When the government of Canada adopted regulations defining membership of Indian bands in terms of male-centered principles, this temporary matrilocality conflicted with the government's view that the bride should join her husband's band when they came from different reserves. This patrilocal pattern has weakened ties among a grandmother, her married daughter, and grandchildren in many cases. If divorce occurs today (despite church proscriptions), it usually is restricted either to Maliseet with spouses from outside the Indian community or to cases in which one spouse has permanently left the native community.

Domestic Unit. Until recently, three-generation families were very common. Despite European norms favoring the two-generation family, a shortage of housing, the presence of unmarried or divorced mothers, and lack of employment opportunities still encourage the formation of three-generation families.

Inheritance. No set patterns for inheritance exist other than that present in the larger non-Indian community.

Socialization. Generally, children were allowed much freedom. They learned from their mistakes rather than from parental admonition. Education was informal and children acquired the necessary adult skills appropriate to their sex through imitation and practice. The threat of externally sanctioning supernaturals, the equivalent of bogeymen, kept small children away from dangerous places. Contemporary parents sometimes use threats of supernatural punishment following death or punishment by a human agent such as a priest or schoolteacher if the child misbehaves.

Sociopolitical Organization

Social Organization. Class distinctions were not unknown in Maliseet society at the time of White contact, with chieftainships following certain "chiefly" families. These families intermarried both within and outside the society and had more than their share of strong shamans and good hunters, talents that kept the chieftainship in the family. Old age brought respect for both males and females. Women held important positions as herbalists, midwives, and—among the Maliseets' closest relatives, the Passamaquoddy—ceremonial positions in the performance of both secular and sacred group rituals. Slaves taken during the colonial period were often White children from southern Maine. Today education is a source of individual and family status differentials. Persons who have completed high school or university, have permanent employment on or off the reserve, or are elected to or acquire leadership roles in the Indian community are held in high esteem.

Political Organization. At first contact and during the colonial period, there was a supreme chief for all Maliseet. In the colonial period he was assisted by a subchief. Other leading men were designated captains. Decisions of concern to the entire group were made collectively by the supreme chief, his assistant, and the captains. The positions of chief and subchief were held for life and were ratified by the neighboring Micmac, Passamaquoddy, and Penobscot. Leading men from each of these groups also met to discuss matters of concern to two or more groups, such as reaching a common position vis-à-vis the colonial governments. As a component group of the Wabanaki Confederacy, the Maliseet chiefs and leading men and their families assembled periodically at Caughnawaga, Quebec. Canadian regulations imposed in 1896 mandated three-year terms for chiefs, but the practice of selecting chiefs for life continued well into the twentieth century. In 1967, the Union of New Brunswick Indians was founded, binding ties between the Maliseet and Micmac. The close ties the Maliseet had with the Passamaquoddy and Penobscot in Maine have gradually become secondary to ties with the Micmac in New Brunswick.

Social Control. Informal techniques of social control (gossip, ostracism, withdrawal) were more effective deterrents to asocial behavior than formal ones. Fear of retaliation by witchcraft or sorcery helped maintain order in the community, especially when the role of shaman as curer was eclipsed by a disapproving Christian church.

Conflict. The role of the Maliseet in colonial disputes between the French in Acadia and the Massachusetts Bay Colony encouraged Maliseet cohesiveness. Changing fortunes owing to the defeat of their allies and the arrival of Loyalist settlers required the Maliseet to make major adjustments. The cordial relations with the French were replaced by sometimes unsympathetic treatment from the English.

Religion and Expressive Culture

Religious Beliefs. One of the first groups in North America to lose their aboriginal religion because of missionary activity, the Maliseet have generally retained the teachings of the French Roman Catholic missionary priests of the 1600s and 1700s. In the last decade traditional Plains Indian religious practices, involving the reintroduction of the sweatlodge, chanting, drumming, and the burning of sweet hay, have been adopted by some families and have acted as an overlay on Christian practices. Kuloskap (Koluskap) was a culture hero and transformer. Some Maliseet see strong parallels between him and the Christian deity, but insist that Kuloskap was never worshipped. Certainly some syncretism of religious traditions is present. The universe was populated with numerous other supernaturals that took animal or part human, part animal forms. Most were thought detrimental to the welfare of humans and had to be controlled by Kuloskap. From the end of the nineteenth century various forerunners signaled and still continue to signal death, illness, or other misfortune, much as in the folk traditions of the French and the residents of the British Isles whose beliefs have strongly influenced the Maliseet.

Religious Practitioners. With the introduction of Christianity, the role of the shaman (*motewolon*) changed from that of curer to sorcerer, and with further enrichment from European folk tradition by the beginning of the twentieth century, to that of witch. Shamans were traditionally male. Political leaders were invariably motewolon as well. By the beginning of the 1900s most white witches were thought to be women whose powers were said to be psychic.

Ceremonies. The shamans' curing ceremonies were public and drew observers. Feasts were held on the occasion of marriage, upon a young man having killed his first game, on the installation of a chief or his assistant, and on other public occasions when Maliseet from divergent regions came together or hosted leaders from neighboring tribes. Christian ceremonies are important to the present-day Maliseet.

Arts. Traditional dances, formerly performed by adult men and women, are now performed by children and women for Whites and for visitors from neighboring bands and tribes. Drumming and chanting, in some cases from non-Maliseet Indian sources, are being introduced by contemporary traditionalists. On special Christian holidays, Maliseet sing portions of the Mass in the community church service in Maliseet or a related Algonkian language.

Medicine. Herbalists, both male and female, continue to prepare herbal remedies on some reserves. White witches, until recently were thought to be knowledgeable in breaking witchcraft spells, often using iron, sharply pointed objects, or the wood or berries of the mountain ash tree. Traditionally, disrespect for game brought illness or misfortune to the community, and the shaman through his spirit helpers was thought to be able to exorcise the offended spirit. At present the Maliseet utilize hospitals and medical personnel available in neighboring White communities.

Death and Afterlife. Witches and animal spirits until recently were held responsible for death as well as illness, a belief that existed alongside accepted Catholic beliefs and practices. In general, death was associated with much ritual and elicited considerable fear. Some traditional Maliseet have introduced modifications to the Catholic funeral, including placing goods with the corpse to be buried, drumming, chanting, and dancing in a circle around the grave. In short, rituals surrounding death have been a major part of Maliseet religion, from the shamanic rituals of the 1600s through Catholic ritual with an emphasis on singing and praying in an Indian language in the eighteenth through the mid-twentieth century to the practice of the new traditionalists with its emphasis on borrowed or rediscovered ritual.

Bibliography

Erickson, Vincent O. (1978). "Maliseet-Passamaquoddy." In _Handbook of North American Indians._ Vol. 15, _Northeast,_ edited by Bruce G. Trigger, 123–136. Washington, D.C.: Smithsonian Institution.

Erickson, Vincent O. (1978). "The Micmac Bouin: Three Centuries of Cultural and Semantic Change." _Man in the Northeast_ 15:3–41.

Mechling, William H. (1958–1959). "The Malecite Indians, with Notes on the Micmacs." _Anthropologia_ 7:1–160; 8:161–274.

Wallis, W. D., and Ruth S. Wallis (1957). _The Malecite Indians of New Brunswick._ National Museum of Canada Bulletin no. 148. Anthropological Series, no. 40. Ottawa.

VINCENT O. ERICKSON

Mandan

ETHNONYMS: Awigaza, Istopa, Mantannes, Nuitadi, Numangkake, Nuptare

Orientation

Identification. The Mandan are an American Indian group located in North Dakota, their aboriginal home. Unlike many Indian tribes, the "Mandan," despite various spellings, have been known by that name since the earliest contact with non-Indians. Although they were sometimes identified by a name belonging to one of the four divisions of Mandan—Nuitadi, Nuptadi, Awigaxa, or Istopa—or by one of the village names, there is no evidence that these were as significant as "Mandan."

Location. In early historic times, the Mandan lived along the Heart River, a major tributary of the Missouri, in western North Dakota. In 1804, Lewis and Clark found they had moved north and settled on the Knife River. Today, they live in the southern segment of Fort Berthold Indian Reservation, about one hundred miles northwest of their original location.

Demography. Prior to the smallpox epidemic of 1837 there were an estimated one thousand Mandan. Although they are no longer enumerated separately, there are probably that many today.

Linguistic Affiliation. The Mandan language belongs to the Siouan language family.

History and Cultural Relations

Some Mandan say they originated underground near the ocean and migrated from the point where they reached the earth's surface to their historic location on the Missouri River. Other Mandan say they were created on the Missouri River and were living there when the migrants joined them. The Mandan were closely affiliated with the Hidatsa and maintained trade relations with many other tribes of the northern plains. The Assiniboine, Cree, Arikara, and Crow were frequent visitors to the villages, and the Cheyenne, Yanktonai, and Lakota (Teton) were sometimes peaceful, sometimes unfriendly, to the Mandan and their allies. The first known European contact with the Mandan occurred in December 1738 when Pierre Gaultier de Varennes, Sieur de La Verendrye, and his sons visited the villages. Not until the late 1700s are there reports of other visits. One of the best known is the 1797 visit of the Canadian explorer David Thompson. The most famous White visitors to the villages were Lewis and Clark in 1804 and 1806, George Catlin in 1832, and Prince Maximilian of Wied-Neuwied in 1833–1834.

The Mandan and Hidatsa villages on the Knife River became centers of commerce on the upper Missouri and steamboats regularly docked there. But the Sioux and smallpox reduced the number of warriors to the point where defense became difficult, and around 1845 refugee Mandan and Hidatsa moved upriver to establish Like-a-Fishhook Village. In 1862, the Arikara moved into the village, where the three tribes lived until the early 1880s, when government officials convinced them to move to ranches scattered across the Fort Berthold Reservation.

Settlements

Aboriginal settlements of the Mandan are found along the Missouri River in North and South Dakota. Early historic documents suggest that before the smallpox epidemic of 1781 there were from six to nine Mandan villages along the Heart and Missouri rivers. Following the epidemic, these villages merged and moved north to the Knife River where Lewis and Clark found the Mandan living in the villages of Mitutanka and Nuptadi and the Hidatsa living nearby in three villages. David Thompson found the Mandan and Hidatsa sharing villages, but by the time of Lewis and Clark, each village was inhabited primarily by members of a single tribe. The Mandan villages were composed of earthlodges arranged randomly around a central plaza with a shrine and ceremonial earth-lodge. The earthlodges were constructed with four center support posts and an outer wall of smaller logs. Roof beams were laid close together from the wall to the center supports and covered with mats. Everything was covered with sod, so the whole structure took the shape of a windowless earthen dome with an elongated earth-covered entryway. Today, the Mandan and the associated Hidatsa and Arikara live in modern ranch-style houses on the reservation.

Economy

Subsistence and Commercial Activities.   Buffalo or bison hunting formed the primary subsistence activity of the Mandan. The women planted maize, squash, beans, and sunflowers in river-bottom garden plots, but left the crops for part of the summer while the tribe went bison hunting. Tribes that did not grow vegetables often visited the Knife River villages to trade for surplus garden products, and these trade opportunities were enhanced by the fur trade. Fur traders moved into the villages or made regular visits to them to buy furs and hides from the Mandan. The Mandan trapped and prepared furs, but they also acquired furs and hides by trading maize and items received from the traders to the nonagricultural tribes of the region. Acting as middlemen, the Mandan and Hidatsa grew rich and became targets for raids by other tribes. The decline of the fur trade was accompanied by an increased military and bureaucratic presence that provided employment opportunities for men as woodcutters, scouts, teamsters, interpreters, and agency employees. The women continued to plant their gardens.

Eventually agents of the Bureau of Indian Affairs convinced the Mandan men to turn to farming and ranching, and in the late 1880s the reservation was divided into individually owned allotments to be worked by the men. The climate makes agriculture risky, and today many Indian people prefer to lease their land to White ranchers. Some Mandan make a living as farmer-ranchers, and others work for the Bureau of Indian Affairs or tribal government, teach in the local schools, or work in nearby towns. Those Mandan who cannot find work have income from various federal, state, and tribal assistance programs.

Industrial Arts.   Traditionally, the Mandan wove willow baskets, made unpainted pottery from local clays, and embroidered hides with porcupine quills and beads. These and other arts were done by people who acquired the right to do them through ceremonial purchase. The introduction of trade goods and the prohibition of ceremonies resulted in the disappearance of these arts, and recent attempts to revive them have not been successful.

Trade.   Prehistorically, the Mandan villages were trade centers that attracted many different tribes and, later, White traders. Goods from the Rocky Mountain tribes were passed to the eastern Plains tribes, while items from the east went west. Even the tribes that maintained hostile relations with the Mandan were welcomed during trade fairs.

Division of Labor.   Men were hunters and warriors, and the women were responsible for home and garden. The women constructed and owned the earthlodges as well as the results of their labor. Men and women could own the rights to certain skills and were paid by others wishing to learn those skills. Ownership of major medicine bundles and most ritual activities were the prerogative of the men, but women also held bundles and directed two important ceremonies. Under the influence of Indian agents, the men turned to the more mechanized forms of agriculture and ranching, and the women continued their household and social activities. In recent times, some women have worked as teachers, nurses, and tribal employees and have been elected to tribal offices.

Land Tenure.   The Mandan shared a large buffalo-hunting territory with other tribes of the region. The Fort Laramie Treaty of 1851 recognized Mandan, Hidatsa, and Arikara claims to 12 million acres of hunting land. In the bottomlands near the village, garden plots were marked out by the leading man of the family and cleared and worked by the women. The products of the gardens belonged to the women. In 1886 some Mandan moved across the Missouri River and established farms that were later allotted to them. In 1954 Garrison Dam flooded the bottomlands where most of the people lived and forced people to take new lands away from the Missouri River. Today, some Mandan still live on their family's allotment, but most of the reservation land has been sold to non-Indians.

Kinship

Kin Groups and Descent.   Aboriginally, Mandan society was divided into thirteen clans, but by early historic times, only four were still functioning. These remaining four, the WaxikEna, the Tamisik, the Prairie Chicken, and the Speckled Eagle, formed two moieties, the west side and east side. These exogamous, matrilineal clans owned earthlodges and sacred bundles, assisted their young men in achieving military and ceremonial recognition, cared for orphans and the elderly, and avenged murders. Intermarriage with non-Mandan and the influence of non-Indian religious and social mores brought about a change in the clan system, and today clans are primarily social groups that sponsor reservation events.

Kinship Terminology.   The Mandan used a Crow-type kinship terminology.

Marriage and Family

Marriage.   The major consideration in a marriage was ownership of sacred bundles. A household with an important clan bundle usually selected a son-in-law from the same clan as the daughter's father. A family with an important bundle might arrange a marriage by presenting a sacred white buffalo cow robe to the prospective son-in-law, thereby committing him to sponsoring sacred ceremonies that eventually finalized the marriage. Families with less important bundles simply exchanged gifts, or, more simply, the young woman moved in with her husband. The ideal marriage was matrilocal, where the young man moved in with the young woman's family, but residence was quite flexible and depended on the type of marriage ceremony, the amount of space available in a lodge, and relationships within the family. A man could have more than one wife and, in the ceremonial form of marriage, the bride's sisters were contracted to the groom, but most men found one wife sufficient.

Domestic Unit.   Until the dispersal to the farmsteads, the basic unit was the lodge group composed of several families of related women who occupied the same earthlodge. Following the dispersal, related families settled near each other, and the extended family continues to be an important factor in Mandan life.

Inheritance. Traditionally, the most important property belonged to the lodge group or the clan and inheritance passed from mother to daughter or father to son. The allotment act contained provisions for inheritance of allotted land and, unless the owner leaves a will, property is now divided equally among the heirs.

Socialization. Children were praised and encouraged and never punished by their parents. When discipline was necessary, the mother's brother or another clan member living outside the lodge was asked. Today Mandan children attend school on or off the reservation and some continue through college.

Sociopolitical Organization

Social Organization. In the early historic period, the Mandan men and women had similar ways of attaining recognition. Age accompanied by success in warfare and acquisition of sacred bundles brought prestige to the men and membership in one of the men's societies; women received acclaim for success in women's arts and sponsorship of sacred ceremonies. The oldest women became members of the important White Buffalo Cow Society. The shift from the hunting-gardening economy to farming and ranching resulted in a decline in the status of women.

Political Organization. The early villages were autonomous units united by the clans. Each village elected two leaders from the council of men who owned sacred bundles. These men represented different qualities of leadership in war and ritual. They had no power to force anyone to obey their commands, but their oratorical skills could convince the council to follow them. White traders and others identified certain men as chiefs and provided them with symbols of their authority. In 1934, under the provisions of the Indian Reorganization Act, the Three Affiliated Tribes adopted a constitutional form of government with an elected council.

Social Control. Under normal circumstances, behavior was regulated by tradition, and bad luck would come to anyone who broke from tradition. When necessary, pressure was exerted by the family and clan. For ceremonial occasions, the Black Mouth men's society acted as village police. In 1885 the Major Crimes Act placed major crimes committed by Indians under the jurisdiction of federal courts, and in 1890 the Indian agent at Fort Berthold appointed three men to act as tribal court judges to deal with minor crimes. Today the Three Affiliated Tribes maintain a tribal court system for those crimes not described in the Major Crimes Act.

Conflict. Traditionally, the Mandan had a strong belief in internal harmony and intravillage disagreements usually resulted in the unhappy segment moving to another village. With the establishment of the reservation, the disagreements between conservatives and progressives intensified. Today, these divisions have virtually disappeared.

Religion and Expressive Culture

Religious Beliefs. Aboriginal Mandan religion centered around a belief in supernatural powers that were shared by all living things. Sacred bundles represented some of the powers that could be obtained through participation in ceremonies. In the mid-1800s Father DeSmet, a Catholic priest, made regular visits to Like-a-Fishhook Village where he taught Christianity and baptized children. In 1876, a Congregational missionary established a permanent mission and school that attracted a number of converts. Today, Mandan participate in both Indian and non-Indian religions. The Mandan believed in First Creator who contested with Lone Man to make the region around the Missouri River. Lone Man traveled around, making tobacco and people and precipitating events that resulted in ceremonies. Other people came from above and below bringing other supernatural beings and ceremonies with them. Of these other sacred beings, Old Woman Who Never Dies, the Sun, the Moon, Black Medicine, and Sweet Medicine were most important.

Religious Practitioners. Ownership of sacred bundles, acquired either through a vision or by ceremonial purchase, committed individuals to act as priests during ceremonies and sometimes provided instructions for curing.

Ceremonies. Mandan life was filled with private and public rituals. The principal public ceremonies were held to make the crops grow, to bring buffalo to the village, to ensure success in warfare, and to cure. The Okipa, held in summer, was a four-day event dramatizing the creation of the earth and promoting general well-being and buffalo fertility.

Medicine. The Mandan distinguished between illness from natural causes and ill health brought about by breaking a supernatural instruction. In cases of supernaturally caused illness, a bundle owner was called in to diagnose the cause and prescribe treatment. The bundle owner would pray and give herbal medicines to the patient. Today, people may seek a traditional healer for some health problems, but most go to the Indian Health Clinic or to one of the physicians living on or near the reservation.

Death and Afterlife. Although death was caused by not following tribal customs, it was considered normal because Lone Man decreed that people would die. People had four souls: two went to the spirit world and two stayed on earth. Funerals were conducted by the father's clan. Burial was usually on a scaffold in a cemetery near the village.

Bibliography

Bowers, Alfred (1973). *Mandan Social and Ceremonial Organization.* Chicago: University of Chicago Press, Midway Reprints.

Meyers, Roy (1976). *Village Indians of the Upper Missouri.* Lincoln: University of Nebraska Press.

Wood, W. Raymond (1967). *An Interpretation of Mandan Culture History.* U.S. Bureau of American Ethnology Bulletin no. 198. Washington, D.C.

MARY JANE SCHNEIDER

Maricopa

ETHNONYMS: Cocomaricopa, Papatsje

The Maricopa are an American Indian group whose two hundred or so members live with members of the Pima tribe on and near the Gila River Indian Reservation and the Salt River Indian Reservation in Arizona. In the late 1700s the Maricopa numbered about three thousand and were located along the middle Gila River in south-central Arizona. The tribal government at Gila River consists of a seventeen-member popularly elected tribal council governed by a constitution adopted and approved in accordance with the Indian Reorganization Act of 1934. The Maricopa language is classified in the Yuman group of the Hokan language family.

Tribal income is primarily from agricultural and business leases and tribal farming operations. They grew maize, beans, pumpkins, and cotton, gathered beans, nuts, and berries, fished, and hunted rabbits in communal drives. Clans were patrilineal, clan exogamy was practiced, and polygyny, particularly of the sororal type, was allowed. The tribe was led by a chief who lived in the strongest village and whose position was sometimes inherited through the male line. According to custom, the dead were cremated and a horse was slain to enable the deceased to ride westward into the land of the dead.

Bibliography

Ezell, Paul H. (1961). *The Hispanic Acculturation of the Gila River Pimas.* Menasha, Wis.: American Anthropological Association.

Spier, Leslie. (1933). *Yuman Tribes of the Gila River.* Chicago: University of Chicago Press.

Massachuset

The Massachuset, with the Nauset (Cape Indians), Nipmuc, Wampanoag, and Natick (Praying Indians), lived in eastern Massachusetts south to the eastern shores of Narragansett Bay. Descendants of these groups now live in the Nipmuc Community near Worcester, Massachusetts, on Martha's Vineyard, Massachusetts (Gay Head), and on Cape Cod, Massachusetts (Mashpee). They spoke Algonkian languages and now number about eight hundred.

Bibliography

Conkey, Laura E., Ethel Boissevain, and Ives Goddard (1978). "Indians of Southern New England: Late Period." In *Handbook of North American Indians.* Vol. 15, *Northeast,* edited by Bruce G. Trigger, 177–189. Washington, D.C.: Smithsonian Institution.

Salwen, Bert (1978). "Indians of Southern New England and Long Island: Early Period." In *Handbook of North American Indians.* Vol. 15, *Northeast,* edited by Bruce G. Trigger, 160–176. Washington, D.C.: Smithsonian Institution.

Mennonites

ETHNONYMS: Anabaptists, Doopgesinden, Mennists, Mennonists, Pennsylvania Dutch, the Plain People, Swiss Brethren, Taufgesinnten, Wiedertaufer

Orientation

Identification.   The name "Mennist" or "Mennonite" was first used in the Netherlands during the sixteenth-century Protestant Reformation when it was applied to the followers of Menno Simons, a disaffected Roman Catholic priest who was influenced by the left-wing Anabaptist reformers. Excluding the related groups, the Amish and Hutterite, there are today eighteen distinct Mennonite groups in North America: Chortitzer Mennonite Church, Conference of Mennonite in Canada, Evangelical Mennonite Conference, Evangelical Mennonite Mission Conference, Old Colony Mennonite Church (Manitoba), Reinlander Mennonite Church, Old Colony (outside Manitoba), Old Order Mennonite, Sommerfelder Mennonite Church, Church of God in Christ Mennonite (Holdeman), Evangelical Mennonite Brethren, Brethren in Christ Church, Mennonite Brethren Churches of North America, Mennonite Church, Evangelical Mennonite Church, General Conference Mennonite Church, Old Order River Brethren, and Old Order Mennonite. Other communities, congregations, and denominations related to the above have been established throughout the world.

Location.   The Dutch Mennonite movement originated in Emden, East Friesland, and from there spread to Groningen, Friesland, and other Dutch and adjoining Belgian provinces. In northern Germany, Mennonite communities were founded in Schleswig-Holstein, Westphalia, and the Rhineland. In Switzerland, Anabaptist leaders had organized congregations more than a decade before Simons joined the movement in 1536. Currently, the major concentrations of Mennonite populations are, however, not in those areas where they originated. As early as the sixteenth and seventeenth centuries, Mennonites often left these European countries to escape severe persecution. The first community of Mennonites (1683, Germantown, Pennsylvania) was established by a Dutch group from Krefeld, Germany. In 1710, the largest colonial settlement was established in Lancaster County, Pennsylvania, by Swiss and South German Mennonites. Even earlier migrations in the 1500s and 1600s from the Netherlands and Germany led to the formation of large Mennonite settlements in the Polish-Prussian region of Danzig and the Vistula Delta. During the late 1700s some left Prussia for the Russian Ukraine where they had been invited to organize agricultural settlements. Again in the nineteenth and twentieth centuries, Mennonites left Prussia, Poland, and Russia to settle in North and South America. After World War I, many from Russia, Canada, and Germany emigrated to Latin America. Presently, Mennonite congregations and communities are found throughout the world: the Soviet Union, China, Western and Eastern Europe, Asia, Africa, and North, Central, and South America.

Demography. The world Mennonite population in 1984 was approximately 700,000: North America, 310,000; Africa, 107,300; Asia, 113,600; Australia, 100; Caribbean, Central and South America, 76,300; Europe, 38,700; and Soviet Union, 55,000.

Linguistic Affiliation. Owing to the dispersion of Mennonite communities and their missionary activities, linguistic affiliation is diverse. Some American communities (including Latin America) use Plattdeutsch (Low German) in daily conversation, and High German for religious functions. Often, English is the only language spoken, especially in North America, and others speak French, Swiss, or predominantly High German (Switzerland, France, and West Germany). In Latin America, Mennonites often speak German, Spanish, and English. Elsewhere, various African and Asian languages are spoken.

History and Cultural Relations

Anabaptist historians have in the past tended to view Zurich, Switzerland, as the epicenter from which the movement extended to the Swiss Confederation, the Netherlands, Austria, Bavaria, Wurttemberg, and the Palatinate. Today, it is argued that this view oversimplifies an otherwise socially, politically, and ideologically diverse movement. Mennonite Anabaptism was a product of both the sixteenth-century Protestant reforms and the fundamental changes taking place in politics and economics across Europe. Thus, like other Reformation religions, they were contending not only with the Roman church but also with changing and discontinuous feudal forces. Unlike mainstream reformers, however, they rejected infant baptism and called for a community of believers or "rebaptizers" (thus, anabaptists)—those who subscribed to the practice of adult baptism upon the confession of faith. The rejection of infant baptism was more than symbolic; it was a challenge to both church and civil authority—a violation of ecclesiastical and civil law. Baptism signified the voluntary commitment of the adult believer not only to the church but also to the closed community of believers, or Gemeinde. Adult baptism symbolized a contract or covenant with God and community—an agreement to respect the Gemeinde and its binding authority. Unlike the more radical contingents of the Anabaptist movement (especially the Hutterian Brethren), the Mennonites embraced the emerging ideology of private property. The ideological roots of contemporary Mennonites can be traced to the Swiss Brethren (in Switzerland and South Germany) and the North German and Netherlands Mennonites.

Interaction with non-Mennonites varies with the group in question. For example, the Holdeman strictly limit interaction not only with non-Mennonites but with members of other Mennonite groups. The General Conference Mennonite Church or the Mennonite Brethren are less concerned, if at all, with limiting interaction with outsiders. Relations with governments and non-Mennonites have frequently been strained during wartime as most are conscientious objectors. During World War I, they were severely treated by the United States government and their neighbors who often perceived them as German sympathizers. In some cases, they were forbidden the use of the German language, their parochial schools were closed, and their barns or homes painted yellow. Still today, most refuse military service and others refuse to take oaths, vote, or serve in public office.

Settlements

Historically, the Mennonites were settled as peasants on feudal estates, as yeomanry on independent farms, and as artisans and merchants in the towns of feudal Europe. Early in the movement, many were driven from the towns and forced into agricultural areas and pursuits. The city of Danzig, for example, refused some habitation. As Mennonites migrated from the Netherlands and other places around Europe and settled in Prussia, Poland, and Russia, they endeavored to establish village settlements. In Poland, they became distinguished and were known as Hollanderdorfer. But as private property in land increasingly replaced (feudal) usufruct rights, these traditional settlement patterns were disrupted. Yet, with each move, they sought again to reestablish villages, especially in Russia. In North America, a few village settlements were established but were soon threatened, as they had been elsewhere, by private property in land and private household accumulation. Only in the less developed areas of the world (in particular, Belize) have these village settlement patterns survived into the present day.

In rural North America today, Mennonites are settled in a manner not unlike other farms—as dispersed private family farms. Swiss Mennonites established a settlement pattern known as the Hof. In the Jura Mountains of Switzerland and in southern parts of Germany they were independent yeomanry who sometimes settled compact or cluster villages (Haufendorfer). The Swiss and German Mennonites settling in Pennsylvania, Ohio, Indiana, and Kansas lived on isolated private farms—Germantown, Pennsylvania, was one exception. Among the largest population concentrations today are Lancaster County, Pennsylvania, and south-central Kansas. Throughout the twentieth century, increasing numbers of Mennonites in North America have settled in urban areas. Today, less than one-third of Mennonites live on farms, one-third in rural communities (but nonfarm), and one-third in large urban areas.

Economy

Subsistence and Commercial Activities. From their beginnings, the Mennonites have been known for their agricultural skills. In the Netherlands and Prussia they drained swamps and built and maintained sophisticated canal systems. The Swiss Mennonites bred exceptionally productive dairy cattle. In the eighteenth century, the Russian state recruited Prussian Mennonites to assist in developing agriculture in the Ukraine. Some became known for their dairy herds, merino sheep raising, and orchards, and the Russian Mennonites were pioneers in the production and marketing of the famous hard winter (turkey red) wheat, which later brought them to the attention of land agents in the United

States and Canada. Today, most have become wage laborers, successful entrepreneurs, educators, or professionals, and only a minority earn a living by farming. Yet in Africa and Asia, many are still agrarian producers, and in Belize, the Mennonites provide nearly all the food consumed and marketed in the country.

Industrial Arts.   In Russia, they manufactured farm equipment for local use as well as for marketing. Among those groups discouraging commercial activity there are many who are skilled carpenters and cabinet and furniture makers.

Trade.   Throughout their history, the Mennonites have depended on trade. In the Baltic, they were involved in the cereal grain trade. In Russia, they sold wool, wheat, and farm equipment. In North America, many become known not only for grain production but for processing and storage of grain. Although their communities have often been extensively involved in commercial activities, they have also been quite self-sufficient. Some of the more conservative groups such as the Holdeman strongly discourage wage labor or commercial occupations. In some cases, they are forbidden to earn interest or carry insurance.

Division of Labor.   In Poland, Prussia, and Russia, the low level of development of technology required a community division of labor—farming or dike construction and maintenance necessitated a degree of cooperation that families alone could not provide. Otherwise, within households, there has been and for some, such as the Holdeman, there remains a strict division of labor between the sexes.

Land Tenure.   In feudal societies, Mennonites normally held usufruct rights to land and allocated some for communal and family use. As peasants were emancipated and land was transformed into a commodity throughout the eighteenth and nineteenth centuries, communities played increasingly smaller roles in the allocation and management of land. In North America, however, during the last part of the 1880s, some settlements of Russian origin continued to distribute and use land in a manner contrary to the prevailing private farmstead. The Swiss Mennonites had established early in their North American experience a freehold land tenure pattern that emphasized the individual private farmstead.

Kinship, Marriage and Family

Kinship   The Mennonites practice bilateral descent and use kin terms typical of bilateral kindreds.

Marriage.   Historically, Mennonites were forbidden to marry non-Mennonites and, in some cases, members of other Mennonite groups. Presently, only the more conservative ones proscribe marriage outside the group. Marriage is strictly monogamous, and historically families negotiated the conditions of marriage (again, arrangements varied from group to group). Currently, only among the more conservative Mennonites are such arrangements made. The *Umbitter* (matchmaker) was usually a role played by the church pastor or elders among the Dutch, Prussian, and Russian Mennonites. Among the Old Colony and Holdeman Mennonites a form of matchmaking continues. Yet, even among the more liberal denominations, informal marriage arrangements and a concern for selection of partners from within the church continue through church-sponsored events like camps, retreats, and institutions of higher education. Among all these groups

the marriage ceremony is taken as seriously as baptism and is a ritual centered in the congregation and performed by church elders or pastors. The Swiss Mennonites, unlike those descended from the Netherlandish wing, have historically conducted the marriage ritual in the home. Although most currently conduct church weddings, they tend to be simpler than typical Protestant ceremonies. Presently, residence is neolocal, and only the more strict of the denominations strongly discourage and sometimes sanction divorce. In former times, it was common for the bride and her family to assemble a dowry. Historically, there have often been cousin marriages.

Domestic Unit.   Until recently, small extended families were common and are still typical among some groups. Among contemporary Mennonites the nuclear family tends to predominate. New households are typically created in each generation, usually but not necessarily at marriage, and are ordinarily dissolved at the death of the last spouse.

Inheritance.   Inheritance practices vary from group to group and through time. In the past, both rules of primogeniture and partibility are found. Today, however, property devolves bilaterally. In rural areas, it is often the case that property passes to persons who have taken care of the owners in their later years.

Socialization.   Generally, children were and continue to be raised according to strict codes of conduct. Among some, dress codes are strictly enforced for all age groups. Still in the twentieth century, many insist on providing their own educational institutions, and some withdraw their children from school beginning in the eighth grade. Among most groups, however, parents encourage their offspring to remain in school and continue with postsecondary education. Throughout North America, there are numerous four-year colleges affiliated with the various denominations.

Sociopolitical Organization

Social Organization.   Two social institutions, church and education, have played dominant roles in Mennonite life. This is as true for the present as for the past. But between the sixteenth and twentieth centuries, these institutions were far more influential and had not, as is more recently evident, incorporated mainstream values and ideas. In fact, not until the twentieth century were women, in some denominations and congregations, permitted or encouraged to assume the roles of church elder (*Aeltester*) or bishop, minister, or teacher. This effectively removed women from major decision-making bodies and relegated them to ancillary roles within the community. The church or congregation was the most powerful institution—it sanctioned marriage, negotiated with secular authorities, and established codes of conduct (*Ordnung*) governing all aspects of life. Church elders were the ultimate authority, and no secular agency could rule on matters pertaining to community life. This, however, was impossible to maintain, as economic and political changes associated with the transition from feudal to capitalist-dominated governments often undermined church authority and led members to capitulate to local and state authorities. In the present, some conservative Mennonites continue to resist participation in government.

Similarly, Mennonites have always recognized the need

to provide their own schooling. In Prussia, Russia, and the United States, they held tenaciously to the right to educate their own; yet state bureaucracies pressured them to concede partial control. As was true for most Anabaptist groups, Mennonites did not believe that children should receive education beyond reading, writing, and arithmetic. Life in agrarian communities was, according to their teaching, potentially jeopardized by knowledge of "worldly" affairs. Although many of the more conservative Mennonite groups retain control of their educational institutions, the majority use the public schools. In fact, at the level of postsecondary education, some have distinguished themselves—there are several major Mennonite colleges and Bible institutes throughout the world, and their historical archives are among the finest.

Political Organization. Their ideological insistence on the strict separation of church and state meant that members did not participate in political organizations outside of the community. Within the Gemeinde a hierarchical distribution of power was highly suspect, but nevertheless a three-tiered ministry emerged. The highest and most revered was that of elder (Aeltester) who was elected by Gemeinde members and who, among other things, had exclusive authority to ordain new elders. Among the Swiss and German Mennonites the elder position was occupied by a bishop who held the same authority. In addition to elders, there were preachers and ministers (*Dienaren*) who were also chosen by the congregation. The former were allowed only to preach, whereas the minister could not only preach but also baptize new members. Deacons were likewise appointed by the congregation to serve the poor and care for widows, elderly, and orphans. Most important, Mennonites strongly believed that Gemeinde authorities should serve; therefore, they were not to be differentiated from other members. For this reason, they were not compensated for their service, and a professional clergy is, for the most part, a recent phenomenon, although some continue to insist upon a lay clergy.

Among Mennonites in Prussia and Russia, the Bruderschaft (brotherhood meetings) were occasionally convened by the elders. In these meetings, the men from the congregation discussed and resolved matters related to congregational life. It was often the case that the Bruderschaft assisted in the resolution of private household matters and conflicts between households. In particular, the Bruderschaft decided if a member was to be disciplined by temporary banishment or expulsion. Imposed on the Mennonites in Russia, and to a lesser extent in Prussia, was a particular form of village political organization.

Among the early Pennsylvania Mennonites a conference was started (1711) to provide leadership and continuity between various Gemeinde. Beginning in the mid-nineteenth century, other Mennonite communities and congregations began to form umbrella organizations or conferences. The General Conference of Mennonite Brethren Churches and the General Conference Mennonite Church are among the largest today. In 1920, an inter-Mennonite organization, the Mennonite Central Committee, was formed to serve as a cooperative agency for a larger Mennonite constituency. This organization is best known for its disaster relief programs.

Social Control. In the past, social control was accomplished through application of the ban and avoidance. If members were not sufficiently repentant, they were banned (excommunicated) or shunned and denied access to the Gemeinde. Still today, some of the more conservative groups strictly apply these mechanisms of social control.

Conflict. Throughout their history there have been numerous churchwide schisms. The most notable of the historical schisms have been the sixteenth-century Netherlands Frisian-Flemish; the Amish division from the Swiss Brethren; the Mennonite Brethren schism in Russia; and the Holdeman Mennonite division.

Religion and Expressive Culture

Religious Beliefs. One of the most important points of difference between Anabaptism and the state churches in the sixteenth century was over the proper role of the church. The church was to be a voluntary association of believers who chose to freely but obediently submit to the community (Gemeinde). The church, they argued, must remain separate from the state and secular or worldly affairs. Special emphasis has been given to the ethical teachings in the New Testament and, in particular, the Sermon on the Mount. Christians were to gather in communities, reject the outside world, war, violence, and refuse to take oaths. Life in the community was to be simple and individual differences in wealth and status deemphasized. Mennonites, however, rejected the radical Anabaptist teachings on the "community of goods," a practice among the Hutterites. Instead, they believed that followers should voluntarily limit their private property insofar as it undermined the common aims, faith, and practices of the Gemeinde; individual self-interest was to remain subordinate to the interests of the community. Mennonites interpret the Bible to mean that Christians may possess property, but it must be recognized that all things come from God; he is the one and only proprietor of goods—all that one can do is practice effective stewardship.

Religious Practitioners. Historically no particular consideration or training has been given to religious leaders. In recent times, however, seminaries have been founded and clergy have received specialized training. The more conservative groups retain a lay ministry.

Ceremonies. In addition to the ceremonies found in most Protestant religions, the Mennonites give special consideration to the rituals of baptism and footwashing at Communion. The rite of entrance into the community was symbolized by baptism, and footwashing (often the cause of some controversy) was a way of symbolizing that no one person was better than another.

Arts. Music, among the Mennonites, has often been controversial. Some denominations exclude musical instruments and allow only singing (often without harmony), whereas others lay a strong emphasis on classical church music. Only among the more conservative groups is singing done in the German language.

Medicine. Late in the nineteenth century, some Mennonites adhered to what could be described as Galenic humoral medicine and extensively utilized midwives. Soon, however, most accepted the allopathic medical tradition, and today Mennonites are well known for their hospitals (medical and mental).

Death and Afterlife.   Access to heaven was not predetermined. One is assured an afterlife only after having been a disciplined member of the community. Historically, some have given emphasis to the Gemeinde in their mortuary tradition by burying their members in the order of their dying—deemphasizing family membership.

Bibliography

Dyck, Cornelius J. (1981) *An Introduction to Mennonite History.* Scottdale, Pa.: Herald Press.

Kraybill, Paul N., ed. (1984) *Mennonite World Handbook.* Lombard, Ill.: Mennonite World Conference.

The Mennonite Encyclopedia: A Comprehensive Reference Work on the Anabaptist-Mennonite Movement (1955–59). 4 vols. Hillsboro, Kans.: Mennonite Brethren Publishing House.

Redekop, Calvin (1989). *Mennonite Society.* Baltimore: Johns Hopkins University Press.

Smith, Henry C. (1981) *Story of the Mennonites.* Newton, Kans.: Faith and Life Press.

Urry, James (1989). *None but Saints: The Transformation of Mennonite Life in Russia, 1789–1889.* Winnipeg: Hyperion Press.

JEFFREY L. LONGHOFER

Menominee

ETHNONYM: Menomini

Orientation

Identification.   The name of this American Indian group, "Menominee," derives from the Chippewa *mano mini,* meaning "wild rice people."

Location.   In the seventeenth century the Menominee inhabited the region bounded by Green Bay, Lake Michigan, and Lake Superior. Since the mid-nineteenth century they have occupied a reservation on the Wolf River in northeastern Wisconsin. The region is dominated by northern hardwood forests, mixed with spruce forests north of the Menominee River. Annual precipitation averages about thirty inches per year. Temperatures may reach as high as 90° F in the summer and dip as low as −30° F in the winter.

Demography.   The first estimates of the Menominee population are late and postdate a long decline following exposure to European disease. In 1820 the Menominee numbered 3,900. In 1834, following a smallpox epidemic, the population dropped to 2,500. By 1915 the population was increasing because of a declining death rate and the addition to the tribal rolls of mixed-bloods and persons married to Menominee. The Menominee numbered 2,917 in 1956 and about 2,700 in the late 1970s.

Linguistic Affiliation.   Menominee is an Algonkian language. It has been classified as a member of the Central Algonkian subgroup, but is not closely related to any other distinct language in the subgroup.

History and Cultural Relations

In the mid-seventeenth century the native groups neighboring the Menominee included the Chippewa to the north, the Winnebago to the south, and the Sauk, Fox, and Kickapoo to the west. The tribes that maintained the closest relations with the Menominee until immediately prior to the reservation period were the Winnebago and Chippewa. Intermarriage with these groups was so extensive that close links have continued through the modern period. Contact with French fur traders occurred about 1667 and with Jesuit missionaries in 1671. As close allies of the French, the Menominee prospered in the fur trade and by 1736 had become one of the dominant tribes in the region. In 1815 the Menominee came under the control of the United States. At about this time, game in the Menominee territory was being rapidly depleted, and consequently the Menominee began ceding their lands to the United States. By 1854 the Menominee had ceded all of their lands and were removed to a four-hundred-square-mile reservation along the upper Wolf River in the heart of their former territory. In 1961 federal jurisdiction over the Menominee reservation, guaranteed by treaty in 1854, was terminated and then restored in 1973.

Settlements

In aboriginal times the Menominee followed a semisedentary seasonal village pattern organized around hunting, fishing, gathering, and horticulture. As a result of Menominee involvement in the fur trade, the village pattern disintegrated and was replaced by a more nomadic way of life oriented toward hunting, trapping, and trading. When the Menominee were removed to their reservation in 1854 a more sedentary settlement pattern was required. For a half century the Menominee dispersed widely across the reservation, but since 1900 they have tended to concentrate in the village centers of Neopit and Keshena, the latter being the location for the buildings and operations of the U.S. Indian Service.

Economy

Subsistence and Commercial Activities.   The precontact Menominee had small gardens in which they grew squash, beans, and maize, but they were basically hunters and gatherers. They also harvested wild rice and made extensive use of the resources of streams, particularly sturgeon. Hunting was done by individuals and small groups, with occasional larger hunts for deer and bison. After contact with the French the Menominee became heavily involved in trapping and trading activities and remained so until the early part of the nineteenth century. Since game and fish were not available in sufficient quantities on their reservation, after 1854 some Menominee turned to farming, although this never proved to be a successful activity. Beginning in the late nineteenth century and up to the present day lumbering has been the primary source of subsistence for many Menominee. In the 1950s, incomes from lumbering were supplemented by seasonal agricultural work and a wide range of relatively minor economic activities, including farming, hunting, fishing, trapping, and gathering wild fruits.

Industrial Arts. The precontact Menominee made birchbark and dugout canoes. They wove bags and baskets of vegetable fiber, bark, and bison hair, and manufactured pottery and bark and reed mats.

Trade. In precontact times the Menominee obtained catlinite originating from the Sioux quarries in present-day Minnesota and copper from the Lake Superior region and traded stone and wood manufactures to the Winnebago.

Division of Labor. Traditionally, men's responsibilities included hunting and fishing, warfare, ceremonial activities, preparing sacred artifacts, and manufacturing canoes and hunting and fishing equipment. Women's responsibilities included cooking, caring for children, collecting wild foods, gathering firewood, carrying water, dressing skins, making clothing, weaving mats and bags, and manufacturing pottery and household utensils. In the 1950s there was extensive sharing of economic roles between men and women among traditional Menominee. In addition, there was considerable occupational diversity among Menominee, most of it related to the lumber industry.

Land Tenure. During the fur trade period families claimed customary rights over particular river paths and hunting territories, as game was depleted and hunting parties were forced to range over progressively wider territories.

Kinship

Kin Groups and Descent. In aboriginal and early contact times the Menominee were organized into two moieties subdivided into totemic descent groups or clans. This system began to disintegrate in the 1700s under the impact of European contact and the nomadic way of life required by involvement in the fur trade. Totemic descent groups were patrilineal.

Kinship Terminology. Kinship terminology is of the Omaha type. One of the main features of Menominee family relationships was a classificatory system of terminology that was still in use in the 1960s.

Marriage and Family

Marriage. In aboriginal and early historic times marriages were arranged by kin groups and polygyny was practiced. A newly married couple usually lived with the husband's parents. With the growing emphasis on mobility and smaller groups accompanying involvement in the fur trade, monogamous marriages gradually became the norm.

Domestic Unit. The large extended family groups characteristic of the aboriginal and early historic Menominee were replaced during the fur trade period by small nomadic family hunting groups. In the 1950s Menominee were divided into approximately 550 households, most consisting of a nuclear family or an old couple with grandchildren or an unmarried daughter and her child.

Inheritance. Inheritance is bilateral. Sacred objects of the totem group are inherited from either the paternal or the maternal side.

Socialization. Traditionally, children were believed to be close to the supernatural through the event of birth and thus were considered extremely important. Infants were usually kept in cradle boards until the age of two or until they were able to walk and were nursed for as long as they would reach for the breast. Child training often took the form of storytelling, a common theme of which was constraint and self-control. Disciplining of children was left largely to the women. There was a distinct sanction against striking any child until he or she was eight years old. For punishment a child might be whipped about the legs, but never struck around the head, for it was believed that to do so would make the child dumb. Other punishments included throwing cold water in the child's face, scolding, or immersion in water. The favored form of coercion consisted of threats by reference to the owl or other creatures of the night. Many of these values and practices persisted in the 1950s among the traditional Menominee.

Sociopolitical Organization

Social Organization. Prior to contact with Europeans the Menominee were organized into semisedentary villages of extended family groups. Involvement in the fur trade undermined this system and led to the development of a band system of social organization that persisted until the reservation period. After their arrival on the reservation many Menominee grouped according to their band affiliations, but with a more sedentary way of life, band identities gradually disappeared.

Political Organization. The formal political structure of the aboriginal Menominee consisted of a tribal chief, who was the head of the Bear moiety and whose position was inherited, and several lesser hereditary chiefs, who were heads of the various totemic descent groups. Descent group chiefs constituted a village council and regulated civil affairs to a limited extent. In addition, there were chiefs who won prestige through dreams or special prowess and who served as keepers of the war medicines and as public spokesmen for the hereditary leaders. Under the influence of the fur trade, leadership qualifications were modified to include success in obtaining furs, directing hunting and trading expeditions, obtaining credit, public speaking, and getting along well with Whites and other Indian tribes.

Social Control. A strong belief in witchcraft functioned as a form of social control among the aboriginal and historic Menominee and persists today among traditional Menominee. The witch could be any powerful elder, and his victims, deviant members of the group who failed to observe the group's prescriptions for behavior.

Conflict. The Menominee were unprepared for self-government when their reservation status was terminated in 1961, and significant health, housing, education, and general welfare problems developed as a result. In the 1970s, after tribal status was restored, severe intratribal differences emerged, as the Menominee sought to find solutions to these problems.

Religion and Expressive Culture

Religious Beliefs. The Menominee belief system was dualistic, with a continuing cosmic conflict between good spirits above the earth and evil spirits below. The highest tier of the universe above the earth was the home of the supreme deity, Mecawetok, and below him were the Thunderbirds or Thunderers, the gods of war, and the Morning Star. Beneath the earth and in the lowest tier was Great White Bear, the main power of evil. Others who resided in the evil underworld were Underground Panther, White Deer, and Horned Hairy Serpent, who inhabited the lakes and streams and tried to capsize boats in order to drag people to the underworld. The earth itself was believed to be peopled with evil spirits and hobgoblins. The central experience of Menominee religion was the dream revelation, in which individuals obtained special power in the form of a guardian spirit. With some changes, the pattern of securing a guardian spirit through fasting and dreaming persisted among traditional Menominee in 1960.

Religious Practitioners. Medicine men and diviners possessing powers obtained from their guardian spirits were organized into ceremonial societies, but worked more or less as individuals.

Ceremonies. A variety of ceremonial organizations developed among the Menominee after European contact, and some of these persisted in varying forms among traditional Menominee in the mid-1900s. These included the Medicine Lodge Society, whose ceremonies are intended to prolong the life and ensure the good health of the members; the Dream Dance or Drum Dance, which involved petitioning the spirits for help in the activities of everyday life; and the Warrior's Dance, borrowed from the Chippewa in 1925 and intended to protect men being drafted and participating in contemporary wars.

Arts. Precontact art forms show a well-developed geometric art and indicate the use of highly conventionalized figures. Postcontact art forms included work with porcupine quills and animal hair with a religious motif. About 1830 a new phase in Menominee art was initiated in which the older geometric motifs were replaced with elaborate floral and realistic designs and the skin and quill work was replaced by cloth and beadwork with new color pigments. This art form persists in special events and dancing for tourists.

Medicine. Illness was believed to be the result of the loss of one's soul through witchcraft. Diviners with special powers consulted with the spirits to find the source of the illness and then would attempt to coax the soul of the patient to return and enter a small wooden cylinder where it was imprisoned and delivered to the patient's relatives. The cylinder was then attached to the patient's breast for four days so that the soul could return to the body.

Death and Afterlife. Traditionally, after death the deceased was placed on a scaffolding or buried beneath logs on the ground. Grave goods included the deceased's weapons, tools, and ornaments. Early observers of the Menominee reported that a corpse was painted red to signify happiness at the privilege of the soul in departing to the spirit land. The ghosts of the dead were believed to linger around the grave indefinitely and to have a strong influence on the living. In spite of the fear of ghosts, mourners visited the burial place to offer food and games, and ritual activities were performed to keep the ghosts contented. Until the mid-twentieth century it was a common practice for the deceased to have his totem painted, usually upside down, on a grave stick at his place of burial. In modern times the dead are buried in a coffin in the ground beneath a small houselike structure with an opening through which food and other offerings can be placed.

Bibliography

Hoffman, Walter J. (1896). *The Menomini Indians.* U.S. Bureau of American Ethnology, 14th Annual Report (1892–1893), Pt. 1, 3–328. Washington, D.C.

Keesing, Felix M. (1939). *The Menomini Indians of Wisconsin: A Study of Three Centuries of Cultural Contact and Change.* Memoirs of the American Philosophical Society, no. 10. Philadelphia.

Skinner, Alanson B. (1913). *Social Life and Ceremonial Bundles of the Menomini Indians.* American Museum of Natural History, Anthropological Papers 13, 1–165. New York.

Skinner, Alanson B. (1921). "Material Culture of the Menomini." *Indian Notes and Monographs* (Museum of the American Indian, Heye Foundation), misc. ser. 20(1). New York.

Spindler, George D. (1955). *Sociocultural and Psychological Processes in Menomini Acculturation.* University of California Publications in Culture and Society, no. 5. Berkeley.

Spindler, Louise S. (1962). *Menomini Women and Culture Change.* American Anthropologial Association, Memoir 91. Menasha, Wis.

Spindler, Louise S. (1978). "Menominee." In *Handbook of North American Indians.* Vol. 15, *Northeast,* edited by Bruce G. Trigger, 708–725. Washington, D.C.: Smithsonian Institution.

LOUISE S. SPINDLER AND GEORGE D. SPINDLER

Mescalero Apache

ETHNONYMS: Apaches de Cuartelejo, Apaches del Rio Grande, Apachi, Faraones, Mezcaleros, Natage, Natahene, Querechos, Sierra Blanca Apaches, Teyas, Tularosa Apaches, Vaqueros

Orientation

Identification. "Mescalero" is from the Spanish: *-ero,* "people of," and *mescale,* "agave" (the century plant). They were so named for their reliance on the huge roasted and preserved root of the plant they used as their primary carbohydrate source. *Apache* is not an aboriginal Southern Athapaskan word. The term seems to have been applied by outsiders to groups of non-Puebloan hunters and gatherers/foragers who entered the Southwest at least a couple of centuries, if not several centuries, prior to the mid-sixteenth-century arrival of the Spanish conquistadores-explorers. Some few contemporary Mescalero aver that the word _Apache_ could have come from ' _abesh' zhi,_ a term referring to those who came from above (to the north of) the Black Rock place, which is thought today to be around Yellowstone. The Mescalero refer to themselves as "_Ndé_" (The People). Often they will also include a band name or a location name to further qualify their identity, as in "Dzithinahndé" (Mountain Ridge Band People) or "Ch' laandé" (Antelope Band People).

Location. Since May 27, 1873, and the establishment of their reservation by executive order of President U. S. Grant, the Mescalero Apache have lived in south-central New Mexico between 33°00′ and 33°23′ N and 105°18′ and 105°56′ W. At the time of Spanish contact, they ranged between southern Colorado and central Chihuahua, Mexico and from central Texas to the Gila River in New Mexico. Today their reservation encompasses approximately 720 square miles and varies in elevation from 3,400 feet to slightly more than 12,000 feet. Terrain is mountainous with some high desert plateaus. There is a summer rainy season and heavy snowfall most winters in the higher elevations. Temperatures rarely exceed 85° F in summer, and winter temperatures below freezing are common.

Demography. The Mescalero Apache Tribe includes Chiricahuas and Lipans. Tribal figures cite slightly more than 2,500 (official designation) enrolled members in 1988. There is no breakdown available on relative numbers of Mescalero to Chiricahua, but popular belief maintains there are approximately equal numbers of those two groups, with perhaps two dozen or so Lipan. There were 468 enrolled Mescalero when the reservation was established in 1873. Between 1903 and 1905 the remnants of the Lipan, said to be just a few wagonloads of people (about 40), joined their Mescalero "cousins," and in 1912 several hundred Chiricahua, or Fort Sill Apache, moved to Mescalero after their imprisonment in Alabama, Florida, and Oklahoma. Population estimates for the period from the mid-sixteenth century until 1873 are difficult to interpret, since often they were inflated for various strategic or political reasons. Because the Apache were not sedentary, they were difficult to count accurately; for example, a Spanish governor, Ugarte, boasted in 1790 that he had secured peace with 3,000 Apache, including Mescalero. It seems plausible to estimate that the group we call Mescalero today probably never numbered more than 6,500–7,000, even when considering all the bands scattered over a very large area.

Linguistic Affiliation. Mescalero Apache is one of the Southern Athapaskan languages. It is mutually intelligible to speakers of other Apachean languages and Navajo and is related to Athapaskan languages in Alaska, western parts of Canada, and the northern California and Oregon coast.

History and Cultural Relations

Coronado's 1540 expedition through central Mexico and into the contemporary American Southwest noted that there were Querechos, generally acknowledged to be ancestral to Eastern Apache, on the Llano Estacado, a vast plains area of eastern New Mexico, western Texas, and southwestern Oklahoma. The Querechos were described as being tall and intelligent; they lived in tents, said to be like those of Arabs, and followed the bison herds, from which they secured food, fuel, implements, clothing, and tipi covers—all of which was transported using dogs and the travois. These Querechos traded with agricultural Puebloan peoples. Initial contact was peaceful, but by the mid-seventeenth century there was all-out war between the Spanish and the Apache. During the seventeenth century, Spanish suzerainty in the Southwest was being enforced with often impossible demands on the Pueblos who, in turn, found themselves subject to Apachean raids when Spanish exploitation left nothing to trade. At the same time, all native people were being decimated by diseases for which they had no immunity. There was also pressure from the Ute and Comanche who were moving southward into the area previously held by Apache. Documentary evidence suggests that the Spanish were arming Comanche to assist in their unsuccessful efforts to subdue and control the Apache.

The Mescalero quickly picked up horses from the Spanish, making their hunting, trading, and raiding infinitely easier. They also borrowed the Spanish practice of slave trading and thus gave the Spanish a weapon to use against them in that Spanish colonists, while taking slaves from Apache captives, raised fear in the Pueblos that they would be the next slaves the Apache sought. In fact, the Apache began to rely less upon trade with Pueblos and more on raids against Spanish colonists.

Despite the Spanish policy of pitting tribes against each other, the latter joined together in 1680 in the Pueblo Revolt and successfully removed the Spanish from New Mexico. Many Puebloan people, who had fled the Spanish by going to live with Apache and Navajo, returned home and it seems the older pattern of Plains hunting and Puebloan trading was reinstituted. In 1692 the colonists returned and the pace of war with Apache quickened.

The history of the eighteenth and early nineteenth centuries was written in blood and broken promises. Treachery was rampant and peace treaties were not worth the ink necessary to write them. Mescalero were routinely referred to as "the enemy, heathen, Apache" and were blamed for practically every disaster that befell Spanish colonists. The real effect of Spain was minimal and Mexico was not yet an independent country. The northern frontier of New Spain was entrusted to a few soldiers of fortune, an inadequately supplied and trained military, mercenary traders, jealous sets of Catholic missionaries, and intrepid civilians trying to wrest a living from unforgiving land. In the midst of this, Spanish regents insisted on treating the Apache as a unified group of people when they were very much several bands, each under the nominal control of a headman; a treaty signed with such a headman bound no one to peace, despite Spanish wishes to the contrary.

In 1821 Mexico became independent from Spain and inherited the Apache problem—at least for a couple of decades. Slavery, on the part of all parties, and debt peonage reached its zenith during this period. By 1846, Gen. Stephen Watts Kearney had taken control of the northernmost portions of the Mexican frontier and established headquarters at Fort Marcy in Santa Fe, New Mexico. The Treaty of Guadelupe Hidalgo in 1848 formally ceded large portions of what is now the American Southwest to the United States and more was added in 1853 with the Gadsden Purchase, transferring "the Apache problem" to the United States. The 1848 treaty guaranteed colonists protection from Indians, the Mescalero; there was no mention of Indian rights. Congress, in 1867, abolished peonage in New Mexico, and an 1868 Joint Resolution (65) finally ended bondage and slavery. The Apache problem remained, however.

Mescalero had been rounded up (frequently) and held (infrequently) at the Bosque Redondo of Fort Sumner, New Mexico, since 1865, although army agents in charge of them continually complained that they came and went with alarming frequency. Four centuries of almost constant conflict and decimation by disease along with the loss of the land base that had sustained them all combined to reduce the Mescalero to a pitiful few by the time their reservation was established.

The late 1870s through the teens of the twentieth century was a particularly difficult time, because of inadequate food, shelter, and clothing. Despite their own suffering, they accepted their "relatives," first the Lipan and later the Chiricahua, onto their reservation. By the 1920s there was a small but significant improvement in the standard of living, although attempts at making Mescalero farmers have never succeeded. The 1934 Indian Reorganization Act found the Mescalero eager and fully able to assume control over their own lives, a fight they still wage through the courts today on issues of land use, water rights, legal jurisdiction, and wardship. Although the arena of the fight for survival has moved from horseback to a Tribal plane that makes frequent trips to Washington, the Apache are still formidable foes.

Economy

Subsistence and Commercial Activities. The traditional subsistence base was one of hunting and gathering/foraging with primary reliance on the bison and mescal. Seeds, nuts, tubers, fruits, and wild plants formed important parts of the diet along with meat from deer, antelope, rabbit, and elk. Neither fish nor bear meat were consumed. Some sources maintain that Plains Apache would occasionally plant maize, but the Mescalero themselves deny this, maintaining they traded with the Pueblos for maize as well as beans, squashes, turkeys, and cotton. From the Spaniards they took not only horses but also cattle whenever possible as they were much easier to hunt than wild animals.

In this century there has been a steady increase in wage work on and off reservation. Tribal enterprises practice Indian preference in hiring. On the reservation, people work in a variety of jobs: accounting, carpentry, child care, clerical, community health, computer programming and operation, conservation, cow punching, services for the elderly, fishery, forestry, housing, hunting guides, lumbering and sawmill operation, maintenance, nursing, recreation, rehabilitation services, skiing operations, social work, stable hands, teaching, and so on. There are also those who choose a military career and those with law and other advanced degrees who have been unable to find work on the reservation. Arts and crafts, especially bead, skin, and woodwork, are practiced but do not form significant economic activities. Although they were once known for their exquisite basketry, it is now almost a forgotten art. Bead and leatherwork as well as wood carving and

other artistic endeavors provide a few with sufficient income. Tribal goals include providing on-reservation jobs for all those who wish them as well as adequate housing for all families; the latter goal appears more in reach. For some, the most stable income source is through tribally generated income. Each enrolled member of the Mescalero Apache Tribe has one share of stock in the Tribal Enterprises that are run as a corporation; profits are periodically divided into equal share dividends. This income, however, is aperiodic and varies with each payment. A few people subsist on tribal or state welfare, but most work.

Division of Labor. In general, men hunted and women gathered and foraged. But women also hunted, particularly small game, and men participated heavily in mescal making as well as occasionally gathering. Both men and women achieve status through being successful parents; it is not unusual to see men as primary caretakers of infants and children.

Kinship

Kin Groups and Descent. Mescalero Apache are matrilineal; however, men are not ignored, especially if one's lineage includes an important warrior. People today use surnames that are sometimes of one's mother's band or family, sometimes of one's father's, and sometimes a transliteration of a famous ancestor's name into English. People consider as siblings all the children of one's mother as well as the children of one's mother's sisters. Sometimes a distinction is made among siblings with the phrase, "same mother, same father"; however, the crucial link is through the mother and laterally from her. Today, with the mid-1980s adoption of a new Tribal Law Code, there seems to be a shift to patrilineal surnames and bilateral descent, although the emphasis is still on the mother's side of the family. Inheritance of material items also seems to be moving to a bilateral model, although here, too, the emphasis is still through the matrilineage, especially for things considered traditional or esoteric. Band membership is no longer of consequence and is preserved primarily through stories and few lexical items or shifts in pronunciation.

Kinship Terminology. There is an elaborate set of kinship terms allowing one to distinguish between relatives through one's mother as distinct from those through one's father; siblings and first cousins through the matrilineage are referred to by the same term, and other cousins are terminologically distinct. When speaking English, however, Eskimo-type rules are used.

Marriage and Family

Marriage. Although polygyny, especially sororal, was practiced, the new law code forbids it. Until very recently those men having more than one wife would marry one "in the White man's way" (legally, according to American law) and other(s) "in the Indian way" (with a formal ritual uniting two families). Even today, if a man is widowed and there is a marriageable woman in his dead wife's matrilineage, it is expected that the man will seriously consider marrying again within the lineage. Divorce used to be by mutual consent or by the wife simply removing her husband's belongings from her house; now, of course, American law is followed. Mother-in-law avoidance was standard practice for men even into the mid-1950s; however, it seems no longer to be practiced even though men still often report feeling "uncomfortable" around their mothers-in-law.

Domestic Unit. A woman owns the family home and everything in it; she and any brothers and sisters share primary responsibility for raising the children, including discipline; the father is friend, confidant, and protector. It is common for a household to be comprised of a woman and her children, children of her sisters, her husband or consort, her unmarried brothers and sisters (especially if the parental home is unavailable for any reason), children of her unmarried children, and often a "grandparent," who may be a biological grandparent or an aunt or uncle of the mother through her matrilineage. Children have a great deal of freedom concerning with whom they will live; often the choice is to live with a maternal aunt. Foster parenting is common, and frequently older children are sent to live with grandparents if the older people are living alone. It is considered especially appropriate to have been raised by one's grandparents.

Socialization. Socialization is through the matrilateral extended family; any older person has the license to correct those younger. Children are expected to learn through observation and practice rather than through questioning or direct verbal instruction. Even today, much of moral and social significance is taught by "elderlies" through stories. Individual rights are respected, even those of small children; the elderly are accorded great respect, even when they claim no special knowledge.

Sociopolitical Organization

Social Organization. The matrilateral extended family is the primary social unit. Bands are no longer of significance and clans were never a part of the Mescalero social fabric.

Political Organization. The 1934 Indian Reorganization Act resulted in the establishment of the Tribal Business Committee, which later became the Tribal Council. The council consists of ten members, each elected, in staggered fashion, for two years. The position of president of the Tribal Council, one of the ten positions, is also open for election every two years; the president serves as president of the tribe as well. Other officers are agreed upon within the council. The council prefers to achieve consensus rather than majority agreement. Committees and subcommittees within the council administer the affairs of the tribe from road maintenance to forestry management to social services.

Social Control. Social control is managed through a tribal court system that operates on a combination of traditional and Anglo law. Minor issues are often handled by families. Public talk is also used to control antisocial behavior.

Conflict. Conflict may be managed within families, between families, by appeal to the president of the tribe, through the tribal court, or through the U.S. judicial system for some federal crimes. Alcoholism continues to escalate and contributes to increased intratribal conflict.

Religion and Expressive Culture

Religious Beliefs. In traditional belief, a Creator (neither male nor female), which is beyond human comprehension but is manifested in natural phenomena, made the world in four days. Portions of the Creator may be seen in the natural universe (thunder, wind, and so on), and the physical representation is said to be the sun. In addition, there are two culture heroes, the Twin War Gods, Born for Water and Killer of Enemies, as well as a heroine, White Painted Woman. Power suffuses the universe and can be employed for good or ill. There are now many Christian denominations on the reservation; most people compartmentalize and maintain both religious systems.

Religious Practitioners. Singers are the traditional practitioners and are so named for they sing ceremonies, complex recitations, and rituals. There are also medicine people, skilled in herbal and psychological healing. _Gaʔhé_, Mountain Gods, are impersonated in complex rituals; they may dance to conduct a blessing or healing.

Ceremonies. The primary extant ceremony is the girls' puberty ceremony, sung any time after initial menses. Singers also sing blessing ceremonies, sometimes in concert with the Mountain God dancers, who are often called upon to bless endeavors and give thanks for success.

Arts. See **Economy**.

Medicine. There is a Public Health Service hospital on the reservation as well as community health representatives who offer in-home services and training. Additionally, people use traditional medicine and blessing dancers and singers.

Death and Afterlife. The world of humans is the world of illusion and shadow; reality resides in the other world of Power and Creator. Upon death a soul remains close to home for four days; if a proper funeral and burial is held, the soul is freed to make its way to the Land of Ever Summer, as some call it. There is disagreement about whether reincarnation is possible, although most traditional people believe it is.

Bibliography

Forbes, Jack D. (1960). _Apache, Navajo, and Spaniard_. Norman: University of Oklahoma Press.

Opler, Morris E. (1983). "Mescalero Apache." In _Handbook of North American Indians_. Vol. 10, _Southwest_, edited by Alphonso Ortiz, 419–439. Washington, D.C.: Smithsonian Institution.

Opler, Morris E., and Catherine H. Opler (1950). "Mescalero Apache History in the Southwest." _New Mexico Historical Review_ 25:1–36.

Sonnichsen, Charles L. (1972). _The Mescalero Apaches_. 2nd ed. Norman: University of Oklahoma Press.

CLAIRE R. FARRER

Metis of Western Canada

ETHNONYMS: Bois Brulé, Chicots, Halfbreeds, Métis, Michif

Orientation

Identification.   Scholars use *metis*, originally a French term meaning "mixed," to designate individuals and communities who identify their ancestors with historical fur trade communities. These metis communities were distinct from indigenous Indian bands and from the trading posts. Some of these communities used "Metis" (pronounced May-tees) to identify themselves. In recent years native peoples of other origins have chosen to apply the term to themselves. Patrilineally, the Metis acknowledge ethnic origins such as French-Canadian, Highland Scot, Orcadian, and English, among others. Equally important for the Metis of the West were "Eastern Indians" including some Iroquois peoples and various Ojibwa peoples, including the Nipissings, Ottawas, and Saulteaux. Matrilineally, the Metis look to indigenous Indian bands; largely Ojibwa in the region of the upper Great Lakes, largely Cree on the northern plains and the southern regions of the boreal forest, and largely Dene down the valleys of the Mackenzie River system to the Arctic Ocean. Individuals of mixed European and Indian ancestry who identify with, and are accepted by, Indian bands are viewed as Indians, not Metis.

Location.   The Great Lakes Metis appeared in the region of the upper Great Lakes in the first quarter of the eighteenth century. A century later, with their dispersal in the face of American settlement, individuals and families journeyed westward to the Missouri River and to the Red River of the North and beyond. By 1800, Plains Metis were emerging in the valleys of the Athabaska, North Saskatchewan, Assiniboine, and Red rivers. Over the next half-century they extended their presence southward toward the Missouri River and westward to the foothills of the Rocky Mountains. Today the largest concentration of Metis families and communities is found in the parkland and boreal forest regions of Canada, particularly the prairie provinces, the Northwest Territories, and northern Ontario.

Demography.   Before the demise of the buffalo, the Plains Metis were doubling their numbers every twenty years. By the third quarter of the nineteenth century, Louis Riel, the noted Metis leader, estimated the Metis population of the West at 10,000 to 12,000. At the same time in the Red River Settlement, metis peoples numbered 10,000 to 11,000. Of this number, over 50 percent could be identified as Metis. While the bulk of the Metis traced their origins to the St. Lawrence–Great Lakes fur trade tradition, with its familiarity with the French language and Roman Catholicism, another group of metis people traced their origins to the Hudson Bay fur trade tradition and its familiarity with the English language and Protestantism. These people did *not* term themselves Metis. They were known variously as "Hudson Bay English," "Country-born," "Red River Halfbreed," and, by some writers, "English metis." They were concentrated in the area of the Red River Settlement and in the valley of the North Saskatchewan River. In latter years, many were absorbed into the settler society. The 1981 census places the metis population

in Canada at 98,260, one-quarter of the Indian population. The majority are found in the provinces of Manitoba (20,485), Saskatchewan (17,455), and Alberta (27,135). Many of these metis would identify themselves as Metis.

Linguistic Affiliation.   In the nineteenth century, most Metis grew to maturity speaking either Cree or Saulteaux, the language of their mothers. It was the language of the bush as well. Males particularly learned French as a language of "work." Under the influence of Roman Catholic missionaries, French became the language of the community for those families settled near permanent missions. With the advent of settlement at the end of the nineteenth century, English became the language of "business" (outsiders). Until recently, many Metis were trilingual. Today, renewed interest in speaking "better" Cree or Saulteaux accompanies the use of English. In a few communities, Michif, a language with a Cree and Saulteaux structure and grammar, together with Cree or Saulteaux and French terms, is encountered.

History and Cultural Relations

In the latter half of the seventeenth century in the Great Lakes region, the factory system of trading fur ended. To sustain their interests, the French took over the role of the trade chief and his followers in gathering furs from different bands, transporting them to the coastal factory to be exchanged for European manufactured goods and carrying the goods inland to be distributed to the Indian bands with the next spring trade. The *en derouine* trade (itinerant peddling) that emerged saw a *bourgeois* (merchant), one among several in a principal post, dispatch small parties of men, led by a *commis* (clerk), to trade with Indian bands on their own territory. To cement commercial relations with a band, the commis frequently would take a "country wife." In time, should he become a bourgeois, he would gather some of his "country children," particularly first-born males, to join his family in the trading post. By 1725, this two-generation process had established the Great Lakes Metis. Half a century later, farther west, in the river valleys of the northern plains and southern boreal forest, "free men," former *engagés* (servants) of the trading companies, with their "country families" appeared as *les gens libres* (the free folk). The traders encouraged them in their pursuit of bison (provisions) and furs. The Indian bands of the region, as kinsmen of the free men's country wives, accepted their presence. In accommodating to a provisioning and trapping niche in the northern plains fur trade, les gens libres emerged as the Plains Metis. By the 1840s, the buffalo robe trade complemented the summer provisioning hunt with family bands of Metis joining with others to establish sizable winter villages in wooded oases on the prairie. They became known as *hivernants* (winterers).

With time, the Metis found their economic interests tied to commercial capitalist interests outside of the region and witnessed the resurgence of a Metis trading class. These Metis traders were invariably the patriarchal heads of wintering villages on the prairies. It was this new commercial and trading interest that was at the root of the free trade controversy, culminating with the Sayer trial in 1849. The trial saw the Red River Metis successfully challenge the Hudson's Bay Company's use of its royal charter to protect its commercial interests from competition.

On both the summer hunts and the robe hunts, violent

incidents could occur, involving the Dakota southwest of the Red River Settlement and, farther west, members of the Blackfoot Confederacy. The most famous incident was the Battle of Grand Coteau, June 16–19, 1851. Metis from White Horse Plains, a community on the Assiniboine River on the western extremity of the Red River Settlement, came under sustained attack from Yankton Dakota near Dog Den Butte close to the Missouri River. Circling their two-wheeled red river carts to corral their oxen and horses and shelter the women and children, the men charged forth the distance of a gun shot to scrape gun pits in the prairie sod. From these vantage points they inflicted casualties that the Dakota found unacceptable and thus broke off the action. Although conflict would continue into the 1870s, the Metis saw themselves as paramount on the northern plains. It was also as guides and interpreters in the fur trade and later with missionaries and in government service that the Metis gained recognition. Many officials considered them indispensable in conducting negotiations with Indians.

With "the transfer" in 1869–1870, the Colony of Canada replaced the Hudson's Bay Company as the political authority in British North West America. Under the leadership of Louis Riel, the Metis in Red River initiated a political movement to ensure their interests in the era of settlement. The college-educated Riel garnered sufficient support to establish a provisional government and subsequently to negotiate an agreement with the Canadians that became the Manitoba Act. Riel believed he had negotiated a position of continuing political relevance for the Metis. The surge of settlement in the decade that followed demonstrated otherwise. With the rewards of the robe trade still evident farther west and experiencing discrimination at the hands of Protestant immigrants, many Red River Metis sold their river lots to incoming Canadians and journeyed westward to join existing settlements or to found new ones. Fifteen years later, Louis Riel, now as a religious prophet, led a movement seeking to recapture the political position lost in Red River. Centered in the village of Batoche in the settlement of St-Laurent on the South Saskatchewan River, events progressed to rebellion, ending with the Battle of Batoche, May 12, 1885. Riel was captured, tried, and hanged on November 16, 1885. After the rebellion, the Metis were dispersed northward and westward, and survived into the twentieth century owning little land and frequently squatting on Crown land (comparable with public land in the United States).

In the 1930s, the Metis in Alberta persuaded the provincial government to enact legislation creating ten (later eight) "colonies" in the boreal forest region. Similar to Indian reserves, the colonies were to facilitate Metis assimilation into the larger population. Other provincial governments have since initiated a number of programs to address problems of disease, poverty, unemployment, substance abuse, and fairness in the judicial process. With the 1950s, Metis organizations agitated for a decision-making role in programs directed at them. Recently, in Alberta, the Federation of Metis Settlements (formerly colonies) and the separate Metis Association have negotiated relationships with the provincial government that suggest that Riel's objective, Metis survival as a recognized political entity, may be realized. Similar understandings may be emerging in other Canadian jurisdictions. In the United States, some Metis communities in Montana and North Dakota have seen Indian status as a vehicle to achieve recognition as a corporate entity in relations with governments. In a few instances, this view has gained adherents in Canada. At present, however, increasing numbers of Metis are taking purposeful steps to acknowledge a Metis heritage.

Settlements

When warfare abated in the middle of the eighteenth century in the immediate region of the upper Great Lakes, several trading families left the trading posts to establish extended-family villages. Numbers in these villages are difficult to determine, but they would mirror those of neighboring Indian bands, reflecting hunting resources supplemented with subsistence horticulture. Besides settlements near the major forts at Michilimackimac, Sault Ste-Marie, Fort William, and Dearborn, other villages appeared at locations such as Chebougamon, Green Bay, and Prairie du Chien. With the advent of settlement, families dispersed westward, some to the valley of the Red River. By the late 1820s, the Red River Settlement contained the largest Metis community in the nineteenth century. By the 1840s, settlements had emerged at Pembina and St-Joseph in Dakota Territory. In the succeeding decade, settlement emerged farther west at Lac Ste-Anne, later moved to St-Albert near Fort Edmonton, and Lac la Biche. With the robe trade, wintering villages appeared in the Qu'Appelle River valley, at Turtle, Moose, and Wood mountains, and in the valley of the South Saskatchewan River and its principal tributaries. For brief periods, communities such as La Petite Ville, Round Plain, Buffalo Lake, and Tail Creek could number as many as several hundred inhabitants. At the time the bison herds collapsed in the early 1880s, wintering villages were found in the Cypress Hills, south of the Missouri River in the Judith Basin in Montana Territory, and westward in the foothills. The wintering villages disappeared with the bison. Settlements about the missions were absorbed into the communities of the settler society.

Economy

Subsistence and Commercial Activities. The Metis were hunters and trappers who practiced subsistence horticulture, raising cereal and vegetable crops on river lots. Bison meat, fresh and processed as pemmican, was the principal food and surplus product generated for sale in the fur trade. Later, the cow's hide taken in winter, the robe, would be the principal surplus product traded. The summer hunt saw the Metis of a particular region gather at a central rendezvous to establish the temporary government of the hunt. By election, the heads of families chose le chef (chief) to be assisted by seven to ten capitaines (captains), each with requisite soldats (soldiers). Rules for the hunt, emphasizing the collective interest over that of the individual, with sanctions, were promulgated. With the end of the hunt, the authority of le chef and les capitaines ended, although they continued to be men of influence and consequence. The format of the summer hunt was followed in the winter village.

In return for the surplus provisions, furs, and robes the Metis supplied to the trader, they consumed products additional to those available in the Indian trade. Besides guns, shot, powder, knives, axes, and blankets, the Metis were heavy consumers of cloth and clothing. Accouterments such as caps, shawls, beads, jewelry, and sleigh bells and pom-poms for dog harnesses found ready buyers. At some locations, fisheries (using nets) from late fall to early winter were of critical importance. With the collapse of robe prices in the 1870s, followed by the collapse of the herds themselves, the Metis shifted to carting and day labor. With the granting of "Half-breed Scrip" in Canada from the 1870s through to the 1900s, some Metis acquired land in addition to being eligible for homestead entry. Many more took money to finance itinerant farming and hunting. Today, many Metis are successful farmers. Many more, as employers and employees, are involved in small businesses and government service in the boreal forest region. Seasonal labor and government assistance continue to be significant sources of income.

Industrial Arts. The Metis incorporated many of the bush skills and products of their Indian kin into their way of life. The distinguishing feature in their behavior was the emphasis they placed on generating a surplus of selected products. Also, from the world of "work" in the fur trade, many men were skilled fishermen, boatmen, and teamsters. As cartwrights they created, without metal parts, the two-wheeled prairie vehicle, the red river cart. As carpenters they built one-room cabins in a matter of days. On occasion, leather garments cut in a European manner, but beaded in the tradition of the woodlands, was their clothing. An assumption sash, a woven belt, extended across the body from shoulder to waist. A cap or hat of distinction (a tam-o'-shanter at midcentury) completed costuming.

Division of Labor. In their skills and roles, the women reflected their cultural antecedents. In appropriate circumstances they could snare small game, although their activities emphasized the manufacture of clothing and the preparation and preservation of food, in addition to some gardening. The men hunted and trapped, and the women played a critical role in processing pemmican and tanning pelts and robes in surplus amounts for trade. Men skinned and butchered carcasses, but it was the women who produced the final product for trade.

Land Tenure. The Metis in Red River squatted with Hudson's Bay Company approval on river lots of a few rods frontage and extending a mile back from the river. By custom, the subsequent two miles were deemed the "hay privilege" of the river-lot resident. Beyond the hay privilege was common land where, for purposes of haying, local decision governed utilization. The pattern in Red River was reflected in other mission settlements, eventually to be recognized by government survey. Transfers of residence involved compensation for improvements, but not the land itself, until resettlement, surveys, and titles conveyed ownership. With the transfer in 1869–1870 and subsequent legislation, the Metis heads of families were granted rights to the land on which they resided and scrip to the amount of $160 or 160 acres. All Metis children were granted 240 acres of land. Over the years, much of this land and scrip fell into the hands of speculators, leaving large numbers of Metis landless. A dimension of Metis activism today aspires to establish a land base in areas where they have been residents for generations.

Kinship

The Metis reflected the kinship practices of their cultural antecedents insofar as existing circumstances made this behavior possible. Free men leaving the fur trade frequently maintained social relations with former workmates living either in the posts or as free men. Marriages among their children were instrumental in defining socially les gens libres and succeeding generations of Metis. The kin ties of the country wives of the free men were instrumental in establishing a relationship of tolerance and, in numerous instances, support from neighboring Indian bands. In their behavior, free men acted in a manner that preserved the kin ties of their wives and children with the bands. Both European and Indian practices influenced Metis behavior, but the exigencies of local circumstances dictated practice.

Marriage and Family

Marriage. Few fur trade engagés had the ability to emerge as free men. For those who did, a country wife closely connected with the leading family of a prominent Indian band seems to have been instrumental in ensuring survival. The fur trade practice of "turning off" could see a free man, because of age, injury, or illness, decide to leave "Indian country." He would give his family and country outfit to a younger man in exchange for the younger man's willingness to serve as husband and father in the family. In some instances, fur trade officers turned off their country families to skilled servants of ability or to free men. Although some individuals, male and female, continued to find marriage partners in Indian bands, second-generation marriages among les gens libres emphasized themselves as the primary sociocultural entity. Courting and the marriage ceremony involved the exchange of gifts between the couple and their families. Residence after marriage was a function of particular circumstances, with all forms being observed.

Domestic Unit. In the bison days, related nuclear families grouped around the patriarch could be observed. Individual families tended to interests on their own river lots but shared garden produce and the returns of the hunt. They also cooperated in joint activities such as the hunt or the fishery. Such family patterns are still evident today. In areas of poverty and high unemployment, three-generational households reflecting female linkages appear.

Inheritance. Property appears to have been passed to those who provided care to children. In most instances, this was the surviving spouse. Should a widow remarry, however, the property passed to the children.

Socialization. Generally speaking, children were raised permissively, with greater restrictions placed on girls. Ostracism, ridicule, and the threat of external malevolent spirits were used to discipline children. Although aggression was discouraged, males particularly were encouraged to be assertive. Mission schools enjoyed very limited success. Many parents have acknowledged the value of education, but it is only recently that significant numbers of youths are appearing in senior high school classrooms and postsecondary institutions.

Sociopolitical Organization

Social Organization.   The preeminence of the active older male has been a hallmark of Metis behavior since the era of the free man. By the same token, women were of critical importance not only for their social links with Indian bands but for their essential skills in preparing surplus amounts of provision and pelts for trade. As neither the Roman Catholic church nor the women themselves approved of polygyny, the importance of women who exercised these skills in the family was enhanced. The elderly who were capable, as well as children of both sexes, were expected to lend a hand at critical times in the production of provisions and robes. With the collapse of both the provision and the robe trade, men attempted to sustain their position by working as freighters, teamsters, and day laborers. This adaptability allowed some men to continue their leading position, but in other families it was the woman and her kinsmen who became preeminent. This latter development may explain in part why in some Metis communities an emphasis is placed upon "Indian," as opposed to "European-Canadian," traditions in acknowledging their heritage. Today, however, numbers of men as well as women demonstrate assertive entrepreneurial abilities in the many small businesses they have established. They are emerging as a social elite of political consequence.

Political Organization.   Family units were the political entity except for the temporary "government" of the bison hunt and the wintering village. In the selection of the temporary chef and other officers, an interplay of ability, social reputation, and family connections seem to explain choices. Not to go unnoticed is the similarity between the conduct of the bison hunt and that of the militia in New France and Lower Canada. In the Red River Settlement, the Metis appear to have remained apart from the Hudson's Bay Company-appointed Council of Assiniboia and the local courts. After 1850, however, members of their community were found on both bodies. With the transfer and the establishment of Riel's provisional government, Metis were involved on both sides in the resulting political conflict. By the end of the decade of the 1870s, the Canadians had largely displaced them in the governments of Manitoba and the Northwest Territories. Farther west, Roman Catholic missionaries encouraged local government activism. But the independence of families outside of the hunt seems to have remained an enduring political tradition. Following the Saskatchewan Rebellion of 1885, the Metis appear to have abandoned political activity until the 1930s. The formation of the Metis Association of Alberta to lobby for government action in their interests was mirrored in other jurisdictions with Metis populations. With the post–World War II era, numbers of organizations, sometimes competing, have emerged at both the national and regional level. Family connections are not without importance in many organizations. Yet, increasingly, it is the successful hunter and trader in relations with government who wins elections at the local level. Women as well as men are active in these organizations.

Conflict.   In the fur trade, fighting among the men was sanctioned only on occasions such as a _boisson_ or _régale_ (celebration), not at work. Among les gens libres, such fights could prove far more disruptive. As a result, avoidance seems to have been the means of resolving disputes involving those other than young men. On the hunt, social pressure demanded that conflict be avoided. Violent clashes did occur with the Dakota and Blackfoot. The Metis, however, would observe Indian practice in relations with Indians in invoking the pipe ceremony and in offering and receiving gift compensation. Among themselves, these practices are not evident. The entrepreneurial success of particular extended families demarked social and political consequences. Such families were valued in forming marriage alliances. In the Red River in 1869–1870, and later in the Saskatchewan Rebellion, some evidence suggests antagonism between the entrepreneurially successful and those who saw themselves excluded from opportunity in the settled West. Some suggest that this pattern, redefined generationally, has continued to this day. There are tensions as well between those Metis who identify a heritage very closely with past practices in association with the Roman Catholic church and those who argue for a much stronger aboriginal component and in some instances a rejection of European-Canadian elements.

Religion and Expressive Culture

Metis display a wide variation of religious beliefs and practices. Prior to the arrival of missionaries, women followed religious and medical practices appropriate to their gender in the Cree and Ojibwa traditions. The men intertwined a folk Catholicism with various Indian practices and beliefs. Subsequently, both sexes were significantly influenced by Roman Catholic rituals. Since much of this variation occurs at the family and community levels, no all-encompassing set of beliefs and practices can be described for the Metis.

Bibliography

Brown, Jennifer S. H. (1988). "Metis." In _The Canadian Encyclopedia_. 2nd ed. Vol. 2, 1343–1347. Edmonton, Alberta: Hurtig Publishers.

Foster, John E. (1986). "The Plains Metis." In _Native Peoples: The Canadian Experience_, edited by R. Bruce Morrison and C. Rod Wilson, 375–404. Toronto, Ontario: McClelland & Stewart.

Giraud, Marcel (1945). _Le Metis Canadien_. Paris: Institut d'Ethnologie, Musée Nationale d'Histoire Naturelle.

Giraud, Marcel (1986). _The Metis in the Canadian West_. Translated by George Woodcock. Edmonton: University of Alberta Press.

JOHN E. FOSTER AND GERHARD J. ENS

Metoac

The Metoac (Long Island Indians), including the Montauk, Corchaug, Shinnecock, Manhasset, Rockaway, and Patchogue, lived in the eastern and central parts of Long Island, New York. Their descendants now live in small communities in the area or have been absorbed into other groups who removed to the West in the late 1700s. They spoke Algonkian languages and numbered about five hundred in 1970.

Bibliography

Conkey, Laura E., Ethel Boissevain, and Ives Goddard (1978). "Indians of Southern New England: Late Period." In *Handbook of North American Indians*. Vol. 15, *Northeast*, edited by Bruce G. Trigger, 177–189. Washington, D.C.: Smithsonian Institution.

Salwen, Bert (1978). "Indians of Southern New England and Long Island: Early Period." In *Handbook of North American Indians*. Vol. 15, *Northeast*, edited by Bruce G. Trigger, 160–176. Washington, D.C.: Smithsonian Institution.

Miami

ETHNONYMS: Miamiouek, Maumee, Oumami, Twightwees

Orientation

Identification. The Miami are an Algonkian people, closely related to the Illinois. They inhabited the area to the south and west of Lake Michigan in mid-continental North America when Europeans first entered the region in the late 1600s. They subsequently moved south into Indiana and were finally removed to Oklahoma in the mid-1800s. Six Miami subgroups were the Wea, Piankashaw, Pepikokia, Kilatika, Mengakonkia, and Atchatchakangouen, each with many variations in spelling.

Location. Throughout their history the Miami have lived in temperate forest and prairie areas of the midwestern United States. Fish, mollusks, and migratory wildfowl are plentiful on the rivers, and deer, elk, bear, and numerous small mammals thrive in the rich deciduous forests. Bison were also common on the prairie peninsula to the west and south of Lake Michigan prior to European settlement. There are two main groups of Miami today: the Miami Tribe of Oklahoma, recognized by the U.S. government, and the Miami Nation in Indiana.

Demography. In the late 1600s it was estimated that there were about five thousand Miami. Rapid decreases in population followed American colonization of the Illinois country in the late 1700s, and the recorded Miami population had fallen below one hundred by 1890. Today, there are several thousand Miami registered at the tribal office in Peru, Indiana (although they are largely acculturated into the White population), and several thousand others listed as members of the Miami Tribe in Oklahoma.

Linguistic Affiliation. The Miami language is classified in the lower tier of the Central Algonkian linguistic group, and is closely related to the Illinois language, the two having only slight dialectical differences. The Miami language has been considered extinct since about 1965, although some Miami still employ a limited vocabulary and attempts have been made to revive the language as part of a recent cultural revival effort.

History and Cultural Relations

The Miami evolved out of the prehistoric Fisher and Huber cultures of the southern Lake Michigan region. In the late 1660s fear of Iroquois raids prompted them to move west of the Mississippi with the Illinois people. At the same time a group of Miami took up residence with a large group of similarly displaced people around Green Bay, Wisconsin. These Green Bay Miami were visited frequently by Jesuit missionaries during the 1670s. In the 1680s the Miami began to move back to the southern end of Lake Michigan. This trend southward continued, and by 1750 large numbers of Miami peoples could be found near the present-day Indiana cities of Fort Wayne, Lafayette, and Vincennes.

The Miami were allied with the English during the American Revolution, and some (most notably Little Turtle and his followers) continued to fight the Americans until the Greenville Treaty was signed in 1795. By 1820 most Miamis had sold their land to American settlers and moved to reservations in Missouri. The majority of the remaining Miami were forcibly removed from Indiana in 1846 and resettled in Kansas, moving finally to Oklahoma in the 1870s to live with other Miami and Illinois people who had settled there.

Settlements

Summer agricultural villages ranged in population from several hundred to perhaps several thousand people, consisting of some dozen or more nuclear and extended family groups. Villages were typically located near a river and often close to open prairie. Villages were frequently palisaded and were apparently kept immaculately clean. In some cases the Miami shared a single palisaded village with another group. Within the palisade were circular or elliptical houses for each nuclear or extended family. These were fashioned from tightly woven reed mats laid over each other on a wooden frame. The doorways were covered with bison skins, which were also used to line the floor. A central hearth provided light, heat, and fire for cooking, the smoke escaping from a hole in the roof. In the center of the village was a larger structure that served as the village chief's house and as a meeting place. Agricultural fields were located outside of the palisade, but within easy walking distance. Winter camps consisted of one or more nuclear and extended family groups, probably never having a population of more than a few dozen people. Winter camps were distributed around Miami territory and may have been moved frequently. Houses in winter camps were similar to those in summer villages.

Economy

Subsistence and Commercial Activities. Simple horticulture and hunting provided the basis of Miami subsistence. Crops grown included maize, beans, squash, pumpkins, melons, and tobacco. Fields were cleared by the slash-and-burn technique, and planting was done using digging sticks and hoes fashioned of stone or bison scapulae. Nuts and fruits were also collected from the forests and prairies. Deer and bison were major sources of meat, although small game were trapped or hunted with bow and arrow. Soon after planting, usually in early June, the majority of a Miami village would leave in a group to hunt bison on the plains. This communal hunt usually lasted five weeks or more. Bison were hunted by ambush or fire drive. The meat from this hunt was used for subsistence until the village's crops matured. Following the harvest in the fall, families would leave the village alone or in small groups to hunt deer and small game in the forests during the winter, although some families remained in the village and hunted in its immediate vicinity. The Miami kept dogs as companions and sacrificial animals.

Today, the Miami are completely acculturated and work as farmers, factory workers, and businessmen.

Industrial Arts. Clothing was fashioned from deer or bison skin, and was often dyed black, yellow, or red. Bison hair was also woven into bags and belts. Cooking and storage pots were made of fired clay. Bowls and spoons were carved from wood. Arrows, axes, hoes, and pipes were fashioned from stone by either chipping or grinding.

Trade. With the coming of Europeans, some Miami became specialists in the fur trade. But trade between the Miami and surrounding groups, even some geographically quite distant, had always been common. Items traded were generally nonlocal raw materials such as copper, obsidian, and unusual chert and stone.

Division of Labor. There was a marked division of labor by sex. Women were expected to take care of the house (including making and repairing the reed mats, supplying water and wood for the fire, and cleaning), make clothing for the family, prepare game that the men brought in (including hide preparation), gather wild plant foods (such as berries, nuts, and roots) and make the baskets and clay pots with which to gather them, weed and cultivate the fields, prepare meals, and take care of children. Men, on the other hand, spent most of their time hunting, warring, gaming, or discussing village matters.

Land Tenure. Until formal land tenure was established by the U.S. government, the control of land was informal. Each village used the land that surrounded it and moved when the land became unmanageable or unproductive.

Kinship

Kin Groups and Descent. The basic kinship unit was the nuclear family consisting of a man, his wife (or wives), and their children. A more inclusive unit was the clan, whose members were determined patrilineally. Clans were exogamous, and their names included the bear, deer, elk, crane, snake, and acorn. More inclusive than the clan was a moiety division in each Miami village.

Kinship Terminology. Kinship terms followed the Omaha system.

Marriage and Family

Marriage. Polygynous marriages were accepted if a man could support more than one wife, but marriages were more often monogamous. Marriage was clan exogamous. Marriages could either be arranged or decided upon by the individuals, but all had to be approved by the individuals' families. Brideprice payments were made by the husband's family to the wife's. If the payment was accepted, the individuals were considered married, although further presentations would be made by both families. Less formal marriage arrangements were also common. Couples were expected to set up their own homes once married, usually near the husband's family. Divorce was common and often resulted from adultery on the part of the wife.

Domestic Unit. The nuclear family of a husband, wife, and children formed the basic domestic unit. They shared a house, fire, food, and household chores. The nuclear family might be extended by the addition of co-wives, parents, grandparents, and perhaps other relatives.

Inheritance. There were apparently no formal rules of inheritance, although a person could be ceremonially adopted to fill the place of an individual who died, and this person would acquire the dead individual's possessions.

Socialization. Mothers gave birth in seclusion and remained secluded with the infant for several weeks. Most of a Miami child's life was spent in close proximity to its mother, often bound in a cradle board. The Miami were concerned and affectionate parents and allowed their children great freedom. At puberty, both boys and girls secluded themselves and fasted, seeking contact with a guardian spirit. The onset of menses apparently marked a girl's becoming a woman, but a boy had to go on at least one war party before he could paint his face red, the symbol of male adulthood. Some boys did not follow the male pattern of maturation, but adopted the women's instead, becoming berdaches who were thought to have great spiritual power and knowledge.

Sociopolitical Organization

Social and Political Organization. Village leaders were also the heads of the various village clans. The village chief was the head of the highest ranking clan. Although clan heads and village chiefs were generally recognized as such because of their wisdom, respect, and speaking ability, the sons of chiefs usually became chiefs themselves. Village chiefs were responsible for day-to-day affairs of the village, settling disputes and maintaining relationships with other groups. Miami village chiefs were paralleled by war chiefs, who organized and carried out raids on other groups. War chiefs were recognized solely according to their success in war. If a war chief organized a raid that failed, his status as a chief would be threatened or lost. Members of raiding parties could not be conscripted, but had to volunteer, so a war chief's ability to conduct raids was dependent on the trust Miami men had in him and his ability to conduct a raid successfully.

Social Control. Internal disputes were handled informally by the families involved or by the village council of clan chiefs. Gossip and the threat of sorcery were probably strong means of social control, although some crimes, such as murder and adultery, carried severe punishments.

Conflict. Intergroup warfare could be initiated for a variety of reasons, from revenge for murder to the desire of young men to gain prestige. The decision to go to war was decided upon by the war chiefs, and once decided, the initiating chief would put together a raiding party of perhaps twelve men. This party would attack a chosen village, attempt to kill one or more men or to take them prisoner, and then retreat quickly. A raid was successful if no one in the raiding party was killed or taken prisoner, and it was considered a great victory if an enemy was killed or taken prisoner. Since war chiefs could lose their power and prestige if too many of their men were killed, Miami war chiefs were very cautious. Raids were often called off just outside an enemy village, and retreat after a raid was always well planned and swift. Prisoners were treated with extreme cruelty, although they could be adopted into the group to take the place of someone who had died or been killed. More frequently, however, prisoners were slowly tortured to death and were sometimes eaten.

Religion and Expressive Culture

Religious Beliefs. Miami religion centered around individual and group attempts to gain power from spirits known as *manitous*. The Miami believed that manitous roamed the world and could take the form of humans, animals, and perhaps even plants or nuts. The source of the manitou's power was known as the *kitchi manitou* and was often equated with the sun, although the kitchi manitou was apparently not considered to be animate. From youth, women and particularly men were instructed to seclude themselves, fast, and try to contact a manitou in a dream. Once contacted, a manitou became the individual's guardian spirit, giving the person power in return for respect and sacrifices. Feasts were given and public and private sacrifices of food or tobacco were made to gain power from or appease specific manitous.

Religious Practitioners. Shamans were considered to be closer to manitous than ordinary people and could gain power from them either to heal or to kill. Shamans also participated in the *Midewiwin* and in unabashed displays of their strength: they would fight and kill each other using supernatural power to throw bones, shells, and other charmed objects into the adversary and then try to bring the dead back to life.

Ceremonies. The Calumet Dance was held to gain power from manitous, usually before going to war. It provided a means to publicly offer tobacco to manitous by the members of a raiding party. The calumet was a stone pipe with a long wooden stem, decorated with paint and feathers. Members of the raiding party would make the calumet "dance" in their hands and then smoke it and offer the smoke to a manitou. "Striking the pole" was also done by members of a raiding party. Each would strike a post with his hatchet or war club, and relate a tale of his own bravery, dancing between the tales. Feasts were also given for manitous, particularly before going to war. There were two types of feasts: one, which was a simple dinner with speeches and dancing rituals, and another in which all the food, frequently in copious amounts, had to be consumed before the feastgoers could leave.

Arts. Miami men were tattooed head to foot, and women were tattooed on their arms, face, and chest. The Miami used paint or painted porcupine quills to decorate their clothes and shoes. Music and song accompanied dances, and dance was probably considered both a form of entertainment and a way of showing respect to a manitou.

Medicine. The Miami employed a wide variety of plant materials in making remedies for common ailments, which apparently provided effective treatments for cuts, fractures, and even arrow and gunshot wounds. Shamans were called in if these remedies failed. The shaman healed by using his supernatural power to expel or pull illness out of an individual. Often this illness was embodied as a small bone or shell which the shaman pretended to physically suck out of the sick person.

Death and Afterlife. Ritualized lamentations and weeping accompanied a friend's or relative's death, and women whose husbands died were required to follow a number of strict taboos. The body of the dead individual was cleaned and decorated, wrapped in skins, and placed on a scaffold or in a tree, sometimes with small presents or food. After the interment a game might be played or a dance performed that the individual had particularly liked, but the body was apparently not visited again. The Miami believed that upon death individuals enter another world, where they find themselves walking down a road. The dead are tempted as they walk, and they must cross several obstacles before reaching a beautiful country where there is great abundance and everyone is happy.

Bibliography

Anson, Burt (1970). *The Miami Indians.* Norman: University of Oklahoma Press.

Callender, Charles. (1978). "Miami." In *Handbook of North American Indians.* Vol. 15, *Northeast,* edited by Bruce G. Trigger, 681–689. Washington, D.C.: Smithsonian Institution.

Kinietz, Vernon (1965). *Indians of the Western Great Lakes, 1615–1760.* Ann Arbor: University of Michigan Press.

Trowbridge, Charles (1938). *Meearmeer Traditions,* edited by Vernon Kinietz. University of Michigan Museum of Anthropology, Occasional Contributions, no. 7. Ann Arbor.

PETER PEREGRINE

Micmac

ETHNONYMS: Gaspesians (Quebec Micmac), Mikmaw, Migmagi, Mickmakiques, Souriquois (Nova Scotia Micmac), Tarrantines

Orientation

Identification. The Micmac are a Canadian Indian group living in eastern Canada. The name "Micmac" is from the Micmac Mi:'maq, the plural form of Mi:k'mawaj, "one of high ability," a word derived from Mi"k'amwesu, the name of a legendary forest dweller with supernatural power.

Location. At the time of contact, the Micmac occupied what is now eastern New Brunswick, Nova Scotia, Prince Edward Island, and the Gaspé Peninsula of Quebec. In historic times, the Micmac colonized Newfoundland. Presently, Micmac also migrate in significant numbers from their Canadian reserves to cities and towns in Ontario, Quebec, Maine, New Hampshire, Massachusetts, Connecticut, New York, and New Jersey; they often spend years or decades in these places before returning to the reserves, often to retire.

Demography. In 1972, the number of registered Micmac was 9,805, with 1,943 in Quebec, 2,645 in New Brunswick, 4,769 in Nova Scotia, and 448 in Prince Edward Island. There is also a small number of Micmac in Newfoundland who have only recently been legally registered as Indians. Owing to natural increase, the Micmac population has been growing rapidly; by 1985, the Nova Scotia figure alone had reached 6,781.

Linguistic Affiliation. Micmac belongs to the Eastern Algonkian branch of the Algonkian division of the Algonkian-Ritwan family. The 3 major dialects are the Nova Scotia, the New Brunswick, and the Quebec.

History and Cultural Relations

Archaeological and linguistic evidence indicate that the Micmac arrived in eastern Canada from the north. The Micmac were perhaps the first American Indian people on the North American continent to be contacted, first by the Vikings and then by John Cabot in 1497. First colonized by the French, the Micmac were converted to Catholicism by the Jesuits beginning in 1611. A traditional enemy was the Maliseet, called the *Ejemin*, with whom the Micmac frequently fought. Alongside their French allies, the Micmac defeated and incorporated another traditional enemy, the Beothuk of Newfoundland. Later, along with the other members of the Wabanaki Confederacy (Penobscot Abenaki, Passamaquoddy, Maliseet) and the French, the Micmac fought the British and their allies the Iroquois. Following the French defeat, the Micmac military leadership and many other Micmac went to Cape Breton Island, which remained French until 1763. During the American Revolution, the Micmac allied themselves with the Americans. After that war, the Micmac became itinerant peddlers, and the British established Indian reserves at traditional Micmac meeting places.

Settlements

Just before 1900 the Micmac began to become sedentary. Prior to this time, they were migratory hunter/gatherers and itinerant peddlers of baskets and axe handles. Although reserves had been established since the late eighteenth century, they were temporary meeting places rather than permanent settlements until the turn of the twentieth century. By that time, railroads obviated the need to migrate to sell handicrafts. There are presently twenty-nine inhabited reserves—thirteen in Nova Scotia, nine in New Brunswick, four in Quebec, two in Prince Edward Island, and one in Newfoundland. Three of these reserves have populations of two thousand people or more, but several have fewer than one hundred.

Economy

Subsistence and Commercial Activities. The Micmac hunted caribou, moose, deer, and bear primarily. They fished for cod, eel, clams, oysters, lobster, smelt, salmon, trout, and other fish. They gathered berries and wild potatoes. In the early contact period, the fur trade was very important. European trade provided metal tools, which improved hunting and fishing, but European efforts to make farmers of the Micmac failed. Only the potato was a successful introduction; potatoes provided valuable food in the winter, and raising them did not interfere with other activities. Most Micmac cash income has come from wage labor and the sale of handicrafts and fish. There have recently been numerous failed attempts by the federal government to develop manufacturing industries. Micmac have owned and operated gift shops, convenience stores, garages, and logging and construction companies, which have done well for the most part. Presently, welfare and work projects are the major sources of income on most reserves; on a few, many of the men travel to cities to work in construction or factories.

Industrial Arts. Aboriginal crafts included stone toolmaking, woodworking, bone and antler working, skin and leatherwork, and the construction of bark housing, cookware, containers, and canoes. The major items of manufacture in the later postcontact period were ash-splint baskets, axe handles, and butter tubs. Presently, only a few people still produce baskets.

Trade. There is archeological and historical evidence of precontact and contact-era trade with peoples to the west and the south. The Micmac were among the first to engage in the fur trade with the Europeans, and consequently they depleted their stock of fur-bearing animals early. Later they peddled baskets and axe handles. They also caught and sold fish and in some places hunted porpoises for oil, which was sold. When temporarily settled, they traded butter tubs to nearby stores for food and manufactured items. Trading activities essentially ceased when welfare payments were increased in the 1950s.

Division of Labor. In early historical times, men hunted, trapped, fished, moved their families, made wooden and bone tools, wigwams and canoes, and carried on warfare. Political and ritual activities were also primarily performed by men. Women brought water and firewood, prepared skins and made clothing, cooked, made bark containers, cared for the children, and retrieved game that the men had killed. In later postcontact times, men cut and split the wood used in baskets, and women wove it. Women also did most of the selling of baskets. Men would work as laborers on nearby farms, and women as domestic laborers. In contemporary times, women keep house while men work at casual labor as lumberjacks and carpenters. The governing of the bands is still largely a male task.

Land Tenure. At contact, Micmac were mobile, though some leaders regulated hunting territories within their sphere of control. After this, Whites slowly took control of the lands, until it became necessary to create reserves, and Whites encroached on many of these. Reserve land is vested in the Crown in right of the dominion, with Indians holding a beneficial interest. Band members may lawfully possess lots on reserves, if so approved by the band's council and the minister of Indian affairs.

Kinship

Kin Groups and Descent. The only universal functioning kin group was and is the nuclear family, although two-generation and three-generation families occasionally function as a temporary unit. Nuclear families related by kinship or marriage often cooperate in mutual ventures, at least temporarily.

Kinship Terminology. Traditional kinship terminology is cognatic, reflecting generation and gender. Presently, Micmac terms have taken the meanings of English terms, and Micmac terms that make distinctions not present in the English system are rarely used. Distinctions in English that are not present in Micmac are largely ignored.

Marriage and Family

Marriage. Traditionally, it is likely that cross-cousin marriage was preferred; polygyny was acceptable. A groom would have to perform bride-service during a probationary period. Nowadays, Micmac follow Roman Catholic rules of prohibition; ideally one should never marry kin of any degree of relatedness. Until 1970 or so, parents would often arrange marriages or persuade their offspring to marry their boyfriends or girlfriends. Neolocal residence was and is the norm, though now that the Micmac are sedentary, newlywed couples usually live on the husband's reserve, often near his parents' house.

Domestic Unit. The traditional domestic unit was the nuclear family, though it sometimes included an aged parent or grandparent as well. Today this is still true. Increased illegitimacy, however, has led to households of one mother and her children, and the raising of children by their mothers' mothers. Also a shortage of housing has resulted in many young married couples living with parents.

Inheritance. Traditionally, real property played no part in inheritance, and personal items were buried with their owner. Since the end of the nineteenth century, at least, the wishes of the decedent concerning the disposition of personal and real property have been respected. Presently, a few Micmac use wills, which are usually executed by the Department of Indian Affairs, according to the provisions of the Indian Act.

Socialization. Parents and other family members treat children tolerantly and provide love and support under nearly all circumstances. It is frequently left to people outside of the family to admonish children when they misbehave. Parents

teach their children by having them assist them in their own tasks and by example. Formal education is not highly valued, and few children complete high school.

Sociopolitical Organization

Social Organization. In early postcontact times, men held superior status, though women had equality and greater status in some respects. Elder men and women were sought for their advice and approval. Presently, ability with the English language and success off the reserve or in business brings the most prestige. Although men have lost status since they ceased subsistence hunting and fishing, they still hold the bulk of political and domestic authority. As in early postcontact times, identification as a member of an extended family is of central importance. There are no economic classes. Micmac are organized by the federal government into bands; usually, one reserve is assigned to each band.

Political Organization. The traditional *saqmaw* (sachem or sagamore), translated by the Micmac as "chief," was actually a headman or big man who ruled a particular area demarcated by bays or rivers. His power came from his position in a large, wealthy, well-allied family and sometimes as well from his ability to instill fear in his followers through sorcery. His activities included the redistribution of wealth, the leading of war parties, the conclusion of agreements with other chiefs, other Indian peoples, and colonial governments, and the adjudication of intragroup civil disputes. Preponderantly, chiefs gave their positions to their sons. There is evidence that Micmac individuals and nuclear families were often quite mobile, not always remaining within the territory of a single chief. After the end of the colonial wars, the British banished most Roman Catholic priests from the region, and the prime duty of the chiefs became to lead prayer and speak on religious subjects. From the late nineteenth through the mid-twentieth centuries, traditional chiefs were replaced one by one with chiefs elected under the provisions of the Indian Act; the last traditional chiefs to be replaced were the members of the Grand Council, a unified body of chiefs who governed the Micmac of Cape Breton Island, the traditional Micmac "head district." The Grand Council survives, but has lost real authority. The Indian Act chiefs, and the councilors who assist them, are democratically elected and work as employees of the Department of Indian Affairs primarily as bureaucratic administrators of government aid.

Social Control. Ostracism remains the most important form of social control. In cases of serious wrongdoing, it usually results in the offender leaving the community for months or years. Otherwise, the saqmaw lectured wrongdoers and, in later times, brought them to the police. Today, Micmac police officers control criminal behavior. Revenge has traditionally played a great role in social control, and the threat of revenge serves to circumscribe the offender's social circle.

Conflict. Politically, divisiveness occurs along geographic-linguistic lines. The Union of Nova Scotia Indians, created by the federal government, is often split into two factions: one lives on Cape Breton and speaks Micmac; the other lives on the mainland and most of its members do not speak Micmac. The Union of New Brunswick Indians often experiences schisms along Micmac-Maliseet lines. These disputes are usually over allocations of federal funds and Micmac representation to the federal government. There are also rivalries between bands, usually played out among young adults in organized sporting events and occasionally in fights. In matters of love, some women will occasionally fight over men, though men almost never fight over women. Most violence involves alcohol. When interpersonal conflict occurs, the extended family functions as a group to ostracize the outsider or to exact revenge.

Religion and Expressive Culture

Religious Beliefs. Traditionally, the Micmac had two major deities, Khimintu (Manitou) the creator, and Glooscap, a legendary hero of supernatural power who taught and protected the Micmac; only the former was an object of worship. (Kji)Mintu became the term for the Christian devil when the Micmac converted to Catholicism, and Glooscap presently awaits to appear to the Micmac when they are most in need. Micmac religious belief is highly syncretic, and other non-Christian supernatural beings also live on in tandem with Christian belief. These include Kukwes, a giant cannibal, Wiklatmuj, little forest people, Jenu, northern ice giants, and the Kinap, a person of extraordinary or supernatural ability, among others.

Religious Practitioners. The literature records no priests. There were and are, however, male and female sorcerers who used supernatural power to their own advantage. The sorcerer, _puoin,_ traditionally healed or injured, and a male puoin used his powers to make himself or other men leaders. Presently, sorcerers use their powers primarily to bring misfortune or injury to others.

Ceremonies. Presently, Roman Catholic ceremonies are most important. In addition to the common ceremonies, the Micmac celebrate the feast day of St. Ann, the Micmac patron saint, at several central locations throughout their territory. During most of the last 350 years, when priests were usually unavailable, funerals and weddings were held during the St. Ann's Mission, a celebration of several days ending with the St. Ann's Day Mass.

Arts. Historically, the material arts have been important, including the incision of designs in birchbark baskets, the dyeing and weaving of porcupine quills in birchbark, as well as the sewing of Micmac motifs on clothing, especially the characteristic double-curve motif. Presently, Indian music, some Micmac and some not, is making a resurgence. A few painters, employing Indian motifs, have had much commercial success.

Medicine. In aboriginal culture, disease was attributed to the influence of malevolent spirits, which were removed by a puoin by blowing or sucking, and using medicinal herbs. The puoin was well paid for his or her services. Today, Canadian clinical treatment and prayer are the first lines of defense, and traditional herbal medicines are used when clinical treatment fails. Abortion is not acceptable to the Micmac. Recently, Micmac-oriented drug and alcohol treatment has become available.

Death and Afterlife. Traditionally, the Micmac believed that all things have souls, and that human beings have two types of souls, one connected with the body and one that held the life of the individual. At death, both souls were affected, the body soul perishing and the life soul becoming a skate:kmuj, which traveled to the land of the souls. The souls of grave goods traveled with the human soul to assist it in the afterlife. Presently, the house of the deceased must be inhabited until burial in order to prevent the skate:kmuj from returning to it, and Micmac believe that to see a skate:kmuj signals one's own impending death. Catholic beliefs now exist syncretistically with Micmac beliefs.

Bibliography

Bock, Philip K. (1966). _The Micmac Indians of Restigouche: History and Contemporary Description._ National Museum of Canada Bulletin no. 213, Anthropological Series, no. 77. Ottawa.

Bock, Philip K. (1978). "Micmac." In _Handbook of North American Indians._ Vol. 15, _Northeast,_ edited by Bruce G. Trigger, 109–122. Washington, D.C.: Smithsonian Institution.

Hoffman, Bernard G. (1955). "The Historical Ethnography of the Micmac of the Sixteenth and Seventeenth Centuries." Ph.D. diss., University of California, Berkeley.

Upton, Leslie F. S. (1979). _Micmacs and Colonists: Indian-White Relations in the Maritimes, 1713–1867._ Vancouver: University of British Columbia Press.

Wallis, Wilson D., and Ruth Sawtell Wallis (1955). _The Micmac Indians of Eastern Canada._ Minneapolis: University of Minnesota Press.

DANIEL STROUTHES

Micronesians

ETHNONYMS: Carolinians, Chamorros, Chuukese (Trukese), Guamanians, I-Kiribati (Gilbertese), Kosraeans, Marshallese, Micronesian Americans, Pacific Islanders, Palauans, Pohnpeians, Nauruans, Yapese

Orientation

Identification. Micronesians of North America are Pacific Islanders whose homeland comprises over twenty-five hundred minuscule coral islets and volcanic islands of the western Pacific. The term _Micronesia,_ meaning "tiny islands," was coined by the French geographer Domeny de Rienzi in 1831 and used by subsequent explorers and cartographers. Geographically, the area includes three great archipelagoes, the Mariana, Caroline, and Marshall Islands, covering an ocean expanse equal to the continental United States. Anthropologists define Micronesia as one of the three "culture areas" of Oceania, which also includes Polynesia and Melanesia. The "culture area" identification, however, cloaks considerable diversity among different island societies within Micronesia. Politically also the Micronesian area is diverse and includes seven entities: two are independent republics (Kiribati and Nauru); two are in a unique "free association" with the United States (the Federated States of Micronesia and the Republic of the Marshall Islands); one is a commonwealth (the Northern Mariana Islands); one is an unincorporated territory of the United States (Guam); and one (the Republic of Belau) has yet to finalize a treaty defining its relationship to the United States as of late 1990. The ethnonym "Micronesia" is primarily an artifact of European cultural categories and geographic divisions imposed as part of a larger heuristic upon the multitudinous island societies of Oceania. There is very little if any common ethnic identification or shared cultural heritage among the different island groups subsumed under this term.

Location. Micronesians in the United States and Canada are one of the smallest and most recent immigrant groups, and its characteristics are changing quickly. Very little research has been directed toward Micronesians in the United States, and it was not until the 1980 census that Micronesians were enumerated separately from other Asian and Pacific Islanders. Consequently, geographic and demographic information on Micronesians in the United States is very sketchy. Most of the Micronesians immigrating to the United States initially take up residence in Hawaii or on the Pacific Coast. The 1980 census indicated that 55 percent of Guamanians (or Chamorros, as the indigenous people of Guam are called) in the United States reside in California. Other Micronesians, such as Chuukese, Marshallese, and Palauans, have formed small pockets of settlement in Washington, Oregon, southern California, and Texas, but the non-Guamanian Micronesians probably reside in largest numbers in Hawaii. These Pacific Islanders prefer West Coast and southern states with sunny climates similar to the tropical Pacific. Micronesians live predominantly in urban or suburban areas where they have access to the employment and educational opportunities that motivated their migration. Although the earlier immigrants—mainly the Guamanians who came to the United States in the 1950s and 1960s—may own homes in working-class suburban neighborhoods, the more recent Micronesians are mainly apartment renters in lower-class urban neighborhoods.

In Canada, the majority of immigrants from the Pacific Islands are Asian Indians who emigrated from Fiji. Pacific Islanders in Canada reside almost exclusively in British Columbia, with less than one thousand in Ontario and Manitoba.

Demography. The 1990 estimated population of the seven island entities composing Micronesia is roughly 375,000, of which the great majority are ethnic Micronesians. On the larger U.S.-affiliated islands in Micronesia there are minority communities of Americans, Filipinos, and Asians who hold professional and technical positions. Guam and the Commonwealth of the Northern Mariana Islands, currently enjoying an economic surge of tourism-related growth, employ sizable numbers of Korean, Chinese, and other Asian construction workers on short-term contracts. In much of Micronesia the population was declining from the mid-nineteenth to the mid-twentieth century, owing mainly to the effects of introduced diseases in small, vulnerable populations. Since the advent of antibiotics, Micronesia has undergone a dramatic demographic reversal, and the population today is young and highly fertile. The Federated States of Mi-

cronesia (FSM) and the Republic of the Marshall Islands (RMI) currently have annual population growth rates of over 3 percent, and the resultant population pressure is one major incentive for increasing migration to Guam, Hawaii, and the U.S. mainland. Micronesians in the United States probably numbered no more than 60,000 in 1990, of which about 85 percent were Guamanians. Demographically, Micronesians in the United States show aspects typical of new migrant populations: a low median age (less than twenty-three, compared with the U.S. median age of thirty) and a preponderance of males over females. The largest concentration of Micronesians—roughly 20,000—is in Long Beach, California, where the naval base has attracted large numbers of Guamanians. Since November 1986, when the United States signed Compacts of Free Association giving citizens of the FSM and RMI the privilege of free immigration to the United States, there has been a surge of emigrants from these two island countries. A sizable Marshallese community has grown up in Costa Mesa outside of Los Angeles. The numbers are nearly inconsequential by U.S. national standards, but the thousand or so emigrants annually from Micronesia to the United States since 1986 represents a significant outflow of people from these small island communities.

In Canada, estimates from the 1986 census indicated that there were 5,305 residents of Pacific Island origin, about 90 percent of them from Micronesia or Melanesia. Whether this figure accounts for just native Pacific Islanders or includes some Fijian Indians is unclear.

Linguistic Affiliation. All Micronesian languages are part of the Austronesian family of languages, which is dispersed over nearly one-third of the globe and includes language communities as widely separated as Madagascar, Easter Island, Hawaii, and the Philippines. None of the Micronesian languages has a writing system that predates European contact. Even today there are very few written materials in these languages, and orthographies are not well standardized or widely accepted. Consequently there are very few contexts outside of the family where Micronesians speak, read, or write their own languages. Guamanians born in the United States usually do not speak their language fluently. According to the 1980 U.S. census, over 50 percent of Guamanians in the United States speak only English at home. Non-Guamanian Micronesians represent a much more recent immigration, and include a larger percentage of first-generation migrants. In the 1980 census, nearly 10 percent of non-Guamanian Micronesians indicated that they speak English "not well" or "not at all."

History and Cultural Relations

The first Micronesian immigrants to the United States were a very few islanders, known as "Bajinerus" in Guam, who shipped out from home as whalers or crewmen on merchant ships in the mid-nineteenth century. In 1898 the United States took possession of Guam as a booty of the Spanish-American War, and prior to World War II, young Guamanian men became eligible for the draft. Military service and the subsequent relocation of families in the 1940s and 1950s provided the first avenue for significant Micronesian immigration to the United States, although this route was limited entirely to Guamanians. This wave of migration reached its peak during the 1950s and 1960s, owing to the Korean and Vietnam wars. The U.S. Naval Base in Long Beach, California, has been the primary employer of Guamanians as navy enlisted personnel and as civilians.

After World War II, the United States received trusteeship of the remainder of the Mariana Islands, the Caroline Islands, and the Marshall Islands, and the entire territory except for Guam became the United Nations Trust Territory of the Pacific Islands. As the Americanization of Guam and the other Micronesian islands accelerated during the postwar decades, education gained increasing importance. American-style schools were built throughout Micronesia, and growing numbers of young Micronesian high school graduates arrived in the United States to pursue college education. This accounted for a second wave of Micronesian migrants. In 1972, U.S. Federal scholarship assistance in the form of grant and loan programs was extended to Micronesians, which considerably increased the tide of college-bound islanders coming to the United States. By the early 1980s, however, this stream of migration peaked. At its height, there were perhaps a maximum of five-thousand Micronesian college-age individuals (not counting Guamanians) in the United States, which represented a sizable percentage of the home population in this age bracket.

The third and most recent wave of Micronesian migration to the United States comprises individuals and families who have left their homes out of dissatisfaction with the economic and social constraints of life in small island communities and have come to the United States to seek a better life. This third wave is significantly different from the first two. The individuals are older, and rather than intending a short-term circular migration for military service or educational training, these migrants usually intend to settle permanently or for a long period in the United States. The third wave shows aspects typical of chain migration. Often the migrants follow relatives or friends who had previously migrated for military or educational reasons, and they rely heavily on their social relations or kinship with previous migrants in order to find jobs and housing, and generally receive assistance in accommodating to their new life. Among Guamanians, this stream began in the 1960s and now accounts for the largest number of immigrants to the United States.

Other Micronesians gained unrestricted immigration into the United States only in 1986 when the Compacts of Free Association were signed, leading to a migration of islanders seeking a better life during the past few years. Micronesian settlement in the United States still reflects the importance of military and educational centers of opportunity. Guamanians are concentrated around military bases in southern California and in the south bay cities of Long Beach, Carson, and Wilmington; settlement extends to border cities of Orange County such as Garden Grove and Buena Park. Other Micronesians tend to cluster around university and community college centers in Washington, Oregon, California, and Texas.

Economy

Micronesians in the United States mostly hold low-paying, semi-skilled or unskilled jobs in service industries such as restaurants and hotels, in the construction industry, and in factories. Some have attained middle-level management positions, but very few hold professional jobs, even among the Guamanians who came to the United States in the 1950s and 1960s. Per capita income of Guamanians and other Micronesians in the United States is about 25 percent below the national average, according to 1980 census data. Lack of education and specialized training, recency of migration, and the low median age are the main factors in Micronesians' marginal integration into the economy. Also, there is no cultural tradition of capital accumulation or mercantile entrepreneurship in the Micronesian societies, and strong kinship pressure still exists for the sharing and redistribution of resources. Many Micronesians send money and material goods back to relatives at home and help finance the migration and education of other relatives.

Kinship, Marriage and Family

Kinship. Micronesian kinship groups and descent vary from one island society to another, but generally give primacy to the female line. The most important kinship group above the level of the domestic unit is the matrilineage, a group of women closely related through their mothers. Kinship terminology reflects the authority of the female line. Micronesian kinship is complex, however, and relatedness is considered through a wide circle of relatives on both the mother's and the father's sides, as well as through "fictive" or constructed kin relations such as customary adoption of children.

Marriage. Micronesian marriages are monogamous and in general are quite stable after the couple has begun having children. There is no particular preference for ethnic group endogamy, especially among the younger Micronesian college-age migrants to the United States. Micronesian marriages to White and Latino spouses are fairly common.

Domestic Unit. In Micronesia, the domestic unit has narrowed considerably within the past two generations. Cash economy has replaced much of the subsistence fishing and gardening activities of the past that provided the rationale for larger, extended domestic groups who resided and worked together and shared subsistence resources. Nevertheless, family structure among Micronesians in the United States is still close-knit and multigenerational. The average number of persons per household among Guamanian and other Micronesian migrants is significantly higher (3.57 and 3.88, respectively) than the U.S. average (2.74).

Inheritance. Traditional inheritance of family land and group membership in most Micronesian societies is matrilineal, and married couples typically reside on the wife's land. But the succession of foreign colonial administrations in Micronesia—Spain, Germany, Japan, and the United States—has greatly altered the customary patterns of land ownership and inheritance, postmarital residence, and the transmission of surnames. Micronesians in the United States have largely adopted the American legal practice of children carrying their father's surname. Frequently the father's given name becomes the family surname in the United States, a practice foreign to Micronesian custom.

Socialization. Micronesian patterns of socialization are highly indulgent during the early years, and children are trained to be respectful toward older family members and to be sensitive toward harmonious social relationships. Responsibilities for infant and child caretaking frequently fall upon young adolescents, especially girls. This practice of multiple caretakers and early child-care responsibilities among older children may help foster socially affiliative and accommodating behavior among adults. Some high school–aged Guamanian youth have formed Chamorro youth clubs to promote ethnic identification, but generally there is very little formal socialization into the ethnic group among Micronesians in the United States.

Sociopolitical Organization

Social and Political Organization. Primary loyalty and identification traditionally among Micronesians are with individual islands and villages. State and national allegiance within Micronesia is a recent political concept and is not strongly developed. In the United States, Guamanians have taken the lead in forming community associations, but other Micronesians are not especially well organized at the community level. There are about a dozen large community organizations of Chamorros in California encompassing Chamorros from San Diego to Sacramento. Annual Chamorro cultural celebrations have recently been organized in Vallejo, and the Chamorro community also shares in the annual celebration of Guam liberation from Japan by U.S. forces following World War II. Some other Micronesian groups have organized community associations in Hawaii and the U.S. West Coast; these often center around a church organization and primarily involve social and recreational activities such as picnics and sports by college-aged individuals and their families. The Marshallese community in Costa Mesa is perhaps the only such Micronesian community association to have received substantial support from its home government and to have constructed a community center building. There is no political association that unifies the various Micronesian groups in the United States. In California, Chamorro community organizations formed the Federation of Guamanian Associations in 1977, aimed at promoting and supporting Chamorro needs and concerns through community organizations and political action. No such overarching political structure exists for other Micronesian groups in the United States.

Social Control and Conflict. In Micronesian islands, social control and conflict resolution customarily were in the hands of traditional chiefs and lineage leaders. Formal legal litigation and arbitration of disputes is a rather newly imposed judicial system in Micronesia and is not entirely understood or accepted. In the United States, many Micronesians feel alienated from the political and legal system, preferring to settle disputes in informal ways. Micronesians in the United States seem to be involved in a disproportionate amount of police trouble relating to drunken and disorderly conduct and alcohol-related vehicular accidents. One factor in this pattern of criminal activity is the preponderance of young males in the migrant population. Within many Micronesian islands, the per capita consumption of alcohol is high by world standards, and roughly 90 percent of arrests and emergency hospitalizations are alcohol-related.

Religion and Expressive Culture

Religious Beliefs. Guam was invaded and conquered by Spanish soldiers and missionized by Catholic priests beginning in 1668, making the island the first Pacific outpost of European colonization and religion. All the Chamorro people from Guam and the neighboring islands were forcibly resettled into mission villages. Within the first forty years of Spanish missionization on Guam, the Chamorro people suffered catastrophic depopulation, losing perhaps 90 percent of their population to disease, warfare, and the hardships brought about by resettlement and forced labor on plantations. Protestant and Catholic missions were established elsewhere throughout the Micronesian islands during the mid-1800s, and a similar pattern of depopulation from introduced diseases ensued on Yap, Pohnpei, and other Micronesian islands. All of the larger islands of Micronesia have been Christianized for at least a century, and in no place was local resistance successfully maintained for very long. Chamorros today are nearly entirely Roman Catholic, while in other areas of Micronesia, Protestants slightly outnumber Catholics. During the past twenty years a number of Christian sects have gained a small foothold, including Baptists, Mormons, Seventh-Day Adventists, and Jehovah's Witnesses. In Guam, Catholic beliefs and practices are heavily flavored with elements from Filipino animism and spiritualism, indigenous Chamorro ancestor veneration, and medieval European idolizing of religious icons. Elsewhere in Micronesia, there is a similar syncretic mix of modern Christian theology and practice with indigenous beliefs in animism and many varieties of magic.

Religious Practitioners. Religious leaders in Micronesia command considerable respect in the wider social and political arena and are frequently called upon as advisers for government planning and development and as mediators in political disputes. Although American and other foreign priests and ministers are working in all the larger islands in Micronesia, indigenous religious practitioners are being trained and are assuming leadership of churches throughout the area.

Ceremonies. Micronesians are faithful churchgoers, and in many communities the church functions as a focus of sociability and cohesion. But Chamorros and other Micronesians who have recently immigrated to the United States for educational reasons or to seek a better life are much less dedicated to churchgoing than the earlier immigrants who came for military service. Nevertheless, ceremonial occasions such as weddings, christenings, and funerals play an important role among Micronesians in the United States not only as occasions for religious observance but, more important, as ceremonies that promote social interdependence and ethnic cohesion. Among Guamanians, one example of this is the prevalent custom of *chinchule*—giving money, food, or other gifts to a family at weddings, christenings, or deaths to assist the family in meeting the costs of the ceremony or to repay a prior gift. This practice reinforces the socioeconomic indebtedness and reciprocity that permeate Micronesian family relationships.

Arts. In traditional Micronesian societies, arts were closely integrated into functional and subsistence aspects of life, such as house building, weaving of clothing, and construction and embellishment of sailing canoes. There was no class of people who worked solely as specialist craftspersons or artists. Performing arts such as dance were also closely integrated into the agricultural calendar and into the cycle of arrivals and departures of people from their home islands. Among Micronesian immigrants in the United States, there are very few if any professional performers who sustain Micronesian arts, but there are frequent informal presentations of Micronesian singing and dancing at community gatherings and family social events.

Medicine. Medical knowledge traditionally was shared fairly widely in Micronesian communities. Although some individuals could gain a reputation for being especially knowledgeable in administering therapeutic massage, setting bones, practicing midwifery, or preparing herbal remedies, there were no specialist healers who were recognized and supported as such. Both magical and efficacious aspects of medical treatment were often used together and were inseparable in actual practice. Among Micronesians in the United States, there is still frequent resort to non-Western explanations of illness causation and to alternative treatments.

Death and Afterlife. Contemporary Micronesian beliefs about the afterlife are a syncretic mix of Christian and indigenous ideas. Christian dogma regarding rewards and punishments in the afterlife is more explicitly formulated than indigenous Micronesian notions, but corresponds with and reinforces some indigenous beliefs in spirit worlds beneath the sea and beyond the horizon. Experiences of spirit possession and communication from the dead are rather widely believed and sometimes are given as an explanation for unnatural deaths such as suicide. Funerals are very important not only as occasions for community and family reintegration involving several days of ceremonial feasts and speeches but also as rituals to mark the departure of the dead properly and to put the person's spirit to rest. Among many Micronesians in the United States, great expense is incurred to return the body of the deceased to his or her home island and to provide a proper burial on family land.

Bibliography

Hezel, Francis X., and Michael J. Levin (1987). "Micronesian Emigration: The Brain Drain in Palau, Marshalls, and the Federated States." _Journal of the Pacific Society_ 10:16–34.

Hezel, Francis X., and Michael J. Levin (1990). "Micronesian Emigration: Beyond the Brain Drain." In _Migration and Development in the South Pacific_, edited by John Connell, 42–60. Pacific Research Monograph no. 24. Canberra: National Centre for Development Studies, Research School of Pacific Studies, Australian National University.

Leon Guerrero, Ramon (1972). "An Exploratory Study of Life-Style Adjustments of Guamanians." Master's thesis, San Diego State University.

Levin, Michael J. (1984). "Pacific Islanders in the United States." Paper presented at the conference on Asia-Pacific Immigration to the United States Honolulu: East-West Population Institute.

Munoz, Faye Untalan (1979). "An Exploratory Study of Island Migration: Chamorros of Guam." Ph.D. diss., University of California, Los Angeles.

Shimizu, D. (1982). "Mental Health Needs Assessment: The Guamanians in California." Ed.D. diss., University of Massachusetts, Amherst.

Underwood, Robert A. (1985). "Excursions into Inauthenticity: The Chamorros of Guam." In Mobility and Identity in the Island Pacific, edited by Murray Chapman and Philip S. Morrison. Special issue of _Pacific Viewpoint_ 26:160–184.

DONALD H. RUBINSTEIN

Missouri

The Missouri (Niutachi) lived in north central Missouri along the Missouri River, including one probable village in Saline County. Their descendants now have been assimilated into and live with the Oto in a federal trust area in north central Oklahoma. They spoke a Chiwere Siouan language.

Bibliography

Chapman, Carl Haley, and Eleanor F. Chapman (1983). _Indians and Archaeology of Missouri_. Rev. ed. Columbia: University of Missouri Press.

Edmunds, R. David (1976). _The Otoe-Missouria People_. Phoenix, Ariz.: Indian Tribal Series.

Miwok

The Miwok are a Penutian-speaking group of American Indians who formerly occupied the coastal region of present-day California between San Francisco and Monterey. In 1800 the Miwok numbered about twenty-two thousand, but their numbers were reduced to five thousand by the mid-nineteenth century as a result of disease and hardship encountered at the hands of the Spanish. In the early eighteenth century thousands of Miwok were forced to settle on Spanish mission posts where many of them succumbed to diseases or were worked to death. During the middle of the nineteenth century they were overwhelmed by gold seekers, fur trappers, ranchers, and settlers. By the early 1900s the population had declined to about seven hundred who were located on several small rancherias purchased for them by the U.S. government. In the late 1970s there were about one hundred Miwok located on several California reservations and probably several times that number mixed with the general population of California.

The Miwok were primarily settled gatherers and hunters who traveled seasonally to harvest wild plant foods. Their staple food was acorns, but various other nuts and a variety of greens, berries, seeds, wild grains, and roots were gathered and accounted for major contributions to the diet. Among the Coast Miwok kelp was a staple food along with acorns. Game animals included deer, antelope, elk, bear, rabbits, beaver, squirrels, and quail. Fishing for salmon, trout, sturgeon, and lamprey eels was also important among some groups, particularly the Coast Miwok.

Miwok society was characterized by a moiety organization, each half of which was identified with the land or water and a representative animal. Local lineage segments cooperated in the exploitation of economic resources and the conduct of certain ceremonies. Politically, the Miwok were organized into tribelets of villages or hamlets. Each tribelet occupied a definite territory and was headed by a chief who inherited his office patrilineally and was responsible for coordinating acorn harvests, settling disputes, and sponsoring ceremonies. Among the Coast Miwok overarching tribal organization was lacking. Instead, each village was headed by a chief whose position was not inherited.

Several types of shamans were recognized in Miwok society for the purposes of curing sickness and disease and divining the location of game animals and lost objects. Shamans inherited their position patrilineally, and their skills derived from instruction by an older shaman and supernatural power obtained through dreaming.

Bibliography

Bates, C. (1984) "Making Miwok Baskets." *American Indian Basketry* 4:15–18.

Corrotto, Eugene L. (1973) *Miwok Means People.* Fresno, Calif.: Valley Publishers.

Kroeber, Alfred L. (1925). *Handbook of the Indians of California.* U.S. Bureau of American Ethnology Bulletin no. 78, 272–278, 442–461. Washington, D.C.

Levy, Richard (1978). "Eastern Miwok." In *Handbook of North American Indians.* Vol. 8, *California,* edited by Robert F. Heizer, 398–413. Washington, D.C.: Smithsonian Institution.

Mohave

ETHNONYMS: Amojave, Jamajabs, Soyopas

Orientation

Identification.   The Mohave were a farming people whose name for themselves, "Hamakhav," has been translated to mean "people who live along the water." In the 1970s, two thousand Mohave lived on the Colorado Indian Reservation and the Fort Mohave Reservation, both located along the Colorado River at the Arizona-California border.

Location.   Aboriginally, the Mohave occupied both sides of the lower Colorado River, roughly the region along the border between the present-day states of Arizona and California. The center of their homeland was the Mohave Valley. Mild winters, hot summers, and low annual precipitation characterize the climate of this region. The central geographical feature is the Colorado River, which flows southwest through canyons and floodplains to the Gulf of California. Before the river was dammed in the twentieth century it overflowed its banks each spring, depositing rich silt on the floodplains cultivated by the Mohave. Cane and arrowweed and cottonwood and willow groves grew along the river bottoms. Rabbits were common at the lower elevations inhabited by the Mohave, while large game such as deer were scarce.

Demography.   The Mohave numbered about 3,000 in 1770, 4,000 in 1872, and only 1,050 in 1910. The dramatic population loss at the end of the nineteenth and beginning of the twentieth centuries was due to disease and poverty stemming from their subjugation by the U.S. government in 1859. The population had increased to 1,500 by 1965 and to 2,000 in the 1980s.

Linguistic Affiliation.   The Mohave speak a dialect of the Yuman language, which is classified in the Hokan-Siouan language family.

History and Cultural Relations

The ancestors of the Mohave are believed to have migrated to the Mohave Valley from the Mohave Desert well before European contact, perhaps as early as A.D. 1150. First White contact was with Spanish explorers in 1604, but from that time until the 1820s the Mohave remained relatively free from and unchanged by European influences. In the 1820s European-American trappers and traders entered the Mohave country, and their encounters with the Mohave were sometimes violent. In 1858 the Mohave attacked a wagon train of White settlers in response partly to intrusions into their territory. A year later they were dealt a disastrous defeat by federal troops. They subsequently were relocated to the Colorado Indian Reservation, established in 1867, and the Fort Mohave Indian Reservation, established in 1880.

The Mohave were allies of the Quechan and Yavapai, but enemies of the other River Yuman peoples, the Halchidhoma, Maricopa, and Cocopa. The Pima and Papago were also counted as traditional enemies. During the nineteenth century the Mohave engaged in a long period of warfare with their enemies, which came to an end when they were defeated by the Pima and Maricopa in 1857.

Settlements

Mohave dwellings consisted of open, pole-framed ramadas for use in warm weather and low, log-framed, thatch-roofed houses covered with a layer of sand for use in the winter. Settlements were neighborhoods of dispersed homesteads situated above the floodplains where crops were planted. Generally, settlements were several miles apart from each other.

Economy

Subsistence and Commercial Activities.   The Mohave planted maize, beans, pumpkins, and melons. The rich silt deposited on their farmlands by spring floods made crop rotation and fertilization unnecessary. The basic farming tools were a planting stick with a wedge-shaped point and a slightly curved wooden weed cutter. Fish were the primary source of animal protein in the diet and were caught with nets, weirs, and scooplike baskets. Deer, rabbits, and other animals, hunted with bow and arrow, and gathered beans, seeds, and fruits supplemented the diet. In recent times the Mohave have practiced irrigation farming and earned income from leases of their reservation lands.

Industrial Arts. Industrial arts were not well developed. They made crude willow twig sieves, scoops, and baskets for use in fishing. Coiled pots of clay tempered with sandstone were also manufactured. These were fired in open wood fires and used as water jars, cooking pots, platters, plates, and bowls. The Mohave also built crude reed rafts for crossing rivers.

Trade. The Mohave participated in an extensive trade network that brought them abalone shells from native peoples in southern California, cotton cloth from the Pueblos to the east, and deer meat from their Walapai neighbors in return for agricultural produce.

Division of Labor. Men cleared land for planting and women harvested the crops; both men and women participated in planting and cultivation. Women were also responsible for collecting wild foods, food preparation, and making baskets, and men were responsible for hunting and fishing, working skins and making skin clothing, making tools and weapons, and building houses.

Land Tenure. Farmland belonged to those who cultivated it. Land could be sold and could be appropriated if unused simply by clearing it and beginning cultivation.

Kinship

Kin Groups and Descent. Patrilineal exogamous clans existed, but they were without leaders and played no role in the ceremonial life of the Mohave. Clan names had totemic import, but totemic taboos were either insignificant or lacking. Descent was patrilineal.

Kinship Terminology. Mohave kinship terminology followed the Hawaiian system.

Marriage and Family

Marriage. Marriage involved neither formal ceremony nor significant property transaction. Clan exogamy prevailed in the choice of spouse, but beyond that individuals were free to arrange their own marriages. Polygynous marriages were permitted, but not common. Postmarital residence was either matrilocal or patrilocal, depending on personal preferences and individual circumstances. Divorce was a simple affair, involving only the separation of the couple at the will of either partner.

Domestic Unit. The nuclear family was the basic unit of Mohave economy and society. Extended family members sometimes cooperated in farming activities.

Inheritance. No personal property was inherited since personal possessions were burned at death. In the twentieth century land was loosely inherited through the male line. Theoretically, daughters had a claim on their father's land as well, but rarely exercised it.

Socialization. Parents were indulgent and permissive with their children; discipline was mild and rarely physical. The young were allowed considerable sexual freedom and were encouraged to enjoy sexual pleasures. As knowledge and skills were thought to be obtained from dreams, education and instruction were informal. Girls were secluded for a short period of time at their first menstruation; dreams during this period of seclusion were considered to be important omens.

Sociopolitical Organization

Social Organization. Mohave settlements constituted local groups or neighborhoods, the cores of which were patrilocal and bilocal extended families. Women occupied a relatively high status in day-to-day life, but in the religious realm they held a distinctly subordinate position.

Political Organization. The Mohave were loosely organized into three regional groupings or bands, each composed of several local groups. A head chief, whose position was inherited patrilineally, existed; however, he exerted little authority. Other influential men in Mohave society were war leaders, religious leaders who were the managers of entertainment and festivals, and shamans, each of whom gained prominence and influence through dreaming. Below the head chief were subchiefs of the various regional bands and, below them, local group leaders who gained influence through dreaming and demonstration of oratorical skills.

Social Control. Scorn and ridicule was heaped on those whose dreams proved false when their enterprises failed. Shamans who consistently failed in their charge to cure the sick or who were suspected of witchcraft might be put to death.

Conflict. Disputes often occurred when the periodic river flooding obliterated property boundary markers. Such disputes were sometimes settled in pushing matches or stick fights on the contested property.

Religion and Expressive Culture

Religious Beliefs. A deity named Mastamho was believed to have been responsible for the creation of the land and teaching the people how to live. When his work was complete, Mastamho transformed himself into a nondeity fish eagle. Other supernaturals were few and were not worshiped nor the object of prayer. Dreaming and dream interpretation were the foundation of Mohave life. Dreams were believed to be the source of knowledge, skills, courage, success in love and war, and shamanistic power. Dreams were of two types: omen dreams, which foretold the future, and great dreams, which were the source of power and were obtained by select individuals before birth and rediscovered in adolescence. During the nineteenth century many Mohave converted to Christianity.

Religious Practitioners. The main religious leaders were men who organized feasts and celebrations and performed ceremonies believed to strengthen the solidarity of the tribe.

Ceremonies. Religious ceremonies were limited to the recitation of dreams and the singing of song cycles received in dreams. In the singing of song cycles ceremonial paraphernalia consisted of gourd rattles and baskets used as drums for accompaniment.

Arts. Pottery was painted with a yellow ocher applied with a small stick. Tattooing was a common practice, as was face painting, especially among the women. Both sexes were commonly tattooed with lines or rows of dots down the chin, and women sometimes added lines across their cheeks and forearms. Since the close of the nineteenth century Mohave women have sold decorated pottery and animal figurines to tourists in Needles, California, near the Fort Mohave Reservation.

Medicine. Illness was believed to derive from a number of sources, including contact with aliens, dreaming, loss of one's soul, ghosts, and sorcery, in addition to physical wounds from arrows and poisonous animals. Illnesses were cured by shamans who were specialists in specific types of illness and who possessed the ability to cure by means of power obtained in "great dreams". Shamans were also believed to be capable of causing disease and death through sorcery.

Death and Afterlife. Funeral ceremonies consisted of the cremation of the deceased and his or her possessions, speeches concerning the deceased, and the singing of song cycles. Wailing accompanied the approach of death and cremation. In addition, mourning ceremonies consisting of ritual reenactments of warfare were held to honor important warriors and chiefs. Mentioning of the names of the dead was taboo. The Mohave believed that after death the soul or ghost of the deceased remained for four days before journeying to the land of the dead, where it was greeted by the souls of deceased relatives and underwent a series of cremations and transformations after which it ceased to exist.

Bibliography

Castetter, Edward F., and Willis H. Bell (1951). *Yuman Indian Agriculture: Primitive Subsistence on the Lower Colorado and Gila Rivers.* Albuquerque: University of New Mexico Press.

Dutton, Bertha (1976). *The Rancheria, Ute, and Southern Paiute Peoples.* Englewood Cliffs, N.J.: Prentice-Hall.

Kroeber, Alfred L. (1953). *Handbook of the Indians of California*, 726–780. Berkeley: California Book Co.

Stewart, Kenneth M. (1983). "Mohave." In *Handbook of North American Indians*. Vol. 10, *Southwest*, edited by Alfonso Ortiz, 55–70. Washington, D.C.: Smithsonian Institution.

GERALD F. REID

Mohawk

The Mohawk were one of the original member tribes of the League of the Iroquois or Five Nations Confederacy. The Mohawk live mostly in Ontario and Quebec in Canada and New York and Oklahoma in the United States and numbered about ten thousand on six reservations in the 1980s. They were the easternmost tribe of the Iroquois Confederacy and in late aboriginal and early historic times occupied the region of present-day New York State bounded by the Mohawk and Hudson river valleys in the south and east and the St. Lawrence River in the north. In 1650 they numbered approximately nine thousand.

In the late 1600s a group of Mohawk who favored the French migrated north to Canada and helped establish the community of Caughnawaga near Montreal. At about this time a second northern Mohawk community was established at Oka, also near Montreal. In 1881 some of the Oka Mohawk established a new settlement at Gibson Reserve east of Georgian Bay in Ontario. In the mid-eighteenth century factional disputes and overcrowding at Caughnawage led to the establishment of a third northern Mohawk community at St. Regis on the St. Lawrence River. In the early nineteenth century some of the Caughnawaga Mohawk joined the Iroquois in migrating to Ohio and later to Indian Territory (Oklahoma). After the American Revolution the Mohawk remaining in New York resettled on the Six Nations and Tyendinaga reserves in Ontario.

Traditionally, the Mohawk were a hunting and farming people, but fishing and gathering were also important subsistence activities. They held nine of the fifty hereditary sachem positions in the council of the League of the Iroquois and were known as the Keepers of the Eastern Door.
See also Iroquois

Bibliography

Blanchard, David (1983). "Entertainment, Dance, and Northern Mohawk Showmanship." *American Indian Quarterly* 7:2–26.

Carse, Mary (Rowell) (1949). "The Mohawk Iroquois." *Bulletin of the Archaeological Society of Connecticut* 23:3–53.

Freilich, Morris (1958) "Cultural Persistence among the Modern Iroquois." *Anthropos* 53:473–483.

Frisch, Jack A. (1970). "Tribalism among the St. Regis Mohawks: A Search for Self-Identity." *Anthropologica* 12:207–219.

Mohegan

The Mohegan, with the Pequot, Narragansett, and Niantic (Nehantic), lived in western Rhode Island and in Connecticut east of the Connecticut River. They now live on some small reservations in the area and in nearby communities. They spoke Algonkian languages and numbered about one thousand in 1980.

Bibliography

Conkey, Laura E., Ethel Boissevain, and Ives Goddard (1978). "Indians of Southern New England: Late Period." In *Handbook of North American Indians*. Vol. 15, *Northeast*, edited by Bruce G. Trigger, 177–189. Washington, D.C.: Smithsonian Institution.

Salwen, Bert (1978). "Indians of Southern New England and Long Island: Early Period." In *Handbook of North American Indians*. Vol. 15, *Northeast*, edited by Bruce G. Trigger, 160–176. Washington, D.C.: Smithsonian Institution.

Simmons, William S. (1978). "Narragansett." In *Handbook of North American Indians*. Vol. 15, *Northeast*, edited by Bruce G. Trigger, 190–197. Washington, D.C.: Smithsonian Institution.

Molokans

ETHNONYM: Spiritual Christians

The Molokans are a Russian fundamental Christian sect. Numbering perhaps as many as a million prior to the Russian Revolution, about thirty-five hundred Molokans immigrated to the United States between 1901 and 1911 to seek religious freedom and economic opportunity and to escape military service in the Russian Empire. Molokans see themselves as ethnically Russian and are related to and perhaps an offshoot of the Doukhobors, whom they followed to North America. The Doukhobors settled in western Canada, but the Molokans preferred the warmer climate first of Hawaii and then of California. In 1970 there were about twenty thousand Molokans in the United States, mainly in Los Angeles and San Francisco, with some also in the San Joaquin Valley and Arizona and Oregon. Two groups are represented in the United States, the Pryguny (Jumpers) centered in Los Angeles and the Postoiannye (Steadfast) in San Francisco. The groups differ mainly in the conduct of religious services, with the most notable difference being that the Pryguny jump during services and the Postoiannye do not.

In Russia the Molokans were essentially peasants, though they were considerably more capitalistic in orientation and life-style than other peasants, which put them at odds with the tsarist regime. This led to forced relocations and the ultimate emigration of some.

In the United States, they have attempted to retain their Russian ethnic identity and fundamentalist beliefs, though the earlier communities have now largely disappeared or been absorbed into the larger Russian communities. In the 1970s, the community on Potrero Hill in San Franciso was still viable, but the original Los Angeles settlement near Union Station had disappeared. Traditional ways are described as surviving mainly in the church context, in the form of the use of Russian in church services, community dinners (*obed*), kin ties, and diet. Economically and politically, they are largely assimilated into American society.

Bibliography

Dunn, Ethel, and Stephen P. Dunn (1977). "Religion and Ethnicity: The Case of the American Molokans." *Ethnicity* 4:370–379.

Young, Pauline V. (1932). *The Pilgrims of Russian-Town: The Community of Christian Spiritual Jumpers in America*. Chicago: University of Chicago Press.

Mono

The Mono, including the Eastern Mono (Owens Valley Paiute) and the Western Mono (Monache) lived in eastern California near the Nevada border, in Owens Valley, and the country to the west, near Bishop, California. They speak a Shoshonean language. There may be as many as six hundred now living in a number of communities and on the Tule River Indian Reservation. They are culturally closest to the Yokuts to the west.

Bibliography

Liljeblad, Sven, and Catherine S. Fowler. (1986) "Owens Valley Paiute." In *Handbook of North American Indians*. Vol. 11, *Great Basin*, edited by Warren L. d'Azevedo, 412–434. Washington, D.C.: Smithsonian Institution.

Montagnais-Naskapi

ETHNONYMS: East Main Cree, Montagnais, Naskapi

Orientation

Identification. In its broadest sense the name "Montagnais-Naskapi" refers to all of the nomadic hunting and fishing Algonkian peoples inhabiting the Labrador Peninsula of Newfoundland and Quebec since at least early historic times. Used in this sense, the name includes those groups referred to historically as the Montagnais, Naskapi, and East Main Cree.

Location. The Montagnais-Naskapi occupied a vast area of the Labrador Peninsula extending from the Gulf of St. Lawrence and the lower St. Lawrence River north to Ungava

Bay and northwest to James and Hudson bays. The Montagnais occupied the southern part of this region, the Naskapi the northern part, and the East Main Cree the western part. The Labrador Peninsula, with its barren coasts and spruce-dominant forested interior, rises from south to north to a rolling, glaciated plateau dotted by numerous lakes, swamps, and bogs. To the extreme north of the plateau the tree line is reached and eventually the plateau is devoid of all plant life except lichens. Winters in Labrador are long and cold, summers cool and short. Precipitation on the peninsula is relatively high for its altitude and tends to be highest near the coasts.

Demography. The Montagnais-Naskapi numbered approximately fifty-five hundred in the early 1600s. From that time until about 1925, their population declined almost continuously because of European diseases, warfare, alcoholism, and starvation owing to fluctuations in game animal densities and overhunting and trapping of game animals. In the mid-nineteenth century the Montagnais-Naskapi numbered about four thousand, decreasing to between three thousand and thirty-five hundred by the end of the century. In the twentieth century the availability of medical supplies and store-bought foods helped reverse the long period of population decline. Today the Montagnais-Naskapi number more than twelve thousand.

Linguistic Affiliation. The Montagnais-Naskapi speak a dialect of the Cree language of the Algonkian language family.

History and Cultural Relations

Hunting peoples long occupied Labrador, but it is not known when the ancestors of the Montagnais-Naskapi arrived in the region. By the mid-sixteenth century the Montagnais-Naskapi were in frequent contact with European traders who took beaver pelts and other furs in exchange for cloth, copper kettles, knives, and other European trade goods. During the sixteenth and seventeenth centuries the development of the fur trading economy served to draw the native population toward the trading centers on the St. Lawrence River. During the eighteenth and nineteenth centuries, White settlement along the St. Lawrence and the establishment by the Hudson's Bay Company of trading posts in the central and eastern parts of Labrador Peninsula combined to encourage the movement of Montagnais-Naskapi groups back inland.

Settlements

The Montagnais built conical, pole-framed, birchbark wigwams, and the Naskapi built conical, caribou-skin-covered tipis; both dwelling types featured a smoke-hole located over a central fireplace. Traditionally, the Montagnais-Naskapi were seminomadic peoples whose seasonal pattern of movement brought them together from dispersed bands and lodge groups into large festive gatherings during the short Labrador summer. The locations of the summer gatherings were the shores of the large interior lakes and the mouths of the rivers that emptied into the St. Lawrence River and Gulf, Hudson and James bays, and Davis and Hamilton inlets. At the end of the summer the Montagnais-Naskapi moved inland for the long winter season and dispersed into smaller regional bands and lodge groups. Following contact, European trading posts became the focus of the summer gatherings. As the importance of the trade in furs and European goods grew in the Montagnais-Naskapi economy, seasonal movements centered increasingly on maintaining access to the trading posts. Eventually, groups attached themselves to specific trading posts, and by the mid-1900s permanent native settlements had emerged.

Economy

Subsistence and Commercial Activities. All Montagnais-Naskapi followed a general pattern of hunting and fishing. Regional variations existed, however, with a greater emphasis on caribou hunting among the Naskapi in the North, on fishing among the East Main Cree in the West, and on moose hunting among the Montagnais in the South. Caribou and moose were the principal food resources during the winter; bear, beaver, and fowl during the spring and summer; eel in the fall; and beaver, porcupine, and smoked eel during the early winter. Bows and arrows and spears were the traditional hunting weapons. Caribou were hunted by driving them into lakes and pursuing them in canoes and by pursuing them on snowshoes through deep snow; moose were also hunted by the latter method. Bears were killed while hibernating or by means of deadfalls and snares. Eels were speared and in the early fall were taken using stone weirs. Other fish taken by the Montagnais-Naskapi included salmon, lake trout, pike, walleye, sucker, sturgeon, whitefish, catfish, and smelt. In the more southerly areas of the Labrador Peninsula various types of fruits and berries, nuts, and tubers were gathered in the summer to supplement the diet.

Fur trapping and trading became central to the Montagnais-Naskapi economy during the eighteenth and nineteenth centuries and remained so until very recent times. The animals trapped included beaver, fox, marten, wolves, wolverine, and muskrat. Today, many families continue to hunt and trap as a supplement to income from seasonal wage labor and government support programs.

Industrial Arts. The nomadic way of life of the Montagnais-Naskapi placed a premium on mobility. Cedar-ribbed birchbark canoes were used for traveling streams and lakes in the summer, and in the winter the deep snows were traversed by means of snowshoes and toboggans. Snowshoes were made in several styles for use in differing terrains and snow depths and conditions. Canvas coverings obtained from Europeans eventually replaced the traditional birchbark covering of canoes. The Montagnais-Naskapi adopted many practical items of European manufacture, although long after contact they continued to make many of their own tools and equipment out of traditional materials such as wood, bone, and antler.

Trade. Within the region of the Labrador Peninsula cedar and birchbark for canoe construction were traded from indigenous groups in the South to those in the North, where those resources were unavailable. The groups of the St. Lawrence region traded moose hides to the Huron for maize and tobacco. At the large summer gatherings, Montagnais-Naskapi on the St. Lawrence River traded with Abnaki, Algonkin, and Huron.

Division of Labor. A sexual division of labor characterized Montagnais-Naskapi society. Males hunted and trapped and were primarily responsible for trading; females processed animal hides, made clothing and birchbark baskets, prepared food, and cared for children. Both men and women fished and together they manufactured canoes and snowshoes.

Land Tenure. Aboriginally and in early historic times Montagnais-Naskapi hunting groups were associated with and occupied a particular territory, but without any defined notion of ownership or restrictive use rights. With the development of the trapping and trading economy and particularly with the emergence of the less nomadic trading post band, notions of territoriality and use rights developed, but in a way that reflected both the traditional and the new economic realities. Hunting and trapping territories had diffuse boundaries, and different types of resource use were recognized: resources exploited for group subsistence needs were available to any who needed them, whereas those resources exploited for sale or trade to Europeans belonged to the individual or group on whose territory they were found.

Kinship

Kin Groups and Descent. No formal kin groups, such as clans, existed among the seventeenth-century Montagnais. Consanguineal and affinal ties linked the members of the trading post bands that emerged as a characteristic form of social organization during the eighteenth and nineteenth centuries. Bilateral descent is inferred for the Montagnais-Naskapi owing to the absence of reported ambilineal, matrilineal, or patrilineal kin groups.

Kinship Terminology. Kinship terms followed the Iroquoian system.

Marriage and Family

Marriage. Bilateral cross-cousin marriage was preferred among the early Montagnais-Naskapi, but this has been discouraged since the beginning of the twentieth century as a result of Roman Catholic influences. Neither band endogamy nor exogamy was preferred. Polygyny was practiced in a limited way, sororate marriages were common, and levirate marriages were permitted. Among the seventeenth-century Montagnais a well-defined rule of postmarital residence appears not to have existed, but among later Mistassini trading post bands patrilocality was the norm.

Domestic Unit. Traditionally, lodge groups of three or four families numbering fifteen to twenty people were the basic units of Montagnais-Naskapi socioeconomic organization. Later, in the 1700s and 1800s, similar-sized hunting groups formed the basis of trading post bands. Among Mistassini hunting groups the individual family units occupied separate dwellings during the hunting and trapping season, but shared a communal lodge following the onset of winter freeze-up.

Inheritance. Inheritance among seventeenth-century Montagnais appears to have exhibited no clear pattern, although, there may have been a preference for a sister's children as a man's heirs. Following the development of trading post bands and hunting territories, hunting privileges within specified tracts of a band's hunting territory were inherited patrilineally.

Socialization. The social ethic of the Montagnais-Naskapi emphasized generosity, and this ideal was instilled in children at a young age. Children shared in the work of the family, including the care of younger siblings. The Montagnais-Naskapi favored strong social pressure over physical punishment in disciplining their children.

Sociopolitical Organization

Social Organization. During the winter season several multifamily lodge groups of about fifty individuals remained in close proximity to one another and traveled and hunted together. Several multilodge groups, in turn, formed named regional bands of between 150 and 300 people who joined together when attending festive summer gatherings. When trapping and trading furs for European goods became the focus of the Montagnais-Naskapi economy during the eighteenth and nineteenth centuries, seasonal band movements revolved increasingly around trips to European trading posts. Gradually, native groups attached themselves to a particular post, and the trading post band emerged as a characteristic form of social organization. During the second half of the nineteenth century, interior trading posts were closed as the fur trade declined, and as a result trading post bands merged into larger groups at mission stations and coastal trading centers. By the middle decades of the twentieth century, relatively large centers of permanent settlement had replaced the trading post band form of social organization.

Political Organization. Within the lodge group and, later, within the hunting group, important matters were resolved through group discussion. Above this no formal decision-making structure existed. Leadership within the lodge-hunting group was ephemeral and fell to those most knowledgeable or skilled in the particular task at hand. In Mistassini hunting groups leaders were men, usually forty years of age or older, who possessed considerable religious and practical knowledge. If a leader was sensitive to the wishes of others in his group and did not attempt to force his own will (action that would result in an immediate loss of his prestige and influence), the group usually followed his initiative. Seventeenth-century Jesuit missionaries attempted to introduce formal chieftainships among the Montagnais-Naskapi as a way to facilitate Christianization and acculturation, but with very little success.

Social Control. Generosity, cooperation, harmony, and patience were key elements in the fabric of Montagnais-Naskapi society. Those who failed to contribute their fair share of goods and services to the group or to those in need were not respected and were the object of ridicule and scorn.

Conflict. The harmony and cooperation central to Montagnais-Naskapi society unraveled under the impact of European contact. Confrontations with European settlers and missionaries, the spread of epidemic diseases, the easy availability of alcohol through French traders, and the concentration of people at trading posts and mission stations all contributed to an increase in social friction and conflict. After the development of trapping rights in defined hunting territories, trespass with the intent of trapping was resented, with retaliation sought through shamanistic performances.

Religion and Expressive Culture

Religious Beliefs. The Montagnais-Naskapi believed that every object and animal in the world around them had its own spirit. Belief in a supreme deity appears not to have been a part of the aboriginal culture, but was evident after missionization. Religion among the Montagnais-Naskapi was an individualistic affair. It was believed that those who conducted their lives appropriately acquired increasing powers of communication with the spirit world as they grew older. Beginning with Jesuit missionization in the early 1600s, Christian and native religious beliefs existed side by side and eventually were integrated into a hybrid system of beliefs and practices reflecting both native and Christian elements.

Religious Practitioners. Shamans used their power to communicate with the spirit world to heal the sick and to divine through scapulimancy and dream interpretation the whereabouts of game. Traditionally, through conscious effort at communicating with the spirits, both men and women could become shamans. Generally it was the case that each hunting group or band had at least one shaman.

Ceremonies. The Montagnais-Naskapi showed respect for the spirits of the animals they killed in ritual practices that included food taboos and respectful disposal of the animals' bones. Shamans conversed with supernatural spirits in specially constructed lodges in a practice known as the shaking tent rite. In Mistassini hunting groups autumn drumming rituals in which individuals sang songs given to them by spirits were performed as a means to obtain knowledge about future events. Among the Davis Inlet Naskapi in the 1960s, ritual feasts in which hunters and their families consumed the marrow of caribou bones expressed Naskapi unity and their relationship to the natural world, its animals, and their spirits.

Art. Animal hide and fur robes and detachable leather sleeves of the traditional Montagnais-Naskapi costume were painted with long stripes. Robes, in particular, were often painted with designs in a double-curve motif. Among Mistassini hunting groups songs given to hunters by spirits were sung in drumming rituals in order to forecast future events.

Medicine. Disease was believed to be the result of the invasion of the body by malevolent spirits and a direct consequence of failing to observe the appropriate behaviors regarding the spirit world. Traditionally, shamans employed their power to communicate with the spirit world to help heal the sick. Other curing methods reported among the Montagnais-Naskapi during the early historic period included sweating, blood-letting, and the drinking of specially concocted emetics.

Death and Afterlife. At death the deceased were wrapped in robes or birchbark and buried along with their personal possessions. In winter corpses were placed on a scaffold and buried later; deposition of the deceased on scaffolds may have been a regular funeral practice among the Naskapi. The dead were buried facing west, the direction of the home of the dead in the sky to which the deceased's soul journeyed after death.

Bibliography

Henriksen, Georg (1973). *Hunters in the Barrens: The Naskapi on the Edge of the White Man's World.* Newfoundland Social and Economic Studies, no. 12. St. John's: Institute for Social and Economic Research, Memorial University of Newfoundland.

Johnson, Frederick, ed. (1946). *Man in Northeastern North America.* Papers of the Robert S. Peabody Foundation for Archaeology, no. 3. Andover, Mass.

LeJeune, Paul (1973). *Le missionaire, l'apostat, le sorcier: Relation de 1634 de Paul LeJeune.* Édition critique par Guy Lafleche. Montreal: Presses de l'Université de Montréal.

Rogers, Edward S., and Eleanor Leacock (1981). "Montagnais-Naskapi." In *Handbook of North American Indians.* Vol. 6, *Subarctic,* edited by June Helm, 169–189. Washington, D.C.: Smithsonian Institution.

Speck, Frank G. (1935). *Naskapi: Savage Hunters of the Labrador Peninsula.* Norman: University of Oklahoma Press.

GERALD F. REID

Mormons

ETHNONYMS: Latter-day Saints, LDS, Saints

Orientation

Identification. The Mormons are a religious-based cultural group founded in western New York State in 1830. They were one of a number of such groups founded in this part of the country during the first half of the nineteenth century. Others included the Shakers, Campbellites, the Oneida Community, and the Community of the Publick Universal Friend. All groups were based in part on a communal lifestyle or value system and a reemphasis of New England Puritan beliefs. Unlike the other groups, however, Mormonism has flourished and is now a worldwide religion. The name "Mormon" is commonly applied to members of the Church of Jesus Christ of Latter-day Saints and splinter groups such as the Reorganized Church of Jesus Christ of Latter-day Saints (founded in 1860) and the Church of Jesus Christ (Bickertonites). The Mormons apply the term *Gentile* to all those who are not members of the church and often refer to themselves as LDS or Saints.

Location. The majority of the Mormon population is located in the intermountain region of the western United States, especially in the state of Utah, in a distinct cultural region labeled by cultural geographers as the Mormon Region. The region consists of a core, domain, and sphere. The core is the zone of the most dense, continuous Mormon population and runs about sixty-five miles north to south in the Wasatch Oasis, centered on Salt Lake City. The domain runs from the upper Snake River country of Idaho south to the lower Virgin River area and southeast Nevada and includes most of west-central Utah and sizable sections of southeast and northeast

Utah. The sphere encompasses those areas where Mormons live in clustered communities within the general population. In addition to Utah, it includes parts of Oregon, Idaho, Montana, Nevada, Colorado, New Mexico, and Arizona. Finally, many Mormons live among the general population, especially in urban areas, with sizable numbers in Los Angeles, San Francisco, and Portland. There are also significant numbers of members in South America, Asia, Africa, Europe, and Oceania.

Demography.   As of the 1980s the church claimed more than 5 million members around the world. Because of a high birth rate, longer than average life expectancy in the United States, and recruitment of new members through worldwide missionary work, the Mormon church has a very high growth rate. In 1989, there were about 4 million members of the Church of Jesus Christ of Latter-day Saints in the United States and over 200,000 in splinter groups.

Linguistic Affiliation.   Mormons in the United States speak English and the basic church documents are written in English. In other nations, members usually speak the native language of the country or of their cultural group.

History and Cultural Relations

The church was officially organized in 1830 by Joseph Smith, Jr., and five followers. Smith, known as "The Prophet," claimed to receive his authority and guidance through divine revelation, and he taught that he was the instrument through which God had restored the church instituted by Jesus Christ. He called others to join him in building the "City of Zion" in preparation for the second coming of Christ. The early years of the church were marked by a series of migrations as hostilities between Mormons and their non-Mormon neighbors caused the Mormons to abandon settlements and move westward. The first temple was built in Kirtland, Ohio, in 1836. In 1841 the group moved to Independence, Missouri, then to northern Missouri, and then across the Mississippi River to what became the Mormon settlement of Nauvoo. In 1844 Joseph Smith was killed by a Gentile mob in Illinois. His death was followed by a brief period of division and dissension within the church over the election of his successor.

Eventually the majority coalesced behind Brigham Young who headed the church until his death in 1877. Under his leadership the Mormons undertook their last forced migration, arriving in the Salt Lake Valley of Utah in 1847. Young named the region "Deseret" and in 1849 sought recognition from the federal government as a state. Congress refused, and designated a much smaller region as Utah Territory. Troubles with the government, other settlers, and Indians continued, and in 1857, the U.S. Army was sent to the area to confront Young and the Mormons he had gathered together in Salt Lake City. The confrontation was peaceful, though the federal presence was continued through the establishment of Fort Douglas overlooking Salt Lake City in the 1860s.

From this base the Mormons then spread and settled throughout the intermountain region, primarily through the formation of farming communities and towns. The church hierarchy played a key role in planning and organizing the settlement and development of this region. An important factor in the growth and development of the church and the Mormon settlement of the West was the large influx of migrants assisted by the church's Perpetual Emigrating Fund. Converts were actively sought and encouraged to migrate to Utah. It is estimated that between 1850 and 1900 the church helped some 90,000–100,000 people immigrate to the United States, primarily from England, Denmark, and Switzerland. Today, there are a number of counties within the Mormon region with markedly high Danish and Swiss-ancestry populations.

The Mormons remained fairly isolated in Utah and adjacent areas until the late 1860s when mining, railroads, and manufacturing attracted non-Mormons to the area in ever-increasing numbers, leading once again to conflicts over social, political, economic, and religious matters. Major issues included the church's role in political affairs, the church's financial holdings and policies, and polygynous marriage by Mormons. This time the U.S. government became actively involved, passing and enforcing legislation aimed at restricting the church's financial practices and Mormon polygyny. By the end of the nineteenth century, the church had made major concessions in its policies as an accommodation to the non-Mormon society within which it had to operate. The conflicts that marked Mormon-Gentile relations over the first seventy years of the church's existence then gave way to the peaceful relations that have existed since. By 1900 the Mormon region as it now exists was basically settled, with the possibility of future expansion limited by the surrounding Gentile settlements.

Settlements

Mormon communities established in the 1800s in Utah and Mormon buildings displayed stylistic features that have been identified as uniquely Mormon. These included a N-S-E-W grid plan with large rectangular blocks, wide streets, roadside irrigation ditches, open fields around towns, cattle and sheep pastured together, unpainted farm buildings, red and light-brown or white houses, brick houses, hay derricks, central-hall house plans, tree-lined streets, and Mormon-style chapels. Buildings constructed since about 1900 generally lack these features and more often reflect outside architectural and stylistic influences.

Economy

Commercial and Subsistence Activities.   The Mormons are participants in the U.S. economy. Historically, however, the Mormons attempted to develop their own economic system and to achieve economic independence from non-Mormons. The Mormon economic ideal, based on the biblical notion of stewardship, was communal ownership. According to this ideal, church members would consecrate all their property and surplus earnings to the church. The church in turn would distribute to each member household that which it needed to survive. Although this ideal was never fully implemented, the values placed on communalism and cooperation and the central economic function of the church were influential in Mormon economic activities and experiments. At present, Mormons in good standing give tithes (10 percent of their income) to the church and 2 percent to the ward, but private property is the norm. In the initial phases of settling the Utah territory, the development of irrigation and agriculture were of primary importance. Mormon leaders were also concerned with developing essential small-scale industries. As the U.S. economy has grown and industrialized, so has the economy of Utah. At present, the majority of Mormons work in industry, commerce, and the professions with agriculture remaining an important though secondary source of income.

The church is often reported to be enormously wealthy, although the actual value of church property and investments is unknown. Still, it is no secret that the church owns considerable real estate in the western and southern United States and a variety of businesses such as banks, insurance companies, hotels, newspapers, and radio stations. The church also has large expenses involved in constructing and maintaining church property and in supporting missionary activities around the world.

Division of Labor.   Mormons have tended to follow societal norms with men working outside the home and women responsible for most domestic tasks. Since the beginning, Mormons have stressed sexual equality, and though women cannot be priests, they are actively involved in other church organizations. There is also an emphasis on age, as reflected in the power held by older men in the church hierarchy.

Land Tenure.   Property rights are seen as a temporary trust held by humans as stewards for the Lord. Individual property ownership is the norm, with a strong value placed on communal effort under church authority.

Kinship, Marriage and Family

Marriage and Family.   Mormons place high values on marriage and family and kinship ties, with large, close-knit, nuclear families the ideal. These values are supported by customs such as annual family reunions, weekly home nights for family activities, and group rather than individually oriented recreational activities. The practice of polygyny was a matter of church doctrine and commonly practiced in the nineteenth century. Harassment from non-Mormons and the U.S. government over the issue led church officials to renounce the teaching in 1890. The practice of polygyny persists among some fundamentalists, but they are subject to excommunication from the official church, and the overwhelming majority of Mormons are opposed to polygyny.

Socialization.   Mormons stress education and have perhaps the highest percentage of college graduates among their members of any religious group in the United States. Early socialization takes place within the family, extended kin network, and church framework. Regular involvement in group activities with other Mormons is perhaps the most important activity. Many Mormons attend college at Brigham Young University, the largest church-affiliated university in the United States. High school and college programs are supplemented by seminary and institute programs, both designed to stress Mormon beliefs and values and to keep the adolescents involved in Mormon group activities.

Sociopolitical Organization

Social Organization.   The Mormons emphasize close relationships among church members and social distance between themselves and nonmembers. The church sponsors a number of social groups and social occasions for its members.

Particularly important groups are the church auxiliary organizations such as the Women's Relief Society, the Young Men's Mutual Improvement Association, and the Young Women's Mutual Improvement Association. These organizations combine social, recreational, educational, and religious functions. Although a formal class structure is absent within the church framework, wealth differences between Mormons or between families are noted, and those among the very wealthy enjoy access to the leaders of the church. Although Mormons, in a general sense, are part of the American class system, their self-identity as Mormons is far more important and takes precedence in social situations. The place of American Indians and African-Americans in the church for some time has been equivocal. Both groups are represented in the membership, but not in the church hierarchy. Similarly, the leaders have always been men.

Political Organization.   The organization of the Church of Jesus Christ of Latter-day Saints is both lateral and hierarchical and exceedingly complex. Laterally, the church is organized territorially into wards and stakes (called respectively branches and missions in areas where membership is too small to warrant full-scale organization). Wards are local-level units, roughly equivalent to a parish, with an average of about six hundred members each and presided over by a ward bishop and his two counsellors. Wards are organized into stakes, with an average of about five thousand members each, which are governed by stake presidents, his two counsellors, and a stake council. Above the stakes are the general authorities of the church, who include the First Presidency (the first president and his two counsellors), the Quorum of the Twelve (the Apostles), the First Council (the Council of the Seventies), the presiding bishopric, and the patriarch of the church. The first president is the apex of religious and administrative authority within the church. He is considered the successor to Joseph Smith, Jr., bears Smith's title—"prophet, seer, and revelator"—and holds office for life. When the office of the first president falls vacant, the senior member of the Quorum of the Twelve succeeds to the office which he holds until he dies. Since the founding of the church, authority has rested with White males, a source of discord today, particularly among some women and African-American members.

Mormons have always been involved in local, state, and national politics and are a major force in Utah politics. They have usually managed to achieve a workable balance between loyalties to the state and to the church, both on the group and individual levels.

Social Control and Conflict.   As noted above, it was not until about 1900 that Mormon conflicts with Gentiles and the federal government were resolved. Mormon relations with Indians (the Ute in Utah) were generally friendlier than between Indians and other settlers. This arose mostly from the Mormons' belief that American Indians are of Hebraic origin and that one goal of Mormonism is to reconvert Indians to Christianity. The Mormons and the Ute were also allies in conflicts with non-Mormon settlers. The Mormons emphasize work and personal development and discourage activities such as alcohol and tobacco consumption that might interfere with that goal. Drinking coffee and tea are also discouraged. As marriage and the family are key social institutions, divorce and birth control are also discouraged, although neither is uncommon. In general, internal social control is achieved through lifelong involvement in Mormonism.

Religion

Religious Beliefs. The Mormon religion is based on Judeo-Christian Scriptures (the Old and New Testaments), the Book of Mormon, said to be a scriptural account of events in the New World between 600 B.C. and A.D. 421, and teaching believed to have come to their prophets through divine revelation as reported in the Doctrine and Covenants and the Pearl of Great Price. The Mormons believe in a three-person Godhead, the immortality of the human spirit, and salvation of the soul through baptism, proper behavior, and repentance of sin. They believe they have the "gifts" or powers outlined in the New Testament including those of healing, speaking in tongues, and prophecy. They also believe that Jesus Christ will return to rule the earth. Like many modern religions, there are conflicts within the church regarding religious interpretation and the degree of literalness with which the Scriptures should be regarded.

Religious Practitioners. There is no professional priesthood within the Mormon church. Rather, any "worthy" practicing Mormon male may become a priest when he reaches the age of twelve or so. There are two levels of the priesthood: the Aaronic, or lower, priesthood and the Melchizidek, or higher, priesthood. Ideally, boys enter the Aaronic priesthood at the age of twelve and move through the three offices within this priesthood (deacon, teacher, priest) by the age of twenty. "Worthy" adult males enter the Melchizidek priesthood, which also has three offices (elder, seventy, and high priest). Members of the higher priesthood have greater authority and wider ritual prerogatives than do members of the lesser priesthood.

Ceremonies. Mormons believe that "worship is the voluntary homage of the soul." Religious services are relatively sedate and involve prayer, singing, and blessings. Baptism and the marriage ceremony are particularly important ceremonies, and individual prayer is a central element of many Mormons' lives. Private religious ceremonies may be more elaborate and emotional than public ones.

Bibliography

Arrington, Leonard J. (1966). *Great Basin Kingdom: An Economic History of the Latter-day Saints, 1830–1900*. Lincoln: University of Nebraska Press.

Francaviglia, Richard V. (1978). *The Mormon Landscape.* New York: AMS Press.

Green, Doyle L., and Randall L. Green (1974). *Meet the Mormons: A Pictorial Introduction to the Church of Jesus Christ of Latter-day Saints and Its People.* Salt Lake City: Deseret Book Co.

Meinig, D. W. (1965). "The Mormon Culture Region: Strategies and Patterns in the Geography of the American West, 1847–1964." *Annals of the Association of American Geographers* 55:191–220.

O'Dea, Thomas F. (1957). *The Mormons.* Chicago: University of Chicago Press.

Shipps, Jan (1985). *Mormonism: The Story of a New Religious Tradition.* Urbana: University of Illinois Press.

Talmage, James E. (1976). *A Study of the Articles of Faith; Being a Consideration of the Principal Doctrines of the Church of Jesus Christ of Latter-day Saints.* 51st ed. Salt Lake City: Church of Jesus Christ of Latter-day Saints.

Turner, Wallace (1966). *Mormon Establishment.* Boston: Houghton Mifflin Co.

Mountain

The Mountain (Tsethaottine, Chitra-Gottineke), an Athapaskan-speaking group, live in the Mackenzie Mountains in the basin of the Keele (Gravel) River, the region of Willow Lake, and the country between the Mackenzie River and Lakes La Martre, Grandin, and Tache, in the western part of the Mackenzie District in the Northwest Territories of Canada. There were about one hundred Mountain Indians in 1971.

Bibliography

Gillespie, Beryl C. (1981). "Mountain Indians." In *Handbook of North American Indians.* Vol. 6, *Subarctic*, edited by June Helm, 326–337. Washington, D.C.: Smithsonian Institution.

Nabesna

The Nabesna (Nebesnatana, Upper Tanana), an Athapaskan-speaking group, live in the basins of the Nabesna and Chitana rivers in southeastern Alaska.
See Tanana

Bibliography

Guédon, Marie-Françoise (1981). "Upper Tanana River Potlatch." In *Handbook of North American Indians*. Vol. 6, *Subarctic*, edited by June Helm, 577–581. Washington, D.C.: Smithsonian Institution.

McKennan, Robert A. (1981). "Tanana." In *Handbook of North American Indians*, Vol. 6, *Subarctic*, edited by June Helm, 562–576. Washington, D.C.: Smithsonian Institution.

Nanticoke

The Nanticoke (Nentego), with the Conoy (Piscataway), lived on the eastern and western shores of Chesapeake Bay in Maryland and in southern Delaware. They spoke Algonkian languages. Their descendants now live in the Nanticoke Community in Sussex County, Delaware, in Canada, and with the Delaware in Oklahoma.

Bibliography

Feest, Christian F. (1978). "Nanticoke and Neighboring Tribes." In *Handbook of North American Indians*. Vol. 15, *Northeast*, edited by Bruce G. Trigger, 240–252. Washington, D.C.: Smithsonian Institution.

Navajo

ETHNONYMS: Apaches de Nabaju, Dine, Dineh, Dinneh, Navaho, Nabajo, Nabaju

Orientation

Identification. The Navajo are a large American Indian group currently located in Arizona and New Mexico. In sixteenth-century Spanish documents the Navajo are referred to simply as "Apaches," along with all the other Athapaskan-speaking peoples of the New Mexico province. The more specific designation "Apaches de Nabaju" appears for the first time in 1626 and sporadically thereafter until the end of the seventeenth century. From about 1700 on, the people are always called "Navajo" (or "Nabajo") in Spanish documents, and the name has been retained throughout the Anglo-American period. The source of the name is uncertain, but is believed to derive from a Tewa Pueblo Indian word for "cultivated fields," in recognition of the fact that the Navajo were more dependent on agriculture than were other Athapaskan peoples. The spelling "Navaho" is common in English-language literature, but "Navajo" is officially preferred by the Navajo Tribe itself. In their own language, however, the Navajo refer to themselves as "Dine," meaning simply "the people."

Location. In the Southwest, the traditional home of the Navajo has been on the Colorado Plateau—the arid and deeply dissected upland of northwestern New Mexico and northeastern Arizona. Elevations range from thirty-five hundred to more than ten thousand feet, with hot summers, cold winters, and relatively scant rainfall. Most of the area is covered by a scattered growth of piñon and juniper trees and sagebrush, but there are also extensive pine forests at the highest elevations and open grasslands at the lowest. The earliest known home of the Navajos was in the area between the Jemez and Lukachukai mountains, in what today is northwestern New Mexico, but subsequently the people expanded westward and northward into portions of present-day Arizona and Utah. The present Navajo Reservation occupies about twenty-five thousand square miles in the Four Corners area where Arizona, New Mexico, Utah, and Colorado come together.

Demography. The Navajo population in 1864 was probably somewhere between 16,000 and 20,000. By 1945 it had increased to about 55,000, and in 1988 it was estimated at about 200,000. The Navajo are the largest Indian tribe in North America today. There are large off-reservation Navajo populations in many cities of the Southwest, but the great majority of Navajo still live on the Navajo Reservation.

Linguistic Affiliation. The Navajo language belongs to the Apachean branch of the Athapaskan family and is particularly close to the languages of the Tonto and Cibecue Apache tribes.

History and Cultural Relations

Ancestors of the Navajo and Apache peoples are thought to have migrated to the Southwest within the last one thousand years, probably from somewhere in the prairie regions of western Canada. They were originally hunters and foragers, but some of the groups, most particularly the Navajo, quickly adopted agriculture, weaving, and other arts from the sedentary Pueblo peoples of the Southwest. There then developed a kind of symbiotic relationship in which the Navajo supplied hides, piñon nuts, and other goods to the Pueblo villages in exchange for agricultural products, woven goods, and pottery. The coming of Spanish rule in 1598 created a new political and economic order, in which the Pueblos were directly under

Spanish rule, whereas the Navajo and Apache were never subjugated but remained intermittently at war with the colonial overlords for the next two and a half centuries. From the newcomers the Navajo soon acquired sheep and goats, which provided them with a new basis of livelihood, and also horses, which greatly increased their ability to raid the settled communities both of the Pueblo Indians and of the Spanish settlers. By the end of the seventeenth century, the Navajo as well as the Apache had become widely feared raiders throughout the Southwest. The American annexation of New Mexico in 1848 did not immediately alter the pattern of Navajo raiding on the settlements of the Rio Grande Valley, and it was not until a decisive military campaign in 1864, led by Col. Kit Carson, that the Navajo were finally brought under military control, and the Navajo wars came to an end. About half the tribe was held in military captivity at Fort Sumner, in eastern New Mexico, until 1868, when a treaty was signed that allowed the people to return to their original homeland along the Arizona–New Mexico border. Since that time the tribe has steadily increased both in numbers and in territory, and the original Navajo Reservation has been enlarged to more than four times its original size.

Modern Navajo culture exhibits a unique blend of Athapaskan, Puebloan, Mexican, and Anglo-American influences. The Navajo preference for a scattered and semimobile mode of existence, in marked contrast to the Pueblo neighbors, is part of the original Athapaskan legacy, as is the ceremonial complex centering on the treatment of disease. On the other hand, much of the Navajos' actual mythology and ritual is clearly borrowed from the Pueblos, along with the arts of farming and weaving. From the Mexicans came the dependence on a livestock economy and the making of silver jewelry, which has become one of the most renowned of Navajo crafts. From the early Anglo-American frontier settlers the Navajo borrowed what has become their traditional mode of dress, as well as an increasing dependence on a market economy in which lambs, wool, and woven blankets are exchanged for manufactured goods.

Settlements

Unlike other agricultural peoples of the Southwest, the Navajo have never been town dwellers. In the late prehistoric and early historic periods they lived in small encampments clustered within a fairly restricted area in northwestern New Mexico. Later, increasing warfare with the Spanish forced them to adopt a more mobile existence, and bands of Navajo might range over hundreds of miles between the Rio Grande and the Colorado River. Since their pacification in the 1860s, the Navajo have lived in extended-family encampments, usually numbering from two to four individual households, that are scattered over the length and breadth of the vast Navajo Reservation. Many extended families maintain two residential encampments a few miles apart. The summer camps are located close to maize fields and therefore are concentrated to some extent in the more arable parts of the reservation; the winter camps are more scattered and are located primarily for easy access to wood and water.

Economy

Subsistence and Commercial Activities. The society and economy of the Navajo have been continually evolving in response to new opportunities and challenges since their first arrival in the Southwest, so that it is difficult to speak of any traditional economy. During most of the reservation period, from 1868 to about 1960, the people depended on a combination of farming, animal husbandry, and the sale of various products to traders. The cultivation of maize was considered by the Navajo to be the most basic and essential of all their economic pursuits, although it made only a relatively small contribution to the Navajo diet. The raising of sheep and goats provided substantial quantities of meat and milk, as well as hides, wool, and lambs that were exchanged for manufactured goods at any of the numerous trading posts scattered throughout the Navajo country. Additional income was derived from the sale or exchange of various craft products, especially rugs, and of piñon nuts. Beginning in the early 1900s, a few Navajo were employed by the Bureau of Indian Affairs and in off-reservation towns and ranches, but wage work did not become a significant feature of the Navajo economy until after World War II. By the 1980s, wage work was contributing about 75 percent of all Navajo income, although the more traditional farming and livestock economies were still being maintained throughout the reservation as well. Tourism, mineral production, and lumbering are the main sources of cash income on the Navajo Reservation.

Industrial Arts. The oldest of surviving Navajo crafts is probably that of pottery making. Only a few women still make pottery, but they continue to produce vessels of a very ancient and distinctive type, unlike the decorated wares of their Pueblo neighbors. The art of weaving was learned early from the Pueblos, but the weaving of wool into heavy and durable rugs in elaborate multicolored patterns is a development of the reservation period and was very much stimulated by the Indian traders. For a time in the late nineteenth century the sale of rugs became the main source of cash income for the Navajo. While the economic importance of weaving has very much declined in the twentieth century, most older Navajo women and many younger ones still do some weaving. Apart from woven goods, the most celebrated of Navajo craft products were items of silver and turquoise jewelry, combining Mexican and aboriginal Southwestern traditions. Although many Navajo still possess substantial quantities of jewelry, the silversmith's art itself has nearly died out. Other craft products that are still made in small quantities are baskets and brightly colored cotton sashes, both of which play a part in Navajo ceremonies.

Trade. In the prehistoric and early historic periods there was a substantial institutionalized trade between the Navajo and many of the Pueblo villages, and this persists on a small scale today. Since the later nineteenth century, however, most Navajo trade has been funneled through the trading post, which in most respects resembles the old country general store. Here clothing, housewares, bedding, hardware, and most of the other material needs of the Navajo are supplied in exchange for livestock products or, more recently, are sold for cash. Traditionally, most Navajo families lived on credit for much of the year, paying off their accounts with wool in the spring and with lambs in the fall.

Division of Labor. In the traditional Navajo economy there was a rigid though not total division between male and female tasks. Farming and the care of horses were male activities; weaving and most household tasks were female activities.

More recently, however, both sexes have collaborated in lambing, shearing, and herding activities, and both men and women are now heavily involved in wage work. Although males played the dominant roles in Navajo ritual activities, there has always been an important place for females as well.

Land Tenure. Families traditionally have exclusive use rights to agricultural land as long as they actually farm it; if it lies uncultivated for more than two years another family may take possession. All range land, however, is treated as common and collective property of the whole community and is unfenced.

Kinship

Kin Groups and Descent. Every Navajo belongs to one of sixty-four matrilineal clans, but is also said to be "born for" the clan of his or her father. Strict exogamy is practiced on both sides. Apart from the clans, there are no formally designated units of kinship in Navajo society; people are known by the household or extended family in which they reside rather than by membership in a named kin group. Property, like clan membership, is inherited mainly in the female line.

Kinship Terminology. Kin terms conform to the basic Iroquoian system.

Marriage and Family

Marriage. Navajo marriages are the result of economic arrangements between kin groups. The great majority of marriages were always monogamous, but polygyny was permitted until recently, and it is estimated that about 10 percent of Navajo men had two or more wives. By far the most common form of polygyny was sororal. Residence for newly married couples was ideally uxorilocal, but there were many departures from this practice when economic circumstances made another arrangement preferable. It was also fairly common for couples to move from the wife's to the husband's residence group, or vice versa, at some time after their marriage. Neolocal residence was very unusual in the past, but is becoming increasingly common today, as couples settle close to where there are wage work opportunities. Both marriage and divorce involve very little formality, and the rate of divorce is fairly high. But the great majority of divorces take place between spouses who have been married less than two years.

Domestic Unit. The basic domestic unit in Navajo society is the biological or nuclear family. Its members traditionally live together in a single hogan (an earth-covered log dwelling) and take their meals together. The basic economic unit is the extended family, a group of biological families who live close together and share productive resources such as a maize field and a flock of sheep and goats in common. An extended family unit most commonly comprises the household of an older couple, plus the households of one or more of their married daughters, all situated "within shouting distance" of one another.

Inheritance. Basic productive resources are the collective property of the extended family and are not alienable by individuals; they are passed on from generation to generation within the group. Jewelry, saddles, horses, and many kinds of ceremonial knowledge are treated as personal property, however. Individuals have considerable freedom in disposal of

these, although it is always expected that a woman will leave most of her personal property to her daughters and that a man will leave much of his property to his sister's children.

Socialization. Children were and are raised permissively, and there is a marked respect for the personal integrity even of very young children. The main sanctioning punishments are shaming and ridicule. Children receive a good deal of formal training in various technical and craft activities from their parents, and boys may be schooled in ceremonial lore and ritual practice by their fathers or by their mothers' brothers. The recitation of myths by grandparents and other elders also contributes to the education of Navajo children.

Sociopolitical Organization

Social Organization. There was no ranking in traditional Navajo society; social obligations were determined entirely by kinship and residence. Both men and women had fairly specific, lifelong obligations toward the family into which they were born as well as toward the family into which they were married. The father in each household was the recognized household head, and the father in the oldest household was the headman of each residence group, with considerable authority over the allocation of labor and resources among all the members of the group. The status of women was notably high.

Political Organization. There was no system of formal authority among the Navajo except that embodied in kinship relationships. In the prereservation period, however, the population was divided into a number of localized bands, and each of these had its recognized leader, although he had no coercive powers. In the reservation period, the organization into bands disappeared, but respected singers (medicine men) may act informally as local community leaders and as arbitrators of disputes. Political organization of the tribe as a whole was instituted only in 1923 and is modeled on the institutions of European and American parliamentary democracy rather than on aboriginal tradition. There is a tribal chairman and a vice chairman, elected by reservationwide popular ballot for four-year terms, a Tribal Council made up of elected delegates from each of about one hundred local "chapters," and an Executive Committee elected by the members of the council. In most parts of the reservation there are also locally elected chapter officers who attend to the political needs of the local community.

Social Control. The principal mechanism for the maintenance of order has always been the concept of collective responsibility, which makes all members of a family, or even of a clan, responsible for the good behavior of any individual member. Maintaining the good name of the family or clan within the community is an important consideration for all Navajo. In addition, the accusation of witchcraft was likely to be directed against persons who were considered to be "bad characters"; this in effect defined them as public enemies.

Conflict. Conflict between individuals or families might arise for a variety of reasons. Disputes over the possession of farmland and disputes arising from poor marital relations were especially common in earlier times. All infractions except incest and witchcraft were treated as private wrongs, to be settled by negotiation between the kin groups involved. Locally respected medicine men might be called upon to arbitrate or advise in these disputes. There is, in addition, a system of Navajo Tribal Courts and a code of offenses adopted by the Navajo Tribal Council, but most Navajo still prefer to settle disputes without recourse to these institutions.

Religion and Expressive Culture

Religious Beliefs. Navajo gods and other supernatural powers are many and varied. Most important among them are a group of anthropomorphic deities, and especially Changing Woman or Spider Woman, the consort of the Sun God, and her twin sons, the Monster Slayers. Other supernatural powers include animal, bird, and reptile spirits, and natural phenomena or wind, weather, light and darkness, celestial bodies, and monsters. There is a special class of deities, the _Yei_, who can be summoned by masked dancers to be present when major ceremonies are in progress. Most of the Navajo deities can be either beneficial or harmful to the Earth Surface People, depending on their caprice or on how they are approached. Navajo mythology is enormously rich and poetically expressive. According to basic cosmological belief, all of existence is divided between the Holy People (supernaturals) and the Earth Surface People. The Holy People passed through a succession of underworlds, each of which was destroyed by a flood, until they arrived in the present world. Here they created First Man and First Woman, the ancestors of all the Earth Surface People. The Holy People gave to the Earth Surface People all the practical and ritual knowledge necessary for their survival in this world and then moved away to dwell in other realms above the earth. However, they remain keenly interested in the day-to-day doings of the Earth Surface People, and constant attention to ceremonies and taboos is required in order to keep in harmony with them. The condition of _hozoji_, or being in harmony with the supernatural powers, is the single most important ideal sought by the Navajo people.

Religious Practitioners. The most respected of Navajo ritual practitioners are called "singers." These are men (or, very occasionally, women) who can perform in their entirety one or more of the major Navajo ceremonies. They are not shamans but priests who have acquired their knowledge and skills through long apprenticeship to an established singer. They are the most highly respected individuals in traditional Navajo society and frequently act as informal community leaders. Men with a lesser degree of ritual knowledge who can perform only short or incomplete ceremonies are referred to by another term, which might be translated as "curers." There is in addition a special class of diagnosticians, or diviners, who use various shamanistic techniques to discover the source of a person's illness or misfortune and who then prescribe the appropriate ceremonial treatment.

Ceremonies. In aboriginal times there were important Navajo ceremonies connected with war, hunting, agriculture, and the treatment of illness. In the reservation period, nearly all of the major public ceremonies have come to focus on curing in the broadest sense—that is, on the restoration of harmony with the supernaturals. There are, or have been, at least sixty major ceremonies, most of which involve an intricate combination of songs, prayers, magical rituals, the making of prayer-sticks and other paraphernalia, and the making of an elaborate dry-painting using colored sands. Masked dancers also play a part in some ceremonies. Ceremonies may last for two, three, five, or nine nights, depending partly on the seriousness of the condition being treated.

Arts. The artistic creativity of the Navajo finds expression in a wide variety of media, including poetry, song, dance, and costume. The most celebrated of Navajo artistic productions are the brightly colored rugs woven by women, and the intricate dry-painting designs executed by the singers as a part of each major ceremony. Dry-paintings were traditionally destroyed at the conclusion of each ceremony, but permanent reproductions of many of the designs are now being made on boards for sale commercially. In the present century, a number of Navajo have also achieved recognition as painters and have set up commercial studios in various western cities.

Medicine. In traditional Navajo belief, all illness or misfortune arises from transgressions against the supernaturals or from witchcraft. Consequently, medical practice is essentially synonymous with ceremonial practice. There are particular kinds of ceremonies designed to treat illnesses caused by the patient's transgressions, by accidents, and by different kinds of witchcraft. Apart from ceremonial practices, there was formerly a fairly extensive materia medica of herbs, potions, ointments, and fumigants, and there were specialists who collected and applied these.

Death and Afterlife. Traditionally, Navajo were morbidly afraid of death and the dead and spoke about them as little as possible. The dead were buried promptly and without public ceremony, although a great many ritual taboos were observed by the close kin of the deceased and by those who handled the corpse. Ideas about the afterlife were not codified in a systematic way, but varied from individual to individual. There was no concept of rewards and punishments for deeds done in this life; it seems that the afterworld was not thought of as a happy or desirable place for anyone.

Bibliography

Kluckhohn, Clyde, and Dorothea Leighton (1946). _The Navaho_. Cambridge: Harvard University Press.

Leighton, Dorothea, and Clyde Kluckhohn (1948). _Children of the People_. Cambridge: Harvard University Press.

Locke, Raymond F. (1976). _The Book of the Navajo_. Los Angeles: Mankind Publishing Co.

Ortiz, Alfonso, ed. (1983). _Handbook of North American Indians_. Vol. 10, _Southwest_, 489–683. Washington, D.C.: Smithsonian Institution.

Underhill, Ruth (1956). _The Navajos_. Norman: University of Oklahoma Press.

WILLIAM Y. ADAMS

Netsilik Inuit

ETHNONYMS: Arveqtormiut, Kungmiut, Pelly Bay Eskimo, Sinimiut, Ugyuligmiut

The Netsilik Inuit are a group of several hundred Inuit who live in the Canadian Arctic north of Hudson Bay on the Boothia Peninsula, King William Island, and the Adelaide Peninsula. In the nineteenth century the Netsilik occupied the same Canadian Arctic area and numbered about five hundred.

Change induced by White contact was limited until the mid-twentieth century, although the Netsilik were involved in fur trapping and trading in the 1920s and several missions were established among them in the 1930s. In the 1950s the first schools, established by the Canadian government, proved to be a significant agent of acculturation. In the 1970s sealing was practiced in the summer and caribou were hunted in both summer and winter. The use of firearms has resulted in more individualized hunting, which increased importance of the nuclear family at the expense of the traditional extended family unit.

The Netsilik were hunters who followed a seasonal subsistence cycle of harpooning seals on the sea ice in winter and fishing and communal hunting of caribou from kayaks during the summer. Extended families formed the basic subsistence unit and tended to be exogamous. The Netsilik were divided in numerous small, fluid hunting bands, each identified with a particular geographical area. They believed in numerous deities, spirits, and monsters and observed many taboos to propitiate a female deity whom they believed to control all animals. Religious leadership was provided by shamans who cured the sick by invoking the aid of protecting spirits.

Bibliography

Balikci, Asen (1970). *The Netsilik Eskimo.* Garden City, N.Y.: Natural History Press.

Rasmussen, Knud (1931). *The Netsilik Eskimos.* Report of the Fifth Thule Expedition, 1921–24. Vol. 8, 1–542. Copenhagen, Denmark.

Taylor, J. Garth (1974). *Netsilik Eskimo Material Culture: The Roald Amundsen Collection from King William Island.* Oslo: Universitetsforlaget.

Nez Percé

ETHNONYMS: Blue Muds, Chopunnish, Kamuinu, Nimipu, Pierced Noses, Tsoop-Nit-Pa-Loo, Tsutpeli

The Nez Percé are a tribe of Sahaptian-speaking Indians who occupied central Idaho, north of the Northern Shoshone, and parts of southeastern Washington and northeastern Oregon. They are now found principally on the Nez Percé Reservation centered in Lapwai, Idaho. Others live on the Colville Reservation in Washington. The area is generally mountainous, interspersed with river valleys, and fairly arid, receiving about fifteen inches of rainfall a year. In the census of 1980, 2,222 people were entered as Nez Percé.

Before their acquisition of horses around 1720, they lived in separate but related villages. After acquiring the horse they tended to group into larger and more unified settlements. During the early historic period, around the end of the eighteenth century, the Nez Percés were involved in numerous conflicts with the Plains tribes (such as the Blackfoot) and with the Basin Shoshonean groups to the south, with the conflicts centering around bison hunting and horse thefts. The Lewis and Clark expedition, which passed through their territory in 1805, noted much evidence of trade goods from White mariners on the Pacific Coast and Spaniards to the south.

Several Protestant missions were established among them beginning in the early 1830s, with many of the tribe being converted. This, as well as disputes about the various treaties signed with the U.S. government, resulted in conflict between the traditionalists and the converts. Following the discovery of gold in the area in the early 1860s, the territory was overrun by gold prospectors and settlers. Most of the tribe was induced to settle on the present reservation in the 1870s, but the band under Chief Joseph refused and fought the U.S. Army in the Nez Percé War of 1877. The remnants of Joseph's band finally settled on the Colville Reservation.

The historical Nez Percé were composed of many small, local bands, each consisting of one or more villages and fishing camps. The bands generally had elected nonhereditary chiefs. The subsistence basis of the society was salmon fishing and/or bison hunting. The more eastern of the groups tended to depend more on bison as the basis of their subsistence than their relatives to the west who depended more on fishing and hunting other types of game. Trout, eel, and sturgeon were also caught and preserved. Gathering of wild vegetable foods by the women was also important.

Before the agglomeration into larger villages, communities usually had fewer than one hundred inhabitants. They lived in a variety of dwellings, from square and conical mat houses to communal longhouses up to 150 feet long, and also had sweat houses and dance lodges. They had large extended families, and polygyny was relatively common. Descent was bilateral with kindreds present. Although the Nez Percé had no metallurgy, weaving, ceramics, or agriculture, their fine basketry skills provided them with hats, bowls, mats, watertight vessels, and shirts, leggings, breechclouts, moccasins, dresses, and women's caps; elk and buffalo robes were used for warmth.

Important in the religious life was the vision quest for a guardian spirit. Shamans provided religious leadership, presiding at ceremonies, exorcising ghosts, and curing the sick. The religion was animistic; Coyote was important in the mythology. The tribal religion is still observed among the traditionalists.

The governing body on the present Nez Percé Reservation is the Nez Percé Tribal Executive Committee, with nine persons being elected at large but distributed geographically. The tribe has presented and won several claims before the

U.S. Indian Claims Commission. Contemporary Nez Percés are heavily involved in the mainstream culture, attending schools, leasing farm and timberlands, and operating a printing plant and a marina. The tribe holds numerous religious and secular events during the year, including games, war-dance contests, religious services, parades, and tribal exhibits.

Bibliography

Haines, Francis (1955). *The Nez Percés*. Norman: University of Oklahoma Press.

Josephy, Alvin M., Jr. (1965). *The Nez Percé Indians and the Opening of the Northwest*. New Haven: Yale University Press.

Slickpoo, Allen P. (1973). *Noon nee-me-poo* (We, the Nez Percés). Lapwai, Idaho: Nez Percé Tribe of Idaho.

Spinden, Herbert J. (1908). *The Nez Percé Indians*. American Anthropological Association, Memoir 2, 165–274. Menasha, Wis.

Walker, Deward E., Jr. (1968). *Conflict and Schism in Nez Percé Acculturation: A Study of Religion and Politics*. Pullman: Washington State University Press.

Nootka

ETHNONYM: Westcoast People

Orientation

Identification.   The Nootka are an American Indian group located mainly on Vancouver Island. The term *nootka* is not a native one, but seems to refer to Captain Cook's rendering of what he thought the native people were calling themselves or their territory. Nootka people are customarily divided into three groups known as the Northern, Central, and Southern Nootkan tribes. Today, the Nootka people as a group prefer to call themselves Westcoast People.

Location.   Aboriginally, the Nootka lived on Vancouver Island, British Columbia, from Cape Cook in the north to Sheringham Point in the south and across the Strait of Juan de Fuca at Cape Flattery on the Olympic Peninsula of Washington State. Today, some Nootkans still live on Westcoast reserves for native people, but many Nootkans have moved to Vancouver Island's urban areas to find employment. For many years, scholars at the Provincial Museum in Victoria, British Columbia, have been assisting local Nootkan groups in their effort to preserve native cultural and language traditions.

Demography.   Aboriginally, there were approximately ten thousand Nootkans. Today, there are probably about five thousand.

Linguistic Affiliation.   Nootka is the language of the Northern, Central, and Southern Nootkan tribes. Numerous geographic dialects correspond to the two hundred-mile or so cultural distribution of Nootkan people on Vancouver Island. The language of the Nitinat, a Southern Nootkan tribe, is sometimes, but not always, distinguished from Nootkan dialects as a separate language. The Makah are Nootkans living on the Olympic Peninsula at Neah Bay, Washington; they spoke a language separate from Nootka and Nitinat. Together, the languages Nootka, Nitinat, and Makah are called Nootkan; they are related to Kwakiutl, the Nootkans' neighbors to the north, and belong to the Wakashan language family.

History and Cultural Relations

A small party of Russian sailors, the earliest European explorers in Nootka territory, arrived on July 17, 1741, but weren't heard from again. On March 29, 1778, Captain James Cook was the first European to walk through a Nootka village at Nootka Bay. In 1803, John Jewitt, a sailor aboard the English ship *Boston*, was captured by Chief Maquinna at Nootka Sound and lived there for more than two years, working as Maquinna's slave. Beginning around 1800 the Nootka were drawn into the fur trade, first with the British and later with the European-Americans. Shaker and Presbyterian missionaries came to Neah Bay in about 1903 and some from the Apostolic Church arrived in the 1930s. Presbyterian missionaries also lived among other Nootka groups.

Settlements

The primary Nootkan settlement was a social unit known as a local group (also called a band). Each local group had one or more clusters of cedar-plank houses (called longhouses), which were as large as forty by one hundred feet. Nootkans moved between winter and summer settlements, with each local group having at least one longhouse for use in the summer at one site and another longhouse for winter use at another site. Up to thirty-five related people (a house-group) lived in a longhouse. Within the longhouse, each house-group family had its own cooking hearth and living area. In the winter, several local groups formed a larger winter village. There, each local group had its own important ceremonial art. The focal point of each was a family of chiefs who owned the houses as well as the territorial rights to exploit local resources. The local group took its name from the place it was located, such as a fishing site; sometimes it was named after a chief. Villages were situated near sources of firewood and fresh water, as well as for shelter from surprise raids. Today there are numerous Nootka reserves dotting Vancouver Island's west coast. The physical isolation of most of these reserves makes year-round living there impractical. Victoria, British Columbia, and Vancouver Island towns are now home for many Nootka. The Makah, who live on Washington State's Olympic Peninsula, live year-round at coastal Neah Bay, which is connected by road to the rest of the peninsula.

Economy

Subsistence and Commercial Activities.   The Nootka were fishermen and whalers. Salmon was the most stable food source and was obtained in large numbers in the fall and stored for the winter months; herring and salmon roe, cod, halibut, sardines, and herring complemented salmon supplies. Wooden fishing weirs were placed in rivers, and tidal fish traps were used in the sea; nets, hooks, lines, herring rakes, gigs, fishing spears, and harpoons, as well as dip nets for smaller fish, such as smelt, were also used. Seals, sea lions, whales, and porpoises were also important food sources; whales were valued for their ceremonial use as well. Land animals, such as deer, bear, and elk, were hunted or occasionally trapped. Wild plants and roots added to the Nootkan diet. Reliable food preservation techniques were vital to maintain adequate food supplies during winter months as well as in lean periods. Herring and sardines, for example, were eaten fresh as well as dried and smoked. Many Nootka return to their aboriginal coastal villages during the summer months to enjoy the pleasure of "going home" to fish, commercially or privately, and to hunt and gather plant and sea foods. Neah Bay is a well-known sport-fishing port and for decades was a prospering commercial fishing port.

Industrial Arts. Traditionally, the Nootka were master wood carvers. Houses, furniture, canoes, containers, masks, headdresses, and many similar objects were made of wood. Wooden boxes of various sizes, for example, were used by house-group families to store food and possessions. Wood in another form was used for clothing. In cold weather, men wore robes woven out of shredded cedar bark; women's robes were similar to men's, and they always wore an apron of shredded cedar bark. Highly prized ceremonial robes had mountain-goat wool woven into the shredded cedar bark. Over the past fifteen years, many Nootka carvers and silkscreen artists have become well-known Indian artists and have drawn critical acclaim for their work.

Trade. Principal trading relations with outsiders, established on Captain Cook's third expedition to Vancouver Island, took place at Nootka Sound. Sea otter pelts were in demand by Chinese merchants at Canton and were bartered at Nootka Sound. British and American vessels in Nootka territory became frequent sights as the fur trade expanded. As traders bartered for valuable native goods, the Nootka began to acquire firearms and ammunition, and hostilities eventually broke out between the Nootka and British and American traders. Trade dwindled progressively in the nineteenth century, as sea otters were hunted nearly to extinction.

Division of Labor. Men fished and hunted for land and sea animals and did the wood carving. Women gathered plant foods, such as elderberries, gooseberries, and currants, and sea food, such as sea urchins and mussels. They usually did the everyday cooking, although young men often prepared food at feasts. Women cured fish such as sardines and salmon. They wove garments, using simple frames, out of yellow cedar bark, which was stripped off of trees with an adze. Pine tree bark was used for clothing, too. Women also wove baskets using grasses.

Land Tenure. Inheritance was the basis of ownership, which in Nootka society went well beyond control of land. Chiefs inherited their right to own and control all economic and ceremonial property as well as the privilege of using those properties. Economic privileges included the ownership of habitation sites, as well as places to fish, hunt, and gather roots and berries; longhouses and living spots within them;

and the salvage rights to beached whales. Chiefs' ceremonial privileges included the right to conduct certain rituals and to perform particular dances or songs, the ownership of dances and songs, and the ritual names that accompanied each privilege. A chief's most important property was his salmon streams. Chiefs not only gave the right to set salmon traps in particular locations; they also had the right to claim the fishermen's entire first salmon catch. By accepting the privilege to fish at certain places, a local-group member publicly acknowledged the chief's right of ownership of those places, and a chief exercised his right to collect a "tribute" during the fishing season. The chief held a feast with his tributes, during which time he announced his hereditary right to collect it.

Kinship

Kin Groups and Descent. Kinship groups were based on ambilineal descent: a person could choose one or more lines of descent on his or her mother's or father's side of the family, or both. Descent was the basis for social as well as political rank, which was determined by birth order; the descent line of the first-born child was ranked highest, and the lowest rank went to the last-born in a family. Economic rights were also accorded to individuals based on their birth order.

Kinship Terminology. Nootka kinship terminology follows the Hawaiian system. Relative age was distinguished among individuals in one's generation as well as between older and younger siblings.

Marriage and Family

Marriage. A boy's preferred marriage partner was a distant relative in his tribe. Marriage was a formal alliance between a bride's and groom's social group and was initiated by the groom's parents. Marriages, particularly those between high-ranking families, were carefully arranged by a group's elders, since significant privileges were passed from parents to children.

Domestic Unit. A nuclear family's right to reside in a house-group was determined by tracing their kinship connections back to an ancestor of the group that controlled the house. Once that social link was made, a family was allowed to reside within a house-group, but had to participate in that group's social and economic activities during its residency there. Families changed house-groups by following the same procedure.

Inheritance. Access to economic property, such as fishing and hunting grounds, as well as ceremonial rights and privileges were inherited through ambilineal kinship lines. Ceremonial names were one of the most important inherited properties.

Socialization. Childbirth was a private matter; dietary restrictions were observed by both parents. Magic was used to ensure a child's healthy development. Infants were placed on a cradle board and wrapped in shredded cedar-bark cloth. As a mark of beauty, young children had their foreheads slightly flattened by a cedar-bark pad attached to the cradle board. The Nootka were affectionate and indulgent parents. Shame, not slapping or spanking, was a common method used to modify children's behavior.

Sociopolitical Organization

Social Organization. Nootka political organization was integrally tied to economics, kinship, and descent. In Nootka society, each person had an inherited social rank, and all Nootka were rank-ordered in relation to each other. Most generally, communities were divided into nobles and commoners. In the noble families, rank was inherited by the rule of primogeniture, or primacy of the first-born. The first-born son of a high-ranking chief not only succeeded his father in their community's sociopolitical organization but also inherited his most important and prestigious rights and privileges. Social rank was visible in numerous ways. For example, each house-group had four ranked chiefs, who were brothers or close kinsmen. Living places within a longhouse were determined by social rank. The highest ranking house-group chief owned and lived in his house's right rear corner; other corners were not owned, even though chiefs of lesser rank lived in them. Commoners lived between the corners. Nootka chiefs kept slaves (war captives) and every village had slaves who performed its heavy labor. Slaves had no rights or privileges.

Political Organization. The Nootka did not constitute a single political entity; however, their cultural patterns as well as the intensity of social interactions between local groups made them a definable social unit. Anthropologists customarily divide Nootka society into a hierarchy of sociopolitical units. The basic political unit was the local group. A tribe was a larger social unit composed of local groups that shared a common winter settlement; the chiefs of a tribe were rank-ordered. Tribes that united to share a common summer village site at which to hunt and fish formed a confederacy, which took the name of one of its tribes. Sometimes confederacies were formed as the result of tribes coming together for warfare. Confederacies correspond to the Nootka's major geographic divisions.

Social Control. There was no formal Nootka legal system. Everyday social control was a face-to-face matter, as kinsmen and friends within a local group or house-group informally settled minor interpersonal problems. On the other hand, a local group protected its members from outside aggressors. The assurance of local-group retaliation acted as an informal deterrent to external attack. When that failed, social control between local groups was based on blood revenge and property settlements (the aggressor's relatives paid valuables and wealth to the victim's family). In a case of death by black magic (witchcraft), the witch was killed, and the death went unavenged.

Conflict. Wars and feuds were distinguished by their scale and motivation. Feuds were small-scale events that occurred to settle minor problems or to punish an offense. Wars, on the other hand, secured slaves or booty, or both. Slings, bows and arrows, and stone clubs were the warriors' favorite weapons. Only chiefs wore body armor.

Religion and Expressive Culture

Religious Beliefs. The Nootka believed in supernatural forces, which they tried to control with public or private rituals. Nootka rituals sought to secure good luck with nature, as in their magical attempts to control the weather. Still other rituals tried to cure sickness. The Nootka conception of the supernatural did not include gods and was in general vague and unsystematic. Nootkans believed in numerous spirits, some malevolent, others not. Men acquired supernatural powers by undertaking vision quests, during which time they came into face-to-face contact with a spirit. That spirit then became a man's ally, or spirit-helper, and bestowed upon him special powers and abilities. Successful whalers, warriors, and fishermen, among others, had supernatural helpers. The traditional religion has been modified by the decades of European-American contact, and today few Nootka follow traditional beliefs.

Religious Practitioners. Shamans, the most powerful supernatural practitioners, acquired their special powers to cure illnesses during a vision quest.

Ceremonies. The Nootkans' main ceremony was the Dancing Society (the English translation of the word for it was "The Shamans," although initiation into it was not restricted only to shamans); the performance of the Dancing Society was called the Wolf Dance because dancers wore wolf masks. Feasts and potlatches were also performed. Four main groups of people attended Nootka potlatches: the host/giver, the people in whose honor the potlatch was given, the guests who attended and witnessed the transfer of rights, and the groups who helped the host by contributing goods and services. The Nootka always potlatched to their relatives. After a cash economy had been established, many potlatch gifts were European (dressers, woven blankets, sewing machines). In traditional days, goods were native (canoes, cured animal skins, large quantities of food). During a potlatch, the social status of the host was elevated, and rights and privileges were transferred, often to children. Potlatch guests publicly witnessed and confirmed the validity of those changes. High-ranking chiefs possessed numerous titles, prerogatives, and privileges, and held many potlatches. Acculturation has altered the social role and symbolism of the potlatch, with today's feasts and dances only reminiscent of the great traditional potlatches. Intertribal dances have become a meaningful social event as well as a means of maintaining contact between the Nootka and non-Nootka neighbors.

Arts. The best known Nootka art is their woven conical hat displaying whale-hunting scenes. The distinctive Nootka wood sculpture was the giant figure carved into longhouse support posts. Ceremonial masks carved without the color and fantasy of other Northwest Coast cultures were a hallmark of Nootka art. The Nootka also excelled at carving red-cedar canoes; canoe carvers were thought to be inspired by a woodpecker spirit-helper. The accomplishments of a carver were publicly recognized at feasts and potlatches. Nootkans also transformed themselves into objects of symbolic expression. Men painted their faces with colors, including black, red, white, and brown; they pierced their ears, often several times, and wore earpieces of abalone shell, bone, quills, shells, or pieces of copper; and they wore their hair in many styles, including pulled to the back of the head and tied English-style. Men also wore woven hats, bracelets, and anklets.

Medicine. Cuts and bruises were treated with home remedies. Serious illnesses were treated by shamans.

Death and Afterlife. The Nootka feared the dead, and handling a corpse was taken seriously. They believed that the dead had some power over whales. A corpse was placed into a wooden box and taken to a burial place distant from their villages.

Bibliography

Colson, Elizabeth (1953). *The Makah Indians.* Manchester, England, and Minneapolis: Manchester University Press and the University of Minnesota Press.

Drucker, Philip (1951). *The Northern and Central Nootkan Tribes.* U.S. Bureau of American Ethnology Bulletin no. 144. Washington, D.C.

Jewitt, John R. (1824). *A Narrative of the Adventures of John R. Jewitt.* Edinburgh: Constable.

Sproat, Gilbert Malcolm (1868). *Scenes and Studies of Savage Life.* London: Smith, Elder & Co.

MARK S. FLEISHER

North Alaskan Eskimos

ETHNONYMS: Iñupiat, Malemiut, Nunamiut, Tariurmiut

Orientation

Identification. The North Alaskan Eskimos are located along the coast of northern Alaska. The name "Eskimo" is of foreign derivation, although there is considerable disagreement about where and when it originated. The North Alaskan Eskimos refer to themselves collectively as "Iñupiat," or "authentic people." "Nunamiut" was and is used as a general designation for people who spend the winter inland, and "Tariurmiut" is the corresponding term for coast dwellers. "Malemiut" is derived from a Yup'ik Eskimo word from Norton Sound that was formerly used to denote the speakers of an Iñuit dialect from Kotzebue Sound. The term was frequently used erroneously in late-nineteenth-century and early-twentieth-century literature to refer to a tribal entity of some kind. Its use is now restricted in the technical literature to the name for a regional dialect.

Location. Aboriginally, the North Alaskan Eskimos occupied the coast of northern Alaska from the western tip of Kotzebue Sound to the mouth of the Colville River, and the entire hinterland drained by rivers reaching the sea between those two points. In the late nineteenth century they expanded eastward along the Arctic coast to beyond what is now the Canadian border, and southward to the eastern shore of Norton Sound.

Demography. The population at the beginning of the 1800s was probably about eight thousand to nine thousand people. There was a decline of some 75 percent in the last quarter of that century, but the population began to recover early in the twentieth century. By about 1975 it had reached its traditional level, and it has continued to grow since.

Linguistic Affiliation. The language of the North Alaskan Eskimos belongs to the Eskimo branch of the Eskaleut language family. More specifically, it is an Iñuit Eskimo language, which is spoken from Bering Strait across northern North America to Greenland. Within North Alaska, the Malemiut dialect is spoken in eleven villages of the Kotzebue Sound drainage and three on the shore of Norton Sound, and the North Slope dialect is spoken in the eight villages north of Kotzebue Sound.

History and Cultural Relations

When they were first encountered by Europeans in the second decade of the nineteenth century, the people were organized in nineteen autonomous societies, or tribes. They welcomed the few explorers and shipborne traders who ventured into their area as long as they were interested in trade. Otherwise, they tended to be hostile, although bloodshed was rare. Relations with Europeans improved with more familiarity. A greater threat to native life was posed by American whalers after 1848; over the next two decades they decimated the bowhead whale and walrus populations, which previously had been major sources of food and other raw materials. In the 1870s the natives themselves decimated the caribou population with newly introduced firearms. Widespread famine followed. European epidemic diseases also arrived about this time, with catastrophic effect. The demographic decline and ensuing chaos resulted in the destruction of the traditional social boundaries and in extensive interregional movement of families trying to find productive hunting and fishing grounds.

In the late nineteenth century, missionaries and miners made their way to the region. Between about 1900 and 1910, schools were established at several locations. The new mission-school villages subsequently became focal points for the natives, resulting eventually in the formation of twenty-two permanent villages distributed across their expanded late-nineteenth-century territory. Domesticated reindeer were introduced to fill the void left by the nearly extinct caribou, and reindeer herding and fur trapping became the basis of a new economic order lasting until the 1930s. The fur trade collapsed during the Great Depression, and reindeer herding declined as the caribou population began to recover. Welfare payments and seasonal wage employment for men, usually far from home, subsequently became the major sources of cash income, while hunting and fishing continued to provide the raw materials for food and some clothing. Increasing economic and political stability, combined with improved medical care, has resulted in a steady population increase since 1910.

The period 1960–1990 has seen major economic and social changes. The Alaska Native Claims Settlement Act (ANCSA) led to the formation of two native regional corporations, NANA Corporation, in the region focused on Kotzebue Sound, and the Arctic Slope Regional Corporation (ASRC) to the north. Oil and mineral development provided a substantial tax base leading to the formation of modern political units: the North Slope Borough (in the general territory of the ASRC) and the Northwest Arctic Borough (in the general territory of NANA). As they approach the end of the twentieth century the people are involved in the general political and economic life of Alaska, but continue to rely to a considerable extent on hunting and fishing for food. Increasing numbers of nonnatives have moved into North Alaska since the 1960s, but Eskimos still constitute a substantial majority of the permanent resident population.

Settlements

During the early contact period each society had a distinctive settlement pattern, but the several forms can be grouped into two broad categories, a whaling pattern and a nonwhaling pattern. In the former, relatively large villages were located at Point Hope, Icy Cape, Ukpiarvik, and Point Barrow, places where spring ice conditions favored hunting the bowhead whale. Smaller satellite villages were distributed along the coast and on the lower reaches of rivers elsewhere within the societal territory. In both types of settlement, the semisubterranean sod house was the sole type of dwelling. After the conclusion of whaling, in June, the inhabitants of these villages dispersed to spring seal-hunting camps scattered along the coast. After the sea ice left in late June or early July, they dispersed even more widely to hunt caribou and fish along the rivers or to trade at one of the annual trade fairs. These travels usually concluded in late August or early September, at which time people returned to their winter villages.

The nonwhaling settlement pattern was characterized by the autumn dispersal of the population in small villages, primarily along rivers, but in a few cases along the coast or around lakes. These villages were usually located in areas likely to be visited by caribou, but at specific sites that were particularly well suited for fishing; in a few instances, they were at good fall seal-hunting locations. Houses in these settlements were constructed of wooden frames covered by one of a variety of materials: sod, moss, or a tarpaulin made of skins. As the winter progressed, people stayed in their fall settlements if food supplies lasted, but they usually had to move around eventually in search of game. In the spring, there was a fair amount of variation. In some societies, people moved to the coast to hunt seals; in others, they moved to lakes and sloughs to hunt muskrats and migratory waterfowl and/or to fish. After the river ice broke up, the members of several societies moved to the coast to trade, hunt sea mammals, and fish, but the members of several others remained inland to fish and to hunt caribou. In all areas summer was a time of movement during which people lived in tents. The two patterns persisted into the twentieth century, but the native population gradually became more sedentary, especially after the end of the reindeer herding and trapping era.

Economy

Subsistence and Commercial Activities. The entire economy was based on hunting and fishing and, to a much more moderate extent, on the gathering of plant products. Whales, seals, caribou, several species of fish, and a variety of fur-bearing animals, small game, and birds provided them with all the raw materials they needed for food and clothing and, to a significant extent, for tools, weapons, and utensils as well. Wood was used in house construction and in the manufacture of some weapons and tools; leaves, berries, and some roots were collected for food. Hunting, fishing, and gathering continue to be important sources of food today, but

are significantly supplemented by foodstuffs imported from regions farther south. Gardening is carried on to a very limited extent in a few villages where soil and summer weather conditions permit. Cash income is derived from welfare payments and by employment in a variety of private commercial enterprises—particularly in the oil, mining, and service industries—and government agencies. Traditionally, the only domesticated animals were large dogs. In winter they were used to pull sleds; in summer, to track boats along the seacoast and rivers and as pack animals. For about half a century, beginning in the 1890s, imported reindeer were raised on a relatively large scale, but that industry has declined to only a few small herds today. Cats and dogs are now kept as pets; teams of sled dogs are kept only for racing.

Industrial Arts. The North Alaskan Eskimos were noted for the quality of their work in ivory and flint. Skin sewing was developed to a high level. Beautiful birchbark baskets were made in the southern interior. Except for work in flint, these traditional manufactures are perpetuated today, skin sewing primarily for personal or family use, ivory and bone carving and basket making as a source of cash income.

Trade. Aboriginally there was a well-developed intersocietal trade network in North Alaska. It was based upon trading partnerships and implemented through two major summer fairs and a system of winter feasts during both of which partners from different societies came together. The whole system was connected by similar links with Athapaskan Indian societies in the Alaskan interior, with other Eskimos in the Bering Strait area and southwestern Alaska, and with Eskimos and Chuckchees in easternmost Asia.

Division of Labor. Aboriginally there was a sharp division of labor based on gender. Men hunted big game, built houses, and manufactured weapons, tools, and utensils. Women looked after most game from the time it was killed: retrieving it, storing it, and performing whatever processing chores were required prior to ultimate consumption. Women also did the sewing and child rearing. Fishing, trapping, and hunting birds and small game were either men's work or women's work, with regional and seasonal variations in the precise allocation of duties. The traditional division of labor based on gender persisted with only a few modifications until the 1960s. Since then, although the pursuit of large game is still carried out primarily by men, the great increase in the opportunities for local employment in teaching, government, and service industries has changed the primary basis of the division of labor to one's level of education and technical training rather than gender.

Land Tenure. Aboriginally, land ownership was vested at the societal level; it was owned in common by all the members of the society. Within the territory of a society, its members were free to live, hunt, and fish where they wished, subject only to the provision that people who first occupied a place had the primary right to use it until they abandoned it. There was no other private ownership of land, nor were there individual or family hunting or fishing territories. Today land ownership in North Alaska follows the pattern that exists generally in the United States; the region is a patchwork of properties owned by individuals and corporations—much of it by native corporations established under ANCSA, local governments, the state of Alaska, and various agencies of the U.S. government.

Kinship

Kin Groups and Descent.   Traditionally, the North Alaskan Eskimos were organized in terms of bilocal extended families. Typically they involved about a dozen people, but many were larger, and some involved as many as sixty to eighty. Unilineal descent groups were absent. Bilocal extended families are still important today, although in recent decades the conjugal family has become the dominant kinship unit.

Kinship Terminology.   In the nineteenth century kinship terminology conformed to the Yuman type. Today, as a result of acculturation, the Eskimo type is beginning to predominate.

Marriage and Family

Marriage.   Traditionally, incest prohibitions applied absolutely to siblings, strongly to first cousins, and rather weakly beyond that. Parents attempted to control, and certainly to influence, their children's choice of a spouse, but there was no institutionalized betrothal system. Monogamy predominated, with polygyny practiced by a few wealthy men, most of whom had two wives, but a few of whom had as many as five. Polyandry was permitted, but was extremely rare. Postmarital residence was bilocal. Divorce was common, especially during the early years of adult life. It could be effected by either party.

Domestic Unit.   A household could consist of a single conjugal family, but usually comprised two or more conjugal families connected by sibling or cousin ties reckoned through either the female or male lines, or both. Adjacent houses were usually occupied by people who were closely related and often were connected to one another by tunnels or passageways, the whole being a single economic and political unit managed by the family head and his wife. Three-generation households were common. This general pattern prevailed until the late 1960s, after which the population increase and the imposition of the U.S. system of land ownership and of clearly bounded property lines in the villages made it difficult to perpetuate.

Inheritance.   Individually owned movable property was buried with the deceased. Houses, boats, and other items owned by the family as a whole continued to be used by the surviving members of that family.

Socialization.   Traditionally, the ratio of adults to children was high, and children received a great deal of individual attention and supervision. Discipline was permissive. Children were encouraged to learn by a combination of admonition, example, and especially practice. The traditional approach is still preferred in native households. As the ratio of children to adults increased in the twentieth century, however, it became less effective because there were too many children to look after with the same level of care. Jobs now take one or more parents out of the house for several hours each day, and much socialization takes place outside the family context, primarily in schools.

Sociopolitical Organization

Social and Political Organization.   Aboriginally, there were no governments, tribal councils, chiefs, or other forms of centralized authority. The traditional societies were organized in terms of large extended families that were politically and economically self-sufficient to a high degree. The several families were linked to one another by various kinship, namesake, and partnership ties to form the society as a whole. Most settlements were occupied by the members of only a single extended family. Larger settlements, including each of the whaling villages, were occupied by the members of several families who lived in close proximity to one another, but who maintained a high level of autonomy nevertheless. Each extended family served as a redistribution network in which the family head and his wife served as foci. Men who demonstrated superior hunting, managerial, and leadership skills, and who were married to women of commensurate ability, attracted more and more relatives to join their family groups. The heads of large families were often wealthy, and they typically had at least two wives. At the opposite extreme, couples who were lazy or incompetent either had to shift for themselves or become affiliated with a large family in some kind of marginal and subservient capacity.

Social Control.   Affiliation with a particular family head was voluntary; both individuals and conjugal families could strike out on their own whenever they wished. This served as a check on disruptive behavior by the family head. Life in isolation was precarious, however, and the only realistic option to belonging to one extended family was to belong to a different one. These facts, which were well understood, served as important constraints on disruptive behavior by ordinary family members. Additional constraints took the form of admonition by family elders, ridicule, and gossip. In cases where these were ineffective, family members might shun an individual or, in extreme cases, even kill the person. There were fewer controls on disruptive behavior between families, since there were no individuals or organizations with authority to mediate interfamily disputes. Over the decades a kind of balance of power seems to have developed among the families in a given society, with smaller units forming alliances to offset the dominance of larger ones. Interfamily relations in traditional times were often tense, especially in the whaling villages, but only rarely erupted into violence.

Conflict.   Within societies, interfamily feuds did occasionally result in murder. When that occurred, the male relative closest to the deceased had the obligation to kill the assassin. If he was successful, the obligation for vengeance passed back to a man on the other side. At the intersocietal level, warfare was relatively common. It seems to have been undertaken solely for the purpose of avenging a wrong of some kind, and the objective was the death of as many people as possible on the enemy side—men, women, and children. War was not conducted for the purpose of acquiring territory, booty, or slaves. Nighttime raids were the preferred form of attack, although organized warfare, with battle lines, tactical maneuvers, and clearly developed fire and shock tactics, also occurred.

Religion and Expressive Culture

Religious Beliefs.   The traditional religion was animistic. Everything was believed to be imbued with a spirit. There was, in addition, an array of spirits that were not associated with any specific material form. Some of these spirits looked kindly on humans, but most of them had to be placated in order for human activities to proceed without difficulty. Harmony with the spirit world was maintained through the wearing of amulets, the observance of a vast number of taboos, and participation in a number of ceremonies relating primarily to the hunt, food, birth, death, the life cycle, and the seasonal round. In the 1890s a few natives from Southwest Alaska who had been converted by Swedish missionaries began evangelical work in the Kotzebue Sound area. About the same time, Episcopal and Presbyterian missionaries from the continental United States began work in Point Hope and Barrow, followed by members of the California Annual Meeting of Friends in the Kotzebue Sound area. After some difficulties, the Friends were successful in converting a large number of people, and these converts laid the foundation for widespread conversions to Christianity throughout North Alaska. Today, practically every Christian denomination and faith is represented in the region.

Religious Practitioners.   In traditional times, shamans interceded between the human and spirit worlds. They divined the concerns of the spirits and advised their fellow humans of the modes of behavior required to placate them. They also healed the sick, foretold the future results of a particular course of action, made spirit flights to the sun and the moon, and attempted to intercede with the spirits when ordinary means proved ineffective. Around 1900, the shamans were replaced by American missionaries. Most of them, in turn, have been replaced by natives ordained as ministers or priests in the Christian faiths to which they adhere.

Ceremonies.   The traditional ceremonial cycle consisted of a series of rituals and festivals related primarily to ensuring success in the hunt. Such events were most numerous and most elaborate in the societies in which whaling was of major importance, but they occurred to some degree throughout the region. Intersocietal trading festivals were also important. The traditional cycle has been replaced by the contemporary American sequence of political and Christian holidays.

Arts.   Traditional arts consisted primarily of the following: (1) making essentially utilitarian objects (such as tools, weapons, and clothes) in a particularly elegant fashion; (2) storytelling; and (3) song and dance. Since the advent of store-bought products and television, all the traditional art forms have declined considerably.

Medicine.   There were two forms of traditional medicine. One, which involved divination and intercession with the spirits, was conducted by shamans. The second involved the massage and/or manipulation of various body parts, particularly the internal organs. The former has given way to Western clinical medicine. The latter, after several decades of being practiced in secret, has recently experienced a revival.

Death and Afterlife.   Life and death were believed to be a perpetual cycle through which a given individual passed. When a person died, his or her personal possessions were placed on the grave for use in the afterlife, although it was understood that, in due course, the soul of everyone who died would be reanimated in the form of a newborn infant. The traditional beliefs about death and the afterworld have been replaced by an array of Christian beliefs. Whereas funerals were not well defined or important rituals in traditional times—the observance of special taboos was much more important—they have in recent decades become elaborate events in which hundreds of people from several villages often participate, particularly when the death of an elder is involved.

Bibliography

Burch, Ernest S., Jr. (1975). _Eskimo Kinsmen: Changing Family Relationships in Northwest Alaska_. St. Paul, Minn.: West Publishing Co.

Burch, Ernest S., Jr. (1980). "Traditional Eskimo Societies in Northwest Alaska." In _Alaska Native Culture and History_, edited by Yoshinobu Kotani and William Workman, 253–304. Suita, Osaka, Japan: National Museum of Ethnology.

Gubser, Nicholas J. (1965). _The Nunamiut Eskimos: Hunters of Caribou_. New Haven, Conn.: Yale University Press.

Rainey, Froelich G. (1947). "The Whale Hunters of Tigara." _Anthropological Papers of the American Museum of Natural History_ 41 (2):230–283.

Spencer, Robert F. (1959). _The North Alaskan Eskimo: A Study in Ecology and Society_. U.S. Bureau of American Ethnology Bulletin no. 171. Washington, D.C.

ERNEST S. BURCH, JR.

Northern Metis

Most of the Northern Metis live in the lower Mackenzie River region in the Mackenzie District of the Northwest Territories of Canada, from Fort Simpson northward. Others live in the northern Yukon Territory and in eastern Alaska. They are dispersed through numerous communities in the region, in most of which they are a minority.

They do not at present form an ethnic group as such and have no collective legal identity. But their sociocultural characteristics, their traditions, and especially the discrimination against them by other groups have in recent years combined to give them a sense of social identity as Metis. They are of a comparatively recent origin as a group, most of them being descendants of mixed unions that took place after the middle of the nineteenth century. They generally have an Athapaskan Indian maternal ancestry and northern European paternal ancestry.

It is difficult to form an estimate of how many Northern Metis exist—probably more than one thousand and fewer than ten thousand. Their social organization is little, if at all, different from that of the other groups in the region. The nuclear family is dominant, with European-American kin terms used in common discourse, and the appropriate Indian or Eskimo kinship patterns expressed with Native American kinsmen. Their church affiliation is mainly Protestant with a large Roman Catholic minority.

Individuals have great physical mobility and wide-ranging social ties, with much community exogamy and neolocal residence after marriage. There are perhaps two dozen family surnames among the Metis in the Mackenzie District with affiliation being determined genealogically. Family stories and traditions often deal with service with various commercial companies. Most Metis have worked at many kinds of jobs, often connected with transportation and the fur trade. Subsistence hunting and fishing, and trapping have been important through the years.

See also Metis of Western Canada

Bibliography

Burger, Joanne O., and Allan Clovis, eds. (1976). *A Portrayal of Our Métis Heritage.* Yellowknife, Northwest Territories: Métis Association of the Northwest Territories.

Slobodin, Richard (1966). *Métis of the Mackenzie District.* Ottawa, Ontario: Saint Paul University, Canadian Research Centre for Anthropology.

Slobodin, Richard (1981). "Subarctic Métis." In *Handbook of North American Indians.* Vol. 6, *Subarctic,* edited by June Helm, 361–371. Washington, D.C.: Smithsonian Institution.

Smith, David Merrill (1981). "Fort Resolution, Northwest Territories." In *Handbook of North American Indians.* Vol. 6, *Subarctic,* edited by June Helm, 683–693. Washington, D.C.: Smithsonian Institution.

Smith, Derek G. (1975). *Natives and Outsiders: Pluralism in the Mackenzie River Delta, Northwest Territories.* Ottawa, Ontario: Department of Indian Affairs and Northern Development, Northern Research Division, Mackenzie Delta Research Project, 12.

Northern Paiute

ETHNONYMS: Mono Pi-Utes, Numa, Oregon Snakes, Paiute, Paviotso, Py-utes

Orientation

Identification.   The people designated here as "Northern Paiute" call themselves nɨmɨ "people." They are sometimes also referred to as "Paviotso" or merely "Paiute"—their name has long been a source of confusion. "Paviotso," derived from Western Shoshone *pabiocco,* who used the term to apply only

to the Nevada Northern Paiute, is too narrow. It also has a slightly derogatory ring among those who use it. "Paiute," of uncertain origin, is too broad, as it also covers groups that speak two other languages—Southern Paiute, and Owens Valley Paiute. "Northern Paiute," which has been in the literature for roughly seventy-five years, is the clearest alternative. But the Indian people when speaking English often use only "Paiute," or they modify it with the name of a reservation or community.

Location.   The Northern Paiute held lands from just south of Mono Lake in California, southeastern Oregon, and immediately adjacent Idaho. Linguistic relatives adjoined the people of the South and East: the Owens Valley Paiute along the narrow southern border and the Northern and Western Shoshone along the long eastern one. The western border was shared with groups speaking Hokan and Penutian languages. The region as a whole is diverse environmentally, but largely classified as desert steppe. Rainfall is scant, and water resources are dependent on winter snowpack in the ranges.

Demography.   Population figures for people identified as Northern Paiute are largely inaccurate, owing to the uncertain number of persons living off-reservation and the growing number of members of other tribes on reservations. The 1980 census suggests that there are roughly five thousand persons on traditionally Northern Paiute reserved lands, and roughly another thirty-five hundred people residing off-reservation. The population at the time of contact (1830s) has been estimated at sixty-five hundred.

Linguistic Affiliation.   The Northern Paiute language belongs to the widespread Uto-Aztecan family. It is more closely related to other languages in the Great Basin that together form the Numic branch of the family, and most closely to Owens Valley Paiute, the other language member of the Western Numic subbranch. The Owens Valley Paiute are close enough culturally to be included in this sketch, although linguistically they are part of a single language with the Monache (the language referred to as Mono). The Bannock of Idaho also speak Northern Paiute. Native language fluency over much of the region is now diminished, although some communities have attempted language salvage programs.

History and Cultural Relations

Linguistic, and to some degree archaeological, evidence suggests that the ancestors of the Northern Paiute expanded into their ethnographically known range within the last two thousand years. Although these data are controversial, they support a generally northward movement from some as yet undetermined homeland in the South, perhaps in southeastern California. Arguing against this view are a number of tribal traditions that tie groups to local features (especially mountain peaks) for origins. With neighbors to the east there was considerable intermarriage and exchange, so that bilingualism prevailed in an ever-widening band as one moved northward. With people on the west, relations were less friendly. First encounters with non-Indian fur trappers and explorers in the 1820s and 1830s were on occasion hostile, prefiguring events to come near mid-century. With the discovery of gold in California in 1848, and gold and silver in western Nevada in 1859, floods of immigrants traversed fragile riverbottom trails across Northern Paiute territory and also settled in equally fragile and important subsistence localities. Environmental destruction led a number of groups to adopt a pattern of mounted raiding for subsistence and booty. Scattered depredations on both sides led to clashes with troops beginning in 1860. After that time, reservations were established to settle the people, principally at Pyramid Lake and Walker River. Those who did not settle on the reservations continued to live near emerging towns and on ranches where wage labor provided a meager living. In the early twentieth century, populations at several of these localities were given small tracts of federal land, generally referred to as "colonies." Both reservations and colonies persist to the present, although few are economically well developed or self-sustaining.

Settlements

In aboriginal and early historic times, the Northern Paiute lived by hunting, gathering, and fishing in recognized subareas within their broader territory. Given that natural resources were not equally distributed across the landscape, there were some variations in settlement systems and sizes of local groups. The large lake basins (Pyramid Lake, Walker Lake) had extensive fisheries and supported people in most seasons of the year. Major marshes (Stillwater, Humboldt, Surprise Valley, Warner Valley, Malheur) also served as settlement foci. Within these areas, people usually resided in more or less fixed locations, at least during the winter. They established temporary camps away from these locations during spring and fall in order to harvest seeds, roots, and if present, piñon nuts. Camp sizes in settled seasons varied, but probably fifty persons constituted the norm. During periods of greater mobility two or three families often camped together (ten to fifteen persons). In areas other than those with lakes or marshes, settlements were less fixed, with the exception of winter camps. In the Owens Valley, a unique area for the proximity of a number of resources, settled villages of one hundred to two hundred persons were reported, all located in the valley bottom. With the establishment of reservations and colonies, these patterns were greatly altered. Clustered housing prevails on colonies with a small land base, and allotment of lands on reservations allows for a more dispersed pattern.

In aboriginal times, houses of different types were built according to the season and degree of mobility of the group. The common winter dwelling, especially near wetland areas, was a dome-shaped or conical house made of cattail or tule mats over a framework of willow poles. Cooking was done outside the house in an adjacent semicircular windbreak of brush, which also served as a sleeping area during the summer. The windbreak was the primary shelter at temporary camps, unless people chose to overwinter in the mountains near cached piñon reserves. In that case, they built a more substantial conical log structure covered with brush and earth. In the 1870s these traditional house types gave way to gabled one- to two-room single-family dwellings of boards on reservations and colonies. Today nearly all these early houses are gone from Indian lands, replaced by modern multiroomed structures with all conveniences.

Economy

Subsistence and Commercial Activities. In the pre- and immediately postcontact periods, the Northern Paiute lived by hunting a variety of large and small game, gathering numerous vegetable products, and fishing where possible. Local seasonal rounds were conditioned by the particular mix of resources present. Names of subgroups (such as "trout eaters") often reflected a common subsistence item, but nowhere was the named resource used to the exclusion of a mix of others. Some people today hunt and collect a few of their former resources, but for the most part, they are engaged in ranching and wage labor and thus purchase food. Although the large reservations support some agriculture, most of it is oriented toward hay and grain production to feed cattle. Except for dogs, there were no domesticated animals in aboriginal times. Today, horses are common in areas where cattle ranching is possible, and a number of people keep them as pleasure animals.

Industrial Arts. Aboriginal arts included extensive work in basketry, and less extensively in crafts such as bead making, feather work, and stone sculpture. Baskets were primarily utilitarian, being used in harvesting and processing plant foods, storage of food and water, trapping fish and birds, and so on. Beads were made of duck bones, local shells, and shells traded into the region from the west. Feather working was related to that complex in California and included the manufacture of mosaic headbands and belts and dance outfits. Stone sculpture was confined to smoking pipes and small effigies. Pottery was present only in Owens Valley. In the historic period, work in buckskin and glass beads became prominent, as the influence of the Plains Culture filtered into the region from the north. Presently basketry, hide working, and beading are the most common, although all except beading have declined within the past twenty years.

Trade. An active trade in shells was maintained in aboriginal times with groups in California. Obsidian trafficking was also important internally, as major sources were not equally distributed. Some trade in pinenuts for acorns occurred across the Sierra Nevada. In historic times, people sold or traded buckskin gloves and wash and sewing baskets to ranchers and townspeople. An active market in fine basketry developed for the Mono Lake and Owens Valley people from the turn of the century to the 1930s.

Division of Labor. In the precontact period, men were hunters and fishermen, and women, plant food gatherers. Women prepared foods and reared the children, although the latter was also the province of grandparents. Both sexes harvested pinenuts and cooperated in house building. In historic times, men have taken primary responsibility for ranching duties. Wage labor was done about equally by the sexes in early historic times as well as at present.

Land Tenure. Lands were not considered to be private property in aboriginal times, but rather for the use of all Northern Paiute. Subgroups exercised some rights to hunt, fish, and gather in their districts, with people from outside usually required to ask permission of the local group. Usufruct rights occurred, especially in Owens Valley and the central Northern Paiute area. Rights to harvest piñons in certain tracts, and to erect fishing platforms or game traps at certain locations, were included. In Owens Valley, these rights extended to harvesting wild seed tracts, especially those purposefully irrigated. A few people today attempt to maintain piñon rights. Otherwise, land tenure on reservations and colonies is determined by tribal and federal regulations.

Kinship

Kin Groups and Descent.   From birth to death, an individual was surrounded by a network of kin and friends that included the immediate family, a larger group of close relatives (the kindred), the camp group of which the family was a part, associated camp groups in the district, and individuals (kin, non-kin) who resided outside the local area. Of all these units, the most important were the immediate family—at base nuclear, but often including one or more relatives or friends, especially grandparents or single siblings of parents—and the kindred—a bilaterally defined unit that functioned to allow the individual access to subsistence but inside of which marriage was prohibited. Only the former was a residence unit, the latter being likely to include people even outside the local subarea. Today the family and the kindred are still the primary functional units.

Kinship Terminology.   Kinship terminology is of the Eskimo type, for those who are still able to recall the native forms.

Marriage and Family

Marriage.   Prohibitions against marriage of any kinsperson, no matter how distant, were formerly the reported norm. Parents attempted to arrange suitable matches, using communal hunts and festivals as opportunities for children to meet. Token gifts were exchanged by the two sets of parents, but little by way of ceremony occurred. Most marriages were initially monogamous, but later a man might take another wife, often his first wife's younger sister. Fraternal polyandry was reported, but thought to have been rare. Initial matrilocal residence as a type of bride-service was common. Marriages were intended to be permanent unions, but little onus attached to either party if divorce occurred. Children always had a place with either side.

Domestic Unit.   The nuclear to small extended family was formerly the norm and remains so today. Most families can and do incorporate relatives and friends, but the arrangement is more temporary than in former times.

Inheritance.   Given bilaterality, usufruct rights came from either side of the family. In some areas, however (for example, Owens Valley), a matrilineal preference was reported for the inheritance of piñon trees.

Socialization.   In precontact times, given the subsistence duties of both parents, children often spent a great deal of time with grandparents. Children were considered to be responsible for their own actions from an early age, thus parents and grandparents advised more than sanctioned beyond that point.

Sociopolitical Organization

Social Organization.   In aboriginal times, age conferred the greatest status on individuals. Younger men and women participated about equally in decision making, given that each had important roles in subsistence. Distinctions based on wealth were lacking. Only the shaman was in part supported by the group. Generosity and sharing, as primary values, function even today as leveling mechanisms.

Political Organization.   Prior to contact, political authority was vested in local headmen. These individuals served as advisers, reminding people about proper behavior toward others and often suggesting the subsistence activities for the day. Occasionally such persons were leaders of communal hunts, although headmanship and task leadership might not be coterminous. Headmen tried to get the individual parties involved in disputes to settle their differences on their own, but if that were not possible they rendered decisions. Most decisions were reached through consensus, achieved in discussions with all adults. Modern tribal councils, most organized under the Indian Rights Act, also attempt to govern by consensus. Each operates independently on its own reservation or colony.

Social Control.   Shame and ridicule by relatives and peers were effective means to bring about conformity.

Conflict.   Precontact conflicts were primarily with tribes to the west and north, but were characterized by raids and skirmishes rather than large-scale battles. Postcontact relationships with Whites were likewise sometimes hostile, although this varied from area to area. In the North, and as far south as central Nevada, small groups of mounted raiders operated from roughly the 1850s to the mid-1870s. A few of the leaders of these groups, such as Winnemucca, Ocheo, Egan, and others, achieved a degree of prominence for their prowess in warfare. In Owens Valley, with displacement of the people from rich irrigated wild seed lands by ranchers, open conflict flared from 1861 to 1863. Troops finally waged a scorched earth policy against the people, and in 1863, nine hundred prisoners were marched to Fort Tejon in California's Central Valley. After three years they were returned to their own valley to eke out a living as best they could. Raiding groups in the North were induced to settle on reserved lands, especially at McDermitt, Nevada, and Surprise Valley, California. After that time, individuals and groups had to adjust to more subtle types of conflict over land, water, access to jobs, and the exercise of personal rights. In recent years, several groups have been engaged in lengthy court battles over land and water.

Religion and Expressive Culture

Religious Beliefs.   The Northern Paiute believed that power (*puha*) could reside in any natural object and that it habitually resided in natural phenomena such as the sun, moon, thunder, clouds, stars, and wind. Any individual could seek power for purposes such as hunting and gambling, but only shamans possessed enough to call on it to do good for others. Supernatural beings could include any or all of those who acted in myths and tales. Not all modern representatives of animal species were necessarily supernaturals, but occasionally such a special animal was encountered. Anthropomorphic beings, such as water babies, dwarfs, and the "bone crusher," could also be encountered in the real world. Water babies, in particular, were very powerful and often feared by those other than a shaman who might acquire their power. Prayers were addressed each morning to the sun for a successful day. Ghosts could remain in this world and plague the living, but specific ghosts could also be sources of power for the shaman. Personal relationships with power sources were private matters. Leaders of communal hunts usually had power—for antelope, always. A rich body of myth and legend, the former involving the activities of animal ancestors, set values and taught a moral and ethical code. Today, people remember parts of these old narratives and often mix them with various Christian beliefs. The Native American Church is active in a few areas, as are the more recent Sweat Lodge and Sun Dance movements.

Religious Practitioners. The shaman was the primary person who put his power to use to benefit others, particularly for healing. Shamans could be either men or women. They acquired their first power unsought, usually in a dream. After that time, and an apprenticeship under a practicing shaman, they might acquire other powers either unsought or courted. Powers were highly specific, and the instructions they gave regarding food taboos and other activities had to be followed to the letter or the power would be withdrawn.

Ceremonies. Group approaches to the supernatural were limited. In all areas dances and prayers were offered prior to communal food-getting efforts. Most of these activities were directed by specialists. All times of group prayer and dancing were also times for merriment. Night dances were followed by gambling, foot races, and other forms of secular entertainment.

Arts. Oral tradition was a major area for the development of personal skill and expression. Gifted narrators were recognized among all groups, and people would spend many winter evenings listening to their performances. Singers were also greatly respected. Some songs, especially round dance songs, have lovely imagery in their texts.

Medicine. The primary function of shamans was the curing of serious illness, which was accomplished in ceremonies held at night in the home of the patient with relatives and friends attending. The shaman went into a trance and attempted to find the cause of the illness and then a prescription for a cure. Since 1900, the number of shamans has been declining, and today very few are active, modern Western medicine prevailing. Less serious illness was formerly treated with home remedies made from over one hundred species of plants. Some families still use plants from this repertoire.

Death and Afterlife. At death the person was buried in the hills along with his or her personal possessions. Cremation was reserved for individuals suspected of witchcraft. In Owens Valley and the extreme southern portion of the Northern Paiute area, the Mourning Ceremony of southern California tribes has been practiced since about 1900. This is accompanied by stylized singing and the burning of the personal property of the deceased. In all areas, funerals remain the most important events of the life cycle.

Bibliography

Fowler, Catherine S., and Sven Liljeblad (1986). "The Northern Paiute." In *Handbook of North American Indians.* Vol. 11, *Great Basin,* edited by Warren L. d'Azevedo, 435-465. Washington, D.C.: Smithsonian Institution.

Kelley, Isabel T. (1932). *Ethnography of the Surprise Valley Paiute.* University of California Publications in American Archaeology and Ethnology 31(3), 67-210. Berkeley.

Liljeblad, Sven, and Catherine S. Fowler (1986). "The Owens Valley Paiute." In *Handbook of North American Indians.* Vol. 11, *Great Basin,* edited by Warren L. d'Azevedo, 412-434. Washington, D.C.: Smithsonian Institution.

Steward, Julian (1933). *Ethnography of the Owens Valley Paiute.* University of California Publications in American Archaeology and Ethnology 33(3), 233-350. Berkeley.

Stewart, Omer C. (1941). *Culture Element Distributions, XIV: Northern Paiute.* University of California Anthropological Records 4(3), 361-446. Berkeley.

CATHERINE S. FOWLER

Northern Shoshone and Bannock

ETHNONYMS: Northern Shoshoni, Ponasht, Snake

Orientation

Identification. The Northern Shoshone (Nimi, Wihinaitti) and Bannock (Banakwut, Nimi, Pan'akwati, Pannaitti) lived in an area roughly within the present boundaries of the state of Idaho, south of the Salmon River, but at times extending slightly into northern Utah. The names do not describe discrete sociopolitical groups, but serve to separate the Shoshonean-speaking groups in this area from those in western Wyoming (Eastern Shoshone) and those in Nevada and Utah (Western Shoshone and Northern Paiute). The Northern Shoshone are distinguished from the Western Shoshone mainly in having had many horses in late aboriginal times, and from the Eastern Shoshone in having had an economy based more on salmon fishing than on bison hunting. The Bannock are distinct from the Northern Shoshone in being Northern Paiute speakers. But they lived with the Northern Shoshone in Idaho for a long period and are similar to them culturally, having adopted the horse and participated with them in organized bison hunts. There are, however, no really clear cultural boundaries between all of these groups. The Northern Shoshone have been divided into six local groupings that are not political divisions. The subgroups are Agaideka (Agaidüka), "Salmon Eaters"; Kammedeka (Kamadüka), "Eaters of Jackrabbits"; Lemhi, Pohogwe (Bohogue, Fort Hall Shoshone, and Bannock), "People of Sagebrush Butte"; Tukudeka, (Tukadüka), "Eaters of Mountain Sheep"; and Yahandeka (Yahandüka), "Eaters of Groundhogs." Most of them are included among the Shoshone-Bannock Tribes of the Fort Hall Reservation, Idaho.

Location. The area they live in belongs to the Columbia Plateau physiographic region, having a generally low precipitation of less than fifteen inches a year. There are two major mountain ranges, the Sawtooth and the Bitterroot, plus the Snake River plains, which provided ecological diversity.

Demography. There were 2,542 Indians living on the reservation in 1980, with many more living in the area. It is estimated that there were about 3,900 in 1984.

Linguistic Affiliation. Both the Northern Shoshone and Bannock languages are members of the Numic branch of the Uto-Aztecan language family. The Bannock speak a dialect of Northern Paiute, a Western Numic language; the Northern Shoshone speak a Central Numic dialect related to Eastern Shoshone, Western Shoshone, and Comanche. There is considerable Northern Shoshone–Bannock bilingualism.

History and Cultural Relations

Little is known of these peoples before the early nineteenth century. The horse probably reached the Shoshone in the late seventeenth century, perhaps from the Spanish settlements in the Southwest. With the aid of the horse, they spread as far as the Canadian border of Montana where they met the Blackfoot, who pushed them back to their present area by the mid-eighteenth century. In contrast, relations with the Flathead to the north and the Nez Percé to the northwest were generally friendly and peaceful, although relations with the latter may not always have been so. They were also on friendly terms with their linguistic relatives, the Western Shoshone to the south and the Northern Paiute to the west. Fur trappers and traders came into their territory in the early nineteenth century, reaching Lake Pend Oreille in the first decade. American expeditions and traders from the time of Lewis and Clark (1803–1804) moved westward from the Missouri River, with various trading posts being established in the period 1807–1832, all with fairly negative implications for Shoshone life. The fur trade had collapsed by 1840, and by 1860 the local bison herds had been almost extinguished. White settlers were moving through the area in fairly large numbers, beginning about 1840. Mormons began moving into the southern areas in 1860, followed by other settlers and gold miners, which resulted in several wars.

Treaties with the United States were signed in 1863 and 1864, and the Fort Hall Reservation in southeastern Idaho was established in 1867. The Lemhi Reservation to the north was established in 1875, but was terminated and the inhabitants removed to Fort Hall in 1907. Because of the demands of a subsidiary of the Union Pacific Railroad and the establishment of the city of Pocatello, as well as the Dawes Act of 1887, the lands of the Fort Hall Reservation were much diminished. Day and boarding schools were established in the 1870s and 1880s.

After the Indian Reorganization Act of 1934, the Shoshone and Bannock of the Fort Hall Reservation approved a constitution and by-laws in 1936 and ratified a corporate charter in 1937. The Fort Hall Business Council consists of individuals elected from the reservation to two-year terms. The council has authority over purchases, borrowing, engaging in business, performing contracts, and other normal business procedures. The tribes are actively trying to increase and to buy land for the reservation. Phosphate deposits on the reservation are being mined and a tribal trading post has been established. There is an annual tribal festival held in mid-August, as well as Sun Dances, an all-Indian rodeo, an Indian Day in late September, and other traditional dances throughout the year.

Settlements

Both groups were seminomadic, ranging over fairly large territories in the warmer months, but returning to protected winter quarters. The major foci of population were the upper Snake River valley in the general region surrounding Fort Hall, the Lemhi River valley, the Sawtooth range, the Boise, Payette, and Weiser River valleys, and the valley of the Bruneau River. The Fort Hall and Lemhi peoples originally lived in tipis, first of hide and later built of canvas. Through the rest of the area, the standard summer dwelling was a small conical lodge or tipi made of sagebrush, grass, or woven willow branches. Small versions of these were used as menstrual huts and sweat houses. Today, they live in typical mainstream society wooden houses and bungalows.

Economy

Subsistence and Commercial Activities. Bison were hunted by groups using the Plains Indians' technique of flanking the herds on horses and shooting them with bows and arrows or rifles. The summer was spent collecting wild foods and hunting. The mounted Shoshone of the Boise, Payette, and Weiser rivers in southwestern Idaho depended on the spring and fall salmon runs for most of their subsistence, but sometimes they took part in the Fort Hall bison hunt. The remainder of the Idaho Shoshone population was largely unmounted, did not participate in the bison hunt, were largely peaceful. Antelope were taken by individual hunters and by running them on horses. Elk, mountain sheep, and deer were pursued by individuals or small parties of hunters. Salmon fishing was basic all through the area, and salmon was the principal food source below Shoshone Falls (near Twin Falls in south-central Idaho) and in the western Idaho region. Salmon were speared from platforms in the streams or while wading, or were captured in weirs built across small streams and channels. Sturgeon, suckers, perch, and trout were also caught. Principal vegetables collected included camas bulbs, yampa roots, tobacco-root, and bitterroot, all dug from the ground by women using digging sticks. Some residents south of Bannock Creek, and south of Fort Hall, relied on pine nuts. Chokecherries, service berries, sunflower seeds, and roots, such as prairie turnips, were also collected, often incidental to hunting expeditions. All the groups had horses, introduced from the south and the Plains, with dogs also available. Nowadays, they engage in farming, livestock raising, and other agriculturally related enterprises, and are heavily involved with the mainstream economy.

Industrial Arts. Among the mounted people in the east, who were influenced by Plains Indians, both sexes wore bison robes in the winter and dressed elk skins with the hair removed in the summer. Both men and women at Lemhi added leggings and breechclouts to their dress. Breechclouts and robes of the fur of smaller animals were standard farther west. Moccasins were made of elk, deer, and bison hide, although people often went barefoot. Some crude pottery was made, but baskets, both coiled and woven, were more common and important. They were made watertight by applying pitch on the interiors. Rawhide containers were important among the eastern groups. Among other manufactures were steatite cups, bowls, and pipe bowls; cradle boards of willow sticks and buckskin; and leather snow goggles. They had arrowheads and knives made from chipped obsidian and, in later times, from metal. High-wheeled wooden wagons drawn by horses were a basic mode of transport from the later nineteenth century to modern times.

Trade. Trade was extensive throughout the region, with the Western Shoshone to the south and the Paiute to the west, as well as with the Nez Percé and Flathead to the north. By the 1820s, the fur trade had become important to some groups, particularly the mounted peoples. The Nez Percé joined the Cayuse, the Umatilla, and the Shoshone at an annual trading market on the Weiser River in the far northwest of Shoshone territory, and some mixed villages of Nez Percé and Shoshone have been reported.

Division of Labor. Women took care of leather- and hideworking, house construction, and most of the gathering. Men did the hunting and fishing, took care of the horses, and engaged in warfare.

Land Tenure. Both groups apparently lacked any form of ownership of land or of the resources upon it. But tools, weapons, and other artifacts, as well as foods after they were obtained were considered private property.

Kinship

Kin Groups and Descent. The Shoshone and Bannock had bilateral descent without kindreds or other kin groups. The basic unit of the society was the bilateral family group, composed of four or five nuclear families that maintained relatively close and continuing association.

Kinship Terminology. The Shoshone and Bannock used a Hawaiian type of kinship terminology, with a fairly consistent pattern of terminological merging of the mother's sister with the mother and the father's brother with the father. There was no distinction between cross and parallel cousins, all being addressed by brother and sister terms. The terminology was of the Dakota type on the first ascending generation, and grandparents and grandchildren addressed each other by the same terms, distinguished only by sex.

Marriage and Family

There were no strict rules on postmarital residence; couples could live with the relatives of the husband or wife and occasionally with more distant relatives. Depending on the group, there were tendencies toward matrilocality or bilocality, the latter probably being more common. Marriages were most often monogamous, but polygamy, usually polygyny, was possible. Some informal polyandry has been noted. Sororal polygyny occurred, and the levirate and sororate were common. Divorce was simple, fairly common, and without formal rules. The usual domestic unit was the independent nuclear family. There seems to have been no concept of inheritance.

Sociopolitical Organization

Social Organization. The main feature of their social organization was a looseness and lack of definition of groups. The presence or absence of bands or chieftains depended upon the type of economic pursuit in which the people were engaged. Organization was needed for the bison hunts and for protection from tribal enemies.

Political Organization. The Northern Shoshone and Bannock showed a wide range of types of political organization and grouping from bands to villages to the scattered groups of foot-going families living in the Sawtooth Range and south of the Snake River. The Shoshone and Bannock of the upper Snake River formed into large composite bands of varying composition and leadership. The Shoshone were always the majority, but the chieftaincy was sometimes held by a Bannock. Most of the Fort Hall and Lemhi peoples formed into single groups each fall to hunt bison in the east and returned west for the winter. The large bands split into smaller groups for the spring salmon fishing. Apart from Fort Hall and Lemhi, the population was widely scattered and villages were small, with chieftainship and larger forms of political organization being absent. The power of the chiefs was limited by camp or band councils which existed among the bison hunters. The office of chief was an achieved role and was not firmly institutionalized, and his powers were quite limited. Band organization in the western part of the region was almost nonexistent. At the base of organization were the basic Shoshone characteristics of loose and shifting group association and individual autonomy.

Social Control and Conflict. A few "police" were needed to keep order in the larger bands, but there were no police societies or sodalities. They shared in the warfare practices of the Plains Indians, counting coup and taking the scalps of enemies. They also borrowed the Scalp Dance from the Plains Indians. There was periodic conflict with the Blackfeet, usually at the time of bison hunts. Otherwise, contacts with neighboring tribes were peaceful.

Religion and Expressive Culture

Religious Beliefs. The basis of their religion seems to have been a belief in the effectiveness of dreams and visions. These were used in acquiring the assistance of guardian spirits. They shared a modified version of the vision quest of the Plains Indians for spirits and other manifestations that gave the questor powers and medicines and imposed food and other taboos. They believed in Appi, a creator, but the principal mythological figures were Wolf and Coyote. The benevolent Wolf created people and the solar system, and Coyote was a trickster who brought disorder. Also known were ogres and animal creatures. Nowadays, over half of the tribes belong to a Christian church—Baptist, Episcopal, Mormon, and Roman Catholic—and others belong to the Native American church.

Religious Practitioners. All men were shamans to some degree.

Ceremonies. Most ceremonialism took the form of dances. Ceremonies were held to ensure the return of the salmon and at the actual time of the run. The Round Dance was used to seek blessings, usually in time of adversity.

Medicine. There was a category of medicine men, who specialized in curing. In addition, they possessed much practical knowledge of plant remedies.

Death and Afterlife.   Aboriginally, the dead were wrapped in blankets and deposited in rock crevices. The souls of the dead went to the Land of Wolf and Coyote.

Bibliography

Liljebad, Sven (1972). *The Idaho Indians in Transition, 1805–1960.* Pocatello: Idaho State Museum.

Lowie, Robert H. (1909). *The Northern Shoshone.* American Museum of Natural History, Anthropologial Papers 2(2). New York.

Madsen, Brigham D. (1958). *The Bannock of Idaho.* Caldwell, Idaho: Caxton Printers.

Madsen, Brigham D. (1980). *The Northern Shoshone.* Caldwell, Idaho: Caxton Printers.

Murphy, Robert F., and Yolanda Murphy (1986). "Northern Shoshone and Bannock." In *Handbook of North American Indians.* Vol. 11, *Great Basin,* edited by Warren L. d'Azevedo, 284–307. Washington, D.C.: Smithsonian Institution.

Steward, Julian H. (1938). *Basin-Plateau Aboriginal Sociopolitical Groups.* U.S. Bureau of American Ethnology Bulletin 120. Washington, D.C. Reprint. Salt Lake City: University of Utah Press, 1970.

Ojibwa

ETHNONYMS: Anishinabe, Bungee, Bungi, Chippewa, Mississauga, Northern Ojibwa, Plains Ojibwa, Saulteaux, Southwestern Chippewa, Southeastern Ojibwa

Orientation

Identification.   The Ojibwa are a large American Indian group located in the northern Midwest in the United States and south-central Canada. "Ojibwa" means "puckered up," a reference to the Ojibwa style of moccasin. The Ojibwa name for themselves is "Anishinabe," meaning "human being."

Location.   Aboriginally, the Ojibwa occupied an extensive area north of Lakes Superior and Huron. A geographical expansion beginning in the seventeenth century resulted in a four-part division of the Ojibwa. The four main groups are the Northern Ojibwa, or Saulteaux; the Plains Ojibwa, or Bungee; the Southeastern Ojibwa; and the Southwestern Chippewa. At the end of the eighteenth century the Northern Ojibwa were located on the Canadian Shield north of Lake Superior and south and west of Hudson and James bays; the Plains Ojibwa, in southern Saskatchewan and Manitoba; the Southeastern Ojibwa, on the lower peninsula of Michigan and adjacent areas of Ontario; and the Southwestern Chippewa, in northern Minnesota, extreme northern Wisconsin, and Ontario between Lake Superior and the Manitoba border. The Canadian Shield country is a flat land of meager soil and many lakes and swamps. The country of the Plains Ojibwa is an environment of rolling hills and forests dominated by oak, ash, and whitewood. The homeland of the Southeastern Ojibwa and the Southwestern Chippewa, also a country of rolling hills, includes marshy valleys, upland prairie, rivers and lakes, and forests of maple, birch, poplar, oak, and other deciduous species. Throughout the region, winters are long and cold and summers short and hot.

Demography.   The Ojibwa are one of the largest American Indian groups north of Mexico. In the mid-seventeenth century they numbered at least 35,000, perhaps many more. Today the Ojibwa who are located in Ontario, Manitoba, and Saskatchewan in Canada and Michigan, Wisconsin, Minnesota, North Dakota, Montana, and Oklahoma in the United States, number about 160,000; the majority of them live in the Canadian provinces.

Linguistic Affiliation.   The Ojibwa languages are classified in the Algonkian language family.

History and Cultural Relations

Contact with Europeans was initiated in the early 1600s, and by the end of the century the Ojibwa were deeply involved in the fur trade and heavily dependent on European trade goods. As a result, the Ojibwa underwent a major geographical expansion that by the end of the eighteenth century had resulted in the four-part division of the tribe. Their migration in some cases led to significant modifications in their aboriginal hunting, fishing, and gathering subsistence pattern. These modifications were most evident among the Northern Ojibwa, who borrowed extensively from the Cree and adopted a subarctic culture pattern, and the Plains Ojibwa, who took up many elements of the Plains Indian way of life. During the first half of the nineteenth century the Southeastern Ojibwa were forced by White demands for farmland to cede their territory for reservation status. Similarly, in the mid-nineteenth century the Southwestern Chippewa and in the late nineteenth and early twentieth centuries the Plains Ojibwa and the Northern Ojibwa were resettled on reservations and reserves in the United States and Canada. Since the 1950s a major theme of Ojibwa cultural change has been migration off the reservations to urban centers where the people have become integrated into the Canadian and American work forces. The 1960s, however, saw a resurgence of native consciousness among the Ojibwa on many of the reservations in the United States and Canada, as the people saw their traditional culture eroding under the impact of government education programs, urban migration, and other acculturative forces.

Aboriginally and in the early historic period the Ojibwa were closely tied to the Huron to their south. After the Huron were defeated by the Iroquois in 1649–1650 in their contest for control of the western fur trade, the Ojibwa came under strong pressure from the Iroquois. By the end of the seventeenth century, however, some Ojibwa were pushing southeastward, sometimes by force, at the expense of the Iroquois. Those who moved into the lower peninsula of Michigan became closely allied with the Ottawa and Potawatomi. During the eighteenth century Ojibwa, who had obtained European firearms from French traders, expanded to the southwest where they had a strategic military advantage over their neighbors and displaced the Dakota, Cheyenne, Hidatsa, and other groups from their traditional homelands. Intermittent and sometimes costly warfare between the Southwestern Ojibwa and the Dakota persisted for more than a century until ended by U.S. government–enforced treaties in the 1850s. The Northern Ojibwa who moved onto the Canadian Shield became closely associated with the Cree peoples to their north and west. With the acquisition of the horse, the westernmost of the Ojibwa had by 1830 evolved a pattern of seasonal migration to the open plains and adopted many elements of the Plains Indian way of life, including the preoccupation with bison hunting, the Sun Dance, and decorative tailored skin clothing.

Settlements

The prehistoric and early historic Ojibwa maintained semipermanent villages for summer use and temporary camps during the remainder of the year, as they moved to exploit fish, game, and wild plant resources. This pattern of seasonal settlement and movement persisted to some extent among all the Ojibwa groups, but especially so among the nineteenth-century Southeastern Ojibwa and Southwestern Chippewa, who in their seasonal round returned each summer to permanent village bases to plant gardens. The typical dwelling of the early Southeastern Ojibwa was the traditional conical hide-covered lodge, but as they adopted farming and a more settled way of life, log cabins and wood frame houses came into widespread use. Among the Southwestern Chippewa the most common dwelling was a dome-shaped wigwam covered with birchbark and cattail matting. The Northern Ojibwa spent much of their year moving in dispersed groups in search of subsistence, but during the summer they congregated at fishing sites in close proximity to trading posts, where they procured their supplies for the coming year. Their basic dwelling was a conical or ridge pole lodge covered with birch and birchbark. A high degree of mobility also characterized the Plains Ojibwa, who adopted bison-skin tipis and a pattern of seasonal movement involving concentration on the open plains in the summer to harvest the bison herds.

Economy

Subsistence and Commercial Activities. In the summer when they gathered in their villages, the aboriginal and early historic Ojibwa fished, collected wild nuts and berries, and planted small gardens of maize, beans, squash, and pumpkins. In some areas wild rice was harvested in the fall. In the winter the bands dispersed and moved to hunting grounds where they subsisted on deer, moose, bear, and a variety of small game. In the spring maple sap was gathered and boiled to produce maple syrup. By the late 1600s, the Ojibwa were heavily involved in the exchange of mink, muskrat, beaver, and other animal pelts for European trade goods. Among the Southeastern Ojibwa and the Southwestern Chippewa this subsistence pattern persisted, but with a greater emphasis on wild rice harvesting among the latter and more intensive farming among the former. Among the Plains Ojibwa bison and bison hunting became the basis of life. The Northern Ojibwa fished, gathered wild foods, and hunted game and waterfowl, but were beyond the environmental range of wild rice and the sugar maple, and so the exploitation of those resources was not part of their subsistence pattern.

Industrial Arts. Birchbark was a multipurpose resource for most of the Ojibwa, providing the raw material for canoes, lodge coverings, and storage and cooking containers. Various types of wood were used for snowshoes, canoe frames, lacrosse racquets, bows and arrows, bowls, ladles, flutes, drums, and fishing lures. Among the Plains Ojibwa bison were the principal source of raw materials for clothing, shelter, and tools.

Trade. Aboriginally, furs and maple sugar were traded to the Huron for maize and tobacco. After becoming involved in the European fur trade Ojibwa traders made annual treks to Quebec and later to Montreal to trade furs for blankets, firearms, liquor, tools, kettles, and clothing. As trading posts were established by the French at Detroit and other closer points the distance of the trading expeditions was gradually reduced. Fur trapping and trading remained an important source of income among the Northern Ojibwa until the mid-twentieth century.

Division of Labor. Men and women shared responsibility for numerous economic activities, such as fishing and trapping, and sometimes cooperated in the same tasks, such as canoe construction. Men's labor focused on hunting, trapping, and trading, and women's labor was most concerned with processing hides, making clothes, preparing food, caring for children, and collecting plant foods and firewood.

Land Tenure. With the development of the European fur trade, bands tended to exploit a particular hunting and trapping territory. Gradually, these vaguely defined areas evolved into territories in which hunting and trapping groups had exclusive rights over fur resources.

Kinship

Kin Groups and Descent. Except for the Northern Ojibwa, Ojibwa society was divided into numerous exogamous totemic clans. Among the nineteenth-century Southwestern Chippewa in Minnesota there were twenty-three such clans, groups of which were linked and divided into five phratries. Clan membership was reckoned patrilineally.

Kinship Terminology. Ojibwa kinship terminology followed the Iroquois pattern. Parallel cousins were merged terminologically with siblings and cross cousins were classed separately. Parallel aunts and uncles were merged terminologically by sex with mother and father and cross aunts and uncles were classed separately.

Marriage and Family

Marriage. Marriages were arranged by parents or guardians and involved little formal ceremony. Cross-cousin marriage was practiced, but not preferred. Polygyny was possible, but most marriages were monogamous. Divorce was permitted and a simple matter to effect for either husband or wife. Remarriage was permitted after divorce and after the death of a spouse following a mourning period of one year.

Domestic Unit. Traditionally, the basic social unit was the extended family. Over time, however, it has given way to the nuclear family.

Inheritance. No single principle of inheritance appears to have prevailed among the Ojibwa. Instead, it seems to have been bilateral and a matter of residence and affection.

Socialization. Children were raised in a permissive fashion and rarely reprimanded or punished physically. The most important phase of a boy's life occurred at puberty when he sought a guardian spirit through a vision quest. The quest involved several days (ideally four) of isolation, fasting, prayer, and dreaming undertaken to contact a guardian spirit to provide aid and protection. Through frequent offerings of food and tobacco the boy could maintain rapport with his guardian spirit and retain its aid and protection throughout his life. At the time of first menstruation the girl was isolated, but not required to undergo a vision quest. If, however, she did receive a vision during her isolation, it was regarded as a special blessing. Among the Plains Ojibwa girls visited by a spirit in this way were believed to possess curing powers.

Sociopolitical Organization

Social Organization. In aboriginal and early historic times the Ojibwa were divided into small autonomous bands of interrelated families. Band organization was loose and flexible, and social relations, apart from divisions along the lines of age and sex, were egalitarian. With involvement in the European fur trade, band organization was modified. Among eighteenth-century Southeastern Ojibwa and Southwestern Chippewa, bands numbered several hundred people; among the Northern Ojibwa, bands were smaller, with about fifty to seventy-five members. Plains Ojibwa bands were loose, shifting units.

Political Organization. Each Ojibwa band was headed by a chief whose position was earned on the basis of hunting ability, personal appeal, and religious knowledge, but was also dependent on kinship connections. Shamans were respected and feared individuals who sometimes also functioned as band leaders. Among the eighteenth-century Southeastern Ojibwa, bands were headed by chiefs, but as farming and a more permanent settlement pattern were adopted local political organization evolved to include an elected chief, assistant chiefs, and a local council. This form of political organization was in part a government-imposed system. Among the Northern Ojibwa band leadership was supplied by a senior male whose kin group formed the basis of the band's membership. In addition, he was usually also a skilled trader. Among the Plains Ojibwa each band had several chiefs, one of whom was recognized as the head chief. The head chief usually inherited his position, held it for life, and was assisted by councillors elected by the adult male members of the band. Secondary chiefs among the Plains Ojibwa achieved their position by virtue of their deeds in war, skills in hunting, generosity, and leadership ability.

Social Control. Censure by means of ridicule and ostracism was the primary mechanism of social control. In addition, among some Ojibwa groups mutilation and execution were punishments for certain offenses. Among the Plains Ojibwa a wife found to have committed adultery could be mutilated or killed by her husband, and among the Southeastern Ojibwa mutilation was the prescribed punishment for violating mourning taboos. Chiefs among Plains Ojibwa sometimes mediated serious disputes, and when the people gathered on the open plains, camp police, or *okitsita*, composed of war heroes, maintained peace and order.

Conflict. Overt face-to-face hostility was rare in Ojibwa society. However, alcohol consumption seems to have increased the frequency and intensity of interpersonal conflict and physical violence. The Ojibwa believed sorcery to be the cause of individual misfortune and often employed sorcery in retaliation against their enemies. Suspicion of sorcery was a cause of conflict and could result in long-lasting feuds between families. Conflict also stemmed from encroachments on hunting and trapping territories.

Religion and Expressive Culture

Religious Beliefs. For the Ojibwa the supernatural world held a multitude of spiritual beings and forces. Some of these beings and forces—Sun, Moon, Four Winds, Thunder, and Lightning—were benign, but others—ghosts, witches, and Windigo, a supernatural cannibalistic giant—were malevolent and feared. Presiding over all other spirits was Kiccimanito, or Great Spirit, although this belief may have been a product of European influence. Ojibwa religion was very much an individual affair and centered on the belief in power received from spirits during dreams and visions. For this reason, dreams and visions were accorded great significance and much effort was given to their interpretation. The power obtained through them could be used to manipulate the natural and supernatural environments and employed for either good or evil purposes. Missionization by the Anglican and Roman Catholic churches began during the nineteenth century, but conversion and Christian influence were limited prior to the twentieth century. In the mid-twentieth century the religious orientation of many Ojibwa was a mixture of Christian and traditional native elements.

Religious Practitioners. In their vision quests, some young men received more spiritual power than others, and it was they who in later life became shamans. Several different types of shamans existed, the type being determined by the sort of spiritual power received.

Ceremonies. The most important religious ceremony for the Southeastern Ojibwa and the Southwestern Chippewa was the Midewiwin, or Medicine Dance, of the Medicine Lodge Society. The Midewiwin ceremony was held semiannually (in the late spring and early fall among the nineteenth-century Wisconsin Chippewa) and lasted for several days. The Northern Ojibwa did not practice the Midewiwin ceremony, although the Plains Ojibwa did. Among the latter, however, it was exceeded in importance by the Sun Dance, performed annually in mid-June in order to bring rain, good health, and good fortune.

Arts. Ojibwa music was individualistic. Musical instruments included tambourines, water drums, rattles, and flutes. Songs were derived from dreams and had magical purposes, such as ensuring success in hunting and other economic activities, invoking guardian spirits, and curing sickness. Among the Southwestern Chippewa porcupine quill work employing a floral motif was an important technique in the decoration of buckskin clothing and leather bags. After European contact glass beads replaced quills in decorative applications, although the floral motif was maintained.

Medicine. Disease and illness were thought to be caused by sorcery or as retribution for improper conduct toward the supernatural or some social transgression. Curing was performed by members of the Midewiwin, or Medicine Lodge Society, into which both men and women were inducted after instruction by Mide priests, payment of fees, and formal initiation. Shamans, with their powers derived from dreams and visions, were curers of sickness, but so, too, were others knowledgeable in the use of medicinal plants.

Death and Afterlife. Upon death the corpse was washed, groomed, dressed in fine clothing, and wrapped in birchbark before burial in a shallow grave. Following death, the soul of the deceased was believed to journey westward for four days to an afterlife in the sky. Among the Southwestern Chippewa the deceased was also painted prior to burial and lay in state in a wigwam. The funeral ceremony was attended by friends and relatives and was conducted by a Mide priest, who talked to the deceased and offered tobacco to the spirits. After the ceremony was concluded the body was removed through a hole in the west side of the wigwam to the grave site, where it was buried along with personal possessions. The door of the wigwam was not used when removing the deceased for fear that the departed soul would return through the door. In later times a long, low, gabled plank house was constructed over the grave. The Plains Ojibwa also employed the gabled grave house and left offerings of food and water at the grave house for four days after burial for the soul's subsistence on its journey to the afterlife.

Bibliography

Barnouw, Victor (1977). _Wisconsin Chippewa Myths and Tales and Their Relation to Chippewa Life._ Madison: University of Wisconsin Press.

Buffalohead, Patricia (1986). "Farmers, Warriors, Traders: A Fresh Look at Ojibway Women." In _The American Indian_, edited by Roger L. Nichols, 28–38. 3rd ed. New York: Alfred A. Knopf.

Densmore, Frances (1979). _Chippewa Customs._ St. Paul: Minnesota Historical Society. Originally published, 1929.

Howard, James H. (1965). _The Plains Ojibwa or Bungi: Hunters and Warriors of the Northern Prairie, with Special Reference to the Turtle Mountain Band._ University of South Dakota, South Dakota Museum, Anthropological Papers, no. 1. Vermillion, S.D.

Ritzenthaler, Robert E. (1978). "Southwestern Chippewa." In _Handbook of North American Indians._ Vol. 15, _Northeast_, edited by Bruce G. Trigger, 743–759. Washington, D.C.: Smithsonian Institution.

Rogers, Edward S. (1978). "Southeastern Ojibwa." In _Handbook of North American Indians._ Vol. 15, _Northeast_, edited by Bruce G. Trigger, 760–771. Washington, D.C.: Smithsonian Institution.

Rogers, Edward S., and J. Garth Taylor (1981). "Northern Ojibwa." In _Handbook of North American Indians._ Vol. 6, _Subarctic_, edited by June Helm, 231–243. Washington, D.C.: Smithsonian Institution.

GERALD F. REID

Okanagon

ETHNONYMS: Isonkuaíli, Okinagan, Okinaken

The Okanagon (Isonkuaíli), including the Northern Okanagon and the Sinkaietk (Southern Okanagon, Lower Okanagon), live along the Okanagan River from its confluence with the Columbia River in north-central Washington to the Okanagan Lake region of south-central British Columbia. They speak an Interior Salish language and today number about twenty-one hundred. Their history differs little from that of neighboring groups such as the Thompson except that their traditional territory was on both sides of what became the boundary between the United States and Canada. Over the last two centuries, beginning with their acquisition of the horse, the Okanagon have slowly moved north and have displaced the Shuswap who once hunted in the environs of Okanagan Lake and the Stuwik and Thompson from the Similkameen Valley. The traditional culture was gravely affected by the invasion of gold miners and settlers in the gold rush of 1858 and by resulting smallpox epidemics. The Sinkaietk are now mainly settled on the Colville Reservation in Washington, and the remainder of the Okanagon are on several reserves in British Columbia.

Prior to being placed on the reservations, the Okanagon

were divided into bands, each of which had a civil chief, usually hereditary, and one or more war chiefs, with power vested in a council of mature men. Like other Plateau groups, the Okanagon relied on salmon as the basis of subsistence; the fish were caught in traps with dip nets and spears, in weirs and traps, and by other methods. Game animals were of secondary importance as a source of food, with deer, elk, and sometimes bison hunted. Camas bulbs and bitterroot, fruits such as chokecherries, huckleberries, and serviceberries, nuts, and other plant foods were gathered by women. Like other groups in the region, they were seminomadic, following food sources as they became available. During the summer they used portable, conical dwellings covered by mats and later by skins or canvas. Winter dwellings were semisubterranean earthlodges.

Dome-shaped sweatlodges were used by both sexes for purification, seclusion, and the quest for guardian spirits. The material culture included bark canoes, snowshoes, double-curved bows, cedar bark and spruce baskets, and goat wool blankets. The traditional religion was animistic, centered around spirits residing in natural objects, animals, plants, and clouds. Guardian spirits were important as, among other things, a source of power for shamans to use to cure the sick. Important ceremonies included the First Fruit Festival, the Sun Dance, and other dances.

Bibliography

Cline, Walter, et al. (1938). *The Sinkaietk or Southern Okanagon of Washington.* Edited by Leslie Spier. General Series in Anthropology no. 6. Menasha, Wisc.

Teit, James A. (1930). *The Salishan Tribes of the Western Plateaus.* U.S. Bureau of American Ethnology, 45th Annual Report (1927–1928), 198–294. Washington, D.C.

Turner, Nancy J., et al. (1977). *The Ethnobotany of the Okanagan Indians of British Columbia and Washington State.* Victoria: British Columbia Language Project.

Old Believers

ETHNONYMS: Old Ritualists, Raskol'niks

Orientation

Identification.　Old Believers are a religious group of people who pattern their worship and way of life on the Old Rite of the Russian Orthodox church. The vast majority are ethnic Russian. In North America, there are two independent groups of Old Believers: a "priestless" group (*Bexpopovtsy*) centered in the eastern part of the United States, and a "chapel" group (*Chasovanniye*) in the western United States, with kin groups of the latter also in Canada and Alaska. The two groups tend to be mutually exclusive, which stems from the particular characteristic of Old Believers. Even at its inception in the seventeenth century, Old Believerism was not,

and indeed has never been, a coordinated movement or a cohesive, consolidated religion, although all advocates observe the same religious rite. Instead, the term *Old Believerism* refers to large numbers of Russian peasants and many of their village priests who, on a person-to-person and family-to-family basis, refuse to conform to the church reforms of the mid-seventeenth century. Characteristically, various groups agree on doctrinal decisions in order to cope with their existing realities. The variations in doctrinal practices ("agreements") give rise to differing branches of Old Believers. Often groups of differing agreements do not consider themselves "in union," which is to say they do not recognize the doctrinal validity of each other. This article refers mostly to the Chasovanniye, Old Believers in the western United States, inasmuch as they are recent immigrants to North America and more closely portray the original ethic of Old Believers.

Location and Demography.　The "priestless" group that settled in the area of Erie, Pennsylvania, arrived first in North America around 1913. They number approximately fifteen hundred. In 1964, quite independently, "chapel" groups of Old Believers settled in Oregon. Originally three thousand, they now have grown to some five thousand. Several families of the Oregon group moved on to the Kenai Peninsula of Alaska in 1969 to establish a more remote village. There are now a number of small villages in that area, with an overall population of some seven hundred. Several years later, another group of families established a village near Edmonton, Alberta, Canada. The population there is about three hundred. In addition, there are families and small groups of families affiliated with one or the other of the above groups who live separately but maintain contact on principal religious holidays.

Linguistic Affiliation.　Old Believers speak a fairly standard Russian, a Slavic Indo-European language. Their religious services are read in Church Slavonic, an early version of Russian, but differing to the extent that special training for the young is required in order to master the orthography as well as differences in pronunciation and some word usage. With the extended residency in North America, however, there has been a tendency among the Oregon group to use English more and more in everyday conversation. In Pennsylvania, conversion to English is complete; services are, for the most part, in English.

History and Cultural Relations

The historical event that gave rise to the Old Believers is known in Russian history as the Great Schism, or *Raskol*. At root in the schism was the introduction of church reforms during the period 1651–1667. The patriarch of the Russian Orthodox church, Patriarch Nikon, assumed the responsibility for revising the church books in use at the time. The reforms transcended the written word, for Nikon extended the reforms to include matters of the service ritual. Large segments of the populace, deeply offended by being told they must change aspects of their traditional ritual, rebelled and remained faithful to the Old Rite. Of the items reformed, one in particular became an identifying symbol of Old Believers, namely, crossing oneself with two fingers instead of the reform-mandated three fingers. Peasant attitudes were strong in opposition to other issues of the reforms as well.

This quickly led to social strife that was so serious that Tsar Alexei exiled Nikon. Nonetheless, in one of history's ironic twists, the tsar approved the reforms. Refusal to accept the reforms became a violation not only of church law but also of civil law. Those refusing to adopt the reforms were considered separatists (_raskolniki_). Priests who refused were arrested and often executed. The Old Ritual became synonymously referred to as the Old Belief. Hence, adherents called themselves and became known as Old Ritualists or Old Believers, and the reformers called them raskolniki.

Old Believers, fleeing persecution, established themselves in remote areas, and they still tend to eschew contact with surrounding populations. After the communist revolution in Russia, many escaped over the border into China where they settled in remote areas of Manchuria and Sinkiang. Some years after the communist revolution in China, Old Believers were able to escape to, or received permission to exit to, Hong Kong. The vast majority went on to South America, principally Brazil. After four discouraging years of poor agricultural conditions, many were able to secure voluntary passage to the United States and eventually settled in an ever-growing community of Old Believers located in Oregon. Here they were joined by another recent immigrant group of Old Believers who had been residents in Turkey and Romania for some two hundred years.

Settlements

Old Believers prefer to build a typical Russian village, with homes along each side of a long street and a prayer hall in the center of the village. Villages in Alaska and Canada, and one location in Oregon, are of this type. But for the most part, Old Believers in Oregon have purchased farms and other real estate in towns. They gather in several prayer halls for worship and meetings. Composition of congregations reflect the different points of origin of Old Believers before they came to North America.

Economy

Subsistence and Commercial Activities. Old Believers are principally oriented toward agriculture but are also interested in marketable activities to earn money to buy materials, needles, and other essentials, now including homes and automobiles. The commercial activities vary widely from area to area. While living in China, groups of Old Believers learned how to catch live tigers for zoos. They also hunted deer and sold the horns to the Chinese. These activities alternated with farming. In Oregon, the farms are devoted to the commercial growing of berries, fruits, and nuts. Individual farms also keep beehives and cattle for their own use. During the off-season, they form teams of workers to do preindustrial thinning in the woods. Others take jobs in furniture factories, men serving as carpenters and the women applying their sewing skills. When they found that factory work paid well, they decided to keep their jobs while continuing to operate their farms full time as well. In Alaska, Old Believers learned the trades of fishing and boat building and in a few years began building boats for themselves and others. Their off-time is spent in maintenance of equipment, some farming, and hunt-

ing. Old Believers are normally diligent and hard-working folk. All members of the family assist in the domestic chores as well as gathering the harvest.

Industrial Arts. Many people engage in part-time craft work, either sewing or carpentry, as stated above.

Trade. Old Believers prefer to be self-sufficient in terms of food products and domestic items, but during scarcities, they buy fruits and vegetables in stores. As the traditional ways give way to convenience, more and more items are bought from stores, and they are not reluctant to acquire technological items that make work lighter and more efficient. The communities in Oregon, Canada, and Alaska trade among themselves, sending berries and nuts north to Alaska and fish and caviar to Oregon. Also, the white honey produced in Canada is highly prized in the other locations.

Division of Labor. Labor is divided in accordance with traditional patriarchal family rules, with domestic tasks done by women. They prepare all meals, keeping track of the church calendar to ensure that fasting is observed. They also produce, through skills in sewing and embroidery, much, if not all, of the clothing for the family and decorations for the home. Girls are encouraged to begin sewing and weaving while young, in order to accumulate a trunkful of decorations and presents for their wedding dowry. Older children look after the younger. Women also do many of the chores on the farm like milking and feeding cattle. The men farm, build, and work outside the home. Young boys usually accompany the older men to learn what is to be done.

Land Tenure. Each family strives to own its own home or farm. In several of the remote settlements in China and Brazil, the land was free. On this land they built their homes and considered it their own. Today, kin groups often pool money to assist a family in purchasing a home or farm in order to become self-sufficient.

Kinship

Kin Groups and Descent. The family forms the basic unit, with kin relations of the extended family an important adjunct. Kinship is traced through the male family name, with a version of the father's name used as the middle name of all children. In accordance with their church writings, people closer than eight steps of kinship are not permitted to marry. Since few records are kept, a young couple deciding to marry must seek out elder members of their families to determine if the proper distance exists. The family of a godparent is also considered kin, hence ineligible for marriage. Therefore, Old Believers assign actual kin, often brothers or sisters, to be the godparents of the young. Living memory of the ancestors usually extends back at least three generations.

Kinship Terminology. Since the extended kin of the family are important in work teams and cooperative efforts, the kinship terminology is specific and intricate. One set of terms is used for consanguineal kin, and another set for all inmarrying members. The latter also differs depending on whether the relative by marriage is male or female.

Marriage and Family

Marriage. Marriage in the Russian Orthodox Old Rite is meant to be permanent. The age at marriage has traditionally been seventeen or eighteen, with males usually a year or two older than the females. But in an effort to preserve their traditional ways in a modern setting and to protect the young from becoming attracted to an outsider, the adults have tended to have the young drop out of school after learning the basic educational skills of reading, writing, and figuring. They are often encouraged to marry early, at fourteen to sixteen. The competition for eligible brides in a kin-restricted environment also encourages early marriage. Confronting the young with the adult responsibilities of marriage had the result at first of keeping them traditionally oriented in the faith for the blessing of their marriage and the baptism of their children. Initially effective, it later became a factor in a rise in divorce, a phenomenon for which there is no ready answer in a patriarchal and traditionally religious society. There has been a subsequent effort to discourage early marriage and encourage instead educational achievement in school. Newlyweds remain in the home of the groom's parents until a child arrives. The new family then builds its own home on the father's land or seeks to buy a home elsewhere.

Domestic Unit.   Each family member shares in the domestic operation of the family and usually contributes money earned from outside work, as long as they are active members of the household. It is common for kin to assist each other within the extended family.

Inheritance.   Land is divided among the males of the family as they acquire families of their own. The youngest male characteristically stays in the parental home, takes care of the aging parents, and inherits the parental home with remaining land. Females of the family may receive livestock, beehives, and so on, but usually not land. In contemporary times, money has become an acceptable form of inheritance or gift.

Socialization.   Emphasis is placed on domestic activities, skills, and respect for work ("It is better to work for free than to sit idle for free"). By their early teens, girls are prepared to cook, sew, and rear children, and boys are skilled with tools and machinery. All can read Church Slavonic. Discipline is a domestic and religiously respected virtue. It is authoritatively maintained by denial and punishment of improper behavior. Good behavior is evidenced by proper activities and humility. Television and radios are discouraged. The young, especially males, are allowed some discreet deviations in the larger society before marriage. But once married, they must assume the traditional way of life.

Sociopolitical Organization

Social Organization.   While the Old Believers are scrupulous in paying taxes and strive to obey laws, they are not interested in becoming involved in local or regional affairs. Many seek U.S. citizenship out of a sense of respect and a desire to belong. Citizenship also allows them easier travel to overseas kin and the ability to register commercial equipment, such as fishing boats. Children attend public school but rarely finish. Only a few have chosen to go on to higher education.

Political Organization.   The congregation of the prayer hall or church remains the central focus of community organization. The lay leader (*nastavnik* or *nastoiatel'*) and his assistants are chosen by unanimous consent of the congregation. Leaders from all the congregations counsel on larger questions that affect the overall Old Believer community.

Social Control.   Improper social behavior automatically violates one religious sanction or another. The violator is "separated" from the congregation and must ask forgiveness to return. This entails a penance and a forty-day period of purification to rejoin "in union." A person not in union is prohibited from eating or praying with those in union. Unrepentant or serious violators can be excommunicated. At death, those not in union are buried in the Old Believers cemetery separately from those in union. In recent cases where the religious sanctions were slow or ineffective, individuals turned to the agencies of the host society for more immediate help.

Religion and Expressive Culture

Religious Beliefs.   An Old Believer considers Eastern Orthodox Christianity as expressed in the enculturated Russian Old Rite to be the true religion. It is a solemn obligation for a man and his family to preserve the faith as they await the end of the earth. Those who practice other religions, other rites, or other versions of the Old Rite must be avoided as ritually unclean. One cannot eat or drink from the same bowl or cup with unclean outsiders or pray with them. Services approximate the Orthodox monastic schedule. The faithful abstain from all animal products, including milk and eggs, usually every Wednesday and Friday and during long fasts throughout the year before the holidays of Christmas, Easter, Peter and Paul, and the Dormition of the Holy Mother. No celebrations or entertainments are permitted during fasting periods. Old Believers shun tobacco and may not drink tea, coffee, or any hard liquor. Instead, they make their own *braga,* either from bread or from fruit and berries. Men wear their hair shorn, but their beards untrimmed. Women do not cut their hair, and after marriage, they bind and cover it. Many of the Oregon kin groups prefer to wear the old-style Russian clothing: tunic shirt for men and shirt with *sarafan* jumper for women, both with a mandatory woven belt. Men don black prayer robes for services.

Ceremonies.   The Orthodox church calendar requires frequent holidays, some major, some minor. These are celebrated at early morning services (from 2 to 8 A.M.). Later in the afternoon of the holiday, family and friends pay social visits to other in union friends. Christmas and Easter are celebrated in this manner for an entire week after the actual holiday. Baptism occurs within the first eight days of life, with the lay leader and the chosen godparent administering. Marriages are blessed in the prayer hall or church and celebrated for two to three days at the home of the groom's parents. The bride's trousseau and dowry trunk contains embroidery and woven presents for the new family, as well as embroidery decorations for the in-laws' living room of her new home.

Arts.   For their own purposes, Old Believers have often had to copy church books, paint icons on wood, or cast metal icons. These activities are performed in a posture of prayer. For domestic decoration, men are skilled at carving and women at weaving and embroidery.

Medicine.   Old Believers prefer to receive care in the following hierarchy: herb medicines and the healing touch of one of their own who is thought to have special competence; a chiropractor; and last, a physician with medicines. Old Believer midwives attend at the majority of births with complicated births referred to a hospital.

Death and Afterlife. Burial services occur within a day after death, attended by the congregation and all who wish to say farewell. The burial is followed by a funeral dinner at the home of the family which has been prepared by the kinfolk. Upon departing, each guest is given a gift (*milostinya*) with a request to pray for the salvation of the deceased. Characteristically, memorial services are held again on the third day after death, the ninth day, the fortieth day, and the year anniversary. The first forty days after death are considered a time of intense prayer in behalf of the deceased. It is on the fortieth day that they believe the soul is given final judgment and, if deserving, enters into heaven.

Bibliography

Billington, James H. (1966). *The Icon and the Axe: An Interpretive History of Russian Culture*. New York: Alfred A. Knopf.

Crummey, Robert O. (1970). *The Old Believers and the World of the Antichrist: The Vyg Community and the Russian State, 1664–1855*. Madison: University of Wisconsin Press.

Fedotov, G. P. (1966). *The Russian Religious Mind*. 2 vols. Cambridge: Harvard University Press.

Morris, Richard A. (1990). *Old Russian Ways: A Comparison of Three Russian Groups in Oregon*. New York: AMS Press.

Robson, Roy R. (1985). "The Other Russians: Old Believer Community Development in Erie, Pennsylvania." Unpublished manuscript, Allegheny College, Meadville, Penn.

RICHARD A. MORRIS

contact with Whites. In 1854 they ceded their land to the federal government and in 1855 were placed on the Omaha Reservation in Nebraska. Ten years later the northern section of the reservation was sold to the Winnebago for their reservation. Then and now the Omaha and Winnebago have enjoyed friendly relations. There are currently about three thousand Omaha in Nebraska.

The Omaha occupy a place of considerable importance in cultural anthropology, as their systems of patrilineal descent, kin terms, and alliances have often been used as models for other such systems in cultures around the world.

The traditional Omaha culture was a mix of Midwest and Plains American Indian cultural patterns. Their settlements were earthlodge villages and in the warmer months tipis, where they lived while hunting bison on the plains. They also gathered food and grew maize, squash, and beans. Omaha society was divided into two divisions, five patrilineal clans, and a number of warrior and religious societies. Tribal unity was symbolized by a sacred pole, with governance resting with a council of seven chiefs. The Omaha Tribe of Nebraska is today governed by an elected council of seven members, officers, and a committee. The traditional religion centered on the creator, Wakonda, and on dreams and visions.

Bibliography

Barnes, R. H. (1984). *Two Crows Denies It: A History of Controversy in Omaha Sociology*. Lincoln: University of Nebraska Press.

Fletcher, Alice C., and Francis LaFlesche (1911). *The Omaha Tribe*. U.S. Bureau of American Ethnology, 27th Annual Report (1905–1906), 17–654. Washington, D.C.

Omaha

ETHNONYM: Maha

The Omaha are a Plains-Prairie Indian group who were located aboriginally in the upper Missouri Valley, between the Platte and Big Sioux rivers, in the present-day states of Nebraska and Iowa. Along with the Kansa, Osage, Ponca, and Quapaw, they spoke dialects of the Dhegiha language of the Siouan language family. They were culturally and linguistically most closely related to the Ponca. They probably numbered about three thousand at the time of contact. According to their tradition, the ancestors of the contemporary five Dhegiha-speaking groups originally migrated from the southeast, with the Quapaw going downstream at the confluence of the Ohio and Mississippi rivers, and the four other groups going north. All then eventually settled in the territories they occupied at contact. Beginning with a severe population loss in a smallpox epidemic in 1802, the Omaha were in sustained

Oneida

The Oneida were one of the original member tribes of the League of the Iroquois or the Five Nations Confederacy. The Oneida live mostly in Wisconsin and New York in the United States and Ontario in Canada and numbered approximately five thousand in the 1980s. In late aboriginal and early historic times the Oneida occupied the region of present-day New York State bounded by the Oneida River in the North and the upper waters of the Susquehanna River in the South. In 1677, after significant losses of population in disease epidemics and warfare, they numbered about one thousand.

In the mid-eighteenth century some Oneida migrated west into the Ohio Valley. During the American Revolution the Oneida attempted to remain neutral, but eventually many sided with the American colonists and as a result were able to retain their lands in New York. In the 1820s the Oneida purchased land near Green Bay, Wisconsin, and between 1823 and 1838 about 654 moved to that location. After 1823 much of the purchased land in Wisconsin was lost through legal battles, treaties, and swindles. Between 1839 and 1845 most of the Oneida remaining in New York resettled on lands purchased on the Thames River near London, Ontario, although they have been in a protracted legal battle with New York State over the return of aboriginal land in central New York.

Traditionally, the Oneida were a hunting and farming people, but also practiced some fishing and gathering. They held nine of the fifty hereditary sachem positions on the council of the League of the Iroquois and, along with the Cayuga, were known as the "Younger Brothers" of the confederacy.

See also Iroquois.

Bibliography

Hazlett, Wayne J. (1981). "Changes in Oneida Indian Crafts in Wisconsin 1916–1949." *Wisconsin Archaeologist* 62:527–532.

Ricciardelli, Alex F. (1963). "The Adoption of White Agriculture by the Oneida Indians." *Ethnohistory* 10:309–328.

Richards, Cara E. (1974). *The Oneida People.* Phoenix: Indian Tribal Series.

Onondaga

The Onondaga were one of the original member tribes of the League of the Iroquois or the Five Nations Confederacy. The Onondaga live mostly on Six Nations Reserve in Ontario, Canada, and the Onondaga Indian Reservation in New York State. In the 1980s they numbered approximately 1,500. In late aboriginal and early historic times the Onondaga occupied a narrow strip of territory extending from the extreme southeastern shore of Lake Ontario south to the upper waters of the Susquehanna River. In 1650 they numbered about 1,750.

During the American Revolution the Onondaga were forced by circumstances to side with the British and subsequently had to cede much of their territory in New York to the United States. Between 1788 and 1842 their remaining lands, which formed the Onondaga Indian Reservation, located south of Syracuse, New York, were gradually reduced through treaties and land sales. In the mid-nineteenth century the majority of Onondaga sold their remaining New York lands and resettled on Six Nations Reserve.

Traditionally, the Onondaga were a hunting and farming people, but gathering and fishing were also important subsistence activities. Onondaga village was the site of the founding of the Iroquois Confederacy and was considered to be its capital. The Onondaga held fourteen of the fifty hereditary sachem positions in the council of the League of the Iroquois, one of which was the chief of the council, and were known as the "Keepers of the Council Fire."

See also Iroquois

Bibliography

Blau, Harold (1967). "Mythology, Prestige and Politics: A Case for Onondaga Cultural Persistence." *New York Folklore Quarterly* 23:45–51.

Bradley, James W. (1987). *Evolution of the Onondaga Iroquois: Accommodating Change, 1500–1655.* Syracuse: Syracuse University Press.

Tuck, James A. (1971). *Onondaga Iroquois Prehistory: A Study in Settlement Archaeology.* Syracuse: Syracuse University Press.

Osage

ETHNONYMS: A-ha-chae, Bone Indians, Crevas, Huzaas, Ouchage, Wasashe, Wasbasha

Orientation

Identification. The Osage are an American Indian group who currently live mainly in Oklahoma. The name "Osage" is derived from "Wa-sha-she," or "water people," the name of one of the Osage phratries. The original Osage name for themselves was "Ni-u-ko'n-ska," or "people of the middle water."

Location. At the time of earliest European contact, the Osage villages were located along the Osage river in what is today southwestern Missouri. During the late eighteenth century, the Osage hunting territory encompassed most of southern and western Missouri, northern and western Arkansas, eastern Oklahoma, and eastern Kansas. Today, most Osage live in Oklahoma.

Demography. In 1976 the Osage population numbered 8,842. Of this number, only 156 were full-blood Osage, while over 75 percent of the population was less than one-fourth degree Osage in ancestry. During the late eighteenth century, the Osage numbered about 6,500.

Linguistic Affiliation. The Osage language belongs to the Dhegiha branch of the Siouan family.

History and Cultural Relations

Linguistic, archaeological, and mythological data present an unclear picture of precontact Osage history. The Osage, Kansa, Omaha, Ponca, and Quapaw collectively constitute the Dhegihan Siouan speakers. These languages are so close as to be mutually intelligible. The myths of these groups describe a westward migration out of the Ohio valley and define the order in which the groups split off from one another. Precisely when this migration took place is not clear, since archaeological data seem to indicate that the Osage had lived in southwestern Missouri for some time prior to French contact in 1673. Native groups bordering the Osage in 1673 included the Caddoan-speaking Pawnee, Wichita, and Mento in the Arkansas River valley to the south and west, the Siouan-speaking Oto, Missouri, and Kansa along the Missouri River to the north and west, and the Algonkian-speaking Illini peoples far to the east along the Mississippi River. During the early historic period, Osage relations with most of these peoples were volatile. The greatest conflict was with the Caddoan-speaking peoples with whom they were at war from the late seventeenth until the late nineteenth centuries. Starting in the 1680s, the Osage were in regular contact with French traders, whose supply of guns made them the most militarily powerful tribe in French Louisiana.

In 1803 Louisiana was purchased by the United States. To find homes for dislocated eastern tribes as well as European-American settlers, the United States negotiated a series of treaties with the Osage. In 1808 the Osage ceded most of their lands in present-day Missouri and Arkansas. The Western Cherokee were given a reservation in Arkansas and quickly came into conflict with the Osage over hunting territory. In 1817 a Cherokee war party attacked an Osage village, killing eighty-three men, women, and children and taking over one hundred captive. The following year a new treaty was negotiated, and the Osage ceded much of eastern Oklahoma. In 1821 the Cherokee again attacked an Osage village, and in 1825 a new treaty ceded all the Osage lands except for a tract in what is now southern Kansas.

In 1870 the Osage agreed to allow the government to sell their Kansas reservation to White settlers for $1.25 per acre. Part of the money was used to purchase a new, smaller reservation in Indian Territory (Oklahoma), where they moved in 1871. The remainder of the money was deposited in the U.S. Treasury, and the interest used for the betterment of the Osage. In 1897 oil was discovered on the Osage reservation. In 1906 the Osage allotment act was passed, and the reservation opened to White settlers. Surface rights were divided among tribal members, but the tribe retained and still retains title to mineral rights, including the vast oil and natural gas deposits. The Osage reservation also retained its legal status as an allotted reservation.

Settlements

The Osage were divided into five bands; the Upland Forest, the Big Hills, the Thorny Thickets, the Hearts-Stays, and the Little Osage. Each of these bands occupied a permanent village located in the bottomlands near their fields. Each village was arranged symmetrically with a main east-west path that separated it into a northern and a southern half. In the very middle of the village, on opposite sides of the path, were the houses of the two village chiefs. Warfare and removal during the early nineteenth century led to fragmentation of the villages, until at one time there were seventeen. Each village, however, remained identified with one of the bands. After the move to Oklahoma in 1871, the five band-village communities were reestablished. Osage dwellings were originally rectangular wigwam-type structures covered with mats, hides, and/or bark. Today three bands exist, the Thorny-Thickets at Pawhuska, the Big Hills at Gray Horse, and the Upland Forest at Hominy. The Hearts-Stays and the Little Osage were absorbed by the Thorny Thickets. Each band has a 160-acre

village with a dance arbor and community building. All families live in American-style houses, some in the band village but most in nearby towns or on rural farms and ranches.

Economy

Subsistence and Commercial Activities. The early Osage economy was based on horticulture, hunting, and the collection of wild food plants. Maize, beans, and squash were the most important crops. Although bison were the most important game animals, elk, deer, and bear were also significant. Persimmons, prairie potatoes, and water lily roots were staples in their diet. During the eighteenth century, the fur trade and Indian slave trade became important aspects of their economy. Horses, first adopted by the Osage in the late seventeenth century, facilitated bison hunting, which became the dominant feature of the Osage economy in the mid-nineteenth century. The last Osage bison hunt took place in 1875. In the last quarter of the nineteenth century, they were dependent upon per capita payments from interest paid on the Kansas land sale money in the federal Treasury. This income and other properties made the Osage the "richest people per capita in the world." Oil income from the 1897 discovery peaked in 1924. In 1906 each of the 2,229 allotees had received a headright, which entitled its owner to 1/2229th of the income from tribal mineral rights. Individuals born after the roll was closed could acquire a headright only by inheritance or purchase. Headrights can be divided, but today only a minority own any part of one, though a few individuals own multiple headrights. Most of the wealthier individuals today are older women. The present economy is based on oil income and wage labor.

Industrial Arts. Historic crafts included leatherwork, beading, finger weaving, ribbonwork, and some metalwork using German silver. Today a limited amount of weaving, ribbonwork, and beading is produced for domestic use.

Trade. From the late seventeenth until the late nineteenth centuries, trade was a critical part of their economy. During the first half of the eighteenth century, they were a major supplier of Indian slaves to the French. Starting in the last half of the eighteenth century, the trade shifted to horses, beaver pelts, and deer and bear skins. By the mid-nineteenth century, they were trading primarily in bison robes and hides.

Division of Labor. Farming, collection of wild food plants, and their preparation and storage were primarily the work of women. Women were also primarily responsible for hide work, making clothes, cooking, and raising children. Hunting was a male activity, and politics, warfare, and ritual activities were dominated by men. Important ritual positions are still limited to males, and few women have held tribal political offices.

Land Tenure. Aboriginally, each of the five bands appears to have had its own hunting territory. At least within their band's territory, individuals had rights to hunt where they wished. Farmland was owned by the family who cleared the land. In 1906 tribal reservation land was allotted to individuals, with each man, woman, and child receiving 658 acres. The tribe reserved three 160-acre "Indian villages" where any member of the tribe could claim an unoccupied lot and build a house. Individual trust land amounts to about 200,000 acres today.

Kinship

Kin Groups and Descent. The Osage were divided into twenty-four patrilineal clans. These clans were grouped into phratries and exogamous moieties. Fifteen clans formed the *hon-qa* or "earth" moiety, which included the *wa-sha-she* or "water" phratry and the *hon-ga* or "land" phratry. Nine clans formed the *tsi-zhu* or "sky" moiety. Each clan had between three and five hierarchically ranked subclans. Most political positions as well as ritual positions and prerogatives were considered the property of particular clans. Each also had its own prescribed area in the village. Clans owned sets of male and female personal names that were given to their members. Today, the only significant function of the clans is in the naming of children.

Kinship Terminology. Traditionally, Osage kin terms were of the Omaha type.

Marriage and Family

Marriage. Individuals could not marry into either their own moiety or their mother's clan. Ideally, marriages were arranged by the extended families of both individuals, commonly without their knowledge. Marriages were important and elaborate social affairs with major gift exchanges between the families. The husband of the oldest sister in a family had a prior claim on all younger sisters, and sororal polygyny was common. Both the levirate and the sororate were also common practices. Traditionally, the Osage may have been patrilocal in residence; however, by the early nineteenth century matrilocal residence was typical.

Domestic Unit. The ideal family lived in an extended family unit headed by the son-in-law. Today, most are nuclear families, with extended family households usually found only among the wealthier families.

Inheritance. Traditionally, household property was passed to the son-in-law upon marriage. Ritual positions and items were usually passed from father to eldest son. Women normally favored their oldest daughters. Today there is still some bias favoring the oldest children. Most property is inherited bilaterally, conforming to laws of the state of Oklahoma.

Socialization. Children were raised in a world with well-defined rules of behavior. Physical punishment was rare, and children were controlled through a combination of ridicule and rewards.

Sociopolitical Organization

Social Organization. Status was conferred on the basis of birth order, age, subclan membership, and personal conduct. Birth order was of major significance, and the first, second, and third sons and daughters had names indicative of their position. A woman's status was in large part dependent upon her husband's status. Since mixed-bloods were usually the children of non-Osage fathers, they did not have a clan affiliation and thus no position within society. By the late nineteenth century, mixed-bloods formed a separate and distinct group whose life-style and values were basically European-American. Today, status is based in part on the prestige of the family and in part on relative wealth.

Political Organization. The five bands were autonomous units. Although there was no overriding political structure, band leaders frequently conferred and acted in concert. Each band had two *ga-hi-ge*, or chiefs, a *tzi-zhu*, or sky chief, and a *hon-ga*, or earth chief. The chiefs were chosen from among the male members of particular lineages and clans. To assist them, the chiefs had ten *a-ki-da*, or "soldiers," who were also chosen from particular clans. The chiefs and soldiers dealt only with day-to-day problems and led the village on hunts. The true power was in the collective decisions of the *non-hon-zhin-ga*, or "little old men," individuals who had been initiated into the clan rituals and had the right to perform such rituals. Each of the clans had its own set of "little old men." They were responsible for and controlled all religious rituals and all external relations including warfare. During the early nineteenth century, the Osage began to fragment politically. Some families continued to follow traditional hereditary chiefs, but others turned to "big man" war leaders. The "little old men" lost influence to younger aggressive warriors. In 1881 the Osage Nation was organized with a constitution based on that of the Cherokee. In 1900 the Indian Service unilaterally abolished the national government. The 1906 Allotment Act provided for a new tribal council to be elected by adult headright owners who vote the number of headrights they own.

Social Control. Gossip and ostracism were and are two informal forms of control. Little is known about witchcraft other than that the last witch died in the early part of the twentieth century. The chiefs and their soldiers were primarily responsible for the maintenance of peace within the village. Physical force and punishment could be used, and on occasion individuals were executed for murder. The 1881 constitution established courts and police. The 1906 Allotment Act made no provision for a tribal judicial system.

Conflict. There were and are sharp political divisions and bitter disputes among the Osage. These disputes, however, have rarely threatened the overall cohesiveness of the tribe. The major division today is between the descendants of the turn-of-the-century mixed-blood and full-blood families. Since today there are few actual full-bloods, the division is based more on social and cultural differences than on biology.

Religion and Expressive Culture

Religious Beliefs. The Osage religion was pantheistic. All life forms and changes in the universe were the product of a single mysterious life-giving force called *Wa-kon-tah*. Humans were merely one manifestation of Wa-kon-tah. Clans were totemic, in that the members of a particular clan were more closely associated or linked to some manifestation of Wa-kon-tah than others. The Osage never claimed to fully understand this force and how it worked. There were spirits, and through visions humans communicated with them and gained their support. Some humans could turn themselves into animals. Power derived from supernatural knowledge was neither "good" nor "evil." The Peyote religion was brought to them in the 1890s. The Osage Peyote church was based on Christianity and totally rejected traditional religious beliefs and practices. By the 1910s, traditional religious ceremonies were gone. Only a few Osage Peyote churches exist today, and these are now affiliated with the Native American church. Most Osages belong to main-line Christian churches—Catholic, Baptist, and Quaker.

Religious Practitioners. The "little-old-men" were formally trained and initiated priests. Every major ritual consisted of prayers, and certain acts and items. The rituals had twenty-four parts, one for each clan, and only a "little-old-man" from that clan had the authority to perform his clan's portion of the ritual. The last of the "little-old-men" died in the early 1970s. The Peyote churches were established on the basis of extended families, and the head of a family was usually formally installed as "road man" for the church. Only certain men had the authority to create new churches and install "road men"; the last man who undisputably had such authority died in the early 1960s. Today the Peyote churches follow the Native American church structure.

Ceremonies. The Osage had both crisis and calendrical rituals. Most of what is known concerns crisis rituals—child naming, mourning, war, peace, and initiation rituals for "little-old-men." Little is known about calendrical rituals. A spring ritual cleansed the village and prepared for planting. There was a planting ritual and in the late summer a green corn ceremony. The Osage had sacred fires and at one time a ritual renewal of fires. There is even some mention of human sacrifice during the early historic period.

Medicine. Little is known about traditional medicine. There were rituals designed to promote long life and health. A wide variety of herbs were used in treatment of illness.

Death and Afterlife. Death was natural in that all things die. What they feared was premature death of a child or young adult. Traditional Osage religion focused on living, not death. The Osage sought continuity through their children and family. Death was associated with night, and they had no well-developed concept of what happened after death. One appeal of the Peyote religion was that it gave them an explanation for what happened after death.

Bibliography

Bailey, Garrick (1973). _Changes in Osage Social Organization, 1673–1906._ University of Oregon Anthropological Papers, no. 5. Eugene: University of Oregon Press.

La Flesche, Francis (1921). _The Osage Tribe: Rite of the Chiefs; Sayings of the Ancient Men._ U.S. Bureau of American Ethnology, 36th Annual Report (1914–1915), 35–604. Washington, D.C.

La Flesche, Francis (1939). _War Ceremony and Peace Ceremony of the Osage Indians._ U.S. Bureau of American Ethnology Bulletin no. 59. Washington, D.C.

Mathews, John Joseph (1961). _The Osages, Children of the Middle Waters._ Norman: University of Oklahoma Press.

GARRICK BAILEY

Oto

The Oto (Chewaere, Hoctatas, Octatas) lived in eastern Nebraska on the lower course of the Platte River and along the Missouri River. They now live in a federal trust area in north-central Oklahoma together with the Missouri. They speak a Chiwere Siouan language and number close to two thousand.

Bibliography

Whitman, William (1937). "The Oto." _Columbia University Contributions to Anthropology_ 23:1–32.

Ottawa

ETHNONYMS: Courtes Oreilles, Odawa

The Ottawa, who speak a southeastern dialect of Ojibwa, an Algonkian language, at the time of first European contact about 1615 were located on Manitoulin Island in Lake Huron and on adjacent areas of the Ontario mainland. In about 1650 some of the group moved westward, away from the Iroquois, and many eventually settled in the coastal areas of the lower peninsula of Michigan and neighboring areas of Ontario, Wisconsin, Illinois, Indiana, and Ohio, with Michigan being the central area for the next three hundred years. In the early 1830s, several groups of Ottawa living in Ohio moved to a reservation in northeastern Kansas. In 1857, this group moved again to a reservation near Miami, Oklahoma, where they are now known as the Ottawa Tribe of Oklahoma. A large number of Ottawa (particularly the Roman Catholic Ottawa) have moved back again to Manitoulin Island in Ontario, their original homeland. The great mobility of the Ottawa during early contact times makes it difficult to locate village sites from that period. After 1650, however, their settlements are fairly well documented. There are probably close to ten thousand descendants of the aboriginal Ottawa now living in the United States and Canada, with most located in northern Michigan, about two thousand enrolled in Oklahoma, and three thousand in Canada.

Like most Indian groups in the Great Lakes area, the Ottawa had a mixed, seasonal economy based on hunting, fishing (which was of primary importance), horticulture, and the gathering of wild vegetable foods. In the warmer seasons, women grew the basic maize, beans, and squash and collected wild foods. The men fished in streams and lakes, generally with nets. They also hunted and trapped deer, bear, beaver, and other game. In the winter smaller groups settled in smaller camps for the hunting of large game, usually deer. A family hunting territory system was developed in the late seventeenth century.

They had large, permanent, sometimes palisaded villages located near river banks and lake shores. They used rectangular houses with half-barrel shaped roofs covered with sheets of fir or cedar bark. On extended hunting trips, matcovered conical tents were used. The villages often had people of other, non-Ottawa groups, such as the Huron, Ojibwa, and Potawatomi, living with them.

In the late seventeenth and early eighteenth centuries, the Ottawa had four main subgroups (Kiskakon, Sinago, Sable, and Nassauakueton) with other minor groups also existing. In the late eighteenth and early nineteenth centuries, sources indicate that the tribe had a number of local units that were autonomous and acted independently of each other. In the modern period, these distinctions have largely disappeared, although adopted tribal organizations still function in Oklahoma and Canada.

The Ottawa believed in a supreme being (the "Master of Life"), as well as many good and evil spirits. Among them were the Underwater Panther, a being of the waters, and the Great Hare, believed to have created the world. Individuals tried to acquire guardian spirits through dreams or the vision quest. Shamans existed generally for curing purposes. Early efforts at Christianization by the Jesuits and Recollects were not successful. But in the early nineteenth century, Roman Catholic, Church of England, Presbyterian, and Baptist missionaries enjoyed great success. A large proportion of Canadian Ottawa today are Roman Catholic.

In modern times, most Ottawa have depended upon farming and wage labor, with the men in Canada also working in the lumber industry. There has also been a significant movement of the population away from rural to urban areas. The Ottawa language has largely been forgotten in Oklahoma, but large numbers still speak the language in Michigan and Ontario.

Bibliography

Feest, Johanna E., and Christian F. Feest (1978). "Ottawa." In *Handbook of North American Indians*. Vol. 15, *Northeast*, edited by Bruce G. Trigger, 772–786. Washington, D.C.: Smithsonian Institution.

Kurath, Gertrude P. (1966). *Michigan Indian Festivals*. Ann Arbor, Mich.: Ann Arbor Publishers.

Ozarks

ETHNONYM: Hillbillies

Orientation

Identification. The Ozarks is a geographical-cultural region in southern Missouri and northern Arkansas in the United States. The residents of the region have traditionally viewed themselves and have been viewed by outsiders as forming a distinct culture based on self-identity as "Ozarkers," a rural life-style, descent from immigrants from southern Appalachia, and a generally traditional-conservative outlook. Since the end of World War II, the region has experienced considerable population and economic expansion, and the traditional way of life is no longer as common or as obvious as in the past. A notable current feature of the population is that it is divided between "traditionalists" who resist externally imposed change and "progressives" who encourage such change. For all Ozarkers, Ozark identity is traced patrilineally—if one's father is a native-born Ozarker, one is then an Ozarker; otherwise one is an outsider or a "furriner." In general, this summary focuses on the traditional way of life.

Location. The Ozark region covers some sixty thousand square miles, primarily in southern Missouri and northern Arkansas, and small sections of eastern Kansas and Missouri. The region is roughly bounded by the Missouri River on the north, the Mississippi River on the east, the Arkansas River on the south and the Grand River on the west. It is an upland plateau covered by a mix of hills, valleys, grasslands, and forests. Running roughly north to south and west to east, the region can be subdivided into a number of geographical zones: Missouri River Border, Osage-Gasconade Hills, St. Francis Mountains, Courtois Hills, Central Plateau, Springfield Plain, White River Hills, and Boston Mountains. The region is largely rural, with urban centers at Jefferson City, Springfield, and Joplin, Missouri, and Fayettville, Arkansas. Average winter temperatures range from 30° to 40° F and summer temperatures from 70° to 75° F. Average annual precipitation is about forty inches.

Demography. The population of the Ozark region is about 2 million, which represents a tenfold increase since 1850. Since the mid-1960s the region has experienced rapid population growth at a rate about three times above the national average. Most of the growth is attributable to in-migration. Since the turn of the century, population shifts have resulted in a number of urbanized settlements near major lakes, existing cities, and transportation routes.

Linguistic Affiliation. Residents of the Ozarks speak a regional dialect of American English, classified as South Midland English or as Northern Midland English in the northernmost sections. Use of regional or local dialect words and colloquial expressions is an important marker of Ozark identity.

History and Cultural Relations

The first inhabitants of the Ozarks were the ancestors of contemporary American Indians who arrived in the region as long as twelve thousand years ago. At the time of European contact, the major Indian groups in the region were Osage, Illinois, Missouri, and Caddo, all of whom eventually ceded their lands and moved west. At later dates Kickapoo and Cherokee occupied western areas of the region, although they, too, eventually settled in Oklahoma. The first Europeans were the Spanish in the mid-1500s, but the area was not settled until the French established Ste. Genevieve in 1735, followed by other French settlements in the eastern Ozarks. It was not until after the Louisiana Purchase in 1803 that large-scale immigration and settlement began. Many of these settlers were native-born Americans of Scots-Irish ancestry who migrated west from Kentucky and Tennessee and the Appalachian region in general. Wealthier migrants settled in the border areas; others, in the interior regions where the soil was poor and land cheaper. The population of the Ozarks was eventually dominated by these settlers, producing an Ozark regional culture similar in many ways to the Appalachian regional culture.

Although the Ozarks is thought of and is largely populated by Whites of British ancestry, other groups also have settled there. In the north are a number of German communities, and there are an identifiable population of African-American Ozarkers (many of whose ancestors entered the region during the first years of settlement), a few Italian and Swedish communities, and, in the last 20 years, some Amish and Mennonite communities.

Settlements

The traditional settlement pattern was of isolated family farms located on what seemed to be the best farmland available. In recent years, there has been a clear pattern of movement to towns and cities along transportation routes, leading to the appearance of eight primary regional centers: Jefferson City, St. Louis, Cape Girardeau, Poplar Bluff, Springfield, Joplin, Northwest Arkansas City, and Batesville. Three house types predominate throughout the Ozarks. Shacks are found mainly in rural, undeveloped areas; two-story houses predominate in the northern and west-central areas; and contemporary-style houses are found in areas of recent development or growth. Trailers have become common in recent years, especially as a means of establishing a second home in the rural areas. The one-room schoolhouse is now all but extinct. Traditionalists tend to live in the rural, more heavily forested areas, in isolated valleys, and in culturally defined traditional neighborhoods in larger towns.

Economy

Subsistence and Commercial Activities. The economy of the first generation or two of settlers was essentially subsistence farming and herding with maize, wheat, tobacco, and hemp the major crops and pigs and sheep the major livestock. By the close of the 1800s, subsistence farming had given way to general farming, which rapidly declined after 1930, being replaced, in part, by more specialized farming such as dairy and fruit farming and livestock raising. Other major industries are mining (iron, lead, zinc, barite), lumbering, recreation, tourism, and various service and transportation industries. Agriculture is now a part-time activity for most Ozark residents who continue to farm. With poverty still a problem in some rural areas and in some cities, government assistance is a source of income for some families.

Industrial Arts. The production and repair of all material objects needed for the family farm was a major activity for both men and women in the past and reflected the core value of self-reliance. Although many of these crafts have fallen into disuse, the methods and designs have been kept alive through organized efforts such as the _Bittersweet_ magazine and book series and regional Ozark cultural centers.

Division of Labor. The division of labor by sex was clearly marked, with much of women's work restricted to women, but men's work open to both sexes. Women's work included most domestic chores as well as employment outside the home. Men's work included planting and harvesting the fields, tend-

ing the livestock, cutting and hauling wood and ice, hunting, distilling whiskey, and employment outside the home. Hunting and fishing are important male activities.

Land Tenure. Ownership of land was and remains an important source of Ozark identity and status. Since immigration has increased, land prices have increased, too, making the sale of land an important source of income for some families.

Kinship, Marriage and Family

Kinship. Although the nuclear family is the basic domestic and residential unit and Ozarkers share a sense of Ozark identity, their ties to the bilateral kinship network integrate individuals into the community. Children are taught their family genealogies, and individuals place considerable importance on being descendants of native Ozarkers. Kin terms follow the typical North American system, although children sometimes identify themselves to others as the son or daughter of "so-and-so."

Marriage and Family. Marriage in the past usually followed dating in the context of group activities. Today, courtship and marriage practices are typical of those in mainstream America. Marriage was seen as a partnership, with the husband and wife each taking responsibility for culturally defined male and female tasks. Postmarital residence was neolocal, although the couple might reside with one set of parents or the other until they could afford a home of their own. Men and women spent little time together, given the rigid division of labor by sex and the common practice of men socializing with other men at the country store or blacksmith's shop.

Socialization. The home, the church, and organized group activities were the major arenas for socialization. The extended kin network often played a central role in child rearing and education. Until fairly recently, formal education and especially college education were resisted by many.

Sociopolitical Organization

The key social distinctions are between Ozarkers and outsiders and between traditional and progressive Ozarkers. Other distinctions are based on wealth, rural versus urban residence (which is related to traditional versus progressive), and possession of traditional knowledge and skills. Whatever their political party affiliation, Ozarkers have a reputation for being on the conservative side of the issues. Traditionalists believe that local problems should be dealt with in accordance with local beliefs and customs. To some extent, this is made possible by the relative isolation of some communities and the use of local police officers.

Religion and Expressive Culture

Religious Beliefs. Religion occupies a central place in Ozark life. Protestantism is the major religion, with traditionalists generally belonging to the more fundamentalist denominations such as the Church of Christ or Baptist church and progressives belonging to the Presbyterian, Episcopal, or Methodist denominations. For traditionalists church attendance and church-sponsored events are of considerable importance. Beyond the services that often involve group singing and emotional displays, camp meetings, outdoor baptisms, community suppers, picnics, and other church events provide an opportunity for social interaction and the reinforcement of Ozark beliefs and customs.

Arts.   Music and dancing are central features of Ozark life. Children routinely attend singing classes, singing is a basic component of church services, dulcimer making and playing have undergone a recent revival, and bluegrass music and square dancing are common entertainments. Some utilitarian crafts such as rug making and quilting have been reborn as art forms for personal enjoyment and the craft trade.

Medicine.   Although most Ozarkers have access to and use modern medical care, there was a rich folk pharmacopeia of herbal and vegetable oils, tonics, and potions to treat most ailments. Traditionally, the midwife was a person of considerable importance in the community.

Death and Afterlife.   In the past, all activities concerning death and preparation for burial took place in the home of the deceased. Today, these matters are left to funeral homes and their directors, though the tradition of neighbors cooking a midday meal for the relatives on the day of the burial continues. In the past, widows were forbidden to remarry for one year.

Bibliography

Gerlach, Russel L. (1976). *Immigrants in the Ozarks: A Study in Ethnic Geography.* Columbia: University of Missouri Press.

Gilmore, Robert K. (1984). *Ozark Baptisms, Hangings, and Other Diversions: Theatrical Folkways of Rural Missouri, 1885–1910.* Norman: University of Oklahoma Press.

Martin, Gladys, and Donnis Martin (1972). *Ozark Idyll: Life at the Turn of the Century in the Missouri Ozarks.* Point Lookout, Mo.: School of the Ozarks Press.

Massey, Ellen G., ed. (1978). *Bittersweet Country.* Garden City, N.Y.: Anchor Books.

Morgan, Gordon D. (1973). *Black Hillbillies of the Arkansas Ozarks.* Fayetteville: Department of Sociology, University of Arkansas.

Rafferty, Milton D. (1980). *The Ozarks: Land and Life.* Norman: University of Oklahoma Press.

Pacific Eskimo

ETHNONYMS: Aleut, Alutiiq, Pacific Gulf Eskimo, Pacific Yup'ik Eskimo, South Alaska Eskimo

Orientation

Identification.   The three major groups lumped under the label "Pacific Eskimo" live on the south coast of Alaska, from the Alaska Peninsula, where they border the Aleut, east to the Copper River, where they border the Tlingit and Eyak. The Pacific Eskimo include the Koniag (Kanagist, Kanjagi, Koniagi, Kychtagmytt, Qiqtarmiut), Chugach (Chiugachi, Shugarski), and the inhabitants of the lower Kenai Peninsula, now called the "Unegkurmiut." Locally, the groups were called the "Aleut" as the Russians lumped the two together. More recently, "Alutiiq" has been used as a collective name for the three groups.

Location.   The Koniag live on Kodiak Island and the eastern section of the Alaska Peninsula. The Chugach live along the coast of Prince William Sound and on offshore islands. The Unegkurmiut live on the lower Kenai Peninsula. Aboriginally and today all settlements were either on the coast or on inlets, as the economy is based on the exploitation of sea mammals and fish. The region is a major center of earthquake activity with at least twenty-two occurring in historic times including a major one in 1964.

Demography.   At the time of first contact in about 1784 there were an estimated nine thousand Pacific Eskimo. By 1800 the population had dropped to six thousand and then, following a smallpox epidemic, three thousand in 1850. Today, there are about two thousand Pacific Eskimo, with the Koniag the largest group and the majority living on Kodiak Island.

Linguistic Affiliation.   The Pacific Eskimo speak Pacific Yup'ik, one of the five Yup'ik languages. There were dialect differences from one locale to another. Today all Pacific Eskimo speak English and only about 25 percent speak Pacific Yup'ik.

History and Cultural Relations

The Pacific Eskimo were first sighted by Vitus Bering in 1741, which led to some forty years of limited and often hostile contact until the Russians established trading posts beginning in 1784. By 1800, posts were established in various locales and the Pacific Eskimo were drawn into the fur trade as workers in procuring and processing salmon meat and furs. The Russian Orthodox church was also established during the Russian period and remains an important influence today. After the close of the Russian period, Americans moved into the region and by 1880 had established canneries that led to a consolidation of the Pacific Eskimo into cannery villages and made them economically dependent on salmon fishing and wage labor. Overfishing led to a demise of the canning industry after 1900. The Alaska Native Claims Settlement Act of 1971 and the Alaska National Interest Lands Conservation Act of 1980 resulted in eligible villages being incorporated as landowning business corporations. In precontact times, the Pacific Eskimo traded with as well as fought with the Aleut, Tlingit, and Tanaina.

Settlements

Traditionally, the Pacific Eskimo had winter and summer villages, the latter usually more temporary in nature and located near salmon streams. Dwellings were semisubterranean lodges with a common room and private rooms that housed up to twenty people. Villages typically had from one hundred to two hundred inhabitants. Today, modern housing has replaced traditional forms. Since the cannery era, there has been considerable shifting, abandonment, and development of new villages, a process recently fueled by the earthquake of 1964, the act of 1971, and the use of South Alaskan towns as oil industry terminals.

Economy

The traditional subsistence economy was based on the hunting of whales, sea otters, and seals and fishing for salmon in streams and saltwater fish in the bays. These activities were supplemented by the hunting of land animals and the collecting of berries, roots, and bulbs. The material culture included the two-hatch kayak, harpoon arrows, darts, twined baskets, and stone, bone, and wooden utensils. Beginning with involvement in the Russian fur trade and then through the cannery period up to the present the Pacific Eskimo have been involved in the cash economy. They usually worked for cash and provided the canneries with salmon, and later crabs, as well as working in the processing plants. The incorporation of the villages as corporate entities has involved them further in the state, regional, and national economies.

Kinship, Marriage and Family

Marriage was marked by a gift exchange followed by a period of matrilocal residence. Polygyny and polyandry were permitted. The nuclear family was the basic social unit, with four or five families occupying a dwelling. Descent was matrilineal, with kin groups above the clan level absent. The Russian Orthodox church introduced godparent relations, which remain important today.

Sociopolitical Organization

Aboriginally, none of three Pacific Eskimo groupings formed a cohesive group. Rather, the local village was the basic sociopolitical entity. There was a class structure of nobles, commoners, and slaves, and the village leadership was inherited by men of the noble class. Some chiefs evidently ruled more than one village. In 1980, the Pacific Eskimo lived in fifteen villages, five towns, and cities in Alaska. Incorporation as business entities has involved the village corporations in new forms of social and political relationships with one another and with American Indian groups, the state government, the federal government, and various business interests.

Religion and Expressive Culture

The traditional religion was evidently similar to Eskimo religion in general with an emphasis on spirit owners of the air, sea, and land, and shamanistic diviners who used spirit help-ers to foretell the future. The Russian Orthodox church has had a major affect on Pacific Eskimo life. Each major settlement has a church and lay leaders who conduct the services, and major social events are scheduled around the church calendar. Baptists have been active since the late nineteenth century, though all villages except one are predominantly Russian Orthodox.

Bibliography

Birket-Smith, Kaj (1953). _The Chugach Eskimo_. Nationalmuseets Skrifter, Etnografisk Raekke 6. Copenhagen, Denmark.

Clark, Donald W. (1984). "Pacific Eskimo: Historical Ethnography." In _Handbook of North American Indians_. Vol. 5, _Arctic_, edited by David Damas, 185–197. Washington, D.C.: Smithsonian Institution.

Davis, Nancy Y. (1984). "Contemporary Pacific Eskimo." In _Handbook of North American Indians_. Vol. 5, _Arctic_, edited by David Damas, 198–204. Washington, D.C.: Smithsonian Institution.

Passamaquoddy

The Passamaquoddy are an American Indian group who aboriginally and today number about one thousand and live in northern Maine.
See Maliseet

Pawnee

ETHNONYMS: Pani, Panzas, Pawni

Orientation

Identification. The Pawnee are an American Indian group currently living in Oklahoma. The name "Pawnee" comes from the term _pariki_, or "horn," and refers to the traditional manner of dressing the hair in which the scalp-lock is stiffened with fat and paint and made to stand erect like a curved horn. The Pawnee called themselves "Chahiksichahiks," meaning "men of men."

Location. Throughout much of the historic period the Pawnee inhabited the territory centered in the valleys of the Loup and Platte rivers and along the Republican River in what is now the state of Nebraska in the central United

States. In 1874–1875 they moved from this territory to reservation lands in Indian Territory (now Oklahoma). The region of the Loup, Platte, and Republican rivers consists largely of high and dry grass-covered plains interrupted by rivers and river valleys and is characterized by a subhumid climate. Trees are nearly absent except along the river courses.

Demography. In the early part of the nineteenth century the Pawnee numbered between 9,000 and 10,000. Subsequently, the population declined because of warfare and European diseases; smallpox epidemics in 1803 and 1825 were especially devastating. In 1859 the population was estimated at 4,000, in 1876 at 2,000, and in 1900 at 650. The population subsequently increased to over 2,000 today.

Linguistic Affiliation. The Pawnee language belongs to the Caddoan linguistic family.

History and Cultural Relations

The ancestors of the Pawnee inhabited the plains region of North America since at least A.D. 1100 and migrated to the region of the Loup, Platte and Republican rivers from a southeasterly direction sometime prior to European contact. Contact with Spanish explorers may have occurred as early as 1541, but direct and sustained contact with Europeans did not come until the eighteenth century. During the contact period the native groups neighboring the Pawnee included the Arapaho and Teton to the west, the Ponca to the north, the Omaha, Oto, and Kansa to the east, and the Kiowa to the south. In 1803 the Pawnee territory passed under the control of the U.S. government through the Louisiana Purchase. In a series of treaties between 1833 and 1876 the Pawnee ceded their lands to the federal government and in 1874–1876 removed to Indian Territory. The gradual ceding of territory to the United States was done reluctantly, but out of necessity as White migration, depletion of the bison herds, and warfare on the plains between native peoples made it increasingly difficult for the Pawnee to carry on the hunting and farming way of life in their traditional territory. In 1870 the Pawnee split over the question of resettlement, but the issue was decided when they were forced to seek the protection of federal authorities after a massacre of Pawnee by the Dakota in 1873. In 1892 their reservation lands were allotted on an individual basis and the Pawnee became citizens of the United States. The transition to individual land ownership proved difficult, as the Pawnee tradition of village living proved inconsistent with individual farming.

Settlements

In the historic period prior to 1833 the Pawnee bands were settled in four groups of villages in valleys along the Platte River. Villages were large and relatively permanent, and consisted of clusters of earthlodges surrounded by fields. In the nineteenth century some villages were surrounded by a sod wall three to four feet high for defensive purposes. Earthlodges were circular and constructed of a log frame plastered over with layers of grass and packed earth. Lodges varied in size according to the number of occupants, but averaged fifteen feet in height and forty feet in diameter. In the summer the occupants of the earthlodge moved outdoors and slept under a brush arbor. Tipis of bison hide were used for shelter on the hunt.

Economy

Subsistence and Commercial Activities. In the historic period until the latter part of the nineteenth century the Pawnee subsistence pattern consisted of farming and hunting, with a minimal amount of gathering. The principal crops were maize, beans, squash, and pumpkins; the principal game animal was the bison. Horses acquired from the Spanish, starting in the late seventeenth century, stimulated the development of a more nomadic, hunting way of life, but this never supplanted the farming basis of life to the degree that it did among other Plains Indian groups. At about the same time European firearms were acquired from the French, but these had less economic impact; even into the nineteenth century the bow and arrow was the weapon of choice among bison hunters. Throughout the nineteenth century the Pawnee were under constant pressure by the U.S. government to give up hunting and adopt European methods of farming. The Pawnee resisted this pressure for a time until White migration, dwindling bison herds, increased population pressure on food resources, and finally resettlement in Indian Territory made the traditional hunting and farming way of life impossible.

Industrial Arts. Work in skins, particularly bison skins, was highly developed and provided the Pawnee with tents, ropes, rawhide, containers, blankets, robes, clothing, and footwear. Other by-products of the bison were used for bows, bowstring, thread, hammers, scrapers, awls, and fuel. Pottery making was not a highly developed skill, but did exist and persisted into the nineteenth century when clay pots were replaced by copper and iron vessels obtained from European-Americans.

Trade. Virtually self-sufficient in aboriginal times, Pawnee trade with neighboring groups was limited. After contact they traded with Whites for horses, firearms and ammunition, steel knives, axes, hoes, brass kettles, and whiskey.

Division of Labor. Traditionally, women tended the fields and men were responsible for hunting, but this division of labor broke down during the second half of the nineteenth century with the decline of bison hunting and the gradual acceptance of plow agriculture as the basis of subsistence.

Land Tenure. Each village traditionally possessed its own fields, the use of which was allotted to individuals by the village chief. Upon the individual's death the lands reverted to the village and were re-allotted.

Kinship

Kin Groups and Descent. The basic kinship grouping among the Pawnee was a division into north and south, or winter and summer people. Membership in these divisions was inherited matrilineally. In games, religious ceremonies, and other social gatherings, the people were divided along hereditary lines.

Kinship Terminology. Kin terms followed the Crow system.

Marriage and Family

Marriage. Marriages were arranged and negotiated primarily by the mother's brother. First-cousin marriages were prohibited, and village endogamy generally prevailed. Polygyny was practiced and as a rule was strictly sororal. Residence was matrilocal. Strong emotional ties generally did not exist between husband and wife, and though divorce was rare, it could be effected by either party.

Domestic Unit. Although nuclear families occasionally lived alone, most often several such families lived together in the earthlodge.

Inheritance. Traditionally, property passed to the oldest male. Theoretically, women had no rights to property, but, in fact, were generally considered to be the owners of lodges, tipis, and their own tools and utensils.

Socialization. Traditionally, early childhood training was in the hands of the grandparents, with strict discipline and harsh punishment the norm. Youths were allowed considerable sexual freedom until puberty, after which time separation of the sexes was enforced until marriage. A mother's brother's wife often served as a sexual partner for a young man from the time of puberty until he married.

Sociopolitical Organization

Social Organization. Nineteenth-century Pawnee society included a series of classlike hierarchical divisions. Highest in rank were chiefs, followed by warriors, priests, and medicine men. Next in rank were common people without power or influence, and below them were semioutcastes, persons who had violated tribal laws and lived on the outskirts of the villages. There was also a category of captured non-Pawnee slaves. Men's societies concerned with warfare and hunting were a prominent feature of Pawnee society. In addition, there were eight medicine men's societies and numerous private organizations that functioned for the public good in times of need.

Political Organization. The Pawnee were divided into four main groups or bands: (1) the Skidi, or Wolf, the largest band, (2) the Chaui, or Grand, (3) Kitkehahki, or Republican, and (4) the Pitahauerat, or Tappage. The Chaui were generally recognized as the leading band; however, the nature of the relationship of the four groups is not clear. Aboriginally the four bands may have been independent of one another, with greater political unity developing in response to the pressures of acculturation. As exhibited by the Skidi Pawnee in the early nineteenth century, band political structure consisted of federated villages held together by a governing council of chiefs and common participation in a ceremonial cycle. Within the band, authority resided with four chiefs, the position of which was inherited matrilineally. Each band consisted of one or more villages. But with the pressures of acculturation and European contact there was a progressive diminution of the number of villages occupied, and in later history two or more bands frequently dwelt together in the same village. Each component village had a chief whose responsibilities included the allotting of village lands to individual users. The position of village chief was inherited, generally by the eldest son, but subject to the approval of a council of chiefs and other leading men.

Social Control. The Pawnee considered violence within the village a serious matter and generally made every attempt to avoid it or stop it when it occurred. For the most part, public opinion acted as the mechanism of social control, but to ensure order each village had a small police society whose head was an old warrior selected by the village chief. On the communal bison hunts held in the late summer and autumn of each year, a special society of military police or soldiers was selected to prevent individual hunters from leaving the camp and disturbing the bison herds.

Conflict. In prehistoric and early historic times interband disputes and violence were not uncommon, particularly between the Skidi and Grand Pawnee.

Religion and Expressive Culture

Religious Beliefs. The Pawnee had a highly integrated system of religious beliefs that resisted European missionization until well into the nineteenth century. In this system of beliefs all life was understood to have derived from the meeting of male (east) and female (west) forces in the sky. The supernatural power at the zenith of the sky where these forces met was known as Tirawa. Tirawa produced the world through a series of violent storms and created star gods, who in turn created humanity. In 1891, along with other Plains Indian groups, the Pawnee participated in the Ghost Dance, a revitalization movement envisioning the return of the dead from the spirit world and the disappearance of the White man from the land. The two most prominent star powers were the Evening Star, the goddess of darkness and fertility who lived in the western sky, and Morning Star, the god of fire and light who was located in the eastern sky. Next in rank to Tirawa, Evening Star and Morning Star were the gods of the four world quarters in the northeast, southeast, northwest, and southwest who supported the heavens.

Religious Practitioners. Pawnee religious specialists consisted of a group of wise men who derived their power and authority from a star planet and held their position as a matter of heredity. They were understood to stand between normal men and Tirawa and supervised a yearly round of religious ceremonies conducted to bring success in farming, hunting, and warfare.

Ceremonies. The foci of Pawnee religious ceremonies were sacred bundles of religious objects believed to have been passed down a line of ancestors. Each village had its own sacred bundle with which its members identified strongly, and each sacred bundle was a medium through which the people communicated with Tirawa. The annual ceremonial cycle began with the first thunder in the spring and concluded with the harvest of maize in the autumn. The climax of the cycle was the sacrifice of a young woman to the Morning Star at the time of the summer solstice in order to ensure prosperity and long life. The sacrifice to the Morning Star persisted until about 1838. Another important ceremonial event concerned preparations for the buffalo hunt. The ceremony began with fasting, prayer, and sacrifice by the priests, followed by a public ritual in which the priests appealed to Tirawa for aid. The ritual concluded with three days of uninterrupted dancing.

Arts. Pawnee music was simple in its melody and rhythm and was an important part of Pawnee ceremonial activities. At the time of the Ghost Dance songs secured in dreams or visions emphasized memories of former days, reunion with the dead, and other aspects of the Ghost Dance revitalization movement.

Medicine. The Pawnee recognized witchcraft and, ultimately, anger and hostility to be major causes of disease.

Pawnee religious specialists also included shamans who cured the sick through powers believed to have been acquired from animal spirits. Shamans were organized into societies with specific rituals performed twice each year in order to perpetuate and renew their powers.

Death and Afterlife.   As with disease, death was believed to sometimes be the result of hostility and witchcraft. Burial preparations varied according to the rank and position of the deceased. Individuals of importance and those who died in extreme old age were painted with a sacred red ointment, dressed in their best costumes, and wrapped in a bison robe before burial. It was believed that after death the soul of the deceased ascended to heaven to become a star or, in the case of those who were diseased or died in a cowardly manner in battle, traveled to a village of spirits in the south.

Bibliography

Hyde, George E. (1951). *Pawnee Indians.* Denver: University of Denver Press.

Murie, James R. (1914). *Pawnee Indian Societies.* American Museum of Natural History, Anthropological Papers 11(4). New York.

Oswalt, Wendell H. (1966). "The Pawnee." In *This Land Was Theirs: A Study of the North American Indian,* edited by Wendell H. Oswalt, 239–289. New York: John Wiley.

Weltfish, Gene (1965). *The Lost Universe.* New York: Basic Books.

GERALD F. REID

Pennacook

The Pennacook (Western Abenaki) lived in the valleys of the Merrimac River in New Hampshire and the Connecticut River in Vermont, New Hampshire, and northern Massachusetts, and in neighboring areas. They were a confederacy of Algonkian-speaking groups; most, such as the Wamesit, Agawam, Nashua, and Winnepesaukee, are now extinct. Some Pennacook descendants live today with the St. Francis Abenaki in Quebec.
See Abenaki

Bibliography

Day, Gordon M. (1978). "Western Abenaki." In *Handbook of North American Indians.* Vol. 15, *Northeast,* edited by Bruce G. Trigger, 148–159. Washington, D.C.: Smithsonian Institution.

Penobscot

The Penobscot are an American Indian group who aboriginally and today number about one thousand and live in northern Maine.
See Abenaki

Peripatetics

ETHNONYMS: Gypsies, Irish Travelers, Rom, Romnichels, Ludars, Scottish Travelers

Peripatetic peoples consist of small, ethnically recruited, kinship-based bands who make their living by providing goods and services to the larger population. These groups are often called "Gypsies." Instead of relying directly on natural resources, peripatetics exploit a social resource base that, although ubiquitous and relatively predictable overall, is characterized by intermittent demand and patchy geographical distribution. Peripatetics usually utilize a wide range of procurement and maintenance strategies. Their relations with the surrounding populations are marked by opportunistic and shifting economic responses, ethnic separation, and ideological opposition that sanctions the economic exploitation of the host population. Although these peripatetic groups are ubiquitous in North America, being present in every state of the Union and in Canada, they are few in number and scattered in distribution; because they maintain a low profile, they go largely unnoticed by the majority of the population. Each constitutes a separate ethnic entity maintaining its identity and distance from the larger society as well as from other peripatetic groups. Each also has its own history, cultural traditions, and a language or dialect that protect against assimilation. Kinship-based and largely egalitarian, their social organization recognizes no leaders beyond an occasional "big man." Most viable social units consist of endogamous family bands whose composition and distribution fluctuates according to concentration of exploitable resources and the degree of amity among members.

A variety of groups in North America can be said to have been traditionally peripatetic, and among them are many families who still continue a peripatetic life-style. These include non-Gypsy Irish and Scottish Travelers and four Gypsy groups: the Rom (of which there are several subgroups), Romnichels, or English Gypsies, Ludar, or Rumanian Gypsies, and a group of German Gypsies calling itself the Black Dutch. The category of peripatetic groups overlaps that of groups who identify themselves as "Gypsies." Some peripatetic groups, such as the Irish and Scottish Travelers, do not call themselves Gypsies and are apparently of indigenous Irish or Scottish ancestry. One American Gypsy group which is sedentary, and perhaps has been for generations, is the

Hungarian-Slovak Gypsies, some of whom are called Romungri and who have traditionally provided professional musical entertainment to the Central European immigrant communities of the northern industrial cities. In addition, there are families not belonging to any of the above-mentioned groups, but who currently follow a peripatetic life-style; they are disdainfully called "Refs" by the members of the other groups.

North America received its first viable group of peripatetics with the arrival of the Romnichels, whose immigration began in 1850. They soon found a lucrative trade in the rapidly increasing demand for horses, first in agriculture and then in urbanizing areas before the advent of tractors and automobiles. After the rapid decline of horse trade following the First World War, most Romnichels relied on previously secondary enterprises, such as basket making, manufacture and sale of rustic furniture, and fortune-telling. Their reliance on horse and mule trading continued longer in the South where poverty and terrain slowed the adoption of mechanized agriculture. Today, most are engaged in a variety of home-repair trades among which roofing, spray painting, and seal coating are the main pursuits.

Although their history has not yet been fully explored, the Irish and Scottish Travelers seem to have arrived shortly after the Romnichels and followed similar pursuits. They are the offshoots of groups commonly called tinkers in the old country after their main means of livelihood; after arriving in North America, however, most pursued a wide range of peripatetic strategies before concentrating on the horse and mule trade after the Civil War. After the decline of that trade, many families relied on the sale of various items, among which linoleum seems to have been prominent. Today, spray painting is a major occupation.

The next large influx of peripatetics into the New World began in the 1880s with the arrival of the Rom and Ludar Gypsy groups interspersed among the waves of other immigrants from Eastern Europe. The Rom at first relied heavily on itinerant copper-smithing work, although horse trading and fortune-telling also remained situationally significant pursuits. After the replacement of copper vats in small businesses and industry by stainless steel and Monel metal, the Rom came to rely more and more on their women's fortune-telling as a main strategy. This emphasis continues today, supplemented by the men's car and trailer sales, fender repairs, black-topping, and roofing work.

Upon their arrival, most of the Ludar were engaged in animal exhibitions and other work related to traveling entertainment. In fact, passenger manifests show bears and monkeys as a major part of their baggage. Although continuing to travel widely throughout North America, the Ludar have also formed concentrated settlements comprising related families, such as shantytowns in the 1930s and, more recently, trailer parks. Today, many Ludar are also in the black-topping and roofing trades. Some remain in the entertainment industry and continue to travel with carnivals. Still others manufacture rustic furniture, which is then sold door-to-door.

Regardless of current specializations or strategies favored by the peripatetic groups, each retains a built-in flexibility to adapt as its environment changes. Most individuals are masters of several trades; even where some families have seemingly "settled down," readiness for mobility remains a viable alternative. In contrast to the ever-changing economic strategies, little change is noted in the ethnocentric ideology, social separation from the majority population, endogamy, and other factors that contribute to the maintenance of a strong ethnic identity.

See also Irish Travelers, Rom

MATT SALO

Pima-Papago

ETHNONYMS: O'odham, Upper Pimas; including, at different times, peoples called Papabota, Sobaipuri, Soba, Gileno, Piato, Areneno, Pima, Papago, Sand Papago, Akimel O'odham (river people), and Tohono O'odham (desert people)

Orientation

Identification and Location. Aboriginally, the Pima-Papagos/Upper Pimas occupied about forty thousand square miles of the Sonoran Desert of the present states of Sonora, Mexico, and Arizona, United States. This territory lies between 30° and 33° N and 112° and 115° W. Today's Pima-Papago are the remnant and consolidation of that territory's earlier occupants whom the Spaniards called the "Upper Pimas." During the nineteenth century, at the time of the U.S. entry into the region, a portion of the Upper Pimas was called the "Gila River Pimas" and most others were called "Papagos." Although many historians and anthropologists have treated the two as separate peoples, we bring them together because so much that is true of the one people is true of the other. Furthermore, in writing of the varieties of Pima-Papagos, we will frequently make use of a three-part division by settlement pattern, which pertains to the two peoples as follows: One Village (sedentary)—Pimas; Two Villagers (seasonal oscillation between lowland field and highland well villages)—most Papagos; and No Villagers (completely migratory campers opposed to villagers)—a few Papagos. There were perhaps five thousand One Villagers, seven thousand Two Villagers, and five hundred No Villagers (the so-called Sand Papagos).

Linguistic Affiliation. These people spoke closely related dialects of Pima-Papago, a Uto-Aztecan language. In the late nineteenth century, the One Villagers spoke one dialect, the Two Villagers about five, and the No Villagers one.

History and Cultural Relations

Archeological evidence is inconclusive on the origins of the Upper Pima/Pima-Papago. It is not clear if they are the descendants of the Hohokam or of some other pre-European culture such as the Mogollon. In early post-European times, they bordered various Apache tribes to the east; the Opata, Lower Pima, and Seri to the south; the Cocopa, Quechan (or Yuma), and Maricopa to the west; and the Yavapai to the north. In the premodern period, relations with the Apache, Quechan, and Yavapai were warlike, those with the Cocopa and Maricopa were peaceful, and those with other peoples were ruled by the Pax Hispanica.

The periods of post-European history are scant European contact (c. 1550–1700), premodern (1700–1900), and modern (1900–the present). Contact began soon after Columbus, but Spanish mission and secular (military, ranching, mining) settlement did not enter Upper Pima territory until nearly 1700. Throughout the premodern period those settlements, whether Spanish, Mexican, or European-American, remained sparse and remote from centers of White culture. For their part, the Upper Pima/Pima-Papago tended to accept European-Americanization whenever it was offered. In premodern times they fought for Spain, Mexico, and the United States against Apaches and Yavapais. When the United States entered and brought peace to the region, from 1850 to 1880, ushering in the modern period, the economic pace quickened on both sides of the new U.S.-Mexican border that divided Pima-Papago territory. These post-1850 developments did not cost the Pima-Papago much additional territory. Except for a town-studded railroad swath that also passed through their territory, separating the Gila River Pimas from the Papagos, the new non-Indian settlements were on land that had earlier been ceded to Spain, Mexico, Yavapais, or Apaches. The unceded Pima-Papago territory (except for the most arid western extremity of it, the home of the Sand Papagos) was incorporated into Indian reservations between 1875 and 1925. From the largest in territory to the smallest, the reservations are Sells, Gila River, San Xavier, Salt River, Ak Chin, and Gila Bend.

Settlements

The One, Two, and No Village settlement patterns existed through the scant contact and premodern periods. Villages were a collection of household buildings (a household had separate sleeping, cooking, and storage structures), plus a central meeting house and an associated central dance ground. Prior to the 1850s, the most substantial village buildings had earth roofs and circular brush walls; mud was not, or not commonly, a building material. The No Villagers had ephemeral versions of the same building types. In particular, they had no earth-roofed buildings. On the other hand, part way through the premodern period, beginning around 1850, the One and Two Villagers added rectangular mud-walled houses to their older mudless form, and they added mud-walled Christian churches, with associated mud-walled feast houses and European-style dance grounds, to their inventory of village public buildings. These new substantial buildings were native or folk copies of Spanish prototypes. During the modern period the Gila River and Salt River reservations of traditionally One Villager People were largely divided into separate household farm allotments producing a dispersed, road-gridded settlement pattern. The largest reservation in the Two Villager tradition, the Sells Reservation, was not so divided. Its villages remained nucleated with wide open spaces between them.

In some respects, however, all reservations, large or small, allotted or not, and whatever their prior settlement pattern, have now become like dispersed small American towns. The downtown is the reservation or tribal headquarters and the distinct villages, or grid of allotments, are the neighborhoods. Like a small town, the reservation is a bounded, self-governing, self-serving social entity of a few thousand people. Unlike a typical U.S. town, however, there is very little commercial (buying and selling) activity. As in previous eras, the gift, not the sale, is the dominant Indian-to-Indian mode of exchange. Therefore, there is nothing in a reservation resembling a business district. Nowadays people buy most of their necessities, but they do so in White towns off the reservation, and they sell little among themselves.

Economy

Subsistence and Commercial Activities. Prior to the modern period, the No Villagers subsisted on a few highly specialized plants as well as some game animals. The Two Villagers had slightly more abundant wild plant food, better hunting opportunities, and cultivable fields in which they grew tepary beans, maize, and squash. The One Villagers had access to fertile river flood plains which provided them with surplus crops. The Spanish brought horses, cattle, wheat, and much else to Pima-Papago awareness, but it was only with the Pax Americana that the Indians could safely cultivate those plants. Two and No Villagers then labored for the geographically better endowed One Villagers, as well as for incoming European-Americans. Since the 1960s, welfare payments and reservation service-sector jobs (working for "the town"—see above) have supplemented the older migratory day-work practice; the traditional food-getting economy is nearly extinct. In aboriginal times, only the dog was domesticated. Cattle, horses, chickens, and so on were introduced early by Europeans and remain important today.

Industrial Arts. Aboriginal crafts included pottery, basketry, and cotton weaving. Pima-Papago arts were utilitarian. Pottery was used for hauling water and cooking. Baskets were used for food storage and preparation. Iron and steel were early adopted for cutting and digging, but stone was retained into the twentieth century for pounding and grinding foodstuffs. By the 1960s, nearly all pottery and baskets were produced for sale to White-Indian traders, not for home use.

Trade. There was aboriginal trade in raw materials among the One, Two, and No Villagers, and among them and other Indian groups. No and Two Villagers exchanged their labor for the grains of the One Villagers. During the last half of the nineteenth century, the One Villagers along the Gila River enjoyed a prosperous trade with White settlers and migrants (such as journeyers to California). As White settlers diverted the river water for their own crops, the One Villagers' farming boom ceased.

Division of Labor. In all periods, men did most of the hunting, farming, and building, and women gathered wild foods and fetched water, made baskets and pottery, cooked, and cared for the young children. Native ritual and curing practices were assigned primarily to men, but women dominated the premodern folk Christian liturgies. Both sexes worked as migrant cash laborers, and both work in the contemporary tribal service economies.

Land Tenure. Land was abundant and fields and houses were easy to make (fifty person hours for an earth-covered house, five hours for a No Villager house). There was a tendency toward patrilineal inheritance of fields and house sites and to patrilocal postmarital residence, but few people felt constrained by those tendencies. Men could reside matrilocally and people could relocate with cousins.

Kinship

Kin Groups and Descent. There were pan-Pima-Papago patrimoieties whose totems were the Coyote and Buzzard. There were five pan-Pima-Papago patrilineal sibs, three Buzzard, and two Coyote. Neither moiety nor sib membership had much effect on marriage, material property, or religious or political office. Sib membership did determine one form of intimate behavior: the word a child used to address his or her father. People without a Pima-Papago father lacked a socially proper way to say "my daddy." In effect this was a pan-Pima-Papago endogamy enforcer. The important economic grouping was the bilateral kindred. A person's kindred extended outside the local community. A prohibition against marrying close relatives (up to second cousins) encouraged this tendency and resulted in households with far-reaching bilateral ties.

Kinship Terminology. Pima-Papago parental generation kin terms were of the lineal type, which uses a distinct term for each relative. For one's own generation two distinct terms were used, which is characteristic of the Eskimo and Iroquois types, but the logic of the Pima-Papago deployment conforms to neither type. The Pima-Papago logic pertains to the relative age either of a sister (by English reckoning) or female cousin to oneself or of a female cousin's parent relative to one's own parent. One term means "younger sister, or child of my parent's younger brother or sister," and the other term means "older sister, or child of my parent's older brother or sister." It is a relative age-sensitive version of the Hawaiian type of same-generation terminology.

Marriage and Family

Marriage. Marriage was permitted with nonrelatives and relatives more remote than second cousins, with marriages arranged by the bride's parents soon after puberty. The levirate and sororate were practiced and polygyny permitted. The husband's first marriage was at sixteen or seventeen years of age. Patrilocal residence was the norm until a couple had several children, when they then built their own house. The primary cause of divorce was a bad temper; next came infidelity. Couples could take their dispute to the Keeper of the Smoke at the central village meeting house (see below). After divorce, men and women tended to remarry quickly.

Domestic Unit. The aboriginal standard was the extended family. Among contemporary Pima-Papago the nuclear family is the norm, yet extended family members usually live nearby.

Inheritance. In aboriginal times individual property, including the deceased's house, was destroyed or buried with the dead. Since land is indestructible and was held not individually but through layers of collective rights, tracts of land, including fields, were neither destroyed after death nor simply transferred to single inheritors. Earth-bound productive resources were constantly but slowly redealt and reshuffled. This is less true today as U.S. probate procedures and inheritance law are used in each reservation's tribal court. Besides land (primarily on the allotted reservations where land is now leased to outsiders), horses (formerly destroyed), cattle (primarily on unallotted reservations), and bank savings are now probated.

Socialization. Child rearing discouraged boisterous or affrontive expressions of hostility or anger. As they matured, children were trained to be modest and retiring. Young people were continually taught a moral code of industry, fortitude, and swiftness of foot.

Sociopolitical Organization

Social Organization. In early times, class distinctions were absent. Status came with heading a large family. The various language dialect groups comprised politically autonomous local or regional bands. There was some intermixing of these bands at ceremonies, and by the mid-nineteenth century there was a pan-Pima-Papago native-centered mythology with public commemorations at two known pan-Pima-Papago ceremonial centers. The ceremony was called the _wi:gita_ (see below).

Political Organization. Aboriginally the Pima-Papago had no centralized regulation of production, exchange, war, or diplomacy. Each village was autonomous but joined with other villages of the regional band for war and ceremonies. Villages had headmen (Keepers of the Smoke) who were at the center of local public life. The headmen ideally were generous, soft-spoken, and humorous. Synonyms for the headman were the "Wise Speaker," "Fire Maker," "Keeper of the Basket," "One Above," "One Ahead," and "One Made Big." Other offices were War Leader, Hunt Leader, Irrigation Ditch Leader, and Song Leader. Shamans, as seers, were none of the above. The above offices pertained to talking and to gaining consensus through talk, not to seeing in the dark (the shaman's specialty). Shamans were thought to have personalities different from politicians. Village council matters concerned agriculture, hunting, war, and dates for ceremonies and games to be held with other villages. The headmen did not pronounce a decision unless there was consensus.

All the reservations adopted U.S.-modeled constitutions in the 1930s (some were grouped under single tribal jurisdictions, however). These constitutions connected villages to districts and then to tribes by establishing elected offices or councilmen (now men and women) at district and tribal levels. The constitutions produced office-rich, high-participation governments, since the tribes had populations equivalent to small U.S. towns. Most matters for council consideration arise from outside (White) initiative; the councils primarily carry White (Bureau of Indian Affairs, private corporate) proposals to grass-root respondents.

Social Control and Conflict. Traditional society operated with a minimum of overt control. Conflicts were glossed over in an attempt to maintain order. Peaceableness was a virtue. For minor offenses, the fear of gossip was a control, as was the fear of witchcraft or sorcery. (One never knew who might be a shaman, at least a bad shaman.) Major offenders might be banished by council decision and bad shamans might be executed, allegedly after village council discussion. Mystical punishments for the violation of taboos were also believed in, and many native sicknesses (see below) were said to result from such violations. Conflict with non-Pima-Papagos was minimized. Warfare was rationalized as defensive. Pima-Papagos fought as mercenaries for Spain, Mexico, and the United States in defense of the latter's frontiers. They sold captive Apaches and Yavapais to Spaniards and Mexicans, and they continued to hold their warrior initiation ceremonies, as "mock battles," long after the Pax Americana.

Religion and Expressive Culture

Religious Beliefs.　Little is known of Pima-Papago beliefs prior to the nineteenth century, which saw, as noted above, a remarkable pan-Pima-Papago pagan religious synthesis. This synthesis was certainly achieved in the knowledge of Christianity and may have been at least partly a response to it. The myth synthesis featured a murdered man-god analogous to Jesus, and the corresponding public ceremony (the wi:gita) was analogous to, and echoed, neighboring Christian tribes' (such as Yaqui) Easter ceremonies. Meanwhile, and probably before this pagan synthesis, God, the devil, the saints, heaven, and hell were all acknowledged. Folk Christianity preceded mission-led Christianity in the northern Upper Pima/Pima-Papago area.

The nineteenth-century pagan prose mythology has as its principal characters two man-gods (a Creator and a Culture Hero), one of whom was murdered by public consent like Jesus; Coyote and Buzzard (moiety totems); a female monster; a race of exterminated humans; and the ancestral Pima-Papagos as the exterminators (this mythology is currently under tribal revision in the direction of pacifism among ancient Indians). The Christian pantheon has long been recognized. Shaman seers and gifted nonshamans dream songs from all the above, Christian and pagan, and from many other things and spirits as well. The songs constitute a literature supplementary to, and actually greater than, the prose mythology. Finally, well into the twentieth century and continuing in parts today, there were native traditional (pagan) public ceremonies for rain, farming, hunting, war, and other activities; and there was an elaborate, generally private (performed at home) development of ritual cures for sicknesses caused by taboo violations.

Religious Practitioners.　Shamans divined for both public ceremonies and private cures. Shamans do not divine for Christian rituals nor for traditional or constitutional governmental deliberations. There were and are non-shaman singers and chanters-orators for all pagan and church religious observances. Certain ceremonies required nonspeaking, sometimes dancing, sometimes costumed, functionaries as well.

Medicine.　"Staying sickness," a class of illness considered to be unique to the Pima-Papago, is an important contemporary religious expression. The sicknesses come from breaking taboos associated with many animals, some plants, unbaptized saints' images, Christian devils, and the wi:gita ceremony. Over a lifetime an individual becomes the host of many such maladies. When a sickness builds to an intolerable level, a shaman is called to make a diagnosis. The shaman then performs a "seeing," with singing, sucking, and blowing, and announces the cause—the violated "way" of the "dangerous object" (from the above list of types). The shaman either sings (and blows) the required liturgy or advises another ritual curer who can do so. This cure originates in and belongs to the offended "way." Upon hearing or feeling the cure, this "way" lifts its power from the sick person.

Death and Afterlife.　The death of others is feared by the living. The spirit of the dead is to proceed to a land of the dead "below the east." The dead live in a community like that of the living yet free from hardships. Burial was formerly at a distance from the village in a rock-covered enclosure or a cave that faced east. A person's possessions were buried with the deceased, placed on top of the mound or destroyed at home. Funeral practices now have a Christian form, with consecrated cemeteries. A one-year death anniversary is observed for the deceased. In addition, on All Souls' Day a feast is prepared by families who vacate their homes to allow the spirits of the dead to visit the household in peace.

Bibliography

Bahr, Donald M. (1988). "Pima-Papago Christianity." *Journal of the Southwest* 30:133–147.

Bahr, Donald M., J. Gregorio, D. Lopez, and A. Alvarez (1974). *Piman Shamanism and Staying Sickness*. Tucson: University of Arizona Press.

Ortiz, Alfonso, ed. (1983). *Handbook of North American Indians*. Vol. 10, *Southwest*, 125–229. Washington D.C.: Smithsonian Institution.

Russell, Frank (1980). *The Pima Indians*. Tucson: University of Arizona Press.

Underhill, Ruth (1939). *Social Organization of the Papago Indians*. New York: Columbia University Press.

Underhill, Ruth (1946). *Papago Indian Religion*. New York: Columbia University Press.

DONALD M. BAHR and DAVID L. KOZAK

Polynesians

ETHNONYM: Pacific Islanders

Orientation

Identification.　Polynesia is the culture area of the Pacific Ocean that lies roughly between 170° and 110° E and 40° to 20° S. It is a vast area with a relatively small population occupying a number of coral and volcanic islands. Only the Hawaiian and Line islands are north of the Equator. Despite the large area and geographical spread of the islands, traditional Polynesian cultures were similar linguistically and culturally. The major island groupings, most of which were and are now distinct political entities, are American Samoa, Cook Islands, French Polynesia, the Hawaiian Islands, Niue, Pitcairn Island, Tokelau, Tonga, Wallis, Futuna, and Western Samoa. In some classification schemes, Fiji and the Ellice Islands are included in Polynesia, but more often they are classified in

Melanesia. Most Polynesians who have immigrated to and settled in North America have done so in the last thirty or so years and live almost exclusively in the United States. They are mainly from American Samoa, Western Samoa, Tonga, and Hawaii.

Location. Polynesians in North America live mainly on the West Coast. The major Samoan communities are in the Los Angeles and San Francisco areas, with smaller communities in San Diego and Seattle. There are also several thousand Samoans in St. Louis and Salt Lake City, most of whom are Mormons. Tongans live mainly near Los Angeles and San Francisco with a smaller community in Salt Lake City. Hawaiians live mostly in California.

Demography. Estimates for 1982 indicate that in the United States there were 24,000 American Samoans, 20,000 Western Samoans, 10,000 Tongans, 1,200 French Polynesians, and 510 Cook Islanders, Niueans, and Tokelauans. In 1981 there were 515 Polynesians in Canada.

Linguistic Affiliation. Because of the long political and economic affiliation with the United States and the British Empire, most Polynesians enter North America already speaking English as well as their native language. There are language education programs in both the Samoan and the Tongan communities designed to maintain the native language in North America, although the majority of U.S.-born Polynesians speak only English fluently.

History and Cultural Relations

For most Polynesian islands, contact with the Western world goes back to the eighteenth and nineteenth centuries when explorers, missionaries, and business interests visited and eventually settled on the major islands. Hawaii was visited by Congregational ministers in 1819. Later in the century the native rulers were overthrown and the economy and political structure came under control of American business interests, with Hawaii formally annexed by the United States in 1898. It became the fiftieth state in 1959. Because of the long and intense contact with the United States, native Hawaiians who immigrated to the mainland arrrived already assimilated into mainstream American society. American Samoa was claimed by the United States in 1900, and other island cultures were claimed at various times by Germany, France, and New Zealand. Today, Western Samoa, Tonga, and Tuvalu are independent nations; American Samoa is a territory of the United States; Wallis, Futuna, and French Polynesia are territories of France; Tokelau is governed by New Zealand; and the Cook Islands and Niue are independent though affiliated with New Zealand.

Samoan immigration to the United States began in the 1950s and is part of a broader diaspora of Pacific Island peoples to cities in their own islands, to other islands, New Zealand, Australia and the United States. Tongan migration to the United States began in the 1960s. On some islands, such as the Cook Islands, out-migration is so great that now more people live away from the islands than on them. The major factor pushing people off the islands is the lack of economic opportunity, and the major pull factor is economic opportunity in the cities or in developed nations. The actual host nation one migrates to is determined mainly by the historical ties between an island and the developed nation and the cur-

rent immigration policies of the host nation. Thus, American Samoans can enter the United States freely, but Tongans and Western Samoans are subject to immigration restrictions. Cook Islanders and others with ties to New Zealand are more likely to migrate there, although some are now moving on to the United States where economic prospects seem brighter. Most immigration has been in the form of chain migrations, with relatives assisting others who follow them to the United States. In the past, overseas immigration was cyclical; today, most immigrants settle permanently in the United States. It has been suggested that those who do return to the islands are mostly people who have failed economically overseas.

Within the United States, Polynesians remain an economically disadvantaged group. Their cultural identity is ambiguous, as they are rarely identified by other Americans as being from a specific island or even as Polynesians or Pacific Islanders. Rather, they are more often lumped with Filipinos or Asians in general or with Latinos or African-Americans.

Settlements

As mentioned above, Polynesians are settled in urban areas, mainly on the West Coast. They do not form distinct ethnic neighborhoods, although there is a marked preference for extended family living arrangements and for relatives to live near one another.

Economy

In traditional Polynesia, farming and fishing were the major subsistence activities. But skills associated with farming and fishing are of little value in the urban United States and most Polynesians find employment in unskilled and semiskilled jobs. Men work mainly in construction and in factories, and women work in such low-level service jobs as maids or hospital aides. The unemployment rate among Polynesian men in the 1970s was 25 percent. Recently, more Polynesians are attending college, suggesting the possibility of greater Polynesian involvement in the professional and business sectors in future years. Although Polynesians as a group are economically disadvantaged in the United States, they perceive their situation there as more favorable than it would be in the islands. An important feature of the Polynesian economy in the United States is the economic ties maintained with the homeland. These include ownership of island property and regular cash remittances sent to kin on the islands. These transfers are used to pay debts, to support the emigration of kin, to purchase goods, and to finance development projects. In Polynesian nations with a large out-migration, these remittances are a major economic resource and benefit the nation by raising living standards, increasing employment, and reducing balance of payment problems. They are not exclusively an economic boon, however, as they tend to inflate prices in the local economy.

Kinship, Marriage and Family

Most initial immigrants were young men who after finding a job and a place to live arranged for other family members to follow. The initial stage of this chain migration process is now nearly complete, with the sex ratio in Polynesian communities nearly balanced. Extended family households are a basic feature of the islands' economic and social systems. In the

United States, the extended family serves as a major adaptive mechanism for Polynesians. Domestic groups tend to be large and flexible, readily accepting newcomers to the United States or others in need. In addition, ties are maintained with other kin within the larger Samoan or Tongan community. The household unit also serves a basic economic function, as a mechanism through which money and material goods can be shared and distributed within the extended family and as an employment center for recent arrivals in need of work. Ties to kin in the islands are maintained through visits to the homeland and the remittances. Socialization for life in the United States begins for many Polynesians in their native countries, where formal education outside the home usually emphasizes Western culture and teaches skills useful in the U.S. economy. In America, formal education and the church play major socialization roles, with the latter providing education in the traditional culture.

Sociopolitical Organization

Relationships between individuals and between groups in traditional Polynesian societies rest on an interlocking and intricate set of relations and identities based on reciprocity, land ownership, status, place of residence (island and village), and kinship. To some extent, Polynesians immigrating to the United States, because they are younger, better educated, and more likely to come from cities or towns, are less involved in the traditional social and political structure than those who stay behind. Still, various traditional beliefs and practices, especially those concerning generosity, obligations to kin, and traditional sources of authority, remain important for the first generation of immigrants, especially within the Polynesian communities. For the second generation, more involved in mainstream society with the emphasis on achievement and status differentials based on wealth, adherence to traditional beliefs and customs is more difficult.

The various churches play a central social and political role in the Samoan and Tongan communities in the United States. With missionary activities going back to the early 1800s in Polynesia, Polynesians who immigrate to the United States are almost all Christians and all were involved in the church community on their island. In the United States, churches remain the center of Polynesian social life, with ministers often playing the role of culture broker in smoothing adaptation to American life while providing continuity with the traditional culture left behind. Samoans, Hawaiians, and Tongans have also formed social, recreational, cultural, and political interest groups outside the church, with a pan-Polynesian identity and movement emerging in the 1970s.

Religion and Expressive Culture

The majority of Tongans in the United States are Mormons, that church's missionaries having been active in Tonga. Some are Methodists, since the Methodist church is the state church in Tonga. The Tongan communities in St. Louis and Salt Lake City are heavily involved with the Mormon church. Samoans are mostly Protestants (Methodist, Congregationalist, Presbyterian, Pentecostal), though some are Mormons, Catholics, and Seventh-Day Adventists. As noted above, the function of churches in Polynesian communities goes well beyond religion with much of the community social and political organization centered on the local church.

Bibliography

Ablon, Joan (1971). "The Social Organization of an Urban Samoan Community." *Southwestern Journal of Anthropology* 27:75–96.

Connell, John (1987). "Paradise Left? Pacific Island Voyagers in the Modern World." In *Pacific Bridges: The New Immigration from Asia and the Pacific Islands,* edited by James T. Fawcett and Benjamin V. Cariño, 375–404. Staten Island, N.Y.: Center for Migration Studies.

Doi, Mary L., Chien Lin, and Indu Vohra-Sahu (1981). *Pacific/Asian American Research: An Annotated Bibliography.* Chicago: Pacific/Asian American Mental Health Research Center.

Macpherson, Cluny, Bradd Shore, and Robert Franco, eds. (1978). *New Neighbors: Islanders in Adaptation.* Santa Cruz, Calif.: Center for South Pacific Studies.

Shore, Bradd (1980). "Pacific Islanders." In *Harvard Encyclopedia of American Ethnic Groups,* edited by Stephan Thernstrom, 763–768. Cambridge: Harvard University Press, Belknap Press.

Pomo

ETHNONYMS: Bidakamtata, Boya, Che'e Foka, Gallinomero, Habenapo, Kale, Kashaya, Konhomtata, Kuhlanapo, Shokowa, Yokaya

Orientation

Identification. "Pomo" and "Pomoan" refer to a family of seven California Indian languages and to their speakers. The seven are often differentiated by placing a direction before the word *Pomo*: Southwestern Pomo, Southern Pomo, Central Pomo, Northern Pomo, Northeastern Pomo, Eastern Pomo, and Southeastern Pomo. Two of these seven groups had a name for themselves as a whole and thus can be referred to by adaptations of their self-designations: "Kashaya" (Southwestern Pomo) and "Salt Pomo" (Northeastern Pomo). The others had names for their politically separate village communities but not for the language groups as a whole. The name "Pomo" arises from a blend of two terms in the Northern Pomo language: the common noun $p^h\bar{o}'$ *ma'*, "inhabitants," and $p^h o\bullet$ *mo•*, "at red earth hole," a specific village.

Location. Six of the linguistic groups lived in a compact area of northern California with a southern boundary fifty miles north of San Francisco (about 38°20′ N), extending northward for ninety miles (to about 39°20′ N), and from the Pacific Ocean inland for fifty miles to Clear Lake. The seventh group, the Salt Pomo, lived in a small detached area on the east side of the Inner Coast Range, about twenty miles to the northeast of the main body. The climate is of the Mediterranean type, with rainy winters and dry summers. Along the coast, the summers are foggy and cool, ideal for the redwood forests. In the interior, the summers are very hot and dry.

Demography. The aboriginal population of all the Pomo has been variously estimated at from eight thousand to twenty-one thousand. The numbers were not evenly distributed among the seven linguistic groups: the Kashaya, Salt Pomo, and Southeastern Pomo were the smallest at about 5 percent each of the total. The Eastern were about 10 percent, the Central Pomo about 15 percent, and the Southern and Northern about 30 percent each. The more numerous linguistic groups were divided into a larger number of politically independent village communities. In the devastation of the nineteenth century, over 90 percent of the population was lost, down to a nadir of about eight hundred. The population recovered somewhat, to twelve hundred by 1910 and has increased steadily since. Later censuses are quite inadequate, as they count only residents of current reservations and omit the great majority of the Pomo who live either on land whose reserved status has been terminated or at other sites.

Linguistic Affiliation. The seven languages of the Pomoan family are quite distinct; at the maximum divergence they are more different from each other than are English and German. At a deeper time depth the Pomoan family is postulated to have been related to other Indian languages, scattered from northern California southward into Mexico, in the Hokan linguistic stock.

History and Cultural Relations

The Pomo were bordered on the north by the three Yukian groups—Coast Yuki, Yuki, Huchnom—on the northeast by the Patwin, on the southeast by the Wappo and Lake Miwok, and on the south by the Coast Miwok. The diversity of languages in a compact area suggests that the Pomo have lived somewhere in their present territory, developing their unique speech forms, for a very long time, on the order of fifteen hundred years. The Salt Pomo have a legend of migrating from a place next to other Pomo across the Inner Coast Range to their present location in recent prehistoric times. If this is so, they must have already possessed a distinct language, as its divergence from the other Pomoan languages is so great as normally to have taken a millennium or so.

The destruction of the Pomo began with the founding of the San Rafael Mission in 1817 and the Sonoma Mission in 1823, with the Southern Pomo the first to be severely affected. In the Russian River and Clear Lake regions, Mexican land grants, rapid settlement, and conversion of the land to grazing and farming deprived the Indians of their former livelihood. In 1833, an epidemic, possibly cholera, took many; in 1838–1839, many more died of smallpox. From 1834 to 1847, thousands died from these causes and from Mexican military campaigns. Survivors were pressed into forced labor, both locally and, later, in distant gold mines. Two White settlers particularly abusive of the Clear Lake Indians were killed in 1849; a U.S. cavalry punitive force swept through the area, northward along the lake and westward to the Russian River valleys, massacring along the way Southeastern, Eastern,

Northern, and Central Pomo, most of whom had nothing to do with the killing of the pair of men. Especially infamous was the slaughter of an innocent fishing party at a place known since as Bloody Island. In the next few years, the surviving Pomo were rounded up and forced onto the Mendocino Indian Reserve and the Round Valley Reservation (considerably north of Pomo territory and mixed with non-Pomo groups). Some escaped to return to their ancestral homes, and the Mendocino Reserve was disbanded. These Indians could not renew their earlier life and became agricultural workers.

The Kashaya have a unique history among the Pomo. Their first contact with Europeans was not with Hispanic or Anglo-Americans but with Russians at the Fort Ross colony, 1811–1842. Because of their relative freedom from forced removal to missions and reservations and their isolation from the regions of densest settlement, they are now the culturally best preserved of the Pomo groups, with more speakers of their language (perhaps sixty) than all the rest of the Pomo combined.

Settlements

The Pomo groups lived in three ecological regions: coast-redwood, river valley, and lake. Each region had hinterland mountainous areas used for hunting and gathering plant food. The Kashaya lived in the coast-redwood region, and the Southern, Central, and Northern Pomo, in the succession of valleys along the Russian River drainage, with territorial extensions to the coast. The Eastern Pomo lived on easterly and northerly shores of Clear Lake. The Southeastern Pomo lived on three islands in the southeastern part of Clear Lake, with ownership and use of adjacent mainland. One Northern Pomo community had an extension to a portion of the northwestern shore of the lake. The Northeastern Pomo lived on the east side of the Inner Coast Range. There were about seventy-five tribelets and several hundred named former settlement sites, not all occupied at one time. The village sizes varied from hamlets of fifty to major centers of over five hundred. In the middle of the twentieth century there were twenty-one small reservations, some bought by the government and others by Pomo groups for themselves. In the 1960s fifteen of these were terminated. Many Pomo still live in their ancestral territory in small rancherias or in adjacent towns where work is available; others are scattered across the United States. Three types of houses were constructed: large semisubterranean ceremonial houses, semisubterranean sweat houses, and dwellings. The dwellings on the coast were conical lean-tos of slabs of redwood bark, suitable for one family only; elsewhere the dwellings could hold several families and consisted of a framework of willow poles with grass thatching in the valleys and tule thatching near Clear Lake.

Economy

Subsistence and Commercial Activities. The Pomo were hunters and gatherers. From the coast, fish were taken, and shellfish and edible seaweed gathered. In the hills, valleys, and coastal plains, edible bulbs, seeds, nuts, and greens were collected, and deer, elk, rabbits, and squirrels hunted or trapped. From the rivers and streams fish were taken. In the lake, fish were plentiful, and in winter the migratory waterfowl numbered in the millions. The staple food for all the

Pomo was the acorn. Both the coastal and lake dwellers allowed others to fish and take food from their unique environments. Most now work for wages and buy their food in a grocery, though many still like to gather old-time foods like acorns and seaweed. The commonest wage work in the past century has been as laborers in agricultural fields or canneries. Coastal Indians have had better paying work in lumber camps. With more education, many are now moving on to better jobs. In daily life, little clothing was worn: men usually went naked but in cold weather might wrap themselves in a robe or mantle of skin or tule; women wore a skirt of skins or of shredded bark or tule. Elaborate costumes of feathers and shells were, and still are, worn on ceremonial occasions.

Industrial Arts.   As money and as gifts, beads were produced in large numbers: most common were beads made from clam shells collected principally at Bodega Bay in Coast Miwok territory. More valuable were larger beads of magnesite, known as "Indian gold." Pendants of abalone were also appreciated. Mortars and pestles of stone were shaped for grinding acorns and various seeds. Knives and arrowheads were of obsidian and chert. Boats of bundled tule were used on Clear Lake; only rafts were used on the coast. The Pomo are famous for their fine baskets.

Trade.   There was aboriginally a considerable amount of trade among the various Pomo communities and with neighboring non-Pomo. Items traded included salt from the Salt Pomo, and from the coastal groups came shells, magnesite, finished beads, obsidian, tools, basketry materials, skins, and food that one group might have in excess and another need. Beads were the measure of value, and the Pomo were adept in counting them to the tens of thousands.

Division of Labor.   The men did the hunting, fishing, and fighting. Women gathered the plant food and prepared the food; especially time consuming was the grinding and leaching of the staple acorn. Men made the beads, rabbit-skin blankets, weapons, coarsely twined burden baskets, and quail and fish traps. Women wove the fine baskets.

Land Tenure.   Aboriginally, with few exceptions, land and hunting and gathering rights were possessed by the village community. Some Central Pomo had family ownership of certain oak trees, berry bushes, and bulb fields. For the Southeastern Pomo, land around their island villages was communally owned, but named tracts of land on the mainland were owned by individual families, who had exclusive gathering rights, although others might be allowed to hunt there. Of twenty-one small reservations existing in the middle of the twentieth century, fourteen were terminated in the 1960s and the land allocated to individual ownership. Many sold their land, and thus outsiders are living among these groups. Many have also left these reservations and bought homes in towns near and far.

Kinship

Kin Groups and Descent.   Kin groups were the most important social unit. Such groups shared, and many still share, labor and its fruits, and support each other politically. There was an institution of "special friend" (with a term that worked like kin terms), which could be established between two individuals by a ritual exchange of gifts. The chief with the largest kin group was usually the most powerful. Having no kin was

the ultimate in poverty: there was no social security, no one to provide food when one's own efforts failed. The kinless person was fair game for any aggressor as there was no one to avenge a wrong.

Kinship Terminology.   The Pomo groups have elaborate systems of kin terms, distinguishing father's father from mother's father, and father's mother from mother's mother. Although there are distinct forms for grandchildren, in many families reciprocal terms are used. For example, in Southern Pomo, a woman who addresses or refers to her maternal grandmother by a word built on the root *-ka-*, or her paternal grandmother by one with *-ma-*, would in turn be addressed or referred to with words constructed with *-ka-* and *-ma-*, respectively. The parents of the grandparents are often designated by the grandparent terms, or more specifically by a phrase, but Southeastern Pomo has unique terms for great-grandfather and great-grandmother. The Kashaya kinship system has been labeled as of the Hawaiian type, that of the Southern Pomo as Crow, and the rest as Omaha. Nevertheless, most share certain features: siblings of grandparents are called by the same terms as the grandparents. At the parent level, most of the languages have separate terms for one's father's older and younger brothers, and for mother's older and younger sisters, but only one term for father's older and younger sisters and one for mother's older and younger brothers. Descent is reckoned evenly on both the paternal and maternal sides. It was a grave insult to say the name of the dead in the presence of a living relative. In Kashaya, however, the dead could be referred to by a kinship term suffixed by *-ya'*, to indicate respect.

Marriage and Family

Marriage.   Marriage partners could be arranged either by the young couple or by their families, though usually all parties would have to concur. The couple could be from the same village or different ones. The man's parents presented gifts (food, beads, blankets, baskets) to the bride's parents, and gifts of nearly equal value were later returned. The young couple could take up residence with either set of parents, and they often moved from one to the other, returning to the woman's parents for the birth of the first child. Divorce was as simple as one party moving out. The levirate and sororate were both known; in fact, the word for stepfather is usually the same as the term for father's younger brother, and stepmother the same as mother's younger sister.

Domestic Unit.   Three- and even four-generation households were and still are common.

Inheritance.   Land belonged to the community or family. Homes were usually burned after a death, and personal possessions were cremated with the deceased, so that there was little to bequeath. Ceremonial paraphernalia might be passed on to an apprentice.

Socialization.   Children are raised permissively; threats and warnings are used much more than chastisement. Behavioral restrictions are often taught by means of stories in which the principal character breaks a rule and suffers through supernatural means, severe retribution, or often death. Children are often raised by their grandparents. Households unable to care for all their children might let some be raised by related couples who are otherwise childless.

Sociopolitical Organization

Social Organization.   The family and extended kin group was the most important social unit. Women had equal status.

Political Organization.   The largest political unit was the tribelet or village community, which could consist of several villages. There were chiefs on several levels, hereditary and elected. There were kin group chiefs and assistant chiefs; if there were several such units in a village or village community, one might be chosen as head chief. Duties varied and included giving counsel, negotiating with other groups, presiding over ceremonies, feasts, and work parties, and distributing the fruits of communal labor.

Social Control.   Breaking any of a vast array of restrictions or taboos could lead to sickness from supernatural agents; death could be averted only by timely treatment by a shaman. The kin group controlled the actions of its members. In case of transgression against non-kin by any group member, the kin group would have to pay compensation, and failure to do so would call forth a revenge attack, either a clandestine killing or magical poisoning. Death of any kin group member, not only of the individual transgressor, was proper vengeance.

Conflict.   Most conflict was in the form of feuds between kin groups and might arise from poaching or suspicion of causing sickness by magical poisoning. Alliances with other communities, even non-Pomo, might be made to carry out conflict on a larger scale. Peace was brought about by negotiation and the payment of reparations to the relatives of those killed.

Religion and Expressive Culture

Religious Beliefs.   All the Pomo believed in a creator who made the world. Most equated this creator with Coyote, the animal and the mythological trickster. Some Eastern Pomo gave the creator a different name, separating him from the other roles of Coyote. All believed that there was a time in the distant past when animals could speak and had other human as well as animal attributes. Then all creatures changed to their present forms. Supernatural forces abided in everything; specific named supernatural beings could appear to one who broke a rule, such as a childbirth or menstrual taboo on a woman or her husband, and by fright cause coma and death. In the early historical period, the Pomo were performing a Kuksu ceremony, in which dancers impersonated certain spirits. In 1871, the Ghost Dance swept in from Nevada across northern California, predicting the return of the dead and the elimination of White people. This reached the Pomo in 1872 in a modification called the Earth Lodge Cult, which stressed a destruction of the world from which the faithful could be protected by gathering in subterranean lodges. Pomo from as far away as the Kashaya streamed into the Clear Lake region to await this event. When the end did not come, the participants suffered great hardship and starvation, not being prepared for life to go on. A development, known as the Bole-Maru, abandoned the belief in imminent catastrophe and stressed belief in an afterlife and a supreme being. Local dreamers and prophets among the various Pomo groups have guided further evolution, even to this day. Most Pomo now belong to some Christian church, but many still fear the consequences of breaking old restrictions.

Religious Practitioners.   Shamans may conduct ceremonies and preach and prophesy or they may doctor. They may specialize in one function or the other, or do both. In the past, they may have inherited the position, but now the powers are usually received through dream inspiration plus apprenticeship. It is said that before 1870 most shamans were men, but now women predominate.

Ceremonies.   Ceremonies were held for certain annual occasions. The Kashaya still hold some of these: in May the strawberry festival for the blessing of the first fruits of the year; in the fall an acorn festival; in summer four nights of sacred dances ending with a feast on the Fourth of July; and in winter possibly another dance. At any time a feast might be pledged, conditional on a sick family member recovering, and then the pledge is carried out by the kin group. The Pomo had a great variety of amusements, games, and sports. One rough team sport that could involve an entire village was a game similar to lacrosse. But, the game in which they took the most passionate interest was that called the hand game (it involves guessing which hand of the opponent holds a marked bone). This they could play all night and would often wager all their possessions on its outcome.

Arts.   Pomo baskets are considered by many to be the finest in the world. They are admired for the great variety of weaves and styles; the delicacy, evenness, and tightness of the stitching; and the artistry of the design. Most spectacular is the sun basket whose surface pattern is made of feathers of different natural colors. The art form still lives and appears to be expanding; the finer work sells for very high prices. In the past century the women have vied in producing the largest baskets (which take many years to complete) and the smallest (which approach pinhead size). The art of singing is well developed for almost any occasion: ceremonial dancing, blessing, doctoring, warding off evil, bringing good luck in the harvest, hunting, attracting a mate, gambling, and so on. Two-part singing is common: one sings the melody while another, called the "rock," keeps the rhythm vocally. Rhythm was also kept with a split-stick rattle, a foot drum, and a two-toned whistle. Tattooing of both the face and body were formerly common, but now the type and frequency of tattoos are no more than among the rest of the populace.

Medicine.   Minor physical ailments like rashes, boils, sore eyes, diarrhea, constipation, or indigestion are often treated herbally by poultices or infusions of various plants and plant parts. For obvious physical injuries and recognized diseases, a White doctor is now usually consulted. Other ailments of unobvious origin might be attributed to the consequences of breaking some taboo or to poisoning (more magical than chemical) by enemies. A shaman, locally called an Indian doctor, is often successful in treating the latter problems by singing powerful songs, by the laying on of hands, or by sucking out the disease or poison. Indian doctors still practice their profession and are sometimes called in by local White people for relief of chronic ailments not helped by modern medicine.

Death and Afterlife.   The deceased were formerly cremated, but about 1870 a shift was made to burial. Mourners would bring gifts (beads, baskets, robes), some specifically designated to be burned with the dead, some to be distributed later; the bereaved family would later return an equivalent in value. The house and personal property of the deceased were also burned, lest the ghost linger around the objects. The supernatural paraphernalia of a doctor, however, might be turned over to a successor apprentice. One year after the funeral, the bones of the deceased were dug up and burned again, along with more gifts, thus terminating the period of mourning. Even now, after the shift to burial, valuable gifts may be thrown into the grave. All the Pomo believed in an afterworld. It was important to have a sacred Indian name, bestowed from the family's ancestral stock (from either the maternal or paternal side, or from both), to announce on reaching the afterworld so that ancestors who were already there could greet the newly arrived family member.

Bibliography

Barrett, Samuel A. (1952). *Material Aspects of Pomo Culture.* Milwaukee: Bulletin of the Public Museum of the City of Milwaukee, no. 20.

Bean, Lowell John, and Dorothea Theodoratus (1978). "Western Pomo and Northeastern Pomo." In *Handbook of North American Indians.* Vol. 8, *California,* edited by Robert F. Heizer, 289–305. Washington, D.C.: Smithsonian Institution.

Gifford, Edward W. (1922). *California Kinship Terminologies.* University of California Publications in American Archaeology and Ethnology, 18, 1–285. Berkeley.

Kroeber, Alfred L. (1925). *Handbook of the Indians of California.* U.S. Bureau of American Ethnology Bulletin no. 78. Washington, D.C. Reprinted, 1953.

Loeb, Edwin M. (1926). *Pomo Folkways.* University of California Publications in American Archaeology and Ethnology, 19(2), 149–405. Berkeley.

McLendon, Sally, and Robert L. Oswalt (1978). "Pomo: Introduction." In *Handbook of North American Indians.* Vol. 8, *California,* edited by Robert F. Heizer, 274–288. Washington, D.C.: Smithsonian Institution.

McLendon, Sally, and Michael J. Lowy (1978). "Eastern Pomo and Southeastern Pomo." In *Handbook of North American Indians.* Vol. 8, *California,* edited by Robert F. Heizer, 306–323. Washington, D.C.: Smithsonian Institution.

ROBERT L. OSWALT

Ponca

The Ponca are a Plains-Prairie Indian group who were located aboriginally in present-day southern South Dakota and northern Nebraska. Their name for themselves is "Ponka," the derivation of which is unknown. Along with the Kansa, Omaha, Osage, and Quapaw, they spoke a dialect of the Dhegiha language of the Siouan language family. They were culturally and linguistically most closely related to the Omaha and may have at one time been an Omaha band. Never a large group, they probably numbered about eight hundred at the time of contact. In 1877 they were removed to Indian Territory (now Oklahoma). But public concern about the conditions of their removal led to a federal agreement resulting in about one-third of the group returning to their traditional land near Niobrara, Nebraska, in 1880. This northern group is now largely assimilated into the neighboring White society and numbered about four hundred in 1980. The southern group in Oklahoma numbered about two thousand in 1980 and lives primarily on allotted land, where they maintain much of their traditional culture despite assimilation into the local economy.

Prior to removal, the Ponca were divided into two bands: the "Gray-blanket" band and the "Fish-smell" band. The traditional economy rested on a combination of hunting (bison were especially important), fishing, gathering, and horticulture (maize, beans, squash, tobacco). Four types of dwelling were used: earthlodges, tipis, wigwams, and elongated lodges. Traditionally, they were organized into four clans, each led by a chief with military, political, and religious authority. The Ponca Tribe of Oklahoma is today governed by elected officers and a committee. The traditional religion centered on the creator, Wakánda, and beliefs in the supernatural forces present in all things. The Peyote religion is still active among the Oklahoma Ponca.

Bibliography

Fletcher, Alice C., and Francis LaFlesche (1911). *The Omaha Tribe.* U.S. Bureau of American Ethnology, 27th Annual Report (1905–1906), 17–654. Washington, D.C.

Howard, James H. (1965). *The Ponca Tribe.* U.S. Bureau of American Ethnology Bulletin no. 195. Washington, D.C.

Potawatomi

ETHNONYM: Potewatmi

In early historic times, the Potawatomi, an Algonkian-speaking tribe closely related to the Ottawa and the Ojibwa, lived in the lower peninsula of Michigan, eastern Wisconsin, northeastern Illinois, and northwestern Indiana. Between 1836 and 1841 a large segment of the tribe moved west of the Mississippi to Iowa, Kansas, or ultimately Oklahoma. Others moved to Canada and Wisconsin, and still others chose to remain in lower Michigan. Their descendants now live on a number of reserves in Canada, intermingled with other Canadian Indian groups, and on a number of reservations and trust areas in the United States. These include the Potawatomi Indian Reservation in Kansas (the Prairie Potawatomi, a very conservative group), the Citizen Band Potawatomi Tribe of Oklahoma, the Potawatomi Indian Reservation in Wisconsin, and the Hannahville Community in Wilson, Michigan. In addition, many Potawatomi have merged with the general U.S. population or with other Indian groups—for example, with the Kickapoo in Mexico and the United States. Their estimated population in 1600 was about 4,000; in the first half of the nineteenth century there were probably 9,000–10,000 Potawatomi. The population in recent times is difficult to establish, with estimates ranging from about 2,700 to about 13,500. It is not possible to make meaningful comparisons of these latter figures with earlier estimates because of the lack of comparability of degree of blood or sociocultural characteristics between the groups.

The Potawatomi do not seem to have had an overarching tribal organization. The most important political unit was the village, which was moved periodically. Each village had its own chief who was assisted by a village council and a specialized warrior sodality, which acted as a police force. An important local chief might dominate a large number of villages. There was a strongly functioning patrilineal corporate clan system, with a secondary emphasis on matrilineal bonds. There may have been as many as thirty clans, later organized into six phratries or larger units. At one time the clans may have been localized, but with the historical population movements they became distributed among numerous villages. The clan system added cohesion to the tribe as a whole and acted as a means of social placement.

Villages were shifted annually from summer to winter quarters and varied greatly in size, from fifty inhabitants to more than a thousand. Nuclear and extended families existed, with some of the larger extended families running to four generations under the same roof. Polygyny was the preferred form of marriage.

Subsistence was based on a seasonal mixed economy with the summer devoted to horticulture (maize, beans, melons, and squash), the collection of a variety of plant foods, hunting of large game (deer, bear, and in some areas bison), and some fishing. In the winter they dispersed to smaller camps where they continued to hunt. The winter camps combined in the spring for communal hunting drives and fishing expeditions.

Each clan had an associated medicine bundle, origin myth, ritual practices, and obligations. Clans had sodalities (including the Midewiwin, a society of influential sorcerers) and various types of shamans and diviners. The individual vision quest was very important. In later years, they were heavily missionized by several religious denominations.

Bibliography

Clifton, James A. (1977). _The Prairie People: Continuity and Change in Potawatomi Culture, 1665–1965_. Lawrence: Regents Press of Kansas.

Clifton, James A. (1978). "Potawatomi." In _Handbook of North American Indians_. Vol. 15, _Northeast_, edited by Bruce G. Trigger, 725–742. Washington, D.C.: Smithsonian Institution.

Landes, Ruth (1970). _The Prairie Potawatomi: Tradition and Ritual in the Twentieth Century_. Madison: University of Wisconsin Press.

Powhatan

ETHNONYM: Pouhatan

The Powhatan are an American Indian group whose members live on the Mattoponi and Pamunkey state reservations in Virginia and in nearby communities. At the beginning of the sixteenth century the Powhatan were a confederacy of thirty tribes numbering nine thousand people in two hundred villages located on the southeastern and southwestern sides of Chesapeake Bay in Maryland and northeastern Virginia. Numbered among the Powhatan subgroups were the Appomattac, Chesapeake, Chickahominy, Mattapony, Pamunkey, Pianketank, Potomac, and Rappahannock.

The Powhatan were agriculturalists, growing maize, beans, pumpkins, and various fruits. They practiced an animistic religion and believed in the immortality of the soul. When a chief died his body was wrapped in skins, placed on a scaffold, and burned. The bodies of others were buried in the ground. The Powhatan confederacy ended in 1644 following a period of hostilities with English colonists resulting from Powhatan raids in 1622 that nearly wiped out the English settlements in Virginia. Subsequent English hostilities decimated the tribes, so that by 1705 the Powhatan were reduced to only twelve villages. The Powhatan languages belonged to the Algonkian family and were out of use by the end of the eighteenth century.

Bibliography

Sheehan, Bernard W. (1980). _Savagism and Civility: Indians and Englishmen in Colonial Virginia_. Cambridge: Cambridge University Press.

Speck, Frank G. (1928). _Chapters on the Ethnology of the Powhatan Tribes of Virginia_. New York: Museum of the American Indian.

Stern, T. (1952). "Chickahominy." _American Philosophical Society, Proceedings_ 96:176–225.

Pueblo Indians

"Pueblo Indians" is the generic label for American Indian groups of the Southwest who are descended from the Anasazi peoples who inhabited the American Southwest continuously from the eighth century A.D. Prior to Spanish arrival in and settlement of the Southwest beginning with Francisco Vásquez Coronado's expedition of 1540–1542 there were ninety or more Pueblo groups in northern Arizona and New Mexico. Today, twenty-one groups still exist, with all but two (the Hopi in Arizona and the Tigua in Texas) in northern New Mexico. Among distinguishing features of the Pueblo culture are long-term occupation of the region, permanent villages, distinctive stone or adobe pueblo dwellings built around central plazas, semisubterranean ceremonial chambers (*kivas*), a traditional subsistence economy based on the irrigated cultivation of maize, squash, and beans, and extensive use of highly stylized coiled pottery. Of the extant Pueblo groups, seven speak Keresan, six speak Tewa, five speak Tiwa, and one each speak Hopi, Towa, and Zuni languages. For the purpose of discussion, the Pueblo groups are categorized on the basis of location: Eastern (near the Rio Grande in New Mexico) or Western (in mesa and canyon country in western New Mexico and eastern Arizona). Cultural variations among groups, however, do not conform neatly to these linguistic and geographical divisions.

Extensive archaeological research indicates that ancestors of some contemporary Pueblo groups had moved north from Mexico by at least 1000 B.C. Descendants of these groups then progressed through a series of cultural traditions culminating in the distinctive Anasazi culture, whose most notable feature was the cliff dwellings found in canyons in northern Arizona and New Mexico and southern Utah and Colorado. The contemporary cultures of the surviving Pueblo groups are an amalgam of the traditional culture as modified by Mexican, Spanish, Roman Catholic, Protestant, and European-American influences. Despite centuries of external influence, however, each group has maintained its identity as a distinct people. There are important differences among groups and sometimes within groups as regards adherence to traditional beliefs and practices, degree of integration into European-American society, and economic well-being. Today, Pueblo groups and manifestations of their culture, such as pottery, jewelry, dances, and so on, are an important tourist attraction and a major element in the New Mexico State economy. Pan-Pueblo interests are represented by the All Pueblo Council, though each group retains and emphasizes its cultural and political autonomy.

Acoma. There were 2,681 Indian inhabitants of the 245,672-acre Acoma Indian Reservation in 1980. The reservation is located about sixty-five miles west of Albuquerque, New Mexico. Acoma Pueblo, located atop a 350-foot mesa, has been occupied for as long as a thousand years, making it, along with Oraibi, a Hopi village in Arizona, the two oldest, continuously occupied settlements in North America. Acoma is a western Keresan language and is still spoken, along with English. The current economy rests on cattle raising, tourism, the sale of pottery and other craft items, and mining on reservation land. The Acoma have retained much of their traditional culture. *See* Keres

Cochiti. There were 613 Indian inhabitants of the 28,776-acre Cochiti Indian Reservation in 1980. The reservation is about thirty miles southwest of Santa Fe, New Mexico. Cochiti is an eastern Keresan language and is spoken today, along with Spanish and English. Much of the traditional culture is still followed, including the traditional form of government, religious and other ceremonies open only to the Cochiti, and the wearing of traditional-style clothing. At the same time, attempts have been made at economic development to take advantage of mineral wealth on reservation land. *See* Keres

Laguna. There were 3,564 Indian inhabitants of the 412,211-acre Laguna Indian Reservation in 1980 (the reservation is actually in three parcels). It is located about forty-five miles west of Albuquerque, New Mexico. The major segment of the Acoma Reservation borders the Laguna Reservation on the west. Their name for themselves is "Kawiak," and Laguna is a western Keresan language. Laguna was settled by migrants from a number of other pueblos in 1697. Unlike other groups who live primarily in or near one village, the Laguna live in more than a half-dozen villages on the reservation. The group derives much income from royalties on uranium ore–mining leases and has invested strongly in economic development. Although more assimilated into Anglo society than most other Pueblo groups, the traditional language, religion, crafts, and ties to other groups are maintained. *See* Keres

San Felipe. There were 1,789 Indian inhabitants of the 48,853-acre San Felipe Indian Reservation in 1980. It is located twenty-five miles north of Albuquerque, New Mexico. Their name for themselves is "Katishtya." The San Felipe speak an eastern Keresan language. The contemporary culture represents a mix of the traditional culture, modern Anglo culture, and Roman Catholicism. *See* Keres

Santa Ana. There were 407 Indian inhabitants of the 45,527-acre Santa Ana Indian Reservation in 1980. It is located twenty-three miles north of Albuquerque, New Mexico. The Santa Ana name for themselves is "Tanava," and they speak an eastern Keresan language. They now live mainly in the village of Ranchos de Santa Ana on the reservation, returning to the traditional village for religious ceremonies. *See* Keres

Santo Domingo. There were 2,139 Indian inhabitants of the 69,260-acre Santo Domingo Indian Reservation in 1980. It is located about twenty-five miles southwest of Santa Fe, New Mexico. The Santo Damingo name for themselves is "Kiua," and they speak an eastern Keresan langauge. Despite regular contact with outsiders and participation in the regional and national pottery and silver jewelry market, Santo Domingo remains one of the most conservative of the Pueblo groups. Their adherence to tradtional ways is manifested in the strength of the traditional religion, the regular use of the native language, the retention of traditional clothing, and the maintenance of traditional kin ties. *See* Keres

Zia. There were 524 Indian inhabitants of the 112,511-acre Zia Indian Reservation in 1980. It is located about twenty miles southwest of Santa Fe, New Mexico. Their name for themselves is "Tseya," and they speak an eastern Keresan language. The Zia are known for their distinctive pottery and for the accommodation they have forged between their traditional culture and Roman Catholicism. *See* Keres

Nambe. There were 188 Indian inhabitants of the 19,073-acre Nambe Indian Reservation in 1980. It is located fifteen miles northeast of Santa Fe, New Mexico. The Nambe speak Tewa, a Tanoan language. The Nambe were much influenced by neighboring Spanish communities, and much of the traditional culture has disappeared. *See* Tewa

Pojoaque. There were 94 Indian residents of the 11,599-acre Pojoaque Indian Reservation in 1980. It is located fifteen miles north of Santa Fe, New Mexico. They speak Tewa, a Tanoan language. Almost extinct in the late 1800s, the Pojoaque have slowly increased in numbers, although they are largely assimilated into Anglo society. *See* Tewa

San Ildefonso. There were 488 Indian inhabitants of the 26,192-acre San Ildefonso Indian Reservation in 1980. It is located eighteen miles northwest of Santa Fe, New Mexico. The San Ildefonso name for themselves is "Poxwogeh," and they have lived in their current location for seven hundred years. They speak Tewa, a Tanoan language. San Ildefonso was the center of the rebirth of American Indian arts and crafts in the 1920s, primarily through the world-famous black-on-black pottery of Maria Martinez. The modern pueblo combines traditional beliefs and practices with integration into the local economy and modern, adobe-style community buildings. *See* Tewa

San Juan. There were 851 Indian inhabitants of the 12,232-acre San Juan Indian Reservation in 1980. It is located twenty-four miles northwest of Santa Fe, New Mexico. The San Juan name for themselves is "Okeh," and they speak Tewa, a Tanoan language. They are closely related to the neighboring Santa Clara. The San Juan have intermarried more with the Spanish than any other Pueblo group, though the traditional culture and language remain strong. *See* Tewa

Santa Clara. There were 1,839 Indian inhabitants of the 45,744-acre Santa Clara Indian Reservation in 1980. It is located thirty miles northwest of Santa Fe, New Mexico. The Santa Clara name for themselves is "Xapogeh," and they speak Tewa, a Tanoan language. Although the language is still spoken and the traditional religion is practiced, the Santa Clara have been much involved in the external economy, primarily through tourism and the sale of Santa Clara pottery. *See* Tewa

Tesuque. There were 236 Indian inhabitants of the 16,810-acre Tesuque Indian Reservation in 1980. It is located ten miles north of Santa Fe, New Mexico. Their name for themselves is "Tetsugeh," and they speak Tewa, a Tanoan language. The Tesuque have lived in their current location for over seven hundred years. Roman Catholicism is followed, though it exists alongside the traditional religion. The Tesuque operate a large bingo hall and campground for tourists. *See* Tewa

Isleta. There were 2,289 Indian inhabitants of the 210,937-acre Isleta Indian Reservation in 1980. It is located fifteen miles south of Albuquerque, New Mexico. Their name for themselves is "Tuei," and they speak southern Tiwa, a Tanoan language. The Pueblo was built around 1709 and counts as its current residents descendants of a number of Pueblo groups including the Hopi, Laguna, Acoma, and Isleta. Despite the closeness to Albuquerque, the Isleta have managed to maintain much of their traditional culture.

Picuris. There were 125 Indian inhabitants of the 14,947-acre Picuris Indian Reservation in 1980. It is located forty miles northeast of Santa Fe, New Mexico. Picuris Pueblo was founded nearly seven hundred years ago. The Picuris were influenced by the Spanish, Plains Indians, and Apache and have been attempting to maintain the traditional culture. They speak northern Tiwa, a Tanoan language and are closely related to the nearby Taos. *See* Taos

Sandia. There were 227 Indian inhabitants of the 22,884-acre Sandia Indian Reservation in 1980. It is located fifteen miles north of Albuquerque, New Mexico. The Sandia name for themselves is "Nafiat," and they speak southern Tiwa, a Tanoan language. Although much of the traditional culture survives, it is under increasing pressure since the Sandia are much involved in tourism.

Taos. *See* Taos

Jemez. There were 1,504 Indian inhabitants of the 88,860-acre Jemez Indian Reservation in 1980. It is located forty-five miles northwest of Albuquerque, New Mexico. The Jemez name for themselves is "Walatowa," and they speak Towa, a Tanoan language. Jemez is also the home of the descendants of the people of Pecos Pueblo, southeast of Santa Fe, which was abandoned in the late 1880s. The Jemez were active participants in the Pueblo Revolt of 1680 amd subsequent revolts. The Jemez maintain ties to the Navajo, which can be traced back to their alliance in the 1696 revolt against the Spanish.

Hopi. *See* Hopi

Zuni. *See* Zuni

Tigua. There were 365 Indian inhabitants on or near the three small (73 acres in all) state reservations near El Paso, Texas, in 1980. The Tigua migrated from Isleta in 1862 and are therefore not considered a distinct group by some experts. The Tigua have been much influenced by the nearby Mexican society and have retained less of the traditional culture than the other Pueblo groups to the north.

See also Keres, Tewa

Bibliography

Ortiz, Alfonso, ed. (1979). *Handbook of Indians of North America.* Vol. 9, *Southwest.* Washington, D.C.: Smithsonian Institution.

Quapaw

The Quapaw (Kwapa, Akansa, Arkansas) lived at or near the mouth of the Arkansas River where it meets the Mississippi River in southeastern Arkansas. They now live on a federal trust area in northeastern Oklahoma. They speak a Dhegiha Siouan language and numbered over twelve hundred in the 1980s.

Bibliography

Baird, W. David (1979). *The Quapaw Indians: A History of the Downstream People*. Norman: University of Oklahoma Press.

Thompson, V. H. (1955). "A History of the Quapaw." *Chronicles of Oklahoma* 33:360–383.

Quechan

ETHNONYMS: Cuchano, Cuchan, Cushan, Yum, Yuma

Orientation

Identification. The Quechan are an American Indian group located in western Arizona and eastern California. "Quechan," meaning "those who descended," is a shortening of the name that the Quechan believe was given to them and to other lower Colorado peoples at the time of creation on the sacred mountain Avikwame: "Xám Kwacán," meaning "those who descended by a different way" or "those who descended by way of the water."

Location. Aboriginally the Quechan lived along the lower Colorado River, north and south of its junction with the Gila River. This area lies primarily within the present states of California and Arizona. Their reservation today is a small portion of their aboriginal territory.

Demography. The population may have been about four thousand prior to contact with Spaniards in 1540. By the early 1900s there were fewer than a thousand. In 1988 the Quechan population was estimated at two thousand, about two-thirds of whom lived on or adjacent to the reservation.

Linguistic Affiliation. Quechan is classified in the Yuman subfamily of the Hokan language family. Those living in the extreme southern portions of their territory may have spoken a distinct dialect of Quechan.

History and Cultural Relations

Quechan tradition describes their creation, along with that of other lower Colorado River tribes, by their culture hero, Kukumat. After Kukumat died, his son Kumastamxo took the people to the sacred mountain Avikwame, near the present city of Needles, California. There he gave them bows and arrows and taught them how to cure illness and then sent them down from the mountain in various directions. The ancestors of the Quechan settled along the Colorado River to the south of the Mohave. Little archaeological evidence of the Quechan past has survived the Colorado's flooding. The Quechan and some of the other lower Colorado tribes may have begun as rather small patrilineal bands that gradually grew into larger "tribal" groupings. What caused the formation of these tribes is not altogether clear; the interrelated factors probably included population increase from a generally reliable and abundant riverbottom horticulture; competition with neighboring riverine groups for control of lucrative trade routes between the Pacific Coast and cultures to the east of the Colorado (including, for a time, the great Hohokam culture between about A.D. 1050 and 1200); and increasingly strong social bonds between small groups living next to one another along the river's banks.

In 1540 a Spanish expedition under Hernando de Alarcón was the first group of Europeans to reach Quechan territory. For the next three and a half centuries the Quechans were in intermittent contact with various Spanish, Mexican, and American expeditions intent on developing the land route between southern California and the interior to the east of the Colorado River. The Quechan controlled the best crossing point along the lower Colorado, just to the south of where it is joined by the Gila. During this time, too, warfare was endemic between the Quechan and other tribes living along the Colorado and Gila rivers. No permanent White settlements were attempted at the crossing until 1779, when Spanish settlers and soldiers arrived. In 1781, after two years of Spanish depredations, the Quechans attacked them, killing some and driving the others away. The tribe retained control of the area until the early 1850s, when the U.S. Army defeated them and established Fort Yuma at the crossing. Just across the river from the fort a small White American town soon sprang up to cash in on the increasing overland traffic between California and the East, and to the north and south along the Colorado itself.

A reservation was set aside for the Quechan on the west (California) side of the river in 1884, but most of its acreage, including some of its best farmland, was lost to the tribe by the fraudulent 1893 agreement with the U.S. government. The government restored twenty-five thousand acres of the original reservation in 1978, minus most of the best farmland taken earlier. For most of the twentieth century the tribe has been attempting to create a secure economic base for the reservation, one to replace the relative abundance of the traditional riverbottom farming that gave out in the early 1900s.

Settlements

The Quechan lived in settlements or rancherias scattered along the Colorado to the north of the Gila confluence for about sixty miles and to the southwest for about ten miles, and for about twenty-six miles eastward along the Gila itself. But the number and precise locations of these rancherias shifted from time to time, perhaps partly in response to warfare with other groups. In the nineteenth century there were six Quechan rancherias, each located on an elevated area above the river floodplain, safe from the spring floods. For much of the agricultural season from spring to fall, the people of the rancheria dispersed to family farm plots along the riverbottoms, where they lived in dome-shaped arrowweed shelters. The rancherias were gradually abandoned after the reservation was created in 1887, and families moved within the reservation boundaries to receive individual ten-acre plots of farmland allotted to them by the federal government. Today households are scattered primarily along the main roads linking the reservation with the nearby city of Yuma, Arizona, and the smaller town of Winterhaven, California.

Economy

Subsistence and Commercial Activities.   Traditionally the Quechan farmed the rich riverbottom lands, growing mainly maize, squash, and beans. The cultivated crops probably accounted for about 50 percent of the Quechan diet. The remainder came from gathered wild foods such as mesquite and screwbean pods and from river fish. Hunting was not very productive. Occasional irregularities in the river floods lent some uncertainty to the supply of cultivated foods. After White Americans developed the crossing into a transportation center, Quechans worked as unskilled wage laborers in the town or on river steamers. By the 1950s there were virtually no Quechans still farming; they worked as wage laborers and/or received income from leasing their land allotments to non-Indian farmers. Presently the tribe leases farm acreage and operates a bingo hall and two modern trailer parks.

Industrial Arts.   In the nineteenth and early twentieth centuries Quechan women made pottery utensils, distinctive clay dolls, and beaded shawls; only the shawls are still made. Men made tools, weapons, and gourd rattles and other ritual paraphernalia. In general the Quechans were little concerned with embellishment of material culture beyond utilitarian needs.

Trade.   The Colorado River crossing in Quechan territory was along one of the main precontact trade routes linking coastal California tribes with the center of the great Hohokam culture in southern Arizona (A.D. 1000–1200), and later with Pima, Pagago, and others after the Hohokam declined. The Quechan likely acted as middlemen and/or extracted a portion of the trade goods in exchange for safe passage across the crossing. In lean years foodstuffs were traded. It is likely that control of this trade route was one of the issues in persistent intertribal warfare until the 1860s.

Division of Labor.   Both men and women worked the riverbottom fields, the men doing the heavier work of clearing brush, and both sexes helped with the harvest. Several related extended family households joined forces at clearing or harvest times. Men did most of the fishing, women the gathering. Males waged war, although there were typically warriorwomen accompanying each major war party. The elderly are still important economic and teaching assets in households where both parents work.

Land Tenure.   Traditionally, farm plots were considered the property of the household. The household's lands were abandoned at the death of one of its adult members, and they sought unoccupied land elsewhere in the vicinity. Ownership rules were not elaborately developed, and there was no inheritance. This changed radically after the reservation was created and the individual members of the tribe were each as-

signed a ten-acre allotment. As the original and successive owners died, the plots were divided, and then repeatedly redivided, creating a major heirship crisis in some cases. The reservation land is still held in trust and cannot be sold. Most of the plots are presently leased to non-Indian farmers.

Kinship

Kin Groups and Descent.   The Quechan recognize a series of exogamous patrilineal clans. Clan functions besides regulating marriage are no longer clearly known. Each has one or more namesakes (totemic animals or plants) associated with it (such as frog, maize, snake, red ant). Some clan names are considered foreign to the Quechan, indicating perhaps some earlier incorporation of alien groups into the tribal structure. Presently younger tribal members are only vaguely aware of the clan names and do not follow the rule of exogamy.

Kinship Terminology.   The traditional kinship terms followed the bifurcate collateral avuncular and Iroquois cousin patterns, with major terminological emphasis on age and gender distinctions.

Marriage and Family

Marriage.   Sometimes parents arranged betrothals followed by periods of gift giving and feasting. But there was apparently considerable flexibility in betrothal and marriage patterns. A man often courted a woman by playing a wooden flute outside her shelter at night, and she might invite him in to sleep with her (without having intercourse). After four nights of sleeping together, the couple was considered married. Ideally, postmarital residence was patrilocal. The typical marriage was monogamous, but polygyny was permitted. Marriages could be dissolved by either partner.

Domestic Unit.   Despite the patrilocal preference, the ambilocal extended family was the predominant household unit until the 1920s, when the effects of land allotment and wage-based subsistence undermined the extended family's importance. Nuclear family households then became numerous. Yet the extended household has remained a popular option for families who have elderly relatives to care for or who want to try to ease the burden of poverty by pooling the resources of the larger household group. And even nuclear family households are frequently but a few acres away from those of close kin.

Inheritance.   Until recently there was no inheritance of deceased's property; it was either destroyed (goods) or abandoned (land), lest the survivors be constantly reminded of their loss. The allotment of land and the construction of substantial housing has changed this pattern somewhat, but there is still the feeling that a deceased's personal property should be destroyed after death.

Socialization.   The elders in the extended family household traditionally played a major part in the socialization of the young. Children were and are raised permissively. During their first menstruation, girls were lectured by older women about the proper adult female role; boys went through an initiation ritual in which they were made to run long distances after having their nasal septa pierced and were lectured on the ideal traits of adult Quechan males.

Sociopolitical Organization

Social Organization. There may have been gradations of status in Quechan families, but the basis for them is not clear. Individual ritualists and leaders possessing dream power had high prestige, as did warriors of exceptional bravery. The several rancherias were largely autonomous social units for much of the year. Quechan tribal structure became apparent during large war expeditions, harvest festivals, and major rituals mourning the death of prominent people. On the modern reservation the tribal identity has replaced most of the older rancheria identity. The elderly as a group are publicly treated with respect.

Political Organization. Most of the time the rancherias operated as autonomous political entities, each with a headman noted for his wisdom and speaking ability. He served at the will of his rancheria and was expected to be generous with his time and property. The key to leaders' effectiveness was the special power derived from dreams; this power was manifest in their performance. There were both civil leaders and war leaders. Traditionally these leadership positions were held by males. Since 1938 the tribe has been governed by an elected seven-member tribal council. Women have often been elected to the council, and the first woman tribal president was elected in 1987.

Social Control. Gossip was probably a frequently used mechanism of social control in the past; it continues to be the most popular means. Sorcery and occasionally murder were used against repeated and flagrant social deviance. Late in the 1800s a Quechan leader reportedly ordered public floggings for drunkards, but such punishment of misbehavior may not be traditional. Children were and are scolded for misbehavior, but seldom spanked. In the late nineteenth and early twentieth centuries government superintendents, with their appointed agency police force, upheld federal law on the reservation. Responsibility for both civil and criminal cases now lies with the Imperial County, California, sheriff's office; the federal government remains the law enforcement authority for major crimes on the reservation.

Conflict. The natural lines of conflict traditionally were between rancherias, and after European contact the most serious conflicts erupted over how best to deal with Whites. Despite changes in specific issues, this has persisted as a fundamental source of political factionalism. Another is the performance of elected tribal officials. Now factions consist of clusters of close relatives.

Religion and Expressive Culture

Religious Beliefs. The elemental Quechan beliefs involve a spiritual power derived from special dreams and a continuing interaction with the souls of the dead. The dream power is bestowed by the first men, created by Kukumat but imbued with spiritual power and culture by Kukumat's son Kumastamxo. Dream power was essential for successful leaders, curers, warriors, and the various ritual specialists. There was as well a collective tribal spiritual power that was renewed and increased through war with enemy tribes. Instead of prayers or sacrifices, there were formulas and purification through smoking and abstinence that produced more or less automatic results. Protestant and Catholic doctrine has become popular, but there is still an active core of men who preserve the traditional beliefs and an even larger group who combine elements of both traditional and Christian belief. Many people had guardian spirits manifest as special voices that spoke to them from time to time. These spirits, and those of the first people, lived either on the sacred mountain Avikwame or on one of the other sacred heights in the region.

Religious Practitioners. Men with unusually potent dream power were given a special title: $k^w ax\acute{o}t^i$. There were also individual speakers and singers who collectively possessed the knowledge of rituals.

Ceremonies. The major tribal ceremony was the *kar'úk*, held to honor the memory of deceased tribal members. It was conceived as a reenactment of the original mourning ceremony following creator Kukumat's death. In the late nineteenth and early twentieth centuries it featured carved wooden images of the deceased along with displays of new clothing laid out as offerings to the spirits of the dead. A major portion of the ritual scenario involved a battle reenactment; its climax was a large fire that consumed the ritual shelter and the offerings. Other "religious" ceremonies were more like large-scale feasts. Even abbreviated kar'úk rituals are now rarely held.

Medicine. Quechans traditionally believed disease could be caused by inadvertently ingesting a poisonous substance or by soul loss. Hostile sorcerers could cause either malady, as could the violation of a mourning, warfare, or menstrual taboo. Dream power was the source of a curer's abilities. Techniques included blowing smoke upon and massaging the patient, and sucking out the intrusive substance.

Death and Afterlife. The souls of the dead pass through four layers, each more distant from the living world. The fourth is the land of the dead, far to the south, a land of plenty and happiness, with the best times enjoyed by those killed in battle. The body is cremated along with personal effects, and others wishing to commemorate deceased relatives at the time may burn offerings of clothing as well. Spirits of some of the dead also return to receive the offerings to them burned during the kar'úk ritual. The traditional funeral ritual still predominates.

Bibliography

Bee, Robert L. (1981). *Crosscurrents along the Colorado: The Impact of Government Policy on the Quechan Indians.* Tucson: University of Arizona Press.

Bee, Robert L. (1983). "Quechan." In *Handbook of North American Indians.* Vol. 10, *Southwest,* edited by Alfonso Ortiz 86–98. Washington, D.C.: Smithsonian Institution.

Forbes, Jack D. (1965). *Warriors of the Colorado: The Yumas of the Quechan Nation and Their Neighbors.* Norman: University of Oklahoma Press.

Forde, C. Daryll (1931). "Ethnography of the Yuma Indians." *University of California Publications in American Archaeology and Ethnology* 28:85–278.

ROBERT L. BEE

Quileute

The Quileute (Quillayute), including the Hoh, live on the west coast of the Olympic Peninsula in northwestern Washington to the south of Cape Flattery. Today they live mainly on the Quileute and Hoh Indian reservations in Washington. The Quileute make a strong effort to preserve the culture, requiring, for example, that tribal membership be given only to those with 50 percent Quileute ancestry and birth on the reservation. They spoke Quileute, a language of the Chimakuan family and numbered about four hundred in the mid-1980s.

Bibliography

Pettit, George Albert (1950). "The Quileute of La Push, 1775–1945." _University of California Anthropological Records_ 14:1–120.

Powell, Jay, and Vickie Jenson (1976). _Quileute: An Introduction to the Indians of La Push_. Seattle: University of Washington Press.

Quinault

The Quinault (Quinaelt, Quinaielt), including the Queets (Quaitso), live on the west coast of the Olympic Peninsula in northwestern Washington to the south of the Quileute and Hoh. They spoke Coast Salish languages and numbered about sixteen hundred in 1984. They now live with the Chehalis, Chinook, and Cowlitz on the Quinault Indian Reservation in Washington.

Bibliography

Barsh, Russell Lawrence (1982). "The Economics of a Traditional Coastal Indian Fishery." _Human Organization_ 41:170–176.

Olson, Ronald L. (1936). "The Quinault Indians." _University of Washington Publications in Anthropology_ 6:1–190.

Rom

ETHNONYMS: Gypsy, or subgroup appellations: Kalderash, Machwaya

Orientation

Identification.   The Rom speaking a Vlach (Vlax) Gypsy dialect have representatives over most of the world including the United States, Canada, Mexico, and much of Central and South America. _Rom_ means "human being," "man," and "husband," thus paralleling the use of the word "man" in English. "Rom" and "Gypsy" are used interchangeably because for the Rom the English term carries none of the negative connotations it has for many non-Gypsies.

Location.   The Rom are found in every state, and although some continue to be seminomadic, traveling throughout the country and into Canada, Mexico, the Caribbean, and occasionally to Europe, most families strive to control a territory focused on a pool of fortune-telling clientele. Most Rom are urban dwellers, found primarily in the larger metropolitan centers; fewer live in small towns and on busy main roads throughout rural America.

Demography.   My enumeration of the Rom population in several states and large cities, and interviews with the Rom about their knowledge of where different families live, resulted in a figure of less than twenty thousand. The New York metropolitan area has the largest concentration, with perhaps as many as four hundred to five hundred families. Los Angeles, Chicago, and other cities have lesser concentrations corresponding primarily to their population size.

Linguistic Affiliation.   The Rom speak a dialect of a language belonging to the Indic branch of the Indo-European language family. They refer to it adverbially as speaking _romanes_, "in the Gypsy way"; in English the language is called "Gypsy." Linguists refer to it and other related but not always mutually intelligible dialects as "Romani." The dialect spoken by the Rom falls into a category of Vlach, or Romanian-influenced Gypsy dialects.

History and Cultural Relations

On the basis of linguistic evidence, the ancestors of the Rom and other Gypsy groups are thought to have left India sometime before A.D. 1000. Loan words in the Gypsy language indicate they passed through Persian- and Greek-speaking areas. The first records that can reasonably be thought to apply to Gypsies come from early-fourteenth-century Greece. After the arrival of Gypsies in Europe, some groups spread west and north, whereas the ancestors of the Rom appear to have stayed in the Balkans, especially in the Serbian and Romanian-speaking areas, until the middle of the nineteenth century, at which time they began another series of migrations, culminating in the distribution of Rom families all over the world. This major split, often referred to as the first and second waves of migrations, is also reflected in the Vlach–non-Vlach dialect division. Before coming to North America, most of the families had traveled widely; group designations reflect the countries with which they were associated, such as Rusuya, Grekuya, Arxentinuya, Meksikaya, and so on. The tribal name of Machwaya derives from the Serbian area from which they emigrated.

My research places the first arrival of Rom in the United States in 1881, but the real influx did not begin until about 1895. It was during this period, from 1895 until immigration was slowed down by World War I and halted by the literacy requirement of 1918, that the ancestors of most of the Rom families currently in the United States and Canada arrived here. The more recent Lovara Rom, who first arrived from Europe in 1973, are not discussed here, as they have not been here long enough yet to be considered "American Rom."

Settlements

Owing to economic competition over fortune-telling territory, Rom in the United States and Canada have evolved a scattered distribution roughly correlated with the density of the non-Gypsy population, especially that portion of it perceived by the Rom to comprise the best clientele. Larger cities are divided into areas of influence in which certain families hold sway, sometimes for decades or until displaced by another family. Some smaller towns are said to be "owned" by a single family, and extended families often lay claim to a portion of a state with rural areas and a number of small towns. This is especially true in the southern states. "Ownership" may consist of informal arrangements with local law enforcement officials, possession of a fortune-telling license, influence with welfare authorities, or a patronage relationship with some influential local person.

Economy

Subsistence and Commercial Activities.   The economic organization of the Rom, like that of most Gypsies, has been characterized by what in recent years has come to be called a "peripatetic adaptation," or sometimes "commercial nomadism." Although much less nomadic and more urbanized today, the adaptation of the Rom remains an ethnically organized, opportunistic exploitation of the human resource base by means of a wide variety of strategies. Non-Gypsies form the clientele; no similar economic relationship is sanctioned among the Rom. This adaptation is unusually stable in its overall relationship to non-Gypsy society, although the specific strategies utilized are readily accommodated to regional differences and changing times. This very flexibility is highly valued by the Rom. The principal trades the Rom have engaged in over the years have alternated between women's fortune-telling and the men's sales and service activities. Today fortune-telling is the primary subsistence activity and influences population distribution and social relations. Whenever possible, the Rom try to operate as independent entrepreneurs, thus avoiding the proletarianization of their labor.

Industrial Arts.   As independent traveling traders and service providers the Rom engaged little in primary productive activities or manufacturing. They were everywhere dependent on the surrounding population for their subsistence. In spite of increased sedentism, the only relationship the Rom have to industry is by means of semiskilled repair trades, formerly as copper- and tinsmiths, today as auto-body workers, electroplaters, metal burnishers, and so on.

Trade.   Rom have always been alert to opportunities to engage in buying, selling, or trading whatever goods seem to be in demand at any particular time. Shrewd tradesmanship is part of the self-definition of a Gypsy. Men generally deal in larger merchandise, formerly horses, today cars and trailers; women tell fortunes or sell smaller items, such as decorative objects; and children engage in occasional productive activities such as shining shoes or hawking flowers on the streets.

Division of Labor.   Sexual dichotomy among the Rom extends to types of work that are considered proper for men and women. Fortune-telling is women's work par excellence, although it's the men who control and protect the territory. Men's work is more variable, but at any particular time and place there is a range of pursuits that are considered properly "Gypsy." By the same token there are jobs, such as plumbing, that contravene the group's pollution taboos and that a Rom should not perform.

Land Tenure.   There is no traditional form of land tenure because there is no traditional attachment to land. Fortune-telling locations and the rights to the local clientele are often bought and sold as businesses, however. Today, real estate also may be purchased either as an investment or as a base for service operations.

Kinship

Kin Groups and Descent.   The Rom population in North America is organized almost entirely on basis of kinship. Students of American Rom disagree in their interpretations of kinship. Gropper and Sutherland describe descent as cognatic or bilateral; Gropper, however, recognizes the patrilineal emphasis in rules of residence. In my view, descent ideology is patrilineal, as expressed frequently by the statement: "We always go by the father." In practice, rare exceptions occur. The patrilineally extended family is generally the largest functioning unit in the society. Patrilineally related males work together, pool their money for bride-price, defend common fortune-telling territories against outside threats, and exhibit solidarity at public gatherings. Women's lineages are considered not to matter, as expressed by the statement referring to marriage: "The girls are thrown away." Above the family are the lineage and the clan, which generally give the group its name; sometimes the names of lineage founders are used in addition to the clan name. Thus an individual may identify himself as being a Rom of the Kalderash tribe, Mineshti clan, Demitro lineage, the son of Zurka, known by the name of Wasso. Both the clan and the lineage are referred to by the term *vitsa*, which originates in the Romanian word meaning a "stem."

Kinship Terminology.   Eskimo-type kinship terms are used. Most of the terminology derives from Indic roots, although some has been borrowed from Romanian and possibly from other European languages. It differs from common European kinship terms primarily by equating grandchildren with nieces and nephews and in emphasizing terms defining relationships among affines, the parties to marriage contracts.

Marriage and Family

Marriage.   Within living memory, most marriages have been arranged by the families of the boy and the girl, the initiative being with the boy's parents. Formerly the young people were rarely consulted in the matter; today their wishes may be taken into consideration, especially if they are strongly opposed to the proposed match. Elopement, which may have been an earlier form of marriage, is occasionally resorted to as an alternative form. Marriage is viewed as a contract between the two families with bride-price as the cement to solidify the agreement. At the wedding, formerly an elaborate three-day series of ceremonies now collapsed to one, the bride is transferred to the groom's family, and money is collected from the guests to defray the costs borne by them. Over the generations, patterns of bride exchange have developed between certain patrilineages amounting to a loose form of alliance. The members of such lineage pairs often say that the frequent intermarriages practically make them into one vitsa. Marriages between cousins once removed are common, but may also occur between first cousins, especially cross cousins. After marriage the couple traditionally resides patrilocally until other brothers in the family get married, at which time the first one may move out to begin an independent nuclear household. The relationship to the husband's paternal household remains strong, however; meals may still be taken there and often the households are in close proximity by choice. Divorce requires the return of a portion of the bride-price, the amount depending on the length of time the couple stayed together.

Domestic Unit. The primary social unit among the Rom is the patrilineally extended family. Formerly this constituted a camping unit, but today it is difficult for such a large number of people to obtain single or adjacent housing. As much as possible, however, the extended family attempts to function as a domestic unit—for example, by visiting daily, sharing meals, and otherwise considering one another's homes as extensions of one's own household.

Inheritance. Typically at the time of death there used to be very little to inherit and a great reluctance to possess items belonging to the deceased; most personal belongings would have been burned, broken, or discarded to avoid possible visits by the spirit of the deceased. Today, increasing ownership of real estate and bank accounts is bringing more mainstream inheritance rules to bear on disposal of property.

Socialization. Children are raised in an extended family setting with all older females sharing in child-caring activities. Children are indulged, protected, and treasured. They grow up feeling secure in, but dependent on, the protection they receive from the extended family. But they often seem at a loss in new situations without the support of the relatives. Even adults consider long separation from the family to be the worst kind of deprivation that could occur.

Sociopolitical Organization

Social Organization. The Rom function on a band level with family elders and influential "big men" as the only type of leadership. Rom society is organized primarily on the basis of kinship, with sex, age, ability, wealth, and family membership used to rank individuals. It is patrifocal in that all important decisions are ultimately made by the adult males, although the advice of women may be considered. Age is generally accorded high respect, but ability may sometimes count for more. Women defer to their men. Wealth is seen as proof of ability and luck and is highly esteemed. Prestige is based on a combination of wealth, ability, and good conduct.

Political Organization. Lacking formal leadership, Rom political organization consists of loose federations, or shifting alliances between lineages, which generally are united by marriage ties. Charismatic individuals, those who have become wealthy or who have influential friends among non-Gypsies, may for a while possess certain power to influence others; however, their power is generally nontransferable. At the death of a "big man," his sons do not necessarily inherit his status. Each has to earn his own status.

Social Control. Social control is ultimately in the hands of one's peers and elders who happen to be in a position to command respect at the particular time. Most of the time, social control consists of discussion and evaluation, gossip, ridicule, and similar informal pressure tactics. In more serious cases a _divano_, a gathering of friends, relatives, and available local elders, may be called first to discuss and attempt to solve the problem in order to avoid the expense and trouble of resorting to a Gypsy court. If this fails, the _Kris_, an ad hoc court of arbitration, is convened, generally by the party that feels it has been wronged. The judges are chosen from among available respected elders, who are felt to be objective and are expected not to favor one side over another. Sanctions may consist of monetary fines or, more rarely, formal ostracism. Charges of contravention of pollution taboos, more frequently used in the past, are among the strongest forms of social control. A person or family labeled unclean, _marime_, is effectively banned from further contact with other Rom until cleared by the Kris. Non-Gypsy law enforcement is also called upon as an adjunct to internal forms of conflict resolution, albeit mostly for the harassment of enemies.

Conflict. Conflicts—which may begin with individual disagreements over division of earnings, disputes over bride-price or daughters-in-law, or competition over fortune-telling territory—are often expressed on another level as disagreements between families or lineages. Patrilineally related individuals are expected to band together to defend the family against outsiders. Women whose natal lineages are in conflict with those of their husbands are sometimes put in an awkward position of having to choose between them.

Religion and Expressive Culture

Religious Beliefs. In addition to traditions that may have earlier roots, the religion of the Rom incorporates elements from Eastern European folk religions, Eastern Orthodoxy, and Roman Catholicism. Today, although most consider themselves Catholic, large numbers have turned toward evangelical Protestant sects such as Pentecostalism. Beliefs are derived partly from indigenous traditions and partly from the official and folk religions of the countries among which the Rom have lived. God, _O Del_, and saints are venerated, and numerous spirits, some associated with natural elements such as wind or water, are recognized. Some are anthropomorphized; others more manlike in their expression. Luck, _Bax_, especially is considered an active supernatural force, closely bound with the notion of fate. Symbolic uncleanness is sometimes also reified as an incarnation of evil. Pollution, or marime taboos based on the symbolic impurity of the lower body, especially of women, dictates proper behavior between the sexes, older and younger people, food and laundry handling, and the arrangement of household furnishings. The same separation of clean from unclean also dictates the kinds of social and economic relations permissible between the Rom and non-Gypsies.

Religious Practitioners. No formal priests, shamans, or other religious specialists exist among the Rom. A few women are noted as interpreters of dreams; others may be feared as witches because of their age or ability to cast curses.

Ceremonies. Major ceremonies with religious components include saint's day feasts, baptisms, funerals, feasts of honor, weddings, and Easter, Thanksgiving, and Christmas celebrations. All celebrate the Rom as a people; by the giving of feasts, respect is demonstrated to both the supernaturals and other Rom.

Arts. Arts consist of music, including recent musical compositions and adaptations, dance, folk songs, legends, and family history. Oratory, especially at a Kris, may also be considered among the artistic expressions of the Rom. Folklore serves educational, evaluative, and prescriptive roles of major importance in the absence of writing and more formal education.

Medicine. There is some evidence that the Rom once possessed a rich body of folk medicines, remedies, and cures, most of which by now have fallen into disuse. There do not appear to have been any internally recognized medical specialists, although the older women served as multipurpose ethnopsychiatrists, herbalists, and curers for outside clients. Modern medicine is accepted, and in cases of serious illness the best physicians and hospitals are sought regardless of the cost or distance.

Death and Afterlife. Spirits of the dead are believed to survive death. The deceased are provided with money, a new suit of clothes, and travel necessities. Their spirits roam the earth for one year after death, retracing the steps traveled during life. The year after death is punctuated by a series of memorial feasts, with the last one after a year formally concluding the journey with a ceremony of "Opening the Road," presumably to heaven, *raio*, and the liberation of the spirit from any further earthly obligations. Anniversaries of death are also commemorated with food offerings, generally by an extra place setting at a table. There is no corresponding belief in hell. Death is considered as polluting, and the appearance of spirits of the dead is generally feared unless the one perceiving the ghost had an especially close and good relationship with the person while alive. Nevertheless, one's ancestors may be invoked to intercede on one's behalf at a time of great need. Those Rom who have recently become Pentecostals have renounced most of these beliefs and practices as "pagan."

Bibliography

Gropper, Rena C. (1975). *Gypsies in the City: Culture Patterns and Survival.* Princeton: Darwin Press.

Miller, Carol J. (1968) "Macvaja Gypsy Marime." M.A. thesis, University of Washington, Seattle.

Pickett, David (1970). "The Gypsies: An International Community of Wandering Thieves." Ph.D. diss., Syracuse University.

Salo, Matt T., and Sheila Salo (1977). *The Kalderas in Eastern Canada.* Folk Culture Studies, no. 21. Ottawa: National Museums of Canada.

Silverman, Carol T. (1979). "Expressive Behavior as Adaptive Strategy among American Gypsies." Ph.D. diss., University of Pennsylvania.

Sutherland, Anne (1975). *Gypsies: The Hidden Americans.* New York: Free Press.

MATT T. SALO

Sanpoil

The Sanpoil (Nesilextcin, N'Puchle), including the Nespelem and the Colville (Skoylpeli, Kettle Falls Indians), lived in northwestern Washington along the Columbia River from Kettle Falls to the vicinity of Grand Coulee and north of the Columbia in the Sanpoil and Nespelem River basins. They now live on the Colville Indian Reservation with the Colville and other Plateau groups in Washington. They speak an Interior Salish language and probably number about one thousand.

Bibliography

Chance, David H. (1973). _Balancing the Fur Trade at Fort Colville._ Record of Washington State University, no. 34. Pullman.

Ray, Verne F. (1954). _The Sanpoil and Nespelem: Salishan Tribes of Northeastern Washington._ New Haven: Human Relations Area Files.

Santee

ETHNONYMS: Eastern Dakota, Isanyati, Mississippi Sioux

The Santee are an American Indian group consisting of the Mdewakanton, Sisseton, Wahpekute, and Wahpeton, four of the seven divisions of the Dakota. The other three divisions are the Teton, Yankton, and Yanktonai. The Santee spoke dialects of the Siouan Eastern Dakota language, which is closely related to Lakota (spoken by the Teton) and Nakota (spoken by the Yankton and Yanktonai). At the time of contact they lived mainly in what are today Minnesota, northern Iowa, and eastern South Dakota. Today they live on a number of reservations, principally in the northern Midwest, including the Santee Reservation in Nebraska, the Flandreau and Sisseton reservations in South Dakota, the Fort Totten Reservation in North Dakota, the Lower Sioux and Prairie Island communities and Prior Lake and Upper Sioux reservations in Minnesota, and several reserves in Canada. There are about six thousand Santee Sioux today.

The first historical mention of these Dakota is in the _Jesuit Relations_ for 1640, when they were probably living in eastern Minnesota and western Wisconsin. Their traditions point to an origin to the northeast and suggest that they once lived about the "Lake of the Woods." There is also strong evidence indicating that they moved north at some point from the Southeast, as there were numerous Siouan-speaking groups in the Carolinas at the time of contact. They were evidently forced out of their historic homeland to the west and south by the expanding Ojibwa. In 1862, the Santee, under Little Crow, rose up against the Whites, and as a result of losing the war, they also lost all their remaining land in Minnesota. Many fled to Canada, and others moved south and southwest to the plains.

Aboriginally, the Santee had numerous subdivisions and bands, the latter often led by hereditary chiefs. They had two basic types of dwellings—gabled summer houses made of bark on a pole framework and conical winter houses covered with mats or skins. Hunting, fishing, and agriculture all contributed to subsistence, with maize, beans, and squash grown and fruits, berries, and wild rice gathered. At times, major bison hunts were conducted on the plains, under the leadership of shamans and various hunt leaders. Women helped the men construct the houses and also grew the crops and gathered wild foods; men hunted, fished, and made war. Both male and female shamans interpreted visions, cured the sick, and prophesized. The Santee believed in a single creator of the universe as well as numerous gods and spirits. In the 1860s they had to adapt to a Plains type of existence, based on hunting bison and other large mammals and on trade with Whites with a reduced role for agriculture. In modern times, on the reservations and reserves, they have been drawn into a wage-labor economy and are assimilating into mainstream society.

Bibliography

Landes, Ruth (1968). _The Mystic Lake Sioux; Sociology of the Mdewakanton-Santee._ Madison: University of Wisconsin Press.

Meyer, Roy W. (1968). _History of the Santee Sioux: United States Indian Policy on Trial._ Lincoln: University of Nebraska Press.

Wallis, Wilson D. (1947). _The Canadian Dakota._ American Museum of Natural History, Anthropological Papers 41(1). New York.

Sarsi

ETHNONYM: Sarcee

The Sarsi are an Athapaskan-speaking American Indian group with close linguistic relationships to the Sekani and Beaver to the west and northwest. They now number about five hundred and live on the Sarcee Reserve just southwest of Calgary, Alberta. At the time of contact, with Matthew Cocking in 1772–1773 and Alexander Mackenzie in 1789, the Sarsi inhabited the drainage area of the Athabaska River south to the North Saskatchewan River. At the beginning of the nineteenth century their main hunting grounds were around the latter river. They differed culturally from the neighboring Athapaskan-speaking groups in being heavily infused with Plains Indian cultural features, owing to their long association with the Blood and Northern Blackfoot. By the early nineteenth century they had obtained horses and guns.

The Sarsi were organized into bands, each composed of several closely related families who hunted and camped together. Band membership was fluid with much splitting and movement of families. Band leadership rested on individual prestige, with no leader holding absolute powers. The bands coalesced in the summer to hunt and hold ceremonies. During the rest of the year the bands or small hunting parties functioned on their own. Bison were the major aboriginal food source—often hunted in communal drives. Bison skin tipis were made by the women. In the twentieth century, many Sarsi have engaged in farming, stock raising, lumbering, and wage-labor work in Calgary.

Marriages were marked by gift exchanges. Polygyny was practiced as were the levirate, sororate, and mother-in-law avoidance for men. In 1897, two divisions of the Sarsi were reported, one at the reserve at Fort Calgary on the Bow River and the other at Battleford in western Saskatchewan. Five bands were counted: the Bloods (Big Plume's Band consisting of mixed Cree and Blood Indians), the Broad Grass (consisting of mixed Cree and Sarsi Indians), People Who Hold Aloof (nearly all Sarsi), Uterus (Blackfoot and Sarsi), and the Young Buffalo Robe. The dances of the male societies, as well as the Sun Dance, were the most important tribal ceremonies. The dead were given scaffold burials with their clothing and personal possessions. Personal horses were killed. Band leaders or noted warriors were left in abandoned tipis. Personal power was obtained in dreams and visions. In the past, the Sarsi were allied with the Blackfoot against the Assiniboin and Cree.

Bibliography

Dempsey, Hugh A. (1978) *The Indian Tribes of Alberta*. Calgary: Glenbow-Alberta Institute.

Jenness, Diamond (1938). *The Sarcee Indians of Alberta*. National Museum of Canada Bulletin no. 90. Ottawa.

Sauk

The Sauk (Sac) lived around the upper part of Green Bay and the lower Fox River in northeastern Wisconsin, but moved over a large part of eastern Wisconsin and northwestern Illinois during the historic period. Most of the Sauk now live with the Fox on the Sac and Fox Indian Reservation in Tama, Iowa; the Sac and Fox Tribe of Missouri (living in Kansas and Nebraska); and the former Sac and Fox Indian Reservation in east-central Oklahoma. They speak an Algonkian language. *See* Fox

Bibliography

Hagan, William T. (1958). *The Sac and Fox Indians*. Norman: University of Oklahoma Press.

Sea Islanders

ETHNONYMS: Gullah-speaking African Americans

Orientation

Identification.   The name "Sea Islanders" refers to the African American inhabitants of the coastal islands of the southeastern United States. The population is characterized by a distinctive Creole language, Gullah or Geechee, and by a long history of land ownership and autonomy from mainland authorities. The region is often cited as a repository of African cultural survivals among New World peoples of African descent.

Location.   The Sea Islands are a series of over one thousand transgressive barrier islands extending from South Carolina to the northern border of Florida. Although most are small and uninhabited, the largest and most densely populated (including John's, St. Helena, Port Royal, and Hilton Head) lie between the cities of Charleston, South Carolina, and Savannah, Georgia. The major islands are today connected to the mainland by bridges, and, on many, the African American population has been displaced by White-owned resort and residential developments. The islands are topographically flat, climatically semitropical, and subject to periodic flooding during hurricanes and other storms. The maze of rivers, estuaries, and tidal marshes separating the islands from the mainland provide a rich wetlands environment for a variety of plant and animal species, some of them endangered.

Demography.   The population of the islands has varied considerably through the years, along with economic cycles of prosperity and hardship. The region has, since the beginning of the eighteenth century, been characterized by an African American majority on the islands and in some coastal mainland communities. African slaves were imported into the area as early as 1682 and the trade had reached a peak of over eleven thousand by 1773. This high rate of importation, coupled with a tendency toward large, concentrated land holdings, resulted in a greatly unbalanced population. According to Rose, by 1861 almost 83 percent of the coastal population consisted of slaves. Entire islands and their populations belonged to single landowners and were worked under the supervision of one or two white overseers.

After the Civil War, much of the former plantation land passed into the hands of the freedmen in the form of small parcels (see below). Sea Islanders participated in the general trend of African American migration from rural to urban areas that characterized the early years of this century. St. Helena Island, for example, saw a population decline of approximately 45 percent between 1900 and 1930. Jones-Jackson reports that African Americans constituted more than 50 percent of Charleston County in 1930 but only 31.4 percent in 1970. Since resort development accelerated in the 1960s and 1970s, the White population has been growing rapidly. Hilton Head Island, which was almost entirely inhabited by African Americans in 1950, has undergone a particularly dramatic shift, with Whites now holding an eight-to-one majority.

Linguistic Affiliation. The distinctive Creole language spoken by Sea Islanders has long attracted researchers. The terms _Gullah_ or _Geechee_ are conventionally used to refer to this language (although not to Sea Islanders themselves, by whom they are taken as terms of abuse). Linguists believe that Gullah is the only surviving form of a generalized Plantation Creole which at one time was widespread in the southern United States. Creole undoubtedly originated as a pidgin, or trade language, from the practical necessity for communication between Africans and Europeans engaged in the West African coastal economy. Gullah is a true Creole in that it differs from other African American dialects of English, which do not vary from the standard in phonology, vocabulary, or syntax and are thus intelligible to speakers of the standard dialect. Creole languages, on the other hand, may be similar to the "primary" language in vocabulary but differ significantly in grammar and syntax; while the Gullah lexicon is composed of mostly English words, its grammatical rules are demonstrably closer to West African languages such as Ewe, Mandinka, Igbo, Twi, and Yoruba. It is on the basis of these grammatical features and on the lack of intelligibility to English speakers that Gullah is considered a language in its own right and not a regional dialect of English. Sea Islanders, however, speak a variety of English dialects as well as using Gullah as the first language at home. Choice of language used varies with social context, with "true" or "deep" Gullah reserved for the primary community. Sea Islanders use various dialects of Black American English in their economic or bureaucratic dealings with non-Islanders. It is important to note that there is considerable ambivalence attached to the use of Gullah in public contexts at which outsiders are present. The use of the language is negatively sanctioned by mainlanders, both African American and White, as denoting backwardness, poverty, and rural lack of sophistication. To be called a "Gullah" or "Geech" is to be insulted, inferring that one can neither "talk right" nor understand what others say. With the recent increase in White tourism has come increasing curiosity about the language, and tourists often express surprise that Sea Islanders can "speak English." Islanders frequently find that visitors speak slowly, loudly, and deliberately to them, as if they were deaf or mentally incompetent, and they quite rightly resent such treatment. Yet Gullah remains the primary language associated with home, family, and an independent life-style, in spite of the obvious impact of mass media, schools, and out-migration. Children are still taught Gullah as a first language, and Jones-Jackson speculates that, for the near future at least, "some version of Gullah will probably continue to exist."

History and Cultural Relations

The strategic location of the Sea Islands is reflected in the history of conflict in the region. Port Royal Sound is the deepest and most accessible harbor on the east coast south of Chesapeake Bay; consequently, Spanish, French, and English colonizers all competed for control of the area. Fierce resistance by the indigenous Yemassee peoples made stable European settlement on the southernmost islands impossible until the early eighteenth century. Early British planters came from Barbados, bringing with them a plantation system based on monocrop agriculture and African slavery. The original cash crop, indigo, was replaced by long-staple cotton after the

American Revolution. This Sea Island cotton produced huge fortunes for the White planters and the region developed a reputation for wealth and luxury.

All this came to an end on November 6, 1861, when the federal fleet, moving north to blockade Charleston, attacked the two small Confederate forts on Hilton Head. The planters evacuated inland, leaving behind their slaves and the year's cotton crop still in the field. This constellation of events set the stage for the famous "Sea Island Experiment" (or Port Royal Experiment), a federal program to determine whether or not ex-slaves could function as free, small-holding citizens. The experiment, sponsored by the secretary of the treasury and administered by a young abolitionist lawyer from Boston, envisioned freed slaves working for wages on government-owned cotton plantations while being prepared for eventual citizenship. Missionaries, teachers, and agricultural specialists were provided by northern benevolent societies, bringing an influx of young, well-educated, fiercely abolitionist men and women from the North behind the battle lines of the Civil War. As the Reconstruction promise of "40 acres and a mule" was revealed as a myth throughout the rest of the South, Sea Islanders, working with northern advisers, managed to gain legal title to most of the land they had formerly worked as slaves. In the words of Willie Lee Rose, the Sea Island Experiment was indeed a "rehearsal for reconstruction" and one of the few places in the South where African Americans emerged from the war with a secure land base.

Although many researchers have stressed the physical isolation of the Sea Islands and imply that their people have been "cut off" since the nineteenth century from mainland U.S. history, this is clearly not the case. In actuality, the islands have never been fully self-sufficient, and periodic male labor migration has been an important source of income since boll weevil infestations at the turn of the century destroyed small-holder cotton production. Sea Islanders have historically produced and sold agricultural products in the markets of cities like Savannah and Charleston, and the men have worked as commercial fishermen and longshoremen up and down the eastern seaboard for generations. What is unique to the island communities is not their geographic isolation but their economic and cultural autonomy. The ownership of land appears to be the crucial variable in Sea Islanders' ability to choose what off-island work they will accept and for how long. Many of the islands instituted their own legal and criminal codes, administered through the churches, allowing them to bypass the White-controlled "unjust law" of the mainland. Since the 1950s, much of the traditional land base has been eroded by out-migration, rising property taxes, forced sheriff's sales, and other coercive practices employed by White developers. As a result, the remaining African American population is increasingly dependent upon wages earned in the service sector of the seasonal tourist economy.

Settlements

Settlement on the islands follows a dispersed pattern with few nucleated centers or villages. On some islands, notably St. Helena, the boundaries of former plantations remain important community markers and define local identity in significant ways. Adult sons strive to acquire land adjacent to their parents on which to build a house and raise their own families; this practice results, over time, in kin-based clusters or compounds of dwellings around a parental "yard." Guthrie has argued that households as social units (as opposed to physical structures) are defined by the presence of a stove and a woman to cook on it; families are defined as those who "eat from the same pot," regardless of where they physically reside. Mobile homes now provide a low-cost alternative to new home construction, although many of the older dwellings conform to the model of the shotgun house, indigenous to the American South. As waterfront property was the first to rise in value (with concomitant increases in taxes), most of the remaining land owned by African Americans is located in the interior, less desirable, portions of the islands.

Economy

Subsistence and Commercial Activities. After the Civil War and prior to the erosion of the land base, the islands supported a mixed economy of small farmers and fishermen who produced both for subsistence and for the urban markets of Savannah and Charleston. Infusions of cash were provided by the seasonal employment of men in off-island occupations such as commercial fishing, logging, and dock work. Outside employment was necessary for paying the all-important property taxes and for buying the staple foods of rice and grits, which were not produced on the islands. Fish, shellfish, game, garden vegetables, and domestic animals produced on the islands provided the rest of the diet. Industrial pollutants have seriously reduced marine resources (particularly the oyster and shrimp populations) and have placed severe limits on the ability of small, independent fishermen to meet subsistence needs. The identification of island men as "fishermen" or "rivermen," however, remains ideologically important. Full-time employment in the service economy, especially in the resort industry, has now become the major source of income.

Industrial Arts. A number of distinctive island crafts have recently become items of interest to tourists. The well-known coiled baskets, made of local materials like pine needles and sweet grass, are an especially popular art form for both domestic use and for sale. Some communities have become specialized in the production of distinctive foods and as destinations for urban excursion boats.

Kinship, Marriage and Family

Marriage and Domestic Unit. Kinship among Sea Islanders generally follows American cognatic descent. A married couple constitutes the basic unit of the household, which may also contain their direct descendants, together or separately, and adopted and foster children and their partners. Formalized marriages are preferred and can be documented as far back as the census of 1880, clearly contradicting the popular notion of African American families as "destroyed" by slavery. Children are considered members of their parents' households until marriage, at which time residence is ideally virilocal. Newly married sons bring their brides into their parents' household until a new dwelling can be provided, preferably in the yard or nearby. Additional household members are added through informal adoption and fosterage and by the tendency of young adults working in mainland cities to send their small children to be raised by grandparents in relative rural safety. Households headed by single women typically represent the end of domestic group cycles and consist of widows living alone or with their grandchildren.

Inheritance. Inheritance descends to all children of a married pair equally, although "outside" children whose parents have not married inherit only from their mothers. The increasing number of off-island heirs who hold rights in small parcels of island property has contributed to the acquisition of formerly African American-owned land by White developers.

Sociopolitical Organization

Social and Political Organization. On St. Helena Island, former plantations serve as important sociopolitical units. Island citizenship is determined through membership in a particular plantation, acquired not by birth or filiation but through "catching sense" in a specific community. Guthrie defines *catching sense* as a process by which children between the ages of two and ten begin to "understand and remember the meaning of social relationships." One's having caught sense on a particular plantation confers eligibility for participation in the system of dispute management and litigation that operates through the Baptist churches and their affiliated "praise houses." The church hierarchy, consisting of the ministers, deacons, and local praise house leaders and their committees, also functions as the politicojural structure.

Social Control and Conflict. Disputes between islanders can go through a series of levels within the religious court system; the goal is to achieve confession and reconciliation between the parties rather than punishment. Islanders who insist on taking cases before the secular courts or "unjust law" of the mainland authorities are sanctioned informally through gossip and general disapproval and may even lose membership in their congregation. Beyond the religious court system, social control is exercised primarily through informal means, such as respect for elders, beliefs in the ability of recently deceased relatives to punish social transgressions, and mechanisms of gossip, reputation, and respect characteristic of small, face-to-face communities.

Religion and Expressive Culture

Religious Beliefs. Most Sea Islanders are at least nominal members of the Baptist or Methodist churches, although many of the smaller island congregations can no longer sustain a full-time minister. The praise house system, as described above for St. Helena, was once widespread on the islands and allowed for immediate, local-level participation in weekday praise meetings which supplemented Sunday services. Praise houses in former times were the settings for "ring shouts," a form of religiously inspired dance. With the decline in the African American population, most praise houses and many churches have fallen into disrepair.

Medicine. Local medical practitioners, primarily women who were also skilled as midwives, or "grannies," are also rapidly disappearing in the face of restrictive state regulations. The grannies are remembered with great affection and respect for their ability to "put you on your feet out of the woods" through the use of locally available herbal medicines. The general feeling is that White-run hospitals and doctors use the same "plants" in their pills as were known to the grannies, but charge much more for their services. The ability to cause others harm through illness as well as the ability to heal is likewise held to be available to skilled and knowledgeable people.

Death and Afterlife. Concepts of death and the afterlife depart from standard Christian doctrine in the belief in multiple souls. While the "soul" leaves the body and returns to God at death, the "spirit" remains on earth, connected to and still interested in its living descendants. Graves are decorated with favorite objects belonging to the deceased in life and elaborate funerals are planned and saved for by the living. Many of the practices relating to the treatment of dead bodies, graves, and burial grounds have clear West African origins. The historical continuity of practices still observable today has been documented by Creel.

Bibliography

Bascom, William R. (1941). "Acculturation among Gullah Negroes." _American Anthropologist_ 43:43–50.

Creel, Margaret Washington (1990). "Gullah Attitudes toward Life and Death." In _Africanisms in American Culture_, edited by Joseph E. Holloway, 69–97. Bloomington: Indiana University Press.

Dillard, J. L. (1970). "Non-standard Negro Dialects: Convergence or Divergence?" In _Afro-American Anthropology_, edited by Norman Whitten and John Szwed, 119–128. New York: Free Press.

Guthrie, Patricia (1977). _Catching Sense: The Meaning of Plantation Membership among Blacks on St. Helena Island, South Carolina_. Ann Arbor, Mich.: University Microfilms.

Guthrie, Patricia (1980). _Praise House Worship and Litigation among Afro-Americans on a South Carolina Sea Island_. Purdue University Africana Studies Occasional Paper no. 80–5. West Lafayette, Ind.

Johnson, Guion Griffis (1930). _A Social History of the Sea Islands_. Chapel Hill: University of North Carolina Press. Jones-Jackson, Patricia (1987). _When Roots Die: Endangered Traditions on the Sea Islands_. Athens: University of Georgia Press.

Kiser, Clyde Vernon (1969). _Sea Island to City_. New York: Atheneum.

Moran, Mary H. (1981). "Meeting the Boat: Afro-American Identity on a South Carolina Sea Island." M.A. thesis, Brown University.

Moran, Mary H. (1986). "Using Census Materials in Ethnohistoric Reconstruction: An Example from South Carolina." In _Ethnohistory: A Researchers' Guide_, edited by Dennis Wiedman, 61–76. Studies in Third World Societies, no. 35. Williamsburg, Va.: Department of Anthropology, College of William and Mary.

Rose, Willie Lee (1964). _Rehearsal for Reconstruction: The Port Royal Experiment_. Indianapolis, Ind.: Bobbs-Merrill.

MARY H. MORAN

Sekani

The Sekani (Sikanee, Thecannies) are an American Indian group who numbered about six hundred in 1978 and are located in the basin of the Peace River and its tributaries in British Columbia. Sekani is an Athapaskan language closely related to Beaver and Sarsi. The Sekani and the Beaver are considered a single culture by some observers, though the northern Sekani more closely resemble the neighboring Kaska. _See_ Beaver

Bibliography

Denniston, Glenda (1981). "Sekani." In _Handbook of Indians of North America_. Vol. 6, _Subarctic_, edited by June Helm, 433–441. Washington, D.C.: Smithsonian Institution.

Jenness, Diamond (1937). _The Sekani Indians of British Columbia_. National Museum of Canada Bulletin no. 84. Anthropological Series, no. 20. Ottawa.

Seminole

ETHNONYMS: Is-te Semihn-ole, Ya-tkitisci, Istica-ti, Simano-li

Orientation

Identification. The Seminole are an American Indian group in southern Florida. The English name "Seminole" is probably derived from the Creek word corrupted from the Spanish _cimarron_, which indicates an animal that was once domesticated but was reverted to a feral state. The Creek Indians applied the term to Indians from a number of broken tribal units in the Southeast that coalesced in what is now the state of Florida after they had abandoned their traditional territories. They refer to themselves as "Red People," or "Ya-tkitisci" in Mikasuki and "Istica-ti" in Muskogee.

Location. Throughout the Southeast, European settlers in the eighteenth century caused massive dislocation among Indian tribes as the newcomers expanded their settlements and agricultural lands. During most of this period, the peninsula of Florida belonged to Spain, and some Indians fled there rather than submit to British and later American efforts to move them off their lands. Forging a political unity, the new arrivals in Florida became known as the Seminole.

Demography. The census data of 1980 indicate about two thousand Seminole in the state of Florida. Seminole also live in Oklahoma. It is believed that at the end of the Third Seminole War in 1856 there were fewer than two hundred Seminole in Florida.

Linguistic Affiliation. Those populations ancestral to the Seminole spoke several mutually nonintelligible languages, but as time passed, two divisions of Muskogean came to predominate: Mikasuki and Muskogee. These two dialects continue to be spoken today, though English is becoming the major language.

History and Cultural Relations

The Seminole as a tribal unit emerged in the mid-eighteenth century from among refugees of a number of southeastern tribes dislocated as a result of European advancement into traditional Indian territory in Georgia and Alabama. Although many tribes contributed to the new entity—for example, Yamassee and Yuchi from north of the Florida peninsula and aboriginal Florida tribes like the Timucua—elements from the Creek Indians became dominant and were strengthened after the Creek war of 1813–1814, so that by the second half of the nineteenth century all members of the group spoke one or the other of the two Creek dialects. The new groups built homes, farms, communities, and functioning societies in Florida, which was ruled by Spain at that time. That country left the Indians in peace, though death from contagious disease decimated the populations. In 1763, England took over the peninsula, and when the Spanish moved to Cuba, some Indians left with them. After England returned Florida to Spain in 1783, new groups of Indians moved into Florida as the United States, now independent, expanded into more southeastern lands. Escaped slaves from plantations joined the Indians in Florida, and U.S. troops raided the Spanish territory pursuing the runaways who had settled in Seminole villages. Andrew Jackson, then a general, fought the first Seminole war in 1818 in northern Florida, where he occupied Spanish installations, seized slaves, and killed Indians. Florida was transferred to the United States by a treaty in 1821.

When the United States took possession, the Seminole were agriculturalists who had added Old World crops like oranges to their traditional crops of maize and beans and pastured their cattle and horses on very desirable land. Settlers from Georgia and other areas coveted the land, and subsequent contention over the area lasted for many decades. The federal government under Jackson, who became president in 1829, devised a plan of removal of all Southeastern Indians to western land acquired under the Louisiana Purchase. The Seminole did not wish to leave Florida, but under pressure to view the western lands and facing hostility from increasing numbers of settlers, they agreed to send a delegation to Indian Territory (now Oklahoma). Although they had no authority to act on behalf of others, some of the delegation signed an agreement to move. Those remaining in Florida were subjected to entreaties and threats, but under the leadership of Osceola, they refused to leave. The deadlock led to the Second Seminole War, 1835–1842, during which the Seminole were pushed ever farther south, finally entering the Everglade-Cypress swamp region at the southern tip of the state. There they stayed, defying U.S. soldiers who could not master the art of fighting in the unmapped, swampy wilderness. The Second Seminole War was the most expensive and exhausting of all Indian wars. It ended inconclusively and without a treaty, leaving the Seminole in Florida where their descendants are still living today.

Living in far less desirable territory than had been theirs to the north, the Seminole remained undisturbed, although there was a brief hostile encounter in 1855–1856, the Third Seminole War. At the end, probably fewer than 200 Seminole remained. They were safe in the wilderness and proved able to adapt, preserving many of their old ways. A few hunters and traders were in contact with them during the last half of the nineteenth century, but little is known about them until 1880, when a researcher from the Bureau of American Ethnology located five small settlements with a total of 208 people.

The federal government set aside trust land for the Seminole in 1891 and added more over the years. The state of Florida also made a large contribution of land abutting the Everglades and extending into Big Cypress Swamp. Today there are four federal reservations and two separate political units: the Seminole Tribe of Florida and the Miccosukee Tribe. Both groups share in the state land.

Settlements

Traditional societies from which the Seminole arose lived in settled towns amid agricultural lands. Those towns had a central plaza or meeting place faced on four sides with housing, religious, and political buildings. After the Seminoles were driven into the peninsula and their population decreased, the towns became little more than clusters of camps. The camps usually contained living quarters with cooking and storage areas for extended families. Aboriginal buildings were of wattle and daub construction with thatched roofs, and summer structures were without walls to let air circulate. The Seminole continued the settlement patterns and building types when they could, but as they moved into tropical regions, they left off the sides and added a platform about thirty inches above the swampy ground. This structure of poles and thatched roof is called a "chickee" (the accent falls on the last syllable).

Economy

Subsistence and Commercial Activities. Field cultivation as in the past was the Seminole mainstay in Florida, with hunting and fishing adding animal proteins, and European crops and animals adding variety to traditional foods. Toward the second half of the nineteenth century, Seminole men occasionally acted as guides for hunters and fishers from the outside, and eventually some found employment as agricultural laborers on farms and plantations around their encampments. Sales of hides, particularly alligator, and plumes from egrets brought money from the fashion industry before World War I, and some men supplied frogs' legs to coastal restaurants. In the twentieth century Seminole found jobs at tourist attractions, and as road building advanced in Florida, some learned to operate heavy machinery. Today they engage in a variety of employments, but agriculture, cattle, and tourist industries remain the significant means of obtaining income.

Industrial Arts and Trade. Aboriginally, the ancestral groups had no metal, but made equipment from wood, stone, bone, hides, clay, and other natural substances. After contact with European traders, metal equipment replaced most of the traditional forms, though some women made baskets well into the twentieth century. Before the turn of the century, Seminole turned to outside traders for tobacco and foodstuffs like coffee and sugar, sometimes paying with currency, sometimes bartering. Today, almost all transactions take place in stores within the money economy. With the advent of woven cloth and the hand-cranked sewing machine in the late nineteenth century, Seminole women developed a distinctive clothing style that is the hallmark of the Florida Seminole even today. The sale of Seminole clothing represents a large part of their tourist trade. Women also make dolls of palmetto fiber, clothe them in their colorful fashions, and sell them to tourists.

Division of Labor. The division of labor traditionally was clear: men hunted, fished, engaged in warfare, and made their equipment. Women raised children, cared for the camp, did the cultivating, and made pottery and baskets. Today the division is blurred. Some women have become cattle owners and a few drive heavy machinery; many men engage in agricultural work or raise cattle. Both sexes freely participate in child rearing and household chores. With higher education, either sex may enter the labor market in a variety of occupations.

Land Tenure. Aboriginally, land was held in clan units or in common as land cultivated under the chief for tribal use. These practices continued where possible when the ancestral Indians were driven into Florida. On the reservations, however, where standard Florida housing was built, the residents of the houses pay for them and are considered owners although the land is in trust. Seminole living off the reservations rent or own properties as any other citizen does. Private personal property is passed on as the owner sees fit.

Kinship

Kin Groups and Descent. The Seminole arose from tribes of the Southeastern matrilineal complex and maintained matriclans during their flight into Florida. The clans were rigidly exogamous until after World War II, and even now, all know their clan membership.

Marriage and Family

Marriage. Traditional marriage was matrilocal, and polygyny—usually sororal—occurred until well within the twentieth century when state laws banning polygyny took precedence. Most today avoid marriage within their clan, with only a few breaking the exogamy ban. Marriage with members of outside communities occurs now, although most Seminole still marry within the Indian group. During the late nineteenth century, outside marriage was looked upon with great disfavor, but much mixed marriage occurred earlier as well as marriage with members of other Indian tribes as the various Southeastern groups joined to create the Seminole in the eighteenth century. Today intermarriage is common. Divorce was simple and at the wish of either partner. Unions under modern law require formal legal divorce for dissolution, but there are many informal liaisons of some duration.

Domestic Unit. The local group today usually comprises nuclear families with older relatives welcome from either side, although relatives of the woman are most common, resulting in a matrilocal extended family. Also common are visiting relatives who may stay for extended periods. Adoption and fostering occur both to give a couple a chance at parenthood and to relieve economic pressures in large families. In camps of chickees, an extra person or so can be housed by constructing another chickee, but in modern housing additional residents make for crowded conditions, and the domestic group tends to be smaller.

Inheritance. Aboriginally, land was controlled through the clan system. Personal property could be passed on according to individual wishes. Today the clans control no property, and inheritance is according to legal wills or by state law under intestacy. Except for houses and automobiles, there is little for anyone to inherit.

Socialization. The mother's brother was the authority figure during the early period. He punished children occasionally by whipping but more often by scratching them with garfish teeth. Less severe punishment came in the form of gossip and ridicule by family and neighbors or ostracism of the miscreant. One's mother's brother is still respected, but today parents are responsible for raising children. Child rearing is generally permissive. Increasingly the school and church have become important agencies in socializing children to fit into outside society.

Sociopolitical Organization

Social and Political Organization. The formal political structures found among the tribes ancestral to the Seminole broke apart under the duress of warfare, disease, and population loss during the migration into Florida. Population movements meant new combinations in new communities, and the leaders eventually became men who had no inherited claim to their positions. The role of chief had been passed on in clans, but that practice ceased as the result of the extinction of some clans and the lack of suitable individuals in others. Leaders became men who were willing, competent, and acceptable. Osceola is an example of such a leader.

Under the Indian Reorganization Act of 1934, the Seminole created a political unit in 1957—the Seminole Tribe of Florida. In 1962 a smaller group of Seminole organized the Miccosukee Tribe. Although not all Seminole belong to one or the other, most have joined. The Seminole Tribe of Florida has three reservations—Hollywood, Brighton, and Big Cypress; the Miccosukee Tribe has a small reservation on the edge of the Everglades.

Social Control. Social control in the clans traditionally lay in the hands of maternal uncles. Gossip, ridicule, and isolation are used to correct antisocial behavior. Supernatural sanctions were important prior to World War I, but are no longer so.

Conflict. Following the formation of the Seminole as a unit, the major conflict was with outsiders and resulted in the three Seminole wars. During this period, the Seminole remaining in Florida greatly disapproved of those moving to Oklahoma. In recent times, intragroup conflict has been insignificant except insofar as the more traditionally oriented people did not join the Seminole Tribe of Florida but created their own group, the Miccosukee Tribe.

Religion and Expressive Culture

Religious Beliefs. Ancestral religion was animistic with natural forces considered far more potent than human ones. Seminole today have scant memory of traditional beliefs, although there is some syncretism that mixes old beliefs with Christianity. Many Seminole belong to Christian churches, primarily Baptist, and a few have become ministers. Although not necessarily church members, Seminole often attend services and events in churches on their reservations. Attendance is a social as much as a religious experience.

Religious Practitioners. The old-time shamans have died without leaving followers or apprentices with the intensive training necessary for the position. Consequently any who claim medicoreligious roles of a traditional sort are self-proclaimed rather than steeped in the lore of the past.

Ceremonies. The Green Corn Dance, or busk, the major ceremony of almost all Southeastern Indians, remains in reduced trivialized form, no longer truly a rite of purification, forgiveness, and renewal, but largely a social event. Only the Miccosukee Tribe has held a busk in recent years, and many Seminole disapprove of the introduction of alcohol into the celebration.

Medicine. With the demise of the shaman who was the healer in Southeastern cultures, much medical lore associated with native plants has been lost. In the 1950s, however, information on medical practices was collected, and some elderly people still perform herbal cures. For the most part, Indians go to Public Health Service physicians, visiting nurses, and local hospitals. Children, for example, are born in hospitals. Public Health nurses and dentists visit the reservations regularly.

Death and Afterlife. Mourning the dead and burial are the responsibility of churches and undertakers in the outer society. Old-time death ceremonials and mourning practices have been all but forgotten. Traditional mortuary practices and religious ceremonials changed or were lost during the long, difficult trek from the original homelands down the peninsula. Since the Seminole during those trying times did not record the changes, we can only surmise what was lost. Probably at one time the ancestral Seminole ascribed illness and death to human failure to observe proper rites concerning nature and the supernatural. Today modern medical theories of disease are acknowledged, and even those not belonging to a church have some notions of an afterlife in a pleasant place.

See also Seminole of Oklahoma

Bibliography

Garbarino, Merwyn S. (1972). *Big Cypress: A Changing Seminole Community*. New York: Holt, Rinehart & Winston.

Garbarino, Merwyn S. (1988). *The Seminole*. New York: Chelsea House.

Hudson, Charles (1976). *The Southeastern Indians*. Knoxville: University of Tennessee Press.

McReynolds, Edwin C. (1957). *The Seminoles*. Norman: University of Oklahoma Press.

Sturtevant, William C. (1971). "Creek into Seminole." In *North American Indians in Historical Perspective*, edited by Eleanor B. Leacock and Nancy O. Lurie, 92–128. New York: Random House.

Sturtevant, William C. (1987). *A Seminole Source Book*. New York: Garland Publishing.

MERWYN S. GARBARINO

Seminole of Oklahoma

The Oklahoma Seminole are the descendants of that segment of the Seminole tribe that was removed from Florida to Indian Territory (now Oklahoma) during and after the Second Seminole War (1836–1842). They are the larger part of the contemporary Seminole people, with a 1977 estimate by the Bureau of Indian Affairs of a population of over 9,000 as against about 2,000 in Florida (with about 1,303 on the Florida reservations in 1980). The two segments have much of their culture in common, but some differences have arisen since the 1840s. The Oklahoma Seminole now live in the prairie and scrub oak hill country of the central part of the state, a very different environment from semitropical Florida. They have maintained much of the traditional Southeastern Indian life-style and have retained some cultural forms mentioned in early accounts, but no longer in use in Florida. In contrast to the Florida group, which has separate Hitchiti- and Muskogee (Creek)-speaking components, almost all contemporary Oklahoma Seminole are Muskogee speakers (almost all speak English as well).

The Oklahoma Seminole today range from very conservative traditionalists to individuals who favor complete assimilation into mainstream American culture. The Seminole Nation of Oklahoma has its capital in Wewoka, Oklahoma. It is governed by a principal chief and secondary chief, who are elected for four-year terms, and by a council of forty-two members, three for each of the fourteen bands or tribal towns. There are twelve recognized bands in the nation. Originally, each was a tribal town and had its own squareground. Today there are nine squaregrounds or tribal town organizations remaining, three of which are dormant and one new. There are twenty-eight matrilineal exogamous clans, which in the past regulated marriage and descent and punished various offenses.

The annual ceremonial cycle is very important. It begins in the spring with an all-night Stomp Dance. Other Stomp Dances follow in May and June. The high point of the cycle is the Green Corn Ceremony (Busk), which renews and purifies the sacred fire, maintains health and prosperity, and purifies the men before eating the ripening green corn; it is the time for bestowing Indian names upon and assigning clan seats to young men not previously initiated, and for recognizing certain tutelary spirits and maintaining their goodwill. This ceremony occurs in June or July; then there are more Stomp Dances in August, and in September the annual tribal holiday, "Seminole Days," held at Seminole, Oklahoma. After this there are various dances until winter.

The traditional Seminole world is suffused with magic, with a type of magic for every occasion. There is a strong belief in witches who cause illness, the latter being treated with magical and herbal remedies. They have a number of supernaturals, including the Great Horned Snake who can give power to individuals, the Little People (who are very small human beings), the Tall Men (ten feet high or more), and Long Ears, an animal with gray hair and ears like a hare, as well as others. They are devoted to sports of all kinds, both traditional and borrowed from mainstream culture. They have borrowed heavily from the non-Indian world, especially in the realm of technology, but they have managed to preserve the core of their traditional value system.

Much of their day-to-day life is that of the mainstream culture—they may be construction workers, rangers, teachers, nurses, shopkeepers—but they return to their traditional world on weekends. Most Seminoles are members of Christian denominations, principally Baptist or Presbyterian, but others follow the traditional religion. All are strongly committed to education and participation in modern economic life. The tribe as a whole was greatly affected by the opening of the Greater Seminole oil field in 1923, which brought prosperity to many Seminole families. The younger people are turning to a form of general American Indian (pan-Indian) culture, exemplified in powwows, war dancing, and the adoption of other American Indian cultural forms, particularly those of the Plains Indians.

See also Seminole

Bibliography

Freeman, Ethel Cutler (1964). "The Least Known of the Five Civilized Tribes: The Seminole of Oklahoma." _Florida Anthropologist_ 17:139–152.

Howard, James H. (1984). _Oklahoma Seminoles: Medicines, Magic, and Religion._ In collaboration with Willie Lena. Norman: University of Oklahoma Press.

Welsh, Louise (1976). "Seminole Colonization in Oklahoma." In _America's Exiles: Indian Colonization in Oklahoma,_ edited by Arrell Morgan Gibson, 77–103. Oklahoma City: Oklahoma Historical Society.

Work, Susan (1978). "The 'Terminated' Five Tribes of Oklahoma: The Effect of Federal Legislation on the Government of the Seminole Nation." _American Indian Law Review_ 6:81–141.

Seneca

The Seneca were one of the original member tribes of the League of the Iroquois or the Five Nations Confederacy. The Seneca live mostly on Six Nations Reserve in Ontario, Canada, and the Allegany, Cattaraugus, and Tonawanda reservations in New York State in the United States. In the 1980s the Seneca on these four reserves numbered approximately forty-five hundred. The Seneca were the western-most tribe of the Iroquois Confederacy and in late aboriginal and early historic times occupied the territory bounded by Lake Ontario in the north, Seneca Lake in the east, the upper waters of the Allegheny and Susquehanna rivers in the south, and Lake Erie in the west.

The Seneca were drawn into the American Revolution on the side of the British and were among their closest Indian allies. Both during and after the war many Seneca migrated north to Canada. In 1797 the Seneca remaining in New York were forced to cede to the United States all their lands except a 200,000-acre reserve, much of which was lost in a treaty in 1838.

Traditionally, the Seneca were a hunting and farming people, but gathering and fishing were also important subsistence activities. The Seneca held eight of the fifty hereditary sachem positions in the Council of the League of the Iroquois and were known as the "Keepers of the Western Door."

See also Iroquois

Bibliography

Abler, Thomas S. (1978). "Seneca." In _Handbook of North American Indians._ Vol. 15, _Northeast,_ edited by Bruce G. Trigger, 505–517. Washington, D.C.: Smithsonian Institution.

Wallace, Anthony F. C. (1970). _The Death and Rebirth of the Seneca._ New York: Alfred A. Knopf.

Serrano

The Serrano, including the Alliklik, Kitanemuk, and Vanyume, lived in a large area to the east and north of Los Angeles, California, in the San Bernardino Range, Tehachapi Mountains, and environs. They spoke Serran languages of the Uto-Aztecan stock. The one hundred or so Serrano descendants live mostly on the Morongo and San Manuel reservations in California.

Bibliography

Bean, Lowell John, and Charles R. Smith (1978). "Serrano." In _Handbook of North American Indians._ Vol. 8, _California,_ edited by Robert F. Heizer, 570–574. Washington, D.C.: Smithsonian Institution.

Blackburn, Thomas C., and Lowell John Bean (1978). "Kitanemuk." In _Handbook of North American Indians._ Vol. 8, _California,_ edited by Robert F. Heizer, 564–569. Washington, D.C.: Smithsonian Institution.

Shakers

ETHNONYM: Believers

The Shakers (the United Society of Believers in Christ's Second Appearing) are a religious sect that began as an offshoot of Protestantism in England in the mid-1700s. Escaping persecution, the Shaker's founder, Mother Ann Lee, and eight followers immigrated to the United States in 1774 and settled in Watervliet, New York, north of Albany. Although not free from persecution in the New World either, Mother Lee was able to attract loyal followers who spread the gospel in New England, the Midwest, and the South. At its height in the mid-1800s, Shakerism numbered over five thousand "brothers and sisters" living in some eighteen communities, or "societies," in Maine, New Hampshire, Vermont, Massachusetts, Connecticut, New York, Pennsylvania, Ohio, Indiana, Kentucky, Georgia, and Florida.

Since that time Shakerism has steadily declined, and today there are only twelve Shakers left, residing at the two communities in Canterbury, New Hampshire, and Sabbathday Lake, Maine. Although the Shakers have largely disappeared, the Shaker way of life remains part of the American scene, primarily through Shaker museums, restored Shaker communities open to tourists, Shaker manufactures such as chairs and oval boxes which command prices of over $100,000 in the antiquities market, and Shaker songs such as "The Gift to Be Simple."

Shaker life is centered on a number of core beliefs and values, including a belief in the second coming of Christ, communal living, celibacy, humility, simplicity, efficiency, hard work, and equality between the sexes. Behaving in accordance with these values is seen as the route to salvation. Although outsiders often attribute the decline of Shakerism to celibacy, the Shakers themselves argued that most people who experimented with Shakerism left the communities because of difficulty in putting aside self-interest for the community's interest.

Although Shakers lived in their own communities in the form of large farms with multiple buildings and considerable acreage, did not vote, and were pacifists, they did not live totally outside mainstream society. In fact, Shakers were often the first in their region to use electricity and telephones, often owned cars, trucks, and tractors for community use, and today use televisions, computers, and other modern conveniences. Most important, celibacy required that all new Shakers had to be recruited from the outside world. The Shakers were open to all those interested including American Indians, Jews, and especially orphaned children, although few actually signed the covenant required for a lifelong commitment to Shakerism.

Shaker communities were large self-sufficient farms with a variety of cottage industries such as furniture making, metalworking, seed packaging, basketry, broom making, and weaving. The products of these endeavors were both used within the community and sold to outsiders. Some, such as the sale of seeds in packages, a Shaker innovation, were highly successful. In all their work, simplicity and efficiency were the guiding principles. The Shakers invented a number of objects still in use, including the circular saw, brimstone match, flat broom, and the revolving oven. Although equality between the sexes was stressed, the actual day-to-day work of the communities was divided on traditional sexual lines. Men usually did most of the outside work and heavy manufacturing, and women were responsible for domestic work, cooking, and traditional female work such as cloth making and weaving. As the number of male Shakers decreased over time, female manufactures began to be a major source of income.

At its height with some eighteen active societies, over 100,000 acres of land, and thousands of members, the Shakers constituted a multistate corporation. Central authority rested with the two elders and two elderesses at the New Lebanon society, east of Albany in New York, with the head elder or elderess the official head. Elders appointed their successors. Each Shaker society was governed by two elders and two elderesses assisted by deacons, who managed the day-to-day operation of the society, and trustees, who dealt with the outside world and were essentially the financial managers. Within the communities, the Shakers were divided into families of about one hundred persons each, who lived and worked separately from other families and with strict sexual segregation within the families. Despite the fairly rigid social structure, authoritarian rule was the exception; social cohesion was mostly the result of a shared commitment to Shaker values and beliefs. All property was owned communally, and new members were required to turn over all personal property to the society upon signing the covenant. This was a major source of the large acreage owned by the Shakers, but also the cause of a number of lawsuits by former members and heirs of deceased members. These suits were nearly always decided in favor of the Shakers.

Shaker religious beliefs are essentially fundamental Christianity, although there are some clearly unique beliefs that deviate from the main branches of Christianity and other sects. The Shakers reject the Trinity; instead they believe in a God made up of female and male elements reflected both in the supernatural and the real worlds. The requirement of celibacy is based on the belief that sin arose from Adam and Eve's sexual behavior in the Garden of Eden, although they do not feel that non-Shakers who marry and have sexual relations are sinners. The Shakers were also strong believers in active, direct communication with the deceased, but this practice apparently declined over the years.

Perhaps the feature of Shaker life that has drawn the most attention was their religious services. The services tended to be long, drawn-out events performed by the Shakers, but often with many non-Shaker observers. During the height of Shakerism in the mid-1800s, these services were ecstatic experiences for the participants, involving hand clapping, dancing, singing, stomping, shaking, jumping, shouting, having visions, and speaking in tongues. Some social scientists suggest that these services provided an emotional outlet for the Shakers who otherwise lived an austere life. As Shakerism declined, so too did the fervor of the services.

Bibliography

Hopple, Lee C. (1989–90). "A Religious and Geographical History of The Shakers, 1747–1988." *Pennsylvania Folklife* 39:57–72.

Kephart, William M. (1987). *Extraordinary Groups.* 3rd ed. New York: St. Martin's Press.

Purcell, L. Edward (1988). *The Shakers*. New York: Crescent Books.

Richmond, Mary L. (1977). *Shaker Literature: A Bibliography*. Hanover, N.H.: University Press of New England.

Shasta

The Shasta live in the middle drainage of the Klamath River in northern California and southern Oregon. They speak a language of the Shastan family of the Hokan-Siouan phylum and probably number less than fifty.

Bibliography

Silver, Shirley (1978). "Shastan Peoples." In *Handbook of North American Indians*. Vol. 8, *California*, edited by Robert F. Heizer, 211–224. Washington, D.C.: Smithsonian Institution.

Shawnee

ETHNONYMS: Chaouanons, Satana, Shawanah, Shawano, Shawanwa

The Shawnee are an Algonkian-speaking people whose component divisions have been reported as living in many areas of the eastern United States and who apparently were never united into a single society. At the time of contact in the seventeenth century they were living along the Savannah River on the Georgia–South Carolina border, along the Ohio River, in Illinois, and in Maryland. In the eighteenth century they were in eastern Pennsylvania and southern Ohio, and some were with the Creek in Alabama. Later they tended to cluster in southern Ohio where they were for a time a significant obstacle to European migration westward. Various groups then began to migrate westward, ultimately settling in Oklahoma in three major groupings. These are now known as the Absentee-Shawnee Tribe of Oklahoma, based in Shawnee, Oklahoma, the Eastern Shawnee Tribe of Oklahoma, based in Quapaw, Oklahoma, and the Cherokee Shawnee, now apparently merged with the Cherokee Nation of Oklahoma, based in Tahlequa, Oklahoma. Some Shawnee also live with the Seneca-Cayuga Tribe of Oklahoma, based in Miami, Oklahoma. There are probably about four thousand of the descendants of the historic Shawnee now living in the state.

Aboriginally, the Shawnee were divided into two types of groups. One consisted of five divisions, each of which was a descent group in which membership was inherited patrilineally. Each was a territorial unit centering on a town—Chillicothe, Ohio, was named after one such division. The other type consisted of the geographically defined groups into which the tribe was split at various times in their history. These groups could merge or split at any time. In the late nineteenth century these became the three permanent groups now known as Absentee-Shawnee, Eastern Shawnee, and Cherokee Shawnee noted above.

The record of aboriginal Shawnee culture is fragmentary, so that it cannot be described coherently at any specific time or place. Subsistence combined hunting and maize, squash, and bean horticulture with some gathering of wild foods. The economy was also strongly oriented toward the fur trade, with an emphasis on the trading of deerskins. They lived in semi-permanent settlements (towns) consisting of bark-covered lodges or longhouses. Each settlement had as its center a wooden building used for council meetings, ritual, and ceremony.

The household seems to have consisted of the nuclear family, and there was a system of patrilineal clans. But notable changes occurred in the system in the nineteenth century, the clans no longer being patrilineal or exogamous. After 1859 the clans evolved into a system of six name-groups, which were not descent units. Political activity was divided between peace and war organizations. The former was apparently based on the five divisions, each with its own chief. There was a single tribal chief with overall authority. Each division also apparently had a war chief, with a single tribal war chief in charge. Both types of chiefs formed a tribal council. There also seems to have been a system of women chiefs operating on the town level.

The Shawnee recognized a supreme being, known as Our Grandmother, as well as a large number of other deities. There may, however, have been an earlier tradition of a male supreme being, the later idea perhaps having been borrowed from the Iroquois. Information on this is uncertain. The annual ceremonial dance cycle formed the main forum for communal worship. Another focus was the five sacred packs, one for each division, about which very little is known.

Bibliography

Callender, Charles (1978). "Shawnee." In *Handbook of North American Indians*. Vol. 15, *Northeast*, edited by Bruce G. Trigger, 622–635. Washington, D.C.: Smithsonian Institution.

Trowbridge, Charles C. (1939). *Shawnee Traditions*. Edited by Vernon Kinietz and Erminie W. Voegelin. University of Michigan, Museum of Anthropology, Occasional Contributions, no. 9. Ann Arbor.

Shuswap

ETHNONYMS: Shihwapmukh, Suxwapmux

The Shuswap now live on a number of reserves attached to the Kamloops-Okanagan and Williams Lake agencies in south-central British Columbia in the general area from Kamloops to Revelstoke in parts of the drainages of the Fraser, Thompson, and upper Columbia rivers. They speak an Interior Salish language related to Lillooet, Thompson, and Okanagon and number about four thousand today. First contact with Europeans was probably with Alexander Mackenzie in 1793 and then with Simon Fraser in 1808, with sustained contact beginning about 1816 through involvement in the fur trade with the Hudson's Bay Company. As with other groups in the region, the traditional culture was much changed by the influx of gold miners and settlers in 1858 and the subsequent epidemics that decimated the Shuswap population. Currently, traditional subsistence activities such as hunting, fishing, and trapping are still carried on, though the staple foods are now store-bought potatoes, flour, rice, and beans.

In 1900 the Shuswap were described as being comprised of nineteen bands organized into seven divisions. The divisions were territorial units, with the bands being the basic political units. The seven divisions are no longer recognized, and the nineteen bands are recognized as synonymous with the reserves they occupy. The Shuswap as a whole were never organized as a cohesive political unit. Traditionally, bands had a chief as well as chiefs for war, the hunt, and dance. The bands residing in the northern and western reaches of Shuswap territory were greatly influenced by Northwest Coast groups in the nineteenth century and developed a social class system with nobles, commoners, and slaves. The bands in the southern and eastern regions were not so influenced, but they too had slaves, obtained through trade and warfare. Although the Shuswap never warred as an organized group, individual bands fought with other groups, including the Cree, Sekani, Okanagon, Beaver, and Assiniboin. The Shuswap were more sedentary than groups to the south, spending much of the year in large semisubterranean earthlodges. Today, these lodges have been replaced by canvas tents and log cabins.

Salmon was the staple food for groups near streams, while other groups relied more on hunting deer, elk, moose, bear, and mountain sheep. Both fish and animal meat were dried and smoked. Women collected roots, bulbs, various fruits, nuts, and other plant foods. The traditional religion was animistic, with the vision quest for guardian spirits by adolescent boys being especially important. These spirits were the major sources of power for shamans in their curing and other rites. The mythology was similar to that of other Plateau groups and included dwarfs, giants, cloud people, wind people, Coyote, the trickster, and Old One, a creator.

Bibliography

Brow, James B. (1972). *Shuswap of Canada*. New Haven: Hraflex Books, Human Relations Area Files.

Palmer, Gary B. (1975). "Shuswap Indian Ethnobotany." *Syesis* 8:29–81.

Teit, James A. (1909). *The Shuswap*. American Museum of Natural History, Memoir no. 4, 447–758. New York.

Slavey

ETHNONYMS: Dehghaot'ine, Dene, Etchareottine, Slave

Orientation

Identification. The Slavey are an American Indian group of northern Canada whose name or cultural designation is of foreign origin. "Slavey" derives from a translation of the Algonkian Cree term *awahkaan*, meaning "captive, slave." Traditionally, peoples referred to as Slavey distinguished various groups among themselves, usually on the basis of residence or territory.

Location. Slavey inhabited the Mackenzie River drainage of northern Canada. Their territory was roughly bounded on the south by the Fort Nelson and Hay rivers; on the north by the Great Bear River; on the east by the nearest shores of the Great Slave and Great Bear lakes; and on the west by the peaks of the Mackenzie Mountains. Most Slavey now reside in the communities of Fort Liard, Hay River, Fort Providence, Fort Simpson, Fort Liard, Fort Wrigley, and Fort Norman in the Northwest Territories; Fort Nelson in British Columbia; and near Fort Vermillion in northern Alberta.

Demography. The aboriginal population has been estimated at about twelve hundred. The contemporary population is about five thousand.

Linguistic Affiliation. The term *Slavey* is used to refer to a number of closely related northeastern Athapaskan languages or dialects, including those spoken by Slavey, Bearlake, Mountain, and Hare Indians. Dogrib and Chipewyan are other closely related northeastern Athapaskan languages. These languages are ultimately related to others spoken in northwestern Canada, Alaska, the Pacific Coast, and the American Southwest.

History and Cultural Relations

Alaska (and perhaps part of northwestern Canada) is the homeland of Athapaskan-speaking peoples in the New World. Prehistoric migrations explain their presence in other areas. Although it is difficult to associate specific Athapaskan peoples with particular prehistoric archaeological traditions, it seems reasonable to suggest an Athapaskan presence in Slavey territory since about 50 B.C.—that is, through the encompassing Mackenzie, Spence River, and Fort Liard Complexes. The Slavey would have had relatively few contacts with non-Athapaskan-speaking peoples. First contact with Europeans occurred in June and July of 1789, when Slavey encountered Alexander Mackenzie during his exploration of what would become the Northwest Territories. For the next 125 years knowledge of and contact with the West came primarily through fur traders and Roman Catholic and Anglican missionaries. Between the late 1790s and 1858 a number of trading forts were established in Slavey territory. Between 1900 and 1922 two treaties were signed with the Canadian government. In the 1930s mineral resources were discovered in Slavey territory and have subsequently been developed. Since the 1960s, Canadian government programs have had a great impact on Slavey culture and society. Culturally, Slavey are most closely related to other Dene (Athapaskan Indians) in northwestern Canada—Dogrib, Bearlake, Mountain, and Hare peoples. They are also culturally similar to the Athapaskan-speaking Chipewyan, Beaver, and Kaska Indians from northern Alberta and northern British Columbia.

Settlements

Traditionally, Slavey were highly mobile hunters and fishermen whose seasonal socioeconomic cycle was characterized by periods of in-gathering and dispersal in relation to the availability and productivity of basic resources. For most of the year people dispersed to hunt and fish throughout their territory in groups of approximately 10 to 25 people. When resources were temporarily concentrated (for example, at selected fisheries during spawning), groups as large as 200 to 250 individuals were formed. When trading posts were established in conjunction with the fur trade, Slavey incorporated visits to them in their yearly movements. Over time, Slavey began to settle relatively permanently at the points of trade. Today, they reside on a year-round basis in the communities mentioned earlier and participate in seasonal hunting, fishing, and trapping scheduled around local employment and schooling.

Economy

Subsistence and Commercial Activities. Slavey were hunters and fishermen for whom vegetable products provided little food (perhaps 5 percent of their diet). The basic food resources were moose, woodland caribou, bear, beaver, fish (whitefish, lake trout, grayling, and herring), rabbits, and duck. With the addition of trapping, beaver, marten, mink, fox, muskrat, and lynx became important for their fur. In their economic pursuits people employed snares, clubs, bows and arrows, spears, fishing weirs, and deadfalls. With the fur trade came guns, twine fish nets, metal traps, canvas tents, and assorted metal tools such as ice chisels. Boats and motors and snowmobiles are essential to the contemporary pursuit of traditional resources.

Industrial Arts. Slavey industrial arts were not highly developed, but hides, stone, bone, and wood were finely worked in production of snowshoes, toboggans, bags, drums, and other material items.

Trade. Traditionally, trade was inconsequential. Before contact with Mackenzie, exchange with Cree and Chipewyan middlemen probably introduced some items of Western material culture. Despite participation in the fur trade, the Slavey remained socioeconomically autonomous from the 1790s to the start of World War I. After the war, through the fur trade they became dependent on European goods and

services. Trapping and fur trading continue to provide significant amounts of income in Slavey communities.

Division of Labor. The traditional division of labor was based on sex and age, with little occupational specialization. Men were primarily responsible for hunting, fishing, and trapping; women, for child rearing, maintaining the household, snaring small game, collecting berries, processing food, and manufacturing clothing. Children aided and eventually assumed the roles of their like-sexed parents.

Land Tenure. Land was not owned, with access to resource sites restricted by use principles. Local and regional bands, however, were symbolically associated with the territories they frequented. With the fur trade came some registration of trapping lines.

Kinship

Kin Groups and Descent. The Slavey had no clans or unilineal descent groups. Kinship was reckoned bilaterally and used as a fundamental organizational principle of local bands the social flexibility of which was a key fact of Slavey life. Such groups were formed by tracing ties from either partner in a marriage to a central figure, a good hunter or provider, who led the group. There seems to have been some emphasis on the female line, as exemplified by temporary matrilocal postmarital residence. There were few formal duties and obligations in kinship relationships; rather, there were diffuse principles of solidarity and reciprocity that lessened in intensity as social distance increased.

Kinship Terminology. Kinship is reckoned bilaterally and both teknonymy and fictive kinship are documented. Consanguineal and affinal kin are separated. Terms for the former are characterized by (1) differentiation only by sex for the second ascending generation, (2) bifurcate merging for the first ascending generation, (3) Hawaiian or Iroquoian distinctions for ego's (one's own) generation, (4) Hawaiian or Iroquoian distinctions for the first descending generation, and (5) contrasts by sex and sex of speaker for the second descending generation.

Marriage and Family

Marriage. There were no prescriptive marriage rules, but local group exogamy with nonparallel relatives was seemingly preferred. Close relatives were considered inappropriate marriage partners. Polygyny occurred relatively frequently, was often sororal, and was explained in socioeconomic terms—the successful hunter could support more than one wife. The sororate was practiced, as was pre- and postmarital brideservice. Temporary matrilocal postmarital residence (while "working for" a father-in-law or brother-in-law) was the norm. After the birth of a first child or some other reasonable period, patrilocal and neolocal residence were possible. Divorce was apparently easy—one spouse simply left.

Domestic Unit. The nuclear family household was the primary domestic group. It could be extended by the addition of one or more of the parents of the married couple. Nuclear families, however, rarely traveled alone, as they normally accompanied larger local groups that were kin-based and within which expectations of economic cooperation and generosity were great.

Inheritance. Traditionally, upon death, individually owned personal property was placed with the corpse of the deceased person or was destroyed or was kept by relatives as mementos. If property was inherited, it was usually by a spouse or child on the informal basis of need and appropriateness. The Canadian government has administered the transmission of registered trapping lines from father to son.

Socialization. Like-sexed parents and the rest of the immediate family were fundamental to socialization, which was accomplished with great leniency. The values of industriousness, individual autonomy, generosity, emotional restraint, and control were encouraged. Because noninterference, or "minding one's own business," was valued, intervening with another's children was rare. Disapproval of self-glorification, stinginess, bossiness, gossiping, anger, laziness, fighting, and illicit sexual congress was expressed.

Sociopolitical Organization

Social Organization. Bilateral kinship, marriage, and friendship principles were central to Slavey social organization. Kinship and social distance were informally computed, and rights, duties, and obligations attenuated as distance increased in this fundamentally egalitarian society.

Political Organization. The Slavey were organized into more or less formal bands. Local bands were normally kin-based and leadership was provided by men possessing special abilities as hunters and providers along with unusual generosity. The successful hunter's obligation to distribute his kill among the local group was a basic fact of Slavey social and, ultimately, political life. The leadership of successful providers was informal and situational, and ceased when their skill diminished or they failed in their distributive obligations. Regional bands were focused on the territories they inhabited and existed as groups only when relatively large groups came together at concentrated resource sites. They lacked leaders and were not necessarily composed of local bands. The Slavey "tribe" was a nonfunctioning category of cultural and linguistic identity.

Social Control. Social sanctions were diffuse and informal. Gossip, the reduction of aid and support, "talking to," and avoidance or withdrawal from unpleasant persons were the norm. Perhaps the most extreme sanction was banishment. Sorcery or the threat of sorcery may have played a role in social control.

Conflict. Raiding and warfare were matters for families and local groups, not regional groups or tribes. Revenge for the death of a kinsperson or for the theft of a woman was the primary motive. Disputes over women were more frequent than disputes over resource sites or extractive resources. The fur trade led to hostilities with the Cree and Chipewyan.

Religion and Expressive Culture

Religious Beliefs. Slavey religious beliefs were dominated by concepts of a mythological past, a diffuse power inherent to the world and everything in it, and animal spirits. By reference to the mythological past, people were able to explain many features of the contemporary world. The presence of inherently dangerous, but morally neutral power was also used to explain (and to exert influence over) phenomena in the world. Animal or "medicine" spirits occupied the traditional Slavey universe. Today, the Christian God and other Western supernaturals are also recognized. Individuals could obtain power from animal spirits.

Religious Practitioners. Shamans (usually, but not always men) dreamed and came to "know" about things. Through dreaming they acquired power, which was used for curing and for success at various subsistence activities such as hunting. Acquired power might also be used negatively. Shamanistic techniques included singing, dancing, sucking, dreaming, and incantating. Knowledge of an animal spirit might necessitate an eating taboo.

Ceremonies. Most Slavey ceremonies were relatively informal and not calendrical. Dancing and feasting to celebrate successful hunts or the meeting of groups were common. Girls were secluded at menses and a boy's first kill was celebrated.

Medicine. Curing was primarily the domain of the Slavey shaman. Supernatural techniques predominated, but roots, berries, spruce gum, other plants, and animal products were employed.

Death and Afterlife. For traditional Slavey, death was accompanied by the loss of a "shadow," but further information about this or about concepts of an afterlife is difficult to obtain. Corpses were either placed in trees or buried in the ground. Modern conceptions of death and afterlife are dominated by Christian beliefs.

Bibliography

Asch, Michael I. (1981). "Slavey." In *Handbook of North American Indians*. Vol. 6, *Subarctic*, edited by June Helm, 338–349. Washington, D.C.: Smithsonian Institution.

Helm, June (1961). *The Lynx Point People: The Dynamics of a Northern Athapaskan Band*. National Museum of Canada Bulletin no. 176. Anthropological Series, no. 53. Ottawa.

Honigmann, John J. (1946). *Ethnography and Acculturation of the Fort Nelson Slave*. Yale University Publications in Anthropology, no. 33. New Haven, Conn.: Department of Anthropology, Yale University.

SCOTT RUSHFORTH

Snoqualmie

ETHNONYMS: Snoqualmu, Snoqualmoo, Snoqualmick, Snoqualamuke, Snuqualmi

Traditionally, the Snoqualmie, speakers of a Coast Salishan language, were called "Sduk-al-bixw," meaning "strong people of status." Today there are about fifteen hundred Snoqualmie many of whom reside in their aboriginal territory within the Snoqualmie River drainage system between

Monroe and North Bend, in northwestern Washington. Aboriginally, they inhabited some fifty-eight longhouses in about sixteen villages with a total population of from three thousand to four thousand persons.

During the 1850s the Snoqualmie chiefdom consisted of four districts: Monroe, Tolt (the administrative center), Fall City (the military center), and North Bend. An impenetrable fort on a hill overlooking the confluence of the Tolt and Snoqualmie rivers secured the valley from outsiders. Head Chief Pat Kanin, perhaps the most powerful Indian in the Puget Sound area in the mid-nineteenth century, along with an assistant chief and district chiefs served as the tribal government. Wealth derived from the trade route over Snoqualmie Pass enabled the Snoqualmie to support full-time wood carvers, toolmakers, weapons specialists, and military leaders.

In 1916 the Snoqualmie changed their political system to one based on majority rule through elections, largely to conform to the standards of White society. Four councils form the current tribal organization: General Council of the People, the Council of Elders, the Representative Tribal Council, and the Council of Chiefs.

Bibliography

Haeberlin, Herman K., and Erna Gunther (1930). _The Indians of Puget Sound_. Seattle: University of Washington Press.

Tollefson, Kenneth D. (1987). "The Snoqualmie: A Puget Sound Chiefdom." _Ethnology_ 26:121–136.

KENNETH D. TOLLEFSON

South and Southeast Asians of Canada

ETHNONYMS: South Asians: East Indians, Indians, Pakistanis, Sikhs. Southeast Asians: Indochinese, Vietnamese, Khmer, Lao, Chinese of Southeast Asia

Orientation

Identification. South Asian and Southeast Asian are broad ethnocultural categories. Each refers to a number of ethnic and national groups. All South Asians have roots in India, Pakistan, Sri Lanka, or Bangladesh. One third, though, originate in the South Asian diaspora—in communities in Tanzania, Kenya, Uganda, South Africa, Guyana, Trinidad, Fiji, or Mauritius. Being South Asian is secondary to identification with the more specific, sometimes overlapping ethnic, religious, and national groups. Southeast Asians considered here are immigrants from Vietnam (75 percent), Laos (11 percent), and Cambodia (12 percent). Those from Vietnam are either ethnic Vietnamese or Chinese. Laotians and Cambodians are primarily Lao and Khmer, respectively, though some are Chinese.

Location. Virtually all South and Southeast Asians are urban, and over 85 percent reside in Canada's major metropolitan areas. Of South Asians, 95 percent live in Ontario (51 percent, 80 percent of these in Toronto), British Columbia (26 percent, 62 percent of these in Vancouver), Alberta (11 percent of these in Calgary and Edmonton), or Quebec (7 percent, 90 percent of these in Montreal). Ninety percent of Southeast Asians live in Ontario (33 percent), Quebec (32 percent), Alberta (15 percent), or British Columbia (10 percent). Access to jobs, housing, and community support, as well as chain migration, have resulted in considerable geographical localization. Residential concentration is high for new immigrants and working-class people, but neighborhoods where either constitute more than 10 percent are rare. Most working-class Southeast Asians reside in urban core areas, especially near Chinatowns, whereas South Asians are increasingly suburban. Certain streets and neighborhoods from British Columbia to Quebec have become centers of South Asian and Southeast Asian commercial and institutional development marked by stores, restaurants, and religious facilities.

Linguistic Affiliation. British colonial influence ensured that in all South Asian source societies English is either a lingua franca of the educated classes or a national language. Thus today English is the mother tongue of 40 percent, and 90 percent of South Asian Canadians claim some facility with it. Other mother tongues are Punjabi, Hindi, Urdu, Gujarati, and secondarily Bengali, Sinhala, Malayalam, Tamil, and Telugu, with 40 to 45 percent using one of these as their primary home language; 20 to 30 percent of immigrant women speak only their mother tongue. Sikhism places a priority on knowing Punjabi, and almost all second- and third-generation Sikhs can speak and understand the language. Most Canadian-born whose parents have another South Asian mother tongue can understand it, but few will achieve full speaking fluency. In contrast, few Southeast Asian initially knew English or French, and a majority presently do not have effective command of either. The key exceptions are French-speaking professionals and children. Children nevertheless maintain the spoken tradition of their parents' languages. Virtually all immigrant adults use their mother tongue in the home and community, and often in the workplace—Vietnamese (ethnic Vietnamese and some Vietnamese Chinese), Khmer (most Cambodians), Lao (most Laotians), Cantonese (most Vietnamese Chinese), and Teochiu (some Cambodian and Laotian Chinese). Cantonese operates as a Chinese commercial lingua franca in Cambodia and Laos, and many Chinese from there can speak it as well.

Demography. In 1990 South Asians numbered about 410,000, or 1.5 percent of Canada's population. The largest groups are Sikhs (130,000), Guyanese (50,000), Hindi- and Punjabi-speaking Indian Hindus (40,000), Pakistanis (30,000), Gujarati-speaking Hindus from India and East Africa (25,000), Ismaili Muslims (25,000), culturally North Indian Muslims from India and East Africa (20,000), Fijians (20,000), and Trinidadians (15,000–20,000). Smaller communities include Bangladeshis, Bengalis, Mauritians, Tamils from India and Sri Lanka, Sinhalese, and Malayalam speakers from South India. Three-quarters of South Asians are immigrants, most coming during 1968–1980. Substantial immigration is ongoing (typically 20,000 per year), about 50 percent from India. Over 90 percent of the 150,000–180,000 Southeast Asians in Canada are post-1974 immigrants. Roughly 60,000 are Vietnamese, 60,000 are Vietnamese Chinese, 20,000 are Laotians, and 20,000 are Cambodians. About 10,000 Southeast Asians a year arrive as refugees and as conventional immigrants.

History and Cultural Relations

The first South Asian immigrants were Sikh (and a few other Punjabi and Bengali) men who settled in British Columbia during 1903–1907. Economically driven anti-Asian hostility quickly focused on Sikhs, and in 1907 South Asian immigration was banned. This ban lasted until 1947, but in 1919 aggressive protest secured for Sikhs permission for wives and dependent children to immigrate. Immigrants during 1947–1962 were primarily Sikh chain migrants. In the mid-1960s the last racial, ethnic, and national immigration restrictions were eliminated. Since then, the ethnic, national, and class backgrounds of South Asian immigrants have broadened greatly, though chain migration has kept immigrant flows ethnically and nationally selective. South Asian settlement has been remarkably smooth, including relations with others. Even so, since 1975 South Asians have faced some intolerance manifest in name-calling, vandalism, and denial of jobs and housing. Relations between South Asian groups are weakly developed save for when institutionally linked needs (especially concerning religion) require them, when specific ethnocultural groups are small or when groups share a common or closely related language. Social and cultural links with source countries remain very strong.

A thousand Southeast Asians, mostly students and professionals, lived in Quebec in 1971. Six thousand political refugees came after the fall of Thieu in Vietnam. They, too, were typically well educated and skilled. Sixty thousand boat and land people were accepted as political refugees during 1979–1980, and through government and private settlement schemes initially were spread across the country. Many soon migrated to major cities in search of relatives, community support, and jobs. Subsequent immigrants have primarily been the relatives of those already here and have joined extant big-city communities. Both intra- and intergroup relations were initially chaotic and under rapid flux. Each major ethnocultural group—Vietnamese, Vietnamese Chinese, Cambodians, and Laotians—essentially went their own way, sharing neither language nor identity. Vietnamese Chinese soon established contacts with other Chinese. Most Southeast Asians at first found themselves on the receiving end of well-intentioned but paternalistic, highly asymmetrical relations with Canadians involved in facilitating their settlement. These relations did not persist, and many Southeast Asians are socially and linguistically isolated from those of other backgrounds. School-age children, though, have developed wide-ranging social relations with their peers. Active prejudice against Southeast Asians is minimal, although their stereotypical portrayal as refugees is occasionally problematic.

Economy

Until the 1960s most South Asians in the labor force were Sikh men, who worked at blue-collar jobs in British Columbia's lumber mills and logging camps. Immigrant selection preferences for professionals in the 1960s and 1970s and for skilled blue- and white-collar workers thereafter widened South Asians' range of occupations. Extensive immigrant sponsorship also brought many unskilled people to Canada. South Asians span the educational spectrum; 30 percent claim a B.A. degree or more, and 20 percent have less than a ninth-grade education. There is a great educational disparity between women and men. Today a very high proportion of women (70 percent) and men (90–95 percent) are economically active outside the home—a remarkable shift from patriarchal source cultures, where few women are in the paid work force. One-third of men are in highly skilled occupations, and another third are in primary and secondary industries. Women are involved in clerical, service delivery, fabrication, and health-related work. Women perform virtually all household tasks, as in source cultures. South Asians have achieved at least a normative Canadian material standard of living, compensating for immigrant disabilities with class resources, extensive familial economic pooling, and community support. South Asians have strong entrepreneurial traditions, and small-scale South Asian commercial activities are well developed. These are chiefly community-based storefront businesses such as retail stores, travel and insurance agencies, service stations, and restaurants. Some South Asians are also involved in larger scale mainstream businesses, especially Ismailis, other Gujaratis, and Sikhs.

Forced migration has limited Southeast Asian economic options. By Southeast Asian standards most people are middle class and comparatively well educated (claiming on average ten years of education). Fewer than 15 percent from Vietnam are from rural backgrounds, though this is higher for Cambodians and Laotians. As many as one-half have backgrounds in shopkeeping and small-scale manufacturing; these were Chinese economic specializations throughout Southeast Asia. Even so, Southeast Asians often have fewer occupational, class, and language resources than typical Canadians, and the majority work at relatively unskilled, poorly remunerated jobs in manufacturing and in the provision of food and janitorial services. Still, within two years of their arrival 90 percent of adults were in the labor force. Women do almost all household work, as in Southeast Asia.

Kinship, Marriage and Family

South Asian source cultures are characterized by patrilineality, patrilocality, class and caste endogamy, consanguineal (and where relevant, village) exogamy (some Muslims excepted), arranged marriage, polygyny, familial gender segregation, patriarchy, male inheritance, joint or extended family organization, extensive familial economic pooling, and the subordination of individual and community concerns to those of the family. Kinship terms vary by language, ethnic group, and religion, but typically follow either a Hawaiian or an Iroquois pattern. Lineages are often acknowledged but are not corporate. Kin relations reflect strong age and gender status differences. In Canada, key familial relations have become deeply symbolic of South Asians' continuity with tradition. Some are also of great practical and psychological importance. The maintenance of extant family roles reduces the psychological marginality of immigrant adults brought on by great shifts in public sphere roles; chain migrants inevitably stay with relatives while establishing themselves; household income pooling by parents and children makes possible a high material standard of living; community-based roles and statuses are closely linked to family. Even so, few reestablish permanent fully extended or joint households. Nuclear families with two to three children predominate, but households composed of nuclear families and one or two other relatives are very common. Almost all elderly reside with relatives, and children usually remain part of their parents' household until marriage, and sometimes for years thereafter. Most parents sharply limit relations of their adolescent and young adult children with those of the opposite sex, usually forbidding daughters (and often sons) to date. Many parents arrange their marriages, and most informally guide the process. South Asians commonly object to intermarriage, for it may symbolize the end of the family line or cause a loss of community status. Intermarriage rates are low, but greater among professionals and some diaspora groups like Fijians and Guyanese. Divorce is rare. The massive labor force participation of women is not yet fully reflected in husband-wife roles. Joint decision making has increased, but elements of patriarchy persist. Wives remain responsible for child rearing.

Southeast Asian patterns are broadly similar, but more closely follow Cantonese Chinese practice. The ideal household is patrilineally based, extended, patriarchal, patrilocal (excepting Lao, who are sometimes matrilocal), and a corporate economic unit. Kinship terminology varies by group. In practice, elderly parents usually stay with the eldest son, but children typically establish their own nuclear households after marriage. Southeast Asian women (especially in Cambodia and Laos) have more power and influence than their South Asian or Chinese peers, both in the household and outside. For all groups powerful cultural values imbue in individuals strong feelings of familial responsibility. Many have been unable to fully reestablish their families in Canada, for they have key family members who cannot leave their countries of origin, who have found safe haven elsewhere, or who have been killed in war. Vietnamese Chinese, however, typically do live in nuclear or partially extended households. A significant minority of Southeast Asians without families in Canada continue to live in the households of relatives or have formed households with similar individuals. Intermarriage rates so far have been low.

Socialization. South and Southeast Asians expend only selective effort to enculturate or socialize their young children into their source culture and its social practices. They have a high (though class-dependent) commitment to their children's social and economic success, and know that along with securing the necessary education and skills comes acculturation. In fact, public school participation (nearly universal) and the influences of the mass media and their peers have produced massive second-generation acculturation. Nevertheless, South and Southeast Asians have stressed the maintenance of certain values and practices that symbolize continuity with tradition and past experience. These include family roles, food traditions, religion, and to a varying degree, language.

Sociopolitical Organization

Social Organization. Both populations exhibit extensive informal community organization and considerable institutional development. Informal community networks provide psychological support, continuity of shared experience, and the means to maintain and modify key personal statuses. They are also useful sources of information about jobs, government and private services, housing, and the home country. Residential concentration is high for new immigrants and working-class people. For both populations informal community networks are ethnic group–specific. Individuals typically have far more social relations with other Canadians than with members of other regional ethnic groups. South Asian associations number over three hundred. Most prevalent are ethnic group sociocultural associations and organizations supporting local religious institutions. Helping and pan–South Asian organizations are rare. Formal organizations among Southeast Asians are less numerous, though each ethnocultural group typically will have at least one representative association established in a given city.

Political Organization. Neither population has had much impact on formal Canadian politics. Neither has exerted any special issue political leverage either, excepting South Asians concerning racial intolerance. Both, however, have been at the center of political debate: Southeast Asians over how many should be accepted by Canada as refugees (now more per capita than any other Western country), and South Asians (primarily Sikhs) over whether Canadian ethnic groups should be involved in source country politics. Intragroup political action is nevertheless intense in both populations.

Among South Asians, some individuals are involved in homeland political causes, most notably Sikhs supporting an independent Sikh state (Khalistan) in Punjab. Tamils, Fijians, Guyanese, and others also support home-country minority groups. South Asian communities are highly political, as various individuals, cliques, and groups compete for status, and spokesperson and brokerage roles. Only Ismailis have established representative community leadership structures, which in their case link households to local, regional, national, and international councils. Most South Asian spokespersons are self-appointed, or else represent an organization or association that itself is not widely based.

In the case of Southeast Asians, they can do little to affect home-country politics. Discussion and interpretation of the home situation nevertheless is intense, and political differences, both real and perceived, factionalize all non-Chinese communities. Key individuals contest for brokerage and spokesperson roles in much the same fashion as with South Asians.

Social Control and Conflict. Reconciliation of changes brought on by immigration with personal values and traditions often engenders considerable marital stress, which is typically resolved (if at all) within the household or with the assistance of close relatives. For South Asians the issue of children's cross-sex relations is often contentious, and Southeast Asians increasingly face intergenerational value conflict stemming from great cultural differences. Community and home-country conceptions of appropriate conduct place great conformity pressure on adults, though in no ethnic group save for Ismailis could there be said to be formal institutions of social control. Neither population makes extensive use of the courts, police, or social welfare institutions to address interpersonal conflict.

Religion and Expressive Culture

Religious Beliefs.   These groups all participate in their traditional religions described. Only beliefs and practices specific to Canada are noted here.

Among South Asians, the one-third who are Sikh have been highly committed to their faith. Since 1908 they have founded *gurdwaras* (temples) all across Canada. Each is organizationally independent and dependent on local financial support. Where several exist, membership often reflects class, caste, source locale, political orientation, or degree of acculturation. Sikh religious practice and belief are not markedly different than in urban India, save for minor accommodations made to Canadian dress, work routines, and the like. As in India, there is no consensus as to what marks one as a "true Sikh," and this can be very contentious. Symbolic "retraditionalization" among Sikhs has occurred since 1984 in response to perceived state oppression in Punjab, and more adult men now wear the five *kakkas* that mark their Khalsa commitment. Instruction of children in religion and in Gurmukhi script is increasing and intergenerational transmission of the religion is high.

About 25 percent are Hindus. Hinduism in India and the non-Western diaspora is highly variable and embedded in everyday family and community life. As such, it has faced challenges becoming established in Canada. Adults continue with their private devotions, and most maintain some dietary restrictions and participate in important calendrical celebrations. Commensal and associational rules limiting contact with others have largely disappeared. Multiuse Hindu temples have been established in major cities and offer life-cycle and weekly services. It is unclear to what degree Hinduism is being transmitted to the Canadian-born.

Of the 25–30 percent who are Muslims, Ismailis have the most well-developed religious institutions. Composing a Shia sect following the spiritual leadership of the Aga Khan, they have organized *jamat khana* for worship everywhere there are practitioners. Otherwise highly acculturated, Ismailis effectively have transmitted their religious tradition to the second generation. Almost all other South Asian Muslims are Sunnis. Save for where particular ethnic or national groups are numerous, they use and support multiethnic/national mosques with Arabs and others. They also seem to be effective in teaching their religion to their children.

Roughly 10–15 percent are Christian from Kerala and Goa in India, Sri Lanka, Guyana, Trinidad, Fiji, Mauritius, and Pakistan. Christians tend to become members of established Canadian congregations, and to adjust their religious practice accordingly. About 2 percent are Sinhalese Theravada Buddhists.

Among the Southeast Asians, most Vietnamese and almost all Chinese are at least nominally committed to a mix of Confucianism, Taoism, and Mahayana Buddhism. Most Vietnamese participate in religiously linked celebrations such as the New Year and Veneration of the Dead, and Vietnamese Buddhist temples have been established in several places in Canada. Chinese typically use the religious institutions of extant Chinese communities. Many Vietnamese and Chinese continue to practice ancestor veneration in their homes. A significant minority of Vietnamese are Catholics, who largely have joined mainstream congregations. Lao and Khmer, and some Laotian and Cambodian Chinese are Theravada Buddhists. Few in number, they have not established many permanent temples outside of Quebec. Lao and Khmer monks, however, circulate among communities.

Arts.   South Asians have made a considerable commitment to the arts in Canada. Instruction in Indian classical and folk dance is widespread, and South Asian folk, religious, classical, and popular music groups have been established in many places. South Asian Canadian literature in English and in vernacular is well developed. Among Southeast Asians are many with literary and artistic skills, especially in poetry and singing. Instruction in the arts is, however, not yet extensive. *See also* East Asians of Canada

Bibliography

Buchignani, Norman, and Doreen Indra (1985). *Continuous Journey: A Social History of South Asians in Canada*. Toronto: McClelland & Stewart.

Chan, Kwok B., and Doreen Indra, eds. (1987) *Uprooting, Loss and Adaptation: The Resettlement of Indochinese Refugees in Canada*. Ottawa: Canadian Public Health Association.

Dorais, Louis-Jacques, Kwok B. Chan, and Doreen Indra, eds. (1988). *Ten Years Later: Indochinese Communities in Canada*. Montreal: Canadian Asian Studies Association.

Dorais, Louis-Jacques, Lise Pilon-Le, and Nguyen Huy (1987). *Exile in a Cold Land: A Vietnamese Community in Canada*. New Haven: Yale Southeast Asian Studies.

Israel, Milton, ed. (1987). *The South Asian Diaspora in Canada: Six Essays*. Toronto: Multicultural History Society of Ontario.

Kanungo, Rabindra N., ed. (1984). *South Asians in the Canadian Mosaic*. Montreal: Kala Bharati Foundation.

NORMAN BUCHIGNANI

South and Southeast Asians of the United States

ETHNONYMS: South Asians: Asian Indians, Bangladeshis, Bhutanese, East Indians, Nepalese, Pakistanis, Sri Lankans; specific cultural groups—Gujaratis, Sikhs, Tamils. Southeast Asians: Burmese, Cambodians, Indonesians, Laotians, Malaysians, Thais, Vietnamese; specific cultural groups—Chinese of Southeast Asia, Hmong, Indos, Khmer, Malays

Orientation

Identification.   The terms *South Asian* and *Southeast Asian* refer to broad ethnic and cultural categories, each comprised of a number of ethnic and national groups. Almost all South

Asians in the United States came from or are descendants of those who came from Bangladesh, India, Pakistan, or Sri Lanka. There are a few people from Nepal and Bhutan. A number are secondary migrants from the South Asian diaspora who lived in Africa, South America, and islands in the Indian and Pacific oceans before coming to the United States. Most individuals define themselves as being Indian, Pakistani, Tamil, Bengali, and so on, rather than as being South Asian. Southeast Asians in the United States are mainly immigrants from Cambodia, Laos, and Vietnam, with substantial numbers also coming from Thailand and to a lesser extent from Myanmar (Burma). Those coming from Myanmar, Thailand, and Vietnam are usually either ethnic Burmese, Thai, Vietnamese, or Chinese. Those coming from Laos and Cambodia (Kampuchea) are mainly ethnic Lao or Khmer, respectively, although some are Chinese or of other ethnic groups.

The nations of South and Southeast Asia contain a rich variety of cultural, religious, and occupational groups. Broad labels such as "South Asian" and "Southeast Asian" and even national labels such as "Indonesian" often obscure the variety and complexity of ethnicity in this part of the world as well as the cultural background of immigrants to the United States.

Location. In general, South and Southeast Asian-Americans are concentrated in the warmer areas of the country, particularly California, with local concentrations in large metropolitan areas in other regions. Except for special cases, such as that of Vietnamese refugees after the fall of that country to the Viet Minh, initial settlement by immigrants has usually been in urban centers. Over time, however, secondary migration within the United States generally increases.

Demography. In early 1990, the U.S. Bureau of the Census reported that heavy immigration of Asians from 1980 to 1988 had increased their total population by 70 percent to about 6.5 million. A significant portion of this increase has been South and Southeast Asians and a great number of these have settled in California. In general these new immigrants, particularly the South Asians, have far higher educational and professional qualifications than those of earlier groups. Major factors in immigration to the United States may be the lack of job opportunities for skilled professional workers in the sending nations as well as political violence there. Large numbers of the immigrants were admitted under family reunification priorities in order to join relatives already in the United States.

In 1980 the number of South Asian–Americans was probably underestimated when the U.S. Bureau of the Census counted about 375,000 Indians, 25,000 Pakistanis, and a few thousand each of Bangladeshis and Sri Lankans. Some experts believe that the Indian population at that time alone may have been in excess of 700,000. Most of the approximately 450,000 Southeast Asian–Americans enumerated in the 1980 census were post-1960 immigrants. The proportion of Vietnamese in this group up to the mid-1980s was steadily increasing.

Linguistic Affiliation. Because of British colonial dominance, in most South Asian nations English was used as the language of the educated classes or as a national language. Other major languages used were and are Gujarati, Hindi, Punjabi, Urdu, Bengali, Malayalam, Sinhala, Tamil, and Telugu. Hundreds of other languages are spoken on the sub-

continent. Most U.S.-born South Asian–Americans can understand the mother tongue of their parents, but few are fully fluent in it. The situation with many Southeast Asian–Americans is much the reverse, as few immigrants knew English, and a significant number presently do not have effective command of it. Many of those coming from former Indochina, a French colonial area, have some command of French, but this is of little use in the United States. Among the major languages are Vietnamese, Khmer, Lao, and Cantonese, which is a commercial lingua franca in the area. In the southern part of the area, Malay and Bahasa Indonesia are the major languages. Other languages spoken are Burmese, Thai, and the languages of numerous smaller ethnic groups, with among the latter groups, only Hmong or Yao spoken by significant numbers in the United States.

History and Cultural Relations

Most of the nineteenth- and early-twentieth-century immigrants were South Asians who saw themselves as temporary laborers who would return home after working hard in the United States to make as much money as possible. Most, however, remained. The number of South and Southeast Asian immigrants began increasing in the early 1900s. Asian Indians formed the majority, usually taking low-paying farming and laboring jobs in the western states. Strict immigration laws after the First World War closed off immigration from these areas, and until the 1960s most immigrants were wives or family members of men already in the United States. After the immigration law amendments of 1965, which essentially eliminated the restrictive annual quotas of the earlier laws, immigration increased greatly, especially of Asian Indians and Indochinese.

The more recent migrants from South Asia have included many well-educated middle-class professionals (often doctors, engineers, and nurses). The ethnic, national, and class backgrounds of South Asian immigrants have widened greatly in this recent period. Their resettlement in the United States has mostly been smooth, although there have been instances of prejudice and intolerance. Social and cultural links with the parent countries are usually strong. Relations between the various ethnic and national groups are not strongly developed, however, except where religious and other needs require them. The sharing of common or closely related languages also tends to strengthen relations among groups, particularly when the groups are small.

In contrast to the South Asians, most Southeast Asians have come to the United States since 1965, particularly since the end of the war in Vietnam in 1975. The earlier immigrants in this period were usually well-educated skilled workers. A large proportion of the immigrants since 1975, however, have been poorly educated and unskilled farm workers and laborers escaping from their parent areas. After their initial spread across the United States, most have relocated to major cities and other core areas, particularly on the West Coast, in order to be near relatives and to have better access to jobs and public welfare assistance. Adjustment to life in the United States has been difficult for most of these later immigrants since they had neither desired nor planned to emigrate. In general, there is a greater likelihood of quicker and easier adjustment among voluntary Southeast Asian–Americans than among those forced to flee their homeland. Nevertheless, many have since become U.S. citizens.

Today, South and Southeast Asian–American groups form a heterogeneous population of different cultural groups displaying a wide variety of life-styles and adaptations to life in the United States. Fifteen of these groups are described below.

Bibliography

Allen, James Paul, and Eugene James Turner (1988). *We the People: An Atlas of America's Ethnic Diversity.* New York: Macmillan.

Baizerman, M., and G. Hendricks (1989). *A Study of Southeast Asian Refugee Youth in the Twin Cities of Minneapolis and St. Paul, Minnesota.* Minneapolis: University of Minnesota, Southeast Asian Refugee Project.

Fawcett, James T., and Benjamin V. Cariño, eds. (1987). *Pacific Bridges: The New Immigration from Asia and the Pacific Islands.* Staten Island, N.Y.: Center for Migration Studies.

Haseltine, P., comp. (1989). *East and Southeast Asian Material Culture in North America: Collections, Historical Sites and Festivals.* Westport, Conn.: Greenwood Press.

Thernstrom, Stephan, ed. (1980). *Harvard Encyclopedia of American Ethnic Groups.* Cambridge, Mass.: Harvard University Press, Belknap Press.

Asian Indians. In 1980, about 375,000 Americans claimed Asian Indian ethnic ancestry. This, however, is likely a gross undercount, with the actual population closer to 700,000. There were only about 700 Asian Indians in the United States before 1900 and fewer than 17,000 before 1965. Between 1917 and 1946 almost all Asian Indian immigration was barred. Most immigrants have arrived since 1965, though there have been Asian Indian–American communities in California since the early part of the twentieth century. Asian Indians have come mostly from the Indo-Gangetic plain of northern India, from Gujarat in western India, and from Dravidian southern India. Asian Indian–Americans are concentrated in metropolitan areas with a wide dispersal in the warmer areas. The bulk of the immigrants before 1920, generally Punjabi Sikhs, worked on farms in the Central Valley of California, which enabled some to eventually own their own farms and orchards. The more recent immigrants have tended to settle in urban areas across the country, particularly around New York City, Chicago, San Francisco, and Los Angeles, but also with a large number scattered across the country. Many new immigrants entered the Central Valley of California in the 1970s, with the younger people often moving to the cities in search of commercial or professional jobs. Many of the Sikhs became prosperous farmers and sponsored immigrants, and the Sikhs in California as a whole form a large and separate social community.

The majority of the post-1965 immigrants are Hindus. Caste distinctions are less important than in India, but social bonds are strongest within each of the many language and religious groups. Hindus tend to categorize Asian Indians in terms of region of origin within India, whereas non-Hindus categorize fellow immigrants in terms of religion. Many male

post-1965 immigrants have returned to India to marry and bring their wives back to the United States. A large number of the recent immigrants have completed college and graduate education and have found positions as engineers, doctors, professors, and so on. Many have become small businessmen, travel and insurance agents, restaurant owners, and operators of motels and hotels, particularly in the warmer parts of the United States and in rural areas.

Bibliography

Dasgupta, Sathi (1988). *On the Trail of an Uncertain Dream: Indian Immigrant Experience in America.* New York: AMS Press.

Fenton, John Y. (1988). *Translating Religious Traditions: Asian Indians in America.* New York: Praeger Publishers.

Jain, Usha R. (1988). *The Gujaratis of San Francisco.* New York: AMS Press.

Jensen, Joan M. (1988). *Passage from India: Asian Immigrants in North America.* New Haven, Conn.: Yale University Press.

Saran, Parmatma (1985). *The Asian Indian Experience in the United States.* Cambridge, Mass.: Schenkman Publishing Co.

Saran, Parmatma, and Edwin Eames, eds. (1980). *The New Ethnics: Asian Indians in the United States.* New York: Praeger Publishers.

Xenos, P., H. Barringer, and M. J. Levin (1989). *Asian Indians in the United States.* 1980 Census Profiles, no. 111. Honolulu: East-West Center, East-West Population Institute.

Bangladeshis. There are probably about 8,000 Americans of Bangladeshi origin, with 6,859 immigrants having arrived between 1960 and 1984. The People's Republic of Bangladesh was known as East Pakistan before becoming independent from Pakistan after a civil war in 1971. Eighty-three percent of the population of Bangladesh are Sunni Muslim, with the remaining non-Muslim 17 percent consisting of Hindus, Buddhists, or Christians. The same general distribution holds for the immigrants to the United States. Most immigrants speak Bengali, although English is the official language of Bangladesh. Many of the earlier immigrants were refugees from the civil war of 1971. The more recent immigrants arrive seeking escape from the continuing sociopolitical and economic stresses in the homeland, one of the world's poorest nations. There are Bangladeshi settlers in nearly every state, with the largest concentrations in California, Illinois, Texas, and the New York Metropolitan area. A large proportion of the immigrants are professionals and white-collar urban dwellers. As a result, most of them have had an easier time in finding employment than immigrants and refugees from other Asian countries. The bulk of the immigrants have been under forty years of age. There have been fewer opportunities for women to gain an education or to work in the homeland; thus the women are not well prepared for the competitive way of life in America. Most men and women marry other Bangladeshis in this country or are married when they arrive. As a result of chain migration, there are many extended families among the settled immigrants. Groups living in the same area have tended to form civic associations that form a focus for various activities and mutual support for adapting to life in the United States.

Bibliography

Hossain, M. (1982). "South Asians in California: A Sociological Study of Immigrants from India, Pakistan, and Bangladesh." _South Asia Bulletin_ 2:74–83.

Bhutanese, Maldivians, and Nepalese.   These groups are discussed together, as so few in each have immigrated to the United States. From 1960 through 1984, 90 immigrants arrived from the Kingdom of Bhutan, 12 from the Republic of Maldives, and 977 from the Kingdom of Nepal. Buddhism is the state religion in Bhutan, Sunni Islam in the Maldives, and Hinduism in Nepal. The basic languages are different as well, with Dzongkha being official in Bhutan, a dialect of Sinhalese in the Maldives, and Nepali in Nepal. All three countries maintain close contacts with India, and many immigrants arrived speaking some English. Little is known about the adaptation of these peoples to life in the United States.

Cambodians.   In 1980, 16,052 Americans claimed Cambodian (Kampuchean) ethnic ancestry and another 2,050 claimed Cambodian and other ethnic ancestry. Most people of Cambodian ancestry belong to the Khmer ethnic group, although some Chinese and members of other ethnic groups may have reported themselves as Cambodian. This reporting is a serious undercount, since by September 1986, 138,900 refugees and immigrants had come to the U.S. and certainly a significant number arrived before 1980. Most Cambodian-Americans immigrated after 1970 to escape war, starvation, the Pol Pot–Khmer Rouge reign of terror, and the Vietnamese invasion in 1979. In the United States, Long Beach, California, has been the main Khmer center since 1975. It has a commercial district, with Cambodian markets, tailors, and jewelry stores, but homes, churches, a Buddhist temple, and various organizations are scattered throughout the city. Ethnic Chinese from Cambodia have more often settled in various Chinatowns. There are large Cambodian-ancestry populations in other parts of the Los Angeles area, in San Diego and in or near Seattle, Houston, and Providence. Additional concentrations are found in Texas, Washington State, and Arlington, Virginia. In the early 1980s the U.S. government established a program to settle Cambodian refugees in twelve cities outside California, including Rochester, New York, Richmond, Virginia, Phoenix, Arizona, and a large number of metropolitan centers that did not have a significant number of Cambodians already living there.

The Khmer are overwhelmingly Theravada Buddhists and were peasant farmers in Cambodia. Adjustment to American life has been difficult, and there is a marked tendency to maintain close ties to the extended family and the ethnic communities in order to cope. When problems become overwhelming, they tend to relocate, usually to other low-rent areas or to California to be with friends and relatives.

Bibliography

Ebihara, May M. (1985). "Khmer." In _Refugees in the United States: A Reference Handbook,_ edited by D. W. Haines, 127–147. Westport, Conn.: Greenwood Press.

Gordon, Linda W. (1987). "Southeast Asian Refugee Migration to the United States." In _Pacific Bridges: The New Immigration from Asia and the Pacific Islands,_ edited by James T. Fawcett and Benjamin V. Cariño, 153–174. Staten Island, N.Y.: Center for Migration Studies.

Burmese.   There are about 20,000 Americans of Burmese ethnic ancestry, of whom 13,197 arrived between 1970 and 1984. Immigrants from Myanmar (the official name of Burma since 1989) began to arrive in the United States in the early 1960s, with significant numbers coming in the 1970s. Most of the immigrants have been fairly young professional, technical, and white-collar workers. Since Myanmar has been a politically isolated nation, the number of immigrants has been small. There do not seem to be any sizable Burmese ethnic communities in the United States, with the largest numbers of Burmese-Americans living in California, New York, Illinois, Maryland, Pennsylvania, and Texas. Because of their small numbers and occupational skills, assimilation into mainstream society has been relatively easy.

Bruneians.   Only 164 immigrants arrived in the United States from Brunei between 1975 and 1984, with none identified as having arrived before then. Earlier immigrants may have been attributed to other countries since Brunei became a sovereign and independent state only in 1984. Malay is the official language of the country, with English and Chinese also spoken. Two-thirds of the inhabitants are Muslim, with the remainder being divided among Buddhist, Christian, and other religions. Since so few Bruneians have arrived in this country, there are no data available on their adaptation to life in the United States.

Indonesians.   There are probably a little over 30,000 Americans of Indonesian descent in the United States today, a small portion of them being former Dutch colonials who left Indonesia when the country gained its independence from the Netherlands. Almost all the remainder are native Indonesians who spoke Malay, Bahasa Indonesian (a variety of Malay), Javanese, or one of a number of Austronesian languages in their homeland. Most of the population are Sunni Muslims, although there are small groups of other denominations. The immigrants, except for students, tend to arrive in family groups and are usually professional, technical, or white-collar workers.

There are also about 60,000 "Indos," people of mixed European and Indonesian ethnic ancestry in the United States. Most Indos came prior to 1962 after having fled Indonesia during the domestic crises in 1947 and 1951. For many, the trip to the United States was a secondary migration, as most had initally fled to the Netherlands.

Bibliography

Kwik, Greta (1989). _The Indos in Southern California._ New York: AMS Press.

Laotians.   In the 1980 census, 53,320 Americans claimed Laotian ancestry and another 2,278 claimed Laotian and other ethnic ancestry. This is a serious underreporting, however, since immigration records show that 110,840 Laotians came into the United States during the 1960 to 1984 period, principally as refugees from the wars in Southeast Asia. As of September 1986 about 162,000 refugees, about one-third of whom were of the Hmong ethnic group, had arrived in the United States. Most Laotian-Americans now live on the West Coast and are mainly composed of two distinct ethnic groups, the Lao of the Laotian lowlands and the Highland Hmong, with minor numbers of other ethnic groups also represented.

The distribution of Laotians in the United States in the early 1980s was mainly determined by various voluntary resettlement agencies and the location of sponsoring groups and families. Many found work in low-paying jobs, such as in meat packing and clothing manufacturing. There was much secondary migration after first settlement in the United States, with members of extended families rejoining one another and with the formation of new communities. Linguistic and cultural barriers are the main reasons that Laotian-Americans have generally achieved only slow occupational advancement, have resorted to public welfare, and have remained socially isolated. In addition, many have sought a return to a farming way of life and have moved to smaller towns and rural areas where they garden or work as farm laborers. The major resettlement area has been California, because of the location of relatives and economic opportunities. Many of the Hmong have settled in California's Central Valley, with particular concentrations in the cities of Fresno and Merced. The Hmong in Merced have formed neighborhood, extended family, and church organizations, as well as an official mutual assistance agency. Many Hmong have settled in the Missoula, Montana, area, which is similar to their Laotian homeland. Other centers of settlement have been in or near Portland, Oregon, and Minneapolis–St. Paul.

Bibliography

Dunnigan, Timothy, and D. P. Olney (1985). "Hmong." In *Refugees in the United States: A Reference Handbook*, edited by D. W. Haines, 111–126. Westport, Conn.: Greenwood Press.

Gordon, Linda W. (1987). "Southeast Asian Refugee Migration to the United States." In *Pacific Bridges: The New Immigration from Asia and the Pacific Islands*, edited by James T. Fawcett and Benjamin V. Cariño, 153–174. Staten Island, N.Y.: Center for Migration Studies.

Hendricks, G. L., B. T. Downing, and A. S. Deinard, eds. (1986). *The Hmong in Transition*. Staten Island, N.Y.: Center for Migration Studies.

Schein, Louisa (1987). "Control of Contrast: Lao Hmong Refugees in American Contexts." In *People in Upheaval*, edited by Scott M. Morgan and Elizabeth Colson, 88–107. New York: Center for Migration Studies.

Van Esterik, John L. (1985). "Lao." In *Refugees in the United States: A Reference Handbook*, edited by D. W. Haines, 149–165. Westport, Conn.: Greenwood Press.

Yang, D., and D. North (1988). *Profiles of the Highland Yao Communities in the United States: Final Report*. Washington, D.C.: CZA.

Malaysians.   There are probably fewer than 10,000 Americans of Malaysian ethnic ancestry in the United States today. Between 1960 and 1984 about 8,400 came. Malays make up about 60 percent of the host country's population, Chinese about a third, and East Indians the remainder. They are predominantly Muslim, with many Hindus, Buddhists, Confucians, and Taoists. Most of the immigrants have been professionals, white-collar workers, and students who have settled in urban areas. Little is known about the life of Malaysians in the United States, however.

Pakistanis.   In the 1980 census, 22,615 Americans claimed Pakistani ethnic ancestry and another 3,348 claimed Pakistani and other ethnic ancestry. Most Pakistanis in the United States have entered since 1965. The immigration rate remains high, as evidenced by the more than 56,000 arriving between 1960 and 1984. The distribution of these immigrants in the United States generally follows that of Asian Indians in recent years. Areas with large Pakistani populations include New York City, Los Angeles, Chicago, Houston, and Fairfax, Virginia. The new settlers have generally had high educational and occupational levels and a preference for living in large metropolitan areas. They have usually assimilated easily into the American economic system. Some have not, however, and are working in various unskilled jobs. About three-fourths of Pakistani-Americans are Sunni Muslims, with small percentages following other religions. Most are Punjabi- or Urdu-speaking and have some background in English as well. More than two hundred Pakistani civic and cultural organizations have been established, largely in urban areas, and several Pakistani periodicals are published.

Bibliography

Ghayur, M. Arif (1981). "Muslims in the United States: Settlers and Visitors." *Annals of the American Academy of Political and Social Science* 454:157–177.

Malik, Iftikhar H. (1988). *Pakistanis in Michigan: A Study of Third Culture and Acculturation*. New York: AMS Press.

Sri Lankans.   There are probably about 6,000 Americans who claim Sri Lankan ethnic descent. They are almost all from Tamil- or Sinhalese-speaking ethnic groups. Most have some knowledge of English as well and are Hindu or Buddhist depending on their ethnic affiliation. Many are well educated and have secured professional and white-collar employment. Very little has been published about their life in the United States and their adaptation to American culture. They are identified by many Americans as Asian Indians.

Thais.   In the 1980 census, 52,214 Americans claimed Thai ethnic ancestry and another 11,700 claimed Thai and other ethnic ancestry. The total of 64,000 is probably an undercount since 70,459 immigrants came into the United States between 1960 and 1984. Few Thais immigrated to the United States before the 1960s. The majority of the people of Thailand are ethnic Thai, with Chinese accounting for about 12 percent of the population and tribal peoples making up 11 percent. Most Thais came to the United States not as refugees but as students, temporary visitors, or spouses of U.S.

military personnel (mainly the air force). Generally, the Thais in the United States are ethnic Thai, but others are Thai Dam (usually not from Thailand but from the upland valleys of northern Vietnam and Laos). Some ethnic Chinese from Thailand may also have listed themsleves as Thai. The Los Angeles area has by far the largest concentration of Thais. Other concentrations can be found in Chicago, New York City, and around military bases, such as Fort Bragg, North Carolina, and Fort Huachuca, Arizona. In Los Angeles, Thai businesses and houses have been clustered in the Hollywood area. Thais own banks, gas stations, beauty parlors, and other small businesses, especially Thai restaurants. Most Thai immigrants have been between the ages of twenty and forty upon arrival. In addition to the family members of the servicemen, there have been many students, professional and white-collar workers and most have found employment in America. The major settlement of the Thai Dam has been in the vicinity of Des Moines, Iowa, where most have found work in low-paying jobs with little hope of advancement. Most Thais are Hinayana Buddhists, although some are Muslims.

Bibliography

Desbarats, J. (1979). "Thai Migration to Los Angeles." _Geographical Review_ 69: 302–318.

Vietnamese.   The U.S. Bureau of the Census reported that in 1980 about 260,000 Vietnamese were living in the United States. At that time many were located in southern California (Los Angeles, Orange, and San Diego counties) with concentrations also around Brockport, Texas, Arlington, Virginia, Amarillo, Texas, and Fort Smith, Arkansas. It is reported, however, that in the period 1960–1984 over 387,000 immigrants had arrived from Vietnam, thus making them by far the largest population group in the United States of Southeast Asian origin. A fairly large proportion (as high as 15 percent in California) were Vietnamese Chinese—members of the Chinese minority community in Vietnam. Most of these have settled in various Chinatowns around the country.

The Vietnamese are one of the newest ethnic communities in the United States, most of them having immigrated because of the Vietnam War and its aftermath. As of September 1986, over 500,000 Vietnamese had entered the United States as refugees. They usually have found sponsoring families and communities (many churches were active in sponsoring immigrants) and were originally widely scattered around the country, usually in nuclear family households. This was less than satisfactory, as most had lived their lives as members of extended families. Soon after settlement, they began to reunite their original extended families, with a very large percentage of them resettling in California, with another focus in Texas.

Few refugees were prepared for life in the United States, and they faced serious language and cultural barriers. Many have had difficulties because most of the jobs available to them were low-paying ones like janitor, laborer, busboy, or dishwasher. Some have found work in factories (electronics assembly) or in restaurants and other small businesses. Many of the recent arrivals are supported at least in part by government programs. The unemployment rate of earlier arrivals, who were usually better educated, is quite low, however. Fishermen have concentrated on the Gulf Coast from Texas through northwestern Florida and have done well through a combination of working hard and taking on the less attractive jobs. In the Monterey area of California, fishermen have also done well by not competing for the same species with local fishermen. Vietnamese Catholics made up a large percentage of the early refugees, and many have settled in the New Orleans area. The largest Vietnamese communities in the eastern states are around Washington, D.C., with many working for the government or for international agencies.

Bibliography

Gold, Steven J. (1987). "Dealing with Frustration: A Study of the Interactions between Resettlement Staff and Refugees." In _People in Upheaval_, edited by Scott M. Morgan and Elizabeth Colson, 108–128. New York: Center for Migration Studies.

Gordon, Linda W. (1987). "Southeast Asian Refugee Migration in the United States." In _Pacific Bridges: The New Immigration from Asia and the Pacific Islands_, edited by James T. Fawcett and Benjamin V. Cariño, 153–174. Staten Island, N.Y.: Center for Migration Studies.

Kelly, Gail P. (1977). _From Vietnam to America: A Chronicle of the Vietnamese Immigration to the United States._ Boulder, Colo.: Westview Press.

Montero, Darrel (1979). _Vietnamese Americans: Patterns of Resettlement and Socioeconomic Organization in the United States._ Boulder, Colo.: Westview Press.

Orbach, M. K., and J. Beckwith (1982). "Indochinese Adaptation and Local Government Policy: An Example from Monterey." _Anthropological Quarterly_ 35:135–145.

Southern Paiute (and Chemehuevi)

ETHNONYMS: Cuajala, Pah-Utes, Paiute, Numa, Yuta Payuchis

Orientation

Identification.   The name "Paiute" is of uncertain origin. It first appeared in the Spanish literature (Yutas Payuchis, Payuchas) in the 1770s. Other versions were recorded after U.S. expansion into the region in the 1820s. There is some uncertainty as to its application when other "Paiute" groups speaking different languages were encountered in southern California and western Nevada (Owens Valley Paiute, Northern Paiute). After a period of much confusion, some of which persists in the popular literature today, the name "Southern Paiute" was imposed in the first decade of the twentieth century. "Chemehuevi," the name of a Southern Paiute subgroup that has developed a historically distinct identity, has an origin equally obscure. Although "Paiute" and "Chemehuevi" are used as self-designations when speaking English, the people's native name is nʏ́mʏ́, nʏ́wʏ́ or nʏ́mʏ́nci, "person," depending on dialect.

Location. Aboriginally, the Southern Paiute occupied lands north and west of the Colorado River extending from southern California through southeastern Nevada, northwestern Arizona, and southern and central Utah. The Chemehuevi held the southernmost section. Environmentally, this vast tract is diverse, taking in lands within the Mojave Desert (low, hot, and dry), the adjacent Great Basin Desert (semiarid steppe country), and parts of the Colorado Plateau (unevenly elevated, often forested, but still semidesert).

Demography. Population figures are difficult to evaluate. A major problem is that several subgroups were terminated from federal supervision in 1957, thus deflating federal figures. There has also been migration to urban areas, further deflating figures unless people identify themselves on a general census. Reinstatement of the Southern Paiute in 1980 may have been in time for formerly terminated individuals to have been counted, but probably not with a high level of accuracy. The 1980 census figure for people on or adjacent to reserved lands is roughly 1,400. The total 1980 Southern Paiute population is estimated at 1,750. The population in 1873, approximately thirty years after settlement by non-Indians, was estimated at 2,300.

Linguistic Affiliation. The language belongs to the Numic branch of the widespread Uto-Aztecan family. It is one of two languages within the Southern Numic subbranch, forming a pair with Kawaiisu of southern California. The Southern Paiute language, including Chemehuevi, is itself a dialect of Ute, the latter term often used to designate the other member of the Southern Numic pair (Kawaiisu, Ute). There is, or better, was measurable dialect diversity. Original dialect distributions are obscured today owing to intrasubgroup marriages and language loss.

History and Cultural Relations

Linguistic and archaeological evidence suggests that the Southern Paiute expanded north and eastward to fill their present territory approximately one thousand years ago. Prior to that time, the central and eastern portions were occupied by Puebloan Anasazi groups related to archaeological cultures in the Southwest. Although Southern Paiute-Anasazi relationships are the subject of some debate, the two peoples seem to have been different. Anasazi withdrawal from these lands is placed at roughly A.D. 1200. By the time of first contact by Spaniards in the 1770s, the Southern Paiute were in exclusive possession of their historic territory. Trade relationships were well established with Yuman tribes to the south and west and with the Hopi to the southeast. With the Ute relationships were initially friendly, although beginning in the late 1700s, Ute raids on Southern Paiute camps for children to be sold as slaves in the Spanish and Mexican settlements of Santa Fe and Los Angeles led to enmity. This traffic continued until roughly 1850, when Mormon and U.S. interventions ended it. Mormon settlement of the area in the 1850s to 1870s brought additional hardships, reducing the area available for aboriginal subsistence drastically.

Although a reservation was established at Moapa in southern Nevada in 1872, and it was alternatively proposed to remove all the Southern Paiute there or to the Uintah Ute reservation in northeastern Utah, few people actually settled on reserved lands until after 1900. In 1903 a reservation was established at Shivwits for groups in southwestern Utah and northern Arizona, and in 1907, the Kaibab Reservation was set aside for people around Kanab, Utah. Some Chemehuevi obtained a reserve in Chemehuevi Valley in 1907, and small colonies and reserves were established at Las Vegas, Nevada, and Indian Peaks, Koosharem, and Kanosh, Utah, between 1911 and 1929.

In 1957 the federal government terminated control over several Utah Southern Paiute subgroups and their lands (Shivwits, Kanosh, Koosharem, Indian Peaks). In 1980, these same groups were reinstated, although the intervening years had resulted in the loss of over half of their lands. New lands and federal and tribal programs have improved conditions in recent years, although all admit that there is a long way to go toward economic self-sufficiency and the full development of human potential.

Settlements. Southern Paiute territory has been divided into fifteen subareas within which groups could hunt and gather enough resources to sustain themselves. All groups moved camps according to a seasonal round of resource exploitation. Several subgroups also practiced a limited amount of horticulture. For these groups, summer camps were in proximity to fields so that irrigation and crop protection could be facilitated. Camps in all seasons consisted of a single family or a few related families with friends, roughly ten to thirty persons. Larger groups occurred during the fall pine nut harvest or at the time of communal rabbit hunts. In several subareas, individual ownership of springs determined seasonal shifts of camp groups. Winter was usually the time groups were most sedentary, camping at lower elevations in proximity to water, fuel, and stored foods. Today some individuals know of former camping places and occasionally use them for hunting and pine nut camps.

The common winter house was conical or subconical, made of willow or juniper poles and covered with brush. The doorway faced east, and smoke from an interior fire hearth exited through a smokehole in the roof. The Chemehuevi built gabled houses like the Mohave except that the front was left open. All groups utilized temporary shelters, such as semicircular windbreaks and four-post shades. All reservation communities have participated in housing projects since the 1970s, so that today houses are comparable to those of their non-Indian neighbors.

Economy

Subsistence and Commercial Activities. Given environmental differences across the whole of Southern Paiute territory, local groups had access to different natural foods. Animals hunted included several species of small mammals, including hares and rabbits, marmots, ground squirrels, and so on. In the Mojave Desert area, the chuckawalla, tortoise, and kangaroo mouse were more common, and replaced some of these. Some groups had little access to deer or antelope;

most could get mountain sheep, but numbers might be very low. Land birds were more common as a food source than waterfowl, and few ate fish. Plant products likewise differed across the region, with those in hot desert climates specializing in agave and mesquite harvesting and those in cooler areas piñon and several types of berries. All collected native seeds. More than half of the subgroups farmed at least a little, a few more intensively. Native crops included maize, beans, squash, sunflowers, and amaranth. Ditch irrigation was used in southwestern Utah and southeastern Nevada, and floodwater farming was used by the Chemehuevi along the Colorado River. Fields were small and usually planted and tended by an extended family.

Contact and the establishment of reservations changed most of these patterns. Some groups were able to do a little farming, but most shifted their attention to wage work for local ranchers or in towns. Today tribal businesses (smoke shops, grocery stores, tourist services) employ modest numbers of people, and tribal governments several more. Others continue to do wage labor in a variety of skilled or semiskilled positions. Except for dogs, there were no domesticated animals prior to European contact. Today a few people keep horses to help with ranch work or for pleasure.

Industrial Arts. Aboriginal crafts included principally basketry, pottery, and hide working. Numerous types and styles of baskets were woven for utilitarian purposes, principally food gathering and processing. All basket making was done by women in either twining or coiling. Pottery was low-fired and, except among the Chemehuevi, unpainted. Hide working was found in areas with access to large game and was principally used for clothing. Groups in other areas wore clothing of twisted and twined vegetable fibers. Today basket weaving persists principally among the Chemehuevi and San Juan subgroups, and a few women work hides for moccasins and gloves. Individuals in some areas are highly skilled in beadwork, a postcontact development.

Trade. Intragroup trade helped to even out some subsistence imbalances. Salt, found principally in Moapa territory, was distributed in all directions, including to non–Southern Paiutes. Ochers used in body painting were found on the Colorado Plateau and thus moved largely westward. Cultigens came into the region from the south, including from the Hopi, Havasupai, and Walapai, as well as Yuman groups on the lower Colorado River.

Division of Labor. Hunting was principally the activity of men in aboriginal times and plant food collecting that of women. Both sexes participated in horticulture. Wage work in the postcontact period was done about equally by men and women, with men engaged as ranch and hay hands and women as domestics. Today work activities parallel those of non-Indian neighbors at similar socioeconomic and educational levels.

Kinship

Kin Groups and Descent. The primary social unit in Southern Paiute society was the nuclear or small extended family, and much the same situation obtains today. Families constituted the primary residence and subsistence units, focused as they were in some areas around privately owned springs. Larger units of several families came together in some seasons but had little permanence. An individual's personal kindred served as his or her primary means of integration within the society at large, as relatives were likely to be found beyond the local group or subarea, and even in another tribe. Mutual obligations to one's kin ensured that none went hungry or lacked a place to stay. These values are still primary in Southern Paiute households, where one is likely to find a relative or two in residence for a month or more. The elderly are foci in many such households.

Kinship Terminology. Kinship reckoning is basically bilateral, with Eskimo cousin terminology prevailing in the native system of designation. Among those with few native language skills, English terminology prevails.

Marriage and Family

Marriage. In theory, marriage was prohibited among any who could trace blood relationships. Young people married early, and most unions were monogamous. There was no ceremony. Some polygyny occurred, usually with sisters as co-wives. Polyandry was reported, sometimes by hearsay. The levirate and sororate were obligatory among some subgroups. Marriages were usually thought to be permanent relationships, but divorce brought no shame to either party. Children commonly went with the mother. Initial matrilocal residence often occurred, usually as a form of bride-service. Neolocal residence prevailed after a year or the birth of the first child.

Domestic Unit. The nuclear or small extended family was the former residence unit and remains so today. Many households contain three and occasionally four generations as a temporary or permanent arrangement.

Inheritance. In aboriginal times, land was available for use to all Southern Paiutes. Resource ownership was limited to claims by families in a few subgroups to exclusive use of mesquite groves or agave-collecting areas. Springs, tanks, and potholes were also considered to be private property, so that permission to camp at them was needed. Plant resource areas often passed through female relatives and spring sites through males, but rules were not strict.

Socialization. Grandparents took a major role in child rearing, given that parents might be absent from camp during much of the day engaged in subsistence chores. Children were considered responsible from an early age (about six years), and sanctions after that time might come from any member of the group through gossip or ridicule. Parents today take a much more active role in child rearing, but in households with grandparents, they also so function. Parents and grandparents are more directive than before, but children are still largely on their own to make mistakes or not.

Sociopolitical Organization

Social Organization. Given that men and women contributed about equally to subsistence, there was little status differentiation along sex lines in former times. The elderly were held in high esteem, although if food resources were scarce, they might not take a share or otherwise sacrifice themselves. Sharing still remains a primary value in most households, so that individuals rarely accumulate or hoard if family members are in need.

Political Organization.   Prior to contact with Europeans, each local group had a headman or adviser, but few had leadership positions beyond this. Men who had dreamed of certain large game animals (usually deer, antelope, mountain sheep) were leaders of communal hunts. Headmen, usually senior males or perhaps owners of spring sites, addressed the camp group each morning, suggesting a subsistence routine. They also announced any visitors or special events. With the advent of Europeans, some who learned English early acted as go-betweens and were referred to as "chiefs" or "captains." Some, because of their skills, spoke for larger groups than might have been the case before. The authority of most was minimal, rarely going beyond that of former days. Presently reservation and colony communities are organized under the Indian Reorganization Act of 1934 or the reinstatement legislation of 1980 (Paiute Tribe of Utah). Their councils are duly elected and serve specified terms.

Social Control.   In former times, social control was handled within extended families on a face-to-face basis or by ridicule or, in severe cases, ostracism. Headmen attempted to get conflicting parties to agree to a solution, but they had little ultimate power. Tribal governments today exercise control through their own police or through cooperative agreements with state, county, or city authorities.

Conflict.   In former times, most Southern Paiute were peaceful and rarely engaged in fighting with each other or with neighbors. An exception may be the wars between the Chemehuevi and the Mohave, said to have resulted in the partial extermination of the latter in the eighteenth century. In the historic period, the slave trade brought troubles with the Utes, Navajos, and a variety of non-Indians. There was some raiding by Southern Paiute local groups along the Old Spanish Trail, which operated from roughly 1820 to 1850 in the central and southwestern sections of their territory. Southern Paiutes were also accused of massacring a wagon train of emigrants en route to California near Enterprise, Utah, in 1857, an event that later turned out to have as many Mormon participants as Indian. With Mormons and other settlers, accommodation was generally peaceful and remains so today. Little intermarriage has taken place across ethnic boundaries.

Religion and Expressive Culture

Religious Beliefs.   Southern Paiute people believe that supernatural power resides in all living things and in many nonanimate objects found in nature as well as in the sun, moon, stars, wind, and so on. Persons are free to establish a relationship with objects of power, but only doctors or shamans possess enough of it to aid in healing. Their powers (often multiple) come unsought in dreams, or they could be courted by going to certain places. Ordinary persons rarely spoke of their powers, although the community might know if they had special powers for large game animals. Special classes of anthropomorphic spirits (water babies, dwarfs, changeable beings) resided at various places. Encounters with these were considered dangerous. Today, elderly people and some younger persons believe in these spirits and in the power of living things and the earth. They may also be Christians (especially Mormons) and/or followers of the Native American (Peyote) church. There is little clear evidence that

a supreme being existed in native religion, although some persons feel strongly that one did. Ethnographic description came after a long period of contact and substantial acculturation in religious views. The existence of natural and anthropomorphic spirits is well documented, and these beliefs are still active to varying degrees today.

Religious Practitioners.   In aboriginal times, the principal religious practitioner was the shaman, who held power through tutelaries to cure illness. Native doctors could be either men or women. They cured the patient through a self-induced trance, during which their powers revealed the cause of the illness (ghost or object intrusion, soul loss) and the prognosis for a cure.

Ceremonies.   The principal ceremony today is the Mourning Ceremony, or "Cry," related to that of southern California. The ceremony is held today as a funeral, although in former times it might occur later than the time of a person's actual death. It involves the singing of standardized song cycles, in which a singer usually specializes. Singers are few, as the work is considered a special gift. In former times, people volunteered property to be burned as a show of grief. Today, the immediate possessions of the deceased are commonly offered. A second, or Annual Mourning Ceremony might be held as an anniversary. Sometimes families with relatives deceased within the past year hold one jointly. Apart from funeral observances, celebrations were held in the spring to renew the earth or in the fall when pine nuts were harvested. The spring ceremony usually involved the Bear Dance, learned from the Ute. Pine nut harvest was an occasion for the Circle Dance, but also for offering prayers of thanksgiving for a good year. The Ghost Dance of 1890, a messianic movement begun in western Nevada, reached the Southern Paiute in that year and persisted for a time.

Arts.   Aesthetic expression focused on song, recitatives, and folk tales. Songs often came in dreams, although they could be given to friends and relatives, and some were widely known. The Chemehuevi had cycles of songs, reminiscent of those of the Mohave, that often established hunt territories. Others had texted songs involving animals or natural imagery, and most were highly poetic. Recitatives occurred in the context of myths and tales, where animal actors took speaking or singing parts using stylized voices. Good narrators, most often men, might solicit help from the audience in giving these performances. Tales, sometimes told in long sequences on winter evenings, involved the adventures of animal actors in a time before people. Many of these cycles today are no longer remembered, owing in large part to language loss. Skill at singing is still much valued, and some categories of native songs have persisted.

Medicine.   Diseases cured by shamans or native doctors were thought to be due to supernatural causes. Those less serious were treated by persons knowledgeable in plant remedies. Some persons today still use this pharmacopoeia, but most also depend on Western medicine. The Native American church functions in some areas in curing.

Death and Afterlife.   Little is known about concepts of the afterlife, other than that ghosts and souls can remain in the vicinity and occasionally cause harm to the living. Some people feel that spirits of the deceased go underground to a world where everything is reversed. Others think that the abode of the dead is in the sky, where activities are much as in this world but done in comparative ease. Proper prayers to the spirit of the deceased were and are considered necessary to protect the living, especially children. Some of this is accomplished through the Mourning Ceremony, but others may be required. Traditional families today usually combine aspects of these older beliefs with Christian (usually Mormon) services.

Bibliography

Kelly, Isabel T. (1964). *Southern Paiute Ethnography*. University of Utah Anthropological Papers, no. 69. Salt Lake City.

Kelly, Isabel T., and Catherine S. Fowler (1986). "Southern Paiute." In *Handbook of North American Indians*. Vol. 11, *Great Basin,* edited by Warren L. d'Azevedo, 368–397. Washington, D.C.: Smithsonian Institution.

Knack, Martha (1980). *Life Is with People: Household Organization of the Contemporary Southern Paiute Indians*. Ballena Press Anthropological Papers, no. 19. Socorro, N. Mex.

Laird, Carobeth (1976). *The Chemehuevis*. Banning, Calif.: Malki Museum Press.

CATHERINE S. FOWLER

placement on reservations in 1872, and a series of legal battles to regain lost land and other rights. In recent years the Spokane have benefited from the leasing of rights to mine uranium ore on their land.

The basic social unit was the family, a number of which generally lived in one settlement and formed a band. In the winter several bands might reside together in a single village. The traditional economy was based on hunting (deer, elk, and so on in the mountains and bison on the plains), salmon fishing, and gathering. Religious beliefs centered on guardian spirits, dreaming, and visions.

Bibliography

Drury, Clifford M. (1976). *Nine Years with the Spokane Indians: The Diary, 1938–1948, of Elkanah Walker*. Glendale, Calif.: Arthur H. Clarke Co.

Ruby, Robert H., and John A. Brown (1970). *The Spokane Indians: Children of the Sun*. Norman: University of Oklahoma Press.

Spokane

ETHNONYMS: Spokan, Spukanees, Sun People

The Spokane lived in northeast Washington State in the general vicinity of the Spokane River. They were divided into a number of subtribes, the three major divisions being the Upper, Middle (Southern), and Lower Spokane subtribes. The bands came together for religious and warfare purposes. Although the core of Spokane territory was in present-day Washington, they ranged into and controlled additional territory in Idaho and Montana. Spokane is an Interior Salish language. Estimates of the population at the time of contact range from 1,500 to 2,500. In 1985 there were 1,961 affiliated with the Spokane Indian Reservation, and an undetermined number living with other Indian groups on the neighboring Colville Indian Reservation and the Coeur d'Alene Indian Reservation in Idaho, and in the city of Spokane, Washington. The Spokane Tribe is governed by an elected tribal business council. Although assimilated into the regional economy, the Spokane are considered to be one of the more conservative American Indian groups.

Like many groups in the interior of the United States, the first effects of European settlement, the horse and disease, were received indirectly through other Indian groups. Regular contact began in the early 1880s and progressed through a series of stages involving participation in the fur trade, missionization, warfare with the federal government,

Tahltan

The Tahltan (Western Nahane), an Athapaskan-speaking group, live in the upper basin of the Stikine River and in neighboring areas of northern British Columbia. They numbered 793 in 1978. *See* Nahane

Bibliography

MacLachlan, Bruce B. "Tahltan." In *Handbook of North American Indians.* Vol. 6, *Subarctic*, edited by June Helm, 458–468. Washington, D.C.: Smithsonian Institution.

Tanaina

ETHNONYMS: Dena'ina, Tnaina, Kenaitze, Kenai, Knaiakhotana

Orientation

Identification. The Tanaina are an Athapaskan-speaking American Indian group located in Alaska. Tanaina synonyms are variations of "Dena'ina" (people) or "Kenaitze." The latter may refer only to the people of Kenai Peninsula, but frequently it is extended to include all Tanaina.

Location. Tanaina are located in the Cook Inlet and adjacent areas of southwestern Alaska between 59° and 63° N and 148° and 157° W. Traditionally and today they comprise three subdivisions, or "societies," based on cultural similarities and on levels of interaction and social interchange including intermarriage. The Kenai subdivision occupied the southeastern shore of Cook Inlet including the Kenai Peninsula, except for the Pacific Ocean side. The Susitna subdivision encompassed the Susitna, Matanuska, and Yentna river valleys including the area now occupied by the modern city of Anchorage and the northwest shore of Cook Inlet. The Interior subdivision was northwest of Cook Inlet. Today, some Tanaina are still found on the Stony River, but the Mulchatna villages have been abandoned. The Lake Clark (Kijik) population has moved south to Sixmile Lake (Nondalton). Iliamna Lake has one Tanaina village (Pedro Bay). Only Tyonek Village remains on the northwest shore of Cook Inlet. Tanaina still reside on the Kenai Peninsula, up the Susitna, Matanuska, and Yentna rivers, and around the city of Anchorage. The region is mountainous or hilly with many lakes, rivers, and streams. Boreal spruce forest with some cottonwood and birch stands on the east shift to taiga at the far western perimeter. The climate is mild in summer with a dry early and wet late period. Winters are cold, reaching −20° F.

Demography. Exact population figures for Tanaina are especially difficult to calculate. According to my estimations, precontact Tanaina must have numbered at least four thousand to five thousand. After severe epidemics of the late 1800s, the figure apparently dropped to about fifteen hundred. Modern census figures do not segregate Tanaina ethnically, and many villages are multiethnic. A rough estimate would be at least fifteen hundred.

Linguistic Affiliation. Tanaina speak an Athapaskan language with two dialects: Upper Inlet (Susitna subdivision) and Lower Inlet. Lower Inlet dialect is subdivided into Outer Inlet, Iliamna, and Interior. Today, all except the elderly speak English, and some young people speak no Tanaina. In recent years a resurgence of interest has stimulated its teaching again.

History and Cultural Relations

Tanaina entered their current location, presumably from the interior, in prehistoric times. Russians discovered Alaska in 1741, but the Tanaina's first European contact was with Capt. James Cook in 1778. They had, however, received a few European goods earlier through trade. In spite of opposition, the Russians were able to establish a post on Kodiak Island as the base of their operations in 1784 (after 1799, the Russian-American Company mercantile monopoly) and from that post managed to establish other trading posts. Some Tanaina intermarriage occurred with Russians, but most was with Koniag Eskimos (from Kodiak Island) and Aleuts who worked for the company. The resulting population of Creoles was most often used by the company to trade with other Tanaina groups. As a result, cultural contact was not purely Russian, but was mediated through Eskimo and Aleut cultural perspectives. Western contact was less severe than in other Alaskan groups, and Tanaina society tended to flourish within its own cultural milieu as a result of Russian trade integrated within the already existing trading complex. With the sale of Alaska to the United States in 1867, the Russian trade monopoly was replaced by independent competing traders, but there was little in the way of U.S. government control. Native populations were neglected until well into the twentieth century.

Local education is available today at least through the eighth grade, and children may complete high school at boarding schools or in cities such as Anchorage. A few take advantage of university or trade school training. Following the Alaska Native Claims Settlement Act of 1971, twelve regional corporations were established to represent natives throughout the state. The Kenai and Susitna subdivisions joined the Cook Inlet Region, Inc.; those near Iliamna Lake affiliated with the Bristol Bay Native Corporation. Ahtna territory abuts the Tanaina on the east and northeast. Culturally and linguistically similar, they share a hunting region west of Talkeetna along the Susitna River. Tanaina feel a close relation with Ahtna in part because they believe they share clan affiliations. To the north and northwest are the Kolchan and Ingalik. To the east and southeast are Pacific Eskimo groups. West of the Tanaina are the southwestern mainland Eskimos. Tanaina settlements near Eskimo and Athapaskan groups were active with them in trading and intermarriage as well as raiding.

Settlements

Tanaina villages were located on or near streams and rivers with salmon runs. There were usually at least two lineage houses in a settlement and frequently ten or more. During periods of conflict, a village might be hidden in the woods to guard against attack from enemies. A village population ranged from around fifty to one hundred or more. In spring and summer, people moved into smaller camps—groups of small nuclear or extended family houses or skin tents either at a lake mouth or spread out along a lake or river shore to facilitate salmon fishing. In late prehistoric and historic times winter houses were semisubterranean (up to about three feet deep), lineage-owned structures. There was one large room about twenty feet square with a central fireplace. Each nuclear family had a small compartment for sleeping, and rooms might be attached as sweatlodges or menstrual huts. Summer houses at fish camps and in hunting areas were small, wood, above-ground houses or skin tents for one or two nuclear families. During the second half of the nineteenth century, houses began to be constructed above ground in log-cabin style, and at summer fishing camps commercial canvas tents were often used. Some Tanaina, particularly those in interior villages, continue today to move to "fish camp" in the summer. Winter houses today are of a small European style and usually made of milled lumber with wood floors.

Economy

Subsistence and Commercial Activities. Tanaina have traditionally been hunters, gatherers, and fishermen. Fish, particularly salmon, has been the basis of the subsistence economy both prehistorically and today. The abundance of salmon during the summer runs and fish preservation techniques made possible permanent winter villages in most areas. Freshwater fish were also exploited. Seal hunting was conducted both at Iliamna Lake and in Cook Inlet. Moose, caribou, bear, and mountain sheep were important resources, but small mammals such as porcupine, squirrel, and hares were also significant. Wild berries were abundant in summer; other wild plants were gathered where available. Fur-bearing animals were trapped for personal use and trade. These subsistence activities persist today, particularly in more remote villages, and many villagers maintain small vegetable gardens.

Fish canneries opened after 1880 and monopolized the best salmon-fishing streams. Tanaina began to work for salmon canneries after 1915 and became directly involved in commercial fishing in Bristol Bay and Cook Inlet after 1940; today many obtain a major part of their income from this activity. Game and fur-bearing animals became more scarce from overhunting, but fur trapping still provides supplemental income for some, although its importance has declined. A few own small planes and make commercial flights locally; others guide vacationing hunters and fishers, work for government installations, or take wage employment in larger towns and cities.

The only domestic animal is the dog. It was used for packing and hunting in prehistoric times. Teams of sled dogs were maintained until the mid-twentieth century, and some people still use them.

Trade. Tanaina, like other southern Alaskan societies, maintained extensive intra- and intertribal trade and trade fairs in precontact times. Trade items included furs, caribou skins, native copper, porcupine quills, sea mammal products, dentalium shells, and slaves. After contact, the Russians also supplied dentalium shells from southeastern Alaska as well as glass beads, and metal products, especially iron. During the first half of the nineteenth century, Tanaina began to trade some of their furs to Russians, and trade, especially between the Kenai Tanaina and the Russian-American Company, increased. When Russia sold Alaska to the United States in 1867, the assets of the Russian-American Company were assumed by the Alaska Commercial Company. The price of furs dropped considerably at the end of the nineteenth century. In 1911, the Alaska Commercial Company sold its interests in the area to private traders. Since that time, the fur trade has become almost moribund.

Industrial Arts. Aboriginally, stone flaking and grinding were the techniques for manufacturing cutting and piercing weapons. Hammered copper was also used for arrowheads and knives. Bone and antler were used for tools as well. The sinew-backed bow and arrows and the spear and spear thrower were the primary weapons. Skins were worked into clothes and foot gear. Basketry, birchbark, wood, and hide provided containers. Birchbark canoes, moose-skin boats, and sealskin open and decked-over boats similar to the Eskimo umiak and kayak were used for water transportation. For winter use, snowshoes were made of birch wood, with bear- or moose-skin webbing (*babiche*). Sleds were manufactured from wood and rawhide. Today, most goods are commercially made, but some people continue to make skin boots, sleds, and snowshoes. Locally made wood skiffs have replaced earlier watercraft.

Division of Labor. In prehistoric and historic times, men hunted large game, trapped and fished, and manufactured weapons and tools. Women snared small animals, split and dried fish, prepared other game, collected berries and plants, prepared skins, manufactured clothing, embroidered with porcupine quills, and made some containers. Today men are most active in commercial fishing from boats, and women usually tend commercial set nets and work in canneries. At home, men and sometimes women hunt and trap. Women set and tend subsistence fish nets, as well as split, dry, and smoke salmon. Both sexes are involved in freshwater fishing. Men continue to manufacture sleds, boats, and snowshoes and are most active in trapping, although women assist in the last. Men are usually the pilots and sport hunting/fishing guides. Women sew, prepare and preserve food, and continue to act both as midwives and village first aid practitioners.

Land Tenure. Aboriginally, land use was based on clan-lineage affiliation. In some areas, lineages had fishing rights at specific locales along a stream. Trap lines have never been registered; a person has the right to trap or hunt in an area he or his family has consistently used. Except for Tyonek, on Cook Inlet, no Tanaina land has been a reservation. People could, however, register a house or homesite but few did so. After the Alaska Native Claims Settlement Act, village sites were established and individuals allowed to claim specific tracts of land if they could establish that they are at least one-quarter Alaskan native.

Kinship

Kin Groups and Descent. Tanaina were organized into moieties and between eleven and eighteen matrilineal exogamous clans. Clans often cross-cut societal and language boundaries. Today, some clans remain active during funeral potlatches and influence the selection of marriage partners.

Kinship Terminology. Twentieth-century terminology probably reflects changes over the last two hundred years of European contact as well as the geographic distances between groups. Iliamna dialect uses Iroquois cousin terms and bifurcate merging avuncular (first ascending generation) terms. The Inland dialect uses Crow cousin and bifurcate merging avuncular terms; Upper Inlet is Iroquois and bifurcate collateral; Outer Inlet dialect is Hawaiian cousin and mixed avuncular terms.

Marriage and Family

Marriage. Marriage was moiety and clan exogamous in the past and to some extent today. Cross-cousin marriage, especially of a male to his father's sister's daughter, was preferred, but there was no strict rule regarding village endogamy. Bride-price or -service and polygyny were practiced. Residence was matrilocal in some instances, but particularly after wealth and prestige became significant, avunculocality was practiced. After about 1900, neolocality and bilaterality with some patrilineal emphasis began to appear. Divorce was simple, but apparently not common in traditional times.

Domestic Unit. By the nineteenth century, the residence unit was a lineage segment headed by a "richman" composed of two or more generations of matrilineally related males and their families. Today, the nuclear family predominates.

Inheritance. Inheritance was matrilineal with regard to affiliation and clan property, but personal property was often destroyed or placed in the grave. Recently, except for certain kinds of clan paraphernalia, inheritance has become primarily bilateral within the nuclear family.

Socialization. Children raised in the extended family were socialized by the residence group, but people were generally permissive. Ridicule was a common means of highlighting unacceptable behavior.

Sociopolitical Organization

Social Organization. Tanaina social organization was based on ranking, which was most prominent in the Kenai subdivision and in other villages near the coast. As one moved inland, rank became less crystallized. There were two ranks: richmen and commoners; slaves were outside the system. Women seem always to have held positions equal to men of the same rank and could accumulate wealth in their own right. Each village was composed of one or more local lineage groups of clans. Each lineage was represented by a richman (highest ranking man of the lineage) who was aided by a group of male relatives of his lineage, usually residing avunculocally either within the lineage house or in individual houses nearby. The richman was responsible for the economic, political, and social well-being of his lineage. He led trading expeditions and maintained trade partners in other Tanaina, Indian, and Eskimo villages. Trade partners not only ensured amicable trade but were also used to negotiate peace between warring villages. After the Russian entry into the fur trade, influential men, usually the most prominent richmen, were appointed as "chiefs" to act as liaisons between the Russians and Tanaina and to lead trading expeditions for the Russians. The added wealth that flowed to selected richmen enhanced their prestige further. With the fur price collapse of 1897, the richmen lost the economic prestige base, and the rank system became less important. Slavery was practiced in late precontact times, with Indian and Eskimo slaves acquired through raiding or trading and retained by richmen.

Political Organization. Each Tanaina village was politically autonomous. Leadership, which rested primarily within the lineage, involved authority rather than power. Richmen and elders held primary leadership and decision-making positions, but people were generally free to dissent if they wished. Women and men had complementary authority, but it was related to inherited wealth, prestige, and rank rather than merely gender. Although autonomous, each village maintained close ties with nearby villages with ties based on marriage, presence of the same clans, and trade.

Social Control. The leading richmen of a village acted as authorities. Gossip was and still is one of the most effective means of social control. Ostracism, revenge killing, beating, or paying *wergild* (compensation) could be used if lesser measures failed. If harm occurred within a clan or moiety, it was for the injured person or a close relative to seek revenge. For problems between clans or moieties, members of the aggrieved kin unit took revenge. At times, this resulted in civil war; prisoners were ransomed back by their kin groups.

Conflict. Tanaina conflicts, primarily raids, were village-specific rather than with an entire society. Occasionally conflicts were between Tanaina villages, but most were with neighboring Eskimo or other Indian villages. Thus, an alliance might exist between one Tanaina and one Eskimo village at the same time that the Tanaina village raided another Eskimo village. Minor conflict occurred between Russians and Tanaina during the early years of contact, but overall relations were comparatively amicable because of the economic advantages for both parties during the fur trade.

Religion and Expressive Culture

Religious Beliefs. The concept of a remote supreme deity living in the North Star may have preceded Russian contact. The world was filled with spirit powers. There was a close relationship between humans, animals, and the spirit realm; everyone had a familiar in which his or her soul could travel. A special alliance existed between humans and the highly respected bear; wolf was a brother who would come to the aid of a person who was lost and hungry. The world was peopled with spirits and quasi-spirits. The trickster, Raven, was the mythological creator. Harmful spirits in the woods hurt or kidnapped people and stole fish and other goods. Other woods and mountain spirits were benign in their relation to humans. Another category of quasi-spirits have reportedly been sighted by Eskimo, Tanaina, and European-Americans in recent years. One, called the "Hairy Man," is equivalent to the Sasquatch. Finally, the belief in luck and hunting magic persists in attenuated form. Offerings may be made at special locales for good luck, and magical songs sung to assist in hunting. Omens are believed to foretell the future, especially potentially bad events. Russian Orthodox priests came into the Kenai area in 1794, but it was another thirty years before active missionization began in any locale. By the end of the nineteenth century priests had become accepted and actively attempted to wipe out shamanism. Some former shamans incorporated themselves into the church hierarchy as deacons. Most Tanaina today are nominally Russian Orthodox. Active missionization by more fundamentalist Protestant groups began after the turn of the twentieth century, and some have become aligned with that faction.

Religious Practitioners.   Shamans were the primary religious and medical practitioners. They often were wealthy, holding authority similar to richmen. They could be of either sex and received their calling in dreams. Although normally "good," assisting their people, they occasionally turned evil.

Ceremonies.   A first salmon ceremony was held at the beginning of fishing season. Girls at menarche were confined from forty days to a year during which time they were taught sewing and other women's skills and proper behavior. Potlatches were originally held following a death, but later were held by richmen at trading and other times as a display of wealth to garner prestige.

Arts.   Singing and dancing at potlatches and the singing of magical songs in hunting were common. Clothing was elaborately decorated with porcupine quill embroidery, sometimes incorporating valuable dentalium shells. After contact, glass beads were worked into long belts of dentalium shells for use at potlatches. Animal and human figures were painted on such items as skin quivers. Some rock paintings may be attributed to Tanaina.

Medicine.   The shaman, wearing a mask, used the spirit in a powerful doll to discern and remove the cause of illness. His long staff was also used to assist in driving out illness. Illness might be caused by soul loss or magical intrusion of objects. Helper spirits located lost souls; intrusive objects were sucked out. In addition, herbal medicines, potions, teas, and plant compresses were used by both shamans and lay people to effect cures. Today, Western medicine is the primary recourse in illness. Trained nurses' aides and midwives are found in some villages, but serious illness requires travel to cities with hospitals.

Death and Afterlife.   At death, the "breath-soul" flew away, but the "shadow-soul" might remain to be near friends or to take revenge. Eventually they journeyed to the lower world where they lived in a way similar to that on earth. Before Christians introduced burial, the deceased was cremated and ashes were buried. At least by early contact times, over the grave a small house might be erected in which the deceased's personal goods were placed. Subsequently, food offerings were left. Members of the opposite (father's or spouse's) clan of the deceased took care of the funeral arrangements. Between forty days and a year following the death, a potlatch involving feasting and distribution of valued goods was given by the deceased's clan for the opposite clan in appreciation for assistance. At times, the deceased's spirit would return to relatives and disturb them, especially if he or she thought the potlatch inadequate. Although not yet documented specifically for the Tanaina, there is some indication of a belief in reincarnation.

Bibliography

Fall, James A. (1981). "Patterns of Upper Inlet Tanaina Leadership, 1741–1918." Ph.D. diss., University of Wisconsin.

Osgood, Cornelius (1937). *The Ethnography of the Tanaina.* Yale University Publications in Anthropology, no. 16. New Haven, Conn.: Department of Anthropology, Yale University.

Townsend, Joan B. (1965). "Ethnohistory and Culture Change of the Iliamna Tanaina." Ph.D. diss., University of California.

Townsend, Joan B. (1970). "The Tanaina of Southwestern Alaska: An Historical Synopsis." *Western Canadian Journal of Anthropology* 2:2–16.

Townsend, Joan B. (1980). "Ranked Societies of the Alaskan Pacific Rim." In *Alaskan Native Culture and History,* edited by Y. Kotani and W. Workman, 123–156. Senri Ethnological Studies, no. 4. Osaka, Japan: National Museum of Ethnology.

Townsend, Joan B. (1981). "Tanaina." In *Handbook of North American Indians.* Vol. 6, *Subarctic,* edited by June Helm, 623–640. Washington, D.C.: Smithsonian Institution.

VanStone, James, and Joan B. Townsend (1970). *Kijik: An Historic Tanaina Settlement.* Fieldiana: Anthropology, vol. 59. Chicago: Field Museum of Natural History.

JOAN B. TOWNSEND

Tanana

ETHNONYMS: Gens des Buttes, Tannin-kootchin, Tenankutchin, Tennankutchin, Tennan-tnu-kokhtana

Orientation

Identification.   The Tanana are an American Indian group located in Alaska. The name "Tanana" is a corruption of the Tanana Athapaskan term *Ten Dona'* which refers to the Tanana River valley. Among Tanana Athapaskans the term used for the Tanana River proper is *Tth'eetoo',* meaning "straight water." The names cited in historical accounts reflect the term applied by neighboring Gwich'in ("Kutchin") Athapaskan groups of the Yukon River valley. The Tanana Athapaskans do not refer to themselves by this larger grouping, but rather by the individual band name, such as "*Mentekhut'ana*" (people who inhabit the Minto Lakes). Nowadays "Tanana" is a linguistic term used to refer to Athapaskan-speaking people of the middle Tanana River and should not be confused with Koyukon-speaking Athapaskans who reside at the village of Tanana situated along the middle Yukon River.

Location. At contact the Tanana occupied and used the areas along the middle Tanana River between the Kantishna and Goodpaster rivers, the adjacent areas of the Tanana Lowlands and Minto Flats, as well as the surrounding hills of the Yukon-Tanana Upland north of the Tanana River and the foothills of the Alaska Range south of the Tanana River. This area is part of the boreal forest situated between 64° and 66° N and 144° and 150° W in central Alaska. Currently, most Tanana-speaking Athapaskans reside in the communities of Minto, Nenana, and Fairbanks.

Demography. In the early 1980s the Tanana population numbered about 500–600, residing primarily in the native villages of Minto and Nenana and the urban center of Fairbanks. In 1910, Tanana Athapaskans totaled about 370 (Minto, Nenana, Chena, and Salcha).

Linguistic Affiliation. The Tanana language is one of twenty-three Northern Athapaskan languages of the Athapaskan family. At contact there were three dialects: Minto-Nenana, Chena, and Salcha-Goodpaster. Nowadays only the Minto-Nenana dialect is spoken.

History and Cultural Relations

Prehistoric evidence of human occupation in the area historically occupied by the Tanana extends as far back as eleven thousand years ago at one of the oldest radiocarbon-dated sites in North America. Elsewhere in the area, there have been few archaeological investigations, and little is known of prehistory of the area or the late prehistoric period that might shed light on the precontact culture and origin of the Tanana. The Tanana language reflects contact with neighboring groups to the west, south, and southeast where the Upper Koyukon, Upper Kuskokwim, and Tanacross Athapaskan languages, respectively, are spoken. Social contact with the Upper Koyukon and Tanacross speakers has persisted from the late nineteenth century to the present day. Direct contact with European-Americans dates from the mid-1800s, first with the Russians who established a network of trading stations to the south and west and the English to the north and northeast. Contact with Americans was later when, after the 1867 purchase of Alaska from Russia, commercial activity and exploration expanded. Continuous contact among Tanana and European-Americans dates from the 1902 discovery of gold in the Fairbanks district and the subsequent intensification of mining at the core of the Tanana geographical area. Trading posts, roadhouses, telegraph stations, and commercial centers were established in the Tanana River valley; steamboats plied the Tanana River bringing goods and nonnative residents into the area. Furs were traded and dried salmon and cordwood became products of trade as dog teams and steamboats became central modes of transportation to supply and service mining operations and commercial activity.

Episcopalian missionaries established churches, schools, and medical facilities in the area during the first twenty years of the twentieth century. By the 1950s, the Salcha and Chena bands were nearly extinct and members of the Nenana, Wood River, Toklat, and Minto bands became consolidated at the villages of Nenana and Minto along the Tanana River. This marked the shift from a mobile hunting and gathering band population to a semipermanent village population. Hunting, fishing, and gathering of local fish and wildlife resources, however, continue to play an important role in the village economies of Minto and Nenana.

Settlements

Aboriginally and in early contact times, Tanana Athapaskans traveled in small bands or extended family groups during the course of the year to harvest seasonally available fish and wildlife. Seasonal settlements were situated along salmon-bearing streams and at the mouths of major salmon-spawning streams during summer and early fall. Some bands occupied fishing settlements at the outlets of large lakes to harvest from the large migrations of whitefish during early summer and fall. During late fall and spring, families moved and set up seasonal camps from which they hunted caribou during their seasonal migrations. During winter families moved frequently, hunting moose and trapping fur animals. Some traveled to the foothills of the Alaska Range where they hunted sheep. The fishing stations were essentially semipermanent villages where family groups returned and the band joined together for ceremonial and religious activities. Around 1900 there were about eight semipermanent villages of the Tanana; most were situated along the Tanana or at the mouth of major tributary streams. Numerous seasonal and temporary camps were dispersed throughout the area along lakes and smaller streams and in the flats and foothills. Band size ranged from about fifty to one hundred persons. By 1950 the population resided in two year-round villages as it does today, with many members also residing in the urban center of Fairbanks. Aboriginal housing included the use of semipermanent log and sod houses and caribou- or moose-skin tents. Throughout the twentieth century, canvas tents and log houses have been used for shelter along with wood-frame houses.

Economy

Subsistence and Commercial Activities. The Tanana were a hunting, fishing, and gathering society. They hunted large and small game of the boreal forest, including moose, caribou, bear, sheep, muskrat, beaver, ptarmigan, hare, grouse, porcupine, and waterfowl. Several species of salmon and whitefish were taken by a variety of methods that included traps, fences, gill nets, dip nets, and fish wheels for salmon. Other fish species taken included northern pike, burbot, sheefish, and longnose sucker. Berries, edible plants, and wood were gathered for use. Nowadays, nearly all of these same fish and wildlife resources continue to be harvested for subsistence. In 1984, the village of Minto had among the largest per capita harvest of wild foods in the state—1,015 edible pounds per person. Since contact, fish and wildlife have been used in trade with European-Americans to obtain manufactured goods. Furs, dried salmon, and cordwood were used in trade and for acquiring cash. A mixed subsistence-cash economy is characteristic of present-day Tanana villages. Trapping, commercial salmon fishing, and wage employment, although all limited, are the primary means for earning cash.

Industrial Arts. Handicrafts include the manufacture of birchbark baskets, dog sleds, snowshoes, fur caps and boots, and various articles of beadwork for sale and exchange.

Trade. Little is known of aboriginal trading practices, although an interregional trail network was clearly well developed as evidenced in several historic accounts that reported the presence of imported manufactured items in advance of European-Americans in central Alaska. After contact, trading trips were made regularly by certain band members to posts along the Yukon River and near the mouth of the Copper River to the south. A native trade fair was held frequently at a site near the junction of the Tanana and Yukon rivers, although its antiquity is uncertain. Trading expeditions declined in the twentieth century as goods and products became available at stations and stores in the Tanana Valley proper.

Division of Labor. Aboriginally, men were responsible for hunting, providing firewood, cooking food, and manufacturing tools, snowshoe frames, boats, and canoes. Women tanned skins from which they made clothing, footwear, and tents. They made birchbark utensils and collected water, edible plants, and berries. Women carried the heavy loads and pulled toboggans loaded with gear and equipment. Women, then as now, could and did hunt large and small game. They cut and dried fish and meat, although men often assisted as they do nowadays. Both men and women fished. Now, traditional cooking of food, particularly for ceremonial purposes and in camp is done by men, and European-American-style cooking is done by women. Earlier in the twentieth century both men and women trapped; however, this is virtually a male activity nowadays. Commercial fishing is done primarily by men, although women commonly assist. Both men and women are involved in wage employment.

Land Tenure. Aboriginally, individuals, family groups, or bands did not own property in the Western legal sense. The use and occupancy of lands were guided by usufruct rights based upon kinship and group affiliation. Band territory was open to all members of the band for subsistence use. Members of neighboring bands asked permission to use certain areas. Trapping areas were used by and associated with particular families and were handed down along family lines from one generation to the next as they often are today. The 1906 Alaska Native Allotment Act was extinguished in 1971 by the Alaska Native Claims Settlement Act. Prior to 1971 many natives applied for individual land allotments, although few have received patent to date. Land was granted to natives of Nenana and Minto in the form of profit-making corporations by the 1971 act, but these lands include a relatively small proportion of the land traditionally used and occupied by Tanana Athapaskans.

Kinship

Kin Groups and Descent. Tanana society was divided into exogamous matrilineal kin groups, or sibs. Within each band were one or several sibs that were associated with one of two moieties. Sibs and moieties regulated marriages, partnerships, and economic and ceremonial exchanges. They were not land-holding groups, nor did they act as corporate groups in intraband affairs. Remnant evidence of the sib system nowadays is found primarily in ceremonial and religious activities associated with funerals and funeral and memorial potlatches.

Kinship Terminology. Tanana kinship is characterized by Iroquois cousin terminology and bifurcate collateral terminology in the first ascending generation, although there has been a shift toward Hawaiian cousin terminology.

Marriage and Family

Marriage. Traditional marriage rules precluded marriage within one's matrilineage: cross-cousin marriages were preferred and sib exogamy was the rule. Residence was generally matrilocal. There was no bride-price or dowry, although the future husband was expected to help his parents-in-law and provide them with gifts. Formerly polygamy was practiced. Divorce was not common. Nowadays marriage is monogamous and avoided between first cousins. Residence tends toward matrilocality, and divorce is still rare.

Domestic Unit. Residence units were characteristically small extended families. Although nuclear families predominate today, extended family groups are still common in the residential unit and are characteristic of most task groups for hunting and fishing.

Inheritance. In the past, among the neighboring Upper Tanana, personal belongings were sometimes given to a close relative or friend prior to death or were supposed to be destroyed upon death. Among the Tanana, valuable items and personal belongings now are often given away at the funeral potlatch.

Socialization. Children were raised to exhibit humility and modesty in pursuits and accomplishments. They had freedom in their activities, and independence was valued. These ideals persist. Formal education is now mandatory through age sixteen, and most students complete high school, although few continue their education beyond the secondary level.

Sociopolitical Organization

Social Organization. Leadership was provided by men who held the position of chief either by ascription or achievement. Their status had to be continually validated by their exhibiting qualities associated with chieftainships—wealth, generosity, wisdom, and hunting prowess. In some cases a wealthy woman who had exhibited industriousness and skillfulness in subsistence activities could regulate activities in and out of camp. Both men and women had an equal voice in community affairs, and influential individuals of both sexes in modern communities are respected for their wisdom, industriousness, and generosity.

Political Organization. Prior to contact, bands, like villages today, were politically independent from others. Trading chiefs were prominent during the Russian period (c. 1820–1867), but they had no power unless they also exhibited the qualities of a traditional leader. Similarly, in modern villages an elected chief of a tribal council formed under the provisions of the Indian Reorganization Act may or may not be a leader in the traditional sense. Traditional leaders and chiefs continue to be influential in community matters.

Social Control. Within Tanana society, social control was a family matter, whereas leaders often negotiated with those of other bands to settle disputes between bands. Social avoidance prevented confrontation as did temporary emigration from the camp or village. In some cases, emigration was forced through overt or subtle social pressure by community or family heads. Although members are subject to state and federal laws, traditional social controls often sanction offending persons as well.

Conflict. The Tanana have never entered into overt conflict with European-American society. Rather, individuals were judged on their personal qualities and characteristics. In historic and modern times, Tanana Athapaskans have been at the heart of native efforts to bring about claims settlements. They have been active leaders beginning with the first Tanana Chiefs Conference held in 1915 and, since the late 1960s, within the nonprofit native organization of the same name, which provides health, social, and advocacy services to natives of all of interior Alaska.

Religion and Expressive Culture

Religious Beliefs. Aboriginally and in early historic times the shaman was the central figure of religious life. Magico-religious practices included omens, charms, amulets, songs, taboos, and beliefs about the supernatural. Beliefs and practices were associated with certain animals, and many centered around hunting. Animal spirits appear to have predominated in Tanana spiritual life, although an evil spirit was manifested in a half-man, half-animal being. Spirits were influential in the activities of the living and in guiding the dead to their final resting place. As in other aspects of society, religious beliefs and practices were highly individualized and were a personal matter. Christian missionaries of the Episcopal church established churches and missions in the area beginning in the early 1900s. Several members of Tanana society, including one woman, have become ordained ministers of the Episcopal church. Many traditional beliefs persist, however, and are particularly evident in ritual behavior surrounding death.

Religious Practitioners. Medicine making was carried out by shamans, both male and female, especially in the cure of the sick. They were integral in the society at least until the 1930s and probably much later. Both ordained and lay ministers are central in religious practices today.

Ceremonies. The most important religious ceremonies have been and continue to be potlatches, particularly the funeral and memorial types. Both the ceremony following the death of an individual and the potlatch held one or several years later as a memorial are central to religious, social, and economic life in Tanana society.

Arts. Songs have been associated with supernatural power particularly surrounding hunting activities. Individuals often had their own songs to empower them in dealing with the natural world and its creatures. Songs continue to be composed in the native language and English to mark key events, as storytelling and as mourning songs sung at funeral and memorial potlatches commemorating deceased individuals.

Medicine. Sickness was rare prior to the coming of European-Americans. Both physical medical cures and shamanism were used to treat various ailments and diseases. Some herbal and traditional medicines continue to be used, and a village health aide staffs a medical clinic.

Death and Afterlife. The native attitude toward death is fatalistic, and death is faced with composure. Although there is no belief in an afterlife, appropriate ritualistic behavior by the survivors ensures that the soul of the deceased will be guided to the narrow trail that leads to the afterworld. The activities and behavior surrounding the death of an individual and the funeral potlatch are especially important in this regard.

Bibliography

Andrews, Elizabeth F. (1975). "Salcha: An Athapaskan Band of the Tanana River and Its Culture." M.A. thesis, University of Alaska, Fairbanks.

Andrews, Elizabeth F. (1988). *The Harvest of Fish and Wildlife for Subsistence by the Residents of Minto, Alaska.* Alaska Department of Fish and Game, Division of Subsistence, Technical Paper no. 137. Juneau.

Olson, Wallace M. (1968). "Minto: Cultural and Historical Influences on Group Identity." M.A. thesis, University of Alaska.

Shinkwin, Anne, and Martha Case (1984). *Modern Foragers: Wild Resource Use in Nenana Village, Alaska.* Alaska Department of Fish and Game, Division of Subsistece, Technical Paper no. 91. Juneau.

Toghotthele Corporation (1983). *Nenana Denayee.* Nenana, Alaska: Toghotthele Corporation.

ELIZABETH F. ANDREWS

Taos

ETHNONYMS: Braba, San Geronimo de Taos, Tayberon (early Spanish), Vallodolid, t' óynemą ("the people" in Taos)

Orientation

Identification. Taos Pueblo is located in northern New Mexico. The name "Taos" is an adaptation of tâotho, "in the village," or tâobo, "to or toward the village," the usual references in the Taos language to the Pueblo. The s was the Spanish plural ending. The name "Taos" is invariable today in both Spanish and English.

Location. The most northern of the Rio Grande Pueblos, Taos is seventy miles north of Santa Fe, New Mexico. The Pueblo is at the base of Taos Mountain, sacred to the Indians and one of several prominent peaks in the Sangre de Cristo (Blood of Christ) mountain range. At an elevation of 7,098 feet, Taos Pueblo is surrounded by an extensive well-watered and agriculturally productive plateau into which the Rio Grande has cut a deep gorge only a few miles from the Pueblo. Wild game is abundant and the mountain stream and small rivers that descend into the Rio Grande are well stocked with fish.

Demography.   The reservation population in 1987 was 1,484, with a total tribal population of 1,951. Those who do not reside at the Pueblo live primarily in Santa Fe and Albuquerque and in Colorado, with others scattered mainly in cities in Arizona and California. Since World War II the population has increased dramatically, from 830 in 1942 to 1,457 in 1964 and nearly 2,000 today. The Taos have vigorously opposed intermarriage with other Indian groups, although many such marriages have occurred over the years. Nevertheless, as of 1972 they maintained a mean percent Indian "blood" of 95, which was high even compared to other conservative Eastern Pueblo groups.

Linguistic Affiliation.   The Taos language is one of two Northern Tiwa languages; the other is spoken at Picuris Pueblo twenty-five miles to the south of Taos. These languages plus the two Southern Tiwa languages spoken at Isleta and Sandia Pueblos near Albuquerque constitute the Tiwa branch of the Kiowa-Tanoan language family.

History and Cultural Relations

It is believed that the ancestors of Taos and other Eastern Pueblo groups moved into the Rio Grande area from the north and west, possibly from the Anasazi region of the Four Corners beginning in the 1100s. The Taos creation myth supports a migration from the north, and it is certain that they have been in the Taos Valley since about 1200, first living at the now-ruined Pot Creek Pueblo and others south of their present location, and at the current site since 1350 where they were encountered by the Coronado expedition in 1540. The Taos have figured prominently in every attempt to expel foreigners from their territory. Following Spanish settlement in 1598 resentment against the Europeans intensified, culminating in the Pueblo Revolt of 1680 which was plotted from Taos. After U.S. occupation, the Taos joined with the Mexicans in the 1847 revolt. The governor, Charles Bent, and others were scalped, and the ruins of the old mission at the Pueblo testify to the retaliation by the U.S. Army. In 1906 Blue Lake, twenty miles above the Pueblo in the mountains, and forty-eight thousand acres of surrounding aboriginal-use area were incorporated into the Carson National Forest. The Indians waged a legal battle with the government for the return of these lands to their reservation. In 1971 sovereignty over the Blue Lake area was restored to the Pueblo, marking the first time in U.S.-Indian relations that land was returned, rather than financial compensation paid, on the basis of religious freedom.

Taos shares many cultural features with the other Pueblo communities of New Mexico and Arizona, and contact between Taos and other Pueblos has been frequent if not intensive. Given their northern location and easy access to the Plains, the Taos had significant contacts with southern Plains groups, notably the Comanche in the 1700s and more recently with the Kiowa and Cheyenne in Oklahoma. In spite of many Plains influences—Peyotism, dress style, secular dances and music—Taos has remained distinctly Puebloid. Some customs that appear to be Plains-derived may actually have been elaborated in response to ecological adaptation, including the reliance on hunting and especially bison hunts,

which fostered a major dependence on horses and all the material culture that requires. As is true of all the Pueblos, there is a marked ethnocentrism at Taos, but this is even more pronounced in terms of their quiet disdain for the Spanish and for the White Americans who have settled in increasing numbers in Taos Valley in the twentieth century, although never on Indian land.

Settlements

Taos Pueblo itself is divided into two massive adobe house blocks by the Rio Pueblo de Taos. This small river, spanned by three-foot-long bridges, flows mainly from Blue Lake, which now symbolizes not only the native religion but also the total integrity of the culture. The north-side Pueblo is five stories high, while the south-side is four. As the population increased, what had been summer houses near the corn and wheat fields became year-round residences. Many people still reside in the old pueblo apartment buildings (109 units were occupied in 1971), and they remain the center of the people's on-reservation activity. No other Indian settlements have appeared since Spanish contact, although Taos Valley is now dotted with many small towns and communities inhabited by Hispanics and White Americans. Most important are the town of Taos, New Mexico, 3 miles south of the Pueblo, which is the hub for local commercial and government activities, and the community of Ranchos de Taos three miles farther south. Although there is daily interaction between the Indians and their neighbors, the physical, cultural, and psychological separation between the two groups is profound. Aboriginally, coursed adobe was used to construct Taos Pueblo and later supplemented by Hispanic-introduced sun-dried brick. Most dwellings in the old apartment buildings have two rooms, one serving as a kitchen and eating area and the other for sleeping and socializing. Government-sponsored housing projects have introduced other house styles and building materials in recent years, but all of these units are well out of sight of the old Pueblo. Electricity and running water are not allowed in the old Pueblo.

Economy

Subsistence and Commercial Activities.   The traditional Taos were agriculturalists, depending primarily on maize, beans, and squash. Wheat and other European imports were eagerly adopted, with wheat gaining some commercial importance in the eighteenth and nineteenth centuries. Hunting always supplemented agriculture, with the mountains providing deer, elk, bear, turkey, grouse, and squirrel and the plateau providing antelope and the plains bison in the 1800s. Eagle, hawk, and duck feathers were important in rituals. Rabbits are still hunted on reservation land and figure prominently in summer ceremonies. Many species of wild plants were and are gathered as well as wildflowers that are important in ceremonies. Given the northern location and altitude, the growing season was too short for cotton, so the Taos relied on the more southerly Pueblos for woven goods. Today, wage labor, revenue from tourism, and many forms of government assistance have largely replaced the traditional subsistence base, with agriculture largely replaced by gardening and hunting reduced mostly to a sport or to obtain ritual items. Pigs and chickens are raised by a few households. Sheep and goats were never herded. The dog was ubiquitous, but the most important animal for both practical and prestige purposes was the horse, which figures prominently in myth and legend and is still highly valued. Although never considered prestigious, cattle became important enough for a Cattlemen's Association to be formed at the Pueblo.

Industrial Arts.　Since 1600 the dominant type of pottery and today the only type is a utilitarian ware of micaceous clay. Taos manufactures reflect their reliance on the hunt and include excellent hard-soles moccasins, folded deerskin "boots" worn by mature women, and drums. Buckskin leggings and shirts, bison robes, and rabbit-skin blankets were important in the past. The art of weaving rabbit-skin blankets was revived by Taos women in 1970, and the establishment of a Pueblo arts and crafts center, along with the popularity of Indian crafts in general, has fostered the emergence of a number of skilled craftspeople and artists working in a number of media.

Trade.　Trade was never of any great importance either pre- or postcontact, although trade from as far away as Mexico (for parrot feathers) did occur.

Division of Labor.　Household chores, horticulture, pottery making, the tending of small domestic animals, and the annual remudding of houses were women's concerns. The men farmed, irrigated, hunted, raised livestock, and worked hides. Men also were more involved in ceremonial activities than were women.

Land Tenure.　Theoretically, land is communally owned, and there are pastures and grazing lands on which anyone can run their horses and cattle. Houses, summer houses, and fields are considered to be individual property and are passed down from one generation to the next without regard for the age or sex of the heir. As is true of all reservations, the land is legally held in trust by the federal government. At Taos, land may be sold, traded, or inherited only by and to a tribally recognized Taos Indian.

Kinship

Kin Groups and Descent.　The kinship system lacks clans and is bilateral. Moiety organization is expressed physically and ceremonially, but weakly so. While individuals belong to either the north- or south-side pueblos and there is alternative ceremonial jurisdiction by north- and south-side kivas, residence is not so determined nor is kiva membership so affected.

Kinship Terminology.　Age and sex are reflected in kin terms, with older males accorded somewhat more respect than females.

Marriage and Family

Marriage.　Marriage is monogamous with freedom of choice in the selection of partners. Little was made of the marriage ceremony, which has been celebrated with the sacraments of the Catholic church since conversion. Secular marriages and common-law unions have increased in number in recent years. Postmarital residence is typically neolocal, although the importance of the bilaterally extended family may influence the couple to live with one family or the other for the first few years of marriage. Ideally, this group of kin remains a source of continual security throughout life. Separa-

tion and divorce have increased, but given the influence of the Catholic church they are still regarded as unfortunate decisions. Instances of intramarital conflict resulting in such things as child support claims, formerly taken to the Pueblo governor for resolution, are today more often handled by U.S. courts and social control agencies outside the Pueblo.

Inheritance.　Land, houses, and personal property are bequeathed at will. Fractionalization of the land base has occurred with the increasing population even though there is no rule or strong tendency toward equal inheritance for offspring or others.

Socialization.　Children are greatly valued. Given the strength of the extended family, very few children have ever been given up for adoption. The importance of wage work drawing most young adults of both sexes out of the Pueblo has strengthened the role of grandparents and other older relatives in the early socialization of many Taos infants and young children. Older Indians, particularly women, have often been the primary socializers of even three or four generations of their descendants. This has contributed to the perpetuation of the Taos language as well as many other older traditions.

Sociopolitical Organization

Social Organization.　Knowledge of this aspect of Taos culture is somewhat opaque, since this is generally a subject about which people have been secretive. There is a very strong sense of communality at Taos, expressed most often in terms of community duties, which every able-bodied adult or legitimate substitute from the extended family must perform. Duties include secular work projects, such as cleaning irrigation ditches, repairing fences, and plastering the Catholic church, as well as dance obligations and other ceremonially linked activities. Most Taos believe that a weakening of communality will ultimately spell the passing of Taos culture. Many persons who otherwise deviate from Taos norms, such as refusing to participate in the kiva-based religion, are nevertheless allowed to remain at the Pueblo and are considered in good standing if they faithfully perform their community duties.

Political Organization.　Secular government, partially Spanish-imposed, is closely entwined with the religious kiva organization. The top officials must be kiva-trained and ceremonially active. Annually the Taos Pueblo Council, composed of the kiva leaders and past top secular officials, elects twenty two civil officers. They are divided into the governor, lieutenant governor, and eight staff members, on the one hand, who handle matters pertaining to the Pueblo proper as well as concerns with the wider society off the reservation, and on the other, the war chief, assistant war chief, and ten deputies who are responsible for problems that arise outside the village but generally on reservation land. Serious matters that affect everyone, such as the battle for Blue Lake, are usually council concerns.

Social Control.　Major deviant behavior requires the intervention of legal authority, most often the governor, or in the rare cases of homicide, outside-based agencies, such as the Bureau of Indian Affairs. Minor deviance is controlled in part through gossip and other types of informal sanctions. Given the tight-knit nature of the Pueblo community, very little happens that does not become common knowledge quickly.

Witchcraft formerly played a more prominent role than currently.

Conflict. Recurrent factionalism is certainly the most obvious evidence of conflict as in nearly all the Pueblos of the Southwest. Issues have ranged from the divisiveness caused by the introduction from Oklahoma and establishment of Peyotism (1907) to the rebellion and dissatisfaction of returning World War II veterans (1950s) to the installation of electricity on parts of the reservation but outside the old village (1970s). Factionalism is almost constant in life at Taos, and it predates the conflict generated by acculturation to the Spanish and Anglo worlds. It has been argued that the causes lie deep in the nature of Pueblo culture.

Religion and Expressive Culture

Religious Beliefs. Three religious systems are active at Taos: the kiva-based aboriginal religion, Catholicism to which nearly all belong at least nominally, and Peyotism. Taos is the only Pueblo where the Peyote religion was accepted. Membership today is small. The Indians have been most secretive concerning their kiva religion, so that a full understanding remains impossible. The six active subterranean kivas together with their constituent societies are Big Earring, Day, and Knife on the north side, Water, Old Axe, and Feather on the south. Extended and rigorous male initiation (six–eighteen months) between the ages of seven and ten culminate and are tribally validated at the annual August pilgrimage to Blue Lake. No non-Taos in this century have been permitted to observe these rites. The ceremonial round, with public performances as integral parts, generally follow Catholic ritual observances such as Saints' Days, Christmas, New Year's Day, and the like and are laced with aboriginal elements. They are paralleled by more or less constant kiva activity about which little has been revealed. There are a host of animistic spirits including prominently Father Sun, Mother Earth, and the cloud spirits. Except for the publicly performed ceremonials, the activities of the kiva societies are poorly described. Prayer sticks, corn meal, pollen, and other standard Pueblo ritual equipment, often referred to as "medicine," are used, but little is known of their true role and significance.

Religious Practitioners. Kiva priests conduct rituals aimed at community welfare and rites of intensification directed toward game animals and agriculture. A few men and women are skilled in the arts of individual curing.

Death and Afterlife. A Catholic mass is held at death with the deceased buried immediately following in the open area of the old mission church destroyed in 1847. It has served since then as the Pueblo cemetery. A four-day observance of general inactivity by the deceased's family follows and closes with a feast celebrating the departure of the dead person's soul to the abode of the cloud spirits in the depths of Blue Lake, although some today regard the Christian heaven as the final place for departed souls.

Bibliography

Bodine, John J. (1979). "Taos Pueblo." In *Handbook of North American Indians*. Vol. 9, *Southwest*, edited by Alfonso Ortiz, 255–267. Washington, D.C.: Smithsonian Institution.

Fenton, William N. (1957). *Factionalism at Taos Pueblo, New Mexico*. U.S. Bureau of American Ethnology, Anthropological Paper no. 56. Washington, D.C.

Parsons, Elsie Clews (1936). *Taos Pueblo*. General Series in Anthropology, no. 2. Menasha, Wis.

Smith, M. Estellie (1967). *Governing at Taos Pueblo*. Eastern New Mexico University Contributions in Anthropology, 2(1). Portales, N. Mex.

JOHN J. BODINE

Tenino

The Tenino (Melilema, Warms Springs Sahaptin), including the John Day (Tukspuch), Tyigh (Tygh, Attayes, Iyich), and Waiam (Wayam, Wayampam, Deschutes Indians), lived in north-central Oregon and south-central Washington along the Columbia River from the Deschutes River in the west to the Umatilla River in the east. They moved to the Yakima Indian Reservation in Washington and the Warm Springs Indian Reservation in Oregon. They spoke a Sahaptin language of the Penutian phylum.

Bibliography

Murdock, George Peter (1958). "Social Organization of the Tenino." In *Miscellanea Paul Rivet Octogenario Dicata*. Vol. 1, 299–315. México, D.F.: Editorial Cultura.

Teton

ETHNONYMS: Dakota, Lakota, Sioux, Teton Sioux, Titunwan, Western Sioux

Orientation

Identification. The Teton are an American Indian group now living predominantly on reservations in South Dakota and in Saskatchewan. The name "Teton" is a corruption of *Titunwan*, which conventionally is glossed "dwellers of the prairie" but which actually connotes the setting up of campsites. The root *ti* gives rise to the name of the popular dwelling *tipi*. Teton designates seven subdivisions of Lakota-speakers who migrated from aboriginal homes in the Great Lakes region to the Northern Plains. They are called "Oglala," "Sicangu" (or "Brule"), "Hunkpapa," "Itazipco" (or "Sans

Arcs"), "Sihasapa" (or "Blackfeet Sioux"), "Oohenunpa" (or "Two Kettle"), and "Mnikowoju." The Teton in turn are one of seven larger divisions collectively known as the "Oceti Sakowin," or "Seven Fireplaces," all of which lived originally in the Great Lakes region. The others are known as "Mdewakanton," "Sisseton," "Wahpeton," and "Wahpekute," collectively known as "Santee" and who speak Dakota; and the "Yankton" and "Yanktonais," who are called "Wiciyela" and speak Nakota, a dialect today associated with the Assiniboins. The only proper tribal designation for this group is "Titunwan," the Anglicized form "Teton," or the linguistic designation, "Lakota." All other terms are misnomers or redundant.

Location. Although the Teton's parent stock migrated from the Southeast, arriving in the region of Milles Lacs, Minnesota, in the sixteenth century, the term *Teton* and its variant forms, particularly the erroneous designation *Dakota* (proper for the eastern division only), were not identified until 1640, after which time migrating bands occupied a large swath of the northern plains in what is now North and South Dakota, parts of Montana, Wyoming, Colorado, and Nebraska. Today, most Teton live on reservations in South Dakota, while others, mainly descendants of fugitives of the Custer battle, fled to small reserves in Canada. A large segment of the population lives in urban areas such as Chicago, Denver, Los Angeles, Rapid City (South Dakota), and San Francisco.

Demography. Early population estimates are meager and largely unreliable. In 1825, however, the Brules were estimated at three thousand; the Oglala at fifteen hundred; and the combined other five at three thousand. These estimates are probably much too low. The current population is similarly difficult to estimate because of intermarriage between Teton and other Indians and non-Indians. But based on estimates derived from population figures for the predominantly Teton reservations in South Dakota and Canada, a current population of sixty-five thousand seems reasonable.

Linguistic Affiliation. The Teton speak a dialect of a newly proposed subfamily of the Siouan language family called Shakowinian, whose other two members include Dakota and Nakota. Today Nakota (or Nakoda) is spoken almost exclusively by the Assiniboins, and most Yankton and Yanktonais speak Dakota. Traces of the Nakota dialect, however, are still found among contemporary Lakota- and Dakota-speakers.

History and Cultural Relations

By the beginning of the sixteenth century the Teton and other members of the Oceti Sakowin had established themselves on the headwaters of the Mississippi River, where they lived in semisedentary villages raising maize, squash, and beans and supplementing their diets by hunting and fishing. They were first encountered by Jean Nicolet, who named them "Sioux," a French corruption of an Algonkian word, *Nadowesiih*, meaning "snakes" or "enemies," which, despite its prevalent use in historical and anthropological literature, is a derogatory term.

After wars with Cree and Ojibwa enemies, who by 1750 were better armed through European contact, some of the Oceti Sakowin began migrating onto the prairies and plains.

Within a generation they became acclimated to a nomadic, bison-hunting way of life. By this date they also had obtained horses from the Arikara and other riverine tribes and soon became adapted to an equestrian way of life.

Although the term *Lakota* translates as "allied" or "affiliated," early observers reported that when the Tetons were not fighting other tribes, they were fighting each other. By 1778, according to their own hide-painted calendars known as winter counts, they had chased out almost all aboriginal inhabitants of the Black Hills region except the Cheyenne and Arapaho and had taken over the land as their own.

The Teton are also known for various skirmishes and battles with the U.S. government during the Indian wars of the 1860s and 1870s. Most notable of these was the Battle of the Little Big Horn, or "Custer's Last Stand," when on June 25, 1876, Custer and most of the Seventh Cavalry were annihilated by a combined force of Tetons, Cheyennes, and Arapahos. Most infamous was the Wounded Knee Massacre of December 19, 1890, where 260 men, women, and children mainly of Big Foot's band were massacred by remnants of Custer's Seventh and Ninth Cavalries during the Ghost Dance movement of 1889–1890. The names of great Teton leaders include Red Cloud, Crazy Horse, Sitting Bull, Rain in the Face, Gall, American Horse, and Young Man Afraid of Horse.

Settlements

In aboriginal times, the Teton lived in tipi camps that fluctuated according to the seasons. During winter, camps were smaller and clustered in wooded ravines where small herds of bison and other game were hunted. In summer, the bands joined for their annual religious ceremony, the Sun Dance, and for the communal bison hunt. In 1868, the Treaty of Fort Laramie between the Great Sioux Nation and the U.S. government established the boundaries of the Great Sioux Reservation located primarily in South Dakota. The roving bands settled down to form the nuclei of the present towns on the reservations. After 1887, Indian land was divided into individual ownership and the Great Sioux Reservation was severely diminished. Today, the Teton live predominantly on six reservations: Pine Ridge (the second largest reservation in the United States), Rosebud, Cheyenne River, Lower Brule, Crow Creek, and Standing Rock (the latter lying partly in North Dakota). Other Tetons live on small reserves in Saskatchewan, mainly remnants of Sitting Bull's band, who fled to Canada after the Custer battle. Over time, tipis gave way to four-walled tents, and then to log cabins and frame houses. Although tipis and tents are still used at ceremonial events, most Tetons live in frame and brick houses on the reservations.

Economy

Subsistence and Commercial Activities. The Teton are primarily associated with bison hunting. In aboriginal times, men, women, and children stampeded herds over cliffs where they would be killed in the fall and then butchered. Later, after the advent of the horse, bison hunting was an equestrian pursuit, both dangerous and thrilling. Most bison were originally hunted with bows and arrows and lances, and later with rifles. The entire bison was utilized for food, clothing, and shelter. Additionally, various species of roots and berries, such as *pomme blanche* or prairie turnips, and chokecherries, buffalo berries, and sand cherries were dried and used through the hard winters. Small game, deer, and elk were also stalked by individual hunters, and their meat and hides were utilized.

After the establishment of the reservations and land allotments, many Teton turned to farming and ranching, both successful enterprises until the Great Depression hit, when many lost their source of income and were never able to recoup. Since World War I, many Teton landowners have made their living by leasing their rich pastures to non-Indian ranchers. Others have invested in individual enterprises such as service stations, grocery stores, and small appliance stores, although many of the larger businesses such as supermarkets are owned by non-Indians. Arts and crafts provide a living for a few who continue to make quillwork and beadwork. About one-third of the work force is employed by the federal government in various agencies of the Bureau of Indian Affairs and the Indian Health Service. An undisclosed number are welfare recipients. Pursuant to treaty stipulations, all enrolled members of the various Teton reservations are eligible to receive annuities, mainly in the form of food, each month.

Industrial Arts. Aboriginal crafts include pictographic hide painting and ornamentation with porcupine quillwork. After the introduction of trade goods, Teton women were particularly known for their elaborate and voluminous beadwork. One of the most outstanding art forms associated with Teton today are their handmade star quilts, originally learned while at school and modeled after those made by the Amish of Pennsylvania. The star quilt is used for all sorts of traditional occasions from cradle to grave, and many of them are in great demand by trading posts and stores catering to the South Dakota tourist trade. The Red Cloud Indian Art Show, sponsored by the Holy Rosary Mission at Pine Ridge, is one of the largest in the country and has produced a number of outstanding Teton artists.

Trade. During the latter part of the eighteenth century, the Teton engaged in trade fairs with other Plains tribes. Trade with Europeans began at the turn of the nineteenth century, and for the first quarter of that century trade was monopolized by French traders from St. Louis. Many Teton bear French surnames today as a result of marriages between French traders and Teton women. Later, the Teton traded with the American Fur Company and the Rocky Mountain Fur Company, and by 1850 trade goods such as beads, blankets, hair pipes, and metal axes, blades, and cooking utensils dominated Teton culture.

Division of Labor. The harsh vicissitudes of the plains required cooperation between males and females. Although men actually hunted bison, women and children accompanied them on the hunt to help kill animals wounded in the chase. Butchering was the primary job of women, but men assisted them when necessary. Women were responsible for collecting fruits, berries, and tubers, but some fruits were collected by men. Making the tipi and clothing was in the domain of females, but men made and decorated ceremonial and war objects. After marriage, however, the tipi and its belongings were considered the property of the woman, and hunting and war implements were owned by men. Today, both men and women share equal positions in the business place as well as in tribal politics, the judicial system, the In-

dian Health Service, and the reservation school system. A fairly larger percentage of women attend colleges and universities located on and off the reservations.

Land Tenure. Being nomadic, the Teton did not have a concept of land tenure until after the Indian Allotment Act of 1887, when reservation lands were issued in fee patent.

Kinship

Kin Groups and Descent. Although kinship terminology suggests that the Teton earlier were organized into matrilineal clans, once they had migrated onto the plains their descent system gave way to a bilateral form of organization. Somewhat reminiscent of an earlier clan system is the Teton unit called *tiyospaye*, a named unit into which people are born and within which men and women cannot intermarry. Although age stratification exists among a number of surrounding plains tribes, the Teton do not exhibit such characteristics.

Kinship Terminology. Traditional kinship terminology follows the Iroquoian system.

Marriage and Family

Marriage. Although there is evidence for an earlier form of preferred cross-cousin marriage, once the Teton reached the plains males and females who did not share a common grandfather were eligible to marry. The ceremony itself was essentially an exchange of gifts between the parents of the couple. Frequently, the marriage was solidified when the groom gave horses to his prospective in-laws, and the female made a tipi and moccasins for her intended husband. Occasionally, the husband provided bride-service for his in-laws for a year. Upon marriage, the parents of the couple adopted a special relationship of co-parenthood. Polygyny was socially acceptable but rare.

Domestic Unit. Tiyospayes were divided into groups of extended families called *wicotis*, a pattern maintained today.

Inheritance. Inheritance was irrelevant to nomadic living. After the establishment of the reservation, however, inheritance followed local American law.

Socialization. Values were instilled in girls by their mothers and grandmothers, and in boys, by their fathers and grandfathers. Ridicule was the strongest form of control, and corporal punishment was eschewed.

Sociopolitical Organization

Social Organization. The Teton were divided into seven tiyospayes prior to the reservation period: the *Payabya*, "head circle"; *Tapisleca* "spleen"; *Kiyaksa*, "breakers of the rule"; *Wajaje*, "Osage"; *Itesica* "bad faces"; *Oyuhpe*, "untidy"; and *Wagluhe*, "loafers." Each tiyospaye was in turn divided into a constantly changing number of wicotis, themselves composed of extended monogamous or polygynous families. The minimal social unit is called *tiwahe*, "family."

Political Organization. Prior to contact, Teton wicoti were under the ad hoc leadership of a chief proficient in hunting and warfare. In the summer, however, when the bands came together for the communal hunt, the entire camp was under the supervision of a group of chiefs called *wakicunze*, who determined when the camps should move and hunts and ceremonials begin. After the reservation period, some of these wakicunze represented their tribes in treaties with the United States. But it is generally accepted that the position of head chief never existed in aboriginal times. After the Indian Reorganization Act of 1934, the Teton reservations formed tribal councils whose officers were elected by ballot every two years. This is the present form of government.

Social Control. During the summer encampments, various sodalities called *akicita* (soldier or marshal) were in charge of policing the camp and ensuring that the bison hunt would not be jeopardized by overzealous individuals. Under the authority of the wakicunze, the akicita could severely punish or even kill offenders. A number of these sodalities, known by such names as Strong Hearts, Foxes, Crow-Owners, and Badgers, also waged personal vendettas against tribes in retaliation for those lost in battle. Members were elected, and great prestige accrued to them.

Conflict. After the establishment of the reservation, conflict arose between several of the Teton chiefs. Sitting Bull and Crazy Horse, both heroes of the Custer battle, were assassinated by their own people as a result of jealousy and a rising fear among Whites that they might regain power. Red Cloud was perhaps the most controversial in that he advocated friendly relations with the United States after earning the reputation of being the only Indian to win a war against the U.S. government. A number of tiyospayes engaged in rivalry with each other, and much factionalism on the Teton reservations still persists along earlier lines of social and political organization.

Religion and Expressive Culture

Religious Beliefs. The Teton have a subterranean origin story in which humans were led to the surface of the earth by Inktomi, the trickster-culture hero, who then abandoned them. The earth and sky were formed after the supernaturals were sent there by Takuskanskan, the prime mover, partly as punishments and rewards for social transgressions. All animate and inanimate objects are capable of having a soul, and supernatural beings and objects are propitiated to maintain or restore harmony between good and evil. The earth is called the lodge of the wind, in which reside the Four Directions, the spirits of the zenith and nadir, and the center of the universe, each of which maintains animal and bird guardian spirits whose help may be invoked through smoking the sacred pipe. Although nearly every Christian denomination is represented on the reservations, most Tetons are only nominal Christians and still respect the beliefs of their ancestors.

Religious Practitioners. Teton differentiate between *wapiye,* or people who mediate between the common people and supernaturals through prayer and self-abnegation, and *pejuta wicasa/winyan,* medicine men and women who cure by means of prayer and herbs. Many of the men and women became active in the Ghost Dance movement of 1889–1890, and still later as lay catechists at mainly Jesuit missions. To a much lesser extent, some Teton also conduct meetings of the Native American church.

Ceremonies. There are seven major ceremonies believed to have been brought to the Teton by the White Buffalo Calf Woman in aboriginal times: Sweat Lodge, Vision Quest, Sun Dance, Ghost-Keeping Ceremony, Making of Relatives, Girl's Puberty Ceremony, and Sacred Ball Game. Other contemporary ceremonies include the pipe ceremony and *Yuwipi,* a modern curing ceremony.

Arts. Music and dance play an important part in Teton performance arts. Songs continue to be composed in the native idiom, and the Teton produce some of the best singers on the northern plains. Individual reenactments of visions, such as the Horse Dance, are still occasionally performed.

Medicine. Although the Indian Health Service maintains hospitals and clinics on Teton reservations, Native wapiye and medicine men and women continue to provide treatment to patients through the implementation of at least eighty kinds of herbal medicines. The sweat lodge is still used for spiritual and salutary purposes.

Death and Afterlife. The Teton believe that each individual has four aspects of soul. The last may be inhered in another individual at birth, and thus this constitutes a reincarnation system. Some deceased are forever required to be ghosts. Twins are considered special and are believed to pre-exist and select the families into which they wish to be born. The Milky Way is considered the path of the campfires of the deceased en route to the Spirit Village. In aboriginal times, the dead were buried mainly on scaffolds, but since the reservation, Christian cemeteries have been used. Funeral rites tend to be a mixture of traditional and Christian belief and ritual, and traditionalists continue to ritually keep the spirit of the deceased for one year, after which it is released at a memorial feast.

Bibliography

Hyde, George E. (1937). *Red Cloud's Folk: A History of the Oglala Sioux Indians.* Norman: University of Oklahoma Press.

Hyde, George E. (1961). *Spotted Tail's Folk: A History of the Brule Sioux.* Norman: University of Oklahoma Press.

Powers, Marla N. (1986). *Oglala Women: Myth, Ritual and Reality.* Chicago: University of Chicago Press.

Powers, William K. (1977). *Oglala Religion.* Lincoln: University of Nebraska Press.

Powers, William K. (1982). *Yuwipi: Vision and Experience in Oglala Ritual.* Lincoln: University of Nebraska Press.

Vestal, Stanley (1957). *Sitting Bull: Champion of the Sioux.* 2nd ed. Norman: University of Oklahoma Press.

WILLIAM K. POWERS

Tewa Pueblos

ETHNONYMS: T'owa, Teguas (Spanish), Tano-Tewa

Orientation

Identification. The name "Tewa" refers to linguistically related American Indian peoples who live in seven distinct communities referred to as "pueblos," the name applied to them by the Spanish colonists in the late 1500s.

Location. The Tewa-speaking Pueblo peoples live, as they have since aboriginal times, in the southwestern United States. Six Tewa pueblos are located adjacent to the Rio Grande in central/north-central New Mexico and one is located on a mesa in northeastern Arizona. The New Mexico Tewa pueblos are San Juan Pueblo, Santa Clara Pueblo, San Ildefonso Pueblo, Tesuque Pueblo, Pojoaque Pueblo, and Nambe Pueblo. The Arizona Pueblo, referred to as Hopi-Tewa because their culture is similar to the Hopi on First Mesa, is Hano at First Mesa. The Hano Tewa lived in New Mexico until they fled following the 1696 Pueblo Revolt (_see_ Hopi and Hopi-Tewa for more information).

Demography. In 1988, the total enrolled membership of the New Mexico Tewa reservation populations was 4,546. Individual pueblo enrollments were San Juan Pueblo, 1,936; Santa Clara Pueblo, 1,253; San Ildefonso Pueblo, 556; Tesuque Pueblo, 329; Pojoaque Pueblo, 76; and Nambe Pueblo, 396. In 1975, there were 625 enrolled Hopi-Tewa at Hano. Most Tewa live on or near their home pueblo, but others live in urban areas throughout the United States. In 1630, or about ninety years after Spanish contact, there were about 2,200 Tewa living in the six New Mexico pueblos. In 1900 an estimated 1,200 Tewa lived on these reservations.

Linguistic Affiliation. The Tewa language is one of three Tanoan languages; the other two are Tiwa and Towa. There are dialectical differences among the seven Tewa Pueblos.

History and Cultural Relations

Tewa culture shares many features with other Southwest Pueblos and derives from the pre-Pueblo peoples and cultures known as Anasazi, whose origins are found in archaeological sites at Mesa Verde in southwestern Colorado and extend southward following the courses of the upper Rio Grande and Chama Rivers in New Mexico and the San Juan River in Arizona. In 1598, the Spanish conquistador Juan de Oñate established the Spanish capital of New Mexico at Yungue, a Tewa village located across the river from San Juan Pueblo. The capital was subsequently moved to San Juan Pueblo. From this locale, Oñate and his men subjected the Tewa and other Pueblo peoples to extraordinarily harsh rule in an attempt to force their conversion to Catholicism. Missions were established in all the pueblos. The capital was moved to Santa Fe in 1609 when Pedro de Peralta replaced Oñate. By 1680, the Pueblo peoples had developed a plan to remove the yoke of colonial oppression, successfully forcing the Spanish south of the Rio Grande in the Pueblo Revolt of 1680. In 1692, Diego de Vargas began the reconquest of the Pueblos, securely reestablishing Santa Fe as the Spanish capital in 1694. In 1696, a second Pueblo revolt occurred but was quickly put down. Apache and Navajo raids for food and captives, which had increased during this period, intensified and soon the Pueblos were taking advantage of Spanish military assistance.

When Mexico gained independence from Spain, Christianized Indians were granted citizenship. In 1858, when the United States acquired New Mexico and other Southwestern regions, the Treaty of Guadalupe Hidalgo promised citizenship to all Mexican citizens of the region who wished it, including the Pueblos. In 1912, it was necessary for the Pueblo of San Juan to sue the U.S. government in order to gain the status of American Indian so that native land and water rights and religious and individual rights could be protected. Hispanic and Anglo-Americans had moved onto Pueblo lands, and many Pueblos had lost their best agricultural areas. In 1920, the United States established the Pueblo Lands Board to settle disputed claims. Eventually, the Tewa gained full citizenship status while retaining indigenous rights to land, water, and religious expression, which, however, have most often been secured only through litigation in federal courts.

Settlements

At the time of Oñate's arrival at Yungue, there were unknown numbers of villages occupied by the Tewa. In 1630, Fray Alonso de Benavides is reported to have listed eight Tewa pueblos with a total population as high as six thousand. Today, hundreds of Pueblo ruins in north-central and northwestern New Mexico have been identified by archaeologists as ancestral sites for contemporary Rio Grande Pueblos; at least sixty pueblos were abandoned in historical times. The number of these that can be directly tied to Tewa villages is uncertain because most of the sites have not been fully investigated. Between the arrival of the Spanish and up to the early 1900s population densities within the pueblos fluctuated, with periods of severe decline in numbers owing to diseases first introduced by the Spanish, warfare, and total abandonment of villages as the peace-loving Pueblos sought to escape the pressures brought on by European expansion.

Population density for the Tewa Pueblos began to rise slowly in the early 1900s and showed a steady climb after the Pueblo Lands Board settled the land claims in 1920. Between 1950 and 1964, population in all six of the Tewa Pueblos nearly doubled. Maternal and infant mortality rates were reduced through better health care. Improved nutrition (largely due to an increase in economic opportunities) and water and sewage systems also contributed to lower morbidity rates. Today housing is of several types. Some families live in the center of their pueblo in homes built originally by their ancestors as long as 350 years ago; they retain their original adobe walls but have been modernized with new roofs, windows, electricity, and water and sewage systems. These homes are built in clusters around central plazas where ceremonial activities take place. Other people live in homes built as single-family dwellings at some distance from the pueblo center and are made of cinder blocks covered with stucco, wood, or stabilized adobe. The kivas, or religious centers, are also located near the plazas, as are the tribal offices and Catholic church. All six New Mexico pueblos have most of the following, which may be located in the same area on a given reservation:

arts and crafts store, senior citizen center, schools, recreation center, library, and health clinic.

Economy

Subsistence and Commercial Activities.   The Tewa were horticulturalists who developed hydraulic irrigation to water their principal crops of maize, beans, and squash. They also hunted deer, bison, elk, rabbit, birds, and other animals, and gathered berries, piñon nuts, wild greens, roots, and other fruits and vegetables. They made tea from several herbal plants. The introduction of new crops and animals by the Spanish enlarged their farming activities to include raising cows, pigs, chickens, chili and other spices, wheat, tomatoes, apples, pears, peaches, and other fruits. Iron kettles and pots were readily accepted for cooking, although pottery remained the main form of storage and eating vessels until the early 1920s. In the recent past, and still today, some people, make and sell pottery as their primary source of income; for other people, making pottery, jewelry and woven goods supplies supplemental income. Today, most people depend on wage labor, welfare, or Social Security or other pensions for their income.

Industrial Arts.   Aboriginal crafts included pottery making, weaving, and wood carving. Painted pottery was used for storage, cooking, and eating, as well as for trade with other tribes. Hides from deer, rabbits, and other game were made into clothing and shoes; cotton was woven for clothing. After a period of decline in pottery making, it was revived as a commercial craft in the early twentieth century. Today, needlework, pottery, jewelry, and woven garments (such as belts and leggings) are made for sale or trade, ceremonial or other personal use, or decoration.

Trade.   An extensive trade network existed throughout the Southwest prior to Spanish contact. Items from as far away as California, central Mexico, the lower Mississippi Valley, the Great Plains to the east, and the great basin to the north appear in old Pueblo ruins. Salt was traded into some pueblos. Trading with people of the plains, the great basin, and Mexico as well as with non-Indians continued to take place well into the twentieth century. Basketry from the Apache and Papago are highly prized; feathers, shells, and beads from Mexico are highly prized for religious and decorative purposes. Trading with other tribes continues today at the Eight Northern Indian Pueblos Arts and Crafts Show, the Santa Fe Indian Market, and other such events held each year.

Division of Labor.   Women were responsible for building and maintaining the homes until the mid-1970s. They gathered plants and insects, processed and stored the harvest, prepared the meals and made pottery. Men were responsible for planting, tending, and harvesting the crops and for hunting. They wove cotton for clothing and carved wooden utensils and ceremonial objects. Although women were primarily responsible for child care, it has regularly been noted from the earliest accounts to the present that men also engage in child care on a daily basis. Since World War II, women and men have sought employment in diverse occupations, and many have held professional positions, both on and off the reservations. Men hold most political and religious offices, but both women and men are involved in community political and religious affairs.

Land Tenure.   Land belongs to the tribe but is assigned to Pueblo members on the basis of need for farming or housing. Once a piece of land has been assigned to an individual, it may be passed to offspring for their use or traded to a pueblo member or to the tribe in exchange for another piece of land or other recompense; the tribe may reclaim it for reassignment if it goes unused. Pueblo land cannot be sold to nontribal members.

Kinship

Kin Groups and Descent.   The Tewa of New Mexico reckon kinship bilaterally, while the Hopi-Tewa of Arizona are matrilineal. The kinship grouping of the New Mexico Tewa reflects their dual social organization, which consists of nonexogamous nonunilinear moieties: every Tewa belongs to either the Winter or Summer moiety. These moieties are the largest kin groups for the Tewa; however, moieties are more than kinship entities (see Social Organization and Religion below). Hopi-Tewa society is divided into exogamous matrilineal clans.

Kinship Terminology.   Tewa kinship terms are mostly descriptive and generational and designate the precise relationship to a speaker. Hopi-Tewa terms follow the Crow system.

Marriage and Family

Marriage.   Marriage within one's own moiety is preferred by many Tewa, but in any case a spouse may not be closer than a fourth cousin. The marriage ceremony usually includes a native ritual as well as a church or other nonnative ritual (such as marriage by a justice of the peace). Marriage is monogamous and sexual fidelity is expected, although divorce and infidelity have been known since the time of first contact. There is no official postmarital residence rule, but in some families pressure is put on the couple to spend the first year of marriage in the home of the husband's mother before establishing a neolocal residence.

Domestic Unit.   Small extended families have been the predominant household composition until recently. Since the late 1970s increased numbers of single-family housing units on most Tewa reservations have resulted in younger families establishing homes away from their parents' house. Economic conditions for some families lead to maintenance of a three-generation household, with many older Tewa preferring such an arrangement.

Inheritance.   Inheritance, like kinship reckoning, is bilateral with a preference for dividing property equitably among all offspring. Lands left intestate (that is, without a written or verbal statement or will having been left by the person to whom it was assigned) may be recovered by the tribe, but usually will be divided among the children by a tribal official. Personal property may be divided among relatives and friends following the funeral of a deceased person or it may accompany the deceased to the grave. Traditionally, daughters inherited their mother's house, but this has changed in recent years on some reservations.

Socialization.   Socialization takes place well into the middle years. From birth to middle age, specific rituals move individuals through various states of being and becoming Tewa. Children are raised relatively permissively until about age six.

By age ten girls and boys have been separated into two groups for instruction in the kivas for fulfilling their responsibilities as women and men in their pueblo. Children of Catholic families also send their children to the church for instruction and preparation for First Communion. Today, families also place great emphasis on education for their children and may begin sending them to school in the Head Start program as early as age four. Tribal encouragement for higher education in public or private colleges is noted in educational grants and subsidies available through the Eight Northern Indian Pueblos Council. Both women and men are responsible for child-rearing activities, including nurturing and protecting them, as are all adults residing in the community.

Sociopolitical Organization

Social Organization. Tewa social organization is centered around two nonexogamous nonunilinear complementary moieties: Winter and Summer. People become members of either one through a series of rituals that take place from birth to their early twenties. Tewa place high value on equality and humility. There are, however, differential statuses accorded individuals on the basis of their degree of ascension, through ritual, and placement within the life and spiritual hierarchies. Equality between the sexes is expressed through the complementarity of women's and men's roles and responsibilities: women are responsible for the homes and the inner portions of the pueblo; men are responsible for the fields and the outer portions. Men are also responsible for village decision making, although women participate, too.

Political Organization. Since aboriginal times, the core Tewa governmental structure has been a theocracy, with political and sacred authority vested in the heads of the two moieties and the religious sodalities. In the early 1600s, the Spanish instituted a secular political structure consisting of the following officers who are selected by the tribal council on advice from sodality and moiety heads in all but Santa Clara and Pojoaque Pueblos: governor, first lieutenant governor, second lieutenant governor, war chief, assistant war chief, sheriff, and fiscales. These officers are responsible for daily management of tribal affairs, as well as for special community events. Santa Clara Pueblo has a constitutional government with public officers elected by adult enrolled members. Most Tewa reservations also have tribal managers who are responsible for programmatic and economic maintenance and development on their reservations. The six New Mexico Tewa pueblos are part of the Eight Northern Indian Pueblos Council, a sociopolitical organization that facilitates sharing of economic, political, educational, and development resources among the Pueblos.

Social Control. Social control is exercised through gossip, teasing, mockery by clowns and _abuelos_ at public ceremonial events, and formal visits by officials to homes of individuals who seriously violate social norms. Crimes against property or individuals are adjudicated in tribal or local courts, depending on the nature of the crime. Serious crimes, such as homicide, are tried in a federal court. Accusations of witchcraft (rare today) may be handled by the medicine man or through the tribal court.

Conflict. The Tewa have a reputation for nonviolence and peaceful settlement of disputes. In aboriginal times and until the U.S. government designated the Tewa pueblos to be limited and bounded reservations, internal conflict that resulted in fissioning could be resolved by a group leaving their natal Pueblo and establishing a new one elsewhere. Movement of a whole community to a new locale could also follow severe externally induced conflict (for example, the Hopi-Tewa of Arizona; see Location above). Overall, most Tewa abhor conflict and will avoid it at all cost, although in recent years, domestic and other forms of interpersonal violence seem to have increased. Internal conflict is usually arbitrated or adjudicated by the tribal council or tribal court. Conflict with outsiders is generally resolved through the local court systems, but some cases have gone as far as the U.S. Supreme Court for settlement.

Religion and Expressive Culture

Religious Beliefs. Religion is _the_ pervading aspect of Pueblo life; it encompasses mythology, cosmology, philosophy, and worldview for the Tewa. It is the life-way through which people aspire to live. It is also one of the most sensitive areas of Tewa life, with only the religious sodality leaders in each pueblo knowing details of their respective systems of belief. Some aspects of religious beliefs that have come to be known outside of the sodality environments involve attribution of the sacred to, and respect and reverence for, the earth (from which all people come and to which all people return), the mountains (where dwell the spirits of the _Towa'e_, or founding brothers of the Tewa), the hills, water, and certain animals, birds, and plants. Polytheism is present in the form of belief in a range of supernatural spiritual forces and entities; because of this, Catholicism over the past two hundred years or so has come to fit easily within the native religious framework.

Religious Practitioners. The principal religious practitioners are the Winter and Summer moiety heads and the sodality heads, as established by the Tewa origin story. The sodalities are referred to in English as the Hunt Society, the Medicine Society, the Clown Society, the Scalp Society, and the Women's Society.

Ceremonies. Ritual ceremonies are performed following a calendrical cycle. Some rituals are specifically associated with subsistence, and others are concerned with individual and community developmental cycles. Each ritual is the responsibility of a particular sodality head, and most are not public. Rituals that are public and may be viewed by outsiders are held in the pueblo plazas. A list of dates for such ceremonies is published each year by the Eight Northern Indian Pueblos Council, located at San Juan Pueblo.

Arts. Tewa art includes highly prized black-on-black pottery made by artists at Santa Clara and San Ildefonso Pueblos and red pottery made at San Juan and Santa Clara pueblos, silverwork, silver and turquoise jewelry, paintings, sculpture, and fabric art made by artists at all the pueblos. Ceremonial songs, dances, and clothing are attended to with great aesthetic care.

Medicine. Herbal teas, poultices, massage, and food taboos (observed during various phases of an individual's development cycle) are all part of routine health care and maintenance. A person who becomes ill or suffers an injury may, as has been true since before contact, ask for assistance from one of the medicine men or from a woman healer, or they may go directly to a local Indian health clinic or physician's office for treatment. Often people use a combination of diagnostic and treatment sources.

Death and Afterlife.   Death occurs as a result of old age, disease, accident, maltreatment of one's own body (such as misuse of alcohol or other drugs), and evil spirits. Funerals are held for the deceased as soon as possible, following a day or more of lying in state. During this time, family and friends visit the deceased and their close kin to pay their respects. The funeral ceremony usually combines native and Catholic religious elements, and burial usually takes place in the graveyard at the pueblo where the deceased lived. The spirit of a deceased person is thought to stay close to the pueblo for several days following death. Various measures are used to protect the living from untoward response to such spirits. On the fourth day a releasing rite is held by family and community elders so that the spirit of the deceased is freed and encouraged to join other departed spirits.

Bibliography

Dozier, Edward P. (1966). *Hano: A Tewa Indian Community in Arizona*. New York: Holt, Rinehart & Winston.

Dozier, Edward P. (1970). *The Pueblo Indians of North America*. New York: Holt, Rinehart & Winston.

Ortiz, Alfonso (1969). *The Tewa World: Space, Time, Being and Becoming in a Pueblo Society*. Chicago: University of Chicago Press.

Ortiz, Alfonso, ed. (1972). *New Perspectives on the Pueblos*. Albuquerque: University of New Mexico Press.

Ortiz, Alfonso, ed. (1979). *Handbook of North American Indians*. Vol. 9, *Southwest*. Washington, D.C.: Smithsonian Institution.

Sando, Joe S. (1976). *The Pueblo Indians*. San Francisco: Indian Historian Press.

SUE-ELLEN JACOBS

Thompson

ETHNONYMS: Knife Indians, Snare, Thompson River Indians
    The Thompson (Nlaka'pamux, Ntlakyapamuk) are an American Indian group who live on the Fraser and Thompson rivers in south-central British Columbia. They speak an Interior Salish language closely related to Shuswap and numbered 2,647 in 1967, an increase from the 1902 estimate of 1,825. Internally, they were divided into the Lower Thompson, who lived from just below Spuzzum on the Fraser River nearly to the village of Cisco and the Upper Thompson, whose towns extended from the latter point nearly to Lillooet on the Fraser River, to within a short distance of Ashcroft on the Thompson River, and in the Nicola Valley. Today, about fifteen bands live in the area. The Thompson were probably first contacted by Simon Fraser during his explorations in 1809. The traditional culture was modified by influences from Victoria established in the 1840s, the gold miners and settlers who arrived in increasing numbers in the 1850s, and the smallpox epidemics of 1863 and the 1880s which reduced the aboriginal population of about 5,000. By the turn of century, most Thompson were somewhat assimilated into European-Canadian society, as they moved into areas of White settlement where they worked as wage laborers and farmed, hunted, and fished.

The traditional bands were individual groups of related families with hereditary chiefs with limited authority. More powerful were the councils composed of mature men. Salmon was the staple food, often caught from wooden fishing stages built over fish runs, with dip nets and spears used as well as traps and weirs. The salmon were dried on poles. Various mammals such as deer, bear, beaver, and elk were hunted, and women collected berries, fruits, roots, and nuts.

Traditionally, the Thompson were seminomadic. In the summer, mat tipis (and later canvas tipis and then tents) were moved to different hunting grounds and berry patches as the season progressed. They also used more permanent semi-subterranean earthlodges. The material culture included birchbark canoes, coiled baskets, drums, double-curved bows, snowshoes, goat wool and rabbit fur blankets, and skin clothing.

Pubescent girls were segregated in small tipis, and dome-shaped sweat lodges covered with mats or canvas were also used. The latter were used by adolescent boys during their quest for guardian spirits. Shamans and curers worked with the aid of these spirits, which were generally animal in nature. The Thompson believed in numerous deities, a major one being the Chief of the Dead. Important ceremonials were the puberty rites for girls, the First Salmon Ceremony, and various dances.

Bibliography

Teit, James A. (1898). *Traditions of the Thompson River Indians*. American Folklore Society, Memoir no. 6. Philadelphia, Pa.

Teit, James A. (1900). *The Thompson Indians of British Columbia*. American Museum of Natural History Memoirs, vol. 2, 163–392. New York.

Tepper, Leslie H., ed. (1987). *The Interior Salish Tribes of British Columbia: A Photographic Essay*. Canadian Museum of Civilization, Mercury Series, Canadian Ethnology Service, Paper no. 111. Ottawa.

Tillamook

The Tillamook (Calamox, Gillamooks), including the Nehalem, Nestucca, and Siletz, lived along the northern Oregon coast from the Nehalem River to the Salmon River. They spoke a Coast Salish language and numbered 139 in 1970.

Bibliography

Pearson, Clara (1959). *Nehalem Tillamook Tales*. Edited by Melville Jacobs. University of Oregon Monographs, Studies in Anthropology, no. 5. Eugene.

Sauter, John, and Bruce Merton (1974). *Tillamook Indians of the Oregon Coast*. Portland: Binfords and Mort.

Tlingit

ETHNONYMS: Thlinget, Thlinkets, Tlinkit, Lleeengit

Orientation

Identification. The Tlingit are an American Indian group located in southern Alaska. "Tlingit" means "in the people."

Location. The Tlingit continue to occupy many of their aboriginal village sites along the southeastern coast of Alaska from Ketchikan to Yakutat—54°40′ N to about 60° N—and from the coast to Lake Atlin, or as the Tlingit say, the "second mountain range." This area includes many offshore islands, numerous streams emptying into inlets, and rugged mountains that jut up from the edge of the sea and whose snow-capped serrated peaks cover most of the area.

Demography. Conservative population estimates place the precontact population at ten thousand. The present Tlingit population numbers about twenty-five thousand.

Linguistic Affiliation. The Tlingit language is classified in the Na-Dene phylum. Among the coastal Tlingit, northern, central and southern dialects are still spoken by the elders.

History and Cultural Relations

Archaeological data suggest that a Tlingit or proto-Tlingit population inhabited the coast of southeastern Alaska by seven thousand B.C. Oral history traces several migration routes of Tlingit clans down various rivers that flowed from the interior to the sea, and linguistic data reveal a close affinity with interior groups. While the neighboring Haida and Tsimshian tribes were pushing some southern Tlingit northward, the northern Tlingit were expanding in Eyak and Eskimo territory. British, French, and Russian interests vied for control of Alaska with the United States acquiring final control over the rich Alaskan resources in 1867. Gunboat diplomacy instituted by the United States undermined local Tlingit autonomy and opened up the territory to outside settlers and gold prospectors. Alaskan natives fought back by organizing the Alaskan Native Brotherhood in 1912 to fight for their civil rights and subsistence resources. In 1929 the Tlingit began a struggle to regain control of their natural resources, resulting in the Alaska Native Claims Settlement Act of 1971 transferring some 100 million acres back to Alaskan natives.

Settlements

Early Tlingit settlers selected village sites near heavily resourced areas along protected sections of coastline ideal for beaching canoes, digging clams, acquiring drinking water, and catching migrating salmon. An expanding Tlingit population, increasing competition for local resources, and intensifying patterns of warfare contributed to the progressive development of four types of villages: the local household village, the localized clan village, the local moiety village, and the consolidated clan village. In early times, people lived in one large community longhouse, which served as shelter, storage place, and fort. Population increases and mounting tension contributed to the breakup of the large household into several smaller related lineage households sharing a common fort. Later, in a third settlement stage, two intermarrying clans from the two moieties moved together to reduce distances, share resources, and increase village security. Depopulation and depletion of subsistence resources following European contact contributed to the rise of a fourth settlement pattern, the consolidated clan village, composed of two or more clans from both moieties.

Economy

Subsistence and Commercial Activities. The Tlingit hunted deer, bear, seals, and goats; fished for salmon, halibut, and herring; and gathered roots, berries, and shellfish. Runs of salmon choked the local streams each year as five species of salmon migrated to their spawning grounds. Fishnets and gaffing hooks were used to haul in large quantities of salmon for smoking and drying for winter consumption. The rapid depletion of the population by foreign diseases and Increased reliance upon proceeds from fur trapping reduced subsistence resources while increasing dependence upon foreign trade goods. Today, the Tlingit value education, resulting in many members working in business, industry, government, and the professions.

Industrial Arts. Carving, basket making, Chilkat blanket weaving, beading, and metalworking were sources of income. Gold and silver coins shaped into bracelets, pendants, and rings were embellished with clan symbols. The active arts and crafts trade that began with the arrival of the early steamship tourists has grown in volume over the years, and several Tlingit villages now have dancing groups that perform for local ceremonies and for tourists.

Trade. An aboriginal trade network flourished between the interior Athapaskans and the Tlingit, between coastal and island Tlingit, and with the neighboring Eyak, Haida, Tsimshian, and Kwakiutl. Native trade goods such as coppers, shells, slaves, canoes, carvings, oulachan oil, and furs were later replaced by European trade goods, including guns, ammunition, knives, axes, blankets, and food.

Division of Labor. Prior to the decline of the traditional culture around 1880, Tlingit men hunted, fished, and carved, and women cleaned fish, gathered food, tanned hides, and wove baskets and blankets. Today, men drive diesel-powered boats equipped with hydraulic hoists and large nets, and women work in modern canneries and make button blankets or beaded moccasins from commercial materials.

Land Tenure. The localized clan was the basic holder of rights to fishing streams, tidelands, and hunting grounds in traditional Tlingit villages. Today, clans own ceremonial and symbolic ritual items. The 1971 Alaska Native Claims Settlement Act organized the Alaska Tlingit into one large regional corporation, called Sealaska. Sealaska received title to 330,000 acres of land and 660,000 acres of mineral rights; it had total assets of $216 million as of March 1988. Sealaska governs nine village corporations each of which received title to 20,040 acres of aboriginal land and hundreds of thousands of dollars in cash payments, depending upon the number of tribal members.

Kinship

Kin Groups and Descent. Tlingit society is divided into two large exogamous moieties—Raven-Crow and Eagle-Wolf (Crow for Inland Tlingit and Wolf for Southern Tlingit). Each moiety contains some twenty autonomous matriclans. Aboriginally, each exogamous localized matriclan had its own village and formed marriage alliances with other communities. Matriclans that intermarried with considerable frequency within a given region formed a *Kwaan*, or district, of which there were fourteen. Following depopulation and the depletion of resources, scattered clans within Kwaans moved together to form consolidated clan villages like Angoon, Hoonah, and Yakutat. Local matriclans were corporate groups holding title to property, real estate, and ceremonial objects. A matriclan consisted of one or more community longhouses in which descent was traced matrilineally. Lineage, clan, and moiety affiliations are still important for marriage and ceremonial purposes.

Kinship Terminology. Crow-type kinship terminology, once a characteristic of Tlingit society, is little used by younger members today.

Marriage and Family

Marriage. The preferential marriage pattern was patrilateral cross-cousin marriage—to father's sister's daughter; the second choice was a member of the paternal grandfather's or great-grandfather's clan; and a third choice was a member of any clan in the opposite moiety. Marriage within one's clan and moiety were strictly forbidden under penalty of death or ostracism. Arranged marriages have rapidly decreased during this century, although patrilateral marriages are still encouraged. Monogamy was the general rule among the lower classes, and polygamy was practiced by a few high-status men and women. Divorce was rare, as it was seen as an offense against the clans of both spouses. Marriage prohibitions within the clan and moiety are still subscribed to in principle, though broken frequently in practice.

Domestic Unit. Until the turn of the century, the lineage community longhouse served as the residential unit. Recent government housing projects have largely eliminated the need for community households. Presently, lineage and clan households have more symbolic than economic significance, serving as the repository for the ceremonial objects and as a symbol of clan identity.

Inheritance. Formerly, property was passed on within the matriclan with much of the wealth going from uncle to nephew. Presently, material possessions are inherited in typical American fashion, although ceremonial goods are still expected to be passed on in conformity with traditional rules.

Socialization. Many elders played an active role in the education of Tlingit youth. Aunts extolled the virtues of respectable clan leaders, and maternal uncles rigorously and rigidly guided their nephews through adolescence, teaching them basic hunting, fishing, carving, and fighting skills. Grandmothers or maternal aunts spend considerable time with pubescent girls, preparing them for childbearing and teaching them clan history and domestic skills such as food preparation, basket weaving, and basic hygiene. Elders still maintain a strong influence even among the large number of members who have attended college.

Sociopolitical Organization

Social Organization. The Tlingit were stratified into three social classes: (1) high-class *anyaddi*, (2) commoners, or *kanackideh*, and (3) low-class *nitckakaku*. Individuals and groups were also ranked within the clan and between clans, depending upon their wealth, titles, and achievements. High-class people managed and controlled strategic resources and used them to promote individual and group status. Class and rank remain important in Tlingit villages.

Political Organization. Each aboriginal settlement was owned by a localized clan whose claims were documented through stories and symbols, with other clans residing in their village viewed as guests. Leadership and councils at the household, clan, and local moiety levels were traditional political units and remain influential. Today, three ethnic associations address Tlingit concerns. The Alaska Native Brotherhood serves as cultural broker and advocate; the Tlingit-Haida Organization with some 14,500 members of Tlingit descent promotes housing and social welfare; and Sealaska, the largest corporation in Alaska, provides growing economic and political clout.

Social Control. Shame and rank were powerful motivators for enforcing traditional social norms. Individuals were said to define their status by the way they conducted themselves, with all ill-mannered persons bringing shame upon their lineage and clan. Thus, elders held a tight rein on youths. Fear of accusation of witchcraft or ridicule also influenced behavior. Several Tlingit villages now have their own mayor, city council, police force, and school boards along with other administrative services.

Conflict. Aboriginally, conflicts arose over assaults, insults, or damages suffered by individuals and groups to themselves or their property. Such conflicts were usually resolved through payment of wealth or, in some cases, killing the offender. Conflicts with Whites over the past century centered around aboriginal resources, civil rights, and civil liberties.

The persistence of these conflicts contributes to alcohol abuse and other drug abuse.

Religion and Expressive Culture

Religious Beliefs.   Early records suggest that the Tlingit believed in a creator, Kah-shu-goon-yah, whose name was sacred and never mentioned above a whisper. This primordial grandfather, or "divisible-rich-man," controlled the sun, moon, stars, and daylight in addition to creating all living things. Little more is known of him. The sacred past centers upon Raven (cultural hero, benefactor, trickster, and rascal) who was credited with organizing the world in its present form and in initiating many Tlingit customs. Raven was never represented, symbolized, or made equal with the supreme being who transcended Tlingit legends. The Tlingit inhabited a world filled with spirits, or _jek_. These spirits could manifest their power through individuals, animals, or things. Since every material object or physical force could be inhabited by a spirit, Tlingit were taught to respect everything in the universe. The penalty for disrespect was the loss of ability to obtain food. Properly purified persons could acquire spirit power for curing illnesses, for protection in warfare, for success in obtaining wealth, and for ceremonial prerogatives. Each Tlingit had a mortal and an immortal spirit.

Religious Practitioners.   Two options open to youths were to seek good power and help the community or to seek evil power and threaten the community. Every Tlingit had a personal guardian spirit, or _tu-kina-jek_. Spirit doctors, or _ichet_, received more powerful spirits and therefore could treat the sick with herbs, discern the presence of evil, predict the future, and protect the community from evil forces. Witches, or _nukw-sati_, sought evil power and used it to harm others.

Ceremonies.   Dancing societies never gained a major foothold in Tlingit society as they did in neighboring Northwest Coast tribes. The Tlingit sought their power primarily through their clan spirit doctor whom they trusted to help and not to harm them. Politicoreligious ceremonies called potlatches, or _koolex_, marked significant events in the life of the clan and its members. Sacred songs, dances, symbols, and stories accompanied all changes in social stature, political leadership, and ceremonial objects within the clan.

Arts.   Carving of house posts, heraldic screens, chiefs' hats, chiefs' staffs, and weaving of Chilkat blankets were highly acclaimed. Wood-carvers, metalworkers, and blanket weavers continue to use their traditional clan symbols (_kotea_) to indicate ownership and identity.

Medicine.   Every family possessed a basic knowledge of herbs and principles of hygiene and for the most part were medically self-sufficient. Occasionally, a spirit doctor, who possessed superior knowledge of herbal medicines and special spirit power, was called in for difficult cases after household remedies failed. Contemporary Tlingit do not hesitate to consult modern medical facilities when the need arises.

Death and Afterlife.   Spirits of the dead traveled to the appropriate level of heaven commensurate with their moral conduct in this life. Morally respectable people went to the highest heaven, _Kiwa-a_, a realm of happiness; moral delinquents went to a second level, or Dog Heaven, _Ketl-kiwa_, a place of torment. Individuals remained in the afterworld for a period of time and then returned to this world as a reincarnation of some deceased maternal relative.

Bibliography

Krause, Aurel (1970). _The Tlingit Indians_. Translated by Erna Gunther. Seattle: University of Washington Press. Originally published, 1885.

Laguna, Frederica de. (1972). _Under Mount Saint Elias: The History and Culture of the Yakutat Tlingit_. Washington, D.C.: Smithsonian Institution Press.

Oberg, Kalervo (1973). _The Social Economy of the Tlingit Indians_. Seattle: University of Washington Press. Originally published, 1937.

Tollefson, Kenneth (1976). "_The Cultural Foundations of Political Revitalization among the Tlingit_." Ph.D. diss., University of Washington.

KENNETH TOLLEFSON

Tolowa

ETHNONYMS: Talawa, Tah-le-wah

The Tolowa are an American Indian group numbering about two hundred whose ancestors in the early nineteenth century numbered about twenty-four hundred and were located in the Pacific coast region from the Oregon boundary of California south to Wilson Creek. In 1850 the California gold rush reached the Tolowa area, and in the latter part of the century the Tolowa population was decimated by measles and cholera. Subsequently, they were removed to small reservations and rancherias where most intermarried with other North American Indian groups.

The Tolowa spoke an Athapaskan language and were a fishing and gathering people. Traditionally, in the summers on the coast the Tolowa fished for smelt and hunted sea mammals from forty-foot redwood canoes; in the autumn they moved inland to temporary camps where they fished for salmon and gathered acorns. Prestige was gained through the accumulation of wealth, consisting primarily of obsidian knives, headdresses of red-headed woodpecker scalps and dentalium shell bead necklaces; the wealthiest man in a village was usually its headman.

The important religious ceremonies of the Tolowa were connected with catching the season's first salmon, smelt, or sea lion. Both men and women could serve as shamans and cured the sick by dancing, trancing, magical formulas, and sucking the sources of evil out of the afflicted. The dead were wrapped in tule mats and buried along with shell beads and other objects.

Bibliography

Drucker, Philip (1937). *The Tolowa and Their Southwestern Oregon Kin.* University of California Publications in American Archaeology and Ethnology 36, 221–300. Berkeley.

Gould, Richard (1968). "Seagoing Canoes among the Indians of Northwestern California." *Ethnohistory* 15:11–42.

Tonkawa

ETHNONYM: Konkone

The Tonkawa (Tátskan wátitch) group, which included the Cava, Emet, Ervipiame, Mayeye, Sana, Tohaha, Toho, Tusolivi, Ujuiap, Yojuane, and Tonkawa proper, lived until the mid-nineteenth century in east-central Texas in an area between Cibolo Creek on the southwest and Trinity River on the northeast. They spoke a language that may have been related to Karankawa, Comecrudo, and Cotoname within the Coahuiltecan stock, but is usually classified as a language isolate in the Macro-Algonkian phylum. The Tonkawa now live in a federal trust area in north-central Oklahoma and are known as the Tonkawa Tribe of Oklahoma. There were an estimated 1,600 Tonkawa in the seventeenth century, but epidemics, warfare, and massacres took their toll, and there were only 181 members enrolled in the tribe in 1984.

Although the Tonkawa no doubt encountered Cabeza de Vaca in 1542, sustained contact with Europeans did not begin until 1691. Between 1746 and 1749 the Tonkawa were gathered into missions on the San Xavier (San Gabriel) River, but these were given up in 1756. During the nineteenth century they were often at war with the Comanche, Lipan Apache, and Caddo, as well as with the Spanish. In 1862, 137 of a group of 300 Tonkawa were massacred by a mixed group of Delaware, Caddo, and Shawnee. In 1884, the surviving Tonkawa were given a reservation in Oklahoma, which later became the trust territory where they now reside.

Culturally, the Tonkawa displayed features of the southern Plains and Gulf regions. Their early acquisition of the horse and dependence on the bison and absence of sea resources suggest that during historic times they more closely fit the Plains pattern. The Tonkawa consisted of a number of autonomous bands who led a nomadic hunting and gathering life. The matrilineal clan was the basic social unit, with a number of clans making up a band. Each band was led by a chief, elected by a council of mature men. Polygynous marriage was permitted, and the sororate and levirate were customary. They lived in small, scattered villages and moved often, following large game and searching for other foodstuffs. Prior to contact they probably lived in small, conical huts covered with branches or bison hides. Later, they adopted a smaller version of the hide-covered tipi. Subsistence was based on the bison, which provided food, clothing, utensils, and materials for trade with Whites. They also hunted deer, bear, and small mammals and gathered many wild plant foods. Little is known of the traditional religion, other than that there were several deities.

Bibliography

Hasskarl, Robert A., Jr. (1962). "The Culture and History of the Tonkawa Indians." *Plains Anthropologist* 7:217–231.

Jones, William K. (1969). *Notes on the History and Material Culture of the Tonkawa Indians.* Smithsonian Contributions to Anthropology, 2(5). Washington, D.C.

Newcomb, William W., Jr. (1961). *The Indians of Texas from Prehistoric to Modern Times.* Austin: University of Texas Press.

Sjoberg, Andree F. (1953). "The Culture of the Tonkawa." *Texas Journal of Science* 5:280–304.

Tsimshian

ETHNONYMS: Chimmesyan, Skeena

The Tsimshian are a Northwest Coast group who lived and continue to live along the Nass and Skeena rivers and nearby coastal regions of British Columbia. In the early 1800s, the Tsimshian numbered as many as 10,000. In 1980, there were nearly that number in British Columbia and 942 in the Metlakatla Community on the Annette Island Reserve. The Tsimshian were composed of three subgroups (some experts say they were separate groups): Tsimshian, Niska (Nass River), and Gitksan (Kitksan). Tsimshian is a Penutian language, and four dialects were spoken aboriginally.

Sustained contact with Europeans began in the early 1700s and focused on Tsimshian involvement in the fur trade, first with the Russians and then with the English and the Americans. This involvement brought many Tsimshian closer to the coast and culminated in the formation of the large town of Fort Simpson around the Hudson's Bay Company post of the same name beginning in 1834. In 1887 the missionary William Duncan, seeking political and religious freedom, led a group of 942 Tsimshian to Annette Island where they founded the Metlakatla Community. The community is noted today for its progressive economic policies and relatively high quality of life. The Tsimshian in Canada are now divided into sixteen bands and live on reserves in their traditional territory. In both Alaska and Canada salmon fishing remains an important subsistence and commercial activity, although modern technology such as power boats have replaced the traditional technology.

As with all Northwest Coast groups, the social and political organization of Tsimshian society was multilayered and involved social classes, kin ties, and territorial units. There were four social classes: royalty, nobles, commoners, and slaves. The basic territorial units were the villages, controlled by the matrilineages. Societal-level integration was achieved through affiliation with one of the four matriclans, potlatching, clan exogamy, and patrilocal postmarital residence. The Tsimshian displayed many cultural features typical of the Northwest Coast including potlatches, large plank houses, an economy based on the sea and especially salmon fishing, slavery, and totem poles. The Tsimshian are known for originating the Chilkat blanket, with clan crests woven from mountain goat wool and yellow cedar bark. Once a medium of exchange, the blankets are now valuable collector's items.

Bibliography

Garfield, Viola (1939). _Tsimshian Clan and Society._ University of Washington Publications in Anthropology, no. 7, 167–340. Seattle: University of Washington Press.

Miller, Jay, and Carol M. Eastman (1984). _The Tsimshian and Their Neighbors of the North Pacific Coast._ Seattle: University of Washington Press.

Tubatulabal

ETHNONYMS: Kern River Indians, Te-bot-e-lob-e-lay

The Tubatulabal inhabited the drainage area of the upper Kern River in California's southern Sierra Nevada foothills region. They were loosely organized into three politically discrete bands (Pahkanapil, Palegawan, and Bankalachi [Toloim]) having a high degree of internal unity. They spoke mutually intelligible dialects of Tubatulabal, a Uto-Aztecan language. Only the Pahkanapil survived the intensive White settlement of their territory that began in the 1850s. Each band had a chief (_timiwal_) who, though he had little authority, acted as arbitrator and band representative; he also had some politicoadministrative duties. The timiwal was usually elected by the elder males of the various band hamlets. A number of mobile family groups made up a band. These lived in semipermanent hamlets near the rivers during the winter months but roamed widely during the remainder of the year. The individual households contained a single, biological, bilateral family, but also contained dependents of various types. Marriage was of two forms—gift exchange and groom service. There was no marriage ritual or postmarital residence rules. There was little inheritance since most personal possessions were destroyed after death. Real property was not inherited. Limited warfare occurred with the neighboring Yokuts, Koso, and Kawaiisu, motivated by revenge for attacks by them. The timiwal was expected to settle hostilities. There was much trade, both long and short distance, especially for white clamshell discs, a form of money.

First contact occurred in 1776 with the visit of Francisco Garcés. In the ensuing years the Tubatulabal came into contact with the Spanish on trading trips to the California coast, but they were not missionized by the Spanish. Extensive contact with European-Americans began in the 1850s with the establishment of ranches in the area followed by the 1857 gold rush. Some conflicts with local Whites and the U.S. Army resulted in many deaths. By 1875 most male Tubatulabal were employed by White ranchers, and in 1893 the surviving Pahkanapil and Palegawan were allotted land in the Kern and South Fork valleys. Most still live in the Kern River valley area. In 1972 there were forty-three full- and mixed-bloods living there, with seven that could be counted in other parts of California.

Aboriginal material culture was simple. During winter, circular domed brush- and mud-covered one-family houses were used. Unwalled shelters were used during the warmer months. Most hamlets had an associated sweat house made of branches, poles, and brush, covered with mud and located near a natural or dammed pool. Women made coiled and twined baskets of split willow or yucca roots and deer grass, and coiled pottery. Self- and sinew-backed bows were used for hunting and warfare. Many varieties of nets, traps, snares, and throwing sticks were used in hunting. Basket traps, nets, harpoons, fishhooks, and corrals were used for fishing.

Subsistence was based on hunting, fishing, and gathering; there was no horticulture. Acorns and piñon nuts were staples, with fish second in importance. A variety of small seeds, shoots, leaves, bulbs, tubers, and berries was collected. Most gathering was done by the women. Rock salt, collected by men, was used for seasoning and preserving meat. Large game (deer, bear, mountain lion, mountain sheep, antelope) was hunted. Communal antelope drives were made with the Yokuts and Kawaiisu in the San Joaquin valley. Rabbits were the only small game actually hunted, usually in communal rabbit drives.

The Tubatulabal lacked any concept of a supreme deity, but believed in a number of spirits, both human and animal, and all treated with respect. Both men and women could become shamans. Male shamans had both curing and witching powers; the females had only witching power. Jimsonweed was used to cure sickness and obtain supernatural help. All misfortunes and death were attributed to witchcraft. There were no puberty rites.

Bibliography

Smith, Charles R. (1978). "Tubatulabal." In _Handbook of North American Indians,_ Vol. 8, _California,_ edited by Robert F. Heizer, 437–445. Washington, D.C.: Smithsonian Institution.

Voegelin, Erminie W. (1938). _Tubatulabal Ethnography._ University of California Anthropological Records, 2(1), 1–84. Berkeley.

Tunica

The Tunica, plus the Koroa, Tiou (Tioux), and Yazoo, lived in west-central Mississippi and northeastern Louisiana. Their descendants live in a community near Marksville, Louisiana. They spoke a language isolate in the Macro-Algonkian phylum and numbered only a few dozen in the 1980s.

Bibliography

Brain, Jeffrey P., et al. (1979). *Tunica Treasure*. Harvard University, Peabody Museum of Archaeology and Ethnology, Papers, no. 71. Cambridge.

Tuscarora

The Tuscarora are an American Indian group living on the Tuscarora Indian Reservation in New York State and the Six Nations Reserve in Ontario. In the 1980s the Tuscarora in New York and Ontario numbered approximately fifteen hundred.

In late aboriginal and early historic times the Tuscarora occupied an extensive territory along the Roanoke, Tar, Pamlico, and Neuse rivers in present-day North Carolina. In the early eighteenth century they were driven out of their territory after a series of devastating wars with White colonists. They migrated north, where they were adopted by the Iroquois tribes and accepted as members of the Iroquois Confederacy in 1722. The Tuscarora participated in the councils of the league, but their chiefs were not given the position of sachem in the council. Before migrating north the Tuscarora economy had been based on a combination of horticulture, hunting, gathering, and fishing. Once joined with the Iroquois, they settled on lands given to them by the Seneca and adopted Iroquoian cultural and organizational patterns. During the American Revolution many Tuscarora were forced by circumstances to side with the British and subsequently were granted lands on Six Nations Reserve. Those Tuscarora able to remain neutral during the war were granted the lands they occupied in New York State.
See also Iroquois

Bibliography

Boyce, Douglas W. (1973). "Did a Tuscarora Confederacy Exist?" *Indian Historian* 6:34–40.

Johnson, Frank R. (1967–1968). *The Tuscaroras: Mythology, Medicine, Culture*. Murfreesboro, N.C.: Johnson Publishing Co.

Tutchone

The Tutchone (Tutchonekutchin), an Athapaskan-speaking group, live in the general drainage area of the upper Yukon River in Yukon Territory in Canada and were culturally similar to the Kutchin, their neighbors to the north. They numbered around fifteen hundred in 1974.

Bibliography

McClellan, Catharine (1981). "Tutchone." In *Handbook of North American Indians*, Vol. 6, *Subarctic*, edited by June Helm 493–505. Washington, D.C.: Smithsonian Institution.

Twana

The Twana (Skokomish, Toanhooches) lived on the southeastern side of the Olympic Peninsula in northwestern Washington, on both sides of the Hood Canal. They now live on or near the Skokomish Indian Reservation in Washington. They spoke a Coast Salish language and numbered about one thousand in the 1980s.

Bibliography

Eells, Myron (1985). *The Indians of Puget Sound*. Seattle: University of Washington Press.

Elmendorf, William W. (1960). *The Structure of Twana Culture*. Washington State Research Studies, Monographic Supplement no. 2. Pullman.

Ukrainians of Canada

ETHNONYMS: Bukovynians, Galicians, Ruthenians, Ukrainian-Canadians

Orientation

Identification.   Ukrainian-Canadians are one of the larger and more prominent ethnic groups in Canada. These people, or more likely their ancestors, originated in Ukrainian territory in Eastern Europe. Ukrainian ethnographic territory corresponds roughly (not exactly) with the area of the Ukrainian Soviet Socialist Republic in the Soviet Union. The Black Sea lies to the south of this land, and its northern neighbors include Russia and Poland. The political boundaries of this territory have undergone many changes up to and during the twentieth century. Only rarely throughout these permutations were the governing bodies controlled by Ukrainians themselves. Indeed, Ukrainian immigrants to Canada carried Austrian, Polish, Russian, and other passports, and could be identified better on the basis of their language, culture, and religion than by their citizenship. Ancestry and culture continue to be the primary criteria for the identification of Ukrainian-Canadians. Language and religion have tended to decline as perceived prerequisites for inclusion in the group, replaced somewhat by participation in the organized Ukrainian community and by a personal sense of Ukrainianness. The Ukrainian-Canadian community does not have sharply defined membership. Large segments of its population live more or less closely in relation to it.

Location.   The first settlements of Ukrainians in Canada were concentrated in the prairie provinces of Manitoba, Saskatchewan, and Alberta. In the earlier years, most were rural homesteaders. Although the prairie provinces still maintain large communities, Ukrainians have been spreading somewhat more randomly across the country. Migration within the country reflects the search for economic advantages and the best personal quality of life. The trend to urbanization has been pronounced for a number of decades, and now 75 percent of the Ukrainian population of Canada lives in cities. In this respect, the Ukrainian community now resembles the general population of the country.

Demography.   Ukrainian people have historically been quite sedentary, and only small numbers emigrated beyond Ukrainian territories prior to the end of the nineteenth century. In the last 120 years, however, they have dispersed widely. Some two million live in North America, two million in Siberia, 250,000 in South America, 90,000 in other countries in Europe, and 35,000 in Australia. In the 1981 census, 529,615 Canadians declared Ukrainian ancestry, and another 225,000 claimed partial Ukrainian heritage. Representing some 2.7 percent of the population, Ukrainian-Canadians are the fifth largest ethnic group in the country. Only about 15 percent of these individuals are immigrants themselves; the remainder are Canadian-born. The city of Winnipeg has had a large Ukrainian population since early in this century. In 1981, the major Ukrainian-Canadian urban centers included Edmonton (63,000, 10 percent of the city's population), Winnipeg (59,000, 10 percent), and Toronto (51,000, 2 percent). Over 20,000 additional persons in each of these cities reported partial Ukrainian ancestry. Particularly in the prairies, numerous small towns and rural areas continue to record a high incidence of Ukrainian settlement, sometimes exceeding 50 percent of the local populace.

Linguistic Affiliation.   Ukrainian is a Slavic language. Though many Ukrainians use the more formal literary language, others speak a Galician dialect with varying degrees of English influence. The community is increasingly English-speaking, with Ukrainians in French-speaking Canada often bilingual or trilingual. The percentage of Ukrainian-Canadians who use Ukrainian in the home has decreased in recent decades, dropping below 20 percent. Those who do speak Ukrainian regularly are often older.

History and Cultural Relations

Ukrainian immigration to Canada took place in three major waves. The first and largest influx (170,000 individuals) took place between 1891 and the beginning of World War I. The vast majority of this group left from the provinces of Galicia and Bukovyna, a small segment of western Ukrainian territory controlled by the Austro-Hungarian Empire at that time. They were mostly peasant farmers wanting to escape poverty, exploitation, and overpopulation. Canada was then actively soliciting such agricultural immigrants to develop its vast and empty prairies. Ukrainian immigrants settled in somewhat compact blocks on homesteads across the large belt of aspen parkland spanning the prairies. The 67,000 Ukrainians who arrived in the interwar period composed the second wave of immigrants. Manitoba was the most popular destination for this group. Work in agriculture and railway construction awaited many. The third immigration consisted primarily of persons displaced after World War II, which was particularly devastating in Ukrainian territories. This group of up to 40,000 people tended to be more urban, more educated, and more politically and nationally motivated than their earlier counterparts. They settled primarily in Canada's urban areas, with Ontario receiving almost half of their number. Since 1952, immigration of Ukrainians to Canada has been light.

The general attitude of the Canadian establishment in the earlier years was to anglicize or "Canadianize" the Ukrainians once they arrived. Ukrainian community development was more or less tolerated depending on how the elite perceived that the organizations might help facilitate assimilation. Attitudes also varied according to economic and political trends. "Anti-alien" sentiments rose sharply during World War I. Bilingual education systems were dismantled and thousands of Ukrainians were kept under surveillance, interned, and sometimes deported with little justification. In spite of a few such experiences, however, Ukrainians have been generally quite pro-Canadian. They perceive Canada as a country that treated them much better and offered them greater prospects than Austro-Hungary, Poland, the Russian Empire, or later the Soviet Union. Ukrainians were very instrumental in establishing Canada's policy of multiculturalism in the 1960s. In theory at least, this policy promotes the cultural identity of the myriad of peoples that populate the country, seeing strength in this diversity. Support for multiculturalism seems to be somewhat on the wane in "English" Canada in the 1980s. Cultural relations between Ukrainians in Canada and those in the Soviet Union, at least until recently, have been somewhat distant. They have been deterred by the wars, the distance, and the cold war attitudes on both sides.

Economy

Agriculture was by far the predominant occupation of Ukrainians in the first half of the twentieth century. Other occupations tended to be in the primary sector and included logging, mining, construction, and building railroads. This situation gradually changed, however, and the structure of the Ukrainian-Canadian work force now resembles that of the general population in almost all respects. But Ukrainians are still somewhat overrepresented in agriculture (7 percent work on farms as compared to the 4 percent Canadian average) and underrepresented in most of the elite groups that hold power in the country.

Kinship, Marriage and Family

Ukrainian-Canadian marriage and kinship practices do not differ substantially from general Canadian norms. Predominant are monogamous marriage, nuclear families, and bilateral descent. Ukrainian kinship terms in many dialects exhibit a degree of bifurcation; terms differ for maternal versus paternal uncles and aunts. Such perceptions are being supplanted by a more classical Eskimo-type kinship system, especially since English is now often used. Godparents have traditionally been regarded as significant relatives. In-group marriage was encouraged by Ukrainian-Canadian society, particularly by parent generations, though the rate of intermarriage is high.

Socialization. The means and degree of socialization of Ukrainian-Canadians varies a great deal depending on the size of the local community, the commitment of family members, and personal choice. The church has traditionally played a major role in this process, as has upbringing. More involved families in larger centers often choose to take advantage of Ukrainian kindergartens, Ukrainian schools (and, recently, public bilingual education), Ukrainian scouts, choirs, dance groups, sports organizations, and many other pursuits. The adult community reaffirms itself in many performances, meetings, and other social events.

Sociopolitical Organization

Social Organization. The Ukrainian community has more organizations than any Canadian ethnic group its size. The plethora of organizations reflects the division of the community into Catholic and Orthodox sectors, each with religious and secular institutions, and men's, women's, and youth divisions. Differences in immigration history, region of origin, political views, generation, past membership in military units, professions, and other factors are all reflected in the organizational scheme of the Ukrainian-Canadian community. Recently, a great number of somewhat independent organizations have been set up to deal with academic pursuits, various art forms, local history, and other specific interests. The Ukrainian Canadian Committee was established in 1940 as an umbrella organization for the noncommunist Ukrainian community. It has achieved varying degrees of success in coordinating the diverse groups. There is no specific effective mechanism for exerting social control or resolving conflict in the Ukrainian-Canadian community.

Political Organization. Ukrainians in Canada have no overarching political structure. Most earlier Ukrainian settlers were not politically sophisticated, partly because of their relative exclusion from political power in their native territories. Disenchantment over living and working conditions in Europe (and, later, often in Canada) promoted radical leftist views in the first decades of this century. Later, immigrants tended to the right of the political spectrum. At present, Ukrainians are a complex and varied electoral group, still demonstrating some tendency to marginality on the left and the right in comparison with the general populace. Politicians sometimes perceive the Ukrainian community to be a significant voting block and address it accordingly. The great majority of the Ukrainian community does not approve of the present Soviet Ukrainian state under Russian domination.

Religion and Expressive Culture

Religious Beliefs and Practitioners. The Ukrainian Catholic and Ukrainian Greek Orthodox churches are the predominant traditional denominations in the Ukrainian-Canadian community, claiming some 190,000 and 99,000 adherents, respectively (the latter figure includes a minority of other Orthodox denominations as well). In the 1981 census, Ukrainians also reported adherence to Roman Catholicism (89,000), the United church (71,000), and many other forms of Christianity. Some 42,000 indicated no religious preference. In spite of declining attendance in the two traditional Ukrainian churches, especially among the younger generations, they continue to maintain substantial significance in Ukrainian-Canadian society. The Ukraine adopted the Byzantine form of Christianity one thousand years ago, and thus eastern Christian traditions of worship are followed. Compared to most western Christian practices, the rites are quite ancient and ritualistic. The older Julian calendar is traditionally retained by these churches, and thus Christmas is celebrated on January 7. The Ukrainian Catholic (Uniate, Greek Catholic) church acknowledges the leadership of the pope in Rome, although theoretically it retains its Orthodox rite. The Ukrainian Greek Orthodox church of Canada, established in 1918, is independent. Both the Ukrainian Catholic and the Orthodox communities in Canada have undergone some westernization in terms of their spiritual culture. General acceptance of latinized rituals, the English language, and the newer Gregorian calendar is more widespread among the Catholics.

Ceremonies. Ukrainian culture was very rich in traditional lore into the beginning of the twentieth century, in part, because it was relatively isolated from cosmopolitan influences and the leveling pressures of industrialization. Most emigrants, then, identified with a rich tradition of rituals and customs. Social life was generally disrupted upon migration because of the isolation and because Canadian policies for settling the prairies precluded tight-knit village settlements. Nonetheless, in many communities, various customs were maintained, adapted, and sometimes reconstructed to establish a unique Ukrainian-Canadian ritual culture. The most important ceremony dealing with the life cycle is the wedding, which is often large and features food, drink, socializing, dancing, and gift-giving.

The cultural response to death has been partially influenced by the community's Eastern Christian spirituality as well as by connections with its peasant origins. These factors are reflected in the services conducted during burial, a lessened tendency to isolate the living from the corpse, somewhat particular grave markers, and traditional cemetery visitations at prescribed intervals. In general, however, funeral practices and attitudes now conform closely to those of the Canadian mainstream.

The most important calendar holidays are Christmas (_Rizdvo_) and Easter (_Velykden'_), both of which retain many Ukrainian features. The main focus at Christmas is on the Christmas Eve supper, consisting traditionally of twelve meatless dishes. Caroling, church service, and visiting follow. Christmas is celebrated twice each year by many Ukrainian families in Canada, once on December 25 and again, somewhat differently, on January 7. The highlight at Easter is breaking the Lenten fast with a blessed family meal on Sunday after church service. A pre-Lenten party (_Pushchennia_), New Year's Eve (_Malanka_) on January 13, and harvest festival (_Obzhynky_) celebrations are common in many communities.

Other holidays include Ukrainian Independence Day, the anniversary of Taras Shevchenko (Ukraine's national poet), and numerous smaller religious feasts. Ukrainian-Canadians also participate in Canadian holidays such as Valentine's Day, Canada Day, Halloween, Thanksgiving, and so on.

Arts. The arts are very important to Ukrainian-Canadian culture. Indeed, they compose the most prominent aspect of Ukrainian-Canadian life in the minds of many Ukrainians and non-Ukrainians alike. Many folk arts were brought over from Europe by the early immigrants, as they lived in a culture where domestic objects were mostly handmade and activities were directly organized. In Ukraine, the style and form of these arts were quite specific. The arts came to be closely identified with Ukrainian consciousness itself. With the transition to the urban, technological, and consumer-oriented world of twentieth-century Canada, the old activities and crafts lost much of their practical worth. On the other hand, many retained or even gained value as symbols of Ukrainianness, markers of a special subculture within the Canadian milieu. This function has remained relevant in the contemporary North American context. In association with this process, many of these "folk arts" changed radically in form, materials, and context. The terms "pseudo-folk arts," "national arts" or "Ukrainian pop" have been proposed to reflect some of the contemporary features of this type of activity. Popular contemporary manifestations of Ukrainian-Canadian material culture include folk costumes, weaving, embroidery, Easter egg painting, church architecture, various styles of pottery, and miscellaneous novelty items. The fine arts of literature, painting, and sculpture have vibrant Ukrainian variants in Canada. Staged folk dance and choral singing are extremely popular in many communities. The Ukrainian music industry includes recording artists in many different styles.

Medicine. Folk medicine was strong in western Ukrainian villages and in rural Canada in earlier years. Local specialists developed much knowledge and expertise dealing with a wide variety of health problems. Remnants of this lore exist unofficially, sometimes dealing with problems outside the realm of traditional medicine. Ukrainian-Canadians participate in the Canadian health care system.

Bibliography

Borovsky, V., et al. (1971). "Ukrainians Abroad: In Canada." In _Ukraine: A Concise Encyclopedia_, Vol. 2, edited by Volodymyr Kubijovyc, 1151–1193. Toronto: University of Toronto Press.

Klymasz, Robert B. (1980). _Ukrainian Folklore in Canada: An Immigrant Complex in Transition_. New York: Arno Press.

Luciuk, Lubomyr Y., and Bohdan S. Kordan (1989). _Creating a Landscape: A Geography of Ukrainians in Canada_. Toronto: University of Toronto Press.

Lupul, Manoly R., ed. (1982). _A Heritage in Transition: Essays in the History of Ukrainians in Canada_. Toronto: McClelland & Stewart.

Lupul, Manoly R., ed. (1984). _Visible Symbols: Cultural Expression among Canada's Ukrainians_. Edmonton: Canadian Institute of Ukrainian Studies.

Petryshyn, W. R., ed. (1980). _Changing Realities: Social Trends among Ukrainian Canadians_. Edmonton: Canadian Institute of Ukrainian Studies.

ANDRIY NAHACHEWSKY

Umatilla

The Umatilla lived in the Umatilla River and adjacent parts of the Columbia River drainages in northeastern Oregon. They now live on the Umatilla Indian Reservation in the same area with the Wallawalla Cayuse. They spoke a Sahaptin language of the Penutian phylum and numbered about one thousand in the 1980s.

Bibliography

Kennedy, James Bradford (1977). "The Umatilla Indian Reservation, 1855–1975: Factors Contributing to a Diminished Land Resource Base." _Dissertation Abstracts International_ 38(4):2344A.

Stern, Theodore (1960). "A Umatilla Prophet Cult." _Acts of the International Congress of Anthropological and Ethnological Sciences_ 5:346–350.

Ute

ETHNONYMS: Eutah, Utah, Utaw, Yuta

Orientation

Identification.   The Ute are an American Indian group located in Utah, Colorado, and New Mexico. "Ute" is a shortened version of "Eutah," a term with uncertain origins. The name was likely borrowed by the Spanish from Ute neighbors who referred to the Ute as "Yu Tta Ci" (Southern Paiute), "Yota" (Hopi), and "Yu Hta" (Comanche). The meaning of "Utah" is likewise unclear. The Ute name for themselves is "Nu Ci," meaning "person" or "Indian."

Location.   At the time of European contact in the 1600s and 1700s, the Ute occupied much of central and eastern Utah and all of western Colorado, as well as minor portions of northwestern New Mexico. For ease of discussion, the Colorado and New Mexico groups are often lumped together as Eastern and those from Utah are labeled Western Ute. Physiographically, this Ute homeland is diverse and includes the eastern fringe of the Great Basin, the northern Colorado Plateau, the Rocky Mountains of Colorado, and the east slopes of the Rockies and high plains of Colorado. Latitude and longitude of the region's center is approximately 39° N and 109° W.

Demography.   In 1880, combined population figures for both Colorado and Utah Ute was some 3,975. By 1983 these numbers had increased modestly to 4,905. Precontact levels were likely considerably higher than these historic figures.

Linguistic Affiliation.   The Ute speak Southern Numic, the easternmost of the Numic languages spoken by the majority of the Indians of the Great Basin–Plateau regions of the intermountain west. Numic is a branch of the Uto-Aztekan language family. Other groups speaking Southern Numic are the Southern Paiute and Kawaiisu. Some dialectical differences were present within Southern Numic, but no clear boundaries existed.

History and Cultural Relations

Linguistic and archaeological evidence argue for an arrival of Southern Numic–speakers in the eastern Great Basin and Plateau country about A.D. 1250–1350. At the time of European settlement in New Mexico in the 1600s and Utah in the late 1700s, the Ute were well established, but had developed along somewhat different trajectories. The Eastern Ute had converted to the horse-riding Plains life-style, and the Western Ute retained more traditional Great Basin patterns until the early 1800s when certain central Utah groups also adopted the horse and other Plains cultural trappings. Ute neighbors to the north, west, and east included other Numic-speakers, such as the Northern Shoshone, Western Shoshone, and Southern Paiute. Also to the south were the Pueblos, Navajo, and Apache. To the east were the Plains groups, such as the Wind River Shoshone (Numic-speakers), Arapaho, Comanche (Numic-speakers), and Southern Cheyenne. Relations were amicable with the Western Shoshone, but raids were common between the Ute and other neighbors, especially the Plains peoples, with the exception of the

Comanche. The unmounted Southern Paiute to the south were routinely subjected to raids by all Utes to obtain slaves, especially women and children, to trade to the Spanish.

Mormon immigration to the Great Basin in 1847 marked the beginning of the end for the traditional Western Ute way of life. Serious conflicts began in 1849, when settlers moved into Utah Valley, an important center of Ute settlement. Following the Walker War of 1850s and the Black Hawk War in the 1860s, all Western Ute were displaced from the eastern Great Basin and relocated in the Uinta Basin of northern Utah. For the Eastern Ute the process was slower. Reduction of lands began in the 1850s owing to a series of treaty agreements and continued until the 1880s. The Meeker Massacre of 1879 resulted in most of the northern Colorado Utes being placed on the Uinta Basin reservation. Other Eastern Utes moved to the small Southern Ute and Elk Mountain reservations in southwestern Colorado and northwestern New Mexico.

Settlements

The Ute are traditionally described in terms of geographically designated bands. Both the Eastern and Western groups consisted of five such bands. For the Eastern group they were the Muache, Capote, Uncompahgre, White River, and Weeminuche. The Western bands were the Uintah, Timpanogots, Sanpitch, Pahvant, and Moanunts. Throughout Ute territory settlements tended to consist of a winter and a summer camp. For the Western and other nonequestrian Ute, winter camps were located in the valley bottoms adjacent to lakes, marshes, or streams or, in some cases, in the piñon juniper woodlands of the lower foothills where fuel and shelter were available and close to food caches. Spring in the valleys along the eastern Great Basin was spawning season and a time for many Western Ute to hold festivities, dances, and games and to fish, especially in Utah Valley. In the summer people dispersed to gather ripening plant seeds and pursue individual hunting. In late summer and fall the Utes moved to the uplands for hunting, berry picking, and piñon nut gathering. The Eastern Ute spent summers and early fall on the plains hunting bison, and these events were generally the time of greatest aggregation for the year. Winter camps consisted of smaller residential units located in sheltered areas in the foothills or valleys. Modern reservation towns, such as Fort Duchesne and Roosevelt on the Uintah-Ouray Reservation, are centers of modern Ute community and commercial life and are very much in the pattern of western towns. Dispersed Ute communities, however, such as that seen at White Mesa in southeastern Utah, are also fairly typical.

Economy

Subsistence and Commercial Activity.   All Utes at the time of European contact were hunters and gatherers, although the subsistence focus varied considerably from east to west. In general, Eastern Ute were more committed to a hunting economy, especially bison, whereas Western Ute diets were broader with more emphasis on smaller animals and fish. Important plant foods included piñon nuts, various small seeds, such as grass and bulrush, and roots. With the withdrawal of traditional foraging areas, the Ute turned to subsistence farming following the European pattern. Commercial farming has not been successful, and most modern employment is now in the energy-related fields or service jobs, especially with the federal government. Although numerous business ventures have been attempted, few have succeeded.

Industrial Arts.　Traditional crafts such as basketry, weaving, and hide working persisted into the twentieth century. Beadwork on tanned leather or other materials continues to be produced, especially for the tourist market, but basketry and weaving have largely died out. Pottery was made prehistorically, but was not a well-developed craft.

Trade.　Prehistoric trade is not well documented for the Ute. Obsidian and probably marine shells were likely traded, but the mechanisms are unknown. Following the arrival of European markets, such as the Spanish in New Mexico, the Utes were active in the fur trade and exchanged skins, furs, and slaves for horses, metal tools, beads, and other European goods. This commerce was active into the mid-1800s.

Division of Labor.　Traditionally, economic tasks were segregated by sex. As a general rule, men hunted larger game and fished, and made weapons and tools related to hunting (bows and arrows, various portable traps, drive lines, and catch corrals). Women gathered plant foods and made the items necessary for those activities, especially baskets. Numerous food-related efforts involved both sexes, however, especially with the Western Ute. For example, women made cordage of plant fibers with which the men wove the nets that were used in rabbit or waterfowl drives. Both men and women participated in these drives. Fishing was generally a male activity, but women made some fishing gear such as basketry traps. Women prepared and cooked food, built houses, made clothing, prepared skins, and made pottery. Some blurring of these divisions was common, also. Both men and women participated in shamanistic rituals. Historic employment trends are generally parallel with national patterns with both sexes working, but with more men employed than women. Women usually remain at home, and some pursue craft production for the tourist trade.

Land Tenure.　Aboriginal land ownership was limited to usufruct rights to hunting and gathering for a family. Individual land ownership was apparently unknown. A degree of territoriality was present to the extent that non-Utes (for example, Shoshone) had no access to important resource areas such as the Utah Lake fishery. Anglo settlement and agricultural pursuits removed the more productive lands from Ute use. The Ute were eventually forcibly removed to reservation lands in Colorado and Utah. The Dawes Severalty Act of 1887 further reduced Indian-owned lands and eventually opened Ute lands to Anglo homesteaders. The impact of this bill was reversed by the Indian Reorganization Act of 1934, which allowed for consolidation of Indian properties and acquisition of other lands as well. In 1988 a legal suit brought by the Ute Tribe against counties and cities of the Uinta Basin returned significant portions of Ute lands in Utah, bringing the total held by that group to 4 million acres.

Kinship

Kin Groups and Descent.　No clans or other formal social units are known for the Ute. Residential units tended toward unranked matridemes. These units, which consisted of several related families, were exogamous. Status within residential units was based on age, sex, and generation.

Kinship Terminology.　Ute kin terms followed a skewed bifurcate collateral pattern.

Marriage and Family

Marriage.　Marriages were often arranged by parents and relatives. Marriage to blood relatives (extended to first and second cousins) was forbidden. Wedding ceremonies were informal, and premarital intercourse at the girl's residence was considered marriage. Band exogamy was generally preferred. Polygyny existed and both the levirate and sororate were practiced; however, monogamy was the norm with less than 10 percent practicing polygamy. Divorce for reasons of sterility, infidelity, and incompatibility was and is common. Children usually remain with the mother. Residence was almost always matrilocal. Bride-service is not reported for the Ute, although it was common in other Great Basin groups.

Domestic Unit.　Traditional households often included relatives such as grandparents and occasionally a spouse of one of the children. This pattern continues today. Single-parent families are very common because of high divorce rates. Households are often swelled by near kin as resources are combined in times of economic stress.

Inheritance.　Inheritance patterns were poorly developed, for most personal material goods were burned at the death of the individual. Rights to eagle aeries, springs, and garden plots were passed down to surviving family members.

Socialization.　Children were desirable and much attention was paid to the pregnant mother, birth, and child rearing. Often young children were tended by older siblings and by grandparents. Children were spoiled and indulged in a permissive environment. Ridicule was the primary means of discipline. Puberty rites were observed for both girls and boys. First menses was celebrated by the family by offering instructions to the girl and imposing food taboos and behavioral restrictions until the end of menstruation. Male puberty rites were not so well defined, but they usually revolved around the first killing of a large game animal. The boy was forbidden to eat of this kill, which was often given to an older relative. To celebrate the event further, the boy was bathed by a special hunter and painted red. Traditional education in crafts, subsistence skills, and oral histories were provided to children by the appropriate grandparent. Education levels among Ute youths are low, with only half completing high school.

Sociopolitical Organization

Social Organization.　Ute social life was rooted in the family. Within the family and among family groups elders, male and female, were respected and given special consideration. Prior to European contact, household leadership tended to be male-oriented, but with the growing numbers of single-parent families, females are more often in family leadership roles.

Political Organization.　Band organization was likely present in the pre-horse era. Bands consisted of several residential units (demes) that united under a leader, usually an elder male who had demonstrated prowess as a hunter as well as wisdom in decision making. Leaders often had one or more assistants who served as speakers or in other capacities. The Western Ute had special chiefs selected to lead dances and rabbit, antelope, waterfowl, and bison drives. Utah Valley Ute had a special fishing chief. Councils consisted of deme leaders and usually met at the chief's house. Women were allowed to attend councils, as were men other than chiefs. Political patterns were strengthened after contact as access to the horse and raiding for the slave markets increased, thereby reinforcing the status of the leaders. This trend continued as Anglo culture often demanded a band or tribal spokesperson. Reservation-era tribal affairs have been directed by the tribal committees of the Ute Indian Tribe. Especially influential on the Uintah-Ouray Reservation is the Ute Tribal Business Committee formed in 1937 after the Indian Reorganization Act.

Social Control.   Traditionally, group leaders played an important role in interpersonal altercations, but no formal process existed in the event of a crime or breach of trust. Individual retaliation was common and control difficult, as there were no means other than social for enforcement. Murders, for example, were usually avenged by relatives who killed the offender, an action condoned and expected by the society. Social controls were also sought through the use of myths and legends that depicted appropriate behavior and introduced the threat of ridicule or expulsion for unacceptable actions. As on other reservations, the federal government now has jurisdiction over serious crimes.

Conflict.   Internal Ute conflicts erupted in the 1880s following the Meeker Massacre when White River and Uncompaghre Utes from Colorado were forced onto the Uintah Reservation. Uintahs resented having to share their reservation and further resented inequities in federal distributions of funds. Bad feelings also existed between the White River and Uncompaghre people based on events during and after the Meeker Massacre. In 1905 Ute-Anglo relations were strained by the opening of the Uintah-Ouray Reservation to Anglo use. In reprisal, a large contingent of Utes left the reservation and sought asylum with the Sioux in South Dakota. Failing this they were returned to the Uintah Basin in 1908. Further internal strife stemmed from a rift between mixed- and full-blood people. The former, because of Anglo contacts and better education, developed more political power in tribal affairs. The rift ultimately resulted in the termination (expulsion) of mixed-bloods (less than 50 percent Ute) from the tribal rolls in 1954. Bad feelings extended to the tribal government, and a group known as the True Utes unsuccessfully attempted to disband this polity during the late 1950s.

Religion and Expressive Culture

Religious Beliefs.   Religion was not formalized, but was nonetheless important and pervaded daily Ute life. An integral element of Ute metaphysics was the concept of power obtained from knowledge received through dreams, visions, or from mythical beings. Religion was expressed at the level of the individual rather than through group activity. Senawahv is named as the Ute creator of the land, animals, food, plants, and the Utes themselves. Animals, especially wolf and coyote, were commonly depicted in myths in which they were described as having humanlike traits combined with some mystical powers. Belief in water babies, supernatural beings that lived in springs, was widespread among Great Basin Indians. Ghosts and souls were real and feared. Charms for various purposes were also common. Several Christian religions currently have followings among the Utes as does the Native American church.

Religious Practitioners.   Shamans held the power of healing obtained through dreams or from other shamans. Healing methods involved songs, dances, and various pieces of paraphernalia, the forms for all of which were learned through the dreams. Special shaman designations included weather, bear, evil, sexual, and childbirth. Both men and women practiced shamanism. A payment was expected if the cure was successful.

Ceremonies.   Two ceremonies have dominated Ute social and religious life: the Bear Dance and the Sun Dance. The former is indigenous to the Ute and aboriginally was held in the spring to coincide with the emergence of the bear from hibernation. The dance was held in a large brush enclosure or dance plaza and lasted about ten days. The dancing, which was mostly done by couples, propitiated bears to increase hunting and sexual prowess. A theme of rebirth and fertility is pervasive throughout. This theme was reinforced by the announcement of the completion of a girl's puberty rites during the ceremony. The Sun Dance was borrowed from the Plains tribes between 1880 and 1890. This ceremony was held in July, and the dancing lasted for four days and nights. The emphasis of the Sun Dance was on individual or community esteem and welfare, and its adoption was symptomatic of the feelings of despair held by the Indians at that time. Participants often hoped for a vision or cures for the sick. Consistent with the emphasis of this ceremony was the fact that dancing was by individuals rather than couples as was the case with the Bear Dance. Both ceremonies continue to be held by the Ute, although the timing of the Bear Dance tends to be later in the year. The Ghost Dance was briefly popular during the late 1880s and 1890s on the Uintah-Ouray Reservation.

Arts.   The Ute enjoy singing and many songs are specific to the Bear Dance and curing. The style of singing is reminiscent of Plains groups. Singing and dancing for entertainment continue to be important. Rock art was another form of expression, and both pictographs (painted) and petrogylphs (pecked) of obvious Ute manufacture have been documented.

Medicine.   Curing ceremonies attempted to drive evil forces from the body through songs, sucking tubes, and so on, rather than through the use of medicines. Herbal remedies were also applied, however, and medicinal powers were assigned to a number of plants. These, usually the leaves or roots, were pounded and boiled and the resulting potion drunk.

Death and Afterlife.   Death was a time of community and individual loss and was formally observed by abstentions from certain behaviors and by acts such as hair cutting. Mourning lasted up to a year. Care was taken to ensure that the ghost of the deceased did not return, although it was generally held that the soul lingered near the body for several days. All souls went to an afterlife similar to this world. Burial and funeral customs included burning the house wherein death occurred and the destruction of most personal property, which sometimes included horses, dogs, and slaves. Bodies were washed, dressed, and wrapped and buried, extended, in a rock-covered grave in the mountains.

Bibliography

Callaway, Donald, Joel C. Janetski, and Omer C. Stewart (1986). "Ute." In _Handbook of North American Indians._ Vol. 11, _Great Basin,_ edited by Warren L. d'Azevedo, 336–367. Washington, D.C.: Smithsonian Institution.

Conetah, Fred A. (1982). _A History of the Northern Ute People._ Edited by Katheryn L. MacKay and Floyd A. O'Neil. Salt Lake City, Utah: Uintah-Ouray Tribe.

Jorgensen, Joseph G. (1964). _The Ethnohistory and Acculturation of the Northern Ute._ Ph.D diss., Indiana University.

Smith, Anne M. (1974). _Ethnography of the Northern Ute._ Museum of New Mexico Papers in Anthropology, no. 17. Santa Fe: University of New Mexico Press.

JOEL C. JANETSKI

Wailaki

The Wailaki, including the Kato (Cahto, Tlokeang), Lassik, Mattole (Van Duzen Indians), Nongatl, and Sinkyone, lived along the coast and inland in northwestern California, along the Bear, Mattole, and Eel rivers. They spoke Athapaskan languages and probably number about one hundred today.

Bibliography

Elsasser, Albert B. (1978). "Mattole, Nongatl, Sinkyone, Lassik, and Wailaki." In _Handbook of North American Indians._ Vol. 8, _California,_ edited by Robert F. Heizer, 190–204. Washington, D.C.: Smithsonian Institution.

Myers, James E. (1978). "Cahto." In _Handbook of North American Indians._ Vol. 8, _California,_ edited by Robert F. Heizer, 244–248. Washington, D.C.: Smithsonian Institution.

Walapai

ETHNONYMS: Hualapai, Jaguallapai, Yampai

Orientation

Identification. The Walapai are an American Indian group located in Arizona. "Walapai" is the most common historic and ethnographic label for the group whose official tribal designation is "Hualapai." The term, meaning "Ponderosa Pine People," originally referred to a single band, the first one encountered by explorers and prospectors coming into Walapai territory from the Colorado River. Prior to the administrative division into two reservations in the nineteenth century, the Walapai and the Havasupai constituted a single ethnic group.

Location. Historically, the Walapai inhabited an extensive territory in northwestern Arizona, bounded on the north and west by the Colorado River, and on the south and east by hostile groups of Yavapai. This arid range is characterized by hot summers and mild winters, with frequent and violent thunderstorms throughout July and August. The Walapai now reside on a reservation of approximately 1 million acres within this aboriginal territory, with tribal offices located at Peach Springs, Arizona.

Demography. In the 1980s, the reservation population numbered about 950 Walapais. Accurate reconstruction of the historic size of the population is difficult, owing to the fluid nature of hunting and gathering bands, but it is probable that the group never numbered more than 1,000. By 1900, following a series of epidemics and battles with U.S. troops, the population had been reduced to less than 600.

Linguistic Affiliation.   The Walapai language, along with Havasupai and Yavapai, form the Upland Pai group within the Yuman language family. Mutually intelligible dialects are also spoken by groups along the Colorado River and in southern California and the northern part of Baja California, Mexico.

History and Cultural Relations

The Upland Pai are descendants of the prehistoric Cerbat tradition, inhabiting the present territory of the Pai as early as A.D. 1100. The Walapai origin myth places the creation of all the Yuman groups at a place on the west bank of the Colorado River, where the Great Spirit transformed the canes along the river's edge into humans. Although Spanish explorers and missionaries established relations with the Yumans living along the river in the sixteenth and seventeenth centuries, it was not until 1776 that direct and brief contact with Walapais occurred.

They remained isolated for another seventy years, until the U.S. Army began to sponsor the search through northern Arizona for railroad routes to the West Coast. These explorations initiated two decades of hostilities between the Walapai and Anglos—the soldiers and the settlers who followed closely behind them. The intrusions began with the discovery of gold near Prescott in 1863. In 1866, the respected Walapai leader, Wauba Yuma, was killed. For the next four years, Walapais engaged the better-armed and better-mounted soldiers in battle. Ultimately, the Walapai surrendered and were moved to the inhospitable lowlands of the Colorado River Indian Reservation. Finding conditions there intolerable, they fled back to their customary territory where, in their brief absence, ranchers and miners had appropriated the habitable areas and taken over many of the springs. Conditions did not improve markedly with the establishment of the reservation in 1883, for heavy grazing had already depleted the Walapai range, wiping out several of the food plants upon which the Indians depended. Impoverished and threatened by epidemic diseases, Walapais sought work in the towns on the Santa Fe Railroad and in the mines. Many, too, turned briefly to the millenarian Ghost Dance in the late 1880s, hoping, to no avail, that the magical power of the dance would expel Anglos from the territory.

Aboriginally, the Upland Pai (Walapai and Havasupai) were culturally and linguistically similar to the Yavapai along their southern boundary and to the Colorado River Yumans to the west. Yet these similarities did not lead to a shared sense of identity. Although Walapais intermarried with the Halchidhoma along the river, raiding and warfare characterized their relationships with the powerful Mohaves and the mobile Yavapais. Enmity intensified with the arrival of Anglo miners and settlers, as Indians were recruited to fight their traditional foes. This process led, in postcontact times, to an increased sense of unity within the beleaguered Walapai bands.

Settlements

Walapai settlement patterns have been and continue to be closely tied to the availability of resources. Aboriginally, the "camp," composed of about 25 related individuals, was the primary settlement and subsistence unit. Relying for much of the year on the abundant and varied wild resources of Walapai territory, the camp might join others during some seasons, either to exploit game or farm near springs and washes. During the period of conquest, there is evidence that farming took on increased importance, resulting in larger and more stable settlements of as many as 250 Walapais. With the establishment of the reservation and consequent reduction in the territory available to Walapais for hunting, gathering, and farming, many took jobs and quarters in towns along the railroad. By 1960, only half of the enrolled tribal members resided in the reservation town of Peach Springs.

Archaeological evidence suggests that the primary aboriginal house form was the rough brush wickiup, a circular structure without poles. Habitation debris has also been located in caves and rock shelters. During the postcontact period, Walapais were observed living in more permanent domed houses, thatched with arrowweed or covered with juniper bark. Eight-sided hogans and tar-paper shacks became common during the reservation period. During the 1970s, the tribe undertook a substantial effort to develop adequate housing on the reservation.

Economy

Subsistence and Commercial Activities.   Historically, the Walapai economy was based primarily on hunting and gathering seasonally available wild resources. Moving frequently, the camps visited locations where resources were known to be abundant. This annual round focused on several key plant foods. In the spring, agave or mescal was gathered in canyons and foothills. When baked for several days in an earth oven, the plant's inner core was eaten immediately while the outer layers were crushed into pulp, dried, and stored for future consumption. Following the mescal harvest, the camps or individual families moved down to the valley and basin floors to collect stick-leaf and abundant and protein-rich wild seed. By midsummer, fruits of several cactus species ripened, and in late summer, attention shifted to nut gathering in mountain groves. Few vegetal resources were available during the winter months, but the Walapai survived on wild game and the stored products of the spring and summer. As settlers moved into Walapai territory in the nineteenth century to graze cattle, cut trees for mine timbers, and exploit wild game, this adaptive hunting and gathering economy changed. Walapais, of necessity, turned increasingly to farming the land around springs and the few perennial streams in the region. Walapais constructed diversion dams to irrigate gardens of squash, maize, beans, watermelons, and wheat. But, once again, this response proved to be short-lived. Restricted to the high grasslands of the reservation after 1883, Walapais in the twentieth century have come to rely on cattle (four thousand head in the 1980s), wage employment in tribal and federal agencies, a successful doll factory, and recently, the development of recreational facilities along the Grand Canyon, bordering the reservation. Nonetheless, over 40 percent of reservation residents remain unemployed. The horses and cattle introduced by Europeans were viewed, until the reservation period, as food on the hoof.

Industrial Arts.   Walapai basketry came to be highly valued in the trade network and afforded women a major outlet for artistic expression. Most baskets were functional containers such as large firewood and burden baskets, conical seed-gathering baskets, flat trays for parching and winnowing seeds, and water bottles sealed with pitch from the piñon tree. Walapai pottery, another aboriginal art, did not survive the influx of metal utensils during the postcontact period.

Trade.   The Walapai actively traded the products of hunting and gathering pursuits to their agricultural neighbors during aboriginal and postcontact times. When at peace with the Mohave, they bartered meat for the beans, maize, and pumpkins cultivated along the river's floodplain. Cultivated foods were also obtained from the Havasupai in return for deer and the skins of mountain sheep. Trade linkages extended well beyond adjacent groups, however. Walapai introduced distinctive products—dried mescal, red hematite pigment, and the prized basketry—into an exchange network which linked Indians of the Pacific Coast to the Pueblos of New Mexico.

Division of Labor.   In the traditional hunting and gathering economy, women bore primary responsibility for collecting and processing plant resources, and men hunted. Farming activities were carried out by all members of the family.

Land Tenure.   Prior to the establishment of a reservation, land tenure took the form of a "customary range," an area of habitat diversity within which the bands gathered and hunted wild resources. The boundaries of these ranges were not precisely demarcated, but there was common consent among the Walapai that the various ranges were the primary subsistence grounds of the bands inhabiting them.

Kinship

Kin Groups and Descent.   Historically, the nuclear family of parents and children was seldom an isolated and self-sufficient unit. Rather, camps of about twenty-five individuals, usually several related nuclear families, proved to be necessary for protection against raids, for communal hunts, and for efficient gathering of wild plant resources. While the camp was the primary land-use unit during the historic period, several camps utilizing adjacent territories were grouped into patrilineal bands, headed by the most respected of the leaders of the individual camps. Eligibility for camp leadership, and thus for the headship of the bands, was transmitted patrilineally, but potential leaders won respect more for their bravery, wisdom, and oratorical abilities than for strict genealogical descent.

Kinship Terminology.   Under reservation life, the Yuman-type kinship terminology of the Walapai does not appear to have retained its salience.

Marriage and Family

Marriage.   Traditionally, marriage was not marked by formal ceremony. Rather, the process was initiated through repeated gifts by the male suitor to the girl's father. If the father found the man to be acceptable, he would urge his daughter to receive the man. Upon marriage, a man was expected to live for a time in the camp of his spouse and then return with his wife to his own patrilineal camp. In practice, however, young couples typically joined the camp that was most in need of their help in subsistence activities. Divorce was reported to be frequent in the postcontact era, for reasons of incompatibility, jealousy, and adultery. With settled reservation life, the incidence of divorce has declined substantially.

Domestic Unit.   Several related families joined together to form the basic domestic entity, the camp. Frequently, these families were polygamous, out of the need to ensure sufficient labor for domestic activities.

Inheritance.   Under aboriginal conditions, notions of inheritance of private property were weakly developed, since an individual's possessions were burned upon death. Access to wild resources within the tribal range was, however, a critical right inherited through the patrilineal band.

Socialization.   Historically, the socialization of children and adolescents centered on economic pursuits, training the young in the critical tasks of hunting and gathering. In recent years, a noteworthy interest has been shown by Walapais in documenting and preserving Walapai language and culture. The Peach Springs School, opened on the reservation in the 1950s, has implemented an extensive program in bilingual and bicultural education for its students.

Sociopolitical Organization

Social Organization.   Prior to its disruptive encounter with the U.S. Cavalry in the 1860s, the Walapai tribe was divided into three named subtribes, each encompassing several adjoining patrilineal bands and their constituent camps. These social units tended to be endogamous, since marriage partners were most frequently selected from adjacent camps and bands. But strict territoriality does not appear to have been maintained: subtribes shared land and resources with other Walapais when necessary for survival. The reservation system has transformed this aboriginal social organization. The Havasupai reservation was established for a single band within one subtribe, and the Walapai reservation, drawing its designation from the proper name for another patrilineal band, now houses descendants of twelve other aboriginal bands.

Political Organization and Conflict.   War with the United States, as well as the customary practice of governmental agents to seek "chiefs" as signatories to official documents, elevated several of the camp and band headmen to positions of subtribal leadership. Wauba Yuma, shortly before his murder, put his mark on the toll-road contract on behalf of the Yavapai Fighters subtribe, as did Hitchi Hitchi for the Plateau People. And Cherum, of the Middle Mountain People, took military command in the ensuing war, developing a clever trade network by which he procured arms from Southern Paiutes who had in turn obtained them from Mormons in Utah. With the creation of the reservation, bringing agents of the Indian Service to Truxton Canyon, the incipient tribal leadership fell dormant. The present tribal government, an elective nine-member council, was established under provisions of the Indian Reorganization Act in the late 1930s.

Social Control.   Aboriginally, the wisdom and oratorical skills of the camp and band leaders were marshaled in family disputes. Undoubtedly, too, the fluidity of group membership facilitated resolution, as disputants could join the camps of friends and relatives.

Religion and Expressive Culture

Religious Beliefs.   The Walapai, like other Yuman groups, do not have an elaborate cosmology or a complex ritual cycle.

Spirits to which shamans attach themselves are associated with particular locations within aboriginal Walapai territory. In the twentieth century, they have been subjected to repeated missionary activity, but the Baptists, Mormons, and the revivalist Four Square Gospel mission have met with little success on the reservation. Much of the traditional religious activity, continuing well into the present century, centers around the shaman.

Religious Practitioners and Medicine. A deceased relative's spirit alerts a prospective shaman to his specialty through a series of dreams. Then, during a solitary visit to a mountain, the individual acquires the necessary power from the spirits through additional dream sequences. Thus prepared, the shaman may operate in the realm of curative medicine. Treatment of diseases and snakebites consists of singing over the patient and sucking the wounds. The specialist may then produce a small object from the wound, believed to be the locus of the malignant spirit. By extracting the offending object, the shaman returns the evil spirit to its mountain. It is reported historically that the shaman was liable to be killed by the relatives of a deceased patient or rewarded with buckskins if the patient recovered.

Ceremonies. The individualistic character of the shaman complex gives rise to few groupwide ceremonial occasions among the Walapai. Girls pass through a brief puberty ceremonial following their initial menses, but, historically, marriage was not marked by formal rites.

Arts. Facial painting and shell neck pendants were, historically, important modes of personal decoration and expression. The shells, obtained in trade from Yumans along the Colorado River, functioned as charms or amulets, guarding the wearer against disease.

Death and Afterlife. Traditionally, Walapai dead were cremated along with their material possessions. The souls of the good people departed for the ancestral land on the bank of the Colorado River to the accompaniment of ceremonial crying by living relatives and friends. Late in the nineteenth century, U.S. soldiers attempted to enforce Christian burial practices, and many Walapai partially acquiesced, interring the dead in rock slides and cairns. The mourning ceremony, an elaborate ritual among the Colorado River Yumans, persists in attenuated form among the Walapai.

Bibliography

Dobyns, Henry F., and Robert C. Euler (1970). *Wauba Yuma's People: The Comparative Socio-Political Structure of the Pai Indians of Arizona*. Prescott College Studies in Anthropology, no. 3. Prescott, Ariz.: Prescott College Press.

Kroeber, Alfred L., ed. (1935). *Walapai Ethnography*. American Anthropological Association, Memoir 42. Menasha, Wis.

Martin, John F. (1985). "The Prehistory and Ethnohistory of Havasupai-Hualapai Relations." *Ethnohistory* 32:135–153.

THOMAS R. MCGUIRE

Wallawalla

The Wallawalla (Walula), including the Palouse (Palus) and Wauyukma, lived along the Wallawalla, Palouse, and Snake rivers in southeastern Washington. The Wallawalla now live on the Umatilla Indian Reservation in Oregon with the Umatilla and the Cayuse. They spoke a Sahaptin language of the Penutian phylum and numbered about five hundred in the 1980s.

Bibliography

Gunkel, Alexander (1979). *Culture in Conflict: a Study of Contrasted Interrelations and Reactions between Euroamericans and the Wallawalla Indians of Washington State*. Ann Arbor, Mich.: University Microfilms International.

Wappo

The Wappo (Ashochimi) lived along the headwaters of the Napa River and Pope and Putah creeks to the south of Clear Lake in northern California. They spoke a language of the Yukian family and probably number less than fifty today.

Bibliography

Driver, Harold (1936). *Wappo Ethnography*. University of California Publications in American Archaeology and Ethnology, 36. Berkeley.

Sawyer, Jesse O. (1978). "Wappo." In *Handbook of North American Indians*. Vol. 8, *California*, edited by Robert F. Heizer, 256–263. Washington, D.C.: Smithsonian Institution.

Washoe

ETHNONYMS: Wah-shoes, Wahshoo, Washaws, Washew, Washo, Washoo

Orientation

Identification. The spelling "Washo" became standard in the ethnographic and linguistic literature of the twentieth century, but "Washoe" is the official spelling used by the people and has been firmly established as local usage in Nevada.

The people refer to themselves as wá·šiw or waší·šwíw which appears to mean "people from here."

Location. In early historic times the Washoe inhabited a region of about four thousand square miles between Honey Lake to the north and the upper reaches of the West Walker River to the south. On the east, the Pinenut and Virginia ranges separated them from the Northern Paiute, and on the west the crest of the Sierra Nevada Mountains separated them from the Miwok and Maidu peoples. The state boundary between Nevada and California roughly bisects their ancient territory, running through Lake Tahoe at an approximate center. Their major year-round settlements were in the well-watered valleys along the eastern slopes of the Sierra Nevada Mountains at an altitude of about forty-five hundred feet and where there was an abundance of vegetation and game. They also made extensive use of alpine areas up to elevations of six thousand or more feet for seasonal hunting, fishing, and gathering except during the severest winters. Regular treks were made to the acorn oak groves in the foothills over the crest of the mountains as well as to fishing sites shared with the Northern Paiute at Pyramid, Walker, and Mono lakes. Today, the remaining Washoe live in small colonies and scattered settlements at Reno, Carson City, and Dresslerville, Nevada, and around Woodfords, California. The headquarters of the modern tribal government is at Gardnerville, Nevada.

Demography. The estimates of an aboriginal population of fifteen hundred or so Washoe people are much lower than what might be expected from the size and resources of the area they inhabited. But they did suffer a sharp drop in numbers owing to disease and poverty in the nineteenth and early twentieth centuries, when figures as low as three hundred were reported. After the 1950s, with increased federal support for education and improved economic conditions, there has been a rapid population recovery indicated by the registration of well over fifteen hundred persons on the tribal rolls.

Linguistic Affiliation. Linguists tentatively agree that Washoe (Washo) belongs to the Hokan stock of Amerind languages. Evidence is uncertain for earlier conjectures that the Washoe migrated eastward from a prehistoric association with other Hokan-speaking peoples in what is now California to their present location, or that they represent the remnant of an ancient distribution of Hokan-speakers some one thousand or more years ago. The isolation of Washoe from related languages, together with linguistic and archaeological evidence, suggests that it has been in place for many thousands of years. The language reveals little dialectic differentiation, but some borrowing has occurred with Numic and other neighboring languages. The number of fluent speakers of Washoe has declined drastically in recent times.

History and Cultural Relations

The Washoe people and their country were unknown to Americans until the early nineteenth century when explorers such as Joseph Walker, Jedediah Smith, and John Frémont traversed the central Great Basin seeking direct routes to California. Although they had some earlier contact with the Spanish to the west, actual intrusion of their territory did not occur until the hordes of immigrants began to appear from the east during the gold rush of the 1840s and 1850s. Many

Whites were attracted to the verdant valleys occupied by the Washoe, fencing the lands for cattle, restricting access to water sources, and establishing numerous trading posts and settlements. By the 1870s the lowland forests, grasslands, and the large game so essential to Washoe subsistence had become depleted. The completion of the transcontinental railroad signaled the end of the old life-way and its conquest by a new, alien society. For the next one hundred years, the Washoe were forced into the status of servile, unfranchised dependents in an aggressive frontier world. Appeals by Washoe spokesmen or by the occasional sympathetic Indian agent for aid and lands went unheeded. A reservation was never assigned to them, and the land allotments provided under the Dawes Act of 1887 were largely unfit for habitation or development. Many families leased their allotments at extremely low rates to sheep ranchers, which, in turn, led to the rapid deterioration of the piñon groves whose harvesting had provided one of the major staples in aboriginal times. The people lived in squalid camps on the outskirts of White towns or on the ranches where many were employed.

In 1917, a few small parcels of land with inadequate facilities were set aside at Reno, Carson City, and Dresslerville primarily for Washoe use. Schools for Indian children were segregated, their language and traditional customs were discouraged, and discriminatory policies restricted social interaction. Citizenship was not granted until 1924. Some improvement in conditions began to take place after the Indian Reorganization Act of 1934 when the Washoe became a legally constituted tribe with a written constitution and official tribal council.

Major change, however, did not occur until after 1970 when the Washoe won a compensation of $5 million (of a $43 million claim filed in 1948) before the Indian Claims Commission. Through effective investment of 70 percent of the funds and issuing per capita payments only to older members, considerable advancement has been made in tribal organization and services. With the emergence of new leadership and planning, state and federal funds were procured for housing, employment opportunities, educational programs, tribal businesses, and additional lands. Young people began to remain in the area or to return from relocation with a sense of hope and renewed identity. The Washoe Tribe of Nevada and California has become an active participant in intertribal affairs, and many of its members are pursuing successful careers in the larger local and national communities.

The aboriginal Washoe were a peaceable people who nevertheless staunchly defended their core habitation and subsistence areas from hostile intrusion yet tolerated access by others except in times of extreme scarcity. Likewise, neighboring peoples such as the Northern Paiute, Miwok, and Maidu allowed some use of resources in their own domains. The few brief skirmishes were between small groups over matters of unnegotiated trespass, perceived insult, or revenge. Networks of intermarriage reinforced long-standing friendly relations with families of surrounding peoples, and this practice has continued into historic times. The Washoe at first accommodated incoming Whites during the early nineteenth century and resorted to sporadic resistance only when the intruders threatened their resources and autonomy. But they were quickly overwhelmed and forced into passive acquiescence during a century of frontier conquest.

Settlements

Aboriginal Washoe settlements were generally placed on elevated ground near sources of water. Domiciles tended to be widely spaced for privacy and reduced visibility from afar. Permanent year-round settlements were maintained in traditionally established locations in the six or seven major lowland valleys along the eastern slope of the Sierra Nevada Mountains. Housing sites, or even entire settlements, might be moved about within these areas upon the death of family members, changing relations between households, or other conditions. During seasonal hunting and gathering activities, small groups set up temporary camps in the mountains or while trekking to distant locations in search of desired resources, returning to their permanent settlements for the winter months. This pattern of mobility and option was terminated by White usurpation in the 1850s. Today, the Washoe continue to live mainly in the small colonies established in the early twentieth century, though many live and work in local towns or in other areas. The traditional winter house was most common in permanent settlements and was a conical construction of bark slabs supported by interlocked poles set over a shallow depression in the ground with an entrance facing eastward. Dome-shaped summer houses of willow frame thatched with tule and brush were used as well as the simple lean-to for shade or for temporary shelter on seasonal treks. During the late nineteenth and early twentieth centuries, versions of these structures were made of discarded materials from White settlements. Standard colony housing up to the 1960s involved rows of dilapidated board shacks surrounded by the accumulated rubble of attempted repair and scavenged materials. Owing to the advancements of the past twenty or thirty years, the quality of Washoe housing today exceeds that of most low-income residences in the area.

Economy

Subsistence and Commercial Activities.   Washoe aboriginal economy was based on hunting, fishing, and gathering. The environment provided an abundance of large and small game, fish in the lakes and streams, and seeds and other plant products requiring a highly skilled pattern of seasonal exploitation over the year. Although the local pinenut and the acorn from over the mountains were much desired foods (and continue to be in modern times when available), other food resources provided a major part of the diet. The destruction of the subsistence base in early historic times resulted in a rapid transformation of diet to one of starches, fats, and sweets prevalent among rural western White settlers. During the frontier period many Washoe lived and worked on ranches—the men as laborers and cowhands, and the women as laundresses and cooks. Other men were employed in the mines or the construction of roads and dams. Some brought wood, fish, and game into the towns for sale until they were restricted by local laws. A few women supplemented income by selling baskets and pinenuts or hiring out to domestic service. Most, however, were destitute. Today, many younger Washoe men and women participate in the general economy and are employed in an expanded tribal government or in a number of tribally operated businesses. In precontact times, the dog was the only domesticated animal. A few Washoe had acquired ponies from the Spanish in California and, later, from

American settlers. But conditions did not permit the development of an equestrian mode such as that appearing among their Northern Paiute neighbors in the early nineteenth century. Sporadic attempts to raise cattle and sheep on tribal lands have been unsuccessful.

Industrial Arts.   The aboriginal Washoe produced a range of manufactures in stone, wood, fiber, bone, or skins, and utilized a repertoire of technologies typical of the hunting and gathering economies of the western Great Basin. American implements, utensils, clothing, and ornament quickly replaced the traditional forms. The basketry produced by the women was admired by all surrounding peoples and continued to be developed as an art of renown well into the twentieth century.

Trade.   Aboriginal trade seems not to have been extensive in the region, though the Washoe did exchange by barter and gift giving some salt, pinenuts, and deer and rabbit skins to westward peoples, such as the Miwok and Maidu, for shells, obsidian, certain medicinal plants, and other items which, in turn, were traded eastward to the Northern Paiute for antelope skins, *kutsavi* and *cui-ui* fish. In the early postcontact period, they engaged in a small exchange involving firewood, pinenuts, game, and fish to White settlers.

Division of Labor.   Traditionally, the gathering of plant products was almost exclusively a woman's activity, as were preparation of food and other household tasks. Women might also participate in major fish runs, rabbit drives, and surrounds of large games such as deer or antelope. Hunting and combat, however, were men's activities, as well as the making of weapons and stone implements. Yet considerable cooperation obtained for major tasks requiring group effort. Among the modern Washoe, even when both men and women are wage earners, traditional gender roles tend to be maintained.

Land Tenure.   Except for traditional habitation or hunting and gathering sites in regular use, Washoe territory was an open range accessible to any but hostile or uncooperative trespassers. Individual families claimed rights to certain plots in the Pinenut Range, but these were generally shared in times of abundance. There was no concept of sectional or tribal land ownership but, rather, flexible and traditionally recognized domains of privilege with regard to natural resources. Notions of land ownership imposed by Whites during early contact, and in the arbitrary assignment of land allotments in the late nineteenth century, were alien and continue to engender stress in social relations. Many Washoe now own land individually, and certain new acquisitions are owned by the tribe in federal trust.

Kinship

Kin Groups and Descent.   Variant forms of the bilateral extended family constituted the basic Washoe kin groups. These composed the small local communities that were essentially family compounds referred to as "bunches." Networks of intermarriage in long-established areas of habitation led to the formation of larger regional communities, or "bands," which people identified as places of relatively permanent residence and close kinship. Ties with more distant communities were weaker and relationships less traceable, but conditions of limited population distribution, mobility, and common language and culture induced a sense of "tribal" identity among all sections. Groups were not corporate, and notions of descent functioned mainly to determine the possible range of kinship obligations and of permissible sexual or marital relations.

Kinship Terminology. All siblings and cousins were referred to by the terms for brother and sister (a "generational" system) and further distinguished only by the relative ages of their parents. Terms in the parental generation were bifurcate-collateral; that is, they provided distinct terms for each of the parents and their siblings. Some change toward the general American system has been taking place in the twentieth century.

Marriage and Family

Marriage. No marriage with known consanguineal relatives was permissible. Despite the small population, potentials for marriageability were maintained by the extensive mobility of individuals and groups and shallow genealogical reckoning that limited the tracing of relationships. Monogamy was the most common marital arrangement, but polygyny (both sororal and nonsororal) frequently occurred. The sororate and levirate also were practiced. First marriages were usually arranged by parents. During the first years of marriage, residence was bilocal but with a tendency to matrilocality. Separation because of incompatibility, infidelity, or improvidence could be initiated by either spouse and was recognized by the community. Intermarriage with other Native Americans and with Whites is increasing in recent times, and marriage practices in general follow the American pattern.

Domestic Unit. The members of a localized bilateral extended family together with some affines, distant relatives, and visiting friends formed the minimal domestic unit. Individuals shifted residence frequently to live in communities of relatives or friends elsewhere. Where feasible, modern Washoe residential arrangements follow earlier patterns.

Inheritance. There is no clear evidence that statuses or property were passed down through any rule of inheritance in aboriginal times. Personal possessions were disposed of at death, and headships and other offices were determined by group consensus. Today, the American system of descent and inheritance prevails legally, though the traditional orientation often is expressed in practice.

Socialization. Nurturing and permissive guidance were the model for ideal parenting. Expression of hostility or violence toward children was strongly discouraged. Admonition and punishment were relegated to third persons or to the threat of supernatural intervention. This pattern continues to predominate among modern Washoe families where personal autonomy and individualism are respected and asserted.

Sociopolitical Organization

Social Organization. Washoe society was egalitarian in orientation with no fixed distinctions of wealth or status groups. Leadership and roles of special skill were acquired through demonstrated ability and legitimized by local group recognition. Women frequently attained positions of authority and expert specialization. Personal attributes of generosity, modesty, and wise counsel were expected if the commu-

nity were not to withdraw its support by turning to another. Today, differences in education and income do obtain, but the traditional social values are effective in minimizing the development of class divisions.

Political Organization. Aboriginal Washoe communities were autonomous, each represented by local headmen or headwomen whose role was essentially that of admired adviser or spokesperson. Ties between local communities were voluntary and could be activated for cooperative enterprises such as festivals, game drives, and defense. Renowned shamans, hunters, or warriors sometimes were solicited as temporary leaders for these purposes. Communication was maintained with distant Washoe sections for periodic communal gatherings and, though rarely, during emergencies where additional warriors might be needed. During historic times, the forced concentration of the Washoe in the small areas allocated by Whites disrupted this pattern of organization. Certain spokesmen, either familiar with English or amenable to negotiation with Whites, were designated as "Captains" under the erroneous assumption that they represented most of the people. A few of these men, such as the renowned "Captain Jim" in the late nineteenth century, emerged as vigorous pleaders for the Washoe cause. Attempts at tribal reorganization in the early twentieth century were ineffective because of the strong sense of family autonomy and resistance to centralized representation. In more recent times, however, an elected Washoe Tribal Council representing each of the colonies as well as off-reservation persons has developed a successful tribal government under federal supervision. It administers collective Washoe affairs and relations with state and federal agencies.

Social Control. Internal cohesion was maintained by intensive socialization for group solidarity. Aggressive behavior, except for defense of the group, was rigidly proscribed. Infractions were dealt with by collective avoidance or the threat of supernatural reprisal. Recalcitrant individuals might be driven from the group or even assassinated. Modern Washoe communities have the services of a tribal police force and courts. Law enforcement agencies of local towns and counties exert a degree of jurisdiction.

Conflict. Warfare among aboriginal Washoe subgroups appears to have been absent, though occasional feuds between individuals or families erupted briefly into open violence. These were resolved when a wrong was deemed to have been avenged or through the intervention of elder negotiators on each side. As the first people in the western Great Basin to experience the full brunt of White invasion, the Washoe were quickly reduced to helplessness in defense of their interests. A deep sense of hopelessness and betrayal permeated their lives during most of the postcontact period and conditioned Washoe-White relations. Homicide, factionalism, gambling, suicide, and accusations of witchcraft increased throughout the small Washoe settlements in the late nineteenth and early twentieth centuries. Some individuals and families managed to escape the worst effects of these circumstances, but all endured the stigma of oppression and degradation. Today, the ravages of the recent past are being obliterated by a remarkable economic and social recovery. Internal conflict has greatly diminished and a positive cultural heritage is being reasserted.

Religion and Expressive Culture

Religious Beliefs. Prayers and ritual manipulation of spiritual powers believed to be invested in nature were the active instruments of Washoe religion and were deemed essential to any successful human endeavor. Nature must be propitiated to ensure its bounty and goodwill. All natural phenomena were thought to be imbued with sentient spirit power. Animals in particular were personified as autochthons in myths of geologic and human origins. Spirits of the dead were feared, and there is little evidence that notions of a supreme being existed prior to the historic period. The modern Washoe retain many of these beliefs and the practices associated with them. Some have been participants in the Native American church while the Assembly of God and the Baptist church have attracted others.

Religious Practitioners. In former times, the shamans were the principal specialists in the use of magical powers for rites of diagnosis, curing, and divination. Their skills also might be exerted to defend against the hostile powers of others or to destroy one's enemies. There were many other individuals acknowledged to derive their abilities from tutelary relationships with specific powers of nature, especially those persons exhibiting exceptional skill in subsistence, ceremonial, medicinal, or martial activities, but they did not command the degree of obeisance afforded the shamans. In the 1930s and 1940s the shamans had obtained such a powerful hold among the Washoe that they were finally denounced by an irate community for conspiracy to defraud and for their exorbitant fees. This movement was led by the new local Native American church which was itself under attack by many White as well as Washoe citizens for its use of peyote as a sacrament. Nevertheless, the control of the shamans was weakened and, in recent times, none is acknowledged in the area. Christian ministers, itinerant preachers, and a few remaining roadchiefs of the Native American church continue to provide religious guidance, while Western medical practitioners and some native herbalists administer to the ailing.

Ceremonies. Important annual ceremonies involving large numbers of people took place at the first harvest in the Pinenut Range, in the easternmost extension of the acorn oak groves near Honey Lake, and at the locations of major fish runs associated with the rivers and lakes of the region. A more localized, but equally important rite was the celebration of the commencement of menses by a girl's family and friends. Other special rites also took place at the birth of a child, boy's puberty, marriage, and death. Many of these observances continue today in diminished and variant forms among some families.

Arts. Most expressions of aboriginal artistry disappeared early in the historic period. These included ornament in shell, bone, and seed; distinctive styles of body painting and tattooing; feathered headdresses; decorative skin and fur accessories; and dyed and woven fibers. There was also an extensive repertoire of songs, tales, and legends, very little of which has been retained. The major surviving art has been the exceptionally fine basketry that became internationally renowned in the early twentieth century through the work of the famous Datsolalee and a number of other expert weavers. Elaborate woven cradles still are constructed for infants, and fancy beadwork and some baskets are made for sale.

Medicine. Illness was attributed to the intrusion of alien objects, offended supernatural agencies, sorcery, or bad feeling. A wide range of herbal and mineral substances was employed in treatment by shamans and various categories of curers endowed with special derived powers. Modern Washoe rely mainly on Western medical facilities, but many also utilize traditional knowledge of herbs and customary practices passed down through elder family members.

Death and Afterlife. Except for old age and chronic infirmity, death was seldom attributed to natural causes. Thus, the occasion of a death was fraught with concern for the safety of the living: every effort must be made to protect the immediate family from whatever malevolent forces might be at work. The spirit of the deceased must be pacified by a period of public mourning and prayers beseeching it to leave the area swiftly and without rancor. Burials in a remote place or cremation were the most common. The personal belongings of the deceased were interred or burned with the body. There was a prohibition against speaking the name of the deceased in the presence of close relatives, for this might call the spirit. Ideas of an afterlife were ambiguous: recorded lore suggests variously that the dead live underground, that some are reluctant to leave the area where they died and wander aimlessly about doing inadvertent or purposeful harm, or that there is a land to the south where spirits of the dead reside. The cosmological beliefs of the modern Washoe are generally similar to those of the American society of which they are now a part but also are influenced by the spread of pan-Indian philosophical concepts among Native American communities. Funerals are of major importance, and though they are usually conducted in accordance with the contemporary rites of local Christian churches, traditional prayers and funeral customs are often observed as well.

Bibliography

d'Azevedo, Warren L., ed. (1956). *The Washo Indians of California and Nevada.* University of Utah Anthropological Papers, no. 67. Salt Lake City.

d'Azevedo, Warren L. (1986). "Washoe." In *Handbook of North American Indians.* Vol. 11, *Great Basin,* edited by Warren L. d'Azevedo, 466–498. Washington, D.C.: Smithsonian Institution.

Downs, James F. (1966). *Two Worlds of the Washo.* New York: Holt, Rinehart & Winston.

Nevers, J. Ann (1976). *Wa-She-Shu: A Washo Tribal History.* Reno: Intertribal Council of Nevada.

Price, John A. (1980). *The Washo Indians: History, Life Cycle, Religion, Technology, Economy, and Modern Life.* Nevada State Museum Occasional Papers, no. 4. Carson City.

Siskin, Edgar E. (1983). *Washo Shamans and Peyotists: Religious Conflict in an American Indian Tribe.* Salt Lake City: University of Utah Press.

WARREN L. D'AZEVEDO

Western Apache

ETHNONYMS: Dził ghą'i, Dilzhę'ę, Dził t'aadń, Ndeé

Orientation

Identification.   The name "Apache" first appears in the historical record in 1598. There is no undisputed etymology, although Zuni is often cited as its source. The Western Apache include the subtribes White Mountain, San Carlos, Cibecue, Northern Tonto, and Southern Tonto. They were defined as a single cultural unit because dialect variation among them was minor, they were horticultural to a degree, and they were linked through matrilineal clans, although they themselves recognized no such superordinate level of organization. All used the word *Ndeé*, or "man, person, Indian," to refer to their specific subtribe, but they did not necessarily include the other "Western Apache" in such a designation.

Location.   Since the late seventeenth century the Western Apache have occupied the mountains of the Mogollon Rim, and the high desert transition zone of the Colorado Plateau, including the headwaters of the Verde, Salt, and Little Colorado rivers, and part of the Gila River. The area is between 32° and 35° N and 109° and 112° W. Today, most Western Apache live on the Fort Apache (White Mountain), San Carlos, Camp Verde, and Payson reservations.

Demography.   According to the 1980 census the Indian populations of the three major reservations were Fort Apache, 7,010; San Carlos, 6,013; and Camp Verde, 136. Estimates of the nineteenth-century population total less than 5,000.

Linguistic Affiliation.   Western Apache is one of the Apachean (Southern Athapaskan) languages, classified in the Athapaskan stock of the NaDené phylum.

History and Cultural Relations

Linguistic and cultural evidence indicates that the Western Apache migrated from Canada between A.D. 1400 and 1500 and arrived in Arizona no earlier than the 1600s where they came into contact with the native Pueblo populations. Pueblo influence was particularly strong after the Pueblo Revolt of 1680 when numerous Pueblos took up residence among Apacheans. Severe pressure from Utes in the early 1700s and again in the mid-1800s along with the U.S. campaign led by Kit Carson resulted in groups of Navajo moving south and coming into contact with or even taking up residence among Apaches. It is likely that it was during these times that the Navajo introduced horticulture and matrilineal clans. Relations with both Western Pueblos and the Navajo alternated between trade and raid up through the nineteenth century. Relations with Spain also alternated between war and peace, though relations with Mexico were generally hostile. Although some new technical items were added to the Apache inventory along with their Spanish names, Spanish and Mexican cultures had little significant impact.

The Western Apache were much less affected than other Apacheans by the changes brought about by the 1848 Treaty of Guadalupe Hidalgo and the subsequent Gadsden Purchase of 1853, probably because their lands in north-central Arizona were not astride major routes of travel, nor, except in the Tonto area, were there major mining activities. They accepted without resistance the presence of forts within their territory, and the White Mountain and Cibecue groups in particular made peace and cooperated with the new conquerors. This quiescent state was marred by two major incidents—the Camp Grant Massacre in 1871, in which at least seventy-five San Carlos women and children were killed by residents of Tucson and their Papago allies, and the Cibecue Fight in 1881, which resulted in the death of a prominent shaman along with a number of soldiers and Apache scouts.

Settlements

With the adoption of horticulture Western Apaches became permanently associated with farming sites. This association was seasonal with local groups composed of several matrilineal-matrilocal extended families (*gotah*) moving from place to place in a yearly round of hunting and gathering—returning in the spring and fall to the farm area and in the winter moving to lower elevations. Local groups varied in size from thirty-five to two hundred individuals and had exclusive rights to certain farm sites and hunting localities. Adjacent local groups, loosely linked through marriage, areal proximity, and dialect, formed what have been called bands controlling farming and hunting resources primarily in a single watershed area. There were twenty of these bands in 1850, each composed of about four local groups. Their ethnographic names, such as Cibecue Creek Band or Carrizo Creek Band, reflect their watershed specificity.

Contemporary Apache communities are an amalgam of these older, territorially defined units, which during the reservation period concentrated near agency headquarters, trading posts, schools, and roads. On the White Mountain Apache Reservation there are two major communities at Cibecue and Whiteriver, and on the San Carlos Reservation there are two at San Carlos and Bylas. Traditional housing was the wickiup (*gogha*); contemporary housing consists of a mixture of older frame homes, modern cinder block or frame tract houses, and mobile homes. Some housing is substandard relative to general U.S. standards, though vast improvements have been made in the last twenty years. The White Mountain Apaches have had a particularly aggressive development program and own a shopping center, motel, theater, sawmill, and ski resort.

Economy

Subsistence and Commercial Activities.   In traditional times, about 40 percent of the diet came from gathered wild plant foods, 35 percent from meat (especially deer), and 25 percent from horticulture. Wild food products included sahuaro fruit, mescal (agave), acorns, mesquite beans, juniper berries, and piñon nuts. Horticulture was practiced in fields often less than an acre in size, with small dams and channels used for irrigation. After the establishment of the reservations a few Apaches took advantage of government allotment programs to develop cattle herds, but those who did often came into conflict with Whites who grazed cattle through a permit system on the reservations. By the 1950s most of the non-Indians who were running livestock on Indian land had been forced off, and the tribes themselves started cooperative herding operations with stock owned by individuals but managed by tribal employees.

Subsistence farming has continued up to the present day only on the Fort Apache Reservation. The White Mountain Apache Tribe has started an irrigated farming operation, and both reservations have a variety of tourist facilities to profit from camping, boating, fishing, and hunting by non-Indians along with lumbering. The Fort Apache Reservation has been more successful in these enterprises than San Carlos because it has more resources and a better climate. San Carlos has developed a jojoba nut industry, and some Apaches mine and sell the semiprecious stone peridot, which is found relatively close to the surface in one area of the reservation. All these activities provide jobs and income for at least part of the population. Other income derives from off-reservation employment, government jobs, small businesses, and public assistance.

Industrial Arts. Traditional activities such as tanning skins, basket making, and the manufacture of cradle boards and pitch-lined water jars are still done on a limited basis. Beadwork, painting, and doll making have been added to the repertoire.

Trade. In the past, Apaches traded with some of the surrounding tribes for a variety of items. Individual handicrafts are still occasionally traded to local stores or sold to dealers, but for the most part the economic system on the reservations is part of the larger American cash economy.

Division of Labor. Although hunting, raiding, and warfare were usually men's tasks, and gathering, basket making, child rearing, and cooking, women's, the division of labor was flexible. Both sexes worked fields and continue to do so. Both work at public gatherings. Both could function in leadership roles and as shamans, although men did so more often. Today both sexes run for and are elected to tribal office. There is, however, marked physical separation of men and women in a variety of contexts, and to preserve their reputations a man and a woman must not be alone with each other.

Land Tenure. Aboriginally, the bands controlled resources within their territories, and farmlands were owned by the individuals who were members of the various local groups. Individuals could will their land to any of their offspring or to their surviving spouse and could also lend land to any of their relatives. Only if they wished to lend land to a nonrelative was approval of local leaders needed. Today land is held in trust by the U.S. government, and individual-use rights are controlled by rules based on a mix of tradition and tribal law.

Kinship

Kin Groups and Descent. There are over fifty named exogamous matrilineal clans, which form three unnamed phratries. Clans were named after farm sites, and the phratries no doubt formed as a result of population spread and settlement of new farm sites. Clans functioned to regulate marriage, sponsor and support the ritual activities of their members, enact revenge, and aid in day-to-day cooperative work groups. Since clans tended to be localized within the same band, they operated at a restricted geographic level, but because the phratries were represented in all the subtribes, they provided weak cross-cutting ties among all the Western Apaches. Clans continue today to play some role in Western Apache

politics, feuds, and ritual; the clan, however, is being supplemented by friendships for mutual economic support in ritual activities, and clan endogamous marriages occur.

Kinship Terminology. Cousin terminology is of the Iroquois type, with bifurcate collateral parental generation terms, emphasis being placed on parental-generation matrilateral kin with parental-generation patrilateral kin being merged into one category regardless of gender.

Marriage and the Family

Marriage. Distant patrilateral cross cousins in the father's clan or phratry were considered ideal and some marriage partners reflect such exchange in several successive generations. Sororal polygyny, levirate, and sororate marriages all occurred. Chastity was highly valued and girls were extremely shy when interacting with boys. During the first few days of a marriage the couple did not necessarily sleep together and sometimes were chaperoned by a female relative of the wife. Residence was matrilocal with the son-in-law responsible for hunting, protection, and labor on his in-law's farm. Rather strict mother-in-law avoidance is still practiced by many Apaches. Divorce was easy and could be effected by either party.

Domestic Unit. Gotah were composed of several generations with a core of matrilineally related women. Some contemporary residence units still reflect this structure, but with jobs frequently requiring sons-in-law to be elsewhere, many families have other arrangements. But, even in families living in tract-style houses it is not unusual for a number of matrilineally related relatives to be close neighbors and for unmarried daughters with small children to compose part of a household. This pattern reflects both high rates of illegitimacy and poverty and traditional views of kinship and residence patterns.

Inheritance. Personal property was often destroyed or buried with an individual, but possessions could be given to any close relative or friend prior to death. Today some items are buried with the body, but the bulk of the estate is divided among a person's children.

Socialization. Apaches value above all else the autonomy of the individual. This applies to children as well as adults, and thus children are often indulged.

Sociopolitical Organization

Social Organization. The only groups were those based on kinship, territoriality, and co-residence. Individuals who were leaders of these various units were titled *nant'an*. Occasionally the prestige of some of these leaders exceeded the boundaries of their respective units, and they might be recognized outside their own local group. Depending on the unit involved, leadership was either inherited matrilineally or achieved. Leaders had no power and little formal authority because of the high value placed on individual autonomy, and they were primarily spokespersons and wealthy individuals with the largest farms in their area. Being wealthy gave them economic clout, and their charisma and their ability to talk and make good decisions meant that they were listened to and highly respected. Relatives often supplied labor for their farms in exchange for being provided for. The only other prominent role in the society was that of shaman.

Political Organization. Today San Carlos, Fort Apache, and Camp Verde have tribal councils and governments based on constitutions authorized under the Indian Reorganization Act of 1934. Elections are vigorously contested.

Social Control. The general Athapaskan value of individual autonomy is evidenced here as well. Traditional social control focused heavily on the threat of witchcraft accusation, which if supported by community consensus resulted in execution. Witchcraft accusation still plays a role in social control, and some murders may be explained as witch executions. Positive role models for behavior are provided by stories repeated by elders in reference to events that have taken place at specific locations in the area. Apaches refer to this as being "stalked by stories." Gossip and indirect criticism also are traditional means of enforcing conformity to accepted standards of behavior. Only when under the influence of alcohol do individuals directly confront each other. Both federal and tribal laws and ordinances are enforced by tribal police and government agents.

Conflict. Western Apaches for the most part avoided direct conflict with American settlers and the military after the 1850s. Minor problems were caused by nativistic movements in the late nineteenth and early twentieth centuries. Traditional feuds between territorial or kinship groups sometimes were carried on through shamans trying to counteract the magic believed to be emanating from the adversary groups. In some cases feuds resulted in violence. Contemporary elections often take on an atmosphere that involves conflict, and accusations of ballot stuffing may be leveled. Some contemporary vandalism is rumored to be reflective of old feuds. There has recently been some conflict between the leadership of the White Mountain Apache Tribe and business leaders and citizens in neighboring communities over issues relating to reservation boundaries, income from tourists, and leased land within the reservation. There has also been some conflict over land and water use with the federal government.

Religion and Expressive Culture

Religious Beliefs. Apaches believe that a number of supernatural powers associated with natural phenomena exist. These powers are neutral with respect to good and evil, but they can be used for various individual purposes. Control of these powers can be either sought after and developed or thrust upon one. Belief is supported by a mythology that explains the creation of the world and includes several deities. Most important are Life Giver, sometimes identified with the sun; Changing Woman, a source of eternal youth and life; and her twins, Slayer of Monsters and Child of Water. These are sometimes syncretically identified with God, Mary, and Jesus. Also important are anthropomorphic mountain spirits called *gaan* who in form and symbolism were no doubt borrowed from the Pueblos. Other important figures in myth are Coyote and Old Man Big Owl.

For many Apaches traditional religion has been supplemented or replaced by a variety of Christian sects. Lutherans and Catholics were the first groups to proselytize, and they have been joined by Mormons, Baptists, Assemblies of God, and the pentecostal Miracle church. Wycliffe Bible Translators has provided an Apache translation of the Bible and has an ongoing literacy program to promote it. Various nativistic movements have characterized Apache life, the most recent of which is the Holy Ground cult centering on regular gatherings at specified "holy grounds" and led by individuals who learned specific prayers and songs recorded in an original style of picture writing developed by a leader, Silas John.

Religious Practitioners. Agents of powers are called *diyin* (shaman). Those who have their knowledge secretly and use it for their own ends are witches, *'iłkashn*.

Ceremonies. In the past there were a large number of curing ceremonies each related to a specific power. These were performed as individual treatment seemed warranted. The only major ceremony still performed is the girl's puberty ceremony, both a rite of passage and a community ritual. It harnesses the power of Changing Woman to ensure individual health and long life and community health. In the last twenty years this ceremony has been elaborated, with expensive gift exchanges continuing between relatives of the girl and relatives of her godparents for several years after the initial ceremony.

Medicine. Traditional curing consisted of shamans' singing ceremonies to restore the balance upset by accidental contact with or disrespect shown toward a power to reverse witchcraft attacks. Herbal medicines were also used. In the recent past both Western medicine and traditional ceremonies were used in various combinations. Today contemporary Western medicine is the primary form of medical treatment, although Changing Woman's power is sought after at puberty rites, and some individual Apaches know songs and prayers to powers, which they use primarily within their immediate families.

Death and Afterlife. Everyone is given an allotted life span, which, unless violence or witchcraft intervenes, will end because of old age. Concepts of an afterlife are vague. Special actions are taken to make sure the dead do not return and try to lure the living to come with them.

Bibliography

Basso, Keith H. (1970). *The Cibecue Apache.* New York: Holt, Rinehart and Winston.

Basso, Keith H. (1983). "Western Apache." In *Handbook of North American Indians.* Vol. 10, *Southwest,* edited by Alfonso Ortiz, 462–488. Washington, D.C.: Smithsonian Institution.

Goodwin, Grenville (1942). *Social Organization of the Western Apache.* Chicago: University of Chicago Press.

Kaut, Charles R. (1957). *The Western Apache Clan System: Its Origins and Development.* University of New Mexico Publications in Anthropology, no. 9. Albuquerque: University of New Mexico Press.

PHILIP J. GREENFELD

Western Shoshone

ETHNONYMS: Diggers, Root-Diggers, Shoshocoes, Walkers

Orientation

Identification. The Western Shoshone, including the Gosiute of northwestern Utah, are a group of closely related peoples who live in the arid regions of the western Great Basin.

Location. Their territory stretched from northern Nevada and northwestern Utah, inhabited by the Gosiute, across the state of Nevada to the Death Valley region of southeastern California, inhabited by the Panamint. The area was very lightly inhabited by the Shoshone because of the stringent ecological conditions obtaining during historical times. Forty-three subgroups were named by Steward in his surveys. The names of these subgroups are generally geographical in origin, having been conferred by Europeans, but some are Shoshone names based on notable local food resources. The whole region is arid and desert in character, with generally a very low annual rainfall, intermittent streams feeding into ponds and small lakes without outlets, scrub vegetation, and a varied topography.

Demography. Most Western Shoshone do not live on rancherias, although there are numerous small reserves, generally governed by local councils, in eastern California and Nevada. In the late nineteenth century, the population totaled about 2,400, and in 1980 the population was 2,923 according to the U.S. Bureau of Indian Affairs.

Linguistic Affiliation. The Shoshone all spoke dialects and varieties of Central Numic, a member of the Uto-Aztecan language family. Central Numic has three basic component languages, Panamint (spoken only by the Panamint in the southwestern part of the area), Comanche (spoken on the southern Great Plains), and Shoshone (spoken by all other Shoshone groups).

History and Cultural Relations

The Western Shoshone live in one of the last areas in the United States to be settled by Europeans and Americans, although the southern parts had been reached by Spanish explorers. Jedediah Smith and Peter Skene Ogden both mention encountering Shoshone in the late 1820s. Other explorers in the area in the first half of the nineteenth century included Zenas Leonard, John C. Frémont, James H. Simpson, and Howard R. Egan. A great cultural impact was made by the arrival of the Mormons after 1847, followed by the California and Carson River gold rushes in 1848 and 1849, and the discovery of the Comstock Lode in 1857. Treaties by the U.S. government with various groups were signed in 1863 and began the process of gathering them on to reservations, although nothing much was accomplished in this respect until the late 1870s. Many small reservations were established shortly after the turn of the century and after the beginning of the "Indian New Deal" in 1935. In the 1930s, two competing councils were organized, one not recognized by the federal government, the other, the Te-Moak Bands Council, being sponsored by the government. In 1974, the United Western Shoshone Legal Defense and Education Association (now the Sacred Lands Association) was established. Shoshone title to their lands was finally extinguished with the awarding of $26 million by the Indian Claims Commission in 1979.

Settlements

The settlement pattern was quite variable, depending upon availability of food resources and season of the year. Stable social units generally occurred where resources were stable, with individual families in other areas moving with their annual seasonal round. Families were generally found within a local geographic district, often around a single valley or winter village cluster. Temporary dwellings were favored and dwelling types varied according to availability of building materials, length of stay, and use. The usual winter house, holding a small family, was a conical, bark-covered hut, while semisubterranean, earth-covered winter dwellings have also been reported. Many families sought shelter in caves rather than build huts. Sun shades were in use during the summer. Circular brush dwellings were built by some groups, and others built domed wickiups. Conical or domed sweat houses were in almost universal use, as were huts for secluding menstruating women.

Economy

Subsistence and Commercial Activities. Subsistence adaptations were extremely complex, varying according to the local subsistence base. The collecting of plants was the subsistence mainstay, with edible greens being gathered in the lowlands in early spring; later in the year berries and seeds were collected and cached in various localities for use during the remainder of the year. Piñon nuts were the mainstay in certain areas in the low foothills. Groves in the Reese River valley were owned by individual families, a unique occurrence among these groups. Winter villages were often located near large caches of nuts. In the Death Valley area, mesquite pods were relied upon heavily with several cactus species, agave, and gourds also being collected. Hunting was important, although not basic to the economy. Among large game, bighorn sheep were of primary importance, generally being killed from ambush in particularly advantageous locales, although communal hunts sometimes occurred. On the other hand, communal antelope drives were the rule in the Gosiute area, and such drives also occurred elsewhere. Antelope were sometimes individually stalked. Deer were also hunted, although they were much scarcer than sheep and antelope. There were occasional communal hunts, but individual hunts were much more usual. The fall rabbit hunt was an important source of food and fur, the jackrabbits and other types being driven into nets of grass twine. Snares and deadfalls were used for cottontail rabbits. Pocket gophers and ground squirrels were flooded or smoked out of their burrows or hooked out by means of skewers, with traps and deadfalls also being used. Fishing was very restricted, being possible in only a few localities. They hunted waterfowl, dove, sage hens and quail, and other birds when they were available. Other foods used included black crickets, bee eggs and larvae, and grasshoppers. Dogs were kept and were sometimes used in hunting. There were usually no other domestic animals, although horses were owned by some families.

Industrial Arts. Clothing was scarce. Most common was a sewn or woven fur robe, usually of rabbit skin, but sometimes of sheep, deer, or antelope hide. Hide clothing, skirts, and breechclouts, as well as clothing of grass or bark, were widespread. Various types of moccasins were used. Basketry was important; coiled and twined baskets, seed beaters, trays, and conical carrying baskets were common, as were the sinew-backed bow of juniper (sometimes of mountain mahogany) and horn glue. Quivers were made of wildcat skins. Low-quality pottery of local clays were made, sometimes sparsely decorated with surface impressions.

Division of Labor. Hunting was the primary occupation of the men, and women did most of the gathering. Women made the pottery. Men usually built the dwellings, with women helping in some groups. Both men and women could make clothing, and women usually did whatever weaving was possible.

Land Tenure. There is no information, although individual families did own piñon groves in the Reese River valley.

Kinship

Basically, the Shoshone kinship system functioned as a social network, the relatives passing on to each other information on the status of resource availability. But there were restrictions on sharing depending upon the predictability of resources—the more predictable, the more sharing. They had bilateral descent and used a Hawaiian-type kin terminology for cousins, with kin terms being modified to facilitate cross-cousin marriage.

Marriage and Family

Marriage. Because men generally hunted and women gathered, marriage was essential to form a viable economic unit. Bride-price was common in some groups, but absent in others. If the man was a good hunter, he might have more than one wife. Such polygyny was usually sororal. There was a strong emphasis on the levirate and sororate. Polyandry was present among some of the eastern groups. Brothers in one family often married sisters in another, with the converse being true as well. Postmarital residence varied from group to group, with uxorilocal residence being common. Divorce was common, and so were multiple remarriages.

Domestic Unit. The nuclear family was the common domestic unit, although there were some polygynous families.

Inheritance. There seems to have been an absence of inheritance rules governing real and movable property.

Socialization. Old and handicapped persons looked after children while the parents were obtaining food. Puberty rites were restricted to females, the rites being an individual rather than a group ritual, with moral precepts and attitudes being instilled by the mother.

Sociopolitical Organization

Social Organization. The Western Shoshone had agamous communities without localized clans or any marked tendency toward local exogamy and endogamy. There was a general absence of complex social institutions—no men's or women's societies, age grades, or significant ceremonialism. As noted above, stable families and other social units tended to occur within areas of stable economic resources; otherwise, social groups and practices were quite variable at a low level.

Political Organization. Political organization was also on a low level of integration. Group composition depended on the number of individual families available. The most stable group was the winter village, but even these had little cohesion and the headmen had little authority. Local bands in some areas were probably a development from mainstream society political and economic pressure.

Conflict. Warfare was not common before contact, although killing of individuals did occur. There was some evidence of conflict with the Ute and Northern Paiute. White migrants passing through the area were attacked occasionally, and there were some early attacks on White settlers.

Religion and Expressive Culture

Religious Beliefs. Western Shoshone religion was animistic. Supernatural powers were acquired through dream and vision experiences.

Religious Practitioners. Steward noted three types of shamans: general curers, curers of specific sicknesses, and those who used their abilities for their own benefit only. Both men and women could become shamans, but only men practiced so far as is known. Some groups denied the presence of shamans. Shamans were also used for help in the hunt—for example, an antelope shaman capturing the souls of antelope through dreams and charming them into corrals for slaughter.

Medicine. Injuries and sicknesses that were not thought to be caused by supernaturals were treated with a very large variety of herbal remedies (reaching into the hundreds of different plant medicines). Sicknesses caused by supernatural agencies were cured by shamans, often by sucking out offending objects or blood. An unsuccessful shaman sometimes returned the fee. Shamans were sometimes killed for refusing aid.

Death and Afterlife. Customs at death were variable. Sometimes bodies were buried in caves, rock slides, or talus slopes; at other times the bodies were cremated, abandoned, or burned in their dwellings. Some groups had an annual mourning ceremony; others cut their hair and abstained from remarriage for a time. In times of great food scarcity, the aged and infirm were sometimes abandoned. The ghost was believed to leave the body at death and return to the Land of the Coyote, and was feared by some groups.

Bibliography

Eggan, Fred (1980). "Shoshone Kinship Structures and Their Significance for Anthropological Theory." _Journal of the Steward Anthropological Society_ 11:165–193.

Knack, Martha Carol (1986). "Indian Economics, 1950–1980." In _Handbook of North American Indians._ Vol. 11, _Great Basin,_ edited by Warren L. d'Azevedo, 573–591. Washington, D.C.: Smithsonian Institution.

Steward, Julian Haynes (1938). _Basin-Plateau Aboriginal Sociopolitical Groups._ U.S. Bureau of American Ethnology Bulletin no. 120. Washington, D.C. Reprint. Salt Lake City: University of Utah Press, 1970.

Steward, Julian Haynes (1938). *Culture Element Distributions.* Vol. 13, *Nevada Shoshone.* University of California Anthropological Records, 4(2), 209–360. Berkeley.

Steward, Julian Haynes (1938). *Some Western Shoshone Myths.* U.S. Bureau of American Ethnology, Anthropological Paper no. 18. Washington, D.C.

Stewart, Omer Call (1982). *Indians of the Great Basin: a Critical Bibliography.* Bloomington: Indiana University Press.

Thomas, David Hurst, Lorann S. A. Pendleton, and Stephen C. Cappannari (1986). "Western Shoshone." In *Handbook of North American Indians.* Vol. 11, *Great Basin,* edited by Warren L. d'Azevedo, 262–283. Washington, D.C.: Smithsonian Institution.

West Greenland Inuit

ETHNONYM: Kalaallit

Orientation

Identification.   The origin of the name "Kalaallit" is not certain, but it has been interpreted as derived from Old Norse *skraelling.* It was recorded in South Greenland in the beginning of the eighteenth century. At the close of the nineteenth and the beginning of the twentieth century, "Kalaallit" came in general use all along the coast spread by Greenlandic catechists educated in Nuuk (Godthab) and through publications in Greenlandic. "Inuit" is now being used as the common name for Eskimo.

Location.   The West Greenland Eskimo occupy the west coast of Greenland from Melville Bay to the Kap Farvel area. Only the coast is habitable, 85 percent of Greenland being covered by an ice sheet. Off the coast are numerous islands, and the coast itself is marked by deep fjords. Generally speaking, the winters are long and cold and the summers short and cool, with climatic variation from north to south.

Linguistic Affiliation.   The West Greenlandic language, Kalaallisut, Greenlandic, or Kitaamiutut, West Greenlandic, belongs to the Inuit-Inupiaq (Eastern Eskimo) group. The various dialects of West Greenland are mutually intelligible. Presently the great majority of Greenlanders use Kalaallisut as their first language and Danish as their second; English is also taught at schools. The Greenland Home Rule Act (1978) states that Greenlandic shall be the principal language.

Demography.   According to a census of 1789 the West Greenlanders numbered 5,122, not including small populations in the marginal areas. The population was decimated by epidemics, especially by a smallpox epidemic in 1733–1734. From 1900 to 1950, the population nearly doubled from 11,118 to 20,730, and during the next twenty years it doubled again because of better health services combined with a higher standard of living. From 1975 to 1980, the population was nearly stable owing to contraception and abortions. Since 1980 the population has been slowly increasing. Presently about 80 percent of the population of West Greenland are Greenlanders; 20 percent are Danes, most of whom reside for only a short period of time in Greenland. As of January 1, 1989, 41,633 people, in a population of 49,976, were native-born in Greenland. The great majority of Greenlanders are West Greenlanders. The corresponding figure for the whole of Greenland was 55,171, including the population in East Greenland and the Thule area.

History and Cultural Relations

Groups of Eskimos have at various times migrated via the Canadian Arctic islands into Greenland. The Paleo-Eskimo were represented by the Saqqaq culture and the Dorset culture (c. 3000 B.C. to c. A.D. 900). The Neo-Eskimo, the Thule Eskimo, arrived in Greenland about A.D. 900. They were the first Eskimos encountered by Europeans, Norse settlers from Iceland who lived in Southwest Greenland from about A.D. 982 to 1500. During the sixteenth to nineteenth centuries the West Greenlanders occasionally had contact with European explorers and whalers and some trading took place, but it was the Danish-Norwegian colonization efforts in 1721 that resulted in radical changes of West Greenland culture and society. In the eighteenth century mission and trading stations were established all along the coast. In the eighteenth and nineteenth centuries the population of southern East Greenland settled in southern West Greenland. The colonial administration was paternalistic and the isolationist policy was not abandoned until after World War II, when modernization of the Greenlandic society accelerated as a result of the state-directed development policy.

Settlements

In aboriginal times the population had a differentiated ecological adaptation, but generally speaking people spent the winters in small scattered settlements on the coast, with summers spent in camps in the fjords. Over the years, the number of inhabited places has been decreasing, and the towns growing at the expense of the villages. The largest town, the capital and administrative center, Nuuk (Godthab) is situated on the section of coast where sea travel is possible all year round. In the eighteenth century the winter houses were built of stone and peat. Illumination came from small windows of seal intestines sewn together and from soapstone blubber lamps. These lamps also heated the room, and meat was boiled in soapstone pots suspended over the lamps. Summers were spent in tents of sealskin covering a frame of driftwood, and cooking was done outdoors over an open fire. The big winter longhouses were gradually abandoned in the nineteenth century and replaced by small houses lined with imported wood. Later on these were made only from wood and were often of poor quality. The majority of houses are now of a modern design. The larger towns are dominated by apartment houses, and nearly all houses in the villages are single-family houses.

Economy

Subsistence and Commercial Activities. Traditionally, the West Greenland Eskimos were hunters. The principal prey were various kinds of seals hunted from the kayak or from the ice with highly specialized weapons. Small whales were also hunted from the kayak, and bigger whales were hunted from the umiaq, which was otherwise used for transportation. Catching sea birds and fishing also played a role. During the summer, caribou were hunted inland. Much of the West Greenland population shifted from seal hunting to fishing for cash during the first part of the twentieth century. The fishing industry, which is mostly based on cod, shrimp, and Greenland halibut, is now modernized. It is Greenland's principal industry, but it is highly vulnerable to climatic shifts. Subsistence hunting and fishing are still important, and the sale of sealskins plays a role in northern West Greenland. Greenlandic hunters have been economically affected by the international actions against the killing of "baby" seals, even if these are not killed by Greenlandic hunters. Sheep keeping was introduced in South Greenland at the beginning of the twentieth century, and some families have since had their main income from sheep. In addition to wage labor in the fishing industry, many Greenlanders are employees in trade, restaurants, hotels, transport, building, construction, and public service. The public authorities play a dominating role as employers; about two-thirds of all wage earners are employed by the Greenland Home Rule Government, the municipalities, or the Danish government. Dogs used for sledging were the only domestic animals in aboriginal times. Dog sledges are not found south of Sisimiut (Holsteinsborg). Sheep holders have imported small Icelandic horses. Reindeer breeding was introduced in the Godthabfjord in 1952.

During the colonial period a number of Greenlandic men were trained as catechists for the church and the schools or as artisans, and some women were trained as midwives. The modernization of Greenlandic society after World War II increased the variety of jobs. A growing number of Greenlanders are now completing some sort of vocational training, half of them women.

Industrial Arts. Aboriginal crafts included making stone blades for knives and harpoonheads, soapstone carving for lamps and pots, preparing needles and other items from bone, and making sledges and so on from driftwood. Clothes were primarily made from sealskins, and caribou, dog, and bird skins were also used for winter clothing. Bead collars on women's coats were made from colored glass obtained from Europeans. Dresses combining Greenlandic and European materials and styles are used by both sexes on festive occasions, thereby stressing their Greenlandic national identity.

Trade. Barter took place on a limited scale between people from different localities when they met at summer camps. In South Greenland, West Greenlanders met with East Greenland Eskimos who wanted to obtain European goods. Before the colonial period, West Greenlanders had access to items of metal and so on through contact with European whalers. For nearly two hundred years the Royal Greenland Trade Company had a monopoly both on buying Greenlandic products like skins, blubber, and fish and selling European goods. In the 1980s, the various sectors were taken over by the Greenland Home Rule Government.

Division of Labor. Men were responsible for hunting, both sexes did some fishing, and women flensed the seals and prepared the food and clothing. Men made both their own implements and those used by the women of their family. At present, many women, especially in the towns, have jobs outside the home and at the same time play a central role in the household.

Land Tenure. All inhabitants of a settlement shared the hunting grounds, even if a regular return to a summer camp with limited resources seems to have granted a certain priority right. Even today, all land in Greenland is public property. Free building land is placed at everyone's disposal. The Home Rule Act states that the resident population of Greenland has fundamental rights to the natural resources of Greenland, but prospecting and exploitation of nonliving resources are regulated by an agreement between the Danish government and the Greenlandic government.

Kinship

Kin Groups and Descent. Aboriginal West Greenland Eskimo society was organized on the basis of kinship ties, and kinship is still of great importance even if it has been weakened by acculturation. The nuclear family was the basic unit, but it rarely lived by itself. The Eskimo kinship system is bilateral, and a person's network of relatives comprises both biological and affinal relatives.

Kinship Terminology. The Eskimo terminological system is followed. In daily interaction, personal names are often replaced by kinship terms.

Marriage and Family

Marriage. Most marriages were monogamous, but polygyny was occasionally practiced. No marriage ceremony existed before the advent of Christianity. Divorce was not unusual as long as a couple had no children. After the introduction of Christianity this pattern changed completely, and divorce was not legalized in Greenland until the passage of a marriage code in 1955. Virilocality was predominant, but in case of a shortage of hunters in the wife's family, the young couple might settle there. Today, young couples and many single persons as well move to a home of their own if it is possible to acquire one.

Domestic Unit. Several extended families, who probably often were related, spent the winters together, but during the summer the families who had shared a longhouse lived in separate tents in camps. Over the years, the households have become smaller, with an average of 3.3 persons per dwelling in Greenland in 1988.

Inheritance. When the head of a family died, his personal belongings were usually placed in the grave. If the oldest son was already in possession of an umiaq and a tent, or if he was still a child, these items went to someone else, who was then obliged to support the widow and her small children.

Socialization. Children were and still are given much attention. They were brought up permissively but disciplined by mockery and ostracism, and occasionally by threats of interference by external non-Eskimo agents. They learn from experience to cope with unexpected difficulties. Children must learn to control themselves and not show open aggressiveness. At present, some of the responsibility of the upbringing of children has been transferred to kindergartens and schools where different methods and other values may prevail.

Sociopolitical Organization

Social Organization.   In aboriginal times, no class distinction existed, but great hunters who were generous were afforded much prestige. Various kinds of dyadic relationships were known: there were men who occasionally borrowed each other's wife, and persons who had a joking relationship as regular opponents in song duels or exchanged rare food. Sharing of food was essential for survival. Hunters taking part in the same hunt had the right to certain parts of an animal killed by any of them, and gifts of meat were presented to all families of the settlements. Intermarriage with Danish men between the middle of the eighteenth century and the middle of the nineteenth century resulted in the formation of a specific socioeconomic category with Greenlandic ethnic identity and Greenlandic as its first language. Many members of these families were employed by the mission and the trading company. Since the 1950s, a considerable number of marriages between Greenlanders and Danes, including Greenlandic men and Danish women have taken place.

Political Organization.   Prior to contact with Europeans, centralized political authority did not exist. Danish-Norwegian colonization, which began in 1721, resulted over time in the population scattered along the immense coast being considered as one people. In the early 1860s, a limited kind of municipal self-government was introduced. In 1908, a law secured the establishment of two provincial councils, and in 1950 they were merged into one. According to the Danish constitution of 1953, Greenland became an integrated part of Denmark, and it has since then sent two representatives to the Danish parliament. In 1979, home rule was established within the unity of the Danish realm, and the provincial council was replaced by a home rule parliament and a government. Greenland is a member of the Nordic Council and of the Inuit Circumpolar Conference.

Conflict and Social Control.   Direct confrontation was avoided and still is. In aboriginal times, song duels held in a festive atmosphere were a major mechanism of social control. Opponents from different settlements took turns singing, insulting each other, and praising themselves—behaviors that would be unthinkable in any other social context. The spectators showed their approbation and displeasure of the performance and tension was released. Conflicts might also be resolved simply by withdrawal. The most extreme form was a person leaving for the wilderness as a *qivittoq*, who, it was assumed, received supernatural powers. Leaving human society in this way was a revenge against those who had treated the person badly. A murder was expected to be followed by blood revenge by a near relative, even if many years might pass before it was carried out. It was also considered a duty to kill a sorcerer who was suspected of having caused another person's death. Although incidents of violence occurred between West Greenland Eskimos and European whalers and explorers in the early contact period, the history of colonization is nearly free of incidents of physical violence between Greenlanders and Europeans. Some resistance did take place—for example, as protest movements among converts. In the twentieth century, disagreement both with Danes and among Greenlanders themselves has been expressed within a political framework. A modern criminal code based on resocialization was introduced in 1954. Since then, alcohol abuse has resulted in many social tragedies and violent deaths. At present, nonnatural deaths (accidents, suicides, homicides) constitute about one-third of all deaths in Greenland. The high suicide rate is thought to result from rapid cultural change.

Religion and Expressive Culture

Religious Beliefs.   According to aboriginal belief, every animal had both a soul like a human being and an *inua*, that is, a man, owner, or lord. The sea, the sun, the moon, a cliff, even sleep and laughter, also had a human quality expressed by an inua. Numerous taboos were attached to birth, death, and hunting. Violation of taboos caused harm not only to the violator but also to other persons, even the entire settlement. Revealing the taboo violation had a neutralizing effect. The inua of the sea, or Sea Woman (Sedna), the inua of the air (Sila) and the inua of the moon, or Moon-Man, were very sensitive to transgressions of taboos and rituals concerning the animals and life crises. The first missionary arrived in 1721. At present, the Greenlandic Evangelic Lutheran church is nearly universal.

Religious Practitioners.   Most shamans (*angakkut*)—the religious experts—were men, but women might also become shamans. *Qilallit* were persons, mostly old women, with an ability to get an answer from a spirit by lifting the head of a person lying on the ground. *Ilisiitsut*, sorcerers or witches, mostly old women, were people who secretly, through magical means, tried to destroy the health or hunting luck of others.

Ceremonies.   Given that the people's whole existence depended upon hunting and fishing, a good relationship with animals was of vital importance. Technical skills in hunting, as well as observations of taboos and use of amulets and secret songs, were considered necessary to ensure a good hunt. A ritual distribution of the meat of the first seal killed by a boy would ensure his success as a future hunter. The first kill of the season of certain animals was also distributed. During seances, the shaman's spirit-helpers served as informers and as an entertaining element. According to myths, the shaman might undertake a journey to the Sea Woman to make her release the sea animals she was holding back because of people's violation of taboos.

Arts.   Singing was integrated into many aspects of social life. Most songs were performed by soloists, sometimes accompanied by the audience. The tambourine drum disappeared in most places in the eighteenth century, and music became strongly influenced by European-American music. Storytelling was another important part of aboriginal life. The transition from oral to written culture was encouraged by a journal in Greenlandic, Atuagagdliutit, founded in Nuuk in 1861. A considerable number of novels, songs, psalms, and the like have been published in Greenlandic.

Medicine.   In the aboriginal culture, illness was thought to be the result of taboo violations or to be caused by a sorcerer. It was the shaman's task to make diagnoses and bring back the sick person's missing soul. The cause of illness might also be discovered by a *qilalik*. All this was long ago replaced by a Western understanding of sickness.

Death and Afterlife. When a death occurred, the inhabitants of the settlement, primarily the close relatives, fell under various taboos. The soul would live on in the afterworld either in the sky, which resembled the inland with possibilities for caribou hunting, or in the underworld where the dead hunted marine animals. The last place was the preferred one. It was the way of dying that decided where one would go. Women who died giving birth and those who died at sea went to the lower world. The name of the dead was tabooed until a newborn child was named after him or her. Such renaming is still common in Greenland.

Bibliography

Birker-Smith, Kaj (1924). _Ethnography of the Egedesminde District with Aspects of the General Culture of West Greenland._ Meddelelser om Grønland, vol. 66. Copenhagen, Denmark.

Damas, David, ed. (1984). _Handbook of North American Indians._ Vol. 5, _Arctic._ Washington, D.C.: Smithsonian Institution.

Kleivan, Inge, and Birgitte Sonne (1985). _Eskimos, Greenland, and Canada._ Iconography of Religions 7(2). Institute of Religious Iconography, State University Groningen. Leiden: E. J. Brill.

Kleivan, Inge (1984). "West Greenland before 1950." In _Handbook of North American Indians._ Vol. 5, _Arctic_, edited by David Damas 595–621. Washington, D.C.: Smithsonian Institution.

INGE KLEIVAN

pattern of migrations south under pressure from the Osage, Comanche, and the French. By 1800 these conflicts plus additional ones with the Apache and disease had decimated the Wichita. In 1820 sustained contact with Whites began, leading to further relocations and eventual settlement in southern Oklahoma.

The traditional economy was based on horticulture (maize, squash, beans, tobacco) in the spring and summer and nomadic bison hunting in the fall and winter. In the spring and summer the Wichita lived in villages composed of large, grass-covered longhouses. In the winter months, when they hunted bison on the plains, they lived in tipis. At the time of contact in 1541 the Wichita may have numbered as many as fifty thousand and were composed of at least six subtribes, all of whom spoke dialects of Wichita, a Caddoan language. The traditional religion centered on Kinnikasus, the creator of the universe, lesser male and female deities, and animistic beliefs in the supernatural forces present in many objects. In 1891 the Wichita adopted the Ghost Dance, though it essentially lost importance within a year, and in 1902 they adopted Peyotism, leading to a split between those who were aligned with Christianity and those who chose the Native American church. The Wichita are not legally incorporated as a tribe, though they do have a system of tribal governance based on a tribal chairman, other officers, and a council.

Bibliography

Dorsey, George A. (1904). _The Mythology of the Wichita._ Carnegie Institution of Washington, Publication no. 21. Washington, D.C.

Newcomb, William W., Jr. (1976). _The People Called Wichita._ Phoenix, Ariz.: Indian Tribal Series.

Wichita

ETHNONYMS: Pawnee Piques, Pawnee Picts

The Wichita are a Southern Plains American Indian group located aboriginally in present-day Kansas and Oklahoma in an area encompassing the Arkansas, Cimarron, and Canadian rivers. "Wichita" is evidently derived from the Choctaw word _Wia chitch,_ meaning "big arbor" in reference to the Wichita's large grass lodges, which resembled haystacks. The Wichita name for themselves was "Kitikiti'sh" or "Kirikirish," meaning "Paramount Men." The name "Pawnee Piques" was given by the French in reference to the Wichita practice of heavily tatooing their faces and upper bodies. The Wichita today number about one thousand and are affiliated with the Caddo and Delaware in Caddo County, Oklahoma, where many live on allotted land. They are largely assimilated into European-American society.

First contact was with Coronado in 1541 who was pushing east from New Mexico in search of the "Land of Quivira." By the end of the seventeenth century the Wichita had acquired the horse and shortly thereafter began a hundred-year

Winnebago

ETHNONYMS: Gens des Puants, Hocangra

Orientation

Identification. Located on Green Bay at the time of contact, the Winnebago later expanded across southwestern Wisconsin and northwestern Illinois. They are now two separately organized groups: one on tribal and individual trust lands scattered over a dozen counties in central Wisconsin and the other on a reservation in Nebraska. Linguistically, they are closely related to the Chiwere Siouan-speaking Iowa, Missouri, and Oto.

Location. This historic territory is characterized by numerous lakes and marshes, generally well drained, with part deciduous and part coniferous forests and patches of prairie. It lies within the line of 120 consecutive frost-free days necessary for maize cultivation.

Demography. Estimates place the aboriginal population at thirty-five hundred to four thousand. Large population decreases occurred after contact, but the group's numbers have now risen to more than thirty-five hundred people each in the Nebraska and Wisconsin enclaves, with perhaps another two thousand in urban areas, primarily in the northern Midwest.

History and Cultural Relations

Various clues point to Winnebago intrusion into Wisconsin from the Southeast. At the time of contact, most of the people congregated in a large village, Red Banks, on the south side of Green Bay. The French learned of the Winnebago from the Ottawa in the early 1620s, though it was not until 1665 that documentation of Winnebago history began. At that time they had recently experienced a period of intertribal wars, epidemics, and famine and were reduced to some 450 to 600 people in all. They made peace and intermarried with neighboring tribes, eventually recouping their population loss. Borrowing extensively from other Algonkian-speaking tribes, they reorganized their socioeconomic patterns to engage in the fur trade. By the eighteenth century, the tribe had withdrawn from Green Bay, and the village groups began separating. They eventually gained firm control of an area bounded on the east and south by Lake Winnebago and the Rock River, on the north and east by the Fox-Wisconsin portage route and the Black River, and on the west by the eastern watershed of the Mississippi River, their territory extending to the river north of Prairie du Chien. They occupied more than thirty villages of one hundred to three hundred people each, trading at major fur company posts in Portage and Prairie du Chien and with independent traders.

The Winnebago signed boundary treaties with the United States in 1825, 1827, and 1828, and treaties ceding their southern lands between the Rock and lower Wisconsin rivers in 1829 and 1832. The Winnebagos' remaining Wisconsin land between the Mississippi and upper Wisconsin rivers was not adequate to support all the people and the 1832 treaty provided a reservation along the Mississippi in Iowa. When the government wanted their last Wisconsin land, the Winnebago sent a delegation to Washington to oppose the sale. Pressured to sign a treaty if they hoped to return home, the group agreed to a treaty that gave them only eight months to move, which created a permanent split in the tribe. The southern villagers, whose land had been overrun by lead miners and already ceded had little recourse but to accept removal, but the northern villagers repudiated the treaty and led a fugitive existence in Wisconsin for nearly three decades. The removed group signed treaties in 1846 and 1855 for new reservations, ending up at Blue Earth, Minnesota. The 1862 Sioux uprising in Minnesota prompted an executive order to remove them along with the dissident Sioux. By the summer of 1863, all had fled the barren land assigned to them in South Dakota, with about twelve hundred arriving among the Omaha in Nebraska. In 1865, they ceded their South Dakota land by treaty for a reservation on what had been the northern strip of the Omaha reservation.

The government initiated allotment in 1871 which was completed under the General Indian Allotment Act of 1887. Generally, the people settled in the unallotted timber land along the Missouri River. They leased and later sold their farmland to Whites. By World War I, most of the western two-thirds of the reservation had passed out of Winnebago ownership. The Indian Bureau repressed traditional leadership and social organization. When the Indian Reorganization Act was passed in 1934, the Nebraska Winnebago established a constitutional government under its provisions.

After 1837, the defiant Winnebago hiding out in central Wisconsin were periodically rounded up by the government and moved to whatever reservation the rest of the tribe currently occupied. But they always returned to Wisconsin. When the Homestead Act of 1862 was extended to Indians, some Wisconsin Winnebago took up homesteads after 1874, but many were afraid to appear before White authorities. In 1881, all the Wisconsin Winnebago were assigned homesteads under special legislation. They retained many of their governing and religious structures. Settlements sprang up with a western focus in the Black River Falls area, where the Evangelical and Reform church established a mission and day school in 1878 and later a boarding school at Neillsville, and an eastern focus near Wittenberg, where a Norwegian Lutheran mission and boarding school opened at Tomah in the 1890s. As the twentieth century wore on, traditional religion and with it traditional social organization came under increasing threat from inroads of mission Christianity and the Peyote or Native American Church.

A new sense of tribal unity was set in motion in Wisconsin when the people elected a claims committee in 1947 to work with the Nebraska tribal council on a common claim before the U.S. Indian Claims Commission. The claim of about $4.5 million was not settled until the late 1970s, when both the Nebraska and Wisconsin groups opted for per-capita payments that were soon spent. The Wisconsin group's economic condition had steadily worsened after World War II and led to organization under the Indian Reorganization Act in 1962. They acquired land under tribal trust status at their major settlements to qualify for housing and other federal benefits. Political power struggles occurred over programmed federal funding, but the late 1980s brought increasing stability under new federal policies of self-determination and the generation of unencumbered income from bingo and smoke shops.

Settlements

The villages throughout the Wisconsin-Illinois domain may have been divided into northeastern and southwestern halves. Permanent dwellings were long wigwams covered with bark in summer and cattail mats in winter. Villages also contained long wigwams for councils and religious rites, small menstrual lodges for women, and sweat lodges for men. Bark-covered tipis were built at temporary hunting camps. Winnebago in Nebraska and Wisconsin today live in wooden frame houses often built under government auspices. Some Wisconsin families have roofing paper wigwams for family rituals and to house guests.

Economy

Subsistence and Commercial Activities. The Winnebago originally had a mixed economy heavily dependent on women's gardens of maize, beans, and squash. New fields were cleared every few years with men's help and when unproductive were left to revert to forest and brush. Tobacco, a ceremonial plant, was raised by men. Parties of families gathered wild plants in season and dried them for winter use, particularly blueberries, roots and seeds of the American lotus that grew along the Mississippi, and "Indian potatoes" (_Apios americana_). There are old traditions of parties setting out in dugouts in the late summer for communal deer hunting and also mentions of crossing the Mississippi to hunt bison. Fishing with spears and bows and arrows was important, particularly for sturgeon. Horses were introduced during the eighteenth century and became a necessity for transport. In the early fall, many families moved with ponies and wagons to campsites along waterways to trap for the fur trade; in later times this was largely confined to the area around La Crosse. The Wisconsin Winnebago moved from a trading to a money economy, selling wild blueberries in the summer and cranberries in the fall to Whites. Income from the sale of blueberries was replaced by wage work harvesting cranberries, cherries, corn, potatoes, peas, and other crops for Whites after 1917. After World War II severe financial deprivation set in as crop work became mechanized and required a much smaller labor force. Few people were prepared for other employment. Aboriginally, the dog was the only domestic animal. By the end of the nineteenth century, a few families used horses for plowing as well as transport and kept cows, hogs, and chickens, but for the most part the Wisconsin Winnebago preferred the independence and immediate returns of an itinerant economy.

Industrial Arts. Women tanned hides and made moccasins, but clothing was largely made of trade textiles with beads and later ribbonwork replacing old embellishments of porcupine quillwork. Aboriginal pottery quickly gave way to metal trade kettles. The arts of splint basketry and silver and nickel-silver jewelry were adopted from the Oneida and Stockbridge.

Trade. The Winnebagos' territory was rich in beaver, muskrat, and other fur-bearing animals. The tribe became dependent on the fur trade for traps, guns, textiles, and a variety of metal utensils, but their continued emphasis on gardening saved them from periodic starvation suffered by tribes that sometimes trapped for the fur trade at the expense of subsistence.

Division of Labor. The basic division was between women's gardening and men's hunting and fishing, but both sexes assisted each other as needed on occasion and engaged in gathering wild foods. Women were specialists in tracking the heavens for astronomical information to guide their gardening and other seasonal activities.

Land Tenure. As far as can be determined, land was held tribally, and as tribal hegemony was extended, local villages were spaced to ensure adequate natural resources and land for gardens.

Kinship

Kin Groups and Descent. The twelve Winnebago clans were grouped into the exogamous Sky Clans and Earth Clans moieties. When the tribe resided in Minnesota there was a four-part division of clans, which suggests a Southeastern origin, as four-part organization was common among Southeastern groups. In historical times the Winnebago were patrilineal. If the father was not Winnebago, children could be adopted into the mother's clan with descent in the following generations reckoned patrilineally. Ideally, in adulthood a warm bond exists whereby an uncle gives nieces and nephews whatever they ask for and, in turn, can exact work from them. They also may tease each other. A parallel gift and work reciprocity and teasing occurs between father's sisters and their nieces and nephews. There was avoidance of parents-in-law of the opposite sex, respectful deference between brothers and sisters, and sexual joking between people who stood in a terminological relationship as brother-in-law to sister-in-law. Prescribed kinship reciprocity and joking relationships are still observed in both Nebraska and Wisconsin.

Kinship Terminology. Winnebago kin terms follow the Omaha system. A marked avuncular emphasis reinforces the speculation of an older matrilineal system, as a man is considered more closely related to his sister's children than to his own.

Marriage and Family

Marriage. Moiety, and thus patriclan, exogamy was a defined ideal, but exceptions are not a recent phenomenon. Marriage also was discouraged among people considered close matrilineal relatives. Duolateral cross-cousin marriage was permitted, but parallel-cousin marriage was proscribed. Uxorilocal residence was normal during the beginning of a marriage, when the groom worked for the bride's family, but as children were born residence usually became patrilocal. There was occasional polygyny, usually with the first wife's younger sisters. On the death of either spouse, the ideal replacement was the spouse's same-sex sibling. There appear to have been no strong interdictions regarding divorce for incompatibility.

Domestic Unit. Permanent villages were made up of extended families representing several to all of the clans, each occupying a long multifamily dwelling with the nuclear units having their individual dwelling areas and fireplaces. The Wisconsinites' fugitive years discouraged large settlements. Later, homesteads also contributed to smaller but usually not strictly nuclear family wigwams, with a continuing preference for units of extended families to live near each other.

Inheritance. A deceased person's belongings were and often still are distributed to mourners beyond immediate descendants.

Socialization. Parents and grandparents instructed children with stories told at night, sacred stories in the winter and secular history at any time of the year. Children learned adult tasks through imitative play and close association with adults of the appropriate sex. At puberty, signified by voice change, boys sought visions through fasting in isolation. Young men whose vision came from the moon, which like the earth is a female deity, became berdaches. Menstrual seclusion was the rule for girls and women, with the onset of menstruation marked by special instructions and isolation when a girl might also receive spirit guidance and prophetic dreams. Compulsory schooling contributed to the end of fasting and other puberty rites in both Nebraska and Wisconsin.

Sociopolitical Organization

Social Organization. A disparity in the number of clans in the upper and lower moieties probably reflects an effort to maintain an approximate population balance between the moieties as new clans evolved in the course of the Winnebagos' incorporation of members of alien tribes. The Thunder and Bear Clans were and are regarded as the leading clans of their respective moieties and also provided the dual tribal chieftainship. In the 1830s, the tribal Thunder Clan chief still was nominally recognized. Each clan had its own origin myth, ceremonies, and a large number of customs relating to birth, naming feasts, death and wakes, lists of personal names, obligations, prerogatives, taboos, reciprocal relationships with other clans, and duties to the tribe as a whole.

Political Organization.   Tribal chieftainship was an old organizational principle rather than a function of White influences. The scattered, increasingly autonomous villages generally maintained a localized dual Thunder and Bear leadership. It is not known how people attained the role of chief except that eligibility by clan also required personal exemplariness. By the treaty period, a few non-Thunder clan men were recognized as civil leaders because of their ability. Like Thunder and Bear Clan chiefs, they were "real," unlike the "bread chiefs" that Whites appointed to deal out rations.

Social Control.   The Thunder Clan chief presided over civil functions, and his was a peace lodge where disputes were adjudicated and prisoners or culprits could seek sanctuary. If agreement could not be reached—for example, on indemnities to survivors in the case of murder—the Thunder Chief turned the offender over to the Bear Chief to be killed. Bear Clan men were called *manape* (soldier) probably in analogy to organized, standing army units at forts, but the Bear Clan really carried out internal police and penal functions. Generally, men were expected to be warriors, but the Hawk or Warrior Clan had the special prerogative of initiating and leading war parties. Old informal techniques of social control are still operative to encourage proper behavior of sharing, generosity, modest demeanor, and respect for other people. These include ridicule, gossip, withdrawal from troublemakers, and witchcraft. Evidently, fear of evoking a witch's envy or being suspected of witchcraft became increasingly important to enforce desired norms as formal, clan-based controls eroded.

Conflict.   Early records portray the Winnebago as exceedingly warlike. Men welcomed opportunities to go to war, and the Winnebago fought with the French against the English, with the English against the Americans, in the Union army in the Civil War, as scouts and fighters in federal conflicts with the Dakota Sioux, and in both world wars, Korea, and Vietnam. Veterans who experienced combat are accorded special respect as speakers at wakes and are recipients of kettles of food at feasts.

Religion and Expressive Culture

Religious Beliefs.   Traditional beliefs include a concept of a layered universe, multiple souls, reincarnation, a remote creator called Earth Maker, and a host of more approachable supernaturals representing spiritual expressions of animals, birds, trees, and other natural objects and phenomena. The Morning Star, like the Sun, was a male war deity. A special deity, Disease Giver, meted out life from one side of his body and death from the other. Other spiritual personages were sent to free the world of man-eating giants and other evil spirits and figure in long myth cycles. The benevolent Hare is in charge of the earth in the layered universe, which led early Peyote people to equate him with Jesus Christ. The Winnebago

Medicine Lodge Society derived from Algonkian sources, but it differs in many particulars from the Ojibwa Midé ceremonies and emphasizes reincarnation rather than curing. The pervasive focus on warfare is evident throughout Winnebago religion. War bundles were the tribe's most sacred objects and remain so among traditionalists. The ceremonies differ in particulars among the bundles, but all take special cognizance of certain groups of spirits in songs and orations. Missions established late in the nineteenth century in Wisconsin were slow in making converts. The Nebraska Winnebago were accessible to missionaries and many embraced Christianity, but after a period of prosperity from land leases and sales, they felt a sense of powerlessness and lack of direction. Vision-producing peyote, introduced around 1900, attracted increasing numbers of converts who incorporated the Bible and belief in Christ with pan-Indian symbols as a bridge between Indian and White ways. In 1908, Nebraska people introduced peyote to Wisconsin. In the Wittenberg area, virtually the entire community is now affiliated with the Native American Church, and there are members in other communities as well.

Religious Practitioners.   Radin recognized what he termed a religious elite, almost priestly leaders in hereditary and other religious societies, versed in the deeper meanings and philosophical significance of myth and ritual. In contrast, shamanism, which Radin attributed to Algonkian influences, was based on sleight of hand and the mechanistic formulae of imitative and contagious magic that could be used for good or evil purposes. Witches, literally "poisoners," could be men or women and usually were old. Healers were primarily learned herbalists, a role reserved to the aged to ensure their support since doctoring worked only if recompensed.

Death and Afterlife.   The ideal deaths were either those incurred in warfare or the only kind the Winnebago recognized as natural, which fits the clinical description of extreme osteoporosis when the bones crumble. This was believed to occur at the age of one hundred. Other deaths were believed to be due to witchcraft or breaking taboos, even inadvertently. Old stories indicate scaffolding of the dead, but interment has long been practiced. The decedent is believed to remain in spirit during the course of a four-night wake, when he or she is instructed in the arduous journey to the next world. In traditional cosmology, the next world is an idealized version of life on earth. People whose religious observances, such as Medicine Lodge membership qualify them for reincarnation can live four times on earth, choosing to be reborn much as they were or as an animal, the opposite sex, or even a White person.

Bibliography

Lurie, Nancy Oestreich (1961). *Mountain Wolf Woman: The Autobiography of a Winnebago Indian*. Ann Arbor: University of Michigan Press.

Lurie, Nancy Oestreich (1978). "Winnebago." In *Handbook of North American Indians*. Vol. 15, *Northeast*, edited by Bruce G. Trigger, 690–707. Washington, D.C.: Smithsonian Institution.

Radin, Paul (1926). *Crashing Thunder: The Autobiography of an American Indian*. New York and London: D. Appleton.

Radin, Paul (1949). *The Culture of the Winnebago: As Described by Themselves.* Indiana University Publications in Anthropology and Linguistics, Memoir no. 1. Bloomington.

Radin, Paul (1970). *The Winnebago Tribe.* Lincoln: University of Nebraska Press. Originally published, 1923.

NANCY OESTREICH LURIE

Wintun

ETHNONYM: Wintu

The Wintun are an American Indian group numbering about one thousand who live on several rancherias and reservations in California. The Wintun language belongs to the Penutian language family. In the early nineteenth century the tribe was located in northwestern California and numbered about fourteen thousand.

The Wintun had a varied subsistence economy including collecting and drying acorns, communal deer and rabbit hunts, and communal fish drives to catch salmon and trout. The tribe was divided into nine major geographical regions, but the largest political units were villages, each of which was headed by a chief whose position was usually inherited.

The Wintun worshiped a supreme deity and prayed to the sun each morning. Religious leaders were shamans who acquired their power in an initiation period of fasting, dancing, and instruction and who cured the sick by means of massage, soul capture, and sucking disease-causing objects out of the patient. Between 1830 and 1870 75 percent of the tribe was wiped out by epidemics. Subsequently, the Wintun were harassed and massacred by the hundreds at the hands of White ranchers and miners and finally forced onto reservations.

Bibliography

DuBois, Cora (1935). *Wintu Ethnography.* University of California Publications in American Archaeology and Ethnology, 36, 1–148. Berkeley.

Goldschmidt, Walter (1951). *Nomlaki Ethnography.* University of California Publications in American Archaeology and Ethnology, 42, 303–443.

Wishram

The Wishram (Echeloots, Haxluit, Tlakluit), who with the Wasco (Galasqo) constitute the Upper Chinook, lived around The Dalles on the Columbia River in north-central Oregon and south-central Washington. Today, the Wishram live in their traditional territory and on the Yakima Indian Reservation. The Wasco live with the Northern Paiute and other groups on the Warm Springs Indian Reservation in Oregon. They speak Chinook languages of the Penutian phylum.

Bibliography

French, David H. (1961). "Wasco-Wishram." In *Perspectives in American Indian Culture Change,* edited by Edward H. Spicer, 357–430. Chicago: University of Chicago Press.

French, David H. (1985). "Zebras along the Columbia River: Imaginary Wasco-Wishram Names for Real Animals." *International Journal of American Linguistics* 51:410–412.

Spier, Leslie, and Edward Sapir (1930). "Wishram Ethnography." *University of Wisconsin Publications in Anthropology* 3:151–300. Madison.

Wiyot

ETHNONYMS: Batawat, Du-Sulatelu, Patawát, So-lot-luk, Soo-lah-te-luk, Suláteluk, Viard, Wikí, Wishosk, Wíyat

Orientation

Identification. The Wiyot are an American Indian group located in northern California. "Wíyat" is the name for Eel River delta, south of Humboldt Bay. Other synonyms listed above are variants of "Wiyot," of the name of the language itself, or of one of the three main tribal regional subdivisions.

Location. Centered around Humboldt Bay, the Wiyot occupied a strip of northern California coast about fifty-one miles long by fifteen miles wide between 40° and 41° N and 124° and 125° W. Wiyot territory was almost entirely in the moist redwood forest belt extending from the coast ranges to the coast itself. Fog and clouds are common throughout the year with the annual rainfall varying from thirty to one hundred inches.

Demography. The most reliable estimate for the aboriginal population is about 3,300. The population decreased markedly in the nineteenth century largely because they held land deemed highly valuable by White settlers. The process is exemplified by the well-documented massacre of Indians concentrated on Gunther Island in Humboldt Bay in 1860. The most recent population estimate (ca. 1968) shows about 190 persons of certainly mixed Wiyot ancestry living on small reservations reported to have been terminated by the federal government in 1958.

Linguistic Affiliation.   Along with its northern neighbor, Yurok, Wiyot is classified in the Algonkian language family. The two languages are only distantly related, suggesting a long presence in the region with a degree of isolation from each other.

History and Cultural Relations

Although the linguistic relationship between Wiyot or Yurok suggests a time of initial occupation of their territories around two thousand years ago, radiometric dating of an important Wiyot site shows an early date of A.D. 900. Cultural materials at the site suggest a continuity into historic times. Wiyot territory is located at the southern end of what is called the Northwest Coast culture area, although the absence of certain characteristic elements of the area requires that the Wiyot be classified as "marginal" to the classic culture. Despite the geographical proximity and linguistic affiliation, there are marked differences between the Wiyot and Yurok, with the Wiyot less like the Northwest Coast groups and more like the cultures of central California.

Settlements

Archaeological and historical evidence points to more intensive settlement in tidewater regions such as the lower courses of streams like the Eel and Mad rivers and along the shores of Humboldt Bay. The open Pacific shore was evidently not used to any great extent. Villages were spaced a mile or so apart along the watercourses, with inhabitants numbering 50 to 150 persons. Permanent dwellings, occupied by two or more families, were rectangular and made from split redwood planks with two- or three-pitch roofs, a smoke hole at the top, and side entrances with sliding doors. Each village also usually had a sweat house, shaped like the dwellings but smaller and with only a two-pitch roof. Conical plank huts were used only for camping.

Economy

Subsistence and Commercial Activities.   Humboldt Bay and its associated rivers and creeks made for a predominantly maritime subsistence economy with mollusks, sea mammals, and fish (especially anadromous salmon) all heavily exploited. The fishing technology utilized boats, harpoons, traps, nets, weirs, and platforms. The surrounding forests, with clearings here and there, provided deer and elk as well as acorns, which were gathered, processed, and prepared in the classic central California manner. Dogs were the only domesticated animals and were used in hunting as well as for companions.

Industrial Arts.   Woodworking (canoe carving and the production of split and dressed planks for dwellings), stone working (well-shaped adz handles and bell-shaped mauls), obsidian chipping (large ceremonial blades and projectile points), bone and shell carving (fishing and mammal-hunting equipment, ceremonial beads and pendants), and twined basket weaving (for acorn collection and processing and decorated women's hats) were the principal industrial arts.

Trade.   The Wiyot supplied their southern neighbors like the Mattole with dugout canoes, dentalium beads, and local foods and received in return tobacco, haliotis shells, and local foods. They supplied groups to the north and west such as the Yurok with white deerskins and olivella shells and received iris-fiber rope.

Division of Labor.   The typical dichotomy for much of California obtained, with men hunting large animals and women weaving baskets and processing and preparing plant foods. Both sexes gathered acorns and pinenuts and made rabbit-skin blankets and buckskin moccasins. Curers, sucking- or herb-doctors or shamans could be of either sex, although the little-known "soul-loss" doctors were all men, as were the priests or ceremonial officials.

Land Tenure.   Dwellings, occupied by two or more families, were privately owned, and there was a specific term for a rich man who owned one. Fishing places, hunting and seed-gathering lands, and tobacco plots were also privately held, although particular trees, fishing weirs, and pens on weirs were not. Sweat houses were probably owned by the village, and beaches by the local group.

Kinship

There was no formal tribal organization or clans, nor were there any standards of kin avoidances, especially those pertaining to in-laws. Descent was patrilineal, and there was no development of elaborate kinship terminology.

Marriage and Family

Marriage.   Monogamy was most common, though nonsororal polygyny was often practiced by most prominent men. Bride-price was negotiated, and sororate and levirate were known. Marriage between blood relatives was prohibited, and fathers could not marry stepdaughters. Both first and permanent residences were patrilocal, except that "half-marriages" (those involving a man lacking some usual qualification for marriage such as the requisite bride-price) led to matrilocal residence. Adultery was a grounds for divorce for both husbands and wives, though it was less common for a man to be divorced for this reason. Children could go to either spouse's family, depending on payment to the husband.

Socialization.   Absence of rigorous puberty rites suggests a general permissive attitude in child rearing. Boys' puberty ceremonies were unimportant, with girls' more important than one might expect.

Sociopolitical Organization

Social Organization.   There was no formal or rigid organization at the tribal level. The chief or headman's main function was apparently to receive the largest share of food and property during ceremonies. There were no war chiefs. Social rank was based on wealth and birth, although "common," or poor men were related to "nobles."

Political Organization.   The Wiyot were divided into three separate subgroups occupying the Humboldt Bay (Wikí), Mad River (Batawat), and Eel River (Wiyot) regions. The groups evidently did not unite for common purposes such as war or conflicts with neighboring groups. Within each group, patrilineally related households and communities could form alliances against others when required.

Social Control. Physical and social self-restraint were encouraged as the qualities by which a man could obtain and retain his wealth and become wealthier. A system of fines for violations of the moral code (for example, adultery or seduction) and the low social status of the poor were the principal controls at work for individuals.

Conflict. Murder, insults, and poaching were causes of both internal and external conflicts. Both surprise attacks and staged battles were fought with neighboring groups such as the Whilkut. Warriors used bows and arrows, elkhide body armor, and rawhide shields. Women and children were not killed, and both sides were compensated for destroyed property.

Religion and Expressive Culture

Religious Beliefs. The Wiyot shared with other northern California groups beliefs about creation and culture heroes, although they lacked the latter's belief in a pre-human race. In addition, they had a conception of a supreme deity, "The Above Old Man," and a Noah myth, both without parallel in the Northwest, although the supreme creator belief is found in central California. Powers or guardian spirits allegedly could be heard—that is, sucking healers could be told by the spirit what caused the illness or where the poison objects were located in the body. Ghosts, souls of the dead, were thought to be audible and visible.

Religious Practitioners. Shamans or curers (probably mostly women) were distinguished from priests (men) who directed ceremonies.

Ceremonies. World renewal rites, of much importance elsewhere in northwestern California, were practiced only irregularly by the Wiyot. They did not hold the associated White Deer Dance at all, although the Jumping Dance was performed.

Arts. Apart from the aesthetic expressions described above under Industrial Arts, singing and dancing, especially ceremonial dancing, along with storytelling, were the only other notable art forms. Ceremonial activities were not as flamboyant as those of the neighboring Yurok.

Medicine. Although detailed ethnobotanical information is lacking, it is likely that the Wiyot, like their neighbors, used a wide range of medicinal herbs in the treatment of common maladies. As disease was believed to be caused by the intrusion of poison objects, soul loss, or violation of a taboo, serious illnesses required treatment by sucking with or without herbs.

Death and Afterlife. The corpse was carried on a plank or pole stretcher out through the door of the house to a cemetery outside the village. It was buried in a plank-lined grave along with money and valuables. Houses of the deceased were purified with tobacco or other burning vegetation, and taboos were observed by undertakers, spouses, and blood relatives for five days. Ghosts were believed "to go East, five days after burial and good and bad had different destinations." Ghosts of some "bad" were thought to stay on earth.

Bibliography

Driver, Harold E. (1939). *Culture Element Distributions X: Northwest California*. University of California Anthropological Records, 1(6). Berkeley.

Elsasser, Albert B. (1978). "Wiyot." In *Handbook of North American Indians*. Vol. 8, *California*, edited by Robert F. Heizer, 155–163. Washington, D.C.: Smithsonian Institution.

Kroeber, Alfred L. (1925). "Wiyot." In *Handbook of the Indians of California*. U.S. Bureau of American Ethnology Bulletin no. 78, pp. 112–120. Washington, D.C.

Loud, Llewellyn L. (1918). *Ethnogeography and Archaeology of the Wiyot Territory*. University of California Publications in American Archaeology and Ethnology, 14(3). Berkeley.

ALBERT B. ELSASSER

Yakima

The Yakima (Pakiut'lema) lived on the lower course of the Yakima River in south-central Washington and now live with the Klickitat as the Confederated Tribes of the Yakima Indian Reservation of Washington. They speak a Sahaptin language of the Penutian phylum and numbered over six thousand in the mid-1980s.

Bibliography

Daugherty, Richard D. (1973). *The Yakima Peoples.* Phoenix, Ariz.: Indian Tribal Series.

Schuster, Helen H. (1982). *The Yakimas: A Critical Bibliography.* Bloomington: Indiana University Press.

Yankton

ETHNONYMS: Nakota, Wiciyela

The Yankton are one of the seven main divisions of the Siouan-speaking Dakota (Sioux) Indians. Prior to the early seventeenth century the Yankton were located in present-day southern Minnesota, where they practiced a hunting, farming, and gathering way of life. During the seventeenth century they were forced by the indirect pressures of European contact to migrate from their homeland in a southwesterly direction to the open plains, eventually ending up in present-day southeastern South Dakota.

Beginning in the 1830s disease, declining bison herds, and hostilities with other Plains Indian groups began to take their toll on the Yankton, and the culture was in decline. About this time they numbered around three thousand people. By 1860 the Yankton had ceded all of their lands to the United States government and were settled on reservations in North and South Dakota. In the 1970s Yankton living on the Crow Creek and Yankton reservations in South Dakota and on several reserves in Canada numbered approximately forty-five hundred.

With the move to the plains, bison hunting became the center of Yankton economic life, though gathering and cultivation of maize, beans, squash, and other crops continued to be important. After acquiring horses they extended their range into the Dakotas and northern Minnesota. The Yankton were organized into eight bands, each of which was subdivided into patrilineal clans. Band governance was provided by a band council composed of a hereditary chief and clan elders. They believed in a supreme deity, Wakan Tanka (Great Spirit), and they practiced scaffold and underground burials.

Bibliography

Howard, James H. (1966). *The Dakota or Sioux Indians: A Study in Human Ecology.* Vermillion: University of South Dakota Museum.

Woolworth, Alan R. (1974). *Ethnohistorical Report on the Yankton Sioux.* New York: Garland Publishing.

Yavapai

ETHNONYMS: Apaches-Mohaves, Cruzados, Mohave-Apache

The Yavapai are a Yuman-speaking American Indian group who in the late seventeenth century numbered about 1,200 and ranged over an extensive territory in present-day central and west-central Arizona. Though in contact with the Spanish as early as the late sixteenth century, Yavapai relations with Whites were limited until gold was discovered in Yavapai territory in the 1860s. By the early 1900s, after some resistance and bloodshed, the U.S. government succeeded in settling the Yavapai onto reservations. In 1978 Yavapai located on the reservations in central Arizona numbered 883.

Except for some western bands along the lower Colorado River who practiced limited horticulture, the Yavapai were nomadic hunters and gatherers. Their staple food source was the agave plant, used to make mescal, and their most important animal resources, deer and rabbits, were taken in communal hunts involving men and women. Yavapai society was divided into three subtribes, each of which was further subdivided into local bands. Tribal and subtribal chiefs were lacking, and bands were headed by influential leaders who had distinguished themselves in warfare.

A central feature of Yavapai religion was prayer, particularly for good health. Shamans who provided religious leadership were believed to be knowledgeable in the supernatural forces that influenced people's lives, and thus they were considered effective healers. Of the supernatural forces appealed to in prayers, the most important were Old Lady White Stone, who is believed to have planted all of the healing plants recognized by the Yavapai, and Lofty Wanderer, who is believed to have put the present world into order. Supernatural aid also came from the *qaqaqe,* "little people," who are recognized by some Yavapai as being like the kachinas of the Hopi.

Bibliography

Coffeen, William R. (1972). "The Effects of the Central Arizona Project on the Fort McDowell Indian Community." *Ethnohistory* 19:345–377.

Gifford, Edward W. (1932). "The Southeastern Yavapai." *University of California Publications in American Archaeology and Ethnology* 29:177–252.

Khera, Sigrid, and Patricia S. Mariella (1983). "Yavapai." In *Handbook of North American Indians*. Vol. 9, *Southwest*, edited by Alfonso Ortiz, 38–54. Washington, D.C.: Smithsonian Institution.

Yokuts

ETHNONYMS: Mariposan, Noche

Orientation

Identification. The groups classified under the name "Yokuts" include some forty to fifty subtribes which are usually distinguished by three main cultural and geographical divisions, the Northern Valley Yokuts, the Southern Valley Yokuts, and the Foothills Yokuts. The name "Yokuts" derives from a term in several of the Yokuts dialects that means "people."

Location. The traditional homeland of the Yokuts was the San Joaquin Valley and the adjacent foothills of the Sierra Nevada in south-central California. Their territory extended from the Calaveras River near Stockton south to the Tehachapi Mountains and into the western foothills of the Sierra Nevada between the Fresno and Kern rivers. The climate of the San Joaquin Valley is semiarid, with mild winters and long hot summers, especially in the south. The eastern side of the valley was characterized by extensive marshes that bordered the numerous rivers and streams flowing westward out of the mountains to the San Joaquin River. Fauna, in the form of fish, shellfish, waterfowl, and large and small game, were abundant. The foothills of the Sierra Nevada is a region of irregular and steep ridges and valleys, offering a diversity of ecological zones and varied plant and animal resources.

Demography. Prior to European contact the Yokuts numbered in excess of 18,000 and perhaps as many as 50,000. In 1833 epidemic disease, probably malaria, devastated the Yokuts, claiming as much as 75 percent of the population. In the late 1970s the Yokuts numbered several hundred, including 325 living on the Tule River Reservation and another 100 living on the Santa Rosa Rancheria.

Linguistic Affiliation. Each of the Yokuts subtribes had its own dialect, all of which belong to the California Penutian language family. In the mid-1970s only a few of the many Yokuts dialects were still being spoken.

History and Cultural Relations

Archaeological evidence indicates the presence of small hunter-gatherer bands in the southern part of the San Joaquin Valley dating to at least eight thousand years ago. The aboriginal neighbors of the Yokuts included the Miwok to the north, the Costanoans, Salinans, and Chumash to the west, the Kitanemuk to the south, and the Tubatulabal and Monache to the east. The Southern Valley Yokuts first encountered Europeans in 1772 when Spanish missionaries penetrated the region. Owing to the remoteness and inaccessibility of the region, however, both they and the Foothills Yokuts were spared intensive contact until the 1820s when Mexican settlers began to invade the area. The early contact experience of the Northern Valley Yokuts was quite different. Early in the nineteenth century many of the Northern Valley Yokuts were drawn into the Spanish mission system, and large numbers were lost to the combination of disease and cultural breakdown that was characteristic of the Spanish mission experience. Following the discovery of gold in California in 1848, White settlers flooded into the San Joaquin Valley and carried out a ruthless campaign to drive the Yokuts off their land. In 1851 the remaining Yokuts groups ceded their lands to the United States, and after resistance by Californians was overcome, a reservation system was eventually established for them. The demoralizing conditions suffered by the Yokuts gave way in 1870 to widespread but short-lived participation in the Ghost Dance. The Ghost Dance promised the return of dead relatives, freedom from sickness and death, peace and prosperity, and the disappearance of Whites. By 1875 interest in the Ghost Dance had died after the new world envisioned by the cult failed to materialize. Today the descendants of the Yokuts live on the Tule River Reservation near Porterville, California, established in 1873, and the Santa Rosa Rancheria near Lemoore, California, established in 1921.

Settlements

The Yokuts occupied permanent residences for most of the year, a pattern that stemmed from the abundance and diversity of the plant and animal resources in their environment. Both the Northern Valley and Southern Valley subtribes made use of oval-shaped single-family dwellings constructed of a wooden pole frame covered with tule mats. The Southern Valley Yokuts also used similar, but larger dwellings that housed as many as ten families. Among the Northern Valley subtribes dwellings were scattered in an irregular pattern in close proximity to one another, and among the Southern Valley groups they were arranged in a single, regular row. The Foothills Yokuts followed the irregular pattern of housing arrangement, but dwellings consisted of conical-shaped huts thatched with pine needles, tar weed, and other locally available materials.

Economy

Subsistence and Commercial Activities. The traditional subsistence activities of the Yokuts varied from region to region but in all instances emphasized fishing, hunting, and gathering. Among the Northern Valley Yokuts the major food staples were salmon, taken in great numbers with nets and spears during fall spawning runs, and acorns, gathered in significant quantities in the late spring or early summer and fall. The hunting of waterfowl, such as geese and ducks, was also of major importance. The subsistence pattern of the Southern Valley Yokuts focused on lake and river fishing with nets, basket traps, and spears, hunting waterfowl from tule rafts, and gathering shellfish and tule roots. The Foothills Yokuts emphasized hunting deer by means of stalking, ambush, and collective drive techniques, trapping and shooting quail, and gathering acorns; fishing, employing spears, weirs, and poisons, supplemented this pattern during certain times of the year. The descendants of the Yokuts living on the Tule River

Reservation now find employment in lumbering and farm and ranch work and derive some income from the lease of grazing lands and timber tracts. Yokuts living on the Santa Rosa Rancheria are less fortunate, with many unable to find anything more than seasonal employment as migrant workers.

Industrial Arts. The Valley Yokuts depended to a considerable extent upon tule as a raw material for baskets, cradles, mats for rafts and house coverings, and a variety of other items. Employing twined and coil techniques, the Yokuts wove baskets of a variety of types, including cooking containers, burden baskets, winnowing trays, seed beaters, and water bottles. Simple, functional pottery was produced by some Foothills Yokuts groups.

Trade. The Yokuts were heavily engaged in trade with their neighbors prior to European contact. Among the variety of goods traded by the Yokuts were fish, dog pups, salt, seeds, and tanned antelope and deer hides. In return they received acorns, stone mortars and pestles, obsidian, rabbit-skin blankets, marine shells, shell beads, and dried sea urchins and starfish.

Division of Labor. Both sexes contributed substantially to subsistence, with males primarily responsible for hunting and fishing and females for collecting shellfish and plant foods. In addition, men wove fishing nets and produced wood, bone, and stone tools; women cooked, cared for children, and wove baskets and tule mats.

Land Tenure. Local or subtribal territories were owned collectively. Each member of a local group possessed rights to utilize the resources of the group's territory; however, in some instances some seed-producing areas were owned by individual women.

Kinship

Kin Groups and Descent. Beyond the family, the most important kinship groupings were patrilineal exogamous totemic lineages, each of which was connected to one of two patrilineal moieties; only among some of the Foothills Yokuts subtribes was the moiety organization absent. Subtribal offices and responsibility for certain ceremonial functions passed within lineages. Moiety members had reciprocal ceremonial obligations and formed groups for opposing teams in games such as gambling, races, and hoop and pole contests. Patrilineal descent was the norm.

Kinship Terminology. Valley Yokuts group kin terms followed the Omaha pattern; Foothills Yokuts terms followed the Hawaiian pattern.

Marriage and Family

Marriage. Marriages arranged by families were preceded by gift giving to the family of the future bride and concluded with a feast. Lineage exogamy was enforced, and moiety exogamy was favored but not prescribed. Matrilocality was customary for newlyweds, but after a year the married couple shifted residence to the husband's father's home or set up their own residence nearby in his village. Polygyny was allowed but infrequent, and divorce was an easy matter to effect by either husband or wife.

Domestic Group. The basic economic and social economic unit among the Valley Yokuts was the nuclear family; among the Foothills Yokuts the extended family was the norm. Generally, each family lived separately in its own dwelling, but among some groups of the Southern Valley Yokuts as many as ten families shared a single large communal home.

Inheritance. Subtribal political offices and certain ceremonial functions were inherited patrilineally within lineages.

Socialization. During her first menstruation a girl was isolated in her home and prohibited from consuming certain foods and drinks. Subsequently, a celebratory feast was held to which neighbors were invited. No special puberty or initiation rite was held for boys. Adult status for both sexes was signified by a group ceremony intended to bring long life, happiness, and prosperity. The ritual involved the consumption of a hallucination-producing decoction derived from the root of jimsonweed.

Sociopolitical Organization

Social and Political Organization. Among the Yokuts there was no overarching political authority uniting the numerous subtribes. Rather, each subtribe was an autonomous unit composed of one or a few villages. Leadership within the village units was provided by a headman whose position was inherited patrilineally within a particular lineage and whose responsibilities included directing the annual mourning ceremony, mediating disputes, hosting visitors, sanctioning the execution of social deviants, and assisting the poor. The headman was aided and counseled by a herald or messenger, whose position also was inherited patrilineally. Relations between subtribes were usually peaceful and cooperative, although warfare between local groups was not unknown. In some instances subtribes united in warfare against common enemies.

Social Control and Conflict. Socially disruptive persons, such as shamans believed to practice sorcery, were sometimes murdered by an execution squad hired by the village headman.

Religion and Expressive Culture

Religious Beliefs. The Yokuts origin myth depicts a world covered with water, which is transformed by the action of Eagle, who takes mud brought from the depths by an aquatic bird, mixes it with seeds, and allows it to expand to form the earth. The Yokuts believed in a variety of localized spirits, some of whom were potentially evil.

Religious Practitioners. Part-time religious specialists, or shamans, with powers derived from visions or dreams cured the sick and conducted public rituals and celebrations. Most often males, the shamans were believed to be capable of using their powers for evil purposes and might be executed on suspicion of doing so.

Ceremonies. The most important of the Yokuts religious rituals was the annual mourning ceremony, a six-day rite held in the summer or fall to honor the dead who had passed away during the previous year. The ceremony, which involved the participation of visitors from other villages, included symbolic killing, the destruction of property, and the ritualized washing of mourners, and concluded with feasting and games. Other ceremonies included simple first-fruit rites held for various seeds and berries as they became available for harvest.

Arts. The most important artistic achievement of the Yokuts was in designs woven into their baskets. Musical instruments included rattles, bone and wood whistles, and a musical bow. Music was expressed primarily as an accompaniment to ritual activities.

Medicine. Serious illnesses were treated by shamans employing supernatural powers received in visions and dreams. Cures, effected only for a fee, involved consulting with spiritual helpers and sucking the sickness-causing agents from the patient's body.

Death and Afterlife. Cremation and burials were typical funeral practices for the Yokuts, with the latter becoming more common in the historical period as a result of White contact. After death the corpse was handled by paid undertakers and buried along with personal possessions with the head to the west or northwest in a cemetery outside the village. Among the Southern Valley Yokuts cremation was reserved for shamans and individuals who died while away from home. After cremation, the remains of the deceased were buried in the village cemetery. The Yokuts believed that the soul left the body of the deceased two days after burial and journeyed to an afterworld in the west or northwest. Following a death, close kin maintained a three-month period of mourning, which included ritual abstention from eating meat and burning the hair short.

Bibliography

Gayton, Anna H. (1948). _Yokuts and Western Mono Ethnography._ University of California Anthropological Records, 10, 1–302. Berkeley.

Kroeber, Alfred L. (1925). _Handbook of the Indians of California._ U.S. Bureau of American Ethnology Bulletin no. 78. Washington, D.C.

Latta, Frank F. (1949) _Handbook of Yokuts Indians._ Bakersfield, Calif.: Kern County Museum.

Spier, Robert F. G. (1978). "Foothill Yokuts." In _Handbook of North American Indians._ Vol. 8, _California,_ edited by Robert F. Heizer, 471–484. Washington, D.C.: Smithsonian Institution.

Wallace, William J. (1978). "Northern Valley Yokuts." In _Handbook of North American Indians._ Vol. 8, _California,_ edited by Robert F. Heizer, 462–470. Washington, D.C.: Smithsonian Institution.

Wallace, William J. (1978) "Southern Valley Yokuts" In _Handbook of North American Indians._ Vol. 8, _California,_ edited by Robert F. Heizer, 448–461. Washington, D.C.: Smithsonian Institution.

GERALD F. REID

Yuchi

The Yuchi (Hughchee, Uchi), with the Westo, lived at various times in several places in the southeastern United States, from eastern Tennessee to Florida, with three main bands, one on the Tennessee River, one in northwestern Florida, and one in the middle drainage of the Savannah River in Georgia. Some of their descendants live in the northwestern part of the former Creek Indian Reservation in eastern Oklahoma, although the Yuchi are extinct as a distinct culture unit. They spoke a language isolate in the Macro-Siouan phylum.

Bibliography

Craford, James Mack (1979). "Timucua and Yuchi: Two Language Isolates of the Southeast." In _The Languages of Native America,_ edited by Lyle Campbell and Marianne Mithun, 327–354. Austin: University of Texas Press.

Speck, Frank G. (1909). _Ethnology of the Yuchi Indians._ University of Pennsylvania, University Museum, Anthropological Publications, no. 1, 1–154. Philadelphia.

Yuit

ETHNONYM: Asiatic Eskimos

Orientation

Identification. "Asiatic Eskimos" refers to those living on St. Lawrence Island in the north Bering Sea and on the adjacent Siberian shore. "Yuit" means "the real people" or "authentic human beings" and is comparable to "Inuit" (used among North American Eskimos); both are indigenous terms. In the 1970s the St. Lawrence Islanders applied the name "Sivuqaq" to both the entire island and the town of Gambell, and a derived term, _sivu.qaxMi.t,_ could mean either "St. Lawrence Islanders" or "people of Gambell." Specific locality-based names were more commonly used in differentiating people from the various areas and clans. The Yuit are those Eskimos who speak one of the two major language groups in this broad ethnic category, namely, those living in Southwest Alaska and eastern Siberia, including St. Lawrence Island. This entry deals only with the latter two groups, the "Asiatic" (Yuit) speakers of the language variant "Yup'ik."

Location. For over two thousand years the Asiatic Eskimos have lived on St. Lawrence Island and in several scattered villages rimming the easternmost tip of Siberia, the nearest point being forty miles away. Archaeological remains have provided a rich store of artifacts highly significant in theories dealing with Eskimo origins. The topography is treeless tundra alternating with spectacular mountain scenery (especially in Siberia), and the climate is wet, cold, and frequently stormy.

Demography. In the middle 1980s the population of the Asiatic Eskimos was approximately two thousand, about half living in the Siberian villages. Because of the relocation policies of the Soviet government, the Eskimos since the 1960s have been grouped with other ethnic minorities, such as the Chukchees, in larger villages intermixed with Europeans. It is impossible to estimate the precontact population with any degree of assurance. What is known is that in the late 1880s there was a calamitous decline brought on primarily from sickness and contact with crews of whaling ships. St. Lawrence Island was especially affected, its population dropping from an estimated sixteen hundred in the 1870s to barely six hundred following the Great Starvation of 1878–1879.

Linguistic Affiliation. Asiatic Eskimos speak three dialects or distinct languages of the Yup'ik branch of the Eskimo language: Sirenikski, Central Siberian Yup'ik, and Naukanski. All are spoken in Siberia, with Central Siberian Yup'ik also found in virtually identical form on St. Lawrence Island.

History and Cultural Relations

Asiatic Eskimos are the cultural and biological descendants of highly successful hunter-gatherers who for at least a couple of millennia had been well adapted to the Arctic ecosystem. First contacts with Europeans came during Russian explorations of the seventeenth century and later (such as that of V. J. Bering, who in 1728 "discovered" and named St. Lawrence Island), and navigators of other nationalities soon followed. The opening of the North Pacific whale fishery after the middle of the nineteenth century brought many whaling ships, disease, new hunting equipment, and liquor into the lives of the Asiatic Eskimos. With the U.S. government's purchase of Alaska from Russia in 1867, a formal political boundary separated the St. Lawrence Islanders from their closest cultural relatives in Siberia, a boundary that was only infrequently observed until post–World War II animosities between the Soviet Union and the United States resulted in hostility sometimes and an "ice curtain" preventing centuries-old patterns of trade and intermarriage. In the late 1980s there occurred several friendship visits of Alaskans (including St. Lawrence Islanders) to the Siberian villages, where long-unseen relatives greeted each other and ties of common identity were renewed.

Settlements

Aboriginally, the Yuit lived in permanent settlements, which they left as the season dictated for hunting, fishing, or bird-catching camps nearby. For centuries the basic dwelling was a semisubterranean sod-covered, driftwood structure with a below-ground tunnel entrance designed to conserve heat. Such structures were large enough to house an extended family. During the nineteenth century Yuit living on the Siberian shore began to use the walrus-hide-covered winter structure of the nearby Maritime Chukchee, and this type of housing spread to St. Lawrence Island. For both groups, the typical summer dwelling was a skin tent in both the permanent settlements and seasonal subsistence camps. Houses constructed of imported lumber began to appear early this century in a style and of materials much less well adapted to the severe winter weather than had been the aboriginal dwellings.

Economy

Subsistence and Commercial Activities. Subsistence was based primarily upon sea mammals: seals, walruses, and whales. Flesh of polar bears was only infrequently eaten, the animal being valued more for its fur and the prestige accruing to the successful hunter. Fishing, bird hunting, and gathering plants and littoral edibles supplemented the meat diet. Today the bulk of food still comes from hunting, but there is also much use of store-purchased food. All edible parts of the animals are eaten—not only flesh but also internal organs (heart, lungs, liver, intestines) and, in the case of whales and male walruses, the skin and attached fat (blubber). Animals also provided other materials vital to subsistence: from seals and walruses, skins for clothing, housing, boat covers, and ropes; from walruses, ivory for harpoon heads and sled runners; from whales, baleen for hunting toboggans and jawbones for house frames. Driftwood and various types of stones provided other principal raw materials needed for tools and housing. Except for the dog, aboriginally there were no domesticated animals. Among the St. Lawrence Island Yuit dogs are no longer kept. Today, features of the emergent material culture—rifles, aluminum boats with high-powered motors, snowmobiles and all-terrain vehicles, electronic communication equipment, airplane service, the occasional calling in of helicopters and government vessels to aid in the search for lost hunters, offshore exploration for oil and other natural resources—illustrate the magnitude of change from former times.

Industrial Arts. Carving and shaping of stones and ivory were highly developed for use as harpoon, lance, and arrow heads and other tools, such as knives. Sewing animal skins for clothing was principally the task of women, who used ivory or bone needles and thread derived from animal sinews. In modern times sewing and carving are done primarily for the tourist trade. The St. Lawrence Islanders, in particular, are renowned internationally for their ivory carving.

Trade. Aboriginally trade between the Siberian villages and St. Lawrence Island took the form of exchanges of reindeer skins (from Siberia) for walrus hides and other animal products from the island. Because of distance, little contact occurred with Alaskan Eskimos. With the advent of European-American exploration and whaling in the North Pacific, the intensity of trade increased, the Eskimos wanting rifles and whaling gear (and, for wealthy boat captains, wooden whale boats), tools of various types, and food and liquor. The whaling and commercial ships bartered for baleen, walrus ivory, skin clothing, and the services of Eskimos during the summer whaling voyages. In the present day, trade patterns are predominantly those of a modern consumer culture based on monetary exchange and, to a limited extent, use of subsistence products.

Division of Labor. The division of labor was simple. Because of their greater physical strength, men were the hunters on the winter ice and in whaling and walrus open-boat hunting. Women contributed significantly by picking leaves, roots, and stalks of vegetal products, fishing through holes chopped in the ice, and collecting anything edible found along the beach. The man's job was to provide the bulk of food (primarily meat); the woman's, to distribute seal and walrus (and other) meat brought home. Once inside the house, it was the woman's right—and responsibility—to give some meat to whomever came asking, and such distribution was always in accordance with the Yuit ethos of communal sharing. Elders, both men and women, contributed to subsistence as long as they were able; and children began early on to emulate their parents' economic activities. In today's world, much the same pattern obtains, with the exception that children, school-bound for most of the year, cannot regularly participate in subsistence pursuits.

Land Tenure. Aboriginally land was not "owned" de juris by a person or family. "Use-ownership" is the best term to apply to the habitual use of a particular camping site or residential location in a village by a given family, and such proprietary interests were socially recognized and accepted. The sea and its faunal bounty, not the land and its products, were the key environmental features elaborated in the culture.

Kinship

Kin Groups and Descent. The Asiatic Yuit are unique among Eskimo groups in having clans. On St. Lawrence Island the clans—each with a distinctive name—continue to function in selection of marriage partners, composition of boat crews for hunting, transmission of the "name soul" to newborn clan members, and social support of all kinds. Clan names usually were derived from traditional camping areas; for example, the "Meruchtameit" are the "people of _Meruchta_," a hunting site used for centuries by a particular family group. One of the St. Lawrence clans, the "Aimaramka," is composed of people whose forebears migrated from Siberia, and extended family relatives and fellow clansmen are still found in the nearest coastal Siberian village. Descent was and continues to be patrilineal. Through life a person remains a member of his or her clan of birth. Even though marriage was clan-exogamous, women maintained certain social and religious ties and practices with their natal group.

Kinship Terminology. In addition to clans, the overall pattern of terms used to designate kin also significantly separates the Yuit from most other Eskimo groups. Although the more widespread Eskimo pattern designates all cousins by a single term—as is done in American society—the Asiatic Yuit follow a different model, that of the Iroquois terminological system. Behavior toward one another expected of cross cousins is culturally structured to be the familiar "joking relationship," and patrilineal parallel cousins show unstinting support and help for one another. So close is that relationship, in fact, that the terms for _brother_ and _sister_ are used interchangeably with those for a patrilineal parallel cousin. Relations between a person and his or her mother's sister's children, although not as close as those with patrilineal parallel cousins, are still supportive and nurturant. The Yuit also had the institution of fictive "brothers," by which two unrelated men engaged in drumming and singing contests as well as exchange of goods and sexual access to the partner's wife.

Marriage and Family

Marriage. Traditionally marriage, clan-exogamous, was arranged by elders of the two families involved, an agreement for the union sometimes being formalized during the childhood of the two young people. There was no formal marriage ceremony, marriage had no religious connotations, and the only ritual involved was that the groom's family customarily took a sledload of gifts to the home of the bride. Residence was matri-patrilocal. For the first year or so the groom lived with his wife in the house of his parents-in-law and performed "groom-work" by helping his father-in-law in hunting and household maintenance. After a year the young couple—accompanied by a reciprocal sledload of gifts—returned to take up permanent residence in the groom's family's household. Divorce was socially recognized although not marked by any formal ritual. The wife simply moved out of the husband's (or husband's family's) house. A divorce posed problems of affiliation and loyalty for children involved, since they belonged to their father's clan. A woman usually would return to the home of a clansman, sometimes with younger children accompanying her.

Domestic Unit. The household was usually composed of an extended family of parents, younger married sons and their wives and children, and unmarried children. Older married sons would usually establish their own households as demands on space in the parental home expanded. They would always, however, build their dwelling close to the parents' home. Thus a settlement would consist of several enclaves or neighborhoods of clansmen, a pattern still found, although changing.

Inheritance. Material objects, such as tools, weapons, sewing and cooking utensils, and clothing, were passed on to appropriate users in the family. A boat was inherited by the eldest son. Nonmaterial property was also recognized; for example, the composer of a song was considered its "owner" and it could not be sung without his permission.

Socialization. Child rearing among the Yuit conformed to the pan-Eskimo pattern of extreme permissiveness in the first two to three years. Few demands were made on the child for adherence to toilet training, obedience, or delaying of gratification; and the implicit goal was that of building deep self-confidence and self-reliance. From four to five years of age onward, the child gradually internalized models for appropriate behavior and self-restraint observed in the familial environment.

Sociopolitical Organization

Social and Political Organization. No autonomous institutionalized political or legal system existed. There were no formal "chiefs" or communitywide leaders, and "legality" inhered in diffuse, established norms for conduct understood by all. Clans were the principal social mechanism by which interpersonal predictability and control of disruptive behavior were accomplished.

Social Control. If a dispute did not appear resolvable amicably by the disputants themselves, elders of the extended family or clan groups involved would adjudicate the issue in an effort to prevent its escalating into interclan violence. Great respect was accorded age and seniority. Sometimes, as in other Eskimo groups, an argument would be settled by a "song contest" (the famous "nith" contests), in which the plaintiffs, in front of an audience, performed newly composed songs insulting their opponents. The winner of the argument was decided by the relative plaudits of public acclaim. In addition to song duels, wrestling matches between two male disputants were also commonly used in the service of justice. Such controlled fighting was never allowed to lead to the death of the opponent. A less overt form of anticipatory behavior control was verbal. In any small community, gossip and innuendo critical of a person's actions always get to the ear of the offender. The basic value all such means of social control implemented was the overriding importance of maintaining intragroup harmony and ties of supportive social reciprocity—the stern challenges to survival presented by nature itself underscored the need for cooperation rather than conflict. The most tangible social value contributing to group cohesiveness was sharing food if another household was in need, no matter how small the animal. Clansmen customarily still share the goods of life with relatives without waiting to be asked. Such widespread sharing practices constituted a form of social insurance against the unpredictable fortunes of the morrow.

Conflict.   Beyond relations among clans within a single settlement, there were occasional armed conflicts between villages. In the past such conflicts periodically occurred between the St. Lawrence Islanders and Siberians from the nearest villages (during lulls in the otherwise amicable trading relations). Informants' accounts still tell of raiding parties, walrus-hide armor, and special bow-and-arrow fighting techniques. In the years immediately following World War II, such animosities were inflamed by cold war politics on each side of the strait, and only recently have visits celebrating friendship and common cultural identity been possible. Since establishment of national political infrastructures in both the Soviet Union and the United States and the gaining of statehood for Alaska, local legal and governmental structures reflect national policies and processes.

Religion and Expressive Culture

Religious Beliefs.   The Yuit world was highly animistic. Almost everything observable had an indwelling spirit as its real substance, its owner. Not only did humans have a name soul, an immortal personality that could pass into the body of a newborn infant and *become* that person; but there were other spiritual dimensions as well, such as the breath soul, whose leaving marked the material death of the person. All animals important to survival—seals, walruses, whales, polar bears—had humanlike souls, which had to be appeased before and after the hunt to keep their goodwill. Aside from souls inhabiting living bodies, there were spirits of rocks and other natural features—a flame, the air, the sea, a mountain—as well as disembodied, free-floating spirits, some of which were malevolent to humans. Frequently they were the instruments of misfortune and disease (one cause being theft or wandering of the soul). Sometimes they acted on their own volition; sometimes they were directed toward evil ends by a witch or sorcerer. In modern times, Christian (or, in the Soviet Union, atheistic) beliefs and practices have largely replaced aboriginal spiritual conceptions.

Religious Practitioners.   The principal spiritual protagonist against witches or the threat of disease was the shaman. (In Yup'ik, the term for this familiar religious figure is *aliginalre*). The shaman was the religious functionary who had obtained power through a period of deprivation on the tundra during which he was visited by spirits who would agree to become his helpers in the seance that was part of every healing or divinatory ritual. At the end of such a ceremony (always attended by the patient's family), the shaman would sacrifice tiny bits of valuable goods offered in payment by the family—for example, walrus-hide rope, seal blubber, reindeer hide, tobacco. The shaman's spiritual helpers as well as the supreme being (familiarly called Apa, or "grandfather") were paid for their assistance by the small pieces of payment goods being thrown into the flame of a seal-oil lamp and accompanied by prayers.

During the seance, which was conducted in a darkened room, the shaman would sing to the beat of a tambourine drum. The language used, mainly archaic words and neologisms, created an aura of belief in the shaman's powers. The purpose of such drumming, singing, and dancing was to transport the shaman's soul into the spiritual world to discover the cause of the problem. Once the soul had returned from the search, there would be a dramatic struggle between the shaman and the witch or spirit causing the disease or misfortune. The entire scene—dim and eerie light, other-worldly singing, the throbbing drum, ventriloquially produced sounds appearing to come from all corners of the room—was highly conducive to belief in the shaman's powers. It strongly reinforced compliance with instructions laid down for the patient's and the family's behavior, such as not working for a given period of time and wearing particular amulets on clothing. Aside from using the (unbeknownst to him) powers of psychological medicine, the shaman might also prescribe eating certain types of foods or using particular folk medicinal remedies.

Ceremonies.   Aside from social rituals accompanying trade gatherings, ceremonialism was largely directed at maintaining proper relations with the animal world and preventing or ameliorating baleful actions of witches and malignant spirits. Proper treatment of the souls of animals was particularly important, both in small-scale and major ceremonies. If, for example, animals were not implored prior to the hunt to offer their flesh for human consumption and were not properly thanked after the kill (say, by a seal's not being given a drink of fresh water by the wife of the household when the carcass enters the house), that soul would tell other seals not to let themselves be killed by humans. Offering prayers, practicing taboos and behavioral restrictions (by both the hunter and his wife), and wearing special clothing and amulets were important accessories to the hunt. Major ceremonies of thanksgiving were conducted after the killing of walruses and polar bears; and for whales, elaborate rituals in preparation for the forthcoming hunt, presided over by the boat captain and his wife and attended by the entire boat crew, were enacted as well.

Arts.   Drumming, singing, and dancing were not confined to the shamanistic seance. They were common forms of entertainment generally, along with telling stories and myths. Ivory carving and needlework were highly developed, as were such children's amusements as string-figures.

Medicine. Folk medicine used both plant and animal products to relieve symptoms and assist curing. For example, a widespread remedy for aches and pains was an infusion of willowbark in water; the salicylic acid thus obtained is the active ingredient in aspirin. Pieces of blubber were applied to a wound to staunch the flow of blood, as was fresh human urine. Prior to contact with outsiders and the contagious diseases they brought, death and disability came primarily from hunting accidents and aging. Since the turn of the century the Yuit have been served by modern Soviet and American medicine.

Death and Afterlife. There were no consistent beliefs about an afterlife. The reincarnation of the name soul into a newborn's body was the single most important (and most uniformly held) belief relating to an afterlife.

Bibliography

Hughes, Charles C. (1984). "Saint Lawrence Island Eskimo." In _Handbook of North American Indians_. Vol. 5, _Arctic_, edited by David Damas, 262–277. Washington, D.C.: Smithsonian Institution.

Hughes, Charles C. (1984). "Siberian Eskimo." In _Handbook of North American Indians_. Vol. 5, _Arctic_, edited by David Damas, 247–261. Washington, D.C.: Smithsonian Institution.

VanStone, James W. (1984). "Southwest Alaskan Eskimo: Introduction." In _Handbook of North American Indians_. Vol. 5, _Arctic_, edited by David Damas, 205–208. Washington, D.C.: Smithsonian Institution.

Yevtushenko, Yevgeny. (1988). _Divided Twins: Alaska and Siberia_. New York: Viking Penguin.

CHARLES C. HUGHES

Yuki

The Yuki, including the Coast Yuki (Ukhotnom) and the Huchnom (Redwoods), live on the northwest coast of California between the Wailaki and the Pomo, and in the upper drainage of the Eel River. They spoke languages of the Yukian family. They probably now number less than fifty, living with the Wailaki, Nomlaki, and Pomo on the Round Valley Indian Reservation.

Bibliography

Miller, Virginia P. (1978). "Yuki, Huchnom, and Coast Yuki." In _Handbook of North American Indians_. Vol. 8, _California_, edited by Robert F. Heizer, 249–255. Washington, D.C.: Smithsonian Institution.

Yurok

ETHNONYMS: Alequa, Aliquois, Eurocs, Kanuck, Kyinnaa, Polikla, Tiamath, Ulrucks, Weits-pek, Youruk, Yurock

Orientation

Identification. The name "Yu-rok" is said to be derived from the language of their neighbors, the Karok, who referred to these people as "Yuruk," meaning "downriver." Later ethnologists referred to Yurok language as Weitspekan. It appears that the Yurok had no name for themselves, but rather used the names of their towns when matters of affiliation were concerned.

Location. The ancestral home of the Yurok was on the northwest California Pacific coast, on the lower forty-five miles of the Klamath River. The remaining contemporary Yurok share the Hoopa Valley reservations in Humboldt and Klamath counties on this same part of the California coast with the Hupa. Persons of Yurok ancestry live throughout California, as well as in their ancestral territory.

Demography. As of 1970, it was reported that full-blood Yuroks were very few, though persons of direct ancestry numbered between three thousand and forty-five hundred. This is larger, it appears, than native, pre-1850 population figures, placed at about fifteen hundred; Kroeber felt that it had certainly not been any higher than twenty-five hundred.

Linguistic Affiliation. Early twentieth-century linguists classified Yurok as an Algonkian language, but some scholars claim this affiliation cannot be confirmed. The Yuroks, as late as the 1970s, asserted that there were minor variations in dialect between men and women, between families (especially rich versus poor), and among Yurok villages. In 1917, when Yurok was still commonly spoken, Kroeber recognized three separate regionally specific dialects within Yurok territory.

History and Cultural Relations

The few archaeological investigations in the Yurok area indicate Yurok presence there in late prehistoric times. There was no known historic contact between the Yurok and Europeans prior to 1775, when they were visited by the Spanish. Fur traders from the Hudson's Bay Company ventured into the Yurok area in 1827, and gold rush prospectors entered the lower Klamath River area in 1850-1851. The first Anglo-European settlement began around 1852. There was considerable violence between the Yurok and the gold seekers during this era. After 1855, however, the Yurok were protected by military and government officials in the area. Prior to the advent of Europeans, the Yurok interacted primarily with the Hupa and the Karok, who shared a common northwestern California coast lifestyle. On their periphery, there were contacts with other groups, including the Wiyot, Chilula, Chimariko, Shasta, Tututni, Chetco, and Tolowa. There were extensive kinship and economic ties between the Yurok and their neighbors, yet the Yurok, Hupa, and Karok were fiercely territorial. They would visit one another's villages for ceremonies, but were generally self-sufficient within their territories, except for obsidian and dentalium shell that were obtained through trade. The Yurok were obsessed with amassing and holding wealth and often sued or demanded tribute from other Yuroks or their neighbors for a variety of infractions. Feuds were fought between Yurok villages, and the Yuroks waged wars, albeit small-scale ones, with the Hupa, Chilula, and Tolowa. Tribute was often extracted by the Yurok, but there was also a complex system of compensation for damages inflicted in feuds between Yurok families or villages. Compensation was usually in the form of strings of dentalium shell used by the Yurok as a measure of currency and wealth.

Settlements

All Yurok settlements were either on the Klamath River, up to about thirty miles inland, and extending about twenty-five miles down the seacoast from the mouth of the Klamath. Kroeber described Yurok habitation as occurring in villages, the latter numbering about fifty-four. Most were on high terraces of the Klamath, though others were at lower elevations near the mouth of the river (for example, from elevations of about two hundred feet to twenty feet above sea level). The wood plank houses within Yurok villages were named according to their topographic location, size, ceremonial frontage, or position. Though there was no formal village plan, these villages, with their typical square houses, were usually tightly clustered. Sweat houses were placed both within the residential area and on its periphery. Although few data exist on the population of these villages, there is an 1852 census, which indicates a range of two to thirty houses per village, though seventeen villages (of the twenty-three recorded in that year) had seven or eight houses or fewer. Yurok villages held communal property, such as acorn groves, or claimed rights to certain waters for whaling. There were distinct boundaries between the properties held by one village and those of an adjacent Yurok village. Villages functioned as units in warfare or feuds and would also host ceremonies, providing the regalia and food for guests.

Economy

Subsistence and Commercial Activities. Subsistence tasks involved fishing, hunting, and gathering. Salmon was certainly the most important food source. Using nets, harpoons, weirs, and specially built platforms, the Yurok obtained large numbers of salmon in the spring and autumn runs. Yurok families often had a ton of dried salmon hanging from the house rafters. They also stored the dried salmon in baskets, separating each layer of fish with aromatic tree leaves; they believed the leaves "kept out the moths" (moth larvae would have eaten the fish), although the leaves may have added flavor to the dried fish. Other fish obtained by the Yurok included eels and sturgeon. They also hunted sea lions and prized the meat from stranded whales. Shellfish were collected, as were wild grass seeds, bulbs, and water lilies. Salt was extracted from seaweed. Deer were hunted with the use of dogs and were usually snared rather than shot. Acorns were collected in the fall from groves usually owned by the village, but sometimes individually owned; some oak groves away from the river or between Yurok villages were said to be open to "everybody." Specific rights were held for certain fishing spots, and conflict often erupted if a spot was used without authorization or if a new fishing locale was established downstream. These were time-honored rights, often inherited within family groups.

Contemporary Yurok of both sexes work today as state and college bureaucrats, teachers, military officers, nurses, accountants, and in the fishing and lumber industries.

Industrial Arts. The Yurok were skilled workers of redwood for house planks, boats, paddles, storage boxes, and hunting and fishing devices. Basket weaving was also a major craft, with basketry items used as baby carriers, storage containers, and mush-cooking vessels. Surviving obsidian tools and salmon-butchering knives of flint also attest to their skills in chipping stone. Shells were strung on long cords to serve as currency. There seems to have been little craft specialization, aside from some men who traditionally made boats.

Trade. Obsidian did not occur within Yurok territory and had to be obtained from Medicine Lake, where it was quarried by the Achumawi and then traded through the Shasta and Karok before reaching the Yurok. Given the role of large obsidian bifaces in Yurok ceremony, this was a vital trade item. Additionally, dentalium shell, prized as Yurok currency, was traded down the Pacific coast from deep-water beds at the north end of Vancouver Island. The Yurok traded redwood boats of their manufacture to the Hupa, Tolowa, and Wiyot.

Division of Labor. Shamans could be either men or women. Men traditionally were the hunters, salmon fishers, and woodworkers. Women gathered shellfish and plant foods and used twined burden baskets for gathering firewood. Children collected acorns, roots, edible berries, and wild potatoes. Rich men manufactured ceremonial regalia, and some men specialized in boat making.

Land Tenure. Towns were usually inhabited by groups of related individuals and their families. Subsistence areas, such as fishing spots or acorn groves, could be owned by the town, by a group of men, or by an individual. Well-defined territorial boundaries existed between the Yurok and their neighbors, though some areas were open to all peoples or were neutral areas, and some were sacred zones. In 1875, nearly all of Yurok territory was placed in Humboldt County; today the Hoopa Valley reservations total more than eighty-seven thousand acres.

Kinship

Kin Groups and Descent. Kroeber thought that patrilineal kin groups existed among the Yurok, but were undesignated and unrecognized by them. Kinspeople were spread through Yurok towns and never organized as circumscribed groups such as clans or tribes. Bilateral kinship must have also been present, so that, in Kroeber's words, "a definite unit of kinsmen acting as a group capable of constituted social action did not exist." Descent groups were traced according to the name of its house site in a particular town, and by the late 1960s, Yurok descent groups were labeled as "families." A "house group," as precontact Yurok descent entities might be called, owned rights to certain land, houses, and ceremonial regalia.

Kinship Terminology. Murdock has suggested that the Yurok are one of several California groups with Hawaiian-type kinship systems.

Marriage and Family

Marriage. Kroeber notes that the Yurok married "whom and where they pleased." In the small Yurok villages, however, exogamy was a necessity, but endogamy was common in the larger villages. Social status of the married couple depended on the amount paid for the bride; men of wealth paid great sums, enhancing their rank in the community as well as that of their children. Whether the man was rich or poor, Kroeber relates, "the formality of payment was indispensable to a marriage." In the 1850s, most Yurok married couples lived with the husband's family, with their children having primary affiliation with this house (a "full marriage" in Yurok terms). A much smaller number of couples maintained permanent residence with the wife's family, with the children subsequently linked to that family (to the Yurok, a "half marriage"). Divorce could be initiated by either party, but if the man was the instigator, he had to refund the payment made for his wife. If the woman was the initiator, her kin would have to compensate the husband. If the woman wanted to take any children from the marriage, the husband had to be compensated. Sterility on the part of the woman was the most frequent ground for divorce.

Inheritance. A man's estate went largely to his sons, though the daughters were expected to have a certain share. Additionally, male relatives expected to receive some portion of the estate.

Socialization. Fathers trained their sons to be hunters and warriors, and it is said that daughters were taught by their mothers to be diligent housewives. Children were also taught to be "merry and alert."

Sociopolitical Organization

Social Organization. Yurok society was socially stratified. Persons of wealth, or "aristocrats," were clearly distinguished from "commoners" and the "poor." The aristocrats wore clothing of high style, performed most religious functions, and had a distinctive manner of speech, said to be "rich in its expressiveness." They also owned heirlooms, such as fifteen-inch obsidian bifaces and albino deerskins. Their wealth enabled them to hold dances, providing regalia and food. Other aristocratic "treasure" included many strings of dentalium shell as well as woodpecker scalps. Slavery existed among the Yurok, though it was not an important institution; men became slaves largely through indebtedness.

Political Organization. Although the basic political unit was probably the village, Kroeber reported no sense of community and no encompassing political entity. Only kinship ties at times united some people in separate villages. There were no chiefs or leaders, although a man could sometimes gain importance through great wealth.

Social Control. Since there was no political organization, there existed no central authority. Nevertheless, the Yurok had a series of eleven principles, or "laws," enumerated by Kroeber. The individual had all rights, claims, and privileges; if someone carried out a violent act, there was an elaborate network of compensation claims that could be applied, for example, to an act of revenge. Indeed, the bulk of Yurok law involves the various levels of liability related to any offense. The concept of full compensation involved negotiation and litiga-tion and thus served as the major factor of social control in Yurok life.

Conflict. Disputes could arise among individuals over fishing rights, boundaries of territories, and adultery. So-called warfare involved feuds between large groups of kinsmen in Yurok villages. Raids and retaliation for such raids took place between the Yurok and their neighbors, such as the Hupa. After raids, however, compensation—settlement for damages that occurred—was always required.

Religion and Expressive Culture

Religious Beliefs. Yurok myths ascribed creation to Woh-pekumew, "widower across the ocean." Their world was thought to float on water, and, as Kroeber related, "at the head of the river in the sky, where the Deerskin dance is danced nightly, are a gigantic white coyote and his yellow mate." Yurok dances expressed their beliefs. The motive of such dances was to renew or maintain the world, beginning with the reciting of long formulae, after which a dance ensued. Dances were of various lengths, but could last ten or more days. Each dance had a strict style of regalia, and the wealthy would display their treasures. There were two main kinds of dances: the White Deerskin Dance and the Jumping Dance. The latter usually followed the White Deerskin Dance, and the ceremonies related to the dances intensified as each day passed. A Deerskin Dance also marked the most famous ceremony of the Yurok, the building of a salmon dam at Kepel in early autumn. This preceded the Yurok's first salmon ceremony, held at a small village near the mouth of the Klamath River each April. After days of recitation by a formulist, a salmon was cooked and ritually consumed, thus signifying the opening of the fishing season for upstream Yurok villages.

Religious Practitioners. Among the Yurok were formulists, usually old men who could recite formulae for various events, such as releasing a person from corpse contamination. The Yurok also believed in sorcerers who caused various evil occurrences. Women usually functioned as "doctors," or shamans. They relieved "pain" for high fees; unsuccessful shamans were not killed as they were in some other California Indian groups. True to Yurok law, they were, however, liable for several forms of compensation if the patient died or remained ill.

Ceremonies. In addition to the dances noted above, the Yurok also held "brush dances," apparently designed to cure a sick child, but also held when younger men in the village desired a holiday. The other dances were once held annually but later took place only in alternate years. The last first salmon ceremony took place around 1865. The other dances have not been performed in Yurok territory since 1939, although Pilling has described a revival of Yurok ceremonialism in the 1970s.

Arts. Only men could dance in Yurok ceremonies, and some served as singers who constantly composed new songs during the dances.

Medicine. Women "doctors," or shamans, smoked pipes as part of curing rituals, which also involved sucking out the patient's pain. Disease was caused by breaking taboos or ceremonial regulations. Late in the nineteenth century and early in the twentieth, the sick person "confessed" wrongdoings to the doctor, followed by positive prayer as part of the cure.

Death and Afterlife. At death, the body was painted with soot and a dentalium shell inserted through the nasal septum. Great efforts were made to avoid contamination through contact with the corpse. Burial was in town cemeteries, often in small plots where several bodies might occupy a single grave. The dead were thought to go "below" where the dead Yurok had to cross a river on a boat. If the boat tipped over, the corpse was revived on earth. Once the river had been crossed, however, return was impossible. The dead were ascribed to three types of afterlife: those killed by weapons went to "the willows," forever dancing and shouting in a war dance; thieves and "contentious" persons went to an "inferior place"; and a rich, peaceable man went to "the sky."

Bibliography

Heizer, Robert F., and M. A. Whipple (1971). *The California Indians: A Source Book.* 2nd ed. Berkeley: University of California Press.

Kroeber, Alfred L. (1925). *Handbook of the Indians of California.* U.S. Bureau of American Ethnology Bulletin no. 78, 1–97. Washington, D.C. Reprint, Berkeley: California Book Co., 1953.

Pilling, Arnold R. (1978). "Yurok." In *Handbook of North American Indians.* Vol. 8, *California,* edited by Robert F. Heizer, 137–154. Washington, D.C.: Smithsonian Institution.

Swezey, Sean (1975). "The Energetics of Subsistence-Assurance Ritual in Native California." In *Ethnographic Interpretations: 12–13,* edited by Sean Swezey et al., 1–46. University of California, Archaeological Research Facility, Contributions, no. 23. Berkeley.

THOMAS R. HESTER

Zuni

ETHNONYMS: Ashiwi, Cibola, Cuñi, Narsh-tiz-a (Apache), Nashtezhe (Navajo), Quini, Saray (Tiwa), Seven Cities of Cibola, Siyo (Hopi), Sumi, Sunyitai or Su'nyitsa (Keres)

Orientation

Identification. The Zuni Indians live today on the Zuni Reservation in west-central New Mexico. The name "Zuni" appears to have derived ultimately from Keresan, wherein Acoma and Santa Ana *su'ny* denotes "a Zuni Indian." It first appears in Spanish as Suñi and Zuni in the entrada reports of Augustín Rodriguez and Francisco Sánchez Chamuscado (1581–82). Alternative spellings occur thereafter. The Zuni refer to themselves as "Ashiwi" and their pueblo as "Itiwana" (Middle Place), "Halona:wa," name of Halona Pueblo, or most commonly now, Zuni.

Location. The Zuni have occupied the Zuni River valley of western New Mexico and eastern Arizona since at least A.D. 700. The present reservation comprises approximately 655 square miles divided into three areas: the main reservation, Zuni Salt Lake (one square mile added in 1978), and Zuni Heaven (*Kolhu/wala:wa*) (fourteen square miles added in 1984).

Linguistic Affiliation. The Zuni language is an isolate that may possibly be related to Penutian of central California. If so, glottochronology suggests a separation minimally of seven thousand years.

Demography. Historically, the Zuni population at European contact in 1540 has been estimated at over 6,000. Population was greatly reduced by diseases such as smallpox, influenza, and measles. Since 1903, when medical doctors arrived, the population has steadily increased. Reservation population in February 1988 was 8,299 Zuni (3,984 men, 4,315 women) and 460 non-Indians. Of the Zuni, 2,469 were less than sixteen years old. Many Zuni live off the reservation, but precise figures are lacking.

History and Cultural Relations

Archaeological evidence indicates a resident population within the Zuni River drainage for well over a millennium. In 1540 the Spanish entrada led by Francisco Vásquez de Coronado, came in search of gold to Zuni (the fabled Kingdom of Cibola) described by Fray Marcos de Niza after his 1539 sojourn with Esteban, a Black slave. Coronado and his party defeated the Zuni at Hawikkuh but found that women, children, and most provisions had been removed to the sacred stronghold mesa, Dowa Yalanne. The men escaped and soon followed. The entrada wintered in the Rio Grande, but passed through Zuni again on the way back to Mexico, having found no gold. Several Mexican Indians remained and were reported alive by later Spanish explorers, Chamuscado (1581), Antonio Espejo (1583), and Juan de Oñate (1598). Colonization of the Southwest by the Spaniards under Oñate in 1598 involved the Rio Grande valley. The Zuni were largely unaffected until 1629, when they accepted the Franciscans. A mission was built at Hawikkuh in 1629 and another at Halona:wa by 1632. Hostility toward the friars led to the

Zuni's killing them at Hawikkuh in 1632. Apparently the missions were then left unattended until after 1660. In 1672, Apaches killed the priest at the rebuilt Hawikkuh mission with suggestions of Zuni complicity. The Pueblo Revolt of 1680 drove the remaining Spanish settlers and priests from the Southwest, and missions and their accouterments were destroyed. The reconquest by Diego de Vargas in 1692, however, revealed the Zuni were the only Indians to have preserved Christian ritual objects. De Vargas found the Zuni living atop Dowa Yalanne. They resettled only Halona:wa in 1700, rebuilding the mission. Early in the 1700s, the Zuni killed three Spaniards and briefly fled to Dowa Yalanne. There were also problems with the Hopi, and mutual raiding of villages occurred (the Hopi Wars).

Throughout the eighteenth and most of the nineteenth centuries, Apache and Navajo raiding parties were a problem. Zuni reprisals in a number of instances involved joining with Spanish militia, later Mexican troops (1821 to 1846), and finally the U.S. Army (1846 to 1865). From the outbreak of the Mexican War, the Zuni were allied to the United States and assisted numerous expeditions/militia with food, shelter, and warriors. Stephen Watts Kearny (1846), John Marshall Washington and James H. Simpson (1849), Lorenzo Sitgreaves (1851), Amiel W. Whipple (1858), and Edward F. Beale (1857–1858, with twenty-five camels!) were among those assisted.

With Americanization came tremendous encroachments on what were recognized as Zuni lands during the Spanish and Mexican periods—about 15 million acres were involved. The Zuni reservation boundary was officially established in 1877 and reflected less than 3 percent of the original area utilized. Reservation lands were officially extended beginning as early as 1883 through the assistance of the Bureau of American Ethnology ethnologist Frank Hamilton Cushing. He accompanied Matilda Coxe and James Stevenson, fellow anthropologists, in 1879 and stayed at Zuni for several years, becoming an adopted tribal member and a bow priest. These early anthropologists began a century-plus collaboration with the tribe. Recently, anthropologists have taken an active role in assisting the Zuni in land claims cases and other endeavors.

Settlements

The original area used by the Zuni contains sites indicating Paleo-Indian occupation dating approximately 10000 to 6000 B.C. The Archaic period follows with more numerous sites reflecting a foraging way of life. The introduction of maize from Mexico in 1500 B.C. eventually resulted in a shift from foraging to horticulture. The traditional ancestral Zuni area embraces both Mogollon and Basketmaker-Pueblo (Anasazi) developments, beginning about A.D. 200. At this time, villages of several pit-structures, the introduction of ceramics, and greater dependence on maize are noteworthy. Population and site frequency increased through time. Within the Zuni River drainage proper, painted ceramics developed about A.D. 700, and by 1000, above-ground masonry pueblos appeared. From about 1000 to 1150, the area was incorporated into the Chacoan system centering in Chaco Canyon to the north, with numerous outliers reflecting well-planned masonry structures featuring Great Kivas (one can see, at Zuni, the Village of the Great Kivas and other sites).

With the collapse of the Chacoan system, the ancestral Zuni began to build larger, aggregated pueblos, often with over a thousand rooms. Irrigation to ensure crop production probably began at this time. At Spanish contact the Zuni resided in six pueblos along a twenty-five-mile section of the Zuni River. One of the sites, Halona:wa, is present-day Zuni.

Following reconquest, the present Zuni was the focus for Zuni life and culture, but a number of seasonally occupied sites were constructed and used in the central area early in the seventeenth century. These villages were associated with farming and peach orchards; they were also outposts for grazing livestock and places where religious ceremonies could be held without Spanish interference. During the latter part of the nineteenth century, after Navajo and Apache raiding ceased, farming villages were established at Nutria, Pescado, and Ojo Caliente where excellent springs for irrigation exist. These villages, though largely in ruin, continue to be occupied, as does Tekapo, founded early in the twentieth century at the terminal point of an irrigation canal associated with Blackrock Dam on the Zuni River.

Economy

Subsistence and Commercial Activities. The Zuni were horticulturists, with maize of several colors, beans, and squash as the primary cultigens grown in dry, floodwater, or irrigated fields. Crops were supplemented by the gathering of numerous wild plants and the hunting of animals (mule deer, rabbits, antelope, mountain sheep, and others, including bison on the plains). Communal hunts, which involved considerable ritual activity, were not uncommon. Following Spanish contact, wheat, melons, peaches, and other plants were introduced, as were sheep, goats, cattle, horses, and burros. Aboriginally, turkeys and dogs were domesticated, and eagles were caged or tethered for ritual use of their feathers. Sheep quickly became the dominant animal (for both wool and meat).

Today, all available range land (95 percent of the reservation) has been assigned in ninety-five grazing units/sheep ranches and four cattle pastures operated by two cattlemen's associations. The reservation was fenced in 1934. Range improvements are ongoing, and sheep and cattle provide a growing source of income. Although trading in turquoise, shell, piñon nuts, salt from Zuni Salt Lake, plants/herbs, and other materials has not ceased, with the coming of the railroads (to Gallup in 1882) and Americanization, there was a shift from bartering to a cash economy. Employment on the reservation is limited to positions associated with federally funded tribal programs, trading posts, and other commercial enterprises. During the 1970s a candle factory and a subsidiary plant of a major electronics company were established, but were short-lived. Cottage industry involving jewelry and other craft production began to be an important source of income during the 1920s and reached a zenith in the 1970s; today, most households are involved on either a part- or full-time basis. Events of the 1970s, particularly the "jewelry boom," nearly brought an end to subsistence farming pursuits. Sources of off-reservation employment include fire fighting with the U.S. Forest Service and a variety of jobs in Gallup.

Industrial Arts. Crafts included pottery, blanket and belt weaving, basketry, fetish carving, turquoise (and shell) bead making, and metalworking after Spanish contact. Although silversmithing began in the late nineteenth century, it did not reach major importance until the 1920s with the assistance of reservation and Gallup traders. A progression from cluster-work to mosaic inlay and, more recently, needlepoint and channel work has brought international prominence to Zuni. Fetishes, glass beadwork, kachinas, paintings, prints, and ceramics are available to the trader and tourist market. Sash and belt weaving is being revitalized, but basketry is near extinction.

Trade.   Since prehistoric times, Zuni have maintained an important position in trade with other Pueblos, Navajo, Apache, Mexican Indians, and other groups. Hawikkuh, ethnohistorically, was the nexus of trade; present-day Zuni (Halona:wa) continues the tradition. While major trade in wheat and other crops no longer exists, trade in jewelry and other crafts, as well as salt and piñon nuts, continues.

Division of Labor.   There has been a major shift from traditional patterns (men worked in fields, harvested crops belonged to the women) to a nonagricultural cash economy wherein both women and men are frequently involved in wage earning. Expectations are that a husband will give his wife his earnings. Livestock ownership traditionally resided with males, with related males sharing flock/herd duties and dividing proceeds after sales. Today, women may be involved via inheritance from their fathers. Within households many married couples work together in jewelry production, dividing the work by personal preference. Preparing food for ceremonial occasions and bread baking continues to be women's work, and wood gathering and chopping generally resides with males.

Land Tenure.   Since Americanization, land has been passed down through either male or female lines, rather than being controlled by matrilineal clans. Today, land associated with houses and farming tends to be viewed as personal property with surveyed boundaries. Cattle and sheep grazing areas are divided among tribal members with registered use rights.

Kinship

Kin Groups and Descent.   As of 1977 there were fourteen matrilineal, exogamous, and totemically named clans. A child is born into the clan of his or her mother and is viewed as a child of the father's clan. Clans with large memberships may have subclans within them. Although there has been some intermarriage with non-Zunis, the clan structure remains strong and viable. Its most conspicuous workings may be seen during ceremonies.

Kinship Terminology.   A basic Crow system operates with some modification in kin terms. The Zuni system incorporates blood kin and conjugal relatives, as well as clan and ceremonial kin, and appears highly complex with inconsistencies to non-Zunis.

Marriage and Family

Marriage.   One does not marry within one's clan, and though one should not marry within the father's clan, this does occasionally occur. Marriage traditionally could take place with or without courtship, but it always entailed gifts, discussions with the girl's mother or father, and the girl's own

choice. Since the 1970s, courting has followed basic American mainstream patterns; marriages are formalized by a church ceremony, by a justice of the peace with a tribal marriage license, or by living together. Divorce is easy, although with a cash economy and nontraditional material possessions, separation can be more complicated. A male returns to his mother's house with his personal possessions and little else. Children belong to their mother's matrilineal clan, and therefore illegitimacy does not exist. Alimony payments are unknown.

Domestic Unit.   Traditional extended matrilocal households continue; however, nuclear housing has become common with federal HUD assistance. Subdivisions fan out around the village, and much development has occurred at Black Rock, two miles east of Zuni.

Inheritance.   Matrilineality continues to play a significant role in inheritance of homes and personal property, though males have considerably more say about sheep and cattle disposition. Modernization of the pueblo, especially since the 1970s, has tended to alter traditional division patterns. Bitter disputes within extended families, in part a result of nuclear family housing, are not uncommon.

Socialization.   The "Zuni Way" begins with infants being tightly bound to a hard-backed cradle board. Childhood is characterized by general permissiveness. Mother's brother may be asked to assist in reprimands, and threats of visits by Boogie Man kachinas are not uncommon for repeated naughty behavior. Aggressive and hostile acts are discouraged. Education—from Head Start through high school—is emphasized as a key factor to improved opportunities in life. The University of New Mexico has a vocational branch at Zuni.

Sociopolitical Organization

Social Organization.   The interconnectedness of the Zuni social, political, and religious systems and their complexities have been described as almost impossible for non-Zunis to comprehend. In essence, no part of the system can be isolated. At the base is the maternal household; it is the social, economic, and religious unit composed of elder members of the maternal lineage, their daughters with their children, unmarried sons, and male in-laws. Within this setting, the status of women is high, particularly for matrons. Males joining households as husbands may achieve relatively high status almost immediately because of knowledge and skills that bring financial support to the family, but their ties and obligations to their maternal households continue.

Political Organization.   Aboriginally, members of the bow priesthood controlled both internal and external political matters. The functioning of the bow priests as a council, an arm of the all-powerful religious priests, may date to precontact times. The Spanish instituted the positions of governor (with a cane of office), lieutenant governor, and assistants perhaps as early as the late 1500s and certainly by 1692 (the reconquest). The head bow priest normally would be governor. Installation by the head priests involved presenting the individual with the Spanish cane and, later, another one from Abraham Lincoln (the Lincoln cane). Selection and appointment by the religious hierarchy continued until 1934, when a nominating committee was selected to present two nominees to the priests. At a public meeting, the individual receiving the most "male stand-up" votes was installed as governor; the other, as lieutenant governor. They then had some say about the remaining members of the council. Women, although not officially excluded, did not vote until 1965, when secret balloting was also initiated.

Significant changes occurred in 1970, when the Zuni constitution was ratified. Terms of office for the governor and council were set at four years, and salaries for the first time were guaranteed from federally derived funds via the Bureau of Indian Affairs. On July 1, 1970, the Tribal Council, following application, gained control of all functions of both the Tribal Council and the reservation with an Indian agent (the secretary of the interior's representative) acting as adviser to tribal programs. This was part of an overall comprehensive development plan whereby Zuni would receive increased funds to bring numerous improvements and job opportunities to the reservation. Funding was based on Federal Law 25 U.S.C. 48, passed in 1834; Zuni was the first to apply. The funding led to forty-three modernization programs, and today the pueblo, with its paved streets, sidewalks, and streetlights, appears little different outwardly from other Southwestern communities its size.

Social Control. Aboriginally, the bow priests were central figures in social control. Many infractions were directly tied to accusations of witchcraft; punishments included public whipping and even death. The last public trials of witches were held in 1925, but belief in witchcraft continues. Now it is resolved privately between the person who catches the witch in the act and the witch. Any infractions against the gods are punished directly by them. Gossip and ridicule play an active role in social control; sacred clowns may publicly expose improper behavior in the plaza on various occasions. Zuni also has a tribal police force and jail, as well as access to the state police, the sheriff's office, and federal agents (the FBI in Gallup) as needed.

Conflict. Internal problems appear to have been minimal given the functioning theocratic aboriginal system. During the twentieth century, factionalism, involving pro- and anti-Catholic groups, religious hierarchy versus political groups, and various combinations, has been a problem. Political differences in 1940 resulted in the Sun Priest (highest priest) refusing to serve; he moved to Gallup and the office lapsed with his death in 1952. In 1984, the religious hierarchy, acting on behalf of the people, requested the return of the canes of office from the Tribal Council, citing gross neglect of duty. The priests appointed an interim council, but it was not recognized by the Bureau of Indian Affairs until an election was conducted. Most recently, in 1990, the religious hierarchy objected to the Tribal Council's plan with the National Park Service for the first cultural park on a reservation after it was approved by Congress. A pueblo-wide vote was taken, and negative results ended the plan.

Religion and Expressive Culture

Religious Beliefs. The "Zuni Way" is an all-encompassing approach to the universe. Everything within it is sacred, and through religion, harmony and balance are maintained. Ancestors, nature, and zootheism are major aspects. Offered are numerous prayers and prayersticks and the sprinkling of sacred white maize meal with bits of turquoise, shell, and coral in order to give thanks and to maintain balance and harmony. Disharmony is caused by infractions of proper behavior, and evil per se is equated with witchcraft. Spanish missionaries attempted to destroy the native religion, and some converted to Catholicism and other Christian faiths. But though many have compartmentalized Christianity with Zuni religion, the latter remains strong and viable. Stability is provided through four interlocking subsystems: clans, kivas (kachina society), curing societies, and priesthoods. Each operates independently, but synchronically, to fulfill both psychological and physical Zuni needs. Within the Zuni supernatural order, "The Ones Who Hold Our Roads" are supreme; these are Sun Father and his wife, Moon Mother. Earth Mother is also of great importance. Another deity, Old Lady Salt, is Sun Father's sister, and White Shell Woman is his mother (or maternal grandmother). Other deities include Turquoise Man, War Gods, Beast Gods, and a number of kachinas who require impersonators of the highest character.

Religious Practitioners. In reality, all Zuni are religious practitioners and religion begins in the home. One's clan may determine positions within the religious system. All males are initiated into the kachina society and become members of one of six kiva groups. The father or mother selects his kiva when he is born, but he may change membership. Initiation occurs in two stages: between ages five and nine, and between ten and fourteen; after this, the male can dance and wear a kachina mask. The kachina society is headed by kachina chief and the kachina spokesman, each of whom has a kachina bow priest assistant. There is also a dance chief for each of the six kivas. Twelve curing societies (Cults of the Beast Gods) are open to both male and female members—individuals may join by choice, by being guilty of trespass, or by being cured of illness. Each has four officers. Membership normally is for life. Sixteen rain priesthoods (six daylight and ten night priests) exist; most have from two to five ranked assistants and may also have one or two female assistants. Some priests come from specific clans either because sacred bundles associated with them are housed by these clans or because clan affiliation is mandatory (for example, the sun priest and the house chief). The final two priesthoods are bow priesthoods (cult of the war gods), and the priest must have taken a scalp.

Ceremonies. All of the above groups perform calendrical ceremonies and rituals; some are public, others are secret. Each kiva group normally dances four times a year (summer, prior to the harvest, prior to the winter solstice, and winter proper). The internationally famous Shalako ceremony and feast in late November or early December requires year-long preparation and has reportedly brought five thousand or more visitors annually in recent years. But as of June 1990, Shalako has been closed to the public and non-Indians. In addition to numerous annual pilgrimages, quadrennial rituals and ceremonies include the boys' initiation into the kachina cult and pilgrimages to Zuni heaven, the home of most kachinas and some ancestors.

Arts. Numerous items are made for religious purposes: highly elaborate masks and costumes, kachina dolls presented to girls and women who represent them, bows and arrows to boys, jewelry worn by dancers, moccasins (painted or dyed red), women's leggings, fetishes, prayersticks, images of the war gods (*Ahayuda*), wood slat altars, and various insignia of societal membership. Dancing, religious text recitation, and singing (both newly created kachina songs as well as older ones, some of which are in Keresan or archaic Zuni) are also important.

Medicine. Sickness is caused by taboo infractions or witchcraft. A tremendous variety of medicinal plants, which are either collected or traded for with other tribes, is used in curing. These are administered in a variety of ways—internally, often as teas, rubbed on the skin, or smoked. The curing societies are associated with specific maladies and effect specific cures. A modern hospital (U.S. Public Health Service) is located at Black Rock for general health, dental, and eye care. Serious problems involve ambulance transport to the Gallup Indian Hospital or air service to Albuquerque's Bernalillo County Indian Hospital.

Death and Afterlife. Witchcraft is commonly viewed as causing death; but kachina dances, which continue for an extended series of days, and dreams wherein the dead appear to lure the living can bring about death as well. Infractions of religious rules can cause either the individual or someone close to that person to die. Thunderstorms in January and observed landslides foretell the death of rain priests within a year. Likewise, a Shalako impersonator who falls, especially during the final races, is expected to die within a year. The time of an individual's death is predetermined by a person's "invisible road." If one commits suicide or dies from grief or other premature cause, the individual may not enter the afterworld until "the road" is fully traversed. Following death, the deceased lies in state at home for an evening. During this time, the body is washed by specific female clan relatives and dressed in traditional clothing. Blankets and clothing brought by the assembled group are buried with the individual during the morning. It is preferred that burial occur within twenty-four hours of death. Rather than the overly crowded Campo Santo in front of the mission, the new Panteah cemetery south of the village is the final resting place. The spirit ("wind") of the deceased remains within the home for four days following death. It passes out the open door and resides at one of several locations. Bow priesthood members become lightning makers; rain priests join their kind "in the waters of the world;" medicine society members go to Shipapulima, Place of Emergence. The majority of others go to kachina village/Zuni heaven to participate in activities there or return as clouds or "invisibly" to Zuni while dancing is going on. Following death, the name of the deceased ceases to be used, except for rain priests, whose names are invoked by extant members to bring rain.

Bibliography

Crampton, C. Gregory (1977). *The Zunis of Cibola*. Salt Lake City: University of Utah Press.

Ferguson, T. J., and E. R. Hart (1985). *A Zuni Atlas*. Norman: University of Oklahoma Press.

Leighton, Dorothea C., and John Adair (1966). *People of the Middle Place: A Study of the Zuni Indians*. New Haven, Conn.: Human Relations Area Files Press.

Ortiz, Alfonso, ed. (1979). *Handbook of North American Indians*, Vol. 9, *Southwest*. Washington, D.C.: Smithsonian Institution.

Wright, Barton M. (1985). *Kachinas of the Zuni*. Flagstaff, Ariz.: Northland Press.

THEODORE R. FRISBIE

Appendix: Extinct Native American Cultures

A number of Native American cultures that are known to have existed at the time of or shortly before European contact no longer exist as distinct cultural units. Cultural extinction is indicated by the disappearance of the group's language and cultural repertoire and the assimilation of the surviving members into another culture. Cultural extinction, however, does not necessarily imply physical extinction; for some groups there are still people who identify themselves as members of those groups. Those groups are indicated by italics in the following list.

Acolapissa	Louisiana
Alsea	Oregon
Apalachee	Florida
Atakapa	Louisiana, Texas
Bayogoula	Louisiana
Beothuk	Newfoundland
Biloxi	Mississippi
Calusa	Florida
Cayuse	Oregon, Washington
Chakchiuma	Mississippi
Chastacosta	Oregon
Chawaska	Louisiana
Chimariko	California
Chitimacha	Louisiana
Coahuilteco	Texas
Conestoga	Pennsylvania
Coos	Oregon
Costano	California
Cusabo	South Carolina
Dwamish	Washington
Edisto	South Carolina
Erie	New York, Ohio, Pennsylvania
Hitchiti	Alabama, Georgia
Jumano	New Mexico, Texas
Kamia	California
Karankawa	Texas
Klikitat	Washington
Kwalhiokwa	Washington
Mackenzie Inuit	Northwest Territories
Manso	New Mexico, Texas
Mobile	Alabama, Mississippi
Molala	Oregon
Montauk	New York
Mosopelea	Michigan, Ohio
Mugulasha	Louisiana
Natchez	Louisiana, Mississippi
Neutral	Michigan, New York, Ontario
Nicola	British Columbia
Nipmuc	Massachusetts
Okelousa	Louisiana
Pamlico	North Carolina
Pamunkey	Virginia
Patwin	California
Pennacook	Maine, Massachusetts, New Hampshire, Vermont
Peoria	Illinois
Piro	New Mexico
Quinipissa	Louisiana
Secotan	North Carolina
Shasta	California
Shinnecock	New York
Siuslaw	Oregon
Southampton Inuit	Northwest Territories
Susquehanna	Maryland, Pennsylvania, New York
Takelma	California, Oregon
Tangipahoa	Louisiana
Tillamook	Oregon
Timucua	Florida
Tlatskanai	Oregon
Tolowa	California, Oregon
Tsetsaut	British Columbia
Tunica	Louisiana, Mississippi
Tutelo	Virginia
Umpqua	Oregon
Wappinger	Connecticut, New York
Wappo	California
Washa	Louisiana
Wenrohonron	Ontario
Yamasee	Georgia
Yana	California
Yuchi	Georgia, South Carolina
Yuki	California

Glossary

aborigine. _See_ autochthones

adobe Large, sun-dried bricks made from water, vegetation, and earth used by Pueblo and other Southwestern Indians to build houses and walls.

affine A relative by marriage.

age grade A social category composed of persons who fall within a culturally defined age range.

agnatic descent. _See_ patrilineal descent

allotment A parcel of tribal land of from 40 to 160 acres given to individual Indians and authorized by the Dawes Act of 1887.

ambilineal descent The practice of tracing kinship affiliation through either the male or the female line.

ancestor spirits Ghosts of deceased relatives who are believed to have supernatural powers that can influence the lives of the living.

Anglo A person of European descent. Commonly used to refer to persons of white skin color in the Southwest.

animal husbandry. _See_ pastoralism

animism A belief in spiritual beings.

autochthones The indigenous inhabitants of a region. Often used to refer to the native inhabitants encountered by European explorers or settlers.

avunculocal residence The practice of a newly married couple residing in the community or household of the husband's mother's brother.

band In Canada, refers to a government-recognized group of American Indians who reside on one or more reserves, though some bands have no reserve.

berdache A person who dresses and acts like a member of the opposite sex and is often regarded as such by members of the community.

bilateral descent The practice of tracing kinship affiliation more or less equally through both the male and the female line.

bride-price, bride-wealth The practice of a groom or his kin giving substantial property or wealth to the bride's kin before, at the time of, or after marriage.

bride-service The practice of a groom performing work for his wife's kin for a set period of time either before or after marriage.

cacique A village or tribal leader.

caste An endogamous hereditary group, usually with a distinct hereditary occupation, who has a virtually immutable position in a hierarchy. Although the caste system is most elaborated throughout South Asia, castes have also been reported in Tibet, Japan, Burundi, and the American South.

Chilkat blankets Blankets of goat's hair and cedar bark made principally by the Chilkat tribe of the Tlingit Indians of southern Alaska.

clan, sib A group of unilineally affiliated kin who usually reside in the same community and share common property.

classificatory kin terms Kinship terms, such as aunt, that designate several categories of distinct relatives, such as mother's sister and father's sister.

cognates Words that belong to different languages but have similar sounds and meanings.

collaterals A person's relatives not related to him or her as ascendants or descendants; one's uncle, aunt, cousin, brother, sister, nephew, niece.

consanguine A relative by blood (birth).

counting coup Among the Plains Indians, a practice in which a warrior, while recounting his war deeds at a ceremony, struck a blow (_coup_ in French), usually with a special stick, to a post erected for that purpose. Among the war deeds counted, from most to least prestigious, were touching an enemy during battle while unarmed, stealing a horse from a guarded enemy camp, and taking a scalp.

cousin, cross Children of one's parent's siblings of the opposite sex—one's father's sisters' and mother's brothers' children.

cousin, parallel Children of one's parent's siblings of the same sex—one's father's brothers' and mother's sisters' children.

couvade The practice of the husband acting as if he had given birth at the time his wife gives birth. The husband may take to bed, experience labor pains, or observe taboos associated with childbirth.

creole A general, inconsistently used term usually applied to a spoken language or dialect that is based on grammatical and lexical features combined from two or more natural languages. It is a first language, distinct from a pidgin.

cross cousin. _See_ cousin, cross

cult The beliefs, ideas, and activities associated with the worship of a supernatural force or its representations, such as an ancestor cult or a bear cult.

culture hero A mythical bird, animal, or person who is believed to be the group's protector.

descriptive kin terms Kinship terms that are used to distinguish different categories of relatives such as _mother_ or _father_.

displaced person An individual forced to leave his or her homeland as a result of World War II.

double descent Kinship affiliation by both matrilineal and patrilineal descent.

dowry The practice of a bride's kin giving substantial property or wealth to the groom or to his kin before or at the time of marriage.

earthlodge A large, dome-shaped, partly underground dwelling constructed on a frame of posts and beams, thatched with bundled grass, branches, mats, and so on, and covered with earth.

ego In kinship studies ego is a male or female whom the anthropologist arbitrarily designates as the reference point for a particular kinship diagram or discussion of kinship terminology.

endogamy Marriage within a specific group or social category of which the person is a member, such as one's caste or community.

evil eye The belief that a person can cause harm to another by simply wishing him or her harm (casting the evil eye).

exogamy Marriage outside a specific group or social category of which the person is a member, such as one's clan or community.

extensive cultivation A form of horticulture in which plots of land are cleared and planted for a few years and then left to fallow for a number of years while other plots are used. Also called swidden, shifting, or slash-and-burn cultivation.

fictive kin Individuals referred to or addressed with kin terms and treated as kin, although they are neither affines nor consanguines.

hogan A conical, hexagonal, or octagonal dwelling of the Navajo with a framework of logs and sticks covered with sod, mud, and adobe.

horticulture Plant cultivation carried out by relatively simple means, usually without permanent fields, artificial fertilizers, or plowing.

initiation, or puberty, rites Ceremonies and related activities that mark the transition from childhood to adulthood or from secular status to being a cult-member.

kachina Supernatural persons, often the mythical ancestors of human beings, who visit the earth periodically; a doll, mask, or other object representing such a person, used for ritual purposes by the Hopi and other Pueblo groups.

kin terms, bifurcate-collateral A system of kinship terminology in which all collaterals in the parental generation are referred to by different kin terms.

kin terms, bifurcate-merging A system of kinship terminology in which members of the two descent groups in the parental generation are referred to by different kin terms.

kin terms, Crow A system of kinship terminology in which matrilateral cross cousins are distinguished from each other and from parallel cousins and siblings, but patrilateral cross cousins are referred to by the same terms used for father or father's sister.

kin terms, Dravidian. *See* kin terms, Iroquois

kin terms, Eskimo A system of kinship terminology in which cousins are distinguished from brothers and sisters, but no distinction is made between cross and parallel cousins.

kin terms, generational A system of kinship terminology in which all kin of the same sex in the parental generation are referred to by the same term.

kin terms, Hawaiian A system of kinship terminology in which all male cousins are referred to by the same term used for *brother*, and all female cousins are referred to by the same term used for *sister*.

kin terms, Iroquois A system of kinship terminology in which parallel cousins are referred to by the same terms used

for brothers and sisters but cross cousins are identified by different terms.

kin terms, lineal A system of kinship terminology in which direct descendants or ascendants are distinguished from collateral kin.

kin terms, Omaha A system of kinship terminology in which female matrilateral cross cousins are referred to by the same term used for one's mother, and female patrilateral cross cousins are referred to by the same term used for one's sister's daughter.

kin terms, Sudanese A system of kinship terminology in which there are distinct terms for each category of cousin and sibling, and for aunts, uncles, nieces, and nephews.

kindred The bilateral kin group of near kinsmen who may be expected to be present and participant on important ceremonial occasions, usually in the absence of unilineal descent.

kinship Family relationship, whether traced through marital ties or through blood and descent.

kiva A subterranean chamber used for ritual observances by Pueblo Indians.

legal Indians. *See* status Indians

levirate The practice of requiring a man to marry his brother's widow.

lineage A unilineal (whether patrilineal or matrilineal) kin group that traces kinship affiliation from a common, known ancestor and extends through a number of generations.

longhouse A large, rectangular-shaped dwelling with a wood frame covered by planks, bark, mats, or other siding and usually housing a number of related families.

magic Beliefs and ritual practices designed to harness supernatural forces to achieve the goals of the magician.

manitou An Algonkian term for the powers of the universe and life or the supernatural being that controls those forces.

matrilineal descent, uterine descent The practice of tracing kinship affiliation only through the female line.

matrilocal residence, uxorilocal residence The practice of a newly married couple residing in the community of the wife's kin. *Uxorilocal* is sometimes used in a more restrictive sense to indicate residence in the household of the wife's family.

medicine bundle A skin-covered package of objects thought by the Plains Indians and other groups to have special ritual or magical properties.

moiety A form of social organization in which an entire cultural group is made up of two social groups. Each moiety is often composed of a number of interrelated clans, sibs, or phratries.

monogamy Marriage between one man and one woman at a time.

Native American church An intertribal American Indian religious organization adapting Christianity to native beliefs and practices, including the sacramental use of peyote.

nativism A movement often with social, religious, or political components that centers on the rebirth of the native culture and the demise of the colonizers.

neolocal residence   The practice of a newly-married couple living apart from the immediate kin of either party.

nonstatus Indians.   *See* status Indians

parallel cousin.   *See* cousin, parallel

pastoralism   A type of subsistence economy based on the herding of domesticated grazing animals such as sheep or cattle.

patois   A dialect of a language spoken by a specific social or occupational group in a multi-cultural environment.

patrilineal descent, agnatic descent   The practice of tracing kinship affiliation only through the male line.

patrilocal residence, virilocal residence   The practice of a newly married couple residing in the community of the husband's kin. *Virilocal* is sometimes used in a more restrictive sense to indicate residence in the household of the husband's family.

peasant, peasantry   Small-scale agriculturalists producing only subsistence crops, perhaps in combination with some fishing, animal husbandry, or hunting. They live in villages in a larger state, but participate little in the state's commerce or cultural activities. Today, many peasants rely on mechanized farming and are involved in the national economy, so they are called *post-peasants* by anthropologists.

peyote   Any of several species of cactus (*Lophophora* spp.) found in the Southwest. The downy white tuft (the "button") is used for medicinal and ritual purposes. Also called mescal or mescaline.

Peyotism   A Native American cult that stresses the use of peyote along with prayer and singing in its ritual activities.

phratry   A social group consisting of two or more clans joined by some common bond and standing in opposition to other phratries in the society.

pidgin   A second language very often made up of words and grammatical features from several languages and used as the medium of communication between speakers of different languages.

piñon (pinyon)   Pine trees (*Pinus edulis* and *Pinus monophylla*) of western North America whose large seeds were once an important food source.

polyandry   The marriage of one woman to more than one man at a time.

polygyny   The marriage of one man to more than one woman at a time.

potlatch   A ceremony among Northwest Coast Indians involving the giving away or destruction of property to enhance one's status.

powwow   A council or social meeting of American Indians.

puberty rites.   *See* initiation rites

Pueblo   A term used to refer to a style of architecture, a type of village, or the Pueblo Indians of the Southwest. As an architectural type, a pueblo is an apartment-building structure of stone or adobe, with a flat roof and ladders leading from one level to another. *Pueblo* (Spanish for village) also refers to Southwest Indian communities with pueblo-style structures.

rancheria   A small collection or settlement of crude huts (*ranchos*) or a small American Indian community.

recognized Indians.   *See* status Indians

refugee   An individual who has left his or her homeland as a result of political events in that nation or for other political reasons.

removals   Actions by the federal or state governments involving the forced relocation of American Indian groups from their native lands to other lands, usually to the West and particularly to Indian Territory (present-day Oklahoma).

reservation   Lands in the United States set aside for the exclusive use of American Indians. The land is held in trust by the federal government, or if a state reservation, by the state government.

reserve   Lands in Canada set aside for the exclusive use of status Indians. Title to reserve lands rests with the Canadian government.

sacred bundle   A skin-covered package of objects thought by the Plains Indians and other groups to have special ritual or magical properties.

shaman   A religious practitioner who receives his or her power directly from supernatural forces.

shifting cultivation.   *See* extensive cultivation

sib.   *See* clan

sister exchange   A form of arranged marriage in which two brothers exchange their sisters as wives.

slash-and-burn horticulture   A system of food production that involves burning trees and brush to clear and fertilize a garden plot, and then planting crops. The plot is used for a few years and then left to fallow while other plots are similarly used.

sorcery   The use of supernatural forces to further the interests of the sorcerer, primarily through formulae and the ritual manipulation of material objects.

sororal polygyny   The marriage of one man to two or more sisters at the same time.

sororate   The practice of a woman being required to marry her deceased sister's husband.

status (legal, recognized) Indians   Indians in Canada who are legally defined as Indians by the government. Non-status Indians are those of Indian ancestry who, because of intermarriage, residence in White communities, or other factors, are not legally defined as Indians.

sucking cure   A curing technique often used by shamans which involved sucking out a foreign object from the patient's body through an implement such as a bone tube. The foreign object, a piece of bone or stone, was viewed as the cause of the malady and the sucking out the cure.

Sun Dance   A ceremonial dance, connected with the summer solstice and often associated with Plains Indians, which lasted for four days and sometimes involved dancing until exhausted as well as inflicting wounds on oneself.

sweat lodge A small, sealed hut in which people took sweat baths by means of steam produced by water being sprinkled on hot stones.

swidden The field or garden plot resulting from slash-and-burn field preparation.

teknonymy The practice of addressing a person after the name of his wife or his or her child rather than by the individual name. For example, "Bill" is called "Father of John."

tipi (tepee, teepee) A conical-shaped portable dwelling of skin- or hide-covered poles, associated with the nomadic Plains Indians.

totem A plant or animal emblematic of a clan that usually has special meaning to the group.

transhumance Seasonal movements of a society or community. It may involve seasonal shifts in food production between hunting and gathering and horticulture or the movement of herds to more favorable locations.

tribe Although there is some variation in use, the term usually applies to a distinct people who view themselves and are recognized by outsiders as being a distinct culture. The tribal society has its own name, territory, customs, subsistence activities, and often its own language.

trickster A character in folklore who plays tricks on his enemies. Among many North American Indian groups the trickster is a coyote and is usually portrayed with a combination of human and animal elements.

tule Tall reeds (*Scirpus lacustris* and *Scirpus acutus*) that grow in marshlands in western North America and are widely used for baskets and mats.

unilineal descent The practice of tracing kinship affiliation through only one line, either the matriline or the patriline.

unilocal residence The general term for matrilocal, patrilocal, or avunculocal postmarital residence.

usufruct The right to use land or property without actually owning it.

uterine descent. *See* matrilineal descent

uxorilocal residence. *See* matrilocal residence

virilocal residence. *See* patrilocal residence

weir A wall of sticks or rocks placed in a body of water, river, or stream to prevent fish from passing.

wickiup A beehive-shaped grass hut.

wigwam A dome-shaped dwelling usually covered with bark, woven grass mats, or animal skins.

witchcraft The use of supernatural forces to control or harm another person. Unlike sorcery, witchcraft does not require the use of special rituals, formulae, or ritual objects.

Filmography

Following is a list of films and videos on Native Americans, North American folk cultures, and ethnic groups. This list is not meant to be complete; rather, it is a sampling of the thousands of films and videos available from hundreds of distributors. Listing a film or video here does not constitute an endorsement by the volume editors or the summary authors, nor does the absence of a film represent any sort of nonendorsement. Abbreviations for names of distributors are provided at the end of each citation. The full name and address may be found in the directory of distributors that follows the filmography. Many of these films are also available through the Extension Media Center of the University of California at Berkeley and/or the Audio-Visual Services of the Pennsylvania State University, indicated by (EMC) or (PS) at the end of a citation.

Abenaki: The Native People of Maine. (Abenaki) 1984. Color, 29 minutes, 16mm. (EMC).

Acorns: Staple Food of California Indians. (Pomo) 1962. American Indian Series. Color, 30 minutes, 16mm. EMC (PS).

Again, a Whole Person I've Become. (Wintun, Karok, Tolowa) N.d. Color, 19 minutes, 16mm. SHENFP (PS).

Agueda Martinez—Our People, Our Country. (Navajo) 1977. Color, 16 minutes, 16mm. EDMEDC.

Ain't Gonna Eat My Mind. (African-Americans) 1973. Color, 34 minutes, 16mm. CAROUSEL (EMC).

Alice Elliott. (Pomo) 1977. Color, 11 minutes, 16mm. (EMC).

Always for Pleasure. (African-Americans) 1977. Les Blank. Color, 58 minutes, 16mm. FLOWERF (EMC).

American Chinatown. (Chinese-Americans) 1982. Color, 30 minutes, 16mm, VHS, U-mat. (EMC).

The American Indian Speaks. (Muskogee, Creek, Sioux) 1973. Color, 22 minutes, 16mm. EBEC (EMC) (PS).

American Shoeshine. (African-Americans) 1976. B&W, 30 minutes, 16mm. PERSPF (EMC).

The Amish: A People of Preservation. (Amish) 1977. Edited version. Color, 28 minutes, 16mm. EBEC (EMC).

The Amish: Not to Be Modern. (Amish) N.d. 57 minutes, 16mm, VHS. (FL).

The Amish: People of Preservation. (Amish) 1976. Color, 52 minutes, 16mm. EBEC (PS).

An Ancient Gift. (Navajo) 1983. Color, 16 minutes, 16mm, VHS, U-mat. (EMC).

Another American. (Latinos) 1985. Color, 27 minutes, VHS. FI (PS).

Another Wind Is Moving. (American Indians) 1986. Color, 59 minutes, 16mm. (EMC).

Appalachia: No-Man's-Land. (Appalachians) 1981. Color, 28 minutes, 16mm. MMA (PS).

Appalachia: Rich Land, Poor People. (Appalachians) 1968. Produced by Jack Willis for NET. B&W, 59 minutes, 16mm. IU (PS) (EMC).

At Laskiainen in Palo, Everyone Is a Finn. (Finnish-Americans) 1983. Produced by the Smithsonian Office of Folklife Programs. Color, 58 minutes, 16mm, VHS, U-mat. (PS).

At the Autumn River Camp: Part 1. (Netsilik Inuit) 1967. A. Balikci for the Netsilik Eskimos Series. Color, 30 minutes, 16mm. UEVA (PS).

At the Autumn River Camp: Part 2. (Netsilik Inuit) 1967. A. Balikci for the Netsilik Eskimos Series. Color, 30 minutes, 16mm. UEVA (PS).

At the Caribou Crossing Place: Part 1. (Netsilik Inuit) 1967. A. Balikci for the Netsilik Eskimos Series. Color, 31 minutes, 16mm. UEVA (PS).

At the Caribou Crossing Place: Part 2. (Netsilik Inuit) 1967. A. Balikci for the Netsilik Eskimos Series. Color, 30 minutes, 16mm. UEVA (PS).

At the Spring Sea Ice Camp: Part 1. (Netsilik Inuit) 1968. A. Balikci for the Netsilik Eskimos Series. Color, 27 minutes, 16mm. UEVA (PS).

At the Spring Sea Ice Camp: Part 2. (Netsilik Inuit) 1968. A. Balikci for the Netsilik Eskimos Series. Color, 27 minutes, 16mm. UEVA (PS).

At the Spring Sea Ice Camp: Part 3. (Netsilik Inuit) 1968. A. Balikci for the Netsilik Eskimos Series. Color, 27 minutes, 16mm. UEVA (PS).

At the Time of Whaling. (Eskimos) 1974. Alaskan Native Heritage Film Project. Color, 37 minutes, 16mm. DER (EMC).

At the Winter Sea Ice Camp: Part 1. (Netsilik Inuit) 1967. A. Balikci for the Netsilik Eskimos Series. Color, 30 minutes, 16mm. UEVA (PS).

At the Winter Sea Ice Camp: Part 2. (Netsilik Inuit) 1967. A. Balikci for the Netsilik Eskimos Series. Color, 37 minutes, 16mm. UEVA (PS).

At the Winter Sea Ice Camp: Part 3. (Netsilik Inuit) 1967. A. Balikci for the Netsilik Eskimos Series. Color, 30 minutes, 16mm. UEVA (PS).

At the Winter Sea Ice Camp: Part 4. (Netsilik Inuit) 1967. A. Balikci for the Netsilik Eskimos Series. Color, 35 minutes, 16mm. UEVA (PS).

Ave Maria: The Story of the Fisherman's Feast. (Italian-Americans) 1987. Color, 24 minutes, 16mm. (EMC).

Basketry of the Pomo: Forms and Ornamentation. (Pomo) 1962. American Indian Series. Color, 21 minutes, 16mm. (EMC) (PS).

Basketry of the Pomo: Introductory Film. (Pomo) 1962. American Indian Series. Color, 30 minutes, 16mm. (EMC) (PS).

Basketry of the Pomo: Techniques. (Pomo) 1962. American Indian Series. Color, 33 minutes, 16mm. (EMC) (PS).

Beautiful Tree—Chishkale. (Pomo) 1965. American Indian Series. Color, 20 minutes, 16mm, VHS, U-mat. (EMC).

Becoming American. (Hmong) N.d. Ken and Ivory Waterworth Levine. Color, 58 minutes, 16mm. NEWDAY.

Becoming American. (Laotian-Americans) 1983. Edited version. Color, 30 minutes, 16mm. NEWDAY, UMICH.

Behind the Masks. (Northwest Coast Indians) 1973. Color, 37 minutes, 16mm. NFBC (EMC).

Be-Ta-Ta-Kin. (Pueblo Indians) 1955. Color, 11 minutes, 16mm. NYU (PS).

The Bible and the Distant Time. (Athapaskans) 1987. Make Prayers to the Raven Series. Color, 27 minutes, VHS. UMICH.

Black and White—Uptight. (African-Americans) 1969. Color, 35 minutes, 16mm. BFA (EMC).

The Black Athlete. (African-Americans) 1980. Color, 58 minutes, 16mm. PYRAMID (EMC).

Black Delta Religion. (African-Americans) 1974. Bill and Josette Ferris. B&W, 15 minutes, 16mm. CSF (PS).

Black G.I. (African-Americans) 1970. Black Journal Series. B&W, 55 minutes, 16mm. IU (EMC).

Black Has Always Been Beautiful. (African-Americans) 1971. Black Journal Series. B&W, 17 minutes, 16mm. IU (EMC).

Black History: Lost, Stolen, or Strayed. (African-Americans) 1968. Of Black America Series. B&W, 54 minutes, 16mm. BFA (EMC).

Black Indians of New Orleans. (African-Americans) 1976. Color, 33 minutes, 16mm. UMICH.

Black Music in America: From Then till Now. (African-Americans) 1971. Color, 28 minutes, 16mm. LCA (EMC).

Black Music in America: The Seventies. (African-Americans) 1979. Color, 32 minutes, 16mm. LCA (EMC).

Black Woman. (African-Americans) 1971. Black Journal Series. B&W, 25 minutes, 16mm. IU (EMC).

Black World. (African-Americans) 1968. Of Black America Series. B&W, 53 minutes, 16mm. BFA (EMC).

Blue. (African-Americans) 1970. Color, 23 minutes, 16mm. (EMC).

Blunden Harbor. (Kwakiutl) 1951. B&W, 20 minutes, 16mm. OP, MACMFL (PS).

A Box of Treasures. (Kwakiutl) N.d. Chuck Olin for the U'Mista Cultural Centre. Color, 28 minutes, 16mm, VHS. DER.

Broken Rainbow. (Navajo) 1986. Maria Florio and Victoria Mudd. Color, 69 minutes, 16mm, VHS. (EMC).

Buckdancer. (Sea Islanders) 1980. Black Americana Series. B&W, 6 minutes, 16mm, VHS, U-mat. (EMC).

Buckeyes: Food of California Indians. (California Indians) 1961. American Indian Series. Color, 13 minutes, 16mm. (EMC) (PS).

Building a Kayak: Part 1. (Netsilik Inuit) 1971. A. Balikci for the Netsilik Eskimos Series. Color, 33 minutes, 16mm. UEVA (PS).

Building a Kayak: Part 2. (Netsilik Inuit) 1971. A. Balikci for the Netsilik Eskimos Series. Color, 33 minutes, 16mm. UEVA (PS).

Calling Me Home: Music from the Maryland-Pennsylvania Border. (Appalachians) 1979. Maryland State Arts Council. Color, 22 minutes, 16mm. PSUPCR (PS).

Calumet, Pipe of Peace. (American Indians) 1964. American Indian Series. Color, 23 minutes, 16mm. (EMC) (PS).

Catfish: Man of the Woods. (Appalachians) 1974. Alan Bennett for Appalshop Films. Color, 27 minutes, 16mm. APPAL (PS).

Celebración del Matrimonio. (Latinos) 1986. English version. Color, 30 minutes, 16mm, VHS, U-mat. (EMC).

Celebración del Matrimonio. (Latinos) 1986. Color, 30 minutes, 16mm, VHS, U-mat. (EMC).

Chiang Ching: A Dance Journey. (Chinese-Americans) 1982. Lana Pih Jokel. Color, 30 minutes, 16mm, VHS, U-mat. (EMC).

Chicano. (Mexican-Americans) 1971. Color, 23 minutes, 16mm. BFA (EMC).

Chicano from the Southwest. (Mexican-Americans) 1970. Newcomers to the City Series. Color, 15 minutes, 16mm. EBEC (PS).

Chicken Soup. (Jews) 1973. B&W, 14 minutes, 16mm. CAROUSEL (EMC).

Children's Chants and Games. (African-Americans, Asian-Americans, European-Americans, Latinos) 1972. Color, 15 minutes, 16mm. BFA (EMC).

Christmas in Appalachia. (Appalachians) 1965. B&W, 29 minutes, 16mm. CAROUSEL (PS).

Circle of the Sun. (Blood) 1960. Color, 30 minutes, 16mm. NFBC (EMC).

Coalmining Women. (Appalachians) 1981. Elizabeth Barret for Appalshop Films. Color, 28 minutes, 16mm. APPAL (PS).

A Common Tongue: Part I. (European-Americans) 1979. Color, 28 minutes, 16mm. EBEC (EMC).

A Common Tongue: Part II. (European-Americans) 1979. Color, 30 minutes, 16mm. EBEC (EMC).

Contrary Warriors: A Film of the Crow Tribe. (Crow) 1986. Connie Poten, Pamela Roberts, and Beth Ferris. Color, 60 minutes, 16mm, VHS. DCL.

Corn Is Life. (Hopi) 1983. Color, 19 minutes, 16mm. (EMC).

Cree Hunters of Mistassini. (Cree) 1974. National Film Board of Canada. Color, 58 minutes, 16mm. NFBC, DER (PS) (EMC).

Crooked Beak of Heaven. (Haida) 1975. Color, 52 minutes, 16mm. BBC/TLF, UMICH.

A Day with Darlene. (Appalachians) 1976. P. J. O'Connell for Penn State Television. B&W, 59 minutes, U-mat. PSUPCR (PS).

Diary of a Harlem Family. (African-Americans) 1968. Gordon Parks for NET. B&W, 20 minutes, 16mm. IU (PS) (EMC).

Dineh (The People): Portrait of the Navajo. (Navajo) 1976. Color, 77 minutes, 16mm. (EMC).

Dinshyin. (Navajo) 1974. Color, 22 minutes, 16mm. (EMC).

Discovering American Indian Music. (American Indians) 1971. Color, 24 minutes, 16mm. BARR, UMICH.

Dream Dances of the Kashia Pomo. (Pomo) 1964. Color, 30 minutes, 16mm, VHS, U-mat. (EMC).

The Drummaker. (Ojibwa) 1978. Smithsonian Institution Office of Folklife Programs. B&W, 37 minutes, 16mm. PSUPCR (PS).

Ephesus. (African-Americans) 1966. B&W, 25 minutes, 16mm. MACMFL (EMC).

Eskimo Artist: Kenojuak. (Baffinland Inuit) 1964. National Film Board of Canada. Color, 20 minutes, 16mm. NFBC (PS).

The Eskimo in Life and Legend (Living Stone). (Inuit) 1959. National Film Board of Canada. Color, 22 minutes, 16mm. NFBC (PS).

Ethnic Notions. (African-Americans) 1908. Marion T. Riggs. Color, 58 minutes, VHS. CNEWS (PS).

The Exiles. (American Indians) 1961. Kent MacKenzie. B&W, 70 minutes, 16mm. McG-H (PS).

Faces of Chinatown. (Chinese-Americans) 1963. San Francisco Pageant Series. B&W, 27 minutes, 16mm. (EMC).

Fire on the Water. (Vietnamese-Americans) 1982. Color, 56 minutes, 16mm. HILR (EMC).

Fires of Spring. (Slavey) N.D. Henry T. Lewis. Color, 33 minutes, 16mm. (PS).

First Americans and Their Gods. (American Indians) 1969. Color, 11 minutes, 16mm. IFF, UMICH.

Fishing at the Stone Weir: Part 1. (Netsilik Inuit) 1967. A. Balikci for the Netsilik Eskimos Series. Color, 30 minutes, 16mm. UEVA (PS).

Fishing at the Stone Weir: Part 2. (Netsilik Inuit) 1967. A. Balikci for the Netsilik Eskimos Series. Color, 27 minutes, 16mm. UEVA (PS).

Fishing at the Stone Weir: Parts 1 and 2. (Netsilik Inuit) 1967. A. Balikci for the Netsilik Eskimos Series. Color, 58 minutes, 16mm. NFBC (EMC).

Fonseca: In Search of Coyote. (American Indians) 1983. Pro-duced by Mary Louise King and Fred Aronow. Color, 30 minutes, 16mm, VHS, U-mat. (EMC).

The Forest of Eyes. (Athapaskans) 1987. Make Prayers to the Raven Series. Color, 27 minutes, VHS. UMICH.

The Forgotten American. (American Indians) 1968. CBS. Color, 25 minutes, 16mm. CAROUSEL (PS) (EMC).

Forty-Seven Cents. (Achomawi) 1973. B&W, 25 minutes, 16mm. (EMC).

4-Butte-1: A Lesson in Archaeology. (Maidu) 1968. Color, 33 minutes, 16mm, VHS, U-mat. (EMC).

The Four Corners: A National Sacrifice Area? (Southwest Indians) 1983. Color, 59 minutes, 16mm. BULFRG (EMC).

From the First People. (Eskimos) 1976. Sarah Elder and Leonard Kamerling for the Alaska Native Heritage Film Project. Color, 46 minutes, 16mm. DER (PS).

Game of Staves. (Pomo) 1962. American Indian Series. Color, 10 minutes, 16mm. UC, (EMC) (PS).

Georgia Sea Island Singers. (Sea Islanders) 1980. Bess Lomax Hawes. B&W, 12 minutes, 16mm, VHS, U-mat. (EMC).

Glooscap. (American Indians) 1985. Color, 26 minutes, 16mm. FLMHUM (EMC).

Goodnight Miss Ann. (Mexican-Americans) 1978. Color, 28 minutes, 16mm. PYRAMID (EMC).

Grandpa Joe's Country. (Athapaskans) 1987. Make Prayers to the Raven Series. Color, 27 minutes, VHS. UMICH.

Gravel Springs Fife and Drum. (African-Americans) 1971. Bill Ferris, David Evans, and Judy Peiser. Color, 10 minutes, 16mm. CSF, IU (PS) (EMC).

Group Hunting on the Spring Ice: Part 1. (Netsilik Inuit) 1969. A. Balikci for the Netsilik Eskimos Series. Color, 34 minutes, 16mm. UEVA (PS).

Group Hunting on the Spring Ice: Part 2. (Netsilik Inuit) 1969. A. Balikci for the Netsilik Eskimos Series. Color, 29 minutes, 16mm. UEVA (PS).

Group Hunting on the Spring Ice: Part 3. (Netsilik Inuit) 1969. A. Balikci for the Netsilik Eskimos Series. Color, 33 minutes, 16mm. UEVA (PS).

Gullah Tales (Sea Islanders) 1987. George deGolian and Gary Moss. Color, 30 minutes, 16mm, VHS. DCL.

Haa Shagoon. (Tlingit) 1983. Color, 29 minutes, 16mm. (EMC).

The Heart of Loisaida. (Latinos) 1979. Marci Reaven and Bienvenida Matias. B&W, 25 minutes, 16mm. CINGLD (PS).

Hello Columbus! (With Mal Sharpe) (Italian-Americans) 1987. Color, 27 minutes, 16mm. (EMC).

Heritage: Civilization and the Jews: Part 7, The Golden Land. (Jews) 1984. WNET. Color, 58 minutes, 16mm. FI (PS).

Heritage: Civilization and the Jews: Part 9, Into the Future. (Jews) 1984. WNET. Color, 58 minutes, 16mm. FI (PS).

Heritage in Black. (African-Americans) 1969. Color, 27 minutes, 16mm. EBEC (PS).

The Heritage of Slavery. (African-Americans) 1968. CBS. Of Black America Series. B&W, 53 minutes, 16mm. PHENIX, BFA (PS) (EMC).

Heritage of the Negro. (African-Americans) 1965. NET. History of the Negro People Series. B&W, 30 minutes, 16mm. IU (PS).

High Lonesome Sound. (Appalachians) 1963. B&W, 30 minutes, 16mm. FI (PS) (EMC).

Hispanic America. (Latinos) 1980. CBS with Walter Cronkite. Color, 13 minutes, 16mm. CAROUSEL (PS) (EMC).

Hitch. (African-Americans) 1971. Directed by Irving Jacoby for the Mental Health Film Board. Color, 90 minutes, 16mm. IFB (EMC).

Holy Ghost People. (Appalachians) 1967. B&W, 53 minutes, 16mm. McG-H (EMC).

Hopis: Guardians of the Land. (Hopi) 1971. Color, 10 minutes, 16mm. FILMF (EMC).

Hopi Songs of the Fourth World. (Hopi) 1986. Pat Ferrero. Color, 60 minutes, 16mm. NEWDAY, UMICH.

Hopi Way. (Hopi) 1972. Color, 23 minutes, 16mm. UMICH.

How's School, Enrique? (Chicano) 1970. Color, 18 minutes, 16mm. AIMS (EMC).

Hunger in America. (African-Americans, Mexican-Americans, Navajo) 1968. CBS Reports. Color, 54 minutes, 16mm. CAROUSEL (PS).

Hupa Indian White Deerskin Dance. (Hupa) 1958. Color, 11 minutes, 16mm. BARR (EMC).

Hutterites. (Hutterites) 1964. National Film Board of Canada with John Hostetler. B&W, 28 minutes, 16mm. NFBC, OPENCC (PS) (EMC).

The Hutterites: To Care and Not to Care. (Hutterites) 1984. John Ruth with John Hostetler. Color, 59 minutes, 16mm. BULLER (PS).

The Ice People. (Inuit) 1970. Color, 23 minutes, 16mm. UMICH.

I Heard the Owl Call My Name. (Northwest Coast Indians) 1974. Directed by Daryl Duke. Color, 78 minutes, 16mm. LCA (EMC).

The Immigrant Experience: The Long, Long Journey. (Polish-Americans) 1972. Directed by Joan Micklin Silver. Produced by Linda Gottlieb. Color, 28 minutes, 16mm, VHS. LCA (PS).

Indian Artists of the Southwest. (Zuni, Navajo, Hopi) 1972. Color, 15 minutes, 16mm. EBEC (EMC).

Indian Art of the Pueblos. (Pueblo) 1976. Color, 13 minutes, 16mm. EBEC (EMC).

Indian Legends: Glooscap. (Micmac) 1985. Color, 26 minutes, VHS. FOTH (PS).

Indian Mainstream. (Hupa, Karok, Tolowa, Yurok) 1971. Thomas Parsons. Color, 25 minutes, 16mm. (PS).

Indian Musical Instruments. (Plains Indians) 1955. Plains Indian Culture Series. Color, 13 minutes, 16mm. UOKLA (PS).

Indians. (American Indians) 1970. Produced for the State Historical Society of Colorado. Color, 31 minutes, 16mm. XEROX (EMC).

Indians and Chiefs. (American Indians) 1972. Judith and David MacDougall. B&W, 40 minutes, 16mm. (EMC).

Indian Self-Rule: A Problem of History. (Flathead, Navajo, Quinault) N.d. Selma Thomas. Color, 58 minutes, VHS, U-mat. DER.

Indians of California: Part I, Village Life. (California Indians) 1955. Color, 15 minutes, 16mm. BARR (EMC).

Indians of California: Part II, Food. (California Indians) 1955. Color, 14 minutes, 16mm. BARR (EMC).

Indians of Early America. (American Indians) 1957. B&W, 22 minutes, 16mm. EBEC (PS) (EMC).

Indians of the Plains—Sun Dance Ceremony. (Plains Indians) 1954. B&W, 11 minutes, 16mm. ACA (PS).

In Doig People's Ears: Portrait of a Changing Native Community. (Beaver) N.d. Color, 30 minutes, VHS. UMICH.

In Search of the Bowhead Whale. (Eskimo) 1974. Color, 50 minutes, 16mm. NFBC (EMC).

In Search of the Lost World. (American Indians) 1972. Color, 50 minutes, 16mm. FI (PS).

Inside Chinatown. (Chinese-Americans) 1977. Color, 43 minutes, 16mm. PHENIX (EMC).

In the Land of the War Canoes. (Kwakiutl) 1914. Filmed by Edward S. Curtis, edited by George Quimby and Bill Holm. B&W, 43 minutes, 16mm. UWASH (PS) (EMC).

I Remember Harlem: Part 1, The Early Years, 1600–1930. (African-Americans) 1980. William Miles. Color, 58 minutes, 16mm. (PS).

I Remember Harlem: Part 2, The Depression Years, 1930–1940. (African-Americans) 1980. William Miles. Color, 58 minutes, 16mm. FOTH (PS).

I Remember Harlem: Part 3, Toward Freedom, 1940–1965. (African-Americans) 1980. William Miles. Color, 58 minutes, 16mm. FOTH (PS).

I Remember Harlem: Part 4, Toward a New Day, 1965–1980. (African-Americans) 1980. William Miles. Color, 58 minutes, 16mm. FOTH (PS).

Ishi in Two Worlds. (Yahi) 1967. Written, directed, and produced by Richard C. Tomkins. Color, 19 minutes, 16mm, U-mat. McG-H (PS) (EMC).

An Island in America. (Puerto Ricans) 1972. Produced by the Anti-Defamation League of B'nai B'rith. Color, 28 minutes, 16mm. ADL (PS).

It's Nation Time. (African-Americans) 1971. Black Journal Series. B&W, 21 minutes, 16mm. IU (EMC).

Jigging for Lake Trout. (Netsilik Inuit) 1971. A. Balikci for the Netsilik Eskimos Series. Color, 32 minutes, 16mm. UEVA (PS).

Kashia Men's Dances: Southwestern Pomo Indians. (Pomo) 1963. American Indian Series. Color, 40 minutes, 16mm. EMC (PS).

Latino Profiles: Living in the U.S. Today. (Latinos) 1976. Color, 18 minutes, 16mm. BFA (EMC).

Lay My Burden Down. (African-Americans) 1966. Jack Willis. B&W, 60 minutes, 16mm. IU (EMC).

Legend of Corn. (Ojibwa) 1985. Color, 26 minutes, 16mm. FLMHUM (EMC).

Legend of the Magic Knives. (Northwest Coast Indians) 1971. Color, 11 minutes, 16mm. EBEC (PS).

Life Cycle of the Jews. (Jews) 1965. Produced by the Anti-Defamation League of B'nai B'rith. B&W, 31 minutes, 16mm. ADL (PS).

The Life of the Bear. (Athapaskans) 1987. Make Prayers to the Raven Series. Color, 27 minutes, VHS. (EMC).

Little White Salmon Indian Settlement. (Northwest Coast Indians) 1972. Directed by Harry Dawson. Color, 31 minutes, 16mm. UNIFIL (PS).

Living in America: A Hundred Years of Ybor City. (Cuban-Americans, Spanish-Americans, Italian-Americans) N.d. Color, 53 minutes, VHS. FL.

Living Music for Golden Mountains. (Chinese-Americans) 1982. Color, 27 minutes, 16mm, VHS, U-mat. (EMC).

Living the Life We Sing About. (African-Americans) 1980. Produced by W. Bryce Combs and Burt Feintuch at Western Kentucky University Television Center. Color, 29 minutes, U-mat. PSUPCR (PS).

Long Walk. (Navajo) 1970. Color, 60 minutes, 16mm. FLMWR (EMC).

The Longest Trail. (American Indians) 1986. Alan Lomax and Forrestine Paulay for the Movement Style and Culture Series. Color, 58 minutes, 16mm, VHS, U-mat. (EMC).

Lonnie's Day. (African-Americans) 1969. Color, 14 minutes, 16mm. CORF (PS).

The Loon's Necklace. (American Indians) 1981. Color, 11 minutes, 16mm. EBEC (EMC).

Louise. (African-Americans) 1973. Religious America Series. Color, 27 minutes, 16mm. NORAC (PS).

Louisiana Story. (Cajuns) 1948. Robert Flaherty. B&W, 77 minutes, 16mm. FI (EMC).

Lubavitch. (Hasidic Jews) 1974. Religious America Series. Color, 28 minutes, 16mm. NORAC (PS).

Made in Mississippi: Black Folk Art and Crafts. (African-Americans) 1975. Bill Ferris. Produced by Yale University Media Design Studio with the Center for Southern Folklore. Color, 19 minutes, 16mm. CSF (PS) (EMC).

Make My People Live: The Crisis in Indian Health. (American Indians) 1984. Produced by Linda Harrar for the Nova Series. Color, 57 minutes, 16mm. AMBVP (PS) (EMC).

Maria and Julian's Black Pottery. (San Ildefonso Pueblo) 1977. Arthur E. Baggs, Jr. Color, 11 minutes, 16mm, VHS, U-mat. PSUPCR (PS).

Mermaids, Frog Legs, and Fillets. (African-Americans) 1981. Produced by Jack Santino, Paul Wagner, and Steven Zeitlin for the Columbia Historical Society. Color, 19 minutes, 16mm, U-mat. PSUPCR (PS).

Mexican-Americans: The Invisible Minority. (Mexican-Americans) 1969. NET. Color, 37 minutes, 16mm. IU (PS) (EMC).

Mexican-American Speaks: Heritage in Bronze. (Mexican-Americans) 1972. Color, 20 minutes, 16mm. EBEC (EMC).

Migrant. (African-Americans, Latinos) 1970. NBC. B&W, 53 minutes, 16mm. FI (EMC).

Miles from the Border. (Mexican-American) 1990. 15 minutes, 16mm, VHS. NEWDAY.

Mill Creek Village. (Prairie Indians) 1973. Color, 27 minutes, 16mm. IOWAU (EMC).

Mohawk Basketmaking: A Cultural Profile. (Mohawk) 1980. Frank Semmens. Color, 28 minutes, 16mm, VHS, U-mat. PSUPCR (PS).

Molly's Pilgrim. (Jews) 1985. Color, 24 minutes, 16mm, VHS, U-mat. PHENIX (EMC).

Moontrap. (French-Canadians) 1963. B&W, 84 minutes, 16mm. NFBC (EMC).

More than Bows and Arrows. (American Indians) 1978. Directed by Roy Williams. Color, 55 minutes, 16mm. (PS).

The Mormons, Missionaries to the World. (Mormons) N.d. 58 minutes, VHS. FL.

The Mountain People. (Appalachians) 1976. Color, 24 minutes, 16mm. WOMBAT (PS).

Mountains of Green, Streets of Gold. (Appalachians) 1977. Directed by Dennis Goulden for WKYC. Color, 24 minutes, 16mm. FI (PS).

My Childhood: Part 2, James Baldwin's Harlem. (African-Americans) 1967. B&W, 26 minutes, 16mm. BNCHMK (EMC).

My Hands Are the Tools of My Soul. (American Indians) 1975. Directed by Arthur Barron. Color, 52 minutes, 16mm. TEXFLM (PS).

The Mystery of the Anasazi. (Southwest Indians) 1973. WGBH. Nova Series. Color, 50 minutes, 16mm. TIMLI (PS).

The Mystery of the Lost Red Paint People. (American Indians) 1987. Produced by Ted Timreck and Will Goetzmann for the Nova Series. Color, 56 minutes, 16mm. BFROG (PS).

My Town—Mio Paese. (Italian-Americans) 1988. Color, 26 minutes, 16mm, VHS, U-mat. (EMC).

Nanook of the North. (Eskimos) 1922. Robert Flaherty, restored in 1975 by David Shephard. B&W, 65 minutes, 16mm. KINO, FI (PS) (EMC).

Nanook of the North. (Eskimos) 1948. Robert Flaherty. B&W, 51 minutes, 16mm. McG-H (PS).

Nature's Way. (Appalachians) 1974. Directed by John Long for Appalshop Films. Color, 22 minutes, 16mm. APPAL (PS).

Navajo: A People between Two Worlds. (Navajo) 1958. Color, 18 minutes, 16mm. (PS).

The Navajo: A Study in Cultural Contrast. (Navajo) 1969. Color, 15 minutes, 16mm, VHS. JOU (PS).

Navajo: The Last Red Indians. (Navajo) 1972. BBC. Color, 50 minutes, 16mm. T-L (EMC).

Navajo Girl. (Navajo) 1973. Color, 20 minutes, 16mm. DERPBA/DOCEDR, UMICH.

Navajo Silversmith. (Navajo) N.d. B&W, 21 minutes, 16mm, silent. MOMA (PS).

Navajo Silversmith. (Navajo) 1960. Color, 10 minutes, 16mm. MOMA (PS).

Neshnabek: The People. (Potawatomi) 1979. B&W, 30 minutes, 16mm, VHS, U-mat. (EMC).

The North American Indian: Part 1, Treaties Made, Treaties Broken. (American Indians) 1971. Color, 18 minutes, 16mm. McG-H (PS).

The North American Indian: Part 2, How the West Was Won and Honor Lost. (American Indians) 1971. Color, 25 minutes, 16mm. McG-H (PS).

The North American Indian: Part 3, Lament of the Reservation. (American Indians) 1971. Color, 24 minutes, 16mm. McG-H (PS).

Obsidian Point-Making. (California Indians) 1964. American Indian Series. Color, 13 minutes, 16mm. (PS) (EMC).

Of Land and Life: People of the Klamath. (Karok) 1990. Jim Culp. 28 minutes, VHS. NEWDAY.

Old Believers. (Russian Old Believers) 1986. Color, 29 minutes, 16mm. (EMC).

Old-Fashioned Home Bread Baking in Rural Pennsylvania. (Mennonites) 1965. Produced by D. P. Duvall and L. P. Greenhill for the Pennsylvania State University. B&W, 13 minutes, 16mm. (PS).

The Old Order Amish. (Amish) 1959. Produced by Vincent R. Tortora. Color, 32 minutes, 16mm. APPLAUS (PS).

One River, One Country: The U.S.-Mexico Border. (Mexican Americans) 1986. CBS. Color, 47 minutes, U-mat. CAROUSEL, UMICH.

On the Spring Ice. (Eskimos) 1976. Alaskan Native Heritage Film Project. Color, 45 minutes, 16mm. DER (EMC).

The Other Side of the Ledger: An Indian View of the Hudson's Bay Company. (American Indians) 1972. Color, 42 minutes, 16mm. NFBC (EMC).

Our Land Is Our Life. (Cree) 1975. Color, 58 minutes, 16mm. NFBC, UMICH.

Our Lives in Our Hands. (Micmac) 1985. Harald Prins and Karen Carter. Color, 49 minutes, 16mm, VHS. DER.

Our Totem Is the Raven. (American Indians) 1972. Color, 21 minutes, 16mm. BFA (EMC).

Painting with Sand: A Navajo Ceremony. (Navajo) 1950. Color, 11 minutes, 16mm. OP (EMC).

The Passage of Gifts. (Athapaskans) 1987. Make Prayers to the Raven Series. Color, 27 minutes, VHS. UMICH.

People of the Buffalo. (Plains Indians) 1969. Color, 14 minutes, 16mm. EBEC (EMC).

People of the Yukon Delta. (Eskimos) 1973. Color, 28 minutes, 16mm. (EMC).

The Performed Word. (African-Americans) 1982. Produced by Gerald L. Davis. Color, 59 minutes, 16mm. CSF (PS).

The Phans of Jersey City. (Vietnamese-Americans) 1979. Directed by Stephen Forman and Dennis Lanson. Color, 49 minutes, 16mm. FI (PS).

Pine Nuts. (Washoe, Paiute) 1961. American Indian Series. Color, 13 minutes, 16mm. (PS) (EMC).

Pizza Pizza Daddy-O. (African-Americans) 1969. Black Americana Series. B&W, 18 minutes, 16mm, VHS, U-mat. (EMC).

Play and Cultural Continuity: Part 1, Appalachian Children. (Appalachians) 1975. S. H. Arnaud and N. E. Curry. Color, 23 minutes, 16mm. CAMPUS (PS).

Play and Cultural Continuity: Part 2, Southern Black Children. (African-Americans) 1975. S. H. Arnaud and N. E. Curry. Color, 27 minutes, 16mm. CAMPUS (PS).

Play and Cultural Continuity: Part 3, Mexican-American Children. (Mexican-Americans) 1975. S. H. Arnaud and N. E. Curry. Color, 28 minutes, 16mm. CAMPUS (PS).

Play and Cultural Continuity: Part 4, Montana Indian Children. (Flathead) 1975. S. H. Arnaud and N. E. Curry. Color, 29 minutes, 16mm. CAMPUS (PS).

Pomo Shaman. (Pomo) 1964. B&W, 20 minutes, 16mm, VHS, U-mat. (EMC).

Preserving a Way of Life: People of the Klamath. (Karok) 1990. Jim Culp. 28 minutes, VHS. NEWDAY.

Quilting Women. (Appalachians) 1976. Directed by Elizabeth Barret for Appalshop Films. Color, 27 minutes, 16mm. APPAL (PS).

Relocation and the Navajo-Hopi Land Dispute. (Navajo, Hopi) 1981. Directed and produced by Victoria Mudd. Color, 23 minutes, 16mm. (PS).

Rendezvous with Freedom. (Jews) 1974. Produced and directed by Marc Siegal for ABC. Color, 38 minutes, 16mm. FI (PS).

Resurrection. (Mexican-Americans) 1973. Religious America Series. Color, 27 minutes, 16mm. NORAC (PS).

Return to Sovereignty. (Kickapoo) 1982. Color, 46 minutes, 16mm. (EMC).

Right to Be Different: Culture Classes. (African-Americans, Amish, Mexican-Americans, Navajo) 1972. ABC. Color, 29 minutes, 16mm. XEROX (EMC).

The Right to Be Mohawk. (Mohawk) 1990. George Hornbein, Anne Stanaway, and Lorna Rasmussen. 17 minutes, 16mm, VHS. NEWDAY.

Salazar Family: A Look at Poverty. (Mexican-Americans) 1970. B&W, 14 minutes, 16mm. (EMC).

Salt of the Earth. (Mexican-Americans) 1954. B&W, 94 minutes, 16mm. FI (EMC).

Sam. (Chinese-Americans) 1973. B&W, 20 minutes, 16mm. (EMC).

Sananguagat: Inuit Masterworks of 1,000 Years. (Inuit) 1974. Color, 25 minutes, 16mm. NFBC (PS).

Seeking the First Americans. (American Indians) 1980. Directed and produced by Graham Chedd. Color, 59 minutes, 16mm. DER (PS).

Shadow Catcher. (American Indians) 1975. Color, 88 minutes, 16mm. PHENIX (EMC).

The Shakers. (Shakers) 1974. Directed by Tom Davenport. Color, 30 minutes, 16mm. (PS) (EMC).

Sinew-Backed Bow and Its Arrows. (Yurok) 1961. American Indian Series. Color, 24 minutes, 16mm, VHS, U-mat. (EMC).

Slavery. (African-Americans) 1965. NET. B&W, 30 minutes, 16mm. IU (PS).

Snaketown. (Southwest Indians) 1969. Color, 40 minutes, 16mm. (EMC).

So Far from India. (South Asian–Americans) 1982. Produced by Mira Nair. Color, 49 minutes, 16mm. FL (PS).

Stalking Seal on the Spring Ice: Part 1. (Netsilik Inuit) 1968. A. Balikci for the Netsilik Eskimo Series. Color, 25 minutes, 16mm. UEVA (PS).

Stalking Seal on the Spring Ice: Part 2. (Netsilik Inuit) 1968. A. Balikci for the Netsilik Eskimo Series. Color, 34 minutes, 16mm. UEVA (PS).

A Storm of Strangers: Italian Americans. (Italian-Americans) 1977. Directed by Martin Scorsese. Color, 30 minutes, 16mm. FI (PS).

A Storm of Strangers: Jewish Americans. (Jews) 1969. B&W, 27 minutes, 16mm. AIMS (PS).

A Storm of Strangers: Jung Sai, Chinese Americans. (Chinese-Americans) 1977. Directed by Frieda Lee Mock and Terry Sanders. Color, 29 minutes, 16mm. FI (PS).

A Storm of Strangers: The Irish. (Irish-Americans) 1974. Color, 26 minutes, 16mm. FI (PS) (EMC).

The Story of English: Part 5, Black on White. (African-Americans) 1986. Color, 60 minutes, VHS. FI (PS).

The Story of English: Part 6, Pioneers O! Pioneers. (African-Americans) 1986. Color, 60 minutes, VHS. FI (PS).

Sucking Doctor. (Pomo) 1964. B&W, 50 minutes, 16mm. (PS) (EMC).

Summer of the Loucheux: Portrait of a Northern Indian Family. (American Indians) 1983. Directed and produced by Gradon McCrea. Color, 28 minutes, 16mm. NEWDAY (PS).

The Sun Dagger. (Southwest Indians) 1983. Directed by Albert Ihde. Produced by Anna Sofaer. Color, 59 minutes, 16mm. BULFRG (EMC).

The Sun Dagger. (Southwest Indians) 1982. Edited version. Directed by Albert Ihde. Produced by Anna Sofaer. Color, 30 minutes, 16mm. BULFRG (PS).

Los Sures. (Puerto Ricans) 1983. Directed and produced by Diego Echeverria. Color, 57 minutes, 16mm. CINGLD (PS).

Tenement. (African-Americans) 1967. CBS. B&W, 40 minutes, 16mm. CAROUSEL (EMC).

Ten Thousand Beads for Navaho Sam. (Navajo) 1971. Color, 25 minutes, 16mm. ECCW (EMC).

That's Me. (Puerto Ricans) 1963. B&W, 15 minutes, 16mm. McG-H (EMC).

Three Stone Blades. (Eskimo) 1971. Ira Latour. Color, 15 minutes, 16mm. IFB (EMC).

Totem Pole. (Northwest Coast Indians) 1963. American Indian Series. Color, 27 minutes, 16mm. (PS) (EMC).

Tribute to Malcolm X. (African-Americans) 1971. Black Journal Series. B&W, 15 minutes, 16mm. IU (EMC).

Tule Technology: Northern Paiute Uses of Marsh Resources in Western Nevada. (Northern Paiute) 1983. Produced by the Smithsonian Institution Office of Folklife Programs. Color, 42 minutes, 16mm. PSUPCR (PS).

Tunnel. (Mexican-Americans) 1974. Color, 25 minutes, 16mm. LRF (EMC).

Tununeremiut: The People of Tununak. (Alaska Eskimos) N.d. Alaska Native Heritage Film Project. Color, 35 minutes, 16mm, VHS. DER.

The Unveilings. (American Indians) 1976. Produced by the Center for Medieval and Renaissance Studies at UCLA and the UCLA Media Center. Color, 28 minutes, 16mm. SALENT (PS).

The Vanishing Family: Crisis in Black America. (African-Americans) 1986. Directed and produced by Ruth C. Streeter for the CBS Reports Series. Color, 64 minutes, VHS. CAROUSEL (PS) (EMC).

A Village in Baltimore: Images of Greek American Women. (Greek-Americans) 1981. Directed and produced by Doreen Moses. Color, 63 minutes, 16mm. ICONF (PS).

Vision Quest. (Plains Indians) 1961. Color, 30 minutes, 16mm. McG-H (PS).

Waterborne: Gift of the Indian Canoe. (Northwest Coast Indians) 1990. Anne Rutledge and David Current. 13 minutes, VHS. NEWDAY.

The Water Is So Clear that a Blind Man Could See. (Taos Pueblo) 1970. NET. Color, 30 minutes, 16mm. IU (PS).

Waterloo Farmers. (Mennonites) 1979. Color, 26 minutes, 16mm. BULFRG (EMC).

Way of Our Fathers. (California Indians) 1972. Color, 33 minutes, 16mm. (EMC).

A Weave of Time: The Story of a Navajo Family, 1938–1986. (Navajo) 1987. Susan Fanshel. Color, 60 minutes, 16mm, VHS. DCL.

We're Moving Up! The Hispanic Migration. (Latinos) 1980. Produced by Patricia Creaghan, Jean Venable, and Anne Chambers for the NBC White Paper Series. Color, 80 minutes, U-mat. FI (PS).

Were You There When the Animals Talked? (African-Americans) 1975. Color, 28 minutes, VHS. BEACON (PS).

Who Do You Kill? (African-Americans) 1968. CBS. B&W, 51 minutes, 16mm. CAROUSEL (EMC).

Wooden Box: Made by Steaming and Bending. (Kwakiutl) 1962. American Indian Series. Color, 33 minutes, 16mm. (PS) (EMC).

Woodrow Cornett: Letcher County Butcher. (Appalachians) 1970. Directed by Bill Richardson for Appalshop Films. B&W, 10 minutes, 16mm. APPAL (PS).

The World of Piri Thomas. (Puerto Ricans) 1968. NET. Color, 60 minutes, 16mm. IU (PS).

Yesterday, Today: The Netsilik Eskimo. (Netsilik Inuit) 1973. NFBC. Color, 57 minutes, 16mm. EDC (EMC).

Yo Soy Chicano. (Mexican-Americans) 1972. Color, 59 minutes, 16mm. IU (EMC).

You Are on Indian Land. (Mohawk) 1969. Produced by Canadian Indians for the National Film Board of Canada. B&W, 37 minutes, 16mm. NFBC, McG-H (PS) (EMC).

Directory of Distributors

ACA	Academy Films, 3918 W. Estes Ave., Lincolnwood, IL 60645
ADL	Anti-Defamation League of B'nai B'rith, 823 United Nations Plaza, New York, NY 10017
AIMS	Aims Instructional Media Services, 6901 Woodley Ave., Van Nuys, CA 91406-4878
AMBVP	Ambrose Video Publishing, 381 Park Ave. S., New York, NY 10016
APPAL	Appalshop, Inc., 306 Madison St., Whitesburg, KY 41858
APPLAUS	Applause Productions, Inc., 85 Longview Rd., Port Washington, NY 11050
BARR	Barr Films, Box 7878, 12801 Schabarum Ave., Irwindale, CA 91706-7878
BEACON	Beacon Films, 930 Pitner Ave., Evanston, IL 60202
BFA	*See* PHENIX
BNCHMK	Benchmark Films, Inc., 145 Scarborough Rd., Briarcliff Manor, NY 10510
BULFRG	Bullfrog Films, Inc., Oley, PA 19547
BULLER	Buller Films, Inc., 1053 Main St., Henderson, NE 68371
CAMPUS	Campus Film Productions, 20 E. 46th St., New York, NY 10017
CAROUSEL	Carousel Films, Inc., 241 E. 34th St., Room 304, New York, NY 10016
CINGLD	Cinema Guild, 1697 Broadway, Room 802, New York, NY 10019
CNEWS	California Newsreel, 630 Natoma, San Francisco, CA 94103
CORF	Coronet Films, 3771 Victoria Park Ave., Scarborough, ON M1W 2P9 Canada
CSF	Center for Southern Folklore, Box 40105, Memphis, TN 38014
DER	Documentary Educational Resources, 101 Morse St., Watertown, MA 02172
EBEC	Encyclopaedia Brittanica Educational Corporation, Division of Encyclopaedia Brittanica, 425 N. Michigan Ave., Chicago, IL 60611
EDC	Education Development Center, Inc., 55 Chapel St., Newton, MA 02160
EMC	University of California Extension Media Center, 2176 Shattuck Ave., Berkeley, CA 94704
FI	Films Incorporated, Subsidiary of PMI, 5547 N. Ravenswood Ave., Chicago, IL 60640
FILMF	Film Fair Communications, Division of FilmFair, Inc., Box 1728, 10900 Ventura Blvd., Studio City, CA 91604
FL	Filmmakers Library, Inc., 124 E. 40th St., New York, NY 10016
FLMHUM	Films for the Humanities, 743 Alexander Rd., Princeton, NJ 08540
FLMWR	Films Wrights, 231 State St., San Francisco, CA 94114

FLOWERF   Flower Films, 10341 San Pablo Ave., El Cerrito, CA 94530

ICONF   Icon Films, 717 Lexington Ave., New York, NY 10022

IFB   International Film Bureau, 332 S. Michigan Ave., Chicago, IL 60604

IFF   International Film Foundation, 155 W. 72nd St., Room 306, New York, NY 10023

IOWAU   Iowa State University, 2121 S. State Ave., Ames, IA 50010

IU   Indiana University, A-V Center, Bloomington, IN 47405

JOU   Journal Films, Inc., Division of the Altschul Group, 930 Pitner Ave., Evanston, IL 60202

KINO   Kino International, 333 W. 39th St., Suite 503, New York, NY 10018

LCA   Learning Corporation of America Highgate New World, 130 E. 59th St., 10th Floor, New York, NY 10022

LRF   Little Red Film House, Box 691083, Los Angeles, CA 90069

MACMFL   Macmillan Films, 866 Third Ave., New York, NY 10022

McG-H   McGraw-Hill Films, 11 W. 19th St., New York, NY 10011

MMA   Mass Media Associates, 2116 N. Charles St., Baltimore, MD 21218

MOMA   Museum of Modern Art Film Library, 11 W. 53rd St., New York, NY 10019-5486

NEWDAY   New Day Films, 22 Riverview Dr., Wayne, NJ 07470

NFBC   National Film Board of Canada, Box 6100, Station A, Montreal, PQ, H3C 3A5, Canada

NYU   New York University, Films Division, Division of Center for Media Services, 26 Washington Place, New York, NY 10003

OPENCC   Open Circle Cinema, Box 315, Franklin Lakes, NJ 07417

PERSPF   Perspective Films/Esquire Communications Group, 369 W. Erie St., Chicago, IL 60610

PHENIX   Phoenix/BFA Films and Video, Inc., 468 Park Ave. S., New York, NY 10016

PS   Pennsylvania State University, Audio-Visual Services, Special Services Building, University Park, PA 16802

PSUPCR   Pennsylvania State University, Psych Cinema Register, 6 Willard Building, University Park, PA 16802

PYRAMID   Pyramid Films, Box 1048, Santa Monica, CA 90406

SALENT   Salz Enterprises, Atrium Building, 98 Cutter Mill Rd., Great Neck, NY 10019

SHENFP   Shenandoah Film Productions, 538 G St., Arcata, CA 95521

TEXFLM   Texture Films, 1600 Broadway, New York, NY 10019

TIRESIAS   Tiresias Film Productions

T-L   Time-Life Multimedia, 100 Eisenhower Dr., P.O. Box 644, Paramus, NJ 07653

UEVA   Universal Education and Visual Arts, Division of Universal City Studios, Inc., 100 University City Plaza, University City, CA 91608

UMICH   University of Michigan, 144 Lane Hall, Ann Arbor, MI 48109-1290

UNIFIL   Unifilm International, 1741 N. Ivar St., Suite 102, Hollywood, CA 90026

UOKLA   University of Oklahoma, Box 26901, Library Building, 1000 Stanton L. Young Blvd., Room 251, Oklahoma City, OK 73190

UWASH   University of Washington, Box 50096, Seattle, WA 98145

WOMBAT   Wombat Film Productions, Division of Cortech Communications, Inc., 250 W. 57th St., Suite 916, New York, NY 10019

XEROX   Xerox Films, Department of Xerox Educational Publications, 245 Long Hill Rd., Middletown, CT 06457

Ethnonym Index

This index provides some of the alternative names and the names of major sub-groups for cultures covered in this volume. The culture names that are entry titles are in boldface.

Abenaki
Abenaque—**Abenaki**
Abenaquioicts—**Abenaki**
Abenaquois—**Abenaki**
Abnaki—**Abenaki**
Absarokee—**Crow**
Acadians
Acadians of Louisiana—**Cajuns**
Acadiens—**Acadians**
Achomawi—**Achumawi**
Achumawi
Acoma—**Keres Pueblo Indians; Pueblo Indians**
Adamstown Indians—**American Isolates**
Aframerindians—**American Isolates**
African Americans
African-Canadians—**Blacks in Canada**
Afro-Americans—**African Americans**
Afro-French—**Black Creoles of Louisiana**
Aglurmiut—**Central Yup'ik Eskimos**
Agutchaninnewug—**Hidatsa**
A-ha-chae—**Osage**
Ahtena—**Ahtna**
Ahtna
Ahtnakotana—**Ahtna**
Akulmiut—**Central Yup'ik Eskimos**
Aiaho—**Chiricahua**
Aivilingmiut—**Iglulik Inuit**
Akansa—**Quapaw**
Akimel O'Odham—**Pima-Papago**
Alabama
Alabama-Coushatta—**Alabama**
Albanians—**European-Americans; European-Canadians**
Alequa—**Yurok**
Aleut
Aleut—**Pacific Eskimo**
Aleutian—**Aleut**
Algonkin
Algonquin—**Algonkin**
Alibamu—**Alabama**
Aliquois—**Yurok**
Alliklik—**Serrano**
Alutiiq—**Pacific Eskimo**
Alyoot—**Aleut**

Amelecite—**Maliseet**
American Isolates
Ameshe—**Hidatsa**
Amish
Amojave—**Mohave**
Anabaptists—**Mennonites**
Anishinabe—**Ojibwa**
Anitakwa—**Catawba**
Apaches de Cuartelejo—**Mescalero Apache**
Apaches del Rio Grande—**Mescalero Apache**
Apaches de Nabaju—**Navajo**
Apaches-Mohaves—**Yavapai**
Apachi—**Mescalero Apache**
Appalachians
Apsaalooke—**Crow**
Apsaroke—**Crow**
Arab Americans
Arab Muslims—**Arab Americans**
Arapaho
Arapahoe—**Arapaho**
Arctic Highlanders—**Inughuit**
Areneno—**Pima-Papago**
Arikara
Arkansas—**Quapaw**
Armenians—**European-Americans; European-Canadians**
Arra-Arra—**Karok**
Arveqtormiut—**Netsilik Inuit**
Ashiwi—**Zuni**
Ashkenazim—**Jews**
Ashochimi—**Wappo**
Asian Indians—**South and Southeast Asians of Canada; South and Southeast Asians of the United States**
Asiatic Eskimos—**Yuit**
Askinarmiut—**Central Yup'ik Eskimos**
Assiniboin
Assiniboine—**Assiniboin**
Assinipwat—**Assiniboin**
Atimopiskay—**Dogrib**
Atsina—**Gros Ventre**
Attayes—**Tenino**

Austrians—**European-Americans; European-Canadians**
Avanersuarmiut—**Inughuit**
Awigaza—**Mandan**

Baffinland Inuit
Bahamians—**Black West Indians in the United States**
Banac—**Bannock**
Banakwut—**Bannock**
Bangladeshis—**South and Southeast Asians of the United States**
Bannock—**Northern Shoshone and Bannock**
Bascos—**Basques**
Basques
Batawat—**Wiyot**
Bearlake Indians
Beaver
Belgians—**European-Americans; European-Canadians**
Belhoola—**Bella Coola**
Believers—**Shakers**
Bellabella
Bella Coola
Bellacoola—**Bella Coola**
Belorussians—**European-Americans; European-Canadians**
Bering Sea Eskimos—**Central Yup'ik Eskimos**
Bhutanese—**South and Southeast Asians of the United States**
Bidakamtata—**Pomo**
Bilqula—**Bella Coola**
Black Americans—**African Americans**
Black Coes—**American Isolates**
Black Creoles—**Black Creoles of Louisiana**
Black Creoles of Louisiana
Blackfoot
Black French—**Black Creoles of Louisiana**
Blacks—**Blacks in Canada**
Blacks in Canada
Black West Indians in the United States

417

Soba—**Pima-Papago**
Sobaipuri—**Pima-Papago**
So-lot-luk—**Wiyot**
Songish—**Klallam**
Sooke—**Klallam**
Soo-lah-te-luk—**Wiyot**
Sorbs—**European-Americans**
Souriquois—**Micmac**
South Alaskan Eskimo—**Pacific Eskimo**
South and Southeast Asians of Canada
South and Southeast Asians of the
    United States
Southern Appalachians—**Appalachians**
Southern Kwakiutl—**Kwakiutl**
Southern Maidu—**Maidu**
Southern Mestizos—**American Isolates**
Southern Paiute (and Chemehuevi)
Southern Tonto—**Western Apache**
Southwest Alaska Eskimos—**Central**
    Yup'ik Eskimos
Southwestern Chippewa—**Ojibwa**
Southwestern Ojibwa—**Ojibwa**
Soyopas—**Mohave**
Spaniards—**European-Americans;**
    European-Canadians
Spiritual Christians—**Molokans**
Spokan—**Spokane**
Spokane
Spukanees—**Spokane**
Sri Lankans—**South and Southeast**
    Asians of the United States
Starrahhe—**Arikara**
Stockbridge-Munsee—**Mahican**
Stoneys—**Assiniboin**
Stonies—**Assiniboin**
Submerged Races—**American Isolates**
Suláteluk—**Wiyot**
Sumi—**Zuni**
Sun People—**Spokane**
Supai—**Havasupai**
Suretika—**Arapaho**
Suxwapmux—**Shuswap**
Svobodniki—**Doukhobors**
Swedes—**European-Americans**
Swiss—**European-Americans;**
    European-Canadians
Swiss-Brethren—**Mennonites**
Syrians—**Arab Americans**

Tah-le-wah—**Tolowa**
Tahltan
Taidnapam—**Klikitat**
Takulli—**Carrier**
Talawa—**Tolowa**
Tallige'—**Cherokee**
Taltushtuntude—**Chastacosta**
Tamils—**South and Southeast Asians of**
    the United States
Tanaina
Tanana
Tä-nä-tinne—**Hare**
Tannin-kootchin—**Tanana**
Tano—**Hopi-Tewa; Tewa Pueblos**
Tano-Tewa—**Tewa Pueblos**
Taos
Tariurmiut—**North Alaskan Eskimos**
Tarrantines—**Micmac**
Tátskan wátitch—**Tonkawa**

Taufgesinnten—**Mennonites**
Tayberon—**Taos**
Tchatakes—**Choctaw**
Tchiactas—**Choctaw**
Tchinouks—**Chinook**
Te-bot-e-lob-e-lay—**Tubatulabal**
Teguas—**Tewa Pueblos**
Teja—**Caddo**
Ten'a—**Ingalik**
Tenan-kutchin—**Tanana**
Tenino
Tennankutchin—**Tanana**
Tennan-tnu-kokhtana—**Tanana**
Tesuque—**Pueblo Indians; Tewa Pueblos**
Tête Pelée—**Comanche**
Teton
Teton Sioux—**Teton**
Tewa Pueblos
Teyas—**Mescalero Apache**
Thais—**South and Southeast Asians of**
    the United States
Thecannies—**Sekani**
Thlingchadinne—**Dogrib**
Thlinget—**Tlingit**
Thlinkets—**Tlingit**
Thompson
Thompson River Indians—**Thompson**
Thuleeskimoer—**Inughuit**
Thulegroenlaendere—**Inughuit**
Tiamath—**Yurok**
Tigua—**Pueblo Indians**
Tillamook
Tinde—**Jicarilla**
Tiou—**Tunica**
Tioux—**Tunica**
Tipai—**Kumeyaay**
Tipai-Ipai—**Kumeyaay**
Titunwan—**Teton**
Tlakluit—**Wishram**
Tlalem—**Klallam**
Tlicho—**Dogrib**
Tlingit
Tlinkit—**Tlingit**
Tlokeang—**Wailaki**
Tnaina—**Tanaina**
Toanhooches—**Twana**
Toderichroone—**Catawba**
Tohono O'odham—**Pima-Papago**
Tolowa
Tongans—**Polynesians**
Tonkawa
Travelers—**Irish Travelers**
Trinidadians—**Black West Indians in**
    the United States
Trinity Indians—**Hupa**
Tri-Racial Isolates—**American Isolates**
Tri-Racials—**American Isolates**
Trukese—**Micronesians**
Tsa'lagi—**Cherokee**
Tsa'ragi—**Cherokee**
Tsattine—**Beaver**
Tsethaottine—**Mountain**
Tsilkotin—**Chilcotin**
Tsimshian
Tsniuk—**Chinook**
Tsoop-Nit-Pa-Loo—**Nez Percé**
Tsutpeli—**Nez Percé**
Tubatulabal

Tukspuch—**Tenino**
Tularosa Apache—**Mescalero Apache**
Tunaha—**Kutenai**
Tunica
Tunumiut—**East Greenland Inuit**
Tununirmiut—**Iglulik Inuit**
Turkey Tribe—**Delaware**
Turks—**American Isolates**
Tusayan—**Hopi**
Tuscarora
Tutchone
Tutchonekutchin—**Tutchone**
Tutuni—**Chastacosta**
Tuyurymiut—**Central Yup'ik Eskimos**
Twana
Twightwees—**Miami**
Tygh—**Tenino**
Tyigh—**Tenino**

Uchi—**Yuchi**
Ugyuligmiut—**Netsilik Inuit**
Uhro-Rusyns—**European-Americans**
Ukhotnom—**Yuki**
Ukrainian-Canadians—**Ukrainians of**
    Canada
Ukrainians—**European-Americans**
Ukrainians of Canada
Ulrucks—**Yurok**
Umatilla
Umpqua—**Chastacosta**
Unaliqmiut—**Central Yup'ik Eskimos**
Unami—**Delaware**
Upper Chehalis—**Chehalis**
Upper Chinook—**Wishram**
Upper Pimas—**Pima-Papago**
Upper Tanana—**Nabesna**
Ushery—**Catawba**
Utah—**Ute**
Utaw—**Ute**
Ute

Vallodolid—**Taos**
Van Duzen Indians—**Wailaki**
Vanyume—**Serrano**
Vaqueros—**Mescalero Apache**
Vascos—**Basques**
Viard—**Wiyot**
Vietnamese—**South and Southeast**
    Asians of Canada; South and
    Southeast Asians of the United States
Vinton County Group—**American**
    Isolates

Wδlastδkwiyδk—**Maliseet**
Wabnaki—**Abenaki**
Wah-shoes—**Washoe**
Wahshoo—**Washoe**
Waiam—**Tenino**
Wailaki
Wailatpam—**Cayuse**
Wailatpu—**Cayuse**
Walapai
Walkers—**Western Shoshone**
Wallawalla
Walula—**Wallawalla**
Wampanoag—**Massachuset**
Wanukeyena—**Hidatsa**

The Editors

Editor in Chief
David Levinson (Ph.D., State University of New York at Buffalo) is vice-president of the Human Relations Area Files in New Haven, Connecticut. He is a cultural anthropologist whose primary research interests are in social issues, worldwide comparative research, and social theory. He has conducted research on homelessness, alcohol abuse, aggression, family relations, and ethnicity. Among his dozens of publications are the award-winning text, *Toward Explaining Human Culture* (with Martin J. Malone), *The Tribal Living Book* (with David Sherwood), and *Family Violence in Cross-Cultural Perspective*. Dr. Levinson also teaches anthropology at Albertus Magnus College in New Haven, Connecticut.

Volume Editor
Timothy J. O'Leary (M.Phil., Columbia University and M.L.S., Southern Connecticut State University) is coordinator of archive development and librarian at the Human Relations Area Files. He is an archaeologist and ethnographic bibliographer and has engaged in archaeological research in the New York City area; the Zuni area of New Mexico; northwestern Florida; southern Alberta; Isle au Haut, Maine; southern Rhode Island; and Connecticut. His major publications include the *Ethnographic Bibliography of South America*, *Circum-Mediterranean Peasantry: Introductory Bibliographies* (with Louise E. Sweet), *Ethnographic Bibliography of North America* (with George Peter Murdock), and *Ethnographic Bibliography of North America, Supplement to the 4th Edition* (with M. Marlene Martin).